Contents

REPAIRS & OVERHAUL

Originally introduced in October 2000, the latest Ford Mondeo is available in four-door Saloon, five-door Hatchback and five-door Estate configurations. This manual covers the facelifted range introduced in July 2003 – on the surface, this was merely a cosmetic exercise to refresh the car's appearance, but a number of important revisions were also made. The range was simplified and further revised in May 2005.

The 1.8 and 2.0 litre chain-driven Duratec-HE 16-valve four-cylinder petrol engines continued largely unchanged. Alongside the existing 24-valve 2.5 litre V6, a new 3.0 litre unit was unveiled, offering 200 bhp (and later, 220 bhp) performance. The common-rail TDCi diesel engine range grew from the existing 2.0 litre 16-valve 115 and 130 versions, with the arrival of a new 2.2 litre 155 engine, and an entry-level 2.0 litre 90 TDCi unit.

All engines are equipped with the latest control technology – petrol engines have Ford's Black Oak system, while diesel engines use Ford EEC V management. The transversely-mounted engine drives the front roadwheels through a 5- or 6-speed manual transmission with a hydraulically-operated clutch, or a 4- or 5-speed automatic transmission.

All models feature a high level of equipment, with occupant safety in accidents a high design priority. The Mondeo has two-stage driver and front passenger airbags, front seat side airbags, side curtain airbags, and seat belt tensioners – this forms what Ford call an Intelligent Protection System, which is designed to only deploy as necessary, specific to the number of occupants, and the circumstances and severity of the accident.

The braking system has discs all round, with ABS, Emergency Brake Assist (EBA) and Electronic Brakeforce Distribution (EBD) for extra safety when braking in emergency situations.

The Mondeo features highly-developed fully-independent suspension. All models have MacPherson struts at the front, located by transverse lower wishbones. Saloon and Hatchback models also have struts at the rear, located by Ford's Quadralink arrangement of transverse and trailing arms. The Estate rear suspension features separate springs and shock absorbers, primarily to give maximum loadspace, but also designed to maintain the excellent ride and handling when heavily-loaded. The power steering is speed-sensitive, providing more assistance during parking and at low speeds.

Provided regular servicing is carried out, the Mondeo should prove a reliable and economical car.

Ford Mondeo

Owners Workshop Manual

RM Jex

Models covered *(4619 - 3AN1 - 400)*

Hatchback, Saloon & Estate, including special/limited editions

Petrol: 1.8 litre (1798cc) & 2.0 litre (1999cc) 4-cylinder, 2.5 litre (2499cc*) & 3.0 litre (2967cc) V6, inc. ST220
**also listed as 2495cc or 2544cc*

Turbo-diesel: 2.0 litre (1998cc) & 2.2 litre (2198cc) TDCi

Does NOT cover 1.8 litre SCi direct injection petrol engine

ABCDE
FGHIJ
KLMNO

A book in the **Haynes Owners Workshop Manual Series**

ISBN **978 1 84425 619 8**

British Library Cataloguing in Publication Data
A catalogue record for this book is available from the British Library.

Printed in the USA

Haynes Publishing
Sparkford, Yeovil, Somerset BA22 7JJ, England

Haynes North America, Inc
861 Lawrence Drive, Newbury Park, California 91320, USA

Haynes Publishing Nordiska AB
Box 1504, 751 45 UPPSALA, Sverige

Contents

LIVING WITH YOUR FORD MONDEO

Your Ford Mondeo manual

The aim of this manual is to help you get the best value from your car. It can do so in several ways. It can help you decide what work must be done (even should you choose to get it done by a garage). It will also provide information on routine maintenance and servicing, and give a logical course of action and diagnosis when random faults occur. However, it is hoped that you will use the manual by tackling the work yourself. On simpler jobs it may even be quicker than booking the car into a garage and going there twice, to leave and collect it. Perhaps most important, a lot of money can be saved by avoiding the costs a garage must charge to cover its labour and overheads.

The manual has drawings and descriptions to show the function of the various components so that their layout can be understood. Tasks are described and photographed in a clear step-by-step sequence. The illustrations are numbered by the Section number and paragraph number to which they relate – if there is more than one illustration per paragraph, the sequence is denoted alphabetically.

References to the 'left' and 'right' of the car are in the sense of a person in the driver's seat, facing forwards.

Acknowledgements

Thanks are due to Draper Tools Limited, who provided some of the workshop tools, and to all those people at Sparkford who helped in the production of this manual.

We take great pride in the accuracy of information given in this manual, but car manufacturers make alterations and design changes during the production run of a particular car of which they do not inform us. No liability can be accepted by the authors or publishers for loss, damage or injury caused by any errors in, or omissions from, the information given.

Working on your car can be dangerous. This page shows just some of the potential risks and hazards, with the aim of creating a safety-conscious attitude.

General hazards

Scalding

• Don't remove the radiator or expansion tank cap while the engine is hot.
• Engine oil, automatic transmission fluid or power steering fluid may also be dangerously hot if the engine has recently been running.

Burning

• Beware of burns from the exhaust system and from any part of the engine. Brake discs and drums can also be extremely hot immediately after use.

Crushing

• When working under or near a raised vehicle, always supplement the jack with axle stands, or use drive-on ramps. ***Never venture under a car which is only supported by a jack.***

• Take care if loosening or tightening high-torque nuts when the vehicle is on stands. Initial loosening and final tightening should be done with the wheels on the ground.

Fire

• Fuel is highly flammable; fuel vapour is explosive.
• Don't let fuel spill onto a hot engine.
• Do not smoke or allow naked lights (including pilot lights) anywhere near a vehicle being worked on. Also beware of creating sparks (electrically or by use of tools).
• Fuel vapour is heavier than air, so don't work on the fuel system with the vehicle over an inspection pit.
• Another cause of fire is an electrical overload or short-circuit. Take care when repairing or modifying the vehicle wiring.
• Keep a fire extinguisher handy, of a type suitable for use on fuel and electrical fires.

Electric shock

• Ignition HT voltage can be dangerous, especially to people with heart problems or a pacemaker. Don't work on or near the ignition system with the engine running or the ignition switched on.

• Mains voltage is also dangerous. Make sure that any mains-operated equipment is correctly earthed. Mains power points should be protected by a residual current device (RCD) circuit breaker.

Fume or gas intoxication

• Exhaust fumes are poisonous; they often contain carbon monoxide, which is rapidly fatal if inhaled. Never run the engine in a confined space such as a garage with the doors shut.
• Fuel vapour is also poisonous, as are the vapours from some cleaning solvents and paint thinners.

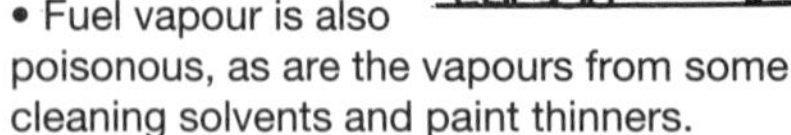

Poisonous or irritant substances

• Avoid skin contact with battery acid and with any fuel, fluid or lubricant, especially antifreeze, brake hydraulic fluid and Diesel fuel. Don't syphon them by mouth. If such a substance is swallowed or gets into the eyes, seek medical advice.
• Prolonged contact with used engine oil can cause skin cancer. Wear gloves or use a barrier cream if necessary. Change out of oil-soaked clothes and do not keep oily rags in your pocket.
• Air conditioning refrigerant forms a poisonous gas if exposed to a naked flame (including a cigarette). It can also cause skin burns on contact.

Asbestos

• Asbestos dust can cause cancer if inhaled or swallowed. Asbestos may be found in gaskets and in brake and clutch linings. When dealing with such components it is safest to assume that they contain asbestos.

Special hazards

Hydrofluoric acid

• This extremely corrosive acid is formed when certain types of synthetic rubber, found in some O-rings, oil seals, fuel hoses etc, are exposed to temperatures above 400ºC. The rubber changes into a charred or sticky substance containing the acid. *Once formed, the acid remains dangerous for years. If it gets onto the skin, it may be necessary to amputate the limb concerned.*
• When dealing with a vehicle which has suffered a fire, or with components salvaged from such a vehicle, wear protective gloves and discard them after use.

The battery

• Batteries contain sulphuric acid, which attacks clothing, eyes and skin. Take care when topping-up or carrying the battery.
• The hydrogen gas given off by the battery is highly explosive. Never cause a spark or allow a naked light nearby. Be careful when connecting and disconnecting battery chargers or jump leads.

Air bags

• Air bags can cause injury if they go off accidentally. Take care when removing the steering wheel and/or facia. Special storage instructions may apply.

Diesel injection equipment

• Diesel injection pumps supply fuel at very high pressure. Take care when working on the fuel injectors and fuel pipes.

Warning: Never expose the hands, face or any other part of the body to injector spray; the fuel can penetrate the skin with potentially fatal results.

Remember...

DO

• Do use eye protection when using power tools, and when working under the vehicle.

• Do wear gloves or use barrier cream to protect your hands when necessary.

• Do get someone to check periodically that all is well when working alone on the vehicle.

• Do keep loose clothing and long hair well out of the way of moving mechanical parts.

• Do remove rings, wristwatch etc, before working on the vehicle – especially the electrical system.

• Do ensure that any lifting or jacking equipment has a safe working load rating adequate for the job.

DON'T

• Don't attempt to lift a heavy component which may be beyond your capability – get assistance.

• Don't rush to finish a job, or take unverified short cuts.

• Don't use ill-fitting tools which may slip and cause injury.

• Don't leave tools or parts lying around where someone can trip over them. Mop up oil and fuel spills at once.

• Don't allow children or pets to play in or near a vehicle being worked on.

The following pages are intended to help in dealing with common roadside emergencies and breakdowns. You will find more detailed fault finding information at the back of the manual, and repair information in the main chapters.

If your car won't start and the starter motor doesn't turn

- ☐ If it's a model with automatic transmission, make sure the selector is in P or N.
- ☐ Open the bonnet and make sure that the battery terminals are clean and tight.
- ☐ Switch on the headlights and try to start the engine. If the headlights go very dim when you're trying to start, the battery is probably flat. Get out of trouble by jump starting (see next page) using a friend's car.

If your car won't start even though the starter motor turns as normal

- ☐ Is there fuel in the tank?
- ☐ Has the engine immobiliser been deactivated? This should happen automatically when the key is inserted and turned to the first position.
- ☐ Is there moisture on electrical components under the bonnet? Switch off the ignition, then wipe off any obvious dampness with a dry cloth. Spray a water-repellent aerosol product (WD-40 or equivalent) on ignition and fuel system electrical connectors like those shown in the photos. (Note that diesel engines don't usually suffer from damp).

A Check the condition and security of the battery connections.

B Check that the HT leads are securely connected to the spark plugs and coils (petrol models).

C Check the engine wiring loom multiplugs for security.

Check that electrical connections are secure (with the ignition switched off) and spray them with a water-dispersant spray like WD-40 if you suspect a problem due to damp

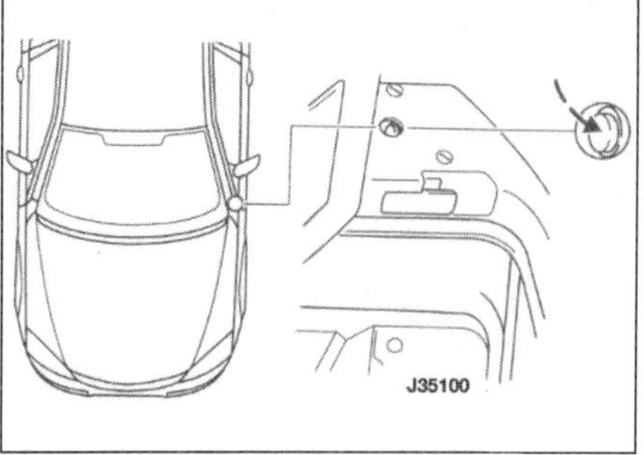

D Check that the fuel cut-off switch has not been activated (diesel models).

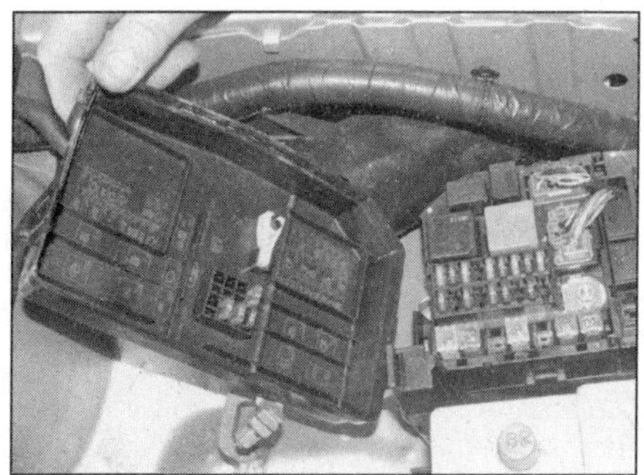

E Check that none of the engine compartment fuses have blown.

Jump starting

When jump-starting a car using a booster battery, observe the following precautions:

- ✔ Before connecting the booster battery, make sure that the ignition is switched off.
- ✔ Ensure that all electrical equipment (lights, heater, wipers, etc) is switched off.
- ✔ Take note of any special precautions printed on the battery case.
- ✔ Make sure that the booster battery is the same voltage as the discharged one in the vehicle.
- ✔ If the battery is being jump-started from the battery in another vehicle, the two vehicles MUST NOT TOUCH each other.
- ✔ Make sure that the transmission is in neutral (or PARK, in the case of automatic transmission).

Jump starting will get you out of trouble, but you must correct whatever made the battery go flat in the first place. There are three possibilities:

1 The battery has been drained by repeated attempts to start, or by leaving the lights on.

2 The charging system is not working properly (alternator drivebelt slack or broken, alternator wiring fault or alternator itself faulty).

3 The battery itself is at fault (electrolyte low, or battery worn out).

1 Connect one end of the red jump lead to the positive (+) terminal of the flat battery

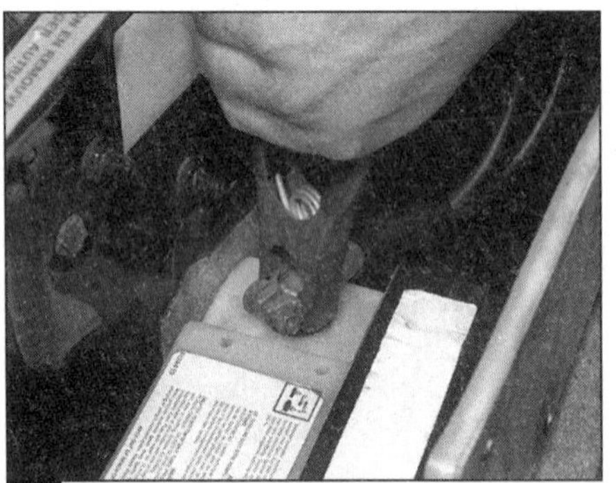

2 Connect the other end of the red lead to the positive (+) terminal of the booster battery.

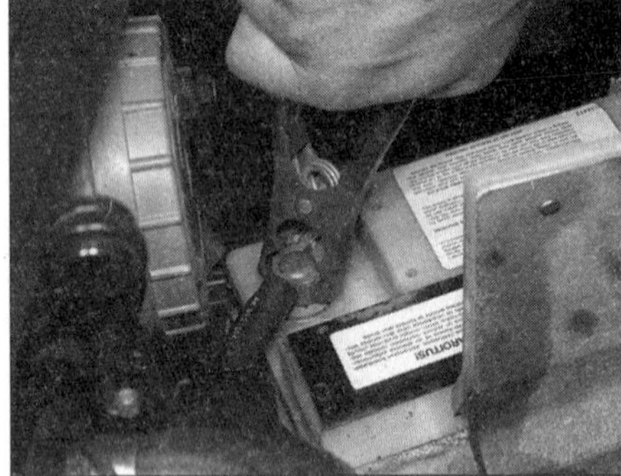

3 Connect one end of the black jump lead to the negative (-) terminal of the booster battery

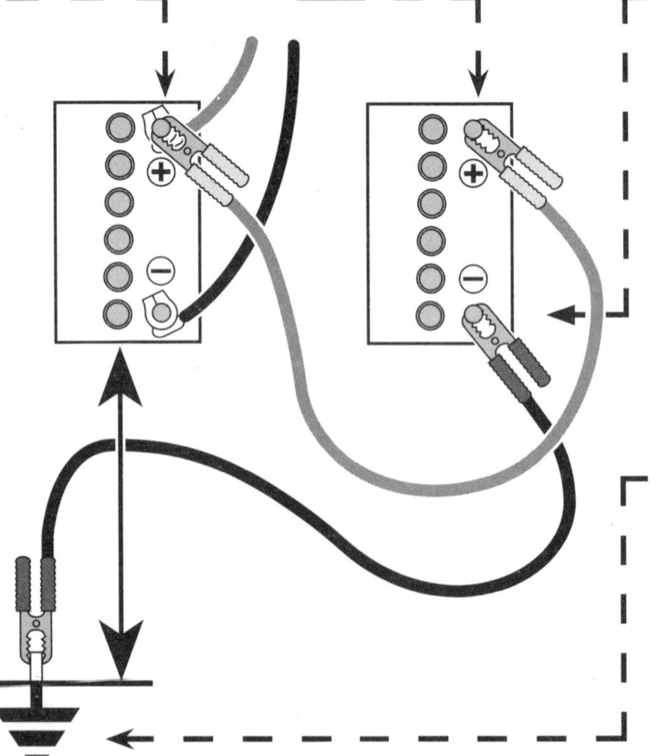

4 Connect the other end of the black jump lead to a bolt or bracket on the engine block, well away from the battery, on the vehicle to be started.

5 Make sure that the jump leads will not come into contact with the fan, drive-belts or other moving parts of the engine.

6 Start the engine using the booster battery and run it at idle speed. Switch on the lights, rear window demister and heater blower motor, then disconnect the jump leads in the reverse order of connection. Turn off the lights etc.

Wheel changing

Warning: Do not change a wheel in a situation where you risk being hit by other traffic. On busy roads, try to stop in a lay-by or a gateway. Be wary of passing traffic while changing the wheel – it is easy to become distracted by the job in hand.

Preparation

- ☐ When a puncture occurs, stop as soon as it is safe to do so.
- ☐ Park on firm level ground, if possible, and well out of the way of other traffic.
- ☐ Use hazard warning lights if necessary.
- ☐ If you have one, use a warning triangle to alert other drivers of your presence.
- ☐ Apply the handbrake and engage first or reverse gear (or P on models with automatic transmission).
- ☐ Chock the wheel diagonally opposite the one being removed – a couple of large stones will do for this.
- ☐ If the ground is soft, use a flat piece of wood to spread the load under the jack.

Changing the wheel

1 The spare wheel and tools are stored in the luggage compartment. Fold back the floor covering and lift up the cover panel, then unscrew the retainer, and lift the spare wheel out.

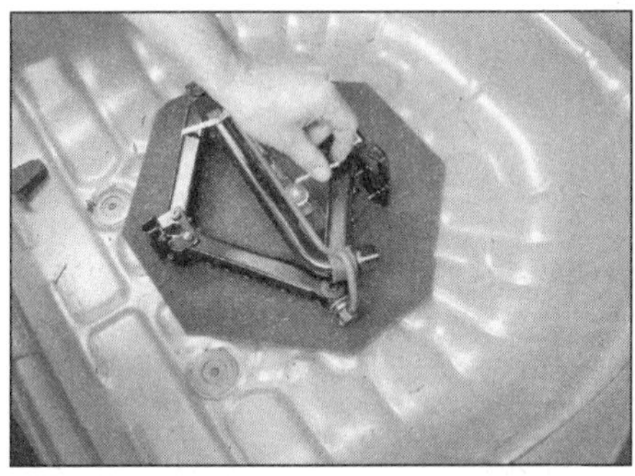

2 Unscrew the retainer, and lift the jack and wheelbrace out of the wheel well. The screw-in towing eye is also provided in the wheel well.

3 If necessary, use the flat end of the wheelbrace to prise off the centre cover or wheel trim to access the wheel nuts. Slacken each nut by a half turn, using the wheelbrace. If the nuts are too tight, DON'T stand on the wheelbrace to undo them – contact a motoring organisation for help.

4 Use the jacking point nearest the punctured wheel. On models with side skirts, unclip the jacking point covers. The front jacking point is 27 cm (11") from the front end of the sill, and the rear one is 10 cm (4") from the rear end. Locate the jack head in the jacking point (don't jack the car anywhere else), and turn the jack handle clockwise until the wheel is off the ground.

5 Unscrew the wheel nuts, noting which way round they fit (tapered side inwards), and remove the wheel. Where a locking wheel nut is fitted, use the special adapter.

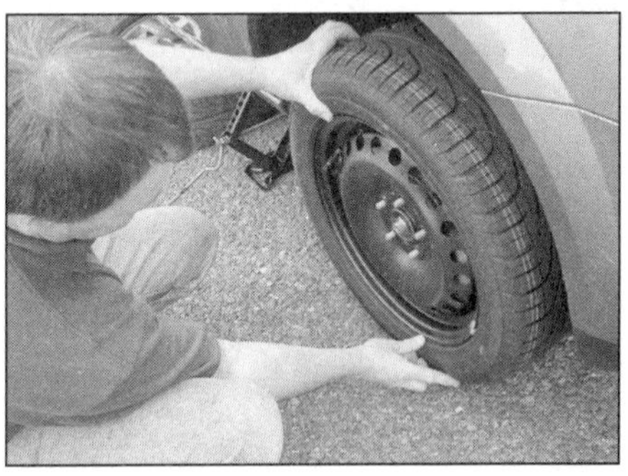

6 Fit the spare wheel, and screw on the nuts. Lightly tighten the nuts with the wheelbrace.

7 Lower the car to the ground and fully tighten the wheel nuts, then refit the wheel trim or centre cover, as applicable. Have the wheel nuts tightened to the correct torque at the earliest opportunity.

Finally . . .

- ☐ Remove the wheel chocks.
- ☐ Stow the jack and tools in the correct locations in the car.
- ☐ Check the tyre pressure on the wheel just fitted. If it is low, or if you don't have a pressure gauge with you, drive slowly to the nearest garage and inflate the tyre to the correct pressure.
- ☐ Have the damaged tyre or wheel repaired as soon as possible.

Caution: If a temporary space-saving spare wheel is fitted, do not exceed 50 mph and do not drive through an automatic car wash.

Identifying leaks

Puddles on the garage floor or drive, or obvious wetness under the bonnet or underneath the car, suggest a leak that needs investigating. It can sometimes be difficult to decide where the leak is coming from, especially if the engine bay is very dirty already. Leaking oil or fluid can also be blown rearwards by the passage of air under the car, giving a false impression of where the problem lies.

Warning: Most automotive oils and fluids are poisonous. Wash them off skin, and change out of contaminated clothing, without delay.

The smell of a fluid leaking from the car may provide a clue to what's leaking. Some fluids are distinctively coloured. It may help to clean the car carefully and to park it over some clean paper overnight as an aid to locating the source of the leak. Remember that some leaks may only occur while the engine is running.

Sump oil

Engine oil may leak from the drain plug...

Oil from filter

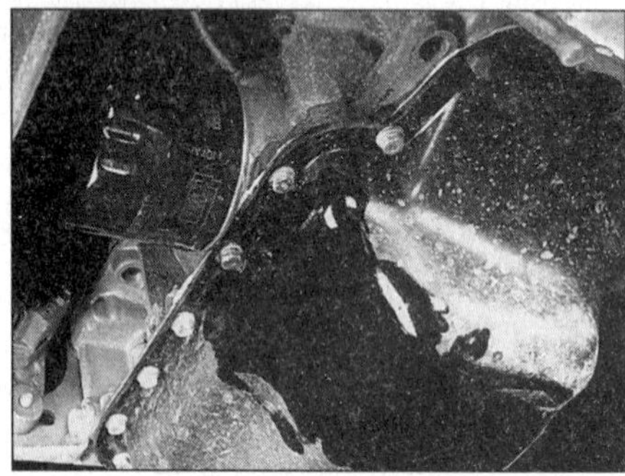

...or from the base of the oil filter.

Gearbox oil

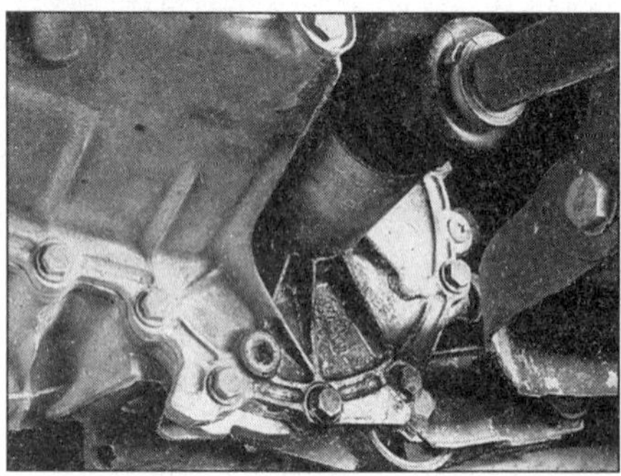

Gearbox oil can leak from the seals at the inboard ends of the driveshafts.

Antifreeze

Leaking antifreeze often leaves a crystalline deposit like this.

Brake fluid

A leak occurring at a wheel is almost certainly brake fluid.

Power steering fluid

Power steering fluid may leak from the pipe connectors on the steering rack.

Towing

When all else fails, you may find yourself having to get a tow home – or of course you may be helping somebody else. Long-distance recovery should only be done by a garage or breakdown service. For shorter distances, DIY towing using another car is easy enough, but observe the following points:

☐ Use a proper tow-rope – they are not expensive. The vehicle being towed must display an ON TOW sign in its rear window.

☐ Always turn the ignition key to the 'On' position when the vehicle is being towed, so that the steering lock is released, and the direction indicator and brake lights work.

☐ The front towing eye is of the screw-in type, and is stored in the spare wheel well. The towing eye screws into the threaded hole below the right-hand headlight, accessible after prising out a cover in the bumper, and has a left-hand thread – ie, it screws in anti-clockwise (see illustration). A similar arrangement is used for the rear towing eye on models with the standard rear bumper. On ST models with the sports rear bumper, the rear towing eye is located on the right-hand side of the lower slot or grille – where necessary, unclip the grille panel for access.

☐ Before being towed, release the handbrake and make sure the transmission is in neutral. On models with automatic transmission, special precautions apply. If in doubt, do not tow, or transmission damage may result.

☐ Note that greater-than-usual pedal pressure will be required to operate the brakes, since the vacuum servo unit is only operational with the engine running.

☐ The driver of the car being towed must keep the tow-rope taut at all times to avoid snatching.

☐ Make sure that both drivers know the route before setting off.

☐ Only drive at moderate speeds and keep the distance towed to a minimum. Drive smoothly and allow plenty of time for slowing down at junctions.

Introduction

There are some very simple checks which need only take a few minutes to carry out, but which could save you a lot of inconvenience and expense.

These *Weekly checks* require no great skill or special tools, and the small amount of time they take to perform could prove to be very well spent, for example:

☐ Keeping an eye on tyre condition and pressures, will not only help to stop them wearing out prematurely, but could also save your life.

☐ Many breakdowns are caused by electrical problems. Battery-related faults are particularly common, and a quick check on a regular basis will often prevent the majority of these.

☐ If your car develops a brake fluid leak, the first time you might know about it is when your brakes don't work properly. Checking the level regularly will give advance warning of this kind of problem.

☐ If the oil or coolant levels run low, the cost of repairing any engine damage will be far greater than fixing the leak, for example.

Underbonnet check points

◀ 1.8 litre petrol engine (2.0 litre similar)

A *Engine oil level dipstick*
B *Engine oil filler cap*
C *Coolant reservoir (expansion tank)*
D *Brake fluid reservoir*
E *Washer fluid reservoir*
F *Battery*
G *Power steering fluid reservoir*

◀ 2.5 litre V6 engine (3.0 litre similar)

A *Engine oil level dipstick*
B *Engine oil filler cap*
C *Coolant reservoir (expansion tank)*
D *Brake fluid reservoir*
E *Washer fluid reservoir*
F *Battery*
G *Power steering fluid reservoir*

◀ 2.0 litre turbo-diesel (2.2 litre similar)

A *Engine oil level dipstick*
B *Engine oil filler cap*
C *Coolant reservoir (expansion tank)*
D *Brake fluid reservoir*
E *Washer fluid reservoir*
F *Battery*
G *Power steering fluid reservoir*

Engine oil level

Before you start

✔ Make sure that the car is on level ground.
✔ Check the oil level before the car is driven, or at least 5 minutes after the engine has been switched off.

If the oil is checked immediately after driving the vehicle, some of the oil will remain in the upper engine components, resulting in an inaccurate reading on the dipstick.

The correct oil

Modern engines place great demands on their oil. It is very important that the correct oil for your car is used (see *Lubricants and fluids*).

Car care

- If you have to add oil frequently, you should check whether you have any oil leaks. Place some clean paper under the car overnight, and check for stains in the morning. If there are no leaks, then the engine may be burning oil (see *Fault finding*).
- Always maintain the level between the upper and lower dipstick marks (see photo 3). If the level is too low, severe engine damage may occur. Oil seal failure may result if the engine is overfilled by adding too much oil.

1 The dipstick is located on the front of the engine (see *Underbonnet Check Points* for exact location). Withdraw the dipstick.

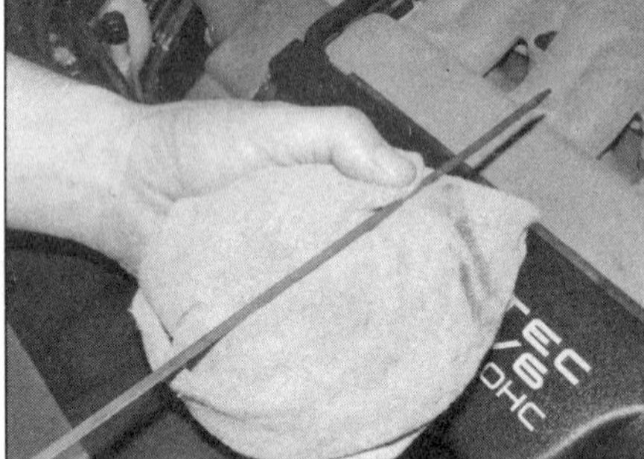

2 Using a clean rag or paper towel remove all oil from the dipstick. Insert the clean dipstick into the tube as far as it will go, then withdraw it again.

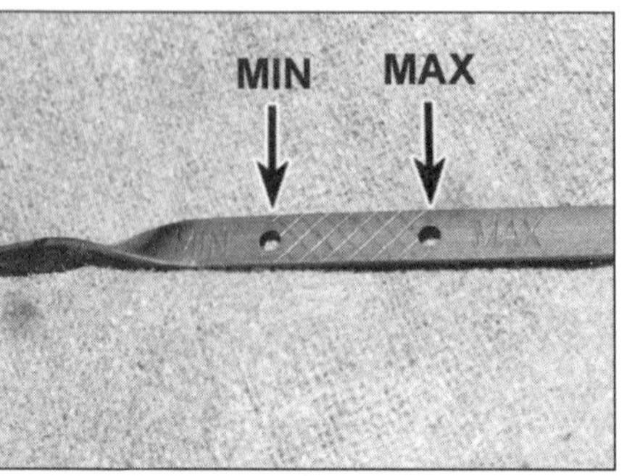

3 Note the oil level on the end of the dipstick, which should be in the hatched area, between the upper (MAX) mark and lower (MIN) mark.

4 Oil is added through the filler cap, located on top of the engine, towards the rear on all except V6 engines. Unscrew and remove the cap. Top-up the level, adding only a small amount of oil at a time. A funnel may help to reduce spillage. Add the oil slowly, checking the level on the dipstick often. Don't overfill.

Coolant level

Warning: Do not attempt to remove the expansion tank pressure cap when the engine is hot, as there is a very great risk of scalding. Do not leave open containers of coolant about, as it is poisonous.

Car Care

● With a sealed-type cooling system, adding coolant should not be necessary on a regular basis. If frequent topping-up is required, it is likely there is a leak. Check the radiator, all hoses and joint faces for signs of staining or wetness, and rectify as necessary.

● It is important that antifreeze is used in the cooling system all year round, not just during the winter months. Don't top up with water alone, as the antifreeze will become diluted.

1 The coolant level varies with the temperature of the engine, and is visible through the expansion tank. When the engine is cold, the coolant level should be between the MAX mark on the side . . .

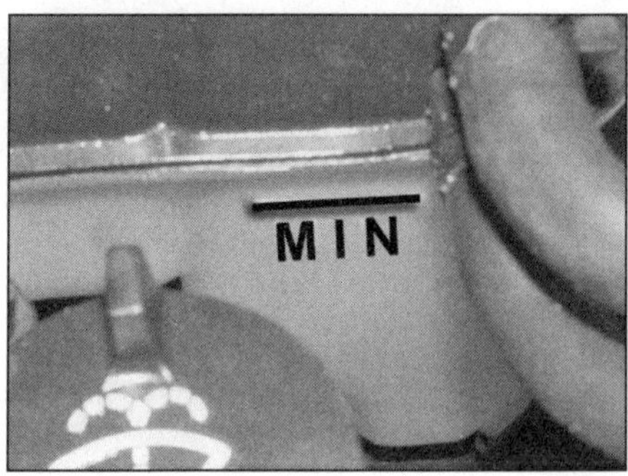

2 . . . and the MIN mark on the front of the reservoir. When the engine is hot, the level may rise slightly above the MAX mark.

3 If topping-up is necessary, wait until the engine is cold. Slowly unscrew the expansion tank cap, to release any pressure present in the cooling system, and remove it.

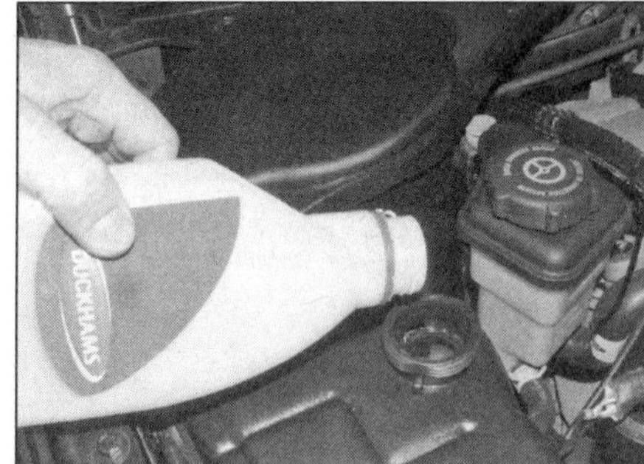

4 Add a mixture of water and antifreeze to the expansion tank, until the coolant is up to the MAX mark. Use antifreeze of the same type (and colour) as that which is already in the system. Refit the cap securely.

Screen washer fluid level

Note: *The underbonnet reservoir also serves the tailgate washer, and the headlight washers, where fitted.*

● Screenwash additives not only keep the windscreen clean during bad weather, they also prevent the washer system freezing in cold weather – which is when you are likely to need it most. Don't top-up using plain water, as the screenwash will become diluted, and will freeze in cold weather.

Warning: On no account use engine coolant antifreeze in the screen washer system – this may damage the paintwork.

1 The screen washer fluid reservoir filler neck is located in the right-hand front corner of the engine compartment, behind the headlight. The fluid level is checked by removing the filler cap and checking the dipstick which is attached to the cap.

2 When topping-up the reservoir, add a screenwash additive in the quantities recommended on the bottle.

Tyre condition and pressure

It is very important that tyres are in good condition, and at the correct pressure - having a tyre failure at any speed is highly dangerous. Tyre wear is influenced by driving style - harsh braking and acceleration, or fast cornering, will all produce more rapid tyre wear. As a general rule, the front tyres wear out faster than the rears. Interchanging the tyres from front to rear ("rotating" the tyres) may result in more even wear. However, if this is completely effective, you may have the expense of replacing all four tyres at once!

Remove any nails or stones embedded in the tread before they penetrate the tyre to cause deflation. If removal of a nail does reveal that the tyre has been punctured, refit the nail so that its point of penetration is marked. Then immediately change the wheel, and have the tyre repaired by a tyre dealer.

Regularly check the tyres for damage in the form of cuts or bulges, especially in the sidewalls. Periodically remove the wheels, and clean any dirt or mud from the inside and outside surfaces. Examine the wheel rims for signs of rusting, corrosion or other damage. Light alloy wheels are easily damaged by "kerbing" whilst parking; steel wheels may also become dented or buckled. A new wheel is very often the only way to overcome severe damage.

New tyres should be balanced when they are fitted, but it may become necessary to re-balance them as they wear, or if the balance weights fitted to the wheel rim should fall off. Unbalanced tyres will wear more quickly, as will the steering and suspension components. Wheel imbalance is normally signified by vibration, particularly at a certain speed (typically around 50 mph). If this vibration is felt only through the steering, then it is likely that just the front wheels need balancing. If, however, the vibration is felt through the whole car, the rear wheels could be out of balance. Wheel balancing should be carried out by a tyre dealer or garage.

1 ***Tread Depth - visual check***
The original tyres have tread wear safety bands (B), which will appear when the tread depth reaches approximately 1.6 mm. The band positions are indicated by a triangular mark on the tyre sidewall (A).

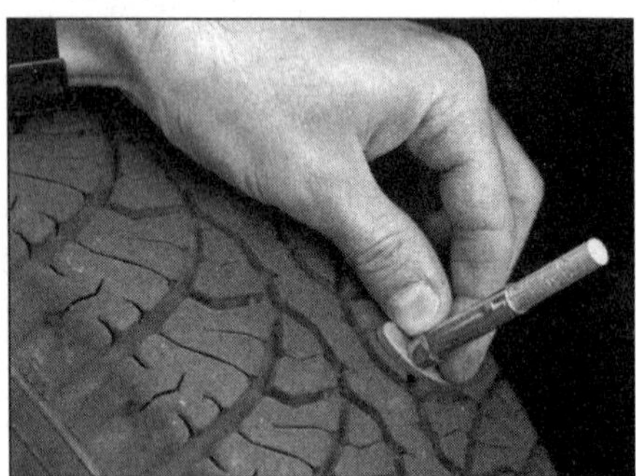

2 ***Tread Depth - manual check***
Alternatively, tread wear can be monitored with a simple, inexpensive device known as a tread depth indicator gauge.

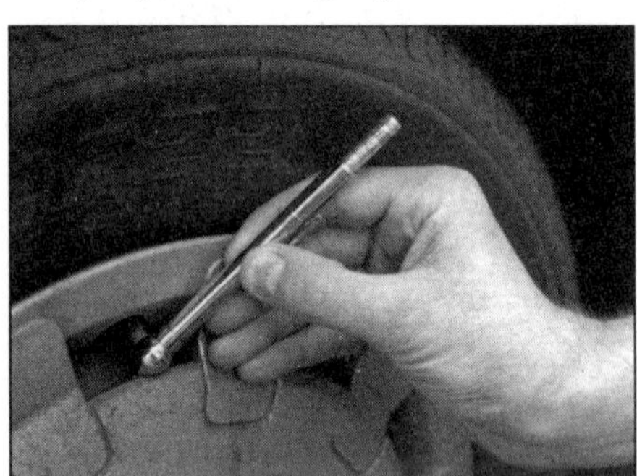

3 ***Tyre Pressure Check***
Check the tyre pressures regularly with the tyres cold. Do not adjust the tyre pressures immediately after the vehicle has been used, or an inaccurate setting will result.

Tyre tread wear patterns

Shoulder Wear

Underinflation (wear on both sides)
Under-inflation will cause overheating of the tyre, because the tyre will flex too much, and the tread will not sit correctly on the road surface. This will cause a loss of grip and excessive wear, not to mention the danger of sudden tyre failure due to heat build-up.
Check and adjust pressures
Incorrect wheel camber (wear on one side)
Repair or renew suspension parts
Hard cornering
Reduce speed!

Centre Wear

Overinflation
Over-inflation will cause rapid wear of the centre part of the tyre tread, coupled with reduced grip, harsher ride, and the danger of shock damage occurring in the tyre casing.
Check and adjust pressures

If you sometimes have to inflate your car's tyres to the higher pressures specified for maximum load or sustained high speed, don't forget to reduce the pressures to normal afterwards.

Uneven Wear

Front tyres may wear unevenly as a result of wheel misalignment. Most tyre dealers and garages can check and adjust the wheel alignment (or "tracking") for a modest charge.
Incorrect camber or castor
Repair or renew suspension parts
Malfunctioning suspension
Repair or renew suspension parts
Unbalanced wheel
Balance tyres
Incorrect toe setting
Adjust front wheel alignment
Note: *The feathered edge of the tread which typifies toe wear is best checked by feel.*

Brake and clutch* fluid level

** The brake fluid reservoir also supplies fluid to the clutch master cylinder on manual transmission models.*

Warning: Brake fluid can harm your eyes and damage painted surfaces, so use extreme caution when handling and pouring it. Do not use fluid which has been standing open for some time, as it absorbs moisture from the air, which can cause a dangerous loss of braking effectiveness.

Before you start

✔ Make sure that the car is on level ground.

✔ Cleanliness is of great importance when dealing with the braking system, so take care to clean around the reservoir cap before topping-up. Use only clean brake fluid.

Safety first!

● If the reservoir requires repeated topping-up, this is an indication of a fluid leak somewhere in the brake or clutch system, which should be investigated immediately.

● If a leak is suspected, the car should not be driven until the braking system has been checked. Never take any risks where brakes are concerned.

● The fluid level in the reservoir will drop slightly as the brake pads wear down, but the fluid level must never be allowed to drop below the MIN mark.

1 The brake fluid reservoir is located on the left-hand side of the engine compartment (left as seen from the driver's seat).

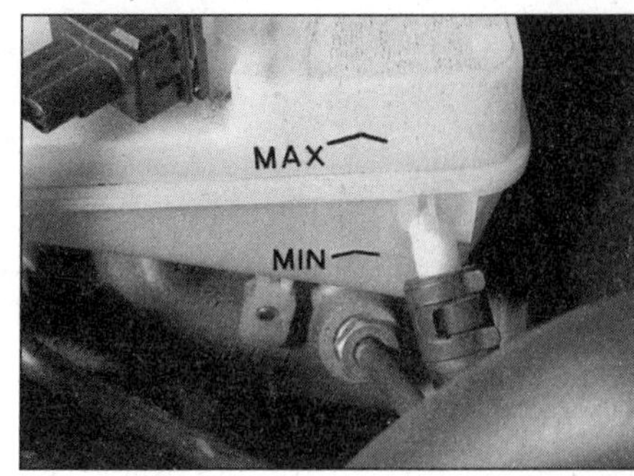

2 The MAX and MIN marks are indicated on the side of the reservoir. The fluid level must be kept between the marks at all times.

3 If topping-up is necessary, first wipe clean the area around the filler cap to prevent dirt entering the hydraulic system, then unscrew and remove the reservoir cap. Inspect the reservoir – the fluid should be changed if it appears to be dark, or if dirt is visible.

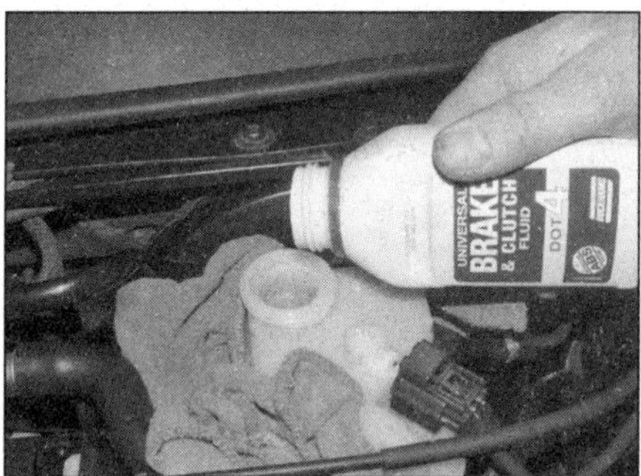

4 Carefully add fluid, taking care not to spill it onto the surrounding components. Use only the specified fluid; mixing different types can cause damage to the system. After topping-up to the correct level, securely refit the cap and wipe off any spilt fluid.

Power steering fluid level

Before you start

✔ The level should be checked when the engine is cold (ie, before the car is driven), with the wheels pointing straight ahead.

✔ For the check to be accurate, the steering must not be turned once the engine has been stopped.

Safety first!

● The need for frequent topping-up indicates a leak, which should be investigated immediately.

1 The fluid level is visible through the reservoir body. When the system is at operating temperature, the level should be up to the MAX mark on the side of the reservoir.

2 If topping-up is required, wipe clean the area around the reservoir filler neck and unscrew the filler cap from the reservoir.

3 When topping-up, use the specified type of fluid and do not overfill the reservoir. When the level is correct, securely refit the cap.

Wiper blades

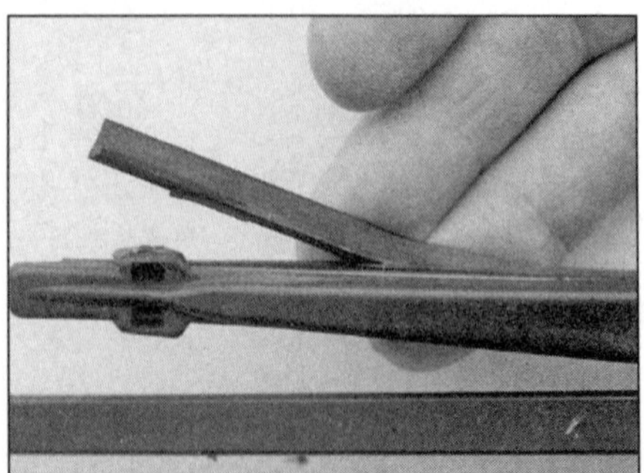

1 Check the condition of the wiper blades; if they are cracked or show any signs of deterioration, or if the glass swept area is smeared, renew them. Wiper blades should be renewed annually.

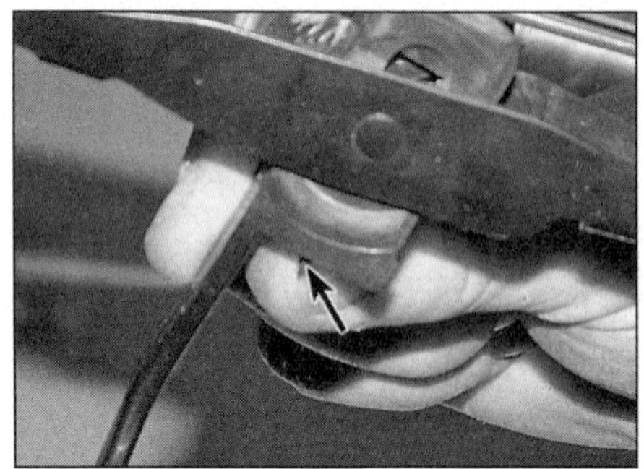

2 To remove a wiper blade, pull the arm fully away from the glass until it locks. Swivel the blade through 90°, then squeeze the locking clip, and detach the blade from the arm. When fitting the new blade, make sure that the blade locks securely into the arm, and that the blade is orientated correctly.

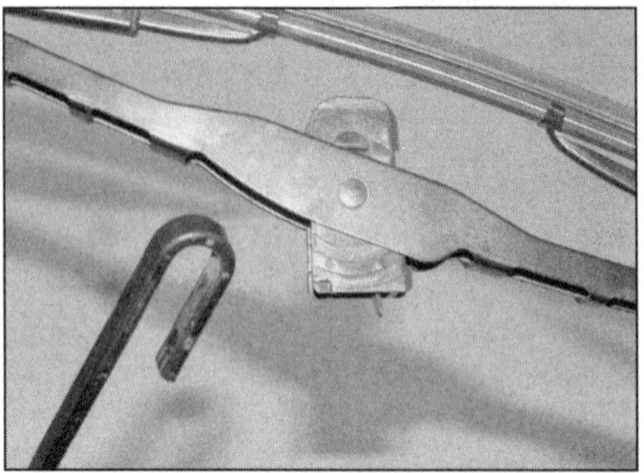

3 Don't forget to check the tailgate wiper blade as well (where applicable). Remove the blade using a similar technique to the windscreen wiper blades.

Battery

Caution: Before carrying out any work on the vehicle battery, read the precautions given in 'Safety first!' at the start of this manual.

✔ Make sure that the battery tray is in good condition, and that the clamp is tight. Corrosion on the tray, retaining clamp and the battery itself can be removed with a solution of water and baking soda. Thoroughly rinse all cleaned areas with water. Any metal parts damaged by corrosion should be covered with a zinc-based primer, then painted.

✔ Periodically (approximately every three months), check the charge condition of the battery as described in Chapter 5A.

✔ If the battery is flat, and you need to jump start your vehicle, see *Roadside Repairs*.

1 The battery is located in the left-hand front corner of the engine compartment. The exterior of the battery should be inspected periodically for damage such as a cracked case or cover.

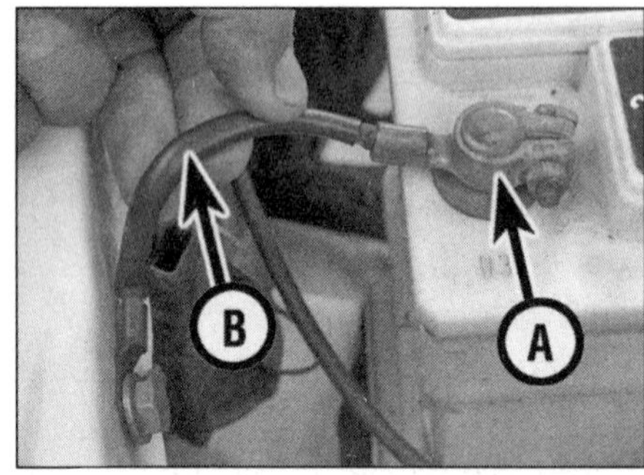

2 Check the tightness of battery clamps (A) to ensure good electrical connections. You should not be able to move them. Also check each cable (B) for cracks and frayed conductors.

Battery corrosion can be kept to a minimum by applying a layer of petroleum jelly to the clamps and terminals after they are reconnected.

3 If corrosion (white, fluffy deposits) is evident, remove the cables from the battery terminals, clean them with a small wire brush, then refit them. Automotive stores sell a tool for cleaning the battery post . . .

4 . . . as well as the battery cable clamps.

Electrical systems

✔ Check all external lights and the horn. Refer to the appropriate Sections of Chapter 12 for details if any of the circuits are found to be inoperative.

✔ Visually check all accessible wiring connectors, harnesses and retaining clips for security, and for signs of chafing or damage.

If you need to check your brake lights and indicators unaided, back up to a wall or garage door and operate the lights. The reflected light should show if they are working properly.

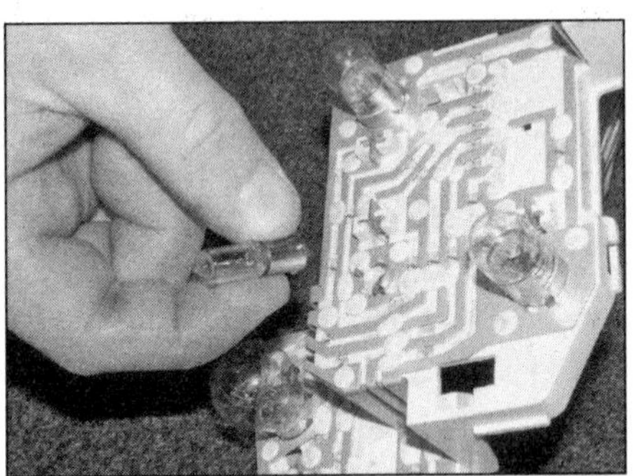

1 If a single indicator light, stop-light or headlight has failed, it is likely that a bulb has blown and will need to be renewed. Refer to Chapter 12 for details. If both stop-lights have failed, it is possible that the switch has failed (see Chapter 9).

2 If more than one indicator light or headlight has failed, it is likely that either a fuse has blown or that there is a fault in the circuit (see Chapter 12). The main fusebox is located below the facia panel on the passenger's side, and is accessed by a lever behind the glovebox. The auxiliary fusebox is located next to the battery – unclip and remove the cover for access.

3 To renew a blown fuse, remove it, where applicable, using the plastic tool provided. Fit a new fuse of the same rating, available from car accessory shops. It is important that you find the reason that the fuse blew (see *Electrical fault finding* in Chapter 12).

Lubricants and fluids

Engine (petrol and diesel)	Multigrade engine oil, viscosity SAE 5W/30, 5W/40 or 10W/40, to Ford specification WSS-M2C913-A or -B, or to ACEA A1/B1, A2/B2, or A3/B3
Cooling system	Motorcraft Super Plus 2000 antifreeze to Ford specification WSS-M97B44-D
Manual transmission	Gear oil to Ford specification WSD-M2C200C
Automatic transmission:	
4-speed	Automatic transmission fluid to Ford specification ESP-M2C 166-H
5-speed	Automatic transmission fluid to Ford specification WSS-M2C922-A1
Power steering system	Hydraulic fluid to Ford specification WSS-M2C204-A
Brake and clutch systems	Brake fluid to Ford specification ESD-M6C57-A, Super DOT 4

Tyre pressures (cold)

Note: *The pressures given here are only a guide, for normal use – always check the vehicle handbook for more detailed information, and for the fully-loaded or high-speed driving pressures. The figures only apply to original-equipment tyres – the recommended pressures may vary if any other make or type of tyre is fitted; check with your tyre dealer.*

	Front	**Rear**
205/50 R 16 tyres:		
4-cylinder petrol engines	2.3 bar (33 psi)	2.1 bar (30 psi)
V6 and diesel engines	2.5 bar (36 psi)	2.2 bar (32 psi)
205/55 R 16 tyres:		
4-cylinder petrol engines	2.1 bar (30 psi)	2.1 bar (30 psi)
V6 and diesel engines	2.3 bar (33 psi)	2.2 bar (32 psi)
205/50 R 17 tyres:		
4-cylinder petrol engines	2.1 bar (30 psi)	2.1 bar (30 psi)
V6 engines	2.3 bar (33 psi)	2.1 bar (30 psi)
Diesel engines	2.4 bar (35 psi)	2.2 bar (32 psi)
225/40 R 18 tyres:		
4-cylinder petrol engines	2.2 bar (32 psi)	2.1 bar (30 psi)
V6 engines	2.4 bar (35 psi)	2.1 bar (30 psi)
Diesel engines	2.5 bar (36 psi)	2.3 bar (33 psi)
Temporary space-saver spare tyre	4.2 bar (61 psi)	4.2 bar (61 psi)

Chapter 1 Part A:
Routine maintenance and servicing – petrol models

Contents

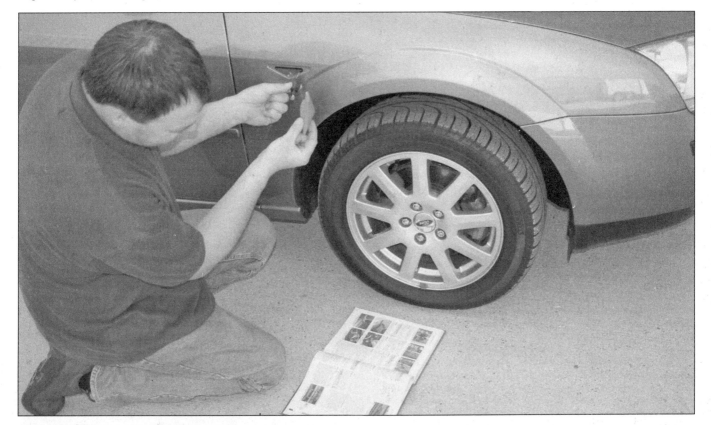

Degrees of difficulty

Easy, suitable for novice with little experience 

Fairly easy, suitable for beginner with some experience

Fairly difficult, suitable for competent DIY mechanic

Difficult, suitable for experienced DIY mechanic 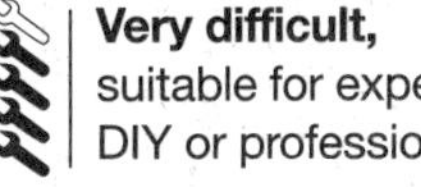

Very difficult, suitable for expert DIY or professional 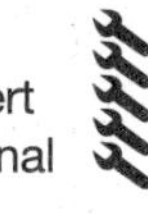

Lubricants and fluids	Refer to the end of *Weekly checks* on page 0•18
Capacities	
Engine oil (with filter):	
1.8 and 2.0 litre engines	4.3 litres
2.5 and 3.0 litre engines	5.7 litres
Difference between dipstick minimum and maximum marks	0.75 to 1.0 litre
Cooling system:	
1.8 litre engine	8.3 litres
2.0 litre engine	8.1 litres
2.5 litre engine:	
Manual transmission	9.5 litres
Automatic transmission	9.7 litres
3.0 litre engine	9.7 litres
Fuel tank	58.5 litres
Manual transmission:	
5-speed	1.9 litres
6-speed	1.75 litres
Automatic transmission:	
4-speed (drain and refill):	
2.0 litre engine	6.0 litres
2.5 litre engine	6.3 litres
5-speed (total capacity – drain and refill not stated)	8.8 litres

Cooling system

Coolant protection at 40% antifreeze/water mixture ratio:	
Slush point	–25°C (–13°F)
Solidifying point	–30°C (–22°F)

Ignition system

Firing order:	
1.8 and 2.0 litre engines	1-3-4-2
2.5 and 3.0 litre engines	1-4-2-5-3-6
No 1 cylinder position	Timing chain end of engine
Spark plugs:	
1.8 and 2.0 litre engines	Motorcraft AGFS 22FE13J
2.5 litre engine	Motorcraft AGSF 32FM
3.0 litre engine	Motorcraft AGSF 22FCSM
Spark plug gap (where adjustable, for the above plugs only)	1.3 mm

Braking system

Note: *No minimum lining thicknesses are given by Ford – the following is given as a general recommendation.*

Minimum front or rear brake pad lining thickness	1.5 mm

Torque wrench settings	**Nm**	**lbf ft**
Automatic transmission drain plug:		
4-speed	27	20
5-speed	45	33
Automatic transmission filler plug (5-speed)	45	33
Automatic transmission selector lever cable cover (5-speed)	22	16
Automatic transmission test plug (5-speed)	15	11
Engine oil drain plug:		
1.8 and 2.0 litre engines	28	21
2.5 and 3.0 litre engines	26	19
Manual transmission filler/level and drain plugs:		
5-speed	45	33
6-speed	35	26
Roadwheel nuts	85	63
Spark plugs:		
1.8 and 2.0 litre engines	12	9
2.5 and 3.0 litre engines	14	10

The maintenance intervals in this manual are provided with the assumption that you, not the dealer, will be carrying out the work. These are the minimum maintenance intervals recommended by us for cars driven daily. If you wish to keep your car in peak condition at all times, you may wish to perform some of these procedures more often. We encourage frequent maintenance, because it enhances the efficiency, performance and resale value of your car.

If the car is driven in dusty areas, used to tow a trailer, or driven frequently at slow speeds (idling in traffic) or on short journeys, more frequent maintenance intervals are recommended.

When the vehicle is new, it should be serviced by a dealer service department (or other workshop recognised by the vehicle manufacturer as providing the same standard of service) in order to preserve the warranty. The vehicle manufacturer may reject warranty claims if you are unable to prove that servicing has been carried out as and when specified, using only original-equipment parts, or parts certified to be of equivalent quality.

Every 250 miles or weekly

- ☐ Refer to Weekly checks

Every 6250 miles or 6 months, whichever occurs first

- ☐ Renew the engine oil and filter (Section 3)

Note: *Frequent oil and filter changes are good for the engine. We recommend changing the oil at the mileage specified here, or at least twice a year if the mileage covered is a less.*

Every 12 500 miles or 12 months, whichever occurs first

In addition to the item listed in the previous service, carry out the following:

- ☐ Check the battery and clean the terminals (Section 4)
- ☐ Check the auxiliary drivebelt (Section 5)
- ☐ Check the electrical system (Section 6)
- ☐ Check under the bonnet for fluid leaks and hose condition (Section 7)
- ☐ Check the condition of all engine compartment wiring (Section 8)
- ☐ Check the condition of all air conditioning system components (Section 9)
- ☐ Check the seat belts (Section 10)
- ☐ Check the antifreeze concentration (Section 11)
- ☐ Check the steering, suspension and roadwheels (Section 12)
- ☐ Check the driveshaft rubber gaiters and CV joints (Section 13)
- ☐ Check the exhaust system (Section 14)
- ☐ Check the underbody, and all fuel/brake lines (Section 15)
- ☐ Check the braking system (Section 16)
- ☐ Check the doors and bonnet, and lubricate their hinges and locks (Section 17)
- ☐ Renew the pollen filter (Section 18)
- ☐ Check the security of all roadwheel nuts (Section 19)
- ☐ Road test (Section 20)

Every 25 000 miles or 2 years, whichever occurs first

In addition to the relevant items listed in the previous services, carry out the following:

- ☐ Check the automatic transmission fluid level (Section 21)

Every 37 500 miles or 3 years, whichever occurs first

In addition to the relevant items listed in the previous services, carry out the following:

- ☐ Renew the spark plugs (Section 22)
- ☐ Renew the air filter element (Section 23). Note that this task must be carried out at more frequent intervals if the car is used in dusty or polluted conditions
- ☐ Check the manual transmission oil level (Section 24)
- ☐ Renew the automatic transmission fluid (Section 25). Note that this task applies to cars used in severe conditions only (short trips of less than 10 miles in freezing conditions, extensive idling, towing a trailer, operating off-road)

Every 3 years (regardless of mileage)

- ☐ Renew the brake fluid (Section 26)
- ☐ Renew the coolant (Section 27)

Every 50 000 miles or 4 years, whichever occurs first

In addition to the relevant items listed in the previous services, carry out the following:

- ☐ Renew the fuel filter (Section 28)
- ☐ Check the valve clearances – 1.8 and 2.0 litre only (Section 29)
- ☐ Renew the auxiliary drivebelts (Section 30)

Underbonnet view of a 2.0 litre engine model

1 *Engine oil filler cap*
2 *Engine oil dipstick*
3 *Power steering hydraulic fluid reservoir*
4 *Washer fluid reservoir*
5 *Coolant expansion tank filler cap*
6 *Front suspension strut upper mounting*
7 *Spark plugs and HT leads*
8 *Ignition coil*
9 *Brake and clutch hydraulic fluid reservoir*
10 *Air cleaner*
11 *Battery*

Underbonnet view of a 2.5 litre V6 engine model

1 *Engine oil filler cap*
2 *Engine oil dipstick*
3 *Power steering hydraulic fluid reservoir*
4 *Washer fluid reservoir*
5 *Coolant expansion tank filler cap*
6 *Front suspension strut upper mounting*
7 *Upper inlet manifold*
8 *Ignition coil*
9 *Brake and clutch hydraulic fluid reservoir*
10 *Air cleaner*
11 *Battery*

Front underbody view of a 2.0 litre engine model

1 *Engine oil drain plug*
2 *Oil filter*
3 *Manual transmission filler/ level plug*
4 *Fuel and brake lines*
5 *Exhaust pipe*
6 *Steering track rods*
7 *Front suspension lower arms*
8 *Rear engine mounting link*
9 *Driveshaft*
10 *Front brake calipers*
11 *Manual transmission*
12 *Front subframe*
13 *Air conditioning compressor*

Front underbody view of a 2.5 litre V6 engine model

1 *Engine oil drain plug*
2 *Oil filter*
3 *Manual transmission filler/ level plug*
4 *Fuel and brake lines*
5 *Exhaust pipe*
6 *Steering track rods*
7 *Front suspension lower arms*
8 *Rear engine mounting link*
9 *Driveshaft*
10 *Front brake calipers*
11 *Manual transmission*
12 *Front subframe*
13 *Air conditioning compressor*

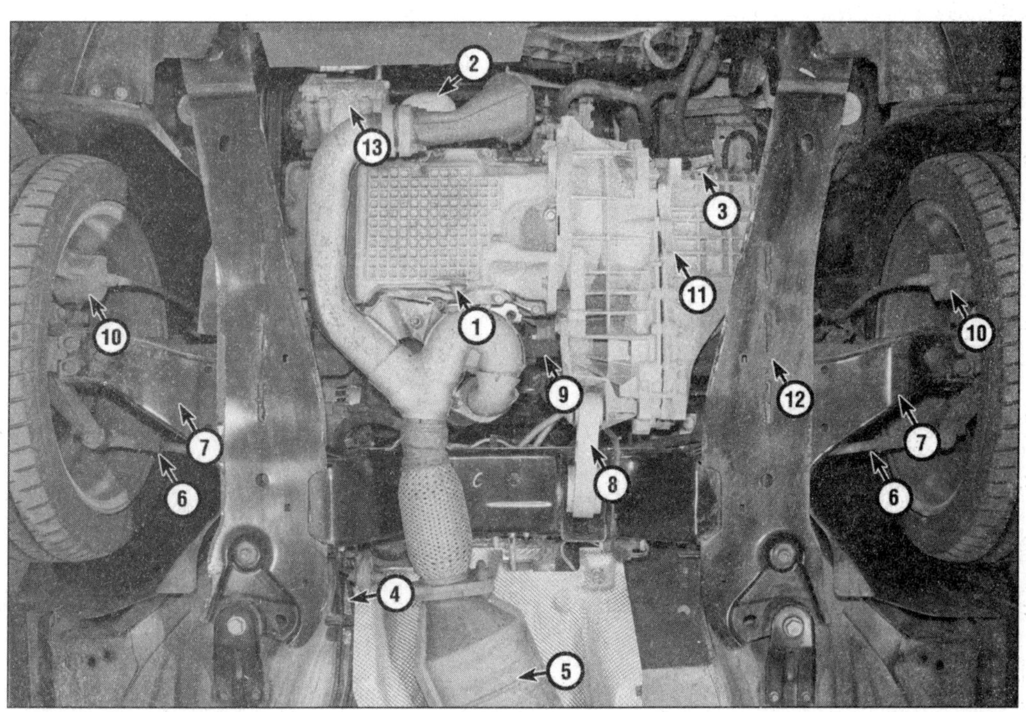

Rear underbody view – Saloon and Hatchback models

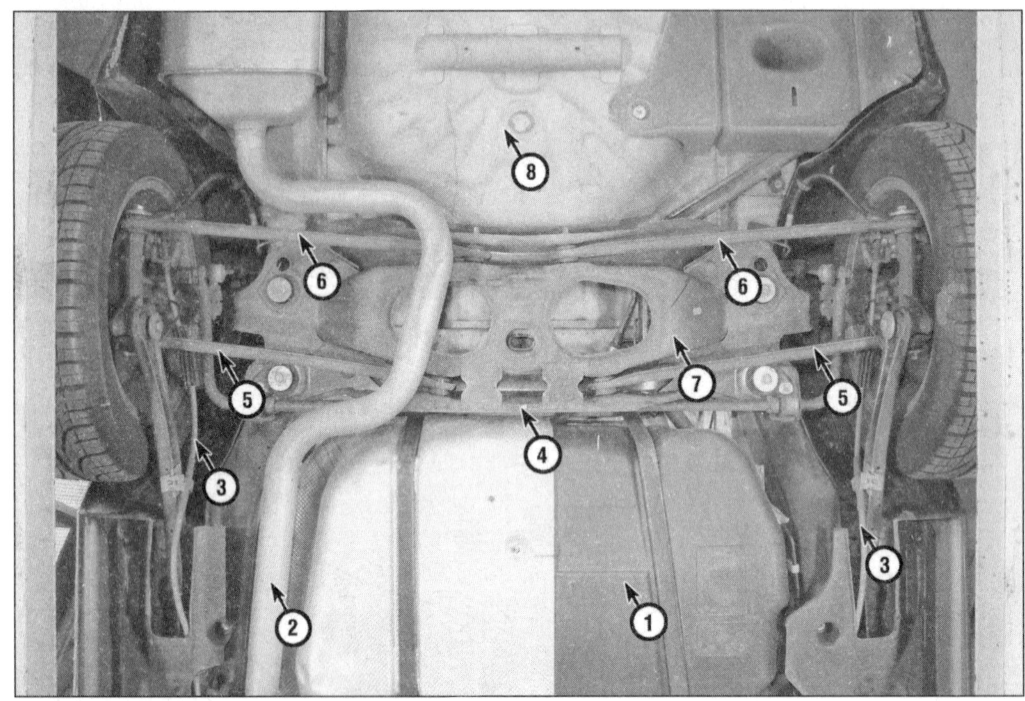

1 *Fuel tank*
2 *Exhaust pipe*
3 *Handbrake cables*
4 *Rear anti-roll bar*
5 *Rear suspension front lower arm*
6 *Rear suspension rear lower arm*
7 *Rear suspension crossmember*
8 *Spare wheel well*

Rear underbody view – Estate models

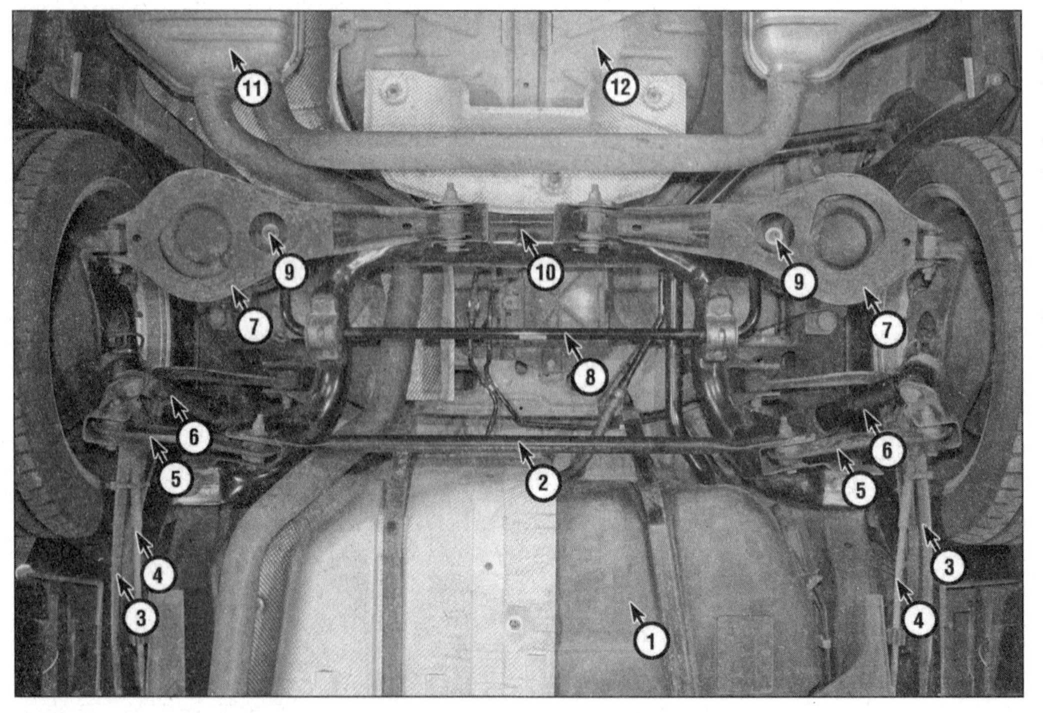

1 *Fuel tank*
2 *Rear suspension brace*
3 *Rear suspension tie bar/ knuckle*
4 *Handbrake cables*
5 *Rear suspension front lower arms*
6 *Rear suspension struts*
7 *Rear suspension lower arms*
8 *Rear anti-roll bar*
9 *Rear anti-roll bar link lower mountings*
10 *Rear suspension crossmember*
11 *Rear exhaust system*
12 *Spare wheel well*

1 General information

1 This Chapter is designed to help the home mechanic maintain his/her car for safety, economy, long life and peak performance.
2 The Chapter contains a master maintenance schedule, followed by Sections dealing specifically with each task in the schedule. Visual checks, adjustments, component renewal and other helpful items are included. Refer to the accompanying illustrations of the engine compartment and the underside of the car for the locations of the various components.
3 Servicing your car in accordance with the mileage/time maintenance schedule and the following Sections will provide a planned maintenance programme, which should result in a long and reliable service life. This is a comprehensive plan, so maintaining some items but not others at the specified service intervals, will not produce the same results.
4 As you service your car, you will discover that many of the procedures can – and should – be grouped together, because of the particular procedure being performed, or because of the proximity of two otherwise-unrelated components to one another. For example, if the car is raised for any reason, the exhaust can be inspected at the same time as the suspension and steering components.
5 The first step in this maintenance programme is to prepare yourself before the actual work begins. Read through all the Sections relevant to the work to be carried out, then make a list and gather all the parts and tools required. If a problem is encountered, seek advice from a parts specialist, or a dealer service department.

2 Regular maintenance

1 If, from the time the car is new, the routine maintenance schedule is followed closely, and frequent checks are made of fluid levels and high-wear items, as suggested throughout this manual, the engine will be kept in relatively good running condition, and the need for additional work will be minimised.
2 It is possible that there will be times when the engine is running poorly due to the lack of regular maintenance. This is even more likely if a used car, which has not received regular and frequent maintenance checks, is purchased. In such cases, additional work may need to be carried out, outside of the regular maintenance intervals.
3 If engine wear is suspected, a compression test (refer to the relevant Part of Chapter 2) will provide valuable information regarding the overall performance of the main internal components. Such a test can be used as a basis to decide on the extent of the work to be carried out. If, for example, a compression test indicates serious internal engine wear, conventional maintenance as described in this Chapter will not greatly improve the performance of the engine, and may prove a waste of time and money, unless extensive overhaul work is carried out first.
4 The following series of operations are those most often required to improve the performance of a generally poor-running engine:

Primary operations

a) Clean, inspect and test the battery (See Weekly checks and Section 4).
b) Check all the engine-related fluids (See Weekly checks).
c) Check the condition and tension of the auxiliary drivebelt (Section 5).
d) Renew the spark plugs (Section 22).
e) Check the condition of the air filter, and renew if necessary (Section 23).
f) Renew the fuel filter (Section 28).
g) Check the condition of all hoses, and check for fluid leaks (Sections 7 and 15).

5 If the above operations do not prove fully effective, carry out the following secondary operations:

Secondary operations

All items listed under *Primary operations*, plus the following:
a) Check the charging system (Chapter 5A).
b) Check the ignition system (Chapter 5B).
c) Check the fuel system (see Chapter 4A).
d) Renew the ignition HT leads (see Chapter 5B).

Every 6250 miles or 6 months

3 Engine oil and filter renewal

1 Frequent oil changes are the most important preventive maintenance the DIY home mechanic can give the engine, because ageing oil becomes diluted and contaminated, which leads to premature engine wear.
2 Before starting this procedure, gather together all the necessary tools and materials. Also make sure that you have plenty of clean rags and newspapers handy, to mop-up any spills. Ideally, the engine oil should be warm, as it will drain more easily and more built-up sludge will be removed with it. Take care not to touch the exhaust or any other hot parts of the engine when working under the car. To avoid any possibility of scalding and to protect yourself from possible skin irritants and other harmful contaminants in used engine oils, it is advisable to wear gloves when carrying out this work.
3 Firmly apply the handbrake then jack up the front of the car and support it on axle stands (see *Jacking and vehicle support*). Where applicable, remove the engine undershield.
4 Remove the oil filler cap, then unscrew the engine oil drain plug (located at the rear of the sump) about half a turn. Position the draining container under the drain plug, then remove the plug completely – recover the sealing washer **(see illustration and Haynes Hint)**.
5 Allow some time for the oil to drain, noting that it may be necessary to reposition the container as the oil flow slows to a trickle.
6 After all the oil has drained, wipe off the drain plug with a clean rag, and fit a new sealing washer. Clean the area around the drain plug opening, and refit the plug. Tighten the plug to the specified torque.
7 Move the container into position under the oil filter, which is located on the front side of the cylinder block.

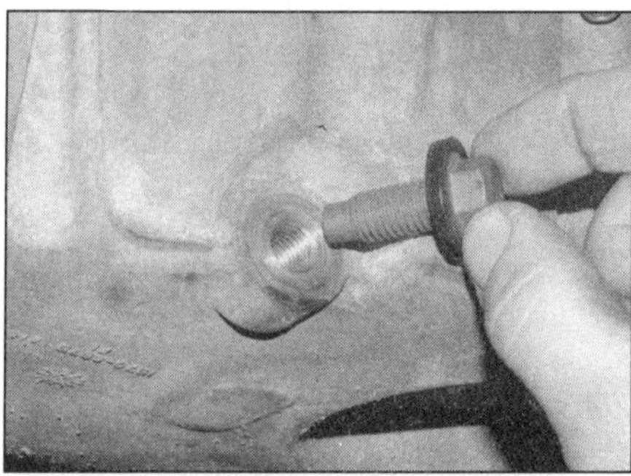

3.4 Removing the engine oil drain plug (2.0 litre engine)

HAYNES HiNT

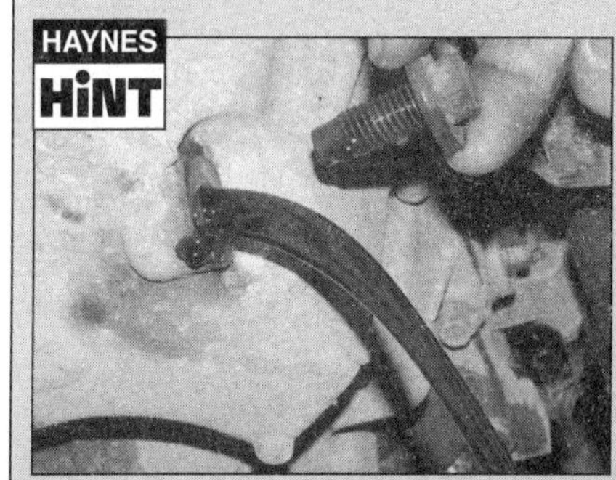

Keep the plug pressed into the sump while unscrewing it by hand the last couple of turns. As the plug releases from the threads, move it away sharply, so the stream of oil issuing from the sump runs into the pan, not up your sleeve.

3.8a Unscrew the oil filter plastic cover . . .

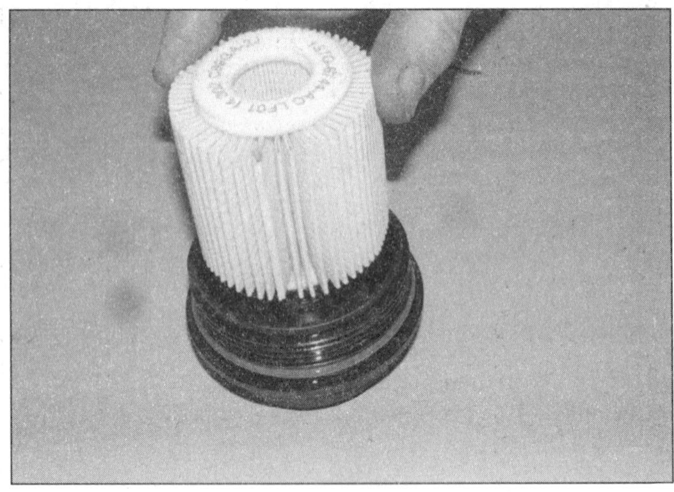

3.8b . . . then remove and discard the paper element (2.0 litre engine)

1.8 and 2.0 litre engines

8 Unscrew the oil filter plastic cover from the bottom of the oil filter housing, then remove and discard the paper element **(see illustrations)**.

9 Remove the O-ring seal and obtain a new one **(see illustration)**. Clean the filter housing and cover.

10 Fit the new O-ring seal onto the cover and lubricate it with a little engine oil **(see illustration)**.

11 Locate the new paper element on the cover, then screw the assembly into the filter housing and tighten securely by hand **(see illustration)**. Where necessary, refit the splash guard under the engine.

3.9 Removing the O-ring seal from the bottom cover (2.0 litre engine)

3.11 Oil filter location (2.0 litre engine)

V6 engines

12 Use an oil filter removal tool to slacken the filter initially, then unscrew it by hand the rest of the way **(see illustration)**. Empty the oil in the old filter into the container.

13 Use a clean rag to remove all oil, dirt and sludge from the filter sealing area on the engine. Check the old filter to make sure that the rubber sealing ring hasn't stuck to the engine. If it has, carefully remove it.

14 Apply a light coating of clean engine oil to the sealing ring on the new filter, then screw it into position on the engine **(see illustration)**. Tighten the filter firmly by hand only – **do not** use any tools. Where necessary, refit the splash guard under the engine.

3.10 Lubricate the new O-ring seal with a little engine oil (2.0 litre engine)

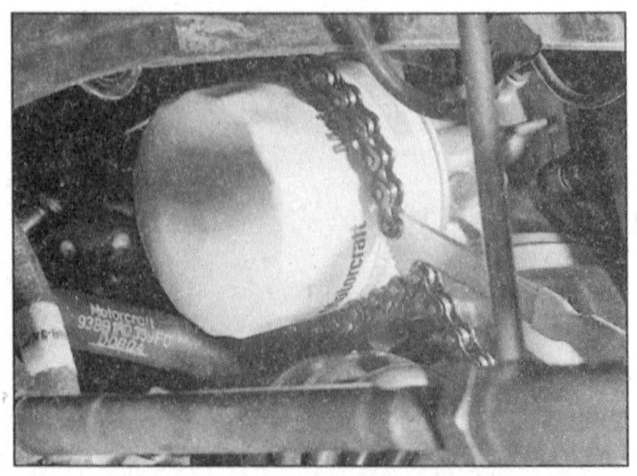

3.12 Using a chain-type wrench to remove the oil filter (V6 engine)

All engines

15 Remove the old oil and all tools from under the car, then lower the car to the ground.

16 Remove the dipstick, then unscrew the oil filler cap from the cylinder head cover. Fill the engine, using the correct grade and type of oil (see *Weekly checks*). An oil can spout or funnel may help to reduce spillage. Pour in half the specified quantity of oil first, then wait a few minutes for the oil to run to the sump. Continue adding oil a small quantity at a time until the level is up to the lower mark on the dipstick. Adding approximately 1.0 litre will bring the level up to the upper mark on the dipstick. Refit the filler cap.

17 Start the engine and run it for a few minutes; check for leaks. Note that there may be a delay of a few seconds before the oil pressure warning light goes out when the engine is first started, as the oil circulates through the engine oil galleries and the new oil filter before the pressure builds-up.

18 Switch off the engine, and wait a few minutes for the oil to settle in the sump once more. With the new oil circulated and the filter completely full, recheck the level on the dipstick, and add more oil as necessary.

19 Dispose of the used engine oil safely, with reference to *General Repair Procedures*.

3.14 Lubricate the filter's sealing ring with clean engine oil before installing the filter on the engine (V6 engine)

Every 12 500 miles or 12 months

4 Battery maintenance and charging

Warning: Certain precautions must be followed when checking and servicing the battery. Hydrogen gas, which is highly flammable, is always present in the battery cells, so keep lighted tobacco and all other open flames and sparks away from the battery. The electrolyte inside the battery is actually dilute sulphuric acid, which will cause injury if splashed on your skin or in your eyes. It will also ruin clothes and painted surfaces. When disconnecting the battery, always detach the negative (earth) lead first and connect it last.

Note: *Before disconnecting the battery, refer to Disconnecting the battery at the end of this manual.*

General

1 A routine preventive maintenance programme for the battery in your car is the only way to ensure quick and reliable starts. For general maintenance, refer to *Weekly checks* at the start of this manual. Also at the front of the manual is information on jump starting. For details of removing and installing the battery, refer to Chapter 5A.

Battery electrolyte level

2 On models not equipped with a sealed or 'maintenance-free' battery, check the electrolyte level of all six battery cells.

3 The level must be approximately 10 mm above the plates; this may be shown by maximum and minimum level lines marked on the battery's casing.

4 If the level is low, use a coin or screwdriver to release the filler/vent cap, and add distilled water. Do not overfill – this can actually render the battery useless. To improve access to the centre caps, it may be helpful to remove the battery hold-down clamp.

5 Install and securely retighten the cap, then wipe up any spillage.

Caution: Overfilling the cells may cause electrolyte to spill over during periods of heavy charging, causing corrosion or damage.

Charging

Warning: When batteries are being charged, hydrogen gas, which is very explosive and flammable, is produced. Do not smoke, or allow open flames, near a charging or a recently-charged battery. If the battery is being charged indoors, ensure this is done in a well-ventilated area. Wear eye protection when near the battery during charging. Also, make sure the charger is unplugged before connecting or disconnecting the battery from the charger.

6 Slow-rate charging is the best way to restore a battery that's discharged to the point where it will not start the engine. It's also a good way to maintain the battery charge in a car that's only driven a few miles between starts. Maintaining the battery charge is particularly important in winter, when the battery must work harder to start the engine, and electrical accessories that drain the battery are in greater use.

7 Check the battery case for any instructions regarding charging the battery. Some maintenance-free batteries may require a particularly low charge rate or other special conditions, if they are not to be damaged.

8 It's best to use a one- or two-amp battery charger (sometimes called a 'trickle' charger). They are the safest, and put the least strain on the battery. They are also the least expensive. For a faster charge, you can use a higher-amperage charger, but don't use one rated more than 1/10th the amp/hour rating of the battery (ie, no more than 5 amps, typically). Rapid boost charges that claim to restore the power of the battery in one to two hours are hardest on the battery, and can damage batteries not in good condition. This type of charging should only be used in emergency situations.

9 The average time necessary to charge a battery should be listed in the instructions that come with the charger. As a general rule, a trickle charger will charge a battery in 12 to 16 hours.

5 Auxiliary drivebelt check

General

1 The main auxiliary drivebelt is of flat, multi-ribbed type, and is located on the right-hand end of the engine. It drives the alternator, water pump (1.8 and 2.0 litre engines), power steering pump and the air conditioning compressor from the engine's crankshaft pulley **(see illustrations)**.

2 On V6 engine models, the water pump is driven by an additional drivebelt at the left-hand end of the engine. The belt is of the multi-ribbed type, and is driven by the front inlet camshaft.

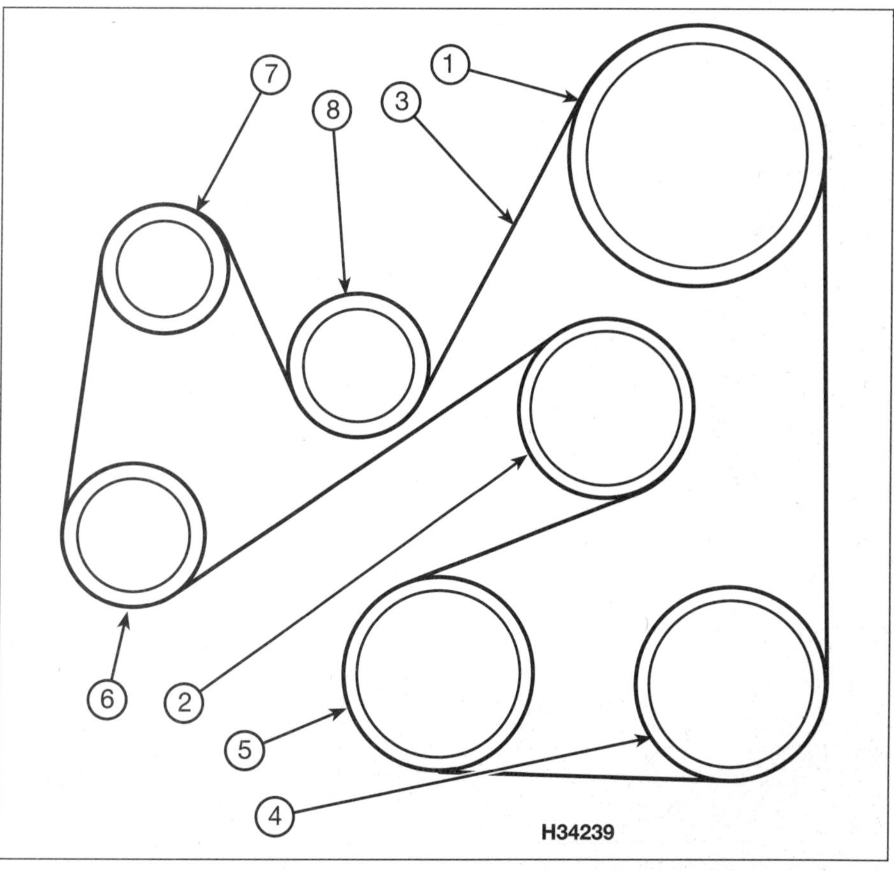

5.1a Auxiliary drivebelt routing (1.8 and 2.0 litre engines)

1 Power steering pump pulley
2 Water pump pulley
3 Auxiliary drivebelt
4 Air conditioning compressor pulley
5 Crankshaft pulley
6 Tensioner pulley
7 Alternator pulley
8 Idler pulley

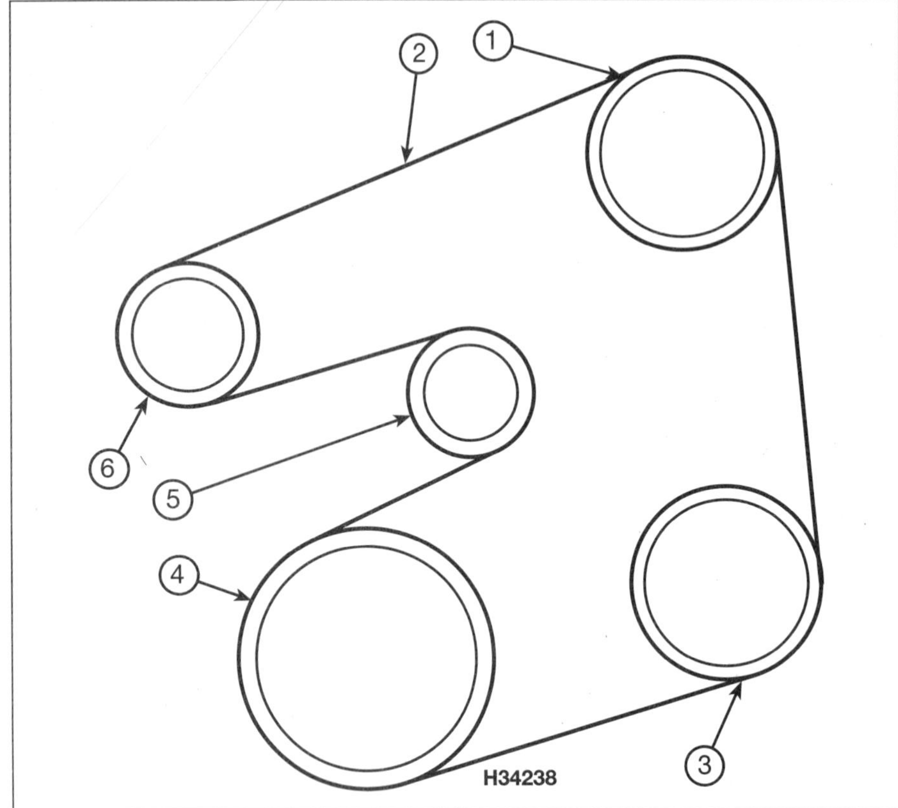

5.1b Auxiliary drivebelt routing (V6 engine)

1 Power steering pump pulley
2 Auxiliary drivebelt
3 Air conditioning compressor pulley
4 Crankshaft pulley
5 Tensioner pulley
6 Alternator pulley

3 The good condition and proper tension of the auxiliary drivebelt is critical to the operation of the engine. Because of their composition and the high stresses to which they are subjected, drivebelts stretch and deteriorate as they get older. They must, therefore, be regularly inspected.

Check

4 With the engine switched off, open and support the bonnet. For improved access to the right-hand end of the engine, first loosen the right-hand front wheel nuts, then jack up the front right-hand side of the car and support it securely on an axle stand (see *Jacking and vehicle support*). Remove the roadwheel, then remove the lower splash shield (three fasteners) from inside the wheel arch.

5 Using an inspection light or a small electric torch, and rotating the engine with a spanner applied to the crankshaft pulley bolt, check the whole length of the drivebelt for cracks, separation of the rubber, and torn or worn ribs. Also check for fraying and glazing, which gives the drivebelt a shiny appearance.

6 Both sides of the drivebelt should be inspected, which means you will have to twist the drivebelt to check the underside. Use your fingers to feel the drivebelt where you can't see it. If you are in any doubt as to the condition of the drivebelt, renew it as described in Section 30.

7 In addition on models with the V6 engine, remove the main cover (or the water pump drivebelt cover) from the top of the engine. Inspect the drivebelt as described in paragraphs 5 and 6.

Drivebelt tension

8 The auxiliary drivebelt is tensioned by an automatic tensioner – regular checks are not required, and manual 'adjustment' is not possible. The only exception is the water pump drivebelt on some V6 engine models – here, an 'elastic' drivebelt is used, with no tensioner.

9 If you suspect that the drivebelt is slipping and/or running slack, or that the tensioner is otherwise faulty, it must be renewed. Refer to Chapter 2A or 2B.

Drivebelt renewal

10 Refer to Section 30.

A leak in the cooling system will usually show up as white – or antifreeze-coloured deposits on the area adjoining the leak.

6 Electrical system check

1 Check the operation of all external lights and indicators (front and rear).

2 Check for satisfactory operation of the instrument panel, its illumination and warning lights, the switches and their function lights.

3 Check the horn(s) for satisfactory operation.

4 Check all other electrical equipment for satisfactory operation.

5 If a fault is suspected, all the main electrical accessories can be checked using the car's own GEM control module, as described in Chapter 12.

7 Underbonnet check for fluid leaks and hose condition

1 Visually inspect the engine joint faces, gaskets and seals for any signs of water or oil leaks. Pay particular attention to the areas around the cylinder head cover, cylinder head, oil filter and sump joint faces. Bear in mind that, over a period of time, some very slight seepage from these areas is to be expected – what you are really looking for is any indication of a serious leak. Should a leak be found, renew the offending gasket or oil seal by referring to the appropriate Chapters in this manual.

2 Also check the security and condition of all the engine-related pipes and hoses, and all braking system pipes and hoses and fuel lines. Ensure that all cable ties or securing clips are in place, and in good condition. Clips which are broken or missing can lead to chafing of the hoses, pipes or wiring, which could cause more serious problems in the future.

3 Carefully check the radiator hoses and heater hoses along their entire length. Renew any hose which is cracked, swollen or deteriorated. Cracks will show up better if the hose is squeezed. Pay close attention to the hose clips that secure the hoses to the cooling system components. Hose clips can pinch and puncture hoses, resulting in cooling system leaks. If the crimped-type hose clips are used, it may be a good idea to update them with Jubilee clips.

4 Inspect all the cooling system components (hoses, joint faces, etc) for leaks **(see Haynes Hint)**.

5 Where any problems are found on system components, renew the component or gasket with reference to Chapter 3.

6 With the car raised, inspect the fuel tank and filler neck for punctures, cracks and other damage. The connection between the filler neck and tank is especially critical. Sometimes a rubber filler neck or connecting hose will leak due to loose retaining clamps or deteriorated rubber.

7 Carefully check all rubber hoses and metal fuel lines leading away from the fuel tank. Check for loose connections, deteriorated hoses, crimped lines, and other damage. Pay particular attention to the vent pipes and hoses, which often loop up around the filler neck and can become blocked or crimped. Follow the lines to the front of the car, carefully inspecting them all the way. Renew damaged sections as necessary. Similarly, whilst the car is raised, take the opportunity to inspect all underbody brake fluid pipes and hoses.

8 From within the engine compartment, check the security of all fuel, vacuum and brake hose attachments and pipe unions, and inspect all hoses for kinks, chafing and deterioration.

9 Check the condition of the power steering and, where applicable, the automatic transmission fluid pipes and hoses.

8 Engine compartment wiring check

1 With the car parked on level ground, apply the handbrake firmly and open the bonnet. Using an inspection light or a small electric torch, check all visible wiring within and beneath the engine compartment.

2 What you are looking for is wiring that is obviously damaged by chafing against sharp edges, or against moving suspension/transmission components and/or the auxiliary drivebelt, by being trapped or crushed between carelessly-refitted components, or melted by being forced into contact with the hot engine castings, coolant pipes, etc. In almost all cases, damage of this sort is caused in the first instance by incorrect routing on reassembly after previous work has been carried out.

3 Depending on the extent of the problem, damaged wiring may be repaired by rejoining the break or splicing-in a new length of wire, using solder to ensure a good connection, and remaking the insulation with adhesive insulating tape or heat-shrink tubing, as appropriate. If the damage is extensive, given the implications for the car's future reliability, the best long-term answer may well be to renew that entire section of the loom, however expensive this may appear.

4 When the actual damage has been repaired, ensure that the wiring loom is rerouted correctly, so that it is clear of other components, and not stretched or kinked, and is secured out of harm's way using the plastic clips, guides and ties provided.

5 Check all electrical connectors, ensuring that they are clean, securely fastened, and that each is locked by its plastic tabs or wire clip, as appropriate. If any connector shows external signs of corrosion (accumulations of white or green deposits, or streaks of 'rust'), or if any is thought to be dirty, it must be unplugged and cleaned using electrical contact cleaner. If the connector pins are severely corroded, the connector must be renewed; note that this may mean the renewal of that entire section of the loom – see your local Ford dealer for details.

6 If the cleaner completely removes the corrosion to leave the connector in a satisfactory condition, it would be wise to pack the connector with a suitable material which will exclude dirt and moisture, preventing the corrosion from occurring again; a Ford dealer may be able to recommend a suitable product.

7 Check the condition of the battery connections – remake the connections or renew the leads if a fault is found (see Chapter 5A). Use the same techniques to ensure that all earth points in the engine compartment provide good electrical contact through clean, metal-to-metal joints, and that all are securely fastened.

9 Air conditioning system check

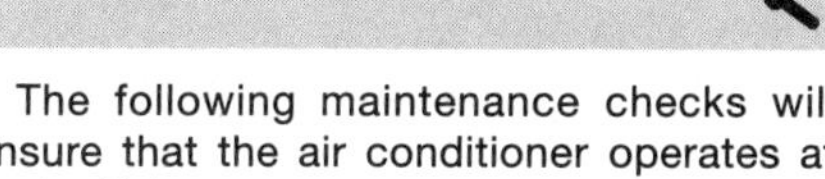

1 The following maintenance checks will ensure that the air conditioner operates at peak efficiency:

a) Check the auxiliary drivebelt (see Section 5).
b) Check the system hoses for damage or leaks.
c) Inspect the condenser fins for leaves, insects and other debris. Use a clean paint brush to clean the condenser. The condenser is mounted in front of the radiator.
d) Check that the drain tube from the front of the evaporator is clear – note that it is normal to have clear fluid (water) dripping from this while the system is in operation, to the extent that quite a large puddle can be left under the car when it is parked.

2 It's a good idea to operate the system for about 30 minutes at least once a month, particularly during the winter. Long term non-use can cause hardening, and subsequent failure, of the seals.

3 Because of the complexity of the air conditioning system and the special equipment necessary to service it, in-depth fault diagnosis and repairs are not included in this manual **(see Tool tip)**.

4 The most common cause of poor cooling is simply a low system refrigerant charge. If a noticeable drop in cool air output occurs, the following quick check will help you determine if the refrigerant level is low.

5 Warm the engine up to normal operating temperature.

6 Place the air conditioning temperature selector at the coldest setting, and put the blower at the highest setting. Open the doors – to make sure the air conditioning system doesn't cycle off as soon as it cools the passenger compartment.

7 With the compressor engaged – the clutch will make an audible click, and the centre of the clutch will rotate – feel the inlet and outlet pipes at the compressor. One side should be cold, and one hot. If there's no perceptible difference between the two pipes, there's something wrong with the compressor or the system. It might be a low charge – it might be something else. Take the car to a dealer service department or an automotive air conditioning specialist.

10 Seat belt check

1 Check the seat belts for satisfactory operation and condition. Inspect the webbing for fraying and cuts. Check that they retract smoothly and without binding into their reels.

2 Check that the seat belt mounting bolts are tight, and if necessary tighten them to the specified torque wrench setting (Chapter 11).

11 Antifreeze concentration check

1 The cooling system should be filled with the recommended antifreeze and corrosion protection fluid. Over a period of time, the concentration of fluid may be reduced due to topping-up (this can be avoided by topping-up with the correct antifreeze mixture) or fluid

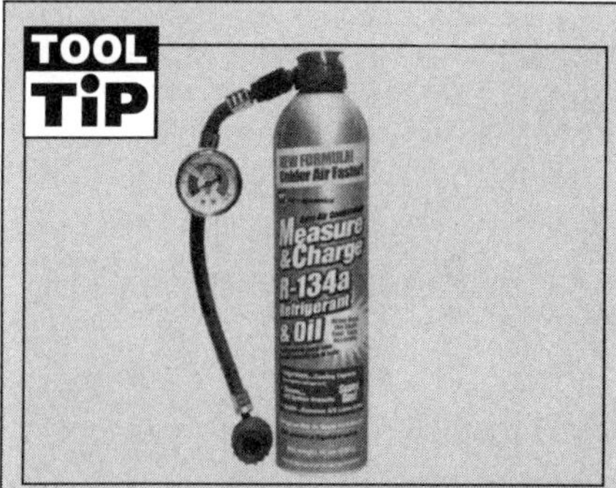

Many car accessory shops sell one-shot air conditioning recharge aerosols. These generally contain refrigerant, compressor oil, leak sealer and system conditioner. Some also have a dye to help pinpoint leaks.

Warning: These products must only be used as directed by the manufacturer, and do not remove the need for regular maintenance.

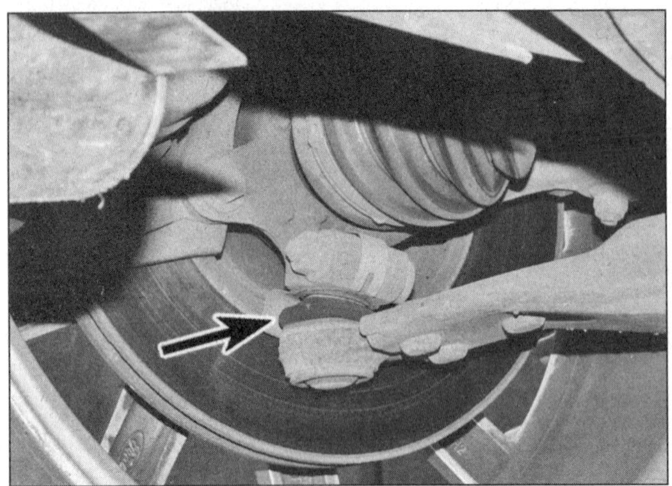

12.2a Check the balljoint dust covers . . .

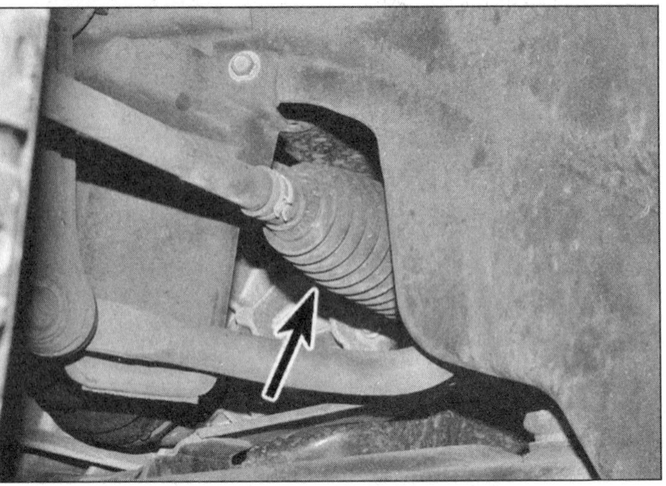

12.2b . . . and the steering rack gaiters for perishing and splits

loss. If loss of coolant has been evident, it is important to make the necessary repair before adding fresh fluid. The exact mixture of antifreeze-to-water which you should use depends on the relative weather conditions. The mixture should contain at least 40% antifreeze, but not more than 70%. Consult the mixture ratio chart on the antifreeze container before adding coolant. Use antifreeze which meets the car manufacturer's specifications.

2 With the engine **cold**, carefully remove the cap from the expansion tank. If the engine is not completely cold, place a cloth rag over the cap before removing it, and remove it slowly to allow any pressure to escape.

3 Antifreeze checkers are available from car accessory shops. Draw some coolant from the expansion tank and observe how many plastic balls are floating in the checker. Usually, 2 or 3 balls must be floating for the correct concentration of antifreeze, but follow the manufacturer's instructions.

4 If the concentration is incorrect, it will be necessary to either withdraw some coolant and add antifreeze, or alternatively drain the old coolant and add fresh coolant of the correct concentration.

12 Steering, suspension and roadwheel check

Front suspension and steering

1 Raise the front of the car, and securely support it on axle stands (see *Jacking and vehicle support*).

2 Visually inspect the balljoint dust covers and the steering rack-and-pinion gaiters for splits, chafing or deterioration **(see illustrations)**. Any wear of these components will cause loss of lubricant, together with dirt and water entry, resulting in rapid deterioration of the balljoints or steering gear.

3 Check the power steering fluid hoses for chafing or deterioration, and the pipe and hose unions for fluid leaks. Also check for signs of fluid leakage under pressure from the steering gear rubber gaiters, which would indicate failed fluid seals within the steering gear.

4 Grasp the roadwheel at the 12 o'clock and 6 o'clock positions, and try to rock it **(see illustration)**. Very slight free play may be felt, but if the movement is appreciable, further investigation is necessary to determine the source. Continue rocking the wheel while an assistant depresses the footbrake. If the movement is now eliminated or significantly reduced, it is likely that the hub bearings are at fault. If the free play is still evident with the footbrake depressed, then there is wear in the suspension joints or mountings.

HAYNES HiNT ***Wheel bearing wear is normally accompanied by a rumbling or droning noise when driving, at a certain speed, or when cornering. If play is found during the check in paragraph 4, with the car out of gear, spin the wheel several times by hand. Though it may be hard to distinguish wheel bearing noise from that of the driveshafts and brake pads, comparison with the other front wheel should reveal if the bearing is worn.***

5 Now grasp the wheel at the 9 o'clock and 3 o'clock positions, and try to rock it as before. Any movement felt now may again be caused by wear in the hub bearings or the steering track rod balljoints. If the outer balljoint is worn, the visual movement will be obvious. If the inner joint is suspect, it can be felt by placing a hand over the rack-and-pinion rubber gaiter and gripping the track rod. If the wheel is now rocked, movement will be felt at the inner joint if wear has taken place.

12.4 Checking for wear in the front suspension and hub bearings

6 Using a large screwdriver or flat bar, check for wear in the suspension mounting bushes by levering between the relevant suspension component and its attachment point. Some movement is to be expected, as the mountings are made of rubber, but excessive wear should be obvious. Also check the condition of any visible rubber bushes, looking for splits, cracks or contamination of the rubber.

7 With the car standing on its wheels, have an assistant turn the steering wheel back-and-forth, about an eighth of a turn each way. There should be very little, if any, lost movement between the steering wheel and roadwheels. If this is not the case, closely observe the joints and mountings previously described. In addition, check the steering column universal joints for wear, and also check the rack-and-pinion steering gear itself.

Rear suspension

8 Chock the front wheels, then jack up the rear of the car and support securely on axle stands (see *Jacking and vehicle support*).

9 Working as described previously for the front suspension, check the rear hub bearings, the suspension bushes and the strut or shock absorber mountings (as applicable) for wear.

Shock absorber

10 Check for any signs of fluid leakage around the shock absorber body, or from the rubber gaiter around the piston rod. Should any fluid be noticed, the shock absorber is defective internally, and should be renewed. **Note:** *Shock absorbers should always be renewed in pairs on the same axle.*

11 The efficiency of the shock absorber may be checked by bouncing the car at each corner. Generally speaking, the body will return to its normal position and stop after being depressed. If it rises and returns on a rebound, the shock absorber is probably suspect. Also examine the shock absorber upper and lower mountings for any signs of wear.

Roadwheels

12 Periodically remove the roadwheels, and clean any dirt or mud from the inside and outside surfaces. Examine the wheel rims for signs of rusting, corrosion or other damage. Light alloy wheels are easily damaged by 'kerbing' whilst parking, and similarly, steel wheels may become dented or buckled. Specialist firms do exist who will repair alloy wheels, but sometimes renewal of the wheel is the only course of remedial action possible.
13 The balance of each wheel and tyre assembly should be maintained, not only to avoid excessive tyre wear, but also to avoid wear in the steering and suspension components. Wheel imbalance is normally signified by vibration through the car's bodyshell, although in many cases it is particularly noticeable through the steering wheel. Conversely, it should be noted that wear or damage in suspension or steering components may cause excessive tyre wear. Out-of-round or out-of-true tyres, damaged wheels and wheel bearing wear/maladjustment also fall into this category. Balancing will not usually cure vibration caused by such wear.
14 Wheel balancing may be carried out with the wheel either on or off the car. If balanced on the car, ensure that the wheel-to-hub relationship is marked in some way prior to subsequent wheel removal, so that it may be refitted in its original position.
15 At this time, also check the spare wheel for damage.

13 Driveshaft rubber gaiter and CV joint check

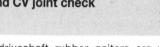

1 The driveshaft rubber gaiters are very important, because they prevent dirt, water and foreign material from entering and damaging the constant velocity (CV) joints. External contamination can cause the gaiter material to deteriorate prematurely, so it's a good idea to wash the gaiters with soap and water occasionally.
2 With the car raised and securely supported on axle stands, turn the steering onto full-lock, then slowly rotate each front wheel in turn. Inspect the condition of the outer constant velocity (CV) joint rubber gaiters, squeezing the gaiters to open out the folds **(see illustration)**. Check for signs of cracking, splits, or deterioration of the rubber, which may allow the escape of grease, and lead to the ingress of water and grit into the joint. Also check the security and condition of the retaining clips. Repeat these checks on the inner CV joints. If any damage or deterioration

13.2 Check the driveshaft gaiters by hand for cracks and/or leaking grease

is found, the gaiters should be renewed as described in Chapter 8.
3 At the same time, check the general condition of the outer CV joints themselves, by first holding the driveshaft and attempting to rotate the wheels. Repeat this check on the inner joints, by holding the inner joint yoke and attempting to rotate the driveshaft.
4 Any appreciable movement in the CV joint indicates wear in the joint, wear in the driveshaft splines, or a loose driveshaft retaining nut.

14 Exhaust system check

1 With the engine cold, check the complete exhaust system, from its starting point at the engine to the end of the tailpipe. If necessary, raise the front and rear of the car and support it on axle stands (see *Jacking and vehicle support*). Remove any engine undershields as necessary for full access to the exhaust system.
2 Check the exhaust pipes and connections for evidence of leaks, severe corrosion, and damage **(see illustration)**. Make sure that all brackets and mountings are in good condition and that all relevant nuts and bolts are tight. Leakage at any of the joints or in other parts of the system will usually show up as a black sooty stain in the vicinity of the leak.
3 Rattles and other noises can often be traced to the exhaust system, especially the brackets and rubber mountings **(see illustration)**. Don't overlook loose exhaust heat shields either, or the

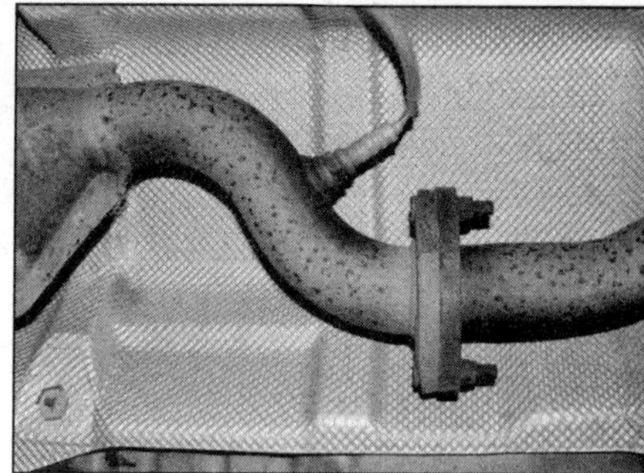

14.2 Check the condition of the exhaust system

possibility that the internal baffles in a silencer box may be the source of a rattle. Try to move the pipes and silencers. If the components are able to come into contact with the body or suspension parts, secure the system with new mountings. Otherwise, separate the joints (if possible) and twist the pipes as necessary to provide additional clearance.

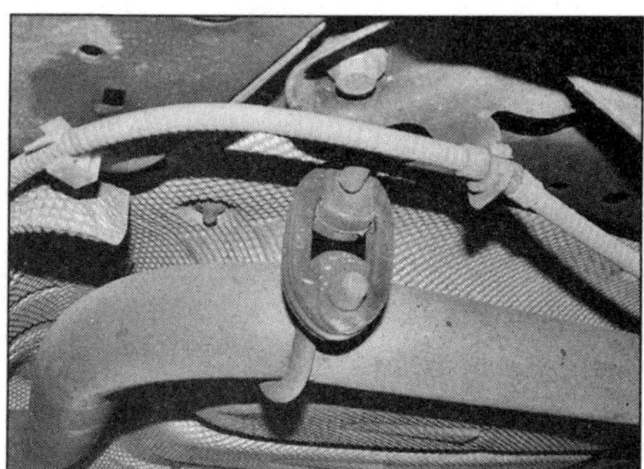

14.3 Don't overlook the exhaust rubber mountings and heat shields

15 Underbody and fuel/brake line check

1 With the car raised and supported on axle stands (see *Jacking and vehicle support*), thoroughly inspect the underbody and wheel arches for signs of damage and corrosion. In particular, examine the bottom of the side sills, and any concealed areas where mud can collect. Also check the inside edges at the base of all doors.
2 Where corrosion and rust is evident, press and tap firmly on the panel with a screwdriver, and check for any serious corrosion which would necessitate repairs.
3 If the panel is not seriously corroded, clean away the rust, and apply a new coating of underseal. Refer to Chapter 11 for more details of body repairs.
4 At the same time, inspect the PVC-coated lower body panels for stone damage and general condition.
5 Inspect all of the fuel and brake lines on the underbody for damage, rust, corrosion and leakage. Particularly check the rear brake pipes where they pass over the fuel tank.

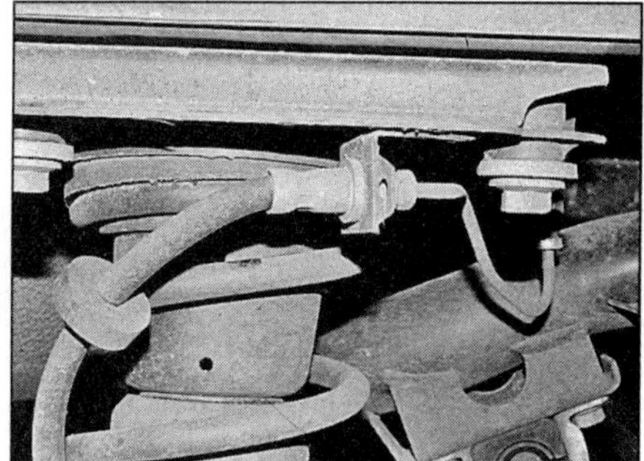

15.5 Check the brake pipes and hoses for condition and security

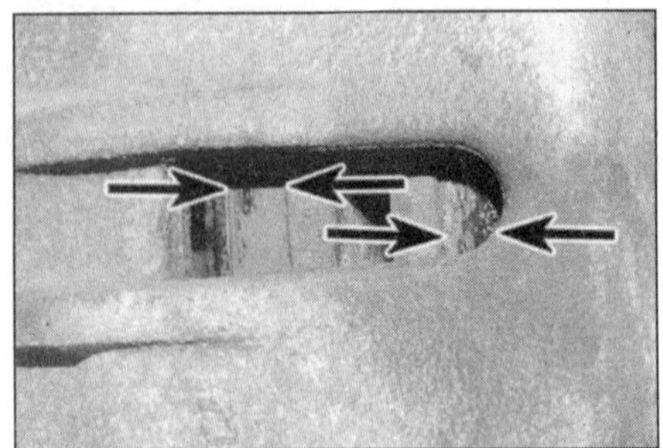

16.2 Check the thickness of the pad friction material through the caliper inspection window

Also make sure that the pipes are correctly supported in their clips **(see illustration)**. Where applicable, check the PVC coating on the lines for damage.

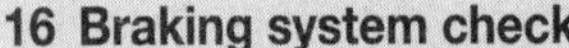

16 Braking system check

Front disc brakes

1 Apply the handbrake, then jack up the front of the car and support it on axle stands (see *Jacking and vehicle support*). For better access to the brake calipers, remove the wheels.

2 Look through the inspection window in the caliper, and check that the thickness of the friction lining material on each of the pads is not less than the recommended minimum thickness given in the Specifications **(see illustration)**.

3 If it is difficult to determine the exact thickness of the pad linings, or if you are at all concerned about the condition of the pads, then remove them from the calipers for further inspection (refer to Chapter 9) **(see illustration)**.

4 Check the caliper on the other side in the same way.

5 If any one of the brake pads has worn down to, or below, the specified limit, *all four* pads at that end of the car must be renewed as a set.

6 Check both front brake discs with reference to Chapter 9.

7 Before refitting the wheels, check all brake lines and flexible hoses with reference to Chapter 9. In particular, check the flexible hoses in the vicinity of the calipers, where they are subjected to most movement. Bend them between the fingers and check that this does not reveal previously-hidden cracks, cuts or splits **(see illustration)**.

8 On completion, refit the wheels and lower the car to the ground. Tighten the wheel nuts to the specified torque.

18.8a Remove the three screws in front of the passenger-side cowl . . .

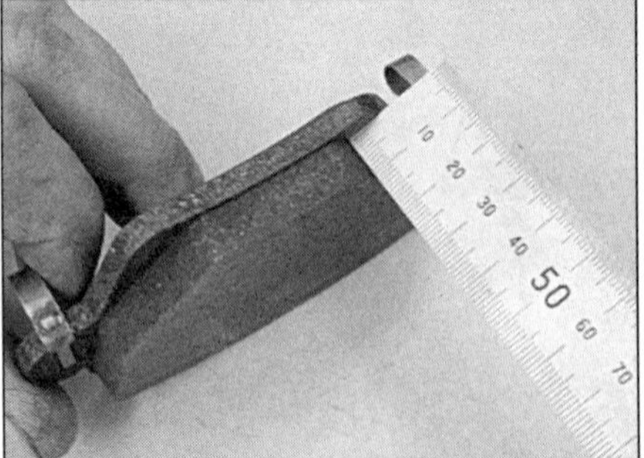

16.3 Checking the thickness of the pad linings with a steel rule

Rear disc brakes

9 Chock the front wheels, then jack up the rear of the car and support on axle stands (see *Jacking and vehicle support*). Remove the rear wheels.

10 The procedure for checking the rear brakes is much the same as described in paragraphs 1 to 8 above.

Handbrake

11 With the car on a slight slope, firmly apply the handbrake lever, and check that it holds the car stationary, then release the lever and check that there is no resistance to movement of the car. If necessary, the handbrake should be adjusted as described in Chapter 9.

17 Door and bonnet check and lubrication

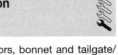

1 Check that the doors, bonnet and tailgate/boot lid close securely. Check that the bonnet safety catch operates correctly. Check the operation of the door check straps.

2 Lubricate the hinges, door check straps, the striker plates and the bonnet catch sparingly with a little oil or grease.

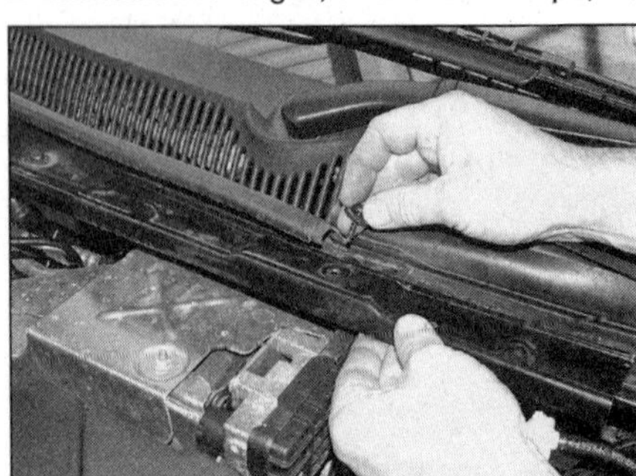

18.8b . . . noting that one of them retains the cowl heat shield

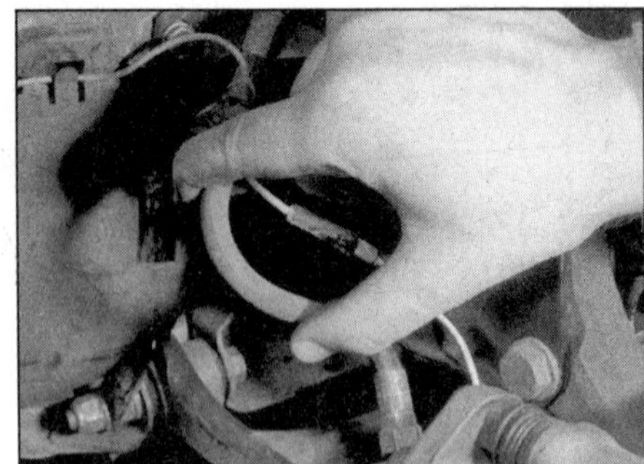

16.7 Checking the condition of a flexible brake hose

18 Pollen filter renewal

1 The air entering the car's ventilation system is passed through a very fine pleated-paper air filter element, which removes particles of pollen, dust and other airborne foreign matter. To ensure its continued effectiveness, this filter's element must be renewed at regular intervals. Failure to renew the element will also result in reduced airflow into the passenger compartment, reducing demisting and ventilation.

2 There are two ways to access the pollen filter for removal. The first method is that recommended by Ford, and is arguably safer. However, we found that the second method also worked fine, when tried on our project cars.

Method 1

3 Remove the windscreen wiper arms as described in Chapter 12.

4 Open the bonnet. Remove a total of five screws, and take off the central joining plate in front of the two windscreen cowl sections. Unclip and remove both the cowl sections from in front of the windscreen, noting that they locate into a grooved strip fitted to the bottom of the windscreen glass.

5 Press and release the two upper retaining clips (where applicable – on later models, the filter appears not to be clipped in place) and withdraw the pollen filter from its housing.

6 Wipe clean the housing, then insert the new filter, observing any direction-of-fitting arrows (arrows indicating airflow should point into the car, ie, rearwards). Check that the clips (where applicable) are correctly engaged.

7 Refit the cowl sections, then refit the wiper arms with reference to Chapter 12.

Method 2

8 With the bonnet open, remove three screws from in front of the passenger-side windscreen cowl. Note that the central screw also retains the cowl's metal heat shield – lift off the heat shield, noting how it fits **(see illustrations)**.

9 The passenger-side cowl must now be lifted upwards at its outer end, to release its locating bead from the grooved strip which is clipped under the base of the windscreen glass **(see illustration)**. With care, if necessary, a small flat-bladed screwdriver can be used to gently prise the cowl's bead upwards – once it has started, it should release along its length as the panel is pulled up. The bead is continuous along the whole length of the cowl panel.
10 When the cowl panel's locating bead is nearly free, slide the panel to the side, to unclip the inner end from the driver's-side cowl panel. It should now be possible to remove the panel completely, for access to the pollen filter **(see illustration)**.
11 Press and release the two upper retaining clips (where applicable – on later models, the filter appears not to be clipped in place) and withdraw the pollen filter from its housing **(see illustration)**.
12 Wipe clean the housing, then insert the new filter, observing any direction-of-fitting arrows (arrows indicating airflow should point into the car, ie, rearwards) **(see illustration)**. Check that the upper clips (where applicable) are correctly engaged.
13 Offer the cowl panel back into place, clipping it first into the driver's-side cowl panel at the inner end. The panel must now be positioned so that its locating bead sits into the groove at the base of the windscreen – this may require some trial-and-error before it fits correctly. The panel may also have to be pressed down gently along its length, to locate the bead into the groove – force should not be used this close to the windscreen glass, obviously.
14 Finally, refit the heat shield at the front of the two cowls, and secure it and the passenger-side cowl with the three screws. Close the bonnet on completion.

19 Roadwheel nut tightness check

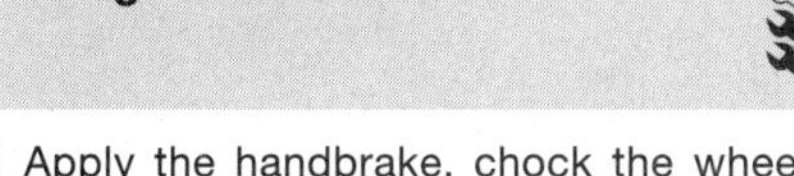

1 Apply the handbrake, chock the wheels, and engage 1st gear (or P).
2 If necessary to gain access to the nuts, remove the wheel cover (or wheel centre cover), using the flat end of the wheelbrace supplied in the tool kit.
3 Check the tightness of all wheel nuts using a torque wrench (refer to the Specifications).

20 Road test

Instruments and electrical equipment

1 Check the operation of all instruments and electrical equipment.

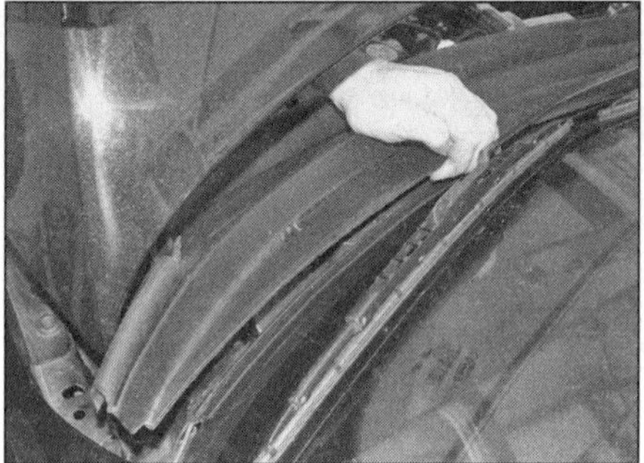

18.9 Lift the cowl panel up at the outer end . . .

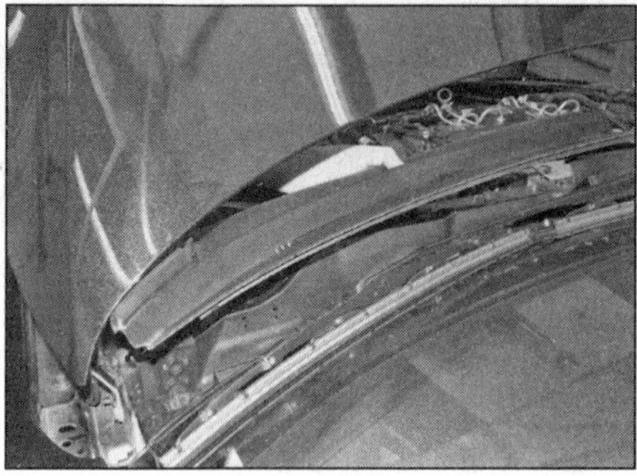

18.10 . . . then separate it in the centre, and remove it

2 Make sure that all instruments read correctly, and switch on all electrical equipment in turn, to check that it functions properly.

Steering and suspension

3 Check for any abnormalities in the steering, suspension, handling or road 'feel'.
4 Drive the car, and check that there are no unusual vibrations or noises.
5 Check that the steering feels positive, with no excessive 'sloppiness', or roughness, and check for any suspension noises when cornering and driving over bumps.

Drivetrain

6 Check the performance of the engine, clutch, transmission and driveshafts.
7 Listen for any unusual noises from the engine, clutch and transmission.
8 Make sure that the engine runs smoothly when idling, and that there is no hesitation when accelerating.
9 Check that, where applicable, the clutch action is smooth and progressive, that the drive is taken up smoothly, and that the pedal travel is not excessive. Also listen for any noises when the clutch pedal is depressed.
10 Check that all gears can be engaged smoothly without noise, and that the gear lever action is smooth and not abnormally vague or 'notchy'.
11 On automatic transmission models, make sure that all gearchanges occur smoothly, without snatching, and without an increase in engine speed between changes. Check that all of the gear positions can be selected with the car at rest.
12 Listen for a metallic clicking sound from the front of the car, as the car is driven slowly in a circle with the steering on full-lock. Carry out this check in both directions. If a clicking noise is heard, this indicates wear in a driveshaft joint (see Chapter 8).

Braking system

13 Make sure that the car does not pull to one side when braking, and that the wheels do not lock when braking hard.
14 Check that there is no vibration through the steering when braking.
15 Check that the handbrake operates correctly, without excessive movement of the lever, and that it holds the car stationary on a slope.
16 Test the operation of the brake servo unit as follows. Depress the footbrake four or five times to exhaust the vacuum, then start the engine. As the engine starts, there should be a noticeable 'give' in the brake pedal as vacuum builds-up. Allow the engine to run for at least two minutes, and then switch it off. If the brake pedal is now depressed again, it should be possible to detect a hiss from the servo as the pedal is depressed. After about four or five applications, no further hissing should be heard, and the pedal should feel considerably harder.

18.11 Removing the pollen filter

18.12 Pollen filter correctly fitted

Every 25 000 miles or 2 years

21 Automatic transmission fluid level check

4-speed transmission

1 The level of the automatic transmission fluid should be carefully maintained. Low fluid level can lead to slipping or loss of drive, while overfilling can cause foaming, loss of fluid and transmission damage.

2 The transmission fluid level should only be checked when the transmission is hot (at its normal operating temperature). If the car has just been driven over 10 miles (15 miles in cold weather), the transmission is hot. **Note:** *If the car has just been driven for a long time at high speed or in city traffic in hot weather, or if it has been pulling a trailer, an accurate fluid level reading cannot be obtained. In these circumstances, allow the fluid to cool down for about 30 minutes.*

3 Park the car on level ground, apply the handbrake firmly, and start the engine. While the engine is idling, depress the brake pedal and move the selector lever through all the positions three times, beginning and ending in P.

21.4 Removing the automatic transmission dipstick from its tube (4-speed)

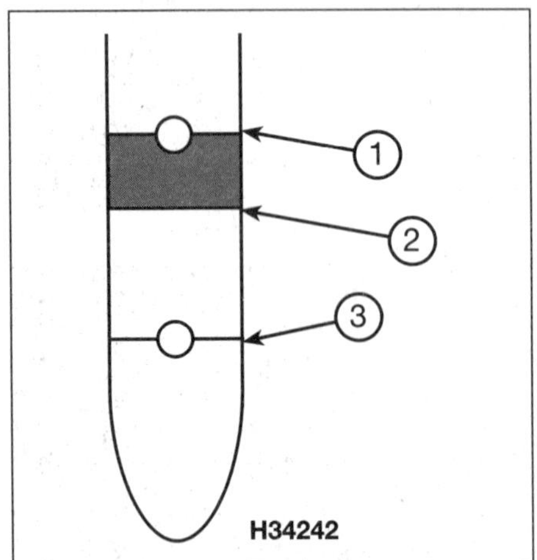

21.6 Transmission fluid dipstick MIN and MAX marks (4-speed)

1 MAX mark
2 MIN mark
3 Lower hole mark (DO NOT DRIVE)

4 Allow the engine to idle, and remove the dipstick from its tube **(see illustration)**. Note the condition and colour of the fluid on the dipstick.

5 Wipe the fluid from the dipstick with a clean rag, and re-insert it into the filler tube until the cap seats.

6 Pull out the dipstick again, and note the fluid level. The level should be between the MIN and MAX marks **(see illustration)**.

7 If the level is on the MIN mark, stop the engine, and add the specified automatic transmission fluid through the dipstick tube, using a clean funnel if necessary **(see illustration)**. It is important not to introduce dirt into the transmission when topping-up.

8 Add the fluid a little at a time, and keep checking the level as previously described until it is correct.

9 The need for regular topping-up of the transmission fluid indicates a leak, which should be found and rectified without delay.

10 The condition of the fluid should also be checked along with the level. If the fluid at the end of the dipstick is black or a dark reddish-brown colour, or if it has a burned smell, the fluid should be changed. If you are in doubt about the condition of the fluid, purchase some new fluid, and compare the two for colour and smell.

5-speed transmission

11 To accurately check the fluid level, a Ford diagnostic tool is necessary to verify the fluid temperature. The DIY mechanic who does not have access to this tool can use the alternative procedure given later, but the fluid level should then be checked by a Ford dealer at the earliest opportunity afterwards.

With diagnostic tool

12 First connect the tool to the diagnostic socket – the transmission fluid temperature must initially be below 30°C.

13 Apply the handbrake firmly, then jack up the front of the car and support it on axle stands (see *Jacking and vehicle support*). Remove the three bolts and take off the selector lever cable cover for access to the test plug, then lower the car to the ground.

21.7 Adding automatic transmission fluid through the dipstick tube (4-speed)

14 Start the engine. While the engine is idling, depress the brake pedal and move the selector lever through all the positions three times, beginning and ending in P. Leave the engine idling until while the fluid level is being checked.

15 When the fluid temperature reaches 30°C, move the selector lever from P to D, and back again to P.

16 With the handbrake still firmly applied, jack up the front and rear of the car and support it securely on axle stands (see *Jacking and vehicle support*). **Note:** *The car must be level for an accurate check, and the car must be supported securely, as the engine will have to be running.*

17 Check that the fluid temperature is between 35°C and 45°C.

18 Position a suitable container beneath the transmission, then unscrew and remove the test plug **(see illustration)**. The test plug is located in the middle of the drain plug, and incorporates a tube extension to the fluid level height inside the transmission. Remove and discard the plug seal.

Caution: Wear suitable gloves as protection against scalding.

19 If no fluid escapes from the test plug, unscrew the filler plug from the top of the transmission and add fresh fluid until it emerges from the test hole. When the fluid ceases to drain, the level is correct.

20 Refit the filler and test plugs together with new seals and tighten to the specified torque. Refit the selector lever cable cover and tighten the bolts to the specified torque.

21 Switch off the engine and lower the car to the ground.

22 Disconnect the diagnostic tool.

Without diagnostic tool

23 To check the fluid level with any degree of accuracy, the fluid must be at operating temperature. One way to achieve this would be to take the car on a short journey (of say 5 to 10 miles) – however, this should not be attempted if the fluid level is known to be low, as damage could be caused.

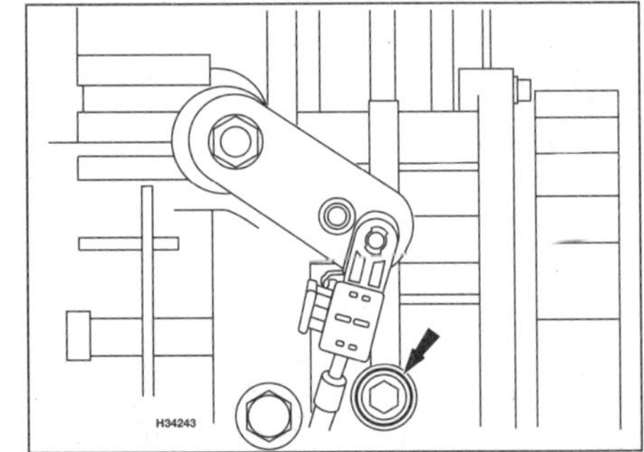

21.18 Test plug (5-speed)

24 Apply the handbrake firmly, then jack up the front of the car and support it securely on axle stands (see *Jacking and vehicle support*). **Note:** *The car must be level for an accurate check, and the car must be supported securely, as the engine will have to be running.*

25 Unbolt the selector lever cable cover for access to the test plug.

26 While the engine is idling, depress the brake pedal and move the selector lever through all the positions three times, beginning and ending in P. Leave the engine idling until while the fluid level is being checked.

27 Finally, press the brake pedal, and move the selector lever from P to D, and back again to P.

28 Position a suitable container beneath the transmission, then unscrew and remove the test plug. The test plug is located in the middle of the drain plug, and incorporates a tube extension to the fluid level height inside the transmission. Remove and discard the plug seal.

Caution: Wear suitable gloves as protection against scalding.

29 If no fluid escapes from the test plug, unscrew the filler plug from the top of the transmission and add fresh fluid until it emerges from the test hole. When the fluid ceases to drain, the level is correct.

30 Refit the filler and test plugs together with new seals and tighten to the specified torque. Refit the selector lever cable cover and tighten the bolts to the specified torque.

31 Switch off the engine and lower the car to the ground.

32 It is advisable to have the fluid level finally confirmed by a Ford dealer, using the diagnostic tool, at the earliest opportunity.

Every 37 500 miles or 3 years

22 Spark plug renewal

1 The correct functioning of the spark plugs is vital for the correct running and efficiency of the engine. It is essential that the plugs fitted are appropriate for the engine; suitable types are specified at the beginning of this Chapter, or in the car's Owner's Handbook. If the correct type is used and the engine is in good condition, the spark plugs should not need attention between scheduled renewal intervals. Spark plug cleaning is rarely necessary, and should not be attempted unless specialised equipment is available, as damage can easily be caused to the firing ends.

2 Remove the engine top cover, with reference to Chapter 2A or 2B if necessary **(see illustration)**.

3 On V6 models, carry out the following:

a) *Remove the water pump drivebelt cover from the transmission end of the engine – the cover is secured by three bolts.*
b) *Remove the upper section of the inlet manifold as described in Chapter 2B.*
c) *To gain access to the plugs on the front bank of cylinders, unscrew the retaining bolts from the Inlet Manifold Runner Control (IMRC) motor. Place the motor out of the way – there is no need to disconnect the wiring or operating cable.*
d) *The spark plugs are numbered from the timing chain end of the engine – 1 to 3 along the rear bank, and 4 to 6 along the front.*

4 Carefully disconnect the HT leads from the spark plugs **(see illustration)**. The original leads are marked for position, however, if they have been previously renewed, mark them to correspond to the cylinder the lead serves.

5 Unscrew the spark plugs from the cylinder head using a spark plug spanner, suitable box spanner or a deep socket and extension bar **(see illustrations)**. Keep the socket aligned with the spark plug – if it is forcibly moved to one side, the ceramic insulator may be broken off.

6 Examination of the spark plugs will give a good indication of the condition of the engine. As each plug is removed, examine it as follows.

7 If the insulator nose of the spark plug is clean and white, with no deposits, this is indicative of a weak mixture or too hot a plug (a hot plug transfers heat away from the electrode slowly, a cold plug transfers heat away quickly).

8 If the tip and insulator nose are covered with hard black-looking deposits, then this is indicative that the mixture is too rich. Should the plug be black and oily, then it is likely that the engine is fairly worn, as well as the mixture being too rich. If the insulator nose is covered with light tan to greyish-brown deposits, then the mixture is correct and it is likely that the engine is in good condition.

9 Where multi-electrode plugs are fitted, the electrode gaps are all preset, and **no** attempt should be made to bend the electrodes – fit the plugs straight out of the packet.

10 If standard single-electrode plugs are fitted, the spark plug electrode gap is of considerable importance. If the gap is too large or too small, the size of the spark and its efficiency will be seriously impaired and it will not perform correctly under all engine speed and load conditions. The gap should be set to the value specified by the manufacturer.

11 To set the gap, measure it with a feeler blade or spark plug gap gauge and then carefully bend the outer plug electrode until

22.2 Removing the engine top cover (2.0 litre engine)

22.4 Disconnecting the HT leads from the spark plugs

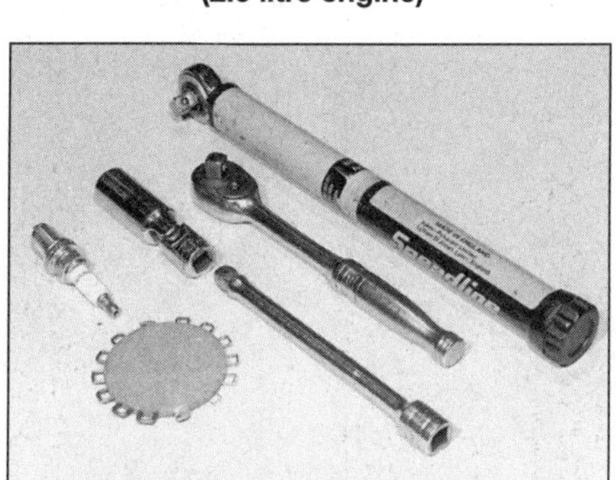

22.5a Tools required for spark plug removal, gap adjustment and refitting

22.5b Removing the spark plugs

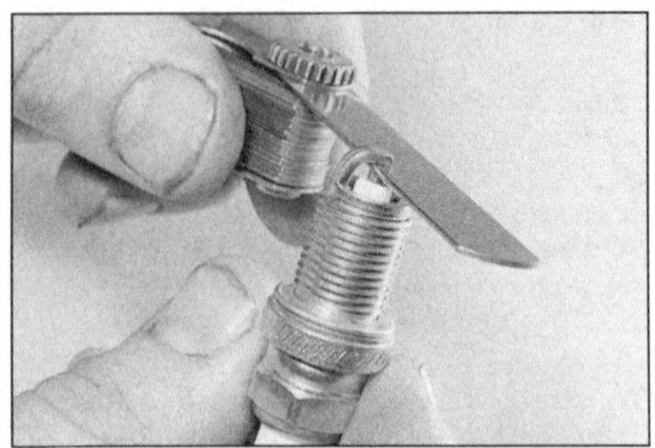
22.11a If single-electrode plugs are being fitted, check the electrode gap using a feeler gauge . . .

22.11b . . . or a wire gauge . . .

22.12 . . . and if necessary adjust the gap by bending the electrode

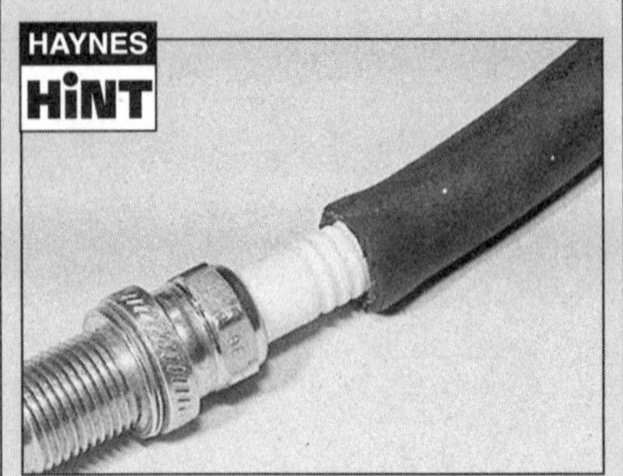
HAYNES HiNT

It is very often difficult to insert spark plugs into their holes without cross-threading them. To avoid this possibility, fit a short length of rubber hose over the end of the spark plug. The flexible hose acts as a universal joint to help align the plug with the plug hole. Should the plug begin to cross-thread, the hose will slip on the spark plug, preventing thread damage to the aluminium cylinder head.

the correct gap is achieved. The centre electrode should never be bent, as this may crack the insulator and cause plug failure, if nothing worse. If using feeler blades, the gap is correct when the appropriate-size blade is a firm sliding fit **(see illustrations)**.

23.1a Air cleaner assembly location (V6 engine)

12 Special spark plug electrode gap adjusting tools are available from most motor accessory shops, or from some spark plug manufacturers **(see illustration).**

13 Before fitting the spark plugs, check that the threaded connector sleeves are tight, and that the plug exterior surfaces and threads are clean **(see Haynes Hint)**.

14 Remove the rubber hose (if used), and tighten the plug to the specified torque using the spark plug socket and a torque wrench. Refit the remaining spark plugs in the same manner.

15 Connect the HT leads to the spark plugs in their correct order.

16 On completion, refit the engine top cover.

23 Air filter element renewal

1 The air filter element is located in the air cleaner assembly on the left-hand side of the engine compartment, behind the battery. Undo the screws and lift up the air cleaner cover **(see illustrations)**.

2 If additional working clearance is required, remove the cover completely; on 1.8 and 2.0 litre models, unclip the cover from the air mass meter, while on the V6 engines, slacken the air inlet hose clip and detach it from the air mass meter.

3 Lift out the element, noting its direction of fitting, and wipe out the housing **(see illustration)**.

4 If carrying out a routine service, the element must be renewed regardless of its apparent condition.

5 On four-cylinder engine models, note that the small foam filter in the rear right-hand corner of the air cleaner housing must be cleaned whenever the air filter element is renewed.

6 If you are checking the element for any other reason, inspect its lower surface; if it is oily or very dirty, renew the element. If it is only moderately dusty, it can be re-used by blowing it clean with compressed air.

23.1b Undo the screws and lift the cover . . .

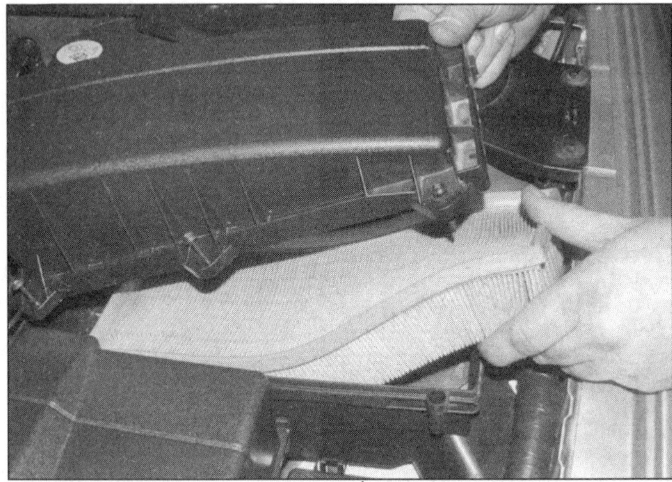
23.3 . . . then remove the air filter element

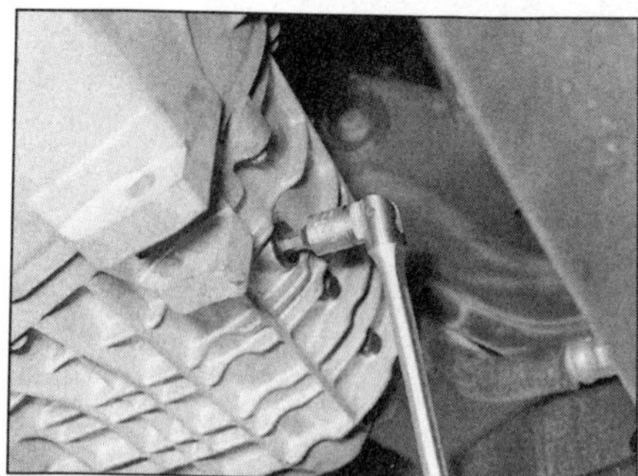

24.3a Using a suitable Allen key or socket, unscrew . . .

7 Fit the new element using a reversal of the removal procedure.

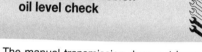

24 Manual transmission oil level check

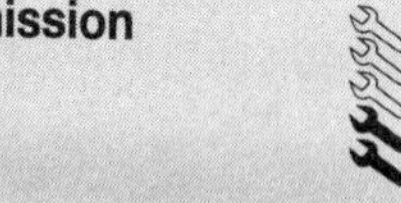

1 The manual transmission does not have a dipstick. To check the oil level, raise the car and support it securely on axle stands, making sure that the car is level.

2 Remove the engine undershields as necessary for access.

3 On 5-speed models, the filler/level plug is located on the lower front side of the transmission housing, while 6-speed models have the plug at the rear, behind the left-hand driveshaft. Using a suitable Allen key or socket, unscrew and remove it – take care, as it will probably be very tight **(see illustrations)**.

4 If the lubricant level is correct, the oil should be up to the lower edge of the hole.

5 If the transmission needs more lubricant (if the oil level is not up to the hole), use a syringe, or a plastic bottle and tube, to add more **(see illustration)**.

6 Stop filling the transmission when the lubricant begins to run out of the hole, then wait until the flow of oil ceases.

7 Refit the filler/level plug, and tighten it to the specified torque wrench setting. Drive the car a short distance, then check for leaks.

8 A need for regular topping-up can only be due to a leak, which should be found and rectified without delay.

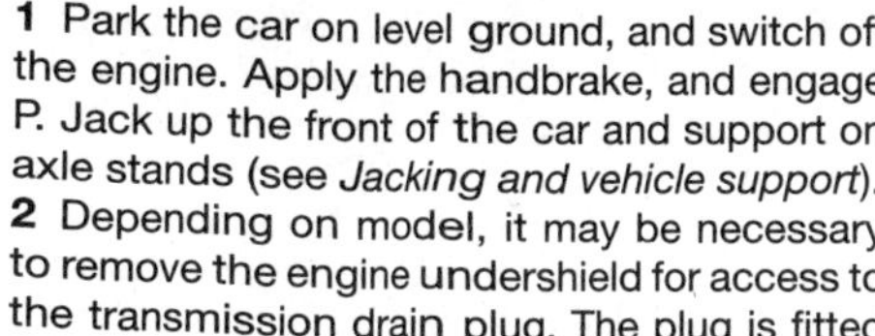

25 Automatic transmission fluid renewal

1 Park the car on level ground, and switch off the engine. Apply the handbrake, and engage P. Jack up the front of the car and support on axle stands (see *Jacking and vehicle support*).

2 Depending on model, it may be necessary to remove the engine undershield for access to the transmission drain plug. The plug is fitted on the base of the transmission housing.

4-speed transmission

3 Remove the transmission fluid dipstick.

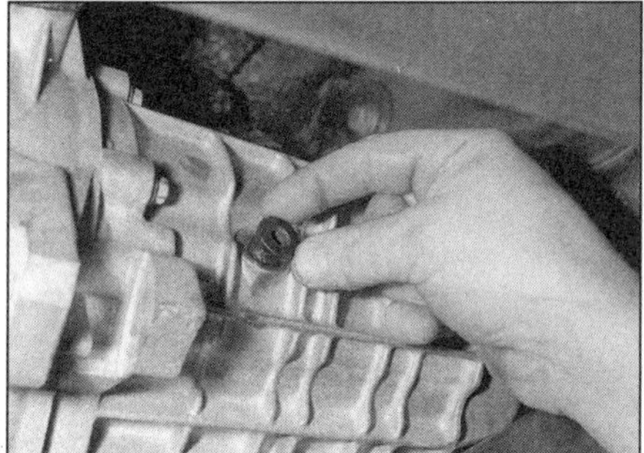

24.3b . . . and remove the transmission oil filler/level plug (5-speed)

4 Taking adequate precautions against burning or scalding if the engine and transmission are hot (wear gloves), position a suitable container below the transmission drain plug.

5 Loosen and remove the drain plug **(see illustration)**, and allow the fluid to drain into the container.

6 Clean the drain plug thoroughly, then when the flow of fluid has ceased, refit the plug and tighten it to the specified torque.

7 Remove the fluid container from under the car.

8 The transmission is filled through the dipstick tube. Use a narrow funnel, and take great care to avoid introducing any kind of dirt into the transmission as it is filled.

9 After about half the specified 'drain and refill' quantity of fluid has been added, refer to Section 21 and complete the level checking procedure.

10 Refit the engine undershield (where removed), then lower the car to the ground.

5-speed transmission

Note: *No fluid dipstick is fitted to this transmission, and the fluid level can only be accurately checked using a special Ford diagnostic tool which monitors the fluid temperature. However, the DIY mechanic can perform an adequate level check, provided the car can be driven to get the fluid up to temperature. Clearly, the car should not be driven with an unknown amount of transmission fluid, as damage may be caused. For this reason, the fluid drained should be stored, and the amount carefully measured, so that the same amount of fresh fluid can be used when refilling.*

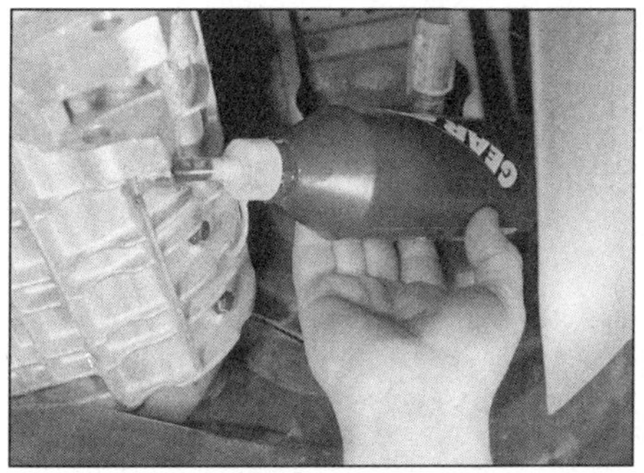

24.5 Topping-up the manual transmission oil (5-speed)

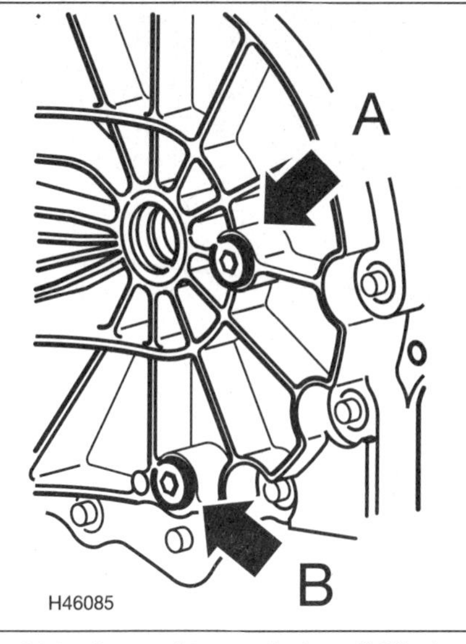

24.3c 6-speed transmission oil filler/level (A) and drain (B) plug locations

11 Taking adequate precautions against burning or scalding if the engine and transmission are hot (wear gloves), position a suitable container below the transmission drain plug. Take care that as little fluid as possible is lost when draining – see the note above.

12 Loosen and remove the drain plug, and allow the fluid to drain into the container. Remove the seal from the plug – a new one should be used when refitting.

13 Unscrew the filler plug from the top of the transmission.

14 Clean the drain plug thoroughly, then when the flow of fluid has ceased, refit the plug (using a new seal) and tighten it to the specified torque.

15 Remove the fluid container from under the car, and measure the amount of fluid drained.

16 The transmission is filled through the filler plug aperture. Use a narrow funnel, and take great care to avoid introducing any kind of dirt into the transmission as it is filled. Fill the transmission with the same amount of fluid as was drained.

17 Refit the engine undershield (where removed), then lower the car to the ground.

18 Refer to Section 21 and complete the level checking procedure.

25.5 Automatic transmission fluid drain plug (4-speed)

Every 3 years (regardless of mileage)

26 Brake fluid renewal

The procedure is similar to that for the bleeding of the hydraulic system as described in Chapter 9, except that the brake fluid reservoir should be emptied by syphoning, and allowance should be made for the old fluid to be removed from the circuit when bleeding a section of the circuit.

Note: *According to Ford, unless the system is bled in conjunction with their WDS2000 diagnostic equipment, old fluid will not be removed from the ABS hydraulic unit. It may therefore be worth considering having this work performed by a Ford dealer, though the amount of old fluid remaining may be quite small.*

27 Coolant renewal

Note: *If the antifreeze used is Ford's own, or of similar quality, Ford state that the coolant need not be renewed for the life of the car. If the car's history is unknown, if the antifreeze is of lesser quality, or if you prefer to follow conventional servicing intervals, the coolant should be changed as follows.*

Warning: Refer to Chapter 3 and observe the warnings given. In particular, never remove the expansion tank filler cap when the engine is running, or has just been switched off, as the cooling system will be hot, and the consequent escaping steam and scalding coolant could cause serious injury. If the engine is hot, the electric cooling fan may start rotating even if the engine is not running, so be careful to keep hands, hair and loose clothing well clear when working in the engine compartment.

Cooling system draining

Warning: Wait until the engine is cold before starting this procedure.

27.3 Radiator drain plug (shown with radiator removed)

1 To drain the system, first remove the expansion tank filler cap. Place a thick cloth over the expansion tank cap, then turn the cap anti-clockwise as far as the first stop and wait for any pressure to be released, then depress it and turn it further anti-clockwise to remove it.

2 If additional working clearance is required, apply the handbrake, then jack up the front of the car and support it on axle stands (see *Jacking and vehicle support*).

3 Remove the radiator undershield, then place a large drain tray underneath, and unscrew the radiator drain plug **(see illustration)**. Allow the coolant to drain into the tray. On completion, retighten the drain plug and refit the undershield. Where necessary, lower the car to the ground.

Cooling system flushing

4 If coolant renewal has been neglected, or if the antifreeze mixture has become diluted, then in time, the cooling system may gradually lose efficiency, as the coolant passages become restricted due to rust, scale deposits, and other sediment. The cooling system efficiency can be restored by flushing the system clean.

5 The radiator should be flushed independently of the engine, to avoid unnecessary contamination.

Radiator flushing

6 Disconnect the top and bottom hoses and any other relevant hoses from the radiator, with reference to Chapter 3.

7 Insert a garden hose into the radiator top inlet. Direct a flow of clean water through the radiator, and continue flushing until clean water emerges from the radiator bottom outlet.

8 If after a reasonable period, the water still does not run clear, the radiator can be flushed with a good proprietary cleaning agent. It is important that the manufacturer's instructions are followed carefully. If the contamination is particularly bad, remove the radiator, insert the hose in the radiator bottom outlet, and reverse-flush the radiator.

Engine flushing

9 Remove the thermostat as described in Chapter 3 then, if the radiator top hose has been disconnected from the engine, temporarily reconnect the hose.

10 With the top and bottom hoses disconnected from the radiator, insert a garden hose into the radiator top hose. Direct a clean flow of water through the engine, and continue flushing until clean water emerges from the radiator bottom hose.

11 On completion of flushing, refit the thermostat and reconnect the hoses with reference to Chapter 3.

Antifreeze mixture

12 Ford state that, if the only antifreeze used is the type with which the system was first filled at the factory (see *Lubricants and fluids*) it will last the lifetime of the car. This is subject to it being used in the recommended concentration, unmixed with any other type of antifreeze or additive, and topped-up when necessary using only that antifreeze mixed with clean water. If any other type of antifreeze is added, the lifetime guarantee no longer applies; to restore the lifetime protection, the system must be drained and thoroughly reverse-flushed before fresh coolant mixture is poured in.

13 If the car's history (and therefore the quality of the antifreeze in it) is unknown, owners who wish to follow Ford's recommendations are advised to drain and thoroughly reverse-flush the system, before refilling with fresh coolant mixture. If the appropriate quality of antifreeze is used, the coolant can then be left for the life of the car.

14 If any antifreeze other than Ford's is to be used, the coolant must be renewed at regular intervals to provide an equivalent degree of protection; the conventional recommendation is to renew the coolant every three years.

15 If the antifreeze used is to Ford's specification, the levels of protection it affords are indicated in the Specifications Section of this Chapter. To give the recommended *standard* mixture ratio for this antifreeze, 40% (by volume) of antifreeze must be mixed with 60% of clean, soft water; if you are using any other type of antifreeze, follow its manufacturer's instructions to achieve the correct ratio **(also see the Haynes Hint)**.

16 Before adding antifreeze, the cooling system should be completely drained, preferably flushed, and all hoses checked for condition and security. Fresh antifreeze will rapidly find any weaknesses in the system.

17 After filling with antifreeze, a label should be attached to the expansion tank, stating the type and concentration of antifreeze used, and the date installed. Any subsequent topping-up should be made with the same type and concentration of antifreeze. If topping-up using antifreeze to Ford's specification, note that a 50/50 mixture is permissible, purely for convenience.

It is rare to ever drain the cooling system completely – a small quantity will remain. If the system has been extensively flushed with clean water, this remaining quantity will in fact be plain water. For this reason, some people will first fill the system with the required quantity of neat antifreeze (half the total system capacity, for a 50% mixture), and then complete the filling process with plain water. This ensures that the resulting coolant (once it has mixed inside the engine) is not 'diluted' by old coolant or water remaining in the system.

Cooling system filling

18 Before attempting to fill the cooling system, make sure that all hoses and clips are in good condition, and that the clips are tight. Note that an antifreeze mixture must be used all year round, to prevent corrosion of the engine components.
19 Slowly fill the system until the coolant level reaches the MAX mark on the side of the expansion tank **(see Haynes Hint)**.

1.8 and 2.0 litre engine models

20 With the filler cap not fitted, start the engine and run it at 2500 rpm for 10 seconds – this will prime the heater circuit.
21 Switch off the engine, then fill the expansion tank to 15 mm over the MAX mark.
22 Refit the filler cap, then start the engine and run it at 2500 rpm for 8 minutes, or until the engine reaches normal operating temperature.
23 Maintain the engine speed at 2500 rpm for a further 3 minutes, then increase the engine speed to 4000 rpm for 5 seconds.
24 Decrease the engine speed to 2500 rpm for 3 minutes and switch off the engine.
25 Check the cooling system for leaks, then allow the engine to cool for at least 30 minutes.
26 Remove the filler cap and top-up the coolant level to the MAX mark on the expansion tank.

V6 engine models

27 Refit expansion tank filler cap.
28 Start the engine and allow it to idle until it reaches its normal operating temperature.
29 Allow the engine to idle for a further 5 minutes, then switch it off.
30 Allow the engine to cool for at least 30 minutes.
31 Remove the filler cap and top-up the coolant level to the MAX mark on the expansion tank.

Airlocks

32 If, after draining and refilling the system, symptoms of overheating are found which did not occur previously, then the fault is almost certainly due to trapped air at some point in the system, causing an airlock and restricting the flow of coolant; usually, the air is trapped because the system was refilled too quickly.
33 If an airlock is suspected, first try gently squeezing all visible coolant hoses. A coolant hose which is full of air feels quite different to one full of coolant, when squeezed. After refilling the system, most airlocks will clear once the system has cooled, and been topped-up.
34 While the engine is running at operating temperature, switch on the heater and heater fan, and check for heat output. Provided there is sufficient coolant in the system, any lack of heat output could be due to an airlock in the system.
35 Airlocks can have more serious effects than simply reducing heater output – a severe airlock could reduce coolant flow around the engine. Check that the radiator top hose is hot when the engine is at operating temperature – a top hose which stays cold could be the result of an airlock (or a non-opening thermostat).
36 If the problem persists, stop the engine and allow it to cool down **completely**, before unscrewing the expansion tank filler cap or loosening the hose clips and squeezing the hoses to bleed out the trapped air. In the worst case, the system will have to be at least partially drained (this time, the coolant can be saved for re-use) and flushed to clear the problem.

Pressure cap check

37 Clean the pressure cap (expansion tank), and inspect the seal inside the cap for damage or deterioration. If there is any sign of damage or deterioration to the seal, fit a new pressure cap. If the cap is old, it is worth considering fitting a new one for peace of mind – they are not expensive. If the pressure cap fails, excess pressure will be allowed into the system, which may result in the failure of hoses, the radiator, or the heater matrix.

Every 50 000 miles or 4 years

28 Fuel filter renewal

Warning: Before carrying out the following operation, refer to the precautions given in Safety first! at the beginning of this manual and follow them implicitly. Petrol is a highly dangerous and volatile liquid, and the precautions necessary when handling it cannot be overstressed.

1 The fuel filter is located by the front right-hand corner of the fuel tank, just forward of the car's right-hand rear jacking point **(see illustration)**. The filter performs a vital role in keeping dirt and other foreign matter out of the fuel system, and so must be renewed at regular intervals, or whenever you have reason to suspect that it may be clogged.
2 Before disturbing any fuel lines, which may contain fuel under pressure, any residual pressure in the system must be relieved as follows.
3 With the ignition switched off, open the engine compartment fusebox and remove the fuel pump fuse.
4 Start the engine, if possible – if the engine will not start, turn it over on the starter for a few seconds.
5 If the engine starts, allow it to idle until it stalls. Turn the engine over once or twice on the starter, to ensure that all pressure is released, then switch off the ignition.

Warning: This procedure will merely relieve the increased pressure necessary for the engine to run – remember that fuel will still be present in the system components, and take precautions accordingly before disconnecting any of them.

6 Disconnect the battery negative lead (refer to *Disconnecting the battery* at the end of this manual).
7 Jack up the rear right-hand side of the car, and support it securely on an axle stand.
8 Using rag to soak up any spilt fuel, release the fuel feed and outlet pipe unions from the filter, by squeezing together the protruding locking lugs on each union, and carefully pulling the union off the filter stub **(see illustration)**. Where the unions are colour-coded, the feed and outlet pipes cannot be confused; where both unions are the same colour, note carefully which pipe is connected to which filter stub, and ensure that they are correctly reconnected on refitting.
9 Noting the arrows and/or other markings on the filter showing the direction of fuel flow (towards the engine), unscrew the filter bracket to underbody bolts, withdraw the bracket,

28.1 Fuel filter location in front of the right-hand side of the fuel tank

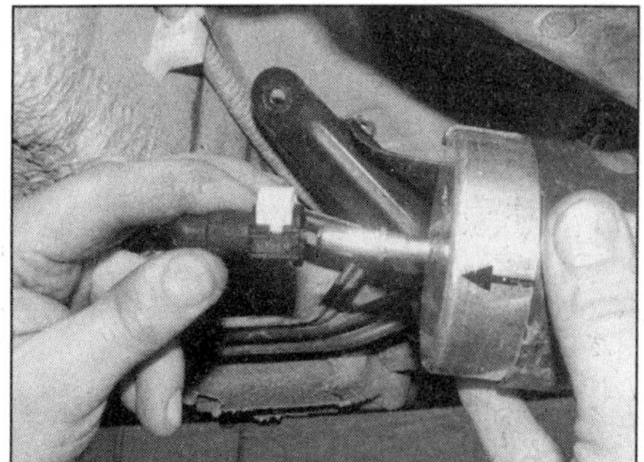

28.8 Disconnecting the fuel lines from the fuel filter

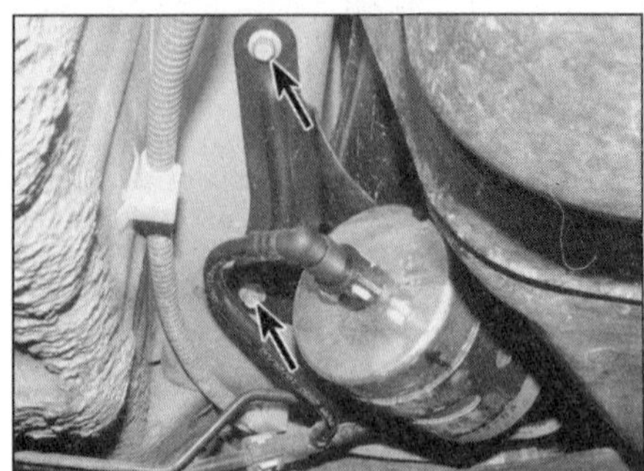
28.9a Fuel filter bracket mounting bolts

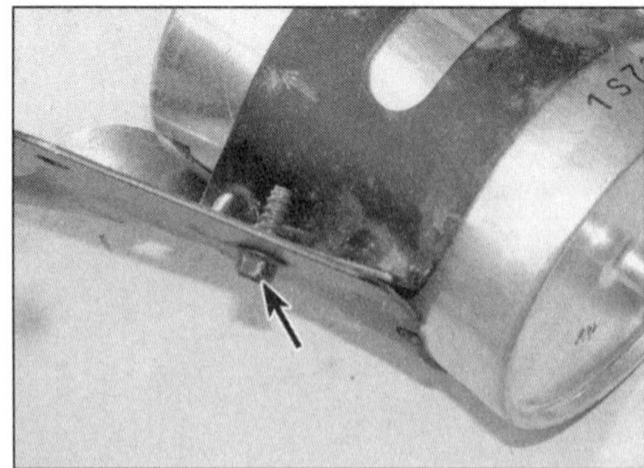
28.9b Fuel filter clamp bolt

30.5 Removing the water pump drivebelt (V6 engine)

then slacken the clamp bolt and slide out the filter **(see illustrations)**. Note that the filter will still contain fuel; care should be taken to avoid spillage and to minimise the risk of fire.

10 On installation, slide the filter into its clamp so that the arrow marked on it faces the same direction as noted when removing the old filter. Tighten the clamp bolt until the filter is just prevented from moving, then refit the bracket to the underbody and tighten the mounting bolts.

11 Slide each pipe union onto its (correct) respective filter stub, and press it down until the locking lugs click into their groove.

12 Refit the fuel pump fuse and reconnect the battery earth terminal, then switch the ignition on and off five times, to pressurise the system. Check for any sign of fuel leakage around the filter unions before lowering the car to the ground and starting the engine.

29 Valve clearance check

Note: *This work applies to the 1.8 and 2.0 litre engines only.*

Refer to Chapter 2A.

30 Auxiliary drivebelt renewal

Note: *This is a precautionary measure, and not part of Ford's schedule. Ford state that the drivebelt should last at least twice this mileage. However, these belts do deteriorate with age, and considering the inconvenience that an in-service failure would cause, it may be wise to fit a new belt at this interval.*

1 With the engine switched off, open and support the bonnet. For improved access to the right-hand end of the engine, first loosen the right-hand front wheel nuts, then jack up the front right-hand side of the car and support it securely on an axle stand (see *Jacking and vehicle support*). Remove the roadwheel, then remove the lower splash shield (three fasteners) from under the wheel arch.

2 If renewing the water pump drivebelt on models with the V6 engine, remove the drivebelt cover from the top of the engine.

3 If the existing drivebelt is to be refitted, mark it, or note the maker's markings on its flat surface, so that it can be installed the same way round.

4 Rotate the tensioner pulley clockwise to release its pressure on the drivebelt. Depending on model and equipment, the tensioner will either have a hex fitting for a spanner or socket, or a square hole into which a ratchet handle from a socket set can be fitted. **Note:** *On some V6 engine models, a tensioner is not fitted to the water pump drivebelt, and the belt has to be cut off to remove it.*

5 Slip the drivebelt off the drive pulley, and release the tensioner again **(see illustration)**. Working from below or from the engine compartment as necessary, and noting its routing, slip the drivebelt off the remaining pulleys and withdraw it.

6 Check all the pulleys, ensuring that their grooves are clean, and removing all traces of oil and grease. Check that the tensioner works properly, with strong spring pressure being felt when its pulley is rotated clockwise, and a smooth return to the limit of its travel when released.

7 If the original drivebelt is being refitted, use the marks or notes made on removal, to ensure that it is installed to run in the same direction as it was previously. To fit the drivebelt, arrange it on the grooved pulleys so that it is centred in their grooves, and not overlapping their raised sides (note that the flat surface of the drivebelt is engaged on one or more pulleys) and routed correctly. Start at the top, and work down to finish at the bottom pulley; rotate the tensioner pulley clockwise, slip the drivebelt onto the bottom pulley, then release the tensioner again.

8 If fitting a new water pump drivebelt on V6 engine models where a tensioner is not used, first fit the belt around the water pump pulley. Fit the belt around the back half of the camshaft pulley as far as possible, trying to ensure that the belt ribs will engage those on the pulley. Have an assistant turn the engine in its normal direction (towards the front of the car), and guide the belt fully onto the pulley as this is done.

9 Using a spanner applied to the crankshaft pulley bolt, rotate the crankshaft through at least two full turns clockwise to settle the drivebelt on the pulleys, then check that the drivebelt is properly installed.

10 Refit the components removed for access, then lower the car to the ground. Refit the roadwheel and tighten the wheel nuts to the specified torque.

Chapter 1 Part B: Routine maintenance and servicing – diesel models

Contents

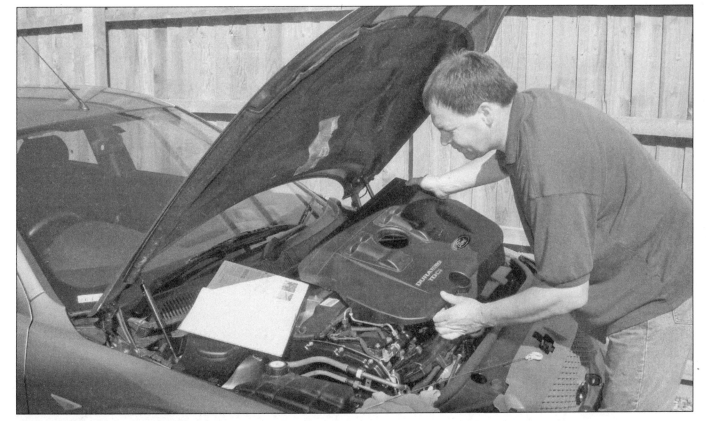

Degrees of difficulty

Easy, suitable for novice with little experience 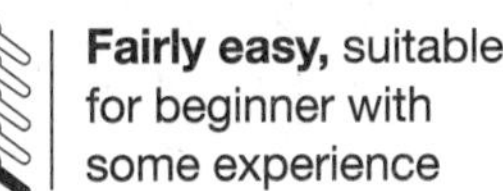	**Fairly easy,** suitable for beginner with some experience	**Fairly difficult,** suitable for competent DIY mechanic 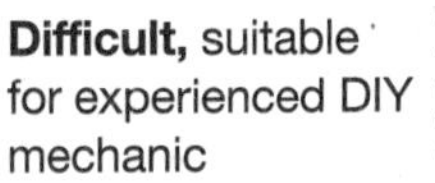	**Difficult,** suitable for experienced DIY mechanic 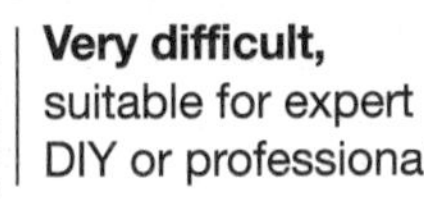	**Very difficult,** suitable for expert DIY or professional 

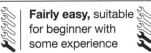

Lubricants and fluids

Lubricants and fluids	Refer to the end of *Weekly checks* on page 0•18

Capacities

Engine oil (with filter)	6.0 litres
Difference between dipstick minimum and maximum marks	2.0 litres
Cooling system (including heating):	
With standard heater	10.4 litres
With auxiliary heater	10.6 litres
Fuel tank	58.5 litres
Manual transmission:	
5-speed	1.9 litres
6-speed	1.75 litres
Automatic transmission (total capacity – drain and refill not stated)	8.8 litres

Cooling system

Coolant protection at 40% antifreeze/water mixture ratio:	
Slush point	–25°C (–13°F)
Solidifying point	–30°C (–22°F)

Braking system

Note: *No minimum lining thicknesses are given by Ford – the following is given as a general recommendation.*

Minimum front or rear brake pad lining thickness	1.5 mm

Torque wrench settings

Torque wrench settings	Nm	lbf ft
Alternator mounting bolt/nuts	47	35
Alternator support bracket bolts	47	35
Automatic transmission drain plug	45	33
Automatic transmission filler plug	45	33
Automatic transmission selector lever cable cover	22	16
Automatic transmission test plug	15	11
Engine oil drain plug	23	17
Manual transmission filler/level and drain plugs:		
5-speed	45	33
6-speed	35	26
Roadwheel nuts	85	63

The maintenance intervals in this manual are provided with the assumption that you, not the dealer, will be carrying out the work. These are the minimum maintenance intervals recommended by us for cars driven daily. If you wish to keep your car in peak condition at all times, you may wish to perform some of these procedures more often. We encourage frequent maintenance, because it enhances the efficiency, performance and resale value of your car.

If the car is driven in dusty areas, used to tow a trailer, or driven frequently at slow speeds (idling in traffic) or on short journeys, more frequent maintenance intervals are recommended.

When the vehicle is new, it should be serviced by a dealer service department (or other workshop recognised by the vehicle manufacturer as providing the same standard of service) in order to preserve the warranty. The vehicle manufacturer may reject warranty claims if you are unable to prove that servicing has been carried out as and when specified, using only original-equipment parts, or parts certified to be of equivalent quality.

Every 250 miles or weekly

- ☐ Refer to *Weekly checks*

Every 6250 miles or 6 months, whichever occurs first

- ☐ Renew the engine oil and filter (Section 3)

Note: *Frequent oil and filter changes are good for the engine. We recommend changing the oil at the mileage specified here, or at least twice a year if the mileage covered is a less.*

Every 12 500 miles or 12 months, whichever occurs first

In addition to the item listed in the previous service, carry out the following:

- ☐ Check the battery and clean the terminals (Section 4)
- ☐ Check the auxiliary drivebelt (Section 5)
- ☐ Check the electrical system (Section 6)
- ☐ Check under the bonnet for fluid leaks and hose condition (Section 7)
- ☐ Check the condition of all engine compartment wiring (Section 8)
- ☐ Check the condition of all air conditioning system components (Section 9)
- ☐ Check the seat belts (Section 10)
- ☐ Check the antifreeze concentration (Section 11)
- ☐ Check the steering, suspension and roadwheels (Section 12)
- ☐ Check the driveshaft rubber gaiters and CV joints (Section 13)
- ☐ Check the exhaust system (Section 14)
- ☐ Check the underbody, and all fuel/brake lines (Section 15)
- ☐ Check the braking system (Section 16)
- ☐ Check the doors and bonnet, and lubricate their hinges and locks (Section 17)
- ☐ Renew the pollen filter (Section 18)
- ☐ Drain any water from the fuel filter – where applicable (Section 19)
- ☐ Check the security of all roadwheel nuts (Section 20)
- ☐ Road test (Section 21)

Every 25 000 miles or 2 years, whichever occurs first

In addition to the relevant items listed in the previous services, carry out the following:

- ☐ Check the automatic transmission fluid level (Section 22)
- ☐ Renew the fuel filter (Section 23)

Every 37 500 miles or 3 years, whichever occurs first

In addition to the relevant items listed in the previous services, carry out the following:

- ☐ Check the glow plugs (Section 24)
- ☐ Renew the air filter element (Section 25). Note that this task must be carried out at more frequent intervals if the car is used in dusty or polluted conditions
- ☐ Check the manual transmission oil level (Section 26)
- ☐ Renew the automatic transmission fluid (Section 27). Note that this task applies to cars used in severe conditions only (short trips of less than 10 miles in freezing conditions, extensive idling, towing a trailer, operating off-road)

Every 3 years (regardless of mileage)

- ☐ Renew the brake fluid (Section 28)
- ☐ Renew the coolant (Section 29)

Every 50 000 miles

In addition to the relevant items listed in the previous services, carry out the following:

- ☐ Renew the auxiliary drivebelt (Section 30)

Component location – diesel models

Underbonnet view of a 2.0 litre model

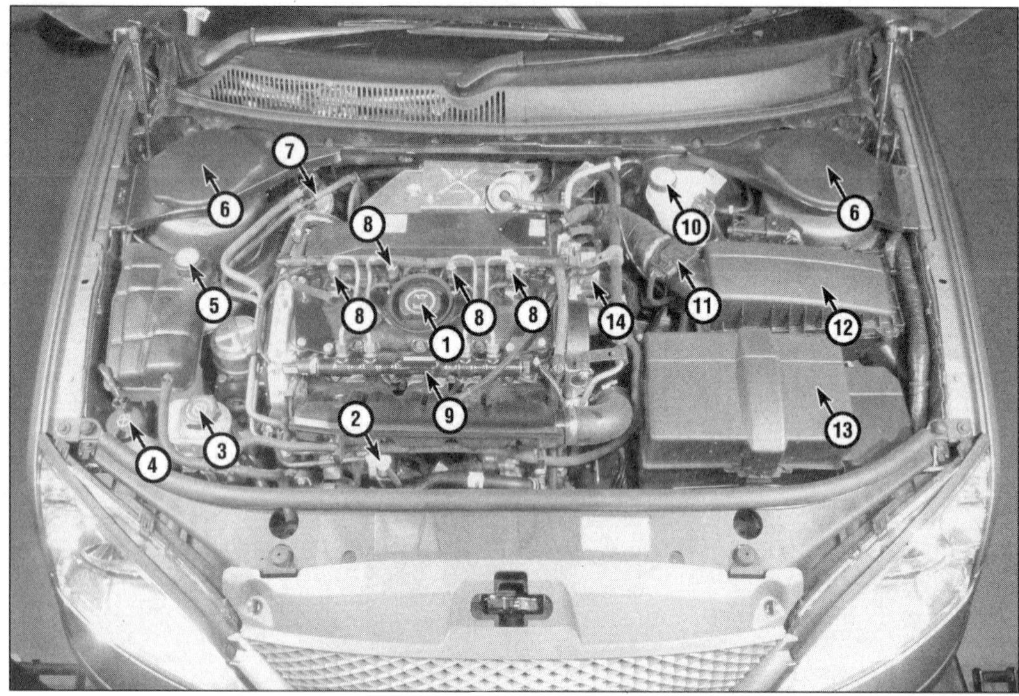

1 *Engine oil filler cap*
2 *Engine oil dipstick*
3 *Power steering hydraulic fluid reservoir*
4 *Washer fluid reservoir*
5 *Coolant expansion tank filler cap*
6 *Front suspension strut upper mounting*
7 *Fuel filter*
8 *Fuel injectors*
9 *Common fuel rail*
10 *Brake fluid reservoir*
11 *Air mass meter*
12 *Air cleaner*
13 *Battery*
14 *Brake vacuum pump*

Front underbody view of a 2.0 litre model

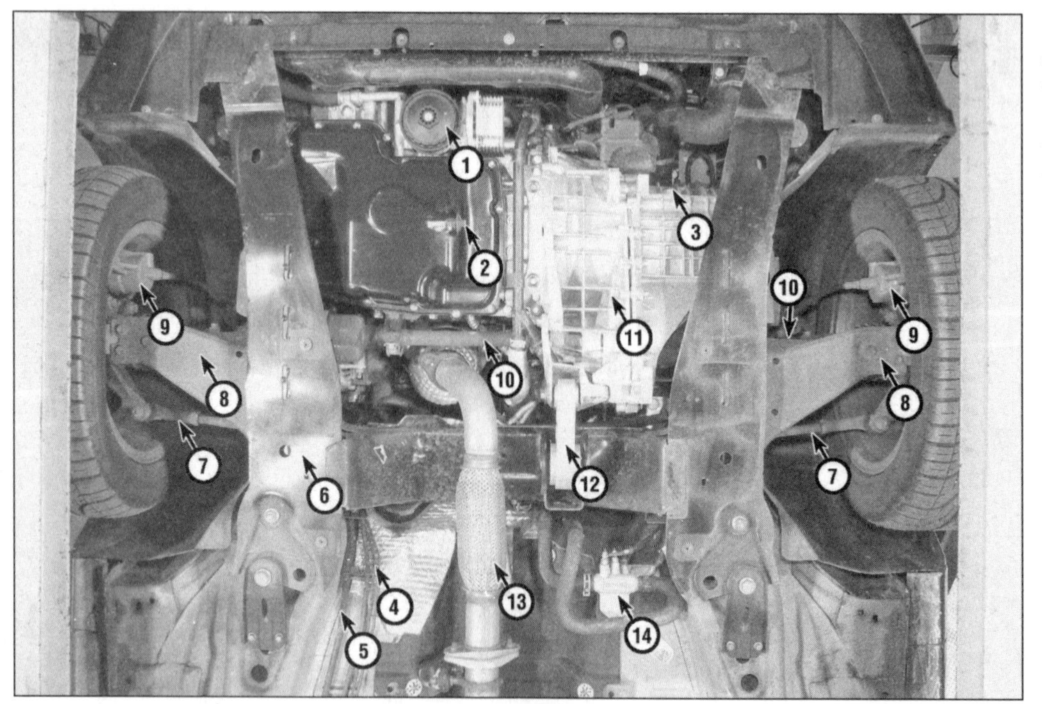

1 *Engine oil filter*
2 *Engine oil drain plug*
3 *Manual transmission filler plug*
4 *Brake lines*
5 *Fuel supply and return lines*
6 *Front subframe*
7 *Steering track rods*
8 *Front suspension lower arms*
9 *Front brake calipers*
10 *Driveshafts*
11 *Manual transmission*
12 *Engine rear mounting/ torque link*
13 *Front exhaust pipe*
14 *Cooling system auxiliary heater*

Rear underbody view – Saloon and Hatchback models

1 *Fuel tank*
2 *Exhaust pipe*
3 *Handbrake cables*
4 *Rear anti-roll bar*
5 *Rear suspension front lower arm*
6 *Rear suspension rear lower arm*
7 *Rear suspension crossmember*
8 *Spare wheel well*

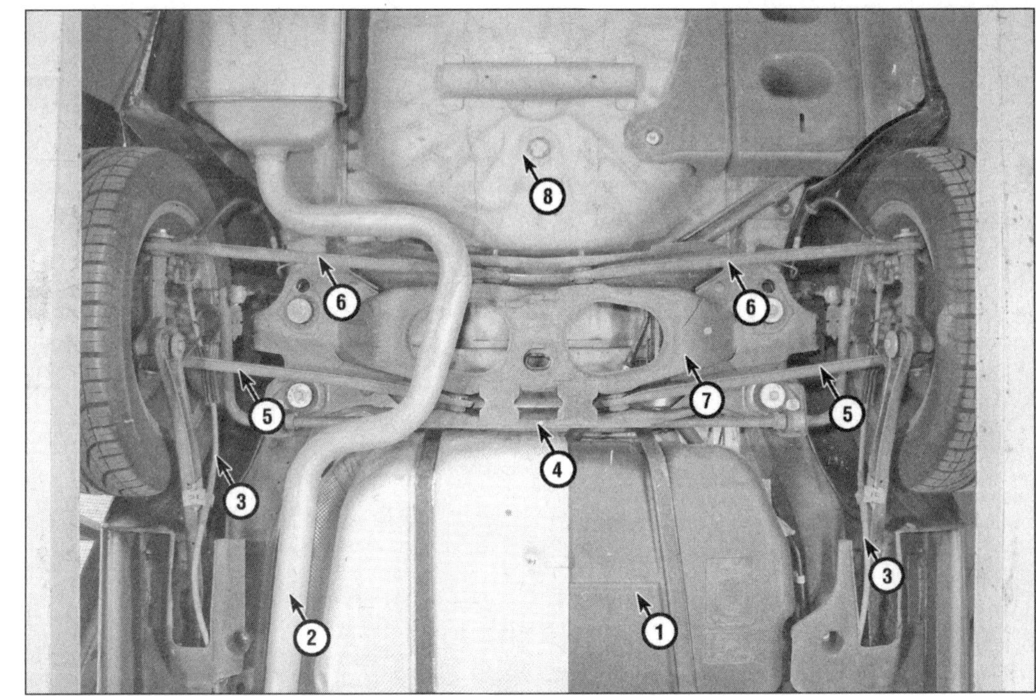

Rear underbody view – Estate models

1 *Fuel tank*
2 *Rear suspension brace*
3 *Rear suspension tie bar/ knuckle*
4 *Handbrake cables*
5 *Rear suspension front lower arms*
6 *Rear suspension struts*
7 *Rear suspension lower arms*
8 *Rear anti-roll bar*
9 *Rear anti-roll bar link lower mountings*
10 *Rear suspension crossmember*
11 *Rear exhaust system*
12 *Spare wheel well*

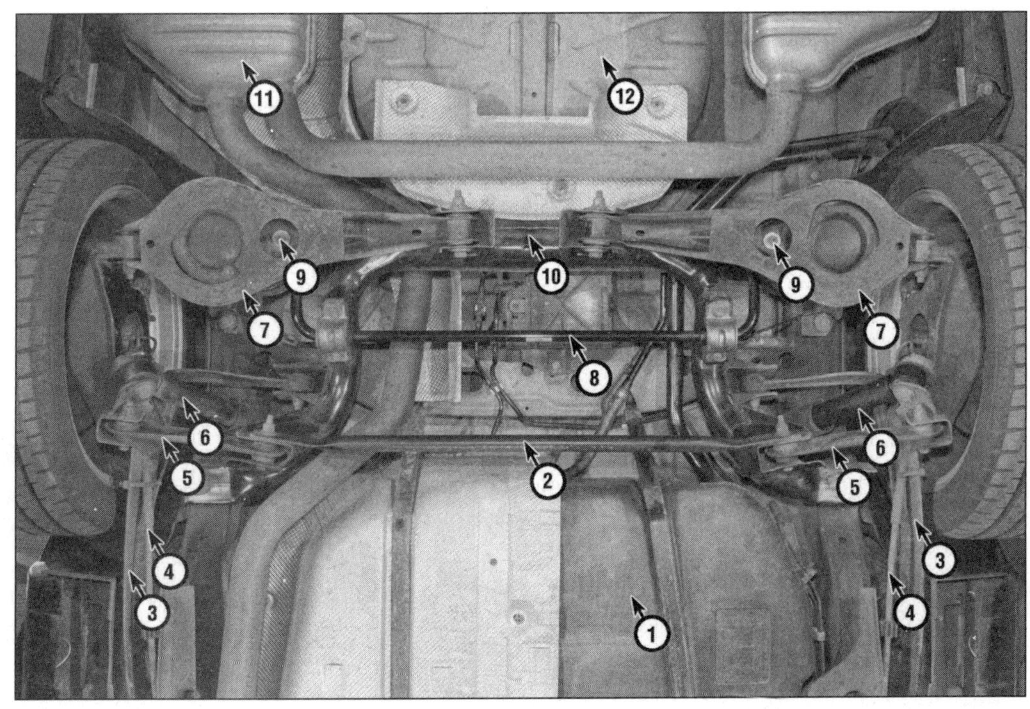

1 General information

1 This Chapter is designed to help the home mechanic maintain his/her car for safety, economy, long life and peak performance.
2 The Chapter contains a master maintenance schedule, followed by Sections dealing specifically with each task in the schedule. Visual checks, adjustments, component renewal and other helpful items are included. Refer to the accompanying illustrations of the engine compartment and the underside of the car for the locations of the various components.
3 Servicing your car in accordance with the mileage/time maintenance schedule and the following Sections will provide a planned maintenance programme, which should result in a long and reliable service life. This is a comprehensive plan, so maintaining some items but not others at the specified service intervals, will not produce the same results.
4 As you service your car, you will discover that many of the procedures can – and should – be grouped together, because of the particular procedure being performed, or because of the proximity of two otherwise-unrelated components to one another. For example, if the car is raised for any reason, the exhaust can be inspected at the same time as the suspension and steering components.
5 The first step in this maintenance programme is to prepare yourself before the actual work begins. Read through all the Sections relevant to the work to be carried out, then make a list and gather all the parts and tools required. If a problem is encountered, seek advice from a parts specialist, or a dealer service department.

2 Regular maintenance

1 If, from the time the car is new, the routine maintenance schedule is followed closely, and frequent checks are made of fluid levels and high-wear items, as suggested throughout this manual, the engine will be kept in relatively good running condition, and the need for additional work will be minimised.
2 It is possible that there will be times when the engine is running poorly due to the lack of regular maintenance. This is even more likely if a used car, which has not received regular and frequent maintenance checks, is purchased. In such cases, additional work may need to be carried out, outside of the regular maintenance intervals.
3 If engine wear is suspected, a compression test or leakdown test (refer to Chapter 2C) will provide valuable information regarding the overall performance of the main internal components. Such a test can be used as a basis to decide on the extent of the work to be carried out. If, for example, a compression or leakdown test indicates serious internal engine wear, conventional maintenance as described in this Chapter will not greatly improve the performance of the engine, and may prove a waste of time and money, unless extensive overhaul work is carried out first.
4 The following series of operations are those most often required to improve the performance of a generally poor-running engine:

Primary operations

a) Clean, inspect and test the battery (See Weekly checks and Section 4).
b) Check all the engine-related fluids (refer to Weekly checks).
c) Check the condition and tension of the auxiliary drivebelt (Section 5).
d) Check the condition of all hoses, and check for fluid leaks (Sections 7 and 15).
e) Renew the fuel filter (Section 23).
f) Check the glow plugs (Chapter 5C).
g) Check the condition of the air filter, and renew if necessary (Section 25).

5 If the above operations do not prove fully effective, carry out the following secondary operations:

Secondary operations

All items listed under *Primary operations*, plus the following:
a) Check the charging system (refer to Chapter 5A).
b) Check the preheating system (refer to Chapter 5C).
c) Check the fuel system (refer to Chapter 4B).

Every 6250 miles or 6 months

3 Engine oil and filter renewal

1 Frequent oil changes are the most important preventive maintenance the DIY home mechanic can give the engine, because ageing oil becomes diluted and contaminated, which leads to premature engine wear.
2 Before starting this procedure, gather together all the necessary tools and materials. Also make sure that you have plenty of clean rags and newspapers handy, to mop-up any spills. Ideally, the engine oil should be warm, as it will drain more easily and more built-up sludge will be removed with it. Take care not to touch the exhaust or any other hot parts of the engine when working under the car. To avoid any possibility of scalding and to protect yourself from possible skin irritants and other harmful contaminants in used engine oils, it is advisable to wear gloves when carrying out this work.

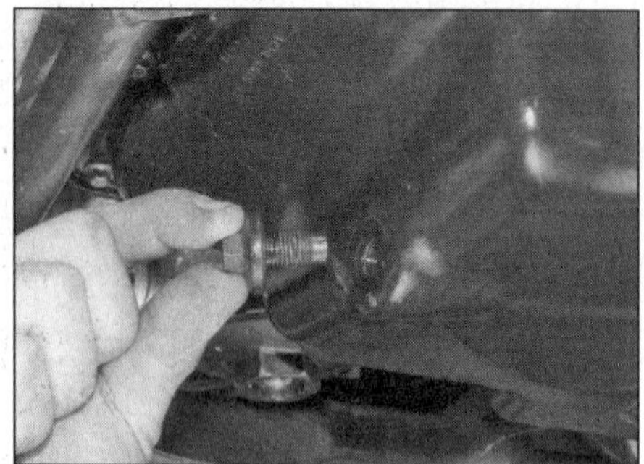

3.4 Removing the engine oil drain plug

3 Firmly apply the handbrake then jack up the front of the car and support it on axle stands (see *Jacking and vehicle support)*. Where applicable, remove the engine undershield.
4 Remove the oil filler cap, then unscrew the engine oil drain plug (located at the lowest point of the sump) about half a turn. Position the draining container under the drain plug, then remove the plug completely – recover the sealing washer **(see illustration and Haynes Hint)**.
5 Allow some time for the oil to drain, noting that it may be necessary to reposition the container as the oil flow slows to a trickle.
6 After all the oil has drained, wipe off the drain plug with a clean rag, and fit a new sealing washer. Clean the area around the drain plug opening, and refit the plug. Tighten the plug to the specified torque.

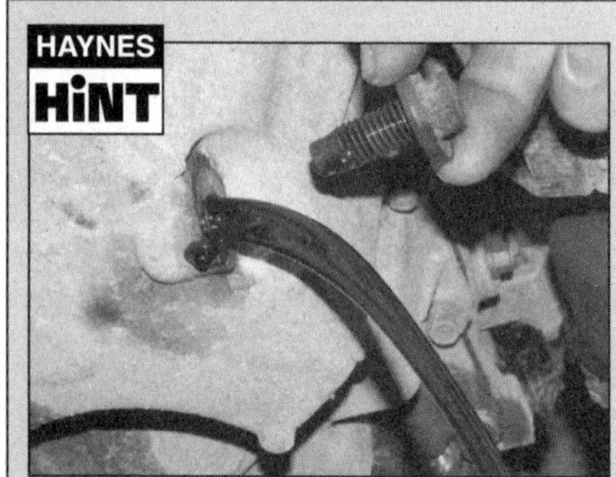

Keep the plug pressed into the sump while unscrewing it by hand the last couple of turns. As the plug releases from the threads, move it away sharply, so the stream of oil issuing from the sump runs into the pan, not up your sleeve.

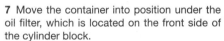

3.8a Unscrew the oil filter housing cover . . .

3.8b . . . and discard the paper element

3.9 Removing the O-ring seal

7 Move the container into position under the oil filter, which is located on the front side of the cylinder block.

8 Unscrew the oil filter plastic cover from the bottom of the oil filter housing, then remove and discard the paper element **(see illustrations)**.

9 Remove the O-ring seal and obtain a new one **(see illustration)**. Clean the filter housing and cover.

10 Fit the new O-ring seal onto the cover and lubricate it with a little engine oil.

11 Locate the new paper element on the cover, then screw the assembly into the filter housing and tighten securely by hand. Where necessary, refit the splash guard under the engine.

12 Remove the old oil and all tools from under the car, then lower the car to the ground.

13 Remove the dipstick, then unscrew the oil filler cap from the cylinder head cover. Fill the engine, using the correct grade and type of oil (*see Weekly checks*). An oil can spout or funnel may help to reduce spillage. Pour in half the specified quantity of oil first, then wait a few minutes for the oil to run to the sump. Continue adding oil a small quantity at a time until the level is up to the lower mark on the dipstick. Refit the filler cap.

14 Start the engine and run it for a few minutes; check for leaks. Note that there may be a delay of a few seconds before the oil pressure warning light goes out when the engine is first started, as the oil circulates through the engine oil galleries and the new oil filter before the pressure builds-up.

15 Switch off the engine, and wait a few minutes for the oil to settle in the sump once more. With the new oil circulated and the filter completely full, recheck the level on the dipstick, and add more oil as necessary.

16 Dispose of the used engine oil safely, with reference to *General Repair Procedures*.

Oil change warning light

17 This warning light is only fitted to models with a diesel particulate filter (DPF) in the exhaust system (see Chapter 4C). The light warns of increased levels of fuel in the engine oil after the DPF has been automatically cleaned. The warning light may come on between normal service intervals, but only indicates the likely need for an engine oil and filter change, which should be carried out as soon as possible.

18 To reset the light after the oil change has been carried out, switch on the ignition to the second position (warning lights on, engine off). Fully depress both the accelerator and brake pedals together, and hold for approximately 20 seconds. The oil change warning light should flash for about 5 seconds, then go out, confirming that it has been reset. If this does not happen, release the pedals, switch off the ignition and try again. On completion, switch off the ignition.

Every 12 500 miles or 12 months

4 Battery maintenance and charging

Warning: Certain precautions must be followed when checking and servicing the battery. Hydrogen gas, which is highly flammable, is always present in the battery cells, so keep lighted tobacco and all other open flames and sparks away from the battery. The electrolyte inside the battery is actually dilute sulphuric acid, which will cause injury if splashed on your skin or in your eyes. It will also ruin clothes and painted surfaces. When disconnecting the battery, always detach the negative (earth) lead first and connect it last.

Note: *Before disconnecting the battery, refer to Disconnecting the battery at the end of this manual.*

General

1 A routine preventive maintenance programme for the battery in your car is the only way to ensure quick and reliable starts. For general maintenance, refer to *Weekly checks* at the start of this manual. Also at the front of the manual is information on jump starting. For details of removing and installing the battery, refer to Chapter 5A.

Battery electrolyte level

2 On models not equipped with a sealed or 'maintenance-free' battery, check the electrolyte level of all six battery cells.

3 The level must be approximately 10 mm above the plates; this may be shown by maximum and minimum level lines marked on the battery's casing.

4 If the level is low, use a coin or screwdriver to release the filler/vent cap, and add distilled water. Do not overfill – this can render the battery useless. To improve access to the centre caps, it may be helpful to remove the battery hold-down clamp.

5 Install and securely retighten the cap, then wipe up any spillage.

Caution: Overfilling the cells may cause electrolyte to spill over during periods of heavy charging, causing corrosion or damage.

Charging

Warning: When batteries are being charged, hydrogen gas, which is very explosive and flammable, is produced. Do not smoke, or allow open flames, near a charging or a recently-charged battery. If the battery is being charged indoors, ensure this is done in a well-ventilated area. Wear eye protection when near the battery during charging. Also, make sure the charger is unplugged before connecting or disconnecting the battery from the charger.

6 Slow-rate charging is the best way to restore a battery that's discharged to the point where it will not start the engine. It's also a good way to maintain the battery charge in a car that's only driven a few miles between starts. Maintaining the battery charge is particularly important in winter, when the battery must work harder to start the engine, and electrical accessories that drain the battery are in greater use.

7 Check the battery case for any instructions regarding charging the battery. Some maintenance-free batteries may require a particularly low charge rate or other special conditions, if they are not to be damaged.

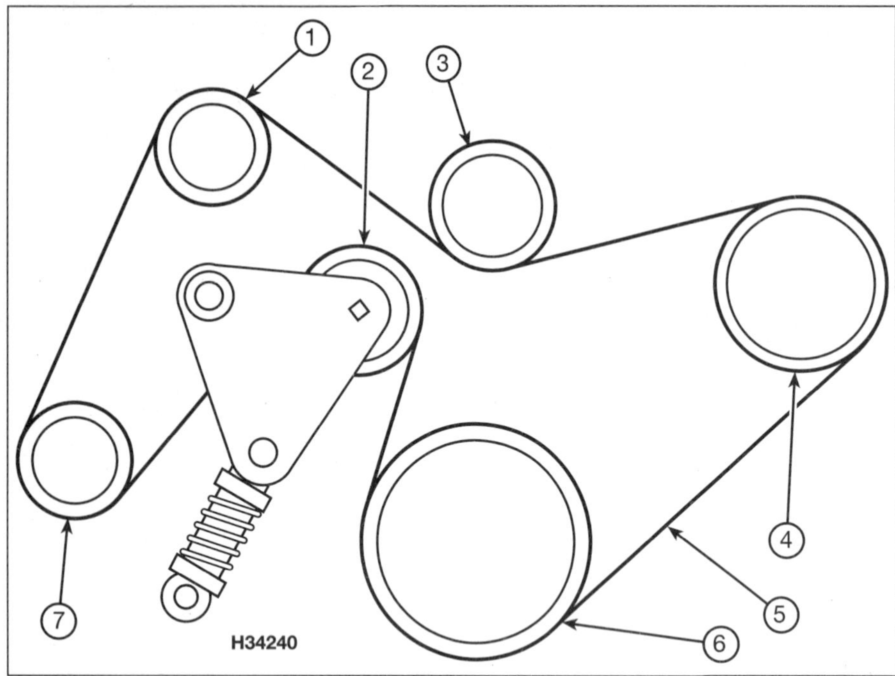

5.1a Main auxiliary drivebelt routing

1 Idler pulley
2 Tensioner pulley
3 Idler pulley
4 Air conditioning compressor pulley
5 Auxiliary drivebelt
6 Crankshaft pulley
7 Alternator pulley

8 It's best to use a one- or two-amp battery charger (sometimes called a 'trickle' charger). They are the safest, and put the least strain on the battery. They are also the least expensive. For a faster charge, you can use a higher-amperage charger, but don't use one rated more than 1/10th the amp/hour rating of the battery (ie, no more than 5 amps, typically). Rapid boost charges that claim to restore the power of the battery in one to two hours are hardest on the battery, and can damage batteries not in good condition. This type of charging should only be used in emergency situations.

9 The average time necessary to charge a battery should be listed in the instructions that come with the charger. As a general rule, a trickle charger will charge a battery in 12 to 16 hours.

5 Auxiliary drivebelt check

General

1 The main auxiliary drivebelt is of flat, multi-ribbed type, and is located on the right-hand end of the engine. It drives the alternator and air conditioning compressor from the engine's crankshaft pulley. A separate multi-ribbed drivebelt drives the power steering pump and water pump from the left-hand end of the inlet camshaft **(see illustrations)**.

2 The good condition and proper tension of the auxiliary drivebelts is critical to the operation of the engine. They must, therefore, be regularly inspected.

Check

3 With the engine switched off, open and support the bonnet. Remove the engine top cover. Also remove the semi-circular drivebelt cover, which is secured by a single nut to the top of the engine.

4 Working at the transmission end of the engine, unclip the small coolant hose from the large-diameter air inlet hose next to the battery. Loosen the clips from each end of the inlet hose, and remove it.

5 For improved access to the right-hand end of the engine, first loosen the right-hand front wheel nuts, then jack up the front right-hand side of the car and support it securely on an axle stand. Remove the roadwheel.

6 Remove the engine undertray, which is secured by a total of eight fasteners. Remove three more bolts, and take off the belt's lower splash shield.

7 Using an inspection light or a small electric torch, and rotating the engine with a spanner applied to the crankshaft pulley bolt, check the whole length of both drivebelts for cracks, separation of the rubber, and torn or worn ribs. Also check for fraying and glazing, which gives the drivebelt a shiny appearance.

8 Both sides of the drivebelt should be inspected, which means you will have to twist the drivebelt to check the underside. Use your fingers to feel the drivebelt where you can't see it. If you are in any doubt as to the condition of either drivebelt, renew it as described in Section 30.

Drivebelt tension

9 The auxiliary drivebelts are tensioned by automatic tensioners; regular checks are not required, and manual 'adjustment' is not possible.

10 If you suspect that a drivebelt is slipping and/or running slack, or that the tensioner is otherwise faulty, it must be renewed.

Drivebelt renewal

11 Refer to Section 30.

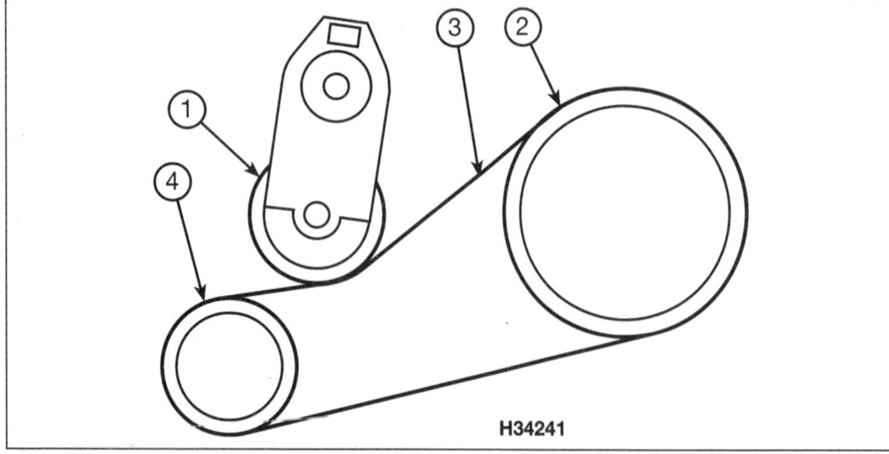

5.1b Water pump drivebelt routing

1 Tensioner pulley
2 Camshaft pulley
3 Auxiliary drivebelt
4 Power steering pump pulley

6 Electrical system check

1 Check the operation of all external lights and indicators (front and rear).

2 Check for satisfactory operation of the instrument panel, its illumination and warning lights, the switches and their function lights.

3 Check the horn(s) for satisfactory operation.
4 Check all other electrical equipment for satisfactory operation.
5 If a fault is suspected, all the main electrical accessories can be checked using the car's own GEM control module, as described in Chapter 12.

7 Underbonnet check for fluid leaks and hose condition

1 Visually inspect the engine joint faces, gaskets and seals for any signs of water or oil leaks. Pay particular attention to the areas around the cylinder head cover, cylinder head, oil filter and sump joint faces. Bear in mind that, over a period of time, some very slight seepage from these areas is to be expected – what you are really looking for is any indication of a serious leak. Should a leak be found, renew the offending gasket or oil seal by referring to the appropriate Chapters in this manual.
2 Also check the security and condition of all the engine-related pipes and hoses, and all braking system pipes and hoses and fuel lines. Ensure that all cable ties or securing clips are in place, and in good condition. Clips which are broken or missing can lead to chafing of the hoses, pipes or wiring, which could cause more serious problems in the future.
3 Carefully check the radiator hoses and heater hoses along their entire length. Renew any hose which is cracked, swollen or deteriorated. Cracks will show up better if the hose is squeezed. Pay close attention to the hose clips that secure the hoses to the cooling system components. Hose clips can pinch and puncture hoses, resulting in cooling system leaks. If the crimped-type hose clips are used, it may be a good idea to update them with Jubilee clips.
4 Inspect all the cooling system components (hoses, joint faces, etc) for leaks **(see Haynes Hint)**.
5 Where any problems are found on system components, renew the component or gasket with reference to Chapter 3.
6 With the car raised, inspect the fuel tank and filler neck for punctures, cracks and other damage. The connection between the filler neck and tank is especially critical. Sometimes a rubber filler neck or connecting hose will leak due to loose retaining clamps or deteriorated rubber.
7 Carefully check all rubber hoses and metal fuel lines leading away from the fuel tank. Check for loose connections, deteriorated hoses, crimped lines, and other damage. Pay particular attention to the vent pipes and hoses, which often loop up around the filler neck and can become blocked or crimped. Follow the lines to the front of the car, carefully inspecting them all the way. Renew damaged sections as necessary. Similarly, whilst the car is raised, take the opportunity to inspect all underbody brake fluid pipes and hoses.
8 From within the engine compartment, check the security of all fuel, vacuum and brake hose attachments and pipe unions, and inspect all hoses for kinks, chafing and deterioration.
9 Check the condition of the power steering and, where applicable, the automatic transmission fluid pipes and hoses.

HAYNES HiNT

A leak in the cooling system will usually show up as white- or antifreeze-coloured deposits on the area adjoining the leak.

8 Engine compartment wiring check

1 With the car parked on level ground, apply the handbrake firmly and open the bonnet. Using an inspection light or a small electric torch, check all visible wiring within and beneath the engine compartment.
2 What you are looking for is wiring that is obviously damaged by chafing against sharp edges, or against moving suspension/transmission components and/or the auxiliary drivebelt, by being trapped or crushed between carelessly-refitted components, or melted by being forced into contact with the hot engine castings, coolant pipes, etc. In almost all cases, damage of this sort is caused in the first instance by incorrect routing on reassembly after previous work has been carried out.
3 Depending on the extent of the problem, damaged wiring may be repaired by rejoining the break or splicing-in a new length of wire, using solder to ensure a good connection, and remaking the insulation with adhesive insulating tape or heat-shrink tubing, as appropriate. If the damage is extensive, given the implications for the car's future reliability, the best long-term answer may well be to renew that entire section of the loom, however expensive this may appear.
4 When the actual damage has been repaired, ensure that the wiring loom is rerouted correctly, so that it is clear of other components, and not stretched or kinked, and is secured out of harm's way using the plastic clips, guides and ties provided.
5 Check all electrical connectors, ensuring that they are clean, securely fastened, and that each is locked by its plastic tabs or wire clip, as appropriate. If any connector shows external signs of corrosion (accumulations of white or green deposits, or streaks of 'rust'), or if any is thought to be dirty, it must be unplugged and cleaned using electrical contact cleaner. If the connector pins are severely corroded, the connector must be renewed; note that this may mean the renewal of that entire section of the loom – see your local Ford dealer for details.
6 If the cleaner completely removes the corrosion to leave the connector in a satisfactory condition, it would be wise to pack the connector with a suitable material which will exclude dirt and moisture, preventing the corrosion from occurring again; a Ford dealer may be able to recommend a suitable product.
7 Check the condition of the battery connections – remake the connections or renew the leads if a fault is found (see Chapter 5A). Use the same techniques to ensure that all earth points in the engine compartment provide good electrical contact through clean, metal-to-metal joints, and that all are securely fastened.

9 Air conditioning system check

1 The following maintenance checks will ensure that the air conditioner operates at peak efficiency:

a) Check the auxiliary drivebelt (see Section 5).
b) Check the system hoses for damage or leaks.
c) Inspect the condenser fins for leaves, insects and other debris. Use a clean paint brush to clean the condenser.
d) Check that the drain tube from the front of the evaporator is clear – note that it is normal to have clear fluid (water) dripping from this while the system is in operation, to the extent that quite a large puddle can be left under the car when it is parked.

2 It's a good idea to operate the system for about 30 minutes at least once a month, particularly during the winter. Long term non-use can cause hardening, and subsequent failure, of the seals.
3 Because of the complexity of the air conditioning system and the special equipment necessary to service it, in-depth fault diagnosis and repairs are not included in this manual **(see Tool tip overleaf)**.
4 The most common cause of poor cooling is simply a low system refrigerant charge. If a noticeable drop in cool air output occurs, the following quick check will help you determine if the refrigerant level is low.
5 Warm the engine up to normal operating temperature.
6 Place the air conditioning temperature

TOOL TIP

Many car accessory shops sell one-shot air conditioning recharge aerosols. These generally contain refrigerant, compressor oil, leak sealer and system conditioner. Some also have a dye to help pinpoint leaks.

Warning: These products must only be used as directed by the manufacturer, and do not remove the need for regular maintenance.

selector at the coldest setting, and put the blower at the highest setting. Open the doors – to make sure the air conditioning system doesn't cycle off as soon as it cools the passenger compartment.

7 With the compressor engaged – the clutch will make an audible click, and the centre of the clutch will rotate – feel the inlet and outlet pipes at the compressor. One side should be cold, and one hot. If there's no perceptible difference between the two pipes, there's something wrong with the compressor or the system. It might be a low charge – it might be something else. Take the car to a dealer service department or an automotive air conditioning specialist.

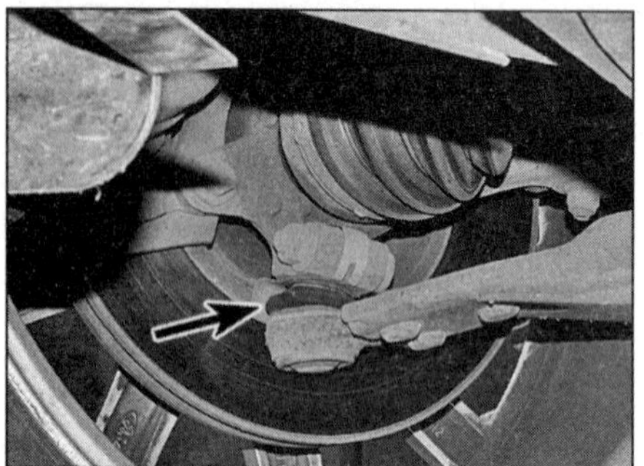

12.2a Check the balljoint dust covers . . .

12.2b . . . and the steering rack gaiters for perishing and splits

10 Seat belt check

1 Check the seat belts for satisfactory operation and condition. Inspect the webbing for fraying and cuts. Check that they retract smoothly and without binding into their reels.

2 Check that the seat belt mounting bolts are tight, and if necessary tighten them to the specified torque wrench setting (Chapter 11).

11 Antifreeze concentration check

1 The cooling system should be filled with the recommended antifreeze and corrosion protection fluid. Over a period of time, the concentration of fluid may be reduced due to topping-up (this can be avoided by topping-up with the correct antifreeze mixture) or fluid loss. If loss of coolant has been evident, it is important to make the necessary repair before adding fresh fluid. The exact mixture of antifreeze-to-water which you should use depends on the relative weather conditions. The mixture should contain at least 40% anti-freeze, but not more than 70%. Consult the mixture ratio chart on the antifreeze container before adding coolant. Use antifreeze which meets the car manufacturer's specifications.

2 With the engine **cold**, carefully remove the cap from the expansion tank. If the engine is not completely cold, place a cloth rag over the cap before removing it, and remove it slowly to allow any pressure to escape.

3 Antifreeze checkers are available from car accessory shops. Draw some coolant from the expansion tank and observe how many plastic balls are floating in the checker. Usually, 2 or 3 balls must be floating for the correct concentration of antifreeze, but follow the manufacturer's instructions.

4 If the concentration is incorrect, it will be necessary to either withdraw some coolant and add antifreeze, or alternatively drain the old coolant and add fresh coolant of the correct concentration.

12.4 Checking for wear in the front suspension and hub bearings

12 Steering, suspension and roadwheel check

Front suspension and steering

1 Raise the front of the car, and securely support it on axle stands (see *Jacking and vehicle support*).

2 Visually inspect the balljoint dust covers and the steering rack-and-pinion gaiters for splits, chafing or deterioration **(see illustrations)**. Any wear of these components will cause loss of lubricant, together with dirt and water entry, resulting in rapid deterioration of the balljoints or steering gear.

3 Check the power steering fluid hoses for chafing or deterioration, and the pipe and hose unions for fluid leaks. Also check for signs of fluid leakage under pressure from the steering gear rubber gaiters, which would indicate failed fluid seals within the steering gear.

4 Grasp the roadwheel at the 12 o'clock and 6 o'clock positions, and try to rock it **(see illustration)**. Very slight free play may be felt, but if the movement is appreciable, further investigation is necessary to determine the source. Continue rocking the wheel while an assistant depresses the footbrake. If the movement is now eliminated or significantly reduced, it is likely that the hub bearings are at fault. If the free play is still evident with the footbrake depressed, then there is wear in the suspension joints or mountings.

Wheel bearing wear is normally accompanied by a rumbling or droning noise when driving, at a certain speed, or when cornering. If play is found during the check in paragraph 4, with the car out of gear, spin the wheel several times by hand. Though it may be hard to distinguish wheel bearing noise from that of the driveshafts and brake pads, comparison with the other front wheel should reveal if the bearing is worn.

5 Now grasp the wheel at the 9 o'clock and 3 o'clock positions, and try to rock it as before. Any movement felt now may again be caused by wear in the hub bearings or the steering track rod balljoints. If the outer balljoint is worn, the visual movement will be obvious. If the inner joint is suspect, it can be felt by placing a hand over the rack-and-pinion rubber gaiter and gripping the track rod. If the wheel is now rocked, movement will be felt at the inner joint if wear has taken place.

6 Using a large screwdriver or flat bar, check

for wear in the suspension mounting bushes by levering between the relevant suspension component and its attachment point. Some movement is to be expected, as the mountings are made of rubber, but excessive wear should be obvious. Also check the condition of any visible rubber bushes, looking for splits, cracks or contamination of the rubber.

7 With the car standing on its wheels, have an assistant turn the steering wheel back-and-forth, about an eighth of a turn each way. There should be very little, if any, lost movement between the steering wheel and roadwheels. If this is not the case, closely observe the joints and mountings previously described. In addition, check the steering column universal joints for wear, and also check the rack-and-pinion steering gear itself.

Rear suspension

8 Chock the front wheels, then jack up the rear of the car and support securely on axle stands (see *Jacking and vehicle support*).

9 Working as described previously for the front suspension, check the rear hub bearings, the suspension bushes and the strut or shock absorber mountings (as applicable) for wear.

Shock absorbers

10 Check for any signs of fluid leakage around the shock absorber body, or from the rubber gaiter around the piston rod. Should any fluid be noticed, the shock absorber is defective internally, and should be renewed. **Note:** *Shock absorbers should always be renewed in pairs on the same axle.*

11 The efficiency of the shock absorber may be checked by bouncing the car at each corner. Generally speaking, the body will return to its normal position and stop after being depressed. If it rises and returns on a rebound, the shock absorber is probably suspect. Also examine the shock absorber upper and lower mountings for any signs of wear.

Roadwheels

12 Periodically remove the roadwheels, and clean any dirt or mud from the inside and outside surfaces. Examine the wheel rims for signs of rusting, corrosion or other damage. Light alloy wheels are easily damaged by 'kerbing' whilst parking, and similarly, steel wheels may become dented or buckled. Specialist firms do exist who will repair alloy wheels, but sometimes renewal of the wheel is the only course of remedial action possible.

13 The balance of each wheel and tyre assembly should be maintained, not only to avoid excessive tyre wear, but also to avoid wear in the steering and suspension components. Wheel imbalance is normally signified by vibration through the car's bodyshell, although in many cases it is particularly noticeable through the steering wheel. Conversely, it should be noted that wear or damage in suspension or steering components may cause excessive tyre wear. Out-of-round or out-of-true tyres, damaged wheels and wheel bearing wear also fall into this category. Balancing will not usually cure vibration caused by such wear.

14 Wheel balancing may be carried out with the wheel either on or off the car. If balanced on the car, ensure that the wheel-to-hub relationship is marked in some way prior to subsequent wheel removal, so that it may be refitted in its original position.

15 At this time, also check the spare wheel for damage.

13 Driveshaft rubber gaiter and CV joint check

1 The driveshaft rubber gaiters are very important, because they prevent dirt, water and foreign material from entering and damaging the constant velocity (CV) joints. External contamination can cause the gaiter material to deteriorate prematurely, so it's a good idea to wash the gaiters with soap and water occasionally.

2 With the car raised and securely supported on axle stands, turn the steering onto full-lock, then slowly rotate each front wheel in turn. Inspect the condition of the outer constant velocity (CV) joint rubber gaiters, squeezing the gaiters to open out the folds **(see illustration)**. Check for signs of cracking, splits, or deterioration of the rubber, which may allow the escape of grease, and lead to the ingress of water and grit into the joint. Also check the security and condition of the retaining clips. Repeat these checks on the inner CV joints. If any damage or deterioration is found, the gaiters should be renewed as described in Chapter 8.

3 At the same time, check the general condition of the outer CV joints themselves, by first holding the driveshaft and attempting to rotate the wheels. Repeat this check on the inner joints, by holding the inner joint yoke and attempting to rotate the driveshaft.

4 Any appreciable movement in the CV joint indicates wear in the joint, wear in the driveshaft splines, or a loose driveshaft retaining nut.

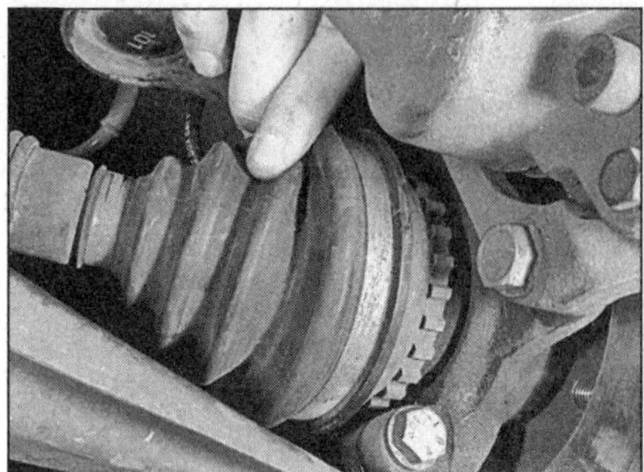

13.2 Check the driveshaft gaiters by hand for cracks and/or leaking grease

14 Exhaust system check

1 With the engine cold, check the complete exhaust system, from its starting point at the engine to the end of the tailpipe. If necessary, raise the front and rear of the car and support it on axle stands (see *Jacking and vehicle support*). Remove any engine undershields as necessary for full access to the exhaust system.

2 Check the exhaust pipes and connections for evidence of leaks, severe corrosion, and damage **(see illustration)**. Make sure that all brackets and mountings are in good condition and that all relevant nuts and bolts are tight. Leakage at any of the joints or in other parts of the system will usually show up as a black sooty stain in the vicinity of the leak.

3 Rattles and other noises can often be traced to the exhaust system, especially the brackets and rubber mountings **(see illustration)**. Don't overlook loose exhaust heat shields either, or the possibility that the internal baffles in a silencer box may be the source of a rattle. Try to move the pipes and silencers. If the components are able to come into contact with the body or suspension parts, secure the system with new mountings. Otherwise, separate the joints (if possible) and twist the pipes as necessary to provide additional clearance.

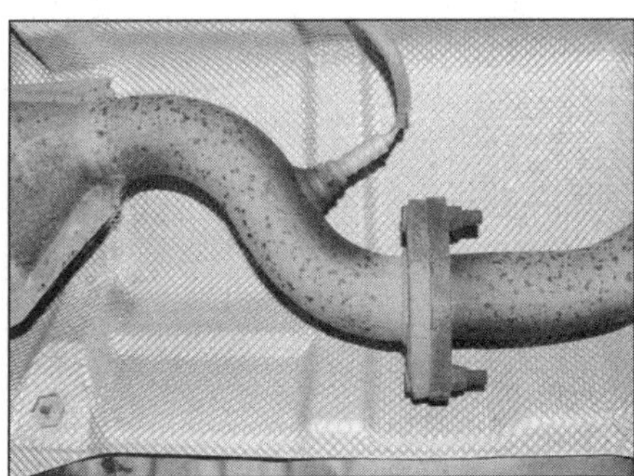

14.2 Check the condition of the exhaust system

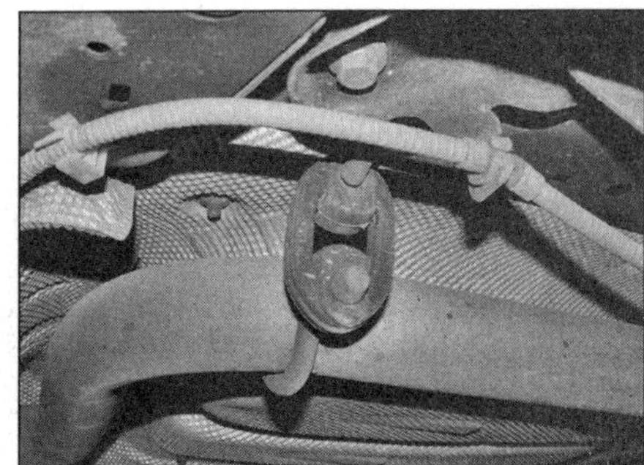

14.3 Don't overlook the exhaust rubber mountings and heat shields

15.5 Check the brake pipes and hoses for condition and security

15 Underbody and fuel/brake line check

1 With the car raised and supported on axle stands (see *Jacking and vehicle support*), thoroughly inspect the underbody and wheel arches for signs of damage and corrosion. In particular, examine the bottom of the side sills, and any concealed areas where mud can collect. Also check the inside edges at the base of all doors.

2 Where corrosion and rust is evident, press and tap firmly on the panel with a screwdriver, and check for any serious corrosion which would necessitate repairs.

3 If the panel is not seriously corroded, clean away the rust, and apply a new coating of underseal. Refer to Chapter 11 for more details of body repairs.

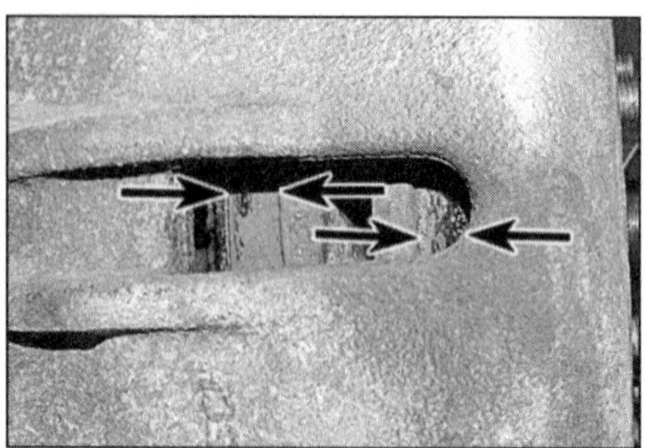

16.2 Check the thickness of the pad friction material through the caliper inspection window

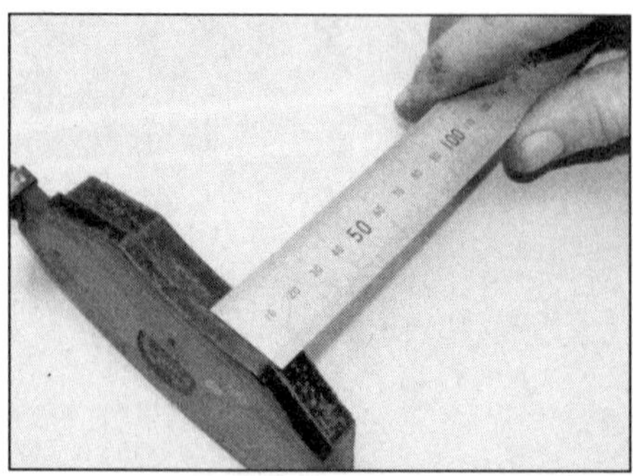

16.3 Checking the thickness of the pad linings with a steel rule

4 At the same time, inspect the PVC-coated lower body panels for stone damage and general condition.

5 Inspect all of the fuel and brake lines on the underbody for damage, rust, corrosion and leakage **(see illustration)**. Particularly check the rear brake pipes where they pass over the fuel tank. Also make sure that the pipes are correctly supported in their clips. Where applicable, check the PVC coating on the lines for damage.

16 Braking system check

Front disc brakes

1 Apply the handbrake, then jack up the front of the car and support it on axle stands (see *Jacking and vehicle support*). For better access to the brake calipers, remove the wheels.

2 Look through the inspection window in the caliper, and check that the thickness of the friction lining material on each of the pads is not less than the recommended minimum thickness given in the Specifications **(see illustration)**.

3 If it is difficult to determine the exact thickness of the pad linings, or if you are at all concerned about the condition of the pads, then remove them from the calipers for further inspection (refer to Chapter 9) **(see illustration)**.

4 Check the caliper on the other side in the same way.

5 If any one of the brake pads has worn down to, or below, the specified limit, *all four* pads at that end of the car must be renewed as a set.

6 Check both front brake discs with reference to Chapter 9.

7 Before refitting the wheels, check all brake lines and flexible hoses with reference to Chapter 9. In particular, check the flexible hoses in the vicinity of the calipers, where they are subjected to most movement. Bend them between the fingers and check that this does not reveal previously-hidden cracks, cuts or splits **(see illustration)**.

8 On completion, refit the wheels and lower the car to the ground. Tighten the wheel nuts to the specified torque.

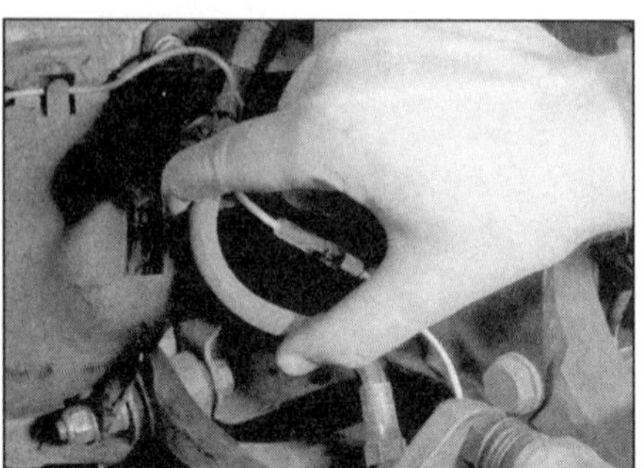

16.7 Checking the condition of a flexible brake hose

Rear disc brakes

9 Chock the front wheels then jack up the rear of the car and support on axle stands (see *Jacking and vehicle support*). Remove the rear wheels.

10 The procedure for checking the rear brakes is much the same as described in paragraphs 1 to 8 above.

Handbrake

11 With the car on a slight slope, firmly apply the handbrake lever, and check that it holds the car stationary, then release the lever and check that there is no resistance to movement of the car. If necessary, the handbrake should be adjusted as described in Chapter 9.

17 Door and bonnet check and lubrication

1 Check that the doors, bonnet and tailgate/boot lid close securely. Check that the bonnet safety catch operates correctly. Check the operation of the door check straps.

2 Lubricate the hinges, door check straps, the striker plates and the bonnet catch sparingly with a little oil or grease.

18 Pollen filter renewal

1 The air entering the car's ventilation system is passed through a very fine pleated-paper air filter element, which removes particles of pollen, dust and other airborne foreign matter. To ensure its continued effectiveness, this filter's element must be renewed at regular intervals. Failure to renew the element will also result in reduced airflow into the passenger compartment, reducing demisting and ventilation.

2 There are two ways to access the pollen filter for removal. The first method is that recommended by Ford, and is arguably safer. However, we found that the second method also worked fine, when tried on our project cars.

Method 1

3 Remove the windscreen wiper arms as described in Chapter 12.

4 Open the bonnet. Remove a total of five screws, and take off the central joining plate in front of the two windscreen cowl sections. Unclip and remove both the cowl sections from in front of the windscreen, noting that they locate into a grooved strip fitted to the bottom of the windscreen glass.

5 Press and release the two upper retaining clips (where applicable – on later models, the filter appears not to be clipped in place) and withdraw the pollen filter from its housing.

18.8a Remove the three screws in front of the passenger-side cowl . . .

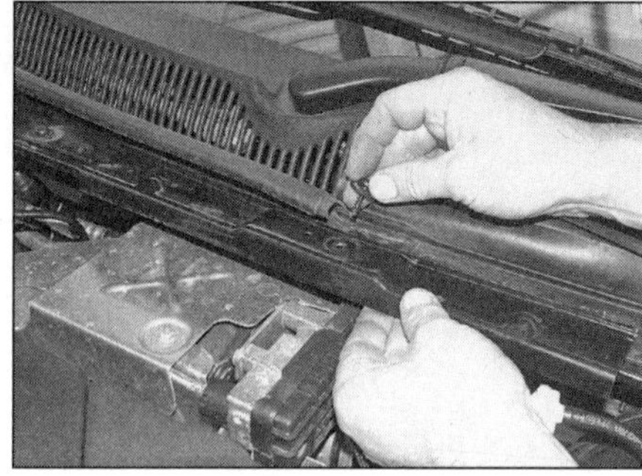
18.8b . . . noting that one of them retains the cowl heat shield

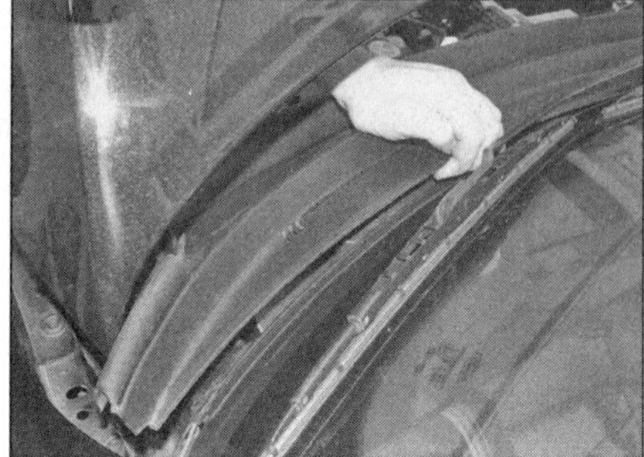
18.9 Lift the cowl panel up at the outer end . . .

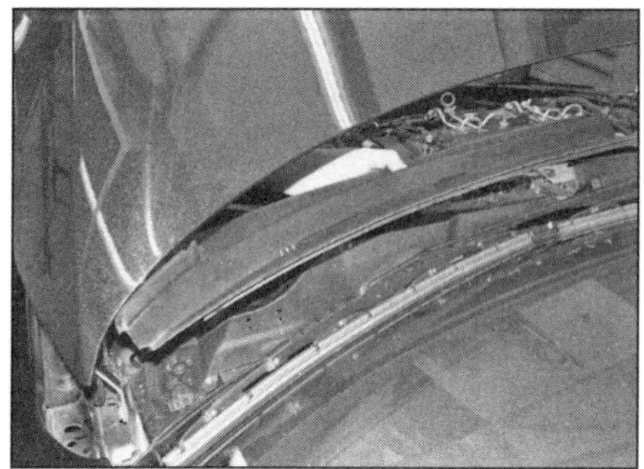
18.10 . . . then separate it in the centre, and remove it

18.11 Removing the pollen filter

18.12 Pollen filter correctly fitted

6 Wipe clean the housing, then insert the new filter, observing any direction-of-fitting arrows (arrows indicating airflow should point into the car, ie, rearwards). Check that the clips (where applicable) are correctly engaged.
7 Refit the cowl sections, then refit the wiper arms with reference to Chapter 12.

Method 2

8 With the bonnet open, remove three screws from in front of the passenger-side windscreen cowl. Note that the central screw also retains the cowl's metal heat shield – lift off the heat shield, noting how it fits **(see illustrations)**.
9 The passenger-side cowl must now be lifted upwards at its outer end, to release its locating bead from the grooved strip which is clipped under the base of the windscreen glass **(see illustration)**. With care, if necessary, a small flat-bladed screwdriver can be used to gently prise the cowl's bead upwards – once it has started, it should release along its length as the panel is pulled up. The bead is continuous along the whole length of the cowl panel.
10 When the cowl panel's locating bead is nearly free, slide the panel to the side, to unclip the inner end from the driver's-side cowl panel. It should now be possible to remove the panel completely, for access to the pollen filter **(see illustration)**.
11 Press and release the two upper retaining clips (where applicable – on later models, the filter appears not to be clipped in place) and withdraw the pollen filter from its housing **(see illustration)**.
12 Wipe clean the housing, then insert the new filter, observing any direction-of-fitting arrows (arrows indicating airflow should point into the car, ie, rearwards) **(see illustration)**. Check that the upper clips (where applicable) are correctly engaged.
13 Offer the cowl panel back into place, clipping it first into the driver's-side cowl panel at the inner end. The panel must now be positioned so that its locating bead sits into the groove at the base of the windscreen – this may require some trial-and-error before it fits correctly. The panel may also have to be pressed down gently along its length, to locate the bead into the groove – force should not be used this close to the windscreen glass, obviously.
14 Finally, refit the heat shield at the front of the two cowls, and secure it and the passenger-side cowl with the three screws. Close the bonnet on completion.

19 Fuel filter water draining

Note: *This procedure is not possible on all Mondeos. It appears that only some models were fitted with filters which have a water drain tap and drain tube on the base – if one is present, the water should be drained from it as described below.*
1 The fuel filter is located in a mounting bracket on the right-hand rear corner of the engine compartment, next to the front suspension strut tower. Working room is limited, and it may be helpful to partly remove the filter from its mounting bracket, using the information in Section 23, to make things easier.
2 Place the end of the drain tube at the base of the filter in a container which is large enough to take the entire contents of the fuel filter (though this should not be necessary). It must be possible to see the tube, to know when the flow of water stops, and fuel starts to emerge.
3 Open the black plastic knurled drain tap on the base of the filter slowly, and allow any water in the filter to flow out into the container. When the flow of water stops, and only fuel emerges, close the drain tap securely.
4 Withdraw the container from the engine compartment, and wipe up any spilt fuel.
5 Switch on the 'ignition', and leave it on for a few seconds to refill the filter before starting the engine. If difficulty is experienced starting the engine, refer to Section 2 of Chapter 4B.

20 Roadwheel nut tightness check

1 Apply the handbrake, chock the wheels, and engage 1st gear (or P).
2 If necessary to gain access to the nuts, remove the wheel cover (or wheel centre cover), using the flat end of the wheelbrace supplied in the tool kit.
3 Check the tightness of all wheel nuts using a torque wrench (refer to the Specifications).

21 Road test

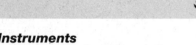

Instruments and electrical equipment

1 Check the operation of all instruments and electrical equipment.

2 Make sure that all instruments read correctly, and switch on all electrical equipment in turn, to check that it functions properly.

Steering and suspension

3 Check for any abnormalities in the steering, suspension, handling or road 'feel'.

4 Drive the car, and check that there are no unusual vibrations or noises.

5 Check that the steering feels positive, with no excessive 'sloppiness', or roughness, and check for any suspension noises when cornering and driving over bumps.

Drivetrain

6 Check the performance of the engine, clutch, transmission and driveshafts.

7 Listen for any unusual noises from the engine, clutch and transmission.

8 Make sure that the engine runs smoothly when idling, and that there is no hesitation when accelerating.

9 Check that, where applicable, the clutch action is smooth and progressive, that the drive is taken up smoothly, and that the pedal travel is not excessive. Also listen for any noises when the clutch pedal is depressed.

10 Check that all gears can be engaged smoothly without noise, and that the gear lever action is smooth and not abnormally vague or 'notchy'.

11 On automatic transmission models, make sure that all gearchanges occur smoothly, without snatching, and without an increase in engine speed between changes. Check that all of the gear positions can be selected with the car at rest.

12 Listen for a metallic clicking sound from the front of the car, as the car is driven slowly in a circle with the steering on full-lock. Carry out this check in both directions. If a clicking noise is heard, this indicates wear in a driveshaft joint (see Chapter 8).

Braking system

13 Make sure that the car does not pull to one side when braking, and that the wheels do not lock when braking hard.

14 Check that there is no vibration through the steering when braking.

15 Check that the handbrake operates correctly, without excessive movement of the lever, and that it holds the car stationary on a slope.

16 Test the operation of the brake servo unit as follows. Depress the footbrake four or five times to exhaust the vacuum, then start the engine. As the engine starts, there should be a noticeable 'give' in the brake pedal as vacuum builds-up. Allow the engine to run for at least two minutes, and then switch it off. If the brake pedal is now depressed again, it should be possible to detect a hiss from the servo as the pedal is depressed. After about four or five applications, no further hissing should be heard, and the pedal should feel considerably harder.

Every 25 000 miles or 2 years

22 Automatic transmission fluid level check

1 To accurately check the fluid level, a Ford diagnostic tool is necessary to verify the fluid temperature. The DIY mechanic who does not have access to this tool can use the alternative procedure given later, but the fluid level should then be checked by a Ford dealer at the earliest opportunity afterwards.

With diagnostic tool

2 First connect the tool to the diagnostic socket – the transmission fluid temperature must initially be below 30°C.

3 Apply the handbrake firmly, then jack up the front of the car and support it on axle stands (see *Jacking and vehicle support*). Unbolt the selector lever cable cover for access to the test plug, then lower the car to the ground.

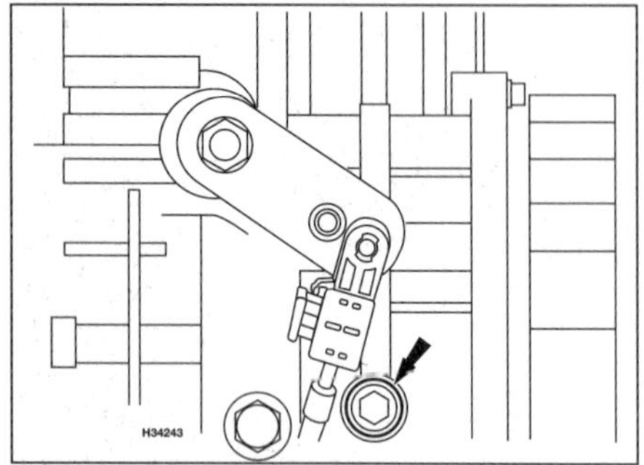

22.8 Automatic transmission fluid level test plug

4 Start the engine. While the engine is idling, depress the brake pedal and move the selector lever through all the positions three times, beginning and ending in P. Leave the engine idling until while the fluid level is being checked.

5 When the fluid temperature reaches 30°C, move the selector lever from P to D, and back again to P.

6 With the handbrake still firmly applied, jack up the front and rear of the car and support it securely on axle stands (see *Jacking and vehicle support*). **Note:** *The car must be level for an accurate check, and the car must be supported securely, as the engine will have to be running.*

7 Check that the fluid temperature is between 35°C and 45°C.

8 Position a suitable container beneath the transmission, then unscrew and remove the test plug **(see illustration)**. The test plug is located in the middle of the drain plug, and incorporates a tube extension to the fluid level height inside the transmission. Remove and discard the plug seal.

Caution: Wear suitable gloves as protection against scalding.

9 If no fluid escapes from the test plug, unscrew the filler plug from the top of the transmission and add fresh fluid until it emerges from the test hole. When the fluid ceases to drain, the level is correct.

10 Refit the filler and test plugs together with new seals and tighten to the specified torque. Refit the selector lever cable cover and tighten the bolts to the specified torque.

11 Switch off the engine and lower the car to the ground.

12 Disconnect the diagnostic tool.

Without diagnostic tool

13 To check the fluid level with any degree of accuracy, the fluid must be at operating temperature. One way to achieve this would be to take the car on a short journey (of say 5 to 10 miles) – however, this should not be attempted if the fluid level is known to be low, as damage could be caused.

14 Apply the handbrake firmly, then jack up the front of the car and support it securely on axle stands (see *Jacking and vehicle support*). **Note:** *The car must be level for an accurate check, and the car must be supported securely, as the engine will have to be running.*

15 Unbolt the selector lever cable cover for access to the test plug.

16 While the engine is idling, depress the brake pedal and move the selector lever through all the positions three times, beginning and ending in P. Leave the engine idling until while the fluid level is being checked.

17 Finally, press the brake pedal, and move the selector lever from P to D, and back again to P.

18 Position a suitable container beneath the transmission, then unscrew and remove the test plug. The test plug is located in the middle of the drain plug, and incorporates a tube extension to the fluid level height inside the transmission. Remove and discard the plug seal.

Caution: Wear suitable gloves as protection against scalding.

19 If no fluid escapes from the test plug, unscrew the filler plug from the top of the transmission and add fresh fluid until it emerges from the test hole. When the fluid ceases to drain, the level is correct.

23.1 The fuel filter is located in the right-hand rear corner of the engine compartment

23.3 Fuel filter quick-release fittings

23.4 Fuel filter retaining spring clip

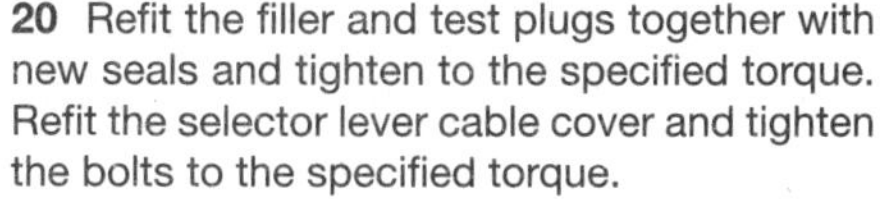

20 Refit the filler and test plugs together with new seals and tighten to the specified torque. Refit the selector lever cable cover and tighten the bolts to the specified torque.

21 Switch off the engine and lower the car to the ground.

22 It is advisable to have the fluid level finally confirmed by a Ford dealer, using the diagnostic tool, at the earliest opportunity.

23 Fuel filter renewal

Note: *Before carrying out the following procedure, read carefully the precautions given in Chapter 4B.*

1 The fuel filter is located in a mounting bracket on the right-hand rear corner of the engine compartment, next to the front suspension strut tower **(see illustration)**.

2 Note the location of the supply and return hoses on the filter, then place some cloth rags beneath it to catch any spilled fuel.

3 Disconnect the quick-release fittings from the filter and position them to one side **(see illustration)**. Be prepared for some loss of fuel. Depending on type, the fittings either release by squeezing the plastic tabs together, or by carefully prising out the coloured plastic section.

4 Push back the spring clip from the top of the filter and remove it from the mounting bracket **(see illustration)**. The fuel filter is supplied as a single renewable unit, and cannot be dismantled.

5 Though not essential, it may help the engine to restart with less effort if the filter can be filled with fresh fuel prior to fitting. Take care not to introduce dirt into the new filter, and avoid spilling fuel over the engine or bodywork.

6 Insert the new filter in the mounting bracket with its stubs in the previously-noted positions, then reconnect the hoses. Make sure that the quick-release fittings have engaged securely – on the type where the plastic section is prised out, reconnect the fitting, then press the section home until flush to secure.

7 Wipe away any spilled fuel, then prime and bleed the fuel system with reference to Chapter 4B.

Every 37 500 miles or 3 years

24 Glow plug check

Refer to Chapter 5C.

25 Air filter element renewal

1 The air filter element is located in the air cleaner assembly on the left-hand side of the engine compartment, behind the battery. Undo the screws and lift up the air cleaner cover **(see illustration)**. If additional working clearance is required, remove the cover completely with reference to Chapter 4B.

2 Lift out the element, noting its direction of fitting, and wipe out the housing **(see illustration)**.

3 If carrying out a routine service, the element must be renewed regardless of its apparent condition.

4 If you are checking the element for any other reason, inspect its lower surface; if it is oily or very dirty, renew the element. If it is only moderately dusty, it can be re-used by blowing it clean with compressed air.

5 Fit the new element using a reversal of the removal procedure.

26 Manual transmission oil level check

1 The manual transmission does not have a dipstick. To check the oil level, raise the car and support it securely on axle stands, making sure that the car is level.

2 Remove the engine undershields as necessary for access.

3 On 5-speed models, the filler/level plug is located on the lower front side of the transmission housing, while 6-speed models have the plug at the rear, behind the left-hand driveshaft. Using a suitable Allen key or socket, unscrew and remove it – take care, as it will probably be very tight **(see illustrations)**.

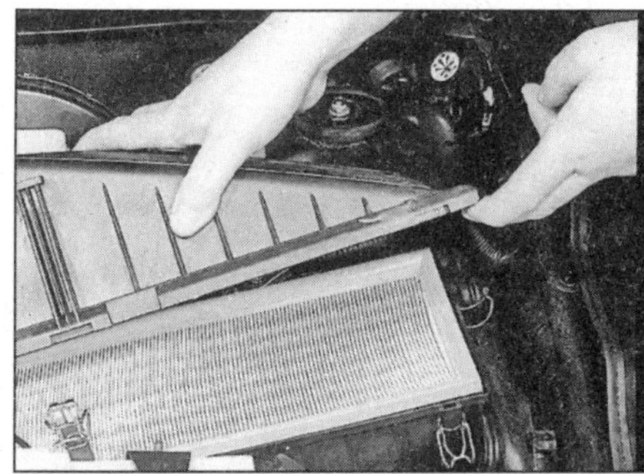

25.1 Remove the cover . . .

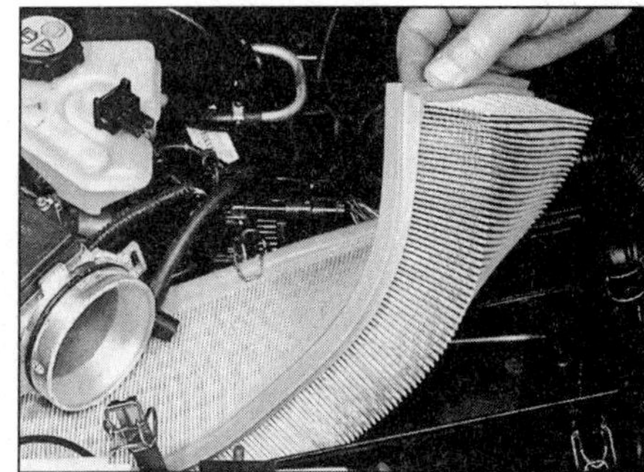

25.2 . . . then lift out the element

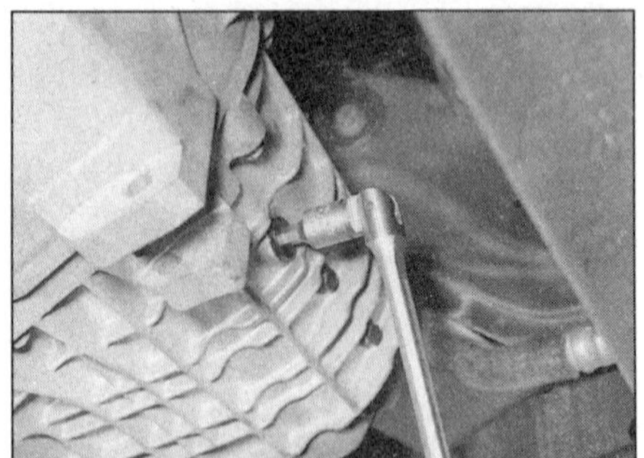

26.3a Using a suitable Allen key or socket, unscrew . . .

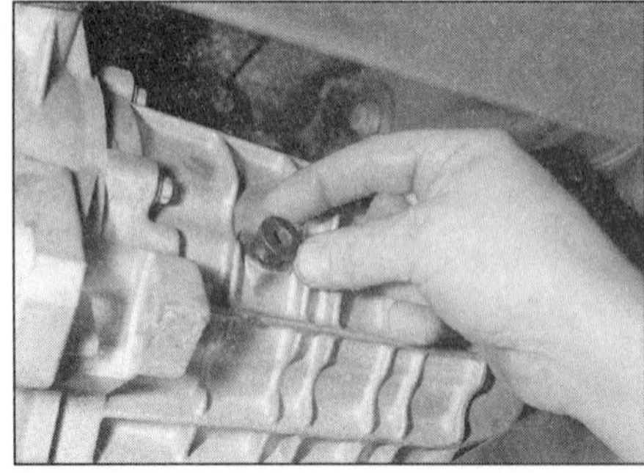

26.3b . . . and remove the transmission oil filler/level plug (5-speed)

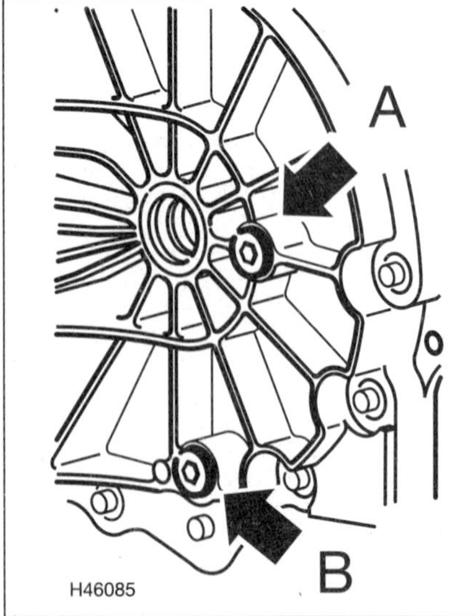

26.3c 6-speed transmission oil filler/ level (A) and drain (B) plug locations

4 If the lubricant level is correct, the oil should be up to the lower edge of the hole.

5 If the transmission needs more lubricant (if the oil level is not up to the hole), use a syringe, or a plastic bottle and tube, to add more **(see illustration)**.

6 Stop filling the transmission when the lubricant begins to run out of the hole, then wait until the flow of oil ceases.

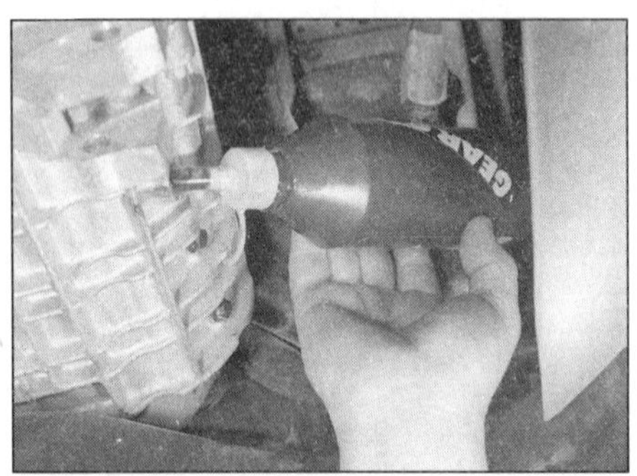

26.5 Topping-up the manual transmission oil (5-speed)

7 Refit the filler/level plug, and tighten it to the specified torque wrench setting. Drive the car a short distance, then check for leaks.

8 A need for regular topping-up can only be due to a leak, which should be found and rectified without delay.

27 Automatic transmission fluid renewal

Note: *No fluid dipstick is fitted to this transmission, and the fluid level can only be accurately checked using a special Ford diagnostic tool which monitors the fluid temperature. However, the DIY mechanic can perform an adequate level check, provided the car can be driven to get the fluid up to temperature. Clearly, the car should not be driven with an unknown amount of transmission fluid, as damage may be caused. For this reason, the fluid drained should be stored, and the amount carefully measured, so that the same amount of fresh fluid can be used when refilling.*

1 Park the car on level ground, and switch off the engine. Apply the handbrake, and engage P. Jack up the front of the car and support on axle stands (see *Jacking and vehicle support*).

2 Depending on model, it may be necessary to remove the engine undershield for access to the transmission drain plug. The plug is fitted on the base of the transmission housing.

3 Taking adequate precautions against burning or scalding if the engine and transmission are hot (wear gloves), position a suitable container below the transmission drain plug. Take care that as little fluid as possible is lost when draining – see the note above.

4 Loosen and remove the drain plug, and allow the fluid to drain into the container. Remove the seal from the plug – a new one should be used when refitting.

5 Unscrew the filler plug from the top of the transmission.

6 Clean the drain plug thoroughly then, when the flow of fluid has ceased, refit the plug (using a new seal) and tighten it to the specified torque.

7 Remove the fluid container from under the car, and measure the amount of fluid drained.

8 The transmission is filled through the filler plug aperture. Use a narrow funnel, and take great care to avoid introducing any kind of dirt into the transmission as it is filled. Fill the transmission with the same amount of fluid as was drained.

9 Refit the engine undershield (where removed), then lower the car to the ground.

10 Refer to Section 22 and complete the level checking procedure.

Every 3 years

28 Brake fluid renewal

The procedure is similar to that for the bleeding of the hydraulic system as described in Chapter 9, except that the brake fluid reservoir should be emptied by syphoning, and allowance should be made for the old fluid to be removed from the circuit when bleeding a section of the circuit.

Note: *According to Ford, unless the system is bled in conjunction with their WDS2000 diagnostic equipment, old fluid will not be removed from the ABS hydraulic unit. It may therefore be worth considering having this work performed by a Ford dealer, though the amount of old fluid remaining may be quite small.*

29 Coolant renewal

Note: *If the antifreeze used is Ford's own, or of similar quality, Ford state that the coolant need not be renewed for the life of the car. If the car's history is unknown, if the antifreeze is of lesser quality, or if you prefer to follow conventional servicing intervals, the coolant should be changed as follows.*

Warning: Refer to Chapter 3 and observe the warnings given. In particular, never remove the expansion tank filler cap when the engine is running, or has just been switched off, as the cooling system will be hot, and the consequent escaping steam and scalding coolant could cause serious injury. If the engine is hot, the electric cooling fan may start rotating even if the engine is not running, so be careful to keep hands, hair and loose clothing well clear when working in the engine compartment.

Cooling system draining

Warning: Wait until the engine is cold before starting this procedure.

1 To drain the system, first remove the expansion tank filler cap. Place a thick cloth over the expansion tank cap, then turn the cap anti-clockwise as far as the first stop and wait for any pressure to be released, then depress it and turn it further anti-clockwise to remove it.
2 If additional working clearance is required, apply the handbrake, then jack up the front of the car and support it on axle stands (see *Jacking and vehicle support*).
3 Remove the radiator undershield, then place a large drain tray underneath, and unscrew the radiator drain plug **(see illustration)**. Allow the coolant to drain into the tray. On completion, retighten the drain plug and refit the undershield. Where necessary, lower the car to the ground.

Cooling system flushing

4 If coolant renewal has been neglected, or if the antifreeze mixture has become diluted, then in time, the cooling system may gradually lose efficiency, as the coolant passages become restricted due to rust, scale deposits, and other sediment. The cooling system efficiency can be restored by flushing the system clean.
5 The radiator should be flushed independently of the engine, to avoid unnecessary contamination.

Radiator flushing

6 Disconnect the top and bottom hoses and any other relevant hoses from the radiator, with reference to Chapter 3.
7 Insert a garden hose into the radiator top inlet. Direct a flow of clean water through the radiator, and continue flushing until clean water emerges from the radiator bottom outlet.
8 If after a reasonable period, the water still does not run clear, the radiator can be flushed with a good proprietary cleaning agent. It is important that the manufacturer's instructions are followed carefully. If the contamination is particularly bad, remove the radiator, insert the hose in the radiator bottom outlet, and reverse-flush the radiator.

Engine flushing

9 Remove the thermostat as described in Chapter 3 then, if the radiator top hose has been disconnected from the engine, temporarily reconnect the hose. The cylinder block may also be drained by removing the drain plug located on the rear left-hand side **(see illustration)**.
10 With the top and bottom hoses disconnected from the radiator, insert a garden hose into the radiator top hose. Direct a clean flow of water through the engine, and continue flushing until clean water emerges from the radiator bottom hose.
11 On completion of flushing, refit the thermostat and reconnect the hoses with reference to Chapter 3.

Antifreeze mixture

12 Ford state that, if the only antifreeze used is the type with which the system was first filled at the factory (see *Lubricants and fluids*) it will last the lifetime of the car. This is subject to it being used in the recommended concentration, unmixed with any other type of antifreeze or additive, and topped-up when necessary using only that antifreeze mixed with clean water. If any other type of antifreeze is added, the lifetime guarantee no longer applies; to restore the lifetime protection, the system must be drained and thoroughly reverse-flushed before fresh coolant mixture is poured in.

29.3 Radiator drain plug (shown with radiator removed)

13 If the car's history (and therefore the quality of the antifreeze in it) is unknown, owners who wish to follow Ford's recommendations are advised to drain and thoroughly reverse-flush the system, before refilling with fresh coolant mixture. If the appropriate quality of antifreeze is used, the coolant can then be left for the life of the car.
14 If any antifreeze other than Ford's is to be used, the coolant must be renewed at regular intervals to provide an equivalent degree of protection; the conventional recommendation is to renew the coolant every three years.
15 If the antifreeze used is to Ford's specification, the levels of protection it affords are indicated in the Specifications Section of this Chapter. To give the recommended *standard* mixture ratio for this antifreeze, 40% (by volume) of antifreeze must be mixed with 60% of clean, soft water; if you are using any other type of antifreeze, follow its manufacturer's instructions to achieve the correct ratio **(also see the Haynes Hint)**.
16 Before adding antifreeze, the cooling system should be completely drained, preferably flushed, and all hoses checked for condition and security. Fresh antifreeze will rapidly find any weaknesses in the system.
17 After filling with antifreeze, a label should be attached to the expansion tank, stating the type and concentration of antifreeze used, and the date installed. Any subsequent topping-up should be made with the same type and concentration of antifreeze. If topping-up using antifreeze to Ford's specification, note that a 50/50 mixture is permissible, purely for convenience.

Cooling system filling

18 Before attempting to fill the cooling system, make sure that all hoses and clips are in good condition, and that the clips are tight.

29.9 Cylinder block drain plug

Note that an antifreeze mixture must be used all year round, to prevent corrosion of the engine components.

HAYNES HiNT ***It is rare to ever drain the cooling system completely – a small quantity will remain. If the system has been extensively flushed with clean water, this remaining quantity will in fact be plain water. For this reason, some people will first fill the system with the required quantity of neat antifreeze (half the total system capacity, for a 50% mixture), and then complete the filling process with plain water. This ensures that the resulting coolant (once it has mixed inside the engine) is not 'diluted' by old coolant or water remaining in the system.***

19 Loosen the bleed valve located on the top of the water pump **(see illustration)**.
20 Slowly fill the system through the expansion tank until coolant emerges from the water pump bleed valve. Tighten the bleed valve.
21 Continue to fill the system until the coolant level reaches the MAX mark on the side of the expansion tank.
22 Start the engine and increase its speed to 1500 rpm for 20 seconds. Switch off the engine.
23 Top-up the coolant in the expansion tank to 15 mm above the MAX mark, then refit the filler cap.

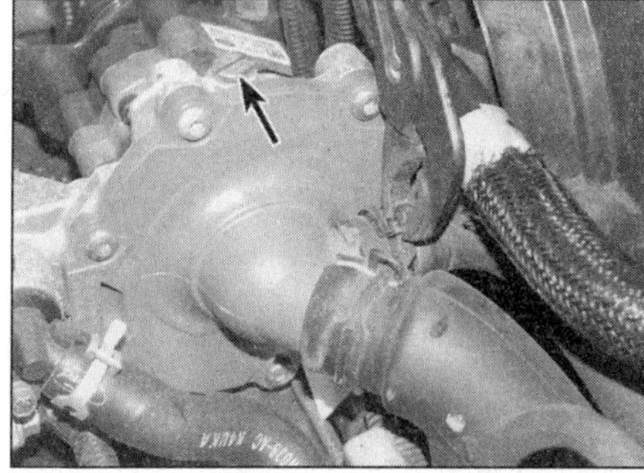

29.19 Bleed valve located on the top of the water pump

24 Start the engine and allow it to idle for 2 minutes.
25 Increase the engine speed to 3000 rpm and hold it at this speed until the electric cooling fan operates. Allow the engine to idle for a further 5 minutes.
26 Switch off the engine and allow it to cool for at least 30 minutes.
27 Remove the filler cap and top-up the coolant level to the MAX mark on the expansion tank. Refit and tighten the cap.

Airlocks

28 If, after draining and refilling the system, symptoms of overheating are found which did not occur previously, then the fault is almost certainly due to trapped air at some point in the system, causing an airlock and restricting the flow of coolant; usually, the air is trapped because the system was refilled too quickly.
29 If an airlock is suspected, first try gently squeezing all visible coolant hoses. A coolant hose which is full of air feels quite different to one full of coolant, when squeezed. After refilling the system, most airlocks will clear once the system has cooled, and been topped-up.
30 While the engine is running at operating temperature, switch on the heater and heater fan, and check for heat output. Provided there is sufficient coolant in the system, any lack of heat output could be due to an airlock in the system.
31 Airlocks can have more serious effects than simply reducing heater output – a severe airlock could reduce coolant flow around the engine. Check that the radiator top hose is hot when the engine is at operating temperature – a top hose which stays cold could be the result of an airlock (or a non-opening thermostat).
32 If the problem persists, stop the engine and allow it to cool down **completely**, before unscrewing the expansion tank filler cap or loosening the hose clips and squeezing the hoses to bleed out the trapped air. In the worst case, the system will have to be at least partially drained (this time, the coolant can be saved for re-use) and flushed to clear the problem.

Pressure cap check

33 Clean the pressure cap (expansion tank), and inspect the seal inside the cap for damage or deterioration. If there is any sign of damage or deterioration to the seal, fit a new pressure cap. If the cap is old, it is worth considering fitting a new one for peace of mind – they are not expensive. If the pressure cap fails, excess pressure will be allowed into the system, which may result in the failure of hoses, the radiator, or the heater matrix.

Every 50 000 miles

30 Auxiliary drivebelt renewal

Note: *This is a precautionary measure, and not part of Ford's schedule. Ford state that the drivebelt should last at least twice this mileage. However, these belts do deteriorate with age, and considering the inconvenience that an in-service failure would cause, it may be wise to fit a new belt at this interval.*

Power steering pump drivebelt

1 Remove the engine top cover. Also remove the semi-circular drivebelt cover, which is secured by a single nut to the top of the engine.
2 Working at the transmission end of the engine, unclip the small coolant hose from the large-diameter air inlet hose next to the battery. Loosen the clips from each end of the inlet hose, and remove it.
3 In the area below the air inlet hose which was removed, remove the two bolts securing the inlet duct and the EGR pipe.
4 If the belt is to be refitted, mark its direction of travel (towards the front of the engine). Using a suitable square drive (such as a socket handle) in the hole at the top of the belt tensioner, turn the tensioner clockwise (towards the back of the engine) to release the belt.
5 Slip the belt off the camshaft pulley, and off the power steering pump pulley, noting how it is fitted. Release the tensioner slowly.
6 When refitting the belt, it is helpful to have an assistant who can hold the tensioner in its released position. Feed the belt onto the camshaft pulley, then hold the tensioner towards the back of the engine while feeding the belt around the power steering pump pulley. Ensure the belt is located correctly in the pulley grooves, then release the tensioner.
7 Refit the two bolts from the inlet duct and EGR pipe, and tighten them securely.
8 Refit the air inlet hose, tightening the hose clips securely, and clip the coolant hose back onto it. Finally, refit the drivebelt cover with its nut, and the engine top cover.

Main drivebelt

9 Remove the engine top cover.
10 Disconnect the battery negative lead, and position the lead away from the battery (also see *Disconnecting the battery*).
11 Working at the back of the engine, unscrew and remove the alternator upper mounting bolt. Note that this bolt also supports a wiring harness bracket, for refitting.
12 Loosen the right-hand front wheel nuts, then jack up the front right-hand side of the car and support it securely on an axle stand. Remove the roadwheel.
13 Remove the engine undertray, which is secured by a total of eight fasteners. Remove three more bolts, and take off the belt's lower splash shield.
14 If the existing drivebelt is to be refitted, mark it, or note the maker's markings on its flat surface, so that it can be installed the same way round.
15 Rotate the tensioner pulley clockwise to release its pressure on the drivebelt. Depending on model and equipment, the tensioner will either have a hex fitting for a spanner or socket, or a square hole into which a ratchet handle from a socket set can be fitted.
16 Slip the drivebelt off the pulleys, noting how it is routed, and release the tensioner again. It will not be possible to remove the belt completely at this stage.
17 Remove the air duct which supplies the alternator with cold air – the duct is secured by a total of four nuts.
18 Disconnect the two wiring plugs from the alternator.
19 Unscrew the alternator's two lower mounting nuts, and move the alternator to one side, to gain access to the support bracket bolts.
20 Remove the three bolts from the alternator support bracket, then move the bracket and tensioner assembly to one side.
21 Withdraw the drivebelt from the car.
22 Refitting is a reversal of removal, noting the following points:

a) *Loosely fit the belt in position, then fit the alternator support bracket and tighten the bolts to the specified torque.*
b) *Fit the alternator lower mounting nuts hand-tight to begin with. Refit the upper mounting bolt (with the wiring harness bracket), and tighten it to the specified torque. Once this is done, tighten the two lower nuts to the specified torque, with the rearmost nut done first.*
c) *Ensure that the alternator wiring plugs are securely reconnected.*
d) *Hold the tensioner in the released position, then slip the belt round all the pulleys. Ensure that it locates correctly in the pulley grooves, then release the tensioner.*
e) *Refit all other removed components, then lower the car to the ground, and tighten the wheel nuts to the specified torque. Reconnect the battery, referring to the information in Disconnecting the battery if necessary.*

Chapter 2 Part A:
1.8 and 2.0 litre petrol engine in-car repair procedures

Contents

Degrees of difficulty

Easy, suitable for novice with little experience	**Fairly easy,** suitable for beginner with some experience	**Fairly difficult,** suitable for competent DIY mechanic	**Difficult,** suitable for experienced DIY mechanic	**Very difficult,** suitable for expert DIY or professional

Specifications

General

Engine type	Four-cylinder, in-line, 16-valve, double overhead camshafts
Engine code:	
1.8 litre models	CDBB, CGBA/B and CHBA/B
2.0 litre models	CJBA/B
Capacity:	
1.8 litre models	1798 cc
2.0 litre models	1999 cc
Bore:	
1.8 litre models	83.0 mm
2.0 litre models	87.5 mm
Stroke – all models	83.1 mm
Compression ratio	10.8 : 1
Power output:	
1.8 litre models:	
CGBA/B	81 kW (110 PS) at 5500 rpm
CDBB and CHBA/B	92 kW (125 PS) at 6000 rpm
2.0 litre models	107 kW (145 PS) at 6000 rpm
Firing order	1-3-4-2 (No 1 cylinder at timing chain end)
Direction of crankshaft rotation	Clockwise (seen from right-hand side of car)

Camshafts

Camshaft endfloat	0.09 to 0.24 mm
Exhaust lobe lift	7.7 mm
Inlet lobe lift :	
1.8 litre:	
CGBA/B	7.4 mm
CDBB and CHBA/B	8.5 mm
2.0 litre	8.8 mm
Camshaft bearing journal diameter	24.96 to 24.98 mm
Camshaft bearing running clearance	0.055 to 0.060 mm

Tappets

Valve clearances (cold):	
Inlet	0.22 to 0.28 mm
Exhaust	0.27 to 0.33 mm

Lubrication

Engine oil capacity (including filter)	See Chapter 1A
Engine oil pressure	3.5 bar @ 2000 rpm
Engine oil type/specification	See end of *Weekly checks*

Torque wrench settings

Torque wrench settings	Nm	lbf ft
Alternator upper bolt	25	18
Auxiliary drivebelt idler pulley	25	18
Camshaft bearing cap bolts:		
Stage 1	7	5
Stage 2	16	12
Camshaft cover bolts	10	7
Camshaft position sensor retaining bolt	6	4
Camshaft sprocket retaining bolts	65	48
Coolant pump pulley bolts	25	18
Crankshaft oil seal carrier bolts	10	7
Crankshaft position sensor retaining bolts	7	5
Crankshaft pulley bolt*:		
Stage 1	100	74
Stage 2	Angle-tighten a further 90°	
Cylinder block timing peg blanking plug	20	15
Cylinder head bolts*:		
Stage 1	5	4
Stage 2	15	11
Stage 3	45	33
Stage 4	Angle-tighten a further 90°	
Stage 5	Angle-tighten a further 90°	
Driveshaft support bearing bracket-to-cylinder block bolts	48	35
Engine/transmission mountings:		
Left-hand mounting bracket-to-transmission bolts:		
Automatic transmission	80	59
Manual transmission	90	66
Left-hand mounting centre nut*	133	98
Left-hand mounting outer nuts*	48	35
Rear mounting link nuts/bolts	80	59
Right-hand mounting-to-inner wing bolts	80	59
Right-hand mounting-to-engine nuts	80	59
Exhaust front pipe to manifold	46	34
Exhaust manifold bracket-to-cylinder block bolts	25	18
Exhaust manifold heat shield bolts	10	7
Exhaust manifold retaining nuts	55	41
Flywheel/driveplate bolts*:		
Stage 1	50	37
Stage 2	80	59
Stage 3	112	83
Inlet manifold retaining bolts	18	13
Knock sensor bolt	20	15
Oil filter housing bolts	25	18
Oil pressure warning light switch	15	11
Oil pump chain guide bolts	10	7
Oil pump chain tensioner bolt	10	7
Oil pump sprocket bolt	25	18
Oil pump-to-cylinder block bolts:		
Stage 1	10	7
Stage 2	23	17
Oil separator-to-cylinder block bolts	10	7
Power steering pump-to-cylinder block bolts	18	13
Roadwheel nuts	85	63
Sump oil drain plug	28	21
Sump-to-cylinder block bolts	25	18
Sump-to-transmission bolts	40	30

Torque wrench settings (continued)	Nm	lbf ft
Timing chain cover:		
Lower blanking plug	12	9
Upper blanking plug	10	7
Timing chain cover bolts:		
Bolts 9, 20, 21 & 22	48	35
All other bolts (including lower bolts)	10	7
Timing chain guide retaining bolts	10	7
Timing chain tensioner bolts	10	7
Torque converter-to-driveplate nuts	36	27
Transmission-to-engine bolts	48	35

** Use new nuts/bolts*

1 General information

How to use this Chapter

This Part of Chapter 2 is devoted to repair procedures possible while the engine is still installed in the car, and includes only the Specifications relevant to those procedures. Since these procedures are based on the assumption that the engine is installed in the car, if the engine has been removed from the car and mounted on a stand, some of the preliminary dismantling steps outlined will not apply.

Information concerning engine/transmission removal and refitting, and engine overhaul, can be found in Part D of this Chapter, which also includes the Specifications relevant to those procedures.

Engine

This is a new engine which has been developed in Japan along with Mazda. Its main objectives were to reduce fuel consumption, engine weight, noise emissions and pollutant levels, It also has increased torque and power output.

The engine, known by Ford's internal code name Duratec-HE, is of four-cylinder, in-line type, mounted transversely at the front of the car, with the (clutch and) transmission on its left-hand end.

Apart from the plastic inlet manifold, the complete engine castings are of aluminium alloy.

The main bearing caps are built into a frame, which holds the crankshaft in the cylinder block to help strengthen the assembly and reduce engine vibration. There are no service operations allowed on the crankshaft assembly, as there is a fine tolerance in the bearing clearances and bearing shells. If there is any reason for repair in this area then the complete cylinder block and crankshaft assembly must be renewed as a unit.

Both camshafts are driven by the same low-noise, maintenance-free, pinned-link timing chain. Each camshaft operates eight valves via conventional bucket tappets without adjusting shims. If there is wear, and the valve clearances require adjustment, then new bucket tappets are available in different sizes to reach the correct clearance.

Each camshaft rotates in five bearings that are line-bored directly in the cylinder head and the (bolted-on) bearing caps; this means that the bearing caps are not available separately from the cylinder head, and must not be interchanged with caps from another engine.

The water pump is bolted to the right-hand end of the cylinder block, and is driven with the power steering pump, air conditioning compressor (where fitted) and alternator by a flat 'polyvee' type auxiliary drivebelt from the crankshaft pulley.

Lubrication system

Lubrication is by means of an eccentric-rotor pump, which is mounted under the right-hand end of the cylinder block, and is driven via a chain from the crankshaft and draws oil through a pick-up pipe located in the sump. The pump forces oil through an externally-mounted element type filter – on some versions of the engine, an oil cooler is fitted to the oil filter mounting, so that clean oil entering the engine's galleries is cooled by the main engine cooling system. From the filter, the oil is pumped into a main gallery in the cylinder block/crankcase, from where it is distributed to the crankshaft (main bearings) and cylinder head.

The big-end bearings are supplied with oil via internal drillings in the crankshaft. While the crankshaft and camshaft bearings and the tappets receive a pressurised supply, the camshaft lobes and valves are lubricated by splash, as are all other engine components.

2 Repair operations possible with the engine in the car

The following major repair operations can be accomplished without removing the engine from the car. However, owners should note that any operation involving the removal of the sump requires careful forethought, depending on the level of skill and the tools and facilities available; refer to the relevant text for details.

a) Compression pressure – testing.
b) Cylinder head valve cover – removal and refitting.
c) Timing chain covers – removal and refitting.
d) Timing chain – renewal.
e) Timing chain tensioner and sprockets – removal and refitting.
f) Camshafts and tappets – removal and refitting.
g) Cylinder head – removal, overhaul and refitting.
h) Cylinder head and pistons – decarbonising.
i) Sump – removal and refitting.
j) Crankshaft oil seals – renewal.
k) Oil pump – removal and refitting.
l) Flywheel/driveplate – removal and refitting.
m) Engine/transmission mountings – removal and refitting.

Clean the engine compartment and the exterior of the engine with some type of degreaser before any work is done. It will make the job easier, and will help to keep dirt out of the internal areas of the engine.

Depending on the components involved, it may be helpful to remove the bonnet, to improve access to the engine as repairs are performed (refer to Chapter 11 if necessary). Cover the wings to prevent damage to the paint; special covers are available, but an old bedspread or blanket will also work.

If vacuum, exhaust, oil or coolant leaks develop, indicating a need for component/ gasket or seal renewal, the repairs can generally be made with the engine in the car. The inlet and exhaust manifold gaskets, sump gasket, crankshaft oil seals and cylinder head gasket are all accessible with the engine in place.

Exterior components such as the inlet and exhaust manifolds, the sump, the oil pump, the water pump, the starter motor, the alternator and the fuel system components can be removed for repair with the engine in place.

Since the cylinder head can be removed without lifting out the engine, camshaft and valve component servicing can also be accomplished with the engine in the car, as can renewal of the timing chain and sprockets.

4.7 TDC sensor (arrowed) under the right-hand wheel arch

3 Compression test – description and interpretation

1 When engine performance is down, or if misfiring occurs which cannot be attributed to the ignition or fuel systems, a compression test can provide diagnostic clues as to the engine's condition. If the test is performed regularly, it can give warning of trouble before any other symptoms become apparent.
2 The engine must be fully warmed-up to normal operating temperature, the oil level must be correct, the battery must be fully charged, and the spark plugs must be removed. The aid of an assistant will be required also.
3 Disable the ignition system by unplugging the ignition coil's electrical connector.
4 Referring to Chapter 12, identify and remove the fuel pump fuse from the fusebox. Now start the engine and allow it to run until it stalls. If the engine will not start, at least keep it cranking for about 10 seconds. The fuel system should now be depressurised, preventing unburnt fuel from soaking the catalytic converter as the engine is turned over during the test.
5 Fit a compression tester to the No 1 cylinder spark plug hole – the type of tester which screws into the plug thread is to be preferred.
6 Have the assistant hold the throttle wide open and crank the engine on the starter motor; after one or two revolutions, the compression pressure should build-up to a maximum figure, and then stabilise. Record the highest reading obtained.
7 Repeat the test on the remaining cylinders, recording the pressure developed in each.
8 Due to the variety of testers available, and the fluctuation of starter motor speed when cranking the engine, different readings are often obtained when carrying out the compression test. For this reason, specific compression pressure figures are not quoted by Ford. However, all cylinders should produce very similar pressures; any difference greater than 10% indicates the existence of a fault.
9 If the pressure in any cylinder is considerably lower than the others, introduce a teaspoonful of clean oil into that cylinder through its spark plug hole, and repeat the test.
10 If the addition of oil temporarily improves the compression pressure, this indicates that bore or piston wear is responsible for the pressure loss. No improvement suggests that leaking or burnt valves, or a blown head gasket, may be to blame.
11 A low reading from two adjacent cylinders is almost certainly due to the head gasket having blown between them; the presence of coolant in the engine oil will confirm this.
12 If one cylinder is about 20 percent lower than the others and the engine has a slightly rough idle, a worn camshaft lobe could be the cause.
13 If the compression is unusually high, the combustion chambers are probably coated with carbon deposits. If this is the case, the cylinder head should be removed and decarbonised.
14 On completion of the test, refit the spark plugs, then reconnect the ignition coil and refit the fuel pump fuse.

4 Top Dead Centre (TDC) for No 1 piston – locating

Note: *Only turn the engine in the normal direction of rotation – clockwise from the right-hand side of the car.*

General

1 Top Dead Centre (TDC) is the highest point in its travel up-and-down its cylinder bore that each piston reaches as the crankshaft rotates. While each piston reaches TDC both at the top of the compression stroke and again at the top of the exhaust stroke, for the purpose of timing the engine, TDC refers to the No 1 piston position at the top of its compression stroke.
2 It is useful for several servicing procedures to be able to position the engine at TDC.
3 No 1 piston and cylinder are at the right-hand (timing chain) end of the engine (right- and left-hand are always quoted as seen from the driver's seat).

Locating TDC

4 Remove all the spark plugs – this will make it easier to turn the engine (Chapter 1A).
5 Disconnect the battery negative (earth) lead (refer to *Disconnecting the battery* at the end of this manual).
6 Apply the handbrake, then jack up the front of the car and support it on axle stands (see *Jacking and vehicle support*). Remove the right-hand front roadwheel.
7 Remove the cover from under the right-hand front wheel arch to expose the crankshaft pulley and TDC sensor **(see illustration)**.
8 There is a timing hole provided on the rear of the cylinder block (below the alternator) to position the crankshaft at TDC **(see illustrations)**. Unscrew the timing hole plug and insert a timing peg (303-507 – obtainable from Ford dealers, or a tool supplier).
9 Using a spanner or socket on the crankshaft

4.8a Remove the timing hole plug . . .

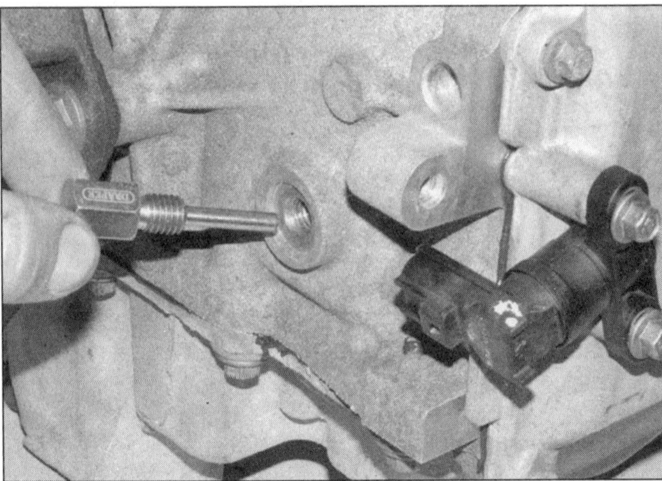
4.8b . . . and insert the timing peg

4.10 Insert an M6 bolt through the pulley to align for TDC

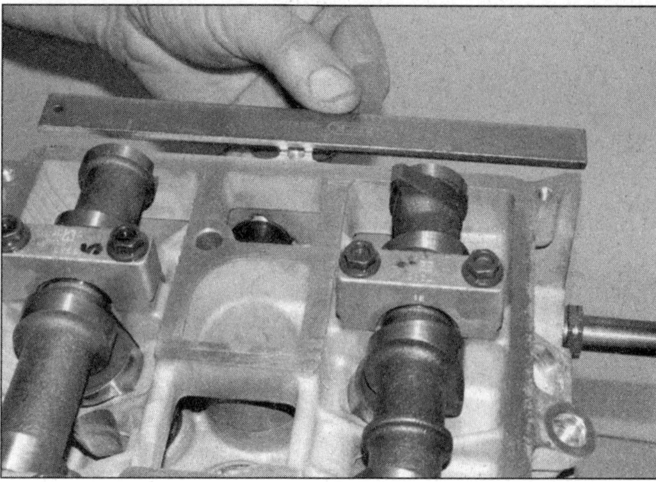
4.12 Slide the tool/metal bar into the slots in the end of the camshafts

pulley bolt, rotate the crankshaft clockwise until it stops against the timing peg.

10 There is a bolt hole in the crankshaft pulley which should align with the thread in the timing chain cover, insert a bolt (M6 x 18 mm) to locate the pulley at TDC **(see illustration)**.

11 Number 1 and 4 pistons are now at TDC, one of them on the compression stroke. To determine which cylinder is on the compression stroke, the camshaft cover will need to be removed (as described in Section 5).

12 Obtain Ford service tool 21-162B, or fabricate a substitute from a strip of metal 5 mm thick (while the strip's thickness is critical, its length and width are not, but should be approximately 180 to 230 mm by 20 to 30 mm). If number 1 cylinder is on the compression stroke – rest the tool on the cylinder head mating surface, and slide it into the slot in the left-hand end of both camshafts **(see illustration)**.

13 The camshaft aligning tool should slip snugly into both slots while resting on the cylinder head mating surface; if one camshaft is only slightly out of alignment, it is permissible to use an open-ended spanner to rotate the camshaft gently and carefully until the tool will fit.

14 If both camshaft slots are below the level of the cylinder head mating surface (they are machined significantly off-centre), rotate the crankshaft through one full turn clockwise and fit the tool again; it should now fit as described in the previous paragraph. **Note:** *The timing peg and crankshaft pulley locking bolt will have to be removed before turning the engine.*

15 Do not use the locked camshafts to prevent the crankshaft from rotating – use only the locking methods described in Section 8 for removing the crankshaft pulley.

16 Once No 1 cylinder has been positioned at TDC on the compression stroke, TDC for any of the other cylinders can then be located by rotating the crankshaft clockwise 180° at a time and following the firing order (see Specifications).

17 Before turning the engine again, make sure that the timing peg and crankshaft pulley locating bolt have been removed.

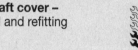

5 Camshaft cover – removal and refitting

Removal

1 Disconnect the battery negative (earth) lead (refer to *Disconnecting the battery* at the end of this manual).

2 Unclip the breather hose from the engine upper plastic cover, then unclip the cover from the top of the engine **(see illustration)**.

3 Disconnect the electrical connector from the camshaft position sensor **(see illustration)**.

4 Detach the wiring harness from the camshaft cover **(see illustration)**.

5 Disconnect the positive crankcase ventilation (PCV) hose from the camshaft cover **(see illustration)**.

6 Unscrew the three engine upper plastic cover retaining pegs from the camshaft cover retaining studs, note the position of the retaining studs.

7 Carefully unplug the HT leads from the

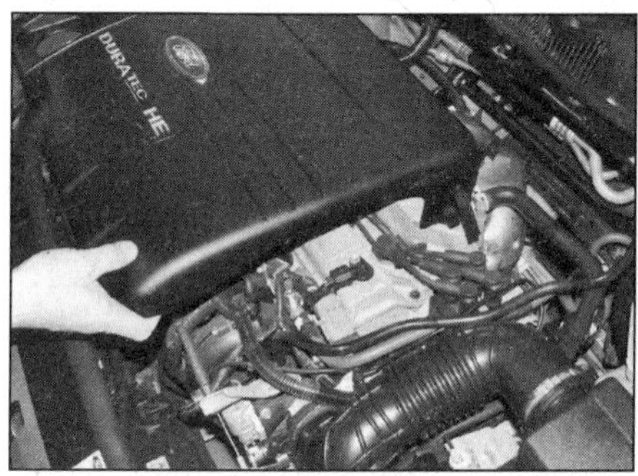

5.2 Unclip the hose and remove the engine upper cover

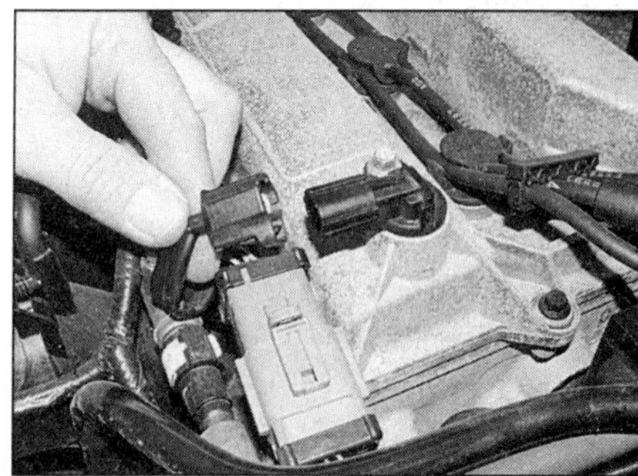
5.3 Disconnect the wiring connector from the camshaft sensor

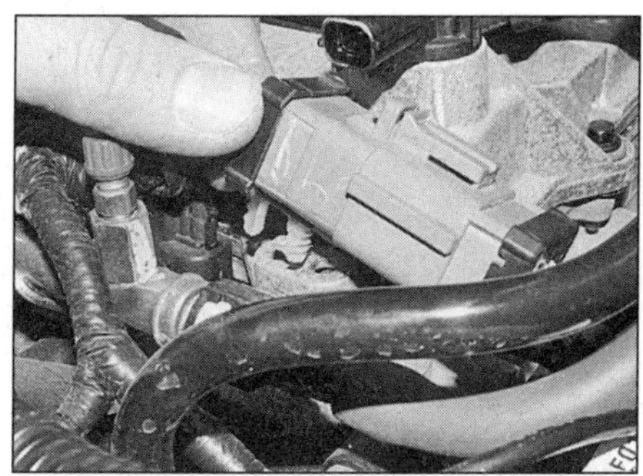
5.4 Unclip the wiring harness from the camshaft cover

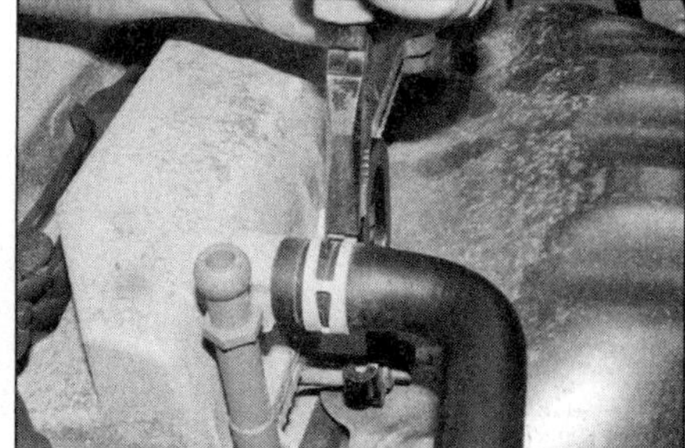
5.5 Using a pair of pliers to remove the crankcase ventilation hose from the rocker cover

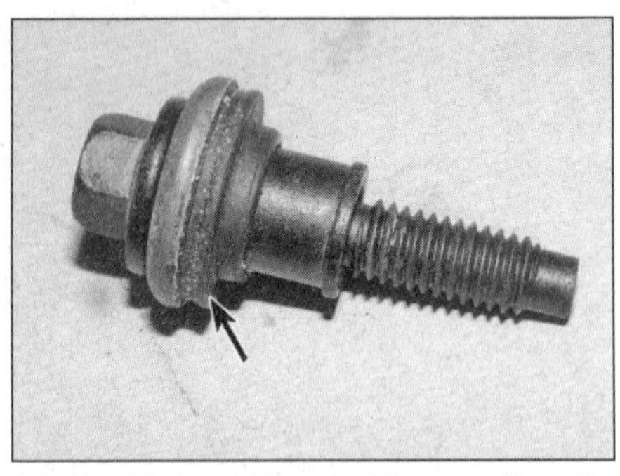

5.9 Check the rubber seal (arrowed) on the camshaft cover retaining bolts for damage

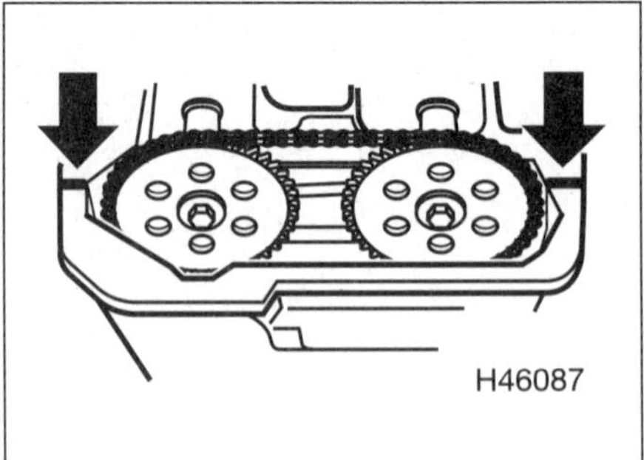

5.11 Apply a thin bead of sealant to the timing cover joints

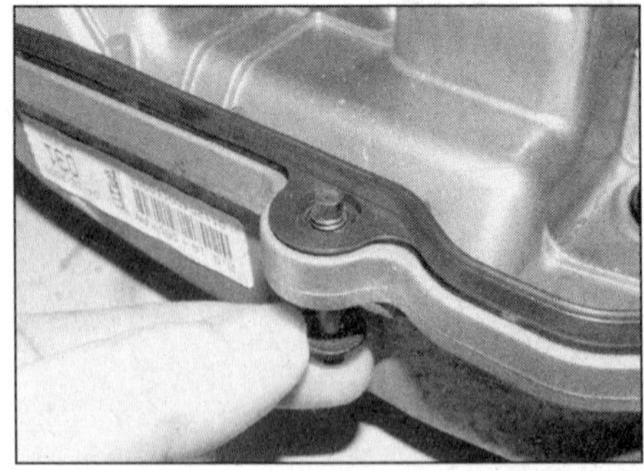

5.12 Insert the bolts into the camshaft cover gasket, ensuring the gasket is in the groove

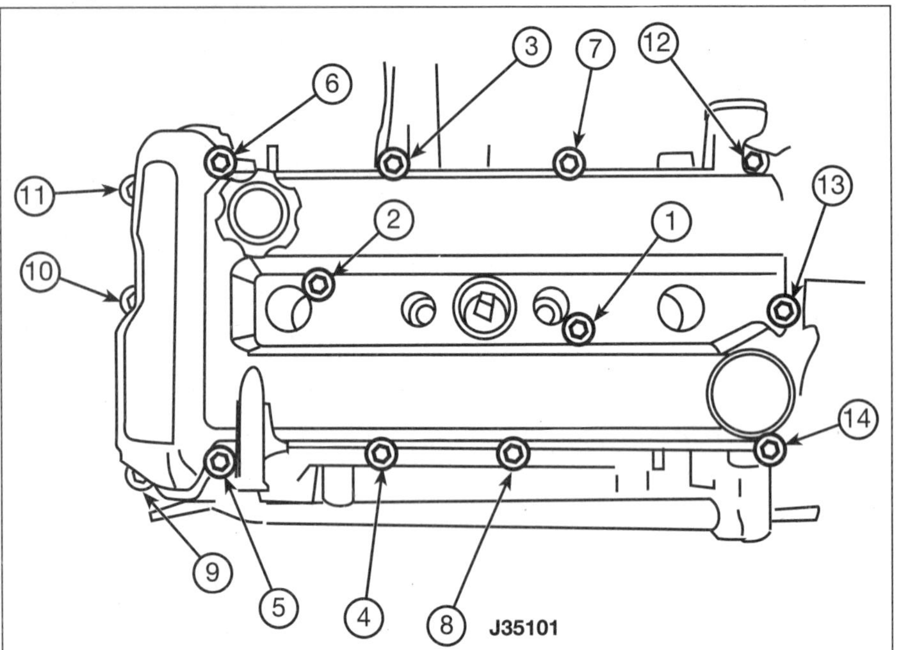

5.13 Sequence for tightening the camshaft cover

spark plugs and withdraw them, unclipping the leads from the cover.

8 Working progressively, unscrew the cylinder head cover retaining bolts and withdraw the cover.

9 Discard the cover gasket; this must be renewed whenever it is disturbed. Check that the sealing faces are undamaged, and that the rubber seal at each retaining bolt is serviceable **(see illustration)**; renew any worn or damaged seals.

Refitting

10 On refitting, clean the cover and cylinder head gasket faces carefully, then fit a new gaskets to the cover, ensuring that they locate correctly in the cover grooves.

11 Apply a thin bead of silicone sealant (Ford part number WSE-M4G323-A6, or equivalent) to the joint between the cylinder head and the timing cover **(see illustration)**.

12 Insert the retaining bolts, complete with rubber seals and spacer at each bolt location then refit the cover to the cylinder head **(see illustration)**. Start all bolts finger-tight, ensuring that the gasket remains seated in its groove.

13 Working in the sequence shown (see illustration), tighten the cover bolts to the specified torque wrench setting. Refit the three engine upper plastic cover retaining pegs to the cover retaining studs noted on removal.

14 The remainder of reassembly is the reverse of the removal procedure. Make sure the HT leads are clipped into place and are correctly routed; each is numbered, and can also be identified by the numbering on its respective coil terminal.

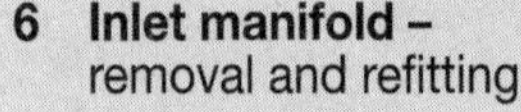

6 Inlet manifold – removal and refitting

Warning: Petrol is extremely flammable, so take extra precautions when disconnecting any part of the fuel system. Don't smoke, or allow naked flames or bare light bulbs in or near the work area. Don't work in a garage where a natural gas appliance (such as a clothes dryer or water heater) is installed. If you spill petrol on your skin, rinse it off immediately. Have a fire extinguisher rated for petrol fires handy, and know how to use it.

Removal

1 Park the car on firm, level ground, apply the handbrake, then jack up the front of the car and support it on axle stands (see *Jacking and vehicle support*).

2 Disconnect the battery negative (earth) lead (refer to *Disconnecting the battery* at the end of this manual).

3 Unclip the breather hose from the engine upper plastic cover, then unclip the cover from the top of the engine.

4 From underneath the car, remove the engine oil dipstick tube lower retaining bolt, and the inlet manifold lower retaining bolt **(see illustration)**.

6.4 Inlet manifold lower retaining bolt (arrowed)

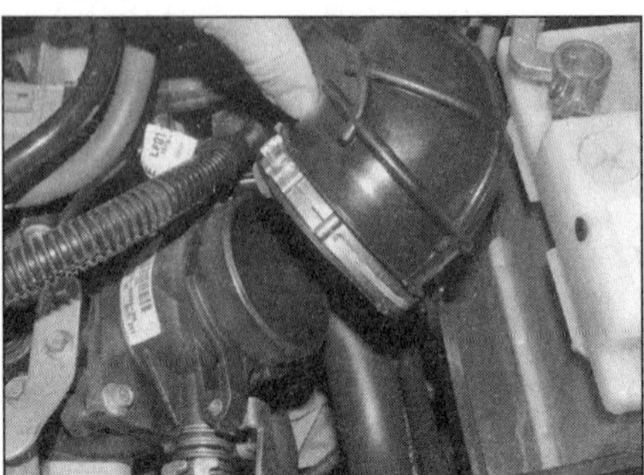

6.5 Release the securing clip and remove the air inlet pipe

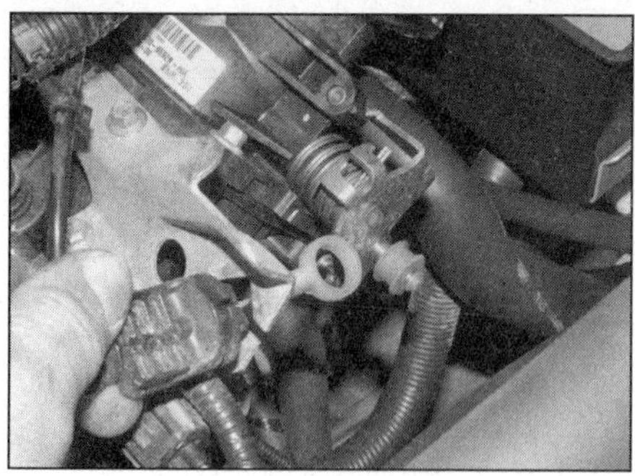
6.6 Twist the outer cable to release it from the mounting bracket

6.7a Disconnect the wiring connector from the throttle position (TP) sensor . . .

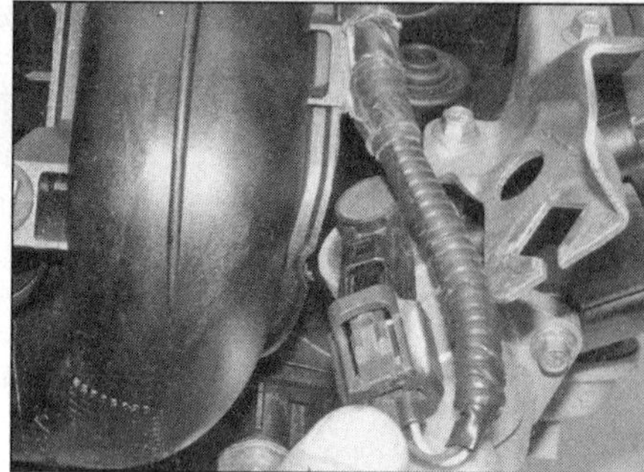
6.7b . . . and the idle air control (IAC) valve

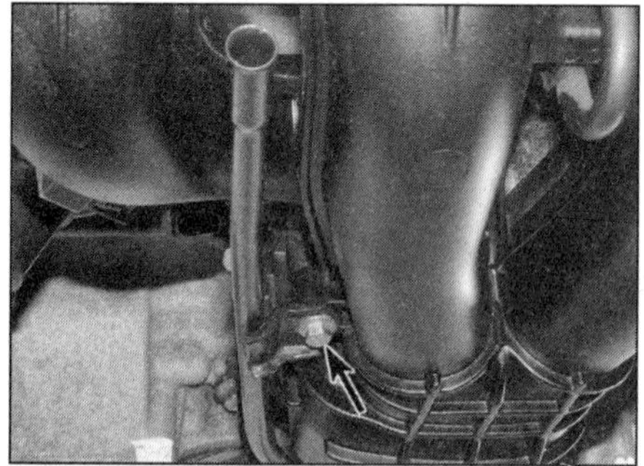
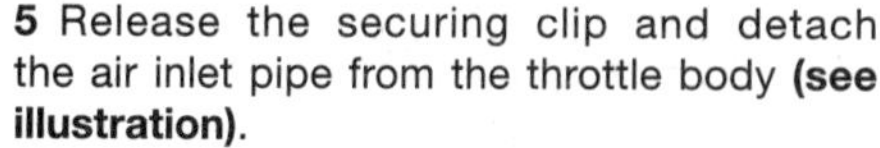
6.10 Remove the oil level dipstick tube upper retaining bolt (arrowed)

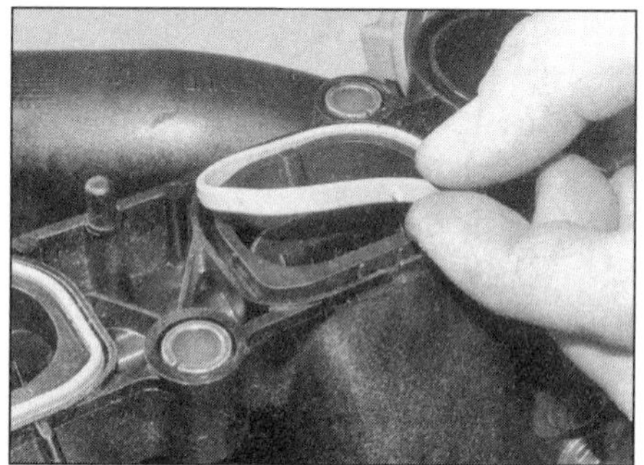
6.12a Fitting one of the four inlet manifold gaskets . . .

6.12b . . . and the EGR gasket to the inlet manifold

5 Release the securing clip and detach the air inlet pipe from the throttle body **(see illustration)**.

6 Unclip the accelerator inner cable from the throttle linkage, then twist the outer cable to release it from the bracket **(see illustration)**.

7 Unplug the two electrical connectors from the throttle position (TP) sensor and the idle air control (IAC) valve **(see illustrations)**.

8 Carefully pull the vacuum hoses (for the brakes, the fuel pulse damper and the purge valve) to release them from the inlet manifold.

9 Detach the wiring harness from across the top of the inlet manifold (releasing it from any relevant connectors and retaining clips, marking or labelling them as they are unplugged), then move the wiring loom to one side of the engine bay.

10 Remove the upper retaining bolt **(see illustration)** and withdraw the engine oil dipstick tube out from the engine. Renew the O-ring at the bottom of the dipstick tube on reassembly.

11 Unscrew the bolts securing the inlet manifold to the cylinder head and withdraw it. Take care not to damage vulnerable components such as the EGR pipe and valve as the manifold assembly is manoeuvred out of the engine compartment.

Refitting

12 Refitting is the reverse of the removal procedure, noting the following points:

a) *Check that the mating faces of the cylinder head and manifold are clean. As rubber gaskets are used, all that should be needed is a wipe over with a suitable solvent. Scraping, or excess use of abrasive material, should be avoided due to the risk of damage to both surfaces.*

b) *Provided the relevant mating surfaces are clean and flat, a new gasket will be sufficient to ensure the joint is gas-tight.* ***Do not*** *use any kind of silicone-based sealant on any part of the fuel system or inlet manifold.*

c) *Fit new gaskets to the four inlet ports and one to the EGR port in the manifold* ***(see illustrations)****, then locate the manifold on the head and install the retaining bolts. Tighten the bolts evenly to the torque listed in the Specifications at the beginning of this Chapter. Work from the centre outwards, to avoid warping the manifold.*

d) *Refit the remaining parts in the reverse order of removal – tighten all fasteners to the torque wrench settings specified.*

e) *Fit a new O-ring seal to the bottom of the dipstick tube.*

f) *Make sure the wiring loom is routed correctly, and all connections securely remade.*

g) *Before starting the engine, check the accelerator cable for correct adjustment and the throttle linkage for smooth operation.*

h) *When the engine is fully warmed-up, check for signs of fuel, inlet and/or vacuum leaks.*

i) *Road test the car, and check for proper operation of all disturbed components.*

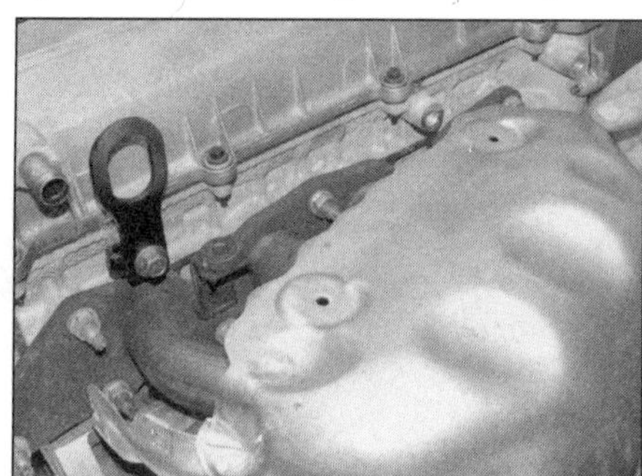
7.4a Remove the upper part of the exhaust manifold heat shield . . .

7 Exhaust manifold – removal, inspection and refitting

Warning: The engine must be completely cool before beginning this procedure.

Removal

1 Park the car on firm, level ground, apply the handbrake, then jack up the front of the car and support it on axle stands (see *Jacking and vehicle support*).

2 Disconnect the battery negative (earth) lead (refer to *Disconnecting the battery* at the end of this manual).

3 Unclip the breather hose from the engine upper plastic cover, then unclip the cover from the top of the engine.

4 Undo the six retaining bolts and withdraw the upper part of the heat shield, then undo the two lower retaining bolts and remove the lower part from the exhaust manifold **(see illustrations)**.

5 Trace the wire back from the oxygen sensor in the manifold downpipe and disconnect

7.4b . . . then remove the lower heat shield retaining bolts (one side – arrowed)

7.5 Undo the two retaining bolts (arrowed) from the exhaust front pipe

7.6 Undo the four bolts (arrowed) to remove the manifold lower retaining bracket

7.7 The studs can be unscrewed using a Torx socket, for additional clearance

the electrical connector. From under the car, unscrew the two retaining nuts to disconnect the exhaust system front downpipe from the manifold **(see illustration)**.

6 Undo the four securing bolts and remove the exhaust manifold lower retaining bracket **(see illustration)**.

7 Remove the nuts and detach the exhaust manifold and gasket. Take care not to damage vulnerable components as the manifold assembly is manoeuvred out of the engine compartment. When removing the manifold with the engine in the car, additional clearance can be obtained by unscrewing the studs from the cylinder head; a female Torx-type socket will be required **(see illustration)**.

Inspection

8 If using a scraper to remove all traces of old gasket material and carbon deposits from the manifold and cylinder head mating surfaces, be careful to ensure that you do not scratch or damage the material of either component – any solvents used must be suitable for this application. If the gasket was leaking, check the manifold and cylinder head for warpage, this may need to be done at an automotive machine shop; resurface if necessary.

Caution: When scraping, be very careful not to gouge or scratch the delicate aluminium alloy cylinder head.

9 Provided both mating surfaces are clean and flat, a new gasket will be sufficient to ensure the joint is gas-tight. Do not use any kind of exhaust sealant upstream of the catalytic converter.

Refitting

10 Refitting is the reverse of the removal procedure, noting the following points:

a) Fit a new manifold gasket over the cylinder head studs.

b) Refit the manifold, and tighten the nuts to the torque listed in the Specifications at the beginning of this Chapter.

c) Fit a new gasket to the front pipe (where fitted).

d) Run the engine, and check for exhaust leaks.

8 Crankshaft pulley – removal and refitting

Caution: The pulley and crankshaft timing gear are not keyed in position – they are held in place by the crankshaft retaining bolt alone, and the timing position will be lost when the bolt is undone. Make sure the engine is set at TDC (see Section 4) before the pulley is removed.

Note: *The crankshaft pulley retaining bolt is very tight, and a holding tool of some kind will be needed to stop the pulley turning as the bolt is undone. Ford use a special tool (205-072/15-030A), but a home-made substitute forked tool can be made from thick metal strip, with bolts at the ends to fit the pulley slots. A new pulley retaining bolt and a friction washer (which fits behind the pulley) will be required on refitting.*

Removal

1 Remove the auxiliary drivebelt – either remove the drivebelt completely, or just secure it clear of the crankshaft pulley, depending on the work to be carried out (see Chapter 1A).

2 Set the engine to TDC (see Section 4). **Note:** *Only turn the engine in the normal direction of rotation – clockwise from the right-hand side of the car.*

3 The crankshaft must now be locked to prevent its rotation while the pulley bolt is unscrewed. If the Ford tool is not available (or a substitute has not been made) proceed as follows:

a) Remove the rubber plug from the transmission bellhousing or, on automatics, unbolt the small metal cover plate from the sump, and use a large screwdriver or similar to lock the flywheel/driveplate ring gear teeth while an assistant slackens the pulley bolt; take care not to damage the teeth or the surrounding castings when using this method.

b) If the engine/transmission has been removed and separated, lock the flywheel/driveplate using a locking tool ***(see illustration).***

4 Unscrew the pulley bolt and remove the pulley. Recover the friction washer fitted behind the pulley, where applicable.

Refitting

5 Refitting is the reverse of the removal procedure; making sure the engine has not moved from its setting at TDC (see Section 4).

6 Ensure that a new retaining bolt is used **(see illustration)**. Where a friction washer

8.3 Using a locking tool to hold the flywheel

8.6 Use a new retaining bolt when refitting the pulley

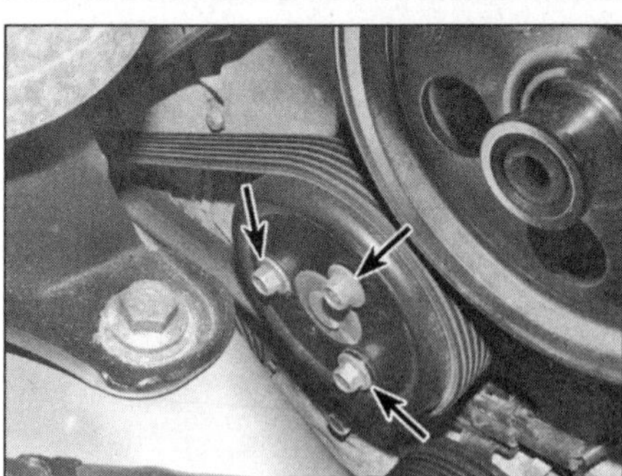

9.3 Slacken the three retaining bolts (arrowed)

9.10 Unscrew the nuts and bolts (arrowed) and remove the engine mounting

was fitted behind the pulley, a new one should be used before refitting the pulley. Ford also state that a friction washer is needed if the new pulley bolt's built-in washer is less than 5.5 mm thick – consult your dealer or parts supplier if clarification is needed.

7 Hold the pulley (or lock the flywheel) using the same method as for bolt removal, and tighten the new bolt to the torque and angle specified at the beginning of this Chapter. It is recommended that an angle gauge is used for the second stage of tightening, to ensure accuracy.

9 Timing chain cover – removal and refitting

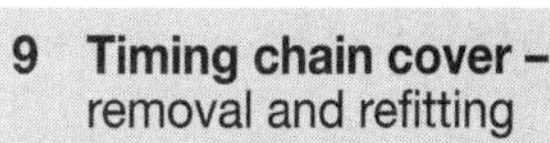

Removal

1 Remove the camshaft cover as described in Section 5.

2 Apply the handbrake, then jack up the front of the car and support it on axle stands (see *Jacking and vehicle support*). Remove the right-hand front road wheel and remove the cover from under the right-hand front wheel arch.

3 Slacken the water pump pulley retaining bolts by approximately three turns **(see illustration)**.

4 Remove the auxiliary drivebelt (Chapter 1A).

5 Remove the power steering pump as described in Chapter 10.

6 Remove the crankshaft pulley (Section 8).

7 Disconnect the crankshaft position (CKP) sensor wiring connector **(see illustration)**.

9.7 Disconnect the wiring connector from the crankshaft position sensor

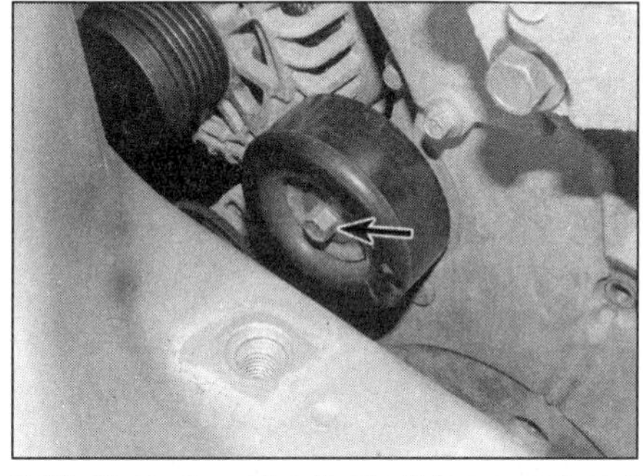

9.11 Undo the retaining bolt (arrowed) and remove the idler pulley

8 Unscrew the retaining bolts and remove the water pump pulley.

9 Undo the retaining bolts and move the coolant expansion tank to one side, disconnect the lower coolant hose if required **(see illustration)**.

10 Support the engine using a trolley jack and block of wood beneath the sump, then unscrew the nuts/bolts securing the engine/transmission right-hand mounting bracket and remove the mounting from the engine **(see illustration)**.

11 Unbolt and remove the auxiliary drivebelt idler **(see illustration)**.

12 Unscrew the timing chain cover retaining bolts (noting their positions for refitting) and withdraw the cover from the engine.

Refitting

13 Refitting is the reverse of the removal procedure (using the relevant Sections), noting the following points:

a) *Clean the sealant from the timing cover, cylinder block and cylinder head mating surfaces. When using a scraper and solvent to remove all traces of old gasket/sealant from the mating surfaces, be careful to ensure that you do not scratch or damage the material of either component – any solvents used must be suitable for this application. If the gasket was leaking, have the mating surfaces checked for warpage – this may need to be done at an automotive machine shop.*

b) *Provided the relevant mating surfaces are clean and flat, apply a (3.0mm) bead of silicone sealant (Ford part number*

9.9 Undo the retaining bolts and move the coolant expansion tank to one side

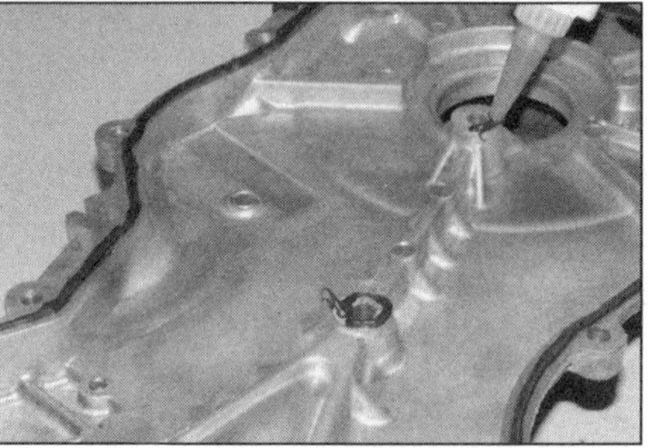

9.13a Apply a 3.0 mm bead of sealant around the timing chain cover, including the inner bolt holes

WSE-M4G323-A6, or equivalent) around the timing chain cover and the inner bolt holes ***(see illustration).*** **Note:** *The cover must be fitted within 10 minutes of applying the sealant.*

c) *Tighten the timing chain cover bolts to the specified torque settings at the beginning of this Chapter, following the sequence shown, noting that not all bolts are tightened to the same torque* ***(see illustration).***

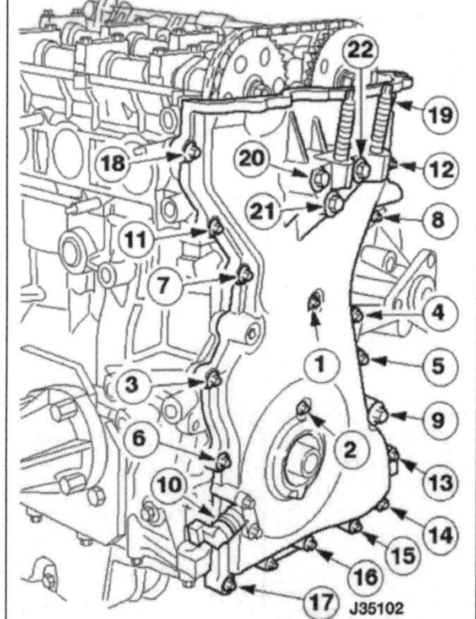

9.13b Tightening sequence for the timing chain cover

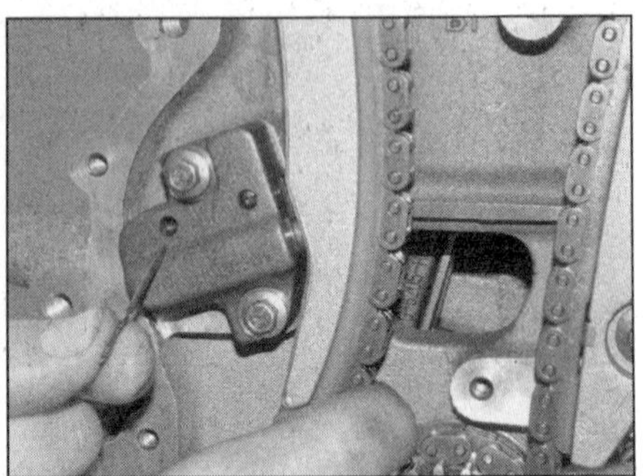
10.4 Press against the timing chain guide and insert a locking pin (approximately 1.5 mm)

10.6 Using a spanner to hold the camshafts, while undoing the retaining bolts

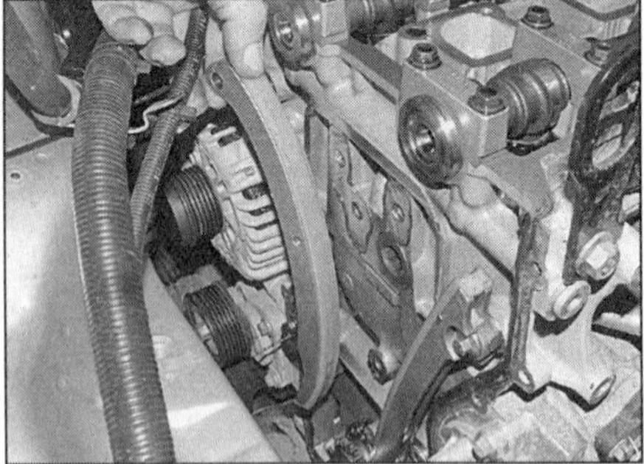
10.7a Withdraw the tensioner guide from the pivot pin . . .

10.7b . . . then undo the retaining bolts (arrowed) to remove the fixed guide

10 Timing chain, tensioner and guides – removal, inspection and refitting

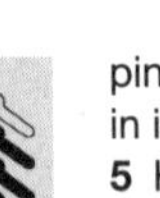

Removal

1 Remove the camshaft cover as described in Section 5.

2 Set the engine to TDC as described in Section 4. **Note:** *Only turn the engine in the normal direction of rotation – clockwise from the right-hand side of the car.*

3 Remove the timing chain cover as described in Section 9.

4 Slacken the timing chain tensioner by inserting a small screwdriver into the access hole in the tensioner and releasing the pawl mechanism. Press against the timing chain guide to depress the piston into the tensioner housing, when fully depressed, insert a locking pin (approximately 1.5 mm) to lock the piston in its compressed position **(see illustration)**.

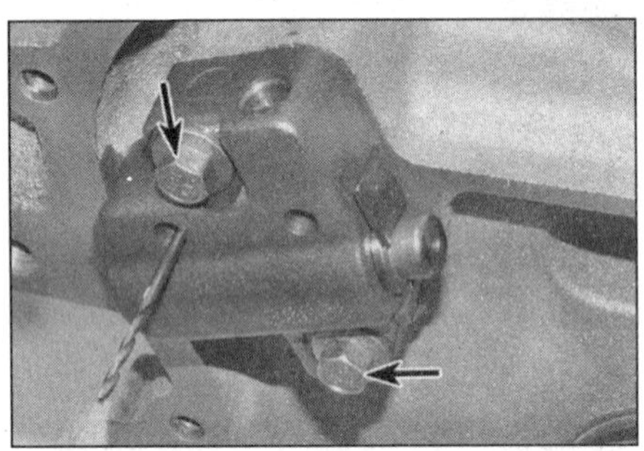
10.8 Undo the two bolts (arrowed) and remove the tensioner, without removing the locking pin (drill bit)

5 Hold the camshafts by the hexagon on the shafts to prevent them from turning, using an open-ended spanner.

6 With the camshafts held in position, undo the camshaft sprocket retaining bolts and remove the camshaft sprockets and timing chain. Do not rotate the crankshaft until the timing chain is refitted **(see illustration)**.

7 If required, unbolt the fixed timing chain guide and withdraw the tensioner timing chain guide from its pivot pin on the cylinder head **(see illustrations)**.

8 To remove the tensioner, undo the two retaining bolts and remove the timing chain tensioner from the cylinder block, taking care not to remove the locking pin **(see illustration)**.

9 To remove the timing chain sprocket from the crankshaft, the oil pump drive chain will need to be removed as described in Section 15. Mark the sprocket to ensure it is refitted the same way round.

Inspection

Note: *Keep all components identified for position to ensure correct refitting.*

10 Clean all components thoroughly and wipe dry.

11 Examine the chain tensioner and tensioner guide for excessive wear or other damage. Check the guides for deep grooves made by the timing chain.

12 Examine the timing chain for excessive wear. Hold it horizontally and check how much movement exists in the chain links. If there is any doubt, compare it to a new chain. Renew as necessary.

13 Examine the teeth of the camshaft and crankshaft sprockets for excessive wear and damage.

14 Before refitting the timing chain tensioner, the piston must be compressed and locked until refitted (if not already done on removal). To do this, insert a small screwdriver into the access hole in the tensioner and release the pawl mechanism. Now lightly clamp the tensioner in a soft-jawed vice and slowly compress the piston. Do not apply excessive force and make sure that the piston remains aligned with its cylinder. When completely compressed, insert a locking pin/1.5 mm diameter wire rod into the special hole to lock the piston in its compressed position.

Refitting

15 If not already fitted, slide the crankshaft drive sprocket (and washer, where fitted) onto the crankshaft. Ensure it is refitted the same way round as noted on removal (see Section 15, for further information on refitting the oil pump drive chain).

16 Refit the tensioner to the cylinder block and tighten the retaining bolts to the specified torque setting. Take care not to remove the locking pin **(see illustration)**.

17 Refit the fixed timing chain guide and tighten the two retaining bolts, then slide the tensioner timing chain guide back into place on the upper pivot pin **(see illustration)**.

18 Refit the inlet camshaft sprocket onto the camshaft, DO NOT tighten the retaining bolt at this stage.

10.16 Refit the timing chain tensioner (still in the locked position) to the cylinder block

10.17 Refitting the timing chain guides to the engine

10.19 Refit the camshaft sprockets into position, complete with timing chain

19 With the timing chain around the exhaust camshaft sprocket refit the timing chain and sprocket, feeding the timing chain around the crankshaft drive sprocket and inlet camshaft sprocket **(see illustration)**.

20 With the timing chain in place, hold pressure against the tensioner guide and withdraw the tensioner locking pin. This will then tension the timing chain **(see illustration)**.

21 Check that the engine is still set to TDC (as described in Section 4).

22 Tighten the both camshaft sprocket retaining bolts, to the torque setting specified in the Specifications at the beginning of this Chapter. **Note:** *Use an open-ended spanner on the hexagon on the camshafts to stop them from turning* ***(see illustration)***.

23 Refit the timing chain cover as described in Section 9.

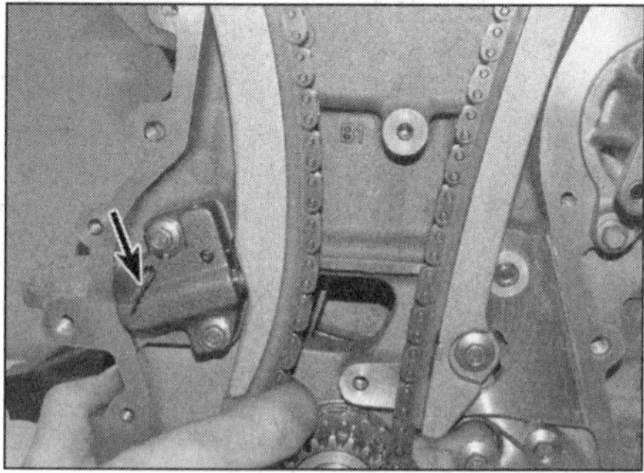

10.20 Hold pressure against the tensioner guide and withdraw the tensioner locking pin (arrowed)

24 Remove the camshaft locking plate and crankshaft timing peg and turn the engine (in the direction of engine rotation) two full turns. Refit the camshaft locking plate and crankshaft timing peg to make sure the engine is still set at TDC (see Section 4 for further information).

25 Refit the camshaft cover as described in Section 5.

11 Camshafts and tappets – removal, inspection and refitting

Removal

1 Remove the camshaft cover as described in Section 5.

2 Remove the timing hole plug and insert a timing peg to position the crankshaft at TDC

10.22 Use an open-ended spanner on the hexagon on the camshafts to stop them from turning

(303-507 – obtainable from Ford dealers, or a tool supplier). For further information on setting the engine to TDC, see Section 4.

3 Remove the timing chain cover lower and upper blanking plugs, to gain access to the timing chain tensioner and guide **(see illustrations)**.

4 Slacken the timing chain tensioner by inserting a small screwdriver into the lower access hole in the timing chain cover and releasing the pawl mechanism in the tensioner **(see illustration)**.

5 Carefully turn the exhaust camshaft (by using an open-ended spanner on the hexagon on the shaft) in the normal direction of rotation, to slacken the timing chain tensioner **(see illustration)**.

6 Holding the exhaust camshaft in position, insert a bolt (M6 x 25 mm) into the upper access hole in the timing chain cover to lock the tensioner guide rail in position **(see illustration)**.

7 With the camshafts held in position (by using an open-ended spanner on the hexagon on the shaft), slacken the camshaft sprocket retaining bolts.

8 Using a cable-tie or similar, fasten the timing chain to the camshaft sprockets.

9 Remove the camshaft sprocket retaining bolts and remove the sprockets, complete with timing chain, away from the camshafts. Using a suitable piece of wire secure the sprockets and timing chain to prevent them dropping into the timing cover.

10 Working in the sequence shown **(see illustration)**, slacken the camshaft bearing

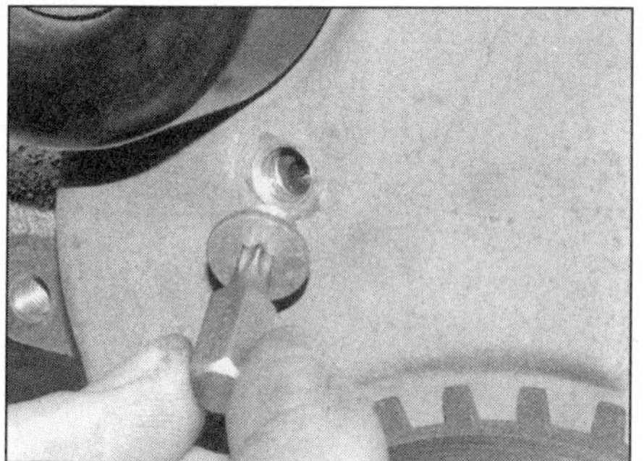

11.3a Remove the timing chain cover lower . . .

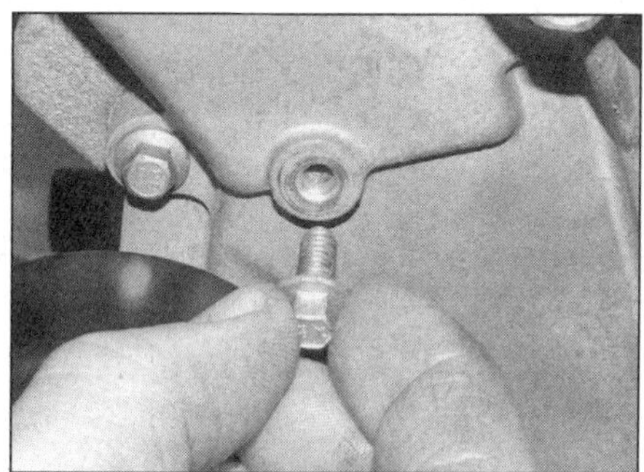

11.3b . . . and upper blanking plugs

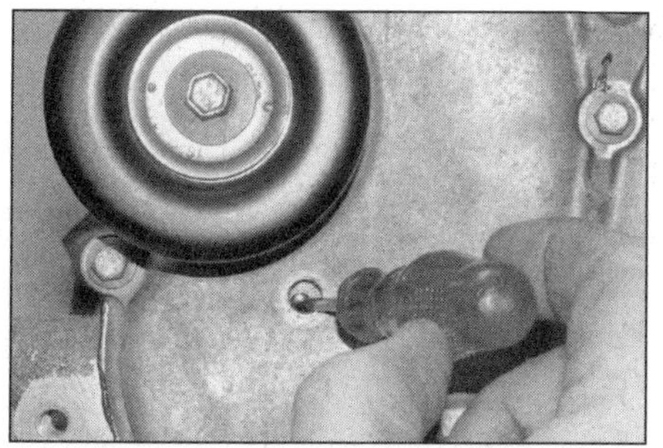

11.4 Inserting a small screwdriver into the lower access hole to release the timing chain tensioner

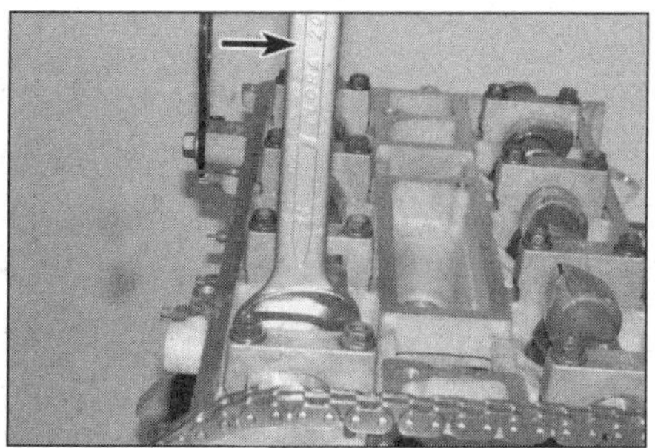

11.5 Turn the exhaust camshaft in the direction of the arrow to slacken the timing chain tensioner

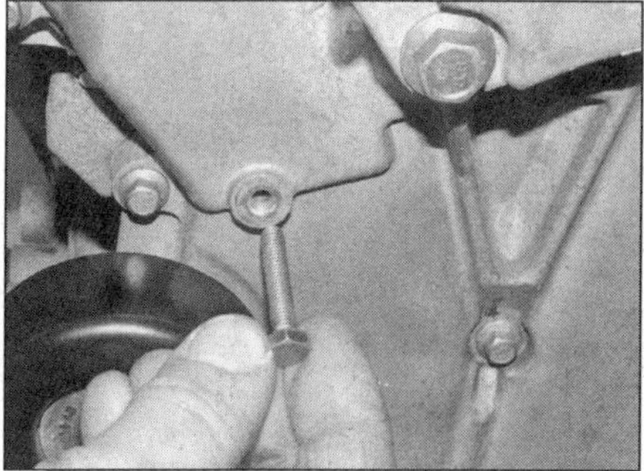

11.6 Holding the exhaust camshaft, insert a bolt to lock the tensioner guide rail

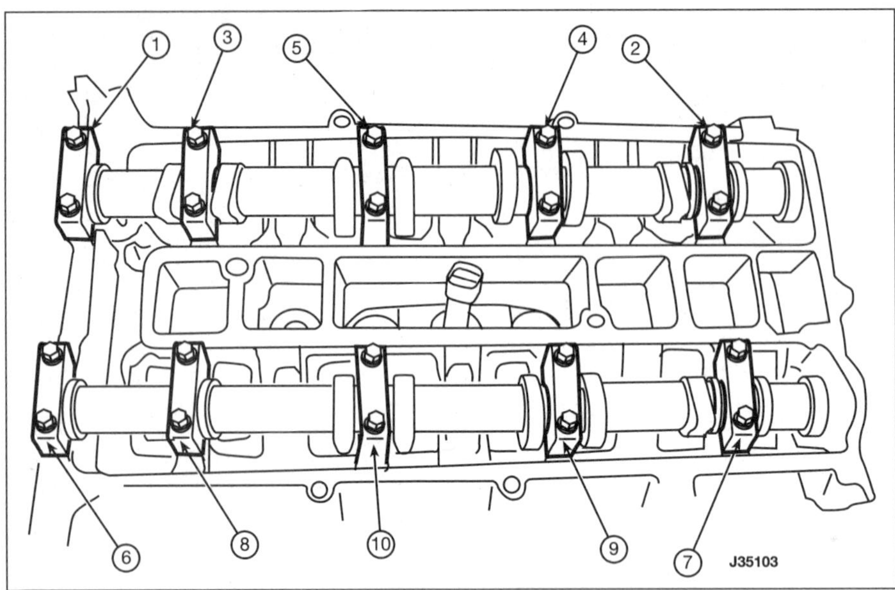

11.10 Sequence for slackening the camshaft bearing cap bolts

cap bolts progressively by half a turn at a time. Work only as described, to release gradually and evenly the pressure of the valve springs on the caps.

11 Withdraw the camshaft bearing caps, noting their markings, then remove the camshafts. The inlet camshaft can be identified by the reference lobe for the camshaft position sensor; therefore, there is no need to mark the camshafts **(see illustrations)**.

12 Obtain sixteen small, clean containers, and number them 1 to 16. Using a rubber sucker, withdraw each bucket tappet in turn and place them in the containers. Do not interchange the bucket tappets as they are of different sizes; the shim is part of the bucket tappet **(see illustrations)**. Different sizes of bucket tappets are available in the event of wear on the valves or repair on the cylinder head assembly.

Inspection

13 With the camshafts and tappets removed, check each for signs of obvious wear (scoring, pitting, etc) and for ovality, and renew if necessary.

14 Measure the outside diameter of each tappet **(see illustration)** – take measurements at the top and bottom of each tappet, then a second set at right-angles to the first; if any measurement is significantly different from the others, the tappet is tapered or oval (as applicable) and must be renewed. If the necessary equipment is available, measure the inside diameter of the corresponding cylinder head bore. If the tappets or the cylinder head bores are excessively worn, new tappets and/or a new cylinder head will be required.

15 Visually examine the camshaft lobes for score marks, pitting, galling (wear due to rubbing) and evidence of overheating (blue, discoloured areas). Look for flaking away of the hardened surface layer of each lobe **(see illustration)**. If any such signs are evident, renew the component concerned.

16 Examine the camshaft bearing journals and the cylinder head bearing surfaces for signs of obvious wear or pitting. If any such signs are evident, renew the component concerned.

17 Using a micrometer, measure the diameter of each journal at several points **(see illustration)**. If any measurement is significantly different from the others, renew the camshaft.

18 To check the bearing journal running clearance, remove the tappets, use a suitable solvent and a clean lint-free rag to clean carefully all bearing surfaces, then refit the camshafts and bearing caps with a strand

11.11a Note the identification markings (arrowed) on the camshaft bearing caps . . .

11.11b . . . and the reference lobe (arrowed) on the inlet camshaft for the position sensor

11.12a Removing the bucket tappet using a rubber sucker

11.12b Note the thickness number under the bucket tappet, different sizes are available

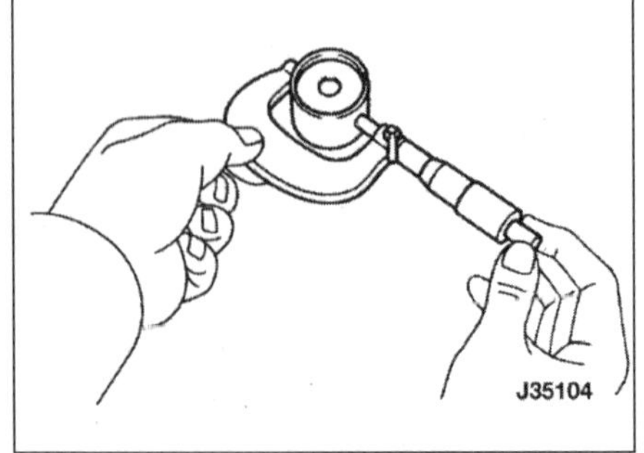

11.14 Use a micrometer to measure diameter of tappets

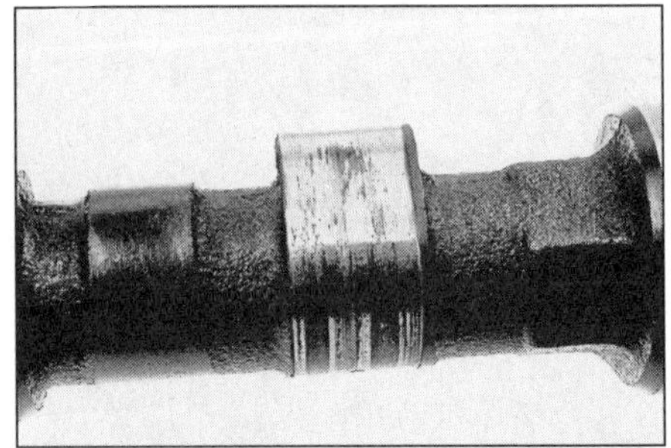

11.15 Check the cam lobes for pitting, wear and score marks – this is excessive scoring

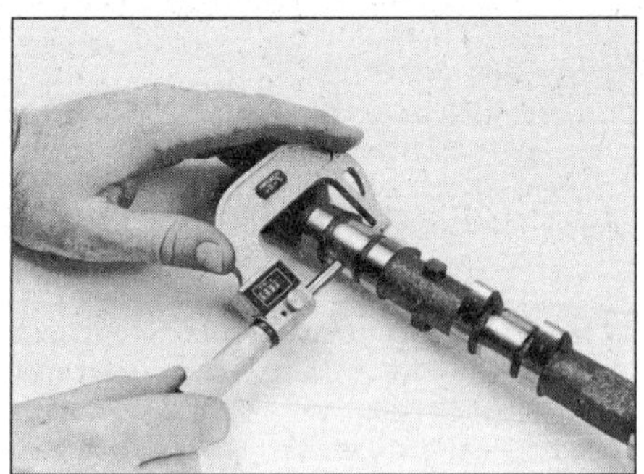
11.17 Measure each journal diameter with a micrometer

11.18a Lay a strip of Plastigauge on each camshaft journal

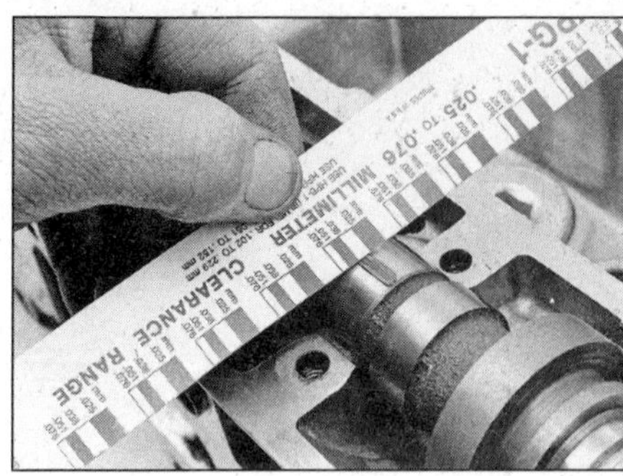
11.18b Compare the width of the crushed Plastigauge to the envelope

of Plastigauge across each journal **(see illustration)**. Tighten the bearing cap bolts to the specified torque wrench setting (do not rotate the camshafts), then remove the bearing caps and use the scale provided to measure the width of the compressed strands **(see illustration)**. Scrape off the Plastigauge with your fingernail or the edge of a credit card – don't scratch or nick the journals or bearing caps.

19 If the running clearance of any bearing is found to be worn to beyond the specified service limits, fit a new camshaft and repeat the check; if the clearance is still excessive, the cylinder head must be renewed.

20 To check camshaft endfloat, remove the tappets, clean the bearing surfaces carefully, and refit the camshafts and bearing caps. Tighten the bearing cap bolts to the specified torque wrench setting, then measure the endfloat using a DTI (Dial Test Indicator, or dial gauge) mounted on the cylinder head so that its tip bears on the camshaft right-hand end.

21 Tap the camshaft fully towards the gauge, zero the gauge, then tap the camshaft fully away from the gauge, and note the gauge reading. If the endfloat measured is found to be at or beyond the specified service limit, fit a new camshaft and repeat the check; if the clearance is still excessive, the cylinder head must be renewed.

Refitting

22 On reassembly, liberally oil the cylinder head tappet bores and the tappets **(see illustration)**. Carefully refit the tappets to the cylinder head, ensuring that each tappet is refitted to its original bore. Some care will be required to enter the tappets squarely into their bores.

23 Turn the engine back approximately 45° so that there are no pistons at the top of the cylinders.

24 Liberally oil the camshaft bearings and lobes **(see illustration)**. Ensuring that each camshaft is in its original location, refit the camshafts, locating each so that the slot in its left-hand end is approximately parallel to, and just above, the cylinder head mating surface.

25 All camshaft bearing caps have an identifying number and letter etched on them. The exhaust camshaft's bearing caps

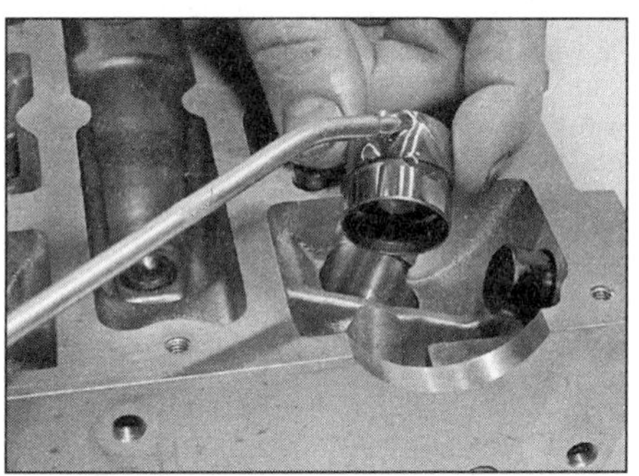
11.22 Oil liberally when refitting hydraulic tappets

11.24 Apply clean engine oil to the cam lobes and journals before refitting a camshaft

are numbered in sequence E1 to E5 and the inlet camshaft's bearing caps I1 to I5 **(see illustration 11.11a)**.

26 Ensuring that each cap is kept square to the cylinder head as it is tightened down, and working in the sequence shown **(see illustration)**, tighten the camshaft bearing cap bolts slowly and by one turn at a time, until each cap touches the cylinder head. Next, go round again in the same sequence, tightening the bolts to the first stage torque wrench setting specified, then once more, tightening them to the second stage setting. Work only as described, to impose gradually and evenly the pressure of the valve springs on the caps.

27 Fit the camshaft aligning tool – it should slip into place as described in Section 4 **(see illustration)**.

28 Refit the camshaft sprockets, complete with timing chain to the ends of the camshafts. DO NOT tighten the camshaft sprocket retaining bolts at this stage. Remove the

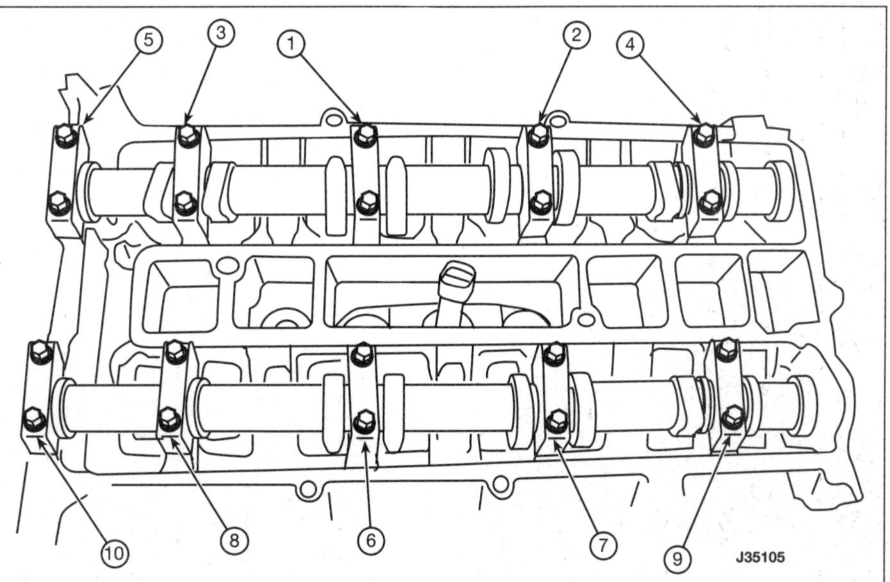

11.26 Sequence for tightening the camshaft bearing cap bolts

11.27 Fit the camshaft aligning tool to set TDC position

cable-ties from the timing chain and camshaft sprockets.

29 Remove the tensioner guide rail locking bolt from the upper access hole in the timing chain cover. It may be necessary to hold some pressure against the tensioner guide rail to remove the locking bolt.

30 Turn the engine (in the direction of rotation) approximately 45° to TDC. For further information on setting the engine to TDC, see Section 4.

31 With the camshafts held in position (by using an open-ended spanner on the hexagon on the shaft), tighten the camshaft sprocket retaining bolts to the specified torque.

32 Remove the camshaft aligning tool and crankshaft timing peg and turn the engine (in the direction of engine rotation – clockwise, or towards the front of the car) two full turns. Refit the camshaft aligning tool and crankshaft timing peg to make sure the engine is still set at TDC (see Section 4 for further information).

33 Refit the timing chain cover upper and lower blanking plugs – coat the blanking plug threads with a suitable sealant to prevent leaks.

34 Refit the camshaft cover as described in Section 5.

12 Valve clearances – checking and adjustment

Checking

1 Remove the camshaft cover as described in Section 5.

12.3 Measure the clearance between the base of the cam lobe and the bucket using feeler blades

2 Set the engine to TDC on cylinder No 1 as described in Section 4. The inlet and exhaust cam lobes of No 1 cylinder will be pointing upwards (though not vertical) and the valve clearances can be checked.

3 Working on each valve, measure the clearance between the base of the cam lobe and the bucket tappet using feeler blades **(see illustration)**. Record the thickness of the blade required to give a firm sliding fit on all the valves of No 1 cylinder. The desired clearances are given in the Specifications. Note that the clearances for inlet and exhaust valves are different. The inlet camshaft is at the front of the engine and the exhaust camshaft at the rear. Record all four clearances.

4 Now turn the crankshaft clockwise through 180° so that the valves of cylinder No 3 are pointing upwards. Check and record the four valve clearances for cylinder No 3. The clearances for cylinders 4 and 2 can be checked after turning the crankshaft through 180° each time.

Adjustment

Note: *Swapping bucket tappets between locations to correct valve clearances will speed up wear because of mis-matched components.*

5 If adjustment is required, the bucket tappets must be changed by removing the camshafts as described in Section 11.

6 If the valve clearance was too small, a thinner bucket tappet must be fitted. If the clearance was too large, a thicker bucket tappet must be fitted. The bucket tappet has a number engraved on the inside **(see illustration)**, if the marking is missing or illegible, a micrometer will be needed to establish bucket tappet thickness.

7 When the bucket tappet thickness and the valve clearance are known, the required thickness of the new bucket tappet can be calculated as follows:

Sample calculation – clearance too small

Desired clearance (A) = 0.25 mm
Measured clearance (B) = 0.20 mm
Tappet thickness found (C) = 2.55 mm
Thickness required (D) = C + B – A
= 2.50 mm

12.6 The bucket tappet has a number engraved on the inside

Sample calculation – clearance too large

Desired clearance (A) = 0.30 mm
Measured clearance (B) = 0.36 mm
Tappet thickness found (C) = 2.19 mm
Thickness required (D) = C + B – A
= 2.25 mm

8 With the correct thickness bucket tappets fitted in the cylinder head, refit the camshafts as described in Section 11.

9 Check the valve clearances are now correct, as described in paragraphs 2 to 4. If any clearances are still not within specification then carry out the adjustment procedure again.

10 It will be helpful for future adjustment if a record is kept of the thickness of bucket fitted at each position. The buckets required for future valve clearance adjustment can be purchased in advance once the clearances and the existing bucket thicknesses are known.

11 When all the clearances are correct, refit the camshaft cover as described in Section 5.

13 Cylinder head – removal and refitting

Removal

1 With the car parked on firm level ground, open the bonnet and disconnect the battery negative (earth) lead (refer to *Disconnecting the battery* at the end of this manual).

2 Whenever you disconnect any vacuum lines, coolant and emissions hoses, wiring loom connectors, earth straps and fuel lines as part of the following procedure, always label them clearly, so that they can be correctly reassembled.

Masking tape and/or a touch-up paint applicator work well for marking items. Take digital photos, or sketch the locations of components and brackets.

3 Drain the cooling system as described in Chapter 1A.

4 Remove the inlet manifold as described in Section 6.

5 Remove the exhaust manifold and heat shields as described in Section 7.

6 Remove the camshaft cover as described in Section 5.

7 Remove the timing chain and sprockets as described in Section 10.

8 Release the pressure in the fuel system by using Method 2 or Method 3 described in Chapter 4A, Section 2.

9 Release the fuel feed pipe from the fuel

injector rail **(see illustration)** – see Chapter 4A for more information. Plug or cap all open fittings, to prevent any ingress of dirt, etc.

10 Disconnect the coolant hoses from the coolant housing on the left-hand end of the cylinder head **(see illustration)**.

11 Slacken and remove the upper retaining bolt from the alternator assembly **(see illustration)**.

12 Undo the securing bolt and disconnect the earth lead from the cylinder head above the alternator assembly **(see illustration)**.

13 Remove the camshafts and tappets as described in Section 11.

14 Working in the sequence shown **(see illustration),** slacken the ten cylinder head bolts progressively and by one turn at a time. Remove each bolt in turn, and ensure that new ones are obtained for reassembly; these bolts are subjected to severe stresses and so must be renewed, regardless of their apparent condition, whenever they are disturbed.

15 Make a final check that nothing is still attached to the head, and that nothing is in the way of its being removed. Lift the cylinder head away; use assistance if possible, as it is a heavy assembly. Remove the gasket and discard it, note the position of the dowels.

Refitting

16 The mating faces of the cylinder head and cylinder block must be perfectly clean before refitting the head. Use a hard plastic or wood scraper to remove all traces of gasket and carbon; also clean the piston crowns. Take particular care, as the soft aluminium alloy is easily damaged. Also, make sure that the carbon is not allowed to enter the oil and water passages – this is particularly important for the lubrication system, as carbon could block the oil supply to any of the engine's components. Using adhesive tape and paper, seal the water, oil and bolt holes in the cylinder block. Clean all the pistons in the same way.

13.9 Release the fuel feed pipe from the fuel injector rail

13.10 Disconnect the hoses from the coolant housing

13.11 Remove the upper retaining bolt from the alternator bracket

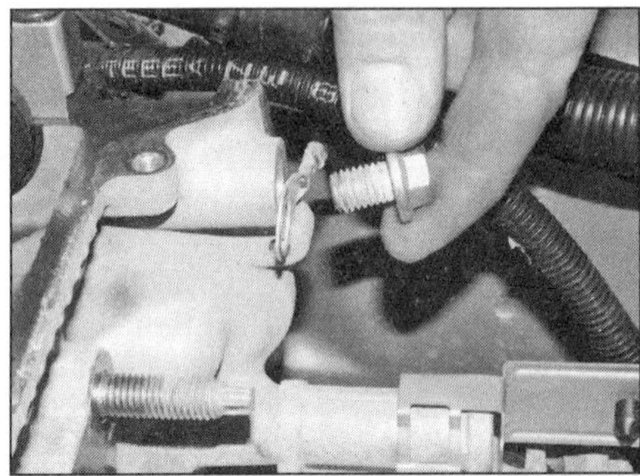

13.12 Disconnect the earth lead from the cylinder head

To prevent carbon entering the gap between the pistons and bores, smear a little grease in the gap. After cleaning each piston, use a small brush to remove all traces of grease and carbon from the gap, then wipe away the remainder with a clean rag.

17 Check the mating surfaces of the cylinder block and the cylinder head for nicks, deep scratches and other damage. If excessive, machining may be the only alternative to renewal.

18 If warpage of the cylinder head gasket surface is suspected, use a straight-edge to check it for distortion. Refer to Part D of this Chapter, if necessary.

19 Wipe clean the mating surfaces of the cylinder head and cylinder block. Check that the locating dowels are in position in the cylinder block, and that all cylinder head bolt holes are free from oil.

20 Position a new gasket over the dowels on the cylinder block surface, making sure it is fitted the correct way around. The trapezoidal tooth (2.0 litre engines) or two trapezoidal teeth (1.8 litre engines) protruding from one edge of the gasket point to the rear of the car **(see illustration)**.

21 Rotate the crankshaft anti-clockwise so that No 1 cylinder's piston is lowered to approximately 20 mm before TDC, thus

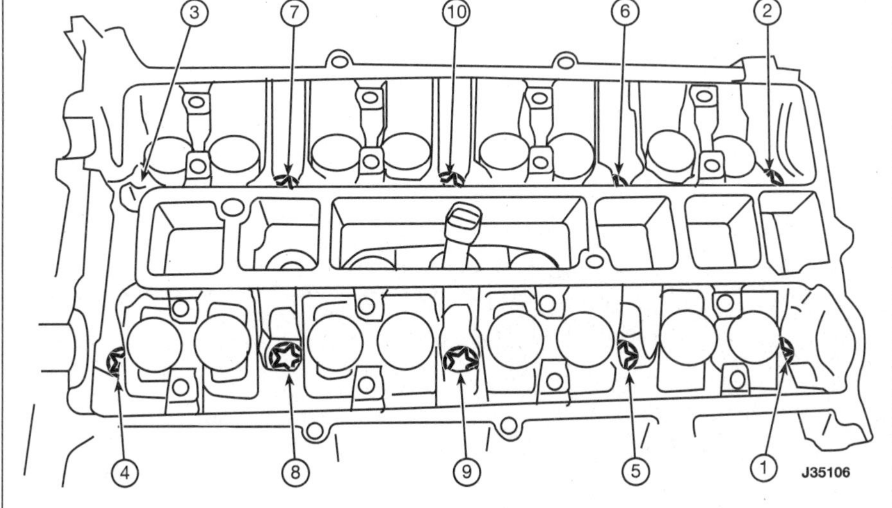

13.14 Sequence for slackening the cylinder head bolts

13.20 Note the trapezoidal tooth (arrowed) on the rear of the head gasket (2.0 litre engine)

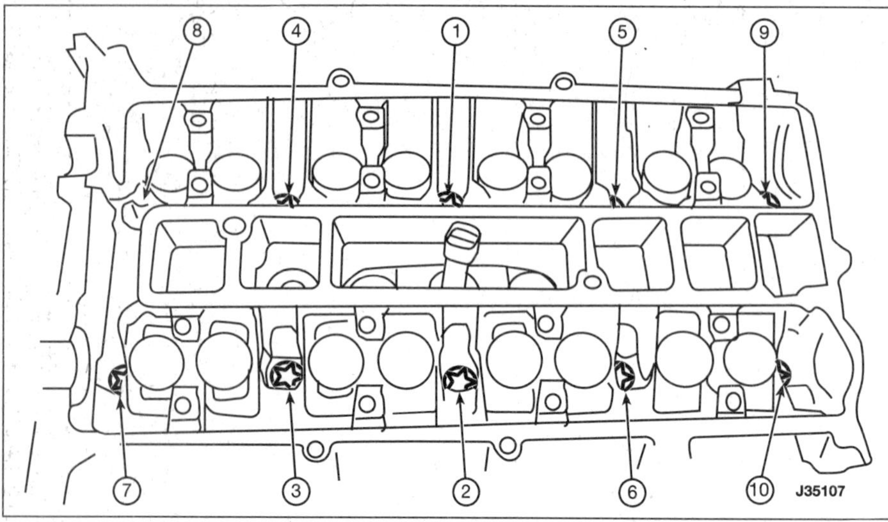

13.23a Tighten the cylinder head bolts in the sequence shown

avoiding any risk of valve/piston contact and damage during reassembly.

22 Refit the cylinder head, locating it on the dowels. Fit the new cylinder head bolts; carefully enter each into its hole and screw it in, by hand only, until finger-tight.

23 Working progressively and in the sequence shown, use first a torque wrench, then an ordinary socket extension bar and an angle gauge to tighten the cylinder head bolts **(see illustrations)**. This is completed in stages given in the Specifications Section at the beginning of this Chapter. **Note:** *Once tightened correctly, following this procedure, the cylinder head bolts do not require check-tightening, and must not be retorqued.*

24 Refit the bucket tappets, the camshafts, and the timing chain as described in Sections 10 and 11.

25 The remainder of reassembly is the reverse of the removal procedure, noting the following points:

a) *See the refitting procedures in the relevant Sections and tighten all nuts and bolts to the torque wrench settings specified.*

b) *Refill the cooling system, and top-up the engine oil.*

c) *Check all disturbed joints for signs of oil or coolant leakage, once the engine has been restarted and warmed-up to normal operating temperature.*

14.9 A support bar is the best way to suspend the engine/transmission for sump removal

14 Sump – removal and refitting

Removal

1 Unclip and remove the engine top cover.

2 Remove the air cleaner assembly and air inlet duct as described in Chapter 4A.

3 Pull out the engine oil dipstick, then remove the dipstick tube upper bolt.

4 Loosen all the transmission-to-engine bolts which are accessible from above, by about 10 mm – do not remove them completely.

5 Loosen the left-hand front wheel nuts. Apply the handbrake, then jack up the front of the car and support it on axle stands (see *Jacking and vehicle support*). Remove the left-hand front wheel.

6 Drain the engine oil, then clean and refit the engine oil drain plug, tightening it to the specified torque wrench setting. **Note:** *If the drain plug seal is damaged, a new drain plug will be required.* Although not strictly necessary as part of the dismantling procedure, owners are advised to remove and discard the oil filter, so that it can be renewed with the oil (see Chapter 1A).

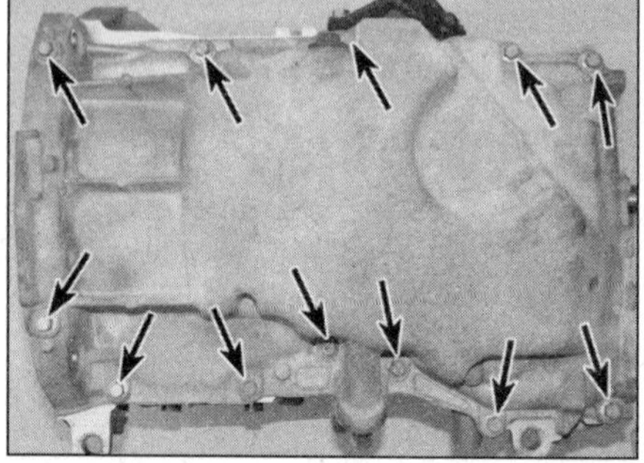

14.15a Unscrew the sump retaining bolts (arrowed) . . .

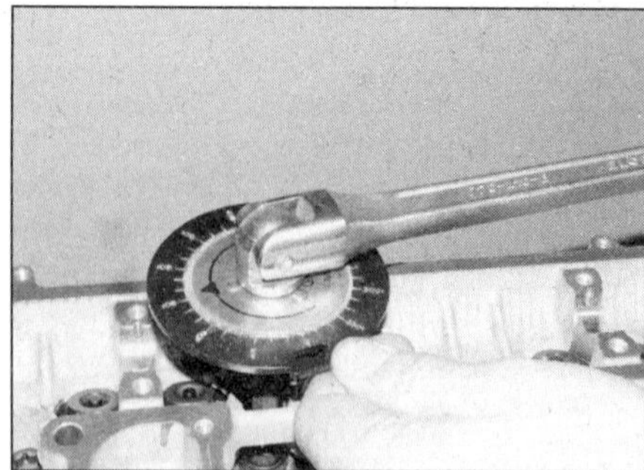

13.23b Use an angle gauge for the final stages

7 Unscrew the dipstick tube lower mounting bolt, and withdraw the dipstick tube out from the engine. Renew the O-ring at the bottom of the dipstick tube on reassembly.

8 Remove the left-hand front wheel arch liner, which is retained by a total of nine fasteners.

9 Referring to Section 20 if necessary, remove the engine rear mounting link. Removing the rear mounting will increase the amount of engine movement, but the engine will still be supported on its right- and left-hand mountings. However, the left-hand mounting bolts must be loosened next, and it is advisable to position a substantial trolley jack under the transmission before this is done. If available, use an engine support bar from above to suspend the engine **(see illustration)**.

10 With a jack placed underneath the transmission as a precaution, just loosen the left-hand mounting bracket bolts from the transmission by a couple of turns. Do not remove the bolts – it is essential for safety that they remain sufficiently fitted to support the transmission. To remove the sump, the transmission must be parted slightly from the engine, and loosening the mounting bolts allows this.

11 Working from below, loosen any remaining transmission-to-engine bolts by about 10 mm – again, do not remove them completely.

12 On automatic transmission models, remove the starter motor as described in Chapter 5A. Remove the rubber cover from the bellhousing to access the four torque converter-to-driveplate nuts – turn the engine using a spanner on the crankshaft pulley until each of the nuts is accessible, and unscrew them one at a time.

13 At the timing chain end of the engine, remove the row of four bolts at the base of the timing chain cover.

14 Keeping the jack under the transmission as a precaution, carefully pull the transmission away from the engine by about 8 mm.

15 Progressively unscrew the sump retaining bolts, including the four bolts between the sump and transmission **(see illustrations)**. Use a scraper or other wide-bladed tool to break the sealant around the sump, taking care not to damage the mating surfaces of the sump and cylinder block. It is not advisable to prise between the mating faces, as this could result in a leak.

> **HAYNES HiNT** ***If the sump is stuck, remove the drain plug, then use a sturdy screwdriver (wrapped in some rag or card to protect the drain plug threads) in the drain plug hole as a prising tool.***

16 Lower the sump and withdraw it with the engine/transmission.

Refitting

17 On reassembly, thoroughly clean and degrease the mating surfaces of the cylinder block/crankcase and sump, then use a clean rag to wipe out the sump.

18 Apply a 3 mm bead of silicone sealant (Ford part number WSE-M4G323-A4, or equivalent) to the sump flange so that the bead is around the inside edge of the bolt holes **(see illustration)**. **Note:** *The sump must be refitted within 5 minutes of applying the sealant.*

19 Offer up the sump and insert the retaining bolts, do not tighten them at this stage.

20 Using a straight-edge, align the sump to the cylinder block on the timing chain end. With the sump held in position, progressively tighten the retaining bolts to the specified torque in the sequence shown **(see illustrations)**.

21 Refit the sump-to-transmission bolts, and tighten them to the specified torque.

22 Tighten all the transmission-to-engine bolts accessible from below to the specified torque.

23 Tighten the left-hand engine mounting bracket bolts to the specified torque. Refit the engine rear mounting link, and tighten its nuts/bolts to the specified torque. Remove the jack from under the transmission (or the engine support bar, if used).

24 On automatic transmission models, refit the torque converter-to-driveplate nuts, and tighten them to the specified torque. Refit the starter motor as described in Chapter 5A.

25 Refit and tighten the four timing chain cover lower bolts to the specified torque.

26 Refit the dipstick tube into the sump, using a new O-ring. Refit and tighten the tube lower mounting bolt.

27 Refit the left-hand wheel arch liner, then refit the left-hand front wheel and lower the car to the ground. Tighten the wheel nuts to the specified torque.

28 Tighten all the transmission-to-engine bolts accessible from above to the specified torque.

29 Refit and tighten the dipstick tube upper bolt, then refit the dipstick.

30 Refit the air cleaner and air inlet duct as described in Chapter 4A.

31 Allow sufficient time for the sealant used on the sump joint to cure before refilling the engine oil.

32 If removed, fit a new oil filter, then refill the engine with oil as described in Chapter 1A.

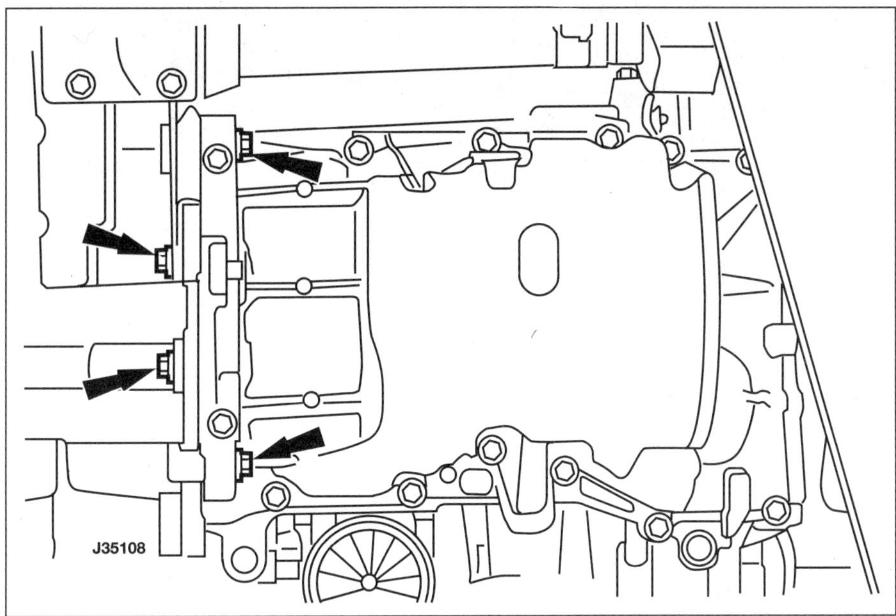

14.15b . . . and the four sump-to-transmission bolts

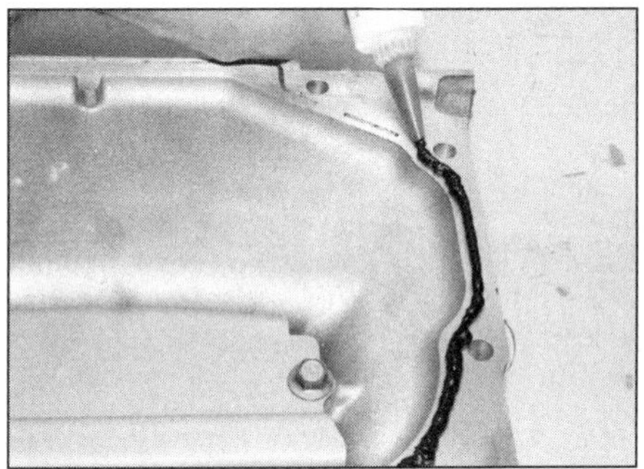

14.18 Apply a 3.0 mm bead of sealant to the sump flange

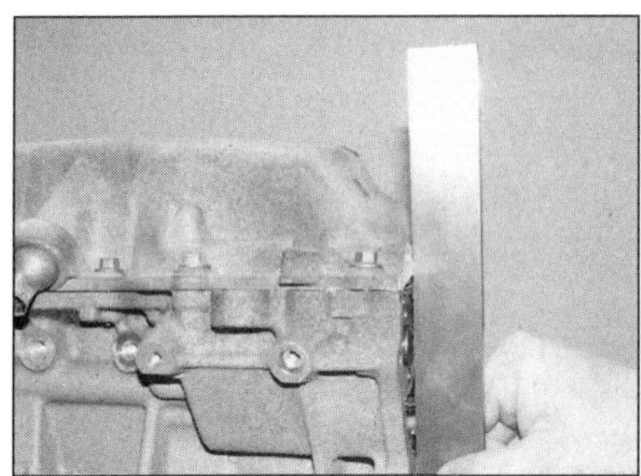

14.20a Using a straight-edge to align the sump to the cylinder block

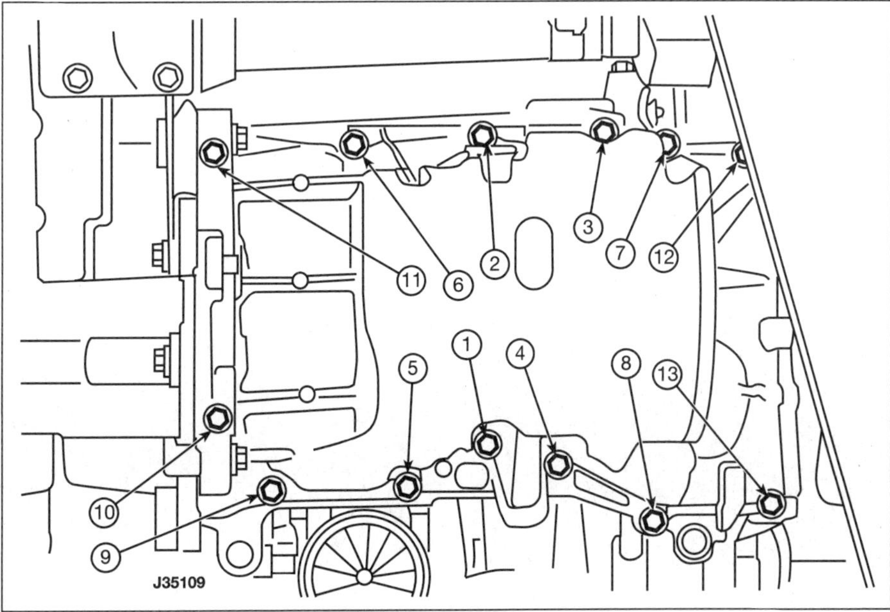

14.20b Sump bolt tightening sequence

15.3 Remove the two bolts securing the oil pump pick-up pipe to the pump

15.4 Undo the retaining bolts (arrowed), then remove the chain guide and tensioner

15.5 Holding the oil pump drive sprocket, while undoing the sprocket retaining bolt

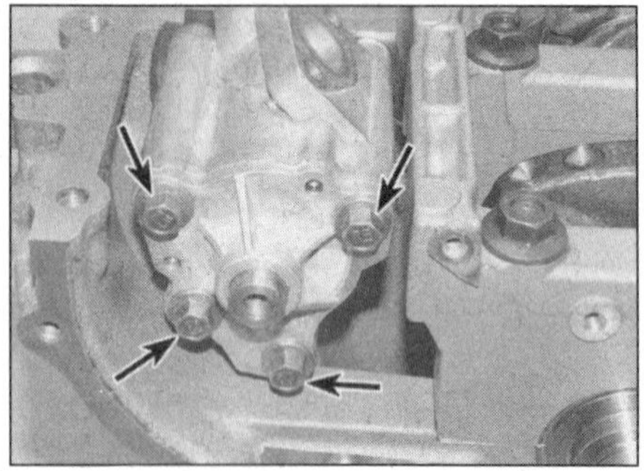

15.7 Undo the four retaining bolts (arrowed) to remove the oil pump

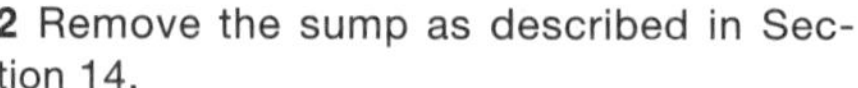

15.11 Using one of the retaining bolts to locate the new gasket in place on the oil pump

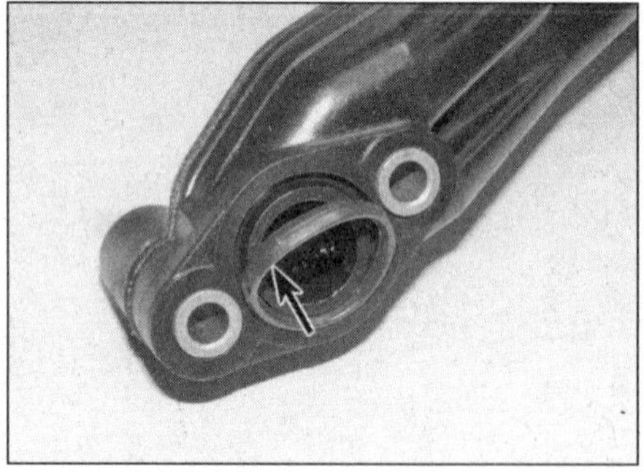

15.12 Fit a new O-ring (arrowed) to the oil pump pick-up pipe

33 Check for signs of oil leaks once the engine has been restarted and warmed-up to normal operating temperature.

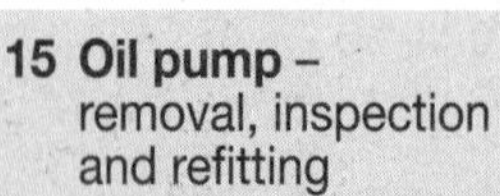

15 Oil pump – removal, inspection and refitting

Note: *While this task is theoretically possible when the engine is in place in the car, in practice, it requires so much preliminary dismantling, and is so difficult to carry out due to the restricted access, that owners are advised to remove the engine from the car first. All the illustrations used in this Section are with the engine out of the car, and the engine upside-down on a work bench.*

Removal

1 Remove the timing chain as described in Section 10.

2 Remove the sump as described in Section 14.

3 Undo the two bolts securing the oil pump pick-up pipe to the pump **(see illustration)**. Discard the O-ring/gasket.

4 Undo the two retaining bolts and remove the oil pump chain guide, then undo the retaining bolt and remove the oil pump chain tensioner **(see illustration)**.

5 Hold the oil pump drive sprocket to prevent it from turning and slacken the sprocket retaining bolt **(see illustration)**.

6 Undo the bolt and remove the oil pump sprocket complete with the oil pump drive chain.

7 Unbolt the pump from the cylinder block/crankcase **(see illustration)**. Withdraw and discard the gasket.

Inspection

8 At the time of writing there was no information on the stripdown of the oil pump. If there is any doubt in the operation of the oil pump, then the complete pump assembly should be renewed. If the engine is being rebuilt after covering a very high mileage, it is considered good practice to fit a new oil pump in any case.

Refitting

9 Thoroughly clean and degrease all components, particularly the mating surfaces of the pump, the sump, and the cylinder block/crankcase. When using a scraper and solvent to remove all traces of old gasket/sealant from the mating surfaces, be careful to ensure that you do not scratch or damage the material of either component – any solvents used must be suitable for this application.

10 The oil pump must be primed on installation, by pouring clean engine oil into it, and rotating its inner rotor a few turns.

11 Fit the new gasket in place on the oil pump using one of the retaining bolts to locate it, refit the pump to the cylinder block/crankcase and insert the retaining bolts, tightening them to the specified torque wrench setting **(see illustration)**.

12 Fit the new O-ring/gasket in place and refit the pump pick-up pipe to the pump, tightening its retaining bolts securely **(see illustration)**.

13 Refit the oil pump drive chain complete with oil pump sprocket **(see illustration)** and tighten the retaining bolt to the specified torque setting. Hold the oil pump drive sprocket (using the same method as removal) to prevent it from turning when tightening the sprocket retaining bolt.

14 Refit the oil pump chain tensioner to the

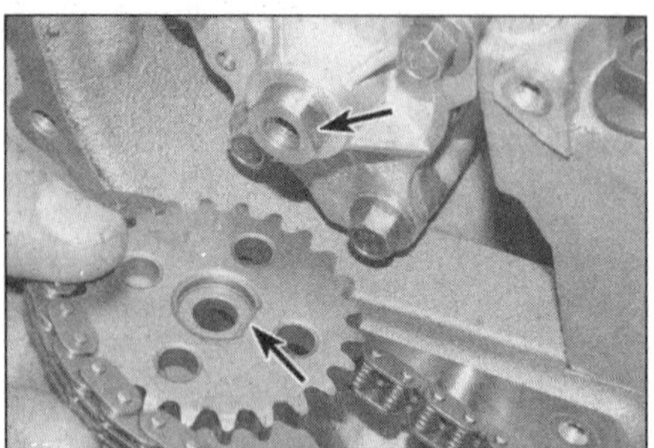

15.13 Align the flats (arrowed) on the oil pump driveshaft and oil pump sprocket when refitting

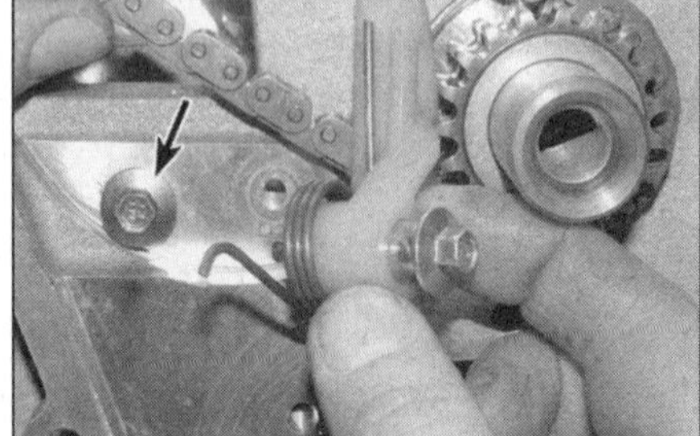

15.14 Make sure the spring on the tensioner is hooked behind the bolt (arrowed) to tension the chain

cylinder block, making sure the spring is located correctly **(see illustration)**. Tighten the retaining bolt to its specified torque setting.

15 Refit the oil pump chain guide to the cylinder block, tightening the two retaining bolts to their specified torque setting.

16 Refit the timing chain as described in Section 10.

17 Refit the sump as described in Section 14.

16 Oil filter housing – removal and refitting

1 Drain the cooling system (see Chapter 1A).

2 If the oil filter element requires renewal, unscrew the oil filter cap from the filter housing (see Chapter 1A) – catch any escaping oil in a drip tray.

3 Disconnect the wiring connector from the oil pressure switch on the filter housing. **Note:** *On some models, a separate oil cooler may be bolted to the top of the oil filter housing, it has two coolant hoses going to it. If required, disconnect the two coolant hoses from the oil cooler, undo the retaining bolt and remove the oil cooler from the top of the filter housing. Renew the o-ring seal on refitting.*

4 Unscrew the four retaining bolts from the filter housing and withdraw the housing from the cylinder block **(see illustration)**, be prepared for coolant loss. Discard the gasket.

5 On reassembly, thoroughly clean any gasket or sealant from the mating surfaces of the cylinder block and oil filter housing.

6 Refitting is the reverse of the removal procedure, noting the following points:

*a) Renew all gaskets **(see illustration)**, O-rings and seals disturbed on removal.*

b) Tighten the housing retaining bolts to the specified torque wrench setting.

c) Refill the cooling system (see Chapter 1A).

d) Refit (or renew) the oil filter, then check the engine oil level, and top-up as necessary (see Weekly checks).

e) Check for signs of oil or coolant leaks once the engine has been restarted and warmed-up to normal operating temperature.

17 Oil pressure warning light switch – removal and refitting

Removal

1 The switch is screwed into the oil filter housing on the front of the cylinder block **(see illustration)**.

2 With the car parked on firm level ground, open the bonnet and disconnect the battery negative (earth) lead (refer to *Disconnecting the battery* at the end of this manual).

3 If required, raise the front of the car, and support it securely on axle stands, this will give better access to the switch.

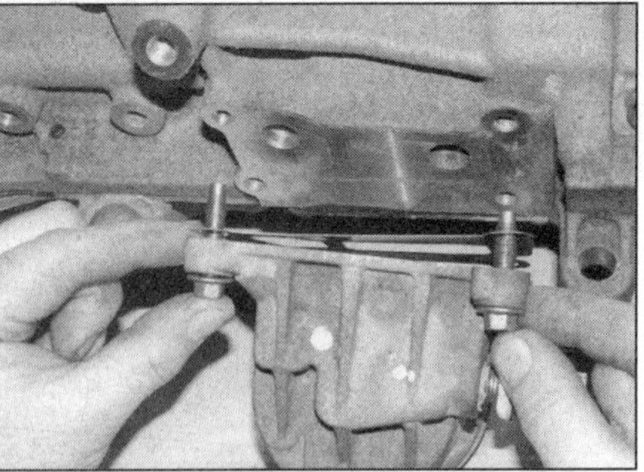

16.4 Undo the retaining bolts and withdraw the filter housing from the cylinder block

4 Disconnect the wiring connector from the switch, and unscrew it; be prepared for some oil loss.

Refitting

5 Refitting is the reverse of the removal procedure; apply a thin smear of suitable sealant to the switch threads, and tighten it to the specified torque wrench setting. Check the engine oil level, and top-up as necessary (see *Weekly checks*). Check for signs of oil leaks once the engine has been restarted and warmed-up to normal operating temperature.

18 Crankshaft oil seals – renewal

Timing chain end oil seal

1 Remove the crankshaft pulley as described in Section 8 of this Chapter.

2 Using a screwdriver, prise the old oil seal from the timing cover. Take care not to damage the surface of the timing cover and crankshaft. If the oil seal is tight, carefully drill two holes diagonally opposite each other in the oil seal, then insert self-tapping screws and use a pair of pliers to pull out the oil seal.

3 Wipe clean the seating in the timing cover and the nose of the crankshaft.

4 Smear clean engine oil on the outer periphery and sealing lips of the new oil seal, then start it into the timing cover by pressing it in squarely. Using a large socket or metal tubing, drive in the oil seal until flush with the outer surface of the timing cover. Make sure the oil seal remains square as it is being inserted. Wipe off any excess oil **(see illustrations)**.

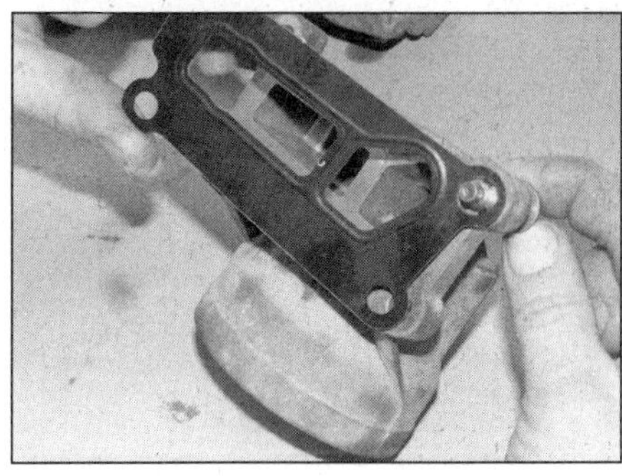

16.6 Using one of the retaining bolts to locate the new gasket in place on the filter housing

5 Refit the crankshaft pulley as described in Section 8 of this Chapter.

Transmission end oil seal

6 Remove the transmission (see the relevant Part of Chapter 7).

7 On manual models, remove the clutch assembly (see Chapter 6).

8 Unbolt the flywheel/driveplate (Section 19).

9 Remove the sump (see Section 14).

10 Undo the six retaining bolts and remove the oil seal carrier from the cylinder block. Where applicable, remove and discard its gasket. **Note:** *The seal and carrier are purchased as a unit.*

17.1 The oil pressure switch (arrowed) is screwed into the oil filter housing

18.4a Make sure the oil seal remains square as it is being inserted into the cover

18.4b A socket of the correct size can be used for fitting of the new seal

11 Clean the seal housing and crankshaft, polishing off any burrs or raised edges, which may have caused the seal to fail in the first place. Where applicable, clean also the mating surfaces of the cylinder block/crankcase, using a scraper to remove all traces of the old gasket/sealant – be careful not to scratch or damage the material of either – then use a suitable solvent to degrease them.

12 Use a special sleeve to slide the seal over the crankshaft, if this is not available, make up a guide from a thin sheet of plastic or similar, lubricate the lips of the new seal and the crankshaft shoulder with oil, then offer up the oil seal carrier, with the guide feeding the seal's lips over the crankshaft shoulder.

13 Being careful not to damage the oil seal, move the carrier into the correct position, and tighten its bolts in the correct sequence to the specified torque wrench setting **(see illustration)**.

14 Wipe off any surplus oil or grease; the remainder of the reassembly procedure is the reverse of dismantling, referring to the relevant text for details where required. Check for signs of oil leakage when the engine is restarted.

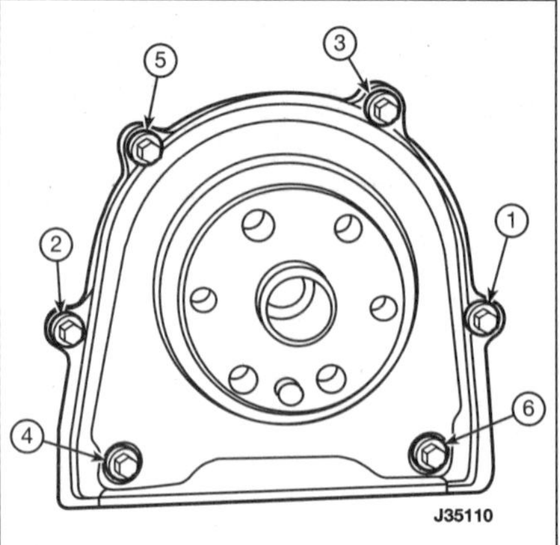

18.13 Tightening sequence for the oil seal carrier retaining bolts

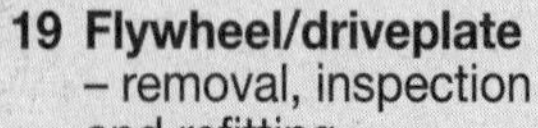

19 Flywheel/driveplate – removal, inspection and refitting

Removal

1 Remove the transmission (see the relevant Part of Chapter 7).

2 Where applicable, remove the clutch (Chapter 6).

3 Use a centre-punch or paint to make alignment marks on the flywheel/driveplate and crankshaft, to ensure correct alignment during refitting.

4 Prevent the flywheel/driveplate from turning by locking the ring gear teeth, or by bolting a strap between the flywheel/driveplate and the cylinder block/crankcase **(see illustration)**. Slacken the bolts evenly until all are free.

5 Remove each bolt in turn, and ensure that new ones are obtained for reassembly; these bolts are subjected to severe stresses, and so must be renewed, regardless of their apparent condition, whenever they are disturbed.

6 Withdraw the flywheel/driveplate from the end of the crankshaft. **Note:** *Take care when removing the flywheel/driveplate as it is a very heavy component.*

Inspection

7 Clean the flywheel/driveplate to remove grease and oil. Inspect the surface for cracks, rivet grooves, burned areas and score marks. Light scoring can be removed with emery cloth. Check for cracked and broken ring gear teeth. Lay the flywheel/driveplate on a flat surface, and use a straight-edge to check for warpage.

8 Clean and inspect the mating surfaces of the flywheel/driveplate and the crankshaft. If the crankshaft left-hand oil seal is leaking, renew it (see Section 18) before refitting the flywheel/driveplate.

9 While the flywheel/driveplate is removed, clean carefully its inboard (right-hand) face. Thoroughly clean the threaded bolt holes in the crankshaft – this is important, since if old sealer remains in the threads, the bolts will settle over a period and will not retain their correct torque wrench settings.

Refitting

10 On refitting, fit the flywheel/driveplate to the crankshaft so that all bolt holes align – it will fit only one way – check this using the marks made on removal. Apply suitable sealer to the threads of the new bolts then insert them **(see illustration)**.

11 Lock the flywheel/driveplate by the method used on dismantling. Working in a diagonal sequence to tighten them evenly, and increasing to the final amount in three stages, tighten the new bolts to the specified torque wrench setting **(see illustration)**.

12 The remainder of reassembly is the reverse of the removal procedure, referring to the relevant text for details where required.

20 Engine/transmission mountings – inspection and renewal

General

1 The engine/transmission mountings seldom require attention, but broken or deteriorated mountings should be renewed immediately, or the added strain placed on the driveline components may cause damage or wear.

2 While separate mountings may be removed and refitted individually, if more than one is disturbed at a time – such as if the engine/transmission unit is removed from its mountings – they must be reassembled and their fasteners tightened in the position marked on removal.

3 On reassembly, the complete weight of the engine/transmission unit must not be taken by the mountings until all are correctly aligned with the marks made on removal. Tighten the engine/transmission mounting fasteners to their specified torque wrench settings.

Inspection

4 During the check, the engine/transmission unit must be raised slightly, to remove its weight from the mountings.

5 Raise the front of the car, and support it securely on axle stands. Position a jack under the sump, with a large block of wood between the jack head and the sump, then carefully raise the engine/transmission just enough to take the weight off the mountings.

Warning: DO NOT place any part of your body under the engine when it is supported only by a jack.

6 Check the mountings to see if the rubber is cracked, hardened or separated from the metal components. Sometimes the rubber will split right down the centre.

19.4 Lock the flywheel/driveplate while the bolts (arrowed) are removed

19.10 Apply suitable locking fluid to the threads of the new bolts on refitting

19.11 Tighten the new bolts, using the method used on dismantling for locking the flywheel/driveplate

20.10a Remove the two locking nuts and the three retaining bolts (arrowed) . . .

20.10b . . . and withdraw the mounting from the vehicle

20.12 Undo the retaining clip and remove the air inlet hose

20.13 Unscrew the centre retaining nut

20.14 Unscrew the four mounting outer retaining nuts (arrowed)

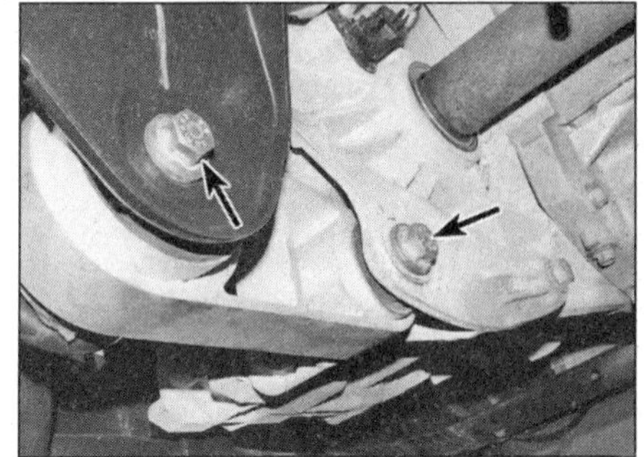

20.16a Unscrew the rear mounting's centre bolts (arrowed) . . .

7 Check for relative movement between each mounting's brackets and the engine/ transmission or body (use a large screwdriver or lever to attempt to move the mountings). If movement is noted, lower the engine and check-tighten the mounting fasteners.

Renewal

Note: *The following paragraphs assume the engine is supported beneath the sump as described earlier.*

Right-hand mounting

8 Remove the coolant expansion bottle from the right-hand inner wing, as described in Chapter 3.

9 Mark the position of the mounting on the right-hand inner wing panel.

10 With the engine/transmission supported, unscrew the two locking nuts from the engine casing, then undo the three retaining bolts to the inner wing panel and withdraw the mounting from the car **(see illustrations)**.

11 On refitting, tighten all fasteners to the torque wrench settings specified. Tighten the two locking nuts to the engine casing first, then release the hoist or jack to allow the mounting bracket to rest on the inner wing panel. Re-align the marks made on removal, then tighten the three mounting bracket-to-inner wing retaining bolts.

Left-hand mounting

Note: *The mounting nuts are self-locking, and must therefore be renewed whenever they are disturbed.*

12 Undo the retaining clip from the air inlet hose **(see illustration),** then lift the complete air cleaner assembly and remove it from the car (see Chapter 4A).

13 With the transmission supported, note the position of the mounting then unscrew the centre retaining nut to release the mounting from the transmission **(see illustration).**

14 Unscrew the four outer retaining nuts to dismantle the mounting from the mounting bracket **(see illustration)**. To remove the mounting bracket, undo the retaining bolts and remove the bracket from the left-hand inner wing panel.

15 On refitting, renew the self-locking nuts. Re-align the mounting in the position noted on removal, then tighten all fasteners to the specified torque wrench settings.

20.16b . . . and remove the mounting from the subframe and the transmission

Rear mounting (roll restrictor)

16 Unbolt the mounting from the subframe and the transmission by unscrewing the mounting's centre bolts **(see illustrations)**. Though removing the rear mounting will increase the amount of engine movement, provided they have not been disturbed, the engine will remain safely supported on its right- and left-hand mountings.

17 On refitting, ensure that the bolts are securely tightened to the specified torque wrench setting.

Notes

Chapter 2 Part B: V6 petrol engine in-car repair procedures

Contents

Degrees of difficulty

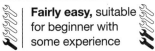

Easy, suitable for novice with little experience	**Fairly easy,** suitable for beginner with some experience	**Fairly difficult,** suitable for competent DIY mechanic	**Difficult,** suitable for experienced DIY mechanic	**Very difficult,** suitable for expert DIY or professional

Specifications

General

Engine type	Six-cylinder, V6 24-valve, in two banks of three cylinders, double overhead camshafts on each bank (four camshafts in total – 'quad-cam')
Engine code:	
2.5 litre, Duratec-VE	LCBD
3.0 litre, Duratec-SE	REBA
3.0 litre, Duratec-ST (ST220)	MEBA
Capacity:	
2.5 litre	2499 cc (sometimes also quoted as 2495 or 2544 cc)
3.0 litre	2967 cc
Bore:	
2.5 litre	81.66 mm
3.0 litre	89.0 mm
Stroke	79.5 mm
Compression ratio:	
2.5 litre	9.7 : 1
3.0 litre	10.0 : 1
Power output:	
2.5 litre, Duratec-VE	125 kW (170 PS) at 6250 rpm
3.0 litre, Duratec-SE (except ST220)	150 kW (204 PS) at 6000 rpm
3.0 litre, Duratec-ST (ST220)	166 kW (226 PS) at 6150 rpm
Firing order	1-4-2-5-3-6 (No 1 cylinder at timing chain end of rear bank)
Direction of crankshaft rotation	Clockwise (seen from right-hand side of car)

Cylinder head

Camshaft bearing diameter	26.987 to 27.012 mm
Hydraulic tappet bore diameter	16.018 to 16.057 mm
Cylinder head warp (maximum)	0.08 mm

Camshafts

Camshaft bearing journal diameter	26.926 to 26.936 mm
Camshaft bearing journal-to-cylinder head running clearance	0.0125 to 0.038 mm
Camshaft endfloat	0.025 to 0.165 mm

Lubrication

Engine oil capacity (including filter)	See Chapter 1A
Oil pressure	3.1 bars @ 1500 rpm
Oil pump clearances (inner to outer rotor max.)	0.18 mm

Torque wrench settings

	Nm	lbf ft
Camshaft bearing cap	10	7
Camshaft oil seal housing to front cylinder head	10	7
Camshaft position sensor	10	7
Coolant pipe to cylinder head	10	7
Coolant transfer pipe to cylinder head	6	4
Crankshaft position sensor to timing cover	10	7
Crankshaft pulley/vibration damper centre bolt*:		
Stage 1	120	89
Stage 2	Loosen 360°	
Stage 3	50	37
Stage 4	Angle-tighten a further 90°	
Cylinder head bolts:		
Stage 1	40	30
Stage 2	Angle-tighten a further 90°	
Stage 3	Loosen 360°	
Stage 4	40	30
Stage 5	Angle-tighten a further 90°	
Stage 6	Angle-tighten a further 90°	
Cylinder head valve cover	10	7
Earth cable-to-transmission bolt	25	18
Engine front lifting eye bolt	112	83
Engine/transmission mountings:		
Front and rear roll restrictors:		
Mounting-to-subframe bolts	48	35
Through-bolt	80	59
Left-hand mounting bracket-to-transmission bolts:		
Automatic transmission	80	59
Manual transmission	90	66
Left-hand mounting centre nut*	133	98
Left-hand mounting outer nuts*	48	35
Right-hand engine mounting*	83	61
Right-hand engine mounting bracket to cylinder block*	47	35
Exhaust front pipe to manifold	40	30
Exhaust manifold	20	15
Flywheel/driveplate to crankshaft	80	59
Front engine roll restrictor to subframe	48	35
Inlet manifolds	10	7
Knock sensor to cylinder head	34	25
Oil baffle to crankcase	10	7
Oil baffle to sump	10	7
Oil cooler pipe to transmission	23	17
Oil cooler to cylinder block	55	41
Oil dipstick tube to transfer pipe	10	7
Oil pressure switch	14	10
Oil pump cover	10	7
Oil pump pick-up tube:		
M6	10	7
M8	25	18
Oil pump to cylinder block	11	8
Oil separator to cylinder block	10	7
Roadwheel nuts	85	63
Sump oil drain plug	26	19
Sump	25	18
Timing chain cover to cylinder block	25	18
Timing chain guides to cylinder block	25	18
Timing chain tensioner to cylinder block	25	18
Torque converter to driveplate	36	27
Transmission-to-engine bolts	48	35

** Use new nuts/bolts*

1 General information

How to use this Chapter

This Part of Chapter 2 is devoted to in-car repair procedures for the engine. All procedures concerning engine removal and refitting, and engine block/cylinder head overhaul can be found in Chapter 2D.

The operations included in this Part are based on the assumption that the engine is still installed in the car. Therefore, if this information is being used during a complete engine overhaul, with the engine already removed, many of the steps included here will not apply.

Engine

The engine, also known by Ford's internal code name Duratec-VE, -SE, or -ST, is of V6 type, mounted transversely at the front of the car, with the transmission on its left-hand end. The engine is of all-aluminium construction, incorporating two banks of three cylinders each. Each cylinder has four valves, two inlet and two exhaust, making a total of 24 valves.

The crankshaft runs in four main bearings, the bearing at the flywheel/driveplate end incorporates thrustwashers at each side of the bearing shell to control crankshaft endfloat. The connecting rods rotate on horizontally-split bearing shells at their big-ends. The pistons are attached to the connecting rods by fully-floating gudgeon pins which are retained by circlips in the pistons. The aluminium alloy pistons are fitted with three piston rings: two compression rings and an oil control ring. After manufacture, the cylinder bores and piston skirts are measured and classified into three grades, which must be carefully matched together, to ensure the correct piston/cylinder clearance; no oversizes are available to permit reboring.

The inlet and exhaust valves are closed by coil springs; they operate in guides which are shrink-fitted into the cylinder heads, as are the valve seat inserts.

The camshafts on each bank are driven by a twin-row timing chain (one to the front bank and another to the rear bank), each operating the twelve valves on each bank via self-adjusting hydraulic tappets, thus eliminating the need for routine checking and adjustment of the valve clearances. Except for the front bank inlet camshaft which rotates in five bearings, the remaining camshafts rotate in four bearings which are line-bored directly in the cylinder head and bearing caps; the bearing caps are not available separately from the cylinder head, and must not be interchanged with caps from another engine.

The water pump is bolted to the transmission end of the cylinder block, and is driven by drivebelt from a pulley attached to the left-hand end of the front bank inlet camshaft.

Lubrication

Lubrication is by means of an eccentric-rotor trochoidal pump, which is mounted on the crankshaft right-hand end, and draws oil through a strainer located in the sump. The pump forces oil through an externally-mounted full-flow cartridge-type filter – on some versions of the engine, an oil cooler is fitted to the oil filter mounting, so that clean oil entering the engine's galleries is cooled by the main engine cooling system. From the filter, the oil is pumped into a main gallery in the cylinder block/crankcase, from where it is distributed to the crankshaft (main bearings) and cylinder head.

The engine covered in this Chapter employs hydraulic tappets which use the lubricating system's oil pressure to take up the clearance between each rocker tip and its respective valve stem. Therefore, there is no need for regular checking and adjustment of the valve clearances, but it is essential that only good-quality oil of the recommended viscosity and specification is used in the engine, and that this oil is always changed at the recommended intervals. On starting the engine from cold, there will be a slight delay while full oil pressure builds-up in all parts of the engine, especially in the tappets; the valve components, therefore, may well 'rattle' for about 10 seconds or so, and then quieten. This is a normal state of affairs, and is nothing to worry about, provided that all tappets quieten quickly and stay quiet.

After the car has been standing for several days, the valve components may 'rattle' for longer than usual, as nearly all the oil will have drained away from the engine's top-end components and bearing surfaces. While this is only to be expected, care must be taken not to damage the engine under these circumstances – avoid high speed running until all the tappets are refilled with oil and operating normally. With the car stationary, hold the engine at no more than a fast idle speed (maximum 2000 to 2500 rpm) for 10 to 15 seconds, or until the noise ceases. *Do not run the engine at more than 3000 rpm until the tappets are fully recharged with oil and the noise has ceased.*

2 Repair operations possible with the engine in the car

1 The following repair operations can be accomplished without removing the engine from the car:

a) Inlet and exhaust manifolds – removal and refitting.
b) Timing chains, tensioners and guide – removal and refitting.
c) Camshafts and hydraulic tappets – removal and refitting.
d) Cylinder heads – removal and refitting.
e) Sump – removal and refitting.
f) Oil pump – removal and refitting.
g) Crankshaft oil seals – renewal.
h) Flywheel/driveplate – removal and refitting.
i) Engine/transmission mounting – removal and refitting.

2 Although it is possible to remove the pistons and connecting rods with the engine installed in the car after removal of the sump, it is better for the engine to be removed, in the interests of cleanliness and improved access. For this reason, the procedure is described in Chapter 2D.

3 Compression test – description and interpretation

1 When engine performance is down, or if misfiring occurs which cannot be attributed to the ignition or fuel systems, a compression test can provide diagnostic clues as to the engine's condition. If the test is performed regularly, it can give warning of trouble before any other symptoms become apparent.

2 The engine must be fully warmed-up to normal operating temperature, the oil level must be correct, the battery must be fully-charged, and the spark plugs must be removed. The aid of an assistant will be required also.

3 Disable the ignition system by unplugging the ignition coil or DIS unit electrical connector.

4 Referring to Chapter 12, identify and remove the fuel pump fuse from the fusebox. Now start the engine and allow it to run until it stalls. If the engine will not start, at least keep it cranking for about 10 seconds. The fuel system should now be depressurised, preventing unburnt fuel from soaking the catalytic converter as the engine is turned over during the test.

5 Fit a compression tester to the No 1 cylinder spark plug hole – the type of tester which screws into the plug thread is to be preferred.

6 Have the assistant hold the accelerator wide open and crank the engine on the starter motor; after one or two revolutions, the compression pressure should build-up to a maximum figure, and then stabilise. Record the highest reading obtained.

7 Repeat the test on the remaining cylinders, recording the pressure developed in each.

8 Due to the variety of testers available, and the fluctuation of starter motor speed when cranking the engine, different readings are often obtained when carrying out the compression test. For this reason, specific compression pressure figures are not quoted by Ford. However, all cylinders should produce very similar pressures; any difference greater than 10% indicates the existence of a fault.

9 If the pressure in any cylinder is considerably lower than the others, introduce a teaspoonful of clean oil into that cylinder through its spark plug hole, and repeat the test. If the addition of oil temporarily improves the compression

4.6a TDC mark on the timing cover

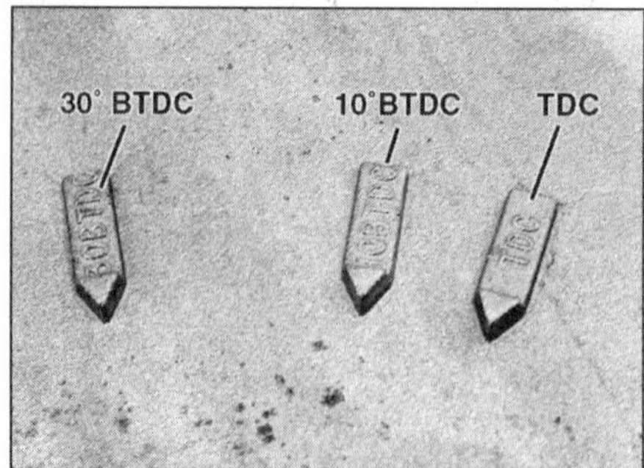

4.6b Timing marks on the timing cover

4.7 With No 1 piston at TDC on compression, these marks must point to each other

pressure, this indicates that bore or piston wear is responsible for the pressure loss. No improvement suggests that leaking or burnt valves, or a blown head gasket, may be to blame.

10 A low reading from two adjacent cylinders is almost certainly due to the head gasket having blown between them; the presence of coolant in the engine oil will confirm this.

11 On completion of the test, refit the spark plugs, then reconnect the ignition system coil and refit the fuel pump fuse.

4 Top Dead Centre (TDC) for No 1 piston – locating

Warning: When turning the engine to locate TDC, always turn it in the normal direction of rotation.

1 Top Dead Centre (TDC) is the highest point in the cylinder that each piston reaches as it travels up-and-down when the crankshaft rotates. Each piston reaches TDC on the compression stroke and again on the exhaust stroke, but TDC generally refers to piston position on the compression stroke. The timing marks on the vibration damper fitted to the front of the crankshaft refer to the number one piston at TDC on the compression stroke.

2 No 1 piston is at the right-hand end of the rear bank, with pistons 2 and 3 on the same bank. No 4 piston is at the right-hand end of the front bank, with pistons 5 and 6 on the same bank.

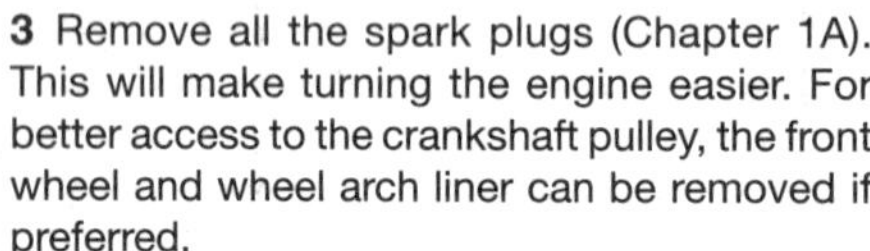

3 Remove all the spark plugs (Chapter 1A). This will make turning the engine easier. For better access to the crankshaft pulley, the front wheel and wheel arch liner can be removed if preferred.

4 The engine may be turned using a socket on the crankshaft pulley centre bolt. Alternatively on a manual transmission model, it may be turned by jacking up the right-hand side of the car so that the wheel is just clear of the ground, and turning the wheel with 4th gear engaged.

5 Turn the engine clockwise and feel for compression from the No 1 spark plug hole. To do this, temporarily insert a suitable plug (such as the handle of a screwdriver) over the spark plug hole. It is important that compression is felt, otherwise the following procedure will position the No 1 piston at TDC on the exhaust stroke instead of the compression stroke.

6 Continue to turn the engine until the crankshaft pulley keyway on the crankshaft is at the 11 o'clock position. The timing mark on the edge of the pulley must be exactly in line with the TDC arrow on the timing cover. **Note:** *On some models, there may be two other timing marks on the timing cover, indicating 10° and 30° before top dead centre* ***(see illustrations).***

7 If necessary, for a further check, the cylinder head covers may be removed (see Section 5) and the position of the timing marks on the rear of the camshaft sprockets checked. With No 1 piston at TDC on compression, the marks must point to each other **(see illustration).**

8 Once the engine has been positioned at TDC for No 1 piston, TDC for any of the remaining cylinders can be located by turning the crankshaft 120° and following the firing order (refer to the Specifications). Mark the crankshaft pulley at 120° intervals past the TDC notch. Turning the engine to the first mark past the No 1 TDC position, will locate No 4 piston at TDC. Another 120° will locate No 2 piston at TDC.

5 Cylinder head cover – removal and refitting

Front cylinder head cover

Removal

1 Remove the upper inlet manifold as described in Section 6 of this Chapter.

2 Unscrew the bolts securing the inlet manifold runner control actuator (IMRC) to the front cylinder head cover and unclip the wiring and cable and position to one side. Disconnect the wiring if necessary **(see illustrations).**

3 Note the location of the HT leads and if necessary identify them. Disconnect the HT leads from the spark plugs and remove the lead support from the right-hand engine mounting **(see illustrations).**

4 Release the crankcase ventilation hose from the top of the valve cover **(see illustration).**

5 At both ends of the cylinder head cover,

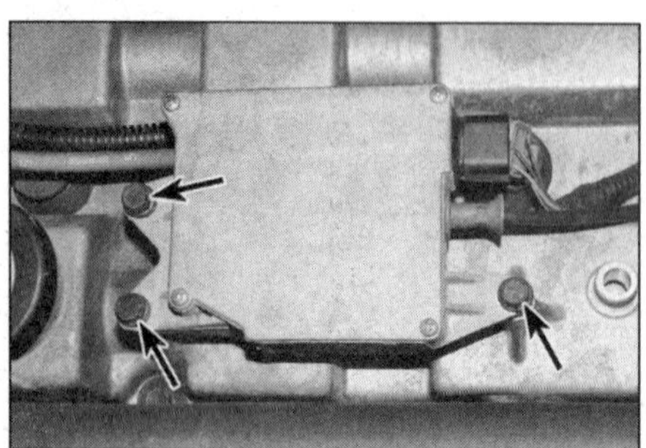
5.2a Unscrew the bolts (arrowed) and remove the IMRC actuator from the valve cover . . .

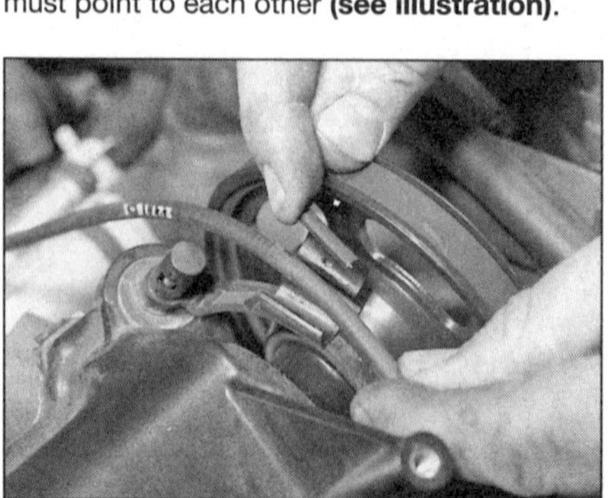
5.2b . . . then release the cable from the clips near the water pump pulley

5.2c If necessary disconnect the wiring from the IMRC actuator

5.3a Disconnect the HT leads from the spark plugs . . .

5.3b . . . and remove the lead support from the top of the right-hand engine mounting

5.4 Disconnect the crankcase ventilation hose from the top of the valve cover

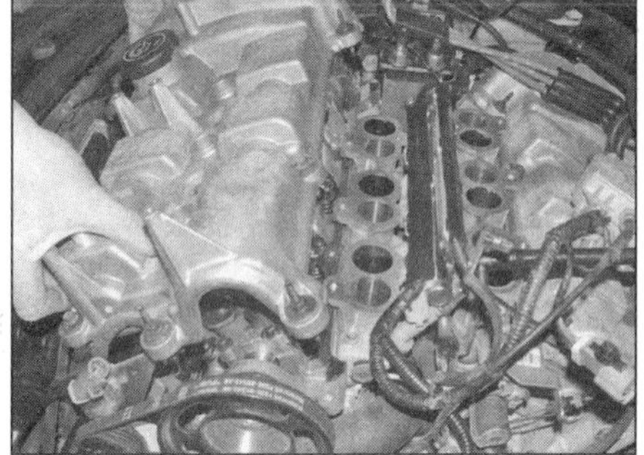
5.6 Removing the front valve cover

5.8a Locate new spark plug hole gaskets in the cylinder head cover . . .

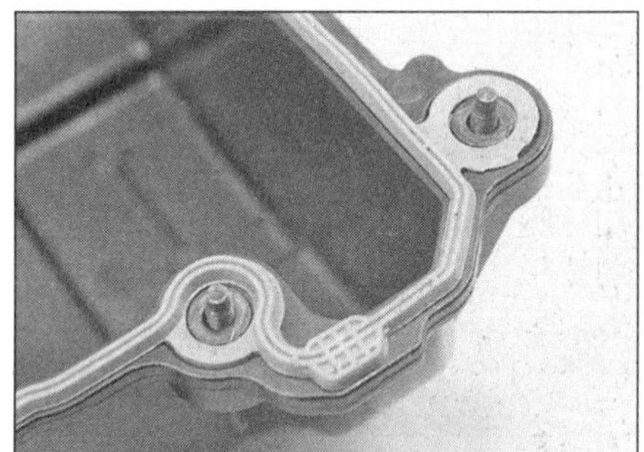
5.8b . . . then fit the outer gasket in the groove

unclip the wiring harness bracket from the cylinder head cover retaining studs.

6 Using the reverse of the sequence shown **(see illustration 5.8c)**, progressively unscrew the cylinder head cover bolts. With all the bolts removed, lift off the cover and remove the gaskets **(see illustration)**.

Refitting

7 Make sure the mating faces of the cover and cylinder head are perfectly clean. Apply an 8 mm diameter bead of silicone sealant (Ford part number WSE-M4G323-A4, or equivalent) to the joints between the timing cover and cylinder head, and the water pump drive pulley housing and cylinder head. Observe the instructions with the sealer, as normally the fitting procedure must be completed within a few minutes of applying the sealer.

8 Locate new spark plug hole gaskets in the cylinder head cover, then fit the outer gasket in the groove **(see illustrations)**. Fit the cylinder head cover and tighten the mounting bolts to the specified torque in the sequence shown **(see illustration)**. Make sure the O-ring seals are correctly fitted to the bolts.

9 Clip the wiring loom to the cylinder head cover retaining studs.

10 Reconnect the HT leads to the spark plugs and to the lead support on the right-hand engine mounting.

11 Refit the inlet manifold runner control actuator (IMRC) wiring and support.

12 Refit the upper inlet manifold together with new gaskets as described in Section 6 of this Chapter. Tighten the retaining bolts in the sequence shown **(see illustration)**.

Rear cylinder head cover

Removal

13 Remove the upper inlet manifold as described in Section 6 of this Chapter.

14 Note the location of the HT leads and if necessary identify them. Disconnect the HT leads from the spark plugs and from the lead support on the right-hand engine mounting.

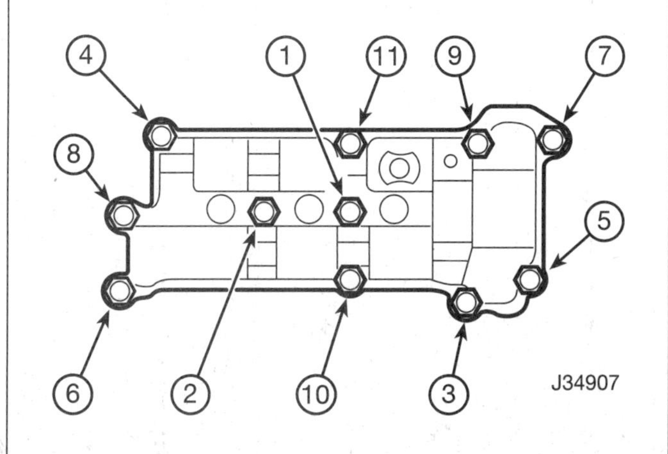

5.8c Tightening sequence for the front cylinder head cover bolts

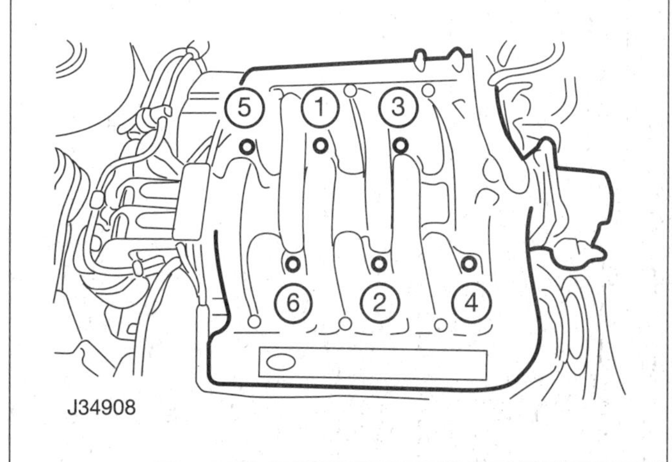

5.12 Tightening sequence for the upper inlet manifold bolts

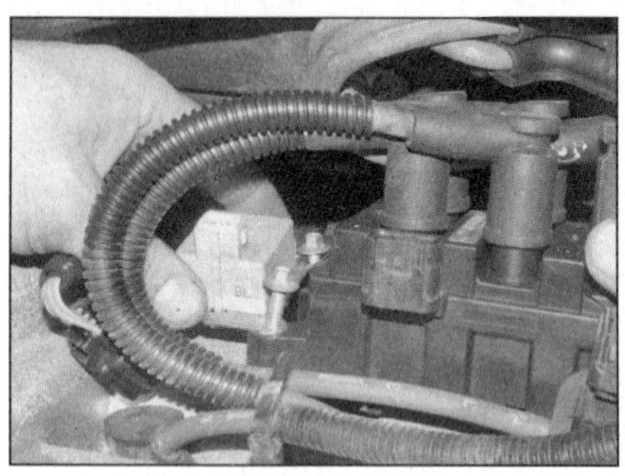
5.15 Remove the ignition coil assembly along with the earth cable and suppressor

5.18 Removing the wiring harness support bracket from the right-hand side of the rear cylinder head cover

5.19 Unscrew the bolts and lift off the rear cylinder head cover

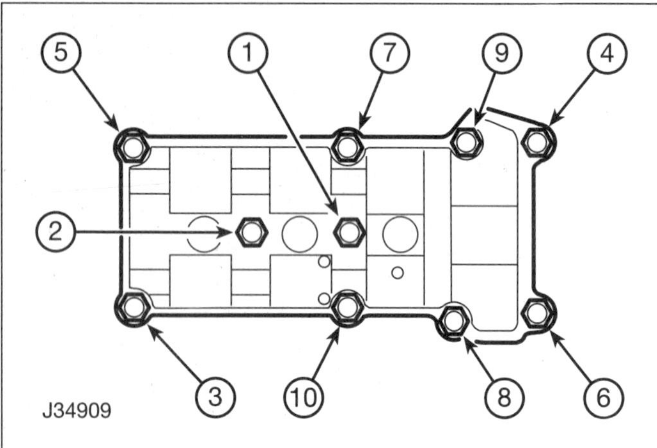

5.21a Tightening sequence for the rear cylinder head cover bolts

5.21b Note the O-ring seals on the cover mounting bolts

15 Unscrew the bolts and remove the ignition coil assembly, also removing the earth cable and suppressor **(see illustration)**.

16 Disconnect the wiring connectors and move the coil and suppressor to one side.

17 At both ends of the cylinder head cover, unclip the wiring harness bracket from the cylinder head cover retaining studs.

18 Disconnect the wiring then unbolt the wiring harness bracket from the rear cylinder head cover **(see illustration)**.

19 Using the reverse of the sequence shown **(see illustration 5.21a)**, progressively unscrew the cylinder head cover bolts. With all the bolts removed, lift off the cover and remove the gasket **(see illustration)**.

Refitting

20 Make sure the mating faces of the cover and cylinder head are perfectly clean. Apply an 8 mm diameter bead of suitable sealer to the joints between the timing cover and cylinder head. Observe the instructions with the sealer, as usually the fitting procedure must be completed within a few minutes of applying the sealer.

21 Locate new spark plug hole gaskets in the cylinder head cover, then fit the outer gasket in the groove. Fit the cylinder head cover and tighten the mounting bolts to the specified torque in the sequence shown **(see illustration)**. Make sure the O-ring seals are correctly fitted to the mounting bolts **(see illustration)**.

22 Refit the wiring harness rail to the rear of the cylinder head cover and tighten the bolt(s).

23 Refit the front wiring harness bracket to the both ends of the cylinder head cover retaining studs.

24 Refit the ignition coil/suppressor assembly and tighten the bolts. Reconnect the wiring and refit the earth cable.

25 Reconnect the HT leads to the spark plugs and to the lead support on the right-hand engine mounting.

26 Refit the upper inlet manifold together with new gaskets, as described in Section 6 of this Chapter.

6.2a One of the cover bolts secures a coolant hose clip

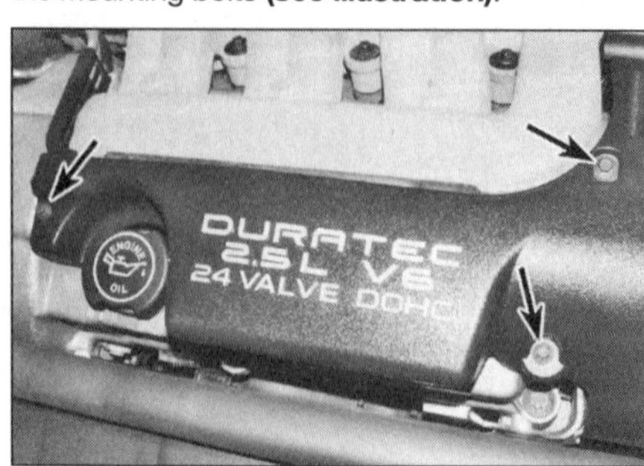

6.2b Undo the bolts (arrowed) and lift the plastic cover from the top of the front cylinder bank

6 Inlet manifolds – removal and refitting

Upper manifold

Removal

1 Disconnect the battery negative (earth) lead (refer to *Disconnecting the battery* at the end of this manual).

2 Undo the three retaining bolts and remove the plastic cover from the top of the front cylinder bank **(see illustrations)**.

3 Disconnect the crankcase ventilation hoses from each side of the air inlet duct leading

6.3a Disconnecting the crankcase ventilation hoses from the front of the air duct . . .

6.3b . . . and the rear of the air duct

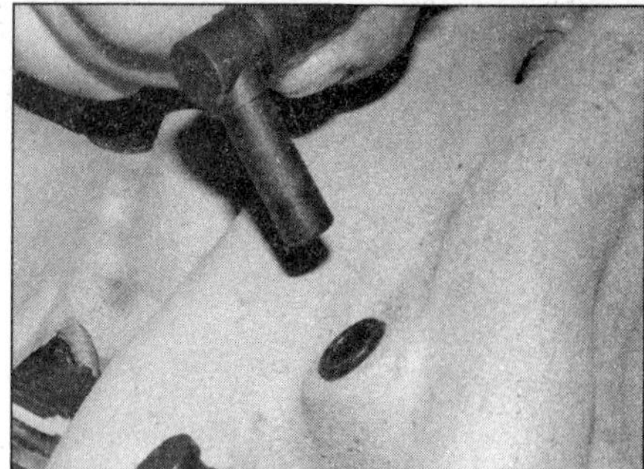
6.5 Disconnecting the vacuum hose from the upper manifold

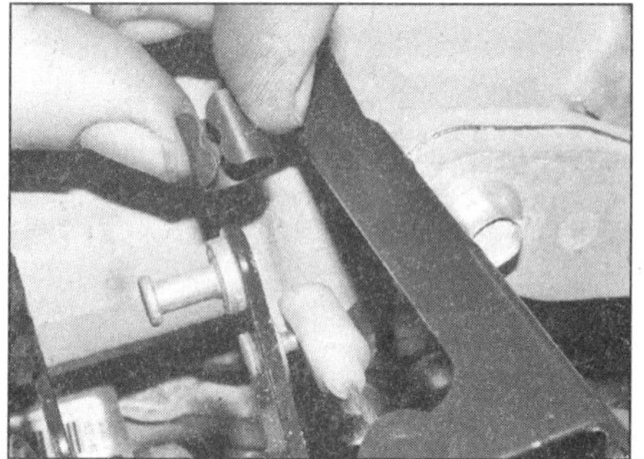
6.6a Disconnecting the retaining clip . . .

6.6b . . . withdraw the locking clip . . .

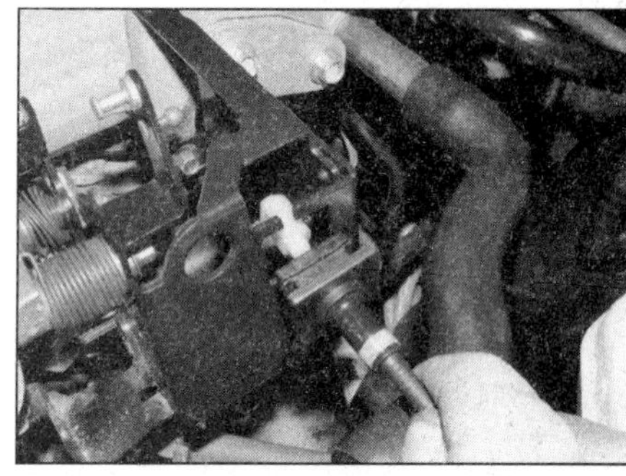
6.6c . . . and remove the accelerator cable

from the air cleaner to the throttle body **(see illustrations)**.

4 Loosen the two clips and disconnect the air inlet duct from the throttle body and air cleaner. Remove the duct.

5 Disconnect the brake vacuum servo hose from the upper inlet manifold **(see illustration)**.

6 Use a screwdriver to prise off the retaining clips, then disconnect the accelerator and speed control cables from the mounting bracket **(see illustrations)**.

7 Unbolt and remove the accelerator cable mounting bracket.

8 Disconnect the wiring from the idle air control (IAC) valve and throttle position (TP) sensor **(see illustrations)**.

9 Where applicable, disconnect the vacuum hose from the EGR valve, then unscrew the valve mounting bolts and recover the gasket. If necessary, remove the valve from the tube **(see illustrations)**.

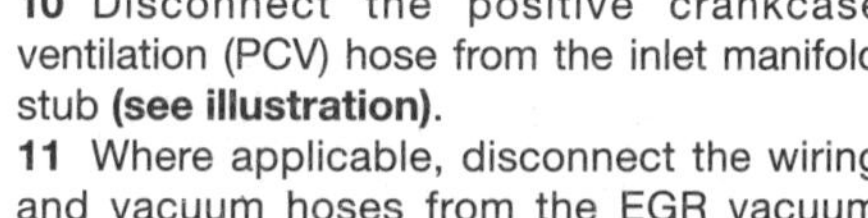

10 Disconnect the positive crankcase ventilation (PCV) hose from the inlet manifold stub **(see illustration)**.

11 Where applicable, disconnect the wiring and vacuum hoses from the EGR vacuum regulator **(see illustrations)**. Also where applicable, detach the canister-purge solenoid valve from its mounting bracket, without disconnecting the hoses.

12 Progressively unscrew the upper inlet

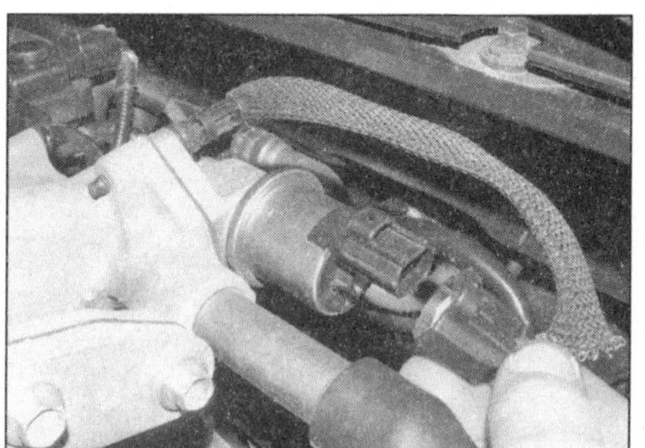
6.8a Disconnecting the wiring from the idle air control valve . . .

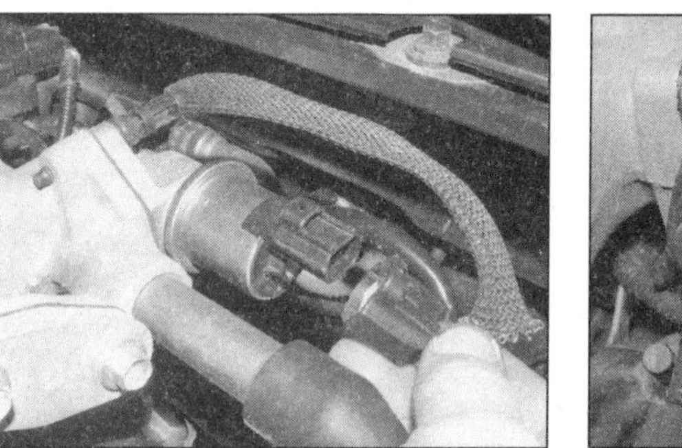
6.8b . . . and throttle position sensor

6.9a Disconnecting the vacuum hose from the EGR valve

6.9b Unscrew the bolts . . .

6.9c . . . and recover the gasket from the EGR valve

6.10 Disconnecting the positive crankcase ventilation (PCV) hose from the upper inlet manifold

6.11a Disconnect the wiring . . .

6.11b . . . and vacuum hoses from the EGR vacuum regulator

manifold mounting bolts in the reverse order to that shown **(see illustration 5.12)** , then remove the upper manifold. Recover the gaskets from the lower inlet manifold. Recover the rubber insulators from the mounting bolts and inspect them – if they are not serviceable, renew them **(see illustrations)**.

Refitting

13 Clean the mating surfaces of the upper and lower inlet manifolds.

14 Locate new gaskets on the lower manifold, then refit the upper manifold. Insert the bolts and tighten to the specified torque in the sequence shown **(see illustration 5.12)**.

15 Reconnect the vacuum hose and wiring to the EGR vacuum regulator. Refit the canister-purge solenoid valve to its bracket, where removed.

16 Reconnect the PCV hose to the inlet manifold stub.

17 Refit the EGR valve together with a new gasket and tighten the bolts. Reconnect the vacuum hose.

18 Reconnect the wiring to the throttle position sensor and idle air control valve.

19 Reconnect the accelerator and speed control cables to the mounting bracket and retain with the clip.

20 Reconnect the brake vacuum servo hose(s) to the upper inlet manifold.

21 Refit the air inlet duct and tighten the securing clips.

22 Reconnect the idle air control valve hose to the air inlet duct.

23 Reconnect the crankcase ventilation hoses each side of the air inlet duct.

24 Refit the plastic cover to the top of the front cylinder bank and tighten the retaining bolts.

25 Reconnect the battery negative (earth) lead on completion.

Lower manifold

Removal

26 Depressurise the fuel system as described in Chapter 4A.

27 Disconnect the battery negative (earth) lead (refer to *Disconnecting the battery* at the end of this manual).

28 Remove the upper inlet manifold as described earlier in this Section.

29 Disconnect the fuel feed and return lines. For further information on fuel lines and fittings see Chapter 4A, Section 3.

30 Disconnect the wiring harness from across the top of the fuel rail and the injectors.

31 Disconnect the vacuum hose from the fuel pressure regulator.

32 Disconnect the inlet manifold runner control (IMRC) actuator rod or cable from the stud and bracket on the front cylinder head cover, and disconnect the vacuum hose from the IMRC vacuum solenoid.

33 Progressively unscrew the lower inlet manifold mounting bolts in the reverse sequence to that shown **(see illustration 6.38)**.

34 With all the bolts removed, lift the lower inlet manifold from the cylinder heads and recover the gaskets **(see illustrations)**.

35 Clean the mating surfaces of the manifold and cylinder head taking care not to damage the aluminium surfaces.

Refitting

36 Place the new gaskets on the cylinder head, making sure that the they are located correctly.

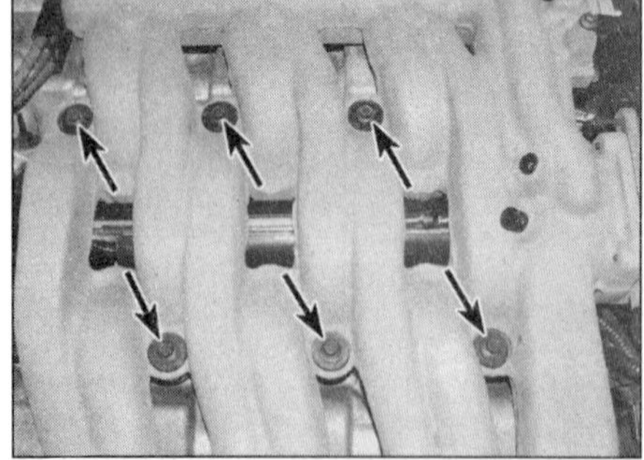
6.12a Upper inlet manifold mounting bolts (arrowed)

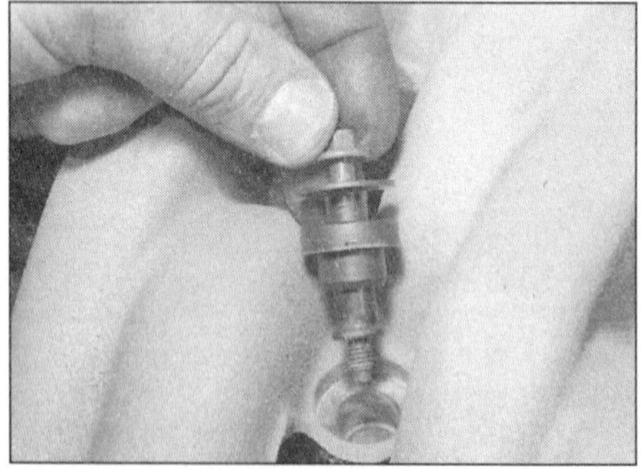
6.12b Mounting bolts and rubber insulators

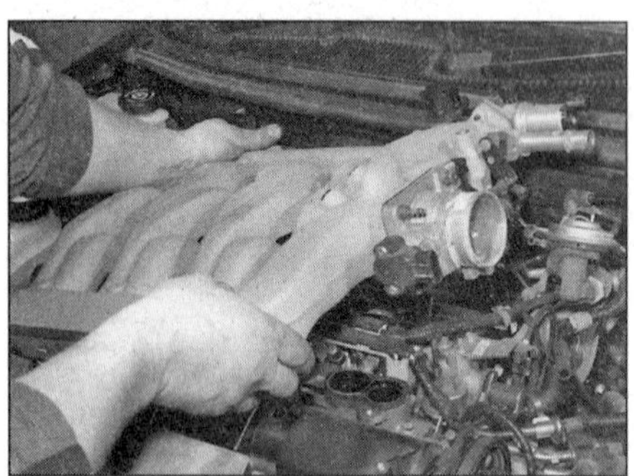
6.12c Removing the upper inlet manifold . . .

6.12d . . . and gaskets

6.34a Unscrew and remove the bolts . . .

6.34b . . . then remove the lower inlet manifold from the cylinder heads . . .

6.34c . . . and recover the gaskets

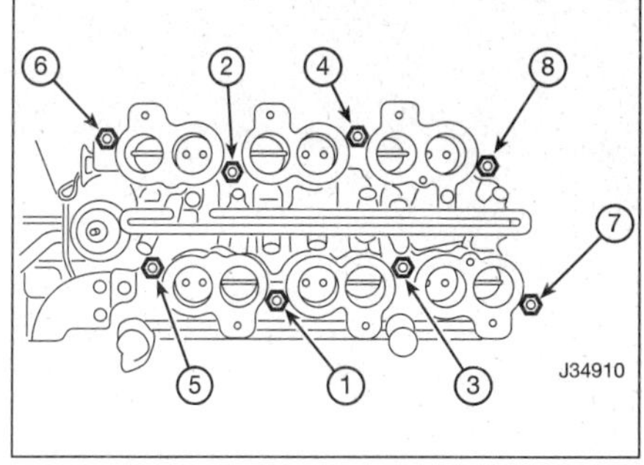

6.38 Tightening sequence for the lower inlet manifold bolts

37 Carefully position the lower inlet manifold on the gaskets making sure that the gaskets are not displaced.

38 Insert the bolts and progressively tighten them to the specified torque in the sequence shown **(see illustration)**.

39 Reconnect the IMRC vacuum hose or actuator rod.

40 Reconnect the vacuum hose to the fuel pressure regulator.

41 Reroute the wiring across the top of the fuel rail and connect the wiring plugs to the injectors, reconnect any other connectors that have been disconnected.

42 Reconnect the fuel line.

43 Reconnect the battery negative (earth) lead on completion.

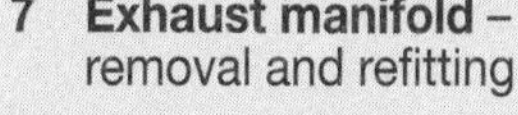

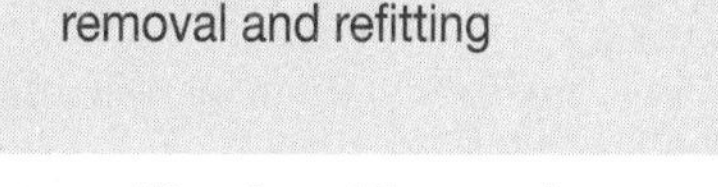

7 Exhaust manifold – removal and refitting

Warning: The engine must be completely cold before starting this procedure.

Front exhaust manifold

Removal

1 Disconnect the battery negative (earth) lead (refer to *Disconnecting the battery* at the end of this manual).

2 Undo the three retaining bolts and remove the plastic cover from the top of the front cylinder bank, then disconnect the oxygen sensor wiring connector at the transmission end of the engine.

3 Where fitted, unscrew the union nut and disconnect the EGR transfer tube from the exhaust manifold.

4 If necessary for additional working room, drain the cooling system and remove the radiator bottom hose. On 3.0 litre engines, remove the radiator cooling fan and shroud as described in Chapter 3.

5 On 2.5 litre engines, unbolt the exhaust front pipe (Y-pipe) from the exhaust manifolds. On 3.0 litre engines, remove the front catalytic converter as described in Chapter 4C.

6 Unscrew the mounting nuts and withdraw the exhaust manifold from the studs on the cylinder head. Remove the gasket and discard it along with the retaining nuts **(see illustrations)**.

7 If necessary, unscrew the oxygen sensor with reference to Chapter 4C.

8 Clean the mating surfaces of the exhaust manifold and cylinder head.

Refitting

9 If removed, refit the oxygen sensor and tighten to the specified torque with reference to Chapter 4C.

10 Position a new gasket on the cylinder head studs.

11 Refit the exhaust manifold and progressively tighten the new mounting nuts to the specified torque.

12 On 2.5 litre engines, reconnect the exhaust front pipe (Y-pipe) to the exhaust manifolds and tighten the bolts to the specified torque. On 3.0 litre engines, refit the front catalytic converter as described in Chapter 4C.

13 Where removed, reconnect the radiator bottom hose and tighten the clip. Refill the cooling system with reference to Chapter 1A. On 3.0 litre engines, refit the radiator cooling fan and shroud as described in Chapter 3.

14 Where applicable, reconnect the EGR transfer tube and tighten the union nut.

15 Reconnect the oxygen sensor wiring, then refit the plastic cover to the top of the front cylinder bank and tighten the retaining bolts.

16 Reconnect the battery negative (earth) lead on completion.

Rear exhaust manifold

Removal

17 Disconnect the battery negative (earth) lead (refer to *Disconnecting the battery* at the end of this manual).

18 Loosen the right-hand front wheel nuts. Apply the handbrake, then jack up the front of the car and support it on axle stands (see *Jacking and vehicle support*). Remove the right-hand front wheel.

19 Remove the alternator as described in Chapter 5A. Also unbolt and remove the alternator mounting bracket from the cylinder block.

20 With reference to Chapter 4C, remove the (rear) catalytic converter from the exhaust system. On 2.5 litre engines, also remove the exhaust front pipe (Y-pipe) from the bottom of the exhaust manifolds.

21 Unscrew and remove the oxygen sensor from the manifold with reference to Chapter 4C.

22 Where fitted, unscrew the union nut and disconnect the EGR transfer tube from the exhaust manifold.

23 Undo the bolt securing the rear engine mounting roll restrictor and move the engine forward slightly, supporting it with a block of wood. **Note:** *Take care not to damage any components when moving the engine forward.*

24 Unscrew the mounting nuts and withdraw the exhaust manifold from the studs on the cylinder head. Remove the gasket and discard it along with the retaining nuts **(see illustrations)**.

7.6a Remove the front exhaust manifold . . .

7.6b . . . and remove the gasket

7.24a Remove the rear exhaust manifold . . .

7.24b . . . and remove the gasket

25 Clean the mating surfaces of the exhaust manifold and cylinder head.

Refitting

26 Position a new gasket on the cylinder head studs.

27 Refit the exhaust manifold and progressively tighten the new mounting nuts to the specified torque.

28 Remove the block of wood, then refit the bolt securing the rear engine/transmission mounting roll restrictor.

29 Where applicable, reconnect the EGR transfer tube and tighten the union nut.

30 Refit the oxygen sensor to the manifold with reference to Chapter 4C.

31 Refit the exhaust front pipe (Y-pipe) and catalytic converter with reference to Chapter 4A and 4C.

32 Refit the alternator mounting bracket and tighten the bolts, then refit the alternator with reference to Chapter 5A.

33 Refit the right-hand wheel and lower the car to the ground. Tighten the wheel nuts to the specified torque.

34 Reconnect the battery negative (earth) lead on completion.

8 Crankshaft pulley – removal and refitting

Removal

1 Disconnect the battery negative (earth) lead (refer to *Disconnecting the battery* at the end of this manual).

2 Loosen the right-hand front wheel nuts. Apply the handbrake, then jack up the front of the car and support it on axle stands (see *Jacking and vehicle support*). Remove the right-hand wheel.

3 Remove the right-hand wheel arch liner with reference to Chapter 11.

4 Using a socket in the square provided, turn the main auxiliary drivebelt tensioner clockwise and slip the belt from the pulleys on the right-hand end of the engine. Carefully release the tensioner.

5 The crankshaft pulley must now be held stationary while the bolt is loosened. On manual transmission models have an assistant engage 4th gear and firmly depress the footbrake pedal. On automatic transmission models, remove the cover from the transmission bellhousing and have an assistant engage a wide-blade screwdriver with the teeth of the starter ring gear. Alternatively, the pulley can be held stationary by bolting a length of metal bar to it using the threaded holes provided, or by using a scissor bar **(see illustration)**.

6 Loosen the bolt then unscrew it completely and remove the washer **(see illustration)**. When fitted, the bolt is torqued-to-yield, and a new bolt must therefore be used on refitting.

7 Using a suitable puller, draw the crankshaft pulley from the end of the crankshaft. If the Woodruff key is loose, remove it from the groove in the crankshaft and keep it in a safe place **(see illustrations)**.

8 Clean the crankshaft pulley and the end of the crankshaft.

Refitting

9 Apply suitable sealer to the key groove on the inside of the pulley. If removed, locate the Woodruff key in the crankshaft groove, making sure that it is parallel with the surface of the crankshaft.

10 Locate the pulley on the crankshaft and engage it with the key. Use the old pulley bolt and washer to draw the pulley fully onto the crankshaft. Unscrew the old bolt and discard it.

11 Insert the new bolt together with the washer, and tighten it to the specified torque and angle while holding the crankshaft stationary using the method described in paragraph 5. Note that the bolt is tightened in four stages as described in the Specifications **(see illustrations)**.

12 Remove the holding tool, and on automatic transmission models refit the cover to the transmission bellhousing.

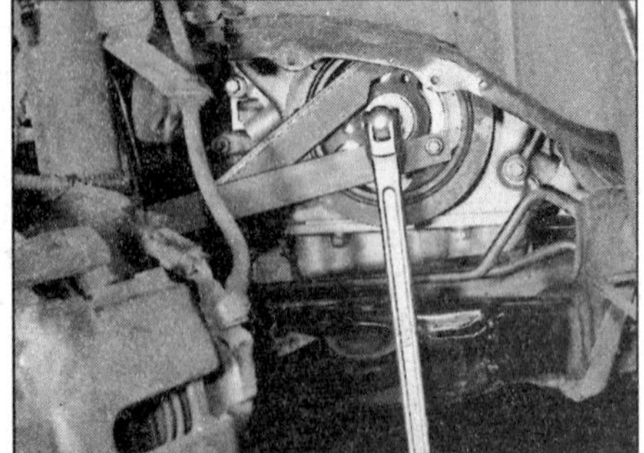

8.5 Hold the crankshaft stationary using a scissor bar while the pulley bolt is loosened

8.6 Removing the crankshaft pulley bolt and washer

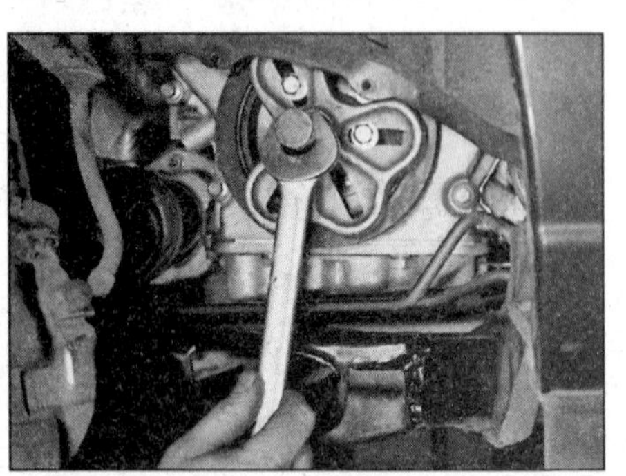

8.7a Using a puller to remove the crankshaft pulley from the end of the crankshaft

8.7b Removing the crankshaft pulley

8.11a Using a torque wrench to tighten the crankshaft pulley bolt

8.11b Using an angle disc to tighten the crankshaft pulley bolt to the specified angle

13 Refit the main auxiliary drivebelt to the right-hand end of the engine with reference to Chapter 1A.

14 Refit the right-hand wheel arch liner with reference to Chapter 11.

15 Refit the right-hand wheel and lower the car to the ground. Tighten the wheel nuts to the specified torque.

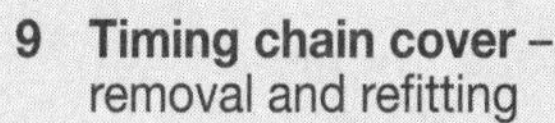

9 Timing chain cover – removal and refitting

Removal

1 Disconnect the battery negative (earth) lead (refer to *Disconnecting the battery* at the end of this manual). Apply the handbrake, then loosen the right-hand front wheel nuts. Jack up the front of the car and support it on axle stands (see *Jacking and vehicle support*). Remove the right-hand front wheel.

9.6 Engine support bar attached to the right-hand mounting bracket on the cylinder block

2 Drain the engine oil (see Chapter 1A).

3 Remove both cylinder head covers as described in Section 5.

4 Remove the alternator as described in Chapter 5A. Also unbolt the alternator mounting bracket from the cylinder block and timing cover.

5 Remove the crankshaft pulley as described in Section 8.

6 Support the weight of the engine with a hoist or engine support bar. If the timing cover is being removed in order to remove the cylinder heads, the hoist must be attached to the right-hand mounting bracket on the cylinder block **(see illustration)**.

7 Disconnect the wiring from the low coolant warning switch (where fitted), then undo the coolant expansion tank mounting screws and position the tank to one side. If the timing cover is being removed in order to remove the cylinder heads, drain the cooling system and remove the expansion tank completely after disconnecting the hoses **(see illustrations)**.

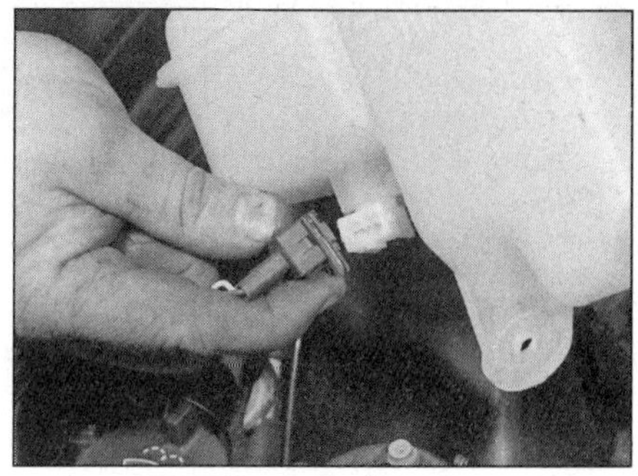

9.7a Disconnecting the low coolant warning switch wiring

8 Mark the position of the engine right-hand mounting, then unscrew the nuts and bolts and remove the mounting and bracket, noting the location of any earth cables.

9 Loosen the bolts securing the pulley to the power steering pump.

10 Using a socket in the square provided, turn the main auxiliary drivebelt tensioner clockwise and slip the belt from the pulleys. Carefully release the tensioner.

11 Fully unscrew the bolts and remove the pulley from the power steering pump, then remove the pump with reference to Chapter 10 but do not disconnect the hydraulic fluid hoses. Position the pump together with the hydraulic lines on the bulkhead **(see illustrations)**.

12 Disconnect the wiring from the camshaft position sensor on the upper part of the

9.7b Coolant hoses on the expansion tank

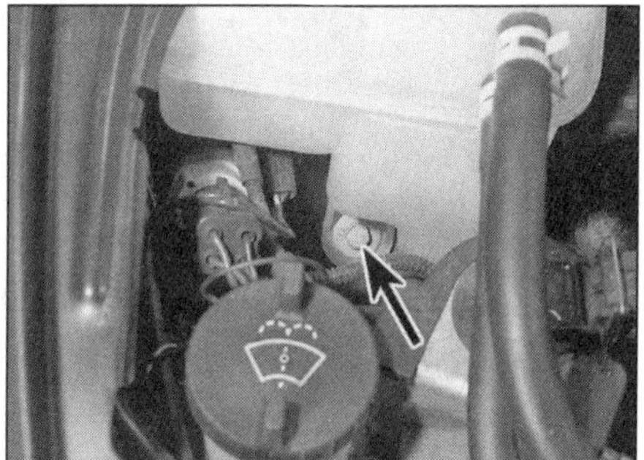

9.7c Expansion tank front mounting bolt

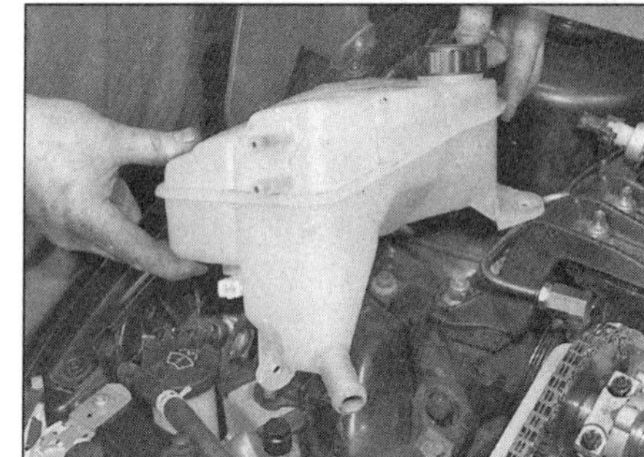

9.7d Removing the expansion tank

9.11a Using a strap wrench to hold the pulley while the bolts are unscrewed

9.11b Removing the power steering pump pulley

9.11c Withdrawing the power steering pump with the hydraulic lines still connected

9.12 Disconnect the wiring connector from the camshaft position sensor (arrowed)

9.16 Stud bolts at the top of the timing cover (power steering pump mounting)

9.17 Removing the timing cover bolts

9.18 Removing the timing cover from the engine

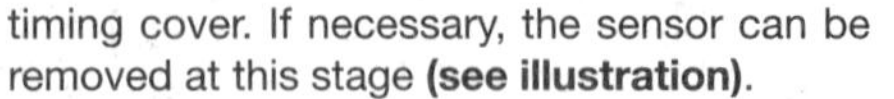

9.20 Fitting a new crankshaft oil seal with the timing cover on the bench

9.21 Apply sealer at the joints between the main bearing ladder and block

timing cover. If necessary, the sensor can be removed at this stage **(see illustration)**.

13 Remove the sump with reference to Section 14.

14 Disconnect the wiring from the crankshaft position sensor on the lower part of the timing cover. If necessary, the sensor can be removed at this stage.

15 If necessary for improved working room, unbolt the air conditioning compressor and position it to one side. Do not disconnect the refrigerant lines from the compressor.

16 Note the location of the bolts and stud bolts on the timing cover to ensure correct refitting. If necessary, make a drawing of the bolt positions **(see illustration)**.

17 Progressively unscrew the bolts from the timing cover in the reverse sequence to that shown **(see illustration and illustration 9.23)**.

18 Remove the timing cover from the location dowels on the engine and withdraw it over the nose of the crankshaft. Carefully remove the cover from the engine compartment, taking care not to damage it as there is very little room to manoeuvre it between the engine and inner wing panel. Remove the gaskets from the cover **(see illustration)**.

19 Clean the contact surfaces of the timing cover, cylinder block and head, taking care not to damage the aluminium faces.

20 If necessary, renew the crankshaft oil seal as described in Section 18. Alternatively, it can be fitted after the timing cover is in position **(see illustration)**. Also if necessary, remove the auxiliary drivebelt tensioner from the timing cover.

Refitting

21 Apply silicone sealant (Ford part number WSE-M4G323-A4, or equivalent) as beads, 6.0 mm long, at the joints between the cylinder head and block, and between the main bearing ladder and cylinder block **(see illustration)**.

22 Locate new gaskets in the timing cover grooves **(see illustration)**.

23 Refit the timing cover with gaskets, making sure that it locates correctly on the dowels.

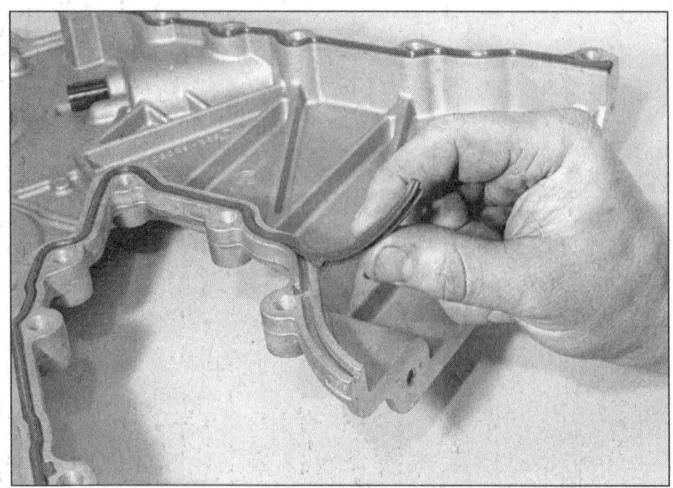

9.22 Locate a new gasket in the timing cover grooves

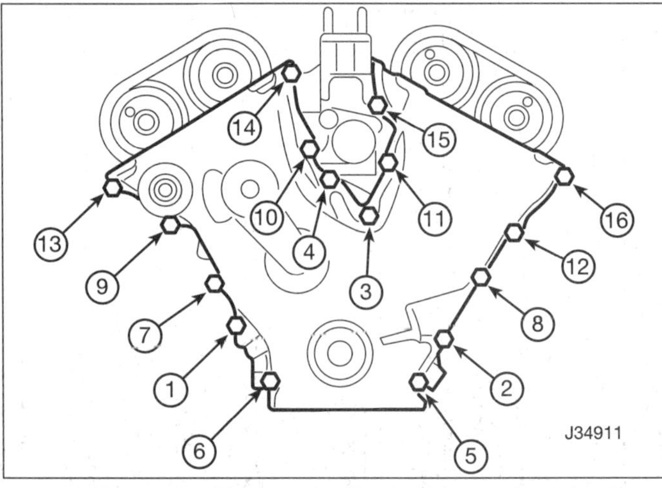

9.23 Tightening sequence for the timing cover bolts/studs

9.24a Refit the auxiliary drivebelt tensioner . . .

9.24b . . . and secure with the special bolt

9.24c Refitting the auxiliary drivebelt idler

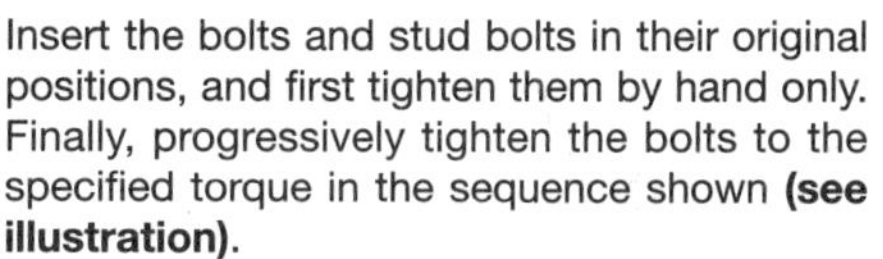

Insert the bolts and stud bolts in their original positions, and first tighten them by hand only. Finally, progressively tighten the bolts to the specified torque in the sequence shown **(see illustration)**.

24 If removed, refit the auxiliary drivebelt tensioner to the timing cover **(see illustrations)**.

25 If removed, refit the air conditioning compressor with reference to Chapter 3 and tighten the bolts.

26 Refit the sump with reference to Section 14.

27 Refit the crankshaft position sensor and the camshaft position sensor, and reconnect the wiring.

28 Refit the power steering pump with reference to Chapter 10 and tighten the bolts to the specified torque. Refit the pulley and tighten the bolts.

29 Locate the main auxiliary drivebelt on its pulleys and release the tensioner with reference to Chapter 1A.

10.3 Slide the crankshaft position sensor pulse ring from the front of the crankshaft

10.7b . . . and remove the rear timing chain tensioner

30 Refit the engine right-hand mounting and bracket in their previously-noted positions, and tighten the nuts and bolts to the specified torque. Make sure that any earth cables that have been removed are refitted back to the engine mounting bracket. Refit the expansion tank and tighten the mounting screws.

31 Remove the engine lifting hoist.

32 Refit the crankshaft pulley with reference to Section 8.

33 Refit the alternator bracket and alternator with reference to Chapter 5A.

34 Refit the cylinder head covers with reference to Section 5.

35 Reconnect the battery negative (earth) lead.

36 Refit the right-hand wheel and lower the car to the ground. Tighten the wheel nuts to the specified torque.

37 Refill the engine with oil (see Chapter 1A).

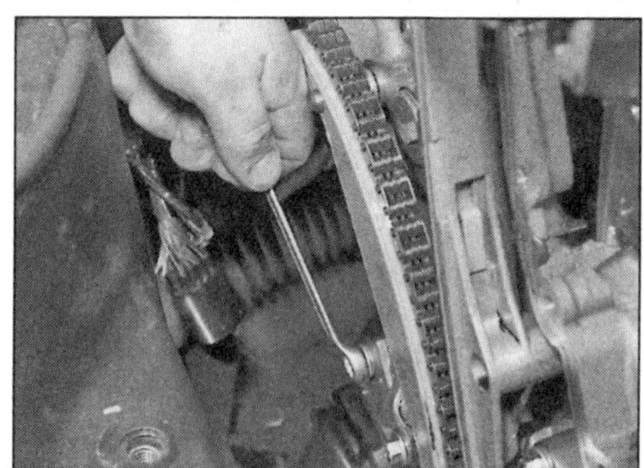

10.7a Unscrew the bolts . . .

10.7c Removing the rear timing chain tensioner guide

10 Timing chains, tensioners and guides – removal, inspection and refitting

Removal

1 Set the engine to TDC on No 1 cylinder as described in Section 4.

2 Remove the timing cover as described in Section 9.

3 Slide the crankshaft position sensor pulse ring from the front of the crankshaft, noting which way round it is fitted. Mark the sensor to ensure it is refitted correctly **(see illustration)**.

4 Temporarily screw the crankshaft pulley bolt in the end of the crankshaft so the crankshaft can be turned with a socket.

5 Note that the timing chain for a particular bank must be removed with the crankshaft at the relevant removal position for that bank. This ensures the camshafts have even valve spring pressure along their lengths. To remove the rear timing chain, turn the crankshaft until the crankshaft pulley keyway is at the 3 o'clock position.

6 If there are no markings on the timing chain, mark the links in relation to the sprocket timing marks with dabs of paint as an aid to refitting. If there are markings on the chain, it is unlikely that they will be aligned with the sprocket marks, however they may be used when refitting the chains. The original marks may be in the form of copper links or white painted dots.

7 Unbolt the rear timing chain tensioner, then remove the tensioner guide from its pivot **(see illustrations)**.

8 Unbolt the fixed timing chain guide for the rear timing chain **(see illustration)**.

9 Disengage the rear timing chain from the crankshaft and camshaft sprockets and remove from the engine **(see illustrations)**. If it is to be re-used, make sure it is identified for the correct fitted position.

10 Remove the crankshaft pulley bolt, then slide the rear timing chain sprocket from the crankshaft, noting which way round it is fitted. Mark the sprocket to ensure it is refitted the same way round **(see illustration)**.

11 Remove the inlet and exhaust camshafts from the rear engine bank as described in

10.8 Removing the fixed timing chain guide for the rear timing chain

10.9a Disconnecting the rear timing chain from the crankshaft sprocket . . .

10.9b . . . and camshaft sprockets

10.10 Removing the rear timing chain crankshaft sprocket

10.14a Unscrew the bolt . . .

10.14b . . . and remove the front timing chain tensioner . . .

Section 12. This is to prevent valve damage when rotating the engine.

12 To remove the front timing chain, first refit the crankshaft pulley bolt, then turn the crankshaft forward one and three quarter turns until the crankshaft pulley keyway is at the 11 o'clock position.

13 If there are no markings on the timing chain, mark the links in relation to the sprocket timing marks with dabs of paint as an aid to refitting. If there are markings on the chain, it is unlikely that they will be aligned with the sprocket marks, however they may be used when refitting the chains. The original marks may be in the form of copper links or white painted dots.

14 Unbolt the front timing chain tensioner, then remove the tensioner guide from its pivot **(see illustrations)**.

15 Disengage the front timing chain from the crankshaft and camshaft sprockets, and remove from the engine **(see illustrations)**. If it is to be re-used, make sure it is identified for the correct fitted position.

16 Unbolt the fixed timing chain guide for the front timing chain **(see illustration)**.

17 Slide the front timing chain sprocket from the crankshaft, noting which way round it is fitted. Mark the sprocket to ensure it is refitted the same way round **(see illustration)**.

10.14c . . . and tensioner guide

10.15a Disengage the front timing chain from the crankshaft sprocket . . .

10.15b . . . and camshaft sprocket

10.16 Fixed timing chain guide for the front timing chain

10.17 Slide the front timing chain sprocket from the crankshaft

10.25 Fit the front timing chain on the camshaft sprockets, ensuring the timing marks are aligned

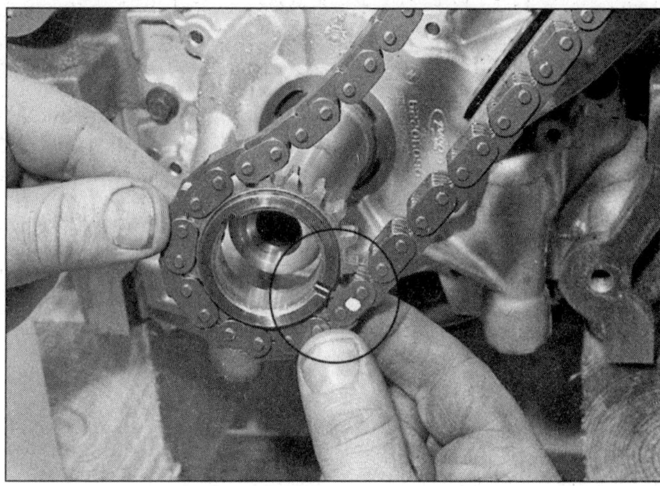

10.26 Locate the sprocket on the front of the crankshaft, ensuring the timing marks are aligned

Inspection

Note: *Keep all components identified for position to ensure correct refitting.*

18 Clean all components thoroughly and wipe dry.

19 Examine the chain tensioners and tensioner guides for excessive wear or other damage. Check the guides for deep grooves made by the timing chains.

20 Examine the timing chains for excessive wear. Hold them horizontally and check how much movement exists in the chain links. If there is any doubt, compare them to new chains. Renew as necessary.

21 Examine the teeth of the camshaft and crankshaft sprockets for excessive wear and damage. Note that the sprockets are integral with the camshafts, and if worn excessively, the complete camshaft must be renewed.

22 Before refitting the timing chain tensioners, their pistons must be compressed and locked until refitted. To do this, insert a small screwdriver into the access hole in the tensioner and release the pawl mechanism. Now lightly clamp the tensioner in a soft-jawed vice and slowly compress the piston. Do not apply excessive force and make sure that the piston remains aligned with its cylinder. When completely compressed, insert a paper clip or similar 1.5 mm diameter wire rod into the special hole to lock the piston in its compressed position.

Refitting

23 If necessary, turn the crankshaft so that the crankshaft pulley keyway is in the 11 o'clock position. This is the position for refitting the front timing chain. **Note:** *The engine should still be in this position, as the front timing chain was the last to be removed.*

24 Refit the fixed timing chain guide for the front timing chain and tighten the mounting bolts.

25 Engage the front timing chain with the camshaft sprockets, making sure that the paint marks/copper links on the timing chain are aligned with the timing marks on the outside of the camshaft sprockets **(see illustration)**.

26 Locate the crankshaft sprocket in the timing chain making sure that the timing marks are correctly aligned, then fit the sprocket onto the crankshaft and engage it with the key **(see illustration)**. The front run of the chain must be against the fixed guide, but the rear run will be loose at this stage.

27 Refit the tensioner guide on its pivot, then refit the tensioner (and adapter plate if fitted) and tighten the mounting bolts to the specified torque. Check that the position marks are still aligned, then remove the 1.5 mm wire rod to release the tensioner. The internal spring is very strong, and it is preferable to hold the chain guide against the tension and release it slowly **(see illustrations)**.

28 Turn the crankshaft clockwise so that the crankshaft pulley key groove is in the 3 o'clock position. This is the position for refitting the rear timing chain.

29 Refit the inlet and exhaust camshafts to the rear engine bank as described in Section 12.

30 Slide the rear timing chain sprocket onto the crankshaft.

31 Refit the fixed timing chain guide for the rear timing chain and tighten the mounting bolts.

32 Engage the rear timing chain with the camshaft and crankshaft sprockets, making sure that the paint marks/copper links are aligned with the timing marks on the outside of the sprockets. The front run of the chain must be against the fixed guide, but the rear run will be loose at this stage.

33 Refit the tensioner guide on its pivot, then refit the tensioner (and adapter plate if fitted) and tighten the mounting bolts to the specified torque. Check that the timing marks are still aligned then remove the wire to release the tensioner.

34 Slide the crankshaft position sensor pulse ring onto the front of the crankshaft making

10.27a Locate the timing chain tensioner on the block. Note the welding rod holding the tensioner plunger

10.27b Tightening the tensioner mounting bolts

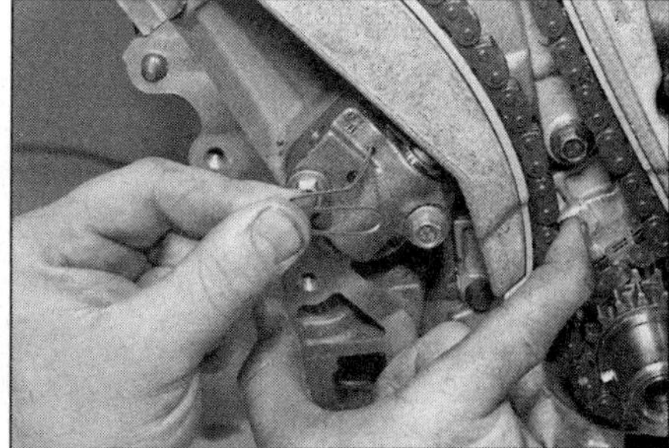

10.27c Hold the chain guide against the spring tension when removing the locking wire rod

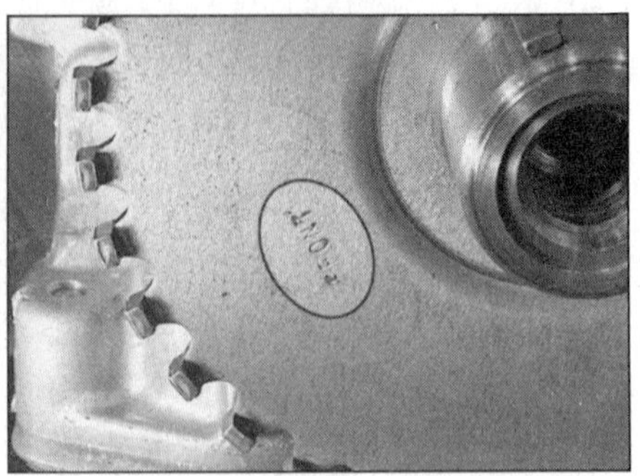

10.34 The crankshaft position sensor pulse ring has a FRONT mark on it

sure that the key groove with the blue painted mark is engaged with the key. The ring may be marked FRONT **(see illustration)**.

35 Temporarily refit the crankshaft pulley bolt, and rotate the engine clockwise two complete turns so that the crankshaft key is located at the 11 o'clock position. **Note:** *After turning the engine, the timing chain timing marks will no longer align with the marks on the sprockets, but the timing marks on the rear of the camshaft sprockets must face each other.*

36 Refit the timing cover with reference to Section 9.

11 Camshaft oil seal – renewal

Note: *There is only one camshaft oil seal located on the left-hand end of the front inlet camshaft. This is because this camshaft drives the water pump by means of a drivebelt. The sprockets at the timing end of the camshafts are enclosed within the timing cover. Check the availability of parts, as the seal may be sold as part of the housing, and not be available as a separate item.*

1 Disconnect the battery negative (earth) lead (refer to *Disconnecting the battery* at the end of this manual).

2 Undo the three retaining bolts and remove the water pump drivebelt cover from the top of the front cylinder bank.

3 Remove the water pump drivebelt by moving the tensioner towards the camshaft. Remove the drivebelt from the pulleys, then carefully release the tensioner. **Note:** *On models where a tensioner is not fitted, the drivebelt will have to be cut off – clearly, a new belt will then be needed for refitting.*

4 The pulley must now be removed from the camshaft. To do this, use a suitable puller.

5 If the seal is available separately, use a screwdriver to carefully prise the oil seal from its bore, taking care not to damage the camshaft or bore.

6 If the seal is supplied together with the housing, it will be necessary to unbolt the housing from the cylinder head and remove the gasket.

7 Wipe clean the camshaft and bore in oil seal housing, or cylinder head face for oil seal housing.

8 Where the seal is available separately, smear clean engine oil on the new oil seal outer periphery and sealing lip, then use a suitable socket or metal tube to drive the oil seal into its bore in the housing, making sure it is kept square. Wipe clean any surplus engine oil.

9 Where the seal is supplied together with the housing, fit a new gasket to the oil seal housing, then smear clean engine oil on the sealing lip of the oil seal. Fit the housing to the cylinder head, while guiding the oil seal onto the end of the camshaft. Then insert and tighten the retaining bolts to the specified torque.

10 Press the pulley onto the camshaft using a bolt screwed into the centre hole, together with a nut and washers. The pulley outer face must be flush with the end of the camshaft to ensure correct alignment with the water pump pulley and tensioner. If the pulley is very tight, preheat it with a heat gun before fitting it.

11 Refit the water pump drivebelt as described in Chapter 1A, Section 30.

12 Refit the plastic cover to the front cylinder bank and tighten the retaining bolts.

13 Reconnect the battery negative (earth) lead on completion.

12.4a Removing the water pump pulley drivebelt

12.4b Unbolt the housing from the left-hand end of the front cylinder head

12.4c Use a puller to pull off the water pump pulley . . .

12.4d . . . then unbolt the housing

12 Camshafts, hydraulic tappets and rocker arms – removal, inspection and refitting

Note: *All camshafts, bearing caps, hydraulic tappets and rocker arms must be marked with their locations, to make sure they are assembled in the original locations in the cylinder head.*

Removal

1 Remove the cylinder head covers and timing cover as described in Sections 5 and 9.

2 Temporarily screw the crankshaft pulley bolt in the end of the crankshaft so the crankshaft can be turned with a socket.

3 Remove the timing chains as described in Section 10. Note that the camshafts for a particular bank must be removed with the crankshaft at the relevant removal position for that bank. This ensures the camshafts have even valve spring pressure along their lengths. If the procedure described in Section 10 is followed correctly, then the camshafts will be at the correct positions.

4 If removing the front bank inlet camshaft, move the water pump drivebelt tensioner towards the camshaft and remove the drivebelt – where a tensioner is not fitted, the drivebelt will have to be cut off. Also unscrew and remove the bolts securing the housing to the left-hand end of the front cylinder head – the water pump pulley may remain in position **(see illustrations)**. Alternatively, pull the water pump pulley from the camshaft, then unbolt the housing **(see illustrations)**.

5 Check that the camshaft bearing caps are marked to indicate their positions. The numbers have the letter R or L to indicate the bank they are fitted to. The 'right-hand' bank is the rear bank, and the 'left-hand' bank is the front bank **(see illustrations)**.

12.5a The camshaft bearing caps are numbered from the timing chain end of the engine . . .

12.5b . . . with corresponding numbers on the cylinder head

12.6 Removing a camshaft bearing cap

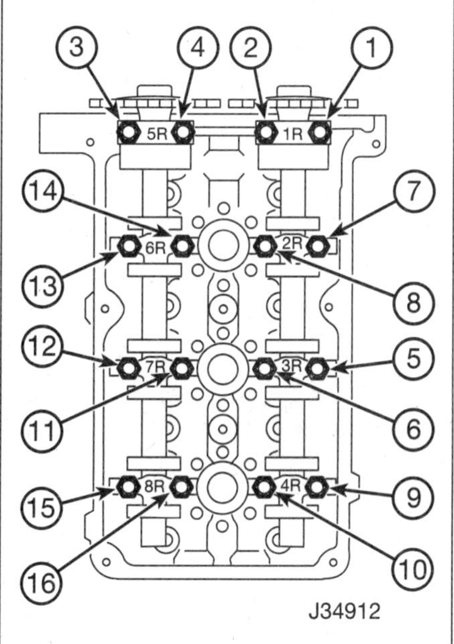

12.7a Loosening sequence for the rear camshaft bearing cap bolts

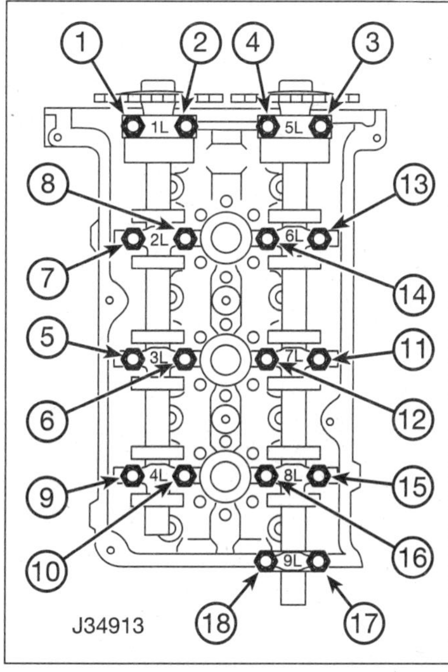

12.7b Loosening sequence for the front camshaft bearing cap bolts

12.7c Unscrewing the camshaft bearing cap bolts

12.8a Front exhaust camshaft sprocket marking

6 Working on one bank at a time, remove the thrust bearing caps first – they are numbered 1L and 5L (or 1R and 5R). These caps must be completely removed before loosening the remaining cap bolts. Unscrew the bolts and remove the thrust bearing caps **(see illustration)**.

7 Using the sequence given, progressively unscrew the bolts securing the camshaft bearing caps to the cylinder head. Make sure the bearing caps lift evenly with the camshafts, then with all the bolts loose, remove the bearing caps **(see illustrations)**. **Note:** *If the bearing caps are tight, tap them lightly with a soft-faced mallet as they are on dowels in the cylinder head.*

8 Identify the camshafts (inlet and exhaust/ front or rear engine bank) and lift them directly from the cylinder head **(see illustrations)**.

9 Note the fitted positions of the rocker arms. Remove the rocker arms from the head,

12.8b Rear inlet camshaft sprocket marking

12.8c Removing the front inlet camshaft . . .

12.8d . . . and front exhaust camshaft

12.9 Removing the rocker arms

12.10 Removing the hydraulic tappets

12.21a Refitting the camshaft bearing caps

keeping them identified for position by placing them in a container marked with their locations **(see illustration)**.

10 Remove the hydraulic tappets from their bores in the cylinder head, and place them in a container marked with their locations **(see illustration)**.

Inspection

11 With the camshafts and hydraulic tappets removed, check each for obvious wear (scoring, pitting and out-of-round). Renew if necessary.

12 Using a micrometer, measure the outside diameter of each tappet – take measurements at the top and bottom of each tappet, then a second set at right-angles to the first. If any measurement is significantly different from the others, the tappet is tapered or out-of-round and must be renewed. If the necessary equipment is available, measure the inside diameter of the corresponding cylinder head bore. Compare the measurements obtained to those given in the Specifications. If the tappets or the cylinder head bores are excessively worn, new tappets and/or a new cylinder head will be required.

13 If a top-end noise is evident, particularly if the noise persists after initial start-up from cold, there is reason to suspect a faulty hydraulic tappet. However, this is best checked with the engine running.

14 Visually examine the camshaft lobes for score marks, pitting, and evidence of overheating. Look for flaking away of the hardened surface layer of each lobe. If necessary renew the camshaft.

15 Examine the camshaft bearing journals and the cylinder head bearing surfaces for obvious wear or pitting. If excessive wear is evident, it may be necessary to obtain a new or reconditioned cylinder head.

16 Using a micrometer, measure the diameter of each journal at several points. If the diameter of any one journal is less than the specified amount, renew the camshaft. If an internal micrometer is available, measure the internal diameters of the bores in the cylinder head and caps.

17 The camshaft endfloat can be checked using a dial gauge in contact with the end of the camshaft. Move the camshaft fully one way and zero the gauge, then move it fully the other way and check the endfloat. If excessive, new thrust caps must be fitted to the relevant camshaft.

Refitting

18 Working on the front bank, lubricate the hydraulic tappets and locate them in their relevant bores in the cylinder head.

19 Lubricate the rocker arms and locate them in their relevant positions in the cylinder head.

20 Lubricate the journals of the inlet and exhaust camshafts, then locate the camshafts in the cylinder head in their relevant positions. Make sure the crankshaft pulley keyway is in the 11 o'clock position before fitting the camshaft bearing caps.

21 Locate the bearing caps in their correct positions on the cylinder head. Insert the bolts and progressively hand-tighten them initially, until they are fully seated. Finally, tighten all the bearing cap bolts to the specified torque in the sequence given **(see illustrations)**.

22 Refit the front timing chain as described in Section 10.

23 Working on the rear bank, lubricate the hydraulic tappets and locate them in their relevant bores in the cylinder head.

24 Lubricate the rocker arms and locate them in their relevant positions in the cylinder head.

25 Lubricate the journals of the inlet and exhaust camshafts, then locate the camshafts in the cylinder head in their relevant positions. Make sure the crankshaft pulley keyway is in the 3 o'clock position before fitting the camshaft bearing caps.

26 Locate the bearing caps in their correct positions on the cylinder head. Insert the bolts and progressively hand-tighten them initially, until they are fully seated. Finally, tighten all the bearing cap bolts to the specified torque in the sequence given **(see illustration)**.

27 Refit the rear timing chain as described in Section 10.

28 Refit the timing cover and cylinder head covers as described in Sections 9 and 5.

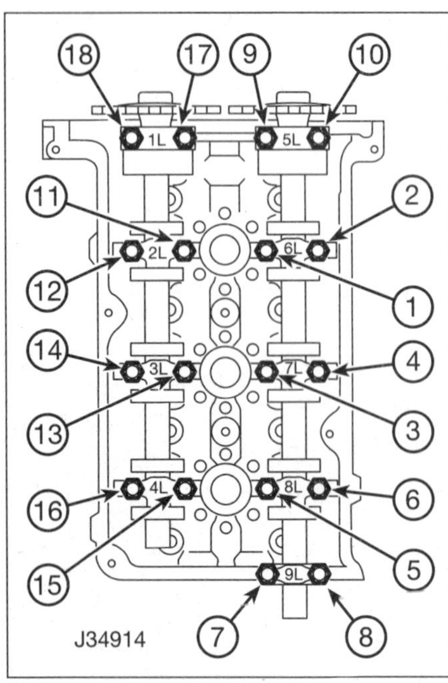

12.21b Tightening sequence for the front camshaft bearing cap bolts

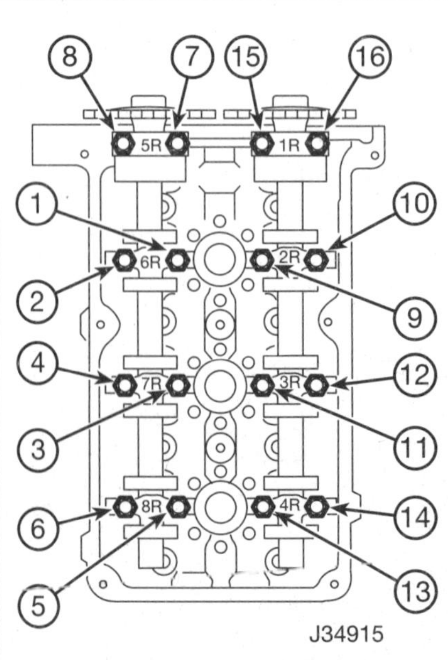

12.26 Tightening sequence for the rear camshaft cap bolts

29 If removed, refit the housing to the front inlet camshaft together with a new gasket, then press on the water pump pulley **(see illustrations)**. Refit the water pump drivebelt as described in Chapter 1A, Section 30.

13 Cylinder heads – removal and refitting

Removal

1 Disconnect the battery negative (earth) lead (refer to *Disconnecting the battery* at the end of this manual). To provide additional working room, remove the battery and the air cleaner assembly.
2 Drain the cooling system as described in Chapter 1A.
3 Remove the upper and lower inlet manifolds as described in Section 6.
4 Drain the engine oil (see Chapter 1A).
5 Remove the timing chains as described in Section 10. **Note:** *If only the rear cylinder head is to be removed, it is only necessary to remove the rear timing chain. If the front cylinder head is to be removed, it is still necessary to remove the rear timing chain.*
6 Temporarily refit the engine right-hand mounting (removed in paragraph 5), and remove the hoist.
7 Remove the camshafts, hydraulic tappets and rocker arms as described in Section 12.

Rear cylinder head

8 Unscrew and remove the oxygen sensor from the rear exhaust manifold (refer to Chapter 4C). Also unbolt the engine rear lifting eye and exhaust gas pressure sensor and bracket from the cylinder head **(see illustration)**.
9 Disconnect the EGR valve back-pressure transducer hoses from the EGR valve-to-exhaust manifold tube.
10 Disconnect the wiring from the EGR valve back-pressure transducer and from the EGR unit.
11 Unscrew the union nut and detach the EGR valve tube from the rear exhaust manifold.
12 Loosen the clips and disconnect the hoses from the coolant connecting pipe at the left-hand end of the cylinder heads. Also disconnect the wiring from the temperature sensors on the pipe.
13 Unscrew the bolts and remove the coolant connecting pipe from the rear cylinder head. Withdraw the pipe from the front cylinder head and recover the O-rings. Note that the upper bolt has a stud extension.
14 The rear exhaust manifold can be removed at this stage, or alternatively it can be removed together with the rear cylinder head and separated on the bench (see Section 7).
15 Loosen each cylinder head bolt, one turn at a time, following the order shown **(see illustration)**. With all the head bolts loose, remove them together with their washers. It is recommended that the head bolts are renewed as a matter of course.
16 Carefully lift the rear cylinder head from the cylinder block and place it on the bench. Recover the gasket from the block.
17 Unbolt the exhaust manifold from the cylinder head and recover the gasket.

Front cylinder head

18 Remove the water pump with reference to Chapter 3. If necessary, also remove the thermostat housing and hoses **(see illustrations)**.
19 Loosen the clips and disconnect the hoses from the coolant connecting pipe at the left-hand end of the cylinder heads. Also disconnect the wiring from the temperature sensors on the pipe **(see illustration)**.
20 Unscrew the bolts and remove the coolant connecting pipe from the rear cylinder head.

12.29a Refitting the housing and new gasket to the front inlet camshaft

12.29b Using a threaded rod and nut to press on the water pump pulley

13.8 Removing the exhaust gas pressure sensor and bracket from the rear cylinder head

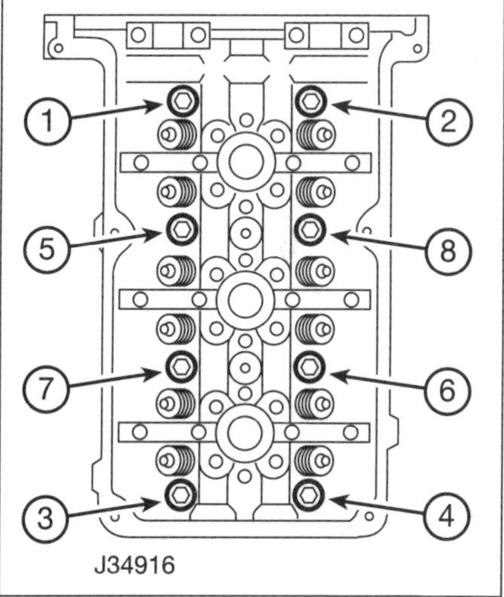

13.15 Loosening sequence for the rear cylinder head bolts

13.18a Removing the water pump

13.18b Removing the thermostat housing and hoses

13.19 Disconnecting the hoses from the coolant connecting pipe

13.20 Removing the coolant connecting pipe

Withdraw the pipe from the front cylinder head and recover the O-rings. Note that the upper bolt has a stud extension **(see illustration)**.

21 Loosen the clip and disconnect the radiator bottom hose from the elbow on the front cylinder head, then unbolt the elbow.

22 Pull out the engine oil level dipstick tube.

23 The front exhaust manifold can be removed at this stage, or alternatively it can be removed together with the front cylinder head and separated on the bench (see Section 7). If it is decided to remove the head together with the manifold, unbolt the air conditioning compressor from the engine block and place it on the front crossmember, and also remove the oil filter. This will provide additional room for the exhaust downpipe to be lifted from the engine compartment.

24 Loosen each cylinder head bolt, one turn at a time, following the order shown **(see illustration)**. With all the head bolts loose,

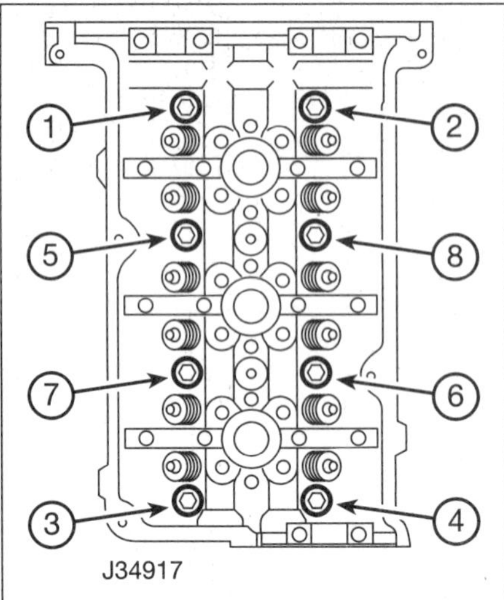

13.24a Loosening sequence for the front cylinder head bolts

remove them together with their washers and check them for damage **(see illustrations)**. It is recommended that the head bolts are renewed as a matter of course.

25 Carefully lift the front cylinder head from the cylinder block and place it on the bench. Recover the gasket from the block **(see illustrations)**.

26 Unbolt the exhaust manifold from the cylinder head and recover the gasket.

Refitting

27 The mating faces of the cylinder heads and cylinder blocks must be perfectly clean

13.24b Unscrew the cylinder head bolts . . .

before refitting the heads. Use a hard plastic or wood scraper to remove all traces of gasket and carbon; also clean the piston crowns. Take particular care, as the soft aluminium alloy is easily damaged. Also, make sure that the carbon is not allowed to enter the oil and water passages – this is particularly important for the lubrication system, as carbon could block the oil supply to any of the engine's components. Using adhesive tape and paper, seal the water, oil and bolt holes in the cylinder block. Clean all the pistons in the same way.

To prevent carbon entering the gap between the pistons and bores, smear a little grease in the gap. After cleaning each piston, use a small brush to remove all traces of grease and carbon from the gap, then wipe away the remainder with a clean rag.

13.24c . . . and remove them together with their washers

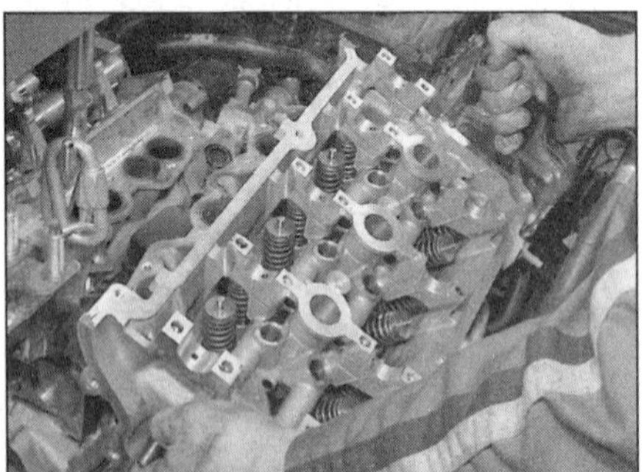
13.25a Lifting the front cylinder head from the cylinder block

13.25b Engine with the front cylinder head and gasket removed

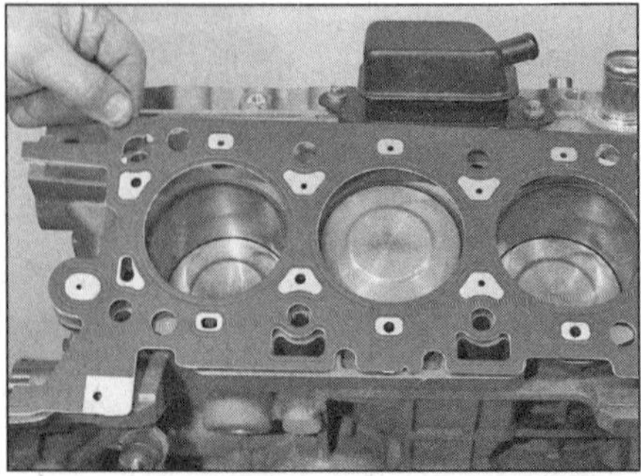
13.31 Locating the front cylinder head gasket on the cylinder block

28 Check the mating surfaces of the cylinder block and the cylinder head for nicks, deep scratches and other damage. If slight, they may be removed carefully with a fine file, but if excessive, machining may be the only alternative to renewal.

29 If warpage of the cylinder head gasket surface is suspected, use a straight-edge to check it for distortion. Refer to Part D of this Chapter if necessary.

30 Wipe clean the mating surfaces of the cylinder heads and cylinder block. Check that the locating dowels are in position in the cylinder block, and that all cylinder head bolt holes are free from oil.

Front cylinder head

31 Locate the front cylinder head gasket on the cylinder block **(see illustration)**.

32 Clean the surfaces of the exhaust manifold and cylinder head, then refit the manifold together with a new gasket and tighten the bolts (see Section 7). Alternatively, the exhaust manifold can be refitted after refitting the cylinder head on the cylinder block.

33 Carefully lower the front cylinder head onto the gasket, making sure that it is aligned with the locating dowels.

34 Insert the head bolts together with washers, and initially hand-tighten them.

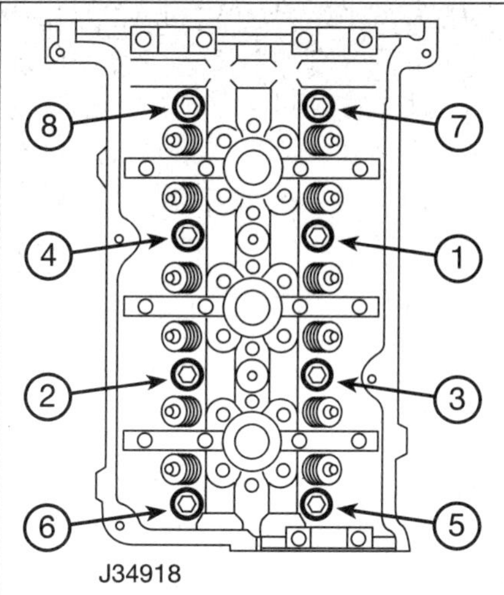

13.35a Tightening sequence for the cylinder head bolts (front shown, rear similar)

35 Using a torque wrench, tighten the head bolts to the Stage 1 torque in the sequence shown **(see illustrations)**.

36 Tighten the bolts in the remaining stages given in the Specifications. For the angle-tightening, use an angle disc socket attachment to ensure the correct angle **(see illustration)**.

37 If applicable, refit the exhaust manifold together with a new gasket.

38 Insert the engine oil level dipstick.

39 Refit the elbow to the front cylinder head together with a new gasket, and tighten the bolts. Reconnect the radiator bottom hose and tighten the clip.

40 Refit the coolant connecting pipe together with a new gasket and O-rings, and tighten the bolts. Reconnect the hoses and tighten the clips. Reconnect the wiring to the temperature sensors, then refit the water pump with reference to Chapter 3.

Rear cylinder head

41 Note: *If this procedure is being used during an engine overhaul, make sure that the engine right-hand mounting bracket is bolted in position on the cylinder block before refitting the rear cylinder head, as it will be impossible to fit the bracket between the front and rear cylinder heads with them already fitted* ***(see illustration)****.*

42 Locate the rear cylinder head gasket on the cylinder block **(see illustration)**.

43 Clean the surfaces of the exhaust manifold and cylinder head, then refit the manifold together with a new gasket and tighten the bolts (see Section 7). Alternatively, the exhaust manifold can be refitted after refitting the cylinder head on the cylinder block.

44 Carefully lower the rear cylinder head onto the gasket, making sure that it is aligned with the locating dowels.

45 Insert the head bolts together with washers, and initially hand-tighten them.

46 Using a torque wrench, tighten the head

13.35b Tightening the head bolts with a torque wrench

13.41 The right-hand engine mounting bracket must be fitted before fitting the rear cylinder head

bolts to the Stage 1 torque in the sequence shown **(see illustration 13.35a)**.

47 Tighten the bolts in the remaining stages given in the Specifications. For the angle-tightening, use an angle disc socket attachment to ensure the correct angle.

48 If applicable, refit the exhaust manifold together with a new gasket.

49 Refit the coolant connecting pipe together with a new gasket and O-rings, and tighten the bolts. Reconnect the hoses and tighten the clips. Reconnect the wiring to the temperature sensors.

50 Refit the EGR valve tube to the rear exhaust manifold and tighten the union nut.

51 Reconnect the wiring to the EGR valve back-pressure transducer.

52 Reconnect the EGR valve back-pressure transducer hoses to the EGR valve-to-exhaust manifold tube.

53 Refit the oxygen sensor to the rear exhaust manifold (refer to Chapter 4C).

Front and rear cylinder heads

54 Refit the camshafts, hydraulic tappets and rocker arms as described in Section 12.

55 Support the weight of the engine with the hoist, then remove the engine right-hand mounting to refit the timing chains and timing cover.

56 Refit the timing chains and cover as described in Section 10, then refit the engine mounting and remove the hoist.

57 Refit the upper and lower inlet manifolds as described in Section 6.

13.36 Using an angle disc socket attachment to angle-tighten the cylinder head bolts

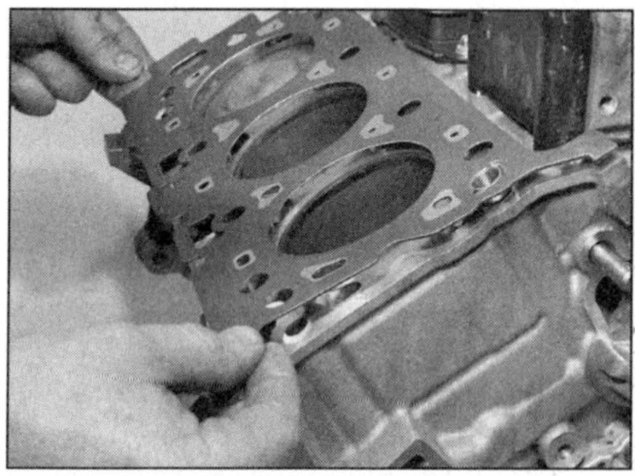

13.42 Locating the rear cylinder head gasket on the cylinder block

58 If removed, refit the battery and air cleaner. Reconnect the battery negative (earth) lead.

59 Refill the engine with oil with reference to Chapter 1A.

60 Refill the cooling system with reference to Chapter 1A.

61 Start the engine and run to normal operating temperature. Check for coolant and oil leaks.

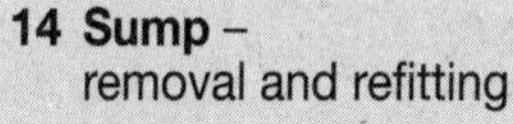

14 Sump – removal and refitting

Removal

1 Apply the handbrake, then jack up the front of the car and support it on axle stands (see *Jacking and vehicle support*).

2 Drain the engine oil as described in Chapter 1A. On completion, clean the drain plug and threaded hole, then refit the plug and tighten to the specified torque.

3 Unscrew the nuts and bolts and remove the exhaust Y-pipe from the bottom of the front downpipes and intermediate exhaust section.

4 Unbolt the exhaust support bracket from the studs on the rear of the sump **(see illustrations)**.

5 Unscrew and remove the lower flange bolts securing the sump to the transmission.

6 Note the location of the stud bolts on the sump, then unscrew and remove the bolts, leaving two opposite ones in place. Finally

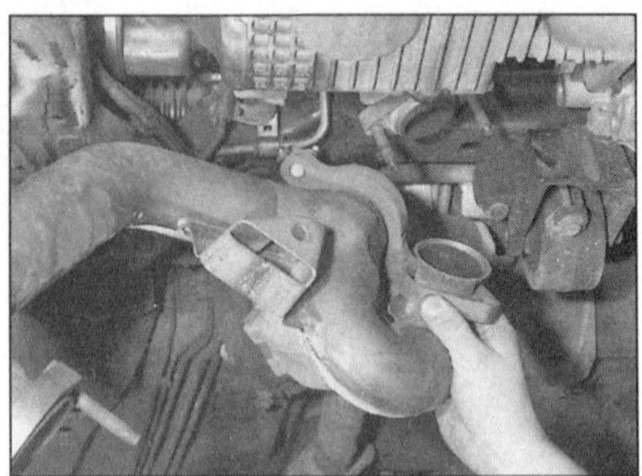
14.4a Removing the exhaust Y-piece from under the sump

14.4b Exhaust support bracket on the rear of the sump

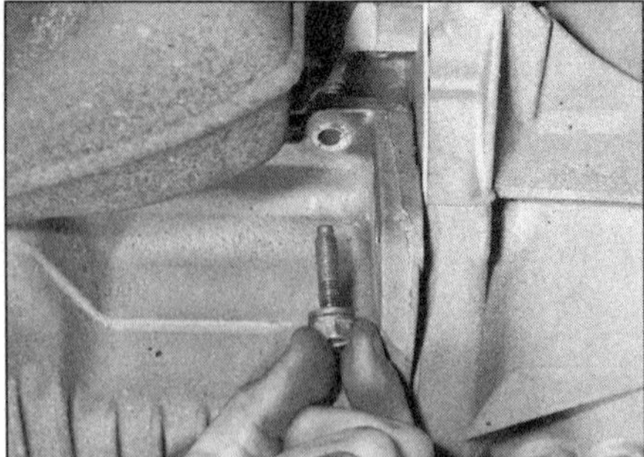
14.6a Unscrew the bolts . . .

14.6b . . . and lower the sump from the cylinder block

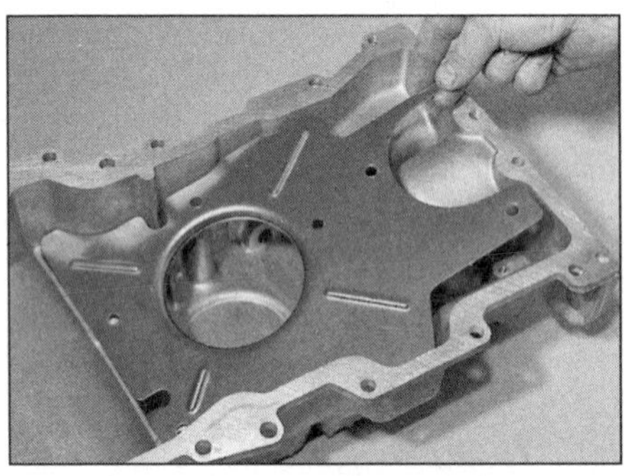
14.7 Removing the baffle plate from the sump

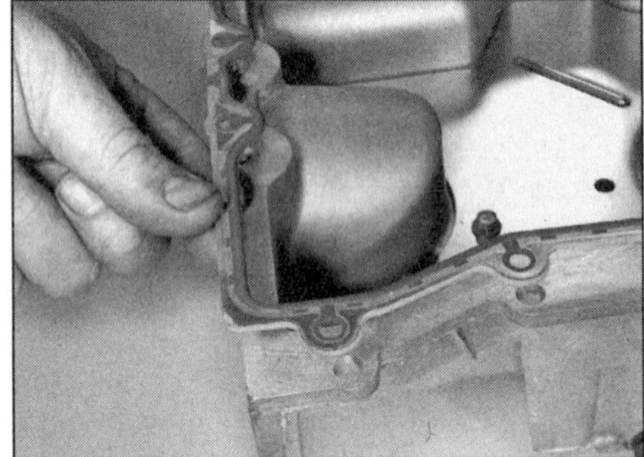
14.9 Locating a new gasket on the sump

support the sump, and remove the last two bolts. Lower the sump from the engine. Remove the gasket and discard it **(see illustrations)**.

Refitting

7 Thoroughly clean the contact surfaces of the sump and cylinder block. Also clean the inside of the sump. If necessary, unbolt and remove the baffle plate **(see illustration)**.

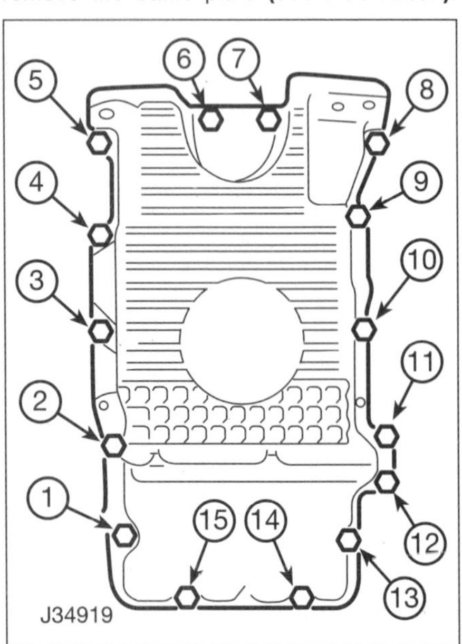

14.11 Tightening sequence for the sump bolts

After cleaning, refit the baffle plate and tighten the bolts.

8 Apply a bead of silicone sealant (Ford part number WSE-M4G323-A4, or equivalent) to the joints between the timing cover and cylinder block, on the bottom of the block.

9 Locate a new gasket on the sump **(see illustration)**. Retain it with a little grease if necessary.

10 Raise the sump and gasket onto the bottom of the cylinder block, and insert several bolts to hold it in position. Make sure the gasket remains in position. Insert the remaining bolts then hand-tighten all the bolts.

11 Tighten the bolts to the specified torque, in the sequence shown **(see illustration)**.

12 Insert and tighten the lower flange bolts securing the sump to the transmission.

13 Refit the exhaust support bracket to the rear of the sump and tighten the bolts **(see illustration)**.

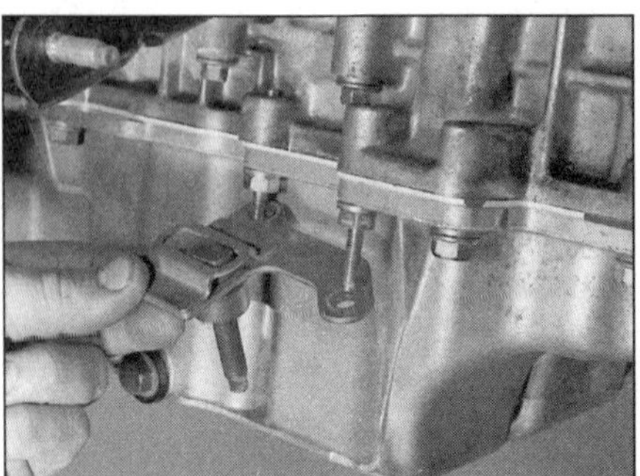
14.13 Refitting the exhaust support bracket

14 Refit the exhaust Y-pipe to the bottom of the front downpipes and intermediate exhaust section, and tighten the new nuts and bolts.

15 Lower the car to the ground, then fill the engine with fresh oil as described in Chapter 1A.

15 Oil pump – removal, inspection and refitting

Removal

1 Remove the timing chains and sprockets as described in Section 10. This procedure includes the removal of the sump as described in Section 14.

2 Unscrew the flange bolts and support nut, and remove the oil pump pick-up tube and filter. Recover the O-ring from the pump.

3 Although not essential at this stage, undo the screws and remove the oil baffle from the crankcase.

4 Progressively loosen the mounting bolts one at a time in the reverse sequence to that shown **(see illustration 15.11)**. With all of the bolts removed, withdraw the oil pump from the cylinder block **(see illustrations)**.

Inspection

5 Using a Torx key, undo the screws and remove the cover from the oil pump **(see illustration)**.

6 Note the location of the identification marks

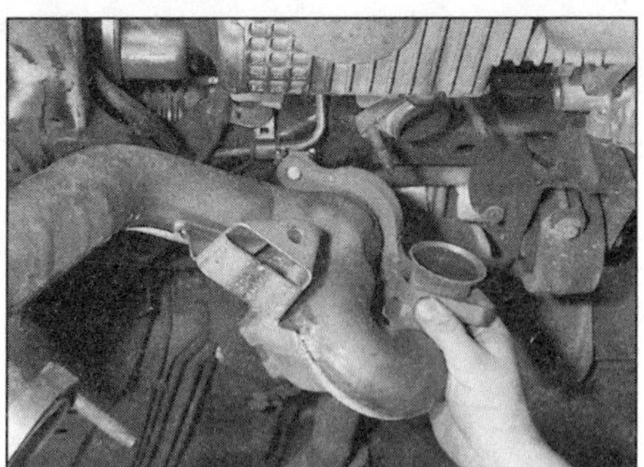
15.4a Unscrew the bolts . . .

15.4b . . . and withdraw the oil pump from the cylinder block

15.5 Removing the cover from the oil pump

15.6a Oil pump and rotors with the cover removed

15.6b Removing the inner rotor . . .

15.6c . . . and outer rotor

on the inner and outer rotors, then remove the rotors. The dot on the outer rotor faces the cover, but the dot on the inner rotor faces the body **(see illustrations)**.

7 Unscrew the plug and remove the pressure relief valve, spring and plunger **(see illustration)**.

8 Clean all the components and examine them for wear and damage. If the rotors or body are excessively scored or damaged, the complete oil pump must be renewed. If the components are still serviceable, first refit the pressure relief valve components and tighten the plug. Lubricate the rotors with fresh engine oil and insert them in the body, making sure that the identification marks are positioned as noted on removal **(see illustration)**.

9 Refit the pump cover and tighten the screws to the specified torque **(see illustration)**.

10 Before refitting the oil pump, prime it by pouring fresh engine oil into the pick-up tube flange port. Turn the rotors by hand so that the oil enters the internal cavities.

Refitting

11 Position the inner rotor so that it will align with the flat on the crankshaft, then locate the oil pump on the cylinder block. Insert the bolts and tighten to the specified torque in the sequence shown **(see illustration)**.

12 If removed, refit the baffle to the crankcase and tighten the bolts.

13 Locate the oil pump pick-up tube and filter in the oil pump together with a new O-ring, then insert the flange bolts and tighten to the specified torque. Refit and tighten the support nut.

14 Refit the timing chains and sprockets as described in Section 10, and the sump as described in Section 14.

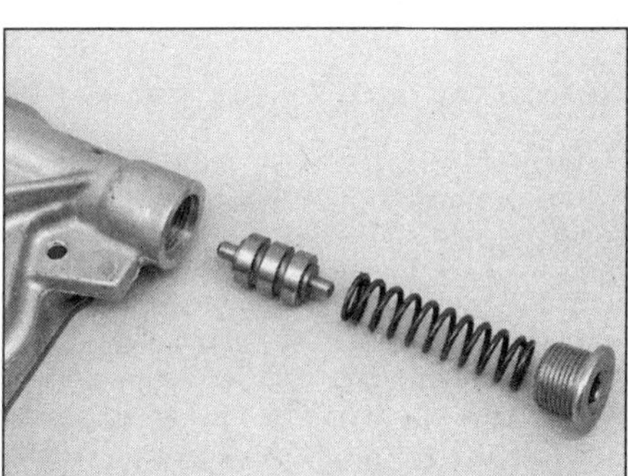
15.7 Pressure relief valve components

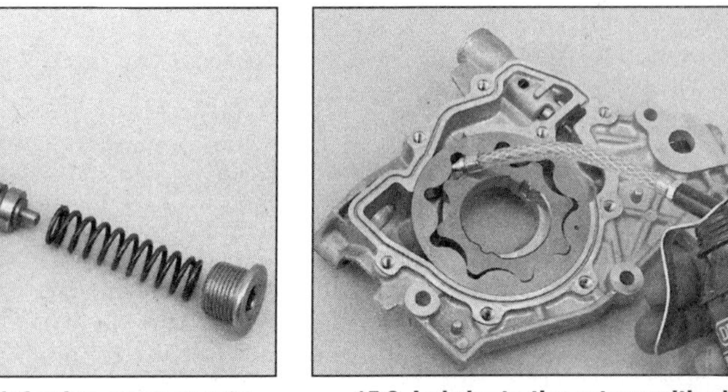

15.8 Lubricate the rotors with clean engine oil before fitting the cover

15.9 Tightening the oil pump cover screws

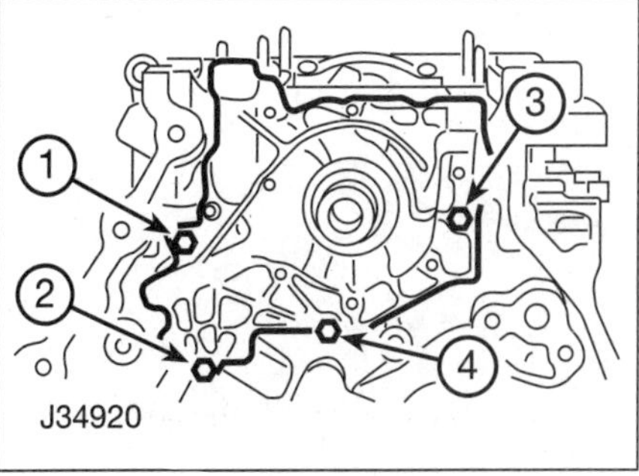

15.11 Tightening sequence for the oil pump mounting bolts

16.5 Removing the oil cooler and O-ring

16 Oil cooler – removal and refitting

Removal

1 The oil cooler is located on the front of the cylinder block between the oil filter and cylinder block. First drain the cooling system as described in Chapter 1A.

2 Apply the handbrake, then jack up the front of the car and support it on axle stands (see *Jacking and vehicle support*). Remove the splash shield from the bottom of the radiator.

3 Loosen the clips and disconnect the coolant hoses from the oil cooler.

4 Position a container beneath the oil filter, then unscrew and remove the oil filter. Keep the oil filter upright to prevent oil spillage.

5 Note the position of the oil cooler stubs, then unscrew the nut and withdraw the oil cooler from the mounting stud. Recover the O-ring **(see illustration)**. Be prepared for loss of oil and coolant.

Refitting

6 Wipe clean the cylinder block and contact surfaces of the oil cooler and oil filter.

7 Locate the oil cooler onto the mounting stub together with a new O-ring. Position the coolant stubs as noted on removal, then tighten the nut to the specified torque.

8 Smear some fresh engine oil onto the sealing ring of the oil filter, then screw it onto the stud and tighten firmly using only the hands. Wipe clean the oil filter and cooler.

19.4 Remove the flywheel bolts . . .

9 Reconnect the hoses and tighten the clips.

10 Refit the splash shield to the bottom of the radiator, and lower the car to the ground.

11 Refill the cooling system with reference to Chapter 1A.

12 Check and if necessary top-up the engine oil level with reference to *Weekly checks*.

17 Oil pressure warning light switch – removal and refitting

Removal

1 The oil pressure warning light switch is located on the front of the cylinder block, next to the oil filter.

2 Apply the handbrake, then jack up the front of the car and support it on axle stands (see *Jacking and vehicle support*). Remove the splash shield from the bottom of the radiator.

3 Disconnect the wiring, then unscrew the switch from the cylinder block.

Refitting

4 Insert the switch and tighten to the specified torque.

5 Reconnect the wiring.

6 Refit the splash shield to the bottom of the radiator, and lower the car to the ground.

7 Check and if necessary top-up the engine oil level as described in *Weekly checks*.

18 Crankshaft oil seals – renewal

Timing chain end oil seal

1 Remove the crankshaft pulley as described in Section 8 of this Chapter.

2 Using a screwdriver, prise the old oil seal from the timing cover. Take care not to damage the surface of the timing cover and crankshaft. If the oil seal is tight, carefully drill two holes diagonally opposite each other in the oil seal, then insert self-tapping screws and use a pair of pliers to pull out the oil seal.

3 Wipe clean the seating in the timing cover and the nose of the crankshaft.

19.5 . . . then lift the flywheel from the crankshaft

4 Smear clean engine oil on the outer periphery and sealing lips of the new oil seal, then start it into the timing cover by pressing it in squarely. Using a large socket or metal tubing, drive in the oil seal until flush with the outer surface of the timing cover. Make sure the oil seal remains square as it is being inserted. Wipe off any excess oil.

5 Refit the crankshaft pulley as described in Section 8 of this Chapter.

Transmission end oil seal

6 Remove the transmission as described in Chapter 7A or 7B.

7 Remove the flywheel or driveplate (as applicable) as described in Section 19.

8 Remove the adapter plate from the engine.

9 Using a screwdriver, prise the old oil seal from the cylinder block. Take care not to damage the surface of the oil seal seating and crankshaft. If the oil seal is tight, carefully drill two holes diagonally opposite each other in the oil seal, then insert self-tapping screws and use a pair of pliers to pull out the oil seal.

10 Wipe clean the seating in the block and the crankshaft.

11 Smear clean engine oil on the outer periphery and sealing lips of the new oil seal, then start it into the cylinder block by pressing it in squarely. Using a large socket or metal tubing, drive in the oil seal until flush with the outer surface of the cylinder block. Make sure the oil seal remains square as it is being inserted. Wipe off any excess oil.

12 Locate the adapter plate on the dowels in the cylinder block.

13 Refit the flywheel or driveplate (as applicable) with reference to Section 19.

14 Refit the transmission as described in Chapter 7A or 7B.

19 Flywheel/driveplate – removal, inspection and refitting

Removal

1 Remove the transmission as described in Chapter 7A or 7B.

2 On manual transmission models, remove the clutch as described in Chapter 6 – now is a good time to check or renew the clutch components.

3 Make alignment marks on the flywheel/driveplate and crankshaft as an aid to refitting.

4 Prevent the flywheel/driveplate from turning by locking the ring gear teeth, or by bolting a strap between the flywheel/driveplate and the cylinder block/crankcase. Unscrew and remove the bolts **(see illustration)**.

5 Withdraw the flywheel/driveplate from the crankshaft, taking care not to drop it – it is very heavy **(see illustration)**. Note that the flywheel on 3.0 litre engines is of the dual-mass type.

6 If necessary, remove the adapter plate from the dowels on the cylinder block **(see illustration)**.

Inspection

7 Clean the flywheel/driveplate to remove grease and oil. Inspect the surface for cracks, rivet grooves, burned areas and score marks. Light scoring can be removed with emery cloth. Check for cracked and broken ring gear teeth. Lay the flywheel/driveplate on a flat surface, and use a straight-edge to check for warpage.

8 Clean and inspect the mating surfaces of the flywheel/driveplate and the crankshaft. If the crankshaft left-hand oil seal is leaking, renew it (see Section 18) before refitting the flywheel/driveplate.

9 While the flywheel/driveplate is removed, clean carefully its inner face. Thoroughly clean the threaded bolt holes in the crankshaft, and also clean the threads of the bolts – this is important, since if old sealer remains in the threads, the bolts will settle over a period and will not retain their correct torque wrench settings.

Refitting

10 Locate the adapter plate on the cylinder block dowels.

11 Refit the flywheel/driveplate on the crankshaft and align the previously-made marks (the bolt holes are arranged so that the flywheel/driveplate will only fit in one position). Apply suitable sealer to the threads of the bolts then insert them and progressively tighten to the specified torque while holding the flywheel/driveplate stationary using the method described in paragraph 4.

12 On manual transmission models, refit the clutch with reference to Chapter 6.

13 Refit the transmission with reference to Chapter 7A or 7B (as applicable).

19.6 Removing the adapter plate

20 Engine/transmission mountings – inspection and renewal

1 The engine/transmission mountings seldom require attention, but broken or deteriorated mountings should be renewed immediately, otherwise the added strain placed on the transmission components may cause damage or wear.

2 While separate mountings may be removed and refitted individually, if more than one is disturbed at a time – such as if the engine/transmission unit is removed – they must be reassembled and tightened in the sequence described in Chapter 2D for engine refitting.

Inspection

3 For access to the engine right-hand mounting, undo the screws securing the coolant expansion tank to the right-hand inner wing panel and temporarily position the tank to one side. For access to the engine left-hand mounting, remove the battery (Chapter 5A) and air cleaner (Chapter 4A). For access to the front and rear engine roll restrictors, apply the handbrake, then jack up the front of the car and support it on axle stands (see *Jacking and vehicle support*). The use of a mirror will help to view the engine mounting from all angles.

4 Check the mounting rubber to see if it is cracked, hardened or separated from the metal at any point; renew the mounting if any such damage or deterioration is evident.

5 Check that all the mounting nuts/bolts are securely tightened; use a torque wrench to check if possible.

6 Using a large screwdriver or lever, check for wear in the mounting by carefully levering against it to check for free play; where this is not possible, enlist the aid of an assistant to move the engine/transmission unit back-and-forth, or from side-to-side, while you watch the mounting. While some free play is to be expected even from new components, excessive wear should be obvious. If excessive free play is found, check first that the nuts/bolts are correctly tightened, then renew any worn components as described below.

Renewal

Right-hand mounting

7 Undo the three retaining bolts and remove the plastic cover from the top of the front cylinder bank.

8 Undo the screws and position the coolant expansion tank to one side.

9 Support the weight of the engine using a suitable hoist. Alternatively, if only the right-hand mounting is to be renewed, it is acceptable to carefully support the weight of the engine using a trolley jack and piece of wood beneath the engine sump.

10 Mark the position of the engine mounting bracket for correct refitting, then unscrew the nuts and remove the bracket. Where applicable, note the position of the earth cable **(see illustrations)**. **Note:** *The nuts are self-locking and must be renewed.*

11 Unbolt the mounting from the body panel.

12 Fit the new mounting to the body panel and tighten the bolts to the specified torque.

13 Locate the bracket on the mounting and engine and position it as noted before removal. Fit the new nuts and tighten to the specified torque. Where applicable, make sure the earth cable is refitted in its correct position.

14 Lower the engine and remove the hoist.

15 Refit the coolant expansion tank and tighten the screws.

16 Refit the plastic cover to the top of the front cylinder bank and tighten the retaining bolts.

Left-hand mounting

17 Remove the battery as described in Chapter 5A.

18 Remove the air filter and housing as described in Chapter 4A.

19 Undo the three retaining bolts and remove the plastic cover from the top of the front cylinder bank.

20 Support the weight of the transmission using a suitable hoist. Alternatively, if only the left-hand mounting is to be renewed, it is acceptable to carefully support the weight of

20.10a Unscrew the right-hand engine mounting bracket nuts and bolts . . .

20.10b . . . noting the location of the earth cable

20.10c Removing the right-hand engine mounting brackets

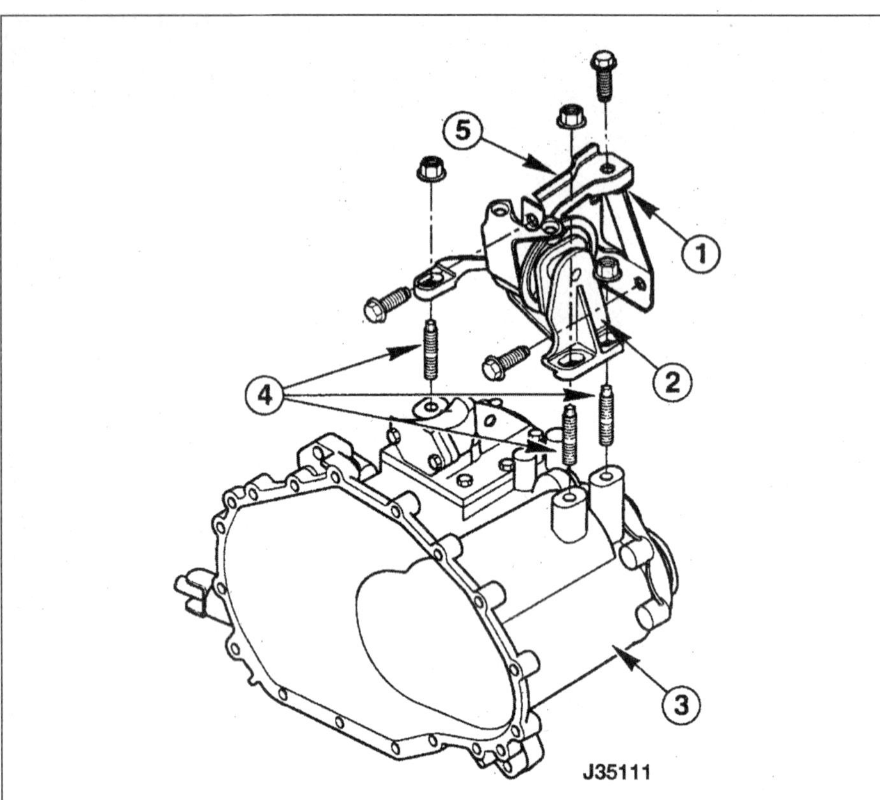

20.21 Left-hand engine/transmission mounting (manual transmission shown – automatic similar)

1 *Body bracket*
2 *Transmission bracket*
3 *Transmission*
4 *Studs*
5 *Plate (if fitted)*

20.22 Left-hand engine mounting body bracket bolt

the transmission using a trolley jack and piece of wood.

21 Mark the position of the engine mounting bracket for correct refitting, then unscrew the nuts securing the mounting to the studs on the transmission **(see illustration)**. **Note:** *The nuts are self-locking and must be renewed.*

22 Unscrew the bolts and remove the mounting from the body panel **(see illustration)**.

23 Fit the new mounting to the body panel and tighten the bolts to the specified torque.

24 Locate the bracket on the mounting and transmission and position it as noted before removal. Fit the new nuts and tighten to the specified torque.

25 Lower the transmission and remove the hoist.

26 Refit the plastic cover to the top of the front cylinder bank and tighten the retaining bolts.

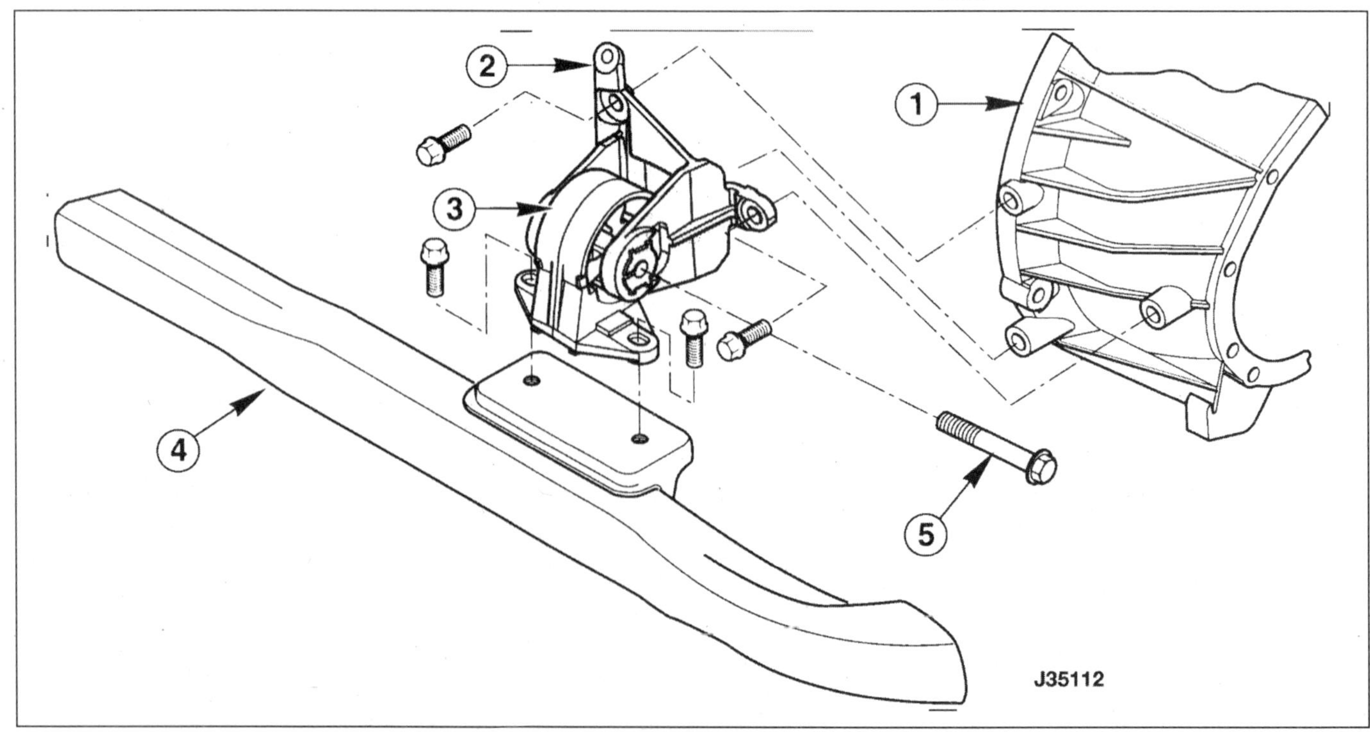

20.30 Front roll restrictor

1 *Transmission*
2 *Mounting bracket*
3 *Mounting*
4 *Subframe*
5 *Centre bolt*

20.38a Rear roll restrictor viewed from under the car

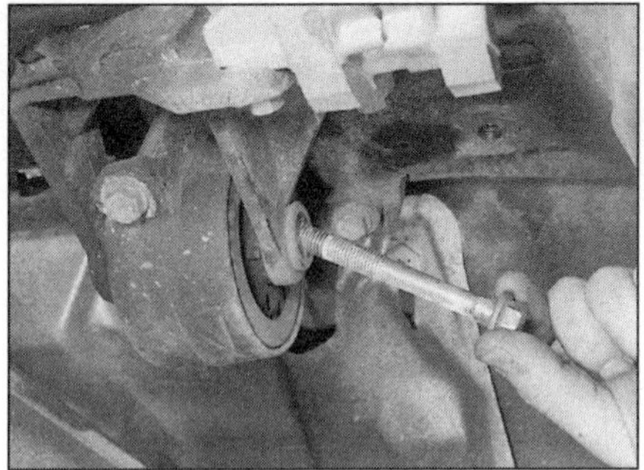

20.38b Removing the rear roll restrictor centre bolt

20.38c Removing the rear roll restrictor

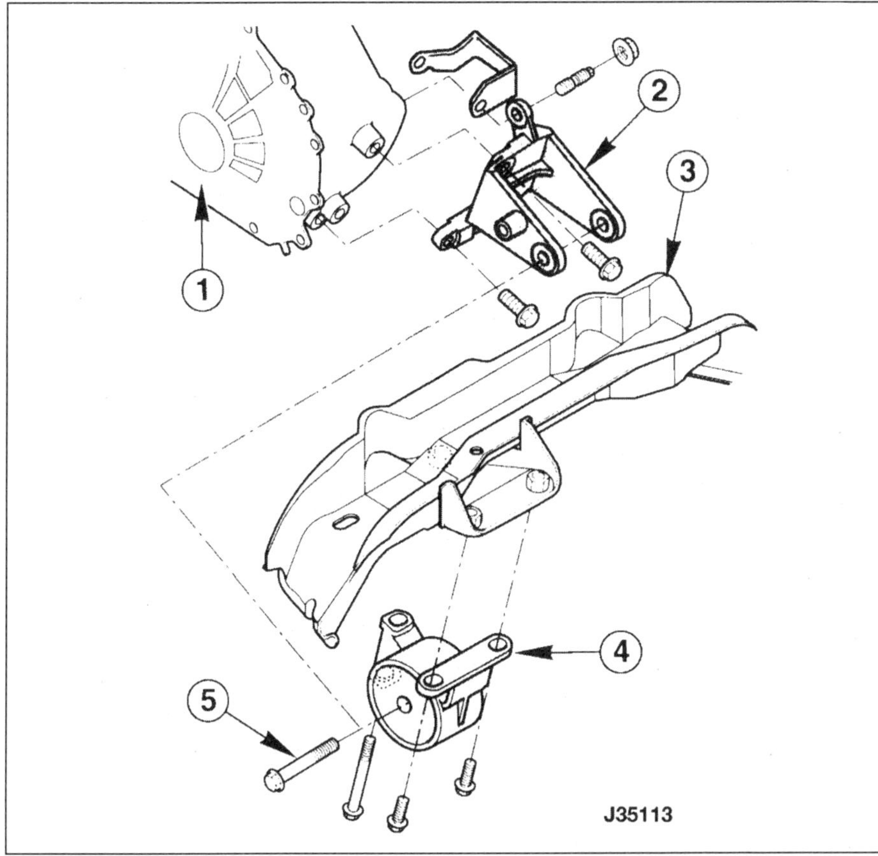

20.38d Rear roll restrictor (manual transmission type)

1 Transmission
2 Mounting bracket
3 Front subframe
4 Mounting
5 Centre bolt

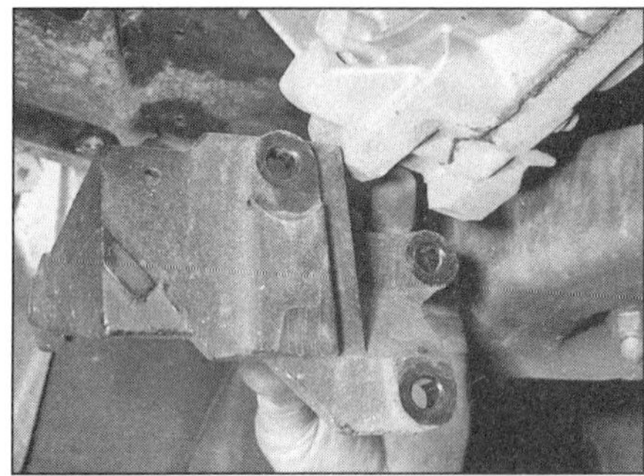

20.39 Removing the rear roll restrictor bracket from the transmission

27 Refit the air filter and housing with reference to Chapter 4A.

28 Refit the battery with reference to Chapter 5A.

Front roll restrictor

29 Apply the handbrake, then jack up the front of the car and support it on axle stands (see *Jacking and vehicle support*).

30 Unscrew the bolts securing the front roll restrictor to the subframe, and also unscrew the through-bolt. Remove the roll restrictor **(see illustration)**.

31 If necessary, unbolt the bracket from the transmission.

32 Refit the bracket to the transmission and tighten the bolts to the specified torque.

33 Locate the new front roll restrictor in the bracket and insert the through-bolt.

34 Insert the bolts securing the front roll restrictor to the subframe, and tighten to the specified torque.

35 Tighten the through-bolt to the specified torque.

36 Lower the car to the ground.

Rear roll restrictor

37 Apply the handbrake, then jack up the front of the car and support it on axle stands (see *Jacking and vehicle support*).

38 Unscrew the nuts/bolts and through-bolt, and remove the rear roll restrictor from its bracket **(see illustrations)**. If necessary, use a trolley jack and block of wood to slightly raise the transmission. Note on certain automatic transmission models, an additional rubber damper is fitted in a bracket below the subframe.

39 If necessary, unbolt the bracket from the transmission **(see illustration)**.

40 Refit the bracket to the transmission and tighten the bolts to the specified torque.

41 Locate the rear roll restrictor in its bracket and tighten the nuts/bolts to the specified torque. On automatic transmission models, locate a new rubber damper to the bracket on the subframe and tighten the nuts to the specified torque.

42 Insert the through-bolt and tighten to the specified torque.

43 Lower the car to the ground.

Chapter 2 Part C:
Diesel engine in-car repair procedures

Contents

Degrees of difficulty

Easy, suitable for novice with little experience	**Fairly easy,** suitable for beginner with some experience	**Fairly difficult,** suitable for competent DIY mechanic	**Difficult,** suitable for experienced DIY mechanic	**Very difficult,** suitable for expert DIY or professional

Specifications

General

Engine type	Four-cylinder, in-line, 16-valve, double overhead camshaft
Designation	DuraTorq TDCi (common-rail injection)
Engine code:	
2.0 litre TDCi, 90 PS	–
2.0 litre TDCi, 115 PS	HJBA/B/C
2.0 litre TDCi, 130 PS	FMBA/B and N7BA
2.2 litre TDCi, 155 PS	QJBA/B
Capacity:	
2.0 litre	1998 cc
2.2 litre	2198 cc
Bore	86.0 mm
Stroke:	
2.0 litre	86.0 mm
2.2 litre	94.6 mm
Compression ratio	19 : 1
Power output:	
– (TDCi 90)	66 kW (90 PS) at 4000 rpm
HJBA/B/C	85 kW (115 PS) at 3800 rpm
FMBA/B and N7BA	96 kW (130 PS) at 3800 rpm
QJBA/B	114 kW (155 PS) at 3800 rpm
Firing order	1-3-4-2 (No 1 cylinder at timing chain end)
Direction of crankshaft rotation	Clockwise (seen from right-hand side of car)

Camshaft

Camshaft bearing journal diameter	26.450 mm
Camshaft bearing journal-to-cylinder head running clearance	0.065 mm
Camshaft endfloat	0.125 mm

Cylinder head

Piston protrusion:	**Thickness of cylinder head gasket**
0.430 to 0.520 mm	1.10 mm (1 hole/tooth)
0.521 to 0.570 mm	1.15 mm (2 holes/teeth)
0.571 to 0.620 mm	1.20 mm (3 holes/teeth)
Maximum permissible gasket surface distortion	0.10 mm

Lubrication

Engine oil capacity	See Chapter 1B	
Oil pressure – maximum (engine at operating temperature):		
At idle	1.25 bars	
At 2000 rpm	2.00 bars	

Torque wrench settings

	Nm	lbf ft
Auxiliary drivebelt idler pulley bolt	43	32
Auxiliary drivebelt tensioner mounting nuts	23	17
Big-end bearing cap bolts:		
Stage 1	30	22
Stage 2	Angle-tighten a further 80°	
Camshaft carrier bolts:		
Bolts 1 to 22	23	17
Bolts 23 to 25	10	7
Camshaft cover	10	7
Camshaft position sensor	10	7
Camshaft sprocket bolts	33	24
Common rail studs	23	17
Coolant pipe bracket to transmission	40	30
Coolant pump	23	17
Crankshaft oil seal carrier	10	7
Crankshaft position sensor	7	5
Crankshaft pulley bolt:		
Stage 1	30	22
Stage 2	Angle-tighten a further 90°	
Cylinder head bolts*:		
Stage 1:		
Bolts 1 to 10	10	7
Bolts 11 to 18	5	4
Stage 2:		
Bolts 1 to 10	20	15
Bolts 11 to 18	10	7
Stage 3:		
Bolts 1 to 10	40	30
Bolts 11 to 18	20	15
Stage 4:		
Bolts 1 to 10	Angle-tighten a further 180°	
Bolts 11 to 18	Angle-tighten a further 180°	
Earth cable-to-transmission bolt	40	30
EGR cooler-to-exhaust manifold bolts	37	27
EGR cooler securing nut and bolt	10	7
EGR pipe union	23	17
Engine/transmission mountings:		
Left-hand mounting bracket-to-transmission bolts:		
Automatic transmission	80	59
Manual transmission	90	66
Left-hand mounting centre nut*	133	98
Left-hand mounting outer nuts*	48	35
Rear mounting link nuts/bolts	80	59
Right-hand mounting bolts	80	59
Exhaust manifold and turbocharger nuts and bolts	40	30
Exhaust manifold bracket to block	46	34
Exhaust manifold heat shield	10	7
Exhaust manifold to catalytic converter	46	34
Flywheel/driveplate bolts:		
Stage 1	25	18
Stage 2	40	30
Stage 3	Angle-tighten a further 48°	
Fuel injection pump mounting bolts	23	17
Fuel injection pump sprocket	32	24
Fuel injectors	47	35
Fuel pressure line unions	40	30
Fuel return line unions	8	6
Glow plugs	13	10
Inlet manifold	16	12
Knock sensor	20	15
Lower crankcase/ladder to cylinder block	23	17

Torque wrench settings (continued)	**Nm**	**lbf ft**
Main bearing cap bolts:		
Stage 1	45	33
Stage 2	80	59
Stage 3	Angle-tighten a further 80°	
Oil cooler	23	17
Oil pump bolts	10	7
Oil pump chain tensioner	16	12
Oil pump pick-up pipe	10	7
Power steering pump	18	13
Power steering pump bracket to block	23	17
Power steering pump belt pulley	64	47
Roadwheel nuts	85	63
Rocker shaft bolts*:		
Stage 1	13	10
Stage 2	Angle-tighten a further 45°	
Starter motor	25	18
Sump bolts:		
Stage 1	7	5
Stage 2	14	10
Sump oil drain plug	23	17
Thermostat housing to cylinder head	23	17
Timing chain cover:		
Nuts	10	7
Bolts	14	10
Timing chain guide retaining bolts	15	11
Timing chain tensioner	15	11
Transmission-to-engine bolts	48	35
Turbocharger oil feed pipe union	14	10
Turbocharger oil return pipe bolts	10	7

** Use new nuts/bolts*

1 General information

How to use this Chapter

This Part of Chapter 2 is devoted to repair procedures possible while the engine is still installed in the car. Since these procedures are based on the assumption that the engine is installed in the car, if the engine has been removed from the car and mounted on a stand, some of the preliminary dismantling steps outlined will not apply.

Information concerning engine/transmission removal and refitting and engine overhaul, can be found in Part D of this Chapter.

Engine

The diesel engines covered in this manual are in-line four-cylinder, turbocharged units, of 16-valve, double overhead camshaft (DOHC) design. They are of the direct fuel injection type, with a modern high-pressure common-rail fuel system. The engine is mounted transversely at the front of the car, with the transmission on its left-hand end.

The engine cylinder block casting is of cast-iron, and has a lower aluminium crankcase which is bolted to the underside of the cylinder block, with an aluminium sump bolted under that. This arrangement offers greater rigidity than the normal sump arrangement, and helps to reduce engine vibration.

The crankshaft runs in five main bearings, the centre main bearing's upper half incorporating thrustwashers to control crankshaft endfloat. The connecting rods rotate on horizontally-split bearing shells at their big-ends. The pistons are attached to the connecting rods by gudgeon pins which are a floating fit in the connecting rod small-end eyes, secured by circlips. The aluminium alloy pistons are fitted with three piston rings: two compression rings and an oil control ring.

The inlet and exhaust valves are each closed by coil springs; they operate in guides which are shrink-fitted into the cylinder head, as are the valve seat inserts.

The double overhead camshaft sprockets and the fuel injection pump are driven by a twin chain from a sprocket on the crankshaft. The camshaft operates the sixteen valves via rockers which are mounted on rocker shafts that run parallel with the camshafts. Each camshaft rotates in five bearings that are machined directly in the cylinder head and the (bolted-on) bearing caps; this means that the bearing caps are not available separately from the cylinder head, and must not be interchanged with caps from another engine.

The vacuum pump (used for the brake servo and other vacuum actuators) is located on the transmission end of the cylinder head, driven by a slot in the end of the exhaust camshaft.

When working on this engine, note that Torx-type (both male and female heads) and hexagon socket (Allen head) fasteners are widely used; a good selection of bits, with the necessary adapters, will be required so that these can be unscrewed without damage and, on reassembly, tightened to the torque wrench settings specified.

Lubrication

Lubrication is by means of a chain-driven oil pump, from a sprocket on the crankshaft. The oil pump is mounted below the lower crankcase, and draws oil through a strainer located in the sump. The pump forces oil through an externally-mounted full-flow cartridge-type filter. From the filter, the oil is pumped into a main gallery in the cylinder block/crankcase, from where it is distributed to the crankshaft (main bearings) and cylinder head. On some models, an oil cooler is fitted next to the oil filter, at the rear of the block. The cooler is supplied with coolant from the engine cooling system.

While the crankshaft and camshaft bearings receive a pressurised supply, the camshaft lobes and valves are lubricated by splash, as are all other engine components. The undersides of the pistons are cooled by oil, sprayed from nozzles fitted above the upper main bearing shells. The turbocharger receives its own pressurised oil supply.

Repairs with engine in car

The following major repair operations can be accomplished without removing the engine from the car. However, owners should note that any operation involving the removal of the timing chain, camshafts or cylinder head require careful forethought, depending on the level of skill and the tools and facilities available; refer to the relevant text for details.

a) Compression pressure – testing.
b) Camshaft cover – removal and refitting.
c) Timing chain cover – removal and refitting.
d) Timing chain – renewal.
e) Timing chain tensioner and sprockets – removal and refitting.
f) Camshaft oil seal – renewal.
g) Camshaft and hydraulic rockers – removal and refitting.
h) Cylinder head – removal, overhaul and refitting.
i) Crankshaft pulley – removal and refitting.
j) Sump – removal and refitting.
k) Crankshaft oil seals – renewal.
l) Oil pump – removal and refitting.
m) Flywheel – removal and refitting.
n) Engine/transmission mountings – removal and refitting.
o) Inlet manifold – removal and refitting.
p) Exhaust manifold – removal and refitting.

Clean the engine compartment and the exterior of the engine with some type of degreaser before any work is done (and/or clean the engine using a steam cleaner). It will make the job easier and will help to keep dirt out of the internal areas of the engine.

Depending on the components involved, it may be helpful to remove the bonnet, to improve access to the engine as repairs are performed (refer to Chapter 11 if necessary). Cover the wings to prevent damage to the paint; special covers are available, but an old bedspread or blanket will also work.

2 Compression and leakdown tests – description and interpretation

Compression test

Note: *A compression tester suitable for use with diesel engines will be required for this test.*

1 When engine performance is down, or if misfiring occurs which cannot be attributed to the fuel or emissions systems, a compression test can provide diagnostic clues as to the engine's condition. If the test is performed regularly, it can give warning of trouble before any other symptoms become apparent.

2 The engine must be fully warmed-up to normal operating temperature, and the battery must be fully-charged. The aid of an assistant will be required.

3 Remove the glow plugs as described in Chapter 5C.

4 Fit a compression tester to the No 1 cylinder glow plug hole. The type of tester which screws into the plug thread is preferred.

5 Crank the engine for several seconds on the starter motor. After one or two revolutions, the compression pressure should build-up to a maximum figure and then stabilise. Record the highest reading obtained.

6 Repeat the test on the remaining cylinders, recording the pressure in each.

7 The cause of poor compression is less easy to establish on a diesel engine than on a petrol engine. The effect of introducing oil into the cylinders (wet testing) is not conclusive, because there is a risk that the oil will sit in the recess on the piston crown, instead of passing to the rings. However, the following can be used as a rough guide to diagnosis.

8 All cylinders should produce very similar pressures. Any difference greater than that specified indicates the existence of a fault. Note that the compression should build-up quickly in a healthy engine. Low compression on the first stroke, followed by gradually increasing pressure on successive strokes, indicates worn piston rings. A low compression reading on the first stroke, which does not build-up during successive strokes, indicates leaking valves or a blown head gasket (a cracked head could also be the cause).

9 A low reading from two adjacent cylinders is almost certainly due to the head gasket having blown between them and the presence of coolant in the engine oil will confirm this.

10 On completion, remove the compression tester, and refit the glow plugs with reference to Chapter 5C.

Leakdown test

11 A leakdown test measures the rate at which compressed air fed into the cylinder is lost. It is an alternative to a compression test, and in many ways it is better, since the escaping air provides easy identification of where pressure loss is occurring (piston rings, valves or head gasket).

12 The equipment required for leakdown testing is unlikely to be available to the home mechanic. If poor compression is suspected, have the test performed by a suitably-equipped garage.

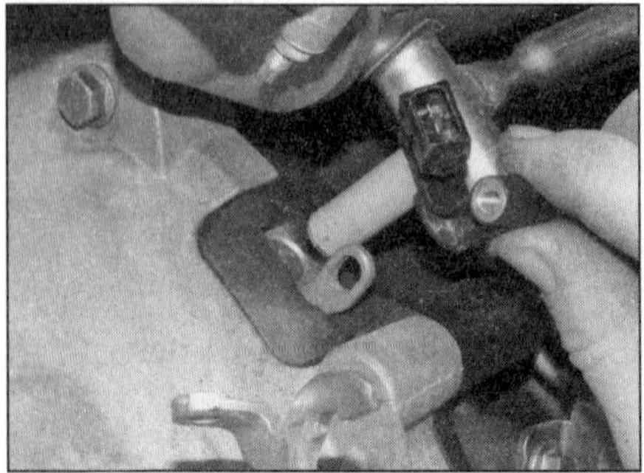

3.10 Undo the retaining bolt and withdraw the crankshaft position sensor

3 Engine timing – setting

Note: *Only turn the engine in the normal direction of rotation – clockwise from the right-hand side of the car.*

General information

1 Top Dead Centre (TDC) is the highest point in the cylinder that each piston reaches as it travels up and down when the crankshaft turns. Each piston reaches TDC at the end of the compression stroke and again at the end of the exhaust stroke, but TDC generally refers to piston position on the compression stroke. No 1 piston is at the timing chain end of the engine.

2 Setting No 1 piston at 50° before top dead centre (BTDC) is an essential part of many procedures, such as timing chain removal, cylinder head removal and camshaft removal.

3 The design of the engines covered in this Chapter is such that piston-to-valve contact may occur if the camshaft or crankshaft is turned with the timing chain removed. For this reason, it is important to ensure that the camshaft and crankshaft do not move in relation to each other once the timing chain has been removed from the engine.

Setting

Note: *Ford service tool 303-698, obtainable from Ford dealers or a tool supplier, will be required to set the timing at 50° BTDC – a tool can be fabricated to set the timing, using a piece of metal bar* ***(see illustrations 3.11a and 3.11b).***

4 Disconnect the battery negative (earth) lead (refer to *Disconnecting the battery*).

5 Loosen the right-hand front wheel nuts, then firmly apply the handbrake. Jack up the front of the car, and support on axle stands (see *Jacking and vehicle support*). Remove the right-hand front wheel.

6 Loosen and remove the retaining screws securing the engine undershield, lower the shield, and remove it.

7 The engine can now be rotated using the crankshaft pulley.

8 A timing hole is provided on the top of the transmission, to permit the crankshaft position sensor to be located.

9 Remove the air cleaner assembly as described in Chapter 4B.

10 Disconnect the wiring connector from the crankshaft position sensor, undo the retaining bolt and withdraw the sensor from the bellhousing **(see illustration)**.

11 The special tool can now be inserted into the sensor hole to set the timing at 50° BTDC **(see illustrations)**.

12 Turn the crankshaft in the direction of engine rotation, until the end of the tool drops into a recess in the outer toothed part of the flywheel, this will be in the 50° BTDC position.

13 If the engine is being set to 50° BTDC

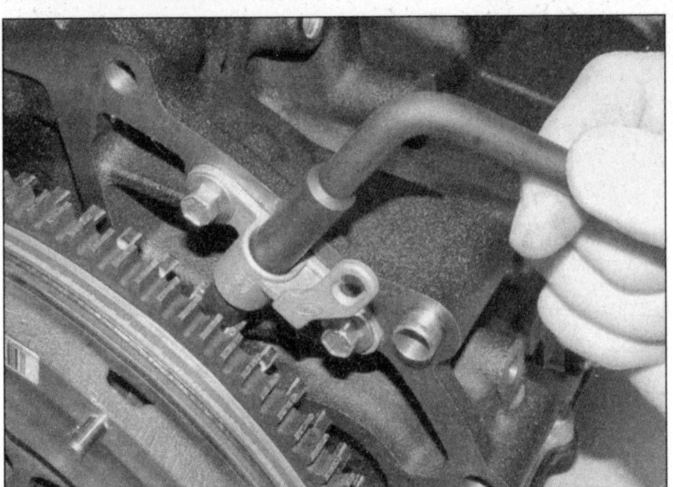
3.11a Ford timing tool inserted into the crankshaft sensor bracket . . .

3.11b . . . a fabricated tool can be used (transmission removed for clarity)

as part of the timing chain removal/renewal procedure, further confirmation of the position can be gained once the timing chain outer cover has been removed. At 50° BTDC, 6 mm timing pins are inserted into the camshaft and fuel pump sprockets, see Section 7.

14 If the holes in the camshaft sprockets do not align, remove the timing pin from the crankshaft and rotate the engine one full turn and re-install the timing pin.

15 Before rotating the crankshaft again, make sure that the timing pin and where fitted the camshaft sprocket timing pins are removed. When operations are complete, refit the crankshaft sensor. **Do not** use the crankshaft timing setting tool to prevent the crankshaft from rotating.

4 Camshaft cover – removal and refitting

Caution: Do not carry out any work on the fuel system with the engine running. Wait for at least 2 minutes after the engine has been stopped before any work is carried out on the fuel system, to make sure the fuel pressure and temperature has dropped sufficiently. Make sure that all the fuel lines are kept clean. Fit blanking plugs to the end of the fuel lines when they are disconnected, to prevent foreign matter entering the components.

Removal

1 Disconnect the battery negative (earth) lead (refer to *Disconnecting the battery*).

2 Remove the oil level dipstick and unclip the engine upper cover.

3 Before proceeding further, use a brush and suitable solvent to clean the area around the injector high-pressure unions. It is essential that no dirt enters the system. Allow time for any solvent used to dry.

4 Disconnect the electrical connectors from the fuel injectors **(see illustration)**, make sure the wiring connectors are kept clean.

5 Release the hinged retaining clip at the front, and withdraw the fuel return lines off the injectors **(see illustrations)**. Discard the O-ring seals – new ones will be required on refitting.

6 Using a spanner to hold the injectors in position, slacken the fuel supply pipes **(see illustration)**. Note the position of the fuel supply pipes before removal.

7 Slacken the high-pressure pipe unions from the fuel supply rail **(see illustration)**.

8 Once the unions are loose, wrap clean absorbent tissue or rag around them briefly, to

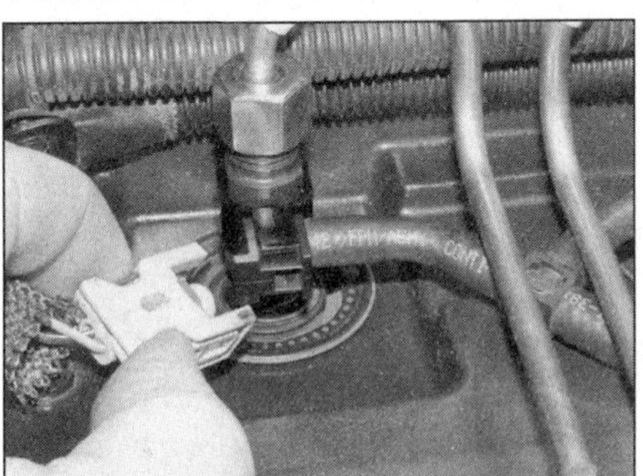
4.4 Disconnecting the electrical connectors from the fuel injectors

4.5a Unclip the hinged collar around the injector . . .

4.5b . . . and withdraw the return pipe

4.6 Use one spanner to hold the injector in position while slackening the union

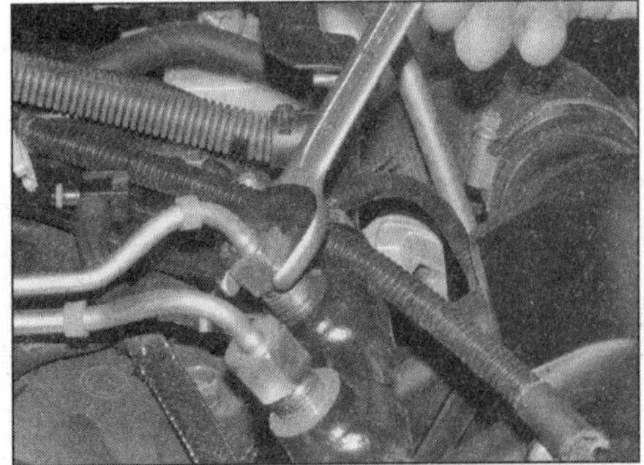
4.7 Slacken the fuel pipes from the supply rail

4.10a Prise out the four fuel injector seals

4.10b Unclip the wiring loom from across the top of the camshaft cover

4.11 Disconnect the crankcase ventilation hose from the camshaft cover

4.12 Remove the securing brackets from the camshaft cover

4.13 Remove the camshaft cover

soak away any dirt which may otherwise enter. If available, Ford recommend using a vacuum line to suck any dirt away from the opening union – do not use an airline, as this may blast dirt inwards, rather than cleaning it away.

9 Disconnect the fuel supply pipes and discard them. New supply pipes will be required for refitting. Fit blanking plugs to the injectors and supply rail unions, to prevent dirt ingress.

10 Carefully prise out the four fuel injector seals from the camshaft cover. Discard the seals – new ones will be required on refitting. Unclip the wiring loom from across the top of the camshaft cover **(see illustrations).**

11 Disconnect the crankcase ventilation hose from the rear of the camshaft cover **(see illustration)**.

12 Unscrew the retaining bolts and remove the two supply rail securing brackets from the camshaft cover **(see illustration)**.

13 Unscrew the retaining bolts and lift the camshaft cover off the cylinder head **(see illustration)**. Recover the gasket and discard it – a new gasket and seals will be required on refitting.

Refitting

14 Clean the sealing surfaces of the cover and the head, and check the condition of the rubber seals fitted to the cover bolts.

15 Refitting is a reversal of removal. Noting the following points:

a) Renew all seals, gaskets and supply pipes as noted on removal.

b) Ensure the gasket is correctly seated on the cylinder head, and take care to avoid displacing it as the camshaft cover is lowered into position.

c) Ensure that the supply pipes are routed as noted on removal.

d) Check the ventilation hose is securely reconnected.

e) Tighten the camshaft cover retaining bolts to the specified torque setting.

16 When the engine has been run for some time, check for signs of oil leakage from the gasket joint.

5 Timing chain cover – removal and refitting

Note: *To carry out this task with the engine/transmission installed in the car it requires the equipment necessary to raise and support the front of the car. Ford technicians use an engine support bar, which locates in the channels at the top of each inner wing, and a further beam attached to this, which rests on the front crossmember. If such an arrangement is not available, use an engine crane; either way, use a suitable length of chain and hooks to attach the lifting gear to the engine lifting eye. If the engine must be supported from below, use a large piece of wood on a trolley jack to spread the load and reduce the chance of damage to the sump. Precise details of the procedure will depend on the equipment available – the following is typical.*

5.8 Undo the retaining bolts and move the coolant expansion tank to one side

Note: *Ford use special tools for removing the oil seal and aligning the timing chain cover – see text. A new timing chain cover will be required on refitting, as the cover will be distorted on removal.*

Removal

1 Disconnect the battery negative (earth) lead (refer to *Disconnecting the battery*).

2 Loosen the right-hand front wheel nuts, then firmly apply the handbrake. Jack up the front of the car, and support on axle stands (see *Jacking and vehicle support*). Remove the right-hand front wheel.

3 Remove the main auxiliary drivebelt as described in Chapter 1B.

4 Remove the crankshaft pulley as described in Section 6.

5 Remove the crankshaft timing chain end oil seal as described in Section 16.

6 Remove the retaining bolts and nuts from the lower part of the timing chain cover.

7 Undo the retaining bolts and remove the auxiliary drivebelt tensioner bracket.

8 Working from inside the engine compartment, undo the retaining bolts and move the coolant expansion tank to one side **(see illustration)**.

9 Disconnect the fuel lines, then undo the retaining nut and bolt and detach the fuel line bracket from the cylinder head **(see illustrations)**.

10 Depending on the equipment available, support the engine either from the top using a support bar or from underneath the sump using a suitable jack.

11 Undo the retaining bolts and nuts, then remove the engine mounting from the right-hand inner front wing panel **(see illustration)**.

5.9a Disconnect the fuel lines (blanking off the open ends) . . .

5.9b . . . undo the retaining nut and bolt and detach the fuel line bracket from the cylinder head

5.11 Undo the retaining bolts/nuts (arrowed) and remove the engine mounting

5.12 Undo the retaining nut (arrowed) and slide the idler pulley away from the engine

Note: *It cannot be removed at this point*

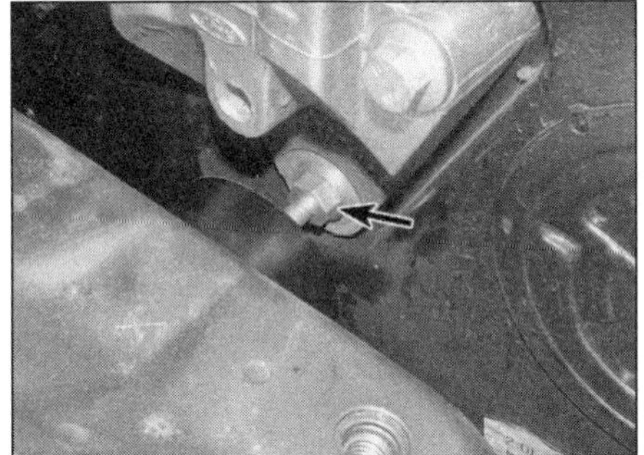

5.13a Undo the retaining bolts, including the one (arrowed) behind the idler pulley . . .

5.13b . . . and remove the mounting bracket, complete with idler pulley

12 Undo the retaining nut and slide the idler pulley from the mounting bracket **(see illustration)**. **Note:** *This will not come all the way off the stud at this point.*

13 Undo the retaining bolts, and remove the mounting bracket, complete with idler pulley from the timing chain cover **(see illustrations)**.

14 Remove the retaining bolts/nuts from the upper part of the timing chain cover.

15 Using a couple of scrapers or similar, carefully work your way around the timing chain cover and prise it away from the engine. The cover will become distorted on removal, discard it, as a new cover must be used on refitting.

Refitting

16 Make sure that the mating surfaces of the cover and the engine casing are clean. Apply a 3 mm bead of silicone sealant (Ford part number WSE-M4G323-A4, or equivalent) around the outer mating surface of the engine casing **(see illustration)**. **Note:** *Install the timing chain cover within 5 minutes of applying the sealer to the engine casing. Make sure the casing does not come into contact with the engine casing, until the correct position for fitting is obtained.*

17 Fit the timing chain cover and install the retaining nuts and bolts hand tight.

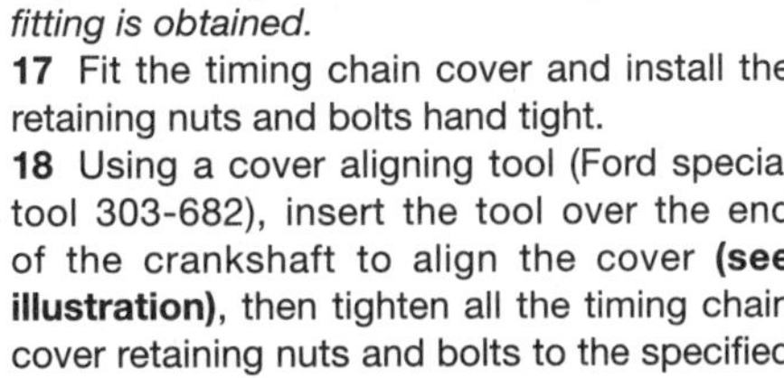

18 Using a cover aligning tool (Ford special tool 303-682), insert the tool over the end of the crankshaft to align the cover **(see illustration)**, then tighten all the timing chain cover retaining nuts and bolts to the specified torque. Remove the tool once the cover is in position.

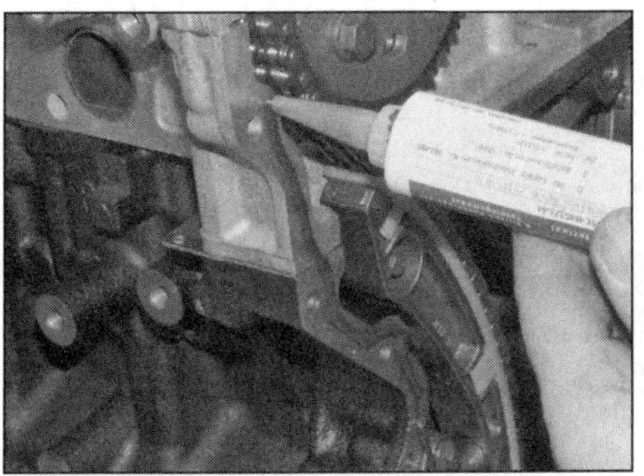

5.16 Apply a 3 mm bead of sealant around the mating surface of the engine casing

5.18 Insert the tool over the end of the crankshaft to align the cover, before tightening the retaining bolts

19 Further refitting is a reversal of removal. Noting the following points:

a) Fit a new crankshaft oil seal as described in Section 16.

b) Refit the crankshaft pulley as described in Section 6.

c) Refit the main auxiliary drivebelt as described in Chapter 1B.

6 Crankshaft pulley – removal and refitting

Removal

1 Disconnect the battery negative (earth) lead (refer to *Disconnecting the battery* at the end of this manual).

2 Loosen the right-hand front wheel nuts, then raise the front of the car, and support securely on axle stands (see *Jacking and vehicle support*). Remove the right-hand front wheel.

3 Remove the retaining screws and withdraw the engine undershield from under the car.

4 Remove the main auxiliary drivebelt, as described in Chapter 1B.

5 The three bolts which secure the crankshaft pulley must now be slackened. Ensure that the car is adequately supported, as considerable effort may be needed to slacken the bolts.

6 Ford technicians use a special holding tool (205-072) which locates in the outer holes of the pulley and prevents it from turning,

6.7 Unscrew the bolts and remove the crankshaft pulley

6.8 Check the crankshaft oil seal for signs of oil leakage

but a home-made substitute forked tool can be made from thick metal strip, with bolts at the ends to fit the pulley slots. If this is not available, select a gear (manual transmission), and have an assistant firmly apply the handbrake and footbrake as the bolts are loosened. On automatic transmission models (or manual transmission models, if necessary), remove the starter motor as described in Chapter 5A, and jam the flywheel ring gear to lock the engine.

7 Unscrew the bolts securing the pulley to the crankshaft, and remove the pulley **(see illustration)**.

8 With the pulley removed, it is advisable to check the crankshaft oil seal for signs of oil leakage **(see illustration)**. If necessary, fit a new seal as described in Section 16.

Refitting

9 Refit the pulley to the end of the crankshaft, then fit the pulley securing bolts and tighten them as far as possible before the crankshaft starts to rotate.

10 Holding the pulley against rotation as for removal, first tighten the bolts to the specified Stage 1 torque.

11 Stage 2 involves tightening the bolts though an angle, rather than to a torque. The bolts must be rotated through the specified angle – special angle gauges are available from tool outlets. As a guide, a 90° angle is equivalent to a quarter-turn, and this is easily judged by assessing the start and end positions of the socket handle or torque wrench.

12 Refit the main auxiliary drivebelt as described in Chapter 1B.

13 Refit the auxiliary drivebelt lower cover, and where removed, the engine undershield(s) and wheel arch liner panels.

14 Refit the wheel, lower the car to the ground, and tighten the wheel nuts to the specified torque. Reconnect the battery negative lead.

7 Timing chain – removal inspection and refitting

Removal

1 Remove the timing chain cover, as described in Section 5.

2 Referring to the information in Section 3, set the engine to 50° BTDC on No 1 cylinder. In this position, insert a 6 mm timing pin (6 mm drill bit) in each camshaft sprocket and one in the fuel pump sprocket **(see illustration)**.

3 If the timing chain is not being fitted straight away (or if the chain is being removed as part of another procedure, such as cylinder head removal), temporarily refit the engine right-hand mounting and tighten the bolts securely **(see illustration)**.

4 Slacken the timing chain tensioner by inserting a small screwdriver into the access hole in the tensioner and releasing the pawl mechanism. Press against the timing chain guide to depress the piston into the tensioner housing, when fully depressed, insert a locking pin (approximately 1.5 mm) to lock the piston in its compressed position **(see illustration)**.

5 To remove the tensioner, undo the two retaining bolts and remove the timing chain tensioner from the cylinder block, taking care not to remove the locking pin **(see illustration)**.

6 Undo the retaining bolts and remove the tensioner timing chain guide and the fixed timing chain guides from the cylinder block **(see illustrations)**.

7 Holding the fuel injection pump sprocket in position, slacken the retaining bolts and remove the sprocket **(see illustration)**. **Note:** *Do not rely on the timing pin (6 mm drill bit) to hold the sprocket in position.*

8 With the camshafts held in position, undo the camshaft sprocket retaining bolts and remove the camshaft sprockets and timing chain. Do not rotate the crankshaft until the timing chain is refitted. **Note:** *Do not rely on the timing pins (6 mm drill bit) to hold the sprockets in position.*

7.2 Insert 6 mm timing pins (6 mm drill bits), to align the camshaft sprockets

7.3 Temporarily refit the engine mounting to support the engine

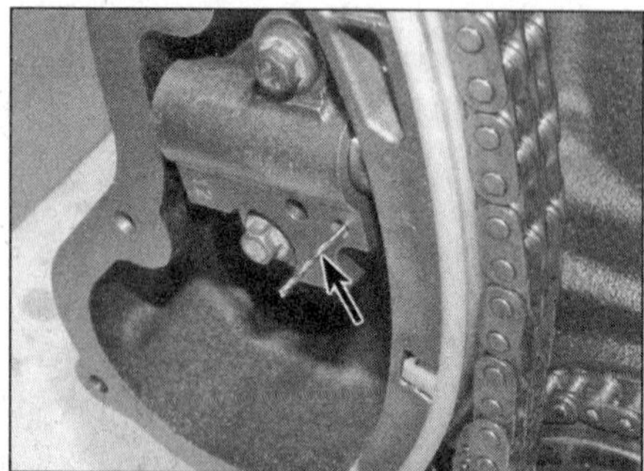
7.4 Insert a pin (arrowed) to lock the piston in its compressed position

7.5 Remove the timing chain tensioner from the cylinder block, taking care not to remove the locking pin

7.6a Undo the retaining bolts and remove the tensioner timing chain guide . . .

7.6b . . . the upper fixed chain guide bolts (arrowed) . . .

7.6c . . . the middle fixed chain guide . . .

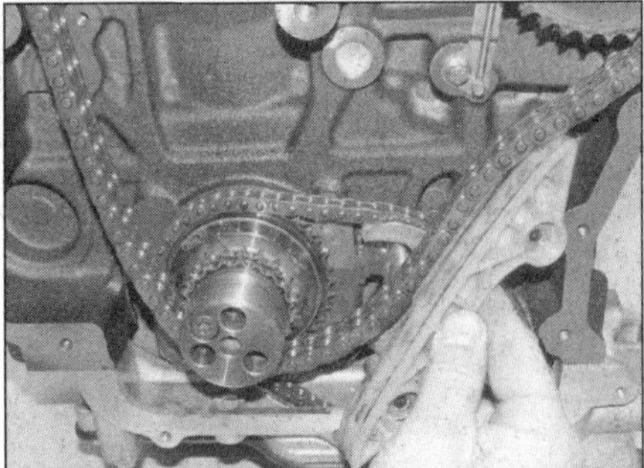

7.6d . . . and the lower fixed timing chain guide

7.7 Remove the fuel pump sprocket

7.10a Insert a locking pin (drill bit) to lock the piston in its compressed position

7.10b Undo the retaining bolt and withdraw the sprocket from the crankshaft

9 Check the condition of the timing chain, tensioner and guides before refitting them. When fitting a new timing chain, a new tensioner should be fitted as a matter of course, especially if the engine has completed a large mileage.

10 To remove the timing chain sprocket from the crankshaft, the oil pump drive chain will need to be removed first, hold the tensioner in and insert a locking pin (approximately 1.5 mm) to lock the piston in its compressed position **(see illustration)**. Undo the two retaining bolts and remove the oil pump drive chain tensioner from the engine. The chain can now be removed from the sprocket. Undo the retaining bolt and withdraw the sprocket from the crankshaft **(see illustration)**.

Inspection

Note: *Keep all components identified for position to ensure correct refitting.*

11 Clean all components thoroughly and wipe dry.

12 Examine the chain tensioner and tensioner guide for excessive wear or other damage. Check the guides for deep grooves made by the timing chain.

13 Examine the timing chain for excessive wear. Hold it horizontally and check how much movement exists in the chain links. If there is any doubt, compare it to a new chain. Renew as necessary.

14 Examine the teeth of the camshaft and crankshaft sprockets for excessive wear and damage.

15 Before refitting the timing chain tensioner, the piston must be compressed and locked until refitted (if not already done on removal). To do this, insert a small screwdriver into the access hole in the tensioner and release the pawl mechanism. Now lightly clamp the tensioner in a soft-jawed vice and slowly compress the piston. Do not apply excessive force and make sure that the piston remains aligned with its cylinder. When completely compressed, insert a locking pin/1.5 mm diameter wire rod into the special hole to lock the piston in its compressed position.

Refitting

16 Ensure that the crankshaft and camshaft are still set to 50° BTDC on No 1 cylinder, as described in Section 3.

17 If not already fitted, refit the crankshaft drive sprocket onto the crankshaft. Refit the oil pump drive chain and tensioner, hold pressure against the tensioner guide and withdraw the tensioner locking pin (see Section 13, for further information on refitting the oil pump).

18 Refit the fuel pump sprocket and the exhaust camshaft sprocket, DO NOT tighten the retaining bolts at this stage.

19 With the timing chain around the inlet camshaft sprocket, refit the timing chain and sprocket, feeding the timing chain around the crankshaft drive sprocket, fuel pump sprocket and exhaust camshaft sprocket **(see illustration)**.

20 With the timing pins (6 mm drill bits) inserted into the sprockets to re-align them, the copper links on the timing chain must line up with the timing marks on the sprockets **(see illustrations)**.

21 Refit the tensioner to the cylinder block and tighten the retaining bolts to the specified torque setting. Take care not to remove the locking pin.

22 Refit the timing chain tensioner guide on

7.19 Refit the timing chain and sprockets

7.20a With the timing pins/6 mm drill bits (arrowed) inserted into the sprockets . . .

7.20b . . . re-align the timing chain copper links with the timing mark (arrowed) on the camshaft sprockets . . .

7.20c . . . and the timing mark (arrowed) on the fuel pump sprocket

7.22 Hold pressure against the tensioner guide (arrowed) and withdraw the locking pin

the upper pivot pin and tighten the retaining bolt to the specified torque setting. Hold pressure against the bottom of the tensioner guide and withdraw the tensioner locking pin. This will then tension the timing chain **(see illustration)**.

23 Refit the three fixed timing chain guides and tighten the retaining bolts to the specified torque setting.

24 Tighten the camshaft sprocket retaining bolts and the fuel injection pump sprocket retaining bolts, to the specified torque setting shown at the beginning of this Chapter. **Note:** *Do not rely on the timing pins (6 mm drill bits) to hold the sprockets in position.*

25 Check that the engine is still set to 50° BTDC (as described in Section 3), and remove the timing pins (6 mm drill bits) from the sprockets and the timing peg from the crankshaft sensor hole.

26 Turn the engine (in the direction of engine rotation) two full turns. Refit the timing pins and crankshaft timing peg to make sure the engine timing is still set at 50° BTDC (see Section 3 for further information).

27 Check the tension of the chain then remove the timing pins (6 mm drill bits) from the sprockets and the timing peg from the crankshaft sensor hole. Refit the crankshaft sensor.

28 Refit the timing chain cover as described in Section 5.

9.6 Marked at the timing chain end of the shafts: IN for inlet shaft

9.7 Removing the upper timing chain guide

8 Timing chain tensioner and sprockets – removal, inspection and refitting

Timing chain tensioner

1 The timing chain tensioner is removed as part of the timing chain renewal procedure, in Section 7.

Camshaft sprocket

2 The camshaft sprocket is removed as part of the timing chain renewal procedure, in Section 7.

Fuel injection pump sprocket

3 Removal of the injection pump sprocket is described as part of the timing chain renewal procedure, in Section 7.

9 Camshaft and hydraulic rockers – removal and refitting

Note: *A new camshaft oil seal and suitable sealant will be required on refitting. New rocker shaft retaining bolts will also be required.*

Removal

1 Remove the timing chain cover, as described in Section 5.

2 Referring to the information in Section 3, set the engine to 50° BTDC on No 1 cylinder. In this position, insert a 6 mm timing pin (6 mm drill bit) in each camshaft sprocket and one in the fuel injection pump sprocket (see Section 7).

3 Remove the camshaft cover, as described in Section 4.

4 Remove the power steering belt as described in Chapter 1B, Section 30. Undo the retaining bolt and remove the power steering pump pulley from the end of the camshaft, see Section 10.

5 Undo the retaining bolts and remove the brake vacuum pump from the transmission end of the exhaust camshaft, as described in Chapter 9.

6 Slacken and remove the rocker shaft retaining bolts, discard them as new ones will be required on refitting. Lift out the rocker shafts, complete with rocker arms and store them in a clean and safe area. **Note:** *They are marked at the timing chain end of the shaft, IN for inlet shaft and EX for exhaust shaft* ***(see illustration)***.

7 Slacken the timing chain tensioner and remove the tensioner timing chain guide, the upper timing chain guide and the camshaft sprockets **(see illustration)** as described in Section 7.

8 Slacken the camshaft carrier retaining bolts in the **reverse** of the sequence shown **(see illustration 9.14),** then lift the camshaft carrier from the cylinder head.

9 Carefully lift out the camshafts, and place them somewhere clean and safe – the lobes must not be scratched. Remove the camshaft oil seals from the transmission end of the camshafts and discard them, new ones will be required for refitting.

10 Before removing the hydraulic rocker arms from the rocker shaft, first mark the rockers so that they are fitted in the same position on re-assembly. The rocker arms can then be withdrawn from the rocker shaft along with the springs.

Refitting

11 Make sure that the top surfaces of the cylinder head, and in particular the camshaft bearing surfaces and the mating surfaces for the camshaft carrier, are completely clean.

12 Lubricate the camshafts and cylinder head bearing journals with clean engine oil, then carefully lower the camshafts into position in the cylinder head **(see illustrations)**.

13 Apply a 2.5 mm bead of sealant (Loctite 510, or equivalent) around the outer mating surface of the camshaft carrier **(see illustration)**. **Note:** *Install the camshaft carrier within 5 minutes of applying the sealer to the*

9.12a Lubricating the cylinder head bearing journals with clean engine oil . . .

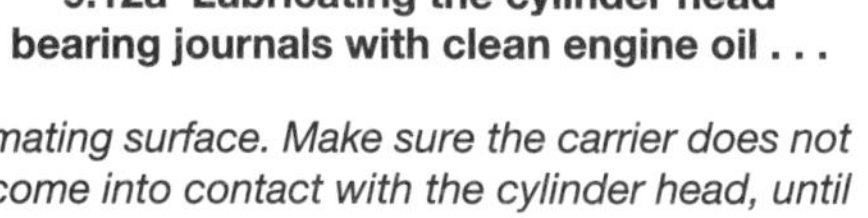

9.12b . . . then carefully lower the camshafts into position

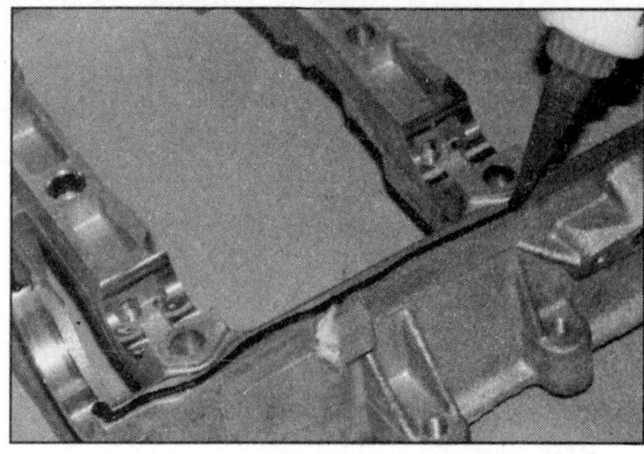

9.13 Apply a 2.5 mm bead of sealant around the outer mating surface of the camshaft carrier

mating surface. Make sure the carrier does not come into contact with the cylinder head, until the correct position for fitting is obtained.

14 Install the camshaft carrier retaining bolts and tighten them in the sequence shown **(see illustration).**

15 Refit the timing chain, sprockets, guides and tensioner as described in Section 7.

16 Install the rocker shafts using new retaining bolts, making sure they are fitted in the correct position as noted on removal (see paragraph 6). Tighten the retaining bolts to the specified torque setting.

17 Fit a new oil seal **(see illustration)**, then refit the brake vacuum pump to the transmission end of the exhaust camshaft, as described in Chapter 9.

18 Fit a new camshaft oil seal and refit the power steering pump pulley to the end of the camshaft as described in Section 10.

19 Refit the camshaft cover, as described in Section 4.

20 Refit the timing chain cover, as described in Section 5.

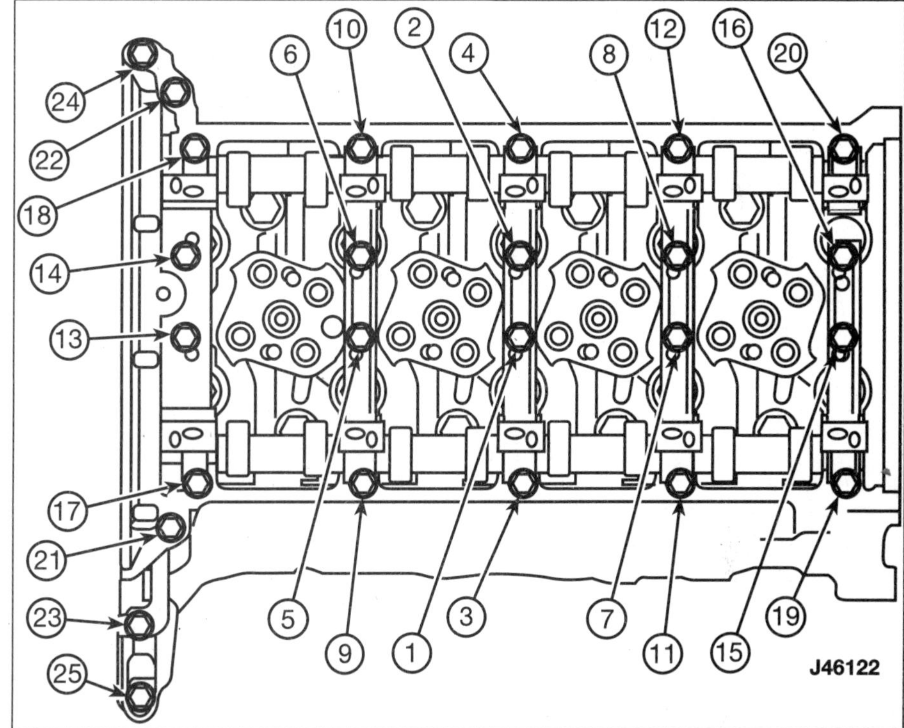

9.14 Tightening sequence for the camshaft carrier retaining bolts

10 Camshaft oil seal – renewal

1 Remove the plastic cover from the power steering belt and slacken the pulley retaining bolt **(see illustration)**.

2 Remove the power steering pump drivebelt as described in Chapter 1B, Section 30.

3 Undo the retaining bolt and remove the power steering pump pulley from the end of the camshaft **(see illustration)**.

4 Remove the camshaft oil seal. Ford dealers use a seal extractor for this (tool No 303-293). In the absence of this tool, do not use any removal method which might damage the sealing surfaces, or a leak will result when the new seal is fitted **(see Haynes Hint)**.

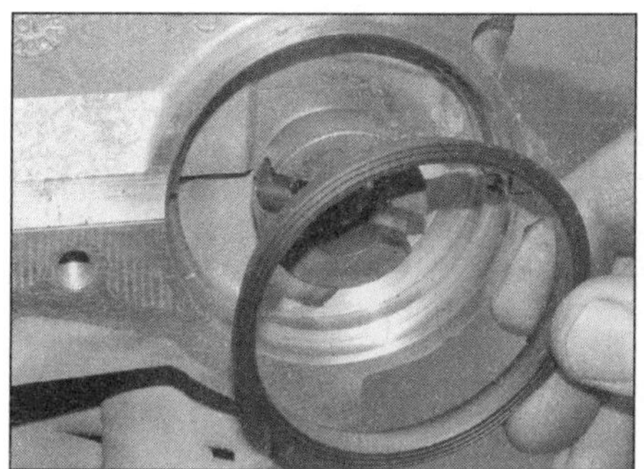

9.17 Fit a new oil seal before refitting the brake vacuum pump

10.1 Undo the retaining nut (arrowed) and remove the pulley plastic cover

10.3 Undo the retaining bolt and remove the power steering pump pulley

10.6 Fitting the oil seal over the end of the camshaft, using the sleeve supplied with the new oil seal

HAYNES HiNT ***One of the best ways to remove an oil seal is to carefully drill or punch two holes through the seal, opposite each other (taking care not to damage the surface behind the seal as this is done). Two self-tapping screws are then screwed into the holes; by pulling on the screw heads alternately with a pair of pliers, the seal can be extracted.***

5 Clean out the seal housing and the sealing surface of the camshaft by wiping it with a lint-free cloth. Remove any swarf or burrs that may cause the seal to leak.

6 Apply a little oil to the new camshaft oil seal, and fit it over the end of the camshaft, using the sleeve supplied with the new oil seal **(see illustration)**. If a sleeve is not supplied, to avoid damaging the seal lips, wrap a little tape over the end of the camshaft.

7 Ford dealers have a special tool for pressing the seal into the cylinder head, but if this is not available, a deep socket of suitable size can be used. **Note:** *Select a socket that bears only on the hard outer surface of the seal, not the inner lip which can easily be damaged.* It is important that the seal is fitted square to the shaft, and is fully seated.

8 Refitting is a reversal of removal.

11 Cylinder head – removal, inspection and refitting

Removal

1 Disconnect the battery negative (earth) lead (refer to *Disconnecting the battery* at the end of this manual).

2 Drain the cooling system as described in Chapter 1B.

3 Remove the alternator as described in Chapter 5A.

4 Remove the camshafts and hydraulic rockers as described in Section 9.

5 Remove the exhaust manifold as described in Section 20.

6 Remove the air cleaner housing assembly, as described in Chapter 4B.

7 Undo the retaining nut and disconnect the bracket for the cylinder head temperature sensor wiring block connector. Unclip the wiring from the end of the cylinder head **(see illustration)**.

8 Undo the retaining bolt and detach the power steering high-pressure pipe upper bracket from the engine lifting eye **(see illustration)**.

9 Undo the retaining bolts and detach the power steering high-pressure pipe lower bracket and release the wiring loom securing clip **(see illustration)**.

10 Disconnect the wiring connector from the end of the fuel supply rail and the camshaft position sensor **(see illustrations)**. Also disconnect the wiring connector from the inlet manifold sensor and the vacuum hose from the inlet manifold.

11 Unclip the coolant hose from under the front of the inlet manifold **(see illustration).**

12 Undo the retaining bolts and remove the inlet manifold.

13 Undo the retaining nut and disconnect the glow plug wiring connector **(see illustration).**

14 Remove the fuel supply pipe clamp and slacken the supply line at the fuel pump. Slacken the fuel supply pipe at the fuel rail, then remove and discard – a new pipe will be required on refitting **(see illustrations)**. Install blanking plugs to the open ports on the fuel pump and supply rail to prevent dirt ingress.

15 Release the retaining clip and disconnect the return pipe from the fuel injection pump – again, discard the return pipe as a new one will be required on refitting **(see illustration)**.

16 Slacken the fuel injector locking sleeves and remove the fuel injectors, for further information see Chapter 4B.

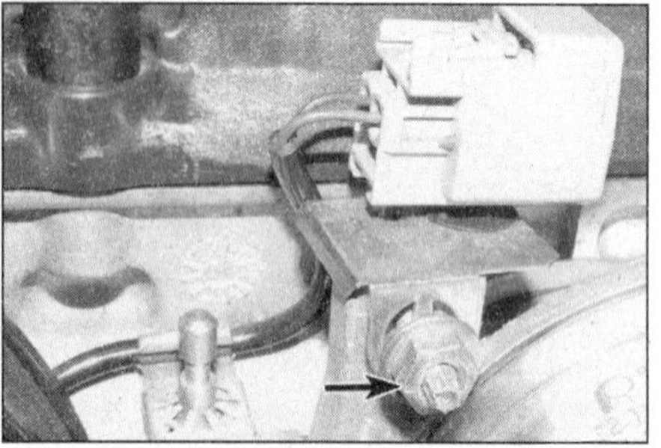

11.7 Undo the retaining nut (arrowed) and remove the bracket for the wiring block connector

11.8 Undo the retaining bolt (arrowed) and detach the bracket from the engine lifting eye

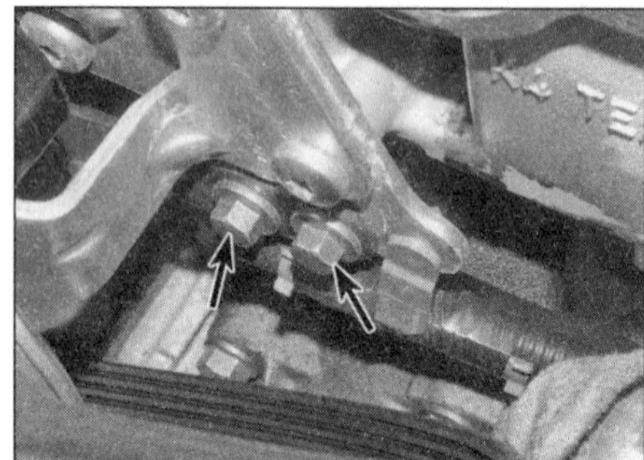

11.9 Undo the retaining bolts (arrowed) and detach the lower bracket

11.10a Disconnect the wiring connector from the end of the fuel supply rail

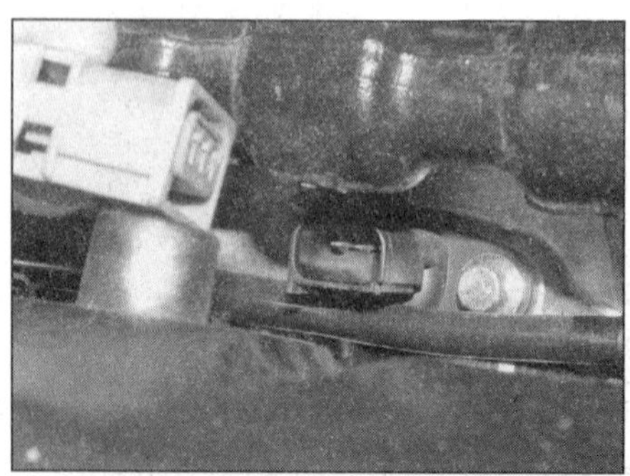

11.10b Disconnect the wiring connector from the camshaft position sensor

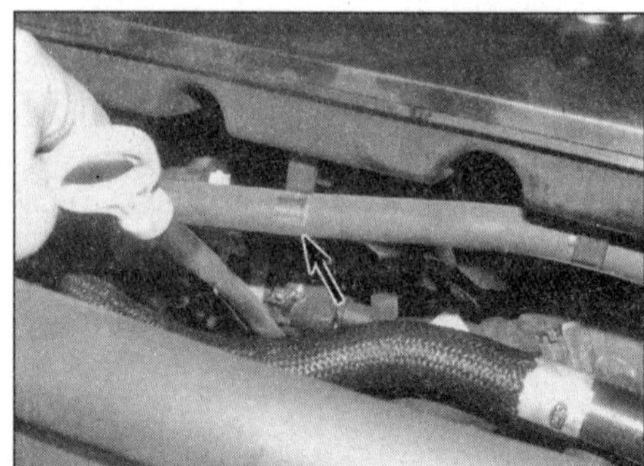

11.11 Unclip the coolant hose (arrowed) from under the front of the inlet manifold

11.13 Undo the retaining nut (arrowed) and disconnect the glow plug wiring connector

11.14a Remove the clamp bolt (arrowed) and slacken the fuel supply pipe union . . .

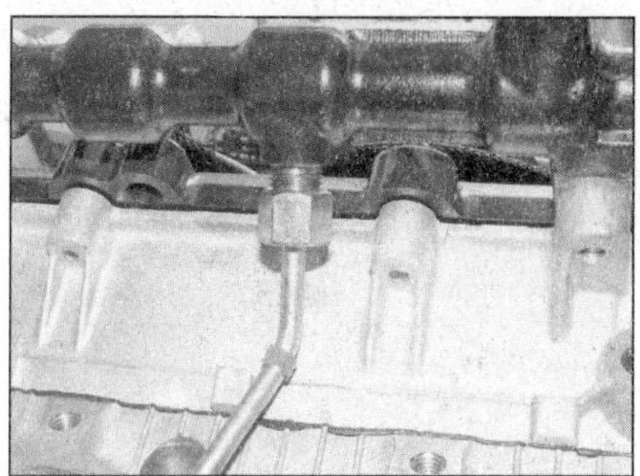
11.14b . . . then slacken the fuel supply pipe at the fuel rail

17 Check around the head and the engine bay that there is nothing still attached to the cylinder head, nor anything which would prevent it from being lifted away.

18 Working in the **reverse** order of the tightening sequence **(see illustration 11.42)**, loosen the cylinder head bolts by half a turn at a time, until they are all loose. Remove the head bolts, and discard them – Ford state that they must not be re-used, even if they appear to be serviceable.

19 Lift the cylinder head away; use assistance if possible, as it is a heavy assembly. Do not, under any circumstances, lever the head between the mating surfaces, as this will certainly damage the sealing surfaces for the gasket, leading to leaks.

20 Once the head has been removed, recover the gasket from the two dowels – discard the gasket, a new one will be required on refitting (see paragraph 22).

Inspection

21 If required, dismantling and inspection of the cylinder head is covered in Part D of this Chapter.

Cylinder head gasket selection

22 Examine the old cylinder head gasket for manufacturer's identification markings. These will be in the form of teeth (one, two or three) on the front edge of the gasket and/or holes in the gasket, which indicate the gasket's thickness **(see illustration).**

23 Unless new components have been fitted, or the cylinder head has been machined (skimmed), the new cylinder head gasket must be of the same type as the old one. Purchase the required gasket, and proceed to paragraph 29.

24 If the head has been machined, or if new pistons have been fitted, it is likely that a head gasket of different thickness to the original will be needed. Gasket selection is made on the basis of the measured piston protrusion above the cylinder head gasket surface (the protrusion must fall within the range specified at the start of this Chapter).

25 To measure the piston protrusion, anchor a dial test indicator (DTI) to the top face (cylinder head gasket mating face) of the cylinder block, and zero the gauge on the gasket mating face **(see illustration)**.

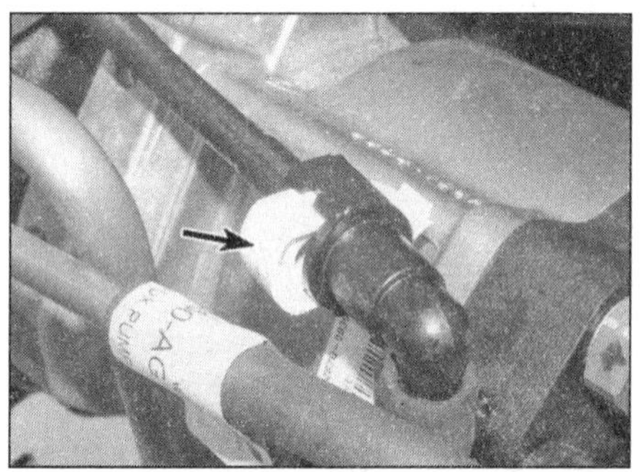
11.15 Release the retaining clip (arrowed) and disconnect the return pipe from the fuel injection pump

26 Rest the gauge probe above No 1 piston crown, and turn the crankshaft slowly by hand until the piston reaches TDC (its maximum height). Measure and record the maximum piston projection at TDC.

27 Repeat the measurement for the remaining pistons, and record the results.

28 If the measurements differ from piston to piston, take the highest figure, and use this to determine the thickness of the head gasket required; see Specifications at the start of this Chapter.

Preparation for refitting

29 The mating faces of the cylinder head and cylinder block must be perfectly clean before refitting the head. Use a hard plastic or wooden scraper to remove all traces of gasket and carbon; also clean the piston crowns. **Note:** *The new head gasket has rubber-coated surfaces, which could be damaged from sharp edges or debris left by a metal scraper.*

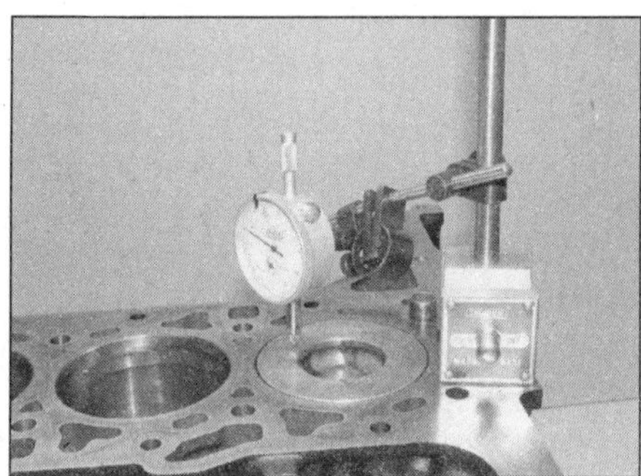
11.25 Using a dial test indicator to measure the piston protrusion

11.22 Teeth and holes in the gasket (arrowed), which indicate the gasket's thickness

30 Take particular care when cleaning the piston crowns, as the soft aluminium alloy is easily damaged.

31 Make sure that the carbon is not allowed to enter the oil and water passages – this is particularly important for the lubrication system, as carbon could block the oil supply to the engine's components. Using adhesive tape and paper, seal the water, oil and bolt holes in the cylinder block.

32 To prevent carbon entering the gap between the pistons and bores, smear a little grease in the gap. After cleaning each piston, use a small brush to remove all traces of grease and carbon from the gap, then wipe away the remainder with a clean rag. Clean all the pistons in the same way.

33 Check the mating surfaces of the cylinder block and the cylinder head for nicks, deep scratches and other damage (refer to the note in paragraph 29). If slight, they may be removed carefully with a file, but if excessive, machining may be the only alternative to renewal.

34 If warpage of the cylinder head gasket surface is suspected, use a straight-edge to check it for distortion. Refer to Part D of this Chapter if necessary.

35 Ensure that the cylinder head bolt holes in the crankcase are clean and free of oil. Syringe or soak up any oil left in the bolt holes. This is most important in order that the correct bolt tightening torque can be applied, and to prevent the possibility of the block being cracked by hydraulic pressure when the bolts are tightened.

Refitting

36 Make sure the timing is still set at 50° BTDC (see Section 3). This will eliminate any risk of piston-to-valve contact as the cylinder head is refitted.

37 To guide the cylinder head into position, screw two long studs (or old cylinder head bolts with the heads cut off, and slots cut in the ends to enable the bolts to be unscrewed) into the end cylinder head bolt locations on the manifold side of the cylinder block.

38 Ensure that the cylinder head locating dowels are in place in the cylinder block, then fit the new cylinder head gasket over the dowels **(see illustration)**. The gasket can only be fitted one way, with the teeth to determine the gasket thickness at the front **(see illustration 11.22)**. Take care to avoid damaging the gasket's rubber coating.

39 Lower the cylinder head into position on the gasket, ensuring that it engages correctly over the guide studs and dowels.

40 Fit the new cylinder head bolts to the remaining bolt locations and screw them in as far as possible by hand.

41 Unscrew the two guide studs from the cylinder block, then screw in the two remaining new cylinder head bolts as far as possible by hand.

42 Working in the sequence shown **(see illustration)**, tighten the cylinder head bolts to the specified torques.

43 Again working in the sequence shown, tighten all the cylinder head bolts through the specified Stages as shown in the specifications at the beginning of this Chapter.

11.38 Locate the new cylinder head gasket over the dowels correctly

44 The last Stages involve tightening the bolts through an angle, rather than to a torque. Each bolt in sequence must be rotated through the specified angle – special angle gauges are available from tool outlets. As a guide, a 180° angle is equivalent to a half-turn, and this is easily judged by assessing the start and end positions of the socket handle or torque wrench.

45 The remainder of the refitting procedure is a reversal of the removal procedure, bearing in mind the following points:

a) Refit the timing chain with reference to Section 7.
b) Refit the camshafts and hydraulic rockers with reference to Section 9.
c) Refit the fuel injectors with reference to Chapter 4B.
d) Reconnect the exhaust manifold with reference to Section 20.
e) Refit the cylinder head cover with reference to Section 4.
f) Refit the alternator with reference to Section 5A.
g) Refit the air cleaner assembly with reference to Chapter 4B.
h) Refill the cooling system with reference to Chapter 1B.
i) Check and if necessary top-up the engine oil level and power steering fluid level as described in Weekly checks.
j) Before starting the engine, read through the section on engine restarting after overhaul, at the end of Chapter 2D.

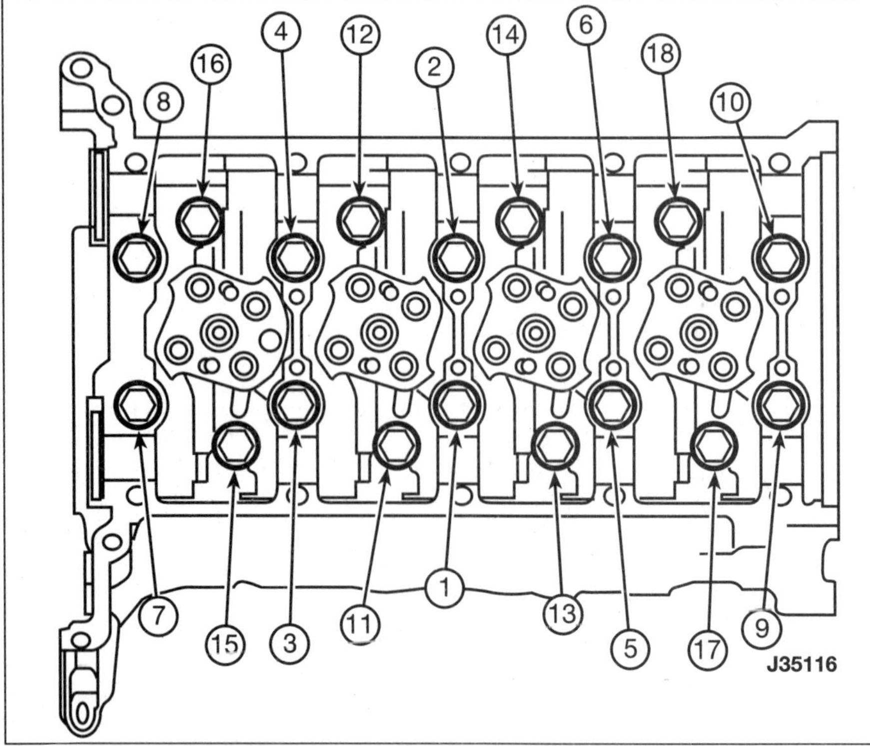

11.42 Tightening sequence for the cylinder head bolts

12 Sump – removal and refitting

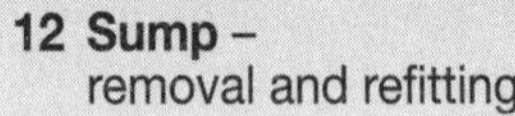

Removal

1 Apply the handbrake, then jack up the front of the car and support it on axle stands (see *Jacking and vehicle support*). Remove the engine undershield.

2 Drain the engine oil, then clean and refit the engine oil drain plug. Inspect the seal for damage, fit a new drain plug and seal if required. Tighten the drain plug to the specified torque wrench setting. Although not strictly necessary as part of the dismantling procedure, owners are advised to remove and discard the oil filter, so that it can be renewed with the oil. Refer to Chapter 1B if necessary.

3 A conventional sump gasket is not used, and sealant is used instead.

4 Progressively unscrew the sump retaining bolts and nuts, break the joint by striking the sump with the palm of the hand, then lower the sump away, turning it as necessary.

5 Unfortunately, the use of sealant can make removal of the sump more difficult. If care is taken not to damage the surfaces, the sealant can be cut around using a scraper or a sharp knife. On no account lever between the mating faces, as this will almost certainly damage them, resulting in leaks when finished.

If the sump is stuck, remove the drain plug, then use a sturdy screwdriver (wrapped in some rag or card to protect the drain plug threads) in the drain plug hole as a prising tool.

Refitting

6 On reassembly, thoroughly clean and degrease the mating surfaces of the cylinder block/crankcase and sump, removing all traces of sealant, then use a clean rag to wipe out the sump and the engine's interior.

7 If the studs have been removed, they must be refitted before the sump is offered up, to ensure that it is aligned correctly. If this is not

12.8 Apply a 3 mm bead of sealant (arrowed) to the lower casing

done, some of the sealant may enter the blind holes for the sump bolts, preventing the bolts from being fully fitted.

8 Apply a 3 mm bead of silicone sealant (Ford part number WSE-M4G323-A4, or equivalent) to the sump flange, making sure the bead is around the inside edge of the bolt holes **(see illustration)**. **Note:** *The sump must be refitted within 5 minutes of applying the sealant.*

9 Fit the sump over the studs, and insert the sump bolts and nuts, tightening them by hand only at this stage.

10 Tighten all the bolts and nuts in the sequence shown **(see illustration)**.

11 Lower the car to the ground, and refill the engine with oil. If removed, fit a new oil filter with reference to Chapter 1B.

13 Oil pump – removal and refitting

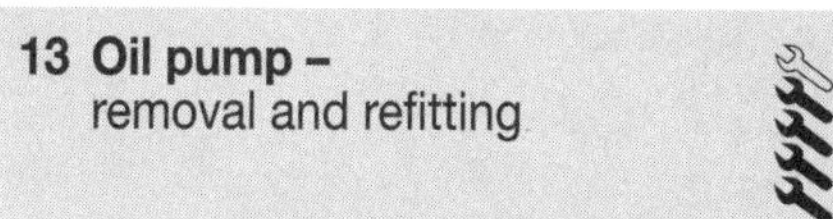

Note: *The following procedure is for removing and refitting of the oil pump. If the oil pump drive chain or tensioner requires renewing, the engine timing chain will need to be removed (see Section 7).*

Removal

1 Remove the sump as described in Section 12.

2 Carefully pull on the oil pump drive chain, to push the oil out of the chain tensioner.

3 Ford special tool (303-705) is used to align the oil pump sprocket; bolt the tool/plate to the sump flange so that it sits flush with oil pump drive sprocket **(see illustration)**.

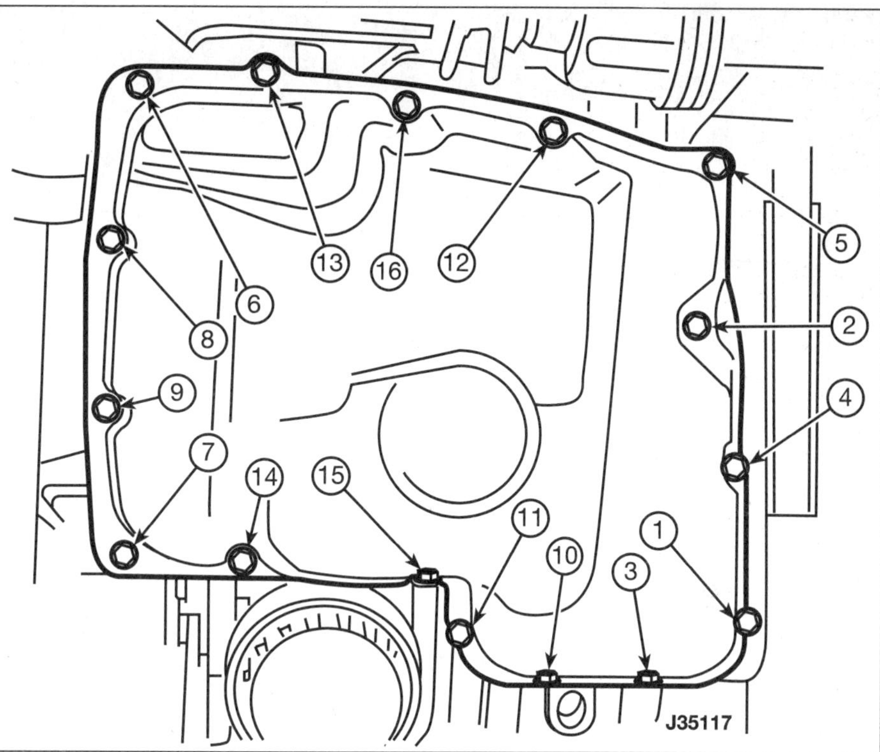

12.10 Tightening sequence for the sump retaining bolts

4 Undo the retaining bolts and remove the pick-up pipe from the oil pump **(see illustration)**.

5 Undo the retaining bolts and remove the oil pump from the lower crankcase, withdraw the chain from the sprocket on removal.

Refitting

6 Refit the oil pump to the lower crankcase, installing the drive chain to the sprocket on the oil pump. Only finger-tighten the oil pump retaining bolts at this stage.

7 Slide the oil pump until the drive sprocket sits flush with the special tool, as aligned on removal **(see illustration 13.3)**. With the oil pump in position, tighten the retaining bolts to the specified torque setting.

Caution: The oil pump sprocket and crankshaft sprocket must be kept in line with each other, so that the chain runs straight. Use Ford's special tool or a DTI gauge to make sure they are aligned correctly.

8 Ensuring that the alignment of the pump is correct, undo the retaining bolts and remove the special tool from the sump flange.

9 Refit the pick-up pipe to the oil pump.

10 Refit the sump with reference to Section 12.

14 Oil pressure warning light switch – removal and refitting

Removal

1 The switch is screwed into the upper part of the oil filter housing **(see illustration)**.

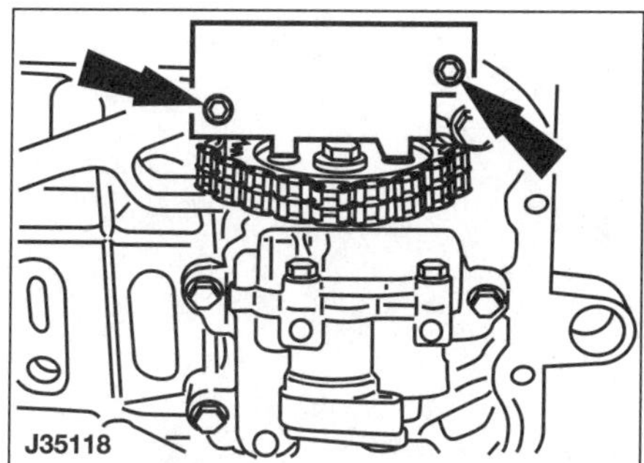

13.3 Aligning the oil pump sprocket using a plate bolted to the lower crankcase

13.4 Removing the oil pick-up pipe from the oil pump

14.1 The oil pressure switch (arrowed) is screwed into the oil filter housing

15.1 The oil cooler (arrowed) is mounted next to the oil filter

2 To improve access to the switch, it may be necessary to apply the handbrake, then jack up the front of the car and support it on axle stands (see *Jacking and vehicle support*). Remove the engine undershield.

3 Unplug the wiring from the switch and unscrew it from the filter housing; be prepared for some oil loss.

Refitting

4 Refitting is the reverse of the removal procedure; apply a thin smear of suitable sealant to the switch threads, and tighten it securely.

5 Check the engine oil level and top-up as necessary (see *Weekly checks*).

6 Check for correct warning light operation, and for signs of oil leaks, once the engine has been restarted and warmed-up to normal operating temperature.

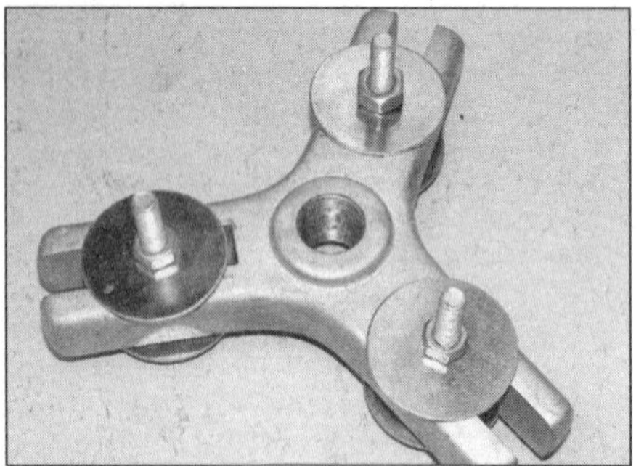

16.2a Tool for removing the oil seal, using a three-legged puller and three bolts . . .

16.2c . . . and rotate the seal anti-clockwise to remove

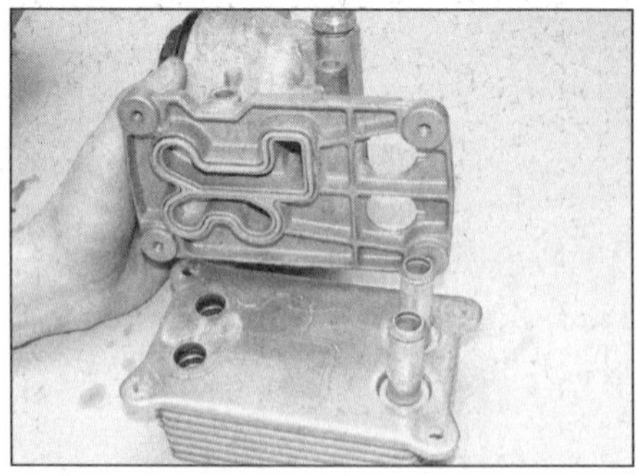

15.4 Unscrew the four bolts and withdraw the oil cooler from the oil filter housing (shown removed for clarity)

15 Oil cooler – removal and refitting

Note: *New sealing rings will be required on refitting.*

Removal

1 The oil cooler is mounted next to the oil filter on the front of the cylinder block **(see illustration)**. Access to the oil cooler is best obtained from below – apply the handbrake, then jack up the front of the car and support it on axle stands (see *Jacking and vehicle support*). Remove the engine undershield.

2 Position a container beneath the oil filter to catch escaping oil and coolant.

3 Clamp the oil cooler coolant hoses to minimise spillage, then remove the clips, and disconnect the hoses from the oil cooler. Be prepared for coolant spillage.

4 Unscrew the four securing bolts and withdraw the oil cooler from the oil filter housing, recover the gasket (a new gasket must be used on refitting) **(see illustration)**.

Refitting

5 Refitting is a reversal of removal, bearing in mind the following points:

a) *Use a new gasket.*
b) *Fit the oil cooler mounting bolts, and tighten them securely.*
c) *On completion, lower the car to the ground. Check and if necessary top-up the oil and coolant levels, then start the engine and check for signs of oil or coolant leakage.*

16.2b . . . insert the bolts into the recesses (arrowed) in the seal . . .

16.5a Locate the new seal over the end of the crankshaft using the locating sleeve . . .

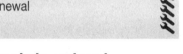

16 Crankshaft oil seals – renewal

Timing chain end seal

1 Remove the crankshaft pulley with reference to Section 6.

2 Ford technicians use a special seal removing and refitting tool (303-679), but an adequate substitute can be achieved using a three-legged puller and three bolts **(see illustrations)**. Turn the seal anti-clockwise, using the tool, to remove the crankshaft oil seal from the timing chain cover.

3 Wipe clean the oil seal contact surfaces and seating, and clean up any sharp edges or burrs which might damage the new seal as it is fitted, or which might cause the seal to leak once in place.

4 The new oil seal may be supplied fitted with a locating sleeve, which must **not** be removed prior to fitting.

5 Locate the new seal (lips facing inwards) over the end of the crankshaft, and press the seal squarely and fully into position in the cover, remove the locating sleeve **(see illustrations)**.

6 Using the special tool used on removal, turn the seal clockwise until it is located securely into the timing chain cover.

7 Refit the crankshaft pulley with reference to Section 6.

16.5b . . . then remove the locating sleeve

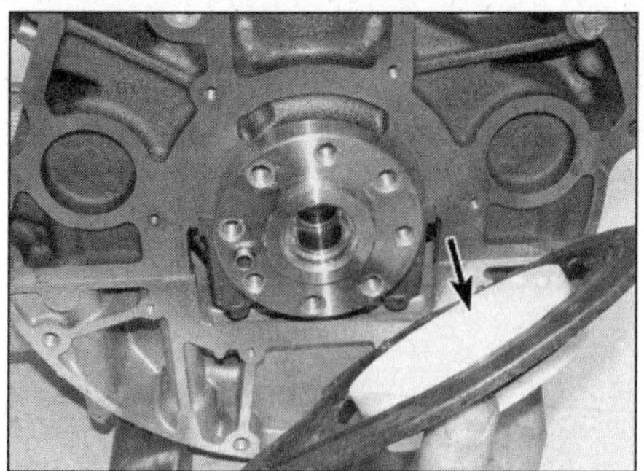

16.12 A locating/centring sleeve (arrowed) is supplied with the new oil seal

16.13a Locate the new seal over the end of the crankshaft using the locating sleeve . . .

16.13b . . . remove the locating sleeve

16.14 Use the centring sleeve to centre the oil seal carrier

16.15 With the oil seal carrier centred around the crankshaft, tighten the retaining bolts

Flywheel end seal

8 Remove the transmission as described in the appropriate Part of Chapter 7, and the clutch assembly as described in Chapter 6 on manual transmission models.

9 Unbolt the flywheel (see Section 17).

10 Unbolt and remove the oil seal carrier; the seal is renewed complete with the carrier, and is not available separately. A complete set of new carrier retaining bolts should also be obtained for reassembly.

11 Clean the end of the crankshaft, polishing off any burrs or raised edges, which may have caused the seal to fail in the first place. Clean also the seal carrier mating face on the engine block, using a suitable solvent for degreasing if necessary.

12 The new oil seal is supplied fitted with a locating sleeve, which must **not** be removed prior to fitting **(see illustration)**. It should also have a centring sleeve supplied with the seal.

13 Offer up the carrier into position, feeding the locating sleeve over the end of the crankshaft **(see illustrations)**. Insert the new seal carrier retaining bolts, and tighten them all by hand. Remove the locating sleeve.

14 Using the special centring sleeve supplied with the seal, centre the oil seal carrier around the end of the crankshaft **(see illustration)**.

15 Ensuring that the correct alignment of the carrier is maintained, work in a diagonal sequence, tightening the retaining bolts to the specified torque **(see illustration)**. Remove the seal centring sleeve.

16 The remainder of the reassembly procedure is the reverse of dismantling, referring to the relevant text for details where required. Check for signs of oil leakage when the engine is restarted.

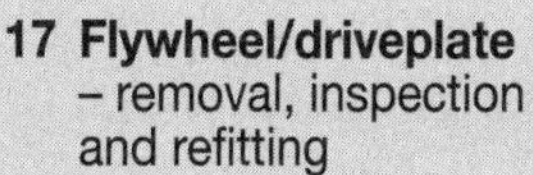

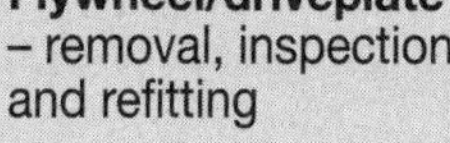

17 Flywheel/driveplate – removal, inspection and refitting

Removal

1 Remove the transmission as described in the appropriate Part of Chapter 7.

2 On manual transmission models, remove the clutch as described in Chapter 6.

3 There is a locating dowel in the end of the crankshaft, to ensure correct alignment during refitting **(see illustration)**.

4 Prevent the flywheel from turning by locking the ring gear teeth, or by bolting a strap between the flywheel and the cylinder block/ crankcase **(see illustration)**. Slacken the bolts evenly until all are free.

5 Remove each bolt in turn and ensure that new replacements are obtained for reassembly; these bolts are subjected to severe stresses and so must be renewed, regardless of their apparent condition, whenever they are disturbed.

6 Withdraw the flywheel, remembering that it is very heavy – do not drop it.

Inspection

7 Clean the flywheel to remove grease and oil. Inspect the surface for cracks, rivet grooves, burned areas and score marks. Light scoring can be removed with emery cloth. Check for cracked and broken ring gear teeth. Lay the flywheel on a flat surface and use a straight-edge to check for warpage.

8 Clean and inspect the mating surfaces of the flywheel and the crankshaft. If the crankshaft seal is leaking, renew it (see Section 16) before refitting the flywheel. If the engine has covered a high mileage, it may be worth fitting a new seal as a matter if course, given the amount of work needed to access it.

9 While the flywheel is removed, clean carefully its inboard (right-hand) face, particularly the recesses which serve as the reference points for the crankshaft speed/ position sensor. Clean the sensor's tip and check that the sensor is securely fastened.

10 Thoroughly clean the threaded bolt holes in the crankshaft, removing all traces of locking compound.

17.3 Locating dowel (arrowed) to align the flywheel when refitting

17.4 Special tool (arrowed) used to lock the flywheel, while the retaining bolts are slackened

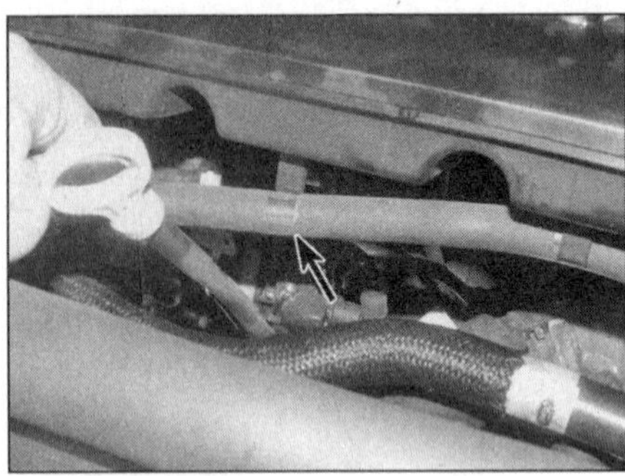

19.3 Unclip the coolant hose (arrowed) from under the inlet manifold

Refitting

11 Fit the flywheel to the crankshaft so that all bolt holes align – it will fit only one way – check the dowel is located correctly. Apply suitable locking compound to the threads of the new bolts, then insert them.

12 Lock the flywheel by the method used on dismantling. Working in a diagonal sequence, tighten the bolts to the specified Stage 1 torque wrench setting.

13 Then working in the same diagonal sequence, tighten them to the specified Stage 2 torque wrench setting.

14 Stage 3 involves tightening the bolts though an angle, rather than to a torque. Each bolt must be rotated through the specified angle – special angle gauges are available from tool outlets.

15 The remainder of reassembly is the reverse of the removal procedure, referring to the relevant text for details where required.

18 Engine/transmission mountings – inspection and renewal

Refer to Chapter 2A, Section 20.

19 Inlet manifold – removal and refitting

Removal

1 Disconnect the battery negative (earth) lead (refer to *Disconnecting the battery* at the end of this manual).

2 Remove the oil level dipstick, then unclip the engine upper plastic cover from the top of the engine.

3 Unclip the coolant hose from under the front of the inlet manifold **(see illustration).**

4 Release the securing clip and detach the turbocharger outlet pipe from the end of the inlet manifold **(see illustration)**.

5 Where applicable, detach any wiring or vacuum hoses from across the inlet manifold (releasing it from any relevant connectors and retaining clips, marking or labelling them as they are unplugged), then move the wiring loom to one side of the engine bay.

19.4 Release the securing clip (arrowed) and detach the outlet pipe from the turbocharger

6 Disconnect the fuel pressure sensor wiring plug (on the end of the fuel rail). Use the quick-release connectors to detach the fuel supply and return pipes from the high-pressure fuel pump, then unclip and move the fuel pipes clear as necessary.

7 Disconnect the exhaust gas recirculation (EGR) solenoid valve wiring plug. Remove the two flange bolts, and separate the EGR pipe from the inlet manifold.

8 Unscrew the bolts securing the inlet manifold to the cylinder head and withdraw it. Take care not to damage vulnerable components as the manifold is being removed.

Refitting

9 Refitting is the reverse of the removal procedure, noting the following points:

a) *If using a scraper or solvent to remove any traces of old gasket material and sealant from the manifold and cylinder head, be careful to ensure that you do not scratch or damage the material of either; the cylinder head is of aluminium alloy, while the manifold is a plastic moulding – any solvents used must be suitable for this application. If the gasket was leaking, have the mating surfaces checked for warpage at an automotive machine shop. While it may be possible to have the cylinder head gasket surface skimmed if necessary, to remove any distortion, the manifold must be renewed if it is found to be warped or cracked – check with special care around the mounting points.*

b) *Provided the relevant mating surfaces are clean and flat, a new gasket will be sufficient to ensure the joint is gas-tight. **Do not** use any kind of silicone-based sealant on any part of the fuel system or inlet manifold.*

c) *Fit new gaskets to the inlet ports in the manifold **(see illustration)**, then locate the manifold on the head and install the retaining bolts.*

d) *Tighten the bolts evenly to the torque listed in the Specifications at the beginning of this Chapter. Work from the centre outwards, to avoid warping the manifold.*

e) *Refit the remaining parts in the reverse order of removal – tighten all fasteners to the torque wrench settings specified.*

f) *If removed, make sure any vacuum hoses and wiring are routed correctly and the connections fitted as labelled up on removal.*

g) *When the engine is fully warmed-up, check for signs of fuel, inlet and/or vacuum leaks.*

h) *Road test the car, and check for proper operation of all disturbed components.*

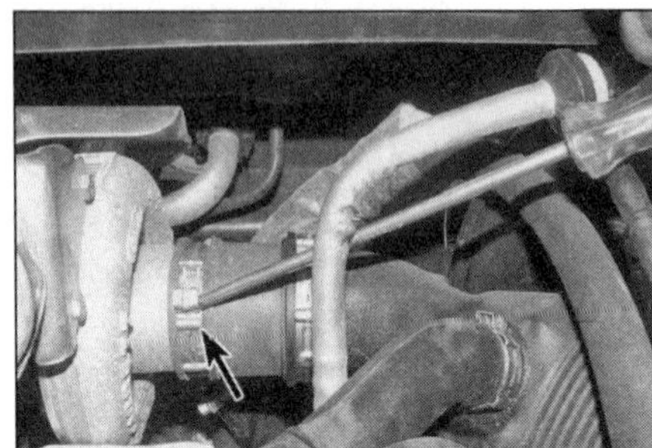

20.4 Release the securing clip (arrowed) and detach the inlet pipe from the turbocharger

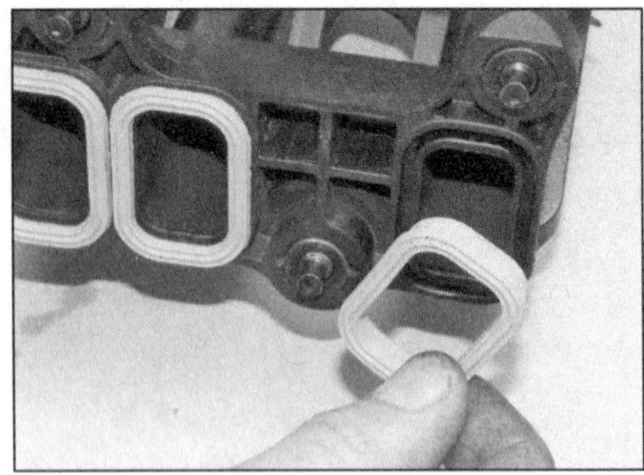

19.9 Fit new gaskets to the inlet ports in the manifold

20 Exhaust manifold – removal, inspection and refitting

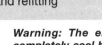

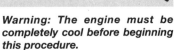

Warning: The engine must be completely cool before beginning this procedure.

Removal

Models up to July 2004

1 Disconnect the battery negative (earth) lead (refer to *Disconnecting the battery* at the end of this manual).

2 Park the car on firm, level ground, apply the handbrake, then jack up the front of the car and support it on axle stands (see *Jacking and vehicle support*). Remove the engine undershield.

3 Remove the catalytic converter as described in Chapter 4C.

4 Release the securing clip and detach the turbocharger inlet pipe from the turbocharger **(see illustration)**.

5 Release the securing clip and detach the charger air cooler inlet pipe from the turbocharger **(see illustration)**.

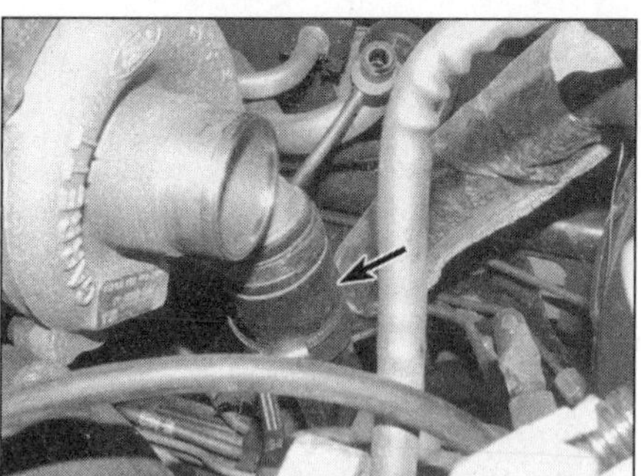
20.5 Release the securing clip and detach the charger air cooler inlet pipe (arrowed)

20.6 Undo the retaining bolts (arrowed) and disconnect the oil return tube

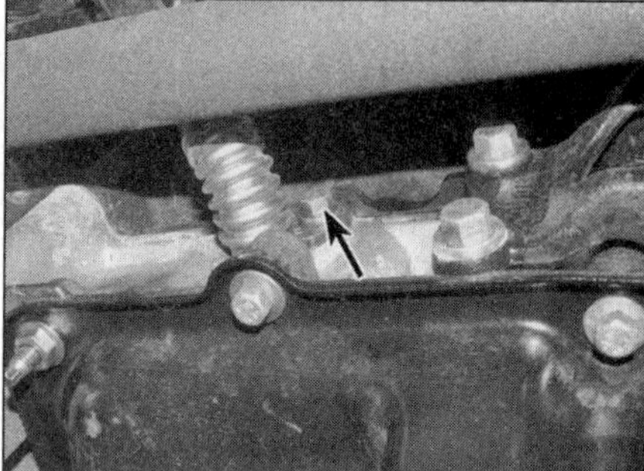
20.7 Remove the oil return tube lower retaining bolt (arrowed)

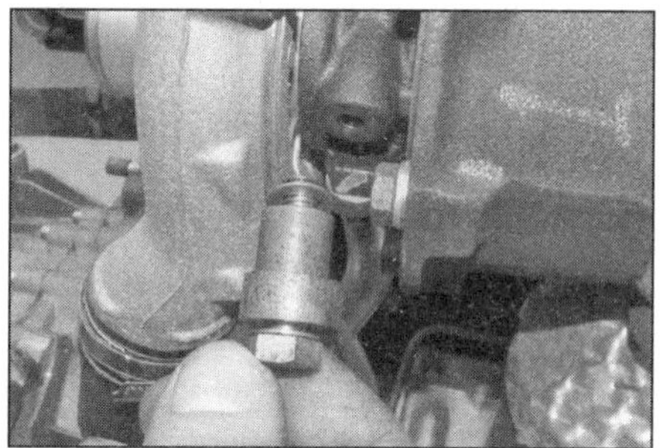
20.8 Disconnect the oil supply tube from the turbocharger (renew the washers on refitting)

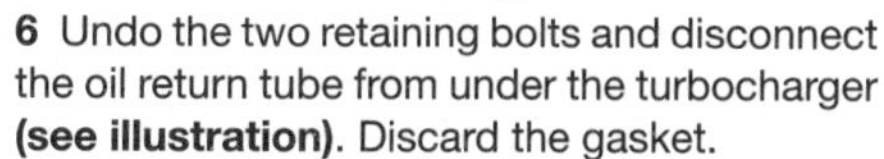

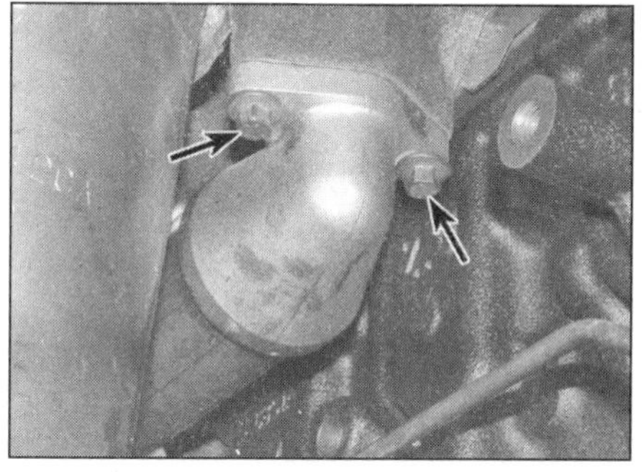
20.9 Undo the retaining bolts (arrowed) and disconnect the EGR cooler

20.10 Remove the nut and bolt (arrowed) to disconnect the EGR cooler from the exhaust manifold

6 Undo the two retaining bolts and disconnect the oil return tube from under the turbocharger **(see illustration)**. Discard the gasket.

7 Remove the oil return tube lower retaining bolt and withdraw it from the engine **(see illustration)**. Discard the O-ring.

8 Undo the retaining bolt and disconnect the oil supply tube from the turbocharger **(see illustration)**. Discard the sealing washers.

9 Undo the two retaining bolts and disconnect the EGR cooler from the exhaust manifold **(see illustration)**. Discard the gasket.

10 Slacken and remove the retaining nut and bolt to disconnect the other end of the EGR cooler from the exhaust manifold **(see illustration)**.

11 As applicable, disconnect the vacuum pipe from the vacuum diaphragm unit, or the wiring plug from the electronic actuator **(see illustration)**.

12 Undo the two retaining bolts and detach the heat shield from the top of the exhaust manifold **(see illustration)**. **Note:** *This cannot completely be removed, until the manifold is withdrawn.*

13 Slacken and remove the retaining bolts along the top of the bulkhead at the back of the engine bay, then withdraw the cowl panel brace bar. This will give more room at the rear of the engine to remove the exhaust manifold.

14 Remove the retaining nuts and bolts from the exhaust manifold. When removing the manifold with the engine in the car, additional clearance can be obtained by unscrewing the studs from the cylinder head; a female Torx-type socket will be required. Discard the nuts and studs, new ones will be required for refitting.

15 Slide the exhaust manifold/turbocharger away from the engine and withdraw the heat shield from the top of the manifold.

16 Rotate the assembly through 180° to remove it, discard the gasket. Take care not to damage vulnerable components as the manifold assembly is manoeuvred out of the engine compartment.

Models from July 2004 onwards

17 Disconnect the battery negative (earth) lead (refer to *Disconnecting the battery* at the end of this manual).

18 Pull out the engine oil dipstick, then unclip and lift off the engine top cover **(see illustration)**.

19 At the back of the engine, remove the turbocharger upper heat shield, which is secured by four screws (three on top, and one at the back). If any of the screws are in poor condition, obtain new ones for reassembly.

20 Disconnect the wiring plug from the electric vane actuator unit on the side of the turbocharger **(see illustration)**.

21 Disconnect the breather hose from the engine top cover, then release the clips and remove the air cleaner duct.

20.11 Disconnecting the vacuum pipe from the vacuum diaphragm unit

20.12 Remove the heat shield retaining bolts (arrowed)

20.18 Removing the engine top cover

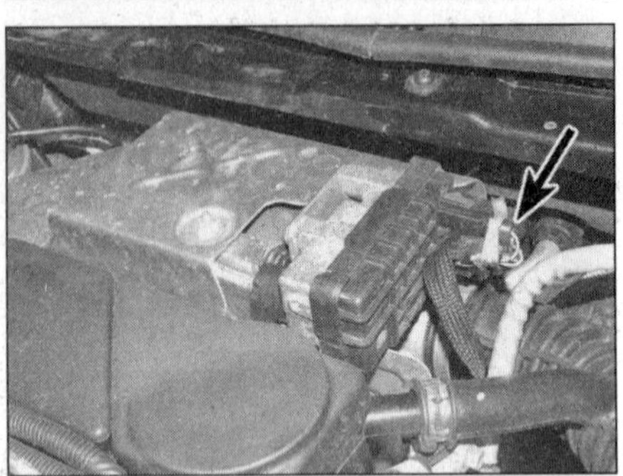

20.20 Disconnect the electric vane actuator unit wiring plug (arrowed)

22 Release the vacuum pipe at the brake vacuum pump by depressing the collar, and remove the pipe.

23 Remove the screws at the front of the windscreen cowl panels securing the metal heat shield and brace bar.

24 Park the car on firm, level ground, apply the handbrake, then jack up the front of the car and support it on axle stands (see *Jacking and vehicle support*). Remove the engine undershield.

25 Remove the catalytic converter as described in Chapter 4C.

26 Remove the alternator as described in Chapter 5A.

27 Release the clips and disconnect the intercooler hose from the turbocharger – this hose runs vertically from the turbocharger to the base of the engine.

28 Undo the two retaining bolts and disconnect the oil return tube from under the turbocharger. Discard the gasket. Remove the oil return tube lower retaining bolt and withdraw the tube from the engine. Discard the O-ring.

29 Undo the retaining bolt and disconnect the oil supply tube from the turbocharger. Note that the sealing washer cannot be removed from the pipe. If required, the pipe can be removed completely – a single bolt secures its support bracket to the back of the engine, and there is a further union bolt behind the alternator location.

30 Unscrew the two bolts from the EGR cooler support bracket (under the exhaust manifold at the turbocharger end). Unscrew the two EGR cooler flange bolts, and separate the cooler from the manifold – move it to one side.

31 Remove the retaining nuts and bolts from the exhaust manifold. When removing the manifold with the engine in the car, additional clearance can be obtained by unscrewing the studs from the cylinder head; a female Torx-type socket will be required. Discard the nuts and studs, new ones will be required for refitting.

32 Lower the car to the ground.

33 Unbolt and withdraw the heat shield from the top of the manifold.

34 Slide the exhaust manifold/turbocharger away from the engine, taking care to avoid damage to the power steering pipes, and manoeuvre it out past the brake servo.

Inspection

35 On models with an electronic vane actuator, the actuator and its bracket can be unbolted and removed from the turbocharger, but Ford state that the actuator must not be separated from its bracket. Problems may also arise if an actuator from another turbocharger is substituted – they are each calibrated to their specific units.

36 If using a scraper to remove all traces of old gasket material and carbon deposits from the manifold and cylinder head mating surfaces, be careful to ensure that you do not scratch or damage the material of either component – any solvents used must be suitable for this application. If the gasket was leaking, check the manifold and cylinder head for warpage, this may need to be done at an automotive machine shop, resurface if necessary.

Caution: When scraping, be very careful not to gouge or scratch the delicate aluminium alloy cylinder head.

37 Provided both mating surfaces are clean and flat, a new gasket will be sufficient to ensure the joint is gas-tight. Do not use any kind of exhaust sealant upstream of the catalytic converter.

Refitting

38 Refitting is the reverse of the removal procedure, noting the following points:

- *a) Fit a new manifold gasket and cylinder head studs and nuts.*
- *b) Refit the manifold, and tighten the nuts to the torque listed in the Specifications at the beginning of this Chapter.*
- *c) Fit new gaskets, O-rings and sealing washers where required.*
- *d) Ensure that the turbocharger oil supply pipe is routed so that it does not contact the turbocharger.*
- *e) Refit the catalytic converter with reference to Chapter 4C.*
- *f) When refitting the intercooler and air cleaner hoses/ducts, wipe any oil residue from inside the end fittings, to ensure that a good fit is made. Also check inside for dirt and foreign material, which could damage the turbocharger if ingested.*
- *g) Run the engine, and check for exhaust leaks.*

Chapter 2 Part D:
Engine removal and overhaul procedures

Contents

Section number

Degrees of difficulty

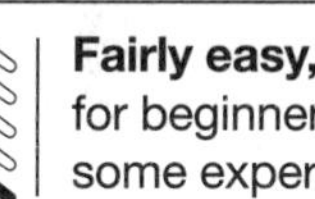

Easy, suitable for novice with little experience	**Fairly easy,** suitable for beginner with some experience	**Fairly difficult,** suitable for competent DIY mechanic	**Difficult,** suitable for experienced DIY mechanic	**Very difficult,** suitable for expert DIY or professional

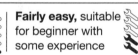

Specifications

Engine codes

Petrol engines

1.8 litre models	CGBA/B (110 PS), CDBB, CHBA/B (125 PS)
2.0 litre models	CJBA/B
2.5 litre	LCBD
3.0 litre:	
Except ST220	REBA
ST220	MEBA

Diesel engines

2.0 litre:	
90 PS	–
115 PS	HJBA, HJBB and HJBC
130 PS	FMBA, FMBB and N7BA
2.2 litre 155 PS	QJBA and QJBB

4-cylinder petrol engines

Note: *Because of the fine tolerances in the bearing shells, no service operations are permitted on the cylinder block/crank assembly. In the event of any failure, the complete cylinder block, pistons and crank assembly must be renewed as a unit.*

Valve lift:	**Inlet**	**Exhaust**
1.8 litre:		
CGBA/B	7.4 mm	7.7 mm
CDBB, CHBA/B	8.5 mm	7.7 mm
2.0 litre	8.8 mm	7.7 mm
Valve stem-to-guide clearance (engine cold)	0.22 to 0.28 mm	0.27 to 0.33 mm
Valve stem diameter	5.465 to 5.480 mm	5.470 to 5.485 mm

V6 engines

Note: *On V6 engines, Ford say that the cylinder bores cannot be rebored or honed, the crankshaft cannot be reground, the main bearings cannot be renewed, and the lower crankcase cannot be re-used once removed. No torque is quoted at the time of writing for the main or big-end bearings.*

Cylinder head		
Maximum permissible gasket surface distortion	0.08 mm	
Valve seat angle	45.5°	
Valve seat included angle	90°	
Valve seat width, inlet	1.1 to 1.4 mm	
Valve seat width, exhaust	1.4 to 1.7 mm	
Valves	**Inlet**	**Exhaust**
Valve head diameter	32.0 mm	26.0 mm
Valve stem-to-guide clearance	0.020 to 0.069 mm	0.045 to 0.094 mm

Diesel engines

Valves – general	**Inlet**	**Exhaust**
Valve stem-to-guide clearance	0.045 mm	0.055 mm
Cylinder block		
Cylinder bore diameter:		
Class 1	86.000 to 86.010 mm	
Class 2	86.010 to 86.020 mm	
Class 3	86.020 to 86.030 mm	
Pistons and piston rings		
Piston diameter:		
Class A	85.94 to 85.95 mm	
Class B	85.95 to 85.96 mm	
Class C	85.96 to 85.97 mm	
Piston-to-cylinder bore clearance	0.05 to 0.07 mm	
Piston ring end gaps*:		
Top compression ring	0.25 to 0.50 mm	
Second compression ring	0.50 to 0.75 mm	
Oil scraper ring	0.25 to 0.50 mm	

***Note:** *Piston ring end gaps should be offset at 120° to one another when fitted*

Gudgeon pin	
Length	66.700 mm
Diameter	30.000 mm
Clearance in piston	0.002 to 0.012 mm
Small-end bore (inside connecting rod) diameter	30.010 to 30.018 mm
Crankshaft and bearings	
Big-end bearing shell standard inside diameter – installed	56.004 to 56.032 mm
Big-end bearing shell running clearance	0.034 mm to 0.100 mm
Big-end bearing journal standard diameter	52.980 to 53.000 mm
Big-end bearing endfloat	0.100 to 0.320 mm
Big-end bore (inside connecting rod) diameter	55.996 to 56.016 mm
Crankshaft endfloat	0.090 to 0.305 mm
Main bearing journals standard diameter:	
1 to 4	64.950 to 64.970 mm
5	69.950 to 69.970 mm
Main bearing shells – installed:	
1 to 4 inside diameter	65.003 to 65.030 mm
5 inside diameter	70.004 to 70.033 mm
Main bearing journal-to-shells – running clearance	0.034 to 0.100 mm
1 to 4	0.033 to 0.080 mm
5	0.034 to 0.083 mm

Torque wrench settings

Refer to Chapter 2A , 2B or 2C Specifications

1 General information and precautions

How to use this Chapter

This Part of Chapter 2 is devoted to engine/transmission removal and refitting, to those repair procedures requiring the removal of the engine/transmission from the car, and to the overhaul of engine components. It includes only the Specifications relevant to those procedures. Refer to Part A, B or C (depending on engine type) for additional Specifications and for all torque wrench settings.

General Information

The information ranges from advice concerning preparation for an overhaul and the purchase of new parts, to detailed step-by-step procedures covering removal and installation of internal engine components and the inspection of parts.

The following Sections have been written based on the assumption that the engine has been removed from the car. For information concerning in-car engine repair, as well as removal and installation of the external components necessary for the overhaul, see Part A, B or C of this Chapter.

When overhauling the engine, it is essential to establish first exactly what parts are available. At the time of writing, very few under- or oversized components are available for engine reconditioning. In many cases, it would appear that the easiest and most economically-sensible course of action is to use an exchange unit.

Caution: Although it is possible to remove the pistons and crankshaft on 4-cylinder petrol engines, it is not possible to carry out any work on the cylinder block. Because of the fine tolerances in the bearing shells, no service operations are permitted on the cylinder block/crank assembly. In the event of any failure, the complete cylinder block, pistons and crank assembly must be renewed as a unit.

Caution: Although it is possible to remove the pistons and crankshaft on the V6 petrol engine, at the time of writing it is not possible to carry out any work on the cylinder block. Ford say that the cylinder bores cannot be rebored or honed, the crankshaft cannot be reground, the main bearings cannot be renewed, and the lower crankcase cannot be re-used once removed. Ford no longer quote tightening torques for the main and big-end bearings.

2 Engine overhaul – general information

It's not always easy to determine when, or if, an engine should be completely overhauled, as a number of factors must be considered.

High mileage is not necessarily an indication that an overhaul is needed, while low mileage doesn't preclude the need for an overhaul. Frequency of servicing is probably the most important consideration. An engine that's had regular and frequent oil and filter changes, as well as other required maintenance, will most likely give many thousands of miles of reliable service. Conversely, a neglected engine may require an overhaul very early in its life.

Excessive oil consumption is an indication that piston rings, valve seals and/or valve guides are in need of attention. Make sure that oil leaks aren't responsible before deciding that the rings and/or guides are worn. Perform a cylinder compression check (Part A, B or C of this Chapter) to determine the extent of the work required.

Loss of power, rough running, knocking or metallic engine noises, excessive valve train noise and high fuel consumption rates may also point to the need for an overhaul, especially if they're all present at the same time. If a full service doesn't remedy the situation, major mechanical work is the only solution.

An engine overhaul involves restoring all internal parts to the specification of a new engine. **Note:** *Always check first what parts are available before planning any overhaul operation – refer to Section 1. Ford dealers, or a good engine reconditioning specialist/ automotive parts supplier may be able to suggest alternatives which will enable you to overcome the lack of parts.*

During an overhaul, it is usual to renew the piston rings, and to rebore and/or hone the cylinder bores; where the rebore is done by an automotive machine shop, new oversize pistons and rings will also be installed – all these operations, of course, assume the availability of suitable parts. The main and big-end bearings are generally renewed and, if necessary, the crankshaft may be reground to restore the journals. However, this work is only permitted by Ford on the diesel engines in the Mondeo range.

Generally, the valves are serviced as well during an overhaul, since they're usually in less-than-perfect condition at this point. While the engine is being overhauled, other components, such as the starter and alternator, can be renewed as well, or rebuilt, if the necessary parts can be found. The end result should be an as-new engine that will give many trouble-free miles. **Note:** *Critical cooling system components such as the hoses, drivebelt, thermostat and water pump MUST have new parts when an engine is overhauled. The radiator should be checked carefully, to ensure that it isn't clogged or leaking (see Chapter 3). Also, as a general rule, the oil pump should be renewed when an engine is rebuilt.*

Before beginning the engine overhaul, read through the entire procedure to familiarise yourself with the scope and requirements of the job. Overhauling an engine isn't difficult, but it is time-consuming. Plan on the car being off the road for a minimum of two weeks, especially if parts must be taken to an automotive machine shop for repair or reconditioning. Check on availability of parts, and make sure that any necessary special tools and equipment are obtained in advance. Most work can be done with typical hand tools, although a number of precision measuring tools are required for inspecting parts to determine if they must be renewed. Often, an automotive machine shop will handle the inspection of parts, and will offer advice concerning reconditioning and renewal. **Note:** *Always wait until the engine has been completely dismantled, and all components, especially the cylinder block/ crankcase, have been inspected, before deciding what service and repair operations must be performed by an automotive machine shop. Since the block's condition will be the major factor to consider when determining whether to overhaul the original engine or buy a rebuilt one, never purchase parts or have machine work done on other components until the cylinder block/crankcase has been thoroughly inspected.* As a general rule, time is the primary cost of an overhaul, so it doesn't pay to install worn or sub-standard parts.

As a final note, to ensure maximum life and minimum trouble from a rebuilt engine, everything must be assembled with care, in a spotlessly-clean environment.

3 Engine/transmission removal – methods and precautions

If you've decided that an engine must be removed for overhaul or major repair work, several preliminary steps should be taken.

Locating a suitable place to work is extremely important. Adequate work space, along with storage space for the car, will be needed. If a workshop or garage isn't available, at the very least, a flat, level, clean work surface made of concrete or asphalt is required.

Cleaning the engine compartment and engine/transmission before beginning the removal procedure will help keep tools clean and organised.

The engine can be withdrawn by removing it complete with the transmission; Ford recommend that the car's body is raised and supported securely, sufficiently high that the engine/transmission can be unbolted as a single unit and lowered to the ground; the engine/transmission unit can then be withdrawn from under the car and separated. An engine hoist or A-frame will therefore be necessary. Make sure the equipment is rated in excess of the combined weight of the engine and transmission. Safety is of primary importance, considering the potential hazards involved in removing the engine/transmission from the car.

If this is the first time you have removed an engine, a helper should ideally be available. Advice and aid from someone more experienced would also be helpful. There are many instances when one person cannot simultaneously perform all of the operations required when removing the engine/ transmission from the car. Safety is of primary importance, considering the potential hazards involved in this kind of operation. A second person should always be in attendance to offer help in any emergency.

Plan the operation ahead of time. Arrange for, or obtain, all of the tools and equipment you'll need prior to beginning the job. Some of the equipment necessary to perform engine/ transmission removal and installation safely and with relative ease, and which may have to be hired or borrowed, includes (in addition to the engine hoist) a heavy-duty trolley jack, a strong pair of axle stands, some wooden blocks, and an engine dolly (a low, wheeled

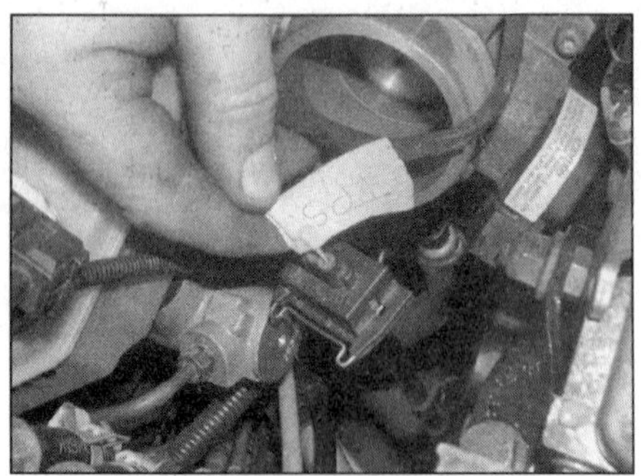

4.5 Label the wiring and hoses as they are disconnected (TPS – Throttle Position Sensor)

platform capable of taking the weight of the engine/transmission, so that it can be moved easily when on the ground). A complete set of spanners and sockets (as described in the rear of this manual) will obviously be needed, together with plenty of rags and cleaning solvent for mopping-up spilled oil, coolant and fuel. If the hoist is to be hired, make sure that you arrange for it in advance, and perform all of the operations possible without it beforehand. This will save you money and time.

Plan for the car to be out of use for quite a while. A machine shop will be required to perform some of the work which the do-it-yourselfer can't accomplish without special equipment. These establishments often have a busy schedule, so it would be a good idea to consult them before removing the engine, to accurately estimate the amount of time required to rebuild or repair components that may need work.

When removing the engine from the car, be methodical about the disconnection of external components. Labelling cables and hoses as they are removed will greatly assist the refitting process.

Always be extremely careful when removing and installing the engine/transmission. Serious injury can result from careless actions. If help is required, it is better to wait until it is available rather than risk personal injury and/or damage to components by continuing alone. By planning ahead and taking your time, the job (although a major task) can be accomplished successfully and without incident.

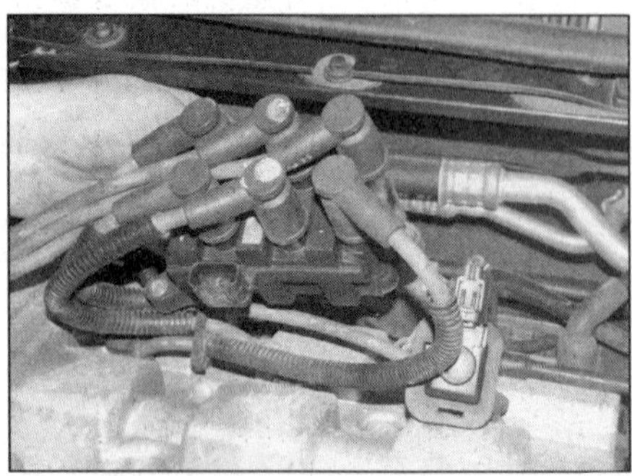

4.11 Remove the ignition coil from the rear camshaft cover (V6 models)

4.7 Unclip the plastic covers and slacken the top mounting retaining nuts

4 Engine/transmission – removal, separation and refitting

Warning: Petrol is extremely flammable, so take extra precautions when disconnecting any part of the fuel system. Don't smoke, or allow naked flames or bare light bulbs in or near the work area, and don't work in a garage where a natural gas appliance (such as a clothes dryer or water heater) is installed. If you spill petrol on your skin, rinse it off immediately. Have a fire extinguisher rated for petrol fires handy, and know how to use it.

Note: *Read through the entire Section, as well as reading the advice in the preceding Section, before beginning this procedure. The engine and transmission are removed as a unit, lowered to the ground and removed from underneath, then separated outside the car.*

Removal

1 Park the car on firm, level ground, apply the handbrake firmly, and slacken the nuts securing both front roadwheels.

2 Place protective covers on the wings and engine compartment front crossmember. For better access to the engine for the engine hoist, remove the bonnet as described in Chapter 11.

3 Disconnect the battery negative (earth) lead (refer to *Disconnecting the battery* at the end of this manual). For better access, the battery may be removed completely (see Chapter 5A).

4.15 Undo the retaining bolt and disconnect the engine wiring loom block connector (diesel models)

4 Depressurise the fuel system pressure (see the relevant Part of Chapter 4).

5 Whenever you disconnect any vacuum lines, coolant and emissions hoses, wiring loom connectors, earth straps and fuel lines as part of the following procedure, always label them clearly, so that they can be correctly reassembled **(see illustration)**.

Whenever any wiring is disconnected, mark or label it, to ensure correct reconnection – vacuum hoses and pipes should be similarly marked. Masking tape and/or a touch-up paint applicator work well for marking items. Take digital photos, or sketch the locations of components and brackets.

6 Where applicable, unclip the breather hose from the engine upper plastic cover, then unclip/unbolt the cover from the top of the engine.

7 Unclip the plastic covers from the top of the suspension struts on both sides of the car, then slacken the three top mounting retaining nuts (**not** the centre nut) by approximately four turns each **(see illustration)**.

8 Drain the cooling system as described in the relevant Part of Chapter 1.

9 Remove the air cleaner assembly and inlet ducting with reference to the relevant part of Chapter 4.

10 On diesel models, undo the retaining clips and remove the turbocharger air inlet hose with reference to Chapter 4B.

11 On V6 petrol engines, undo the retaining bolts and remove the ignition coil from the rear camshaft cover, also unclip the evaporative emissions (EVAP) solenoid valve from the retaining bracket **(see illustration)**.

12 Disconnect the accelerator cable from the throttle linkage as described in Chapter 4A – where fitted, also disconnect the cruise control actuator cable (see Chapter 12). Secure the cable(s) clear of the engine/transmission.

13 Label all the vacuum hoses, wiring connections, and coolant hoses to ensure correct refitment. Follow the engine/transmission hoses and wiring loom unclipping them from any retaining clips, then disconnect them. Pieces of masking tape with numbers or letters written on them work well. If there is a possibility of confusion regarding connections or routing, make a sketch or notes.

14 On V6 petrol models, unbolt the engine wiring harness earth cable from the left-hand inner wing panel, behind the headlight. The engine wiring harness must now be disconnected from the powertrain control module (PCM). It will be necessary to drill out the rivets in order to lift the cover from the module. Unscrew the bolt and disconnect the multiplug. To prevent entry of dust and dirt, cover the multiplug and PCM with polythene sheeting or place it in a polythene bag. Withdraw the wiring harness onto the engine.

15 On diesel models, undo the retaining bolt and disconnect the engine wiring loom block connector from the left-hand front suspension turret, in front of the brake master cylinder **(see illustration)**.

16 On 4-cylinder petrol models, detach the power steering line bracket from the camshaft cover. On V6 petrol models, disconnect the power steering line from by the right-hand engine mounting. On diesel models, detach the power steering line brackets from the transmission end of the cylinder head.

17 Undo the retaining bolts and withdraw the coolant expansion tank from the inner wing panel.

18 With the fuel pressure released (see paragraph 4), disconnect the fuel supply line connection to the engine or high-pressure pump (see Chapter 4A or 4B). Plug or cap all open fittings **(see illustration)**.

19 Remove the cooling fan motor and shroud as described in Chapter 3.

20 On manual transmission models, mark their positions, then disconnect the gearchange linkage cables from the transmission (see Chapter 7A for details). Also prise out the spring clip and disconnect the clutch hydraulic pipe (see Chapter 6), release the pipe from the bracket and plug the pipe opening to prevent dirt ingress and fluid loss.

21 On automatic transmission models, disconnect the selector cable, wiring connectors and the fluid cooler pipe(s) from the transmission with reference to Chapter 7B.

22 On petrol models, disconnect the wiring connector(s) for the oxygen sensor(s).

23 Unbolt the engine/transmission-to-body earth lead(s) from the transmission's top surface. Disconnect the wiring connector from the reversing light switch in the top of the transmission and the wiring connector(s) from the vehicle speed sensor(s) – refer to Chapter 7A or 7B.

24 Raise the car and support it securely on axle stands, there must be sufficient clearance below the car for the engine/transmission to be lowered and removed. Remove both front roadwheels and, where fitted, the engine undertray. If the engine is to be dismantled, drain the engine oil and remove the oil filter (see the relevant Part of Chapter 1). Also drain the transmission as described in the relevant Part of Chapter 7.

25 Remove the front section of the exhaust system with reference to Chapter 4A or 4B.

26 Remove the front subframe with reference to Chapter 10.

27 Remove the driveshafts with reference to Chapter 8. Unbolt the right-hand driveshaft centre bearing bracket from the rear of the cylinder block.

28 Remove the auxiliary drivebelt (see the relevant Part of Chapter 1).

29 On air conditioning models, unplug the compressor's electrical connector, and unbolt the compressor from the engine. Secure it as far as possible (**without** disconnecting the system's hoses) clear of the engine/transmission.

4.18 Note colour-coding on the fuel supply and return lines when disconnecting

30 Unbolt the power steering pump (see Chapter 10); secure it as far as possible (without disconnecting the system's hoses – where possible) clear of the engine/transmission.

31 The engine/transmission unit should now be hanging on the right- and left-hand mountings only, with all components which connect it to the rest of the car disconnected or removed and secured well clear of the unit. Make a final check that this is the case, then ensure that the body is securely supported, high enough to permit the withdrawal of the engine/transmission unit from underneath; allow for the height of the engine lift, if used.

32 Attach lifting chains/straps to the lifting eyes provided on the cylinder head and take the weight of the engine/transmission unit **(see illustration)**. Unscrew the nuts and bolts securing the right-hand mounting bracket and left-hand bracket to the car inner wing panels and remove the mountings from the engine/transmission unit (see the relevant Part of Chapter 2).

33 If available, a low trolley should be placed under the engine/transmission assembly, to facilitate its easy removal from under the car. Alternatively, if the engine is lowered onto some old carpet or card, this will protect it, and make it easier to drag around as necessary.

34 As a precaution against possible damage when removing (and refitting) the engine, attach some thick card across the rear face of the radiator.

35 Make a final check to ensure that nothing else remains connected to the engine/transmission.

4.32 Attach the chains/straps to the lifting eyes on the cylinder head

36 Lower the engine/transmission to the ground, making sure nothing is trapped, taking great care not to damage the radiator assembly. Enlist the help of an assistant during this procedure, as it may be necessary to tilt the assembly slightly to clear the underbody. Great care must be taken to ensure that no components are trapped and damage during the removal procedure.

37 Detach the hoist – be prepared to steady the engine when it touches down, to stop it toppling over. Withdraw the engine/transmission from under the car.

Separation

38 With the engine/transmission assembly removed, support the assembly on suitable blocks of wood, on a work bench (or failing that, on a clean area of the workshop floor).

39 On automatic transmission models, remove the blanking plug to access the torque converter retaining nuts/bolts. Turn the crankshaft to align each one in turn through the access hole – see Chapter 7B.

40 Ensure that engine and transmission are adequately supported, then slacken and remove the remaining bolts securing the transmission housing to the engine. Note the correct fitted positions of each bolt (and relevant brackets) as they are removed, to use as a reference on refitting. Refer to the relevant Part of Chapter 7, when separating the transmission from the engine.

41 Carefully withdraw the transmission from the engine, ensuring that, on manual transmission models, the weight of the transmission is not allowed to hang on the input shaft while it is engaged with the clutch friction disc – see Chapter 7A. On automatic models, make sure the torque converter withdraws from the engine with the transmission – see Chapter 7B.

42 While the engine/transmission is removed, check the mountings; renew them if they are worn or damaged. Similarly, check the condition of all coolant and vacuum hoses and pipes (see the relevant Part of Chapter 1); components that are normally hidden can now be checked properly, and should be renewed if there is any doubt at all about their condition. On manual transmission models, take the opportunity to overhaul the clutch components (see Chapter 6). It is regarded by many as good working practice to renew the clutch assembly as a matter of course, whenever major engine overhaul work is carried out. Check also the condition of all components (such as the transmission oil seals) disturbed on removal, and renew any that are damaged or worn.

Refitting

43 Refitting is the reverse of the removal procedure, noting the following points.

a) *Tighten all fasteners to the torque wrench settings given; where settings are not quoted in the Specifications Sections of Chapter 2A, 2B or 2C, refer to the*

Specifications Section of the relevant Chapter of this manual.

b) In addition to the points noted in paragraph 42 above, always renew any circlips and self-locking nuts disturbed on removal.

c) Where wiring, etc, was secured by cable-ties which had to be cut on removal, ensure that it is secured with new ties on refitting.

d) With all overhaul operations completed, refit the transmission to the engine as described in Chapter 7A or 7B.

e) Manoeuvre the engine/transmission unit under the car, attach the hoist, and lift the unit into position until the right- and left-hand mountings can be reassembled; tighten the (new) nuts only lightly at this stage. Do not yet release the hoist; the weight of the engine/transmission unit must not be taken by the mountings until all are correctly aligned.

f) Refit, and where applicable adjust, all engine-related components and systems with reference to the Chapters concerned.

g) Add coolant, engine oil and transmission fluids as needed (see Weekly checks and the relevant Part of Chapter 1).

h) Run the engine, and check for proper operation and the absence of leaks. Shut off the engine, and recheck the fluid levels.

Note: *Remember that, since the front suspension subframe and steering gear have been disturbed, the wheel alignment and steering angles must be checked fully and carefully as soon as possible, with any necessary adjustments being made. This operation is best carried out by an experienced mechanic, using proper checking equipment; the car should therefore be taken to a Ford dealer or similarly-qualified person for attention.*

5 Engine overhaul – dismantling sequence

Caution: Refer to the Cautions in Section 1 on petrol models.

1 It is much easier to dismantle and work on the engine if it is mounted on a portable engine stand. These stands can often be hired from a tool hire shop. Before the engine is mounted on a stand, the flywheel/driveplate should be removed so that the stand bolts can be tightened into the end of the cylinder block/crankcase.

2 If a stand is not available, it is possible to dismantle the engine with it mounted on blocks, on a sturdy workbench or on the floor. Be extra-careful not to tip or drop the engine when working without a stand.

3 If you are going to obtain a reconditioned engine, all external components must be removed first, to be transferred to the new engine (just as they will if you are doing a complete engine overhaul yourself). **Note:** *When removing the external components from the engine, pay close attention to details that may be helpful or important during refitting. Note the fitted position of gaskets, seals, spacers, pins, washers, bolts and other small items. These external components include the following:*

a) Alternator, starter and mounting brackets (Chapter 5A).

b) The ignition system, HT leads (or ignition coils) and spark plugs, etc – petrol models (Chapters 1A and 5B).

c) The glow plug/preheating system components – diesel models (see Chapter 5C).

d) Cooling system/thermostat housings (Chapter 3).

e) Oil level dipstick and dipstick tube.

f) All fuel injection system components (Chapter 4A – petrol models, 4B – diesel models).

g) Brake vacuum pump – diesel models (Chapter 9).

h) All electrical switches and sensors and engine wiring harness (relevant Parts of Chapters 4 and 5).

i) Inlet and exhaust manifolds (Part A, B or C of this Chapter).

j) Engine/transmission mounting brackets (Part A, B or C of this Chapter).

k) Flywheel/driveplate (Part A, B or C of this Chapter).

4 If you are obtaining a 'short' engine (which consists of the engine cylinder block/crankcase, crankshaft, pistons and connecting rods all assembled), then the cylinder head, sump, oil pump, oil filter cooler/housing and timing chains will have to be removed also.

5 If you are planning a complete overhaul, the engine can be dismantled and the internal components removed in the following order.

a) Inlet and exhaust manifolds (Part A, B or C of this Chapter).

b) Timing chain(s), tensioner(s) and toothed pulleys (Part A, B or C of this Chapter).

c) Cylinder head(s) (Part A, B or C of this Chapter).

d) Flywheel/driveplate (Part A, B or C of this Chapter).

e) Sump (Part A, B or C of this Chapter).

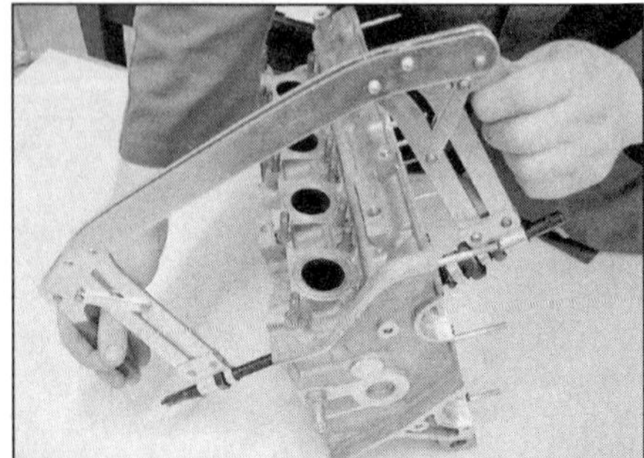

6.4 Compress the valve springs using a spring compressor tool

f) Oil pump (Part A, B or C of this Chapter).

g) Piston/connecting rod assemblies – diesel engines only (Section 9).

h) Crankshaft – diesel engines only (Section 10).

6 Before beginning the dismantling and overhaul procedures, make sure that you have all of the correct tools necessary. Refer to the introductory pages at the end of this manual for further information.

6 Cylinder head – dismantling

Note: *New and reconditioned cylinder heads are available from the manufacturers, and from engine overhaul specialists. Due to the fact that some specialist tools are required for the dismantling and inspection procedures, and new components may not be readily available (refer to Section 1), it may be more practical and economical for the home mechanic to purchase a reconditioned head, rather than to dismantle, inspect and recondition the original head.*

1 If the cylinder head is going to be reconditioned (or machined), remove all external components as necessary, to avoid the risk of damage.

2 On diesel models, remove the injectors and glow plugs (see Chapters 4B and 5C).

3 Where applicable, remove the rear coolant outlet housing together with its gasket/O-ring.

4 With the cylinder head resting on one side, using a valve spring compressor, compress each valve spring in turn until the split collets can be removed. A special valve spring compressor will be required, to reach into the deep wells in the cylinder head without risk of damaging the tappet bores; such compressors are now widely available from most good motor accessory shops. Release the compressor, and lift off the spring upper seat and spring **(see illustration)**.

5 If, when the valve spring compressor is screwed down, the spring upper seat refuses to free and expose the split collets, gently tap the top of the tool, directly over the upper seat, with a light hammer. This will free the seat to remove the collets.

6 Release the valve spring compressor and remove the upper spring seat, and valve spring **(see illustrations)**.

7 Withdraw the valve through the combustion chamber. If it binds in the guide (won't pull through), push it back in, and deburr the area around the collet groove with a fine file or whetstone; on 4-cylinder petrol engines, take care not to mark the tappet bores.

8 Use a pair of pliers or a special tool to extract the valve spring lower seat/stem oil seals from the valve guide **(see illustrations)**. **Note:** *On some models, the seal and lower spring seat are a complete assembly.*

9 It is essential that the valves are kept together with their collets, spring seats and

6.6a Remove the upper spring seat . . .

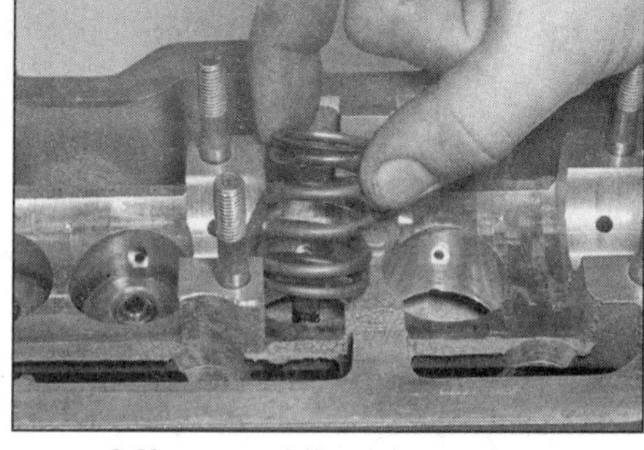

6.6b . . . and the valve springs

6.8a Use a removal tool to extract the stem oil seal . . .

springs, and in their correct sequence (unless they are so badly worn that they are to be renewed). If they are going to be kept and used again, place them in a labelled polythene bag or similar small container **(see illustration)**.

7 Cylinder head and valve components – cleaning and inspection

1 Thorough cleaning of the cylinder head and valve components, followed by a detailed inspection, will enable you to decide how much valve service work must be carried out during the engine overhaul. **Note:** *If the engine has been severely overheated, it is best to assume that the cylinder head is warped, and to check carefully for signs of this.*

Cleaning

2 Using a suitable degreasing agent, remove all traces of oil deposits from the cylinder head, paying particular attention to the journal bearings, cam follower/bucket tappet bores, valve guides, oilways and, where applicable, hydraulic tappet bores.

3 Scrape away all traces of old gasket material and sealing compound from the cylinder head, taking great care not to score or gouge the surfaces.

4 Scrape away the carbon from the combustion chambers and ports, then wash the cylinder head thoroughly with paraffin or a suitable solvent to remove the remaining debris.

5 Scrape off any heavy carbon deposits that may have formed on the valves, then use a power-operated wire brush to remove deposits from the valve heads and stems.

Inspection

Note: *Be sure to perform all the following inspection procedures before concluding that the services of a machine shop or engine overhaul specialist are required. Make a list of all items that require attention.*

Cylinder head

6 Inspect the head very carefully for cracks, evidence of coolant leakage, and other damage. If cracks are found, a new cylinder head should be obtained.

6.8b . . . then remove the lower spring seat (where applicable)

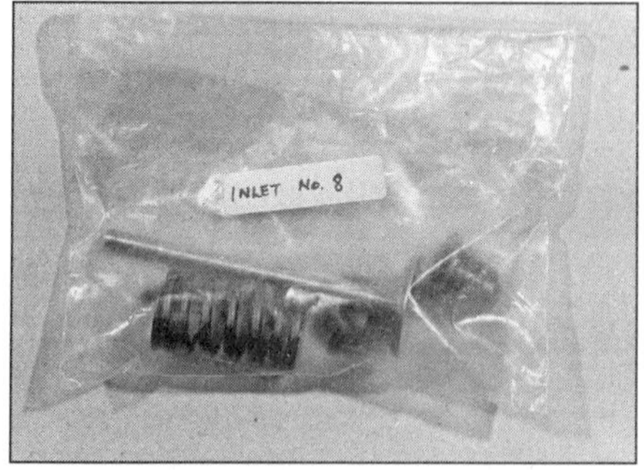

6.9 Use clearly marked containers to identify components and to keep matched assemblies together

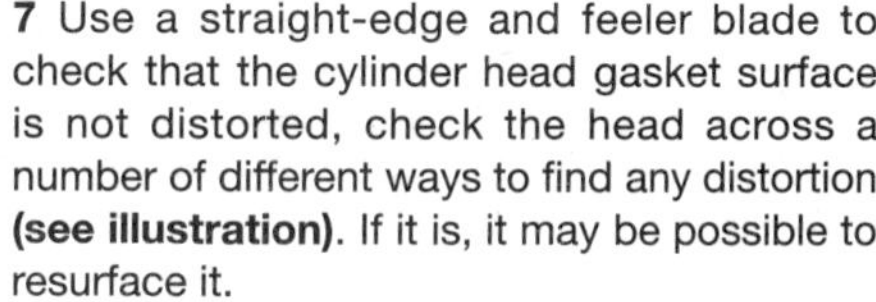

7 Use a straight-edge and feeler blade to check that the cylinder head gasket surface is not distorted, check the head across a number of different ways to find any distortion **(see illustration)**. If it is, it may be possible to resurface it.

8 Examine the valve seats in each of the combustion chambers. If they are severely pitted, cracked or burned, then they will need to be renewed or recut by an engine overhaul specialist. If they are only slightly pitted, this can be removed by grinding-in the valve heads and seats with fine valve-grinding compound, as described below.

9 If the valve guides are worn, indicated by a side-to-side motion of the valve, new guides must be fitted. Measure the diameter of the existing valve stems (see below) and the bore of the guides, then calculate the clearance, and compare the result with the specified value; if the clearance is excessive, renew the valves or guides as necessary.

10 The renewal of valve guides is best carried out by an engine overhaul specialist.

11 If the valve seats are to be recut, this must be done only after the guides have been renewed.

Valves

12 Examine the head of each valve for pitting, burning, cracks and general wear, and check the valve stem for scoring and wear ridges. Rotate the valve, and check for any obvious indication that it is bent. Look for pits and excessive wear on the tip of each valve stem. Renew any valve that shows any such signs of wear or damage.

13 If the valve appears satisfactory at this stage, measure the valve stem diameter at several points, using a micrometer **(see illustration)**. Any significant difference in the

A B C D E F G
J35119

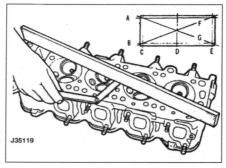

7.7 Check the cylinder head surface for warpage, in the planes indicated

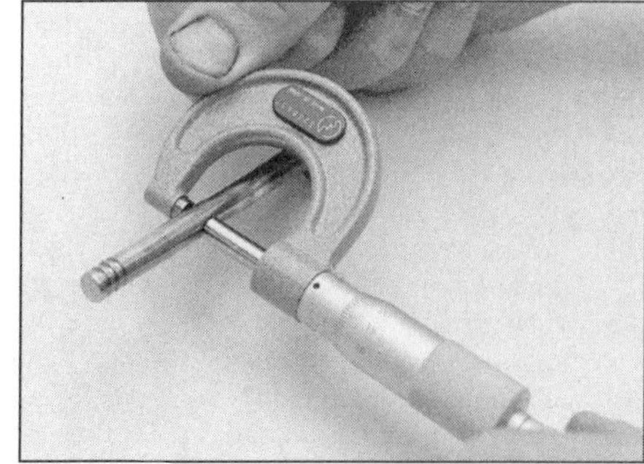

7.13 Measure the diameter of the valve stems with a micrometer

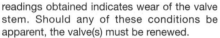

7.16 Grind-in the valves with a reciprocating rotary motion

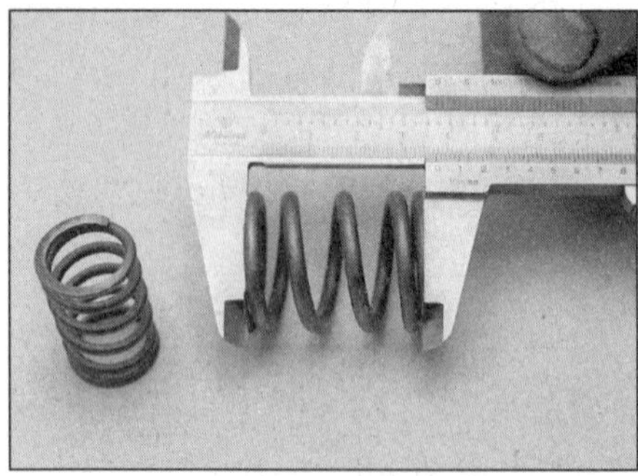
7.19 Measure the free length of each valve spring

7.20 Checking the squareness of the valve springs

readings obtained indicates wear of the valve stem. Should any of these conditions be apparent, the valve(s) must be renewed.

14 If the valves are in satisfactory condition, they should be ground (lapped) into their respective seats, to ensure a smooth gas-tight seal. If the seat is only lightly pitted, or if it has been recut, fine grinding compound only should be used to produce the required finish. Coarse valve-grinding compound should not be used unless a seat is badly burned or deeply pitted; if this is the case, the cylinder head and valves should be inspected by an expert, to decide whether seat recutting, or even the renewal of the valve or seat insert, is required.

15 Valve grinding is carried out as follows. Place the cylinder head upside-down on a bench, with a block of wood at each end to give clearance for the valve stems.

16 Smear a trace of (the appropriate grade of) valve-grinding compound on the seat face, and press a suction grinding tool onto the valve head. With a semi-rotary action, grind the valve head to its seat, lifting the valve occasionally to redistribute the grinding compound **(see illustration)**. A light spring placed under the valve head will greatly ease this operation.

17 If coarse grinding compound is being used, work only until a dull, matt even surface is produced on both the valve seat and the valve, then wipe off the used compound, and repeat the process with fine compound. When a smooth unbroken ring of light grey matt finish is produced on both the valve and seat, the grinding operation is complete. Do not grind in the valves any further than absolutely necessary, or the seat will be prematurely sunk into the cylinder head.

18 When all the valves have been ground-in, carefully wash off all traces of grinding compound, using paraffin or a suitable solvent, before reassembly of the cylinder head.

Valve components

19 Examine the valve springs for signs of damage and discolouration, and also measure their free length by comparing each of the existing springs with a new component **(see illustration)**.

20 Stand each spring on a flat surface, and check it for squareness **(see illustration)**. If any of the springs are damaged, distorted, or have lost their tension, obtain a complete set of new springs.

21 Check the spring upper seats and collets for obvious wear and cracks. Any questionable parts should be renewed, as extensive damage will occur if they fail during engine operation. Any damaged or excessively-worn parts must be renewed; the valve spring lower seat/stem oil seals must be renewed as a matter of course whenever they are disturbed.

22 Check the tappets (hydraulic or conventional) as described in Part A, B or C of this Chapter.

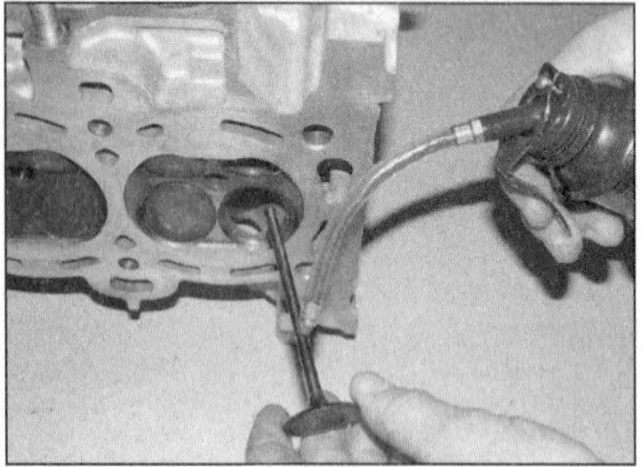
8.2 Oil the valve stems before refitting them

8.3a Fit a protective sleeve over the valve stem before fitting the stem seal

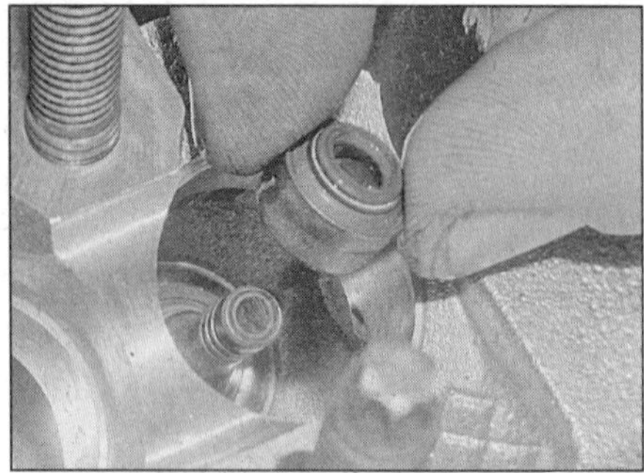
8.3b Push the stem seal over the valve and onto the top of the valve guide . . .

8.3c . . . then use a long reach socket to seat the seal

8 Cylinder head - reassembly

1 Regardless of whether or not the head was sent away for repair work of any sort, make sure that it is clean before beginning reassembly. Be sure to remove any metal particles and abrasive grit that may still be present from operations such as valve grinding or head resurfacing. Use compressed air, if available, to blow out all the oil holes and passages.

Warning: Wear eye protection when using compressed air.

2 Beginning at one end of the head, lubricate and install the first valve. Apply molybdenum disulphide-based grease or clean engine oil to the valve stem, and refit the valve **(see illustration)**. Where the original valves are being re-used, ensure that each is refitted in its original guide. If new valves are being fitted, insert them into the locations to which they have been ground.

3 Where applicable, fit the plastic protector supplied with new valve spring lower seat/stem oil seals to the end of the valve stem.

Dip a new valve stem oil seal in clean engine oil, then put the new seal squarely on top of the guide – take care not to damage the stem seal as it passes over the valve end face. Use a suitable long reach socket or special installer to press it firmly into position **(see illustrations)**, remove the protective sleeve.

4 Refit the valve spring and upper seat **(see illustration)**.

5 Compress the spring with a valve spring compressor, and carefully install the collets in the stem groove. Apply a small dab of grease to each collet to hold it in place if necessary. Slowly release the compressor, and make sure the collets seat properly **(see illustration)**.

6 When the valves are installed, use a hammer and interposed block of wood (to prevent the end of the valve stem being damaged), tap the end of the valve stem gently, to settle the components.

7 Repeat the procedure for the remaining valves. Be sure to return the valve assembly components to their original locations – don't mix them up!

8 Refit the tappets and camshafts as described in Part A, B or C of this Chapter.

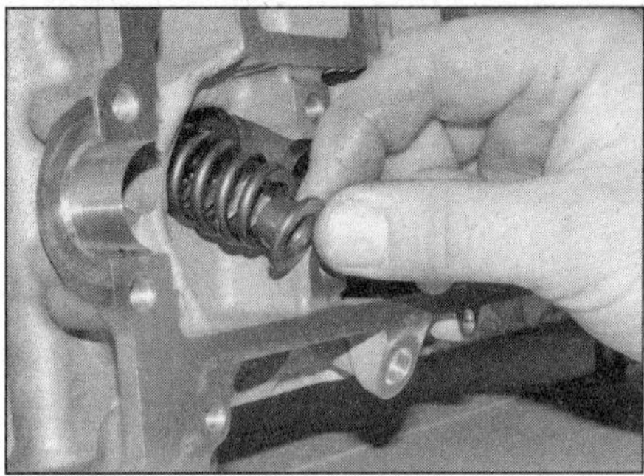

8.4 Fitting the valve spring and upper seat

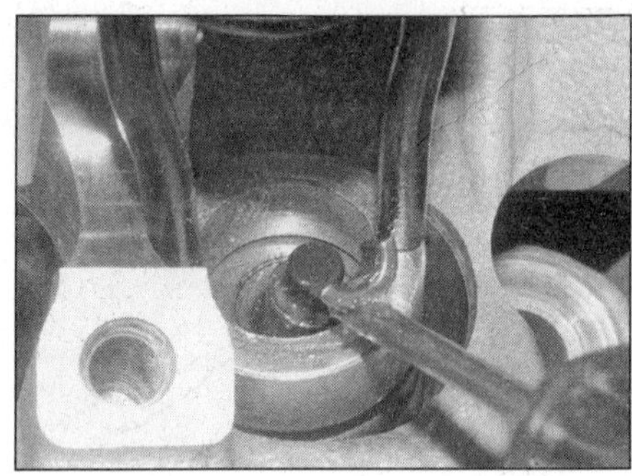

8.5 Use grease to hold the two halves of the split collet in the groove

9 Piston/connecting rods (diesel) – removal and inspection

Caution: Refer to the Caution and Notes in Sections 1 and 2 on models fitted with petrol engines.

Note: *While this task is theoretically possible when the engine is in place in the car, in practice, it requires so much preliminary dismantling, and is so difficult to carry out due to the restricted access, that owners are advised to remove the engine from the car first. The following paragraphs assume the engine is removed from the car.*

Removal

1 Remove the cylinder head and sump with reference to Part C of this Chapter.

2 Unbolt the oil pump pick-up tube and filter, and recover the O-ring from the pump.

3 Unscrew the bolts securing the lower crankcase to the cylinder block. Loosen the bolts gradually and evenly, then separate the lower crankcase from the cylinder block.

4 On diesel engines, the connecting rods and caps are of 'cracked' design. During production, the connecting rod and cap are forged as one piece, then the cap is broken apart from the rod using a special technique. Because of this design, the mating surfaces of each cap and rod is unique and, therefore, nearly impossible to mix up **(see illustration)**.

5 Temporarily refit the crankshaft pulley, so that the crankshaft can be rotated. Note that each piston/connecting rod assembly can be identified by its cylinder number (counting from the timing chain end of the engine) etched into the flat-machined surface of both the connecting rod and its cap. Furthermore, each piston has an arrow stamped into its crown, pointing towards the timing chain end of the engine. If no marks can be seen, make your own before disturbing any of the components, so that you can be certain of refitting each piston/connecting rod assembly the right way round, to its correct (original) bore, with the cap also the right way round **(see illustration)**.

6 Use your fingernail to feel if a ridge has formed at the upper limit of ring travel (about 6 mm down from the top of each cylinder). If carbon deposits or cylinder wear have produced ridges, they must be completely removed with a special tool called a ridge reamer **(see illustration)**. Follow the manufacturer's instructions provided with the tool.

Caution: Failure to remove the ridges before attempting to remove the piston/connecting rod assemblies may result in piston ring breakage.

7 Slacken each of the big-end bearing cap bolts half a turn at a time, until they can be removed by hand. Remove the No 1 cap and bearing shell. Don't drop the shell out of the cap.

8 Remove the upper bearing shell, and push the connecting rod/piston assembly out through the top of the cylinder block. Use a wooden hammer handle to push on the connecting rod's bearing recess. If resistance is felt, double-check that all of the ridge was removed from the cylinder. Repeat the procedure for the remaining cylinders.

9 After removal, reassemble the big-end bearing caps and shells on their respective connecting rods, and refit the bolts finger-tight. Leaving the old shells in place until reassembly will help prevent the bearing recesses from being accidentally nicked or gouged. New shells should be used on reassembly.

10 Remove the retaining screws and withdraw the piston cooling jets from the bottom of the cylinder bores **(see illustrations)**.

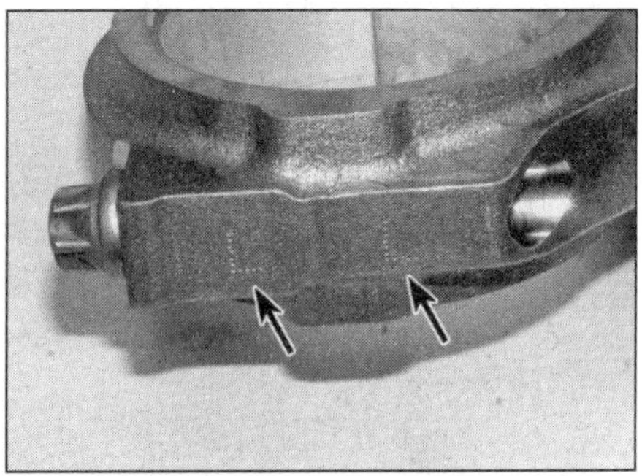

9.4 Note the markings (arrowed) on each part of the connecting rod and cap

9.5 Make your own marks (arrowed) to correspond with the connecting rod location

9.6 A ridge reamer may be required, to remove the ridge from the top of each cylinder

9.10a Remove the piston cooling jet retaining screws . . .

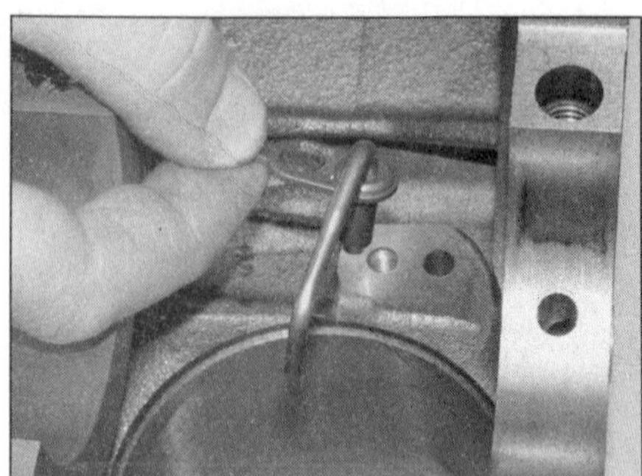

9.10b . . . and remove the jets from their mounting holes

Inspection

11 Before the inspection process can be carried out, the piston/connecting rod assemblies must be cleaned, and the original piston rings removed from the pistons. The rings should have smooth, polished working surfaces, with no dull or carbon-coated sections (showing that the ring is not sealing correctly against the bore wall, so allowing combustion gases to blow by) and no traces of wear on their top and bottom surfaces.

12 The end gaps should be clear of carbon, but not polished (indicating a too-small end gap), and all the rings (including the elements of the oil control ring) should be free to rotate in their grooves, but without excessive up-and-down movement. If the rings appear to be in good condition, they are probably fit for further use; check the end gaps (in an unworn part of the bore) as described in Section 14. If any of the rings appears to be worn or damaged, or has an end gap significantly different from the specified value, the usual course of action is to renew all of them as a set. **Note:** *While it is usual to renew piston rings when an engine is overhauled, they may be re-used if in acceptable condition. If re-using the rings, make sure that each ring is marked during removal to ensure that it is refitted correctly.*

13 Using a piston ring removal tool, carefully remove the rings from the pistons. Be careful not to nick or gouge the pistons in the process, and mark or label each ring as it is removed, so that its original top surface can be identified on reassembly, and so that it can

9.22a Insert a small screwdriver into the slot (arrowed) and prise out the circlips . . .

9.15a The piston ring grooves can be cleaned with a special tool, as shown here . . .

be returned to its original groove. Take care also with your hands – piston rings are sharp **(see Tool Tip)**.

If a piston ring removal tool is not available, the rings can be removed by hand, expanding them over the top of the pistons. The use of two or three old feeler blades will be helpful in preventing the rings dropping into empty grooves.

14 Scrape all traces of carbon from the top of the piston. A hand-held wire brush or a piece of fine emery cloth can be used, once the majority of the deposits have been scraped away. Do not, under any circumstances, use a wire brush mounted in a drill motor to remove deposits from the pistons – the piston material is soft, and may be eroded away by the wire brush.

15 Use a piston ring groove-cleaning tool to remove carbon deposits from the ring grooves. If a tool isn't available, but new rings have been bought, a piece broken off the old ring will do the job. Be very careful to remove only the carbon deposits – don't remove any metal, and do not nick or scratch the sides of the ring grooves **(see illustrations)**. Protect your fingers – piston rings are sharp.

16 Once the deposits have been removed, clean the piston/rod assemblies with solvent, and dry them with compressed air (if available). Make sure the oil return holes in the back

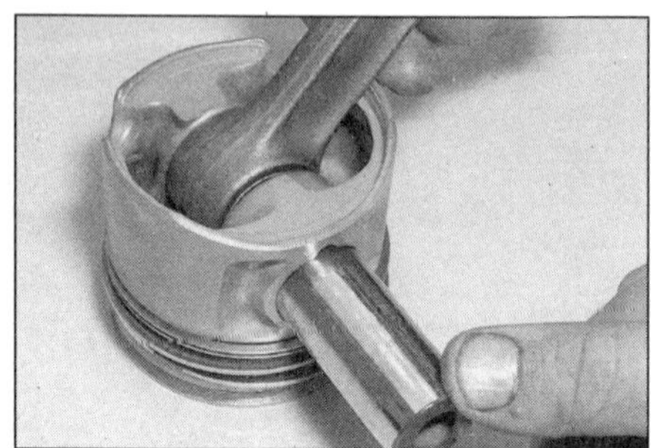

9.22b . . . then push out the gudgeon pin to separate the piston and the connecting rod

9.15b . . . or a section of a broken piston ring, if available

sides of the ring grooves, and the oil hole in the lower end of each rod, are clear.

17 If the pistons and cylinder walls aren't damaged or worn excessively and if the cylinder block/crankcase is not rebored, new pistons won't be necessary. Normal piston wear appears as even vertical wear on the piston thrust surfaces, and slight looseness of the top ring in its groove.

18 Carefully inspect each piston for cracks around the skirt, at the pin bosses, and at the ring lands (between the ring grooves).

19 Look for scoring and scuffing on the thrust faces of the skirt, holes in the piston crown, and burned areas at the edge of the crown. If the skirt is scored or scuffed, the engine may have been suffering from overheating and/or abnormal combustion, which caused excessively-high operating temperatures. The cooling and lubrication systems should be checked thoroughly. A hole in the piston crown is an indication that abnormal combustion (pre-ignition) was occurring. Burned areas at the edge of the piston crown are usually evidence of spark knock (detonation). If any of the above problems exist, the causes must be corrected, or the damage will occur again. The causes may include fuel injection or EGR system malfunctions.

20 Corrosion of the piston, in the form of small pits, indicates that coolant is leaking into the combustion chamber and/or the crankcase. Again, the cause must be corrected, or the problem may persist in the rebuilt engine.

21 Check the piston-to-rod clearance by twisting the piston and rod in opposite directions. Any noticeable play indicates excessive wear, which must be corrected. The piston/connecting rod assemblies should be taken to a Ford dealer or engine reconditioning specialist to have the pistons, gudgeon pins and rods checked, and new components fitted as required.

22 On diesel engines, remove the circlips, push out the gudgeon pin, and separate the piston from the connecting rod **(see illustrations)**. Discard the circlips as new items must be fitted on reassembly. If the pin proves difficult to remove, heat the piston to 60°C with hot water – the resulting expansion will then allow the two components to be separated. Take note of the fitment of the

10.1 Measure the crankshaft endfloat using a DTI gauge

10.2 Fitting the thrust control bearing which is part of the No 3 (centre) main bearing (4-cylinder engines)

10.3 If a DTI gauge is not available, measure the endfloat using feeler gauges

10.4a Note the main bearing caps are numbered to indicate their locations . . .

10.4b . . . the caps may have an embossed arrow pointing to the timing chain end of the engine

10.6 Carefully remove the crankshaft from the cylinder block

piston to the connecting rod, so that it can be refitted in the same position.

23 Check the connecting rods for cracks and other damage. Temporarily remove the big-end bearing caps and the old bearing shells, wipe clean the rod and cap bearing recesses, and inspect them for nicks, gouges and scratches. After checking the rods, refit the old shells, slip the caps into place, and tighten the bolts finger-tight.

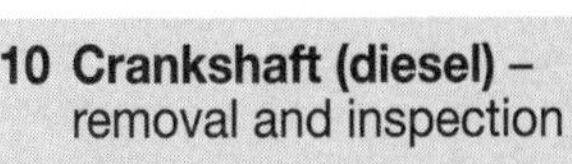

10 Crankshaft (diesel) – removal and inspection

Note: *It is not recommended that the crankshaft be removed on petrol engines – see Section 1.*

Note: *The crankshaft can be removed only after the engine/transmission has been removed from the car. It is assumed that the transmission and flywheel/driveplate, timing chain, lower crankcase, cylinder head, sump, oil pump pick-up/strainer pipe and oil baffle, main oil seal, oil pump, and piston/connecting rod assemblies, have already been removed. The crankshaft oil seal carrier must be unbolted from the cylinder block/crankcase before proceeding with crankshaft removal.*

Removal

1 Before the crankshaft is removed, check the endfloat. Mount a DTI (Dial Test Indicator, or dial gauge) with the probe in line with the crankshaft and just touching the crankshaft **(see illustration)**.

2 Push the crankshaft fully away from the gauge, and zero it. Next, lever the crankshaft towards the gauge as far as possible, and check the reading obtained. The distance that the crankshaft moved is its endfloat; if it is greater than specified, check the crankshaft thrust surfaces for wear. If no wear is evident, new thrustwashers should correct the endfloat – the thrust control bearing is part of the No 3 (centre) main bearing **(see illustration)**.

3 If a dial gauge is not available, feeler gauges can be used. Gently lever or push the crankshaft all the way towards the right-hand end of the engine. Slip feeler gauges between the crankshaft and the right-hand face of the No 3 (centre) main bearing to determine the clearance **(see illustration)**.

4 Check the main bearing caps, to see if they are marked to indicate their locations. They should be numbered consecutively from the timing chain end of the engine – if not, mark them with number-stamping dies or a centre-punch. The caps will also have an embossed arrow pointing to the timing chain end of the engine **(see illustrations)**. Slacken the cap bolts a quarter-turn at a time each, starting with the left- and right-hand end caps and working toward the centre, until they can be removed by hand.

5 Gently tap the caps with a soft-faced hammer, then separate them from the cylinder block/crankcase. If necessary, use the bolts as levers to remove the caps. Take care not to drop the bearing shells as the bearing caps are removed.

6 Carefully lift the crankshaft out of the engine **(see illustration)**. It may be a good idea to have an assistant available, since the crankshaft is quite heavy. With the bearing shells in place in the cylinder block/crankcase and main bearing caps, return the caps to their respective locations on the block, or refit the lower crankcase, and tighten the bolts finger-tight. Leaving the old shells in place until reassembly will help prevent the bearing recesses from being accidentally nicked or gouged. New shells should be used on reassembly.

Inspection

7 Clean the crankshaft, and dry it with compressed air if available. Be sure to clean the oil holes with a pipe cleaner or similar probe.

Warning: Wear eye protection when using compressed air.

8 Check the main and crankpin (big-end) bearing journals carefully. If uneven wear, scoring, pitting and cracking are evident, then the crankshaft should be reground (where possible) by an engineering workshop, and refitted to the engine with new undersize bearings.

9 Rather than attempt to determine the crankshaft journal sizes, and the bearing clearances, take the crankshaft to an automotive engineering workshop. Have them perform the necessary measurements, grind the journals if necessary, and supply the appropriate new shell bearings.

10 Check the oil seal journals at each end of the crankshaft for wear and damage. If either seal has worn an excessive groove in

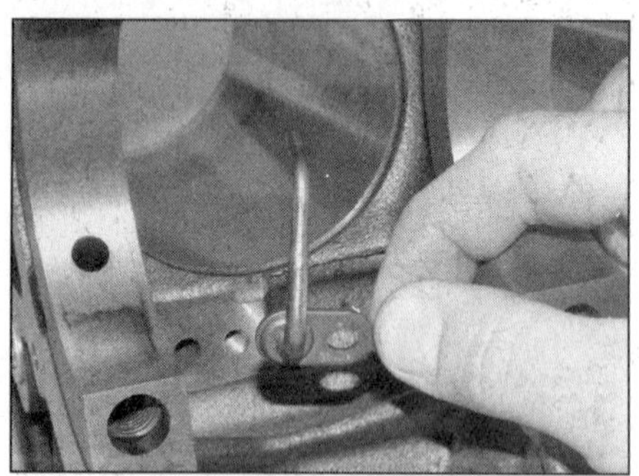

11.1 Where fitted, unbolt the piston-cooling oil jets (or blanking plugs)

11.8 The main bearing cap and head bolt holes especially should be cleaned with a tap

its journal, it may cause the new seals to leak when the engine is reassembled. Consult an engine overhaul specialist, who will be able to advise whether a repair is possible, or whether a new crankshaft is necessary.

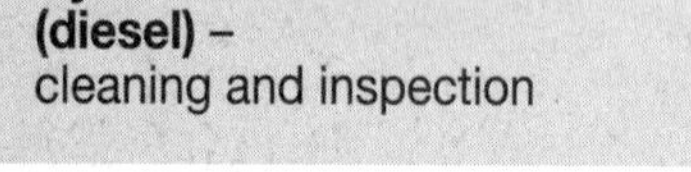

11 Cylinder block/crankcase (diesel) - cleaning and inspection

Cleaning

1 For complete cleaning, make sure that all the external components have been removed, including lifting eyes, mounting brackets, oil cooler and filter housing, fuel injection pump mounting bracket (where applicable) and all electrical switches/sensors. Where fitted, unbolt the piston-cooling oil jets or blanking plugs **(see illustration)**. **Note:** *On some models, Ford state that the piston-cooling oil jets must be renewed whenever the engine is dismantled for full overhaul – check with Ford dealer.*

2 Remove the main bearing caps or lower crankcase, and separate the bearing shells from the caps and the cylinder block. Mark or label the shells, indicating which bearing they were removed from, and whether they were in the cap or the block, then set them aside **(see illustration)**. Wipe clean the block and cap bearing recesses, and inspect them for nicks, gouges and scratches.

3 Scrape all traces of gasket from the cylinder block/lower crankcase, taking care not to damage the sealing surfaces.

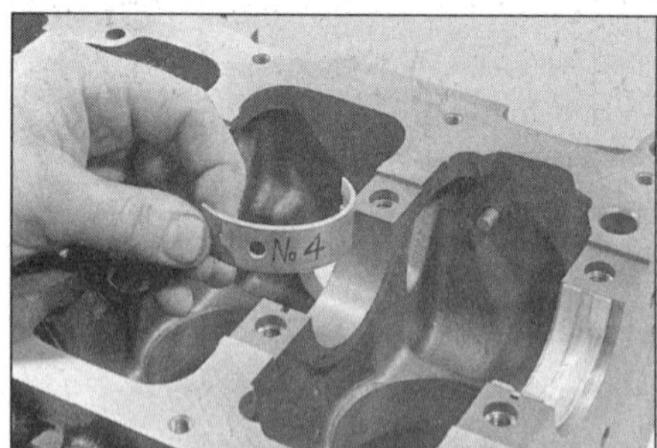

11.2 Felt marker pens can be used as shown to identify bearing shells without damaging them

11.9 A large socket on an extension can be used to drive the new core plugs into their bores

4 Remove all oil gallery plugs (where fitted). The plugs are usually very tight – they may have to be drilled out and the holes retapped. Use new plugs when the engine is reassembled. Remove the core plugs by knocking them sideways in their bores with a hammer and a punch, then grasping them with large pliers and pulling them back through their holes. Alternatively, drill a small hose in the centre of each core plug, and pull them out with a car bodywork dent puller **(see illustration)**. ***Caution: The core plugs (also known as freeze or soft plugs) may be difficult or impossible to retrieve if they are driven into the block coolant passages.***

5 If any of the castings are extremely dirty, they should be steam-cleaned.

6 After the castings are returned from steam-cleaning, clean all oil holes and oil galleries one more time. Flush all internal passages with warm water until the water runs clear, then dry thoroughly, and apply a light film of oil to all machined surfaces, to prevent rusting. If you have access to compressed air, use it to speed the drying process, and to blow out all the oil holes and galleries.

Warning: Wear eye protection when using compressed air.

7 If the castings are not very dirty, you can do an adequate cleaning job with hot soapy water (as hot as you can stand) and a stiff brush. Take plenty of time, and do a thorough job. Regardless of the cleaning method used, be sure to clean all oil holes and galleries very thoroughly, and to dry all components completely; protect the machined surfaces as described above, to prevent rusting.

11.4 The core plugs can be removed with a dent puller

8 All threaded holes must be clean and dry, to ensure accurate torque readings during reassembly; now is also a good time to clean and check the threads of all principal bolts – however, note that some, such as the cylinder head and the flywheel/driveplate bolts, must be renewed as a matter of course whenever they are disturbed. Run the proper-size tap into each of the holes, to remove rust, corrosion, thread sealant or sludge, and to restore damaged threads **(see illustration)**. If possible, use compressed air to clear the holes of debris produced by this operation. **Note:** *Take extra care to exclude all cleaning liquid from blind tapped holes, as the casting may be cracked by hydraulic action if a bolt is threaded into a hole containing liquid.*

9 When all inspection and repair procedures are complete (see below) and the block is ready for reassembly, apply suitable sealant to the new oil gallery plugs, and insert them into the holes in the block. Tighten them securely. After coating the sealing surfaces of the new core plugs with suitable sealant, install them in the cylinder block/crankcase **(see illustration)**. Make sure they are driven in straight and seated properly, or leakage could result. Special tools are available for this purpose, but a large socket with an outside diameter that will just slip into the core plug, used with an extension and hammer, will work just as well.

10 Refit the blanking plugs or (new) piston-cooling oil jets (as applicable), smear a small amount of thread locking fluid onto the retaining screws and tighten the oil jets into position **(see illustrations)**. Also refit all other external components removed, referring to the relevant Chapter of this manual for further details where required. Refit the main bearing caps, and tighten the bolts finger-tight.

11 If the engine is not going to be reassembled right away, cover it with a large plastic bag to keep it clean. Apply a thin coat of engine oil to all machined surfaces to prevent rusting.

Inspection

12 Visually check the castings for cracks

and corrosion. Look for stripped threads in the threaded holes. If there has been any history of internal coolant leakage, it may be worthwhile having an engine overhaul specialist check the cylinder block/crankcase for cracks with special equipment. If defects are found, have them repaired, if possible, or renew the assembly.

13 Check each cylinder bore for scuffing and scoring. Any evidence of this kind of damage should be cross-checked with an inspection of the pistons (see Section 9 of this Chapter). If the damage is in its early stages, it may be possible to repair the block by reboring it. Seek the advice of an engineering workshop.

14 Place the cylinder block on a level surface, crankcase downwards. Use a straight-edge and set of feeler blades to measure the distortion of the cylinder head mating surface in both planes. A maximum figure is not quoted by the manufacturer, but use the figure 0.05 mm as a rough guide. If the measurement exceeds this figure, repair may be possible by machining – consult an engineering workshop for advice.

15 To allow an accurate assessment of the wear in the cylinder bores to be made, take the cylinder block to an automotive engineering workshop, and have them carry out the measurement procedures. If necessary, they will be able to rebore the cylinders, and supply the appropriate piston kits.

16 Even if the cylinder bores are not excessively worn, the cylinder bores must be honed. This process involves using an abrasive tool to produce a fine, cross-hatch pattern on the inner surface of the bore. This has the effect of seating the piston rings, resulting in a good seal between the piston and cylinder. Again, an engineering workshop will be able to carry out the job for you at a reasonable cost.

17 Refit all the components removed in paragraph 1.

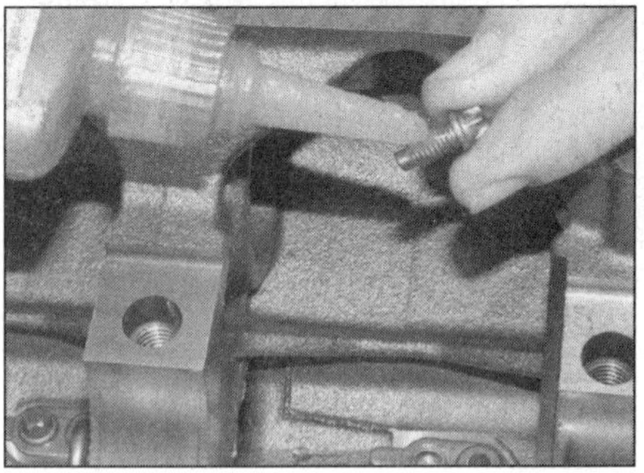

11.10a Apply a small amount of thread locking fluid onto the retaining screws . . .

11.10b . . . and tighten the oil jets into position

12 Main and big-end bearings (diesel) – inspection

1 Even though the main and big-end bearing shells should be renewed during the engine overhaul, the old shells should be retained for close examination, as they may reveal valuable information about the condition of the engine **(see illustration)**.

2 Bearing failure occurs because of lack of lubrication, the presence of dirt or other foreign particles, overloading the engine, and corrosion. Regardless of the cause of bearing failure, it must be corrected before the engine is reassembled, to prevent it from happening again.

3 When examining the bearing shells, remove them from the cylinder block/crankcase and main bearing caps, and from the connecting rods and the big-end bearing caps, then lay them out on a clean surface in the same general position as their location in the engine. This will enable you to match any bearing problems with the corresponding crankshaft journal. Do not touch any shell's bearing surface with your fingers while checking it, or the delicate surface may be scratched.

4 Dirt or other foreign matter gets into the engine in a variety of ways. It may be left in the engine during assembly, or it may pass through filters or the crankcase ventilation system. It may get into the oil, and from there into the bearings. Metal chips from machining operations and normal engine wear are often present. Abrasives are sometimes left in engine components after reconditioning, especially when parts are not thoroughly cleaned using the proper cleaning methods. Whatever the source, these foreign objects often end up embedded in the soft bearing material, and are easily recognised. Large particles will not embed in the material, and will score or gouge the shell and journal. The best prevention for this cause of bearing failure is to clean all parts thoroughly, and to keep everything spotlessly-clean during engine assembly. Frequent and regular engine oil and filter changes are also recommended.

5 Lack of lubrication (or lubrication breakdown) has a number of interrelated causes. Excessive heat (which thins the oil), overloading (which squeezes the oil from the bearing face) and oil leakage (from excessive bearing clearances, worn oil pump or high engine speeds) all contribute to lubrication breakdown. Blocked oil passages, which usually are the result of misaligned oil holes in a bearing shell, will also starve a bearing of oil, and destroy it. When lack of lubrication is the cause of bearing failure, the bearing material is wiped or extruded from the shell's steel backing. Temperatures may increase to the point where the steel backing turns blue from overheating.

6 Driving habits can have a definite effect on bearing life. Full-throttle, low-speed operation (labouring the engine) puts very high loads on bearings, which tends to squeeze out the oil film. These loads cause the shells to flex, which produces fine cracks in the bearing face (fatigue failure). Eventually, the bearing material will loosen in pieces, and tear away from the steel backing.

7 Short-distance driving leads to corrosion of bearings, because insufficient engine heat is produced to drive off condensed water and corrosive gases. These products collect in the engine oil, forming acid and sludge. As the oil is carried to the engine bearings, the acid attacks and corrodes the bearing material.

8 Incorrect shell refitting during engine assembly will lead to bearing failure as well. Tight-fitting shells leave insufficient bearing running clearance, and will result in oil starvation. Dirt or foreign particles trapped behind a bearing shell result in high spots on the bearing, which lead to failure.

9 *Do not* touch any shell's internal bearing surface with your fingers during reassembly; there is a risk of scratching the delicate surface, or of depositing particles of dirt on it.

10 As mentioned at the beginning of this Section, the bearing shells should be renewed as a matter of course during an engine overhaul. To do otherwise is false economy.

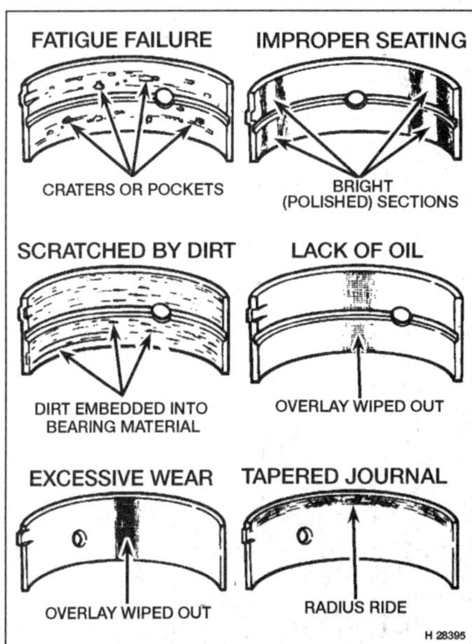

12.1 When inspecting the main and big-end bearings, look for any of these problems

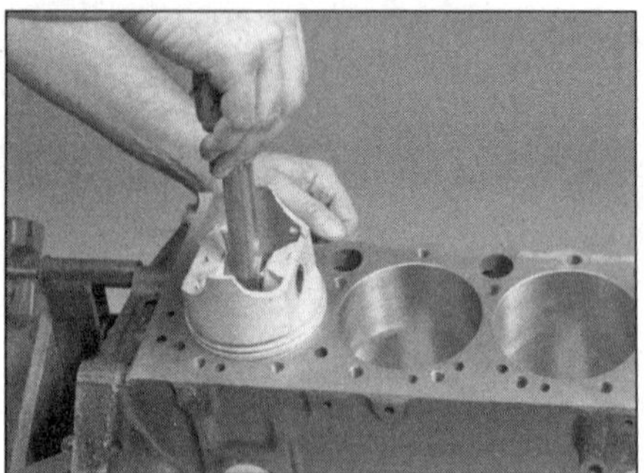
14.2 Square the ring up in the cylinder bore; push the ring down with the top of the piston

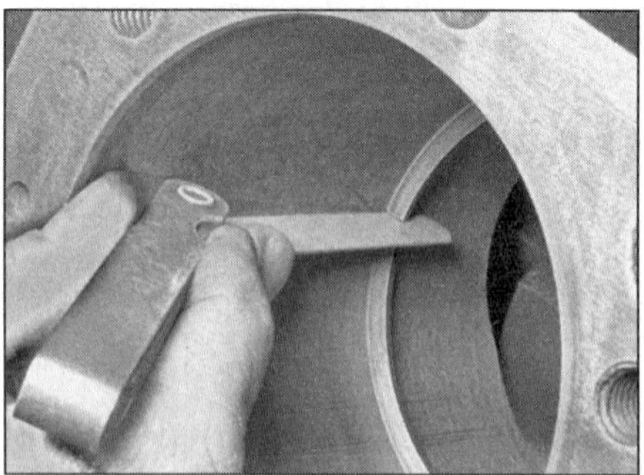
14.3 With the ring square in the bore, measure the end gap with a feeler gauge

13 Engine overhaul – reassembly sequence

1 Before reassembly begins, ensure that all new parts have been obtained, and that all necessary tools are available. Read through the entire procedure, to familiarise yourself with the work involved, and to ensure that all items necessary for reassembly of the engine are at hand. In addition to all normal tools and materials, thread-locking compound will be needed. A suitable tube of sealant will also be required for certain joint faces that are without gaskets. It is recommended that the manufacturers own products are used, which are specially formulated for this purpose.
Caution: Certain types of high-volatility RTV can foul the oxygen sensor and cause it to fail. Be sure that any RTV used is a low-volatility type and meets Ford specifications for use on engines equipped with an oxygen sensor.
2 In order to save time and avoid problems, engine reassembly can be carried out in the following order:
a) Crankshaft (Section 15).
b) Piston/connecting rod assemblies (Section 16).
c) Oil pump (Part A, B, or C of this Chapter).
d) Sump (Part A, B, or C of this Chapter).
e) Flywheel/driveplate (Part A, B, or C of this Chapter).
f) Cylinder head(s) (Part A, B, or C of this Chapter).
g) Timing chain(s), tensioner(s) and toothed pulleys (Part A, B or C of this Chapter).
h) Inlet and exhaust manifolds (Part A, B, or C of this Chapter).
i) Engine external components and ancillaries.

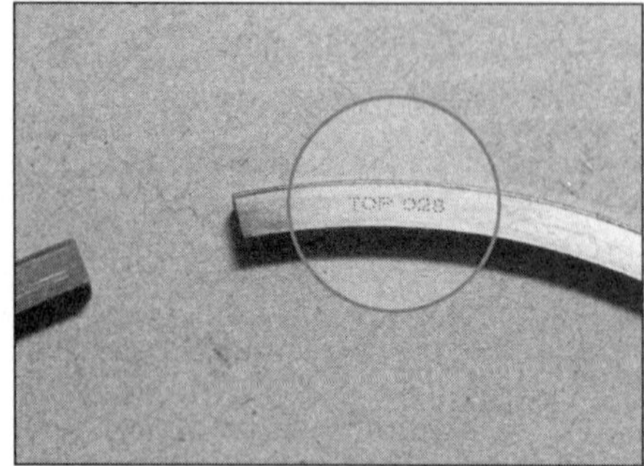

14.6 Piston ring TOP markings

3 At this stage, all engine components should be absolutely clean and dry, with all faults repaired. All components should be neatly arranged on a completely clean work surface or in individual containers.

14 Piston rings (diesel) – refitting

1 Before installing new piston rings, check the end gaps. Lay out each piston set with a piston/connecting rod assembly, and keep them together as a matched set from now on.
2 Insert the top compression ring into the first cylinder, and square it up with the cylinder walls by pushing it in with the top of the piston **(see illustration)**. The ring should be near the bottom of the cylinder, at the lower limit of ring travel.
3 To measure the end gap, slip feeler gauges between the ends of the ring, until a gauge equal to the gap width is found **(see illustration)**. The feeler gauge should slide between the ring ends with a slight amount of drag. Compare the measurement to the value given in the Specifications Section of this Chapter; if the gap is larger or smaller than specified, double-check to make sure you have the correct rings before proceeding. If you are assessing the condition of used rings, have the cylinder bores checked and measured by a Ford dealer or similar engine reconditioning specialist, so that you can be sure of exactly which component is worn, and seek advice as to the best course of action to take.
4 If the end gap is still too small, it must be opened up by careful filing of the ring ends using a fine file. If it is too large, this is not as serious, unless the specified limit is exceeded, in which case very careful checking is required of the dimensions of all components, as well as of the new parts.
5 Repeat the procedure for each ring that will be installed in the first cylinder, and for each ring in the remaining cylinders. Remember to keep rings, pistons and cylinders matched up.
6 Refit the piston rings as follows. Where the original rings are being refitted, use the marks or notes made on removal, to ensure that each ring is refitted to its original groove and the same way up. New rings generally have their top surfaces identified by markings (often an indication of size, such as STD, or the word TOP) – the rings must be fitted with such markings uppermost **(see illustration)**. **Note:** *Always follow the instructions printed on the ring package or box – different manufacturers may require different approaches. Do not mix up the top and second compression rings, as they usually have different cross-sections.*
7 The oil control ring (lowest one on the piston) is usually installed first. It is usually composed of three separate elements. Slip the spacer/expander into the groove. Next, install the lower side rail. Don't use a piston ring installation tool on the oil ring side rails, as they may be damaged. Instead, place one end of the side rail into the groove between the spacer/expander and the ring land, hold it firmly in place, and slide a finger around the piston while pushing the rail into the groove. Next, install the upper side rail in the same manner.
8 After all the oil ring components have been installed, check that both the upper and lower side rails can be turned smoothly in the ring groove.
9 The second compression (middle) ring is installed next, followed by the top compression ring – ensure their marks are uppermost. Don't expand either ring any more than necessary to slide it over the top of the piston.
10 With all the rings in position, space the ring gaps (including the elements of the oil control ring) uniformly around the piston at 120° intervals. Repeat the procedure for the remaining pistons and rings.

15 Crankshaft (diesel) – refitting

1 Crankshaft refitting is the first major step in engine reassembly. It is assumed at this point that the cylinder block/crankcase and crankshaft have been cleaned, inspected and repaired or reconditioned as necessary. Where removed, the oil jets must be refitted at this stage and their mounting bolts tightened securely.
2 Place the cylinder block on a clean, level work surface, with the crankcase facing upwards. Wipe out the inner surfaces of the main bearing caps and crankcase with a clean cloth – they must be kept spotlessly clean.
3 Clean the rear surface of the new main bearing shells with a lint-free (non-fluffy) cloth. Fit the shells with an oil groove in each main bearing location in the block. Note the

15.3a Fitting the shells in each main bearing location

15.3b Note the thrustwashers integral with the No 3 (centre) upper main bearing shell

15.5 Ensure the bearing shells are absolutely clean and lubricate liberally

thrustwashers integral with the No 3 (centre) upper main bearing shell. Fit the other shell from each bearing set in the corresponding main bearing cap. Where applicable, make sure the tab on each bearing shell fits into the notch in the block or cap/lower crankcase. Also, the oil holes in the block must line up with the oil holes in the bearing shell **(see illustrations)**. Don't hammer the shells into place, and don't nick or gouge the bearing faces. It is critically important that the surfaces of the bearings are kept free from damage and contamination.

4 Clean the bearing surfaces of the shells in the block and the crankshaft main bearing journals with a clean, lint-free cloth. Check or clean the oil holes in the crankshaft, as any dirt will become embedded in the new bearings when the engine is first started.

5 Apply a thin, uniform layer of clean molybdenum disulphide-based grease, engine assembly lubricant, or clean engine oil to each surface **(see illustration)**. Coat the thrustwasher surfaces as well.

6 Making sure the crankshaft journals are clean, lay the crankshaft back in place in the block.

7 Lubricate the crankshaft oil seal journals with molybdenum disulphide-based grease, engine assembly lubricant, or clean engine oil.

8 Refit and tighten the main bearing caps as follows:

a) *Clean the bearing surfaces of the shells in the caps, then lubricate them. Refit the caps in their respective positions, with the arrows pointing to the timing chain end of the engine.*

b) *Working on one cap at a time, from the centre main bearing outwards (and ensuring that each cap is tightened down squarely and evenly onto the block), tighten the main bearing cap bolts to the specified torque wrench setting.*

9 Rotate the crankshaft a number of times by hand, to check for any obvious binding.

10 Check the crankshaft endfloat (see Section 10). It should be correct if the crankshaft thrust faces aren't worn or damaged, and if the thrust control bearing(s) has been renewed.

11 Refit the crankshaft oil seal carrier, and install a new seal.

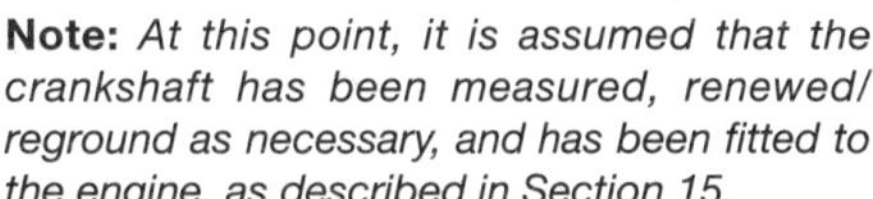

16 Piston/connecting rods (diesel) - refitting

Note: *At this point, it is assumed that the crankshaft has been measured, renewed/reground as necessary, and has been fitted to the engine, as described in Section 15.*

1 Before refitting the piston/connecting rod assemblies, the cylinder bores must be perfectly clean, the top edge of each cylinder must be chamfered, and the crankshaft must be in place.

2 Remove the big-end bearing cap from No 1 cylinder connecting rod (refer to the marks noted or made on removal). Remove the original bearing shells, and wipe the bearing recesses of the connecting rod and cap with a clean, lint-free cloth. They must be kept spotlessly-clean.

3 Lubricate the cylinder bores, the pistons, piston rings and upper bearing shells with clean engine oil. Lay out each piston/connecting rod assembly in order on a clean work surface. Take care not to scratch the crankpins and cylinder bores when the pistons are refitted.

4 Start with piston/connecting rod assembly No 1. Make sure that the piston rings are still spaced as described in Section 14, then clamp them in position with a piston ring compressor.

5 Insert the piston/connecting rod assembly into the top of cylinder No 1. Lower the big-end in first, guiding it to protect the cylinder bores. Where oil jets are located at the bottom of the bores, take particular care not to break them off when guiding the connecting rods onto the crankpins.

6 Ensure that the orientation of the piston in its cylinder is correct – the piston crown, connecting rod and big-end bearing caps should have markings, which must be aligned in the position noted on removal (see Section 9).

7 Using a block of wood or hammer handle against the piston crown, tap the assembly into the cylinder until the piston crown is flush with the top of the cylinder **(see illustration)**.

8 Ensure that the bearing shell is still correctly installed. Liberally lubricate the crankpin and both bearing shells with clean engine oil. Taking care not to mark the cylinder bores, tap the piston/connecting rod assembly down the bore and onto the crankpin. Where applicable, remove the insulating tape from the bolts, then oil the threads and underside of the bolt heads. Fit the big-end bearing cap, tightening its new retaining nuts/bolts finger-tight at first. Note that the orientation of the bearing cap with respect to the connecting rod must be correct when the two components are reassembled **(see illustration)**.

9 Tighten the retaining bolts/nuts to the specified Stage 1 torque. Tighten the retaining bolts/nuts to the specified Stage 2 torque.

10 Repeat the entire procedure for the remaining piston/connecting rod assemblies.

11 After all the piston/connecting rod assemblies have been properly installed, rotate the crankshaft a number of times by hand, to check for any obvious binding or tight spots.

16.7 Using a hammer handle to tap the piston into its bore

16.8 Note the markings on the bearing cap with respect to the connecting rod on refitting

16.12a Place a straight-edge across the transmission mating surface of the cylinder block . . .

16.12b . . . and the side of the lower crankcase-to-cylinder block alignment

16.15 Measure the piston protrusion using a DTI gauge

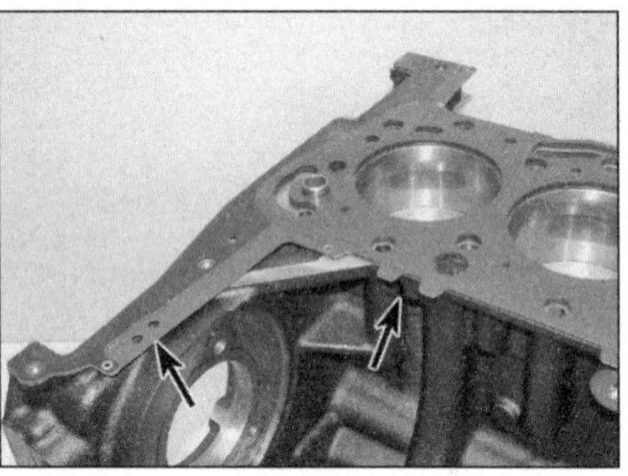

16.16 Note the markings (arrowed) on the cylinder head gasket (diesel engine)

12 Refit the new lower crankcase-to-cylinder block gasket. Refit the lower crankcase to the cylinder block, insert the bolts and hand-tighten. Place a straight-edge across the transmission mating surface of the cylinder block and the lower crankcase to check the lower crankcase-to-cylinder block alignment. The lower crankcase should be flush with the cylinder block. If not flush, the alignment should be within –0.05 mm overlap to a +0.05 mm gap at the rear and side of the cylinder block **(see illustrations)**.

13 Once the alignment is within specifications, tighten the lower crankcase bolts to the specified torque.

14 If new pistons are fitted or a new short engine is installed, the projection of the piston crowns above the cylinder block upper surface at TDC must be measured, to determine the type of head gasket that should be fitted.

15 Turn the cylinder block over (so that the lower crankcase is facing downwards) and rest it on a stand or wooden blocks. Anchor a DTI gauge to the cylinder block, and zero it on the head gasket mating surface. Rest the gauge probe on No 1 piston crown and turn the crankshaft slowly by hand so that the piston reaches TDC. Measure and record the maximum projection at TDC **(see illustration)**.

16 Repeat the procedure for the remaining pistons and record the measurements. If the measurement differs from piston-to-piston, take the highest reading and use this to determine the head gasket type that must be used **(see illustration)** – refer to Chapter 2C, Section 11, for details.

17 Note that if the original pistons have been refitted, then a new head gasket of the same type as the original must be used.

18 Refer to Part of this Chapter and refit the relevant assemblies.

17 Engine – initial start-up after overhaul

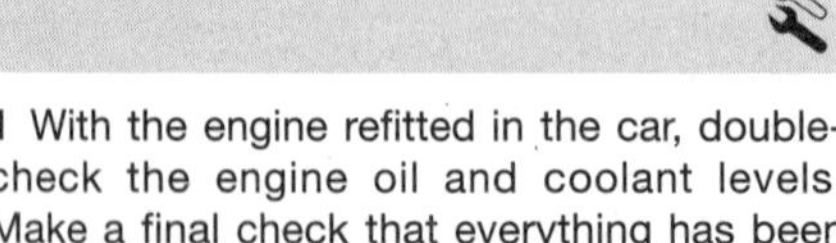

1 With the engine refitted in the car, double-check the engine oil and coolant levels. Make a final check that everything has been reconnected, and that there are no tools or rags left in the engine compartment.

Petrol models

2 Remove the spark plugs (see Chapter 1A).

3 Disable the ignition system by unplugging the ignition coil's electrical connector, remove the fuel pump fuse from the fusebox (see Chapter 12 – wiring diagrams).

Caution: To prevent damage to the catalytic converter, it is important to disable the fuel system.

4 Turn the engine on the starter until the oil pressure warning light goes out. If the light fails to extinguish after several seconds of cranking, check the engine oil level and oil filter security. Assuming these are correct, check the security of the oil pressure switch wiring – do not progress any further until you are satisfied that oil is being pumped around the engine at sufficient pressure.

5 Refit the spark plugs, and connect all the spark plug (HT) leads (Chapter 1A). Reconnect the ignition coil wiring, refit the fuel pump fuse, then switch on the ignition and listen for the fuel pump; it will run for a little longer than usual, due to the lack of pressure in the system.

Diesel models

6 Turn the engine on the starter until the oil pressure warning light goes out. If the light fails to extinguish after several seconds of cranking, check the engine oil level and the oil filter. Assuming these are correct, check the security of the oil pressure switch wiring – do not progress any further until you are satisfied that oil is being pumped around the engine at sufficient pressure.

All models

7 Start the engine, noting that this also may take a little longer than usual, due to the fuel system components being empty.

8 While the engine is idling, check for fuel, coolant and oil leaks. Don't be alarmed if there are some odd smells and smoke from parts getting hot and burning off oil deposits. If the hydraulic tappets have been disturbed, some valve gear noise may be heard at first; this should disappear as the oil circulates fully around the engine, and normal pressure is restored in the tappets.

9 Keep the engine idling until hot water is felt circulating through the top hose, check that it idles reasonably smoothly and at the usual speed, then switch it off.

10 After a few minutes, recheck the oil and coolant levels, and top-up as necessary (*Weekly checks*).

11 If they were tightened as described, there is no need to retighten the cylinder head bolts once the engine has first run after reassembly – in fact, Ford state that the bolts must not be retightened.

12 If new components such as pistons, rings or crankshaft bearings have been fitted, the engine must be run-in for the first 500 miles. Do not operate the engine at full-throttle, or allow it to labour in any gear during this period. It is recommended that the oil and filter be changed at the end of this period.

Chapter 3
Cooling, heating and air conditioning systems

Contents

Degrees of difficulty

Easy, suitable for novice with little experience	**Fairly easy,** suitable for beginner with some experience	**Fairly difficult,** suitable for competent DIY mechanic	**Difficult,** suitable for experienced DIY mechanic	**Very difficult,** suitable for expert DIY or professional

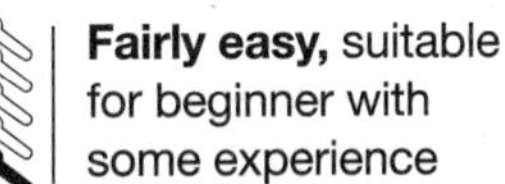

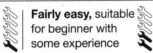

Specifications

Coolant

Antifreeze type	See *Lubricants and fluids* on page 0•18
Cooling system capacity	See Chapter 1A or 1B

Expansion tank filler cap

Pressure rating	18 to 21 psi (124 to 145 kpa)

Air conditioning system

Refrigerant	R134a

Torque wrench settings

Torque wrench settings	Nm	lbf ft
Air conditioning accumulator/dehydrator	8	6
Air conditioning compressor:		
Except V6 engines	25	18
V6 engines	20	15
Air conditioning condenser	10	7
Air conditioning high-pressure cut-off switch	8	6
Air conditioning low-pressure cut-off switch	3	2
Oil temperature control thermostat (diesel engines)	10	7
Radiator support bracket	10	7
Refrigerant union to accumulator	8	6
Refrigerant union to air conditioning compressor	20	15
Thermostat housing:		
1.8 and 2.0 litre petrol engines	10	7
V6 engines	18	13
Diesel engines	23	17
Water pump:		
Petrol engines	10	7
Diesel engines	24	18
Water pump housing (diesel engines)	10	7
Water pump pulley (1.8 and 2.0 litre petrol engines)	25	18

1 General information and precautions

Engine cooling system

All models covered by this manual use a pressurised engine cooling system with thermostatically-controlled coolant circulation. The coolant is circulated by an impeller-type water pump, which is belt-driven from the crankshaft pulley on four-cylinder petrol engines, or belt-driven from a pulley attached to the front inlet camshaft on V6 and diesel engines.

On 1.8 and 2.0 litre petrol engines, the water pump is located on the right-hand front of the engine and is driven by the main auxiliary drivebelt which also drives the alternator, power steering pump and air conditioning compressor. On V6 engines, the water pump is at the left-hand front of the engine, driven by a small drivebelt off the camshaft. On diesel engines, the water pump is bolted to the left-hand front of the engine cylinder block, and is driven off the camshaft, via the power steering pump – the drivebelt drives the power steering pump pulley, and the power steering pump drives the water pump by splines.

On 1.8 and 2.0 litre petrol engines, the thermostat is located on the right-hand rear of the cylinder block, next to the water pump. Unusually, the thermostat is fitted with an engine ECU-controlled heating element, to reduce warm-up times when the engine is started from cold – when the coolant reaches a certain temperature, the element cuts out. On V6 engines, the thermostat is located in the return hose from the cylinder block to the water pump, on the left-hand rear of the engine. On diesel engines, the thermostat is located in a housing on the left-hand end of the cylinder block, beneath the brake vacuum pump.

The coolant flows through the cylinder block around each cylinder; in the cylinder head(s), cast-in coolant passages direct coolant around the inlet and exhaust ports. During warm-up, the closed thermostat prevents coolant from circulating through the radiator. Instead, it returns through the coolant metal pipe running across the front of the engine to the radiator bottom hose. The supply to the heater is made from the rear of the thermostat housing. As the engine reaches normal operating temperature, the thermostat opens and allows hot coolant to travel through the radiator, where it is cooled before returning to the engine.

1.6 Cooling system booster heater located on the lower bulkhead

The radiator is of aluminium construction, and has plastic end tanks. On models with automatic transmission, the fluid cooler is incorporated in the left-hand end tank. The cooling system is sealed by a pressure-type filler cap in the expansion tank. The pressure in the system raises the boiling point of the coolant, and increases the cooling efficiency of the radiator. When the engine is at normal operating temperature, the coolant expands, and the surplus is displaced into the expansion tank. When the system cools, the surplus coolant is automatically drawn back from the tank into the radiator. One or two electric cooling fans (according to model) are mounted behind the radiator and are controlled by a thermostatic switch.

On certain diesel models, a booster heater is fitted into the heater matrix supply hose to quickly supply heat to the heater matrix while the engine is warming-up. In addition to providing hot coolant to the heater, it assists the engine to reach its normal efficient temperature in as short a period as possible. The heater is located at the rear of the engine compartment, on the lower bulkhead **(see illustration)**. It is controlled by the engine ECU, and is switched on when the engine inlet air temperature is approximately 0°C. Three heating plugs are fitted to the heater housing, each one having an output of 250W (750W total).

On diesel models for Scandinavian markets, a fuel-fired booster heater is fitted, having an output of between 2.2kW and 5kW. A fuel pump supplies diesel fuel from the engine supply line to the evaporator section of the heater combustion chamber. The system is activated when the engine is running and the ambient temperature is lower than 5°C, or the coolant temperature is below 75°C.

Heating/ventilation system

The heating system consists of a blower fan and heater matrix (radiator) located in the heater unit, with hoses connecting the heater matrix to the engine cooling system. Hot engine coolant is circulated through the heater matrix. Incoming fresh air for the ventilation system passes through a pollen filter mounted below the windscreen cowl panel. The ventilation system air distribution is controlled by a number of electronically-operated flap doors in the heater housing. When the heater controls are operated, the flap doors open to direct the air to the chosen areas of the passenger compartment. When the blower control is operated, the blower fan forces air through the unit according to the setting selected.

On models equipped with automatic climate control, a digital display indicates the temperature, blower speed, demist/defrost mode, and airflow direction.

Air conditioning system

See Section 10.

Precautions

Cooling system

Do not attempt to remove the expansion tank filler cap or to disturb any part of the cooling system with the engine hot, as there is a risk of scalding. If the expansion tank filler cap must be removed before the engine and radiator have fully cooled down (even though this is not recommended) the pressure in the cooling system must first be released. Cover the cap with a thick layer of cloth, to avoid scalding, and slowly unscrew the filler cap until a hissing sound can be heard. When the hissing has stopped, showing that the pressure is released, slowly unscrew the filler cap until it can be removed. If more hissing sounds are heard, wait until they have stopped before unscrewing the cap completely. At all times keep well away from the filler opening.

Do not allow antifreeze to come in contact with your skin or painted surfaces of the car. Rinse off spills immediately with plenty of water. Never leave antifreeze lying around; as it can be fatal if ingested.

If the engine is hot, the electric cooling fan may start rotating even if the engine is not running, so be careful to keep hands, hair and loose clothing well clear when working in the engine compartment.

Air conditioning system

On models with an air conditioning system, it is necessary to observe special precautions whenever dealing with any part of the system, its associated components and any items which necessitate disconnection of the system. If for any reason the system must be disconnected, entrust this task to a refrigeration engineer.

Refrigerant must not be allowed to come in contact with a naked flame, otherwise a poisonous gas will be created. **Do not** allow the fluid to come in contact with the skin or eyes.

2 Cooling system hoses – disconnection and renewal

Note: *Refer to the precautions in Section 1 of this Chapter before starting work.*

1 If the checks described in the appropriate part of Chapter 1 reveal a faulty hose, it must be renewed as follows.

2 First drain the cooling system (see the appropriate part of Chapter 1); if the antifreeze is not due for renewal, the drained coolant may be re-used, if it is collected in a clean container.

3 Release the hose clips from the hose concerned. Almost all the standard clips fitted at the factory are the spring type, released by squeezing its tangs together with pliers, at the same time working the clip away from the hose stub. These clips can be awkward to use, can pinch old hoses, and may become less effective with age, so may have been updated with Jubilee clips (released by turning the screw).

4 Unclip any wires, cables or other hoses which may be attached to the hose being removed. Make notes for reference when reassembling if necessary.

5 Note that the coolant unions are fragile (most are made of plastic); do not use excessive force when attempting to remove the hoses. If a hose proves to be difficult to remove, try to release it by rotating the hose ends before attempting to free it – if this fails, try gently prising up the end of the hose with a small screwdriver to 'break' the seal.

If the hose is stiff, use a little soapy water as a lubricant, or soften the hose by soaking it with hot water. If all else fails, cut the coolant hose with a sharp knife, then slit it so that it can be peeled off in two pieces. Although this may prove expensive if the hose is otherwise undamaged, it is preferable to buying a new radiator.

6 Before fitting the new hose, smear the stubs with washing-up liquid or a suitable rubber lubricant to aid fitting. **Do not** use oil or grease, which may attack the rubber.

7 Fit the hose clips over the ends of the hose, then fit the hose over its stubs. When refitting hose clips, give some thought to how easy they will be to remove in the future – make sure the screw fitting or spring tangs will be accessible.

8 Work each hose end fully onto its outlet, check that the hose is settled correctly and is properly routed, then slide each clip along the hose until it is behind the outlet flared end before tightening it securely. Spring-type clips must have the ends squeezed together, and the clip positioned over the outlet flared end, then released. Do not overtighten screw-type clips, as this may damage the hoses (and even the unions).

9 Refill the cooling system as described in Chapter 1A or 1B. Run the engine, and check that there are no leaks.

10 Recheck the tightness of the hose clips on any new hoses after a few hundred miles.

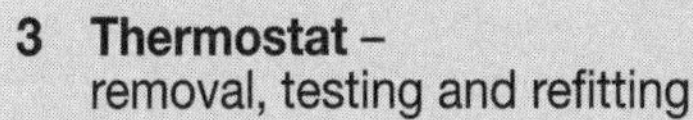

3 Thermostat – removal, testing and refitting

Note: *Refer to the precautions in Section 1 of this Chapter before starting work.*

1 As the thermostat ages, it will become slower to react to changes in water temperature ('lazy'). Ultimately, the unit may stick in the open or closed position, and this causes problems. A thermostat which is stuck open will result in a very slow warm-up; a thermostat which is stuck shut will lead to rapid overheating.

3.19 Thermostat housing on the V6 engine

2 Before assuming the thermostat is to blame for a cooling system problem, check the coolant level. If the system is draining due to a leak, or has not been properly filled, there may be an airlock in the system (refer to the coolant renewal procedure in Chapter 1A or 1B).

3 If the engine seems to be taking a long time to warm up (based on heater output), the thermostat could be stuck open. Don't necessarily believe the temperature gauge reading – some gauges never seem to register very high in normal driving.

4 A lengthy warm-up period might suggest that the thermostat is missing – it may have been removed or inadvertently omitted by a previous owner or mechanic. Don't drive the car without a thermostat – the engine management system's ECU will then stay in warm-up mode for longer than necessary, causing emissions and fuel economy to suffer.

5 If the engine runs hot, use your hand to check the temperature of the radiator top hose. If the hose isn't hot, but the engine clearly is, the thermostat is probably stuck closed, preventing the coolant inside the engine from escaping to the radiator – renew the thermostat. Again, this problem may also be due to an airlock (refer to the coolant renewal procedure in Chapter 1A or 1B).

6 If the radiator top hose is hot, it means that the coolant is flowing (at least as far as the radiator) and the thermostat is open. Consult the *Fault diagnosis* section at the end of this manual to assist in tracing possible cooling system faults, but a lack of heater output would now definitely suggest an airlock or a blockage.

3.21 Purge hose and stub on the thermostat cover

7 To gain a rough idea of whether the thermostat is working properly when the engine is warming-up, without dismantling the system, proceed as follows.

8 With the engine completely cold, start the engine and let it idle, while checking the temperature of the radiator top hose. Periodically check the temperature indicated on the coolant temperature gauge – if overheating is indicated, switch the engine off immediately.

9 The top hose should feel cold for some time as the engine warms-up, and should then get warm quite quickly as the thermostat opens.

10 The above is not a precise or definitive test of thermostat operation, but if the system does not perform as described, remove and test the thermostat as described below.

Removal

11 Drain the cooling system as described in Chapter 1A or 1B. If the coolant is relatively new or in good condition, drain it into a clean container and re-use it.

1.8 and 2.0 litre petrol engines

12 Remove the right-hand headlight as described in Chapter 12, Section 7.

13 Unscrew the nut and detach the power steering pump hydraulic fluid supply line support from the water pump.

14 Disconnect the wiring from the heating element on the thermostat housing.

15 Note the location of the hoses on the thermostat housing, then loosen the clips and disconnect them.

16 Unscrew the bolts and remove the thermostat housing from the cylinder block. Recover the gasket/O-ring seal and discard it; obtain a new one for refitting.

17 It is not possible to separate the thermostat from the housing.

V6 engines

18 Unbolt and remove the top cover from over the water pump pulley.

19 Release the clips and disconnect the hoses from the thermostat housing and cover **(see illustration)**. Remove the housing and cover assembly from the engine compartment.

20 With the assembly on the bench, unscrew the two bolts and remove the cover, then noting how the thermostat is fitted, withdraw it from the housing. Recover the O-ring seal from the perimeter of the thermostat and discard it; obtain a new one for refitting.

Diesel engines

21 Loosen the clips and disconnect the purge and radiator top hoses from the thermostat housing **(see illustration)**. Where spring-type clips are fitted, use a pair of grips or, preferably, obtain a special cable-operated tool to release the clips.

3.22a Unscrew the bolts . . .

3.22b . . . and separate the cover from the thermostat housing

3.23a Remove the thermostat from the housing . . .

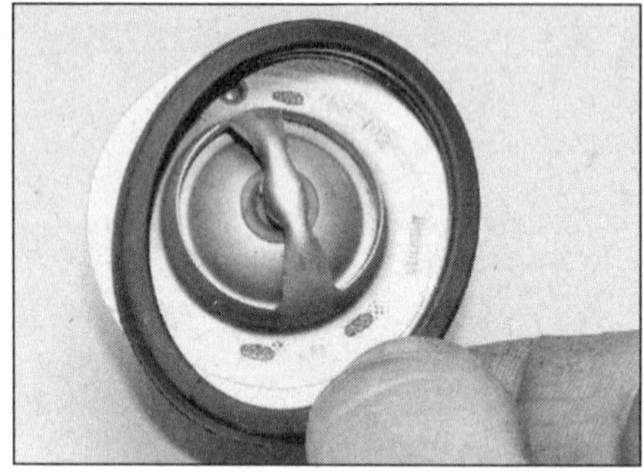
3.23b . . . then remove the O-ring seal

22 Unscrew the bolts and separate the cover from the thermostat housing **(see illustrations)**.

23 Note how the thermostat is fitted and withdraw it from the housing. Recover the O-ring seal and discard it; obtain a new one for refitting **(see illustrations)**.

24 If necessary, the thermostat housing may be removed from the cylinder head outlet elbow. First, disconnect the exhaust gas recirculation (EGR) cooler hose. Unscrew the single bolt and remove the housing. Recover the O-ring seal and discard it; obtain a new one for refitting **(see illustrations)**. Withdraw the housing from the engine compartment.

3.24a Unscrew the single bolt . . .

3.24b . . . remove the housing . . .

3.24c . . . and recover the O-ring seal

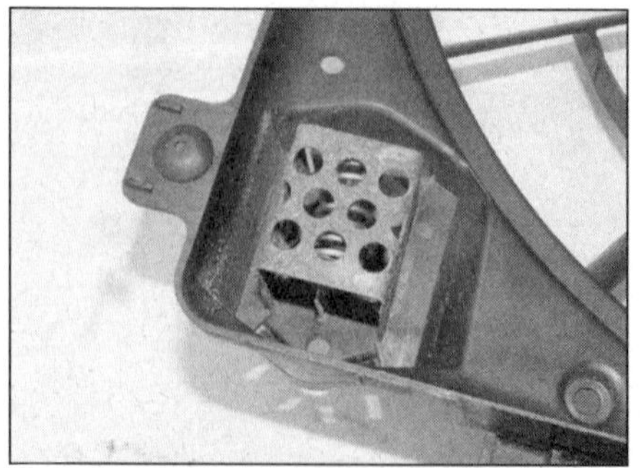
4.1 Fan speed control resistor assembly

Testing

Note: *If there is any question about the operation of the thermostat, it's best to renew it – they are not usually expensive items. Testing involves heating in, or over, an open pan of boiling water, which carries with it the risk of scalding. A thermostat which has seen more than five years' service may well be past its best already.*

25 If the thermostat remains in the open position at room temperature, it is faulty, and must be renewed as a matter of course.

26 Check to see if there's a open temperature marking stamped on the thermostat.

27 Using a thermometer and container of water, heat the water until the temperature corresponds with the temperature marking stamped on the thermostat. If no marking is found, start the test with the water hot, and heat slowly until it boils.

28 Suspend the (closed) thermostat on a length of string in the water, and check that maximum opening occurs within two minutes, or before the water boils.

29 Remove the thermostat and allow it to cool down; check that it closes fully.

30 If the thermostat does not open and close as described, or if it sticks in either position, it must be renewed.

Refitting

31 Refitting is a reversal of removal, but note the following additional points:

a) *Clean all mating surfaces thoroughly before reassembly.*
b) *Renew all seals and gaskets, and smear O-rings with a little rubber grease to aid seating.*
c) *Tighten all bolts to their specified torque wrench settings (where given).*
d) *Ensure the coolant hose clips are positioned so that they do not foul any other components, and so they can easily be removed in future, then tighten them securely.*
e) *Refill the cooling system (see Chapter 1A or 1B).*

4 Radiator cooling fan(s) – testing, removal and refitting

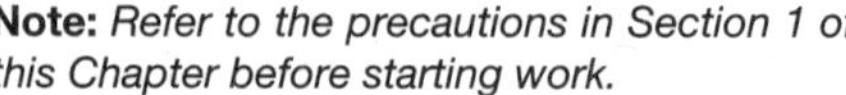

Note: *Refer to the precautions in Section 1 of this Chapter before starting work.*

Testing

1 The radiator cooling fan is controlled by the engine management system's ECU, acting on the information received from the coolant temperature sensor. Twin fans are fitted to all except 1.8 and 2.0 litre petrol models with manual transmission. Where twin fans or two-speed fans are fitted, control is through a resistor assembly secured to the bottom left-hand corner of the fan shroud **(see illustration)** – this can be renewed separately if faulty.

2 First, check the relevant fuses and relays (see Chapter 12).
3 To test the fan motor, unplug the electrical connector and use fused jumper wires to connect the fan directly to the battery. If the fan still does not work, renew the motor.
4 If the motor proved sound, the fault lies in the coolant temperature sensor (see Section 5 for testing details), in the wiring loom (see Chapter 12 for testing details) or in the engine management system (see the appropriate part of Chapter 4).

Removal

Except diesels with auto transmission

5 Disconnect the battery negative lead (refer to *Disconnecting the battery* at the end of this manual).
6 Apply the handbrake, then jack up the front of the car and support it on axle stands (see *Jacking and vehicle support*). Where necessary, remove the engine undertray.
7 Remove the splash shield from beneath the radiator.
8 Using string or cable-ties, support the weight of the radiator, then unscrew the bolts securing the radiator lower mounting brackets to the front suspension subframe. Remove the brackets, noting that they are handed, and are marked to ensure correct refitting **(see illustration)**.
9 Disconnect the wiring from the cooling fan motors and release the wiring harness ties from the shroud and subframe **(see illustrations)**. On V6 models, the wiring plug incorporates a spring clip which must be released.
10 Release the coolant purge hose from the clip on the shroud **(see illustration)**.
11 Unscrew the nuts retaining the cooling fan motors and shroud to the radiator. Carefully slide the electric cooling fan assembly upwards from the side brackets, then lower it downwards and withdraw from under the car **(see illustrations)**.

Diesels with automatic transmission

12 Disconnect the battery negative lead (refer to *Disconnecting the battery* at the end of this manual).
13 Apply the handbrake, then jack up the front of the car and support it on axle stands (see *Jacking and vehicle support*). Remove the engine undertray.
14 Remove the splash shield from beneath the radiator.
15 Using string or plastic cable-ties, support the weight of the radiator, then unscrew the bolts securing the radiator lower mounting brackets to the front suspension subframe. Remove the brackets, noting that they are handed, and are marked to ensure correct refitting.
16 Disconnect the wiring from the cooling fan motors and release the wiring harness from the clip on the front suspension subframe.
17 Unscrew the nuts retaining the cooling fan motors and shroud to the radiator.
18 Carefully slide the electric cooling fan assembly upwards from the side brackets, then lower it until it is possible to reach the cooling fan motor module. Unscrew the module mounting bolts, and position it within the shroud – this will provide additional clearance for removing the assembly.
19 Lower the assembly and withdraw it from under the car.

Refitting

20 Refitting is a reversal of removal.

4.8 Removing the radiator lower mounting brackets

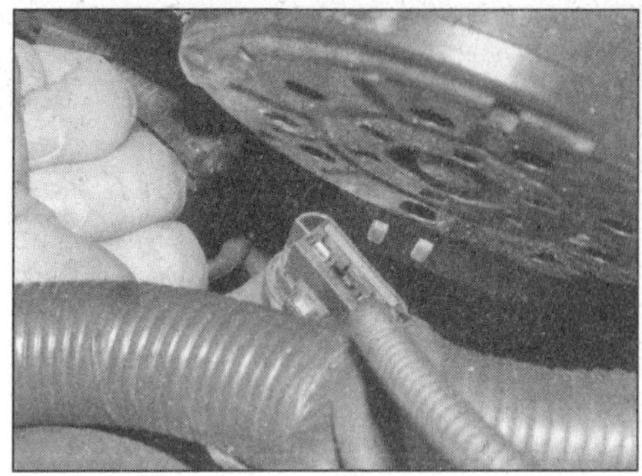
4.9a Disconnect the electric cooling fan motor wiring . . .

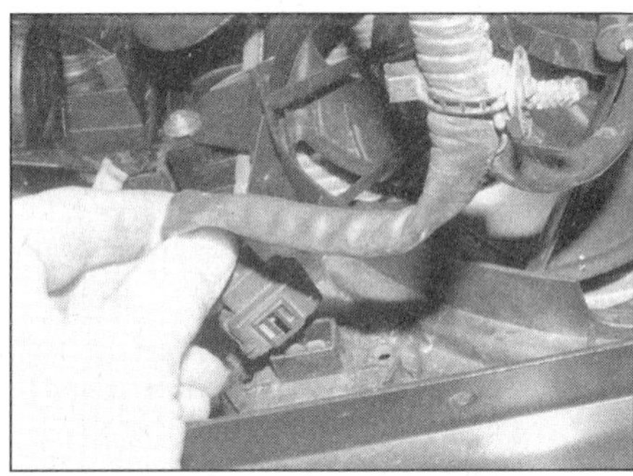
4.9b . . . and loom connector . . .

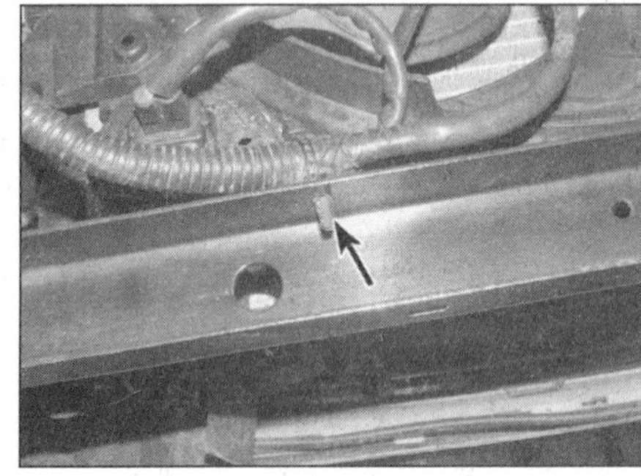
4.9c . . . and release the wiring loom from the subframe

4.10 Release the coolant purge hose from the clip on the shroud

4.11a Unscrew the right-hand mounting nut . . .

4.11b . . . and left-hand mounting nut . . .

4.11c . . . then lower the electric cooling fan assembly from under the vehicle

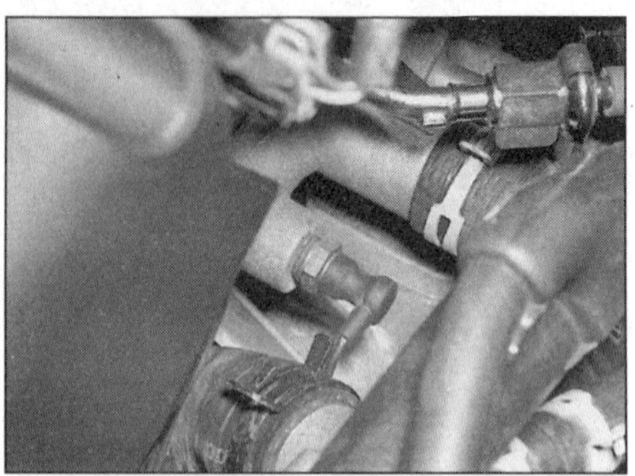
5.2 Coolant temperature sender on the 2.5 litre V6 engine

5 Coolant temperature sensor – testing, removal and refitting

Note: *Refer to the precautions in Section 1 of this Chapter before starting work.*

1 On all except V6 engine models, the sensor is screwed into the outlet housing on the left-hand end of the cylinder head.

2 On V6 engine models, the sensor is at the front of the bypass housing on the left-hand end of the engine **(see illustration)**.

Testing

3 If the coolant temperature gauge is inoperative, check the fuses first (see Chapter 12).

4 If the gauge indicates 'hot' at any time, consult the *Fault finding* Section at the end of this manual, to assist in tracing possible cooling system faults.

5 If the gauge indicates 'hot' shortly after the engine is started from cold, unplug the coolant temperature sensor's electrical connector. If the gauge reading now drops, renew the sensor. If the reading remains high, the wiring to the gauge may be shorted to earth, or the gauge is faulty.

6 If the gauge fails to indicate after the engine has been warmed-up and the fuses are known to be sound, switch off the engine. Unplug the sensor's electrical connector, and use a jumper wire to connect the white/red wire to a clean earth point (bare metal) on the engine. Switch on the ignition without starting the engine. If the gauge now indicates 'hot', renew the sensor.

7 If the gauge still does not work, the circuit may be open, or the gauge may be faulty. See Chapter 12 for additional information.

Removal

8 Drain the cooling system (see Chapter 1A or 1B) and remove the engine top cover.

9 On 1.8 and 2.0 litre petrol engines, remove the ignition coil pack (see Chapter 5B).

10 On V6 and diesel engines, remove the water pump drivebelt cover. Refer to the appropriate part of Chapter 4 and disconnect the air inlet hose from the air cleaner housing. Access will be made easier if the battery is also removed (see Chapter 5A).

11 Unplug the electrical connector from the sensor.

12 Unscrew the sensor and withdraw it.

Refitting

13 Clean any traces of old sealant from the sensor location, then apply a light coat of sealant to the sensor's threads. Screw in the sensor and tighten it securely, and reconnect the wiring.

14 Refill the cooling system as described in Chapter 1A or 1B and run the engine. Check for leaks.

6.3 Disconnecting the radiator top hose

6.4 Expansion tank hose on the radiator

6 Radiator and expansion tank – removal, inspection and refitting

Note: *Refer to the precautions in Section 1 of this Chapter before starting work. If leakage is the reason for removing the radiator, bear in mind that minor leaks can often be cured using a radiator sealant added to the coolant with the radiator in situ.*

Radiator

Removal

1 Drain the cooling system as described in Chapter 1A or 1B. If the coolant is relatively new or in good condition, drain it into a clean container and re-use it.

2 Remove the radiator electric cooling fan assembly as described in Section 4. This procedure includes removing the radiator bottom mounting brackets.

3 Release the clips and disconnect the top and bottom hoses from the radiator **(see illustration)**.

4 Loosen the clip and disconnect the expansion tank hose from the radiator **(see illustration)**.

5 On diesel engine models, position a suitable container beneath the oil cooler coolant hose on the radiator, then loosen the clip and disconnect the hose. Also, release the oil cooler hose from the retaining clip and remove the clip from the front suspension subframe.

6 Support the weight of the air conditioning condenser with cable-ties or string, then unscrew the bolts securing it to the radiator **(see illustrations)**.

Warning: Do not disconnect any of the refrigerant hoses.

7 Release the radiator, then carefully lower it and withdraw it from under the car **(see illustration)**. Take care not to damage the radiator fins, as they are easily bent.

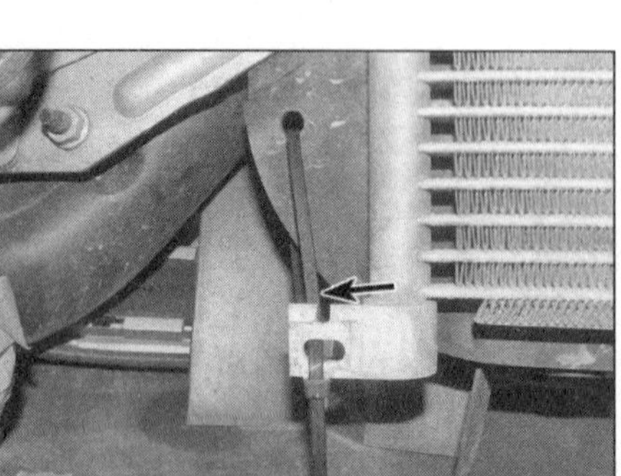
6.6a Support the air conditioning condenser with cable ties . . .

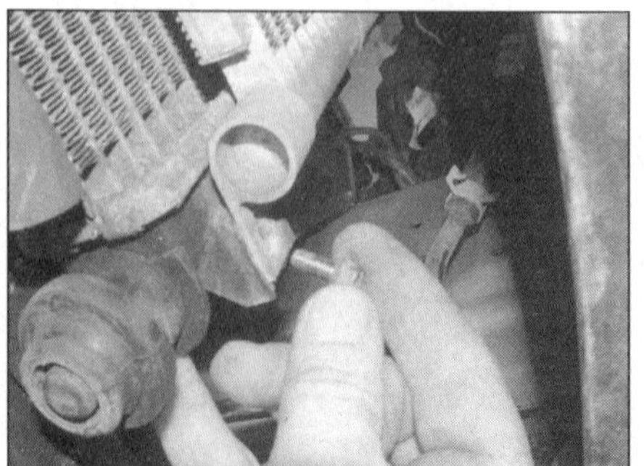
6.6b . . . then unscrew the condenser mounting bolts

6.7 Lowering the radiator from under the vehicle

8 Remove the radiator rubber mounting bushes from the top and bottom brackets, and inspect them for wear and damage **(see illustration)**. If worn excessively, obtain and fit new ones before refitting the radiator.

Inspection

9 With the radiator removed, it can be inspected for leaks and damage. If it needs repair, have a radiator specialist or dealer service department perform the work, as special techniques are required.

10 Insects and dirt can be removed from the radiator with a garden hose or a soft brush. Take care not to bend the cooling fins.

Refitting

11 Refitting is the reverse of the removal procedure, but refill the cooling system as described in Chapter 1A or 1B.

Expansion tank

Removal

12 With the engine completely cool, remove the expansion tank filler cap to release any pressure, then syphon all of the coolant from the tank. If the antifreeze is not due for renewal, the drained coolant may be re-used, if it is kept clean.

13 Disconnect all the hoses from the tank.

14 Unscrew the tank's two mounting bolts and withdraw it, unplugging the coolant low level switch electrical connector (where fitted).

15 Wash out the tank, and inspect it for cracks and chafing – renew it if damaged.

Refitting

16 Refitting is the reverse of the removal procedure. Refill the cooling system with the proper mixture of antifreeze and water with reference to Chapter 1A or 1B.

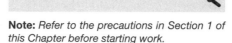

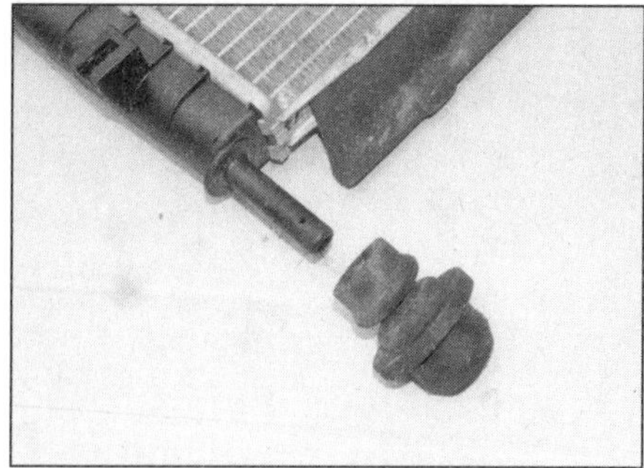

6.8 Check the radiator mounting bushes

7 Water pump – removal and refitting

Note: *Refer to the precautions in Section 1 of this Chapter before starting work.*

Removal

1 Drain the cooling system as described in Chapter 1A or 1B. If the coolant is relatively new or in good condition, drain it into a clean container and re-use it.

1.8 and 2.0 litre petrol engines

2 Before removing the auxiliary drivebelt, loosen the water pump pulley mounting bolts by half a turn. Alternatively, they may be loosened later if a suitable pulley holder is available.

3 Apply the handbrake, then jack up the front of the car and support it on axle stands (see *Jacking and vehicle support*). Remove the right-hand front roadwheel.

4 Working under the right-hand front wheel arch, undo the bolts and remove the splash shield for access to the right-hand end of the engine.

5 Note the routing of the auxiliary drivebelt. Turn the tensioner clockwise, then slip the drivebelt from the pulleys and remove from the engine compartment. If the belt is to be re-used, mark its direction of fitting.

6 Fully unscrew the bolts and remove the pulley from the water pump **(see illustrations)**.

7 Progressively unscrew the three mounting bolts and remove the water pump from the engine. Remove the O-ring seal and discard it **(see illustrations)**. Obtain a new one for the refitting procedure, noting that Ford state that the seal should be lubricated with 'Merpol' grease.

V6 engines

8 Remove the air cleaner as described in Chapter 4A.

9 Remove the thermostat housing as described in Section 3.

10 Remove the water pump drivebelt by turning the tensioner clockwise with a socket **(see illustration)** – on later V6 engines, a tensioner is not used, and the only way to remove the belt is to cut it off. Slip the drivebelt from the pulleys and remove it from the engine compartment.

7.6a Using a pulley holder when removing the water pump pulley (1.8 and 2.0 litre petrol engine)

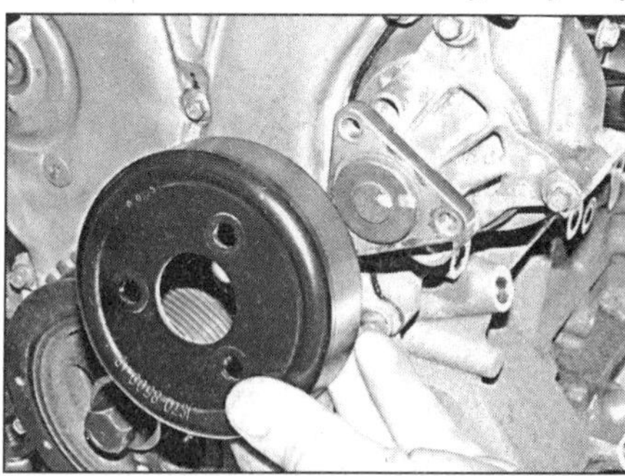

7.6b Removing the water pump pulley (1.8 and 2.0 litre petrol engine)

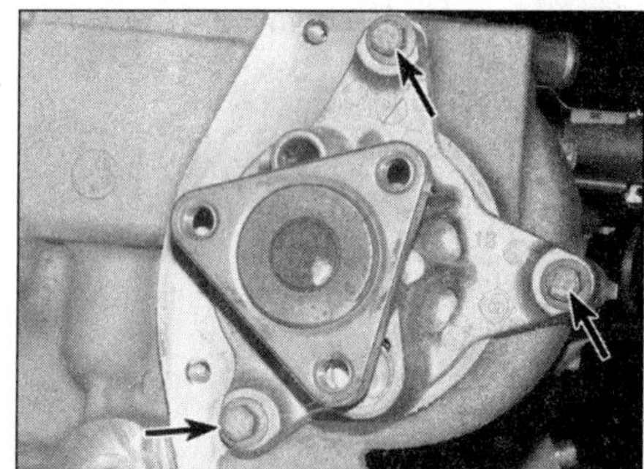

7.7a Unscrew the mounting bolts . . .

7.7b . . . remove the water pump . . .

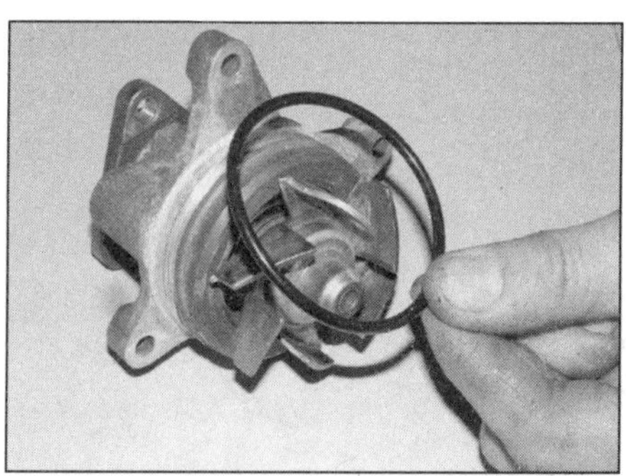

7.7c . . . and remove the O-ring seal (1.8 and 2.0 litre petrol engine)

7.10 Water pump and drivebelt (V6 engine)

7.11 Water pump mounting bolts (V6 engine)

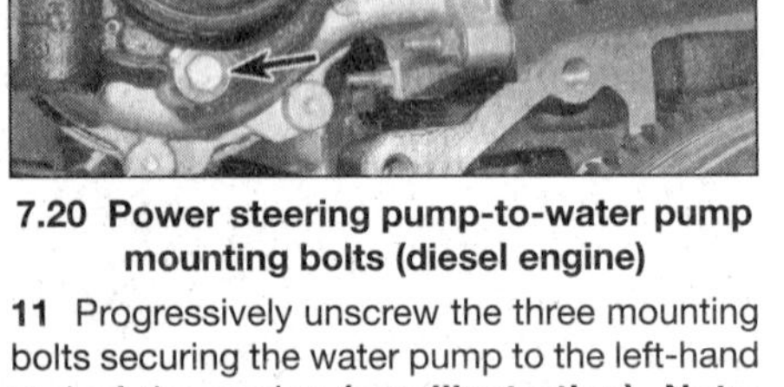

7.20 Power steering pump-to-water pump mounting bolts (diesel engine)

11 Progressively unscrew the three mounting bolts securing the water pump to the left-hand end of the engine **(see illustration)**. **Note:** *The impeller is secured to the housing by the remaining five bolts. Neither the impeller nor its gasket is available separately.*

7.22a Unscrew the water pump housing-to-block bolts . . .

7.22c . . . and remove the gasket

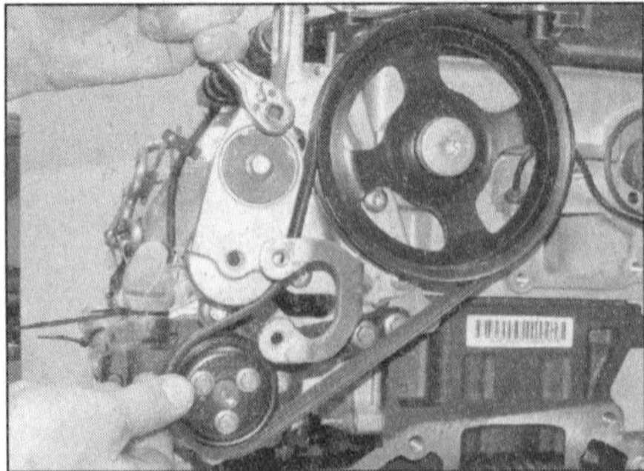

7.16 Removing the drivebelt from the power steering pump pulley

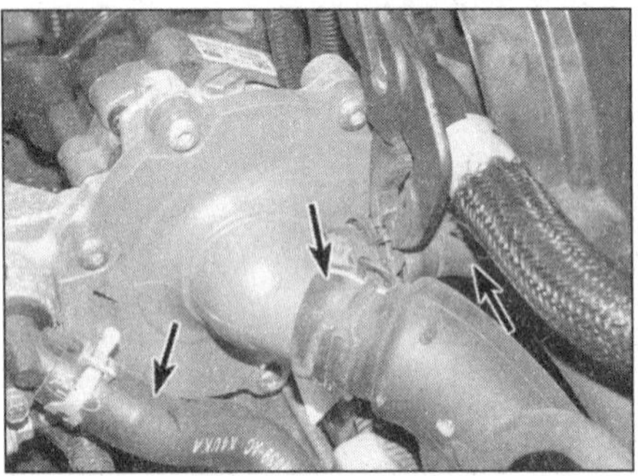

7.21 Disconnecting the hoses from the water pump (diesel engine)

12 Loosen the clips and disconnect the hoses, then withdraw the pump from the engine.

Diesel engines

13 Remove the engine plastic top cover.

14 Remove the air inlet pipe. To do this, first release the coolant pipe from the clip, then loosen the clips and withdraw the inlet pipe.

15 Unscrew the air inlet pipe and exhaust gas recirculation (EGR) tube mounting bolts.

16 Using a suitable square drive in the special hole, turn the tensioner clockwise, then slip the drivebelt from the power steering pump pulley **(see illustration)**. If the belt is to be re-used, mark its direction of fitting. Remove the drivebelt from the engine compartment.

17 Remove the inlet manifold from the engine as described in Chapter 2C.

18 Unscrew the mounting bolt and position the power steering fluid reservoir to one side.

19 Unscrew the bolt securing the power steering fluid line support bracket to the cylinder head.

20 Unscrew the bolts securing the power steering pump to the water pump, and position it to one side **(see illustration)**.

21 Release the clips and disconnect the hoses from the water pump **(see illustration)**.

22 Unscrew and remove the water pump housing-to-block bolts, noting the location of the wiring harness on the lower bolts. Withdraw the pump far enough to disconnect the remaining hose. Remove the gasket and discard it **(see illustrations)**. Obtain a new one for the refitting procedure.

23 Unbolt the engine oil temperature control thermostat from the water pump housing and discard the O-ring seal **(see illustrations)**. Obtain a new one for the refitting procedure.

7.22b . . . withdraw the assembly . . .

7.23a Unscrew the bolt . . .

Refitting

24 Refitting is a reversal of removal, but tighten the mounting bolts/nuts to the specified torque. Refill the cooling system with reference to Chapter 1A or 1B.

8 Heater/ventilation components – removal and refitting

Heater blower motor

Removal

1 Unclip and remove the passenger footwell lower trim panel **(see illustration)**.

2 Remove the glovebox as described in Chapter 11.

7.23b . . . and remove the oil temperature control thermostat from the water pump housing

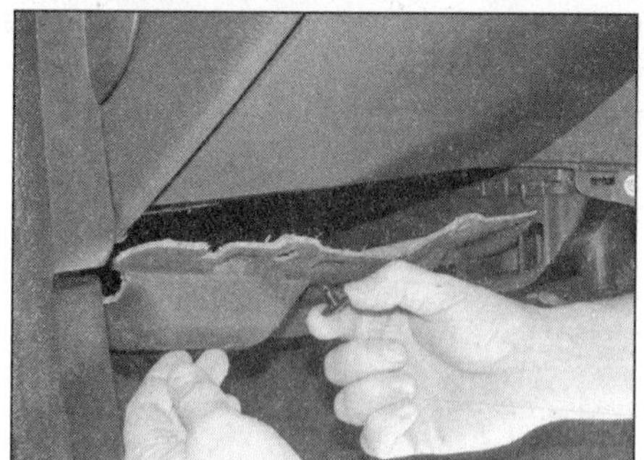

8.1 Removing the passenger footwell lower trim panel

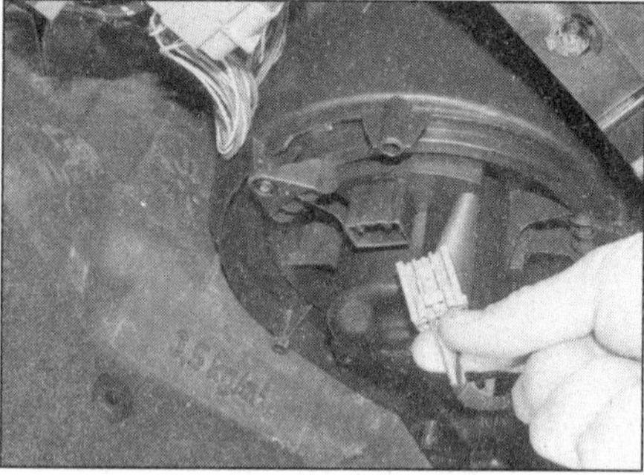
8.3 Disconnect the wiring . . .

8.4a . . . then undo the retaining screws . . .

3 Disconnect the wiring from the heater blower motor **(see illustration)**.

4 Undo the retaining screws and lower the blower motor from the heater casing **(see illustrations)**.

Refitting

5 Refitting is a reversal of removal.

Heater matrix

Removal

6 Apply the handbrake, then jack up the front of the car and support it on axle stands (see *Jacking and vehicle support*). On diesel models, remove the engine undertray.

7 Drain the cooling system as described in Chapter 1A or 1B. If the coolant is relatively new or in good condition, drain it into a clean container and re-use it.

8 On the engine side of the bulkhead, loosen the clips and disconnect the coolant hoses from the matrix stubs **(see illustration)**. Identify the locations of the hoses for correct refitting. Also disconnect the water drain hose from the drain connection on the matrix.

9 Remove the centre console as described in Chapter 11.

10 Undo the two lower and single rear screws securing the rear footwell air guide to the matrix housing, then release the clips and remove the air guide **(see illustrations)**. If the clips are tight, press upwards on the guide while releasing them.

11 Remove the front clips, then release the side clips and lower the matrix and housing to the floor **(see illustrations)**. Withdraw it from inside the car.

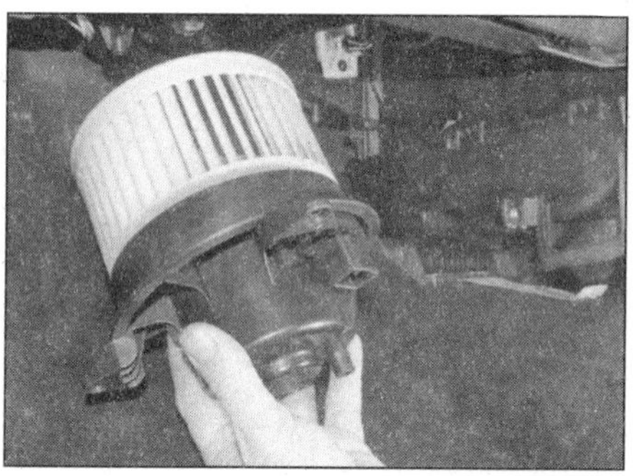
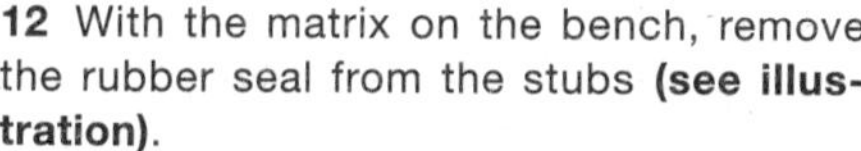
8.4b . . . and lower the heater blower motor from its housing

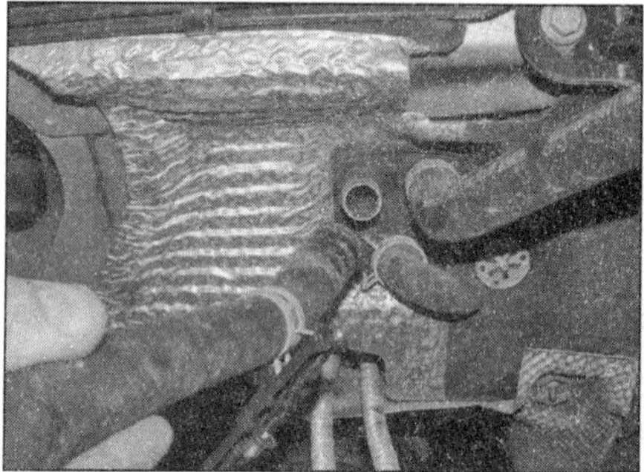
8.8 Disconnecting the hoses from the matrix stubs on the bulkhead

12 With the matrix on the bench, remove the rubber seal from the stubs **(see illustration)**.

13 Undo the screw and remove the plastic clamp, then remove the matrix from its housing **(see illustrations)**. Be prepared for some spillage of coolant by placing cloth rags on the floor of the car.

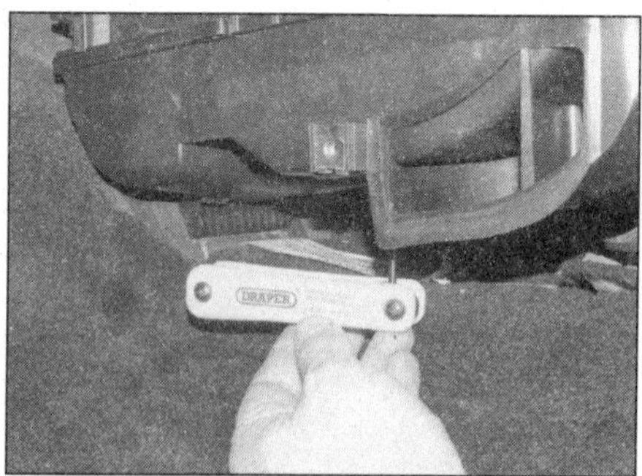
8.10a Undo the lower screws . . .

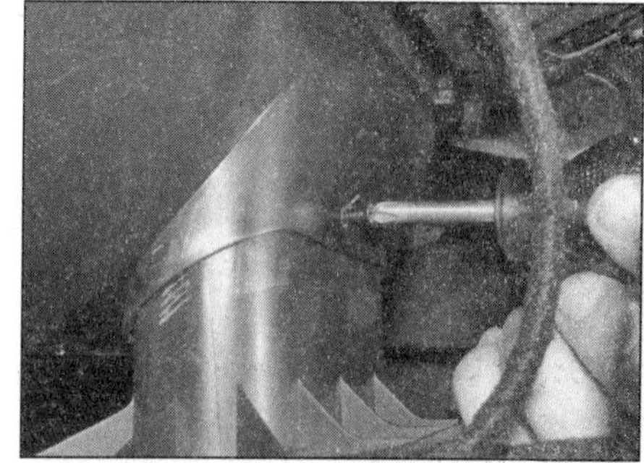
8.10b . . . and single rear screw . . .

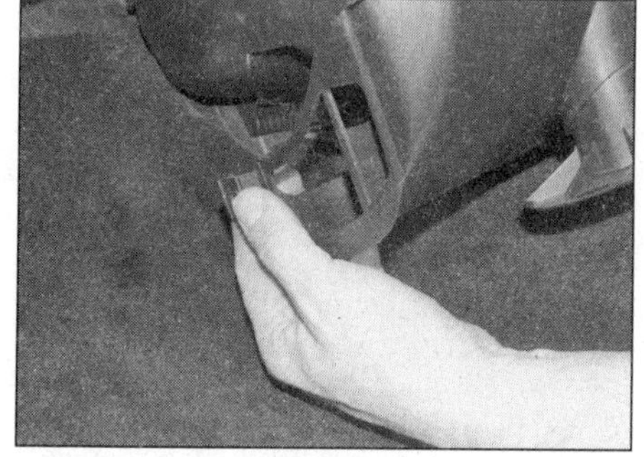
8.10c . . . and remove the rear footwell air guide

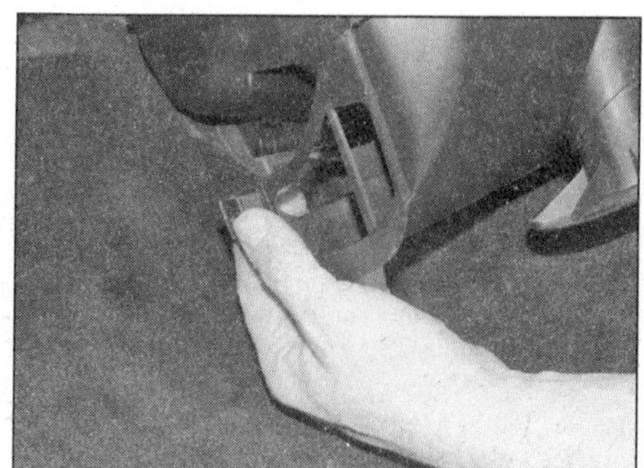
8.11a Remove the front clips . . .

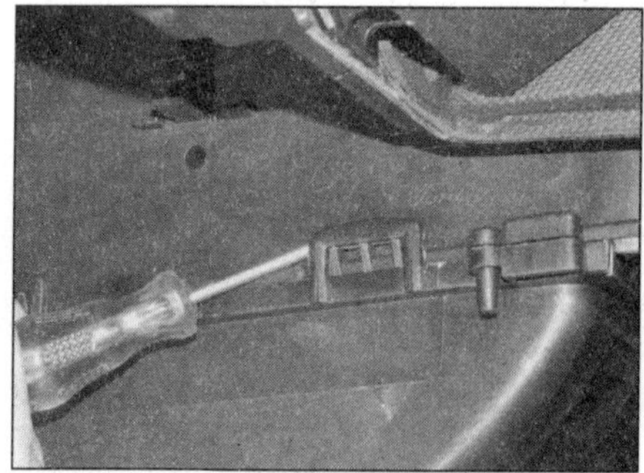
8.11b . . . release the side clips . . .

8.11c . . . and lower the matrix and housing to the floor

8.13b . . . remove the plastic clamp . . .

Refitting

14 Refitting is a reversal of removal. Refill the cooling system with reference to Chapter 1A or 1B.

9.3a There are two facia centre panel screws above the heater control panel . . .

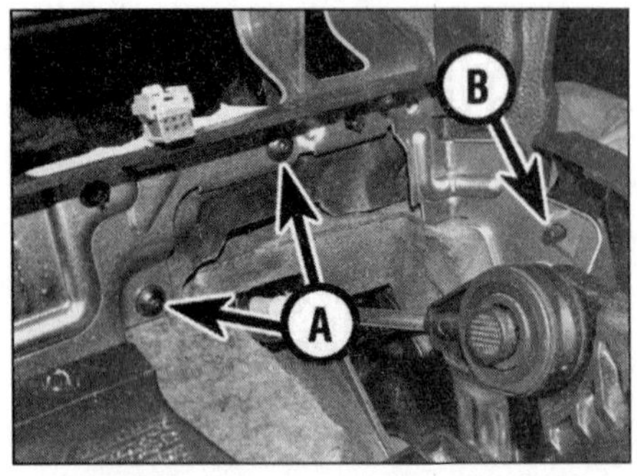

9.6a Metal support bracket's two centre screws (A) – note one side peg (B)

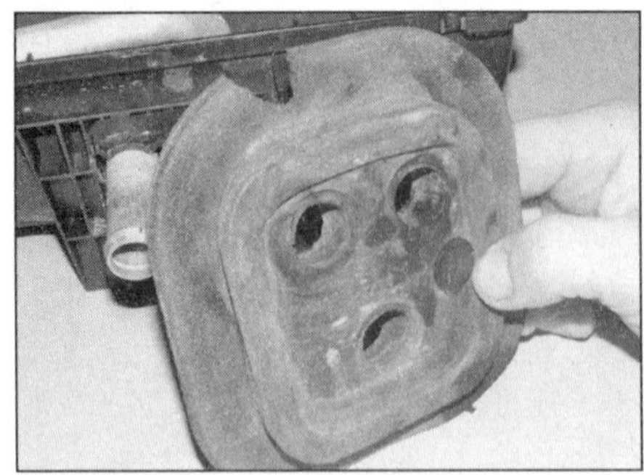
8.12 Removing the rubber seal from the matrix stubs

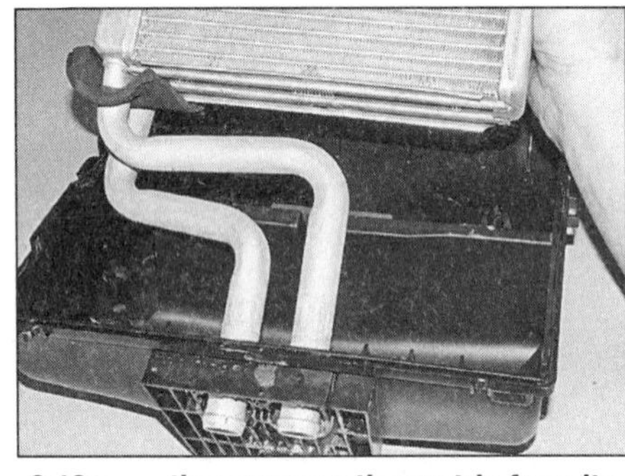
8.13c . . . then remove the matrix from its housing

Heater housing

Removal and refitting

15 The heater housing removal and refitting procedure is similar to that for the air conditioning heater/evaporator housing described in Section 11.

9.3b . . . and two more on each side of the radio aperture

9.6b Console screw on each side also secures the metal support bracket

8.13a Undo the screw . . .

Pollen filter

Removal and refitting

16 Refer to Chapter 1A or 1B.

9 Heater/air conditioning controls – removal and refitting

Note: *On high-specification models with touchscreen satellite navigation, the heater controls are part of the touchscreen unit, and are located down one side. The complete unit can be removed as described in Chapter 12, Section 24, but the heater controls are part of it. The heater control module on the rear of the unit is, however, available separately.*

Removal

1 Disconnect the battery negative lead (refer to *Disconnecting the battery* at the end of this manual).

2 Remove the radio/CD player and the clock as described in Chapter 12 (the clock itself does not have to be unscrewed, but its surround panel must be removed).

3 The screws securing the facia centre panel must now be removed. There are two screws above the heater control panel, and two more on each side of the radio aperture **(see illustrations)**.

4 Working in the footwell on each side, remove the console front side panels. To do this, prise out the cover and undo the front screw located near the bulkhead, then carefully release the five upper clips and one lower clip. Withdraw the panels.

5 Working as described in Chapter 11, Section 29, paragraphs 4 and 5, remove the gear/selector lever trim panel.

6 Remove the metal support bracket at the front of the centre console. This bracket is secured by two screws in the centre, and by the centre console front screw on either side. The bracket is also located on two pegs from the centre console – once the four screws are removed, carefully pull the front 'legs' of the console outwards to release the pegs, and the bracket can be withdrawn **(see illustrations)**.

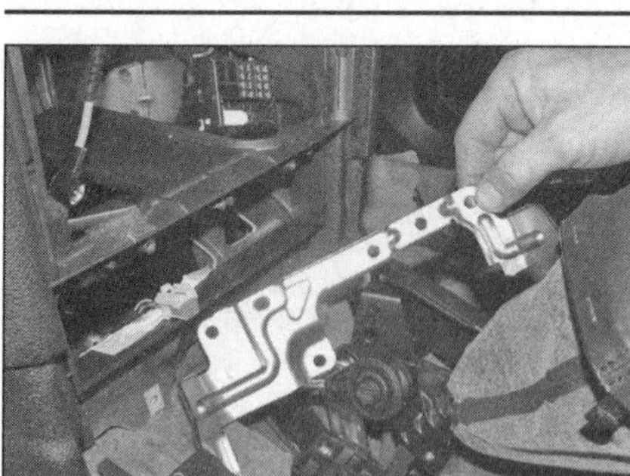

9.6c Removing the metal support bracket

9.7a Pull the facia centre panel out at the base . . .

9.7b . . . then at the top to release the vents

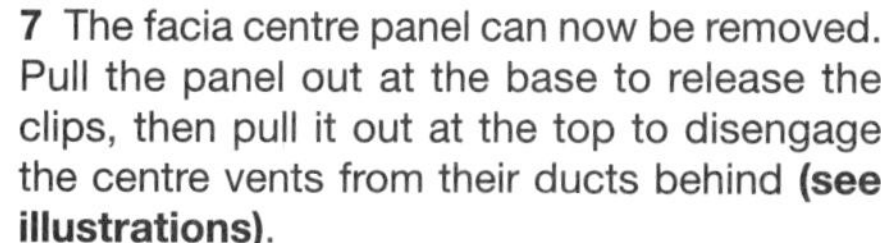

7 The facia centre panel can now be removed. Pull the panel out at the base to release the clips, then pull it out at the top to disengage the centre vents from their ducts behind **(see illustrations)**.

8 When the centre panel is free, reach in behind and disconnect the two wiring plugs from the heater control panel – the plugs are secured using hinged locking levers, which must be pivoted sideways to release them **(see illustration)**.

9 The heater control panel is secured to the inside of the facia centre panel by four screws – remove the screws and withdraw the panel **(see illustration)**. It appears that the panel is a self-contained unit, with no parts (not even bulbs) available separately.

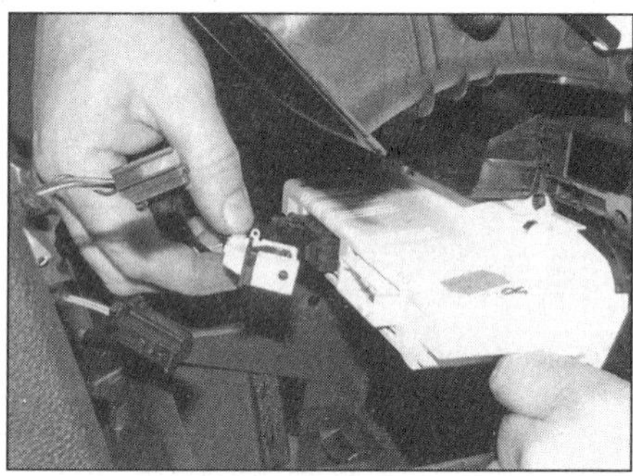

9.8 Disconnecting the heater control panel wiring plugs

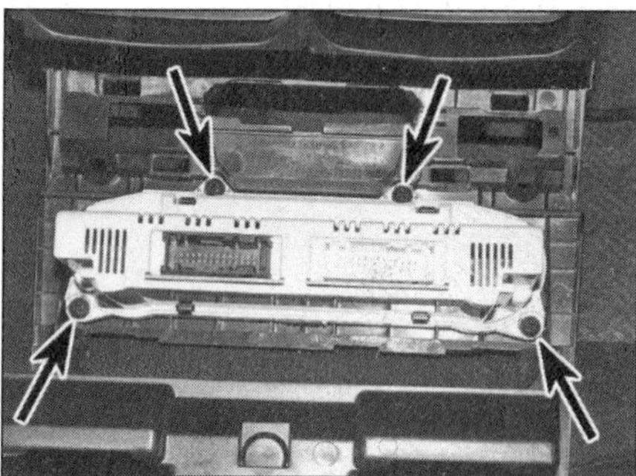

9.9 Heater control panel securing screws

Refitting

10 Refitting is a reversal of removal. Ensure that the wiring plugs on the back of the heater control panel are connected securely, and locked in place using the hinged levers.

10 Air conditioning system – general information and precautions

General information

The air conditioning system consists of a condenser mounted in front of the radiator, an evaporator mounted adjacent to the heater matrix, a compressor driven by an auxiliary drivebelt, an accumulator/dehydrator, and the pipes connecting all of the above components **(see illustration)**.

The cooling side of the system works in the same way as a domestic refrigerator. Refrigerant gas at low pressure is drawn into a belt-driven compressor and passes into a condenser mounted on the front of the radiator, where it loses heat and becomes liquid. The liquid passes through an expansion valve to an evaporator, where it changes from liquid under high pressure to gas under low pressure. This change is accompanied by a drop in temperature, which cools the evaporator. The refrigerant returns to the compressor, and the cycle begins again.

Air blown through the evaporator passes to the air distribution unit, where it is mixed

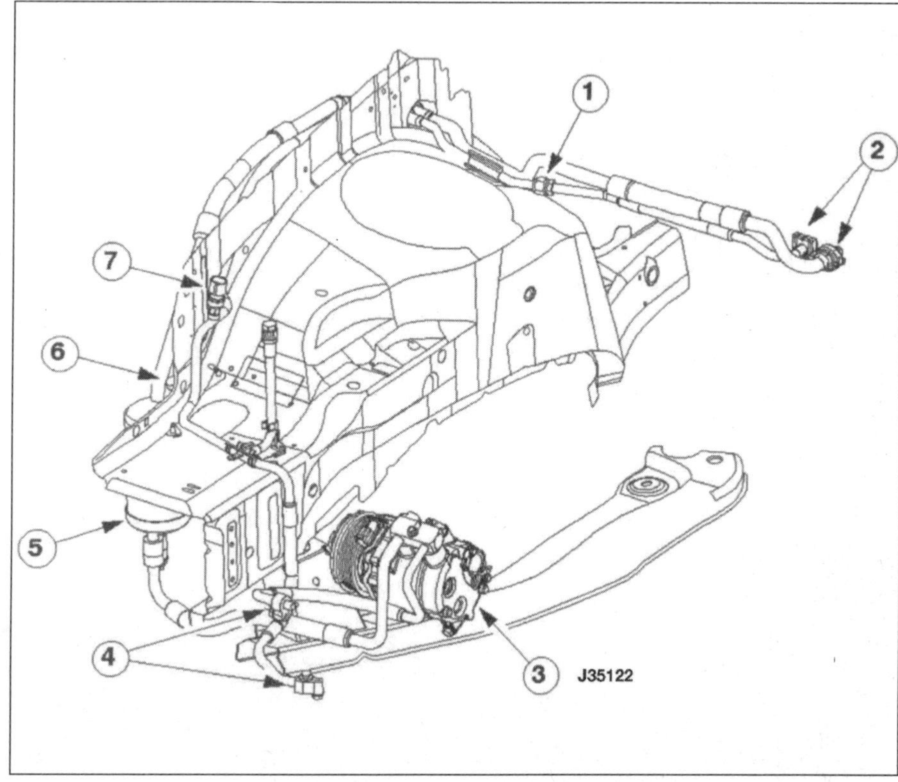

10.1 Air conditioning system components

1 Evaporator matrix orifice
2 Evaporator core connections
3 Air conditioning compressor
4 Condenser matrix connections
5 Suction accumulator/dehydrator
6 Low-pressure cut-off switch
7 High-pressure cut-off switch

TOOL TIP

Many car accessory shops sell one-shot air conditioning recharge aerosols. These generally contain refrigerant, compressor oil, leak sealer and system conditioner. Some also have a dye to help pinpoint leaks.

Warning: These products must only be used as directed by the manufacturer, and do not remove the need for regular maintenance.

with hot air blown through the heater matrix to achieve the desired temperature in the passenger compartment.

The heating side of the system works in the same way as on models without air conditioning.

Precautions

Warning: The air conditioning system is under high pressure. Do not loosen any fittings or remove any components until after the system has been discharged. Air conditioning refrigerant should be properly discharged into an approved type of container, at a dealer service department or an automotive air conditioning repair facility capable of handling R134a refrigerant. Always wear eye protection when disconnecting air conditioning system fittings.

When an air conditioning system is fitted, it is necessary to observe the following special precautions whenever dealing with any part of the system, its associated components, and any items which necessitate disconnection of the system:

a) *While the refrigerant used – R134a – is less damaging to the environment than the previously-used R12, it is still a very dangerous substance. It must not be allowed into contact with the skin or eyes, or there is a risk of frostbite. It must also not be discharged in an enclosed space – while it is not toxic, there is a risk of suffocation. The refrigerant is heavier than air, and so must never be discharged over a pit.*

b) *The refrigerant must not be allowed to come in contact with a naked flame, otherwise a poisonous gas will be created – under certain circumstances, this can form an explosive mixture with air. For similar reasons, smoking in the presence of refrigerant is highly dangerous, particularly if the vapour is inhaled through a lighted cigarette.*

c) *Never discharge the system to the atmosphere – R134a is not an ozone-depleting ChloroFluoroCarbon (CFC) like R12, but is instead a hydrofluorocarbon, which causes environmental damage by contributing to the 'greenhouse effect' if released into the atmosphere.*

d) *R134a refrigerant must not be mixed with R12; the system uses different seals (now green-coloured, previously black) and has different fittings requiring different tools, so that there is no chance of the two types of refrigerant becoming mixed accidentally.*

e) *If for any reason the system must be disconnected, entrust this task to your Ford dealer or a refrigeration engineer.*

f) *It is essential that the system be professionally discharged prior to using any form of heat – welding, soldering, brazing, etc – in the vicinity of the system, before having the car oven-dried at a temperature exceeding 70°C after repainting, and before disconnecting any part of the system.*

11 Air conditioning system components – removal and refitting

Warning: The air conditioning system is under high pressure. Do not loosen any fittings or remove any components until after the system has been discharged. Air conditioning refrigerant should be properly discharged into an approved type of container, at a dealer service department or an automotive air conditioning repair facility capable of handling R134a refrigerant. Cap or plug the pipe lines as soon as they are disconnected, to prevent the entry of moisture. Always wear eye protection when disconnecting air conditioning system fittings.

Note 1: *This Section refers to the components of the air conditioning system itself – refer to Sections 8 and 9 for details of components common to the heating/ventilation system.*

Note 2: *Some diesel models with automatic transmission have their fluid cooler incorporated into the condenser, meaning that the fluid cooler pipes have to be disconnected as part of this procedure. A Ford special tool is needed to separate the pipe quick-release connections – refer to Chapter 7B, Section 12.*

Condenser

Removal

1 Have the refrigerant discharged at a dealer service department or an automotive air conditioning repair facility.

2 On diesel models fitted with automatic transmission, secure the radiator at both sides with cable-ties or string.

3 Apply the handbrake, then jack up the front of the car and support it on axle stands (see *Jacking and vehicle support*).

4 Remove the radiator lower splash shield.

5 Disconnect the refrigerant lines from the condenser, and immediately cap the openings to prevent the entry of dirt and moisture **(see illustrations)**. Discard the O-ring seals and obtain new ones for the refitting procedure.

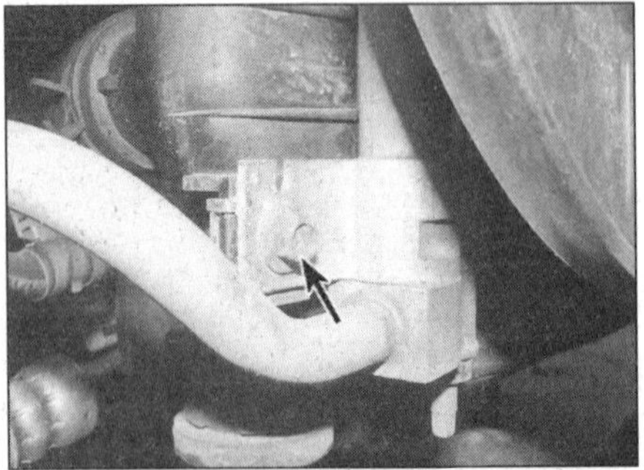

11.5a Disconnect the refrigerant line upper . . .

11.5b . . . and lower retaining nuts

6 On diesel models fitted with automatic transmission, unbolt the radiator lower mounting bracket from the subframe, then mark the automatic transmission fluid cooler hoses for position. Position a suitable container beneath the fluid cooler, then disconnect the hoses and allow the fluid to drain into the container – for more information, refer to Chapter 7B, Section 12.

7 Unscrew the bolts securing the air conditioning condenser to the radiator, then carefully lower it and withdraw from under the car.

Refitting

8 Refitting is a reversal of removal, noting the following points:

a) *Fit new O-ring seals to the refrigerant pipes when reconnecting. The O-ring seals must be coated with clean refrigerant oil before refitting them.*

b) *On diesel models with automatic transmission, refer to Chapter 7B, Section 12, when reconnecting the fluid cooler pipes. Top-up or refill the transmission, then warm-up and check the fluid level, as described in Chapter 1B.*

c) *Have the air conditioning system evacuated, charged and leak-tested by the specialist who discharged it.*

Heater/evaporator housing

Note: *Special tool 412-081 will be required for this work.*

Removal

9 Have the refrigerant discharged at a dealer service department or an automotive air conditioning repair facility.

10 Apply the handbrake, then jack up the front of the car and support it on axle stands (see *Jacking and vehicle support*). On diesel models, remove the engine undertray.

11 Disconnect the battery negative lead (refer to *Disconnecting the battery* at the end of this manual).

12 Drain the cooling system as described in Chapter 1A or 1B. If the coolant is relatively new or in good condition, drain it into a clean container and re-use it.

13 On the engine side of the bulkhead, loosen the clips and disconnect the coolant hoses from the matrix stubs. Identify the locations of the hoses for correct refitting.

14 Disconnect the water drain hose from the drain connection on the matrix.

15 Remove the facia as described in Chapter 11.

16 Remove the air duct, then pull back the weatherstrip from the right-hand door opening and remove the cowl side trim panel.

17 Unbolt the earth cable from the A-pillar, disconnect the main electrical connector and disconnect the two wiring plugs from the generic electronic module (GEM).

18 Release the wiring harness from the heater/evaporator matrix housing. Also unclip and disconnect the vent actuator wiring harness.

19 Disconnect the blower motor and resistor wiring. Also disconnect the temperature sensor and handbrake warning light wiring.

20 Disconnect the adaptive restraint module and central junction box wiring.

21 Undo the screws and remove the windscreen air duct.

22 On V6 engine models, remove the ignition coil.

23 Release the refrigerant line spring lock coupling locking clips **(see illustration)**.

24 Using the special tool 412-081, disconnect the left- and right-hand refrigerant lines from the evaporator matrix. Discard the O-ring seals.

25 Unscrew and remove the heater/evaporator matrix housing mounting nut from the bulkhead.

26 Unclip the wiring harness, and remove the bulkhead cross-beam from inside the car.

27 Withdraw the heater/evaporator housing from inside the car. Be prepared for some spillage of coolant by placing cloth rags on the floor of the car.

Refitting

28 Refitting is a reversal of removal, but fit new O-ring seals. The O-ring seals must be coated with clean refrigerant oil before refitting them. Have the system evacuated, charged and leak-tested by the specialist who discharged it.

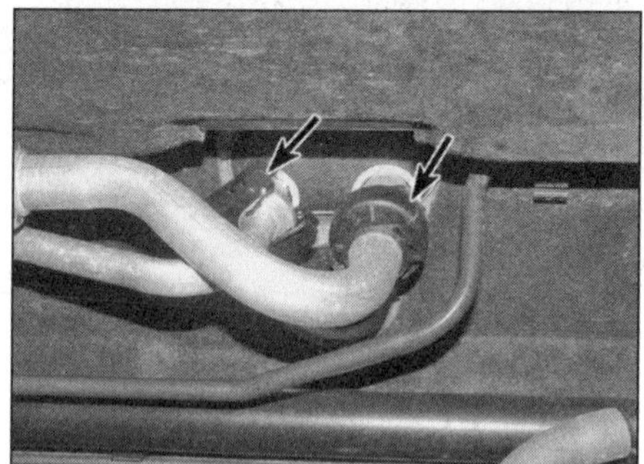

11.23 Air conditioning refrigerant line spring lock coupling locking clips

Compressor

Removal

29 Have the refrigerant discharged at a dealer service department or an automotive air conditioning repair facility.

30 Apply the handbrake, then jack up the front of the car and support it on axle stands (see *Jacking and vehicle support*). Remove the radiator lower splash guard. On diesel models, remove the engine undertray.

31 On V6 models, unbolt and remove the compressor heat shield.

32 On diesel models, loosen the clip and disconnect the intercooler outlet hose from the exhaust gas EGR return valve. Also disconnect the wiring from the mass airflow (MAF) sensor, and remove the intercooler outlet hose after loosening the clips.

33 On diesel models, remove the radiator as described in Section 6.

34 Disconnect the wiring from the air conditioning compressor. Note on diesel models, it is easier to disconnect the wiring as the compressor is being withdrawn from the engine.

35 Remove the main auxiliary drivebelt as described in Chapter 1A or 1B.

36 Unscrew the bolt and disconnect the union block from the compressor. Discard the O-ring seals, and obtain new ones for the refitting procedure. Tape over or plug the compressor apertures and line ends, to prevent entry of dust and dirt.

37 Support the air conditioning compressor, then unscrew the mounting bolts. Lower the compressor from the engine. **Note:** *Keep the compressor level during handling and storage. If the compressor has seized, or if you find metal particles in the refrigerant lines, the system must be flushed out by an air conditioning technician, and the accumulator/dehydrator must be renewed.*

Refitting

38 Refitting is a reversal of removal, but fit new O-ring seals after coating them with clean refrigerant oil, and tighten the mounting bolts to the specified torque.

39 Have the system evacuated, charged and leak-tested by the specialist that discharged it.

Accumulator/dehydrator

Note: *Special tool 412-069 will be required for this work.*

Removal

40 Have the refrigerant discharged at a dealer service department or an automotive air conditioning repair facility.

41 Apply the handbrake, then jack up the front of the car and support it on axle stands (see *Jacking and vehicle support*). Remove the right-hand front roadwheel. Remove the radiator lower splash guard. On diesel models, remove the engine undertray.

42 Remove the wheel arch liner from under the right-hand front wing.

43 Disconnect the wiring from the low-pressure cut-off switch **(see illustration)**.

44 Unscrew the union and disconnect the lower refrigerant line from the accumulator **(see illustration)**. Discard the O-ring seals and obtain new ones for the refitting procedure.

45 Using the Ford special tool 412-069, disconnect the upper refrigerant line from the accumulator. Discard the O-ring seals and obtain new ones for the refitting procedure. Tape over or plug the accumulator apertures and line ends, to prevent entry of dust and dirt.

46 Unbolt the windscreen washer fluid reservoir from the inner wing panel, and position to one side. If required, the front bumper can be removed to provide additional working room (see Chapter 11).

11.43 Air conditioning low pressure cut-off switch

11.44 Lower refrigerant line connection to the accumulator/dehydrator

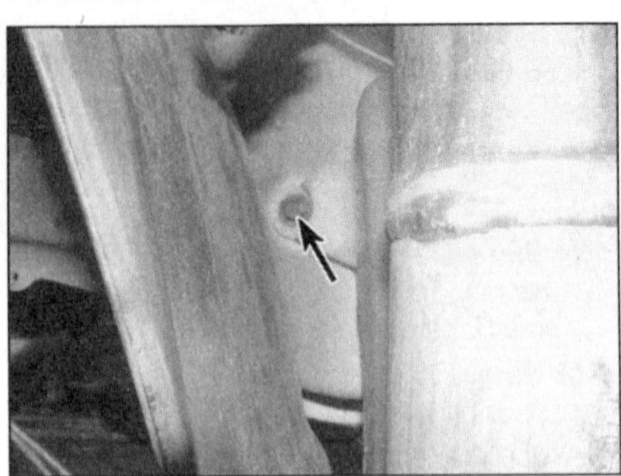

11.47 Undo the accumulator/dehydrator mounting bolts

47 Unscrew the mounting bolts and remove the accumulator/dehydrator from beneath the wing **(see illustration)**.

Refitting

48 Refitting is a reversal of removal, but fit new O-ring seals after coating them with clean refrigerant oil, and tighten the mounting bolts to the specified torque.

49 Have the system evacuated, charged and leak-tested by the specialist who discharged it.

Low-pressure cut-off switch

Warning: This work is best carried out by a dealer service department or an automotive air conditioning repair facility.

Removal

50 Apply the handbrake, then jack up the front of the car and support it on axle stands (see *Jacking and vehicle support*).

51 Unscrew the lower and front bolts securing the right-hand wheel arch liner, and tie the liner to one side for access to the switch.

52 Disconnect the wiring from the switch.

53 Connect a 20-amp fused jumper wire between Pin 1 and Pin 4 of the switch wiring, then start the engine and turn the air conditioning switch to ON. **Note:** *The air conditioning compressor MUST run during removal of the low-pressure cut-off switch.*

54 Unscrew and remove the switch and discard the O-ring seals. **Note:** *Check that the low-pressure cut-off switch valve closes completely after removal of the switch, to prevent loss of refrigerant.* Obtain new seals for the refitting procedure.

Refitting

55 Refitting is a reversal of removal, but fit new O-ring seals after coating them with clean refrigerant oil, and tighten the switch **only** to the specified torque.

High-pressure cut-off switch

Removal

56 The high-pressure cut-off switch is located in the engine compartment, next to the power steering hydraulic fluid reservoir.

57 Disconnect the wiring from the switch.

58 Unscrew and remove the switch and discard the O-ring seals. **Note:** *Check that the high-pressure cut-off switch valve closes completely after removal of the switch, to prevent loss of refrigerant.* Obtain new seals for the refitting procedure.

Refitting

59 Refitting is a reversal of removal, but fit new O-ring seals after coating them with clean refrigerant oil, and tighten the switch **only** to the specified torque.

12 Heater/evaporator housing - dismantling and reassembly

Dismantling

1 With the housing on the bench, undo the four screws and remove the blend door actuator assembly.

2 Undo the three screws and remove the air inlet blend door actuator.

3 Remove the heater matrix with reference to Section 8.

4 Undo the two screws and remove the evaporator matrix upper housing.

5 Remove the rubber seal, then undo the evaporator matrix retaining bolt.

6 Undo the screws and remove the evaporator matrix lower housing.

7 Remove the evaporator matrix.

8 Remove the heater blower motor as described in Section 8.

9 Undo the screw and remove the heater blower motor resistor.

10 Release the clips and retaining tabs, and remove the heater blower motor upper housing.

11 Remove the gasket and release the retaining tabs, then separate the motor upper housing.

12 Remove the clips and release the retaining tabs, then separate the evaporator matrix housing.

13 Remove the clip and release the retaining tabs, then separate the heater and evaporator matrix housings.

14 Note their location, then pull out the three blend doors and shafts.

Reassembly

15 Reassembly is a reversal of dismantling.

Chapter 4 Part A:
Fuel and exhaust systems – petrol models

Contents

Degrees of difficulty

Easy, suitable for novice with little experience 

Fairly easy, suitable for beginner with some experience

Fairly difficult, suitable for competent DIY mechanic

Difficult, suitable for experienced DIY mechanic

Very difficult, suitable for expert DIY or professional

Specifications

General

System type	Sequential multi-point Fuel injection (SFi)
Recommended fuel (minimum octane rating)	95 RON unleaded
Idle speed:	
4-cylinder engines	700± 50 rpm
V6 engine	725± 50 rpm
Idle mixture (CO level):	
4-cylinder engines	0.5% maximum
V6 engine	0.5% maximum

Inlet air temperature sensor

Resistance (at 20°C)	38 kilohms (38 000 ohms) approximately

Torque wrench settings

Torque wrench settings	Nm	lbf ft
Camshaft position sensor (4-cylinder engines)	6	4
Crankshaft speed/position sensor:		
Sensor-to-bracket screw	8	6
Bracket-to-cylinder block crankcase screw	21	15
Exhaust system:		
3.0 litre V6 engine:		
Catalytic converter to manifold	25	18
Catalytic converter to engine	23	17
Flexi-pipe to catalytic converter	55	41
Main system nuts and bolts (unless otherwise specified)	47	35
Fuel filter retaining bolts	10	7
Fuel pressure regulator bolts	6	4
Fuel pressure relief valve (V6 engine)	8	6
Fuel pump/gauge sender unit locking ring	85	63
Fuel rail:		
4-cylinder engines	25	18
V6 engines	10	7
Fuel tank support strap retaining bolts	25	18
Idle air control valve bolts	10	7
Inlet air temperature sensor (V6 engines)	23	17
Inlet manifold tuning valve	10	7
Throttle housing-to-inlet manifold screws	10	7

2.6a Fuel pressure relief valve cap on the fuel rail on the V6 engine

2.6b . . . and on 4-cylinder engines

1 General information and precautions

The fuel system consists of a plastic tank (mounted under the body, beneath the rear seats), fuel hoses and metal lines, an electric fuel pump mounted in the fuel tank, and an electronic fuel injection system (which is described in more detail in Section 11)

The exhaust system consists of an exhaust manifold (two on the V6 engine), front downpipe, catalytic converter(s) and a rear section incorporating two or three silencers. The service replacement exhaust system consists of three or four sections. The system is suspended throughout its entire length by rubber mountings.

Extreme caution should be exercised when dealing with either the fuel or exhaust systems. Fuel is a potentially-explosive liquid, and extreme care should be taken when dealing with the fuel system. The exhaust system is an area for exercising caution, as it operates at very high temperatures. Serious burns can result from even momentary contact with any part of the exhaust system, and the fire risk is ever-present. The catalytic converter in particular runs at very high temperatures.

When removing the powertrain control module (PCM), do not touch the terminals, as there is a chance that static electricity may damage the internal electronic components.

Warning: Many of the procedures in this Chapter require the removal of fuel lines and connections, which may result in some fuel spillage. Before carrying out any operation on the fuel system, refer to the precautions given in Safety first! at the beginning of this manual, and follow them implicitly. Petrol is a highly-dangerous and volatile liquid, and the precautions necessary when handling it cannot be overstressed.

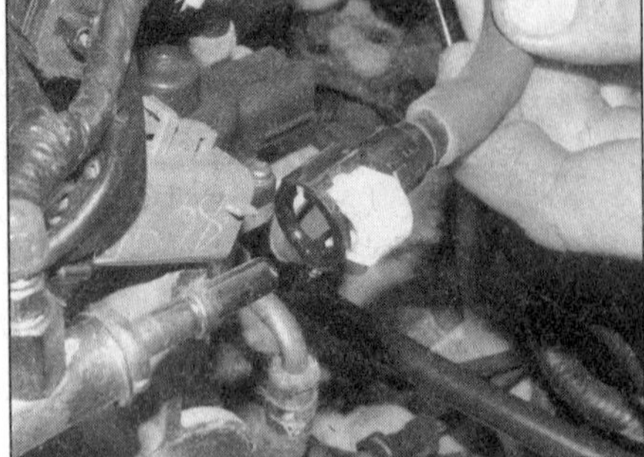

3.3 Disconnect fuel line quick-release coupling

2 Fuel system – depressurisation

Note: *Refer to the warning in Section 1 before proceeding.*

Warning: The following procedures will merely relieve the pressure in the fuel system – remember that fuel will still be present in the system components, and take precautions accordingly before disconnecting any of them.

1 The fuel system referred to in this Chapter is defined as the fuel tank and tank-mounted fuel pump/fuel gauge sender unit, the fuel rail, the fuel injectors, and the metal pipes and flexible hoses of the fuel lines between these components. All these contain fuel which will be under pressure while the engine is running and/or while the ignition is switched on.

2 The pressure will remain for some time after the ignition has been switched off, and must be relieved before any of these components is disturbed for servicing work.

3 Whichever depressurisation method is used, bear in mind the following points:

a) Plug the disconnected pipe ends, to minimise fuel loss and prevent the entry of dirt into the fuel system.

b) Note that, once the fuel system has been depressurised and drained (even partially), it will take significantly longer to restart the engine – perhaps several seconds of cranking – before the system is refilled and pressure restored.

Method 1

4 The simplest depressurisation method is to disconnect the fuel pump electrical supply. With the ignition switched off, remove the fuel pump fuse (refer to the wiring diagrams or the label on the relevant fusebox for exact location) and try to start the engine – allow the engine to idle until it stops through lack of fuel. Turn the engine over once or twice on the starter to ensure that all pressure is released, then switch off the ignition – do not forget to refit the fuse when work is complete.

Method 2

5 Place a suitable container beneath the connection or union to be disconnected, and have a large rag ready to soak up any escaping fuel not being caught by the container. Slowly loosen the connection or union nut to avoid a sudden release of pressure, and position the rag around the connection to catch any fuel spray which may be expelled.

Method 3

6 The Ford method of depressurisation is to use service tool 23-033 fitted to the fuel rail pressure test/release fitting. The fitting consists of a Schrader-type valve with a plastic cap located on the fuel rail **(see illustrations)**, and the tool acts as a tap by depressing the valve core.

3 Fuel lines and fittings – general information

Note: *Refer to the warning in Section 1 before proceeding.*

1 Quick-release couplings are employed at all unions in the fuel feed and return lines. **Note:** *Fuel supply line connectors are identified by white quick-release coupling connector and the return lines are identified by a red quick-release coupling connector.*

2 Before disconnecting any fuel system component, relieve the pressure in the system as described in Section 2, and equalise tank pressure by removing the fuel filler cap.

3 Release the protruding locking lugs on each fuel line union, by squeezing them together and carefully pulling the coupling apart **(see illustration)**. Use rag to soak up any spilt fuel. Where the unions are colour-coded, the pipes cannot be confused. Where both unions are the same colour, note carefully which pipe is connected to which, and ensure that they are correctly reconnected on refitting.

4 Another type of quick-release coupling used on the Mondeo has a plastic clip (often red or white) which is prised out of the coupling to release it. When refitting, press the coupling firmly together, then press the clip back in flush to secure it.

5 If there are no locking lugs on the fuel line union, then a special tool to release the quick-release fitting is required – the tool expands the internal coil spring so that the two sections of the fitting can be disconnected. A home-made tool can be made out of a coiled piece of plastic around the fuel pipe, which may then be slid along the fuel pipe into the union to release the coil spring.

6 To reconnect one of these couplings, press

them together until they are locked. Switch the ignition on to pressurise the system, and check for any sign of fuel leakage around the disturbed coupling before attempting to start the engine.

7 Checking procedures for the fuel lines are included in Chapter 1A.

8 Always use genuine fuel lines and hoses when renewing sections of the fuel system. Do not fit substitutes constructed from inferior or inappropriate material, or you could cause a fuel leak or a fire.

9 Before disconnecting any part of the fuel system, note the routing of all hoses and pipes, and the orientation of all clamps and clips to ensure correct refitting.

4 Air cleaner assembly and ducts – removal and refitting

Air cleaner assembly

4-cylinder engines

1 Disconnect the battery negative (earth) lead (refer to *Disconnecting the battery* at the end of this manual).

2 Undo the retaining clip and disconnect the air outlet pipe and breather hose from the air cleaner upper housing **(see illustration)**.

3 Withdraw the air cleaner assembly, lifting it upwards out of its grommets, and releasing it from the air inlet pipe under the inner wing panel.

4 Refitting is the reverse of the removal procedure. Ensure that the housing pegs seat correctly in their grommets, and that the air inlet pipe is fully engaged with the air cleaner housing.

V6 engine

5 Disconnect the battery negative (earth) lead (refer to *Disconnecting the battery* at the end of this manual).

6 Disconnect the wiring from the airflow sensor **(see illustration)**.

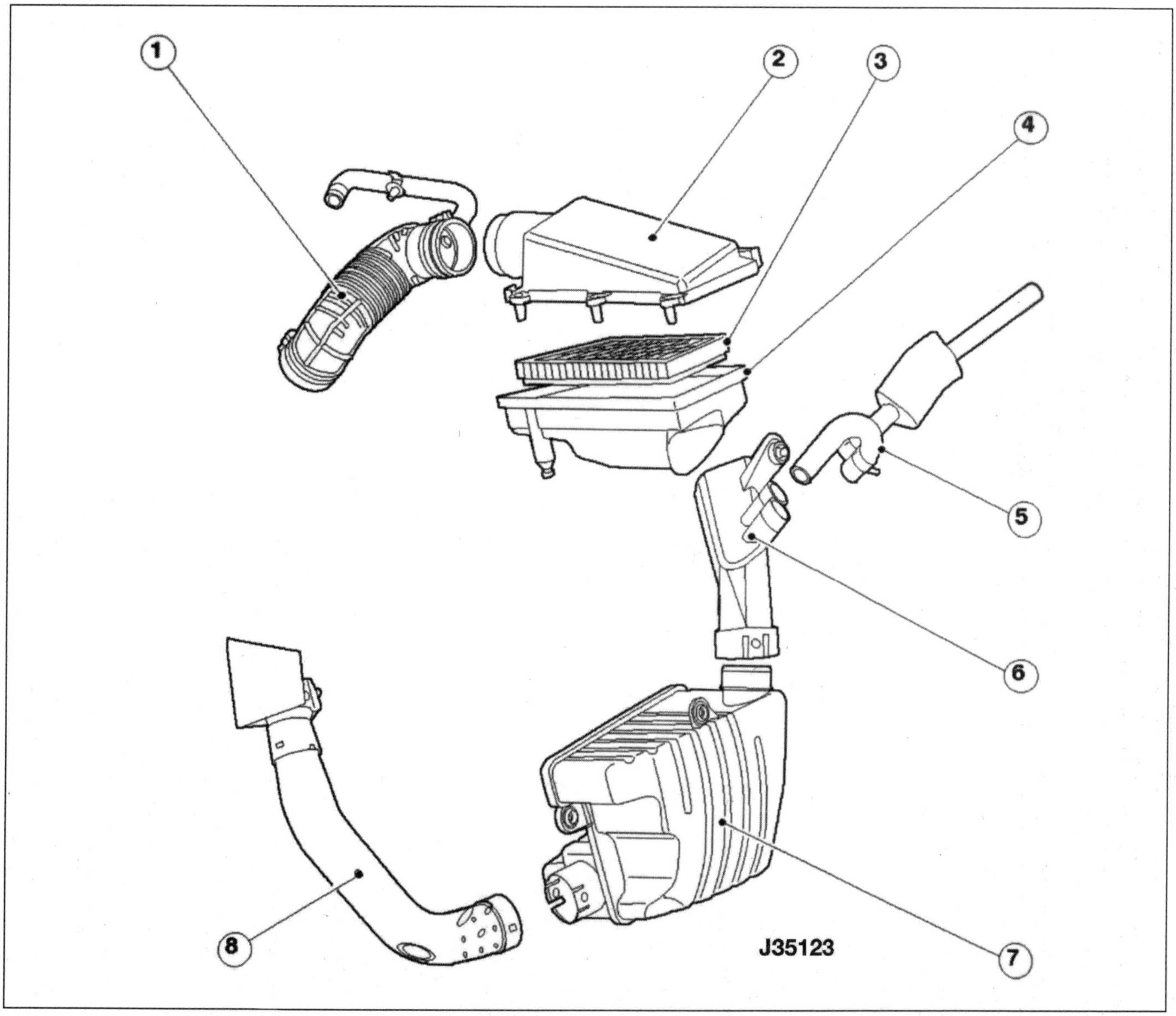

J35123

4.2 Air cleaner assembly and ducts (4-cylinder engines)

1 *Air cleaner outlet pipe*
2 *Air cleaner housing cover*
3 *Air cleaner element*
4 *Air cleaner housing*
5 *Air inlet tuning pipe*
6 *Air cleaner inlet pipe*
7 *Air Inlet resonator box*
8 *Air cleaner inlet pipe*

7 Disconnect the air bypass hose and the crankcase ventilation hoses from the air cleaner assembly.
8 Loosen the securing clip and disconnect the air outlet hose from the air cleaner housing.
9 Lift the air cleaner from its location grommets, and at the same time disconnect the inlet pipe from the left-hand side.
10 Refitting is the reverse of the removal procedure. Ensure that the housing pegs seat correctly in their grommets, and that the air inlet pipe and ventilation hoses are fully engaged with the air cleaner housing assembly.

Air inlet resonator

4-cylinder engine

11 Remove the air cleaner housing as described at the beginning of this Section.
12 Undo the air inlet pipe upper retaining bolt from the left-hand inner wing.
13 Loosen the left-hand front wheel nuts. Chock the rear wheels, then jack up the front of the car and support on axle stands (see *Jacking and vehicle support*).
14 Remove the left-hand front wheel and inner wheel arch liner (Chapter 11).
15 From under the left-hand front wing, withdraw the upper inlet pipe and tuning pipe from the resonator box.
16 Undo the retaining bolts and remove the resonator box from under the left-hand wing. Where applicable, disconnect the foglight's wiring block connector from the clip on the resonator box.
17 To remove the lower air inlet pipe, remove the radiator grille as described in Chapter 11.
18 Refitting is the reverse of the removal procedure.

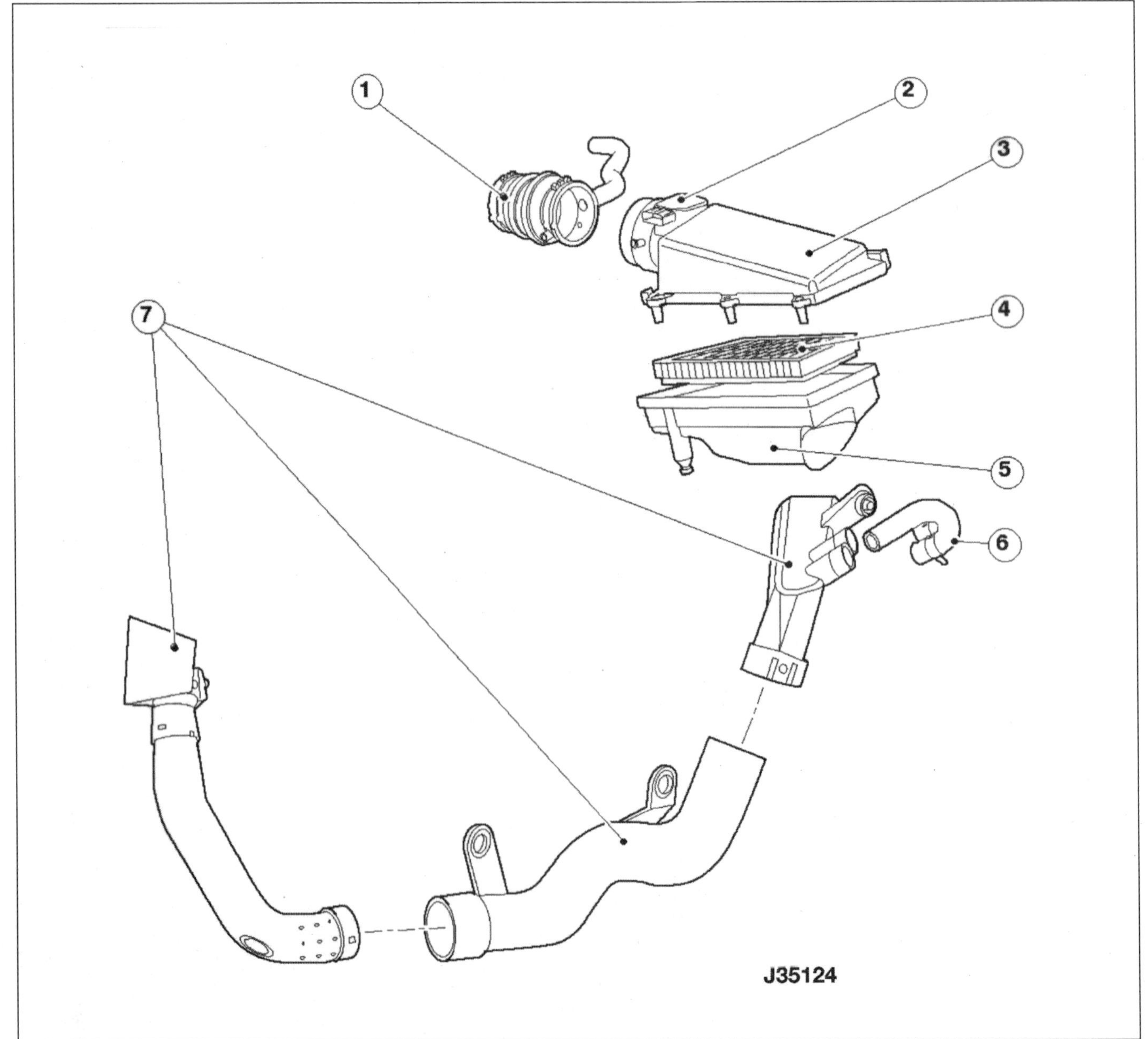

4.6 Air cleaner assembly and ducts (V6 engine)

1 Air cleaner outlet pipe
2 Mass air flow sensor
3 Air cleaner housing cover
4 Air cleaner element
5 Air cleaner housing
6 Air inlet tuning pipe
7 Air cleaner inlet pipes

Air inlet pipes

V6 engine

19 Carry out the procedures for removing and refitting of the resonator box on the 4-cylinder engines in this Section, except in paragraph 16, undo the retaining bolts and remove the air inlet pipes from under the left-hand wing.

20 Refitting is the reverse of the removal procedure.

5 Accelerator cable – removal and refitting

4-cylinder engine

Removal

1 Unclip the breather hose from the engine upper plastic cover, then unclip the cover from the top of the engine.

2 Unclip the accelerator inner cable from the throttle linkage, then twist the outer cable to release it from the bracket **(see illustrations)**. Release the cable from any securing clips or ties.

3 Working in the passenger compartment, reach up to the top of the accelerator pedal. Pull the end fitting and collar out of the pedal, then release the cable inner wire through the slot in the pedal **(see illustration)**. Tie a length of string to the end of the cable.

4 Returning to the engine compartment, pull the cable through the bulkhead until the string can be untied and the cable removed.

Refitting

5 Refitting is the reverse of the removal procedure; use the string to draw the cable through the bulkhead.

V6 engine

Note: *While the following procedure deals with the complete cable, the pedal-to-actuator and actuator-to-throttle housing sections of the cable are available separately, and can be removed and refitted individually. If doing this, modify the procedure as required.*

Removal

6 The accelerator cable consists of a primary and secondary cable. The primary cable is attached to the accelerator pedal and traction control unit actuator. The secondary cable is attached to the traction control unit actuator and throttle housing quadrant.

7 Pull out the clip and lift the secondary outer cable from the support bracket **(see illustration)**.

8 Disconnect the inner cable from the quadrant or lever on the throttle housing. Where necessary, prise off the spring clip first **(see illustrations)**.

9 Unhook the secondary cable from the front support clip.

10 Disconnect the wiring from the traction control motor.

5.2a Unclip the accelerator inner cable from the throttle linkage . . .

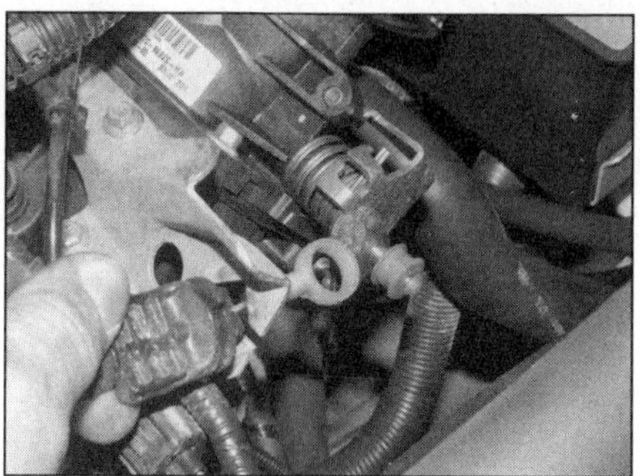

5.2b . . . then twist the outer cable to release it from the bracket

5.3 Release the cable (arrowed) from the slot in the top of the pedal

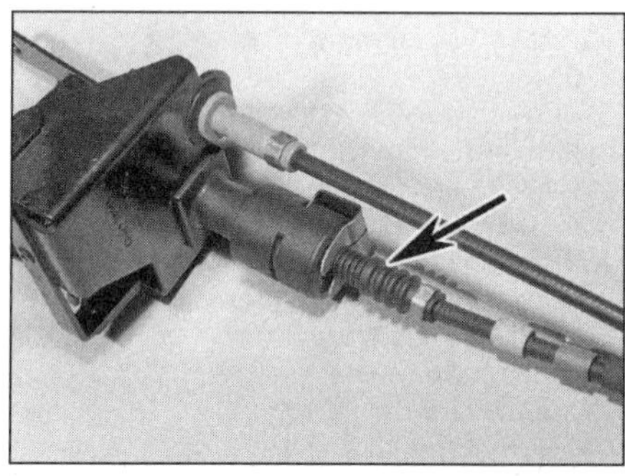

5.7 Outer cable and adjustment ferrule

11 Carefully remove the cover from the traction control motor.

12 Disconnect the secondary inner cable from the motor upper quadrant, then detach the secondary cable from the bracket on the motor.

13 Release the cable-tie, and disconnect the primary inner cable from the motor lower quadrant. Detach the primary cable from the bracket on the motor.

14 Inside the car, disconnect the primary inner cable from the accelerator pedal. Tie a length of string to the end of the cable.

15 Returning to the engine compartment, pull the cable through the bulkhead until the string can be untied and the pedal-to-actuator cable removed.

Refitting

16 Refitting is the reverse of the removal procedure. Use the string to draw the pedal-to-actuator cable through the bulkhead. Ensure that each cable end is connected to the correct actuator quadrant.

Adjustment

Note: *Both sections of the cable must be adjusted together, even if only one has been disturbed.*

17 Remove the metal clip from the adjuster of each cable section **(see illustration)**, and lubricate the adjusters' grommets with soapy water.

18 Remove any slack by pulling both outer cables as far as possible out of their respective adjusters.

19 Unplug the TCS throttle actuator's electrical connector, and prise off its cover. Lock both pulleys together by pushing a locking pin (a pin punch or a similar tool of suitable size) into their alignment holes. Disconnect the actuator-to-throttle housing cable's end nipple from the throttle linkage.

20 Have an assistant depress the accelerator

5.8a Prise off the spring clip . . .

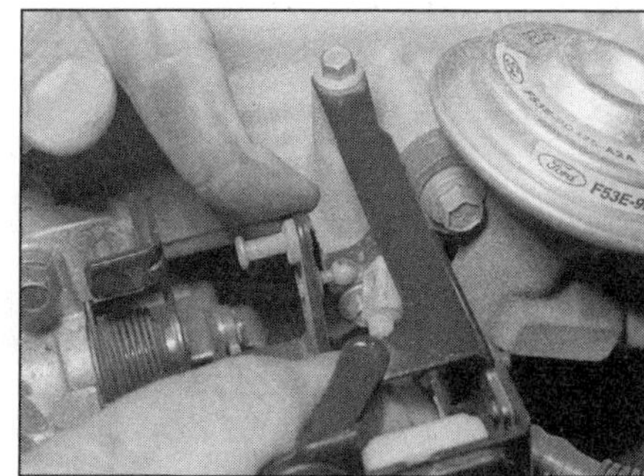

5.8b . . . and disconnect the inner cable from the lever

5.17 Location of TCS throttle actuator-to-throttle housing cable adjuster (arrowed)

pedal fully. The pedal-to-actuator cable outer will move back into the adjuster; hold it there, and refit the clip.

21 Connect the actuator-to-throttle housing cable end nipple to the throttle linkage, and check that the outer cable grommet is correctly secured in the housing bracket.

22 Again have the assistant depress the accelerator pedal fully. The actuator-to-throttle housing cable outer will move back into the adjuster; hold it there, and refit the clip.

23 Remove the locking pin from the pulleys. Check that the throttle valve moves smoothly and easily from the fully-closed to the fully-open position and back again, as the assistant depresses and releases the accelerator pedal. Re-adjust the cable(s) if required.

24 When the setting is correct, refit the TCS throttle actuator's cover and electrical connector.

6 Accelerator pedal – removal and refitting

Removal

1 Working in the driver's footwell, reach up to the top of the accelerator pedal. Pull the end fitting and collar out of the pedal, then release the inner cable from the slot in the pedal.

2 Undo the retaining nuts and bolt, then withdraw the pedal assembly **(see illustration)**.

Refitting

3 Refitting is a reversal of removal. On V6 models, check the correct fitment of the accelerator cable as described in Section 5.

6.2 Undo the retaining nuts and bolt (arrowed) to remove the accelerator pedal assembly

7 Fuel pump/fuel pressure - check

Note: *Refer to the warning in Section 1 before proceeding.*

Fuel pump operation check

1 Switch on the ignition and listen for the fuel pump (the sound of an electric motor running, audible from beneath the rear seats). Assuming there is sufficient fuel in the tank, the pump should start and run for several seconds, then stop. **Note:** *If the pump runs continuously all the time the ignition is switched on, the electronic control system is running in the back-up (or 'limp-home') mode referred to by Ford as 'Limited Operation Strategy' (LOS). This almost certainly indicates a fault in the powertrain control module (PCM) itself, and the car should therefore be taken to a Ford dealer for a full test of the complete system, using the correct diagnostic equipment; do not waste time trying to test the system without such facilities.*

2 Listen for fuel return noises from the fuel pressure regulator. It should be possible to feel the fuel pulsing in the regulator and in the feed hose from the fuel filter. If the pump does not run at all, check the fuse, relay and wiring (see Chapter 12).

Fuel pressure check

3 A fuel pressure gauge, equipped with an adaptor to suit the Schrader-type valve on the fuel rail pressure test/release fitting (identifiable by its blue plastic cap, and located on the union of the fuel feed line and the fuel rail) is required for the following procedure. If the Ford special tool 23-033 is available (see Section 2), the tool can be attached to the valve, and a conventional-type pressure gauge attached to the tool.

4 If using the service tool, ensure that its tap is turned fully anti-clockwise, then attach it to the valve. Connect the pressure gauge to the service tool. If using a fuel pressure gauge with its own adapter, connect it in accordance with its maker's instructions.

5 Start the engine and allow it to idle. Note the gauge reading as soon as the pressure stabilises, and compare it with the manufacturer's recommendations.

a) *If the pressure is high, check for a restricted fuel return line. If the line is clear, where fitted renew the pressure regulator.*

b) *If the pressure is low, pinch the fuel return line. If the pressure now goes up, where fitted renew the fuel pressure regulator. If the pressure does not increase, check the fuel feed line, the fuel pump and the fuel filter.*

6 Where applicable, detach the vacuum hose from the fuel pressure regulator; the pressure shown on the gauge should increase. Note the increase in pressure, and compare it with manufacturer's recommendations. If the pressure increase is not as specified, check the vacuum hose and pressure regulator.

7 Reconnect the regulator vacuum hose, and switch off the engine. Verify that the fuel pressure stays at the specified level for five minutes after the engine is turned off.

8 Carefully disconnect the fuel pressure gauge. Be sure to cover the fitting with a rag before slackening it. Mop-up any spilt petrol.

9 Run the engine, and check that there are no fuel leaks.

8 Fuel pump/gauge sender unit – removal and refitting

Note: *Refer to the warning in Section 1 before proceeding. Ford specify the use of their service tool 310-069 (a large box spanner with projecting teeth to engage the fuel pump/sender unit retaining ring's slots) for this task. While alternatives are possible, as shown below, in view of the difficulty experienced in removing and refitting the pump/sender unit, owners are strongly advised to obtain this tool before starting work. The help of an assistant will be required.*

Removal

1 Remove the fuel tank as described in Section 9.

2 Release the fuel pump/sender unit's retaining ring by turning it anti-clockwise. As noted above, Ford recommend the use of service tool 310-069. For those without access to such equipment, a hammer and drift, or a pair of slip-jointed pliers, may serve as a substitute **(see illustration)**.

3 Rotate the fuel pump/fuel gauge sender unit anti-clockwise and withdraw it from the fuel tank, taking care not to damage the float arm. The float arm is mounted on a spring-loaded extension, to hold it closely against the bottom of the tank. Note the sealing ring; this must be renewed whenever it is disturbed.

Refitting

4 On refitting, ensure that the sender unit is

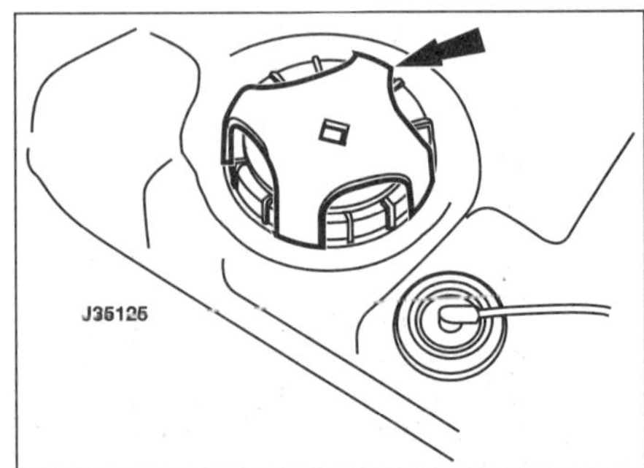

8.2 Ford service tool used to release the fuel pump/sender locking ring

not damaged, and that the gauze filter over the base of the pump pick-up is clean.

5 Insert the fuel pump/sender unit into the fuel tank so that the arrows on the fuel tank and pump/sender unit are correctly aligned.

6 Use a new sealing ring, when refitting the fuel pump/sender unit's retaining ring (Ford service tool provides the best way of holding the ring square to the tank and turning it at the same time).

7 The remainder of the fuel tank refitting procedure is the reverse of removal as described in Section 9.

9 Fuel tank – removal, inspection and refitting

Note: *Refer to the warning in Section 1 before proceeding.*

Removal

1 A fuel tank drain plug is not provided, therefore it is preferable to carry out the removal operation when the tank is nearly empty **(see illustration)**. First depressurise the fuel system as described in Section 2, and equalise the tank pressure by removing the fuel filler cap.

2 Syphon or hand-pump the remaining fuel from the tank. Alternatively, position a clean container beneath the fuel filter, then disconnect the feed pipe and connect a length of hose from the filter to the container. Switch on the ignition and allow the fuel pump to empty the tank into the container. Be sure to take all necessary precautions to prevent the risk of fire. Reconnect the hose after draining the tank.

3 Make sure the ignition is switched off.

4 Unbolt or fold forwards (as appropriate) the rear seat base cushion (see Chapter 11). Prise the grommet from the floor for access to the fuel pump/sender unit **(see illustration)**.

5 Disconnect the wiring from the fuel pump/sender unit, also disconnect the fuel supply and return pipes from the unit **(see illustration)**. If the fuel lines are not marked, clearly label them and their respective unions. Plug the hoses, to prevent leakage and contamination of the fuel system.

6 Chock the front wheels, then jack up the rear of the car and support on axle stands (see *Jacking and vehicle support*).

7 Remove the fuel filter as described in Chapter 1A.

8 Unhook the exhaust system rubber mountings. Lower the system onto a suitable support, so that the front downpipe-to-exhaust manifold joint is not strained, or remove it completely as described in Section 14.

9 Unscrew the retaining nuts, and withdraw the exhaust system's rear heat shield from the underbody.

10 On models with headlight-levelling sensor fitted, remove the sensor as described in Chapter 12.

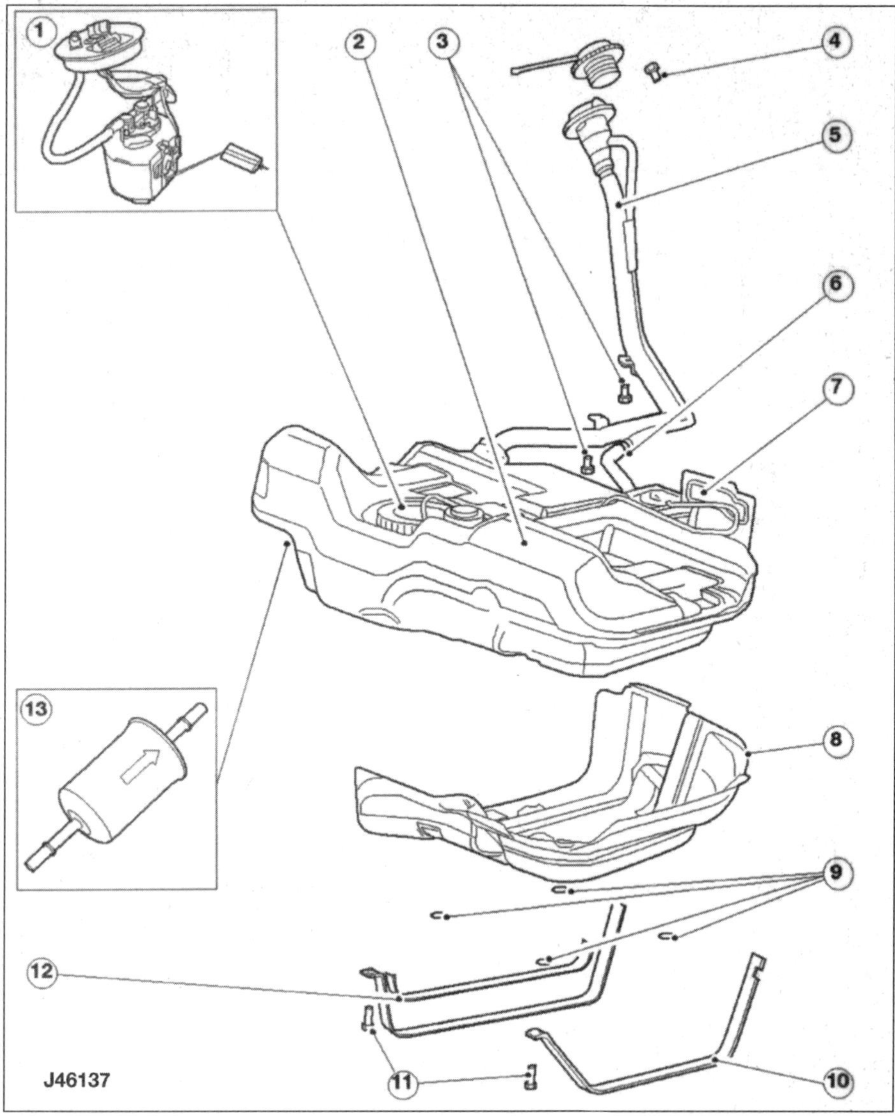

9.1 Fuel tank – system layout

1 *Fuel pump/sender unit*
2 *Fuel tank*
3 *Filler pipe lower retaining bolts*
4 *Filler pipe upper retaining bolt*
5 *Fuel tank filler pipe*
6 *Filler pipe breather hose*
7 *Heat shield – Estate models*
8 *Fuel tank heat shield*
9 *Heat shield retaining clips*
10 *Fuel tank support straps*
11 *Support strap retaining bolts*
12 *Support strap insulator*
13 *Fuel filter – petrol models*

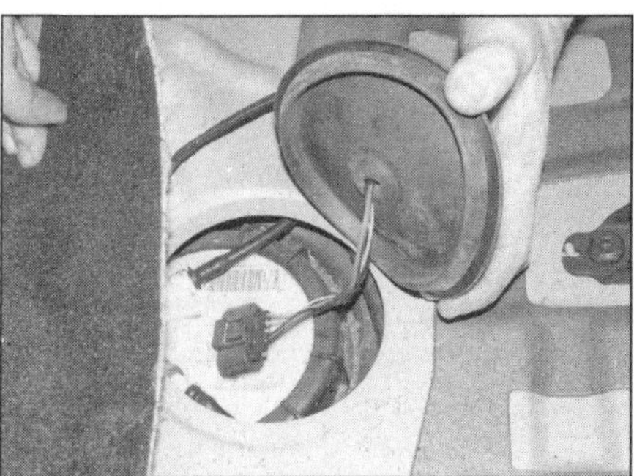

9.4 Prise the grommet from the floor to access to the fuel pump/sender unit wiring

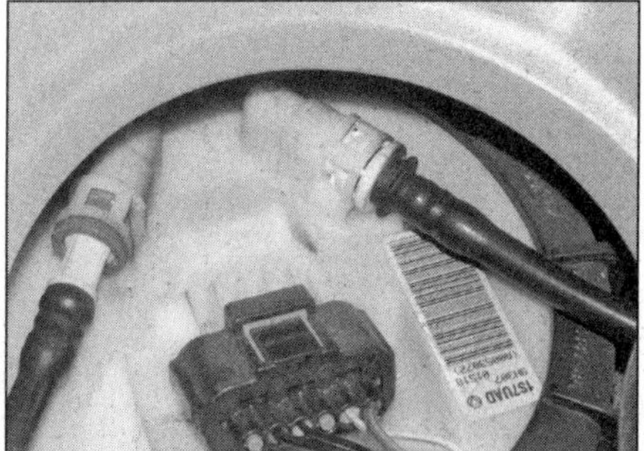

9.5 Note the fuel line ends may be colour-coded to enable refitting

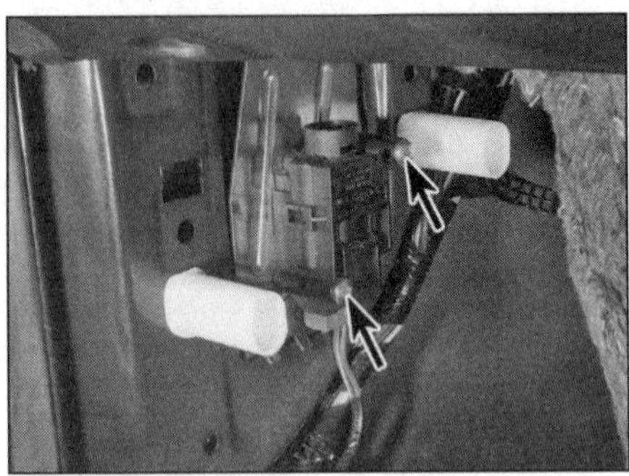

10.3 Fuel cut-off switch retaining screws (arrowed)

11 Unbolt the rear suspension anti-roll bar connecting links. Lower the bar down as far as possible – if preferred, remove the bar completely (see Chapter 10).

12 Support the tank with a trolley jack and block of wood.

13 Unscrew the bolt at the front of each retaining strap, then rotate the straps (twist them through 90°) at the other end to release them from the car. Check that the straps and their locations in the underbody are in good condition.

14 Lower the tank enough to disconnect the charcoal canister's vapour hose from the union at the top rear of the tank. Release the locking lugs and disconnect the fuel filler pipe neck from the fuel tank.

15 Make sure there are no fuel pipes or wiring connectors still connected. Remove the tank from the car, releasing it from the filler neck stub.

Caution: Take care when lowering the fuel tank, as there will still be some fuel left inside. The weight of this fuel will move around as the tank is lowered if the tank is not kept level.

16 If required, the fuel tank filler neck can be removed. It is secured by a single screw in the filler opening, and by two bolts to the underbody. **Note:** *On some models it may be necessary to lower the rear crossmember slightly, to give access for the filler neck to be removed (see Chapter 10, for information on the rear crossmember).*

Inspection

17 Check the fuel tank for damage. Any sediment inside the tank should be removed, either by swilling out with clean fuel or by steam cleaning.

18 Any repairs to the fuel tank or filler neck should be carried out by a professional who has experience in this critical and potentially-dangerous work. Even after cleaning and flushing of the fuel system, explosive fumes can remain and ignite during repair of the tank.

Refitting

19 Refitting is a reversal of removal.

10 Fuel cut-off switch – removal and refitting

Removal

1 Disconnect the battery negative (earth) lead (refer to *Disconnecting the battery* at the end of this manual).

2 Remove the trim panel from the left-hand footwell.

3 Peel back the sound-insulating material from the switch, and undo the two retaining screws **(see illustration)**.

4 Disconnect the wiring, and withdraw the switch.

Refitting

5 Refitting is the reverse of the removal procedure. Ensure that the switch is reset by depressing its red button.

11 Fuel injection system – general description

1 All petrol models are equipped with sequential multi-point fuel injection (SFI), controlled by a Visteon 'Black Oak' engine management system.

Fuel supply and air induction

2 An electric fuel pump located inside the fuel tank supplies fuel under pressure to the fuel rail, which distributes fuel to the injectors. A filter between the fuel pump and the fuel rail protects the components of the system. A pressure regulator controls the system pressure in relation to inlet depression. From the fuel rail, fuel is injected into the inlet ports, just above the inlet valves, by four fuel injectors.

3 The amount of fuel supplied by the injectors is precisely controlled by the Powertrain Control Module (PCM). The PCM uses the signals from the engine speed/crankshaft position sensor and the camshaft position sensor, to trigger each injector separately in cylinder firing order (sequential injection).

4 The air induction system consists of an air

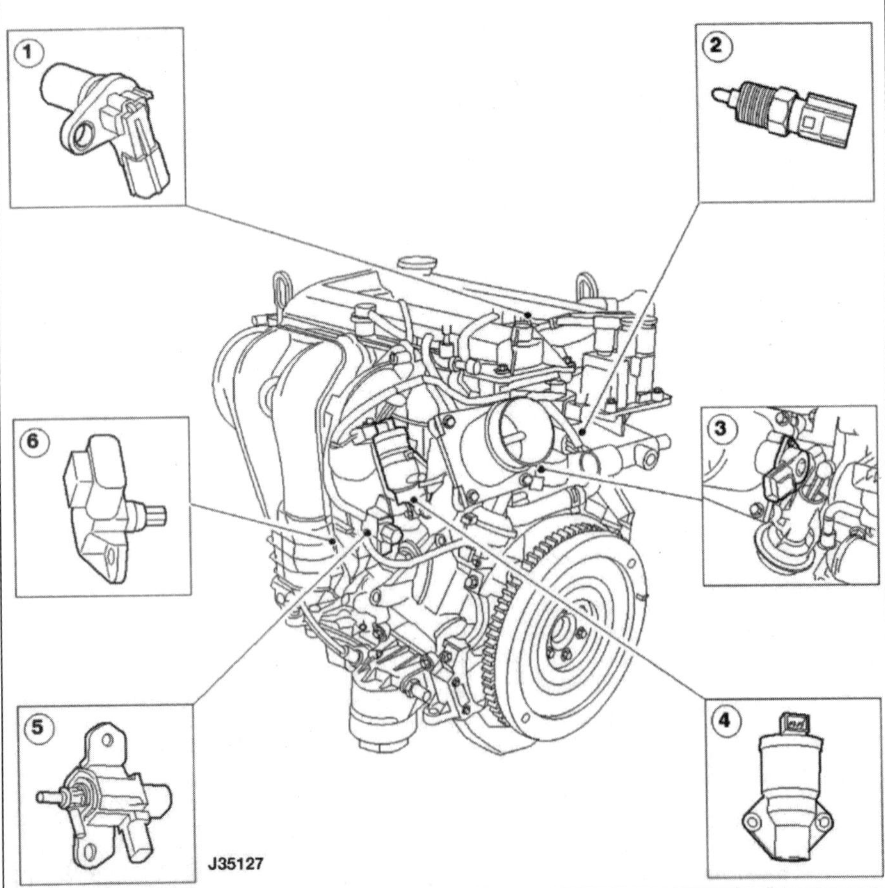

11.6a Location of fuel injection, ignition and emissions system components on 4-cylinder models

1 *Camshaft position sensor*
2 *Engine coolant temperature sensor*
3 *Throttle position sensor*
4 *Idle air control valve*
5 *Inlet manifold tuning valve*
6 *Temperature and manifold absolute pressure sensor*

filter housing, a Mass AirFlow (MAF) sensor on V6 engines, a Temperature and Manifold Absolute Pressure (T-MAP) sensor on 4-cylinder engines, inlet ducting, and a throttle housing. The MAF and T-MAP sensors are information-gathering devices for the PCM. The MAF sensor measures the volume and temperature of the air passing through the air inlet pipe into the engine. The T-MAP sensor measures the air pressure and temperature in the inlet manifold. The PCM uses these signals to calculate the mass/pressure of the air entering the engine.

5 The throttle valve inside the throttle housing is controlled by the driver, through the accelerator pedal. As the valve opens, the quantity of air entering the engine increases. The throttle potentiometer is attached to the throttle valve and informs the PCM of the throttle position. The PCM calculates the relevant period of injection, and controls the injector opening times.

Electronic control system

6 The 'Black Oak' engine management system controls the fuel injection by means of a microcomputer known as the PCM (Powertrain Control Module) **(see illustrations)**. The PCM receives signals from a number of sensors, which monitor the inlet air mass/pressure and

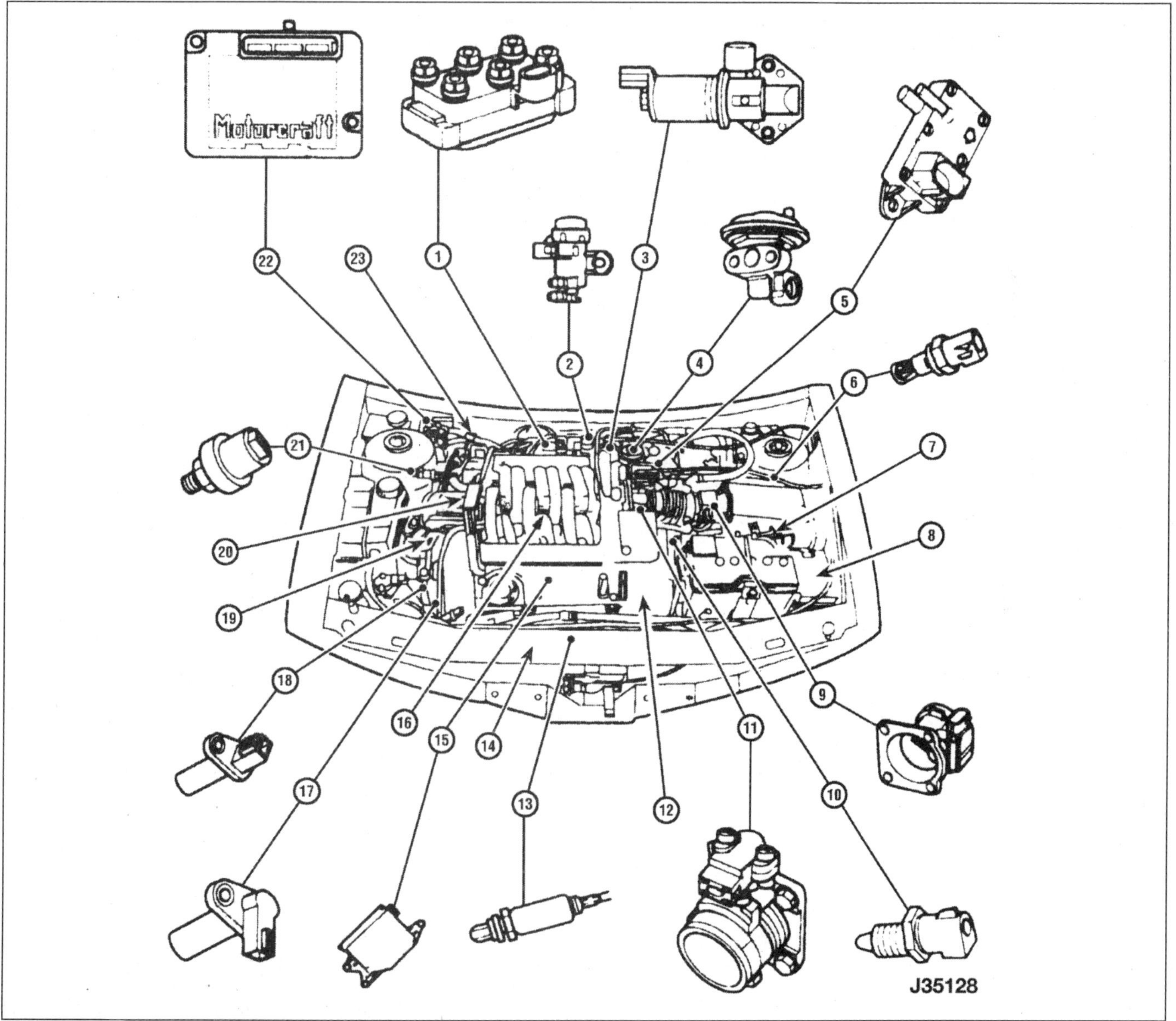

11.6b Location of fuel injection, ignition and emissions system components on V6 models

1 *Ignition coil*
2 *Electronic vacuum regulator*
3 *Idle air control valve (IAC)*
4 *Exhaust Gas Recirculation (EGR) valve*
5 *Electronic differential pressure sensor (DPFE)*
6 *Inlet air temperature sensor (IAT)*
7 *Air cleaner*
8 *Battery junction box*
9 *Mass air flow sensor (MAF)*
10 *Coolant temperature sensor (ECT)*
11 *Throttle housing and throttle position sensor (TP)*
12 *Water pump drivebelt cover*
13 *Heated oxygen sensor (HO_2S)*
14 *Front catalytic converter (rear on rear exhaust manifold)*
15 *Inlet manifold runner control (IMRC)*
16 *Upper inlet manifold*
17 *Camshaft position sensor (CMP)*
18 *Crankshaft position sensor (CKP)*
19 *Hydraulic engine mounting*
20 *Right-hand engine mounting*
21 *Power steering pressure switch (PSPS)*
22 *Power train control module (PCM) or Electronic control unit (ECU)*
23 *Service plug (octane adjustment)*

temperature, coolant temperature, camshaft and crankshaft position, throttle position, and exhaust gas oxygen content. The signals are processed by the PCM to determine the injection duration necessary for the optimum air/fuel ratio. The sensors and associated PCM-controlled relays are located throughout the engine compartment.

7 In the event of a sensor malfunction, a back-up circuit will take over, to provide driveability until the problem is identified and fixed. The following paragraphs describe the components of the electronic control system.

Powertrain control module

8 This component is the heart of the entire engine management system, controlling the fuel injection, ignition and emissions control systems. It also controls sub-systems such as the radiator cooling fan, air conditioning and automatic transmission, where appropriate.

Mass airflow sensor

V6 engine

9 This uses a 'hot-wire' system, sending the PCM a constantly-varying (analogue) voltage signal corresponding to the mass of air passing into the engine. Since air mass varies with temperature (cold air being denser than warm), measuring air mass provides the PCM with a very accurate means of determining the correct amount of fuel required to achieve the ideal air/fuel mixture ratio.

T-MAP sensor

4-cylinder engines

10 The T-MAP sensor measures the temperature and air pressure in the inlet manifold. The PCM then uses these signals to calculate the pressure of the air in the manifold. When the manifold vacuum is high (eg, engine at idle), manifold absolute pressure is low and the PCM provides less fuel. When the manifold vacuum is low (eg, throttle wide open), manifold absolute pressure is high and the PCM provides more fuel.

Crankshaft speed/position sensor

11 This is an inductive pulse generator bolted to the timing chain cover. The sensor scans cut-outs machined on a timing disc located on the timing chain end of the crankshaft. The ridge between the 35th and 36th holes (corresponding to 50° BTDC) is missing – this step in the incoming signals is used by the PCM to determine crankshaft (ie, piston) position.

Camshaft position sensor

12 On 4-cylinder models, the camshaft position sensor is bolted to the front left-hand end of the camshaft cover, and is triggered by a high-point on the inlet camshaft. On V6 models, the camshaft position sensor is mounted on the right-hand side of the front cylinder head and is triggered by a high-point on the front inlet camshaft. The sensor functions in the same way as the crankshaft speed/position sensor, producing a series of pulses. This gives the PCM a reference point, to enable it to determine the firing order, and operate the injectors in the appropriate sequence.

Coolant temperature sensor

13 This component, which is screwed into the coolant housing on the left-hand end of the cylinder head on 4-cylinder models or into the coolant crossover on V6 models, is an NTC (Negative Temperature Coefficient) thermistor – that is, a semi-conductor whose electrical resistance decreases as its temperature increases. It provides the PCM with a constantly-varying (analogue) voltage signal, corresponding to the temperature of the engine coolant. This is used to refine the calculations made by the PCM, when determining the correct amount of fuel required to achieve the ideal air/fuel mixture ratio.

Inlet air temperature sensor

14 On 4-cylinder models, this component is part of the temperature and manifold absolute pressure (T-MAP) sensor which is fitted into the inlet manifold. On V6 models it is located in the air cleaner housing cover with the mass airflow (MAF) sensor. The sensor is an NTC thermistor – see the previous paragraph – providing the PCM with a signal corresponding to the temperature of air passing into the engine. This is used to refine the calculations made by the PCM when determining the correct amount of fuel required to achieve the ideal air/fuel mixture ratio.

Throttle potentiometer

15 This is mounted on the end of the throttle valve spindle, to provide the PCM with a constantly-varying (analogue) voltage signal corresponding to the throttle opening. This allows the PCM to register the driver's input when determining the amount of fuel required by the engine.

ABS wheel sensors

16 Previous Mondeos had a vehicle speed sensor, mounted on the transmission. Now, the sensor has been deleted, and vehicle speed information is instead provided by the car's ABS wheel sensors. The PCM uses the information to determine fuel mapping, and to control features such as the fuel shut-off on the overrun, idle strategy when stationary, and to provide information for the trip computer and cruise control systems (where fitted).

Power steering pressure switch

17 This is a pressure-operated switch, screwed into the power steering system's high-pressure pipe. Its contacts are normally closed, opening when the system reaches the specified pressure – on receiving this signal, the PCM increases the idle speed, to compensate for the additional load on the engine.

Air conditioning system

18 Two pressure-operated switches and the compressor clutch solenoid are connected to the PCM, to enable it to determine how the system is operating. The PCM can increase idle speed or switch off the system, as necessary, so that normal operation and driveability are not impaired. Fault diagnosis and repair should be left to a dealer service department or air conditioning specialist.

Idle air control valve

19 The idle air control (IAC) valve maintains a stable idle speed by varying the quantity of air entering the engine through an auxiliary air passage. The valve is activated by a signal from the PCM.

Inlet manifold runner control actuator

4-cylinder engines

20 The inlet manifold runner control (IMRC) actuator, operates four (one for each cylinder) plates in the passageways of the inlet manifold. These plates are called swirl plates and reduce the cross-section of the inlet passages at low speeds, this increases the inlet air swirl to make the mixture ignite more efficiently around the spark plug area. This in turn will reduce exhaust emissions and fuel consumption.

Inlet manifold tuning valve

4-cylinder engines

21 The inlet manifold tuning (IMT) valve controls the inlet manifold runner control actuator via a vacuum pipe, this will then give the correct position of the swirl plates depending on the vacuum in the inlet manifold.

Automatic transmission sensors

22 In addition to the driver's controls, the 4-speed transmission has a speed sensor, a fluid temperature sensor (built into the solenoid valve unit), and a selector lever position sensor. All of these are connected to the PCM, to enable it to control the transmission through the solenoid valve unit. On 5-speed transmissions, there is a selector lever position sensor and a Transmission Control Module (TCM). See Chapter 7B for further details.

Exhaust gas oxygen sensor

23 The oxygen sensor in the exhaust system provides the PCM with constant feedback – 'closed-loop' control – which enables it to adjust the mixture to provide the best possible conditions for the catalytic converter to operate. Refer to Chapter 4C for more information.

12 Fuel injection system – checking and fault diagnosis

Note: *Refer to the warning in Section 1 before proceeding.*

Checking

1 Check all earth wire connections for tightness. Check all wiring and electrical connectors that are related to the system. Loose electrical connectors and poor earth connections can cause many problems that resemble more serious malfunctions.

2 Check that the battery is fully-charged and its leads tightened correctly. The PCM and sensors depend on an accurate supply voltage to properly meter the fuel.

3 Check the air filter element – a dirty or partially-blocked filter will severely impede performance and economy (see Chapter 1A).

4 Referring to the information given in Chapter 12 and in the wiring diagrams at the back of this manual, check that all fuses protecting the circuits related to the engine management system are in good condition. Fit new fuses if required, and at the same time check that all relays are securely plugged into their sockets.

5 Check the air inlet ducts for leaks. Also check the condition of the vacuum hoses connected to the inlet manifold.

6 Disconnect the air ducting from the throttle housing, and check the throttle valve for dirt, carbon or residue. **Note:** *A warning label on the housing states specifically that the housing bore and the throttle valve have a special coating, and must not be cleaned using solvents such as carburettor cleaner, as this may damage it.*

7 With the engine running, place a screwdriver or a stethoscope against each injector, one at a time. Listen for a clicking sound, indicating correct operation.

8 If an injector is not operating correctly, turn off the engine, and unplug the electrical connector from the injector. Check the resistance across the terminals of the injector, and compare your reading with the relevant Ford specifications. If the resistance is not as specified, consult a Ford dealer before renewing the injector, but a zero or infinite reading is a definite indication of a fault.

9 A rough idle, diminished performance and/or increased fuel consumption could also be caused by clogged or fouled fuel injectors. Fuel additives to clean fouled injectors are available at car accessory shops.

10 If these checks fail to reveal the cause of the problem, the car should be taken to a suitably-equipped Ford dealer for testing. A wiring connector is incorporated in the engine management circuit, into which a special electronic diagnostic tester can be plugged – the connector is located under the steering column. The tester will locate the fault quickly and simply, alleviating the need to test all the system components individually, which is a time-consuming operation that also carries a risk of damaging the PCM.

Powertrain control module

11 Do not attempt to 'test' the PCM with any kind of equipment. If it is thought to be faulty, take the car to a Ford dealer for the entire electronic control system to be checked using the proper diagnostic equipment. Only if all other possibilities have been eliminated should the PCM be considered at fault, and renewed.

Mass airflow sensor

12 Testing of this component is beyond the scope of the DIY mechanic, and should be left to a Ford dealer.

T-MAP sensor

13 Testing of this component is beyond the scope of the DIY mechanic, and should be left to a Ford dealer.

Crankshaft speed/position sensor

14 Unplug the electrical connector from the sensor.

15 Using an ohmmeter, measure the resistance between the sensor terminals. Compare this reading to the one Ford specify, if the indicated resistance is not within the specified range, renew the sensor.

16 Plug in the sensor's electrical connector on completion.

Camshaft position sensor

17 The procedure is as described in paragraphs 14 to 16 above.

Coolant temperature sensor

18 Refer to Chapter 3.

Inlet air temperature sensor

19 Unplug the electrical connector from the sensor.

20 Using an ohmmeter, measure the resistance between the sensor terminals. Depending on the temperature of the sensor tip, the resistance measured will vary, but at 20°C it should be as given in the Specifications Section of this Chapter. If the sensor's temperature is varied – by placing it in a freezer for a while, or by warming it gently – its resistance should alter accordingly.

21 If the results obtained show the sensor to be faulty, renew it.

Throttle potentiometer

22 Remove the engine plastic cover, where necessary, and unplug the potentiometer's electrical connector.

23 Using an ohmmeter, measure the resistance between the unit's terminals – first between the centre terminal and one of the outer two, then from the centre to the remaining outer terminal. The resistance should be within the limits given in Ford specifications, and should alter smoothly as the throttle valve is moved from the fully-closed (idle speed) position to fully open and back again.

24 If the resistance measured is significantly different from the specified value, if there are any breaks in continuity, or if the reading fluctuates erratically as the throttle is operated, the potentiometer is faulty, and must be renewed.

ABS wheel sensor

25 Refer to Chapter 9.

Power steering pressure switch

26 Unplug the electrical connector from the sensor.

27 Using an ohmmeter, measure the resistance between the switch terminals. With the engine switched off, or idling with the roadwheels in the straight-ahead position, little or no resistance should be measured. With the engine running and the steering on full-lock, the pressure increase in the system should open the switch contacts, so that infinite resistance is now measured.

28 If the results obtained show the switch to be faulty, renew it.

Idle air control valve

29 Disconnect the wiring from the idle speed control valve, then connect a 12-volt supply to the valve terminals – positive to terminal 37 and negative to terminal 21. A distinct click should be heard each time contact is made and broken. If not, measure the resistance between the terminals. If the resistance is not as specified, renew the valve.

Inlet manifold runner control actuator

30 The inlet manifold runner control actuator is vacuum operated, check the vacuum pipe for splits and correct fitting, also check to make sure the pipes are not blocked. Check the actuator linkage to the swirl plates for free movement. **Note:** *The swirl plates should be in the closed position, when the engine is switched off.*

Inlet manifold tuning valve

31 The inlet manifold tuning valve is electrically-operated and controls the vacuum, check the vacuum pipes for splits and correct fitting, also check to make sure the pipes are not blocked.

Fault diagnosis

32 The various components of the fuel, ignition and emissions control systems (not forgetting the same PCM's control of sub-systems such as the radiator cooling fan, air conditioning and automatic transmission, where appropriate) are so closely interlinked that diagnosis of a faulty component may be almost impossible to trace using traditional methods.

33 To quickly and accurately find faults, the PCM is provided with a built-in self-diagnosis facility, which detects malfunctions in the system's components. When a fault occurs, the PCM identifies the fault and stores it in its memory, and (in most cases) runs the system using back-up values pre-programmed ('mapped') into its memory. Good driveability is thus maintained, to enable the car to be driven to a garage for attention.

34 Any faults that may have occurred are stored in the PCM, when the system is connected (via the built-in diagnostic socket under the steering column) to special Ford diagnostic equipment (WDS2000) – this points the user in the direction of the faulty circuit, so that further tests can pinpoint the exact location of the fault.

35 Given below is the procedure that would be followed by a Ford technician to trace a fault from scratch. Should your car's engine management system develop a fault, read through the procedure and decide how much you can attempt, depending on your skill and experience and the equipment available to you, or whether it would be simpler to have the car attended to by your local Ford dealer.

a) *Preliminary checks.*
b) *Fault code or description read-out*.*
c) *Check ignition timing and base idle speed. Recheck fault codes to establish whether fault has been cured or not*.*
d) *Carry out basic check of ignition system components. Recheck fault codes to establish whether fault has been cured or not*.*
e) *Carry out basic check of fuel system components. Recheck fault codes to establish whether fault has been cured or not*.*
f) *If fault is still not located, carry out system test*.*

* *Operations marked with an asterisk require special test Ford diagnostic equipment.*

Preliminary checks

Note: *When carrying out these checks to trace a fault, remember that if the fault has appeared only a short time after any part of the car has been serviced or overhauled, the first place to check is where that work was carried out, however unrelated it may appear, to ensure that no carelessly-refitted components are causing the problem.*

36 If you are tracing the cause of a 'partial' engine fault, such as lack of performance, in addition to the checks outlined below, check the compression pressures (see the relevant Part of Chapter 2) and bear in mind the possibility that, on V6 models, one of the hydraulic tappets might be faulty, producing an incorrect valve clearance. Check also that the fuel filter has been renewed at the recommended intervals.

37 If the system appears to be completely dead, remember the possibility that the alarm/inhibitor system may be responsible.

38 The first check for anyone without special test equipment is to switch on the ignition, and to listen for the fuel pump (the sound of an electric motor running, audible from beneath the rear seats); assuming there is sufficient fuel in the tank, the pump should start and run for approximately one or two seconds, then stop. If the pump runs continuously all the time the ignition is switched on, the electronic control system is running in the back-up (or 'limp-home') mode referred to by Ford as 'Limited Operation Strategy' (LOS). This almost certainly indicates a fault in the PCM itself, and the car should therefore be taken to a Ford dealer for a full test of the complete system using the correct diagnostic equipment; do not waste time trying to test the system without such facilities.

39 After checking the fuel pump, a considerable amount of fault diagnosis is still possible without special test equipment. Refer to the information given at the beginning of this Section.

40 Working methodically around the engine compartment, check carefully that all vacuum hoses and pipes are securely fastened and correctly routed, with no signs of cracks, splits or deterioration to cause air leaks, or of hoses that are trapped, kinked, or bent sharply enough to restrict airflow. Check all connections and sharp bends, and renew any damaged or deformed lengths of hose.

41 Working from the fuel tank, via the filter, to the fuel rail (and including the feed and return), check the fuel lines, and renew any that are found to be leaking, trapped or kinked.

42 Check that the accelerator cable is correctly secured and adjusted; renew the cable if there is any doubt about its condition, or if it appears to be stiff or jerky in operation. Refer to the Section 5 for further information, if required.

43 If there is any doubt about the operation of the throttle, remove the air ducting from the throttle housing, and check that the throttle valve moves smoothly and easily from the fully-closed to the fully-open position and back again, as an assistant depresses the accelerator pedal. If the valve shows any sign of stiffness, sticking or otherwise-inhibited movement (and the accelerator cable is known to be in good condition), spray the throttle linkage with penetrating lubricant, allow time for it to work, and repeat the check.

44 Run the engine at idle speed. Working from the air inlet at the inner wing panel, check the air inlet ducting for air leaks. Usually, these will be revealed by sucking or hissing noises. If a leak is found at any point, tighten the fastening clamp and/or renew the faulty components, as applicable.

45 Check the exhaust system for leaks with reference to Section 14.

46 It is possible to make a further check of the electrical connections by wiggling each electrical connector of the system in turn as the engine is idling; a faulty connector will be immediately evident from the engine's response as contact is broken and remade.

47 Switch off the engine. If the fault is not yet identified, the next step is to check the ignition voltages, using an engine analyser with an oscilloscope – without such equipment, the only tests possible are to remove and check each spark plug in turn, to check the spark plug (HT) lead connections and resistances, and to check the connections and resistances of the ignition coil. Refer to the relevant Sections of Chapters 1A and 5B.

48 The final step in these preliminary checks would be to use an exhaust gas analyser to measure the CO level at the exhaust tailpipe. This check cannot be made without special test equipment – see your local Ford dealer for details.

Fault diagnostic equipment

Note: *The Ford WDS 2000 tester must be used, this tester will display the fault without reference to a fault code. Do not use the STAR tester – only use the WDS2000 tester.*

49 The preliminary checks outlined above should eliminate the majority of faults from the engine management system. If the fault is not yet identified, the next step is to connect the (WDS2000) Ford diagnostic equipment. This will guide the technician through a procedure, then direct him to a specific area for investigation and to rectify the fault.

Basic check of fuel system

50 If the checks so far have not eliminated the fault, the next step is to carry out a basic check of the fuel system components.

51 Assuming that the preliminary checks have established that the fuel pump is operating correctly, that the fuel filter is unlikely to be blocked, and also that there are no leaks in the system, the next step is to check the fuel pressure (see Section 7). If this is correct, check the injectors (see beginning of this Section) and the Positive Crankcase Ventilation system.

Idle speed and mixture

52 Both the idle speed and mixture are under the control of the PCM, and cannot be adjusted. The settings can only be checked using special diagnostic equipment.

53 If the idle speed and mixture are thought to be incorrect, take the car to a Ford dealer for the complete system to be tested.

13 Fuel injection system components – removal and refitting

Note: *Refer to the warning in Section 1 before proceeding.*

Powertrain control module

Caution: The PCM is fragile. Take care not to drop it or subject it to any other kind of impact, and do not subject it to extremes of temperature, or allow it to get wet. Do not touch the PCM terminals as there is a chance that static electricity may damage the internal electronic components.

Note: *If renewing the powertrain control module, note that it must be reprogrammed for the specific model by a Ford dealer using the WDS2000 diagnostic equipment. Failure to do so will result in the PCM assuming its limited operating strategy (LOS) settings giving poor performance and economy.*

1 Disconnect the battery negative (earth) lead (refer to *Disconnecting the battery* at the end of this manual).

2 Unclip the plastic cover and remove the three retaining nuts from the right-hand strut top mounting. **Note:** ***DO NOT*** *jack up the front of the car, while these nuts are removed.*
3 Undo the four retaining bolts from the right-hand strut top mounting brace and remove it from the car.
4 A security shield is riveted over the PCM, and it will be necessary to drill out the rivet(s) to remove the shield and earth cable.
Caution: The PCM earth cable is connected behind the security shield rivet. Take care not to damage the earth cable when drilling through the rivet.
5 Unclip the wiring harness from along the right-hand inner wing panel.
6 Undo the retaining bolt and release the wiring connector from the PCM – to prevent dust and dirt entering the multiplug, cover it with a polythene bag.
7 From inside the car, unclip the generic electronic module (GEM) from the PCM bracket (as described in Chapter 12).
8 Undo the retaining nut and withdraw the PCM and mounting bracket from the driver's side footwell.
9 Refitting is the reverse of the removal procedure. Whenever the PCM (or battery) is disconnected, the information relating to idle speed control and other operating values will be lost from its memory until the unit has reprogrammed itself; until then, there may be surging, hesitation, erratic idle and a generally-inferior level of performance. To allow the PCM to relearn these values, start the engine and run it as close to idle speed as possible until it reaches its normal operating temperature, then run it for approximately two minutes at 1200 rpm. Next, drive the car as far as necessary – approximately 5 miles of varied driving conditions is usually sufficient – to complete the relearning process.

Mass airflow sensor

V6 engine

10 Disconnect the battery negative (earth) lead (refer to *Disconnecting the battery* at the end of this manual).
11 Disconnect the wiring connector from the mass airflow sensor **(see illustration)**.
12 Remove the air cleaner assembly as described in Section 4. Unscrew and remove the sensor mounting bolts and withdraw the sensor from the air cleaner cover.
13 Refitting is the reverse of the removal procedure. Ensure that the sensor and air cleaner cover are seated correctly and securely fastened, so that there are no air leaks.

T-MAP sensor

4-cylinder engines

14 Disconnect the battery negative (earth) lead (refer to *Disconnecting the battery* at the end of this manual). Unclip the breather hose from the engine upper plastic cover, then unclip the cover from the top of the engine.
15 Disconnect the wiring connector from the temperature and manifold absolute pressure sensor **(see illustration 11.6a)**.
16 Undo the retaining screw and withdraw the sensor from the inlet manifold **(see illustration)**.

13.11 Disconnecting the wiring connector from the mass airflow sensor (V6 engine)

13.16 Undo the retaining screw (arrowed) to remove the T-MAP sensor (4-cylinder engines)

13.20a Disconnecting the wiring connector from the crankshaft position sensor (4-cylinder engines)

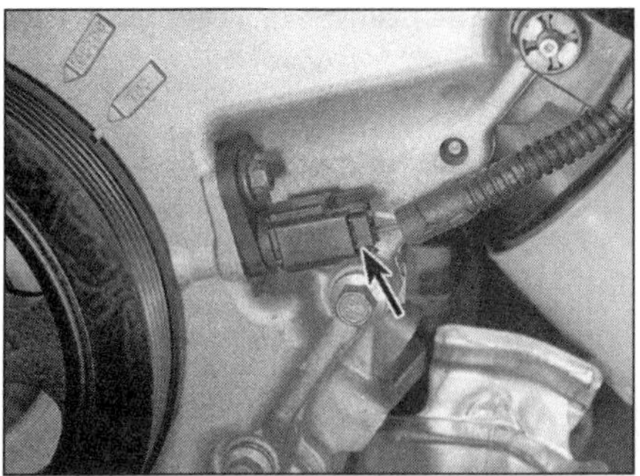
13.20b On V6 engines, the crankshaft position sensor (arrowed) is to the right of the crankshaft pulley

Crankshaft speed/position sensor

17 Disconnect the battery negative (earth) lead (refer to *Disconnecting the battery* at the end of this manual).
18 Apply the handbrake, then jack up the front of the car and support it on axle stands (see *Jacking and vehicle support*).
19 Remove the right-hand front roadwheel, undo the retaining bolts and withdraw the wheel arch liner (see Chapter 11).
20 Disconnect the wiring from the sensor **(see illustrations)**.
21 Undo the retaining bolt and withdraw the sensor.
22 Refitting is the reverse of the removal procedure.

Camshaft position sensor

23 The camshaft sensor is located on the front left-hand end of the camshaft cover on 4-cylinder models. On V6 models, the sensor is located in the timing chain cover, adjacent to the front inlet camshaft sprocket **(see illustrations)**.
24 On 4-cylinder models, unclip the breather hose from the engine upper plastic cover, then unclip the cover from the top of the engine.
25 Disconnect the sensor's electrical connector. Remove the retaining bolt, and withdraw the sensor from the camshaft cover (4-cylinder engines) or timing chain cover (V6 engines); be prepared for slight oil loss.

13.23a Disconnecting the wiring connector from the camshaft position sensor (4-cylinder engines)

13.23b On V6 engines, the camshaft position sensor is at the top front edge of the timing chain cover

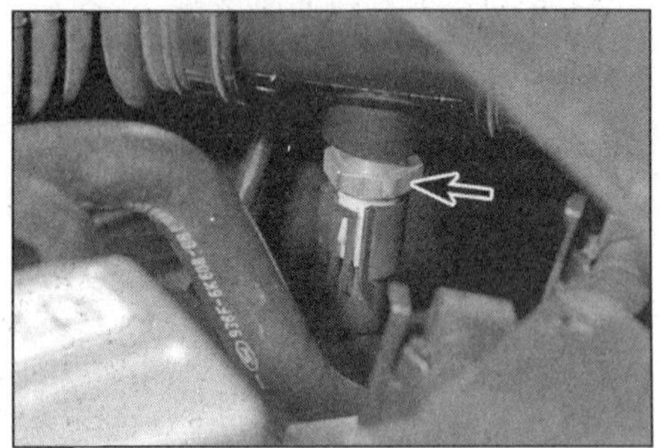
13.28 Inlet air temperature sensor (arrowed) is screwed into the underside of the air inlet resonator

13.33a Disconnecting the throttle sensor wiring plug on a 4-cylinder engine . . .

13.33b . . . and on a V6 engine

26 Refitting is the reverse of the removal procedure, noting the following points:

a) *Apply petroleum jelly or clean engine oil to the sensor's sealing O-ring.*
b) *Locate the sensor fully in the camshaft cover/timing chain cover, and wipe off any surplus lubricant before securing it.*
c) *Tighten the bolt to the specified torque wrench setting.*

Coolant temperature sensor

27 Refer to Chapter 3.

Inlet air temperature sensor

V6 engine

28 Remove the mass airflow sensor to gain access to the temperature sensor **(see illustration)**.

29 Releasing its clip, unplug the sensor's electrical connector, then unscrew the sensor from the resonator, air inlet duct or air cleaner housing.

30 Refitting is the reverse of the removal procedure. Tighten the sensor to the specified torque wrench setting. If it is overtightened, its tapered thread may crack the resonator, duct or air cleaner housing.

Throttle position sensor

31 On 4-cylinder models, unclip the breather hose from the engine upper plastic cover, then unclip the cover from the top of the engine.

32 On V6 models, remove the water pump pulley shield. If necessary, remove the PCV hose from the air inlet duct.

33 Disconnect the wiring plug. Remove the retaining screws, and withdraw the unit from the throttle housing **(see illustrations)**. Do not force the sensor's centre to rotate past its normal operating sweep, otherwise the unit will be seriously damaged.

34 Refitting is the reverse of the removal procedure, noting the following points:

a) *Ensure that the sensor is correctly orientated, by locating its centre on the D-shaped throttle shaft (throttle closed), and aligning the sensor body so that the bolts pass easily into the throttle housing.*
b) *Tighten the screws securely (but do not overtighten them, or the sensor body will be cracked).*

ABS wheel sensors

35 Refer to Chapter 9.

Power steering pressure switch

36 The pressure switch is located in the high-pressure pipe from the power steering pump. Disconnect the wiring connector and unscrew the switch from the pipe.

Throttle housing

4-cylinder engines

37 Disconnect the battery negative (earth) lead (refer to *Disconnecting the battery* at the end of this manual).

38 Unclip the breather hose from the engine upper plastic cover, then unclip the cover from the top of the engine. Slacken the retaining clips and remove the air inlet pipe from the throttle housing.

39 Disconnect the accelerator cable from the throttle linkage (see Section 5). Where fitted, also disconnect the cruise control actuator cable.

13.41 Undo the retaining bolts and remove the throttle housing (4-cylinder engines)

13.48 Undo the retaining bolts (arrowed) and remove the throttle housing (V6 engine)

40 Disconnect the wiring plug from the throttle position sensor's electrical connector.

41 Remove the throttle housing mounting screws **(see illustration)**, then detach the throttle housing and gasket from the inlet manifold. Discard the gasket – this must be renewed whenever it is disturbed.

42 Using a soft brush and a suitable liquid cleaner, thoroughly clean the exterior of the throttle housing, then blow out all passages with compressed air.

Caution: Do not clean the throttle housing's bore, the throttle valve, or the throttle position sensor, either by scraping or with a solvent. Just wipe them over carefully with a clean soft cloth.

43 Refitting is the reverse of the removal procedure. Fit a new gasket, and tighten the housing screws to the specified torque.

V6 engine

44 Disconnect the battery negative (earth) lead (refer to *Disconnecting the battery* at the end of this manual).

45 Remove the air cleaner and air inlet duct (see Section 4). Also remove the water pump pulley shield.

46 Disconnect the wiring from the throttle position sensor and detach the wiring from the stud. Position the wiring to one side.

47 Disconnect the accelerator cable and speed control cable (if fitted) from the throttle housing.

48 Unscrew the mounting bolts and nut, and withdraw the throttle housing from the upper inlet manifold **(see illustration)**. Recover the gasket.

49 Using a soft brush and a suitable liquid cleaner, thoroughly clean the exterior of the throttle housing, then blow out all passages with compressed air.

Caution: Do not clean the throttle housing's bore, the throttle valve, or the throttle position sensor, either by scraping or with a solvent. Just wipe them over carefully with a clean soft cloth.

50 Refitting is the reverse of the removal procedure. Fit a new gasket, and tighten the housing bolts and nut to the specified torque.

Fuel rail and injectors

4-cylinder engines

Note: *The following procedure describes the*

removal of the fuel rail assembly, complete with the injectors and pulse damper, to enable the injectors to be serviced individually on a clean work surface.

51 Depressurise the fuel system as described in Section 2. Also equalise tank pressure by removing the fuel filler cap.

52 Disconnect the battery negative (earth) lead (refer to *Disconnecting the battery* at the end of this manual).

53 Unclip the breather hose from the engine upper plastic cover, then unclip the cover from the top of the engine.

54 Disconnect the wiring from the four fuel injector electrical connectors.

55 Disconnect the fuel supply line at the quick-release coupling from the end of the fuel rail (see Section 3) – use clean rag or paper towel to soak up any spilt fuel **(see illustration)**.

56 Disconnect the vacuum pipe from the fuel pulse damper **(see illustration)**.

57 Unscrew the bolts securing the fuel rail, and withdraw the rail, complete with the injectors, out of the cylinder head. Drain any remaining fuel into a suitable clean container.

58 Recover the fuel rail spacers from the cylinder head **(see illustration)**.

59 Clamp the rail carefully in a vice fitted with soft jaws. Release the locking tangs at the top of the injector to withdraw the injectors from the fuel rail. Place the injectors in a clean storage container **(see illustration)**.

60 Discard the seals/O-rings from the fuel injectors and obtain new ones **(see illustrations)**.

61 Further testing of the injectors is beyond the scope of the home mechanic. If you are in doubt as to the status of any injector, it can be tested at a dealer service department.

62 Refitting is the reverse of the removal procedure, noting the following points:

a) Lubricate each (new) seal/O-ring with clean engine oil before refitting.
b) Locate each injector carefully in the fuel rail recess, ensuring that the retaining clips are located correctly on the top of the injectors.
c) Tighten the fuel rail bolts to the torque wrench setting specified.
d) Reconnect the fuel feed quick-release coupling as described in Section 3.
e) Ensure that the breather hose, vacuum hose and wiring are routed correctly, and secured on reconnection by any clips or ties provided.
f) On completion, switch the ignition on to activate the fuel pump and pressurise the system, without cranking the engine. Check for signs of fuel leaks around all disturbed unions and joints before attempting to start the engine.

V6 engine

63 Depressurise the fuel system as described in Section 2. Also equalise tank pressure by removing the fuel filler cap.

64 Disconnect the battery negative (earth)

13.55 Disconnect fuel line quick-release coupling

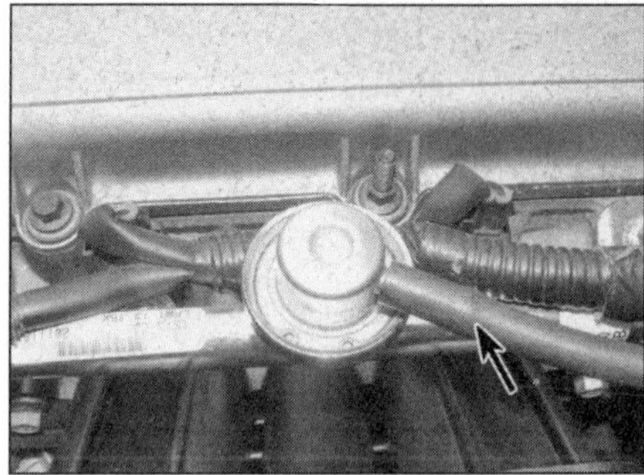

13.56 Disconnect the vacuum pipe (arrowed) from the fuel pulse damper

13.58 Recover the fuel rail spacers from the cylinder head

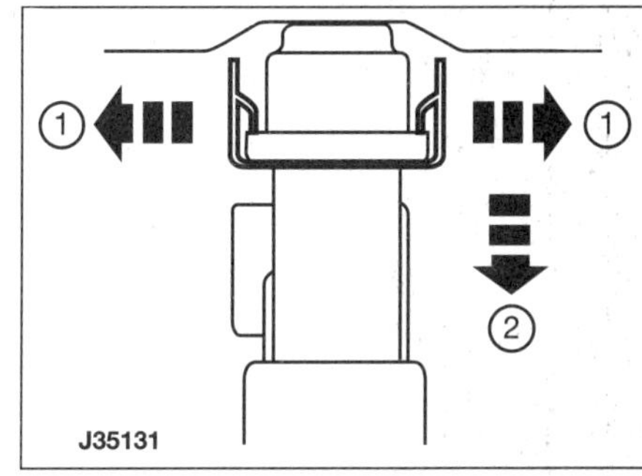

13.59 Unclip the locking tangs to withdraw the injectors

lead (refer to *Disconnecting the battery* at the end of this manual).

65 Remove the upper inlet manifold as described in Chapter 2B.

66 Disconnect the wiring harnesses from the injectors, and position to one side **(see illustrations)**.

67 Disconnect the fuel supply line at the quick-release coupling from the end of the fuel rail (see Section 3).

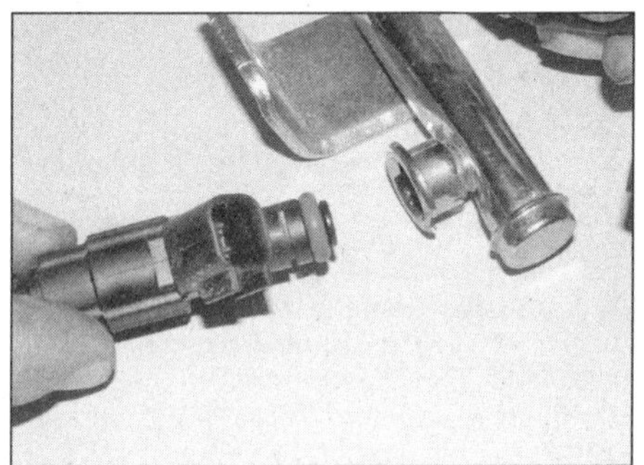

13.60a Withdraw the injectors from the fuel rail . . .

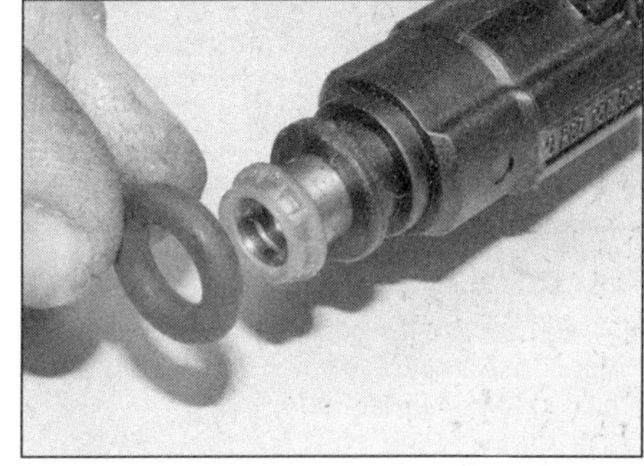

13.60b . . . and remove the O-ring seals

13.66a Use a small screwdriver to release the injector wiring securing clips . . .

13.66b . . . then move the wiring harness to one side

13.68a Unscrew the mounting bolts . . .

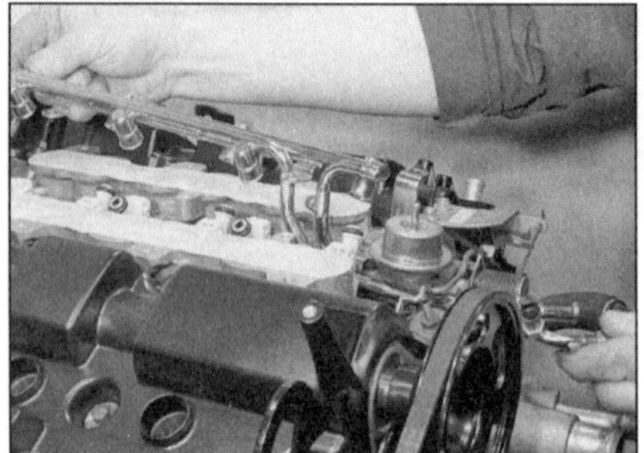
13.68b . . . and remove the fuel rail

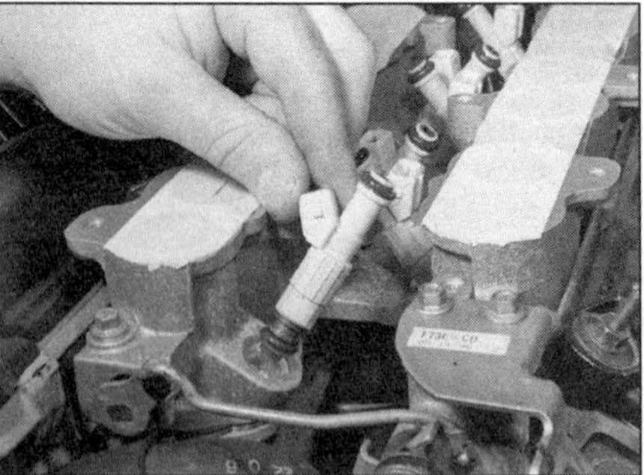
13.71 Inserting the injectors in the lower inlet manifold

68 Unscrew the mounting bolts and remove the fuel rail from the lower inlet manifold **(see illustrations)**. The injectors may come away with the rail or they may remain in the inlet manifold.

69 Where applicable, carefully ease the injectors from the lower inlet manifold or fuel rail and place them in a clean container.

70 Remove and discard all O-ring seals. Further testing of the injectors is beyond the scope of the home mechanic. If you are in doubt as to the status of any injector, it can be tested at a dealer service department.

71 Refitting is the reverse of the removal procedure, noting the following points:

a) *Lubricate each (new) O-ring seal with clean engine oil before refitting, and refit the injectors in the lower inlet manifold before fitting the fuel rail to them* ***(see illustration)****.*

b) *Tighten the fuel rail bolts to the specified torque.*

c) *On completion, switch the ignition on to activate the fuel pump and pressurise the system, without cranking the engine. Check for signs of fuel leaks around the unions and joints before attempting to start the engine.*

Fuel pressure regulator

72 Depressurise the fuel system as described in Section 2. Also equalise tank pressure by removing the fuel filler cap.

73 Disconnect the battery negative (earth) lead (refer to *Disconnecting the battery* at the end of this manual).

74 On V6 models, remove the upper inlet manifold as described in Chapter 2B.

75 Disconnect the vacuum hose from the regulator. Remove the two regulator screws and remove the regulator. Recover the O-ring seal. Soak up spilled fuel using a clean rag.

76 Refitting is the reverse of the removal procedure, noting the following points:

a) *Renew the regulator sealing O-ring whenever the regulator is disturbed. Lubricate the new O-ring with clean engine oil on installation.*

b) *Locate the regulator carefully, and tighten the bolts to the specified torque wrench setting.*

c) *On completion, switch the ignition on and off five times, to activate the fuel pump and pressurise the system, without cranking the engine. Check for signs of fuel leaks around all disturbed unions and joints before attempting to start the engine.*

Idle air control valve

77 Disconnect the battery negative (earth) lead (refer to *Disconnecting the battery* at the end of this manual).

78 On 4-cylinder engines, unclip the breather hose from the engine upper plastic cover, then unclip the cover from the top of the engine.

79 Disconnect the wiring from the idle air control valve **(see illustrations)**.

80 Unscrew the two retaining bolts (4-cylinder) or nuts (V6), and withdraw the valve from the inlet manifold **(see illustration)**. Recover the gasket.

81 Since the valve's individual components are not available separately, and the complete assembly must be renewed if it is thought to be faulty, there is nothing to be lost by attempting to flush out the passages, using carburettor cleaner or similar solvent. This won't take much time or effort, and may well cure the fault.

82 Refitting is the reverse of the removal procedure, noting the following points:

a) *Clean the mating surfaces carefully, and always fit a new gasket whenever the valve is disturbed.*

b) *Tighten the bolts evenly and to the specified torque wrench setting.*

c) *Once the wiring and battery are reconnected, start the engine and allow it to idle. When it has reached normal operating temperature, check that the idle speed is stable, and that no induction (air) leaks are evident. Switch on all electrical loads (headlights, heated rear window, etc), and check that the idle speed is still correct.*

Inlet manifold runner control actuator

4-cylinder engines

83 Remove the throttle housing as described in paragraphs 37 to 42 in this Section.

84 Disconnect the actuator arm from the inlet manifold swirl plate linkage **(see illustration)**.

85 Disconnect the vacuum pipe from the inlet manifold runner control actuator **(see illustration)**.

13.79a Disconnecting the wiring from the idle air control valve (4-cylinder engines)

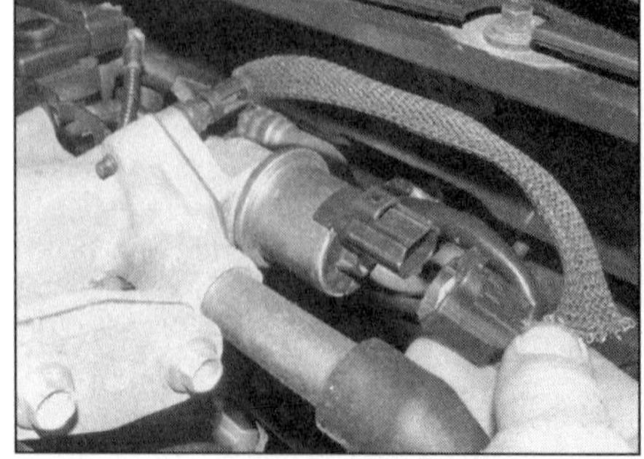
13.79b Disconnecting the wiring from the idle air control valve (V6 engine)

13.80 Unscrew the two retaining bolts (arrowed) (4-cylinder engines)

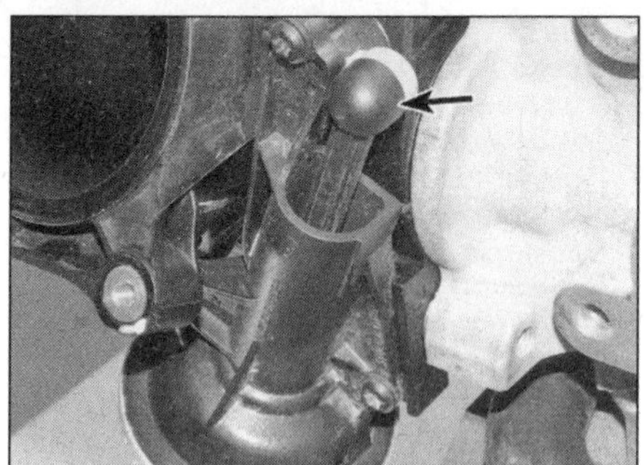
13.84 Disconnect the actuator arm (arrowed) from the linkage

13.85 Disconnect the vacuum pipe (arrowed) from the actuator

13.89 Disconnecting the wiring connector from the inlet manifold runner control unit

86 Undo the three retaining screws and withdraw the inlet manifold runner control actuator from the inlet manifold.

87 Refitting is the reverse of the removal procedure, noting the following points:

a) Clean the mating surfaces carefully, and always fit a new gasket.

b) Tighten the bolts evenly.

c) Once the wiring and battery are reconnected, start the engine and allow it to idle. When it has reached normal operating temperature, check that the idle speed is stable, and that no induction (air) leaks are evident. Switch on all electrical loads (headlights, heated rear window, etc), and check that the idle speed is still correct.

V6 engine

88 Undo the retaining bolts and remove the plastic cover from the front camshaft cover.

89 Disconnect the wiring connector from the inlet manifold runner control unit **(see illustration)**.

90 Undo the three retaining bolts and withdraw the inlet manifold runner control unit from the camshaft cover **(see illustration)**.

91 Disconnect the operating cable from the throttle housing linkage.

92 Refitting is the reverse of the removal procedure.

Inlet manifold tuning valve

4-cylinder engines

93 Disconnect the battery negative (earth) lead (refer to *Disconnecting the battery* at the end of this manual).

94 Unclip the breather hose from the engine upper plastic cover, then unclip the cover from the top of the engine.

95 Disconnect the wiring connector from the inlet manifold tuning valve.

96 Disconnect the vacuum pipes from the inlet manifold tuning valve **(see illustration)**.

97 Undo the two retaining bolts and withdraw the valve from the inlet manifold.

98 Refitting is the reverse of the removal procedure, noting the following points:

a) Clean the mating surfaces carefully, and always fit a new gasket.

b) Tighten the bolts evenly and to the specified torque wrench setting.

13.90 Undo the three retaining bolts (arrowed) and withdraw the control unit

c) Once the wiring and battery are reconnected, start the engine and allow it to idle. When it has reached normal operating temperature, check that the idle speed is stable, and that no induction (air) leaks are evident. Switch on all electrical loads (headlights, heated rear window, etc), and check that the idle speed is still correct.

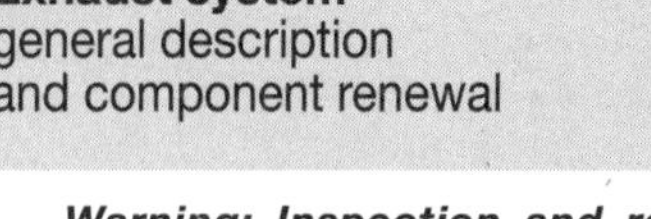

14 Exhaust system – general description and component renewal

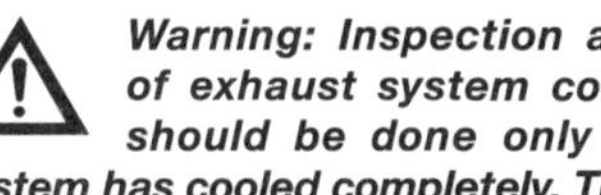

Warning: Inspection and repair of exhaust system components should be done only after the system has cooled completely. This applies particularly to the catalytic converter, which runs at very high temperatures.

General description

1 4-cylinder models are fitted with an exhaust system consisting of a manifold connecting to a front flexible downpipe, catalytic converter, and a rear section incorporating two silencers **(see illustration overleaf)**.

2 On V6 models except the 3.0 litre ST, the exhaust system consists of two exhaust manifolds (one from each bank) with a connecting Y-piece, catalytic converter, and a rear section incorporating three silencers **(see illustration overleaf)**.

3 V6 models with the 3.0 litre ST engine have a new exhaust system, designed to reduce back-pressure, which features two catalytic

13.96 Disconnect the vacuum pipes (arrowed) from the valve

converters – one for each bank of cylinders. A connecting Y-piece feeds to two flexible sections, which then join to the rear system, which has four silencers in total.

4 The exhaust system on all models is suspended throughout its entire length by rubber mounting rings.

Component renewal

5 If any section of the exhaust is damaged or deteriorated, excessive noise and vibration will occur.

6 Carry out regular inspections of the exhaust system, to check security and condition. Look for any damaged or bent parts, open seams, holes, loose connections, excessive corrosion, or other defects which could allow exhaust fumes to enter the car. Deteriorated sections of the exhaust system should be renewed.

7 If the exhaust system components are extremely corroded or rusted together, it may not be possible to separate them. In this case, simply cut off the old components with a hacksaw, and remove any remaining corroded pipe with a cold chisel. Be sure to wear safety glasses to protect your eyes, and wear gloves to protect your hands.

8 Here are some simple guidelines to follow when repairing the exhaust system:

a) Work from the back to the front when removing exhaust system components.

b) Apply penetrating fluid to the flange nuts before unscrewing them.

c) Use new gaskets and rubber mountings when installing exhaust system components.

d) Apply anti-seize compound to the threads of all exhaust system studs during reassembly.

e) Note that on some models, the downpipe is secured to the manifold by two coil springs, spring seats and a self-locking nut on each. Where fitted, tighten the nuts until they stop on the bolt shoulders; the pressure of the springs will then be sufficient to make a leak-proof connection. Do not overtighten the nuts to cure a leak – the studs will shear. Renew the gasket and the springs if a leak is found.

f) Be sure to allow sufficient clearance between newly-installed parts and all points on the underbody, to avoid overheating the floorpan, and possibly damaging the interior carpet and insulation. Pay particularly close attention to the catalytic converter and its heat shield.

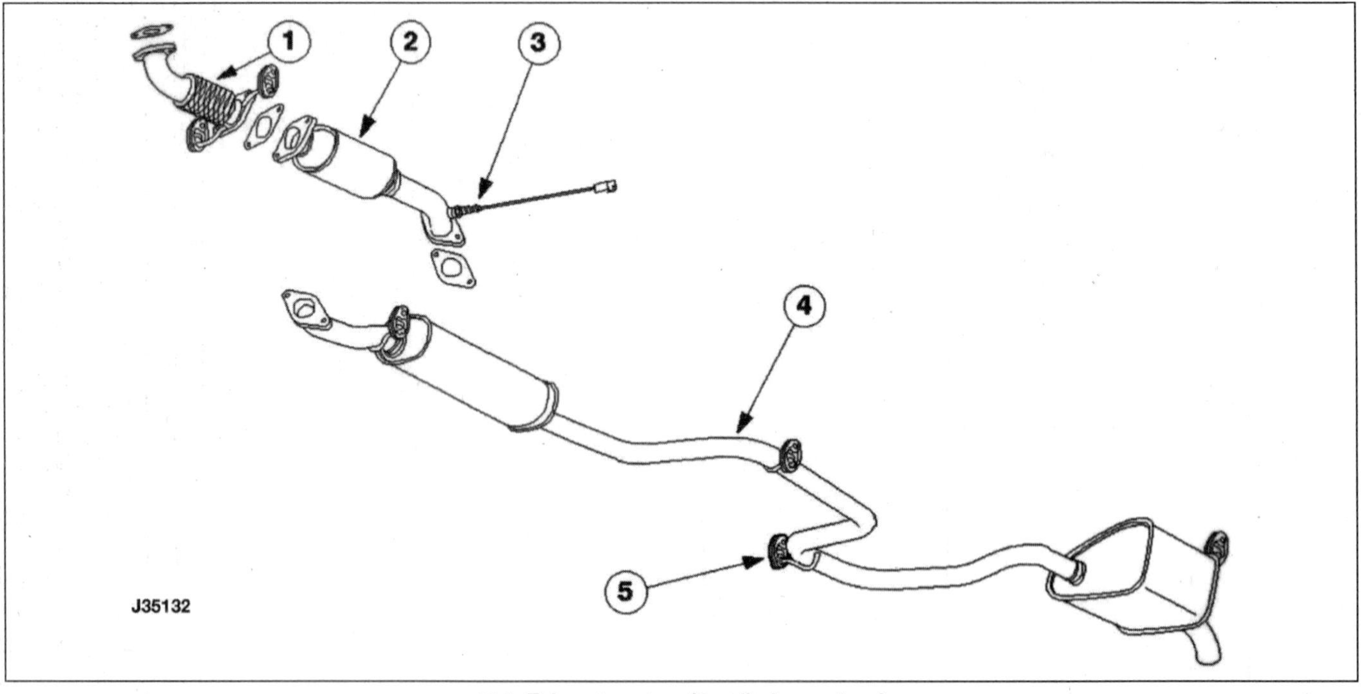

14.1 Exhaust system (4-cylinder engines)

1 *Flexible pipe*
2 *Catalytic converter*
3 *Heated oxygen sensor*
4 *Silencer and tailpipe assembly*
5 *Bracket mounting on Estate only*

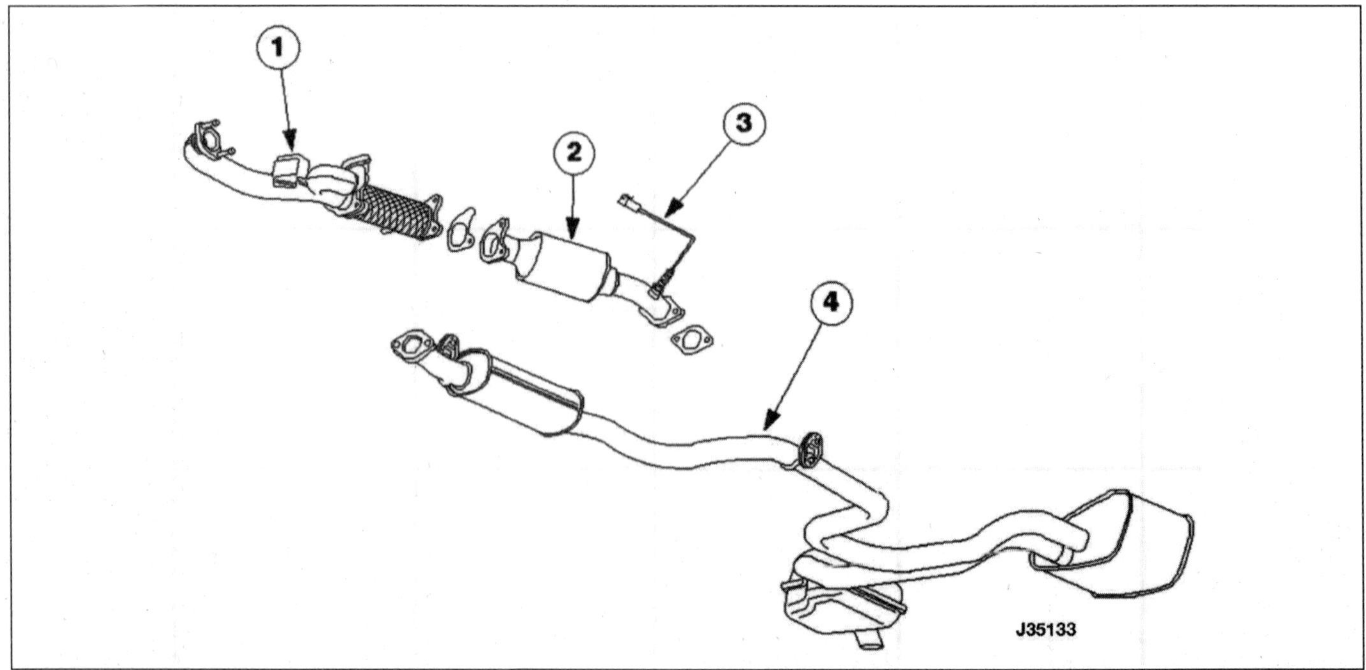

14.2 Exhaust system (V6 engine, except 3.0 litre ST)

1 *Dual flexible pipe/Y-pipe*
2 *Catalytic converter*
3 *Heated oxygen sensor*
4 *Silencer and tailpipe assembly*

Chapter 4 Part B:
Fuel and exhaust systems – diesel models

Contents

Section number

Degrees of difficulty

Easy, suitable for novice with little experience

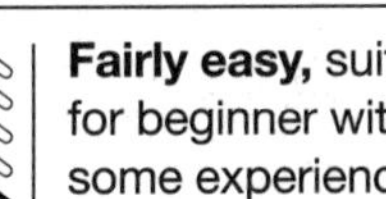

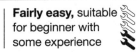

Fairly easy, suitable for beginner with some experience

Fairly difficult, suitable for competent DIY mechanic

Difficult, suitable for experienced DIY mechanic

Very difficult, suitable for expert DIY or professional

Specifications

General

System type	Turbocharged Direct Common-rail injection (TDCi), intercooled, controlled by injection driver module and EEC V PCM, high-pressure pump
Engine codes	Refer to Chapter 2C Specifications
Firing order	1 – 3 – 4 – 2 (No 1 at timing chain end)
Idle speed (engine management-controlled):	
Early 115 PS engine	900 rpm
Later 115 PS engine, and all 130 PS engines	750 rpm
150 PS engines	800 rpm

Glow plugs

Maximum preheat time	8 seconds
Maximum after-glow phase (less than 2500rpm)	30 seconds
Engine above 80°C	No preheating

Injection pump

Make and type	Delphi high-pressure
Rotation (viewed from crankshaft pulley end)	Clockwise
Drive	Twin chain via crankshaft and camshaft sprockets

Torque wrench settings

Torque wrench settings	Nm	lbf ft
Catalytic converter support bracket	46	34
Catalytic converter to front pipe	46	34
Catalytic converter-to-manifold nuts (renew)	46	34
Crankshaft position sensor bolt	7	5
Cylinder head temperature sensor	11	8
DPF flange nuts	46	34
EGR cooler securing nut and bolt	10	7
EGR cooler-to-exhaust manifold bolts	37	27
EGR pipe union	23	17
Exhaust heat shield fasteners	10	7
Exhaust manifold	40	30
Exhaust temperature sensor (models with DPF)	35	26
Fuel injection pump mounting bolts	22	16
Fuel injection pump shield lower bolt	33	24
Fuel injection pump sprocket bolts	33	24
Fuel injection pump support bracket bolts	33	24
Fuel injector locking sleeve	47	35
Fuel rail bolts	23	17
Fuel rail support bracket bolts	14	10
Fuel supply/return pipe unions	24	18
Fuel temperature sensor	15	11
High-pressure pipe unions	36	27
Inlet manifold	15	11
Turbocharger oil supply pipe bolt	14	10
Turbocharger oil return pipe flange bolts	10	7

1 General information and precautions

General information

The fuel system consists of a fuel tank (mounted under the body, beneath the rear seats), fuel gauge sender unit mounted in the fuel tank, fuel filter, high-pressure fuel injection pump, fuel supply rail, fuel pipes, injectors, injector driver module, and EEC-V PCM (powertrain control module).

Fuel is drawn from the tank via a transfer pump, built into and driven from the high-pressure pump, and it then passes through the fuel filter located in the engine bay, where foreign matter and water are removed. The high-pressure injection pump is driven from the crankshaft via the twin-row timing chain which also drives the camshafts.

The pump supplies fuel at high pressure to a common rail supplying all four injectors, which are then opened as signalled by the PCM. On reaching the high-pressure pump, the fuel is pressurised according to demand, and accumulates in the injection common rail, which acts as a fuel reservoir. The pressure in the rail is accurately maintained using a pressure sensor in the end of the rail and the pump's metering valve, with fuel return being controlled according to fuel temperature. The PCM determines the exact timing and duration of the injection period according to engine operating conditions. The four fuel injectors operate sequentially according to the firing order of the cylinders.

There are four pipes from the fuel supply manifold (one for each of the injectors), and one from the supply manifold back to the fuel pump. Each injector disperses the fuel evenly, and sprays fuel directly into the combustion chamber as its piston approaches TDC on the compression stroke. This system is known as direct injection. The pistons have a recess machined into their crowns, the shape of which has been calculated to improve 'swirl' (fuel/air mixing).

The DuraTorq TDCi engine is very much a 'state-of-the-art' unit, in that it features a full electronic engine management system. An extensive array of sensors are fitted, which supply information on many different parameters to the PCM.

Information on crankshaft position and engine speed is generated by a crankshaft position sensor. The inductive head of the sensor runs just above the engine flywheel, and scans a series of 36 protrusions on the flywheel periphery. As the crankshaft rotates, the sensor transmits a pulse every time a protrusion passes it. There is one missing protrusion in the flywheel periphery at a point corresponding to 50° BTDC. The PCM recognises the absence of a pulse from the crankshaft position sensor at this point to establish a reference mark for crankshaft position. Similarly, the time interval between absent pulses is used to determine engine speed.

Information on the quantity and temperature of the inlet air is derived from the T-MAP sensor. The temperature and manifold absolute pressure (or T-MAP) sensor is located in the top of the air inlet duct that runs along the front of the engine subframe below the radiator. It measures the temperature and the pressure of the air in the inlet system. The temperature and quantity of air has a direct bearing on the quantity of fuel to be injected for optimum efficiency.

The traditional coolant temperature sensor has been superseded by a cylinder head temperature sensor. The new sensor is seated in a blind hole in the cylinder head, and measures the temperature of the metal directly. Information on engine temperature is critical for accurate fuelling calculations, and is also used to control the preheating system for cold starts.

The clutch pedal sensor informs the PCM whether the clutch is engaged or disengaged. When the clutch pedal is depressed, the quantity of fuel injected is momentarily reduced, to make gearchanging smoother.

The stop-light switch and separate brake pedal sensor inform the PCM when the brakes are applied – when this signal is received, the PCM puts the engine into idle mode until a signal is received from the accelerator position sensor.

Vehicle speed information is provided by the car's ABS wheel sensors, and is vital to the engine management calculations performed by the PCM.

No accelerator cable is fitted on the DuraTorq engines – instead, a sensor located next to the accelerator pedal informs the PCM of the accelerator position, and this information is used to determine the most appropriate fuelling requirements from the injection pump. The engine idle speed is also controlled by the PCM, and cannot be adjusted. From the signals it receives from the various sensors, the PCM can control the idle speed very accurately, compensating automatically for additional engine loads or unfavourable ambient/engine temperatures.

Cold-starting performance is automatically controlled by the PCM. Under cold start conditions, the cylinder head temperature (CHT) sensor informs the PCM on the engine temperature, this determines the preheat time.

The glow plugs are located in the side of the cylinder head, one to each cylinder, and are electrically-heated. A warning light illuminates when the ignition is switched on, showing that the glow plugs are in operation. When the light goes out, preheating is complete and the engine can be started. The glow plugs have an after-glow phase which only operates under 2500 rpm, and below temperatures of 50°C. This helps the engine to run more smoothly during idling, and reduces exhaust emissions through more efficient combustion just after starting.

The fuel system has a built-in 'strategy' to prevent it from drawing in air, should the car run low on fuel. The PCM monitors the level of fuel in the tank, via the gauge sender unit. After switching on the low fuel level warning light, it will eventually induce a misfire as a further warning to the driver, and lower the engine's maximum speed until the engine stops.

The fuel system on diesel engines is normally very reliable. Provided that clean fuel is used and the specified maintenance is conscientiously carried out, no problems should be experienced. The injection pump and injectors may require overhaul after a high mileage has been covered, but this cannot be done on a DIY basis.

Precautions

Warning: It is necessary to take certain precautions when working on the fuel system components, particularly the fuel injectors. Before carrying out any operations on the fuel system, refer to the precautions given in Safety first! at the beginning of this manual, and to any additional warning notes at the start of the relevant Sections. In particular, note that the injectors on direct-injection diesel engines operate at extremely high pressures, making the injector spray extremely hazardous.

2 Fuel system – priming and bleeding

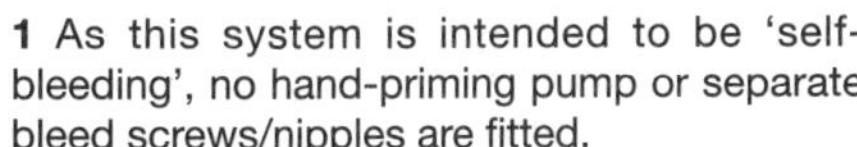

1 As this system is intended to be 'self-bleeding', no hand-priming pump or separate bleed screws/nipples are fitted.

2 When any part of the system has been disturbed therefore, air must be purged from the system by cranking the engine on the starter motor until it starts. When it has started, keep the engine running for approximately 5 minutes to ensure that all air has been removed from the system.

3 To minimise the strain on the battery and starter motor when trying to start the engine, crank it in 10 second bursts, pausing for 30 seconds each time, until the engine starts.

4 Depending on the work that has been carried out, it may be possible to partially prime the system before attempting to start it. For example, fill the fuel filter with clean fuel via one of the top connections – it is essential that no dirt is introduced into the system, and that no diesel fuel is poured over vulnerable components (particularly the alternator) when doing this.

5 Note that the high-pressure injection pump relies on the fuel passing through it for lubrication. It is essential that the pump does not run for any length of time with the fuel tank supply interrupted.

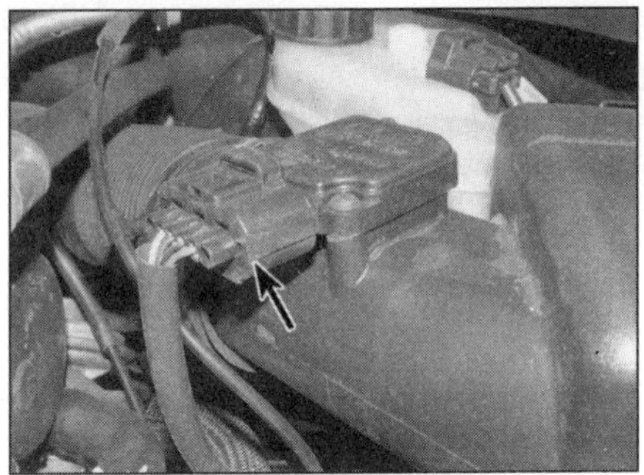

3.1 Disconnect the wiring plug (arrowed) from the mass airflow sensor

3 Air cleaner assembly and air inlet components – removal and refitting

Air cleaner assembly

1 Disconnect the wiring from the mass air flow (MAF) sensor **(see illustration)**.

2 Release the hose clips and disconnect the air inlet duct. Note that the hose clip may not be of the screw type, and will have to be separated by prising the crimped section with a small screwdriver. The clip can be re-used if care is taken, but it may be preferable to fit a screw-drive clip when refitting.

3 Disconnect the breather hose leading to the inlet cleaner housing.

4 Lift and remove the air cleaner assembly to release it from the rubber grommets **(see illustration)**.

5 Check the rubber grommets for deterioration and renew them if necessary.

6 Refitting is the reverse of the removal procedure. Ensure that the air cleaner pegs seat fully in their rubber grommets.

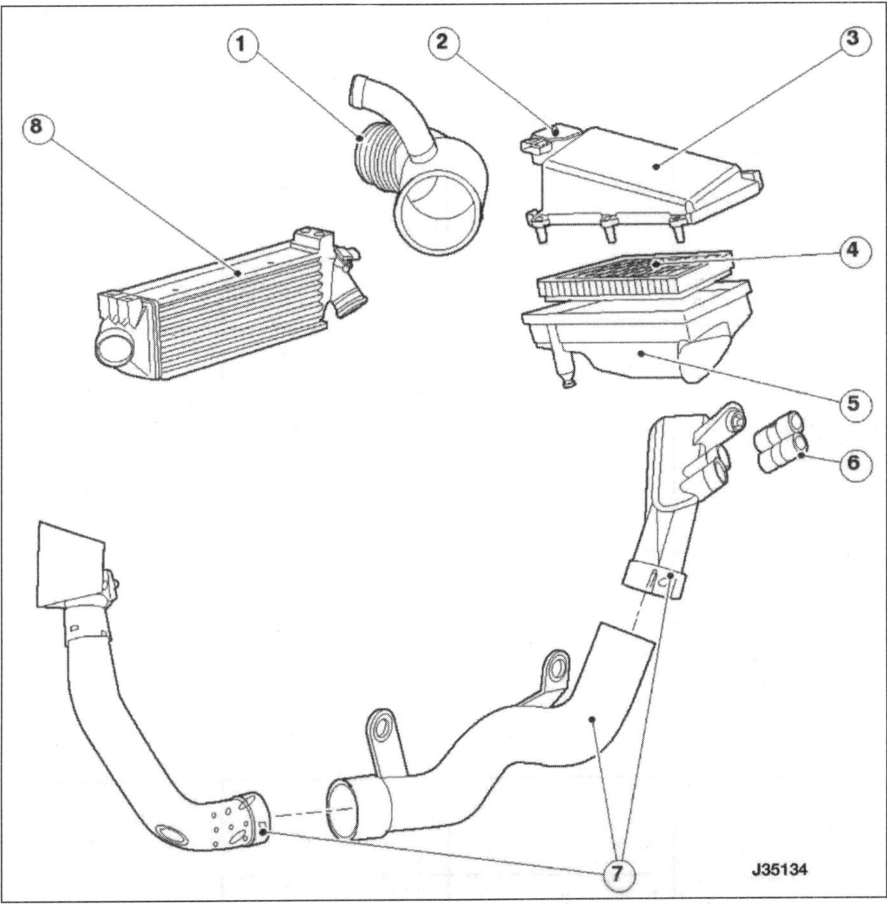

3.4 Air cleaner assembly layout

1 Air cleaner outlet pipe
2 Mass air flow sensor (MAF)
3 Air cleaner housing cover
4 Air cleaner element
5 Air cleaner housing
6 Air cleaner inlet pipe blanking cap
7 Air cleaner inlet pipe
8 Charge air cooler

Air inlet components

7 If removing the inlet duct between the air cleaner and turbocharger, first ensure that the engine is cool. Release the hose clip and carefully ease the duct off the turbocharger. Note that the hose clip may not be of the screw type, and will have to be separated by prising the crimped section with a small screwdriver. The clip can be re-used if care is taken, but it may be preferable to fit a screw-drive clip when refitting.
8 To remove the upper air inlet pipe attached to the air cleaner base, first remove the air cleaner assembly as described in paragraphs 1 to 4.
9 Undo the air inlet pipe upper retaining bolt from the left-hand inner wing.
10 Loosen the left-hand front wheel nuts. Chock the rear wheels and apply the handbrake, jack up the front of the car and support it on axle stands (see *Jacking and vehicle support*).
11 Remove the left-hand front wheel and inner wheel arch liner (Chapter 11).
12 From under the left-hand front wing, withdraw the upper inlet pipe from the middle inlet pipe.
13 Undo the retaining bolts and remove the middle inlet pipe from under the left-hand wing. Where applicable, disconnect the foglight's wiring block connector from the clip on the inlet pipe.
14 To remove the lower air inlet pipe, remove the radiator grille as described in Chapter 11.
15 Refitting is the reverse of the removal procedure.

4 Accelerator pedal – removal and refitting

Removal

1 Remove the driver's side lower facia trim panel, which is secured by four screws and two upper clips. Where applicable, unclip the diagnostic connector plug and/or disconnect the climate control sensor wiring plug as the panel is removed.
2 Disconnect the wiring plug from the accelerator position sensor, then unscrew the bolts and remove the accelerator pedal assembly.

8.5a Unscrew the mounting bolt (arrowed) . . .

Refitting

3 Refit in the reverse order of removal. On completion, check the action of the pedal with the engine running.

5 Fuel tank – removal, inspection and refitting

Note: *Refer to the warning note in Section 1 before proceeding.*

Refer to Chapter 4A, Section 9. The basic procedure for tank removal on diesel models is much the same as that for petrol versions, but ignore the references to the charcoal canister and the fuel filter.

6 Fuel gauge sender unit – removal and refitting

Note: *Refer to the warning note in Section 1 before proceeding. Ford technicians use a special wrench to unscrew the pump/sender unit retaining ring, but ordinary tools can be used successfully.*
1 The fuel gauge sender unit is located in the top face of the fuel tank. The unit can only be detached and withdrawn from the tank after the tank is released and lowered from under the car.
2 Removing the fuel gauge sender unit is a very similar procedure to that for removing the combined fuel pump and sender unit fitted to petrol models, described in Chapter 4A, Section 8.

7 Diesel injection system – checking

Note: *Refer to the warning note in Section 1 before proceeding.*
1 If a fault appears in the diesel injection system, first ensure that all the system wiring connectors are securely connected and free of corrosion. Then ensure that the fault is not due to poor maintenance; ie, check that the air cleaner filter element is clean, the cylinder compression pressures are correct, the fuel filter has been drained (or changed) and the engine breather hoses are clear and undamaged, referring to Chapter 1B or Chapter 2C.
2 If these checks fail to reveal the cause of the problem, the car should be taken to a suitably-equipped Ford dealer for testing. A diagnostic connector is incorporated in the engine management system wiring harness, into which dedicated electronic test equipment can be plugged – the connector is located under the steering column. The test equipment is capable of 'interrogating' the powertrain control module (PCM) electronically and accessing its internal fault log (reading fault codes).
3 Fault codes can only be extracted from the PCM using a dedicated fault code reader. A Ford dealer will obviously have such a reader, but they are also available from other suppliers. It is unlikely to be cost-effective for the private owner to purchase a fault code reader, but a well-equipped local garage or auto-electrical specialist will have one.
4 Using this equipment, faults can be pinpointed quickly and simply, even if their occurrence is intermittent. Testing all the system components individually in an attempt to locate the fault by elimination is a time-consuming operation that is unlikely to be fruitful (particularly if the fault occurs dynamically), and carries a high risk of damage to the PCM's internal components.
5 Experienced home mechanics equipped with a diesel tachometer or other diagnostic equipment may be able to check the engine idle speed; if found to be out of specification, the car must be taken to a suitably-equipped Ford dealer for assessment. The engine idle speed is not manually adjustable; incorrect test results indicate the need for maintenance (possibly, injector cleaning or recalibration) or a fault within the injection system.
6 If excessive smoking or knocking is evident, it may be due to a problem with the fuel injectors. Proprietary treatments are available which can be added to the fuel, in order to clean the injectors. Injectors deteriorate with prolonged use, however, and it is reasonable to expect them to need reconditioning or renewal after 60 000 miles or so. Accurate testing, overhaul and calibration of the injectors must be left to a specialist.

8 Diesel injection system electronic components – removal and refitting

1 Disconnect the battery negative (earth) lead (refer to *Disconnecting the battery* at the end of this manual).
2 Withdraw the oil level dipstick and unclip the engine plastic cover.

Crankshaft position sensor

3 The sensor is located in the top of the bellhousing to the rear.
4 For better access remove the air cleaner assembly as described in Section 3.
5 Disconnect the wiring plug, then unscrew the mounting bolt and withdraw the sensor **(see illustrations)**. **Note:** *Before removing the sensor, mark the position of the retaining bolt, so that it can be refitted in the same place.*
6 Refitting is a reversal of removal.

Cylinder head temperature sensor

7 The switch is screwed into the left-hand (flywheel) end of the cylinder head, behind the power steering pump pulley **(see illustration)**.

8 To improve access to the switch, it will be necessary to remove the power steering pump pulley, referring to Chapter 2C, Section 10.

9 It may also be helpful to release the air inlet hoses and move them to one side, as described in Section 3.

10 Trace the wiring from the sensor, and disconnect it at the plug, which is clipped to the brake vacuum pump **(see illustration)**.

11 The sensor can now be unscrewed and removed **(see illustration)**. However, the length of wiring may make it difficult getting a tool to fit onto it.

12 Ultimately, it may be necessary to cut the sensor wiring, unscrew the sensor using a thin-wall socket or box spanner, then remake the wiring after fitting, using a suitable connector.

13 Refitting is a reversal of removal. Clean the threads of the sensor and mounting hole, then refit the sensor and tighten it to the specified torque.

ABS wheel sensors

14 Previous Mondeos had a vehicle speed sensor, mounted on the transmission. Now, the sensor has been deleted, and vehicle speed information is instead provided by the car's ABS wheel sensors. Refer to Chapter 9.

Temperature and manifold absolute pressure sensor

15 The T-MAP sensor is mounted on the air inlet duct which runs along the front of the engine subframe, below the radiator.

16 Disconnect the wiring plug from the sensor.

17 Unscrew and remove the two mounting bolts, and withdraw the sensor from the inlet duct.

18 Refitting is a reversal of removal, ensuring that the wiring plug is securely reconnected and the sensor is fitted securely to the inlet duct.

EGR valve

19 Refer to Chapter 4C, Section 4.

Clutch pedal position switch

20 Remove the trim panel above the driver's footwell to gain access to the clutch pedal – the panel is secured by four screws and two upper clips. Unclip the diagnostic connector plug, and/or disconnect the climate control temperature sensor as the panel is removed.

21 Reach up and disconnect the wiring from the clutch switch at the top of the pedal bracket.

22 Slide the retaining clip (where fitted) down to release the switch, then twist the switch anti-clockwise and remove it from the pedal bracket.

23 Refitting is a reversal of removal. **Note:** *A new retaining clip will be required.*

Brake pedal position switch

24 Remove the trim panel above the driver's footwell to gain access to the clutch pedal – the panel is secured by four screws and two upper clips. Unclip the diagnostic connector plug, and/or disconnect the climate control temperature sensor as the panel is removed.

8.5b . . . and withdraw the sensor

8.7 The cylinder head temperature sensor (arrowed)

25 Reach up and disconnect the wiring from the switch at the top of the pedal; there are two switches and if both switches are removed at once, take care to note which wiring plug serves which switch.

26 Slide the retaining clip down to release the switch, then twist the switch through 90° and remove it from the pedal bracket.

27 Refitting is a reversal of removal. **Note:** *A new retaining clip will be required.*

Accelerator pedal sensor

28 The accelerator pedal sensor is integral with the pedal assembly, which is removed as described in Section 4.

Powertrain Control Module

Caution: The PCM is fragile. Take care not to drop it or subject it to any other kind of impact, and do not subject it to extremes of temperature, or allow it to get wet. Do not touch the PCM terminals as there is a chance that static electricity may damage the internal electronic components.

Note: *If renewing the powertrain control module, note that it must be reprogrammed for the specific model by a Ford dealer using the WDS2000 diagnostic equipment. Failure to do so will result in the PCM assuming its 'limited operating strategy' (LOS) settings giving poor performance and economy.*

29 Ensure that the 'ignition' is switched off – take out the key. Disconnect the battery negative (earth) lead (refer to *Disconnecting the battery* at the end of this manual). This is **essential** to avoid damaging the module.

30 Unclip the plastic cover and remove the three outer retaining nuts from the right-hand strut top mounting – do not unscrew the strut's centre nut. **Note:** ***DO NOT*** *jack up the front of the car while the strut upper mounting nuts are removed.*

31 Unclip the cover from the right-hand strut top mounting brace and undo the retaining nuts and bolts, then remove it from the car.

32 A security shield is riveted over the PCM, and it will be necessary to drill out the rivet(s) to remove the shield and earth cable **(see illustration overleaf)**.

Caution: The PCM earth cable is connected behind the security shield rivet. Take care not to damage the earth cable when drilling through the rivet.

33 Unclip the wiring harness from along the right-hand inner wing panel.

34 Undo the retaining bolt and release the wiring connector from the PCM – to prevent dust and dirt entering the multiplug, cover it with a polythene bag.

35 From inside the car, unclip the generic electronic module (GEM) from the PCM bracket (as described in Chapter 12).

36 Undo the retaining nut and withdraw the PCM and mounting bracket from the driver's side footwell.

37 Refitting is the reverse of the removal procedure. Whenever the PCM (or battery) is disconnected, the information relating to idle speed control and other operating values will be lost from its memory until the

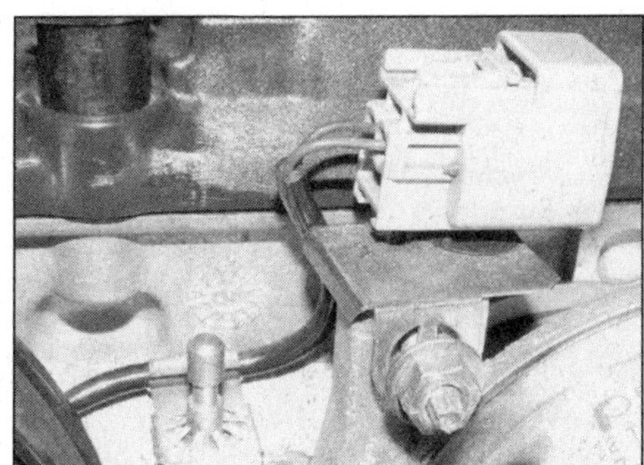

8.10 Detach the wiring connector from the retaining bracket

8.11 Unscrew the sensor (arrowed) – note the wiring is part of the sensor

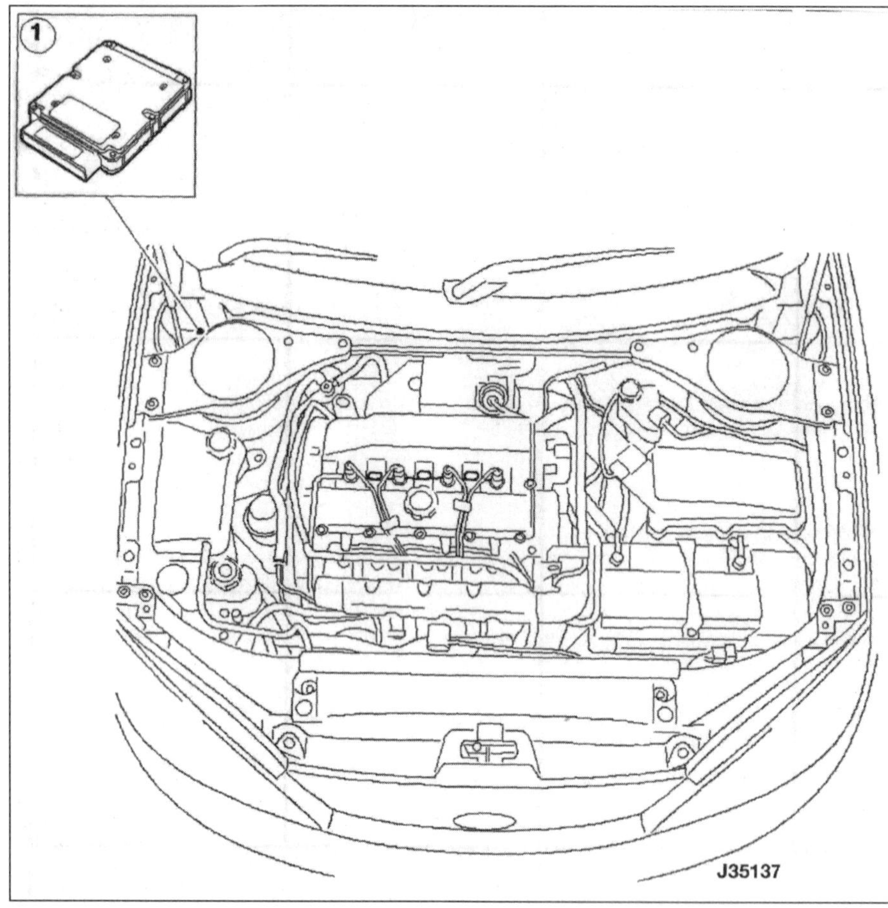

8.32 Powertrain control module (PCM) (1) location

unit has reprogrammed itself; until then, there may be surging, hesitation, erratic idle and a generally-inferior level of performance. To allow the PCM to relearn these values, start the engine and run it as close to idle speed as possible until it reaches its normal operating temperature, then run it for approximately two minutes at 1200 rpm. Next, drive the car as far as necessary – approximately 5 miles of varied driving conditions is usually sufficient – to complete the relearning process.

Injector driver module (IDM)

38 The module is located under the front of the left-hand front wing (as viewed from the driver's seat). **Note:** *On later models, the IDM unit has been integrated into the PCM, and a separate unit is not fitted.*

39 Remove the front bumper as described in Chapter 11.

40 Undo the retaining bolts and remove the inlet pipe from under the left-hand wing **(see illustration)**. Where applicable, disconnect the foglight's wiring block connector from the clip on the inlet pipe.

41 Remove the shear bolts and detach the IDM unit from the housing cover **(see illustration)**.

42 Support the IDM unit and disconnect the wiring connectors from the unit.

8.40 Undo the retaining bolts (arrowed) to remove the air inlet pipe

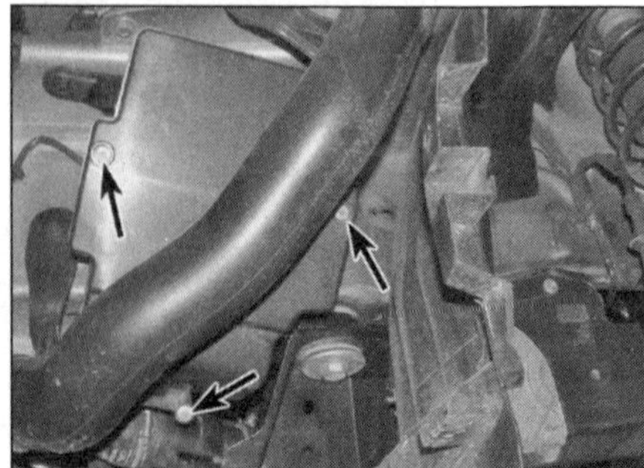

8.41 Remove the shear bolts (arrowed) to release the injector driver module

43 The IDM must be electronically 'configured' to the powertrain control module (PCM), this must be done by your Ford dealer, as specialised electronic equipment is required.

Mass airflow (MAF) sensor

44 Disconnect the battery negative (earth) lead (refer to *Disconnecting the battery* at the end of this manual).

45 Remove the air cleaner assembly as described in Section 3. Unscrew and remove the sensor mounting bolts and withdraw the sensor from the air cleaner cover.

46 Refitting is the reverse of the removal procedure. Ensure that the sensor and air cleaner cover are seated correctly and securely fastened, so that there are no air leaks.

Fuel pressure sensor

47 The fuel pressure sensor is screwed into the fuel rail, and is not intended to be removed.

48 Owing to the difficulty in ensuring a fuel-tight seal, the pressure sensor is not available separately, and can only be renewed with the fuel rail (see Section 11).

Fuel metering valve

49 Remove the engine oil dipstick, then take off the engine's plastic top cover.

50 Referring to Chapter 4C if necessary, remove the EGR cooler tube.

51 Cover the alternator with a plastic bag or similar, to protect it from any fuel which may be lost when the metering valve is removed.

52 Clean the area around the metering valve using a brush and suitable solvent – it is vital that no dirt enters the pump.

53 Disconnect the wiring plug from the fuel temperature sensor and from the metering valve, then remove the two mounting screws and withdraw the valve from the pump. Recover the valve's O-ring seal – a new one must be used when refitting. If the valve will be removed for some time, cover over or plug the valve opening in the pump, to stop dirt getting in.

54 Fit a new O-ring to the valve, and lubricate it lightly with a general-purpose spray lubricant (such as WD-40).

55 Fit the valve in position, and insert the bolts. Tighten them evenly and gently until the valve is secure.

56 Further refitting is a reversal of removal. Refit the EGR cooler tube as described in Chapter 4C.

Fuel temperature sensor

57 Remove the engine oil dipstick, then take off the engine's plastic top cover.

58 Cover the alternator with a plastic bag or similar, to protect it from any fuel which may be lost when the sensor is removed.

59 Clean the area around the sensor using a brush and suitable solvent – it is vital that no dirt enters the pump.

60 Disconnect the wiring plug from the fuel temperature sensor, then unscrew and withdraw the sensor from the pump. If the sensor will be removed for some time, cover over or plug the opening in the pump, to stop dirt getting in.

61 Fit a new O-ring to the sensor, and lubricate it lightly with a general-purpose spray lubricant (such as WD-40).

62 Screw the sensor into position, and tighten it to the specified torque. Reconnect the wiring plug, then refit the engine top cover and dipstick.

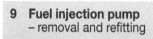

9 Fuel injection pump – removal and refitting

Caution: Be careful not to allow dirt into the injection pump or injector pipes during this procedure.

Note: *If a new injection pump is fitted, there is a possibility that the engine may not run properly (or even at all) until the PCM has been electronically 'configured' using Ford diagnostic equipment. In particular, the immobiliser may not function correctly, leading to the engine not starting. Ford special tools will be required for the removal and refitting procedure of the fuel injection pump – see text.*

Removal

1 Disconnect the battery negative (earth) lead (refer to *Disconnecting the battery* at the end of this manual).

2 Withdraw the oil level dipstick and unclip the engine plastic cover.

3 Undo the retaining bolts and move the coolant expansion bottle to one side.

4 Undo the retaining bolt(s) and move the power steering reservoir to one side.

5 Where applicable, undo the two damper retaining bolts and detach the damper from the engine mounting **(see illustration)**.

6 Using the Ford special tool (303-679), unscrew the access cover anti-clockwise from the timing chain cover. A tool was made up using a three-legged puller and three bolts **(see illustration)**.

7 Turn the engine in the normal direction of rotation (using a spanner or socket on the crankshaft pulley) until the timing hole in the injection pump sprocket is at the 1 o'clock position. Confirm this by temporarily fitting a 6 mm diameter timing pin (such as a drill bit) through the sprocket, as described in Chapter 2C, Section 3 **(see illustration)**.

8 Disconnect the glow plug supply wire, and move it to one side.

9 Referring to Chapter 4C if necessary, remove the EGR cooler tube.

10 Use the quick-release fittings (either by squeezing the catches, or by lifting up the locking clip) to disconnect the two fuel return hoses and the fuel supply hose from the high-pressure pump. Plug or tape over the open connections – dirt must not be allowed to enter the pump. Noting how they are routed, either unclip the hoses and move them aside (models after December 2003), or unbolt the hose support bracket **(see illustration)**.

11 Remove the inlet manifold as described in Chapter 2C.

12 Disconnect the wiring plug from the fuel temperature sensor and from the fuel metering valve **(see illustration)**.

13 Unscrew the nut and release the high-pressure fuel line support clamp.

14 Before proceeding further, use a brush and suitable solvent to clean the area around the pump's high-pressure union, and the area around the pump itself. It is essential that no dirt enters the pump, as this could quickly ruin it. Allow time for any solvent used to dry.

15 Carefully loosen the high-pressure pipe union at the fuel pump and the one to the fuel supply rail. Ford recommend (if possible) that the tool used to loosen these unions is fitted at the **top** of the union, to reduce the chance of damaging the union as it is loosened.

16 Once the unions are loose, wrap clean absorbent tissue or rag around them briefly, to soak away any dirt which may otherwise enter. If available, Ford recommend using a vacuum line to suck any dirt away from the opening union – do not use an airline, as this may blast dirt inwards, rather than cleaning it away.

17 Remove the high-pressure fuel pipe, and discard it – a new one should be used when refitting. Plug or tape over the open connections.

18 Fit Ford special tool 303-1151 to the timing cover, and turn it clockwise to lock the sprocket to the timing cover **(see illustration)**. Make sure this tool does not slip as the pump mounting bolts and sprocket bolts are loosened.

9.5 Removing the damper from the engine mounting

9.6 Using a home-made tool to remove the access cover (engine mounting removed for clarity)

9.7 A 6 mm drill bit (arrowed) locating fuel pump sprocket in the 1 o'clock position

9.10 Removing the fuel line retaining bracket – models up to December 2003

9.12 Disconnect the fuel metering valve wiring connectors (arrowed)

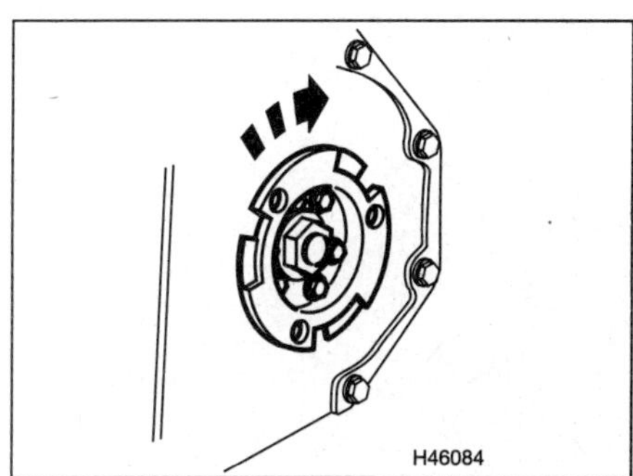

9.18 Special tool used to lock the pump sprocket in place

9.19 Access holes (arrowed) to fuel pump mounting bolts (timing cover removed for clarity)

9.21 Unbolt the pump rear support bracket (arrowed)

9.27 Fitting new gasket – note the cut out (arrowed)

19 Using Ford tool 310-083 (which appears to be a slim box spanner), loosen the three pump mounting bolts, accessible through the holes in the fuel pump sprocket **(see illustration)**. **Note:** *The bolts cannot be completely removed.*

20 Undo the four sprocket retaining bolts, making sure the tool stays in place to lock the sprocket to the timing chain cover.

21 Unbolt and the injection pump rear support bracket from the cylinder block **(see illustration)**.

22 Remove the fuel injection pump from the cylinder block. Recover and discard the gasket – a new one will be required on refitting.

23 On models up to December 2003, unbolt the fuel supply pipe union from the fuel pump.

24 If a new pump is being fitted, unbolt and remove the support bracket and shield from the old unit, and transfer them to the new one – tighten the bolts by hand only at this stage.

Refitting

25 On models up to December 2003, fit the fuel supply pipe to the pump, and tighten the union to the specified torque.

26 Using a 6 mm pin (drill bit), align the hole in the pump drive pulley with the cut-out provided in the pump rotor mounting face. With the cut-out aligned, remove the 6 mm pin.

27 Offer the pump into position, with a new gasket **(see illustration)**. Apply a little thread-locking fluid to the threads of the support bracket bolts, then fit them hand-tight only at this stage.

28 With the fuel pump in position, fit the three fuel pump mounting bolts through the holes provided in the fuel pump sprocket, and tighten them to their specified torque setting, using Ford tool 310-083 if necessary.

29 Install the four sprocket retaining bolts, and tighten them to the specified torque. Remove the sprocket locking tool 303-1151 by unscrewing it anti-clockwise from the timing cover. Refit the timing cover access cover, screwing it clockwise into place, using the same tool as described in paragraph 6.

30 Tighten the fuel pump support bracket bolts (pump-to-bracket and bracket-to-engine) to the specified torque. Where removed, also tighten the pump shield bolts – the larger one of the three should be tightened to the specified torque.

31 Reconnect all the disturbed fuel pipes and hoses, bolting them or clipping them back into place, routed as noted prior to removal.

32 Fit a new high-pressure pipe, and tighten the unions by hand until the pipe support clamp has been refitted and tightened. When refitting, do not bend or strain the pipe, and make sure it is kept clean. Also, do not allow the union nuts to hit the olive-shaped ends of the pipe during fitting, as this may result in damage.

33 Tighten both high-pressure unions to the specified torque, noting the point made in paragraph 15.

34 Further refitting is a reversal of removal. If a new pump has been fitted, fit a new fuel filter as described in Chapter 1B, then prime the fuel system as described in Section 2.

35 Start the engine, and let it idle, noting that it may take a while before a stable idle speed is achieved, as the powertrain control module (PCM) may have to relearn some of the 'adaptive' values. As the engine warms-up, check for signs of leakage from the fuel unions. If no leakage is evident, take the car for a short journey (of at least 5 miles) to allow the PCM to complete its 'learning' process.

36 If a new injection pump has been fitted, refer to the Note at the start of this Section.

10 Injection pipes – removal and refitting

Caution: Be careful not to allow dirt into the injection system during this procedure.

Removal

1 The fuel injection pipes should be removed as a set. At the time of writing, it is not clear whether individual pipes are available.

2 Disconnect the battery negative (earth) lead (refer to *Disconnecting the battery* at the end of this manual).

3 Withdraw the oil level dipstick and unclip the engine plastic cover.

4 Before proceeding further, use a brush and suitable solvent to clean the area around the high-pressure unions. It is essential that no dirt enters the system. Allow time for any solvent used to dry.

5 Using a spanner to hold the injectors from turning, slacken the union at each injector **(see illustration)**.

6 Slacken the four injector supply pipe unions at the fuel supply rail and, if required, the union at either end of the pump-to-rail supply pipe **(see illustrations)**. Unscrew the nut and release the high-pressure fuel line support clamp.

7 Once the unions are loose, wrap clean absorbent tissue or rag around them briefly, to soak away any dirt which may otherwise enter. If available, Ford recommend using a vacuum line to suck any dirt away from the opening union – do not use an airline, as this may blast dirt inwards, rather than cleaning it away.

8 With all the unions slackened, the fuel pipes can now be completely disconnected and

10.5 Hold the injector with one spanner, while slackening the pipe union

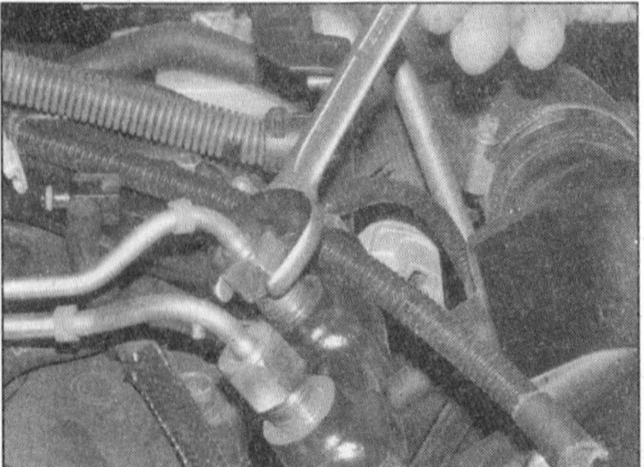
10.6a Disconnecting the injector pipe from the fuel supply rail

removed. Fit blanking plugs to the injectors **(see illustration)**, supply rail and fuel pump unions to prevent dirt ingress.

9 Discard the fuel injection pipes, as Ford recommend that new pipes must always be used when refitting.

Refitting

10 When refitting, do not bend or strain the pipes, and make sure they are kept clean. Also, do not allow the union nuts to hit the olive-shaped ends of the pipes during fitting, as this may result in damage.

11 Refit the pipe assemblies to the injectors, supply rail and injection pump, initially hand-tightening the union nuts. With all the fuel injection pipes in place, fully tighten the union nuts to the specified torque.

Caution: The injectors are not to turn from their position in the cylinder head – a special tool is used to align the injectors (see Section 12)

12 Reconnect the battery negative (earth) lead.

13 If only the pipes have been removed, there should be no need to bleed the system (Section 2).

14 Run the engine and check the disturbed unions for leaks.

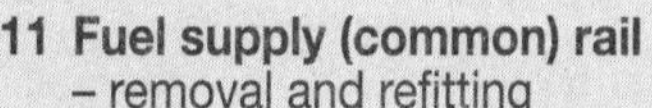

11 Fuel supply (common) rail – removal and refitting

Removal

1 Disconnect the battery negative (earth) lead (refer to *Disconnecting the battery* at the end of this manual).

2 Withdraw the oil level dipstick and unclip the engine plastic cover.

3 Referring to Chapter 4C if necessary, remove the EGR cooler tube.

4 Remove the inlet manifold as described in Chapter 2C.

5 Remove the injection pipes as described in Section 10.

6 Disconnect the wiring plug from the fuel temperature sensor, and from the fuel metering valve.

7 Remove a total of three fuel rail mounting bolts, then remove two further bolts at each end from the rail mounting brackets. Lift off the fuel rail

Refitting

8 Offer the fuel rail into position, then fit the mounting and support bracket bolts, hand-tight only.

9 Fit new high-pressure pipes to the fuel rail, injectors and fuel pump, leaving the union nuts hand-tight only at this stage. Do not bend or strain the pipes, and make sure they are kept clean. Also, do not allow the union nuts to hit the olive-shaped ends of the pipes during fitting, as this may result in damage.

10 Tighten the four fuel rail support bracket

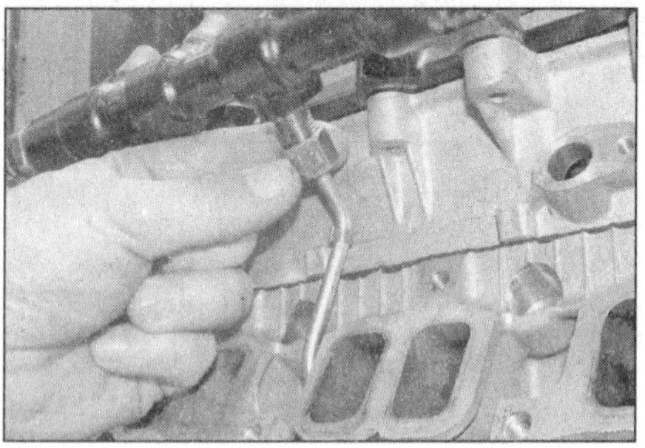

10.6b Disconnect the fuel pump pipe from the fuel rail (inlet manifold removed for clarity)

bolts to the specified torque, then tighten the three fuel rail mounting bolts.

11 With all the fuel injection pipes in place, fully tighten the union nuts to the specified torque.

Caution: The injectors are not to turn from their position in the cylinder head – a special tool is used to align the injectors (see Section 12)

12 Further refitting is a reversal of removal.

12 Fuel injectors – removal, testing and refitting

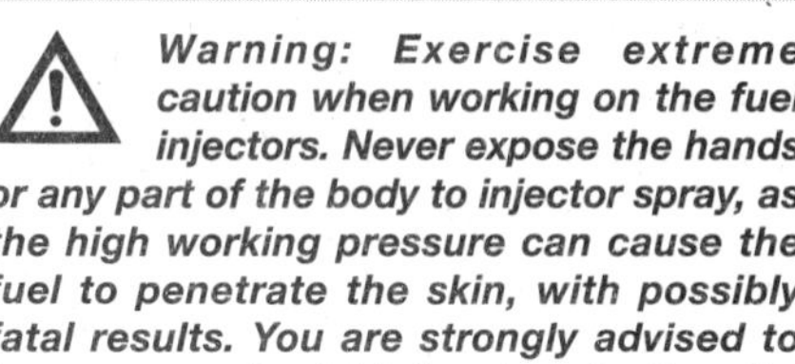

Warning: Exercise extreme caution when working on the fuel injectors. Never expose the hands or any part of the body to injector spray, as the high working pressure can cause the fuel to penetrate the skin, with possibly fatal results. You are strongly advised to have any work which involves testing the injectors under pressure carried out by a dealer or fuel injection specialist.

Caution: Be careful not to allow dirt into the injection system during this procedure.

Note: *Ford special tools will be required for the refitting procedure of the fuel injectors – see text.*

Removal

1 Disconnect the battery negative (earth) lead (refer to *Disconnecting the battery* at the end of this manual). Clean around the injectors and the injection pipe unions.

10.8 Fitting blanking plugs to the injectors

2 Remove the camshaft cover as described in Chapter 2C.

3 Slacken the fuel injector locking sleeves until they are all the way off, then remove the fuel injectors from the cylinder head **(see illustration)**. **Note:** *The injectors may be tight – carefully work them until they can be withdrawn.*

4 Recover the sealing washers and O-rings from each injector **(see illustration)**, and discard them – new washers/O-rings must be used on reassembly.

5 Take care not to drop the injectors, nor allow the needles at their tips to become damaged.

Testing

6 Testing of injectors requires a special high-pressure test rig, and is best left to a professional. If the skin is exposed to spray from the injectors, the pressure is high enough for diesel fuel to penetrate the skin, with potentially fatal results.

7 Defective injectors should be renewed or professionally repaired. DIY repair is not a practical proposition.

Refitting

8 Commence refitting by inserting new washers to the injector bores and fitting O-ring seals to the injectors **(see illustration)**.

9 Insert the injectors, using the Ford tool (303-711) to align the injectors in the cylinder head **(see illustration)**. **Note:** *A flat bar with two cut-outs can be fabricated to lock two of the injectors, to prevent them from turning.*

10 With the injectors held in position, tighten

12.3 Slacken the locking sleeve and remove the fuel injectors

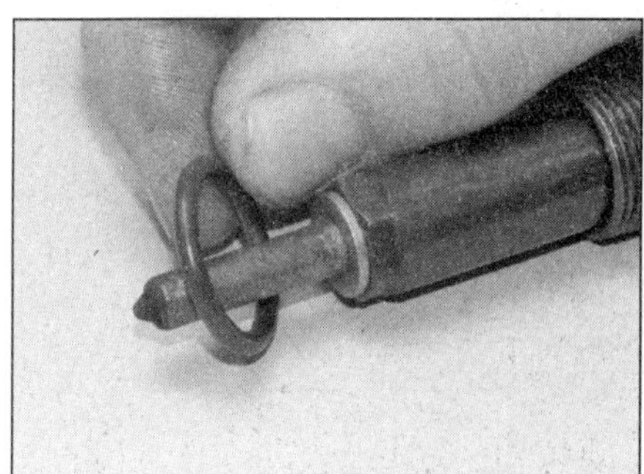

12.4 Remove the O-ring seals and discard them

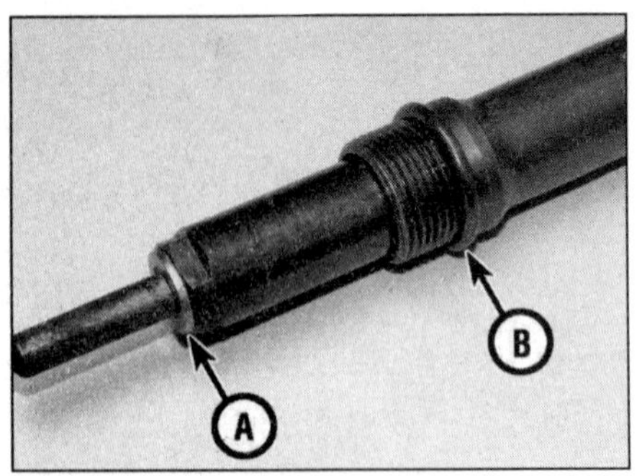

12.8 Renew the injector sealing washer (A) and O-ring seal (B)

12.9 Aligning the injectors using a flat metal bar with two cut-outs

12.12 Checking the position of the injectors using the Ford special tool

the locking sleeve to the correct torque setting, using Ford special socket (303-677).

11 Refit the camshaft cover (Chapter 2C).

12 Check the position of the injectors using the Ford special tool (303-711) or equivalent when refitting the fuel pipes **(see illustration)**.

13 Reconnect the battery negative (earth) lead.

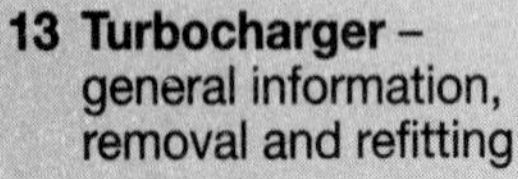

13 Turbocharger – general information, removal and refitting

General information

1 The turbocharger increases engine efficiency by raising the pressure in the inlet manifold above atmospheric pressure. Instead of the air simply being sucked into the cylinders, it is forced in. Additional fuel is supplied by the injectors, in proportion to the increased amount of air.

2 Energy for the operation of the turbocharger comes from the exhaust gases being forced from the combustion chambers. The gas flows through a specially-shaped housing (the turbine housing) and in so doing, spins the turbine wheel. The turbine wheel is attached to a shaft, at the end of which is another vaned wheel, known as the compressor wheel. The compressor wheel spins in its own housing, and compresses the inducted air on the way to the inlet manifold.

3 Between the turbocharger and the inlet manifold, the compressed air passes through an intercooler (see Section 14 for details). The purpose of the intercooler is to remove from the inducted air some of the heat gained in being compressed. Because cooler air is denser, removal of this heat further increases engine efficiency.

4 Boost pressure (the pressure in the inlet manifold) is limited by a wastegate, which diverts the exhaust gas away from the turbine wheel in response to a pressure-sensitive actuator.

5 The turbo shaft is pressure-lubricated by its own dedicated oil feed pipe. The shaft 'floats' on a cushion of oil. Oil is returned to the sump via a return pipe that connects to the sump.

6 The turbocharger on the DuraTorq engine is integral with the exhaust manifold, and is not available separately. There are two types of turbocharger fitted to the DuraTorq engine – a fixed-vane type is fitted to 90 PS engines, with a variable-vane type fitted to all others **(see illustration)**. On the fixed-vane type, there

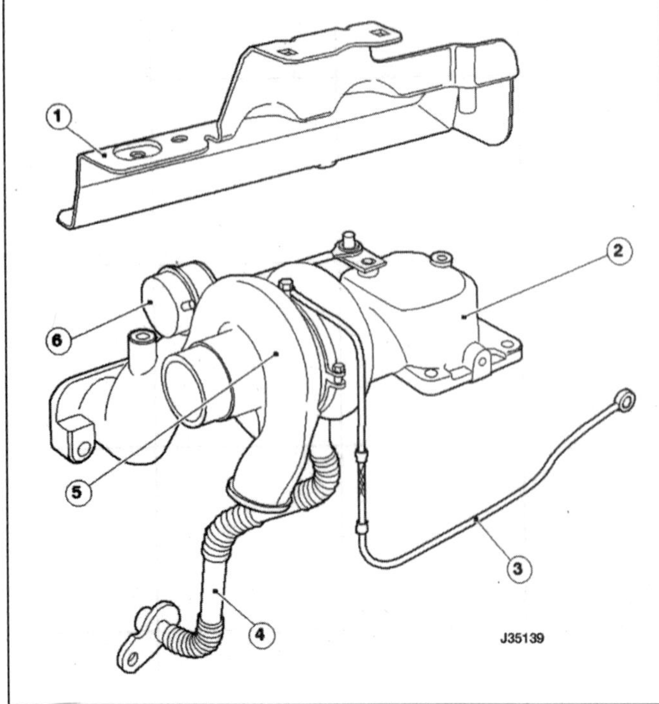

13.6a Fixed-vane turbocharger

1 Exhaust manifold heat shield
2 Exhaust manifold
3 Oil supply tube
4 Oil return tube
5 Turbocharger
6 Wastegate control valve

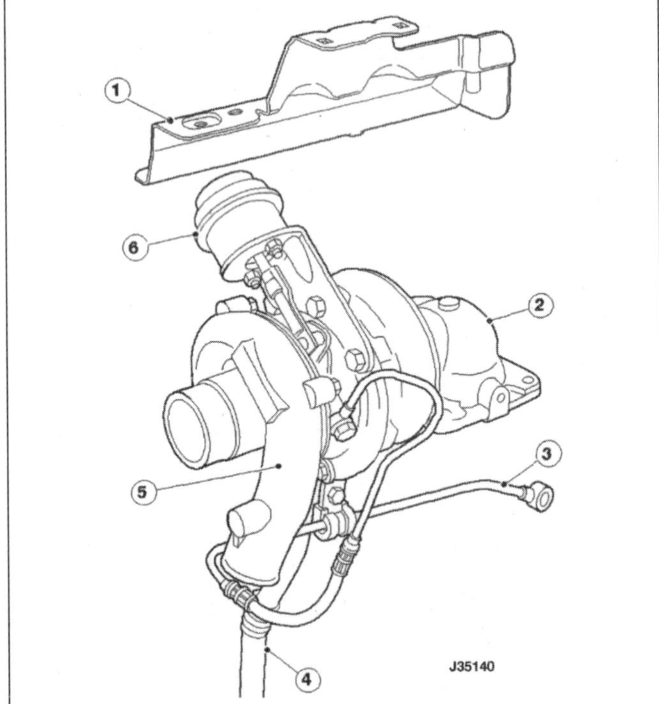

13.6b Variable-vane turbocharger

1 Exhaust manifold heat shield
2 Exhaust manifold
3 Oil supply tube
4 Oil return tube
5 Turbocharger
6 Wastegate

14.6 Slacken the hose clip (arrowed) and disconnect the intercooler air inlet pipes (right-hand side)

is a wastegate control valve, which opens a flap at high engine speeds. On the variable-vane type, as the engine speed increases, the guide vanes in the turbine housing are progressively opened before the wastegate is activated, maintaining boost pressure over a wider operating range.

7 The turbocharger is part of the exhaust manifold assembly. Removal and refitting of the exhaust manifold/turbocharger is covered in Chapter 2C, Section 20.

Precautions

- The turbocharger operates at extremely high speeds and temperatures. Certain precautions must be observed to avoid premature failure of the turbo or injury to the operator.
- Do not race the engine immediately after start-up, especially if it is cold. Give the oil a few seconds to circulate.
- Always allow the engine to return to idle speed before switching it off – do not blip the throttle and switch off, as this will leave the turbo spinning without lubrication.
- Allow the engine to idle for several minutes before switching off after a high-speed run.
- Observe the recommended intervals for oil and filter changing, and use a reputable oil of the specified quality. Neglect of oil changing, or use of inferior oil, can cause carbon formation on the turbo shaft and subsequent failure.

Warning: Do not operate the turbo with any parts exposed. Foreign objects falling onto the rotating vanes could cause excessive damage and (if ejected) personal injury.

14 Intercooler – general information, removal and refitting

General information

1 The intercooler is effectively an 'air radiator', used to cool the pressurised inlet air before it enters the engine.

2 When the turbocharger compresses the inlet air, one side-effect is that the air is heated, causing the air to expand. If the inlet air can be cooled, a greater effective volume of air will be inducted, and the engine will produce more power.

14.7a Remove the retaining bolt (one each side) . . .

3 The compressed air from the turbocharger, which would normally be fed straight into the inlet manifold, is instead ducted forwards around the left side of the engine to the base of the intercooler. The intercooler is mounted at the front of the car, in the airflow. The heated air entering the base of the unit rises upwards, and is cooled by the airflow over the intercooler fins, much as with the radiator. When it reaches the top of the intercooler, the cooled air is then ducted rearwards into the inlet manifold.

Removal

4 Disconnect the battery negative lead, and position the lead away from the battery (refer to *Disconnecting the battery* at the end of this manual).

5 Remove the front bumper as described in Chapter 11.

6 Slacken the hose clips and disconnect the intercooler air inlet pipes from each end of the intercooler **(see illustration)**.

7 Remove the two bolts (one each side) securing the intercooler to the engine compartment front panel. Lift the intercooler away from front panel, and place it somewhere safe (remember that the intercooler fins are just as vulnerable to damage as those on the radiator) **(see illustrations)**.

Refitting

8 Refitting is a reversal of removal. Check the inlet and outlet pipes for signs of damage, and make sure that the pipe clips are securely tightened.

15 Exhaust system – general information and component renewal

Warning: Inspection and repair of exhaust system components should be done only after the system has cooled completely. This applies particularly to the catalytic converter, which runs at very high temperatures.

General information

1 The catalytic converter (see Chapter 4C) is mounted at an angle, directly below the exhaust manifold. Immediately below the

14.7b . . . and remove the intercooler from the car

converter is a short flexible section of pipe, connecting to the factory-fitted one-piece rear section, which contains the centre and rear silencers **(see illustration overleaf)**. Later models may be fitted with a diesel particulate filter (DPF) after the flexible section, and has a flanged joint at either end (see Chapter 4C for more details).

2 To renew either silencer, the original rear section must be cut through mid-way between the centre and rear silencers. Before making any cut, offer up the new exhaust section for comparison and, if necessary, adjust the cutting points as required. Bear in mind that there must be some 'overlap' allowance, as the original and new sections are sleeved together.

3 The system is suspended throughout its entire length by rubber mountings, with a rigid support bracket fitted below the catalytic converter.

4 To remove a part of the system, first jack up the front or rear of the car, and support it on axle stands (see *Jacking and vehicle support*). Alternatively, position the car over an inspection pit, or on car ramps.

5 Ford recommend that all nuts (such as flange joint nuts, clamp joint nuts, or converter-to-manifold nuts) are renewed on reassembly – given that they may be in less-than-perfect condition as a result of corrosion, this seems a good idea, especially as it will make subsequent removal easier.

6 At least on the car seen in our workshop, no gaskets appear to be used on the exhaust system mating surfaces. Make sure that the mating faces of the exhaust system joints are cleaned thoroughly before assembling.

Component renewal

7 If any section of the exhaust is damaged or deteriorated, excessive noise and vibration will occur.

8 Carry out regular inspections of the exhaust system, to check security and condition. Look for any damaged or bent parts, open seams, holes, loose connections, excessive corrosion, or other defects which could allow exhaust fumes to enter the car. Deteriorated sections of the exhaust system should be renewed.

9 If the exhaust system components are extremely corroded or rusted together, it may not be possible to separate them. In this case, simply cut off the old components with a hacksaw, and remove any remaining corroded pipe with a cold chisel. Be sure to wear safety glasses to protect your eyes, and wear gloves to protect your hands.

10 Here are some simple guidelines to follow when repairing the exhaust system:

a) Work from the back to the front when removing exhaust system components.

b) Apply penetrating fluid to the flange nuts before unscrewing them.

c) Use new gaskets and rubber mountings when installing exhaust system components.

d) Apply anti-seize compound (copper brake grease will suffice) to the threads of all exhaust system studs during reassembly.

e) Note that on some models, the downpipe is secured to the manifold by two coil springs, spring seats and a self-locking nut on each. Where fitted, tighten the nuts until they stop on the bolt shoulders; the pressure of the springs will then be sufficient to make a leak-proof connection. Do not overtighten the nuts to cure a leak – the studs will shear. Renew the gasket and the springs if a leak is found.

f) Be sure to allow sufficient clearance between newly-installed parts and all points on the underbody, to avoid overheating the floorpan, and possibly damaging the interior carpet and insulation. Pay particularly close attention to the catalytic converter and its heat shield.

g) The heat shields are secured to the underside of the body by special nuts, or by bolts. They are fitted above the exhaust, to reduce radiated heat affecting the cabin or fuel tank. Each shield can be removed separately, but note that some overlap each other, making it necessary to loosen another section first. If a shield is being removed to gain access to a component located behind it, it may prove sufficient in some cases to remove the retaining nuts and/or bolts, and simply lower the shield, without disturbing the exhaust system. Otherwise, remove the exhaust section as described earlier.

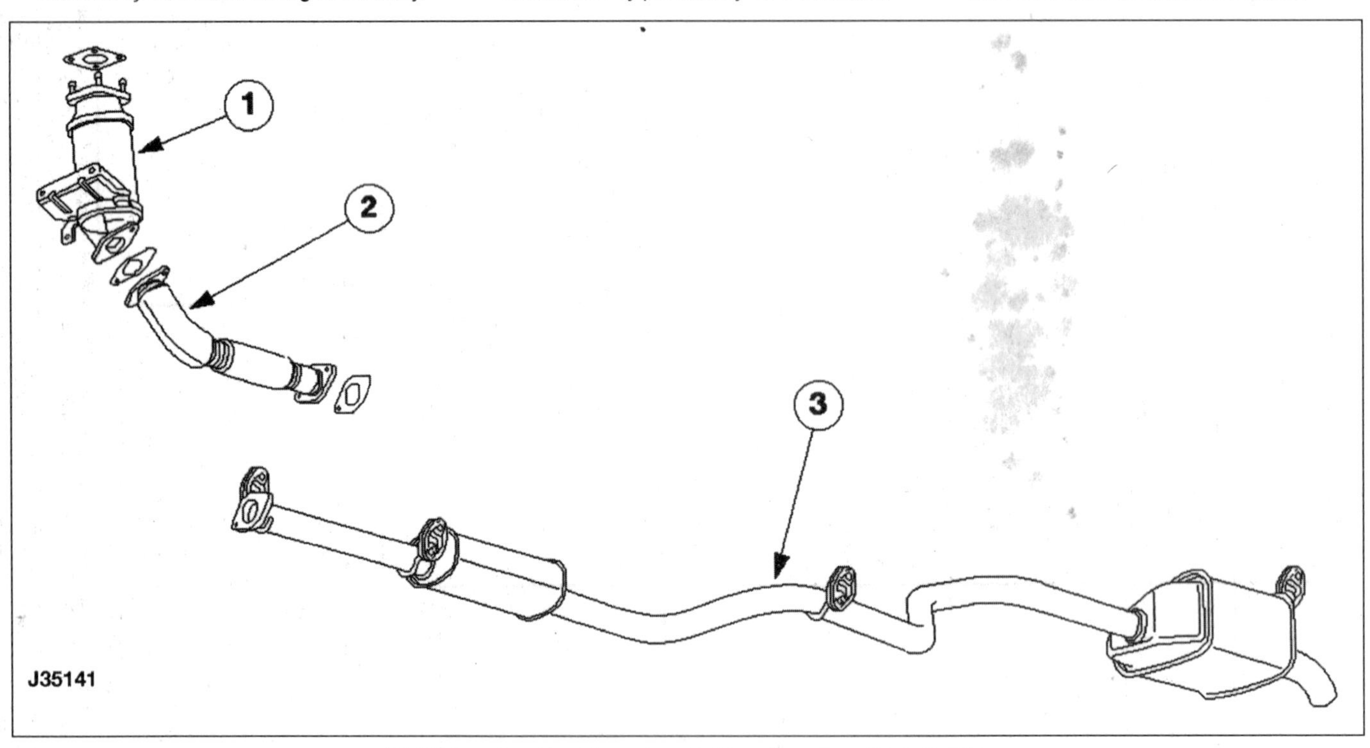

15.1 Exhaust system layout – models without particulate filter

1 *Catalytic converter*
2 *Exhaust flexible pipe*
3 *Silencer and tailpipe assembly*

Chapter 4 Part C: Emission control systems

Contents

Degrees of difficulty

Easy, suitable for novice with little experience 	**Fairly easy,** suitable for beginner with some experience	**Fairly difficult,** suitable for competent DIY mechanic	**Difficult,** suitable for experienced DIY mechanic	**Very difficult,** suitable for expert DIY or professional

Specifications

Torque wrench settings	Nm	lbf ft
Catalytic converter mounting bolts (3.0 litre models)	23	17
Catalytic converter-to-exhaust nuts	46	34
Catalytic converter to manifold:		
3.0 litre models	25	18
Diesel models	46	34
DPF flange nuts	46	34
EGR cooler mounting bracket bolts	10	7
EGR cooler-to-manifold bolts	37	27
EGR tube-to-EGR valve bolts (diesel models)	10	7
EGR valve outlet tube union (1.8 and 2.0 litre petrol models)	55	41
EGR valve mounting bolts:		
Petrol models	25	18
Diesel models	20	15
Exhaust flexible pipe to catalytic converter	46	34
Exhaust flexible pipe to intermediate pipe	46	34
Exhaust gas temperature sensor (models with DPF)	35	26
Heat shield retaining bolts	10	7
Oil separator retaining bolts	10	7
Oxygen sensors	48	35
Strut upper mounting nuts	30	22

1 General information and precautions

Petrol models

1 All petrol engines are designed to use unleaded petrol, and are controlled by the Visteon 'Black Oak' engine management system to give the best compromise between driveability, fuel consumption and exhaust emission production. In addition, a number of systems are fitted that help to minimise other harmful emissions.

2 A Positive Crankcase Ventilation (PCV) control system is fitted, which reduces the release of pollutants from the engine's lubrication system, and a catalytic converter is fitted which reduces exhaust gas pollutants.

3 An exhaust gas recirculation (EGR) system is fitted, to further reduce emissions. Also an evaporative emission control system is fitted which reduces the release of gaseous hydrocarbons from the fuel tank.

Crankcase emissions control

4 On 4-cylinder models, the crankcase ventilation system main components are the oil separator mounted on the front (radiator) side of the cylinder block/crankcase behind the inlet manifold, and the Positive Crankcase Ventilation (PCV) valve set in a rubber grommet in the separator's left-hand upper end. The associated pipework consists of a crankcase breather pipe and two flexible hoses connecting the PCV valve to a union on the left-hand end of the inlet manifold, and a crankcase breather hose connecting the cylinder head cover to the air cleaner assembly. On V6 models, the system is similar, but the oil separator is located on top of the cylinder block between the cylinder heads, below the inlet manifold. A small foam filter in the air cleaner prevents dirt from being drawn directly into the engine.

5 The function of these components is to reduce the emission of unburned hydrocarbons from the crankcase, and to minimise the formation of oil sludge. By ensuring that a depression is created in the crankcase under most operating conditions, particularly at idle, and by positively inducing fresh air into the system, the oil vapours and 'blow-by' gases collected in the crankcase are drawn from the crankcase, through the oil separator, into the inlet tract, to be burned by the engine during normal combustion.

6 The system requires no attention other than to check at regular intervals that the hoses, valve and oil separator are free of blockages and in good condition.

Exhaust emissions control

7 To minimise the amount of pollutants which escape into the atmosphere, all models are fitted with a catalytic converter in the exhaust system. The system is of the closed-loop type, in which two oxygen sensors in the exhaust system provide the fuel injection/ignition system ECU with constant feedback, enabling the ECU to adjust the mixture to provide the best possible conditions for the converter to operate. One oxygen sensor is located in the exhaust manifold, with the second downstream of the catalytic converter, to monitor the converter's efficiency.

8 The oxygen (lambda) sensor has a heating element built-in that is controlled by the ECU through the sensor relay to bring the sensor's tip to an efficient operating temperature quickly. The sensor's tip is sensitive to oxygen and sends the ECU a varying voltage depending on the amount of oxygen in the exhaust gases; if the inlet air/fuel mixture is too rich, the exhaust gases are low in oxygen, so the sensor sends a low voltage signal, the voltage rising as the mixture weakens and the amount of oxygen rises in the exhaust gases.

9 Peak conversion efficiency of all major pollutants occurs if the inlet air/fuel mixture is maintained at the chemically correct ratio for the complete combustion of petrol of 14.7 parts (by weight) of air to 1 part of fuel (the 'stoichiometric' ratio). The sensor output voltage alters in a large step at this point, the ECU using the signal change as a reference point and correcting the inlet air/fuel mixture accordingly by altering the fuel injector pulse width.

Evaporative emissions control

10 The evaporative emission control (EVAP) system fitted to petrol models consists of the purge valve, the activated charcoal filter canister and a series of connecting vacuum hoses. Little is possible by way of routine maintenance, except to check that the vacuum hoses are clear and undamaged. Careless servicing work may lead to the hoses becoming crushed – always take care to route these and other hoses correctly. This system is fitted to minimise the escape of unburned hydrocarbons into the atmosphere.

11 The fuel tank filler cap is sealed, and a charcoal canister is mounted to the rear of the fuel tank. The canister stores petrol vapours generated in the tank when the car is parked. When the engine is running, the vapours are cleared from the canister under the control of the PCM via the canister-purge solenoid valve. The vapours are drawn into the inlet manifold, to be burned by the engine during normal combustion.

12 To ensure that the engine runs correctly when it is cold and/or idling, and to protect the catalytic converter from the effects of an over-rich mixture, the canister-purge solenoid valve is not opened by the PCM until the engine is fully warmed-up and running under part-load. The solenoid valve is then switched on and off, to allow the stored vapour to pass into the inlet manifold. The purge valve is located on a bracket by the ignition coil, at the left-hand rear of the engine on 4-cylinder engines (left as seen from the driver's seat), and on the rear cylinder head cover on V6 engines.

Exhaust gas recirculation

13 To reduce oxides of nitrogen (NOx) emissions, some of the exhaust gases are recirculated through the EGR valve to the inlet manifold. This has the effect of lowering combustion temperatures. The system consists of the EGR valve, the EGR exhaust gas pressure differential sensor, the EGR solenoid valve, the PCM, and various sensors. The PCM is programmed to produce the ideal EGR valve lift for all operating conditions.

14 On 4-cylinder models, the EGR valve is mounted on the transmission end of the cylinder head. On V6 models, an EGR vacuum regulator is located on the bulkhead.

Diesel models

15 All diesel engine models are designed to meet strict emission requirements, and are also equipped with a crankcase emissions control system. In addition to this, all models are fitted with an unregulated catalytic converter to reduce harmful exhaust emissions. To further reduce emissions, an exhaust gas recirculation (EGR) system is also fitted.

Crankcase emissions control

16 To reduce the emission of unburned hydrocarbons from the crankcase into the atmosphere, the engine is sealed. Blow-by gases and oil vapour are drawn from inside the crankcase, through the cylinder head cover, then through a pressure-sensitive recirculation valve into the turbocharger. From the turbocharger, the gases enter the inlet manifold to be burned by the engine during normal combustion.

17 There are no restrictors in the system hoses, since the minimal depression in the inlet manifold remains constant during all engine operating conditions.

Exhaust emissions control

18 To minimise the amount of pollutants which escape into the atmosphere, an unregulated (reduction) catalytic converter is fitted in the exhaust system. The catalytic converter consists of a canister containing a fine mesh impregnated with a catalyst material, over which the exhaust gases pass. The catalyst speeds up the oxidation of harmful carbon monoxide, unburnt hydrocarbons and soot, effectively reducing the quantity of harmful products reaching the atmosphere. The catalytic converter operates remotely in the exhaust system, and there is no oxygen sensor as fitted to the petrol engines.

19 Certain models may additionally be equipped with a diesel particulate filter (DPF), which is fitted after the exhaust flexible section at the front, and has a flanged joint at either end. This filters out the soot particles which may be present in the exhaust. As it is a filter which may become blocked, a pressure differential sensor is fitted in the engine compartment to monitor the exhaust pressure drop across the filter, via pipework fitted to the filter housing. Also fitted to the filter is an exhaust temperature sensor, which monitors the temperature of the exhaust gas leaving the catalytic converter. When the filter needs 'regenerating' (cleaning), this is achieved by the PCM adding excess fuel to raise the exhaust gas temperature and burn off the deposits – the exhaust may emit white smoke when this happens. This cleaning can also be done 'manually', using the Ford WDS2000 diagnostic tool. Models with a DPF have an oil change warning light in the instrument panel, which comes on after the DPF has been cleaned this way enough times, to warn of the risk of fuel in the engine oil.

Exhaust gas recirculation

20 To reduce oxides of nitrogen (NOx) emissions, some of the exhaust gases are recirculated through the EGR valve to the inlet manifold. This has the effect of lowering combustion temperatures. The system consists of the EGR valve, the EGR exhaust gas pressure differential sensor, the EGR solenoid valve, the PCM, and various sensors. The PCM is programmed to produce the ideal EGR valve lift for all operating conditions.

21 On diesel engines, the EGR system is fitted with a cooler fitted across the rear of the engine below the exhaust manifold, supplied from the engine cooling system. The EGR valve is located on the transmission end of the cooler (except on models with the 5-speed automatic transmission – the EGR valve is then located on the front of the engine at the timing chain end).

2 Evaporative emission control system (petrol models) – testing and component renewal

Testing

1 Poor idle, stalling and poor driveability can be caused by an inoperative canister-purge solenoid valve, a damaged canister, split or cracked hoses, or hoses connected to the wrong fittings. Check the fuel filler cap for a damaged or deformed gasket.

2 Fuel loss or fuel odour can be caused by liquid fuel leaking from fuel lines, a cracked or damaged canister, an inoperative canister-purge solenoid valve, and disconnected, incorrectly routed, kinked or damaged vapour or control hoses.

3 Inspect each hose attached to the canister for kinks, leaks and cracks along its entire length. Repair or renew as necessary.

4 Inspect the canister. If it is cracked or damaged, renew it. Look for fuel leaking from the bottom of the canister. If fuel is leaking, renew the canister, and check the hoses and hose routing.

5 If the canister-purge solenoid valve is thought to be faulty, unplug its electrical connector and disconnect its vacuum hoses. Connect a 12 volt battery directly across the valve terminals. Check that air can flow through the valve passages when the solenoid

2.9a Disconnecting the wiring connector from the purge valve (4-cylinder petrol models) . . .

is energised, and that nothing can pass when the solenoid is not energised. Alternatively, connect an ohmmeter to measure the resistance across the solenoid terminals – no reading, or an infinite resistance, suggests a problem. Renew the solenoid valve if it is faulty.

6 Further testing should be left to a dealer service department.

Purge solenoid valve renewal

7 Disconnect the battery negative (earth) lead (refer to *Disconnecting the battery* at the end of this manual). On 4-cylinder models, unclip the breather hose from the engine upper plastic cover, then unclip the cover from the top of the engine.

8 Disconnect the hose(s) from the solenoid valve, noting their positions for refitting.

9 Disconnect the valve's electrical connector, then unclip the solenoid valve from the bracket **(see illustrations)**.

10 Refitting is the reverse of the removal procedure.

Charcoal canister renewal

Saloon and Hatchback models

Note: *Read through this procedure carefully before starting work, and ensure that the equipment is available that is required to carry it out safely and with minimum risk of damage, and to align the crossmember with sufficient accuracy on reassembly.*

11 Loosen the rear wheel nuts. Chock the front wheels, then jack up the rear of the car and support on axle stands (see *Jacking and vehicle support*).

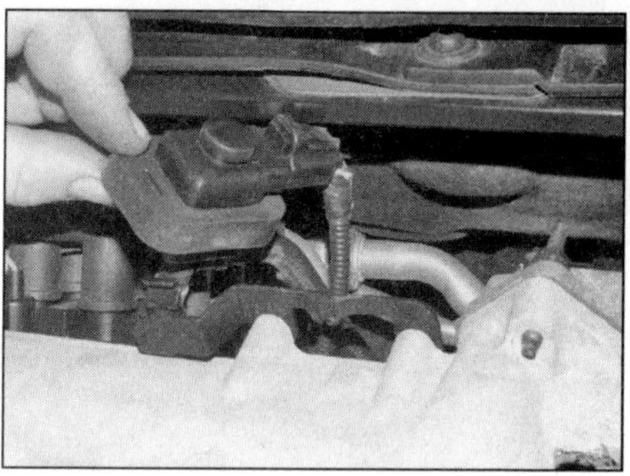

2.9b . . . then unclip the valve from the bracket (V6 models)

12 Remove the exhaust system as described in Chapter 4A.

13 Where fitted, remove the headlight-levelling sensor as described in Chapter 12.

14 Ensure that the rear of the car's body is supported securely on axle stands, then support the rear suspension crossmember with a jack. Remove the roadwheels and unscrew the rear suspension strut top mounting bolts (two per side).

15 Use white paint or similar (do not use a sharp-pointed scriber, which might break the underbody protective coating and cause rusting) to mark the exact relationship of the crossmember to the underbody. Unscrew the four mounting bolts. Lower the crossmember approximately 75 mm on the jack, and support it securely.

Warning: Take care when lowering the crossmember not to place any strain on the brake hoses and suspension components.

16 Unscrew the two rearmost canister bracket retaining bolts.

17 Disconnect the two hoses from the canister assembly, noting which way round they are fitted.

18 Unscrew the canister assembly's front retaining bolt. Withdraw the canister assembly.

19 Unclip the water separator box cover, then release the canister by pushing it to one side and unclipping it from the canister bracket **(see illustrations)**.

20 On reassembly, refit the canister to its bracket and refit the assembly to the car, tightening the retaining bolts securely, and

2.19a Unclip the water separator box cover . . .

2.19b . . . and pushing it to one side, unclip the canister from the bracket

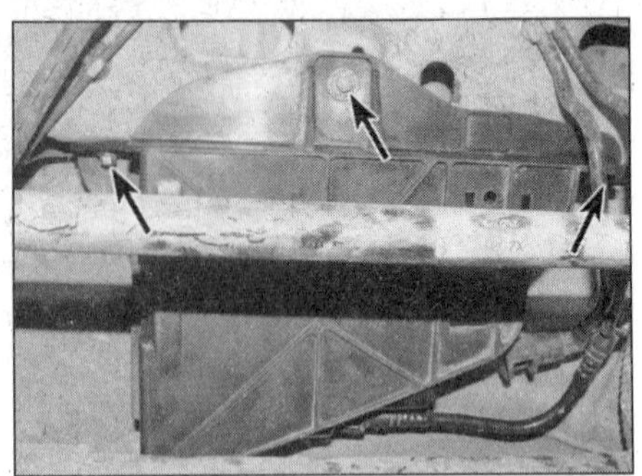

2.28 Undo the retaining bolts (arrowed) to remove the canister assembly

ensuring that the two hoses are securely reconnected to their original unions.

21 Offer up the crossmember and refit the crossmember bolts, tightening them only lightly at this stage. The crossmember must now be aligned on the underbody. Ford specify the use of service tool 205-316 (15-097-A), which is a pair of tapered guides, with attachments to hold them in the crossmember as it is refitted. However, since the working diameter of these tools is 20.4 mm, and since the corresponding aligning holes in the crossmember and underbody are 21 mm and 22 mm in diameter, there is a significant in-built tolerance possible in the crossmember's alignment, even if the correct tools are used.

22 If these tools are not available, align the crossmember by eye, centring the crossmember aligning holes on those of the underbody, and using the marks made on removal for assistance. Alternatively, use a tapered drift such as a clutch-aligning tool, or a deep socket spanner of suitable size. Once the crossmember is aligned as precisely as possible, tighten its bolts to the specified torque (see Chapter 10 Specifications) without disturbing its position. Recheck the alignment once all the bolts are securely tightened.

23 The remainder of the refitting procedure is the reverse of removal.

24 Remember that, if the rear suspension crossmember has been disturbed, the wheel alignment and steering angles must be checked fully and carefully as soon as possible, with any necessary adjustments being made. This operation is best carried out by an experienced mechanic using proper checking equipment; the car should therefore be taken to a Ford dealer or similar for attention.

Estate models

25 Disconnect the battery negative (earth) lead (refer to *Disconnecting the battery* at the end of this manual)..

26 Chock the front wheels, then jack up the rear of the car and support on axle stands (see *Jacking and vehicle support*).

27 Disconnect the two hoses from the canister assembly, noting which way round they are fitted.

28 Unscrew the canister assembly retaining bolts and withdraw the assembly, unclipping it from the front mounting **(see illustration)**.

29 Unclip the water separator box cover, then release the canister by pushing it to one side and unclipping it from the canister bracket **(see illustration 2.19a and 2.19b)**.

30 On refitting, secure the canister to its bracket, and refit the assembly to the car. Tighten the retaining bolt securely, and ensure that the two hoses are securely reconnected to their original unions.

3 Crankcase emission system (petrol models) – component renewal

PCV valve

1 The valve is plugged into the oil separator which is bolted to the cylinder block. Remove the inlet manifold as described in Chapter 2A (4-cylinder engines) or 2B (V6 engines) for access.

2 Release the locking clips with a screwdriver and pull the Positive Crankcase Ventilation (PCV) valve upwards to remove it from the oil separator **(see illustrations)** it can now be flushed, or renewed, as required.

Oil separator

4-cylinder models

3 Remove the inlet manifold (see Chapter 2A).

4 Unbolt the oil separator from the cylinder block/crankcase, and withdraw it. Remove and discard the gasket **(see illustration)**.

5 Flush out or renew the oil separator, as required.

6 On reassembly, fit a new gasket, and tighten the bolts securely **(see illustration)**.

7 The remainder of the refitting procedure is the reverse of removal.

V6 models

8 Remove the inlet manifold (see Chapter 2B).

9 Either disconnect the hose leading to the separator, or pull out the PCV valve.

10 Unscrew the bolts and remove the separator from the top of the cylinder block (between the cylinder heads), recover the gasket **(see illustration)**.

11 If not already done, remove the PCV valve from the separator. Wash out the oil separator using a suitable solvent (such as engine degreaser), and ensure that its passages are clear.

12 Refitting is a reversal of removal. Use a new gasket, and tighten the retaining bolts securely.

3.2a Using a screwdriver to release the clips . . .

3.2b . . . then pull the valve upwards to remove it from the oil separator

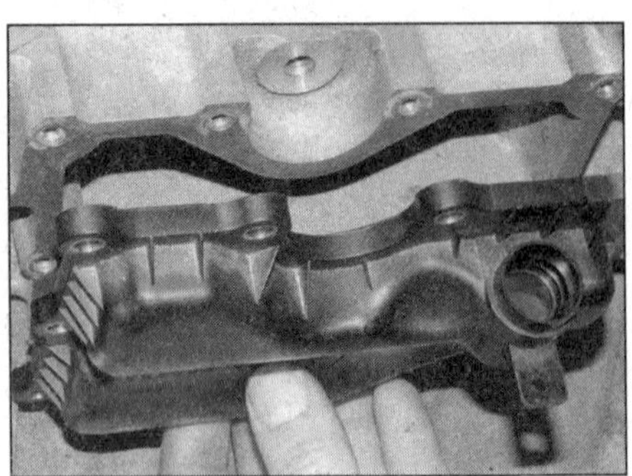

3.4 Unbolt and withdraw the oil separator from the cylinder block

3.6 Make sure the peg (arrowed) on the new gasket is located correctly

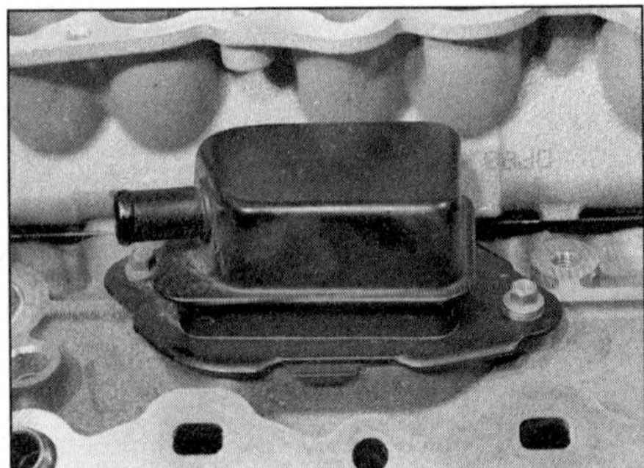

3.10 Oil separator on V6 models

PCV hose(s)

13 The hoses are a push-fit onto the PCV valve and inlet manifold, and can only be renewed once the inlet manifold has been removed (see relevant part of Chapter 2).

14 Wash the oil separator and valve in suitable solvent (such as engine degreaser), and ensure that all passages are clear. Check the hoses for signs of damage, especially at the hose ends. Where an O-ring is used to seal the valve into its location, check the condition of the O-ring before refitting.

15 Refitting is a reversal of removal. Make sure that the hoses are securely and correctly refitted, and that the hoses are routed as before.

4 Exhaust Gas Recirculation (EGR) system – testing and component renewal

Testing

EGR valve

1 Start the engine and allow it to idle.

2 Detach the vacuum hose from the EGR valve, and attach a hand vacuum pump in its place.

3 Apply vacuum to the EGR valve. Vacuum should remain steady, and the engine should run poorly or stall.

a) *If the vacuum doesn't remain steady and the engine doesn't run poorly, renew the EGR valve and recheck it.*

b) *If the vacuum remains steady but the engine doesn't run poorly, remove the EGR valve, and check the valve and the inlet manifold for blockage. Clean or renew parts as necessary, and recheck.*

EGR system

4 Any further checking of the system requires special tools and test equipment. Take the car to a dealer service department for checking.

EGR valve renewal

4-cylinder petrol models

5 Disconnect the battery negative (earth) lead (refer to *Disconnecting the battery* at the end of this manual).

6 Unclip the breather hose from the engine upper plastic cover, then unclip the cover from the top of the engine.

7 Drain the cooling system as described in Chapter 3.

8 Undo the retaining clips and remove the air inlet pipe from the throttle body to the air filter housing **(see illustration)**.

9 Disconnect the electrical connector from the EGR valve **(see illustration)**.

10 Detach the coolant hose from the EGR valve.

11 Remove the two valve mounting bolts, and withdraw the valve from the transmission end of the cylinder head **(see illustration)**.

4.8 Remove the air inlet pipe from the throttle body

V6 models

12 Disconnect the battery negative (earth) lead (refer to *Disconnecting the battery* at the end of this manual).

13 Remove the mass airflow sensor and remove the idle air control valve as described in Chapter 4A, Section 13.

14 Detach the vacuum hose, unscrew the sleeve nut securing the EGR pipe to the valve, remove the two valve mounting bolts, and withdraw the valve from the inlet manifold **(see illustration)**. Ensure that the end of the pipe is not damaged or distorted as the valve is withdrawn, and note the valve's gasket; this must be renewed whenever the valve is disturbed.

15 Note that the metal pipe from the valve to the manifold itself should not be disturbed – it is not available separately from the manifold. However, check whenever the manifold is removed that the pipe's end fitting is securely fastened **(see illustration)**.

4.11 Undo the two mounting bolts and withdraw the EGR valve

4.15 Check end fitting of EGR pipe into inlet manifold whenever manifold is removed, but do not disturb

4.9 Disconnecting the wiring connector from the EGR valve

16 Check the valve for sticking, or heavy carbon deposits. If such is found, clean the valve or renew it.

17 Refitting is the reverse of the removal procedure. Apply a smear of anti-seize compound to the sleeve nut threads, fit a new gasket, and tighten the valve bolts to the specified torque wrench setting.

Diesel models with manual transmission

18 Remove the EGR valve outlet tube as described in paragraphs 39 to 44.

19 Disconnect the vacuum pipe from the EGR valve **(see illustration)**.

20 Where applicable, disconnect the electrical connector from the EGR valve.

21 Undo the two retaining nuts and remove the EGR valve from the cooler **(see illustration)**. Recover the gasket – a new one should be used when refitting.

22 Refitting is a reversal of removal.

4.14 Refitting the EGR valve together with a new gasket

4.19 Disconnect the vacuum pipe (arrowed) from the EGR valve

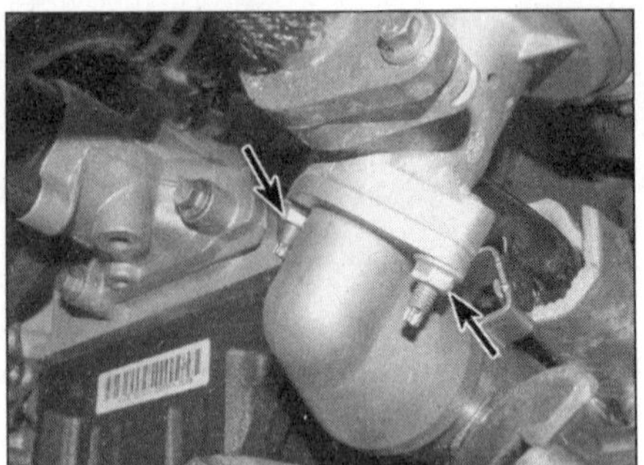
4.21 Undo the two retaining nuts (arrowed) and lift the EGR valve from the cooler

Diesel models with automatic transmission

23 Remove the engine upper cover, undo the two retaining nuts and detach the EGR valve tube from the EGR valve, renew the gasket on refitting.
24 Slacken the securing clip and disconnect the charge air cooler hose from the EGR valve.
25 Disconnect the vacuum pipe from the EGR valve.
26 Undo the two retaining bolts and remove the EGR valve from the inlet manifold – renew the gasket on refitting.
27 Refitting is a reversal of removal.

EGR pipe renewal

V6 models

28 Disconnect the idle air control valve tube from the air cleaner and upper inlet manifold.

4.31 Removing the EGR tube on V6 models

29 Unscrew the EGR tube sleeve nut from the EGR valve and disconnect the tube.
30 Loosen the left-hand front wheel nuts. Chock the front wheels, then jack up the rear of the car and support on axle stands (see *Jacking and vehicle support*). Remove the front left-hand wheel and the wheel arch liner.
31 Remove the EGR tube nut from the rear exhaust manifold and remove the tube **(see illustration)**.
32 Refitting is a reversal of removal. Apply anti-seize compound to the nuts on both ends of the tube.

Exhaust gas pressure differential sensor

V6 models

33 This component measures the difference in pressure of the exhaust gases across a venturi (restriction) in the exhaust gas recirculation (EGR) system's pipe, and sends the PCM a voltage signal corresponding to the pressure difference.

4.37 Disconnecting the wiring plug from the exhaust gas pressure differential sensor

34 Testing of this component is beyond the scope of the DIY mechanic, and should be left to a Ford dealer.

Component renewal

35 The differential pressure sensor is located next to the EGR solenoid, on the left-hand end of the rear cylinder head.
36 Note the positions of the vacuum hoses for refitting (they are of different diameter), then disconnect them from the ports on the sensor.
37 Disconnect the sensor wiring plug, then unscrew the sensor mounting bolts and remove the sensor from its location **(see illustration)**.
38 Refitting is a reversal of removal, making sure that the hoses are correctly refitted. **Note:** *Check the condition of both hoses and renew them if necessary.*

EGR valve outlet tube renewal

Diesel models

39 Disconnect the battery negative (earth) lead (refer to *Disconnecting the battery* at the end of this manual). Remove the engine upper cover.
40 Disconnect the wiring connector from the mass airflow sensor, slacken the air inlet hose retaining clips and remove the complete air cleaner housing from the car (see Chapter 4B).
41 Undo the two retaining bolts and disconnect the outlet tube from the EGR valve **(see illustration)**, renew the gasket on refitting.
42 Unclip the coolant hose, slacken the securing clips and remove the air inlet pipe from the outlet tube **(see illustration)**.
43 Slacken the securing clip and disconnect the charge air cooler hose from the outlet tube **(see illustration)**.
44 Undo the retaining bolts and remove the outlet tube from across the top of the transmission **(see illustration)**.
45 Refitting is a reversal of removal, making sure that the hoses are correctly refitted. **Note:** *Check the condition of the hoses and renew them if necessary.*

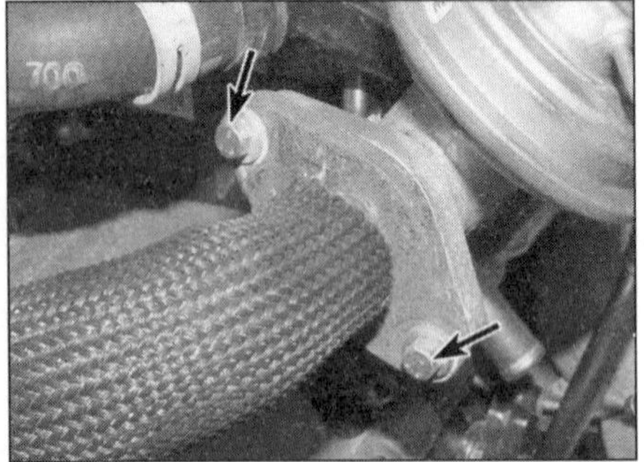
4.41 Undo the two retaining bolts (arrowed) to disconnect the outlet tube

4.42 Slacken the securing clips and remove the air inlet pipe

4.43 Slacken the securing clip (arrowed) and disconnect the charge air cooler hose

4.44 Undo the retaining bolts (arrowed) and remove the outlet tube

EGR tube/cooler renewal

Diesel models

46 The EGR system on diesel models is fitted with a cooler (supplied from the cooling system), which reduces the temperature of the exhaust gas being recycled; the cooler is effectively a water jacket around the pipe connecting the exhaust manifold and the EGR valve.

47 Remove the EGR valve outlet tube (and EGR valve on manual transmission models) as described in paragraphs 39 to 44 and 18 to 22.

48 Drain the cooling system as described in Chapter 1B.

49 To gain better access, remove the catalytic converter as described in Section 6.

50 Slacken the securing clips and disconnect the coolant hose from the thermostat housing and EGR cooler.

51 Depending on model and transmission fitted, the EGR cooler tube routing will vary. Follow the tube and undo the retaining nuts and release any retaining clips to remove the tube.

52 Undo the retaining nut and bolts and remove the cooler **(see illustrations)**, renew the gasket on refitting.

53 Refitting is a reversal of removal, making sure that the hoses are correctly refitted. Check the condition of the hoses and renew them if necessary. Top-up the cooling system as required.

4.52a Undo the retaining nut and bolt (arrowed) . . .

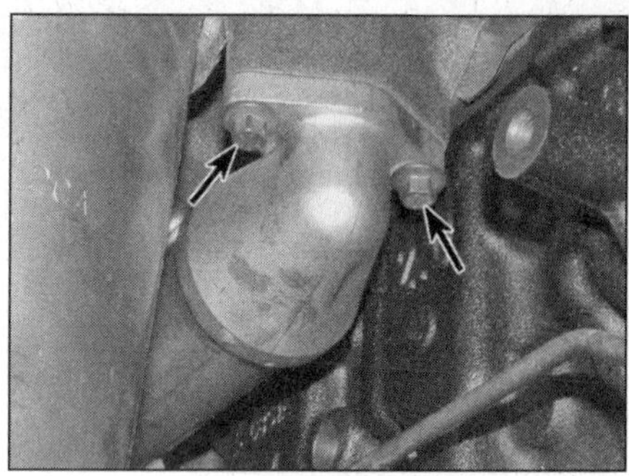

4.52b . . . and the two bolts (arrowed), then remove the cooler

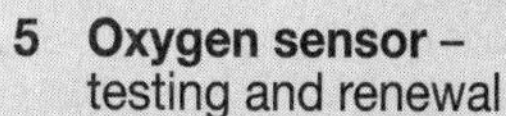

5 Oxygen sensor – testing and renewal

Testing

1 Testing the oxygen sensor is only possible by connecting special diagnostic equipment to the sensor wiring, and checking that the voltage varies from low to high values when the engine is running. **Do not** attempt to 'test' any part of the system with anything other than the correct test equipment. This is beyond the scope of the DIY mechanic, and should be left to a Ford dealer. **Note:** *Most models are fitted with two sensors – one before and one after the catalytic converter. This enables more efficient monitoring of the exhaust gas, allowing a faster response time. The overall efficiency of the converter itself can also be checked. The sensor after the catalytic converter is sometimes known as a monitor sensor.*

Renewal

Note: *The sensor is delicate, and will not work if it is dropped or knocked, or if any cleaning materials are used on it.*

2 Where applicable, remove the bolts securing the heat shield fitted over the exhaust manifold, and lift away the heat shield for access to the sensor.

3 Trace the wiring from the sensor body back to its wiring plug, and disconnect it. On models with two sensors, the wiring plug for the rearmost sensor is usually clipped to the rear of the subframe under the car **(see illustrations)**. Note how the wiring is routed, as it must not come into contact with hot exhaust components.

4 Raise and support the front of the car if required to remove the sensor from underneath. Unscrew the sensor from the exhaust system front downpipe on 4-cylinder models or from each exhaust manifold on V6 models **(see illustration)**. Recover the gasket (where fitted).

5 It may be beneficial to clean the sensor before refitting it, especially if the sensor tip appears to be contaminated. However, great care must be exercised, as the tip will be damaged by any abrasives, and by certain solvents. Seek the advice of a Ford dealer before cleaning the sensor.

6 Refitting is a reversal of removal, noting the following points:

a) *Apply a little anti-seize compound to the sensor threads, taking care not to allow any on the sensor tip, and tighten the sensor to the specified torque.*

b) *Reconnect the wiring, ensuring that it is routed clear of any hot exhaust components.*

c) *If required, proof that the sensor is working can be gained by having the exhaust emissions checked, and compare it with the figure that Ford recommends. Remember that a faulty sensor will have generated a fault code – if this code is still logged in the PCM electronic memory, then see your Ford dealer to read the fault code still in the memory.*

6 Catalytic converter – general information and precautions

General information

1 The catalytic converter reduces harmful exhaust emissions by chemically converting the more poisonous gases to ones which (in theory at least) are less harmful. The chemical reaction is known as an 'oxidising' reaction, or one where oxygen is 'added'.

2 Inside the converter is a honeycomb structure, made of ceramic material and coated with the precious metals palladium, platinum and rhodium (the 'catalyst' which promotes the chemical reaction). The chemical

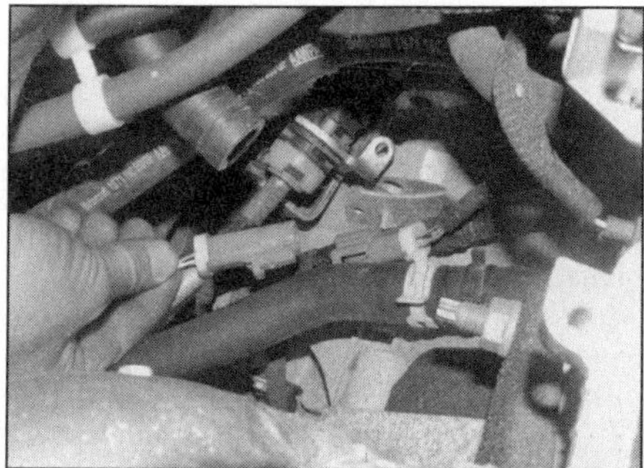

5.3a Disconnecting the oxygen sensor wiring block connector

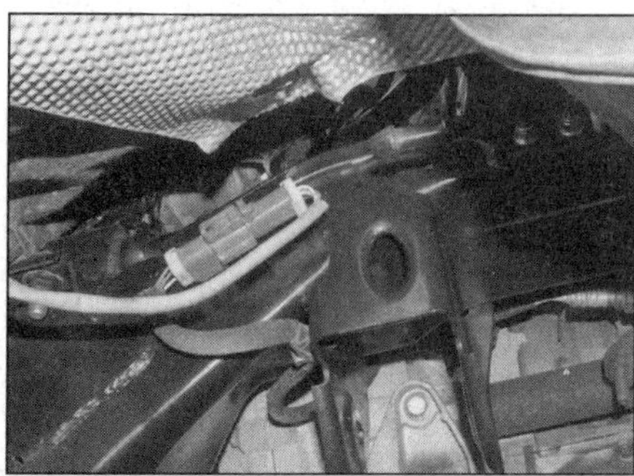

5.3b The rear sensor wiring connector is clipped to the rear of the subframe

5.4 Removing the oxygen sensor from the exhaust manifold on V6 models

reaction generates heat, which itself promotes the reaction – therefore, once the car has been driven several miles, the body of the converter will be very hot.

3 The ceramic structure contained within the converter is understandably fragile, and will not withstand rough treatment. Since the converter runs at a high temperature, driving through deep standing water (in flood conditions, for example) is to be avoided, since the thermal stresses imposed when plunging the hot converter into cold water may well cause the ceramic internals to fracture, resulting in a 'blocked' converter – a common cause of failure. A converter which has been damaged in this way can be checked by shaking it (do not strike it) – if a rattling noise is heard, this indicates probable failure.

Precautions

4 The catalytic converter is a reliable and simple device which needs no maintenance in itself, but there are some facts of which an owner should be aware if the converter is to function properly for its full service life.

Petrol models

a) *DO NOT use leaded petrol (or lead-replacement petrol, LRP) in a car equipped with a catalytic converter – the lead (or other additives) will coat the precious metals, reducing their converting efficiency and will eventually destroy the converter.*
b) *Always keep the ignition and fuel systems well-maintained in accordance with the manufacturer's schedule (see Chapter 1A).*
c) *If the engine develops a misfire, do not drive the car at all (or at least as little as possible) until the fault is cured.*
d) *DO NOT push or tow-start the car – this will soak the catalytic converter in unburned fuel, causing it to overheat when the engine does start.*
e) *DO NOT switch off the ignition at high engine speeds – ie, do not 'blip' the throttle immediately before switching off the engine.*
f) *DO NOT use fuel or engine oil additives – these may contain substances harmful to the catalytic converter.*
g) *DO NOT continue to use the car if the engine burns oil to the extent of leaving a visible trail of blue smoke.*
h) *Remember that the catalytic converter operates at very high temperatures. DO NOT, therefore, park the car on dry undergrowth, over long grass or piles of dead leaves after a long run.*
i) *As mentioned above, driving through deep water should be avoided if possible. The sudden cooling effect may fracture the ceramic honeycomb, damaging it beyond repair.*
j) *Remember that the catalytic converter is FRAGILE – do not strike it with tools during servicing work, and take care handling it when removing it from the car for any reason.*
k) *In some cases, a sulphurous smell (like that of rotten eggs) may be noticed from the exhaust. This is common to many catalytic converter-equipped cars, and has more to do with the sulphur content of the brand of fuel being used than the converter itself.*
l) *If a substantial loss of power is experienced, remember that this could be due to the converter being blocked. This can occur simply as a result of contamination after a high mileage, but may be due to the ceramic element having fractured and collapsed internally (see paragraph 3). A new converter is the only cure in this instance.*
m) *The catalytic converter, used on a well-maintained and well-driven car, should last at least 100 000 miles – if the converter is no longer effective, it must be renewed.*

Diesel models

5 The catalytic converter fitted to diesel models is simpler than that fitted to petrol models, but it still needs to be treated with respect to avoid problems:

a) *DO NOT use fuel or engine oil additives – these may contain substances harmful to the catalytic converter.*
b) *DO NOT continue to use the car if the engine burns (engine) oil to the extent of leaving a visible trail of blue smoke.*
c) *Remember that the catalytic converter operates at very high temperatures. DO NOT, therefore, park the car in dry undergrowth, over long grass or piles of dead leaves after a long run.*
d) *As mentioned above, driving through deep water should be avoided if possible. The sudden cooling effect will fracture the ceramic honeycomb, damaging it beyond repair.*
e) *Remember that the catalytic converter is FRAGILE – do not strike it with tools during servicing work, and take care handling it when removing it from the car for any reason.*
f) *If a substantial loss of power is experienced, remember that this could be due to the converter being blocked. This can occur simply as a result of contamination after a high mileage, but may be due to the ceramic element having fractured and collapsed internally (see paragraph 3). A new converter is the only cure in this instance.*
g) *The catalytic converter, used on a well-maintained and well-driven car, should last at least 100 000 miles – if the converter is no longer effective, it must be renewed.*

7 Catalytic converter – removal and refitting

1 Disconnect the battery negative (earth) lead (refer to *Disconnecting the battery* at the end of this manual).

Petrol models except 3.0 litre ST

2 Chock the rear wheels, then jack up the front of the car and support it on axle stands (see *Jacking and vehicle support*).

3 Disconnect the wiring connector(s) from the oxygen sensor(s), unclip the wiring loom from under the car, where required.

4 Undo the two retaining nuts and disconnect the flexible pipe from the catalytic converter, discard the gasket. To prevent possible damage to the flexible section of pipe behind the flange joint, Ford technicians cable-tie two strips of thick metal on either side, down the length of the flexible section.

5 Undo the two retaining nuts and disconnect the catalytic converter from the exhaust intermediate pipe, discard the gasket.

6 Refitting is a reversal of removal, noting the following points:

a) *Use new nuts, bolts and gaskets as necessary. **Note:** Exhaust sealant paste should not be used on any part of the exhaust system upstream of the catalytic converter (between the engine and the converter) – even if the sealant does not contain additives harmful to the converter, pieces of it may break off and foul the element, causing local overheating.*
b) *Tighten all fasteners to the specified torque.*

3.0 litre ST models

Front converter

7 Remove the three bolts securing the ignition coil pack to the front of the engine, and move it to one side without disconnecting the HT leads.

8 Chock the rear wheels, then jack up the front of the car and support it on axle stands (see *Jacking and vehicle support*).

9 Undo the two retaining nuts and disconnect the flexible pipe from the catalytic converter, discard the gasket. To prevent possible damage to the flexible section of pipe behind the flange joint, Ford technicians cable-tie two strips of thick metal on either side, down the length of the flexible section.

10 Disconnect the wiring connector from the oxygen sensor, and unclip the wiring loom from under the car, where required. To avoid the possibility of damage to the sensor when removing the converter, it is recommended that the sensor be unscrewed and removed first.

11 Remove the single bolt securing the converter to its support bracket.

12 Support the converter, then unscrew the three flange nuts and remove it from under the car. Renew the flange nuts if they are in poor condition.

13 Refitting is a reversal of removal, noting the following points:

a) *Use new nuts, bolts and gaskets as necessary. **Note:** Exhaust sealant paste should not be used on any part of the exhaust system upstream of the catalytic converter (between the engine and the* *converter) – even if the sealant does not contain additives harmful to the converter, pieces of it may break off and foul the element, causing local overheating.*

b) Ford recommend that the three converter studs are unscrewed and renewed whenever the converter is disturbed.

c) Tighten all fasteners to the specified torque.

Rear converter

Note: *Removing the rear converter on 3.0 litre ST models requires that the front subframe is removed, making this a particularly difficult job for the DIY mechanic.*

14 Remove the upper section of the inlet manifold, as described in Chapter 2B.

15 Unscrew the two nuts securing the wiring harness to the rear camshaft cover, and lift it off. Disconnect the wiring plug for the rear oxygen sensor, just above the harness.

16 Unscrew and remove the oxygen sensor from the rear exhaust manifold.

17 Unscrew the three bolts securing the exhaust manifold heat shield.

18 Chock the rear wheels, then jack up the front of the car and support it on axle stands (see *Jacking and vehicle support*).

19 Unscrew the three flange nuts securing the converter to the manifold – renew these nuts if they are in poor condition.

20 Remove the front subframe as described in Chapter 10.

21 Remove the alternator as described in Chapter 5A.

22 Disconnect the wiring plug, then unscrew and remove the downstream oxygen sensor from the converter.

23 Unscrew the nut and two bolts, and remove the converter heat shield, sliding it towards the transmission end of the engine, and then down.

24 Support the converter, then unscrew the two bolts securing the converter to its support bracket. Remove it from under the car, and recover the gasket – a new one must be used when refitting.

25 Refitting is a reversal of removal, noting the following points:

*a) Use new nuts, bolts and gaskets as necessary. **Note:** Exhaust sealant paste should not be used on any part of the exhaust system upstream of the catalytic converter (between the engine and the converter) – even if the sealant does not contain additives harmful to the converter, pieces of it may break off and foul the element, causing local overheating.*

b) Ford recommend that the three converter studs are unscrewed and renewed whenever the converter is disturbed.

c) Tighten all fasteners to the specified torque.

Diesel models

26 Disconnect the battery negative (earth) lead (refer to *Disconnecting the battery* at the end of this manual).

7.27 Removing the heat shield from the top of the exhaust manifold

27 Undo the retaining bolts and remove the heat shield from the top of the exhaust manifold **(see illustration)**.

28 Remove the four nuts securing the top of the catalytic converter to the exhaust manifold **(see illustration)**. Renew these nuts if they are in poor condition.

29 Chock the rear wheels, then jack up the front of the car and support it on axle stands (see *Jacking and vehicle support*).

30 Undo the two retaining nuts and disconnect the flexible pipe from the bottom of the catalytic converter, discard the gasket. To prevent possible damage to the flexible section of pipe behind the flange joint, Ford technicians cable-tie two strips of thick metal on either side, down the length of the flexible section.

31 Support the converter, then remove the retaining bolts from the support bracket at the base of the converter. Alternatively, remove the support bracket completely **(see illustration)**.

32 With the converter supported, lower the converter downwards under the car, taking great care not to drop it or knock it, as the internals are fragile **(see illustration)**. The converter is a bulky component, and it may be necessary to rotate it as it is withdrawn.

33 Refitting is a reversal of removal, noting the following points:

*a) Use new nuts, bolts and gaskets as necessary. **Note:** Exhaust sealant paste should not be used on any part of the exhaust system upstream of the catalytic converter (between the engine and the converter) – even if the sealant does not contain additives harmful to the converter,*

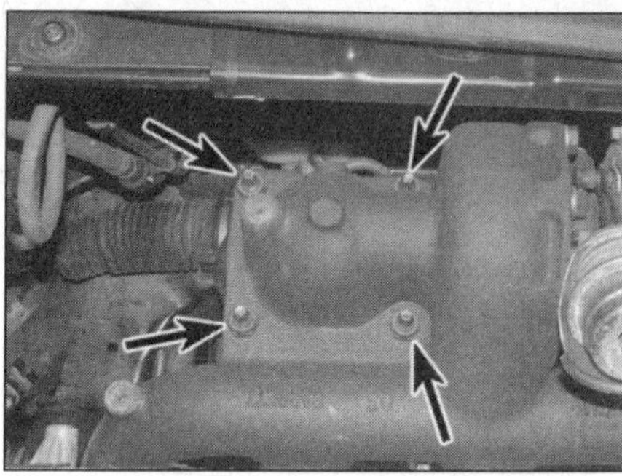

7.28 Remove the four nuts (arrowed) to remove the catalytic converter

pieces of it may break off and foul the element, causing local overheating.

b) Tighten all fasteners to the specified torque.

8 Diesel particulate filter (DPF) components – removal and refitting

Diesel particulate filter

1 Ensure that the ignition is switched off (take out the key).

2 Chock the rear wheels, then jack up the front of the car and support it on axle stands (see *Jacking and vehicle support*).

3 Trace the wiring from the exhaust temperature sensor on the side of the DPF up to its in-line connector, and disconnect it. Note how the wiring is routed, as it must not come into contact with hot exhaust components.

4 Trace the two pressure differential pipes at the front and rear of the DPF to their hose connections – release the hose clips and disconnect them. Note how the hoses are routed, as they must be kept clear of hot exhaust components. If the hose clips are in poor condition, obtain new ones, or use Jubilee clips, for reconnection.

5 Undo the two retaining nuts and disconnect the flexible pipe from the front of the DPF. Discard the gasket – a new one must be used on reassembly. To prevent possible damage to the flexible section of pipe behind the flange joint, Ford technicians cable-tie two strips of

7.31 Support bracket (arrowed) fitted to the lower part of the catalytic converter

7.32 Lowering the converter downwards from the manifold

thick metal on either side, down the length of the flexible section.

6 Support the DPF, then remove the rear flange nuts and separate it from the rear system. Unhook the DPF from its mounting rubber, and remove it from under the car.

7 If the DPF is being removed due to blockage, consult a Ford dealer for advice on how it should best be unblocked without causing damage.

8 Refitting is a reversal of removal, noting the following points:

a) *Use new nuts and gaskets as necessary.* **Note:** *Exhaust sealant paste should not be used on any part of the exhaust system upstream of the DPF (in this case, on the DPF front flange joint) – pieces of it may break off and foul the filter.*
b) *Apply high-temperature grease (such as copper brake grease) to the DPF flange studs.*
c) *Tighten all fasteners to the specified torque.*
d) *Ensure the wiring and hoses are routed clear of the hot exhaust, and that the hoses are not kinked or crushed.*

Differential pressure sensor

9 The differential pressure sensor is mounted on the engine compartment bulkhead, on the right-hand side (right as seen from the driver's seat).

10 Ensure that the ignition is switched off (take out the key).

11 Unclip the plastic cover and remove the three retaining nuts from the right-hand strut top mounting. **Note:** ***DO NOT*** *jack up the front of the car, while these nuts are removed.*

12 Undo the four retaining bolts from the right-hand strut top mounting brace and remove it from the car.

13 Disconnect the wiring plug from the sensor.

14 Note their fitted positions (mark the hoses if necessary) then release the hose clips, and disconnect the two hoses from the sensor. If the clips are in poor condition, obtain new ones, or use Jubilee clips, for reconnection.

15 Unscrew the two sensor mounting bolts, and withdraw the sensor from its location.

16 Refitting is a reversal of removal. Tighten the strut mounting nuts to the specified torque.

Exhaust gas temperature sensor

17 Ensure that the ignition is switched off (take out the key).

18 Chock the rear wheels, then jack up the front of the car and support it on axle stands (see *Jacking and vehicle support*).

19 Trace the wiring from the sensor body at the front of the DPF, back to its wiring plug, and disconnect it. Note how the wiring is routed, as it must not come into contact with hot exhaust components.

20 Taking care that the sensor wiring does not become twisted, unscrew and remove the sensor from the side of the DPF.

21 It may be beneficial to clean the sensor before refitting it, especially if the sensor tip appears to be contaminated. However, great care must be exercised, as the tip will be damaged by any abrasives, and by certain solvents. Seek the advice of a Ford dealer before cleaning the sensor.

22 Refitting is a reversal of removal, noting the following points:

a) *Apply a little anti-seize compound to the sensor threads, taking care not to allow any on the sensor tip, and tighten the sensor to the specified torque.*
b) *Reconnect the wiring, ensuring that it is routed clear of any hot exhaust components.*

Chapter 5 Part A:
Starting and charging systems

Contents

Degrees of difficulty

Easy, suitable for novice with little experience

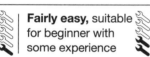

Fairly easy, suitable for beginner with some experience

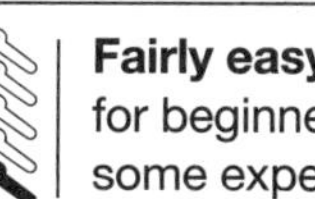

Fairly difficult, suitable for competent DIY mechanic

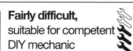

Difficult, suitable for experienced DIY mechanic

Very difficult, suitable for expert DIY or professional

Specifications

General

System type	12 volt, negative-earth	

Battery

Type	Lead-calcium	
Rating	60 to 70 Ah (depending on model)	

Starter motor

Type	Motorcraft, pre-engaged	

Torque wrench settings

	Nm	lbf ft
Alternator mounting nuts/bolts	47	35
Alternator mounting studs (diesel engines)	15	11
Starter motor mounting bolts:		
4-cylinder engines	25	18
V6 engine	35	26

1 General information and precautions

General information

The engine electrical systems include all ignition, charging and starting components. Because of their engine-related functions, these components are discussed separately from body electrical devices such as the lights, the instruments, etc (which are included in Chapter 12).

Precautions

Always observe the following precautions when working on the electrical system:

a) *Be extremely careful when servicing engine electrical components. They are easily damaged if checked, connected or handled improperly.*
b) *Never leave the ignition switched on for long periods of time when the engine is not running.*
c) *Don't disconnect the battery leads while the engine is running.*
d) *Maintain correct polarity when connecting a battery lead from another vehicle during jump starting – see the Jump starting Section at the front of this manual.*
e) *Always disconnect the negative lead first, and reconnect it last, or the battery may be shorted by the tool being used to loosen the lead clamps.*

It's also a good idea to review the safety-related information regarding the engine electrical systems shown in the Safety first! section at the front of this manual, before beginning any operation included in this Chapter.

Battery disconnection

Refer to *Disconnecting the battery* at the end of this manual.

2.2 Always disconnect battery (–) negative lead first

2 Battery – removal and refitting

Removal

1 Unclip the battery cover and withdraw it from the top of the battery.

2 Disconnect the battery negative (earth) lead (refer to *Disconnecting the battery* at the end of this manual) **(see illustration)**.

3 Undo the two retaining nuts and remove the battery hold-down clamp **(see illustration)**.

4 Lift out the battery – be careful, as the battery is heavy. Use the carry handle, if the battery is so equipped.

5 If required, the battery tray and its support bracket can also be removed. Release the two clips in the base of the tray, then lift it out – where necessary, unbolt the engine compartment fusebox from the side. Working from above, remove the two support bracket bolts, and disconnect the two earth cables from the bracket. Noting how it is fitted, detach the wiring harness as necessary from the bracket. Finally, remove the three bolts securing the bracket to the inner wing, and remove the bracket completely.

6 If you are renewing the battery, make sure that you get one that's identical, with the same dimensions, amperage rating, cold cranking rating, etc. Dispose of the old battery in a responsible fashion. Most local authorities have facilities for the collection and disposal of such items – batteries contain sulphuric acid and lead, and should not be simply thrown out with the household rubbish.

2.3 Unscrew hold-down nuts (one of two arrowed)

Refitting

7 Refitting is the reverse of the removal procedure. **Note:** *After the battery has been disconnected, the engine management system requires approximately 5 miles of driving to relearn its optimum settings. During this period, the engine may not perform normally. Also refer to Disconnecting the battery at the end of this manual.*

3 Battery – testing

Testing

1 The simplest way to test a battery is with a voltmeter (or multimeter set to voltage testing) – connect the voltmeter across the battery terminals, observing the correct polarity. The test is only accurate if the battery has not been subjected to any kind of charge for the previous six hours. If this is not the case, switch on the headlights for 30 seconds, then wait four to five minutes before testing the battery after switching off the headlights. All other electrical circuits must be switched off, so check that the doors and tailgate/boot lid are fully shut when making the test.

2 If the voltage reading is less than 12.0 volts, then the battery is less than healthy. Under 11.5 volts, and the battery needs charging. However, as little as 11.0 volts will still usually be enough to start the engine, though a battery in this condition could not be relied on. A reading of around 10.0 volts suggests that one of the six battery cells has died – a common way for modern batteries to fail.

3 If the battery is to be charged, remove it from the car (Section 2) and charge it as described later in this Section.

Low-maintenance battery

4 If the car covers a small annual mileage, it is worthwhile checking the specific gravity of the electrolyte every three months to determine the state of charge of the battery. Use a hydrometer to make the check, and compare the results with the tool maker's instructions (typically, there will be a colour-coded scale on hydrometers sold for battery testing).

5 If the battery condition is suspect, first check the specific gravity of electrolyte in each cell. A significant variation between any cells indicates loss of electrolyte, or deterioration of the internal plates.

6 If the cell variation is satisfactory but the battery is discharged, it should be charged as described later in this Section.

Maintenance-free battery

7 In cases where a 'sealed for life' maintenance-free battery is fitted, topping-up and testing of the electrolyte in each cell is not possible. The condition of the battery can therefore only be tested using a battery condition indicator or a voltmeter.

Charging

Note: *The following is intended as a guide only. Always refer to the manufacturer's recommendations (often printed on a label attached to the battery), and always disconnect both terminal leads before charging a battery.*

Low-maintenance battery

8 It is advisable to remove the cell caps or covers if possible during charging, but note that the battery will be giving off potentially-explosive hydrogen gas while it is being charged. Small amounts of acidic electrolyte may also escape as the battery nears full charge. Removing the cell caps will allow you to check whether all six cells are receiving charge – after a while, the electrolyte should start to bubble. If any cell does not bubble, this may indicate that it has failed, and the battery is no longer fit for use.

9 Charge the battery at a rate of 3.5 to 4 amps, and continue to charge the battery at this rate until no further rise in specific gravity is noted over a four-hour period.

10 Alternatively, a trickle charger charging at the rate of 1.5 amps can safely be used overnight.

11 Specially rapid 'boost' charges which are claimed to restore the power of the battery in 1 to 2 hours are not recommended, as they can cause serious damage to the battery plates through overheating.

12 While charging the battery, note that the temperature of the electrolyte should never exceed 38°C.

Maintenance-free battery

13 This battery type takes considerably longer to fully recharge than the standard type, the time taken being dependent on the extent of discharge, but it can take anything up to three days.

14 A constant-voltage type charger is required, to be set, when connected, to 13.9 to 14.9 volts with a charger current below 25 amps. Using this method, the battery should be usable within three hours, giving a voltage reading of 12.5 volts, but this is for a partially-discharged battery and, as mentioned, full charging can take considerably longer.

15 If the battery is to be charged from a fully-discharged state (condition reading less than 12.2 volts), have it recharged by your local automotive electrician, as the charge rate is higher and constant supervision during charging is necessary.

4 Charging system – general information and precautions

General information

The charging system includes the alternator, an internal voltage regulator, a no-charge (or 'ignition') warning light, the battery, and the wiring between all the components. The charging system supplies electrical power for the ignition system, the lights, the radio, etc. The alternator is driven by the auxiliary drivebelt at the right-hand end of the engine.

The purpose of the voltage regulator is to limit the alternator's voltage to a preset value. This prevents power surges, circuit overloads, etc, during peak voltage output.

The charging system doesn't ordinarily require periodic maintenance. However, the drivebelt, battery and wires and connections should be inspected at the intervals outlined in Chapter 1A or 1B.

The instrument panel warning light should come on when the ignition key is turned to positions II or III, then should go off immediately the engine starts. If it remains on, or if it comes on while the engine is running, there is a malfunction in the charging system. If the light does not come on when the ignition key is turned, and the bulb is sound (see Chapter 12), there is a fault in the alternator.

Precautions

Be very careful when making electrical circuit connections to a car equipped with an alternator, and note the following:

- *a) When reconnecting wires to the alternator from the battery, be sure to note the polarity.*
- *b) Before using arc-welding equipment to repair any part of the car, disconnect the wires from the alternator and the battery terminals.*
- *c) Never start the engine with a battery charger connected.*
- *d) Always disconnect both battery leads before using a battery charger.*
- *e) The alternator is driven by an engine drivebelt which could cause serious injury if your hand, hair or clothes become entangled in it with the engine running.*
- *f) Because the alternator is connected directly to the battery, it could arc or cause a fire if overloaded or shorted-out.*
- *g) Wrap a plastic bag over the alternator, and secure it with rubber bands, before steam-cleaning or pressure-washing the engine* ***(do not forget to remove before restarting the engine).***
- *h) Never disconnect the alternator terminals while the engine is running.*

5 Charging system – testing

1 If a malfunction occurs in the charging circuit, don't automatically assume that the alternator is causing the problem. First check the following items:

- *a) Check the tension and condition of the auxiliary drivebelt – renew it if it is worn or deteriorated (see Chapter 1A or 1B).*
- *b) Ensure the alternator mounting bolts and nuts are tight.*
- *c) Inspect the alternator wiring harness and the electrical connections at the alternator; they must be in good condition, and tight.*
- *d) Check the large main fuses in the engine compartment (see Chapter 12). If any is blown, determine the cause, repair the circuit and renew the fuse (the car won't start and/or the accessories won't work if the fuse is blown).*
- *e) Start the engine and check the alternator for abnormal noises – for example, a shrieking or squealing sound may indicate a badly-worn bearing or bush.*
- *f) Make sure that the battery is fully-charged – one bad cell in a battery can cause overcharging by the alternator.*
- *g) Disconnect the battery leads (negative first, then positive). Inspect the battery posts and the lead clamps for corrosion. Clean them thoroughly if necessary (see Weekly checks). Reconnect the lead to the negative terminal.*
- *h) With the ignition and all accessories switched off, insert a test light between the battery negative post and the disconnected negative lead clamp:*
  - *1) If the test light does not come on, re-attach the clamp and proceed to the next step.*
  - *2) If the test light comes on, there is a short in the electrical system of the car. The short must be repaired before the charging system can be checked.*
  - *3) To find the short, disconnect the alternator wiring harness. If the light goes out, the alternator is at fault. If the light stays on, remove each fuse until it goes out – this will tell you which component is short-circuited.*

2 Using a voltmeter, check the battery voltage with the engine off. It should be approximately 12 volts.

3 Start the engine and check the battery voltage again. Increase engine speed until the voltmeter reading remains steady; it should now be approximately 13.5 to 14.6 volts.

4 Switch on as many electrical accessories (eg, the headlights, heated rear window and heater blower) as possible, and check that the alternator maintains the regulated voltage at around 13 to 14 volts. The voltage may drop and then come back up; it may also be necessary to increase engine speed slightly, even if the charging system is working properly.

5 If the voltage reading is greater than the specified charging voltage, renew the voltage regulator.

6 If the voltmeter reading is less than that specified, the fault may be due to worn brushes, weak brush springs, a faulty voltage regulator, a faulty diode, a severed phase winding, or worn or damaged slip-rings. The brushes and slip-rings may be checked, but if the fault persists, the alternator should be renewed or taken to an auto-electrician for testing and repair.

6 Alternator – removal and refitting

Removal

1 Disconnect the battery negative (earth) lead (refer to *Disconnecting the battery* at the end of this manual).

2 On 4-cylinder engines, remove the upper plastic cover from the engine, and undo the alternator upper retaining bolt **(see illustrations)**. Remove the wiring harness support bracket.

3 Loosen the right-hand front wheel nuts. Apply the handbrake, then jack up the front of the car and support it on axle stands (see *Jacking and vehicle support*). Remove the right-hand front wheel and wheel arch liner – also remove the steering gear gaiter splash shield, which is secured with a single bolt. Where applicable, remove the engine undershield.

4 On 3.0 litre V6 ST engines, carry out the following:

- *a) Referring to Chapter 10 if necessary, detach the top of the front anti-roll bar drop link from the right-hand suspension strut (use a 5 mm Allen key to stop the balljoint turning as the nut is undone).*
- *b) With reference to Chapter 2B, remove the rear through-bolt from the engine rear roll restrictor – this will allow the engine to pivot forwards, creating more room at the rear. Securely wedge the engine forwards temporarily using a piece of wood, but make sure that no pipes or hoses are being strained.*
- *c) Remove the rear catalytic converter heat*

6.2a Removing the alternator upper retaining bolt (4-cylinder models) . . .

6.2b . . . and unclip the wiring harness bracket

6.6 Removing the cooling duct from the rear of the alternator (4-cylinder models)

6.10 Withdrawing the alternator through the right-hand front wheel arch

shield nut and two bolts. Slide the heat shield towards the transmission end of the engine, then down.

5 Remove the (main) auxiliary drivebelt as described in Chapter 1A or 1B.

6 On 4-cylinder engines, release the retaining clips and remove the cooling duct from the rear of the alternator **(see illustration)**.

7 Unplug the wiring connector from the rear of the alternator, then undo the nut to disconnect the wiring terminal from the alternator **(see illustration)**.

8 To create more room for the alternator to be withdrawn, disconnect the outer end of the track rod end, as described in Chapter 10.

6.7 Disconnect the wiring terminals from the alternator

7.2 Remove three screws and withdraw end cover (Bosch alternator) . . .

9 On V6 engines, undo the alternator upper retaining bolt and unclip the wiring harness support bracket.

10 Remove the two lower mounting bolts and remove the alternator out through the right-hand wheel arch **(see illustration)**. **Note:** *On diesel engines the alternator is fastened by studs and nuts, the studs will need to be removed from the cylinder block to allow the alternator to be removed.*

11 If required, undo the four retaining nuts and remove the plastic cover from the rear of the alternator.

12 If you are renewing the alternator, take the old one with you. Make sure that the new or rebuilt unit is identical to the old alternator. Look at the terminals – they should be the same in number, size and location as the terminals on the old alternator. Finally, look at the identification markings – they will be stamped in the housing, or printed on a tag or plaque affixed to the housing. Make sure that these numbers are the same on both alternators and the pulleys are identical.

Refitting

13 Refitting is the reverse of the removal procedure, referring where necessary to the relevant Chapters of this manual. Tighten all nuts and bolts to the specified torque wrench settings.

7 Alternator brushes and voltage regulator – renewal

Note: *This procedure assumes that parts of the correct type have been obtained. At the time of writing, no individual alternator components were available as separate replacement Ford parts. An auto-electrical specialist should be able to supply parts such as brushes.*

1 Remove the alternator from the car (see Section 6) and place it on a clean workbench.

Removal

2 Undo the retaining screws/nuts, and withdraw the alternator end cover **(see illustration)**.

3 Remove the two voltage regulator/brushholder mounting screws and, where applicable, ease the wire from the connector.

4 Remove the regulator/brushholder from the end frame **(see illustrations)**.

5 Measure the exposed length of each brush, and check with an auto-electrical specialist whether they are excessively worn.

6 Make sure that each brush moves smoothly in the brushholder.

7.4a . . . then remove regulator/brushholder assembly (secured by two screws)

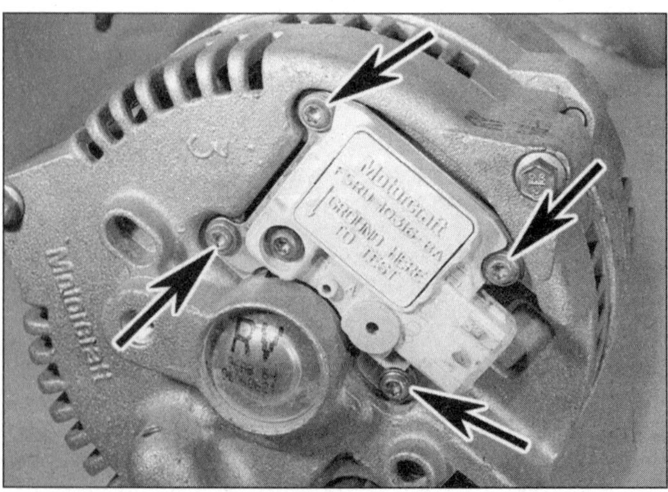

7.4b Regulator/brushholder retaining screws (Motorcraft alternator)

7 Check that the slip-rings – the rings of copper on which each brush bears – are clean **(see illustration)**. Wipe them with a solvent-moistened cloth; if either appears scored or blackened, take the alternator to a repair specialist for advice.

Refitting

8 Fit the voltage regulator/brushholder **(see illustration)**. Ensure the brushes bear correctly on the slip-rings, and that they compress into their holders. Tighten the screws securely and where applicable, refit the wire to its connector

9 Install the rear cover, and tighten the screws/nuts securely.

10 Refit the alternator (see Section 6).

8 Starting system – general information and precautions

General information

The sole function of the starting system is to turn over the engine quickly enough to allow it to start.

The starting system consists of the battery, the starter motor, the starter solenoid, and the wires connecting them. The solenoid is mounted directly on the starter motor.

The solenoid/starter motor assembly is installed on the rear upper part of the transmission on V6 engines except the 3.0 litre ST, and on the front of the cylinder block, next to the transmission bellhousing, on 4-cylinder and 3.0 litre V6 ST engines.

When the ignition key is turned to position III, the starter solenoid is actuated through the starter control circuit. The starter solenoid then connects the battery to the starter. The battery supplies the electrical energy to the starter motor, which does the actual work of cranking the engine.

The starter motor on a car equipped with automatic transmission can be operated only when the selector lever is in Park or Neutral (P or N).

If the alarm system is armed or activated, the starter motor cannot be operated. The same applies with the engine immobiliser system (where fitted).

Precautions

Always observe the following precautions when working on the starting system:

a) *Excessive cranking of the starter motor can overheat it, and cause serious damage. Never operate the starter motor for more than 15 seconds at a time without pausing to allow it to cool for at least two minutes. Excessive starter operation will also risk unburned fuel collecting in the catalytic converter's element, causing it to overheat when the engine does start.*

b) *The starter is connected directly to the battery, and could arc or cause a fire if mishandled, overloaded or shorted-out.*

c) *Always detach the lead from the negative terminal of the battery before working on the starting system (see Section 1).*

7.7 Check that the slip-rings are clean

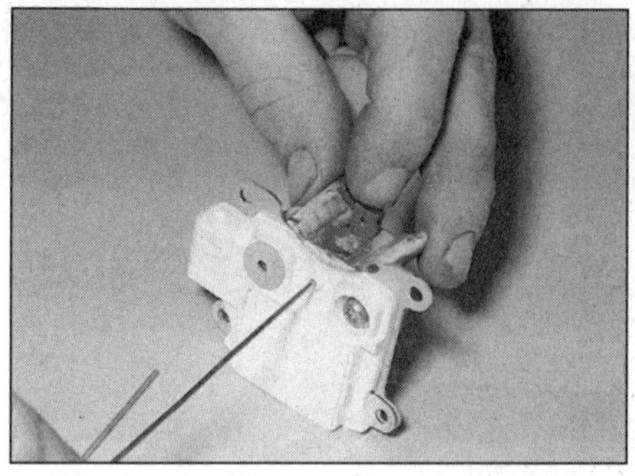

7.8 Insert a rod through the special hole to retain the brushes in their retracted position

9 Starting system – testing

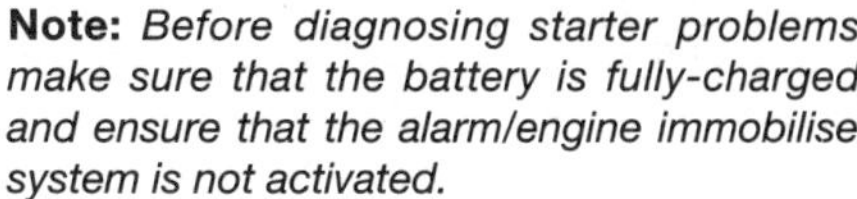

Note: *Before diagnosing starter problems, make sure that the battery is fully-charged, and ensure that the alarm/engine immobiliser system is not activated.*

1 If the starter motor does not turn at all when the switch is operated, make sure that, on automatic transmission models, the selector lever is in Park or Neutral (P or N).

2 Make sure that the battery is fully-charged, and that all leads, both at the battery and starter solenoid terminals, are clean and secure.

3 If the starter motor spins but the engine is not cranking, the overrunning clutch or (when applicable) the reduction gears in the starter motor may be slipping, in which case the starter motor must be overhauled or renewed. (Other possibilities are that the starter motor mounting bolts are very loose, or that teeth are missing from the flywheel/driveplate ring gear.)

4 If, when the switch is actuated, the starter motor does not operate at all but the solenoid clicks, then the problem lies with either the battery, the main solenoid contacts, or the starter motor itself (or the engine is seized).

5 If the solenoid plunger cannot be heard to click when the switch is actuated, the battery is faulty, there is a fault in the circuit, or the solenoid itself is defective.

6 To check the solenoid, connect a fused jumper lead between the battery (+) and the ignition switch terminal (the small terminal) on the solenoid. If the starter motor now operates, the solenoid is OK, and the problem is in the ignition switch, selector lever position sensor (automatic transmission) or in the wiring.

7 If the starter motor still does not operate, remove it. The brushes and commutator may be checked, but if the fault persists, the motor should be renewed, or taken to an auto-electrician for testing and repair.

8 If the starter motor cranks the engine at an abnormally-slow speed, first make sure that the battery is charged, and that all terminal connections are tight. If the engine is partially-seized, or has the wrong viscosity oil in it, it will crank slowly.

9 Run the engine until normal operating temperature is reached, then switch off and disable the ignition system by unplugging the ignition coil's electrical connector; remove the fuel pump fuse – see wiring diagrams in Chapter 12.

10 Connect a voltmeter positive lead to the battery positive terminal, and connect the negative lead to the negative terminal.

11 Crank the engine, and take the voltmeter readings as soon as a steady figure is indicated. Do not allow the starter motor to turn for more than 15 seconds at a time. A reading of 10.5 volts or more, with the starter motor turning at normal cranking speed, is normal. If the reading is 10.5 volts or more but the cranking speed is slow, the solenoid contacts are burned, the motor is faulty, or there is a bad connection. If the reading is less than 10.5 volts and the cranking speed is slow, the starter motor is faulty or there is a problem with the battery.

10 Starter motor – removal and refitting

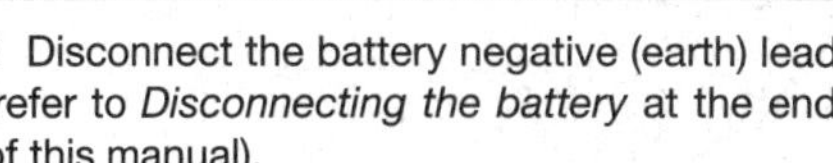

1 Disconnect the battery negative (earth) lead (refer to *Disconnecting the battery* at the end of this manual).

4-cylinder and 3.0 litre ST models

Removal

2 Apply the handbrake, then jack up the front of the car and support it on axle stands (see *Jacking and vehicle support*).

3 Where applicable, remove the engine undershield.

4 Remove the splash shield from across the front of the car under the radiator.

5 On diesel models, disconnect the T-MAP sensor wiring plug from the intercooler inlet pipe which runs across the front subframe. Undo the retaining bolts and hose clips, and remove the inlet pipe.

10.6 Remove the wiring harness bracket from the starter motor retaining studs/bolts

10.8 Undo the retaining bolt (arrowed) from the rear support bracket (4-cylinder petrol models)

6 Undo the two retaining nuts and release the wiring bracket from the starter motor retaining studs/bolts **(see illustration)**.

7 Unscrew the nuts to disconnect the wiring from the starter/solenoid terminals **(see illustration)**.

8 On 4-cylinder petrol models, undo the retaining bolt and remove the starter motor rear support bracket **(see illustration)**.

9 Unscrew the two starter motor mounting studs/bolts, and remove the starter motor **(see illustration)**.

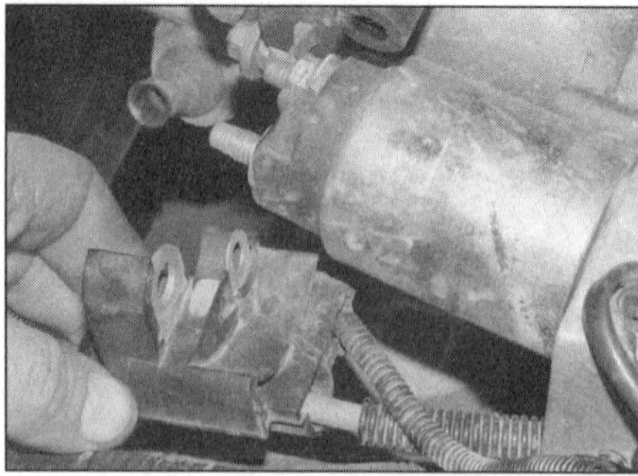
10.7 Disconnecting the wiring from the starter/solenoid terminals

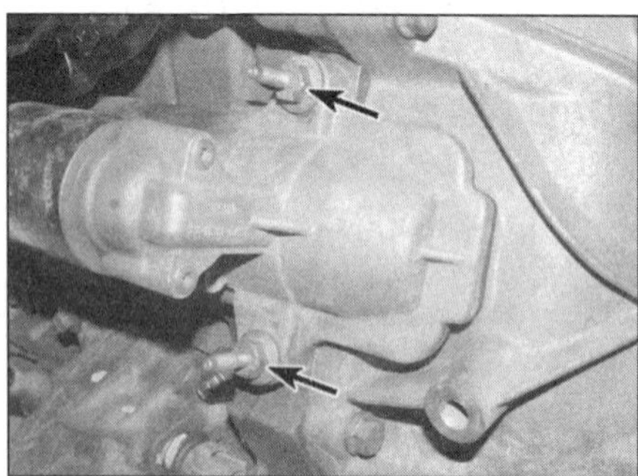
10.9 Unscrew the two starter motor mounting bolts/studs (arrowed)

Refitting

10 Refitting is the reverse of the removal procedure. Tighten the bolts to the specified torque wrench settings.

V6 models except 3.0 litre ST

Removal

11 Release the retaining clips from the air inlet hoses, disconnect the mass airflow (MAF) sensor, then remove the air cleaner and air cleaner mounting bracket.

12 Remove the battery as described in Section 2. Remove the battery tray, which is released using the two clips in the base. Remove the bolt from the air intake pipe, and move the pipe to one side.

13 Disconnect the wiring from the starter motor. Also remove the two nuts and bolt securing the support bracket to the starter motor and transmission housing. Remove the bracket **(see illustration)**.

14 On manual transmission models, disconnect the wiring from the reversing light switch.

15 Unscrew the mounting bolts from the starter motor, then release the starter motor from the dowels on the transmission housing and withdraw from the engine compartment **(see illustrations)**.

Refitting

16 Refitting is a reversal of removal. Tighten the bolts to the specified torque wrench settings.

11 Starter motor – testing and overhaul

Note: *At the time of writing, no individual starter motor components were available as separate Ford parts. An auto-electrical specialist should be able to supply and fit parts such as brushes.*

If the starter motor is thought to be defective, it should be removed from the car (as described in Section 10) and taken to an auto-electrician for assessment. In the majority of cases, new starter motor brushes can be fitted at a reasonable cost. However, check the cost of repairs first, as it may prove more economical to purchase a new or exchange motor.

10.13 Disconnecting the wiring and support bracket from the starter motor

10.15a Unscrew the mounting bolts . . .

10.15b . . . and withdraw the starter motor from the transmission

Chapter 5 Part B: Ignition system – petrol models

Contents

Degrees of difficulty

Easy, suitable for novice with little experience 	**Fairly easy,** suitable for beginner with some experience	**Fairly difficult,** suitable for competent DIY mechanic	**Difficult,** suitable for experienced DIY mechanic	**Very difficult,** suitable for expert DIY or professional 

Specifications

Ignition timing	Not adjustable – PCM (Powertrain Control Module) controlled	
Ignition coil		
Primary resistances – measured at coil connector terminal pins	0.50 ± 0.05 ohms	
Torque wrench settings	**Nm**	**lbf ft**
Knock sensor:		
4-cylinder models	20	15
V6 models	34	25

1 Ignition system – general information and precautions

General information

The ignition system includes the ignition switch, the battery, the crankshaft speed/position sensor, the coil, the primary (low tension/LT) and secondary (high tension/HT) wiring circuits, and the spark plugs. On models with the CD4E (four-speed) automatic transmission, a separate ignition module is also fitted, its functions being incorporated in the PCM on models with manual transmission. The ignition system is controlled by the engine management system's Powertrain Control Module (PCM). Using data provided by information sensors which monitor various engine functions (such as engine speed and piston position, inlet air mass and temperature, engine coolant temperature, etc), the PCM ensures a perfectly-timed spark under all conditions (see Chapter 4A). **Note:** *The ignition timing is under the full control of the PCM, and cannot be adjusted – see Chapter 4A for further details.*

The basic operation is as follows; the module supplies a voltage to the input stage of the ignition coil, which causes the primary windings in the coil to be energised. The supply voltage is periodically interrupted by the PCM, and this results in the collapse of the primary magnetic field, which then induces a much larger voltage in the secondary windings, called the High Tension (HT) voltage. This voltage is directed, via the HT leads, to the spark plugs. The spark plug electrodes form a gap small enough for the HT voltage to arc across, and the resulting spark ignites the fuel/air mixture in the cylinder. The timing sequence of events is critical, and is regulated by the PCM.

Precautions

When working on the ignition system, take the following precautions:

a) Do not keep the ignition switch on for more than 10 seconds if the engine will not start.

b) If a separate tachometer is ever required for servicing work, consult a dealer service department before buying a tachometer for use with this car – some tachometers may be incompatible with this ignition system – and always connect it in accordance with the equipment manufacturer's instructions.

c) Never connect the ignition coil terminals to earth. This could result in damage to the coil and/or the PCM or ignition module (whichever is fitted).

d) Do not disconnect the battery when the engine is running.

e) Make sure that the ignition module (where fitted) is properly earthed.

f) Refer to the warning at the beginning of the next Section concerning HT voltage.

2 Ignition system – testing

Warning: Extreme care must be taken when working on the system with the ignition switched on; it is

possible to get a substantial electric shock from the ignition system. Persons with cardiac pacemaker devices should keep well clear of the ignition circuits, components and test equipment. Always switch off the ignition before disconnecting or connecting any component and when using a multimeter to check the resistances.

Warning: Because of the high voltage generated by the ignition system, extreme care should be taken whenever an operation is performed involving ignition components also. This not only includes the ignition module/PCM, coil and spark plug (HT) leads, but related components such as electrical connectors, tachometer and other test equipment also.

General

Note: *This is an initial check of the 'ignition part' of the main engine management system, to be carried out as part of the preliminary checks of the complete engine management system (see Chapter 4A).*

1 Most ignition system faults are likely to be due to loose or dirty connections or to tracking (unintentional earthing) of the HT voltage due to dirt, dampness or damaged insulation, rather than by the failure of any of the systems components. Always check all the wiring thoroughly before condemning an electrical component and work methodically to eliminate all the other possibilities before deciding that a particular component is faulty.

2 The practise of checking for a spark by holding the live end of an HT lead a short distance away from the engine is definitely not recommended, because of the risk of personal injury, or of damage to the PCM/ ignition module.

Engine will not start

3 If the engine either will not turn over at all, or only turns very slowly, check the battery and the starter motor. Connect a voltmeter across the battery terminals (meter positive probe to battery positive terminal), then disable the ignition by disconnecting the wiring from the coil. Note the voltage reading obtained while turning the engine over on the starter for a maximum of 10 seconds. If the reading obtained is less than approximately 10 volts, first check the battery, starter motor and charging systems (see Chapter 5A).

Checking HT leads and coil

4 Disconnect the (HT) lead from any spark plug, and attach it to a calibrated tester (available at most automotive accessory shops). Connect the clip on the tester to a good earth – a bolt or metal bracket on the engine. If you're unable to obtain a calibrated ignition tester, have the check carried out by a Ford dealer service department or similar. Any other form of testing (such as jumping a spark from the end of an HT lead to earth) is not recommended (see Warnings above and in Section 1).

3.8 Disconnecting the wiring connector for the ignition coil (4-cylinder engine)

5 Crank the engine and watch the end of the tester to see if bright blue, well-defined sparks occur.

6 If sparks occur, sufficient voltage is reaching the plug to fire it. Repeat the check at the remaining plugs, to ensure that all leads are sound and that the coil is serviceable. However, the plugs themselves may be fouled or faulty, so remove and check them as described in Chapter 1A.

7 If no sparks or intermittent sparks occur, the spark plug lead(s) may be defective.

8 If there's still no spark, check the coil's electrical connector, to make sure it's clean and tight. Check for full battery voltage to the coil, at terminal 2 on 4-cylinder engines and at terminal 4 on V6 engines. The coil is earthed through the PCM – do not attempt to check this. Check the coil itself (see Section 3). Make any necessary repairs, then repeat the check again.

9 The remainder of the system checks should be left to a dealer service department or other qualified repair facility, as there is a chance that the PCM may be damaged if tests are not performed properly.

3 Ignition coil – check, removal and refitting

Caution: see Warnings in Section 2 of this Chapter, before proceeding with any work on the ignition system.

3.9 Undo Torx-type screws (arrowed) to release ignition coil assembly

Note the suppressor is held on by two of the screws

Check

1 Having checked that full battery voltage is available at the coil's electrical connector (see Section 2), disconnect the battery negative (earth) lead (refer to *Disconnecting the battery* at the end of this manual).

2 Unplug the coil's electrical connector, if not already disconnected.

3 Using an ohmmeter, measure the resistance of the coil's primary windings, connecting the meter between the coil's terminal pins as follows. Measure first from one outer pin to the centre pin, then from the other outer pin to the centre. Compare your readings with the coil primary resistance listed in the Specifications Section at the beginning of this Chapter.

4 Disconnect the spark plug (HT) leads – note their connections or label them carefully, as described in Chapter 1A. Use the meter to check that there is continuity between each pair of (HT) lead terminals. On 4-cylinder models, coil terminals 1 and 4 are connected by their secondary windings as are terminals 2 and 3. On V6 models, terminals 1 and 5 are connected, terminals 3 and 4 are connected and terminals 2 and 6 are connected. Now switch to the highest resistance scale, and check that there is no continuity between either pair of terminals and the other – ie, on 4-cylinder models, there should be infinite resistance between terminals 1 and 2 or 3 and 4 – also between any terminal and earth.

5 If either of the above tests yield resistance values outside the specified amount, or results other than those described, renew the coil. Any further testing should be left to a dealer service department or other qualified repair facility.

Removal and refitting

4-cylinder models

Note: *On 4-cylinder models, the ignition coil is mounted on the coolant housing located at the left-hand end of the cylinder head.*

6 Disconnect the battery negative (earth) lead (refer to *Disconnecting the battery* at the end of this manual).

7 Unclip the breather hose from the engine upper plastic cover, then unclip the cover from the top of the engine.

8 Unplug the electrical connector from the coil, then disconnect the spark plug (HT) leads – note their connections or label them carefully, as described in Chapter 1A **(see illustration)**.

9 Undo the four (Torx-type) screws securing the coil to the top of the coolant housing **(see illustration)**. Withdraw the coil assembly from the cylinder head. **Note:** *The suppressor on the side of the coil can also be removed, disconnect the wiring connector if required.*

10 Refitting is the reverse of the removal procedure. Ensure that the spark plug (HT) leads are correctly reconnected, and tighten the coil screws securely.

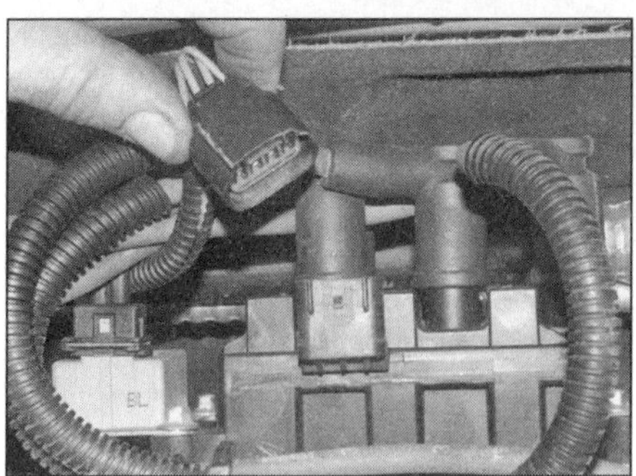

3.12a Disconnecting the wiring from the ignition coil . . .

3.12b . . . and the suppressor (V6 engines)

3.13 Disconnecting the HT leads – each one is marked with its cylinder number

V6 models

Note: *On V6 models, the ignition coil is mounted on the rear valve cover.*

11 Disconnect the battery negative (earth) lead (refer to *Disconnecting the battery* at the end of this manual).

12 Disconnect and unclip the wiring from the ignition coil and suppressor **(see illustrations)**.

13 Note their location, then disconnect the spark plug (HT) leads from the ignition coil. Label the wires for location to ensure correct refitting, each lead is marked with its corresponding cylinder number **(see illustration)**.

14 Unscrew the mounting screws and remove the coil, noting that an earth wire is attached to one of the mounting bolts and the suppressor is attached to two of the bolts **(see illustrations)**.

15 Refitting is a reversal of removal. Make sure the earth wire is attached to one of the coil mounting screws. Also, ensure that the spark plug (HT) leads are connected correctly.

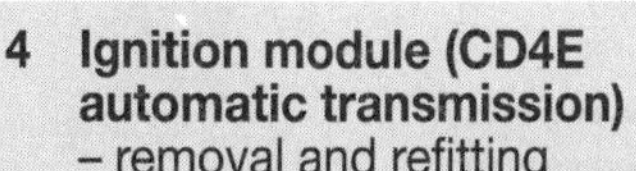

4 Ignition module (CD4E automatic transmission) – removal and refitting

Removal

1 Disconnect the battery negative (earth) lead (refer to *Disconnecting the battery* at the end of this manual).

2 If better access is required, remove the air inlet resonator (see Chapter 4A, Section 4).

3.14a An earth wire is attached to one of the ignition coil mounting bolts . . .

3 Unplug the electrical connector from the module **(see illustration)**.

4 Remove the mounting bolts, and detach the module from the bulkhead mounting bracket.

Refitting

5 Refitting is a reversal of removal.

5 Ignition timing – adjusting and checking

The ignition timing is controlled entirely by the PCM (acting with the ignition module, on models with CD4E automatic transmission), and cannot be adjusted. Not only can the ignition timing not be adjusted, it cannot be checked either, except with the use of special diagnostic equipment – this makes it a task for a Ford dealer service department.

3.14b . . . and a suppressor to two of the mounting bolts

6 Knock sensors – removal and refitting

Removal

1 On 4-cylinder engines, the knock sensor is bolted to the front of the cylinder block under the inlet manifold. On V6 engines, it is bolted to the rear of the engine above the right-hand intermediate driveshaft **(see illustrations)**. **Note:** *On some V6 engines, there may be a second knock sensor fitted to the front bank of cylinders.*

2 On 4-cylinder engines, remove the inlet manifold as described in Chapter 2A.

3 Follow the wiring from the knock sensor and disconnect its wiring block connector, where applicable, unclip the wiring from the cable ties.

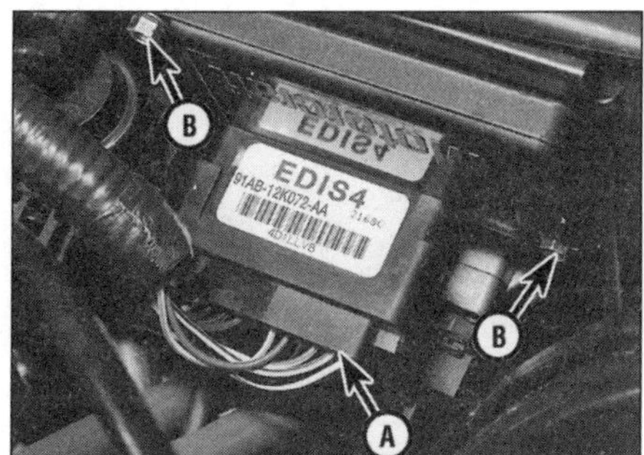

4.3 Separate ignition module on automatic models – wiring plug (A) and bolts (B)

6.1a On 4-cylinder engines, the knock sensor (arrowed) is above the oil separator

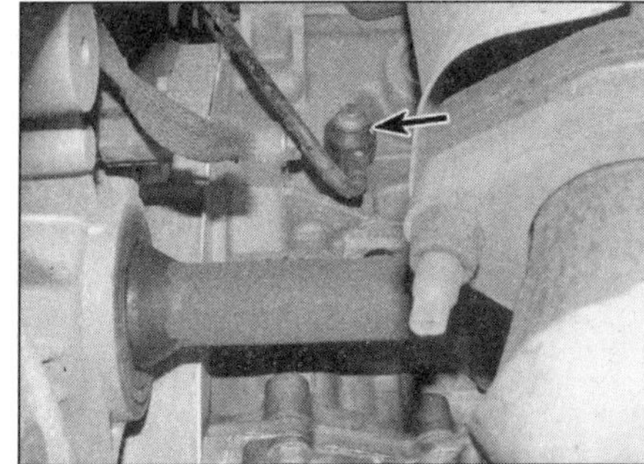

6.1b On V6 engines, the knock sensor (arrowed) is on the rear of the engine

6.4 Removing the knock sensor (4-cylinder engine, head removed for clarity)

6.5 Leave a gap (arrowed) when refitting the knock sensor (4-cylinder engines)

4 Unscrew the centre bolt and remove the knock sensor from the cylinder block **(see illustration)**.

Refitting

5 Refitting is the reversal of the removal procedure; noting the following points:

a) *Clean the sensor and its location on the cylinder block.*

b) *On 4-cylinder models, rotate the sensor as far anti-clockwise as possible, without touching the cylinder head/block or oil separator* ***(see illustration)****.*

c) *The sensor bolt* **must** *be tightened to the specified torque, as this is critical to the sensor's correct operation.*

Chapter 5 Part C:
Preheating system – diesel models

Contents

Degrees of difficulty

Easy, suitable for novice with little experience 	**Fairly easy,** suitable for beginner with some experience	**Fairly difficult,** suitable for competent DIY mechanic	**Difficult,** suitable for experienced DIY mechanic	**Very difficult,** suitable for expert DIY or professional 

Specifications

Torque wrench setting	**Nm**	**lbf ft**
Glow plugs	13	10

1 Preheating system components – general information

General information

Cold-starting performance is automatically controlled by the PCM. Under cold start conditions, the cylinder head temperature (CHT) sensor informs the PCM on the engine temperature, this determines the preheat time.

Each cylinder of the engine is fitted with a heater plug (commonly called a glow plug) screwed into the cylinder head. The plugs are electrically-operated before and during start-up when the engine is cold. Electrical feed to the glow plugs is controlled via the powertrain control module (PCM).

A warning light in the instrument panel tells the driver that preheating is taking place. When the light goes out, the engine is ready to be started. The voltage supply to the glow plugs continues for several seconds after the light goes out. If no attempt is made to start, the timer then cuts off the supply, in order to avoid draining the battery and overheating the glow plugs.

The glow plugs have an after-glow phase which only operates under 2500 rpm, and below temperatures of 50°C. This helps the engine to run more smoothly during idling, and reduces exhaust emissions through more efficient combustion just after starting.

Component locations

1 The preheating is controlled by the powertrain control module (PCM) which is located on the rear right-hand side of the engine compartment (as seen from the driver's seat) where it is mounted with the generic electronic module (GEM). Refer to Chapter 4B, Section 8, for removal and refitting details.

2 The cylinder head temperature switch is screwed into the transmission end of the cylinder head. Refer to Chapter 4B, Section 8, for removal and refitting details.

3 The glow plug relay is located in the fusebox in the engine compartment in front of the battery. Refer to Chapter 12 for further details.

2 Glow plugs – testing, removal and refitting

Testing

1 If the system malfunctions, testing is ultimately by substitution of known good units, but some preliminary checks may be made as follows.

2 Connect a voltmeter or 12 volt test light between the glow plug supply cable and earth (engine or vehicle metal). Make sure that the live connection is kept clear of the engine and bodywork.

3 Have an assistant switch on the ignition and check that voltage is applied to the glow plugs. Note that, after a certain number of seconds, the system cuts out automatically if the engine is not started, to prevent battery drain. Switch off the ignition.

4 If an ammeter of suitable range (0 to 50 amp approx) is available, connect it between the glow plug feed wire and the busbar (the wire which connects the four plugs together). During the preheating period, the ammeter should show a current draw of approximately 8 amps per working plug, ie, 32 amps if all four plugs are working. If one or more plugs appear not to be drawing current, remove the busbar and check each plug separately with a continuity tester or self-powered test light.

5 If there is no supply at all to the glow plugs, the associated wiring may be at fault. Otherwise, this points to a defective cylinder head temperature sensor (see Chapter 4B, Section 8), or to a problem with the powertrain control module (PCM).

6 To locate a defective glow plug, disconnect the main feed wire and the interconnecting busbar from the top of the glow plugs. Be careful not to drop the nuts and washers.

7 Use a continuity tester, or a 12 volt test light connected to the battery positive terminal, to check for continuity between each glow plug terminal and earth. The resistance of a glow plug in good condition is very low (less than 1 ohm), so if the test light does not come on or the continuity tester shows a high resistance, the glow plug is certainly defective.

8 If an ammeter is available, the current draw of each glow plug can be checked. After an initial surge of around 15 to 20 amps, each plug should draw around 10 amps. Any plug which draws much more or less than this is probably defective.

9 As a final check the glow plugs can be removed and inspected as described below.

Removal

Warning: If the glow plug (preheating) system has just been energised, or if the engine has recently been running, the glow plugs may be extremely hot.

10 Ensure that the ignition is switched off (take out the key). Disconnect the battery negative lead, and position the lead away from the battery (also see *Disconnecting the battery*).

11 Withdraw the engine oil dipstick and unclip the engine plastic cover.

12 Remove the inlet manifold as described in Chapter 2C.

13 Unscrew the nut securing each glow plug connector, then lift the wiring away from the plugs **(see illustration)**. Note that the wiring need not be removed completely for access to the plugs.

14 Unscrew the glow plugs, and remove them from the engine for inspection **(see illustration)**.

15 Inspect the glow plug stems for signs of damage. A badly burned or charred stem may be an indication of a faulty fuel injector – consult a diesel specialist for advice if necessary. Otherwise, if one plug is found to be faulty and the engine has completed a high mileage, it is probably worth renewing all four plugs as a set.

Refitting

16 Refitting is a reversal of removal, noting the following points:

a) Apply a little anti-seize compound (or copper brake grease) to the glow plug threads.

b) Make sure when remaking the glow plug wiring connections that the contact surfaces are clean.

c) Tighten the glow plugs to the specified torque.

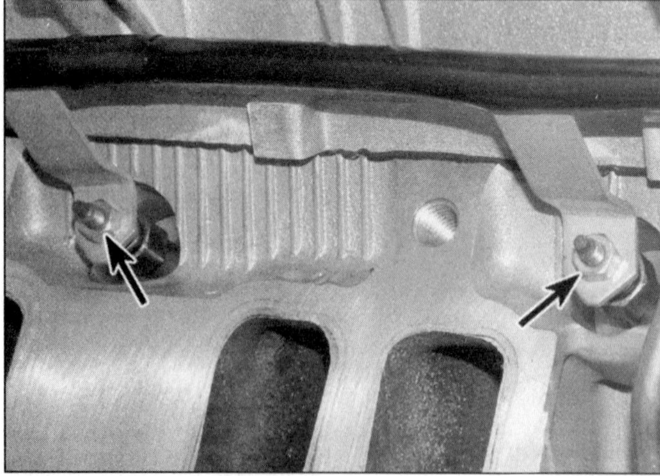

2.13 Unscrew the retaining nut (two of four arrowed) from each glow plug – inlet manifold removed for clarity

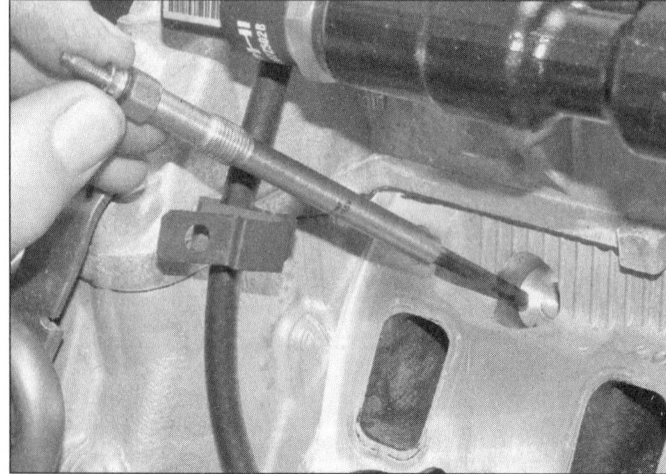

2.14 Remove the glow plug from the cylinder head – inlet manifold removed for clarity

Chapter 6
Clutch

Contents

Degrees of difficulty

Easy, suitable for novice with little experience 	**Fairly easy,** suitable for beginner with some experience	**Fairly difficult,** suitable for competent DIY mechanic	**Difficult,** suitable for experienced DIY mechanic	**Very difficult,** suitable for expert DIY or professional

Specifications

General

Type	Single dry plate, hydraulically-operated with automatic adjustment
Disc diameter:	
Petrol engines:	
1.8 and 2.0 litre	228 mm
2.5 and 3.0 litre	240 mm
Diesel engines	228 mm
Lining thickness:	
New	6.8 mm
Minimum (worn)	6.0 mm

Torque wrench settings

Torque wrench settings	Nm	lbf ft
Clutch cover to flywheel	29	21
Clutch master/slave cylinder mounting nuts/bolts	10	7
Clutch pedal retaining nut	23	17

1 General information

Models with manual transmission are fitted with a hydraulically-operated single dry plate clutch system. When the clutch pedal is depressed, effort is transmitted to the clutch release mechanism via a master cylinder at the pedal end, and a slave cylinder (which is combined with the release bearing) at the transmission end. The release mechanism transfers effort to the pressure plate diaphragm spring, which withdraws from the flywheel and releases the friction disc.

The flywheel is mounted on the crankshaft, with the pressure plate bolted to it. Removal of the flywheel is described in the appropriate part of Chapter 2.

Since many of the procedures covered in this Chapter involve working under the car, make sure that it is securely supported on axle stands placed on a firm, level floor (see *Jacking and vehicle support*).

Warning: The fluid used in the system is brake hydraulic fluid, which is poisonous. Take care to keep it off bare skin, and in particular not to get splashes in your eyes. The fluid also attacks paintwork, and may discolour carpets, etc – keep spillages to a minimum, and wash any off immediately with cold water. Finally, hydraulic fluid is highly inflammable, and should be handled with the same care as petrol.

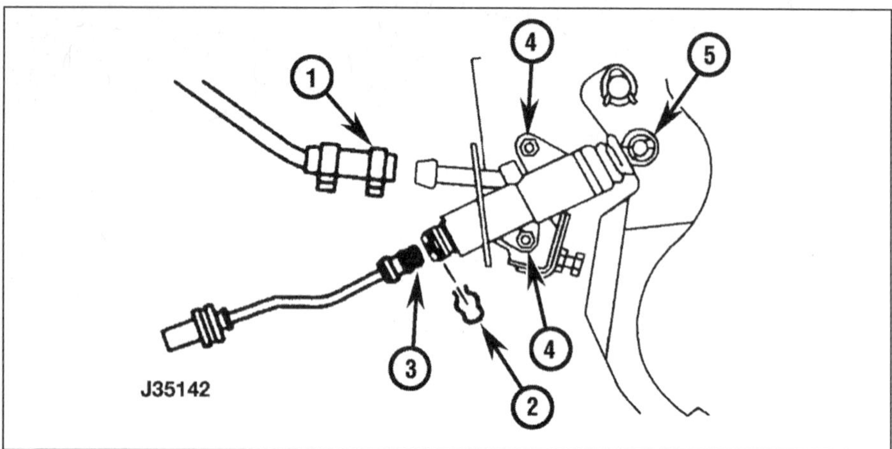

2.5 Clutch master cylinder and related fittings

1 Fluid supply (low-pressure) hose
2 Hose retaining clip
3 High-pressure fluid pipe
4 Master cylinder mounting nuts
5 Master cylinder-to-pedal circlip

2 Clutch – description and checking

Description

1 All manual transmission models are equipped with a single dry plate diaphragm spring clutch assembly. The cover assembly consists of a steel cover (dowelled and bolted to the rear face of the flywheel), the pressure plate, and a diaphragm spring.

2 The clutch friction disc is free to slide along the splines of the transmission input shaft, and is held in position between the flywheel and the pressure plate by the pressure of the diaphragm spring. Friction lining material is bonded or riveted to the friction disc (driven plate), which has a spring-cushioned hub, to absorb transmission shocks and help ensure a smooth take-up of the drive.

3 The centrally-mounted clutch release bearing contacts the fingers of the diaphragm spring. Depressing the clutch pedal pushes the release bearing against the diaphragm fingers, so moving the centre of the diaphragm spring inwards. As the centre of the spring is pushed inwards, the outside of the spring pivots outwards, so moving the pressure plate backwards and disengaging its grip on the friction disc.

4 When the pedal is released, the diaphragm spring forces the pressure plate back into contact with the linings on the clutch friction disc. The disc is now firmly held between the pressure plate and the flywheel, thus transmitting engine power to the transmission.

5 The clutch is hydraulically-operated and has a master cylinder mounted behind the clutch pedal, it takes its hydraulic fluid supply from a chamber in the brake fluid reservoir **(see illustration)**.

6 Depressing the clutch pedal operates the master cylinder pushrod, and the fluid pressure is transferred along the fluid lines to a slave cylinder mounted inside the transmission bellhousing **(see illustration)**.

7 The slave cylinder is incorporated into the release bearing – when the slave cylinder operates, the release bearing moves against the diaphragm spring fingers and disengages the clutch.

8 The hydraulic clutch is self-adjusting.

Checking

9 The following checks may be performed to diagnose a clutch problem:

a) Check the fluid lines from the clutch master cylinder into the bellhousing for damage, signs of leakage, or for kinks or dents which might restrict fluid flow.
b) Slow or poor operation may be due to air being present in the fluid. The system can be bled of air as described in Section 7.
c) Check the clutch pedal for excessive wear of the bushes (where applicable), and for any obstructions which may restrict the pedal movement.

2.6 Clutch release bearing (arrowed) is combined with the slave cylinder

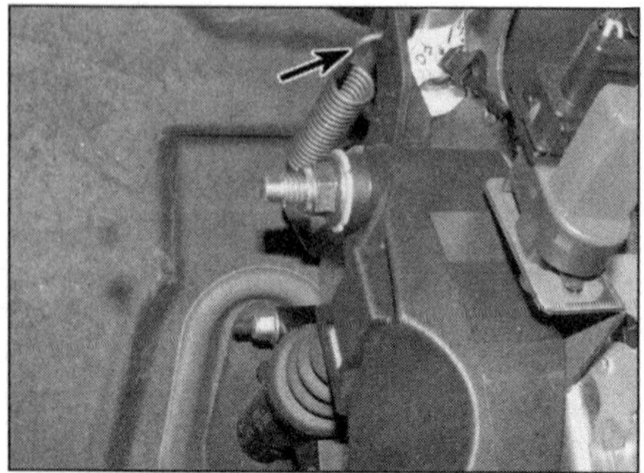

3.3 Unhook the clutch pedal return spring (arrowed) from the bracket

3 Clutch master cylinder – removal and refitting

Note: *Refer to the warning in Section 1 concerning the dangers of hydraulic fluid before proceeding.*

Removal

1 Disconnect the battery negative (earth) lead (refer to *Disconnecting the battery* at the end of this manual).

2 Working inside the car, move the driver's seat fully to the rear, to allow maximum working area. Remove the driver's side lower facia trim panel, which is secured by four screws and two upper clips. Where applicable, unclip the diagnostic connector plug from the panel, and/or disconnect the wiring from the climate control sensor as the panel is removed.

3 Twist the clutch pedal position switch(es) and detach it from the pedal bracket. Depending on model, release either the clutch pedal return spring (5-speed models, at the top) or the clutch pedal support spring (6-speed models, at the side) from the retaining bracket **(see illustration)**.

4 Before proceeding, anticipate some spillage of hydraulic (brake) fluid – most will occur on the engine compartment side but if sufficient fluid comes into contact with the carpet, it may be discoloured or worse. Place a good quantity of clean rags below the clutch pedal, and have a container ready in the engine compartment.

5 Remove the brake fluid reservoir cap, and then tighten it down over a piece of polythene or cling film, to obtain an airtight seal. This may help to reduce the spillage of fluid when the lines are disconnected.

6 To gain access to the fluid connections where they pass through the engine compartment bulkhead, move any wiring and hoses to one side as necessary. On 4-cylinder models, remove the air cleaner inlet hose and plenum chamber as described in the relevant Part of Chapter 4. On V6 models, it may be necessary to remove the upper section of the inlet manifold as described in Chapter 2B.

7 Working in the engine compartment, release the hose clip and disconnect the (upper) fluid supply hose from the clutch master cylinder **(see illustration)**. Plug or clamp the hose end if possible, to reduce fluid loss and to prevent dirt entry.

8 To remove the (lower) fluid pipe, pull out the spring clip to the side, then pull the pipe fitting out of the base of the cylinder **(see illustration)**. Again, plug or tape over the pipe end, to avoid losing fluid, and to prevent dirt entry.

9 Returning to the driver's footwell, undo the two mounting nuts from the clutch master cylinder **(see illustration)**.

10 Undo the clutch pedal retaining nut **(see illustration)** and remove the pedal complete with the clutch master cylinder. Release the retaining clip and detach the master cylinder from the clutch pedal. Take care to avoid spilling any remaining fluid onto the interior fittings.

Refitting

11 Refitting is a reversal of removal, noting the following points:

- *a) Tighten the mounting nuts to the specified torque.*
- *b) Use new clips when refitting the fluid feed hose.*
- *c) Refit any components removed for access.*
- *d) Remove the polythene from under the fluid reservoir cap, and top-up the fluid level (see Weekly checks).*
- *e) Refer to Section 7 and bleed the clutch hydraulic system.*
- *f) If the fluid level in the reservoir fell sufficiently, it may be necessary to bleed the braking system also – refer to Chapter 9.*

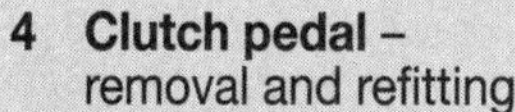

4 Clutch pedal – removal and refitting

Removal

1 Disconnect the battery negative (earth) lead (refer to *Disconnecting the battery* at the end of this manual).

2 Working inside the car, move the driver's seat fully to the rear, to allow maximum working area. Remove the driver's side lower facia trim panel, which is secured by four screws and two upper clips. Where applicable, unclip the diagnostic connector plug from the panel, and/or disconnect the wiring from the climate control sensor as the panel is removed.

3 Twist the clutch pedal position switch and detach it from the pedal bracket. Depending on model, release either the clutch pedal return spring (5-speed models, at the top) or the clutch pedal support spring (6-speed models, at the side) from the retaining bracket **(see illustration 3.3)**.

4 Where possible, prise off the circlip which secures the clutch master cylinder to the clutch pedal. **Note:** *It may be necessary to remove the pedal complete with master cylinder as described in Section 3.*

5 Undo the clutch pedal retaining nut and remove the pedal from the pivot shaft **(see illustration 3.10)**.

3.7 Release the hose clip (arrowed) and disconnect the fluid supply hose

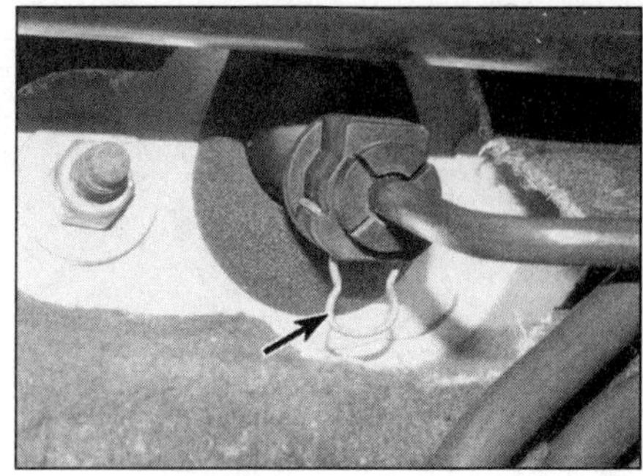

3.8 Withdraw the spring clip (arrowed) and disconnect the pipe

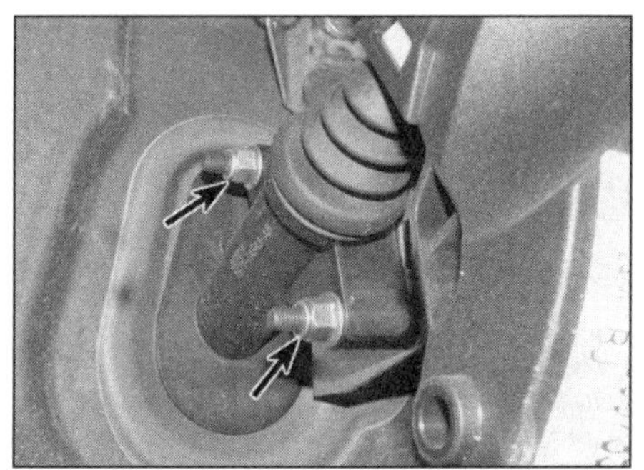

3.9 Undo the two clutch master cylinder mounting nuts (arrowed)

3.10 Undo the clutch pedal retaining nut (arrowed)

Refitting

6 Prior to refitting the pedal, apply a little grease to the pivot shaft.

7 Refitting is a reversal of the removal procedure, making sure that any bushes or spacers (where applicable) are correctly located.

8 If the master cylinder was removed with the clutch pedal, refit as described in Section 3.

5 Clutch components – removal, inspection and refitting

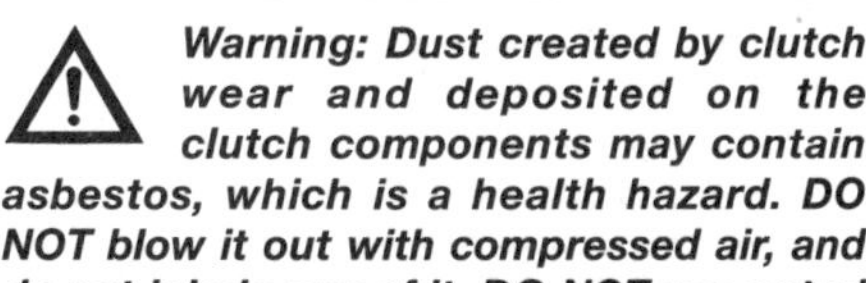

Warning: Dust created by clutch wear and deposited on the clutch components may contain asbestos, which is a health hazard. DO NOT blow it out with compressed air, and do not inhale any of it. DO NOT use petrol or petroleum-based solvents to clean off the dust. Brake system cleaner or methylated spirit should be used to flush the dust into a suitable receptacle. After the clutch components are wiped clean with rags, dispose of the contaminated rags and cleaner in a sealed, marked container.

5.3a Unscrewing the clutch cover bolts . . .

Removal

1 Access to the clutch may be gained in one of two ways. The engine and transmission can be removed together, as described in Chapter 2D, and the transmission separated from the engine on the bench. Alternatively, the engine may be left in the car and the transmission removed independently, as described in Chapter 7A.

2 Having separated the transmission from the engine, check if there are any marks identifying the relation of the clutch cover to the flywheel. If not, make your own marks using a dab of paint or a scriber. These marks will be used if the original cover is refitted, and will help to maintain the balance of the unit. A new cover may be fitted in any position allowed by the locating dowels.

3 Unscrew and remove the six clutch cover retaining bolts, working in a diagonal sequence, and slackening the bolts only a turn at a time. If necessary, the flywheel may be held stationary using a home-made locking tool **(see illustrations)** or a wide-bladed screwdriver, inserted in the teeth of the starter ring gear and resting against part of the cylinder block.

4 Ease the clutch cover off its locating

5.3b . . . using a home-made locking tool to hold the flywheel

5.8 Examine the fingers of the diaphragm spring for wear or scoring

dowels. Be prepared to catch the friction disc, which will drop out as the cover is removed. Note which way round the disc is fitted.

Inspection

5 The most common problem which occurs in the clutch is wear of the friction disc. However, all the clutch components should be inspected at this time, particularly if the engine has covered a high mileage. Unless the clutch components are known to be virtually new, it is worth renewing them all as a set (disc, pressure plate and release bearing). Renewing a worn friction disc by itself is not always satisfactory, especially if the old disc was slipping and causing the pressure plate to overheat.

6 Examine the linings of the friction disc for wear, and the disc hub and rim for distortion, cracks, broken torsion springs, and worn splines. The surface of the friction linings may be highly glazed, but as long as the friction material pattern can be clearly seen (and the thickness of the lining is within the specifications at the beginning of this Chapter), this is satisfactory. The disc must be renewed if the lining thickness has worn down to the minimum thickness in the specifications.

7 If there is any sign of oil contamination, indicated by shiny black discoloration, the disc must be renewed, and the source of the contamination traced and rectified. This will be a leaking crankshaft oil seal or transmission input shaft oil seal. The renewal procedure for the former is given in the relevant Part of Chapter 2. Renewal of the transmission input shaft oil seal is given in Chapter 7A.

8 Check the machined faces of the flywheel and pressure plate. If either is grooved, or heavily scored, renewal is necessary. The pressure plate must also be renewed if any cracks are apparent, or if the diaphragm spring is damaged or its pressure suspect. Pay particular attention to the tips of the spring fingers **(see illustration)**, where the release bearing acts upon them.

9 With the transmission removed, it is also advisable to check the condition of the release bearing, as described in Section 6. Having got this far, it is almost certainly worth renewing it.

Refitting

10 It is important that no oil or grease is allowed to come into contact with the friction material of the clutch disc or the pressure plate and flywheel faces. To ensure this, it is advisable to refit the clutch assembly with clean hands, and to wipe down the pressure plate and flywheel faces with a clean dry rag before assembly begins.

11 Ford technicians use a special tool for centralising the friction disc at this stage. The tool holds the disc centrally on the pressure plate, and locates in the middle of the diaphragm spring fingers **(see illustration)**. If the tool is not available, it will be necessary to centralise the disc after assembling the cover loosely on the flywheel, as described in the following paragraphs.

12 Place the friction disc against the flywheel, ensuring that it is the right way round. It should be marked TRANS-SIDE, but if not, position it so that the raised hub with the cushion springs is facing away from the flywheel **(see illustration)**.

5.11 Using a clutch-aligning tool to centralise the clutch friction disc

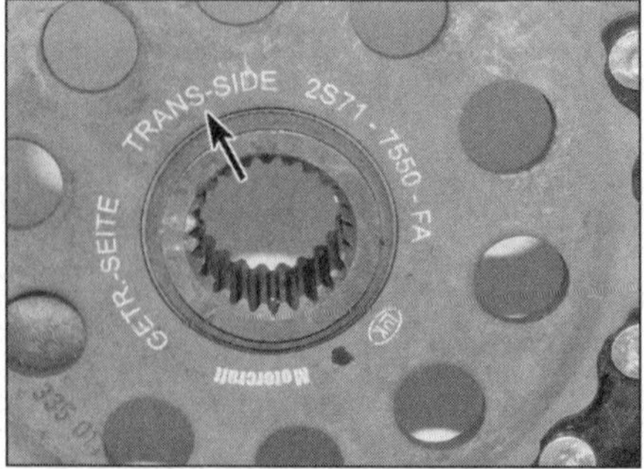

5.12 Transmission side TRANS-SIDE marking on the clutch friction disc

13 Place the clutch cover over the dowels. Refit the retaining bolts, and tighten them finger-tight so that the friction disc is gripped lightly, but can still be moved.

14 The friction disc must now be centralised so that, when the engine and transmission are mated, the splines of the transmission input shaft will pass through the splines in the centre of the disc hub.

15 Centralisation can be carried out by inserting a round bar through the hole in the centre of the friction disc, so that the end of the bar rests in the hole in the rear end of the crankshaft. Move the bar sideways or up-and-down, to move the disc in whichever direction is necessary to achieve centralisation. Centralisation can then be checked by removing the bar and viewing the friction disc hub in relation to the diaphragm spring fingers, or by viewing through the side apertures of the cover, and checking that the disc is central in relation to the outer edge of the pressure plate.

16 An alternative and more accurate method of centralisation is to use a commercially-available clutch-aligning tool, obtainable from most accessory shops **(see illustration 5.11)**.

17 Once the clutch is centralised, progressively tighten the cover bolts in a diagonal sequence to the torque setting given in the Specifications.

18 Ensure that the input shaft splines, clutch disc splines and release bearing guide sleeve are clean. Apply a thin smear of high melting-point grease to the input shaft splines.

19 Refit the transmission to the engine as described in Chapter 7A.

6 Clutch release bearing (and slave cylinder) – removal, inspection and refitting

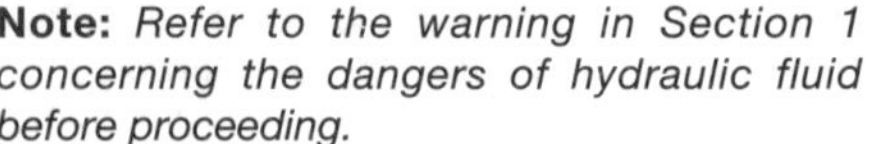

Note: *Refer to the warning in Section 1 concerning the dangers of hydraulic fluid before proceeding.*

Removal

1 Remove the transmission as described in Chapter 7A.

2 The release bearing and slave cylinder are combined into one unit, which is located in the bellhousing of the transmission.

3 Remove the bleed screw dust cap, and prise out the grommet from the top of the transmission housing **(see illustrations)**.

4 Remove the three mounting bolts, and withdraw the slave cylinder and release bearing from the transmission input shaft **(see illustrations)**.

Inspection

5 Check the bearing for smoothness of operation, and renew it if there is any sign

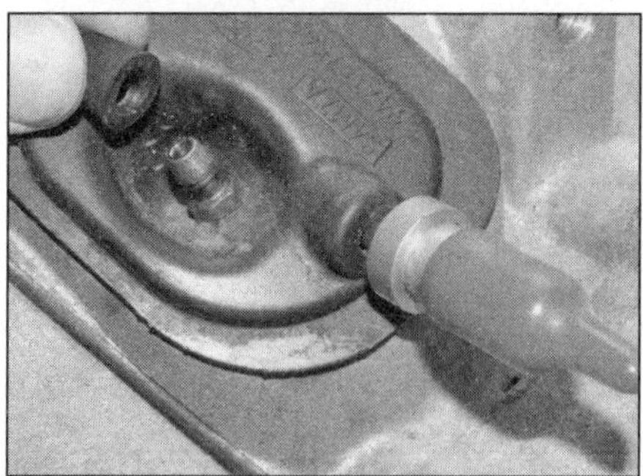
6.3a Take off the bleed screw cap . . .

6.3b . . . then prise out the grommet from the transmission housing

6.4a Remove the three mounting bolts (arrowed) . . .

6.4b . . . and withdraw the slave cylinder/ release bearing assembly

6.7a Renew the large O-ring on the slave cylinder . . .

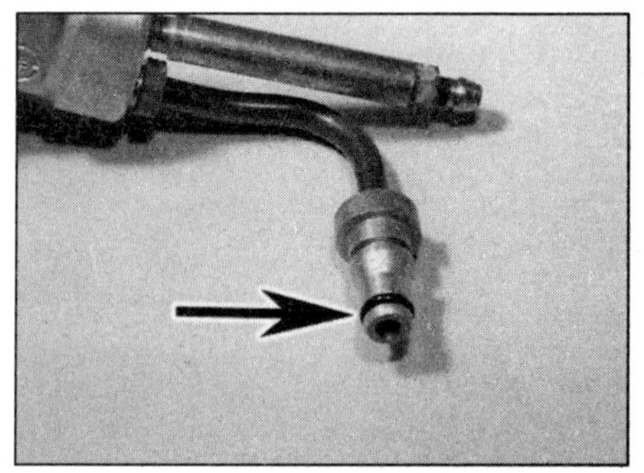
6.7b . . . and of the smaller pipe connection O-rings

of harshness or roughness as the bearing is spun. Do not attempt to dismantle, clean or lubricate the bearing.

6 Repair kits are not available from Ford. If a fault develops, the complete cylinder/release bearing must be renewed. **Note:** *Cylinder assemblies should be supplied with an input shaft seal already fitted. If not, refer to Chapter 7A and fit a new seal.*

7 Check the condition of all seals, and renew if necessary **(see illustrations)**. Considering the difficulty in gaining access to some of the seals if they fail, it would be wise to renew these as a precaution.

Refitting

8 Refitting of the clutch release bearing is a reversal of the removal procedure, noting the following points:

a) Renew the cylinder-to-transmission casing O-ring seal.
b) Tighten the mounting bolts to the specified torque.
c) Refit the transmission as described in Chapter 7A.
d) Bleed the system as described in Section 7.

7 Clutch hydraulic system – bleeding

Note: *Refer to the warning in Section 1 concerning the dangers of hydraulic fluid before proceeding.*

1 The clutch hydraulic system will not normally require bleeding, and this task should only be necessary when the system has been opened for repair work. However, as with the brake pedal, if the clutch pedal feels at all soggy or unresponsive in operation, this may indicate the need for bleeding.

2 The system bleed screw is located on top of the transmission bellhousing.

3 Where applicable, remove the battery as described in Chapter 5A, and the air cleaner as described in the relevant Part of Chapter 4. Move the pipework and wiring harness to one side as necessary to reach the access cover.

4 Remove the bleed screw cap **(see illustration 6.3a)**.

5 Bleeding the clutch is much the same as bleeding the brakes – refer to Chapter 9. Ensure that the level in the brake fluid reservoir is maintained well above the MIN mark at all times, otherwise the clutch and brake hydraulic systems will both need bleeding.

6 If conventional bleeding does not work, it may be necessary to use a vacuum pump kit: Ford tool 416-D001 (23-036A). Syphon some of the fluid out of the reservoir until the level is at the MIN mark, remove the bleed screw dust cap and connect the hose from the hand pump. Fill the hand pump reservoir with new hydraulic fluid, open the bleed screw, and pump the fluid backwards through the slave cylinder/release bearing up to the reservoir until it reaches its MAX mark.

7 On completion, tighten the bleed screw securely, and top-up the brake fluid level to the MAX mark. If possible, test the operation of the clutch before refitting all the components removed for access.

8 Failure to bleed correctly may point to a leak in the system, or to a worn master or slave cylinder. At the time of writing, it appears that the master and slave cylinders are only available as complete assemblies – overhaul is not possible.

Chapter 7 Part A: Manual transmission

Contents

Degrees of difficulty

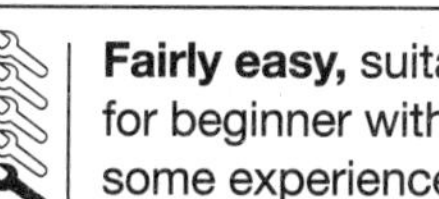

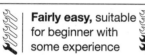

Easy, suitable for novice with little experience	**Fairly easy,** suitable for beginner with some experience	**Fairly difficult,** suitable for competent DIY mechanic	**Difficult,** suitable for experienced DIY mechanic	**Very difficult,** suitable for expert DIY or professional

Specifications

General

Type	Manual, five or six forward gears and reverse. Synchromesh on all forward gears
Identification code:	
Five-speed transmission	MTX-75
Six-speed transmission	MMT-6 (Durashift)

Lubrication

Recommended oil	See *Lubricants and fluids* on page 0•18
Capacity:	
5-speed	1.9 litres
6-speed	1.75 litres

Torque wrench settings

	Nm	lbf ft
Driveshaft/hub retaining nut*	290	214
Gear lever assembly to floor	10	7
Gearchange linkage to selector shaft	23	17
Transmission filler/drain plugs:		
5-speed	45	33
6-speed	35	26
Transmission mounting bracket	90	66
Transmission mounting centre nut*	133	98
Transmission mounting outer nuts*	48	35
Transmission to engine	48	35

* *Use new nuts*

1 General information

The manual transmission is a compact, two-piece, lightweight aluminium alloy housing, containing both the transmission and differential assemblies.

Because of the complexity, possible unavailability of parts and special tools necessary, internal repair procedures for the manual transmission are not recommended for the home mechanic. For readers who wish to tackle a transmission rebuild, brief notes on overhaul are provided in Section 10. The bulk of the information in this Chapter is devoted to removal and refitting procedures.

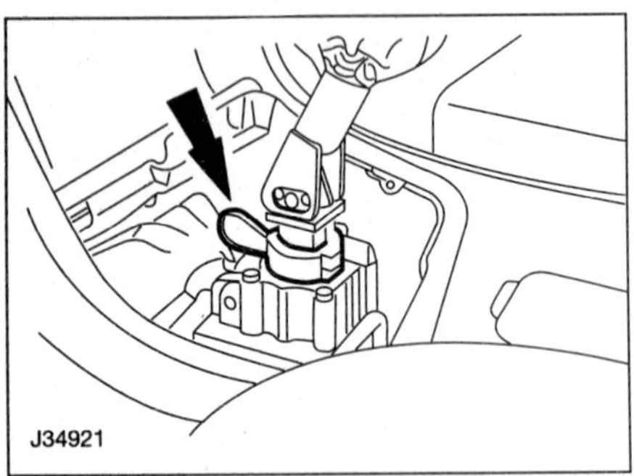

2.3 Ford special tool used to lock the gear lever in neutral (5-speed)

2 Gearchange cables – adjustment

5-speed

Note: *The special Ford tool 308-436 (16-097) will be required in order to carry out the following adjustment. This tool locks the gear lever in the neutral position during adjustment. If the tool is not available, adjustment is still possible by proceeding on a trial-and-error basis, preferably with the help of an assistant to hold the gear lever in the neutral position.*

1 Disconnect the battery negative (earth) lead

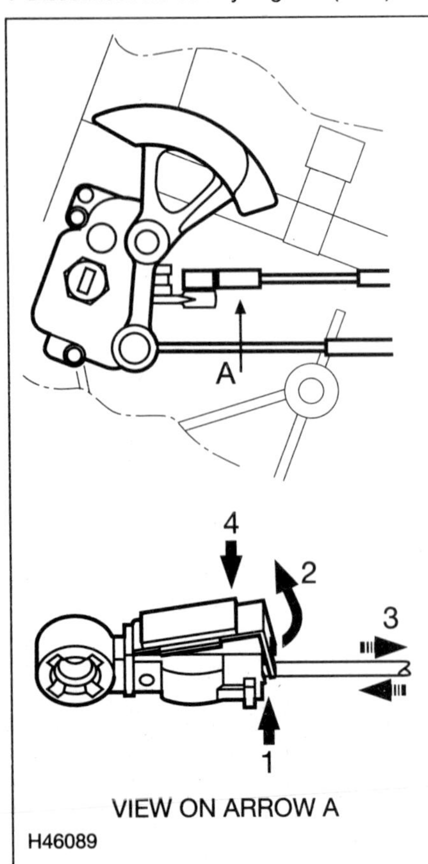

2.15 Releasing the selector lever locking clip (6-speed)

2.5 Disengage the red plastic locking slider (arrowed) to adjust the cable (5-speed)

(refer to *Disconnecting the battery* at the end of this manual) and check the gear lever is the neutral position.

2 Inside the car, prise up the gear lever trim panel at the rear to release the clips, then pull it backwards to release the front clips. Release the gaiter from the gear knob, and lift the panel off. Remove the foam insulation pad around the base of the lever.

3 Lock the gear lever in neutral using the special tool **(see illustration)**.

4 Apply the handbrake, then jack up the front of the car and support it on axle stands (see *Jacking and vehicle support*).

5 On the transmission, release the adjusters on the cables by disengaging the red plastic locking sliders from the cable **(see illustration)**.

6 Make sure that the levers on the transmission are both in the neutral position, then lock the red plastic locking sliders by pressing them back into the cable.

7 Remove the special tool, and check the gear lever can select all the gears.

8 Refit the gaiter and trim to the gearchange lever.

9 Reconnect the battery negative (earth) lead.

6-speed

Note: *The special Ford tool 308-451 will be required in order to carry out the following adjustment. This tool locks the gear lever in the neutral position during adjustment. If the tool is not available, adjustment is still possible by proceeding on a trial-and-error basis, preferably with the help of an assistant to hold the gear lever in the neutral position.*

10 Check the gear lever is the neutral position.

11 Inside the car, prise up the gear lever trim panel at the rear to release the clips, then pull it backwards to release the front clips. Release the gaiter from the gear knob, and lift the panel off. Remove the foam insulation pad around the base of the lever.

12 Lock the gear lever in neutral using the special tool.

13 Remove the air cleaner assembly as described in Chapter 4A or 4B.

14 Using the transmission lever, select 4th gear at the transmission. If necessary, temporarily remove the special tool and have an assistant select 4th gear using the gear lever, while you watch the transmission levers.

15 Ensure that the special tool is in place, locking the gear lever inside the car in neutral. Release the locking clip on the (grey) selector cable only, by pressing the tab inwards at the base, then lifting it up **(see illustration)**.

16 Now the selector cable is released, move it gently in and out of the locking clip until it is settled in place. Lock the cable by pressing the clip down and in at the base.

17 Refit the air cleaner, referring to Chapter 4A or 4B if necessary.

18 Remove the special tool from the gear lever, and refit the gaiter trim panel.

19 Drive the car, and check for correct gear selection. Repeat the adjustment procedure if necessary.

3 Gearchange lever – removal and refitting

Removal

1 Disconnect the battery negative (earth) lead (refer to *Disconnecting the battery* at the end of this manual).

2 Apply the handbrake, then jack up the front of the car and support it on axle stands (see *Jacking and vehicle support*).

3 Where applicable, remove the engine undershield.

4 If required, remove the relevant front part of the exhaust (as described in Chapter 4A or 4B), to gain access to the underside of the gear lever.

5 On petrol models, remove the exhaust front heat shield, disconnecting the oxygen sensor cable on removal.

6 Unscrew the retaining nuts and release the lever assembly from the floor **(see illustration)**.

7 Inside the car, prise up the gear lever trim panel at the rear to release the clips, then pull it backwards to release the front clips. Release the gaiter from the gear knob, and lift the panel off. Remove the foam insulation pad around the base of the lever.

8 Press the side button in to release the cable end fittings from the gear lever stubs – note their fitted locations, then detach the

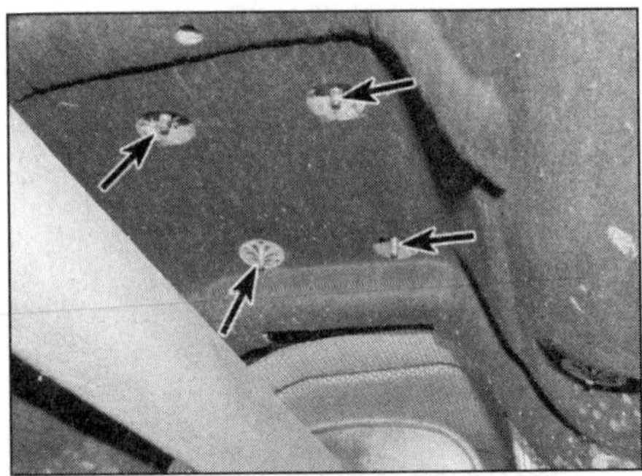

3.6 Unscrew the retaining nuts (arrowed) to release the lever assembly

cable ferrules from the bracket by turning the serrated collars clockwise **(see illustrations)**.

9 Withdraw the gearchange linkage/lever assembly out from the centre console **(see illustration)**.

Refitting

10 Refitting is a reversal of removal, noting the following points:

a) Fit new gasket between the gear lever assembly and the floor.

b) Fit new gear lever assembly retaining nuts.

c) If required, adjust the cables as described in Section 2.

3.8a Press the side button (arrowed) in . . .

3.8b . . . and release the cable from the gear lever stub

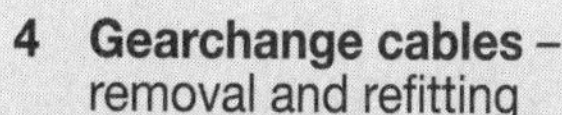

4 Gearchange cables – removal and refitting

Removal

5-speed models

1 The cables are located on the front of the transmission, and access is best from below.

2 Apply the handbrake, then jack up the front of the car and support it on axle stands (see *Jacking and vehicle support*).

3 At the transmission, remove the cables from the support brackets by twisting the spring-loaded knurled collars anti-clockwise. On the 5-speed units, the gearchange cable is white, and the selector cable is black. Press the retaining button at the end of the cables and release them from the transmission lever balljoints – note their fitted locations. Withdraw the cables downwards from the engine compartment **(see illustrations)**.

4 Detach the cables from the retaining clips on the subframe.

6-speed models

5 The cables are on top of the transmission, and access is from above **(see illustration)**.

6 Remove the air cleaner as described in Chapter 4A or 4B.

7 The gearchange cable is black, with the selector cable grey. Disconnect the cables from the ball-and-socket joints on the transmission levers, then further down the cable, squeeze the tabs to disconnect the cables from the support bracket.

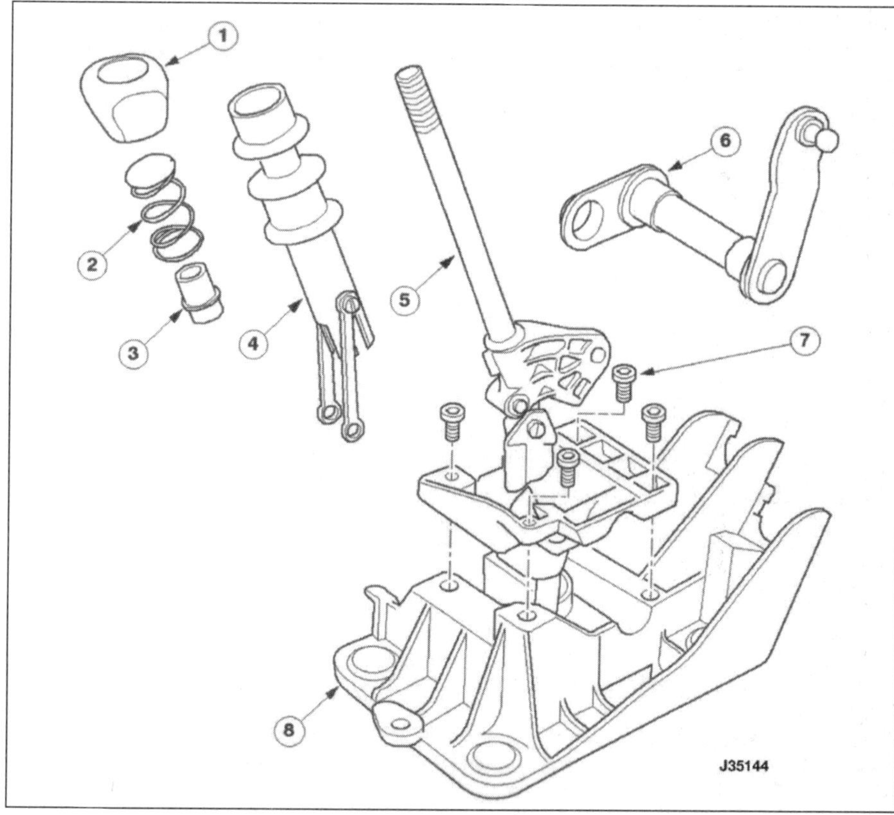

3.9 Gearchange lever and housing

1 Gearshift lever knob
2 Compression spring
3 Spring damper
4 Reverse gear release
5 Gearshift lever/linkage
6 Selector lever
7 Self-tapping screws
8 Gearshift linkage lower housing

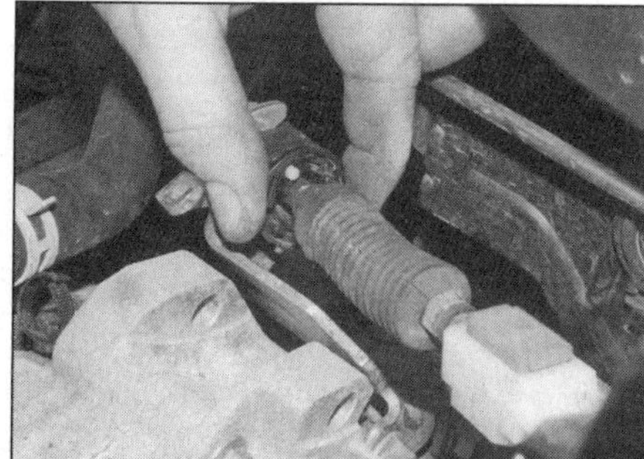

4.3a Twist the spring-loaded knurled collar anti-clockwise . . .

4.3b . . . and withdraw the outer cable from the retaining bracket . . .

4.3c . . . then press the button and release the cable from the transmission lever balljoints

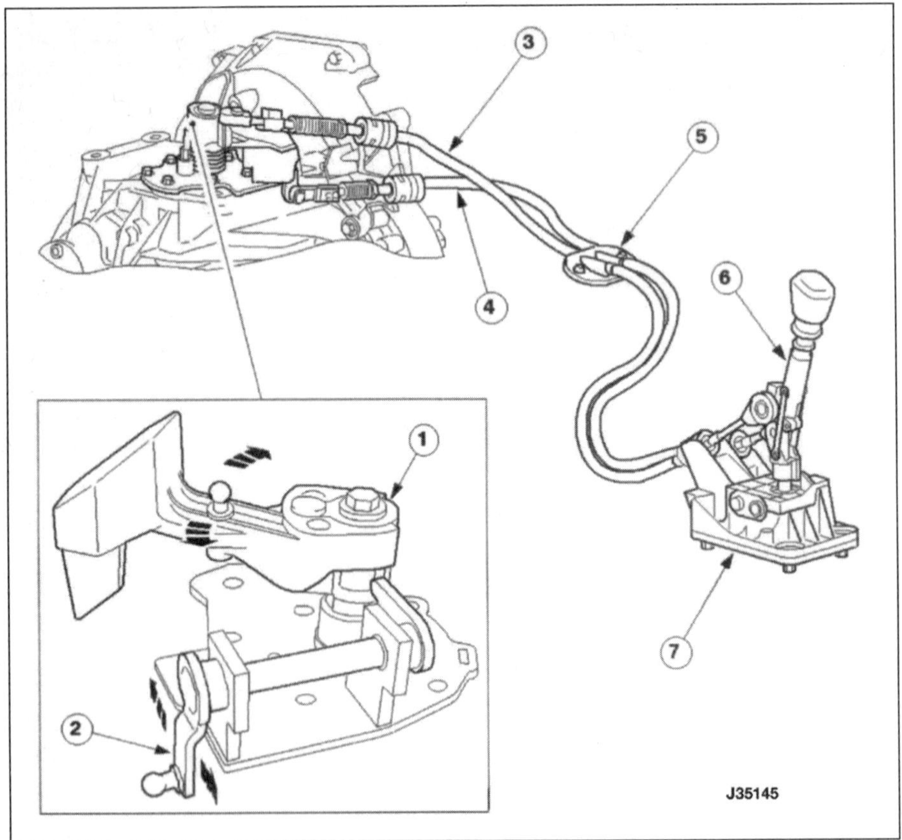

4.3d Gearchange mechanism and cables (5-speed)

1 *Shift lever*
2 *Selector lever*
3 *Shift cable (white)*
4 *Selector cable*
5 *Gearshift cable bushing*
6 *Gearshift lever*
7 *Gearshift linkage*

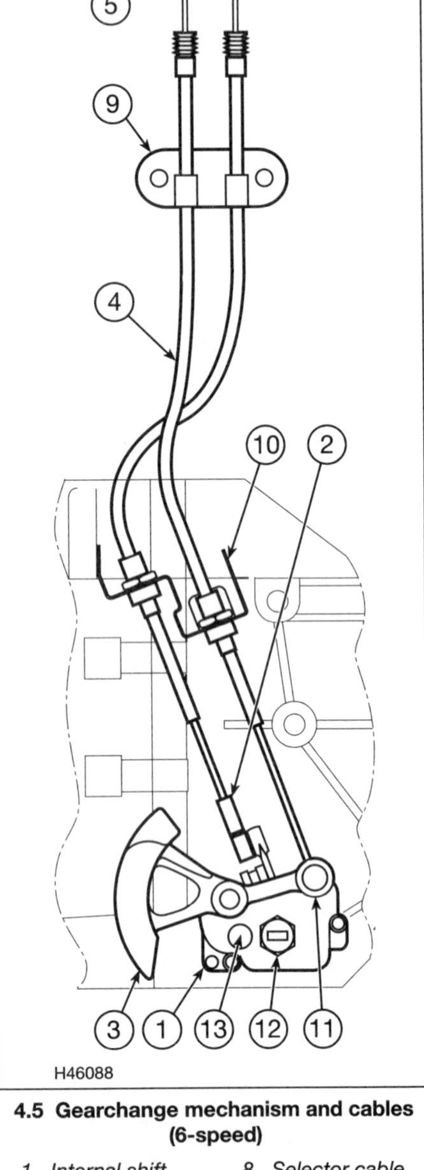

4.5 Gearchange mechanism and cables (6-speed)

1 *Internal shift mechanism*
2 *Selector cable adjuster*
3 *Counterbalance*
4 *Shift cable*
5 *Gear lever housing*
6 *Gear lever*
7 *Selector cable end fitting*
8 *Selector cable*
9 *Floor adapter plate*
10 *Mounting bracket*
11 *Shift cable end fitting*
12 *Reversing light switch*
13 *Transmission vent*

All models

8 Remove the centre console as described in Chapter 11.

9 Remove the gearchange lever assembly as described in Section 3.

10 Pull the carpet to one side (the carpet and insulation may need to be cut slightly to gain access to the cable retaining plate). Unscrew the nuts and release the adapter from the floor, then withdraw the cables through the bulkhead and into the car **(see illustration)**. **Note:** *Do not bend or kink the cables as damage to the cables may occur.*

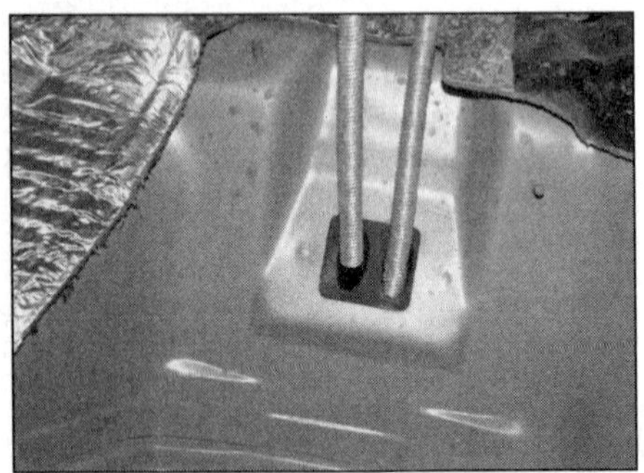

4.10 The cables pass through a rubber adapter in the lower part of the bulkhead

Refitting

11 Refitting is a reversal of removal. **Note:** *If required, adjust the cables as described in Section 2.*

5 Speedometer drive – general information

The Mondeo has an electronic speedometer. Previous models had the vehicle speed signal provided by a sensor attached to the transmission, but this sensor has now been deleted. Instead, the speed signal is generated by the car's ABS wheel sensors.

6 Oil seals – renewal

Differential oil seals

1 The differential oil seals are located at the sides of the transmission, where the driveshafts enter the transmission. If leakage at the seal is suspected, raise the car and support it securely on axle stands. If the seal is leaking, oil will be found on the side of the transmission below the driveshaft.

2 Refer to Chapter 8 and remove the appropriate driveshaft. If removing the right-hand driveshaft, it will be necessary to remove the intermediate shaft as well.

3 Using a large screwdriver or lever, carefully prise the oil seal out of the transmission casing, taking care not to damage the transmission casing **(see illustration)**. **Note:** *To improve access for the right-hand oil seal, it may be helpful to remove the front section of exhaust pipe (see relevant part of Chapter 4)*

4 Wipe clean the oil seal seating area in the transmission casing.

5 Apply a smear of grease to the outer lip of the new oil seal. Ensure the seal is correctly positioned, then press it a little way into the casing by hand, making sure that it is square to its seating.

6 Using suitable tubing or a large socket, carefully drive the oil seal into the casing until it contacts the seating **(see illustration)**.

7 Refit the driveshaft with reference to Chapter 8.

8 Check the oil level in the transmission as described in Chapter 1A or 1B.

Input shaft oil seal

9 The input shaft oil seal is fitted into the rear of the clutch slave cylinder/release bearing. Remove the clutch slave cylinder/release bearing as described in Chapter 6, Section 6.

10 Carefully prise the oil seal out of the slave cylinder using a flat-bladed screwdriver **(see illustration)**.

11 Wipe clean the oil seal seating area in the slave cylinder. Using suitable tubing or a large socket, carefully drive the oil seal into the casing until it contacts the seating **(see illustration)**.

12 Refit the slave cylinder/release bearing with reference to Chapter 6, Section 6.

6.3 Prise out the oil seal with a suitable lever

6.6 Using a socket to drive in the new seal

6.10 Prise the input shaft oil seal from the rear of the slave cylinder

6.11 Using a socket to drive in the new seal

7 Reversing light switch – removal and refitting

Removal

1 The reversing light circuit is controlled by a switch mounted on the gearchange bracket located on the top of the transmission casing.

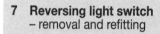

2 Remove the air cleaner as described in Chapter 4A or 4B.

3 Disconnect the wiring leading to the reversing light switch on the top of the gearchange bracket **(see illustration)**.

4 Unscrew the reversing light switch from the cover housing on the transmission.

Refitting

5 Refitting is a reversal of the removal procedure.

8 Transmission – removal and refitting

Note: *Read through this procedure before starting work to see what is involved, particularly in terms of lifting equipment. Depending on the facilities available, the home mechanic may prefer to remove the engine and transmission together, then separate them on the bench, as described in Chapter 2D.*

Removal

1 Remove the battery and its tray as described in Chapter 5A. Also remove the engine top cover.

2 If necessary, the bonnet may be removed as described in Chapter 11 for better access, and for fitting the engine lifting hoist.

3 Hold the radiator in its raised position by using cable-ties to fasten it to the upper crossmember. This is necessary to retain the radiator when the subframe is removed.

4 Remove the mass airflow sensor and air inlet duct with reference to Chapter 4A or 4B. On V6 models, remove the water pump pulley cover.

5 Remove the air cleaner assembly as described in Chapter 4A or 4B.

6 Unclip the plastic covers from the top of the suspension struts on both sides of the car, then slacken the top mounting retaining nuts by approximately four turns each **(see illustrations)**.

7.3 Disconnecting the wiring connector from the reversing light switch (arrowed)

8.6a Unclip the plastic covers . . .

8.6b . . . then slacken the retaining nuts by approximately four turns each

8.8 Undo the retaining bolt and remove the earth terminals

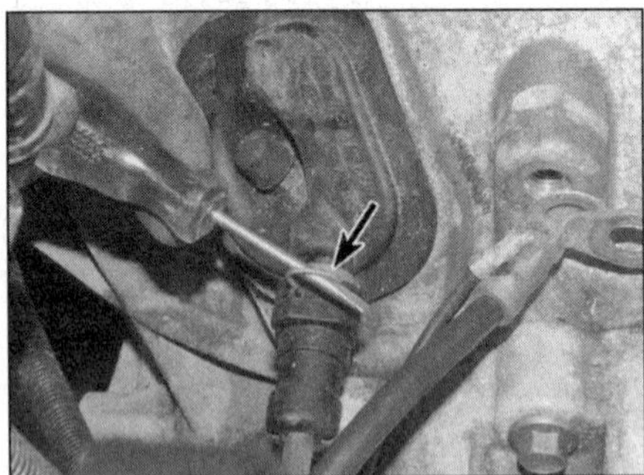
8.9a Prise out the retaining clip (arrowed) . . .

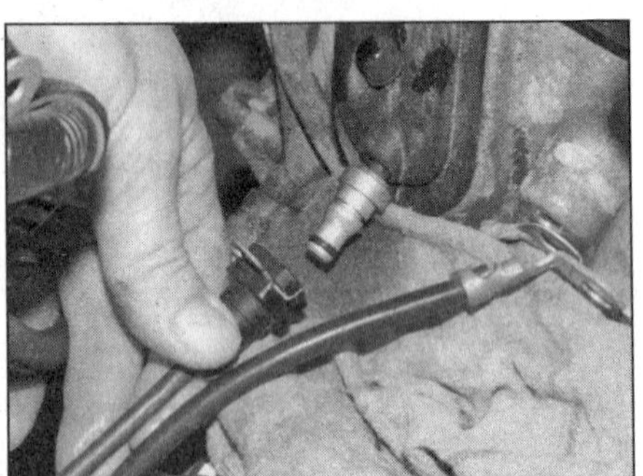
8.9b . . . and disconnect the clutch hydraulic pipe

8.16 Removing the centre retaining nut from the left-hand transmission mounting

7 Disconnect the wiring from the reversing light switch on the transmission.

8 Unscrew the bolt, and remove the earth terminal from the top of the transmission **(see illustration)**.

9 Using a small screwdriver, prise out the retaining clip and disconnect the clutch hydraulic pipe from the transmission (use a suitable clamp on the hydraulic flexible hose to prevent leaks) **(see illustrations).** Cover both the union and the pipe ends to minimise fluid loss and prevent the entry of dirt into the hydraulic system. **Note:** *Whilst the hydraulic hose/pipe is disconnected, DO NOT depress the clutch pedal.*

10 Apply the handbrake, and chock the rear wheels. Slacken both front roadwheel retaining bolts and, where accessible, the driveshaft hub bolts.

11 Jack up the front of the car and support it on axle stands. There must be sufficient clearance below the car for the transmission to be lowered and removed. Remove both front roadwheels and, where fitted, remove the engine undertray.

12 Drain the transmission or be prepared for some oil loss as the driveshafts are removed.

13 The engine and transmission must now be supported, as the left-hand mounting must be disconnected. Ford technicians use a support bar which locates in the tops of the inner wing panels – proprietary engine support bars are available from tool outlets.

14 If a support bar is not available, an engine hoist should be used. With an engine hoist the engine/transmission can be manoeuvred more easily and safely, balancing the engine on a jack is not recommended.

15 Remove the front subframe as described in Chapter 10.

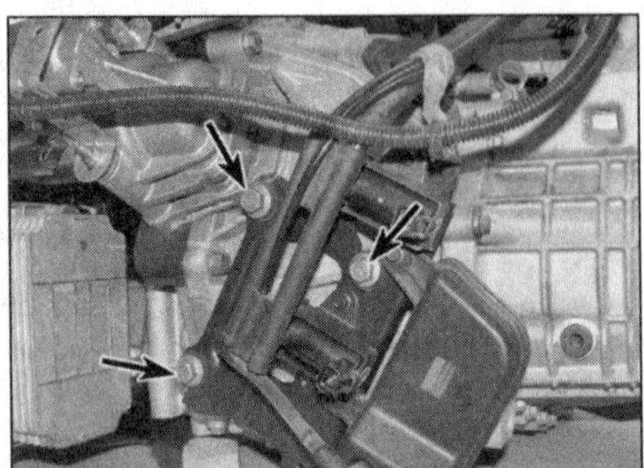
8.19 Undo the bolts (arrowed) to remove the vacuum regulator solenoid valve assembly (diesel models)

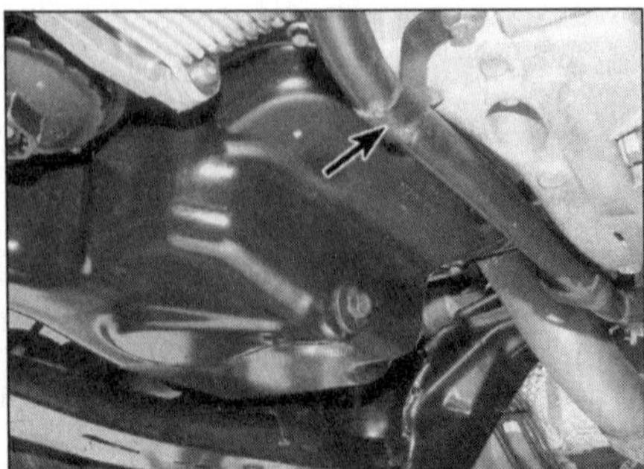
8.22 On diesel models, detach the coolant pipe (arrowed) under the transmission housing

16 Support the transmission with a trolley jack from below, then undo the retaining nut from the left-hand transmission mounting **(see illustration),** then undo the four retaining bolts and remove the mounting bracket from the top of the transmission housing.

17 Remove the gearchange cables from the support brackets by twisting the spring-loaded knurled collars anti-clockwise (see Section 4). Press the retaining clips at the end of the cables and release them from the transmission lever balljoints – note their fitted locations.

18 Remove the starter motor as described in Chapter 5A.

19 On diesel models, undo the three retaining bolts and remove the vacuum regulator solenoid valve assembly from the front of the transmission housing **(see illustration)**.

20 Remove the driveshafts as described in Chapter 8. Plug the transmission to prevent dirt ingress (or oil loss, if the oil has not been drained).

21 Working your way around the transmission casing, slacken and remove the transmission-to-engine securing bolts. Disconnect any wiring loom brackets, where applicable.

22 On diesel models, undo the two retaining bolts and detach the coolant pipe from under the transmission housing **(see illustration)**.

23 With the help of an assistant, withdraw the transmission squarely from the engine, taking care not to allow its weight to hang on the clutch friction disc. Once the transmission is free, lower the transmission on the jack and manoeuvre the unit out from under the car.

24 The clutch components can now be inspected with reference to Chapter 6, and renewed if necessary. (Unless they are virtually new, it is worth renewing the clutch components as a matter of course, even if the transmission has been removed for some other reason.)

Refitting

25 With the transmission secured on the trolley jack as on removal, raise it into position, and then carefully slide it onto the rear of the engine, at the same time engaging the input shaft with the clutch friction disc splines. Do not use excessive force to refit the transmission – if the input shaft does not slide into place easily, readjust the angle of the transmission so that it is level, and/or turn the input shaft so that the splines engage properly with the disc. If problems are still experienced, check that the clutch friction disc is correctly centred (Chapter 6).

26 The transmission is refitted by a reversal of the removal procedure, bearing in mind the following points:

a) *Tighten all nuts and bolts to the specified torque (where given).*
b) *If required, renew the differential oil seals as described in Section 6.*
c) *Refit the driveshafts as described in Chapter 8.*
d) *Refit the front subframe as described in Chapter 10*

e) Check the oil level in the transmission as described in Chapter 1A or 1B.
f) If required, adjust the gearchange cables as described in Section 2.

27 Make a final check that all connections have been made, and all bolts tightened fully. Road test the car to check for proper transmission operation, then check the transmission visually for leakage of oil.

9 Transmission mounting – checking and renewal

This procedure is covered in Chapter 2A, 2B or 2C.

10 Transmission overhaul – general information

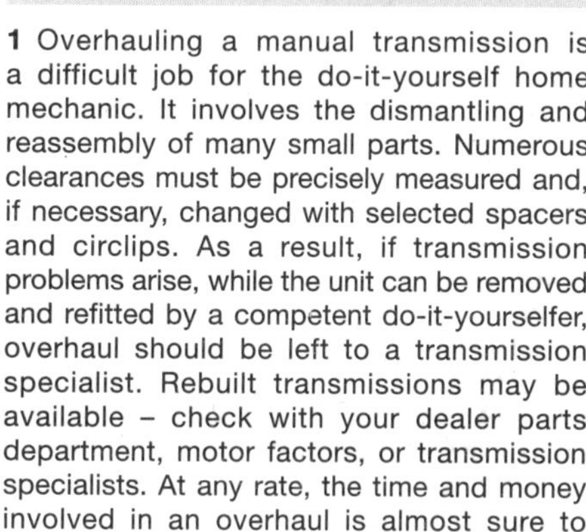

1 Overhauling a manual transmission is a difficult job for the do-it-yourself home mechanic. It involves the dismantling and reassembly of many small parts. Numerous clearances must be precisely measured and, if necessary, changed with selected spacers and circlips. As a result, if transmission problems arise, while the unit can be removed and refitted by a competent do-it-yourselfer, overhaul should be left to a transmission specialist. Rebuilt transmissions may be available – check with your dealer parts department, motor factors, or transmission specialists. At any rate, the time and money involved in an overhaul is almost sure to exceed the cost of a rebuilt unit.

2 Nevertheless, it's not impossible for an inexperienced mechanic to rebuild a transmission, providing the special tools are available, and the job is done in a deliberate step-by-step manner so nothing is overlooked.

3 The tools necessary for an overhaul include: internal and external circlip pliers, a bearing puller, a slide hammer, a set of pin punches, a dial test indicator, and possibly a hydraulic press. In addition, a large, sturdy workbench and a vice or transmission stand will be required.

4 During dismantling of the transmission, make careful notes of how each part comes off, where it fits in relation to other parts, and what holds it in place. Noting how they are fitted when you remove the parts will make it much easier to get the transmission back together.

11.4a Removing the drain plug for the transmission oil to drain (5-speed)

5 Before taking the transmission apart for repair, it will help if you have some idea what area of the transmission is malfunctioning. Certain problems can be closely tied to specific areas in the transmission, which can make component examination and renewal easier. Refer to the *Fault finding* Section at the end of this manual for information regarding possible sources of trouble.

11 Transmission oil – draining and refilling

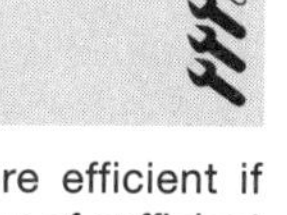

1 This operation is much more efficient if the car is first taken on a journey of sufficient length to warm the engine and transmission up to normal operating temperature.

Caution: If the procedure is to be carried out on when the transmission is hot, take care not to burn yourself on the hot exhaust or other components.

2 Park the car on level ground, switch off the ignition and apply the handbrake firmly. Jack up the front of the car and support it securely on axle stands. Undo the retaining bolts/nuts and remove the undertray (where applicable).

3 Wipe clean the area around the drain plug and position a suitable container underneath.

4 Unscrew the drain plug and allow the transmission oil to drain into the container **(see illustrations)**.

5 Allow the oil to drain completely into the container. If the oil is hot, take precautions against scalding.

6 Once the oil has finished draining, ensure the drain plug is clean and refit it to the transmission with a new washer. Tighten the drain plug to the specified torque. Lower the car to the ground.

7 The transmission is refilled through the level plug hole on the front of the transmission casing **(see illustration)**. Wipe clean the area around the level plug and unscrew it from the casing. Refill the transmission with the specified type and amount of oil given in the specifications, until the oil begins to trickle out of the level hole. Refit the plug and tighten it to the specified torque.

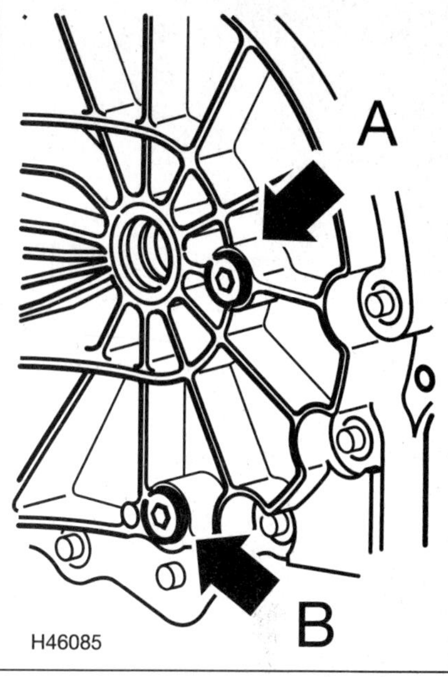

11.4b 6-speed transmission oil filler/ level (A) and drain (B) plug locations

11.7 Oil level plug (arrowed) is on the front of the transmission casing (5-speed)

8 Take the car on a short journey so that the new oil is distributed fully around the transmission components.

9 On your return, park on level ground and check the transmission oil level as described in Chapter 1A or 1B. Refit the engine undertray.

Chapter 7 Part B:
Automatic transmission

Contents

Degrees of difficulty

Easy, suitable for novice with little experience 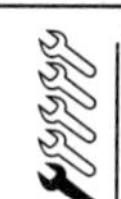	**Fairly easy,** suitable for beginner with some experience	**Fairly difficult,** suitable for competent DIY mechanic	**Difficult,** suitable for experienced DIY mechanic	**Very difficult,** suitable for expert DIY or professional 

Specifications

General

Transmission type:	
2.0 litre petrol	CD4E (4-speed)
2.5 litre V6 petrol and 2.0 litre diesel	5F31J (5-speed)

Torque wrench settings	**Nm**	**lbf ft**
Driveshaft/hub retaining nut*	290	214
Fluid cooler pipes to transmission:		
CD4E	23	17
5F31J	40	30
Selector cable adaptor/grommet	9	7
Selector lever cable cover (5F31J)	22	16
Selector lever position sensor:		
CD4E	12	9
5F31J	6	4
Selector lever to floor	9	7
Speed sensors (CD4E)	13	10
Torque converter-to-driveplate nuts*	36	27
Transmission drain plug:		
CD4E	27	20
5F31J	45	33
Transmission earth cable	20	15
Transmission mounting bracket (5-speed)	80	59
Transmission mounting centre nut*	133	98
Transmission mounting outer nuts*	48	35
Transmission to engine	48	35

* *Use new nuts*

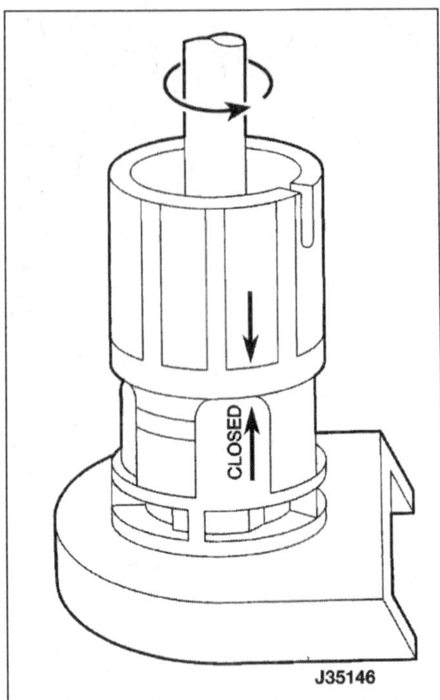

3.3a Cable end fitting arrowhead markings in locked (closed) position

1 General information

CD4E transmission

This well-proven transmission (it has been used on the earliest Mondeos) is controlled electronically by the engine management electronic control unit. There are two operational modes (Economy and Sport), and a driver-operated overdrive inhibit switch which locks out 4th gear during certain conditions. With the Economy mode selected, gearchanges occur at low engine speeds, whereas with the Sport mode selected, the changes occur at high engine speeds.

The transmission incorporates a chain drive between the planetary gear sets and the final drive. The transmission fluid passes through a cooler located within the radiator.

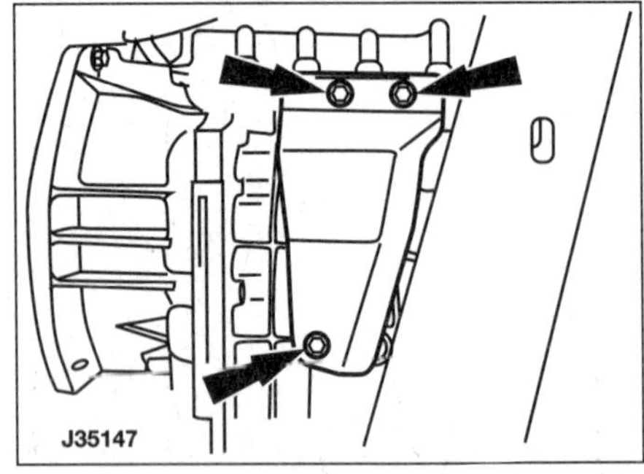

3.3b Remove the retaining bolts (arrowed) to remove cover

There is no kickdown switch, as kickdown is controlled by the throttle position sensor in the engine management system.

The electronic control system has a fail-safe mode, which gives the transmission limited operation in order to drive the car home or to a garage.

5F31J transmission

This transmission is also known under Ford's name Durashift 5-tronic, and was developed by Jatco – a Japanese automatic transmission manufacturer. It is a fully-automatic electronically-controlled design for front-wheel-drive cars.

The transmission ratios are achieved with three planetary gearsets on two shafts. The individual components are driven or held by means of four multi-plate clutches, two multi-plate brakes, one brake band and two roller-type one-way clutches. A torque converter lock-up clutch (TCC) ensures that fuel consumption is optimised, and this is engaged by the transmission control unit, depending on vehicle speed and engine load.

The transmission has a control unit (located behind the facia on the left-hand side) which calculates the gearshift timing according to driving style. Additional driving restrictions (such as towing a trailer or driving uphill/downhill in mountains or steep hills) are also taken into account when calculating the gearshift timing. Gears can be selected either automatically (selector lever position D) or manually by the driver (selected-shift mode), with some models offering steering wheel-mounted shift buttons. The automatic transmission range or the manually-selected gear (select-shift mode) is displayed in the instrument panel.

The transmission fluid passes through a separate cooler located in front of the radiator.

In the event of failure of any electronic components, a hydraulic emergency running programme provides restricted operation of the transmission. If the transmission control unit can no longer ensure that the correct gearshifts are performed, it will automatically switch into emergency running mode, which is indicated by two horizontal lines on the transmission display in the instrument panel. The car will then be able to drive on, but with the following restrictions:

a) In selector lever position D (or in the select-shift gate) – 4th gear is permanently engaged.
b) In selector lever position R – reverse gear can be selected.
c) There is maximum hydraulic line pressure applied – which may give a harsh gearchange.

All transmissions

As a safety measure, it is necessary for the ignition to be switched to position II and for the brake pedal to be depressed in order to move the selector from position P. If the car's battery is discharged, the selector lever release solenoid will not function; if it is required to move the car in this state, remove the cover in the centre console next to the selector lever and insert a key or a similar small instrument into the aperture. Push the locking lever down to allow the selector lever to be moved out of the P position.

2 Fault finding – general

In the event of a fault occurring on the transmission, first check that the fluid level is correct (see Chapter 1A or 1B). If there has been a loss of fluid, check the oil seals as described in Section 7. Also check the hoses to the fluid cooler in the radiator for leaks. The only other checks possible for the home mechanic are the adjustment of the selector cable (Section 3) and the selector lever position sensor (Section 6).

If the fault still persists, it is necessary to determine whether it is of an electrical, mechanical or hydraulic nature; to do this, special test equipment is required. It is therefore essential to have the work carried out by an automatic transmission specialist or Ford dealer if a transmission fault is suspected.

Do not remove the transmission from the car for possible repair before professional fault diagnosis has been carried out, since most tests require the transmission to be in the car.

3 Selector cable – removal, refitting and adjustment

Removal

1 Unclip the breather hose from the engine upper plastic cover, then unclip the cover from the top of the engine.

2 Remove the air cleaner assembly (Chapter 4A or 4B) in order to gain access to the selector cable, which is located on the side of the transmission.

3 Detach the selector inner cable end fitting outwards from the lever on the side of the transmission. Turn the outer cable locking ring anti-clockwise to remove the cable from the bracket. On the 5F31J transmission, remove the selector lever cable cover first **(see illustrations)**.

4 Apply the handbrake, then jack up the front of the car and support it on axle stands (see *Jacking and vehicle support*).

5 Working beneath the car (on petrol models), remove the heat shield from above the catalytic converter, disconnect the wiring connector for the oxygen sensor.

Caution: The catalytic converter operates at very high temperatures, if there is any chance that the system may be still hot, wear suitable safety clothing/gloves.

6 Working along the outer cable, unclip the cable from the retaining clips under the bulkhead.

7 Move the selector lever in the car to the D (drive) position.

8 Remove the centre console as described in Chapter 11.

9 Detach the selector cable retaining clip from the selector lever, pull out the retaining pin and push the cable out from the selector lever.

10 Pull the carpet to one side (the carpet and insulation may need to be cut slightly to gain access to the cable retaining plate).

11 Undo the retaining screw and detach the heater air duct from under the centre of the facia panel.

12 Unscrew the retaining nuts and release the adapter/grommet from the floor, then withdraw the cable through the bulkhead and into the car. **Note:** *Before pulling the cable through the bulkhead, tie a piece of guide-wire to the transmission end of the selector cable and pull it through with the cable. Disconnect the guide-wire leaving it through the bulkhead for refitting.*

Refitting

13 Refitting is a reversal of the removal procedure, but adjust the cable as follows.

Adjustment

CD4E

14 Check that the selector lever in the car is still in the D position.

15 With the inner cable disconnected from the lever on the transmission, check that the lever is in the D position on the transmission. To do this, it will be necessary to move the lever slightly up-and-down until it is positioned correctly **(see illustration)**.

16 Check that the cable locking ring on the transmission end is still unlocked (ie, turned anti-clockwise by 90°).

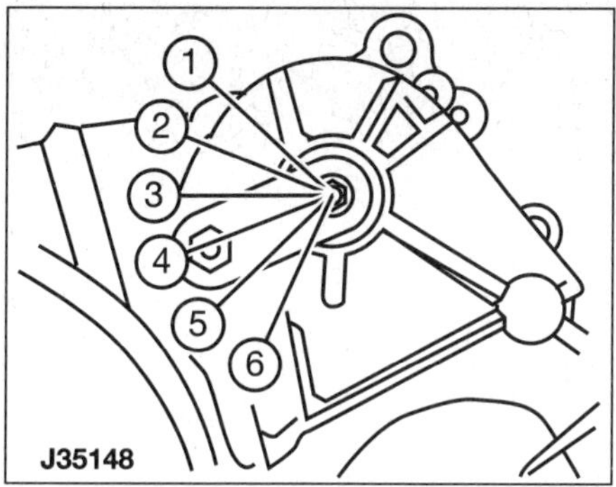

3.15 Lever positions on transmission

1 *First gear*
2 *Second gear*
3 *Drive*
4 *Neutral*
5 *Reverse*
6 *Park*

17 With the selector lever inside the car in position D and the lever on the transmission also in position D, refit the cable end fitting to the transmission lever, then turn the locking ring 90° clockwise to lock it in the selector bracket.

18 With the handbrake applied, start the engine and move the selector lever through all the ranges, allowing enough time for each position to engage.

19 Road test the car to check the transmission for correct operation.

5F31J

20 Check that the selector lever in the car is still in the D position.

21 With the selector lever cover removed, release the yellow locking clip from the selector lever cable adjustment mechanism **(see illustration)**.

22 Move the selector lever on the transmission until it is in the D position **(see illustration)**. **Note:** *The dot on the transmission casing must align with the hole on the selector lever when it is in the D position.*

23 With the selector in the D position, press the yellow locking clip back into the selector lever cable to lock the adjustment mechanism. Refit the selector lever cable cover.

24 With the handbrake applied, start the engine and move the selector lever through all the ranges, allowing enough time for each position to engage.

25 Road test the car to check the transmission for correct operation.

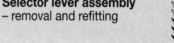

4 Selector lever assembly – removal and refitting

Removal

1 Remove the centre console as described in Chapter 11.

2 Detach the selector cable retaining clip from the selector lever, pull out the retaining pin and push the cable out from the selector lever.

3 Apply the handbrake, then jack up the front of the car and support it on axle stands (see *Jacking and vehicle support*).

4 Working beneath the car (on petrol models), remove the heat shield from above the catalytic converter, disconnect the wiring connector for the oxygen sensor.

Caution: The catalytic converter operates at very high temperatures, if there is any chance that the system may be still hot, wear suitable safety clothing/gloves.

5 Unscrew the mounting nuts securing the selector lever assembly to the floor.

6 Disconnect the selector lever wiring connector, then withdraw the selector lever assembly from inside the car. Where applicable, recover the gasket.

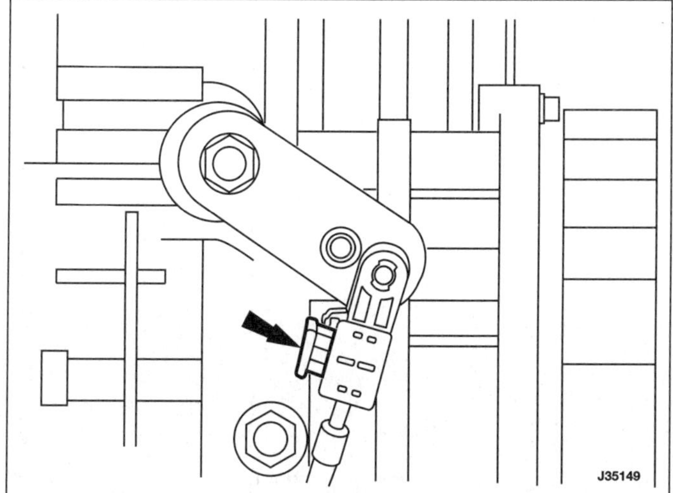

3.21 Release the locking clip (arrowed) from the selector lever cable

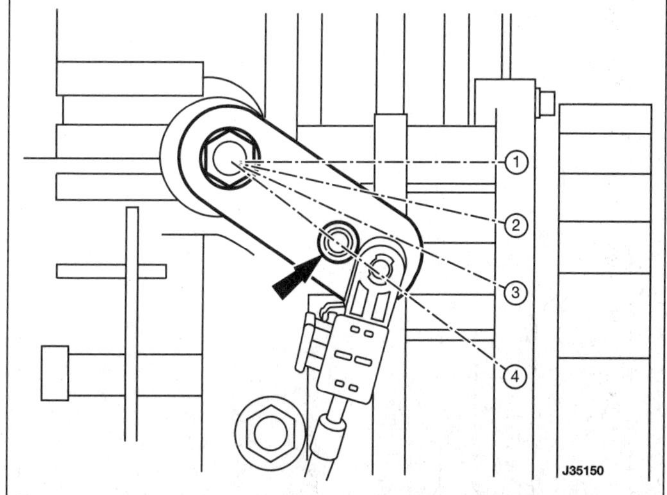

3.22 Align the dot (arrowed) on the transmission housing with the hole in the lever to select the D (drive) position

1 *Park* 2 *Reverse* 3 *Neutral* 4 *Drive*

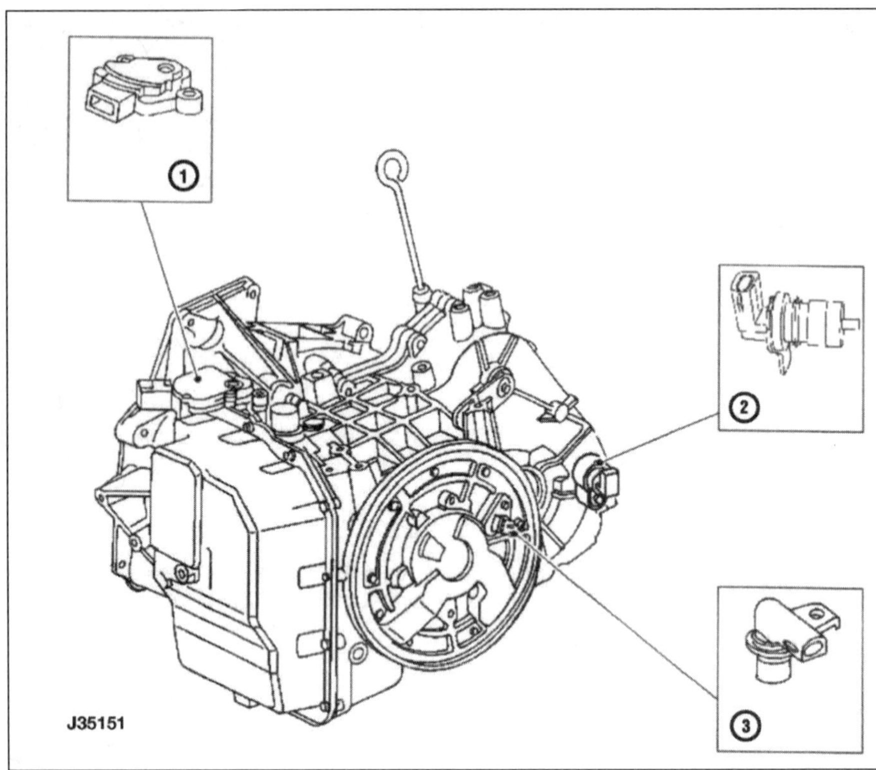

5.2 Sensors fitted to the CD4E transmission

1 *Selector lever position sensor*
2 *Output speed sensor (OSS)*
3 *Turbine shaft speed sensor (TSS)*

Refitting

7 Refitting is a reversal of the removal procedure, but adjust the selector cable as described in Section 3.

5 Speed sensors – removal and refitting

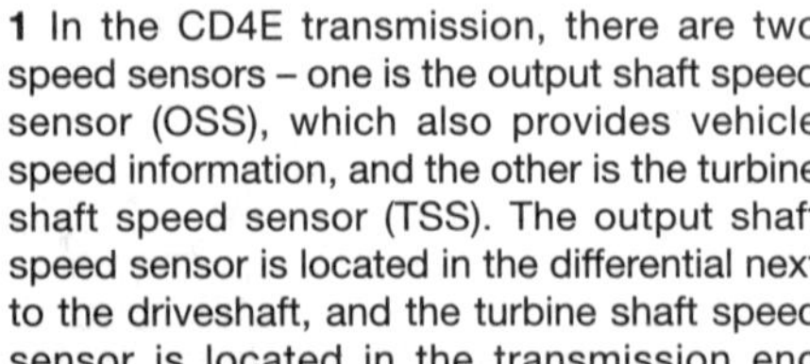

1 In the CD4E transmission, there are two speed sensors – one is the output shaft speed sensor (OSS), which also provides vehicle speed information, and the other is the turbine shaft speed sensor (TSS). The output shaft speed sensor is located in the differential next to the driveshaft, and the turbine shaft speed sensor is located in the transmission end cover. The procedures for the removal and refitting of both speed sensors are the same.

6.4 Multiplug (arrowed) for the selector lever position sensor (CD4E)

2 The same speed sensors are fitted on the 5F31J unit, but both the OSS and TSS are inaccessible without dismantling the transmission, which is judged to be beyond the scope of the DIY mechanic.

CD4E transmission

Removal

3 Apply the handbrake, then jack up the front of the car and support it on axle stands (see *Jacking and vehicle support*).

4 Disconnect the wiring connector from the speed sensor **(see illustration)**. **Note:** *The output shaft speed sensor connector is coloured black and the turbine shaft speed sensor connector is coloured white.*

5 Unscrew the retaining bolt and withdraw the output shaft speed sensor from the transmission.

6 Using a small screwdriver, remove the rubber O-ring from the sensor and discard it; obtain a new one for reassembly.

7 Wipe clean the speed sensor and the seating bore in the transmission casing.

Refitting

8 Refitting is a reversal of the removal procedure noting the following points:

a) Lightly lubricate the new O-ring with petroleum jelly before inserting the assembly in the transmission casing.
b) Tighten the clamp bolt to the specified torque setting.
c) With the handbrake applied, start the engine and move the selector lever through all the ranges, allowing enough time for each position to engage.
d) Select the park P position and check the transmission fluid level as described in Chapter 1A or 1B.

6 Selector lever position sensor – removal, refitting and adjustment

Note: *This is also known as the transmission range sensor.*

Removal

1 Remove the battery and its tray as described in Chapter 5A.

2 In order to gain better access to the selector lever position sensor, which is located on top of the transmission, remove the air cleaner assembly as described in Chapter 4A or 4B.

3 Move the selector lever to the N (neutral) position.

4 Disconnect the wiring multiplug from the position sensor **(see illustration)**.

5 Unscrew the mounting bolts, and remove the sensor.

Refitting and adjustment

6 Refitting is a reversal of the removal procedure, but check the alignment of the sensor as follows before fully tightening the mounting bolts.

7 Check that the transmission is in the N (neutral) position (see Section 3).

8 There is a Ford special tool for aligning the sensor, it consists of a metal plate with pegs to engage with the cut-outs in the sensor and shaft **(see illustrations)**.

9 Twist the sensor on the transmission until the special tool is aligned, this is the neutral N position in the transmission. With the sensor correctly aligned, tighten the bolts, then remove the alignment tool.

10 Reconnect the wiring multiplug to the position sensor.

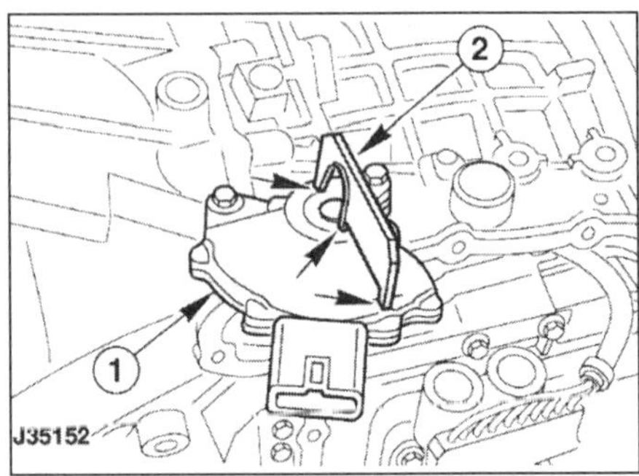

6.8a Alignment tool for the selector lever position sensor (selector in position N) (CD4E transmission)

1 *Sensor*
2 *Alignment tool (pegs arrowed)*

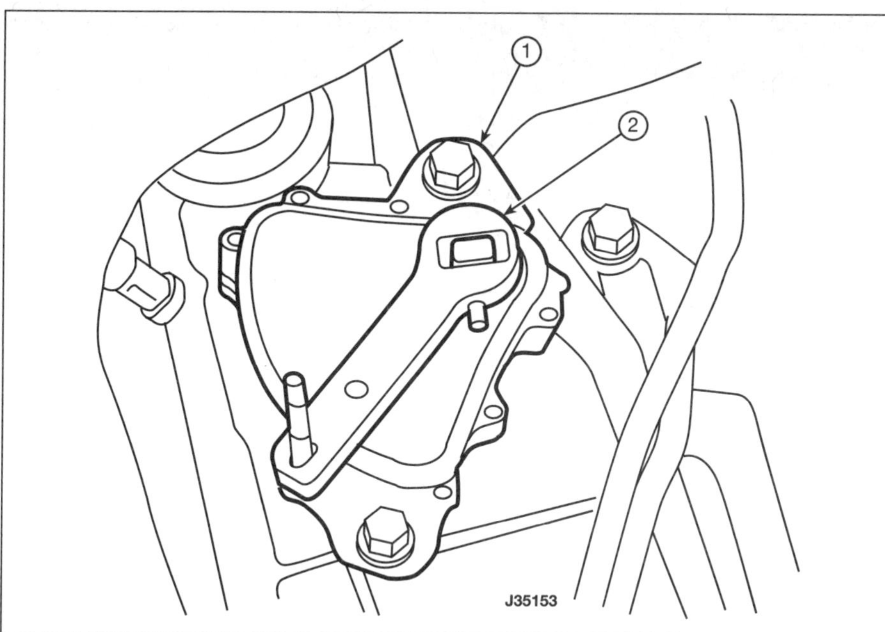

6.8b Alignment tool for the selector lever position sensor (5F31J transmission)

1 Selector lever position sensor *2 Alignment tool*

11 Refit the battery and its tray as described in Chapter 5A, and the air cleaner assembly as described in Chapter 4A or 4B.

12 As a further check, with the handbrake applied, move the selector lever to position park P or neutral N, the engine should start. **Note:** *The car should not be able to start if any other gear is selected.* When reverse R is selected the reversing lights should illuminate.

7 Oil seals – renewal

Differential side gear oil seals

1 The procedure is the same as that for the manual transmission (refer to Chapter 7A). **Note:** *Ford use a special puller tool, to remove the differential seal from the transmission casing.*

Speed sensor oil seals

2 The procedure is covered in Section 5.

8 Transmission – removal and refitting

Note: *Read through this procedure before starting work, to see what is involved, particularly in terms of lifting equipment. Depending on the facilities available, the home mechanic may prefer to remove the engine and transmission together, then separate them on the bench, as described in Chapter 2D.*

Removal

1 Remove the battery and tray as described in Chapter 5A. Also remove the engine top cover.

2 If necessary, remove the bonnet (Chapter 11) for better access, and for fitting the engine lifting hoist.

3 Raise the radiator, and hold it in the raised position by using cable ties through the holes in the upper crossmember. This is necessary to retain the radiator when the subframe is removed.

4 Unclip the plastic covers from the top of the suspension struts on both sides of the car, then slacken the top mounting retaining nuts by approximately four turns each **(see illustrations)**.

5 Remove the air cleaner assembly as described in Chapter 4A or 4B. On diesel models, disconnect the turbocharger air inlet pipe.

6 Drain the cooling system as described in Chapter 1A or 1B.

7 Where applicable, detach the battery earth lead from the transmission **(see illustration)**.

8 Pull the selector cable end fitting from the lever on the transmission and unbolt the support bracket. On the 5F31J transmission, remove the selector lever cable cover first (see Section 3).

9 Apply the handbrake, and chock the rear wheels. Slacken the front roadwheel nuts, and if possible, the driveshaft hub nuts.

10 Jack up the front of the car and support it on axle stands. There must be sufficient clearance below the car for the transmission to be lowered and removed. Remove both front roadwheels and where fitted, the engine undertray.

11 Remove the front lower cover from under the radiator, by prising out the side clips and unscrewing the retaining bolts.

12 Drain the transmission fluid into a suitable container. Where fitted discard the washer/ gasket, refit the plug with a new washer/ gasket and tighten to the specified torque setting on completion.

13 On diesel models undo the retaining bolts, and remove the intercooler inlet hose from across the underside of the engine/ transmission.

14 The engine and transmission must now be supported. Ford technicians use a support bar which locates in the tops of the inner wing panels – proprietary engine support bars are available from tool outlets.

15 If a support bar is not available, an engine hoist should be used. With an engine hoist the engine/transmission can be manoeuvred more easily and safely, balancing the engine on a jack is not recommended.

16 Remove the front subframe as described in Chapter 10.

17 Remove the driveshafts as described in

8.4a Unclip the plastic covers . . .

8.4b . . . then slacken the top strut mounting retaining nuts

8.7 Earth lead attachment (arrowed) on the transmission

8.18a Undo the retaining nut (arrowed) . . .

8.18b . . . then undo the four retaining nuts (arrowed)

Chapter 8. Plug the transmission to prevent dirt ingress (or fluid loss, if the fluid has not been drained).

18 Support the transmission with a trolley jack from below, then undo the retaining nut from the left-hand transmission mounting, then undo the four retaining nuts and remove the mounting from the inner wing panel **(see illustrations)**.

19 On CD4E transmissions, disconnect the wiring connectors from the output speed sensor (OSS), the turbine shaft speed sensor (TSS) and (where fitted) the headlamp-levelling sensor wiring connector.

20 On the 5F31J transmissions, disconnect the three multiplug wiring connectors from the end of the transmission housing. Also disconnect the vent hose from the top of the transmission.

21 Unscrew the union nut securing the automatic transmission fluid cooler pipe to the left-hand side of the transmission and also the cooler return pipe to the transmission. Unclip the pipes, and move them to one side. Plug the end of the pipes, to prevent dust and dirt entering the hydraulic system.

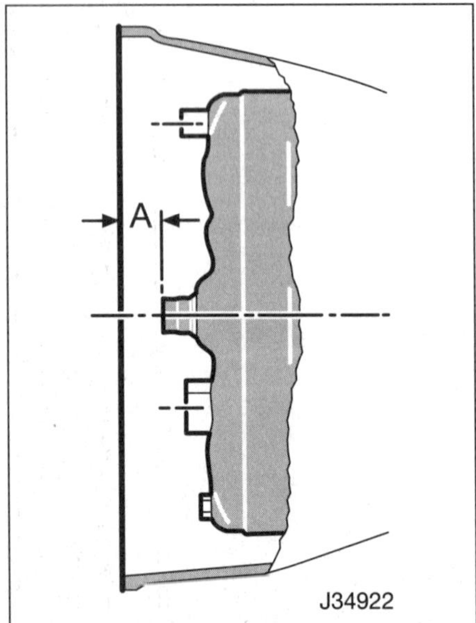

8.33a Torque converter centre spigot must be at least 14 mm below the transmission flange (dimension A) (CD4E transmission)

22 Remove the starter motor as described in Chapter 5A.

23 Disconnect the wiring connectors from the selector lever position sensor, on top of the transmission. On CD4E transmissions, disconnect the transmission control electrical connector from the top of the transmission.

24 On CD4E transmissions, remove the rubber cover from the starter motor recess in the transmission bellhousing, for access to the torque converter retaining bolts.

25 On the 5F31J transmissions, remove the cover in the lower section of the transmission casing to gain access to the torque converter retaining bolts.

26 Unscrew and remove the torque converter retaining bolts. It will be necessary to turn the engine, using the crankshaft pulley bolt, so that each of the four nuts can be unscrewed through the aperture.

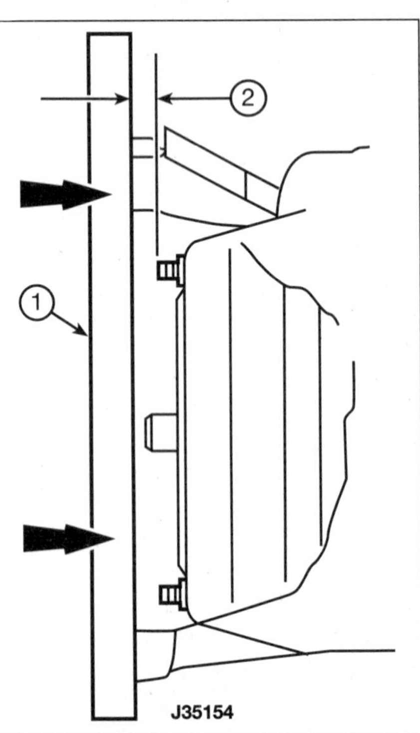

8.33b Torque converter driveplate stud depth (2) must be measured using a straight-edge (1) (5F31J transmission)

1 Straight-edge
2 Depth:
21 mm – diesel engines
15.5 mm – 2.5 litre V6 petrol engines

27 Undo the retaining nuts/bolts and remove transmission mounting bracket from the top of the transmission housing.

28 With the weight of the transmission supported on a trolley jack. Use safety chains or make up a cradle to steady the transmission on the jack.

29 Working your way around the transmission casing, slacken and remove the transmission-to-engine securing bolts. Disconnect any wiring loom brackets, where applicable.

30 With the help of an assistant, withdraw the transmission squarely from the engine, making sure that the torque converter comes away with the transmission, and does not stay in contact with the driveplate. If this precaution is not taken, there is a risk of the torque converter falling out and being damaged.

31 Lower the transmission to the ground.

Refitting

32 Clean the contact surfaces of the driveplate and torque converter.

33 Check that the torque converter is fully entered in the transmission, to do this, place a straight-edge across the transmission flange. Apply a thin layer of high-temperature grease to the centre spigot on the torque converter.

a) On CD4E transmissions, check that the torque converter centre spigot is 14 mm below the straight-edge ***(see illustration)****.*

b) On 5F31J transmissions, check the drive plate studs are:
21 mm below the straight-edge on diesel engines.
15.5 mm below the straight-edge on 2.5 litre V6 petrol engines ***(see illustration)****.*

Caution: This procedure is important, to ensure that the torque converter is fully engaged with the fluid pump. If it is not fully engaged, serious damage will occur.

34 With the help of an assistant, raise the transmission, and locate it on the rear of the driveplate. Ensure the transmission is correctly aligned with the locating dowels, before pushing it fully into engagement with the engine. **Note:** *The torque converter must remain in full engagement with the fluid pump at the correct installation depth throughout the fitting procedure.*

35 Working your way around the transmission casing, refit the transmission-to-engine bolts. Do not fully tighten the retaining bolts until all the bolts are in place, then tighten to the specified torque setting.

36 Using four new retaining nuts, tighten the torque converter retaining nuts to the specified torque. Turn the engine as required to bring each of the nuts into view. **Note:** *Insert all of the new nuts before fully tightening them to the specified torque.*

37 The remainder of the refitting procedure is a reversal of the removal procedure, noting the following special points:

a) Tighten all retaining bolts to their specified torque wrench setting (where given).
b) Reconnect and adjust the selector cable, as described in Section 3.
c) Renew the transmission fluid as described in Chapter 1A or 1B.
d) If a new unit has been fitted, depending on the transmission type, it may be necessary to have the transmission ECU 'matched' to the engine management PCM electronically, to ensure correct operation – seek the advice of your Ford dealer or automatic transmission specialist.
e) After running the engine, recheck the transmission fluid level, and top-up if necessary (refer to Chapter 1A or 1B).
f) Road test the car to check the transmission for correct operation.

9 Transmission fluid – renewal

Refer to Chapter 1A or 1B.

10 Transmission overhaul – general information

In the event of a fault occurring, it will be necessary to establish whether the fault is electrical, mechanical or hydraulic in nature, before repair work can be contemplated. Diagnosis requires detailed knowledge of the transmission's operation and construction, as well as access to specialised test equipment, and so is deemed to be beyond the scope of this manual. It is therefore essential that problems with the automatic transmission are referred to a Ford dealer or automatic transmission specialist for assessment.

A faulty transmission should not be removed before the car has been assessed by a dealer or specialist, as fault diagnosis is carried out with the transmission connected up to the car. Refer to the information given in Section 2 before removing the unit.

Note that, if the car is still within the warranty period, in the event of a fault it is important to take it to a Ford dealer, who will carry out a comprehensive diagnosis procedure using specialist equipment. Failure to do this will invalidate the warranty.

11 Transmission control module (5F31J) – removal and refitting

Note: *The transmission control module (TCM) which is fitted to the 5F31J transmissions, is located on the inner bulkhead behind the facia panel.*

Removal

1 Remove the facia panel as described in Chapter 11.
2 Undo the retaining bolts and remove the crossbeam from across the inside of the bulkhead.
3 Disconnect the wiring connector from the transmission control module.
4 The control module is riveted to a bracket on the inner bulkhead, drill out the rivets and remove the control module from the car.

Refitting

5 Refitting is a reversal of the removal procedure, fit new rivets to the control module retaining bracket.
Caution: Check the correct transmission control module (TCM) for the car is installed, or irregular driving conditions may occur.

12 Transmission fluid cooler (5F31J) – removal and refitting

Note 1: *A Ford special tool is needed to disconnect the cooler's quick-release fittings without damage.*
Note 2: *Some diesel models have the fluid cooler incorporated into the air conditioning condenser – where this is the case, the cooler cannot be removed separately. The condenser can be removed as described in Chapter 3.*

Removal

1 For preference, this procedure should only be carried out when the transmission fluid is cool, and not immediately after a run. If this procedure must be performed when the fluid will be hot, take precautions against scalding (for example, wear gloves).
2 Remove the front bumper as described in Chapter 11.
3 Prise out the two push-in clips, and remove the plastic cover which protects the cooler's fluid connections at one end.
4 Before disconnecting the fluid cooler connections, refer to Chapter 1A or 1B, and consider whether to drain the transmission fluid – this may be advisable, as the quantity of fluid lost must be accurately established for refilling, and the fluid may be released more controllably from the transmission itself. However, even if the transmission is drained first, a small amount of fluid will still be lost when the cooler is opened, and this too should be kept.
5 Ford special tool 307-242 is now needed to disconnect the cooler's two quick-release fittings. This tool is a split collar which slides inside one half of the connection, and releases the internal lugs. If the tool is not available, it may be possible to fabricate something similar, perhaps from an old feeler blade – care must be taken to avoid any damage to the connection, or fluid leaks may result.
6 Once the two pipes have been disconnected, allow the fluid to drain into a suitable container. It is important that the fluid drained is kept, as an identical quantity of fluid must be used when topping-up the transmission (there is no dipstick, nor is there a conventional level plug).
7 Mark the disconnected pipes for their fitted locations, perhaps by wrapping some tape around them – they should not be interchanged when refitting. If the cooler will be removed for some time, plug or tape over the open connections, to prevent dirt ingress or further fluid loss.
8 Remove the upper mounting bolt on either side of the cooler, then lift it out of its mounting bracket, to disengage the two lower locating lugs. Empty any remaining fluid out of the cooler, keeping it with the other fluid which was drained.

Refitting

9 Refitting is a reversal of removal, noting the following points:
a) Offer the cooler into position, and engage the lower mounting lugs with the support bracket. Fit the upper bolts, and tighten securely.
b) Ensure that the cooler connections are securely remade. Unlike removal, reconnecting the pipes does not require the special tool – just press the connection together until the locating lugs are heard or felt to engage. Once connected, gently try and pull the pipes apart, to ensure a good connection.
c) On completion, refill the transmission with the same amount of fluid as was drained. Bring the transmission to operating temperature, then check the fluid level, as described in Chapter 1A or 1B for fluid renewal.

13 Steering wheel shift buttons (5F31J) – general information

Some models with the 5-speed automatic transmission may have steering wheel-mounted manual shift buttons, for use in the selected-shift mode. According to Ford, these buttons cannot be renewed separately, and, if faulty, a new steering wheel will be needed. Once a new wheel has been fitted, there is no need to have the transmission control unit reprogrammed by a Ford dealer – the buttons should work straight away.

Notes

Chapter 8
Driveshafts

Contents

Degrees of difficulty

Easy, suitable for novice with little experience	**Fairly easy,** suitable for beginner with some experience	**Fairly difficult,** suitable for competent DIY mechanic	**Difficult,** suitable for experienced DIY mechanic	**Very difficult,** suitable for expert DIY or professional 

Specifications

Torque wrench settings	Nm	lbf ft
Anti-roll bar link and mounting	48	35
Driveshaft/hub retaining nut*	290	214
Front suspension lower arm balljoint clamp bolt	83	61
Front suspension strut top mount to body	30	22
Front suspension subframe mounting bolts	142	105
Front suspension subframe rear bracket	10	7
Intermediate shaft centre bearing bracket to block	48	35
Intermediate shaft centre bearing retaining nut	25	18
Roadwheel nuts	85	63
Steering column flexible coupling to steering gear pinion shaft*	25	18
Steering column-to-flexible coupling clamp bolt*	20	15

** Use a new nut or bolt*

1 General information

Drive is transmitted from the transmission differential to the front wheels by means of two driveshafts, each incorporating two constant velocity (CV) joints. The right-hand driveshaft is in two sections, and incorporates a support bearing **(see illustration)**. On 1.8 and 2.0 litre petrol models, the driveshaft is of tubular design, while on all other models solid shafts are used.

Each driveshaft consists of three main components: the sliding (tripod type) inner joint, the actual driveshaft, and the outer (fixed ball) joint. The inner (male) end of the left-hand tripod joint is secured in the differential side gear by the engagement of a circlip. The inner (female) end of the right-hand driveshaft is held on the intermediate shaft by the engagement of a circlip. The intermediate shaft is held in the transmission by the support bearing, which in turn is supported by a bracket bolted to the rear of the cylinder block. The outer CV joint on both driveshafts is of fixed ball-bearing type, and is secured in the front hub by the hub nut. **Note:** *Ford state that the driveshaft nut may be re-used up to four times, but we recommend a new nut is fitted every time it is loosened – given the extreme torque it must be tightened to, and the safety consequences of the nut failing, not fitting a new nut is false economy. The driveshaft nut is of laminated design, and with repeated re-use, the nut may split apart.*

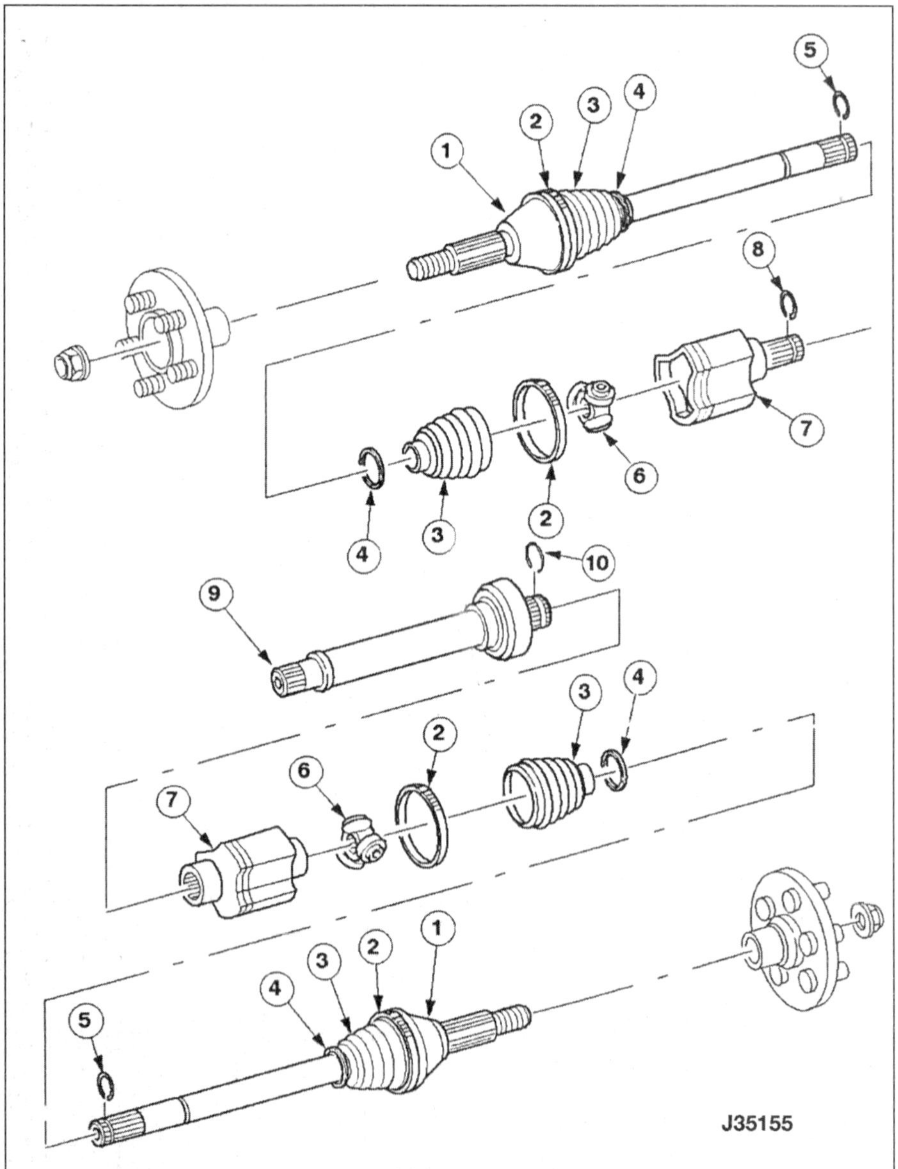

1.1 Exploded view of the driveshafts (1.8 and 2.0 litre engine)

1 Driveshaft with fixed outer CV joint
2 Large gaiter retaining clamp
3 Gaiter
4 Small gaiter retaining clamp
5 Inner joint tripod retaining circlip
6 Inner joint tripod
7 Inner joint housing
8 Driveshaft inner retaining circlip
9 Intermediate shaft
10 Right-hand driveshaft-to-intermediate shaft retaining circlip

2 Driveshafts – removal and refitting

Caution: When removing the driveshafts, the inner CV joint must not be bent by more than 18°, and the outer CV joint must not be bent by more than 45° – in other words, keep the shaft as straight as possible. The outer CV joint must not be dismantled from the driveshaft, as it is a press-fit.

Note: *This procedure includes partially lowering the front suspension subframe.*

Removal

1 Position the front wheels in the straight-ahead position, and centralise the steering wheel. Remove the wheel cover (or centre cover) from the relevant wheel, apply the handbrake, and engage 1st gear (manual transmission) or P (automatic transmission). Loosen the hub nut about half a turn.

2 Loosen the front wheel retaining nuts. Jack up the front of the car and support it on axle stands (see *Jacking and vehicle support*). Remove both front wheels. On diesel models, remove the engine undertray.

3 Working inside the car, unscrew and remove the clamp bolt securing the steering inner column to the splined pinion shaft of the steering gear. Rotate the clamp plate clockwise and detach the clamp from the pinion shaft. Discard the bolt as a new one must be fitted on reassembly.

4 With the bonnet open, unclip the cover from the top of the relevant front suspension strut, then unscrew each of the three mounting nuts four turns only.

5 Unscrew and remove the hub nut **(see illustration)**. It is recommended that a new hub nut is obtained for refitting (see Section 1).

2.5 Removing the hub nut

2.23 Using a lever to remove the left-hand driveshaft from the transmission

2.24 Removing the outer end of the driveshaft from the steering knuckle

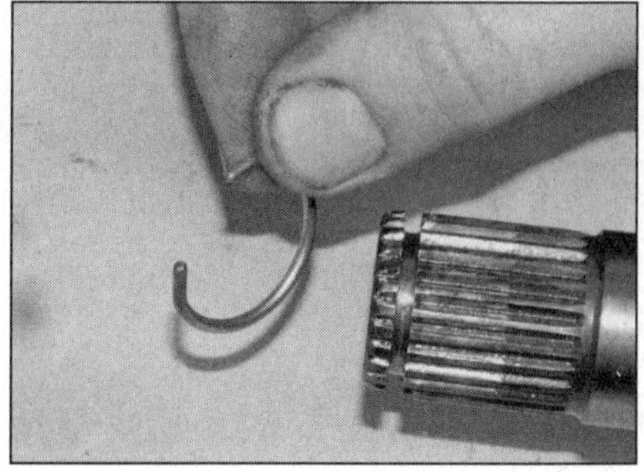

2.26 Removing the circlip from the inner end of the left-hand driveshaft

6 Undo the screws and remove the splash shield from under the radiator position.

7 At the front of the engine compartment, use cable ties to support the radiator on both sides. Alternatively, pins may be inserted through the holes in the radiator upper location tubes. Access to the tubes is gained through the apertures in the front crossmember.

8 Under the front of the car, unbolt the hose bracket (where fitted) next to the left-hand radiator support bracket, then unbolt and remove both radiator support brackets.

9 On diesel models, loosen the clips and disconnect the air inlet hose and turbocharger outlet hose near the front of the subframe.

10 Working beneath each wheel arch in turn, unbolt the anti-roll bar link from the suspension strut.

11 On 1.8 and 2.0 litre petrol engines, and all diesel engines, remove the exhaust flexible pipe from the front of the exhaust system with reference to the appropriate part of Chapter 4.

12 On V6 engines, remove the exhaust front lower Y-pipe with reference to Chapter 4A.

13 Remove the engine rear mounting with reference to the appropriate part of Chapter 2.

14 On petrol models, disconnect the catalytic converter monitor sensor wiring, and unclip the wiring from the subframe.

15 On models with xenon headlights, release the cable-ties and detach the headlight-levelling sensor wiring harness from the subframe.

16 Release the radiator cooling fan wiring harness from the subframe. Check around the subframe that there is nothing left attached to it, which would prevent it from being lowered.

17 Support the front suspension subframe on one or (preferably) two trolley jacks. If necessary, enlist the help of an assistant.

18 Note which way round the front suspension lower arm balljoint clamp bolts are fitted on each side, then unscrew and remove each one from the knuckle assembly.

Caution: Do not pull down on the lower arms at this stage, as the rear hydro-bushes will be damaged.

19 Carefully mark the position of the front suspension subframe on the underbody to ensure correct refitting. **Note:** *Ford technicians use special alignment pins to locate the subframe accurately when refitting – it is recommended that these pins are obtained for the refitting procedure.* Unscrew and remove the subframe rear mounting bolts, then unbolt the rear brackets from the subframe.

20 Unscrew and remove the subframe front mounting bolts.

21 Keeping it as level as possible, lower the subframe approximately 150 mm, making sure that the lower arm rear hydro-bushes are not strained or damaged.

22 Detach the lower arm balljoints from the steering knuckles, and remove the heat shields. If they are tight, carefully tap down the outer ends of the arms with a mallet, or drive a thin metal wedge into the knuckle clamps. Take care not to damage the balljoint rubber boots.

Left-hand driveshaft

23 Insert a lever between the inner driveshaft joint and the transmission case, with a thin piece of wood against the case. Prise free the inner joint from the differential **(see illustration)**. If it proves reluctant to move, strike the lever firmly with the palm of the hand. Be careful not to damage adjacent components, and in particular, make sure that the driveshaft oil seal in the differential is not damaged. Be prepared for some oil spillage from the transmission. Support the inner end of the driveshaft on an axle stand.

24 Press the outer end of the driveshaft through the front hub and steering knuckle **(see illustration)**. If necessary, use a universal puller located on the hub flange.

25 Withdraw the driveshaft from under the car.

26 Extract the circlip from the groove on the inner end of the driveshaft, and obtain a new one **(see illustration)**.

Right-hand driveshaft

Note: *The right-hand driveshaft may either be removed complete with the intermediate shaft from the transmission, or it may be disconnected from the outer end of the intermediate shaft.*

27 Press the outer end of the driveshaft through the front hub and steering knuckle – if necessary, use a universal puller located on the hub flange. Tie the steering knuckle to one side, and support the outer end of the driveshaft on an axle stand.

28 To disconnect the driveshaft from the outer end of the intermediate shaft, insert a lever between the inner driveshaft joint and the intermediate bearing housing, with a thin piece of wood against the housing. Prise free the inner joint from the bearing housing; this will release the internal circlip. Alternatively, use a soft-faced mallet to drive off the housing **(see illustrations)**.

29 To remove the intermediate shaft, unscrew the nuts securing the driveshaft support bearing to the rear of the bracket on the cylinder block and, where fitted, remove the exhaust heat shield. Mark the cap with the normal direction of rotation to ensure correct refitting **(see illustrations)**.

30 Withdraw the intermediate shaft from the transmission **(see illustration)**.

31 Where the driveshaft has been disconnected from the intermediate shaft, extract the circlip from the groove on the

2.28a Using a mallet to drive off the right-hand driveshaft housing

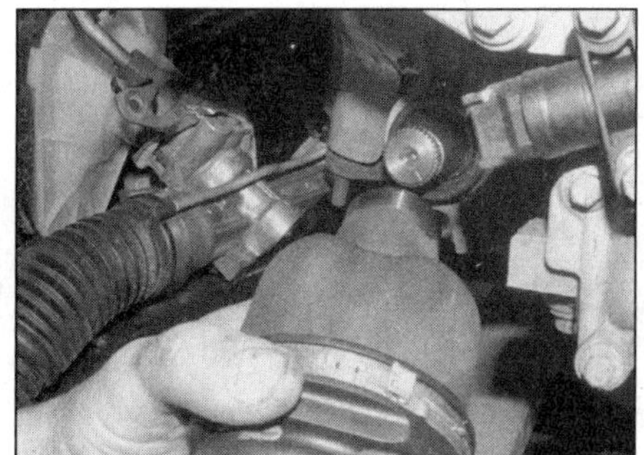

2.28b Disconnecting the right-hand driveshaft from the intermediate shaft

2.29a Mark the cap with the normal direction of rotation . . .

2.29b . . . then remove the cap . . .

2.29c . . . and withdraw the bearing from the bracket

2.29d Intermediate shaft support bearing (V6 engine)

2.29e Exhaust heat shield (2.0 litre engine)

2.30 Withdraw the intermediate shaft from the transmission

splined outer end of the intermediate shaft, and obtain a new one **(see illustration)**.

Both sides

32 Check the condition of the differential oil seals, and if necessary renew them as described in Chapter 7A (manual transmission) or Chapter 7B (automatic transmission) **(see illustrations)**. Check the support bearing, and if necessary renew it as described in Section 5.

2.31 Removing the circlip from the groove on the intermediate shaft

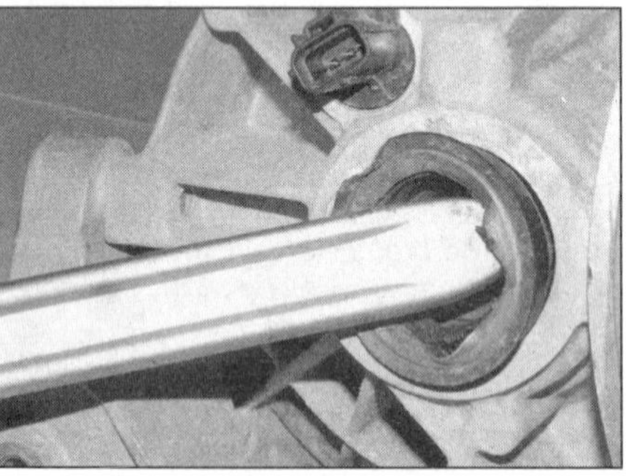
2.32a Prising out the old oil seal

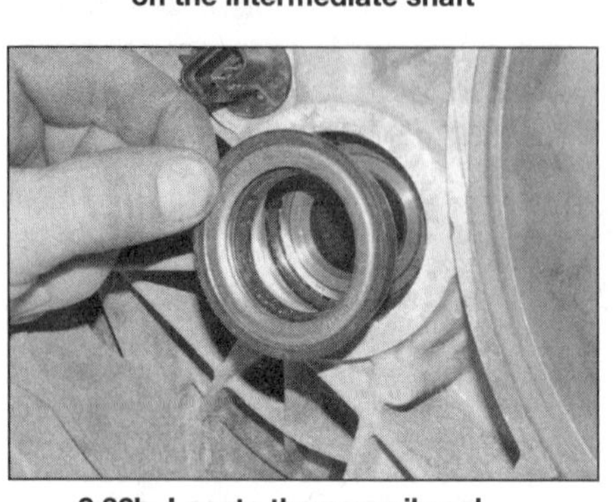
2.32b Locate the new oil seal . . .

2.32c . . . and drive it fully into the transmission casing

Refitting

Left-hand driveshaft

33 Fit the new circlip to the groove on the inner end of the driveshaft, making sure it is correctly seated.

34 Keeping the driveshaft level, insert the splined inner end into the transmission and engage with the splines in the differential sun gear. Take care not to damage the transmission oil seal. Press in the driveshaft until the circlip is fully engaged.

35 Pull the knuckle outwards, and insert the outer end of the driveshaft through the hub. Turn the driveshaft as necessary to engage the splines in the hub, and fully push on the hub. If necessary, use a wooden mallet to tap the hub onto the driveshaft splines until it is possible to screw on the hub nut several threads.

Right-hand driveshaft

36 If the complete driveshaft and intermediate shaft have been removed, insert the inner end of the intermediate shaft into the transmission and engage it with the splines on the differential sun gear, taking care not to damage the oil seal. Locate the intermediate shaft centre bearing on its bracket, refit the cap, and tighten the retaining nuts to the specified torque.

37 Where the intermediate shaft was left in position, locate a new circlip in the groove on the outer end of the intermediate shaft, then locate the driveshaft on the intermediate shaft splines, and push it on until the internal circlip is heard to engage with the groove in the shaft.

38 Pull the knuckle outwards, and insert the outer end of the driveshaft through the hub. Turn the driveshaft as necessary to engage the splines in the hub, and fully push on the hub. If necessary, use a wooden mallet to tap the hub onto the driveshaft splines until it is possible to screw on the hub nut several threads.

Both sides

39 Locate the front suspension lower arm balljoint stubs in the bottom of the knuckles together with the heat shields. Insert the clamp bolts from the rear (heads facing rearwards), screw on the nuts, and tighten it to the specified torque.
40 Raise the subframe against the underbody, and position it accurately with the marks made during removal. If available, use the special Ford alignment pins. Refit the rear brackets, then insert the mounting bolts and tighten to the specified torque. Make sure the subframe does not move when tightening the bolts.
41 Refit the radiator cooling fan wiring harness to the subframe.
42 On models with xenon headlights, attach the headlight-levelling sensor wiring harness to the subframe using cable ties.
43 On petrol models, reconnect the catalytic converter monitor sensor wiring, and secure the wiring to the subframe.
44 Refit the engine rear support/link insulator with reference to the appropriate part of Chapter 2.
45 On 1.8 and 2.0 litre petrol engines, and all diesel engines, refit the exhaust flexible pipe to the front of the exhaust system with reference to the appropriate part of Chapter 4.
46 On V6 engines, refit the exhaust front lower Y-pipe with reference to Chapter 4A.
47 Refit the anti-roll bar link to the suspension strut and tighten the nut to the specified torque.
48 On diesel models, reconnect the air inlet hose and turbocharger outlet hose near the front of the subframe, and tighten the clips.
49 Under the front of the car, refit the hose bracket and the radiator support brackets, making sure that the rubber mountings are located on the radiator correctly, then tighten the bolts. Remove the temporary cable ties or pins from the radiator.
50 Refit the splash shield beneath the radiator and tighten the screws.
51 Tighten the hub nut moderately at this stage.
52 Tighten the front suspension strut upper mounting nuts to the specified torque, then refit the plastic cover.
53 Working inside the car, refit the steering column clamp to the steering gear pinion shaft, taking care not to turn the column from its straight-ahead position. Turn the clamp plate anti-clockwise and insert the **new** clamp bolt. Tighten the bolt to the specified torque.
54 On diesel models, refit the engine undertray.
55 Check, and if necessary top-up the transmission oil or fluid with reference to Chapter 1A or 1B.

3.4a Remove the inner joint gaiter large clip . . .

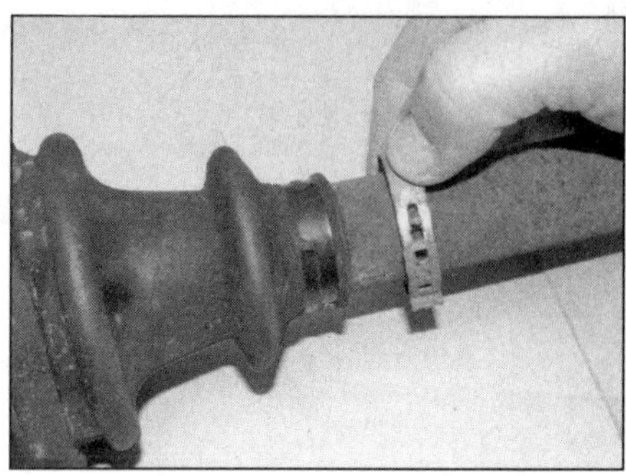

3.4b . . . and small clip, release the gaiter . . .

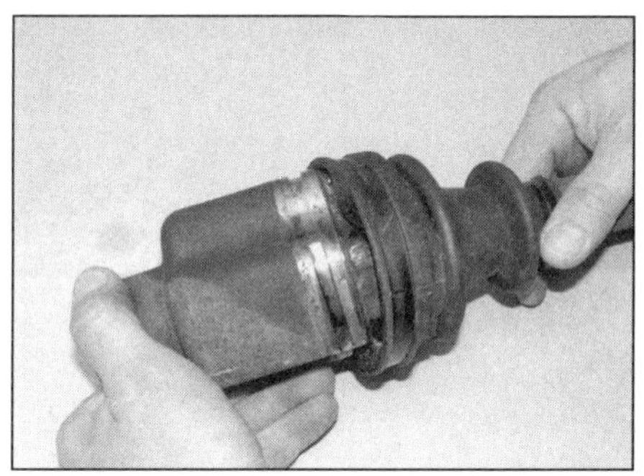

3.5a . . . and withdraw the inner joint housing from the tripod

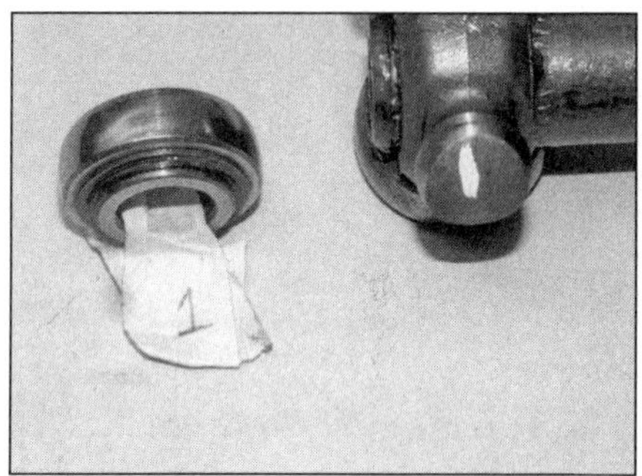

3.5b Identify the rollers for position

56 Refit both front wheels, then lower the front of the car to the ground and tighten the wheel nuts to the specified torque.
57 Fit a new hub nut, and tighten it to the specified torque. Finally, refit the wheel cover (or centre cover).

3 Driveshaft inner CV joint gaiter – renewal

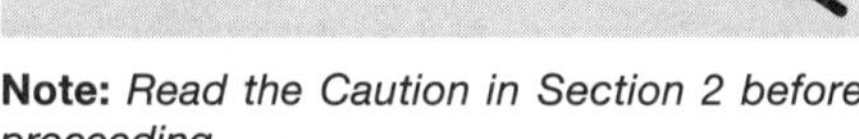

Note: *Read the Caution in Section 2 before proceeding.*

1 Although it is possible to renew the gaiter by just disconnecting the inner end of the driveshaft from the transmission (LH) or intermediate shaft (RH), it is recommended that the driveshaft be removed completely and the work carried out on the bench. If the work is carried out working beneath the car, the CV joints may inadvertently be articulated beyond the maximum angles described in Section 2. Note that if both the inner and outer gaiters are being renewed at the same time, the outer gaiter is removed from the inner end of the driveshaft.
2 Remove the driveshaft as described in Section 2, and mount it in a vice.
3 Mark the driveshaft in relation to the joint housing, to ensure correct refitting.
4 Note the fitted location of both of the inner joint gaiter retaining clips, then release the clips from the gaiter, and slide the gaiter back along the driveshaft a little way **(see illustrations)**.
5 Withdraw the inner joint housing from the tripod. As the housing is being removed, be prepared for some of the bearing rollers to fall out – identify them for position with a dab of paint and tape **(see illustrations)**. Scoop out the grease from the joint and gaiter.
6 Check that the inner end of the driveshaft is marked in relation to the splined tripod hub. If not, carefully centre-punch the two items, to ensure correct refitting. Alternatively, use dabs of paint on the driveshaft and one end of the tripod.
7 Extract the circlip retaining the tripod on the driveshaft **(see illustration)**.
8 Using a puller, remove the tripod from the end of the driveshaft, and slide off the gaiter **(see illustration)**.
9 If the outer gaiter is also to be renewed, remove it and fit the new one with reference to Section 4.

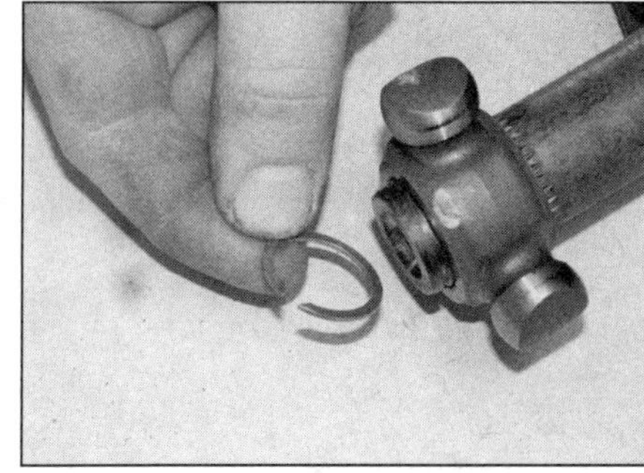

3.7 Removing the circlip retaining the inner tripod on the driveshaft

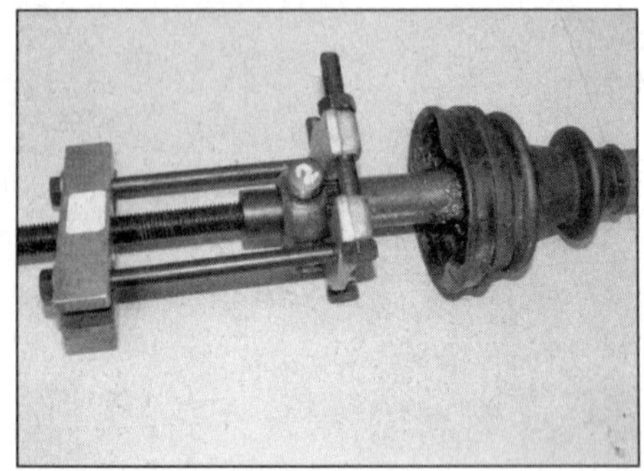
3.8 Using a puller to remove the tripod

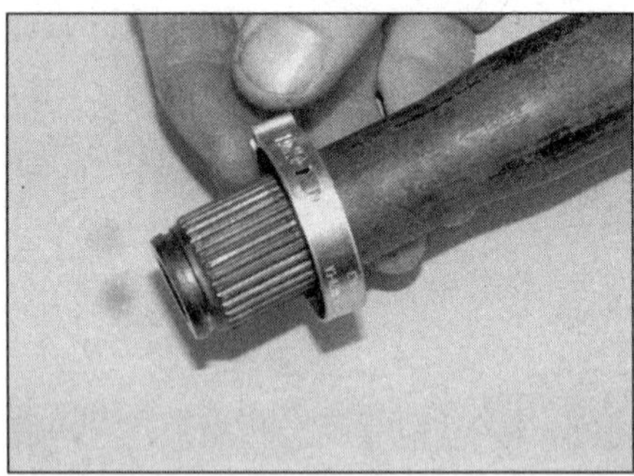
3.11a Slide on the small clip . . .

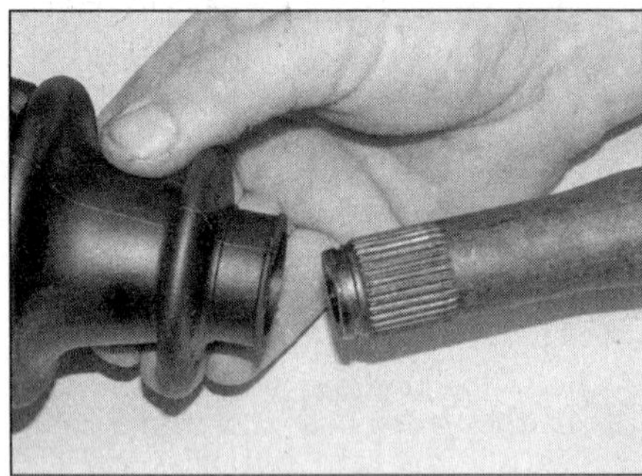
3.11b . . . followed by the gaiter and large clip

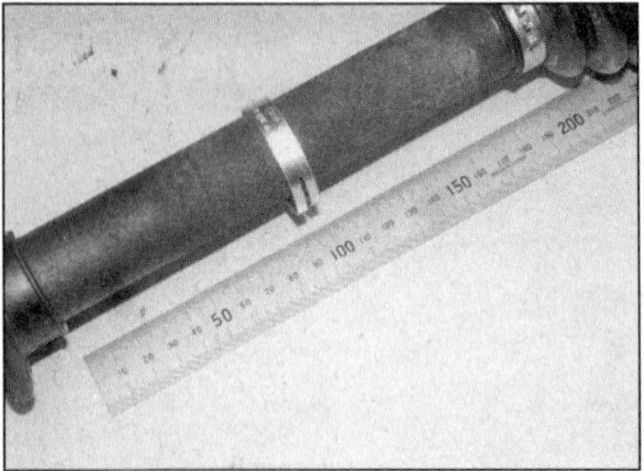

3.11c Checking the distance between the inner and outer gaiters

3.12a Drive the tripod fully onto the driveshaft splines . . .

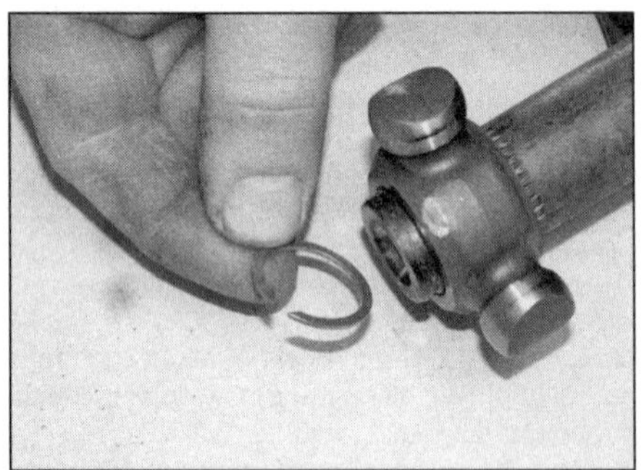
3.12b . . . and fit the new circlip

10 Clean the driveshaft, and obtain a new joint retaining circlip. The gaiter retaining clips must also be renewed.

11 Slide the new gaiter on the driveshaft, together with new clips. Make sure that the gaiter is located at its previously-noted position on the driveshaft, then tighten the small diameter clip **(see illustrations)**. The distance between the inner and outer gaiters must be:

1.8 and 2.0 litre manual transmission models: 180.0 mm

2.0 litre automatic transmission models: 160.0 mm

V6 and all diesel models: 165.5 mm

12 Refit the tripod on the driveshaft splines, if necessary using a soft-faced mallet and a suitable metal tube to drive it fully onto the splines. It must be fitted with the chamfered edge leading (towards the driveshaft), and with the previously-made marks aligned. Secure it in position using a new circlip. Ensure that the circlip is fully engaged in its groove **(see illustrations)**.

13 Locate the bearing rollers on the tripod in their previously-noted positions, using grease to hold them in place **(see illustration)**.

14 Pack sufficient CV joint grease into the tripod and joint housing **(see illustration)**.

15 Guide the joint housing onto the tripod fully, and locate the gaiter in the special groove, ensuring it is not twisted or distorted **(see illustrations)**.

16 Insert a small screwdriver under the lip of the gaiter at the housing end. This will allow trapped air to escape, then withdraw the joint housing by 20 mm from its fully-in position – this is the normal operating position **(see illustrations)**.

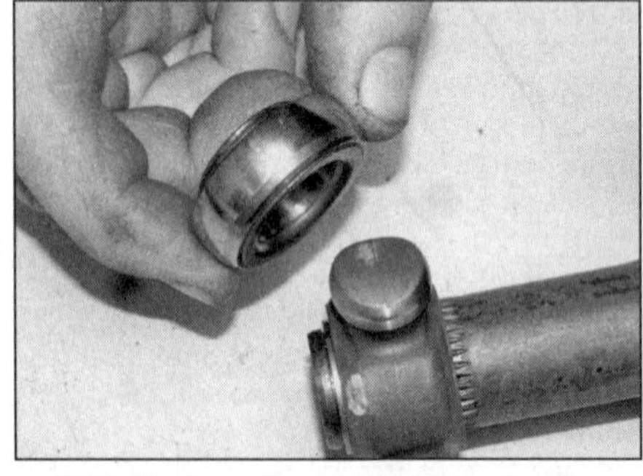
3.13 Fit the rollers in their previously-noted position . . .

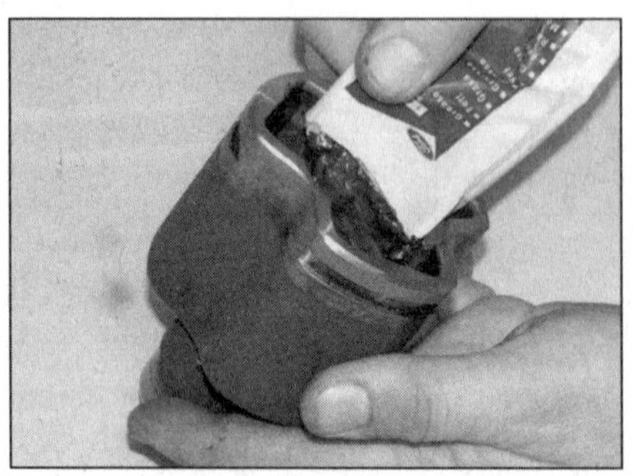
3.14 . . . and pack the joint housing with CV joint grease

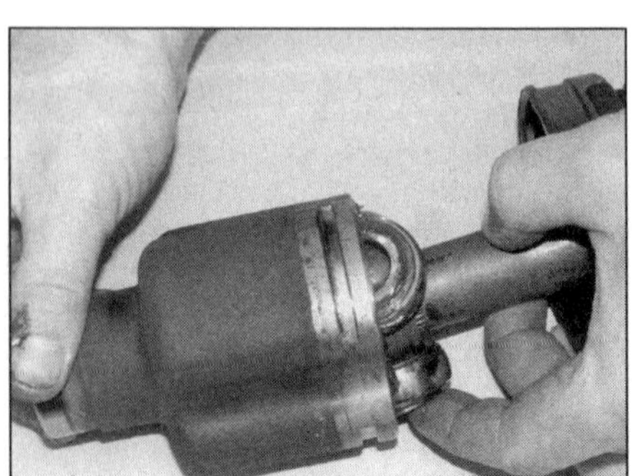
3.15a Guide the housing onto the tripod . . .

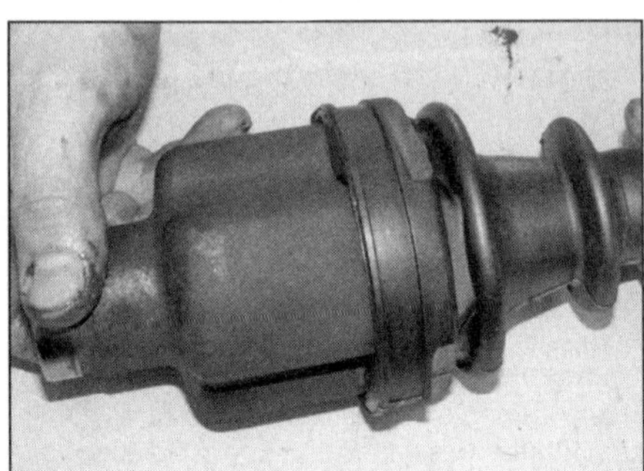
3.15b . . . and locate the gaiter in the special groove

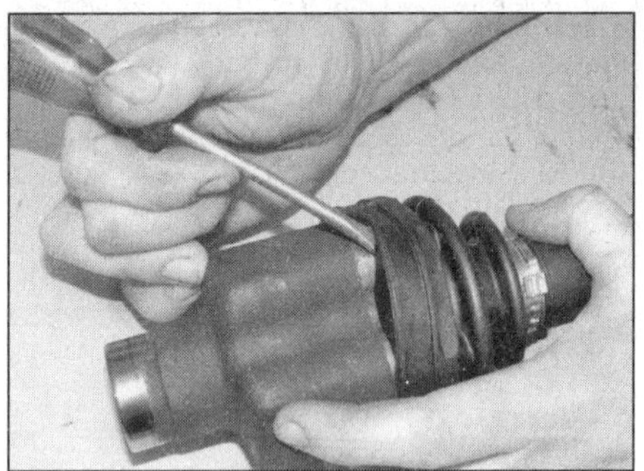
3.16a Use a screwdriver to release the trapped air . . .

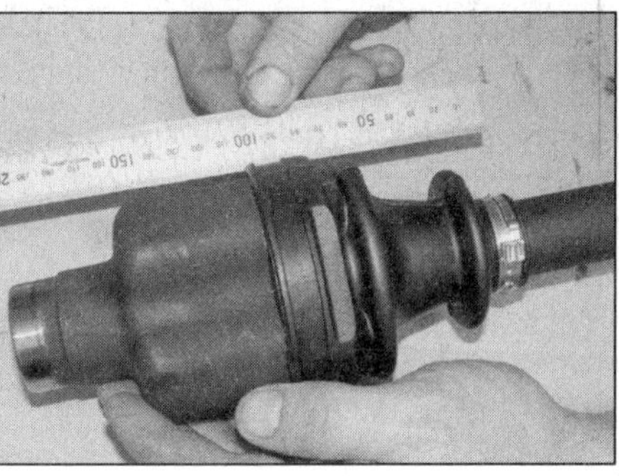
3.16b . . . then withdraw the joint housing by 20 mm

3.17 Using the special tool to tighten the gaiter clips

17 Fit and tighten the retaining clips. If possible, use the special tool to tighten the clips, otherwise, use pincers **(see illustration)**.
18 Refit the driveshaft with reference to Section 2.

4 Driveshaft outer CV joint gaiter – renewal

Note: *Read the Caution in Section 2 before proceeding. The outer CV joint is pressed onto the driveshaft and must not be removed.*
1 The outer CV joint gaiter is removed by first removing the inner gaiter as described in Section 3.
2 Clean the exposed part of the driveshaft to facilitate removal of the balance weight (where fitted) and the outer gaiter.
3 Mark the position of the balance weight (where fitted) and the outer gaiter on the driveshaft. The balance weight is pressed onto the driveshaft, and ideally a puller or press is required to remove it. However, if the weight is supported in a vice, the driveshaft may be driven through it, using a soft-faced mallet on the inner end of the driveshaft.
4 Note the location of both of the outer gaiter retaining clips, then release them. Release the gaiter from the outer CV joint, then slide it off of the inner end of the driveshaft together with the clips **(see illustrations)**. Scoop out the grease from the outer CV joint.
5 Slide the new gaiter, together with the new clips, onto the driveshaft until it is near the outer CV joint.
6 Pack the outer CV joint with sufficient grease, working it well into the rollers – many gaiter kits come with a sachet of grease, but if not, your Ford dealer or parts supplier should be able to suggest a grease type. Pack any excess grease into the gaiter, then slide the gaiter fully onto its previously-noted position on the driveshaft and CV joint housing. Ensure the gaiter is not twisted or distorted.
7 Temporarily insert a small screwdriver under the lip of the gaiter at the housing end. This will allow trapped air to escape.
8 Tighten the gaiter retaining clips.
9 Where a balance weight is fitted, measure its length and add 125 mm to determine the correct fitting position on the driveshaft. The distance must be measured from the inner end of the driveshaft to the further (smaller diameter) edge of the weight **(see illustration)**. Press or drive the weight onto the driveshaft, however, do not exceed a force of 10 kN if supporting the outer end of the driveshaft, otherwise the outer CV joint may be damaged.
10 Refit the inner gaiter with reference to Section 3.

5 Driveshafts – inspection and joint renewal

Note: *Read the Caution in Section 2 before proceeding.*

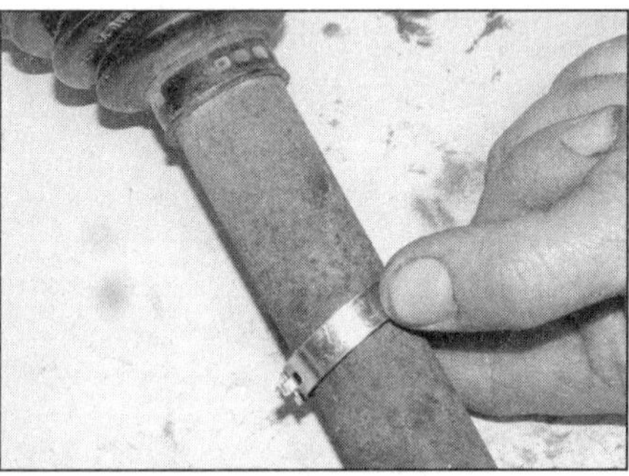
4.4a Remove the small clip . . .

4.4c . . . and slide the gaiter off the inner end of the driveshaft

1 If any of the checks described in the appropriate part of Chapter 1 reveal apparent excessive wear or play in any driveshaft joint, first remove the wheel cover (or centre cover), and check that the hub nut (driveshaft outer nut) is tightened to the specified torque. Repeat this check on the hub nut on the other side.
2 Road test the car, and listen for a metallic clicking from the front as the car is driven slowly in a circle on full-lock. If a clicking noise is heard, this indicates wear in the outer constant velocity joint, which means that the driveshaft and outer joint must be renewed; it is not possible to renew the joint separately.
3 If vibration, consistent with roadspeed, is felt through the car when accelerating, there is a possibility of wear in the inner tripod joints. To renew an inner joint, remove the driveshaft as described in Section 2, then separate the

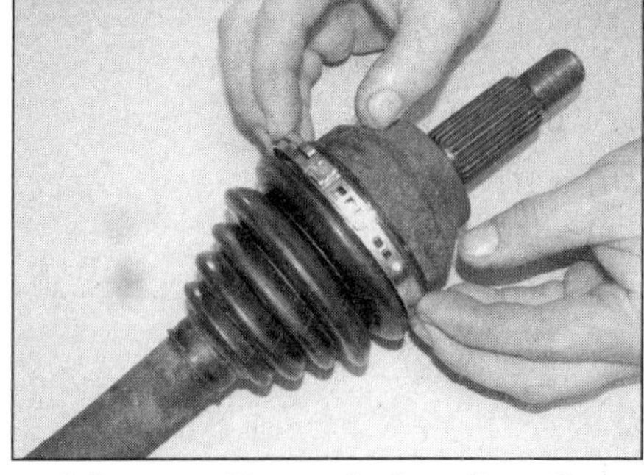
4.4b . . . and large clip from the outer joint . . .

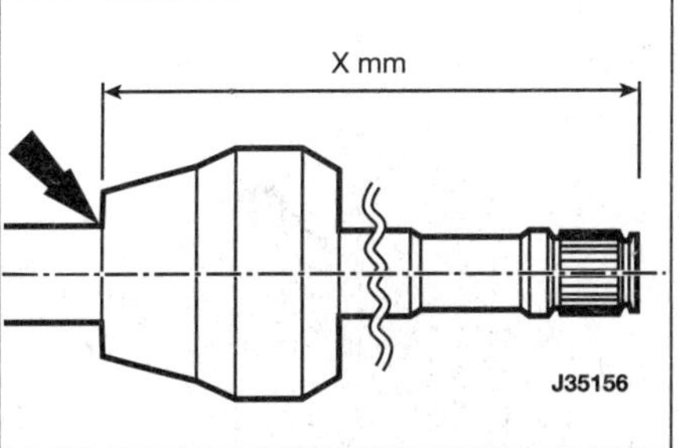

4.9 The fitting position of the balance weight (x) = the length of the weight + 125 mm joint from the driveshaft with reference to Section 3.

4 Continual noise from the right-hand driveshaft, increasing with roadspeed, may indicate wear in the support bearing. To renew this bearing, the driveshaft and intermediate shaft must be removed (see Section 2), and the bearing extracted using a puller.

5 Remove the bearing dust cover, and obtain a new one.

6 Drive or press on the new bearing, applying the pressure to the inner race only. Similarly drive or press on the new dust cover.

7 Refit the driveshaft and intermediate shaft with reference to Section 2.

Chapter 9
Braking system

Contents

Degrees of difficulty

Easy, suitable for novice with little experience	**Fairly easy,** suitable for beginner with some experience	**Fairly difficult,** suitable for competent DIY mechanic	**Difficult,** suitable for experienced DIY mechanic	**Very difficult,** suitable for expert DIY or professional

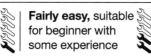

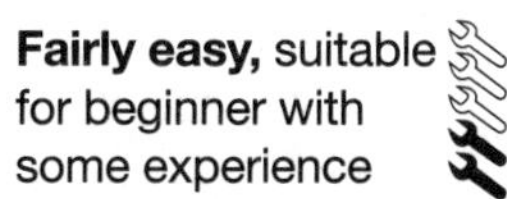

Specifications

Front brakes

Type	Ventilated disc, with single-piston floating caliper
Minimum front brake pad lining thickness	1.5 mm
Disc diameter	300.0 mm
Disc thickness:	
New	24.0 mm
Minimum	22.0 mm
Maximum disc run-out (fitted)	0.15 mm
Maximum disc thickness variation	0.015 mm
Front hub face maximum run-out	0.05 mm

Rear disc brakes

Type	Solid disc, with single-piston floating caliper
Minimum rear brake pad lining thickness	1.5 mm
Disc diameter	280.0 mm
Disc thickness:	
New	12.0 mm
Minimum	10.2 mm
Maximum disc thickness variation	0.015 mm

Torque wrench settings

Torque wrench settings	Nm	lbf ft
ABS hydraulic unit	25	18
Brake line union nuts to ABS hydraulic unit	15	11
Brake pedal bracket	25	18
Brake pedal cross-shaft	25	18
Brake pipe unions to master cylinder	20	15
Caliper guide pin bolts	30	22
Caliper mounting bracket:		
Front	130	96
Rear (up to September 2004)	80	59
Rear (September 2004 onwards)	66	49
Handbrake lever assembly to floor	20	15
In-line brake union nuts	17	13
Master cylinder	20	15
Rear hub retaining bolts	90	66
Roadwheel nuts	85	63
Thermostat housing (diesel models)	22	16
Vacuum pump (diesel models)	22	16
Vacuum servo:		
Bracket to body	25	18
Mounting nuts	20	15

1 General information and precautions

The braking system is of diagonally-split, dual-circuit design, with ventilated discs at the front, and solid discs at the rear. The front and rear calipers are of single-piston, floating design. Models with steel wheels have standard brake discs, whereas models with alloy wheels have anti-corrosion coated brake discs – this is intended to prevent corrosion between the disc and wheel hub, which can make alloy wheels difficult to remove.

The handbrake is cable-operated, with a short primary cable and two rear main cables. Unlike earlier Mondeos, the latest models have reverted to a manual handbrake adjustment system.

All models are fitted with a low-pressure anti-lock braking system (ABS) which uses the basic conventional brake system, together with an ABS hydraulic unit fitted between the master cylinder and the four wheel brakes. If wheel lock-up is detected on a wheel when the vehicle speed is above 3 mph, the valve opens, releasing pressure to the relevant brake until the wheel regains a rotational speed corresponding to the speed of the vehicle. The cycle can be repeated many times a second. In the event of a fault in the ABS system, the conventional braking system is not affected. Diagnosis of a fault in the ABS system requires the use of special equipment, and this work should therefore be left to a Ford dealer.

Besides ABS, all models are equipped with Emergency Brake Assist (EBA). This feature detects when an emergency stop is happening through a fluid pressure sensor, and uses the ABS to generate even greater fluid pressure (or braking effort) without the need for increased driver effort at the brake pedal. This allows maximum braking effort to be generated rapidly by the system when needed, still within the confines of avoiding wheel lock-up.

A brake traction control system (BTCS) is fitted to some models, and uses the basic ABS components, with an additional pump and valves fitted to the hydraulic actuator. If wheelspin (abnormally-high front wheel speed) is detected at a speed below 30 mph, one of the valves opens, to allow the pump to pressurise the relevant brake, until the spinning wheel slows to a rotational speed corresponding to the speed of the vehicle. This has the effect of transferring torque to the wheel with most traction. At the same time, the throttle plate is closed slightly, to reduce the torque from the engine.

Even with ABS and traction control, it is still possible for a vehicle to get out of control and spin, or to slide off the road, especially when braking and cornering at the same time. The Electronic Stability Program (ESP) adds another safety function to the ABS. Sensors measure the position of the steering wheel, the pressure in the brake master cylinder, the yaw velocity/rate (body roll), and the lateral (sideways) acceleration. With this information, the system can compare the driver's intention with the car's movement, and apply the appropriate corrective action – this might be to apply or release an individual brake to steer the car, or to reduce engine power via the engine management system. Though the ESP can be switched off manually, it defaults to the 'on' position whenever the engine is started. On models with ESP, the EBA feature described previously operates in conjunction with the ESP, but the EBA feature is not switched off manually with the ESP facia switch.

In addition to their purely braking system functions, the ABS wheel sensors are also used to provide the engine management system with a vehicle speed signal.

Precautions

The car's braking system is one of its most important safety features. When working on the brakes, there are a number of points to be aware of, to ensure that your health (or even your life) is not being put at risk.

Warning: Brake fluid is poisonous. Take care to keep it off bare skin, and in particular not to get splashes in your eyes. The fluid also attacks paintwork and plastics – wash off spillages immediately with cold water. Finally, brake fluid is highly inflammable, and should be handled with the same care as petrol.

- ***Make sure the ignition is off (take out the key) before disconnecting any braking system hydraulic union, and do not switch it on until after the hydraulic system has been bled. Failure to do this could lead to air entering the ABS hydraulic unit. If air enters the hydraulic unit pump, it will prove very difficult (in some cases impossible) to bleed the unit.***
- ***When servicing any part of the system, work carefully and methodically – do not take short-cuts; also observe scrupulous cleanliness when overhauling any part of the hydraulic system.***
- ***Always renew components in axle sets, where applicable – this means renewing brake pads on BOTH sides, even if only one set of pads is worn, or one wheel cylinder is leaking (for example). In the instance of uneven brake wear, the cause should be investigated and fixed (on front brakes, sticking caliper pistons is a likely problem).***
- ***Use only genuine Ford parts, or at least those of known good quality.***
- ***Although genuine Ford brake pads are asbestos-free, the dust created by wear of non-genuine parts may contain asbestos, which is a health hazard. Never blow it out with compressed air, and don't inhale any of it.***

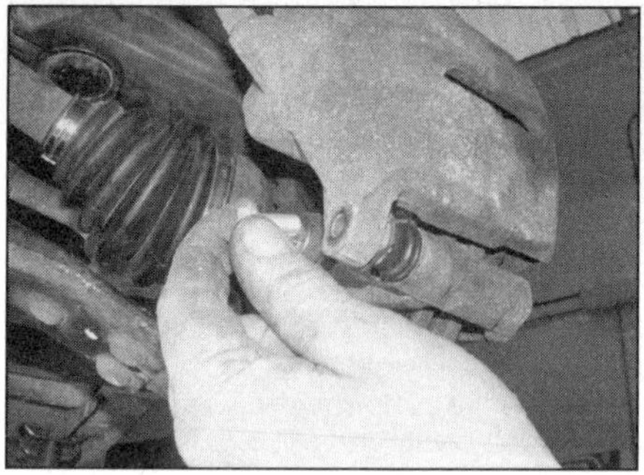
2.3 Unscrewing the caliper lower guide pin bolt

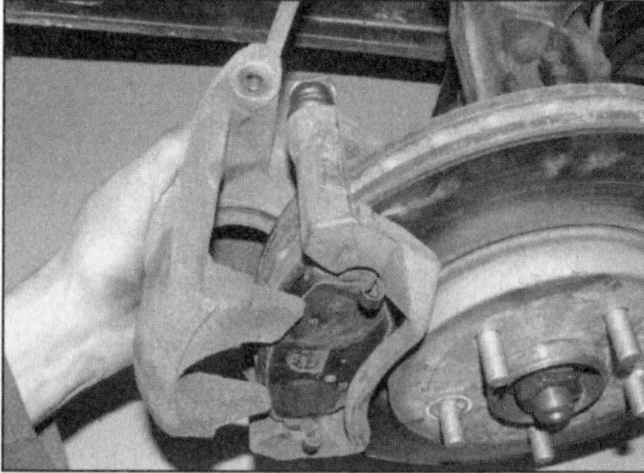
2.4 Removing the caliper from the front brake pads

2.5 Removing the brake pads from the mounting bracket

- ***DO NOT use petroleum-based solvents to clean brake parts; use brake cleaner or methylated spirit only.***
- ***DO NOT allow any brake fluid, oil or grease to contact the brake pads or disc.***
- ***ABS components are subject to near-continuous development, and it is recommended that only new components are fitted when needed. Secondhand parts should be checked carefully, to make sure they are from the same generation of ABS as that fitted to your car (check that the part numbers match), otherwise the system may not function properly after fitting.***

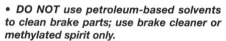

2 Front brake pads – renewal

Note: *Refer to the precautions in Section 1 before proceeding.*

1 Apply the handbrake, then jack up the front of the car and support it on axle stands (see *Jacking and vehicle support*). Remove both front roadwheels. Work on one brake assembly at a time, using the assembled brake for reference if necessary.

2 Push the piston into its bore by pulling the caliper outwards.

3 Unscrew and remove the caliper lower guide pin bolt, using a slim open-ended spanner to prevent the guide pin itself from rotating **(see illustration)**.

4 Pivot the caliper away from the brake pads and mounting bracket, and tie it to the suspension strut using a suitable piece of wire. If the upper guide pin bolt is also removed, do not allow the caliper to hang down by the hose **(see illustration)**.

5 Withdraw the two brake pads from the caliper mounting bracket **(see illustration)**.

6 First measure the thickness of each brake pad lining **(see illustration)**. If either pad is worn at any point to the specified minimum thickness or less, all four pads must be renewed. Note that the pads are fitted with audible warning springs, which are designed to make a warning noise when the linings have reached their minimum thickness. The pads should also be renewed if any are fouled with oil or grease; note that there is no satisfactory way of degreasing friction material. If worn unevenly, or fouled with oil or grease, trace and rectify the cause before reassembly.

7 If the brake pads are still serviceable, carefully clean them using a clean, fine wire brush or similar, paying particular attention to the sides and back of the metal backing. Clean out the grooves in the friction material, and pick out any large embedded particles of dirt or debris. Carefully clean the pad locations in the caliper mounting bracket.

8 Prior to fitting the pads, check that the guide pins are free to slide easily in the caliper mounting bracket, and check that the rubber guide pin gaiters are undamaged. Brush the dust and dirt from the caliper and piston, but **do not** inhale it, as it is a health hazard. Scrape any corrosion from the edge of the disc, taking care not to damage the friction surface and inspect the disc for scoring and cracks. Inspect the dust seal around the piston for damage, and the piston for evidence of fluid leaks, corrosion or damage. If attention to any of these components is necessary, refer to Sections 3 and 4.

9 The caliper piston must be pushed back into the caliper to make room for new pads – this may require considerable effort. Either use a G-clamp, sliding-jaw (water pump) pliers, or suitable pieces of wood as levers **(see illustration)**. Any brake fluid spilt on paintwork should be washed off with clean water without delay – brake fluid is a highly-effective paint-stripper.

Caution: Pushing back the piston causes a reverse-flow of brake fluid, which has been known to 'flip' the master cylinder rubber seals, resulting in a total loss of braking. To avoid this, clamp the caliper flexible hose and open the bleed screw – as the piston is pushed back, the fluid can be directed into a suitable container using a hose attached to the bleed screw. Close the screw just before the piston is pushed fully back, to ensure no air enters the system.

10 If the recommended method of opening a bleed screw before pushing back the piston is not used, the fluid level in the reservoir will rise, and possibly overflow. Make sure that there is sufficient space in the brake fluid reservoir to accept the displaced fluid, and if necessary, syphon some off first. **Note:** *Do not syphon the fluid by mouth, as it is poisonous; use a syringe or an old antifreeze tester.*

11 Smear a little high melting-point brake grease to the metal contact points of each brake pad **(see illustration)**.

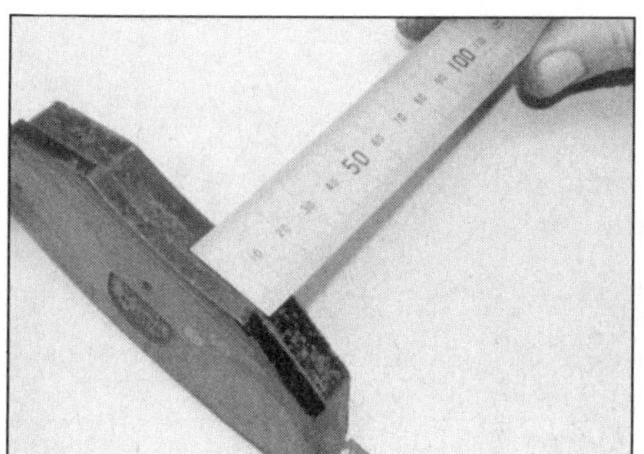
2.6 Measuring the thickness of the front brake pad linings

2.9 Using a special tool to retract the caliper piston

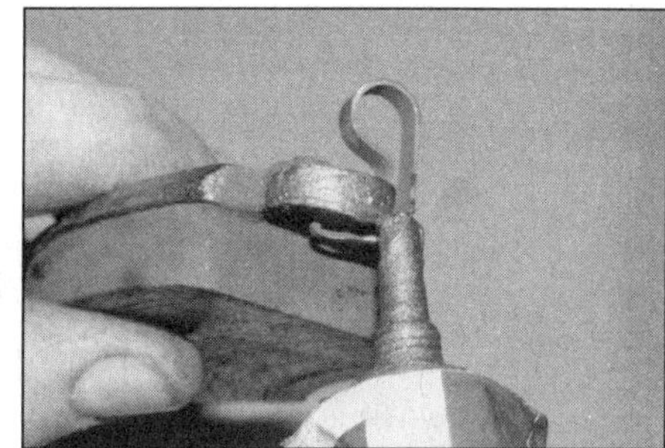
2.11 Apply a little high melting-point brake grease to the contact points of each brake pad

12 Ensuring that the friction material of each pad is against the brake disc, fit the pads to the caliper mounting bracket.
13 Locate the caliper over the pads, then fit the guide pin bolts and tighten them to the specified torque while retaining the guide pin with an open-ended spanner.
14 Depress the brake pedal repeatedly, until the pads are pressed into firm contact with the brake disc, and normal pedal pressure is restored.
15 Repeat the above procedure on the remaining front brake caliper.
16 Refit the roadwheels, then lower the car to the ground and tighten the roadwheel nuts to the specified torque setting.
17 Check the hydraulic fluid level as described in *Weekly checks*.

HAYNES HiNT ***New pads will not give full braking efficiency until they have bedded-in. Be prepared for this, and avoid hard braking as far as possible for the first hundred miles or so after pad renewal.***

3 Front brake caliper – removal, overhaul and refitting

Note: *Refer to the precautions in Section 1 before proceeding.*

Removal

1 Apply the handbrake, then jack up the front of the car and support it on axle stands (see *Jacking and vehicle support*). Remove the appropriate front roadwheel.
2 Fit a brake hose clamp to the flexible hose leading to the front brake caliper. This will minimise brake fluid loss during subsequent operations.
3 Loosen the union on the caliper end of the flexible brake hose. Once loosened, do not try to unscrew the hose at this stage.
4 Remove the caliper guide pin bolts as described in Section 2.
5 Support the caliper in one hand, and prevent the hydraulic hose from turning with the other hand. Unscrew the caliper from the hose, making sure that the hose is not twisted unduly or strained. Once the caliper is detached, plug the open hydraulic unions in the caliper and hose, to keep out dust and dirt.
6 If required, the pads can be removed and the caliper mounting bracket can be unbolted and removed from the steering knuckle **(see illustration)**.

Overhaul

7 With the caliper on the bench, brush away all traces of dust and dirt, but take care not to inhale any dust, as it may be injurious to health.
8 Pull the dust-excluding rubber seal from the end of the piston.
9 Apply low air pressure to the fluid inlet union, and eject the piston. Only low air pressure is required for this, such as is produced by a foot-operated tyre pump.

Caution: The piston may be ejected with some force. Position a thin piece of wood between the piston and the caliper body, to prevent damage to the end face of the piston, in the event of it being ejected suddenly.

10 Using a suitable blunt instrument, prise the piston seal from the groove in the cylinder bore. Take care not to scratch the surface of the bore.
11 Clean the piston and caliper body with methylated spirit, and allow to dry. Examine the surfaces of the piston and cylinder bore for wear, damage and corrosion. If either the cylinder bore or piston is unserviceable, the complete caliper must be renewed. The seals must be renewed, regardless of the condition of the other components.
12 Coat the piston and seals with clean brake fluid, then manipulate the piston seal into the groove in the cylinder bore.
13 Carefully push the piston squarely into its bore.
14 Fit the dust-excluding rubber seal onto the piston and caliper, then depress the piston fully.
15 Release the dust-excluding rubber boots and remove the guide pin components from the mounting bracket. Thoroughly clean the components and examine them for wear and damage. Renew as necessary, and reassemble using a reversal of the removal procedure, using high melting-point grease to lubricate the guide pins **(see illustrations)**.

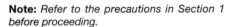

3.6 Front brake caliper mounting bracket bolts

3.15a Front brake caliper mounting bracket components

3.15b Apply high melting-point grease to the bracket bore . . .

3.15c . . . fit the rubber dust cover . . .

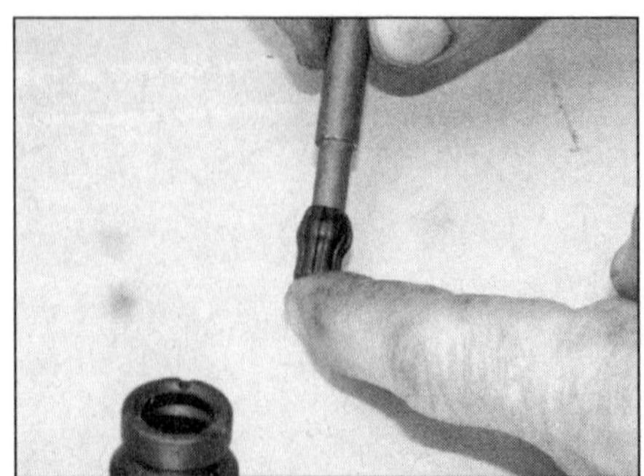

3.15d . . . locate the rubber bush on the lower guide pin . . .

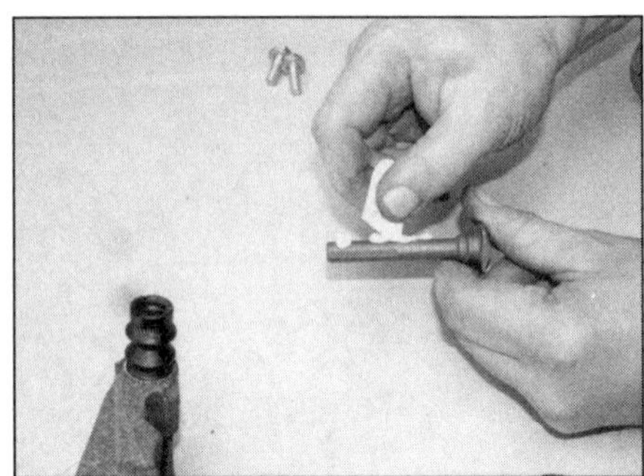

3.15e . . . grease the guide pin . . .

3.15f . . . and refit the guide pin

Refitting

16 Refit the caliper, and where applicable the pads and mounting bracket, by reversing the removal operations. Make sure that the flexible brake hose is not twisted. Tighten the mounting bolts and wheel nuts to the specified torque.

17 Bleed the brake circuit as described in Section 12, remembering to remove the brake hose clamp from the flexible hose. Make sure there are no leaks from the hose connections. Test the brakes carefully before returning the car to normal service.

4 Front brake disc – inspection, removal and refitting

Note: *Refer to the precautions in Section 1 before proceeding.*

Inspection

1 Apply the handbrake. Loosen the relevant wheel nuts, jack up the front of the car and support it on axle stands. Remove the appropriate front wheel.

2 Unscrew the two bolts securing the brake caliper mounting bracket to the steering knuckle, then slide the caliper and brake pads off of the brake disc. Tie the caliper and bracket to the front suspension strut coil spring, taking care not to strain the flexible hydraulic hose.

3 Temporarily refit three of the wheel nuts, with the flat sides of the nuts against the disc. Tighten the nuts progressively, to hold the disc firmly.

4 Scrape any corrosion from the disc. Rotate the disc, and examine it for deep scoring, grooving or cracks. Using a micrometer, measure the thickness of the disc in several places **(see illustration)**. The minimum thickness is stamped on the disc hub. Light wear and scoring is normal, but if excessive, the disc should be removed, and either reground by a specialist, or renewed. If regrinding is undertaken, the minimum thickness must be maintained. Obviously, if the disc is cracked, it must be renewed.

5 Using a dial gauge or a flat metal block and feeler gauges, check that the disc run-out 10 mm from the outer edge does not exceed the limit given in the Specifications **(see illustration)**. To do this, fix the measuring equipment and rotate the disc, noting the variation in measurement as the disc is rotated. The difference between the minimum and maximum measurements recorded is the disc run-out.

6 If the run-out is greater than the specified amount, check for variations of the disc thickness as follows. Mark the disc at eight positions 45° apart, then using a micrometer, measure the disc thickness at the eight positions, 15 mm in from the outer edge. If the variation between the minimum and maximum readings is greater than the specified amount, the disc should be renewed.

7 The hub face run-out can also be checked in a similar way. First remove the disc as described later in this Section, fix the measuring equipment, then slowly rotate the hub, and check that the run-out does not exceed the amount given in the Specifications. If the hub face run-out is excessive, this should be corrected (by renewing the hub bearings – see Chapter 10) before rechecking the disc run-out.

If vibration is felt through the pedal when braking, this could be a sign that the discs are warped. However, if it occurs only under heavy braking, this is a normal feature of the ABS in operation, and does not suggest that the discs should be renewed.

4.4 Checking the thickness of the front brake disc with a micrometer

4.10a Remove the special washers . . .

Removal

8 With the wheel and caliper removed, remove the wheel nuts which were temporarily refitted in paragraph 3.

9 Mark the disc in relation to the hub, if it is to be refitted.

10 Remove the two special washers (where fitted), and withdraw the disc over the wheel studs **(see illustrations)**.

Refitting

11 Make sure that the disc and hub mating surfaces are clean, then locate the disc on the wheel studs. Align the previously-made marks if the original disc is being refitted.

12 Refit the two special washers, where fitted.

13 Refit the brake caliper and mounting bracket with reference to Section 3.

14 Refit the wheel, and lower the car to the ground.

15 Test the brakes carefully before returning the car to normal service.

5 Rear brake pads – renewal

Note: *Refer to the precautions in Section 1 before proceeding.*

1 Work on one brake assembly at a time, using the assembled brake for reference if necessary. Chock the front wheels, loosen the rear wheel nuts, then jack up the rear of the car and support on axle stands (see *Jacking and vehicle support*). Remove the rear wheels, then release the handbrake lever.

4.5 Using a dial gauge to check the brake disc run-out

4.10b . . . and withdraw the brake disc over the wheel studs

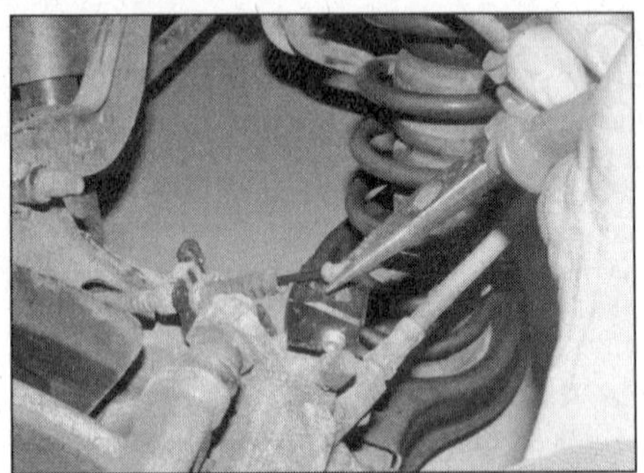

5.2 Disconnecting the handbrake inner cable from the rear caliper lever

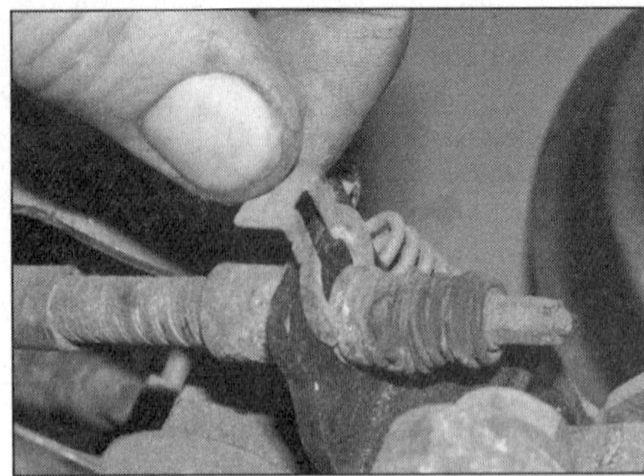

5.3 Disconnecting the handbrake cable from the caliper bracket

5.4 Remove the caliper lower guide pin bolt and swivel the caliper upwards

5.5a Remove the inner disc pad . . .

5.5b . . . followed by the outer disc pad

Models up to September 2004

2 To enable the caliper to pivot upwards for pad removal, the handbrake cable must be disconnected from the caliper. First push the lever forwards, then release the end of the inner cable from the fitting on the lever **(see illustration)**.

3 Release the handbrake outer cable from the caliper bracket and position it to one side. Where a plastic ferrule is fitted to the outer cable, it will be necessary to compress the plastic tangs in order to release it from the bracket. Where a spring clip is fitted, pull it from the outer cable **(see illustration)**.

4 Unscrew and remove the caliper lower guide pin bolt **(see illustration)**. Swivel the caliper upwards, leaving the upper guide pin still entered in the caliper mounting bracket.

5 Remove the pads from the mounting bracket, noting their fitted positions **(see illustrations)**. Brush all dust and dirt from the caliper, pads and disc, but do not inhale it, as it may be harmful to health. Scrape any corrosion from the edge of the disc.

6 Inspect the rear brake disc as described in Section 7.

7 Apply a little copper-based brake grease to the contact areas on the pad backing plates **(see illustration)**, taking care not to get any on the friction material. Fit the new pads onto the mounting bracket, with the friction material facing the brake disc.

8 The self-adjusting piston must be retracted into the caliper, to allow room for the new pads **(see illustration)**. To do this, turn the piston fully into the caliper whilst also applying pressure to it, using an Allen key. On Saloon and Hatchback models, turn the piston anti-clockwise when working on the right-hand rear caliper, and clockwise when working on the left-hand rear caliper. On Estate models, turn the piston anti-clockwise when working on the left-hand rear caliper, and clockwise when working on the right-hand rear caliper.

Caution: Pushing back the piston causes a reverse-flow of brake fluid, which has been known to 'flip' the master cylinder rubber seals, resulting in a total loss of braking. To avoid this, clamp the caliper flexible hose and open the bleed screw – as the piston is pushed back, the fluid can be directed into a suitable container using a hose attached to the bleed screw. Close the screw just before the piston is pushed fully back, to ensure no air enters the system.

9 With the piston screwed in fully, centralise the correct cut-out on the piston with the raised mark on the caliper as shown **(see**

5.7 Apply a little copper-based brake grease to the contact areas on the pad backing plates

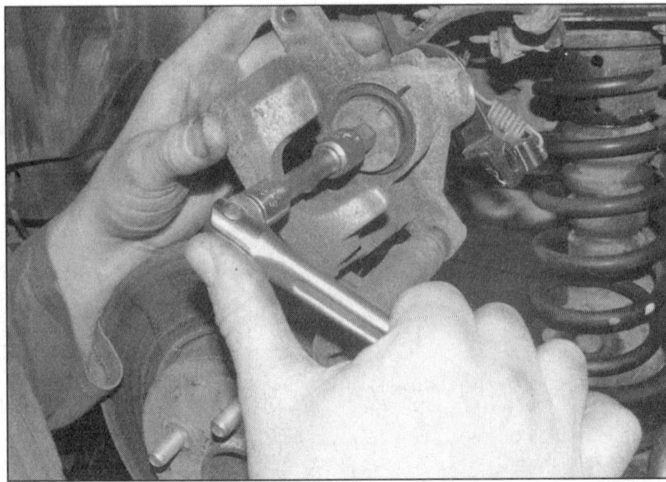

5.8 The self-adjusting piston must be retracted into the caliper to allow room for the new pads

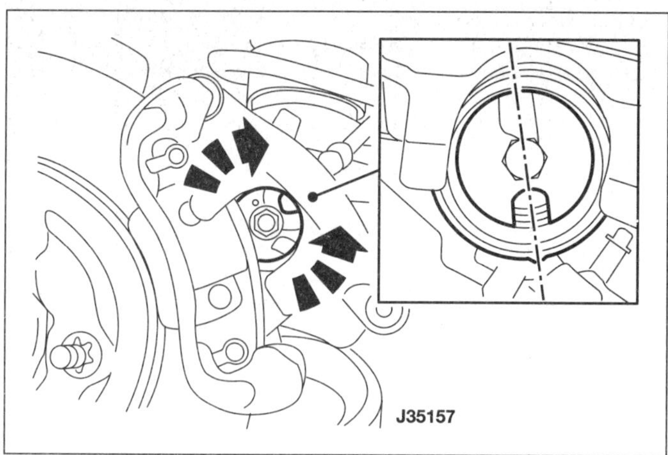

5.9a On the left-hand rear caliper, the 'short' cut-out must align with the raised mark . . .

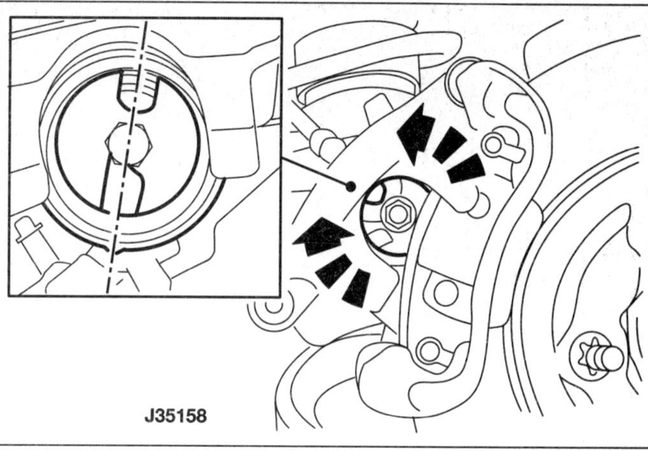

5.9b . . . but on the right-hand rear caliper, the 'long' cut-out must align with the mark

illustrations). On the left-hand rear caliper, the 'short' cut-out must align with the mark, whereas, on the right-hand rear caliper, the 'long' cut-out must align with the mark. Note that the 'pips' on the outer faces of the brake pads locate in these cut-outs.

10 Swivel the caliper down. Apply a little locking fluid to the threads of the lower guide pin bolt, then tighten it to the specified torque.

11 Refit the handbrake outer cable to the bracket, making sure that it is locked firmly in position.

12 Push the handbrake lever forwards, then hook the inner cable on the fitting, and release the lever.

Models from September 2004

13 Unscrew and remove both the rear caliper guide pin bolts, and lift the caliper off the pads and mounting bracket **(see illustrations)**. Note how the handbrake cable sits, so the caliper can be refitted correctly.

14 The self-adjusting piston must be retracted into the caliper, to allow room for the new pads. To do this, turn the piston fully into the caliper whilst also applying pressure to it. Ford dealers use a special tool (206-085) which has two prongs to engage the two indents in the piston – if this tool is not available, various tool companies sell suitable substitutes **(see illustration)**. Since the piston must be pressed back with some force, experience has shown that using pliers for this task rarely works.

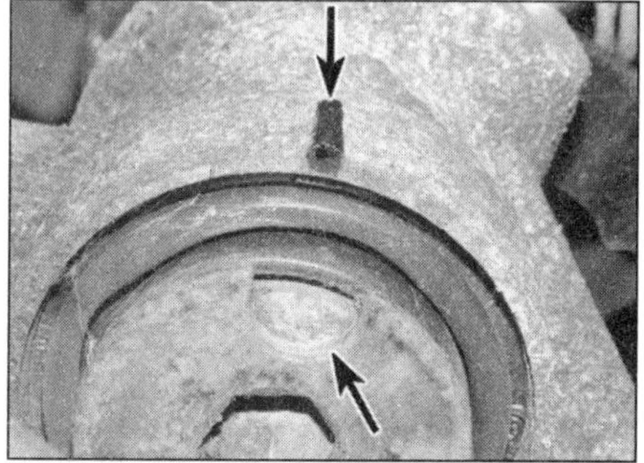

5.9c Piston alignment on the left-hand rear caliper . . .

5.9d . . . and right-hand rear caliper

15 On Saloon and Hatchback models, turn the piston anti-clockwise when working on the right-hand rear caliper, and clockwise when working on the left-hand rear caliper. On Estate models, turn the piston anti-clockwise when working on the left-hand rear caliper, and clockwise when working on the right-hand rear caliper.

Caution: Pushing back the piston causes a reverse-flow of brake fluid, which has been known to 'flip' the master cylinder rubber seals, resulting in a total loss of braking. To avoid this, clamp the caliper flexible hose and open the bleed screw – as the piston is pushed back, the fluid can be directed into a suitable container using a hose attached to the bleed screw. Close the screw just before the piston is pushed fully back, to ensure no air enters the system.

16 When the piston is fully retracted, set the piston indents in the central vertical position, relative to the caliper **(see illustration)**. The back of the inner pad has a raised nib which must sit inside one of the piston indents when the caliper is refitted.

17 Using a piece of wire, string, or cable ties, suspend the caliper so that the flexible hose and handbrake cable are not under strain.

18 Note the positions of the brake pads in the mounting bracket – the inner pad has a

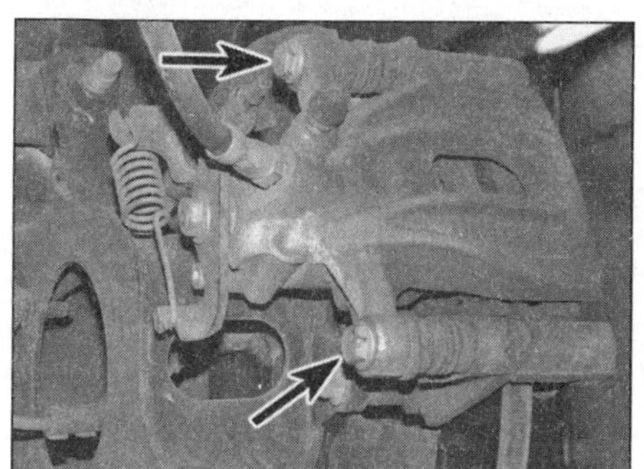

5.13a Unscrew the caliper guide pin bolts . . .

5.13b . . . and lift the caliper off the pads

5.14 Wind the piston back into the caliper using a tool designed for this purpose

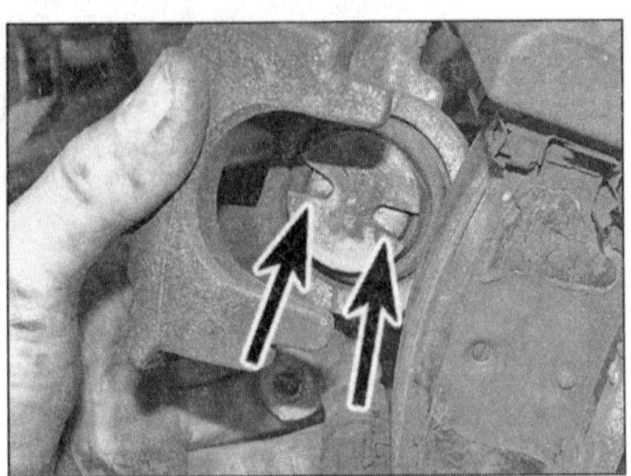

5.16 Showing the caliper piston retracted, with the two indents set 'vertically'

chamfered front (leading) edge, and the outer pad has a shim (which should be removed and re-used if a new one is not supplied with the pads). Remove the pads from the bracket **(see illustrations)**.

19 With the pads removed, check the condition of the two pad retaining springs in the mounting bracket – the long tangs should face away from the brake disc. If this is not the case, or if the springs are damaged, remove the caliper mounting bracket and correct the problem – tighten the two mounting bracket bolts to the specified torque on completion.

20 Fit the inner pad (which has a chamfered leading edge) into the mounting bracket. Note any arrows showing the forward direction of rotation. Rest the pad on the retaining spring's long tang, then press it downwards and twist the pad into place.

21 Remove the adhesive backing from the outer pad, then fit it as described in the previous paragraph. Clean and stick the shim to the back of the pad.

22 Refit the caliper over the pads, making sure that the handbrake cable is routed as before, and is not kinked, twisted or stretched. Refit the guide pin bolts, and tighten them to the specified torque.

All models

23 Repeat the procedure on the remaining rear brake, then refit the rear wheels and lower the car to the ground. Tighten the wheel nuts to the specified torque.

24 Firmly depress the brake pedal a few times, to bring the pads to their normal working position. Check the level of the brake fluid in the reservoir, and top-up if necessary.

25 Give the car a road test, to make sure that the brakes are functioning correctly, and to bed-in the new linings to the contours of the disc. Remember that full braking efficiency will not be obtained until the new linings have bedded-in, and if possible, avoid heavy braking for the first few hundred miles. Check the operation of the handbrake, and adjust if necessary as described in Section 23.

6 Rear brake caliper – removal, overhaul and refitting

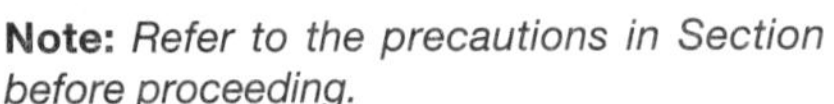

Note: *Refer to the precautions in Section 1 before proceeding.*

Removal

1 Fit a brake hose clamp to the flexible hose leading to the rear brake caliper. This will minimise brake fluid loss during subsequent operations.

2 Loosen the union on the caliper end of the flexible hose, but do not completely unscrew it at this stage.

3 Remove the caliper from the mounting bracket as described in Section 5 – on models up to September 2004, also unscrew the upper guide pin bolt. Do not allow the caliper to hang down unsupported, as this will strain the brake hose.

4 Unscrew the caliper from the hydraulic hose, making sure that the hose is not twisted or strained unduly. Tape over or plug the open hydraulic unions and ports to keep dust and dirt out.

5 Remove the pads and the mounting bracket from the knuckle if necessary.

Overhaul

6 No overhaul procedures were available at the time of writing, so check availability of spares before dismantling the caliper. In principle, the overhaul information given for the front brake caliper will apply, noting that it will be necessary to unscrew the piston from the handbrake mechanism before being able to expel the piston from the caliper.

7 On reassembly, push the piston fully into the caliper, and screw it back onto the handbrake mechanism. Do not attempt to dismantle the handbrake mechanism; if the mechanism is faulty, the complete caliper assembly must be renewed.

8 Release the rubber boots, and slide the guide pins from the mounting bracket. Thoroughly clean the guide pins and their locations in the bracket, then inspect the boots for wear or damage. Renew the boots as necessary. Apply some high-temperature copper grease (or brake grease) to the guide pins, and insert them in the carrier. Locate the boots on the bracket and guide pins.

Refitting

9 Refit the mounting bracket to the knuckle and tighten the bolts to the specified torque. Fit the pads.

10 Remove the temporary plugs, then screw the caliper fully onto the hose.

11 Locate the caliper on the mounting bracket and refit the upper guide pin bolt. Tighten the bolt to the specified torque.

12 Fully tighten the hydraulic flexible hose union. Check that the hose is not twisted; if necessary, remove the caliper from the mounting bracket and reposition it.

13 Remove the brake hose clamp from the flexible hose.

14 Refit the lower guide pin bolt with reference to Section 5.

15 Bleed the brake circuit with reference to Section 12. Make sure there are no leaks from the hose connections. Test the brakes carefully before returning the car to normal service.

7 Rear brake disc – inspection, removal and refitting

Refer to Section 4 (front disc inspection). Once the rear caliper is remcved as described in Section 6, the procedure is the same.

8 Master cylinder – removal and refitting

Warning: Do not fit a standard brake master cylinder to a car equipped with Emergency Brake Assist.

Note: *Refer to the precautions in Section 1 before proceeding.*

Removal

1 Exhaust the vacuum in the servo by pressing the brake pedal a few times, with the engine switched off.

2 Unclip and disconnect the vacuum pipe from the one-way/check valve on the brake servo unit.

3 Disconnect the low fluid level warning light multiplug from the fluid reservoir **(see illustration)**. Unscrew and remove the filler cap.

5.18a Unclip the outer . . .

5.18b . . . and the inner pad from the mounting bracket

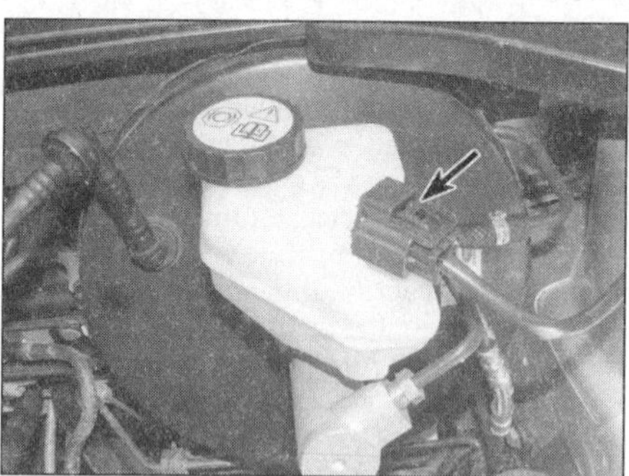
8.3 Low fluid level warning light multiplug

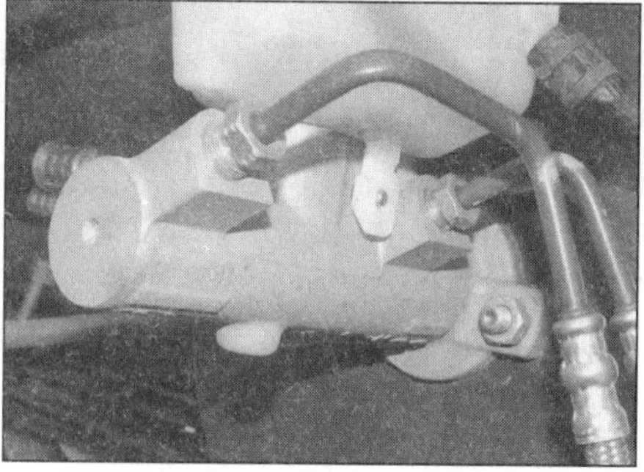
8.8 Brake master cylinder

4 Draw off the hydraulic fluid from the reservoir, using an old battery hydrometer or a poultry baster. If preferred, to reduce fluid spillage, completely drain the fluid as described in the following paragraph.

Warning: Do not syphon the fluid by mouth; it is poisonous.

5 To completely drain the hydraulic fluid from the reservoir and master cylinder, it is necessary to connect a bleed tube to each front brake caliper in turn. Apply the handbrake, then jack up the front of the car and support it on axle stands (see *Jacking and vehicle support*). With the steering on the left-hand lock, connect the tube to the left-hand caliper bleed screw. Loosen the screw and have an assistant depress the footbrake pedal repeatedly until the hydraulic fluid is completely drained from the reservoir. Retighten the bleed screw. Now turn the steering on the right-hand lock and connect the tube to the right-hand caliper bleed screw. Loosen the screw and have the assistant depress the footbrake pedal several times in order to drain the remaining fluid from the reservoir and master cylinder.
6 On manual transmission models, release the clip and disconnect the clutch fluid hose from the brake fluid reservoir. Tape over or plug the hose and reservoir openings.
7 Place rags beneath the master cylinder to catch spilt hydraulic fluid. Identify the locations of the brake pipes on the master cylinder, then unscrew the union nuts and carefully move the pipes to one side without bending them excessively. If the nuts are tight, a split ring spanner should be used in preference to an open-ended spanner. Plug or cap open unions, to keep dust and dirt out.
8 Unscrew the mounting nuts, and withdraw the master cylinder together with the fluid reservoir from the studs on the front of the servo unit **(see illustration)**. Recover the gasket ring.
9 Carefully prise the fluid reservoir from the rubber grommets on the top of the master cylinder, then prise out the grommets and gaskets.
10 If the master cylinder is faulty, it must be renewed. It is not possible to obtain new internal seals.

Refitting

11 Locate the rubber grommets and gaskets in the master cylinder inlet ports.
12 Apply a little brake fluid to the grommets, then press the fluid reservoir fully into position.
13 Clean the contact surfaces of the master cylinder and servo, and fit a new gasket ring.
14 Position the master cylinder on the studs on the servo unit. Refit and tighten the nuts to the specified torque.
15 Carefully insert the hydraulic lines in the apertures in the master cylinder, then tighten the union nuts. Make sure that the nuts enter their threads correctly.
16 On manual transmission models, reconnect the clutch fluid supply hose, then fill the reservoir with fresh brake fluid.
17 Bleed the brake hydraulic system as described in Section 12. On manual transmission models, if fluid has been lost, bleed the clutch hydraulic system as described in Chapter 6.
18 Refit the reservoir filler cap, and reconnect the multiplug for the low fluid level warning light.
19 Reconnect the vacuum pipe to the one-way/check valve on the brake servo unit.
20 Test the brakes carefully before returning the car to normal service.

9 Brake pedal and bracket - removal and refitting

Removal

1 On models with manual transmission, fit a hose clamp to the hydraulic fluid supply hose to the clutch master cylinder on the bulkhead. Alternatively, disconnect the hose from the brake fluid reservoir and plug its end. Loosen the clips and disconnect both hoses from the clutch master cylinder.
2 Working inside the car, move the driver's seat fully to the rear, to allow maximum working area. Remove the driver's side lower facia trim panel, which is secured by four screws and two upper clips. Where applicable, unclip the diagnostic connector plug from the panel, and/or disconnect the wiring from the climate control sensor as the panel is removed.
3 Unscrew the nut and detach the cross-link (RHD) or vacuum servo (LHD) pushrod from the brake pedal **(see illustration)**.
4 Remove the brake pedal position switch retaining clip and discard it **(see illustration)**. A new one must be fitted on reassembly. Disconnect the wiring, then twist the switch anti-clockwise and remove it from the pedal bracket.
5 On manual transmission models, twist the clutch pedal position switch anti-clockwise and remove it from the pedal bracket **(see illustration)**.
6 Release the brake pedal position switch wiring from the bracket.
7 Unhook the accelerator cable from the top of the accelerator pedal **(see illustration)**.
8 On right-hand drive models only, undo the two pedal bracket mounting nuts from the bulkhead inside the car, then, working in the engine compartment, undo the two mounting nuts from the engine side of the bulkhead **(see illustration)**.

9.3 Pushrod-to-brake pedal nut (RHD)

9.4 Brake pedal position switch (RHD)

9.5 Clutch pedal position switch (RHD)

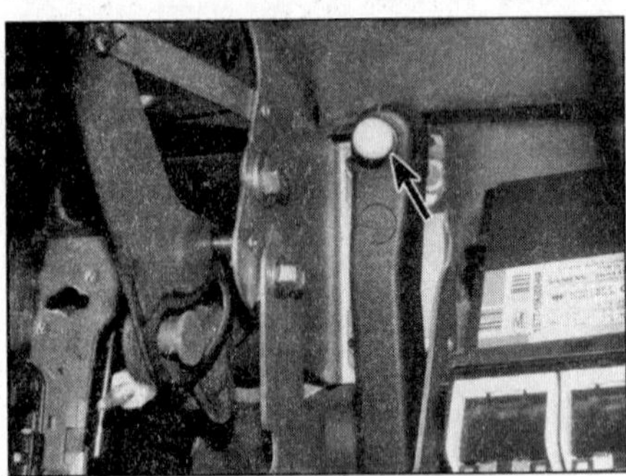

9.7 Accelerator cable connection to the top of the pedal (RHD)

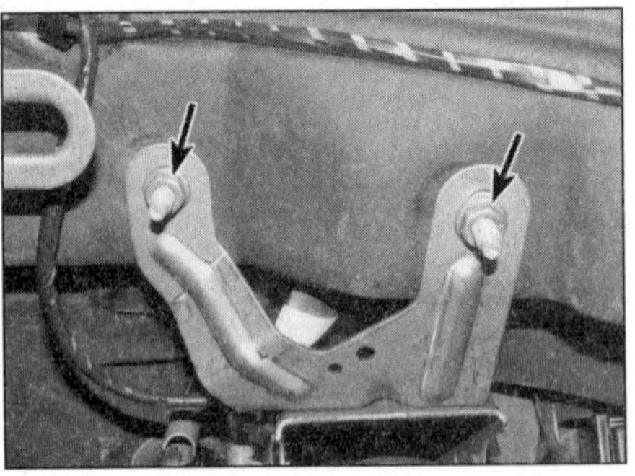

9.8 Pedal bracket top mounting nuts (RHD)

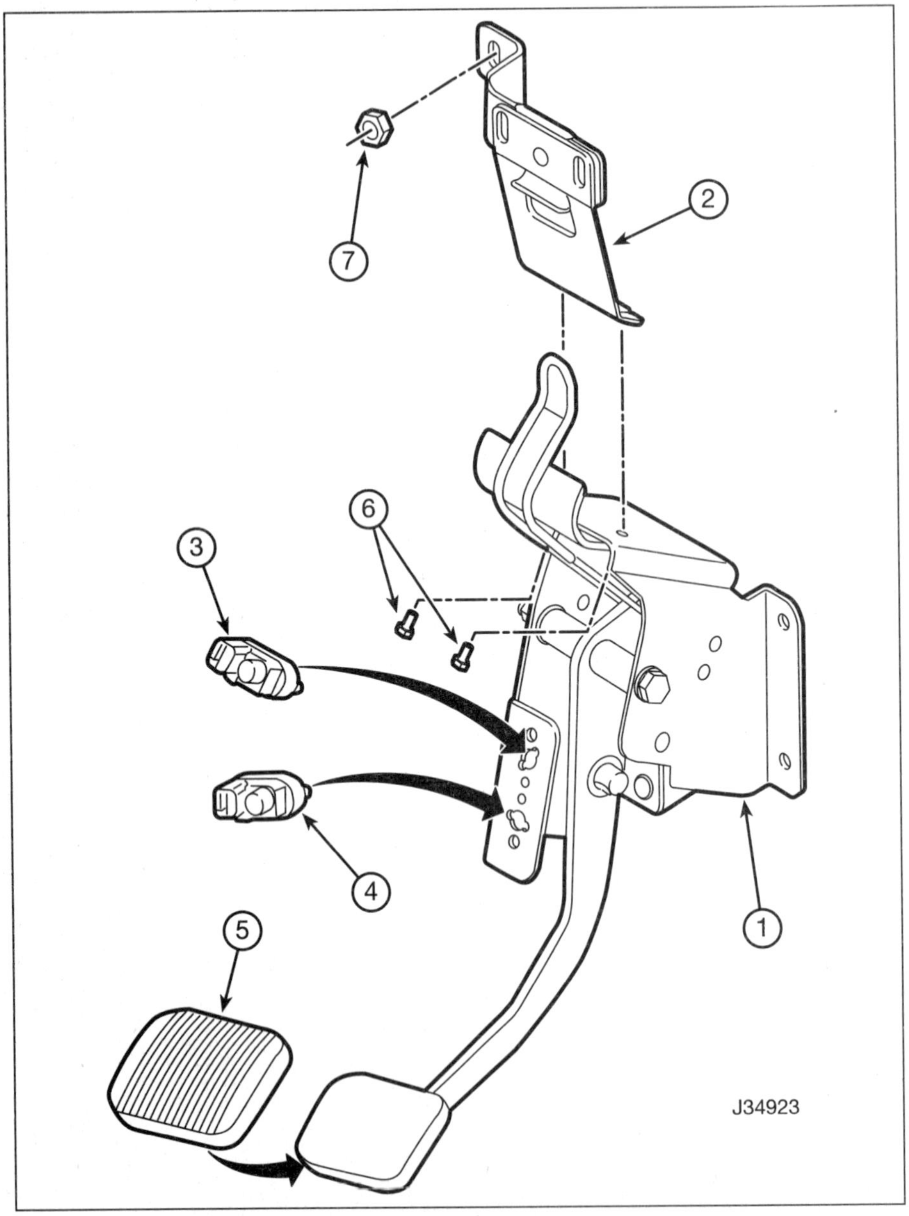

9.9 Brake pedal and bracket components (LHD automatic transmission)

1 *Pedal and bracket assembly*
2 *Upper support bracket*
3 *Speed control inhibitor*
4 *Stop-light switch*
5 *Pedal pad*
6 *Screw*
7 *Nut*

9 On left-hand drive models only, undo the pedal bracket mounting nuts from the bulkhead inside the car **(see illustration)**.

10 Remove the brake pedal and bracket from inside the car and recover the seal and spacer.

11 On manual transmission models, unhook the return spring from the top of the clutch pedal, then unscrew the nut and slide the clutch pedal from the pivot bolt.

12 Unscrew and remove the pivot bolt and remove the brake pedal from the bracket.

Refitting

13 Refitting is a reversal of the removal procedure, but fit a new brake pedal position switch retaining clip, and bleed the clutch hydraulic system as described in Chapter 6.

10 Brake pedal-to-servo cross-link – removal and refitting

Note: *The servo cross-link is only fitted to right-hand-drive (RHD) models.*

Removal

1 Disconnect the battery negative lead (refer to *Disconnecting the battery* at the end of this manual).

2 Remove the master cylinder and the vacuum servo unit as described in Sections 8 and 13.

3 Working inside the car, turn the brake pedal cross-link to release the tension on the return spring, then unhook it, noting how it is fitted.

4 Unscrew the nut and detach the cross-link pushrod from the brake pedal.

5 Loosen the brake vacuum servo mounting nuts.

6 Unscrew and remove the brake pedal bracket mounting nuts.

7 Unscrew and remove the cross-link bracket mounting bolts **(see illustration)**.

8 Move the vacuum servo mounting bracket towards the left-hand side of the engine compartment.

9 Move the cross-link to the right then pull it forward and remove from the engine compartment.

10 Clean the cross-link components, and examine the bushes for wear. Renew the bushes if necessary.

10.7 Brake pedal-to-servo cross-link

Refitting

11 Refitting is a reversal of the removal procedure.

11 Hydraulic pipes and hoses – inspection, removal and refitting

Note: *Refer to the precautions in Section 1 before proceeding.*

Inspection

1 Jack up the front and rear of the car, and support on axle stands.

2 Check for signs of leakage at the pipe unions, then examine the flexible hoses for signs of cracking, chafing and fraying.

3 The brake pipes should be examined carefully for signs of dents, corrosion or other damage. Corrosion should be scraped off and, if the depth of pitting is significant, the pipes renewed. This is particularly likely in those areas underneath the body where the pipes are exposed and unprotected.

4 Renew any defective brake pipes and/or hoses.

Removal

5 If a section of pipe or hose is to be removed, loss of brake fluid can be reduced by unscrewing the filler cap, and completely sealing the top of the reservoir with cling film or adhesive tape. Alternatively, the reservoir can be emptied as described in Section 8.

6 To remove a section of pipe, hold the adjoining hose union nut with a spanner to prevent it from turning, then unscrew the union nut at the end of the pipe, and release it. Repeat the procedure at the other end of the pipe, then release the pipe by pulling out the clips attaching it to the body.

7 Where the union nuts are exposed to the full force of the weather, they can sometimes be quite tight. If an open-ended spanner is used, burring of the flats on the nuts is not uncommon, and for this reason, it is preferable to use a split ring (brake) spanner, which will engage all the flats. If such a spanner is not available, self-locking grips may be used as a last resort; these may well damage the nuts, but if the pipe is to be renewed, this does not matter.

8 To minimise the loss of fluid when disconnecting a downstream rigid pipe from a flexible brake hose, clamp the hose using a brake hose clamp or a pair of self-locking grips with protected jaws.

9 To remove a flexible hose, first clean the ends of the hose and the surrounding area, then unscrew the union nuts from the hose ends. Remove the spring clip, and withdraw the hose from the serrated mounting in the support bracket. Where applicable, unscrew the hose from the caliper.

10 Brake pipes supplied with flared ends and union nuts can be obtained individually or in sets from Ford dealers or accessory shops. The pipe is then bent to shape, using the old pipe as a guide. Be careful not to kink or crimp the pipe when bending it; ideally, a proper pipe-bending tool should be used.

Refitting

11 Refitting of the pipes and hoses is a reversal of removal. Make sure that all brake pipes are securely supported in their clips, and ensure that the hoses are not twisted. Check also that the hoses are clear of all suspension components and underbody fittings, and will remain clear during movement of the suspension and steering.

12 On completion, bleed the brake hydraulic system as described in Section 12 and, where applicable, the clutch hydraulic system as described in Chapter 6.

12 Hydraulic system – bleeding

Note 1: *Refer to the precautions in Section 1 before proceeding.*

Note 2: *If the system is being bled after the ABS hydraulic unit has been disturbed, note that it may be necessary to take the car to a Ford dealer to achieve full system operation. Apparently, unless the hydraulic unit is actuated using Ford's WDS2000 diagnostic equipment, the unit will remain sealed off from the rest of the system, and will not therefore be bled properly.*

1 Disconnect the battery negative lead (refer to *Disconnecting the battery* at the end of this manual).

2 If the master cylinder or ABS unit has been disconnected and reconnected, then the complete system (both circuits) must be bled of air. If a single component of one circuit has been disturbed, then only that particular circuit need be bled.

3 Bleeding should commence on one front brake, followed by the diagonally-opposite rear brake. The remaining front brake should then be bled, followed by its diagonally-opposite rear brake.

4 There is a variety of do-it-yourself 'one-man' brake bleeding kits available from motor accessory shops, and it is recommended that one of these kits be used wherever possible, as they greatly simplify the bleeding operation. Follow the kit manufacturer's instructions in conjunction with the following procedure.

5 During the bleeding operation, do not allow the brake fluid level in the reservoir to drop below the minimum mark. If the level is allowed to fall so far that air is drawn in, the whole procedure will have to be started again from scratch. Only use new fluid for topping-up, preferably from a freshly-opened container. Never re-use fluid bled from the system.

6 Before starting, check that all rigid pipes and flexible hoses are in good condition, and that all hydraulic unions are tight. Take care not to allow hydraulic fluid to come into contact with the vehicle paintwork, otherwise the finish will be seriously damaged. Wash off any spilt fluid immediately with cold water.

7 If a brake bleeding kit is *not* being used, gather together a clean jar, a length of plastic or rubber tubing which is a tight fit over the bleed screw, and a new container of the specified brake fluid (see *Lubricants and fluids*). The help of an assistant will also be required.

8 Clean the area around the bleed screw on the front brake unit to be bled (it is important that no dirt be allowed to enter the hydraulic system), and remove the dust cap. Connect one end of the tubing to the bleed screw, and immerse the other end in the jar, which should be filled with sufficient brake fluid to keep the end of the tube submerged.

9 Open the bleed screw by one or two turns, and have the assistant depress the brake pedal to the floor. Tighten the bleed screw at the end of the downstroke, then have the assistant release the pedal. Continue this procedure until clean brake fluid, free from air bubbles, can be seen flowing into the jar. Finally tighten the bleed screw with the pedal in the fully-depressed position.

10 Remove the tube, and refit the dust cap. Top-up the master cylinder reservoir as necessary, then repeat the procedure on the diagonally-opposite rear brake.

11 Repeat the procedure on the remaining circuit, starting with the front brake, and followed by the diagonally-opposite rear brake.

12 Check the feel of the brake pedal – it should be firm. If it is spongy, there is still some air remaining in the system, and the bleeding procedure should be repeated.

13 When bleeding is complete, top-up the master cylinder reservoir and refit the cap.

14 On completion, check the operation of the hydraulically-operated clutch; if necessary, bleed the clutch hydraulic system as described in Chapter 6.

15 Reconnect the battery negative lead (refer to *Disconnecting the battery* at the end of this manual).

13 Vacuum servo – testing, removal and refitting

Warning: Do not fit a standard vacuum servo unit to a car equipped with Emergency Brake Assist.

Note: *Refer to the precautions in Section 1 before proceeding.*

Testing

1 To test the operation of the servo unit, depress the footbrake four or five times to dissipate the vacuum, then start the engine while keeping the footbrake depressed. As the engine starts, there should be a noticeable 'give' in the brake pedal as vacuum builds-

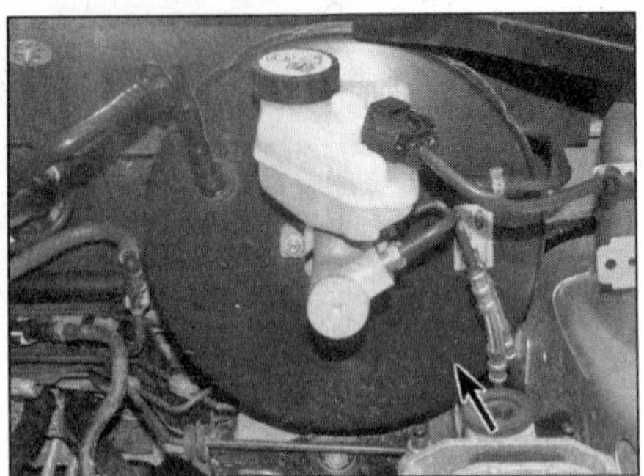
13.3 The vacuum servo unit

13.7 Vacuum servo unit mounting nuts

14.2 Vacuum hose adapter at the servo unit

up. Allow the engine to run for at least two minutes, and then switch it off. If the brake pedal is now depressed again, it should be possible to hear a hiss from the servo when the pedal is depressed. After four or five applications, no further hissing should be heard, and the pedal should feel harder.

2 Before assuming that a problem exists in the servo unit itself, inspect the check valve as described in the next Section.

Removal

3 Refer to Section 8 and remove the master cylinder **(see illustration)**.

4 Unclip the plastic cover from the top of the left-hand front suspension strut.

5 With the weight of the car on the front suspension, unscrew and remove the three mounting nuts from the top of the strut.

6 Unbolt the top mount brace from the bulkhead and inner wing panel.

7 On right-hand drive models, unscrew the nuts securing the brake vacuum servo to its mounting bracket on the left-hand side of the bulkhead **(see illustration)**, then extract the clip and pull out the pin attaching the cross-link to the vacuum servo pushrod. If necessary, have an assistant hold the brake pedal depressed to improve access.

8 On left-hand drive models, working inside the car, unscrew the nut securing the pedal trunnion to the servo unit pushrod, then unscrew the vacuum servo mounting nuts from the inside of the bulkhead.

9 Remove the brake servo unit from the engine compartment.

10 Note that the servo unit cannot be dismantled for repair or overhaul and, if faulty, must be renewed.

Refitting

11 Refitting is a reversal of the removal procedure. Refer to Section 8 for details of refitting the master cylinder.

14 Vacuum servo hose and check valve – removal, testing and refitting

Removal

1 With the engine switched off, depress the brake pedal four or five times, to dissipate any remaining vacuum from the servo unit.

2 Disconnect the vacuum hose adapter at the servo unit **(see illustration)**, by pulling it free from the rubber grommet. If it is reluctant to move, prise it free, using a screwdriver with its blade inserted under the flange.

3 Detach the vacuum hose from the inlet manifold connection, pressing in the collar to disengage the tabs, then withdrawing the collar slowly.

4 If the hose or the fixings are damaged or in poor condition, they must be renewed.

Testing

5 Examine the check valve for damage and signs of deterioration, and renew it if necessary. The valve may be tested by blowing through it in both directions. It should only be possible to blow from the servo end towards the inlet manifold.

Refitting

6 Refitting is a reversal of the removal procedure. If fitting a new check valve, ensure that it is fitted the correct way round.

15 Vacuum pump (diesel models) – removal and refitting

Removal

1 Unclip the plastic cover from the top of the engine.

2 Drain the cooling system as described in Chapter 1B.

3 Disconnect the wiring plug for the cylinder head temperature sensor at the power steering hydraulic fluid line support bracket.

4 Unbolt the power steering line support bracket from the brake vacuum pump on the left-hand end of the cylinder head.

5 Loosen the clip and disconnect the crankcase ventilation hose from the valve cover.

6 Disconnect the vacuum hose from the rear of the vacuum pump **(see illustration)**.

7 Release the clip, and disconnect the coolant hose from the vacuum pump. If the original clip is fitted, use a pair of grips to release it.

8 Disconnect the exhaust gas recirculation coolant hose from the thermostat housing.

9 Unbolt the thermostat housing from the brake vacuum pump and recover the O-ring seal.

10 Unscrew the mounting bolts and withdraw the brake vacuum pump from the end of the cylinder head **(see illustrations)**. Discard the gasket and obtain a new one.

15.6 Vacuum hose connection on the vacuum pump

15.10a Brake vacuum pump mounting bolts

15.10b Removing the vacuum pump and housing from the cylinder head

11 Thoroughly clean the mating surfaces of the vacuum pump, cylinder head and thermostat housing.

Refitting

12 Locate a new gasket on the vacuum pump, then refit the pump to the cylinder head, making sure that the drive dog engages correctly with the end of the camshaft **(see illustrations)**. Insert the mounting bolts and tighten to the specified torque.
13 Refit the thermostat housing to the brake vacuum pump using a new O-ring seal, and tighten the mounting bolts to the specified torque.
14 Reconnect the exhaust gas recirculation coolant hose to the thermostat housing.
15 Reconnect the coolant hose to the vacuum pump and tighten the clip.
16 Reconnect the vacuum hose to the rear of the vacuum pump.
17 Reconnect the crankcase ventilation hose to the valve cover.
18 Refit the power steering line support bracket and tighten the bolts.
19 Reconnect the wiring plug for the cylinder head temperature sensor.
20 Refill the cooling system with reference to Chapter 1B.
21 Refit the plastic cover to the top of the engine.

16 Vacuum pump (diesel models) – testing and overhaul

1 The operation of the braking system vacuum pump can be checked using a vacuum gauge.
2 Disconnect the vacuum pipe from the pump, and connect the gauge to the pump union using a suitable length of hose.
3 Start the engine and allow it to idle, then measure the vacuum created by the pump. As a guide, after one minute, a minimum of approximately 500 mm Hg should be recorded. If the vacuum registered is significantly less than this, it is likely that the pump is faulty. However, seek the advice of a Ford dealer before condemning the pump.
4 Overhaul of the vacuum pump is not possible, since no components are available separately for it. If faulty, the complete pump assembly must be renewed.

17 ABS hydraulic unit – removal and refitting

Note 1: *Refer to the precautions in Section 1, and the notes at the start of Section 12, before proceeding.*
Note 2: *If any part of the ABS hydraulic unit is defective, with the exception of the ESP hydraulic pressure transducer, the unit must be renewed complete.*

15.12a Fit a new vacuum pump housing gasket on the cylinder head

Note 3: *A different hydraulic unit was fitted to models from August 2004. It is vitally important for the correct operation of the system that earlier and later components are not interchanged.*

Removal

1 Disconnect the battery negative lead (refer to *Disconnecting the battery* at the end of this manual).
2 Remove the air cleaner as described in the appropriate part of Chapter 4.
3 Remove the brake vacuum servo unit as described in Section 13.
4 Disconnect the wiring from the ABS hydraulic unit.
5 Make a note of the brake line positions on the ABS hydraulic unit and in-line connectors as an aid to refitting **(see illustration)**.
6 On models up to August 2004, unscrew the union nuts and disconnect the three brake lines from the ABS hydraulic unit at the in-line connectors.
7 Unscrew the union nuts and disconnect the six brake lines from the ABS hydraulic unit. Tape over or plug the ends of the lines and the apertures in the unit to prevent entry of dust and dirt.
8 Release the brake, clutch and fuel lines from their supports on the bulkhead.
9 On manual transmission models, push the clutch master cylinder hydraulic hose and grommet from its support bracket over the transmission and position to one side.
10 Unscrew the four mounting bolts and remove the ABS hydraulic unit and mounting bracket from the bulkhead.

17.5 ABS hydraulic unit location

15.12b Drive dogs on the end of the camshaft

11 Note the position of the insulator pad (rubber collars on later versions), then remove the side clip and separate the hydraulic unit from the bracket.

Refitting

12 Refitting is a reversal of removal, noting the following points:
a) *Make sure that the insulator pad is positioned correctly on the bottom of the hydraulic unit, or that the rubber collars are correctly fitted to the mounting bracket, as applicable.*
b) *Tighten all union nuts securely.*
c) *Refer to Section 13 when refitting the servo unit, and to the appropriate part of Chapter 4 when refitting the air cleaner.*
d) *Bleed the hydraulic system as described in Section 12. If the system does not bleed satisfactorily, or if the ABS warning light remains lit on completion, refer to a Ford dealer – it may be necessary to set the system up using their WDS2000 diagnostic equipment. Bear in mind that air trapped in the hydraulic unit may enter the main braking system, resulting in a dangerous loss of normal braking.*

18 ABS wheel sensor – testing, removal and refitting

Testing

1 Checking of the sensors is done before removal, connecting a voltmeter to the disconnected sensor multiplug. Using an analogue (moving coil) meter is not practical, since the meter does not respond quickly enough. A digital meter having an AC facility may be used to check that the sensor is operating correctly.
2 To do this, raise the relevant wheel, then disconnect the wiring to the ABS sensor and connect the meter to it.
3 Spin the wheel and check that the output voltage is between 1.5 and 2.0 volts, depending on how fast the wheel is spun.
4 Alternatively, an oscilloscope may be used to check the output of the sensor – an alternating current will be traced on the screen, of magnitude depending on the speed of the rotating wheel.

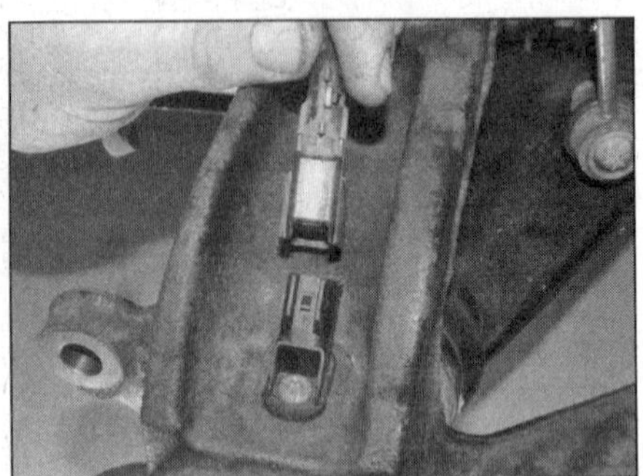
18.7 Disconnect the wiring . . .

18.8a . . . then unscrew the bolt . . .

18.8b . . . and withdraw the ABS front wheel sensor

18.10 Rear wheel sensor wiring plug (Estate model shown)

5 If the sensor output is low or zero, renew the sensor.

HAYNES HiNT ***ABS wheel sensors operate in a harsh environment, and one of the most common reasons for apparent failure is a corroded wiring connector. If corrosion (which often appears as a white or green powder) is found when the plug is disconnected, clean the connector carefully, and apply some water-dispersant aerosol to help prevent further problems.***

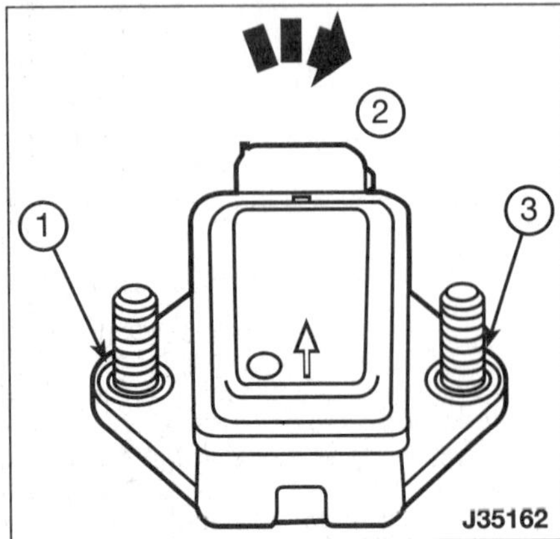

19.8 Yaw rate sensor removal

1 Lift the sensor from the left-hand stud . . .
2 . . . tilt it clockwise . . .
3 . . . and remove it from the right-hand stud

Removal

Front wheel sensor

6 Loosen the front wheel nuts. Apply the handbrake, then jack up the front of the car and support it on axle stands (see *Jacking and vehicle support*). Remove the relevant wheel.

7 Disconnect the wiring from the sensor located on the steering knuckle **(see illustration)**.

8 Unscrew the mounting bolt and withdraw the sensor **(see illustrations)**.

Rear wheel sensor

9 Loosen the rear wheel nuts. Chock the front wheels and engage 1st gear (or P), then jack up the rear of the car and support on axle stands (see *Jacking and vehicle support*). To improve access, remove the rear wheel.

10 Disconnect the wiring from the sensor located on the inner end of the hub. Access is through the hole in the rear suspension lower arm **(see illustration)**.

11 Unscrew the mounting bolt, and withdraw the sensor.

Refitting

12 Refitting is a reversal of the removal procedure. On completion, refit the removed wheel(s), then lower the car to the ground and tighten the wheel bolts to the specified torque.

19 Electronic Stability Program (ESP) components – removal and refitting

Yaw rate sensor

Warning: Never fit a damaged yaw rate sensor, as the car may react dangerously in the event of an emergency. The yaw rate sensor will be damaged if dropped.

Removal

1 Disconnect the battery negative lead (refer to *Disconnecting the battery* at the end of this manual).

2 On automatic transmission models, unclip and remove the selector lever surround trim panel.

3 On manual transmission models, unclip and remove the gear lever surround panel, then remove the insulation pad.

4 Remove the centre console side trim panels as follows. Unscrew the front mounting screws, then carefully prise out the trim panels to release the retaining clips.

5 Disconnect the wiring from the yaw rate sensor.

6 Unscrew and remove the left-hand mounting nut for the sensor. Note the arrow on the top of the sensor faces towards the front of the car.

7 On manual transmission models, prise the gear linkage rod from the balljoint, then rotate the linkage through 90°.

8 Unscrew and remove the right-hand mounting nut, then lift the sensor from the left-hand locating stud, tilt it clockwise, and remove it from the right-hand locating stud **(see illustration)**.

Refitting

9 Refitting is a reversal of removal, but make sure that the sensor is fitted with the arrow facing the front of the car.

Steering wheel rotation sensor

Warning: Never fit a damaged steering wheel rotation sensor, as the car may react dangerously in the event of an emergency. Do not use excessive force when removing or refitting the sensor.

Removal

10 Remove the steering column complete as described in Chapter 10.

11 With the steering column on the bench, undo the three screws and carefully withdraw the sensor from the bottom of the column.

12 Thoroughly check the sensor drive pins and pin locations in the sensor for damage, wear and looseness **(see illustrations)**. The pins must be located correctly in the sensor hub. If necessary, obtain a new sensor otherwise the car may react dangerously in the event of an emergency.

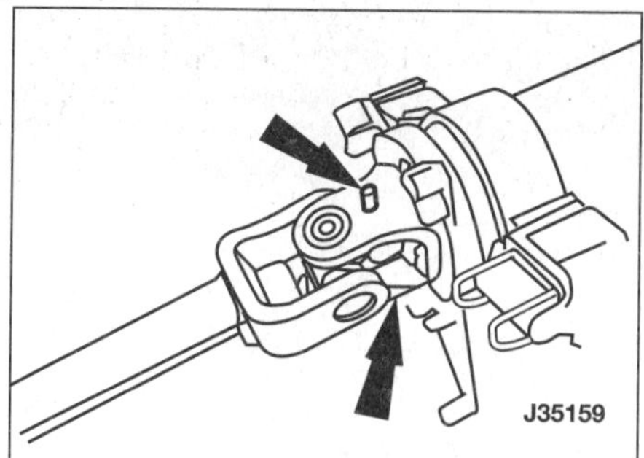

19.12a Drive pins on the steering column intermediate shaft upper UJ . . .

Refitting

13 Carefully locate the sensor over the bottom of the column and onto the base of the upper column. Insert the screws, making sure they are centralised, then tighten them securely, the screw on the flat edge first, followed by the two screws on the curved edge. Check the vertical alignment of the sensor as shown **(see illustration).**

Hydraulic pressure sensor

Note: *Refer to the warning in Section 1 before proceeding.*

Removal and refitting

14 On models with ESP, the pressure sensor is part of the hydraulic unit. On models without ESP, the hydraulic pressure sensor is screwed into the side of the ABS hydraulic unit on the left-hand side of the engine compartment, and can be obtained separately. First, disconnect the wiring from the sensor.

15 Have the new sensor ready to fit, then unscrew the old one using suitable grips, and immediately screw in the new one and tighten securely. If the new unit is not immediately available, plug the hydraulic unit aperture.

16 Bleed the complete brake hydraulic circuit as described in Section 12.

20 Stop-light switch – removal, refitting and adjustment

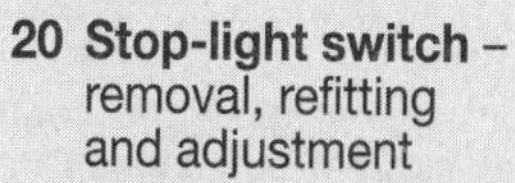

Removal

1 The stop-light switch is located on the pedal bracket. The switch is the lower of the two switches mounted over the brake pedal; the upper switch is the brake pedal position switch or the cruise control inhibitor switch.

2 To improve access, if necessary, remove the driver's side lower facia trim panel, which is secured by four screws and two upper clips. Where applicable, unclip the diagnostic connector plug from the panel, and/or disconnect the wiring from the climate control sensor as the panel is removed.

3 Pull out the switch retaining clip and discard it. A new one must be fitted on reassembly.

4 Disconnect the wiring from the switch.

5 Twist the switch 90° anti-clockwise and withdraw it from the pedal bracket.

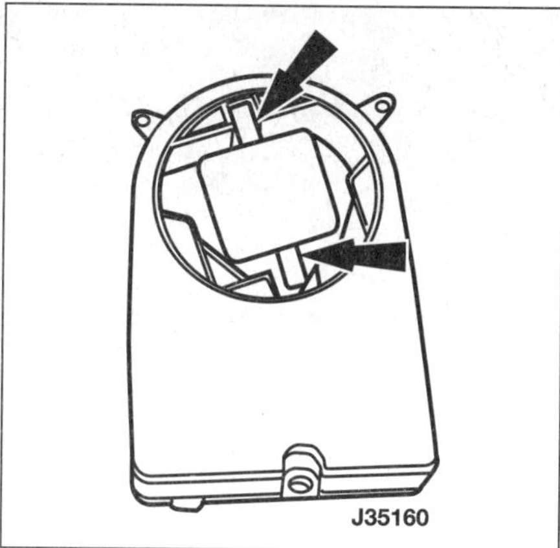

19.12b . . . and the corresponding locations in the steering wheel rotation sensor

Refitting and adjustment

6 Fit a new retaining clip to the bracket.

7 Fully extend the switch plunger.

8 Depress the brake pedal and hold it in this position while refitting the switch.

9 Insert the switch in the pedal bracket and turn it 90° clockwise to lock it.

10 Release the brake pedal; this will automatically adjust the switch plunger.

11 Reconnect the wiring to the switch.

21 Handbrake lever – removal and refitting

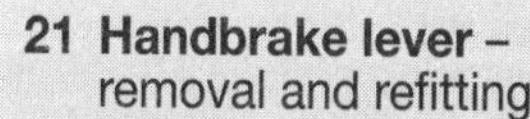

Removal

1 Chock the front wheels, then jack up the rear of the car and support on axle stands (see *Jacking and vehicle support*). For improved access to the underbody, also raise the front of the car and support on axle stands. Fully release the handbrake lever.

2 On petrol models (except 3.0 litre V6 engines), for additional working room it is recommended that the catalytic converter is unbolted from the exhaust front pipe (see Chapter 4C) and supported on an axle stand. However, it is possible to reach the underside of the handbrake lever with the exhaust still *in situ,* provided care is taken not to damage the catalytic converter or wiring when removing the heat shields.

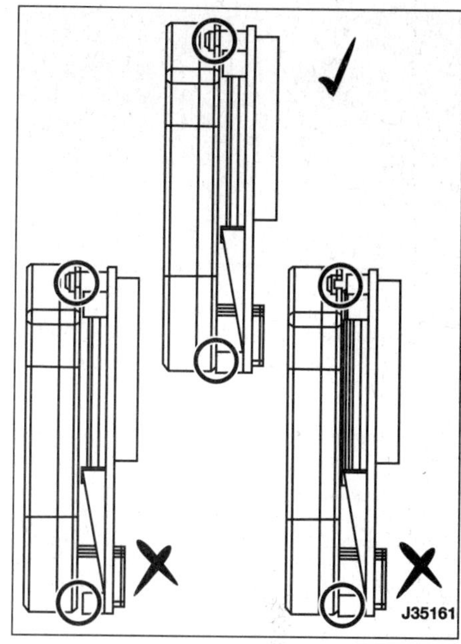

19.13 Make sure that the sensor is correctly positioned on the base of the upper steering column

3 On diesel models, and 3.0 litre V6 engines, unbolt the flexible section(s) from the front exhaust pipe(s) (see Chapter 4A or 4B) and support the front pipe on an axle stand. To prevent damage to the flexible pipe, it is recommended that a splint is attached to it – two or three lengths of wood attached to the pipe with cable ties will be sufficient. On models with a diesel particulate filter, take care that the associated wiring and pipework are not strained.

4 It is recommended that the exhaust gaskets, sealing rings and nuts are all renewed on reassembly.

5 Support the exhaust system, then release the front and intermediate rubber hangers and lower it as far as possible from the underbody. Support the exhaust on an axle stand.

6 Undo the special nuts and remove the intermediate and rear exhaust heat shields from the underbody for access to the handbrake lever mounting nuts **(see illustrations).**

7 Loosen the primary cable adjuster nut

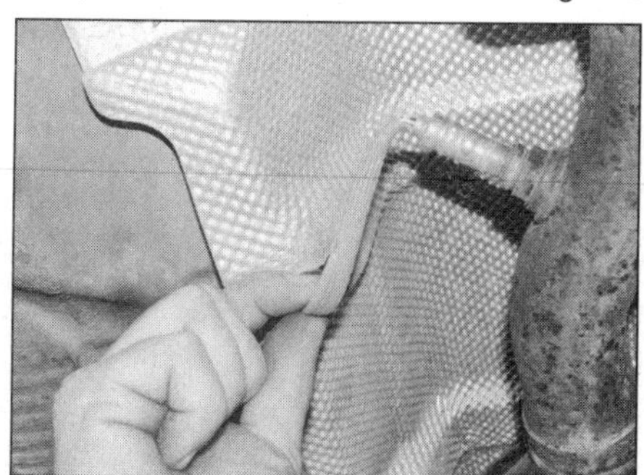

21.6a Release the catalytic converter wiring from the heat shield . . .

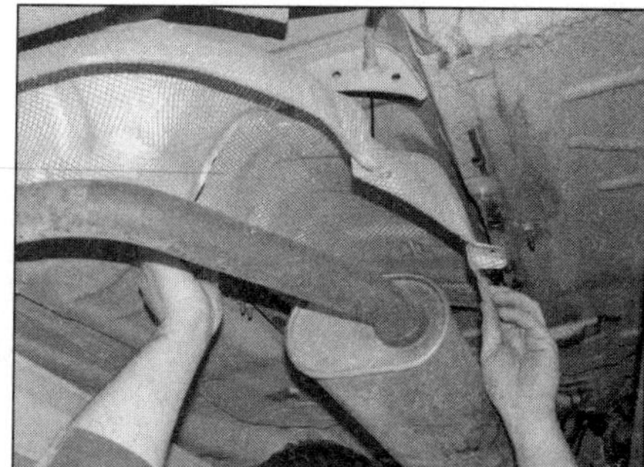

21.6b . . . then remove the heat shields

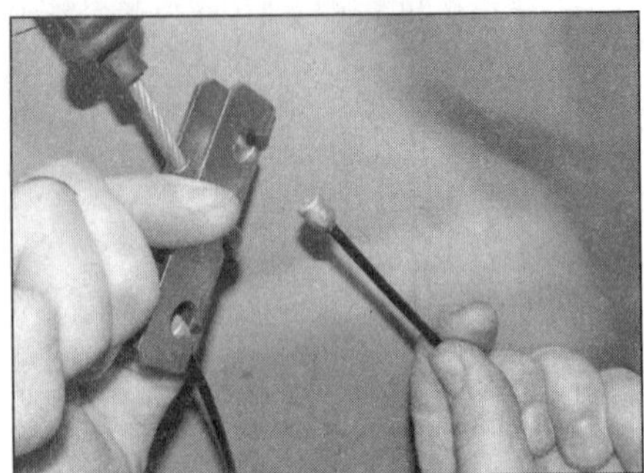
21.7 Disconnecting the handbrake secondary cables from the equaliser bar

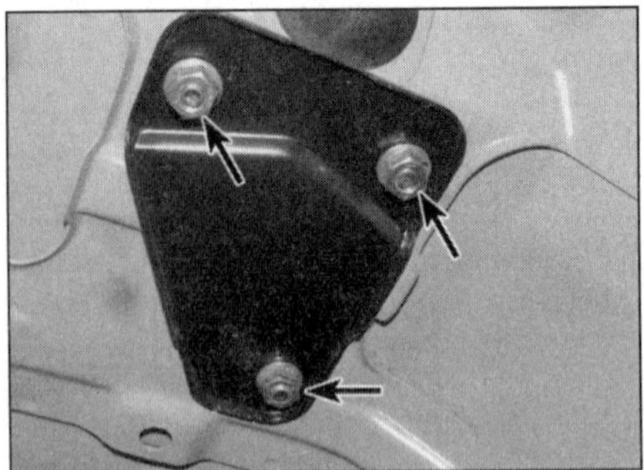
21.8a Unscrew the nuts . . .

21.8b . . . and remove the plate

21.10 Disconnecting the wiring from the handbrake warning light switch

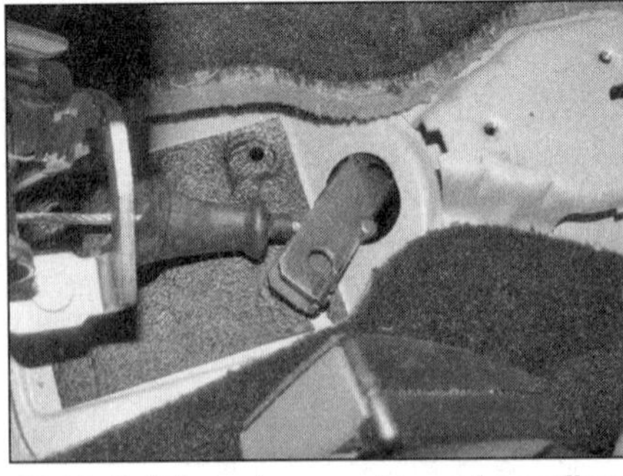
21.11 Pull the primary cable and equaliser bar through the hole in the floor

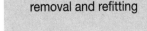

at the rear of the equaliser bar, holding the hex-section of cable in front of the bar with a 6 mm spanner. Disconnect both secondary cables by pulling them slightly forwards and unhooking them **(see illustration)**.

8 Unscrew the nuts securing the handbrake lever assembly to the floor/underbody and remove the plate **(see illustrations)**.

9 Working inside the car, remove the centre console as described in Chapter 11. Take care to release the handbrake warning light switch wiring from the clip inside the console before lifting it.

10 Disconnect the wiring from the warning light switch on the handbrake lever assembly **(see illustration)**.

11 Pull the primary cable and equaliser bar through the hole in the floor and withdraw the lever assembly from inside the car **(see illustration)**. If necessary, have an assistant guide the bar through the hole from underneath. Undo the screw and remove the warning light switch.

12 Examine all components for wear or damage, and renew as necessary.

Refitting

13 Refitting is a reversal of removal, noting the following points:

a) Refit the centre console as described in Chapter 11.

b) Tighten all fasteners to the specified torques, using new nuts, bolts and gaskets as necessary.

c) Before refitting the exhaust system components, adjust the handbrake as described in Section 23.

d) Refer to the relevant Parts of Chapter 4 when refitting the exhaust system components.

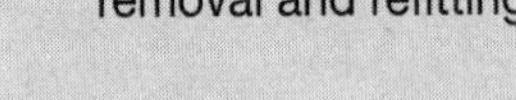

22 Handbrake cables – removal and refitting

Removal

Primary (front)

1 Remove the handbrake lever assembly as described in Section 21.

2 Loosen and remove the adjuster nut, and separate the cable from the equaliser bar. Unhook the front of the cable from the lever, and remove it.

Secondary (rear)

3 Refer to Section 21, paragraphs 2 to 7 inclusive.

4 At the rear brake caliper, push the handbrake operating lever forwards, then unhook the inner cable from the fitting **(see illustration)**.

5 Release the handbrake outer cable from the caliper bracket. Where a plastic ferrule is fitted to the outer cable, it will be necessary to compress the plastic tangs in order to release it from the bracket. Where a spring clip is fitted, pull the clip from the end of the outer cable **(see illustration)**.

6 Release the front end of the outer cable from the underbody support by compressing the plastic tangs **(see illustration)**.

7 Release the outer cable from the support clips and withdraw from under the car **(see illustrations)**.

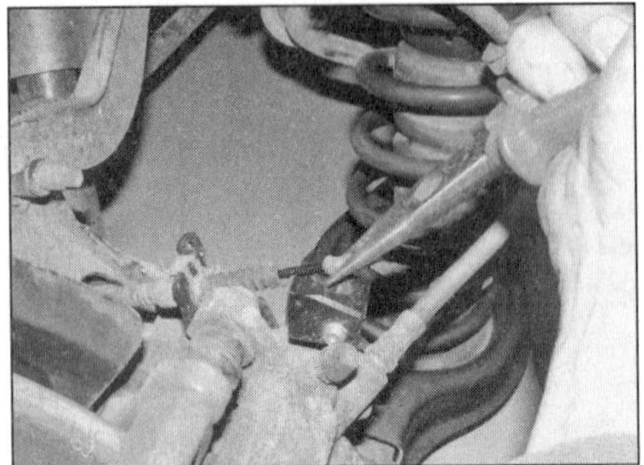
22.4 Unhooking the inner cable from the rear brake caliper fitting

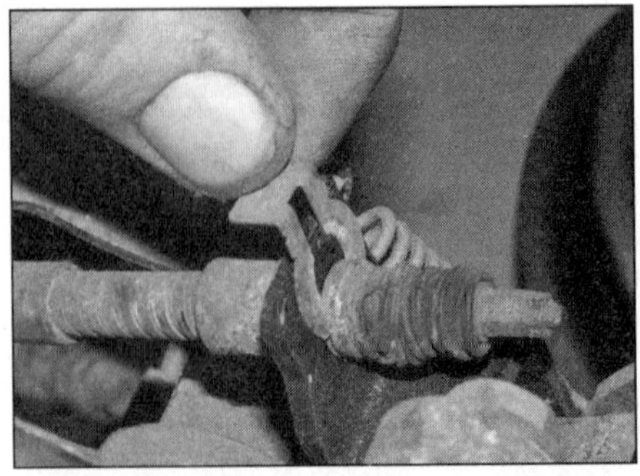
22.5 Pull out the spring clip securing the handbrake cable to the caliper bracket

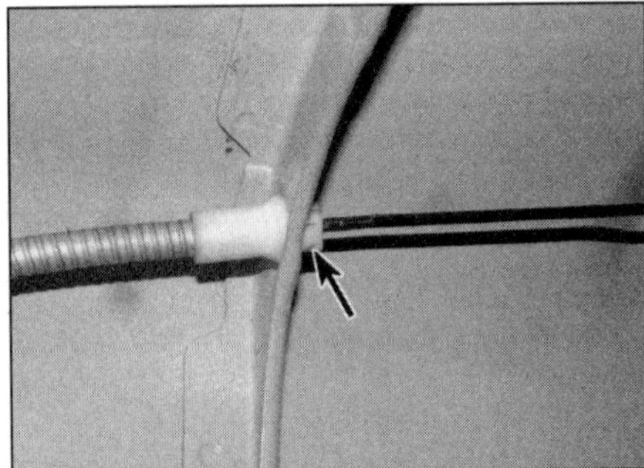
22.6 Compress the plastic tangs to release the handbrake outer cable from the support

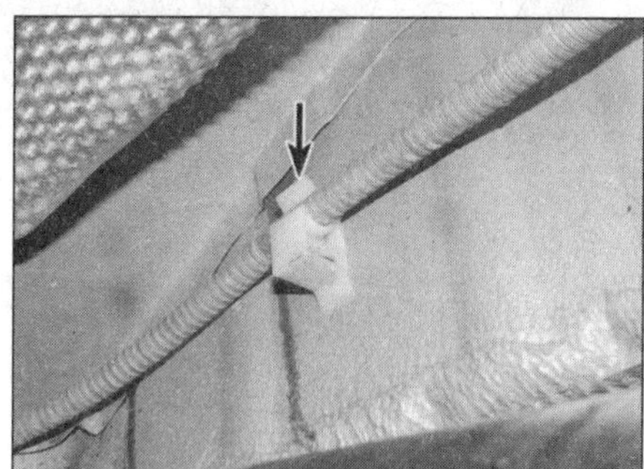
22.7a Handbrake cable underbody support clip

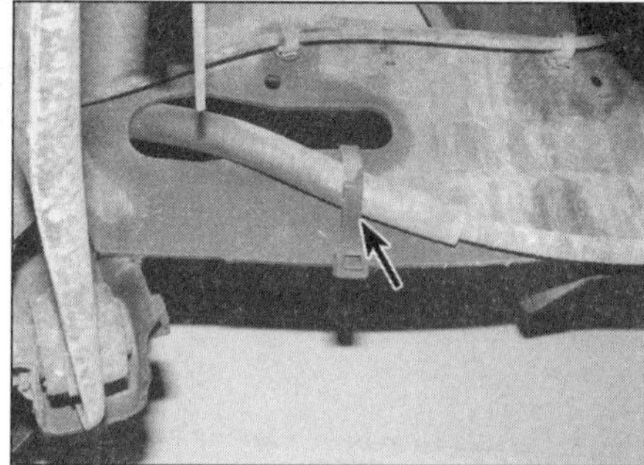
22.7b Cable tie securing the handbrake cable to the rear suspension trailing arm

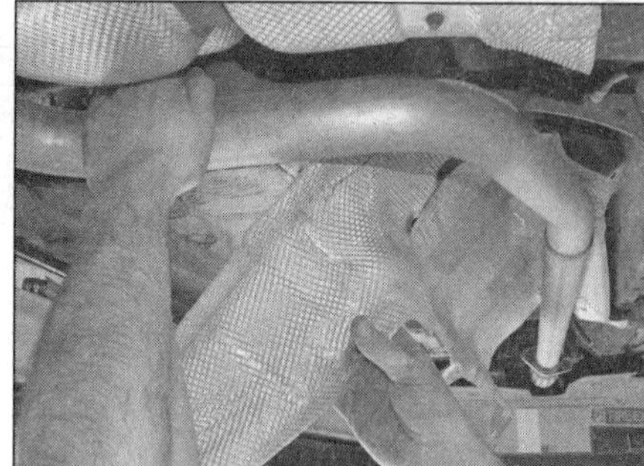
23.3 Removing the exhaust heat shield to access the handbrake adjuster

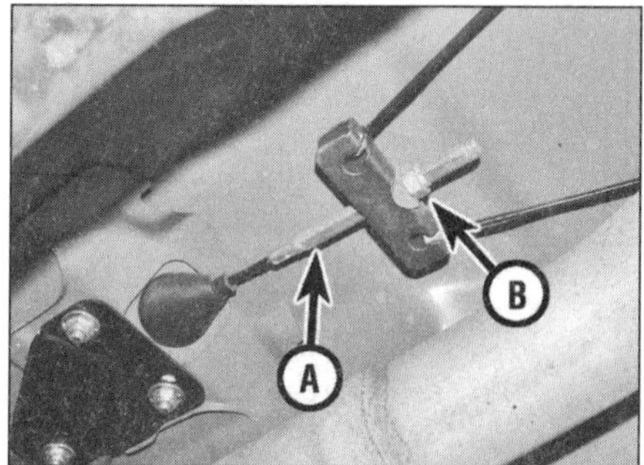

23.5 Handbrake adjuster – hold flat section (A) and adjust nut (B)

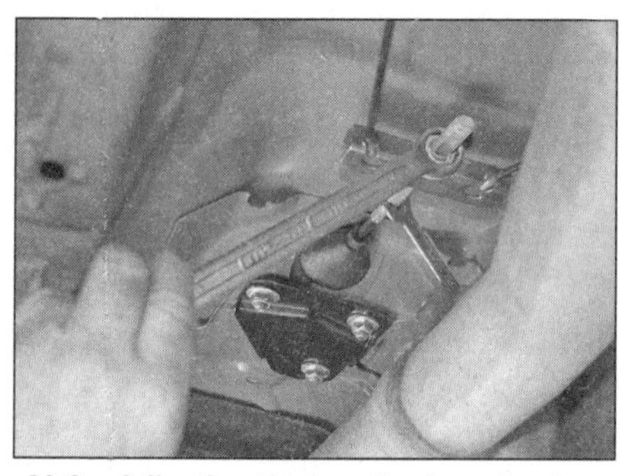
23.6a Adjusting the handbrake using two spanners

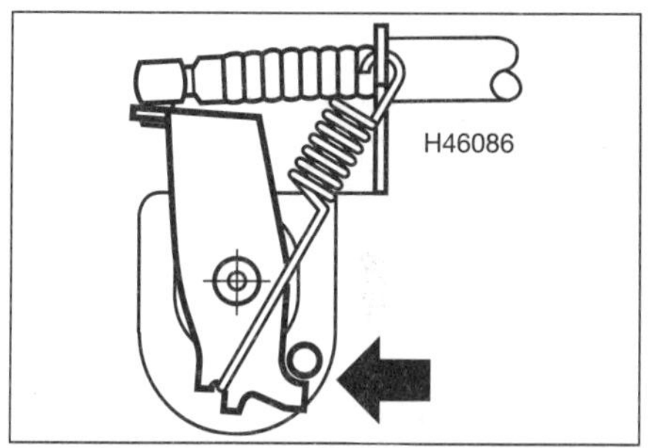

23.6b Adjust until a clearance of 1 mm is obtained between the caliper lever and its stop

Refitting

8 Refitting is a reversal of the removal procedure. Adjust the handbrake on completion as described in Section 23.

23 Handbrake – adjustment

1 Jack up the rear of the car, and support it on axle stands (see *Jacking and vehicle support*).
2 The handbrake adjuster nut is on the back of the cable equaliser bar, which is underneath the car, hidden above the exhaust system heat shields.
3 Undo the special nuts and remove the exhaust heat shields from the underbody as necessary – pull down gently on the exhaust to create extra clearance for the shields to be withdrawn around the pipe **(see illustration)**. Alternatively, if possible, slide the shields rearwards to access the adjuster. Take care as the shields are removed not to catch any wiring for the oxygen sensors (petrol models).
4 Ensure that the handbrake lever inside the car is fully released. Also, if the cables have been disturbed, ensure that they are correctly routed and located, with no kinks or sharp bends.

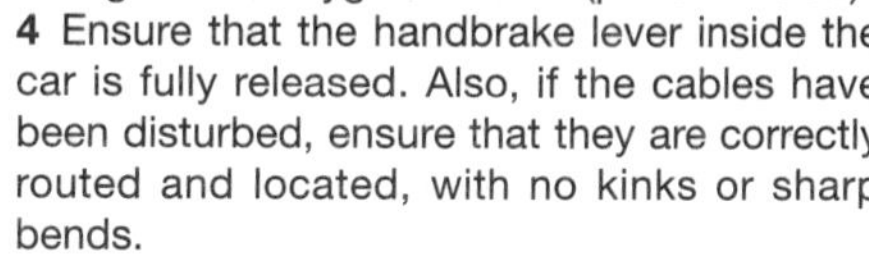

5 Use a 6 mm spanner on the flats provided in front of the equaliser bar, to stop the cable turning during adjustment **(see illustration)**.
6 Loosen the adjuster nut (16 mm on our project car) on the back of the equaliser bar by a few turns. From this position, tighten it again until resistance is felt. Keep tightening the nut slowly, until there is a clearance of 1 mm between one of the rear caliper's handbrake levers and its stop (the opposite caliper should have a clearance of 1 mm or less) **(see illustrations)**.
7 Now settle the cables by applying and releasing the handbrake at least five times – there should be roughly 12 clicks from the handbrake ratchet when this is done. Finally, release the lever completely.
8 Repeat the adjustment procedure given in paragraph 6. Note that the clearance measured at the caliper should not exceed 1 mm on either side – if on completion it does, the cables should be settled as described in paragraph 7, then the adjustment procedure repeated once more.
9 On completion, refit the heat shields and lower the car to the ground. Check that the handbrake is working properly – for example, by trying to drive off gently with the handbrake applied. If the handbrake performs poorly, this may be due to seized, damaged or badly-routed cables, partially-seized caliper handbrake levers, or by rear disc pads which are worn (or new ones which have not bedded-in).

Chapter 10
Suspension and steering

Contents

Degrees of difficulty

Easy, suitable for novice with little experience 	**Fairly easy,** suitable for beginner with some experience	**Fairly difficult,** suitable for competent DIY mechanic	**Difficult,** suitable for experienced DIY mechanic	**Very difficult,** suitable for expert DIY or professional 

Specifications

Wheel alignment

Front wheel toe setting:	
Except 3.0 litre V6 models:	
Checking	0.0 mm ± 2.5 mm (0°00' ± 0°21' or 0.00° ± 0.35°)
Setting	0.0 mm ± 1.0 mm (0°00' ± 0°08' or 0.00° ± 0.14°)
3.0 litre V6 models:	
Checking	0.0 mm ± 2.8 mm (0°00' ± 0°21' or 0.00° ± 0.35°)
Setting	0.0 mm ± 1.1 mm (0°00' ± 0°08' or 0.00° ± 0.14°)
Rear wheel toe setting:	
Except 3.0 litre V6 models:	
Checking	2.0 mm toe-in ± 2.5 mm (0°17' toe-in ± 0°21' or 0.28° toe-in ± 0.35°)
Setting	2.0 mm toe-in ± 1.0 mm (0°17' toe-in ± 0°08' or 0.28° toe-in ± 0.14°)
3.0 litre V6 models:	
Checking	2.2 mm toe-in ± 2.8 mm (0°17' toe-in ± 0°21' or 0.28° toe-in ± 0.35°)
Setting	2.2 mm toe-in ± 1.1 mm (0°17' toe-in ± 0°08' or 0.28° toe-in ± 0.14°)

Roadwheels and tyres

Wheel size (except spare)	16 x 6.5, 17 x 6.5 or 18 x 7
Tyre sizes (depending on model)	205/50R16, 205/55R16, 205/50R17 or 225/40R18
Tyre pressures	See end of *Weekly checks* on page 0•18

Torque wrench settings

	Nm	lbf ft
Front suspension		
Anti-roll bar clamp bolts	48	35
Anti-roll bar link	48	35
Brake caliper mounting bracket to steering knuckle	130	96
Coolant hose support bracket to subframe	10	7
Crossmember mounting bolts	120	89
Engine rear mounting link	80	59
Hub/driveshaft nut*	290	214
Lower arm balljoint to lower arm (service replacement, bolted on)	58	43
Lower arm balljoint-to-steering knuckle pinch-bolt	83	61
Lower arm front bolt*:		
Stage 1	80	59
Stage 2	Angle-tighten by a further 60°	
Lower arm rear bolt*:		
Stage 1	90	66
Stage 2	Angle-tighten by a further 60°	
Radiator mounting bracket to subframe	25	18
Steering knuckle-to-suspension strut pinch-bolt	83	61
Subframe rear mounting brackets to underbody	10	7
Subframe to underbody	142	105
Suspension strut thrust bearing (centre) retaining nut	59	44
Suspension strut top mount to body	30	22
Track rod end to steering arm	40	30
Rear suspension (Saloon/Hatchback)		
ABS sensor to hub	7	5
Anti-roll bar link	48	35
Anti-roll bar to crossmember	25	18
Brake caliper mounting bracket to knuckle/tie-bar:		
Up to September 2004	80	59
September 2004 onwards	66	49
Crossmember bolts to underbody	120	89
Hub to suspension knuckle/tie-bar	70	52
Lower arm to crossmember	103	76
Lower arm to knuckle	120	89
Strut mounting bolts	25	18
Strut to knuckle	85	63
Suspension strut thrust bearing retaining nut	50	37
Tie-bar bracket to underbody	120	89
Tie-bar to bracket	103	76
Tie-bar to knuckle	103	76
Rear suspension (Estate)		
Note: *Same as for Saloon/Hatchback, except for the following.*		
Anti-roll bar mounting	25	18
Anti-roll bar to rear lower arm	48	35
Lower arm to crossmember	103	76
Lower arm to tie-bar/knuckle	84	62
Shock absorber lower mounting bolt	120	89
Shock absorber lower mounting to tie-bar/knuckle	120	89
Shock absorber upper mounting bolt	84	62
Shock absorber upper mounting to crossmember	84	62
Tie-bar/knuckle front mounting bracket to underbody	120	89
Tie-bar/knuckle front mounting to bracket	103	76
Upper arm to crossmember	84	62
Upper arm to knuckle	120	89
Upper arm to tie-bar/knuckle	120	89
Steering (general)		
Flexible coupling to steering gear pinion shaft*	25	18
Steering column mounting bolts*	24	18
Steering column-to-flexible coupling clamp bolt*	20	15
Steering gear mounting bolts*	130	96
Steering gear fluid union bolt*	23	17
Steering wheel	45	33
Track rod end to steering knuckle*	40	30
Track rod end-to-track rod locknut	40	30

Torque wrench settings (continued)

	Nm	lbf ft
Steering (1.8 and 2.0 litre petrol engines)		
Power steering hydraulic fluid reservoir mounting stud/bolts	9	7
Power steering pump high-pressure outlet union nut	65	48
Power steering pump mounting bolts/studs	18	13
Steering (V6 engines)		
Engine right-hand mounting	83	61
Power steering pump elbow	10	7
Power steering pump high-pressure outlet union nut	65	48
Power steering pump mounting bolts	48	35
Power steering pump pulley	25	18
Retaining plate to power steering pump:		
Nuts	10	7
Bolts	25	18
Steering (diesel engines)		
Power steering pump high-pressure outlet union nut	57	42
Power steering pump mounting bolts	18	13
Power steering pump pulley	10	7
Roadwheel nuts	85	63

** Use a new nut or bolt*

1 General information

The independent front suspension is of MacPherson strut type, incorporating coil springs, integral telescopic shock absorbers, and an anti-roll bar. The struts are attached to steering knuckles at their lower ends, and the knuckles are in turn attached to the lower arm by balljoints. The rear bushes of the front lower arms are of hydraulic type, and must not be bent downwards excessively – all procedures involving the lower arms include cautions against excessive movement of the arms (it is not possible to renew these bushes separately). The anti-roll bar is bolted to the rear of the subframe, and is connected to the front struts by link rods **(see illustration)**.

On Saloon/Hatchback models, the independent rear suspension is of 'Quadralink' type, having four mounting points on each side of the car. The two lower arms are attached to the rear knuckle at their outer ends, and to the rear crossmember at their inner ends. A tie-bar, located between the bottom of the knuckle and the floor, counteracts braking and acceleration forces on each side **(see illustration)**.

On Estate models, the independent rear suspension is of 'SLA' (Short and Long Arm) type, with no suspension points projecting into the luggage area. There are three side arms on each side: one forged upper arm, and two pressed-steel lower side arms. A tie-bar on each side supports the rear knuckles. The coil springs are separate from the shock absorbers **(see illustration)**.

A rear anti-roll bar is fitted to all models. Self-levelling rear shock absorbers are available on Estate models. All 3.0 litre ST models feature suspension which has been lowered by 15 mm,

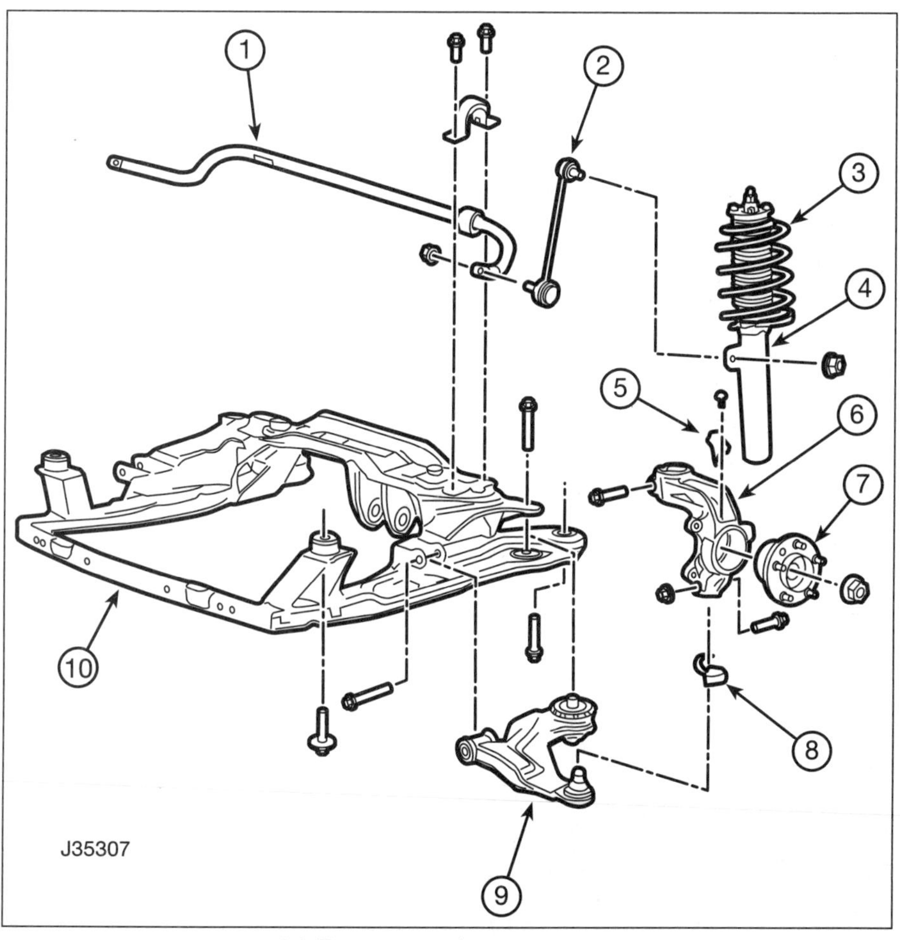

1.1 Front suspension components

1 *Anti-roll bar*
2 *Link*
3 *Front coil spring*
4 *Front suspension strut*
5 *ABS wheel speed sensor*
6 *Knuckle*
7 *Hub*
8 *Balljoint heat shield*
9 *Front suspension lower arm*
10 *Subframe*

with shorter springs and uprated shock absorbers; ST Estates also have uprated front lower arm bushes.

A variable-ratio type rack-and-pinion steering gear is fitted, together with a conventional column and telescopic coupling, incorporating two universal joints. Power-assisted steering is fitted to all models, with the pump being driven from an auxiliary drivebelt. A power steering system fluid cooler is fitted, in front of the cooling system radiator on the crossmember.

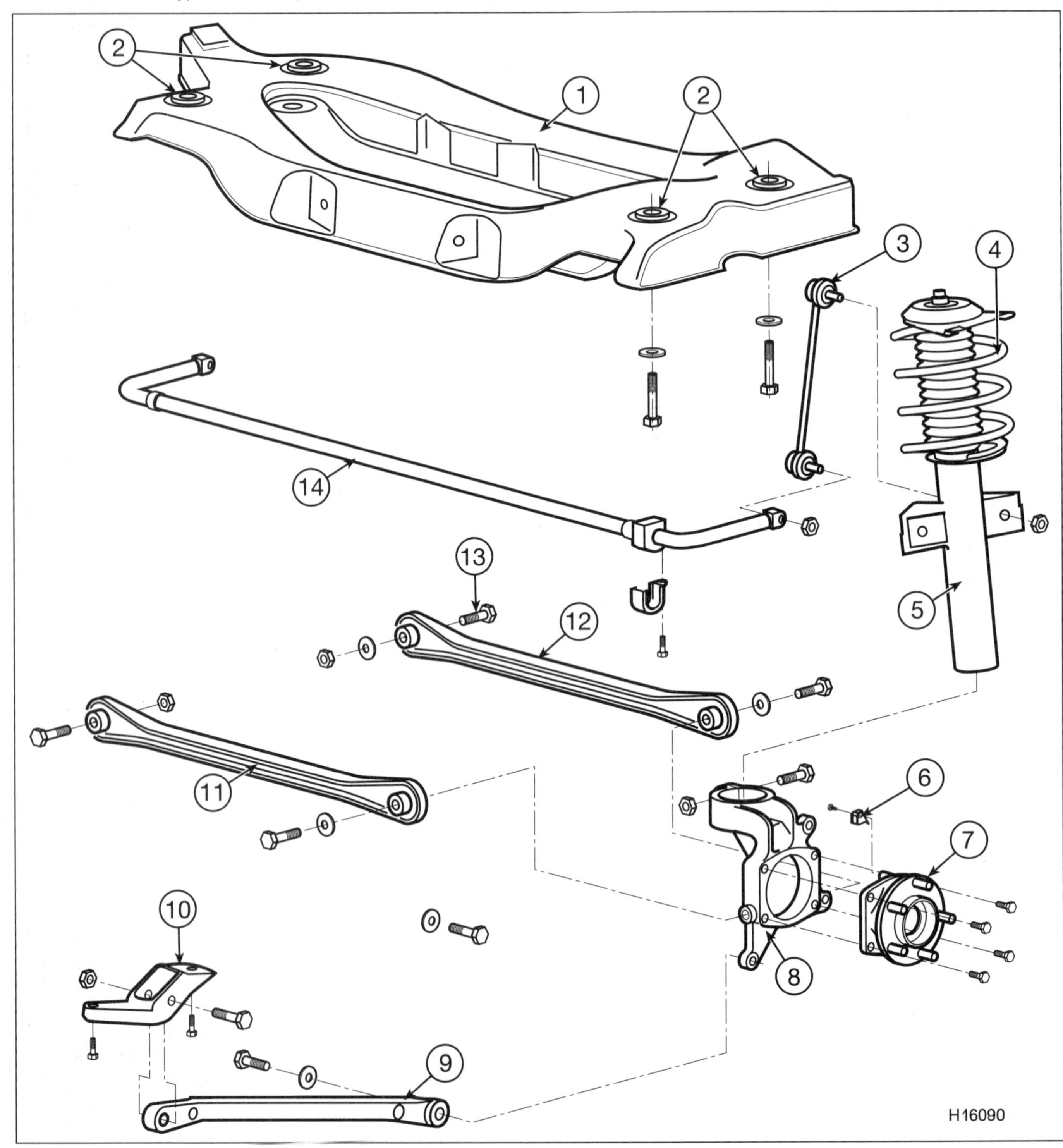

1.2 Rear suspension components (Saloon and Hatchback models)

1 Crossmember
2 Crossmember bush locations
3 Anti-roll bar drop link
4 Rear spring
5 Rear strut/shock absorber
6 ABS wheel sensor
7 Wheel hub/bearing
8 Rear knuckle
9 Rear tie-bar
10 Tie-bar bracket
11 Front lower arm
12 Rear lower arm
13 Eccentric cam bolt
14 Anti-roll bar

2 Steering knuckle and hub assembly – removal and refitting

Removal

1 Remove the wheel cover (or centre cover) from the wheel, apply the handbrake, and engage 1st gear or P. Loosen the hub/driveshaft nut about half a turn.

Warning: The driveshaft nut is done up extremely tight, and considerable effort will be required to loosen it. Do not use poor-quality, badly-fitting tools for this task, due to the risk of personal injury.

2 Working inside the engine compartment, remove the plastic cover from the top of the front strut. Retain the strut piston with an Allen key, then loosen the strut thrust bearing retaining nut by five complete turns. Do not remove the nut completely.

3 Loosen the front wheel nuts, then jack up the front of the car and support it on axle stands (see *Jacking and vehicle support*). Remove the front wheel, then unscrew and remove the hub nut. It is recommended that a new hub nut is obtained for refitting.

4 Disconnect the wiring from the ABS wheel speed sensor located at the top of the steering knuckle.

5 Loosen the track rod end balljoint nut several turns, then use a balljoint removal tool to release the balljoint from the steering arm. If necessary, use a 5 mm Allen key to hold the balljoint spindle while loosening the nut. With the balljoint released, unscrew the nut and disconnect the balljoint from the steering arm. Discard the nut, as a new one must be fitted on reassembly.

6 Unscrew the two bolts securing the brake caliper mounting bracket to the steering

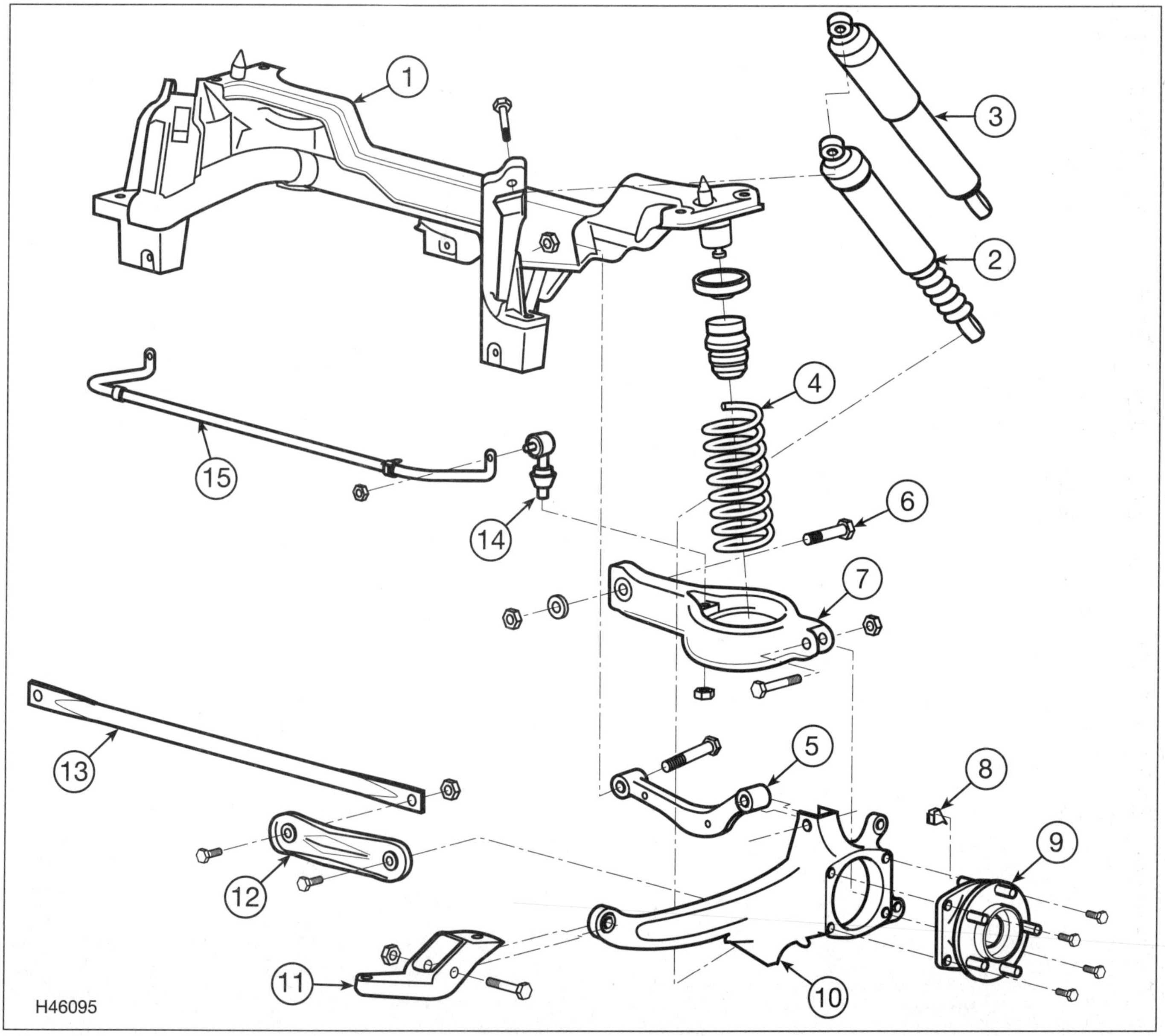

H46095

1.3 Rear suspension components (Estate models)

1 *Crossmember*
2 *Self-levelling shock absorber*
3 *Conventional shock absorber*
4 *Rear spring*
5 *Upper arm*
6 *Eccentric cam bolt*
7 *Rear lower arm*
8 *ABS wheel sensor*
9 *Wheel hub/bearing*
10 *Tie-bar/knuckle*
11 *Tie-bar bracket*
12 *Front lower arm*
13 *Arm brace*
14 *Anti-roll bar drop link*
15 *Anti-roll bar*

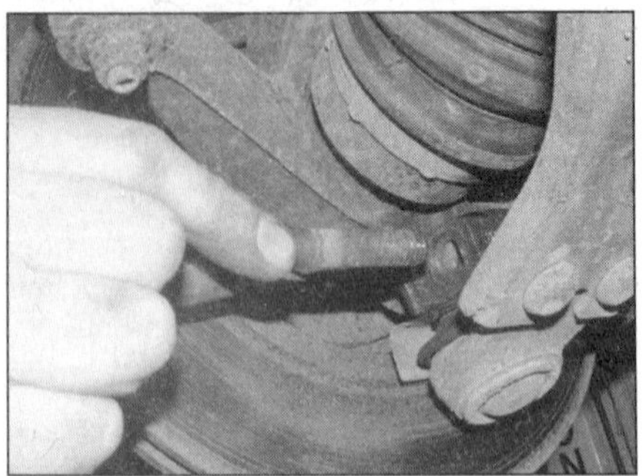
2.12 Removing the balljoint pinch-bolt

2.14 Removing the lower arm balljoint from the steering knuckle

knuckle, then slide the caliper and brake pads off the brake disc. Tie the caliper and bracket to the front strut coil spring, taking care not to strain the flexible hydraulic hose.

7 Undo the screws securing the front splash undershield to the subframe. On diesel engine models, remove the engine undershield complete.

8 Support the subframe next to the relevant lower arm using a trolley jack. **Note:** *Only one side of the subframe needs to be lowered to detach the lower arm balljoint from the steering knuckle.*

9 Carefully mark the position of the front subframe on the underbody to ensure correct relocation. **Note:** *Ford technicians use special alignment pins to locate the subframe accurately.*

10 Unbolt and remove the subframe-to-underbody rear mounting bracket on the side being worked on. Loosen the bolts of the remaining rear mounting bracket by five turns only.

Caution: The subframe MUST be lowered when removing the steering knuckle, otherwise damage will occur to the lower arm rear hydro-bush.

11 Unscrew and remove the subframe front mounting bolt on the side being worked on. Loosen the remaining front mounting bolt by five turns.

12 Note which way round the front lower arm balljoint pinch-bolt is fitted, then unscrew and remove it from the knuckle assembly **(see illustration)**. **Do not** pull down on the lower arm at this stage, as the rear hydro-bush will be damaged.

13 Lower the subframe on the side being worked on, far enough to access the top of the lower arm rear mounting bolt; this will give the necessary room to disconnect the lower arm balljoint. Check that the steering inner column is free to move through the bulkhead.

14 Detach the lower arm balljoint from the steering knuckle, and remove the heat shield **(see illustration)**. If it is tight, carefully tap down the outer end of the arm with a mallet, or prise open the knuckle clamp using a wedge-shaped tool. Take care not to damage the balljoint rubber boot.

15 Remove the brake disc with reference to Chapter 9.

16 Using a universal puller located on the hub flange, press the outer end of the driveshaft through the front hub and steering knuckle. It will help if the knuckle is turned at an angle. Keep the driveshaft joints as straight as possible, or damage may occur.

17 Unscrew and remove the pinch-bolt securing the steering knuckle assembly to the front strut, noting which way round it is fitted. Prise open the clamp using a wedge-shaped tool, and release the knuckle from the strut **(see illustrations)**. If necessary, tap the knuckle downwards with a soft-headed mallet to separate the two components. Remove the knuckle from the car.

Refitting

18 Thoroughly clean the bottom end of the strut and its location in the knuckle. Locate the knuckle onto the strut and over the tab, then insert the pinch-bolt and tighten to the specified torque **(see illustration)**.

19 Pull out the knuckle, and insert the end of the driveshaft through the front hub. Fit the new driveshaft/hub nut, and tighten it moderately at this stage. Final tightening of the nut is made with the car lowered to the ground.

20 Refit the brake disc with reference to Chapter 9.

21 Locate the heat shield on the bottom of the knuckle, then position the knuckle over the lower arm balljoint and lift the balljoint until the spindle is fully entered in the clamp. Tap up the end of the lower arm to make sure it is fully entered. Insert the pinch-bolt from the rear of the knuckle and tighten it to the specified torque.

22 Raise the subframe against the underbody, and position it accurately with the marks made during removal. If available, use the special Ford alignment pins. Refit the rear bracket, then insert the mounting bolts. Tighten all of the subframe and rear bracket bolts to the specified torque. Make sure the subframe does not move when tightening the bolts. If applicable, remove the Ford alignment pins.

23 On diesel models, refit the complete engine undershield. On all models, insert and tighten the screws securing the front splash undershield to the subframe.

24 Locate the brake caliper complete with mounting bracket to the steering knuckle, while guiding the brake pads over the brake disc. Insert the bolts and tighten them to the specified torque.

25 Locate the track rod end balljoint on the steering arm. Screw on a new nut and tighten to the specified torque. If necessary, use a 5 mm Allen key to hold the balljoint spindle while tightening the nut.

26 Reconnect the wiring to the ABS wheel speed sensor on the steering knuckle.

27 Have an assistant apply the brakes, then tighten the hub nut to a preload setting of 100 Nm (74 lbf ft).

28 Refit the front wheel and lower the car to the ground. Fully tighten the wheel nuts, then fully tighten the hub nut to the specified torque. Refit the wheel cover (or centre cover) to the wheel.

29 Hold the strut piston stationary with an Allen key, then tighten the upper mount thrust bearing (centre) nut to the specified torque.

2.17a Prise open the clamp with a cold chisel . . .

2.17b . . . and release the knuckle from the strut

2.18 Locate the knuckle over the tab on the strut

The nut can be tightened initially with a ring spanner while the piston rod is being held, then a torque wrench can be used for the final tightening.

30 Refit the plastic cover to the top of the front strut.

3 Front hub and bearings – inspection and renewal

Inspection

1 The front hub bearings are non-adjustable, and are supplied already greased.

2 To check the bearings for excessive wear, apply the handbrake, then jack up the front of the car and support it on axle stands (see *Jacking and vehicle support*).

3 Grip the front wheel at top and bottom, and attempt to rock it. If excessive movement is noted, it may be that the hub bearings are worn. Do not confuse wear in the driveshaft outer joint or front lower arm balljoint with wear in the bearings. Hub bearing wear will show up as roughness or vibration when the wheel is spun; it will also be noticeable as a rumbling or growling noise when driving.

Renewal

Note: *The ABS wheel speed sensor ring is integral with the hub bearing.*

4 Remove the steering knuckle and hub assembly as described in Section 2.

5 Undo the screw and remove the ABS wheel speed sensor from the knuckle.

6 The hub must now be removed from the bearing. It is preferable to use a press to do this **(see illustration)**, but it is possible to drive out the hub using a length of metal tube of suitable diameter. Part of the inner race will remain on the hub, and the remaining bearing will remain in the knuckle. The bearing will be rendered unserviceable by removing it, and **must not** be re-used.

7 On models with automatic transmission, use suitable circlip pliers to extract the large circlip which is used to retain the bearing. If this circlip is in good condition, it may be re-used.

8 With the hub removed, remove the bearing cage, oil seal and the old bearing inner race by supporting the race and pressing the hub down through it. Alternatively use a puller to withdraw the race **(see illustrations)**. Do not use heat to remove the race.

9 Press or drive the bearing from the steering knuckle, using a length of metal tube of suitable diameter **(see illustration)**.

10 Clean the bearing seating surfaces on the steering knuckle and hub.

11 Press the new bearing into the knuckle until it contacts the shoulder **(see illustration)**, using a length of metal tube of diameter slightly less than the outer race. The wheel speed sensor ring may be damaged if the bearing is driven into position, therefore it is recommended that a press is used. Do not apply any pressure to the inner race.

Caution: The bearing must be fitted with the ABS wheel speed sensor ring, coloured black, towards the wheel speed sensor end of the knuckle. The ABS wheel speed sensor ring must not be subjected to any impact.

12 On models with automatic transmission, refit the large circlip which is used to retain the bearing. Ensure the circlip locates fully into its groove.

13 Support the bearing inner race on a length of metal tube, then press or drive the hub fully into the bearing **(see illustration)**. Alternatively, support the hub and press the bearing inner race onto it.

14 Refit the ABS wheel speed sensor and tighten the screw.

15 Refit the steering knuckle and hub assembly as described in Section 2.

4 Front strut – removal and refitting

Removal

1 Loosen the front wheel nuts. Apply the

3.6 Using a press to remove the front hub from the bearings

3.8a Remove the bearing cage (and oil seal) . . .

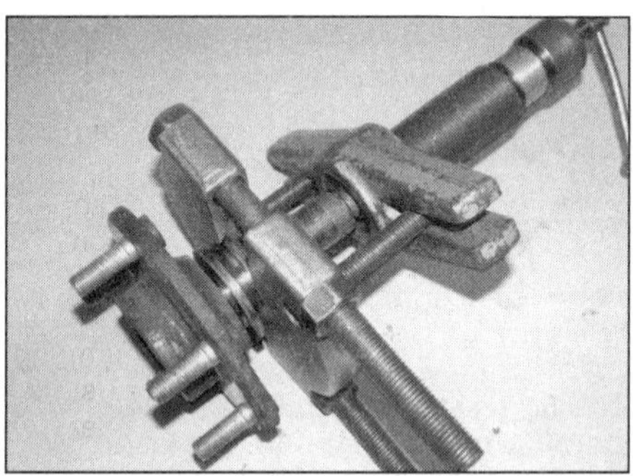

3.8b . . . then use a puller . . .

3.8c . . . to remove the old bearing inner race

3.9 Pressing out the old bearing

3.11 Pressing in the new bearing . . .

3.13 . . . then press the hub through the inner race

4.2 Removing the hydraulic hose support bracket from the strut

handbrake, then jack up the front of the car and support it on axle stands (see *Jacking and vehicle support*). Remove the front wheel.

2 Unbolt the brake hydraulic hose support bracket from the strut **(see illustration)**. Alternatively, unclip the hose from the bracket.

3 Unscrew the nut and disconnect the anti-roll bar link from the strut. If necessary, use a 5 mm Allen key to hold the spindle while the nut is loosened.

4 Unscrew the two bolts securing the brake caliper mounting bracket to the steering knuckle, then slide the caliper and brake pads off the brake disc. Tie the caliper and bracket to one side or support on an axle stand, making sure that the flexible hose is not strained.

5 Undo the screws securing the front splash undershield to the subframe. On diesel engine models, remove the engine undershield complete.

6 Support the subframe on the relevant side using a trolley jack. **Note:** *Only one side of the subframe needs to be lowered to detach the lower arm balljoint from the steering knuckle.*

7 Carefully mark the position of the front subframe on the underbody to ensure correct relocation. **Note:** *Ford technicians use special alignment pins to locate the subframe accurately.*

8 Unbolt and remove the subframe-to-underbody rear mounting bracket on the side being worked on. Loosen the bolts of the remaining rear mounting bracket by five turns only.

9 Unscrew and remove the subframe front mounting bolt on the side being worked on. Loosen the remaining front mounting bolt by five turns.

10 Lower the subframe on the side being worked on, far enough to access the top of the lower arm rear mounting bolt; this will give the necessary room to disconnect the strut from the knuckle without damaging the lower arm rear mounting hydro-bush. Check that the steering inner column is free to move through the bulkhead.

Caution: The subframe MUST be lowered when removing the front strut, otherwise damage will occur to the lower arm rear hydro-bush.

11 Note which way round the front lower arm balljoint pinch-bolt is fitted, then unscrew and remove it from the knuckle assembly.

12 Detach the lower arm balljoint from the steering knuckle, and remove the heat shield. If it is tight, carefully tap down the outer end of the arm with a mallet, or prise open the knuckle clamp using a wedge-shaped tool. Take care not to damage the balljoint rubber boot. Do not press the lower arm down excessively, as the rear hydro-bush will be damaged.

13 Unscrew and remove the pinch-bolt securing the steering knuckle assembly to the front strut, noting which way round it is fitted.

14 Prise open the clamp using a wedge-shaped tool, and release the knuckle from the strut. If necessary, tap the knuckle downwards with a soft-headed mallet to separate the two components. Support the knuckle on an axle stand, taking care not to bend the driveshaft joints excessively – keep the driveshaft as straight as possible.

15 Working inside the engine compartment, remove the plastic cover from the top of the front strut. Note the arrow and white line on the top mount are facing the front of the car **(see illustrations)**.

16 Support the strut, then unscrew the three top mount nuts **(see illustration)**. Lower the strut and withdraw from under the wheel arch.

Refitting

17 Lift the strut into position, and insert the studs through the holes in the body, making sure that the arrow and white line on the top mount are facing the front of the car. Screw on the nuts and tighten them to the specified torque.

18 Refit the plastic cover to the top of the strut.

19 Thoroughly clean the bottom end of the strut and its location in the knuckle. Locate the knuckle onto the strut, then insert the pinch-bolt and tighten to the specified torque.

20 Locate the heat shield on the bottom of the knuckle, then position the knuckle over the lower arm balljoint and lift the balljoint until the spindle is fully entered in the clamp. Tap up the end of the lower arm to make sure it is fully entered. Insert the pinch-bolt from the rear of the knuckle, and tighten it to the specified torque.

21 Raise the subframe against the underbody, and position it accurately with the marks made during removal. If available, use the special Ford alignment pins. Refit the rear bracket, then insert the mounting bolts. Tighten all of the subframe and rear bracket bolts to the specified torque. Make sure the subframe does not move when tightening the bolts. If applicable, remove the Ford alignment pins.

22 On diesel models, refit the complete engine undershield. On all models, insert and tighten the screws securing the front splash undershield to the subframe.

23 Locate the brake caliper complete with mounting bracket to the steering knuckle, while guiding the brake pads over the brake disc. Insert the bolts and tighten them to the specified torque.

24 Refit the anti-roll bar link to the strut. Screw on the nut and tighten to the specified torque. If necessary, use a 5 mm Allen key to hold the spindle.

25 Refit the brake hydraulic hose support bracket to the strut, and tighten the nut securely.

26 Refit the front wheel and lower the car to the ground. Tighten the wheel nuts to the specified torque.

5 Front strut – overhaul

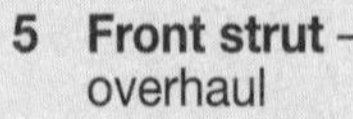

Warning: Before attempting to dismantle the front strut, a spring compressor tool is required to hold the coil spring in compression. Do

4.15a Removing the plastic cover from the top of the strut

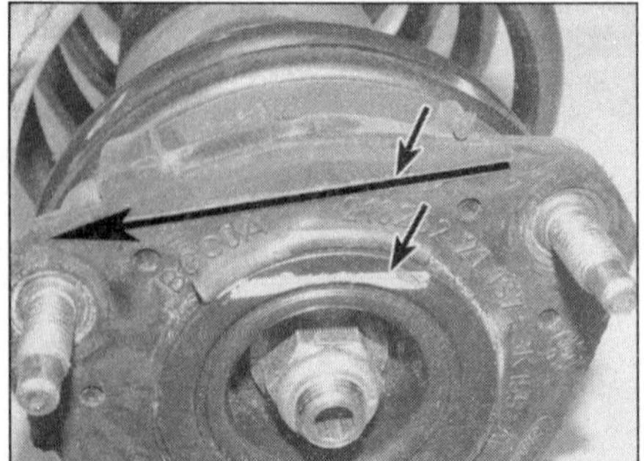

4.15b The arrow and white line on the top mount must face the front of the car

4.16 Unscrewing the front strut top mount nuts

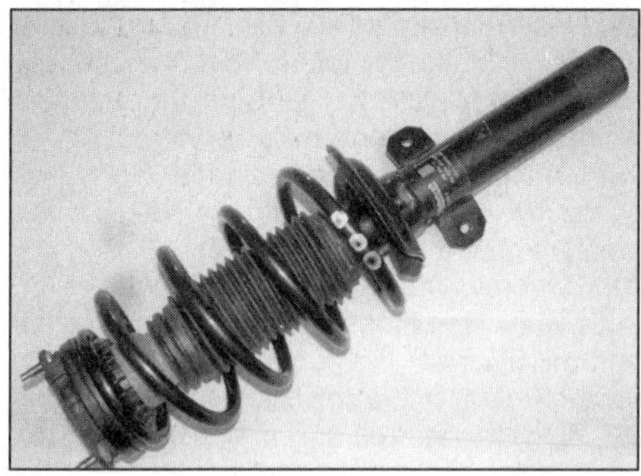

5.2 Front strut and coil spring removed from the car

5.4 Hold the piston with an Allen key while unscrewing the retaining nut

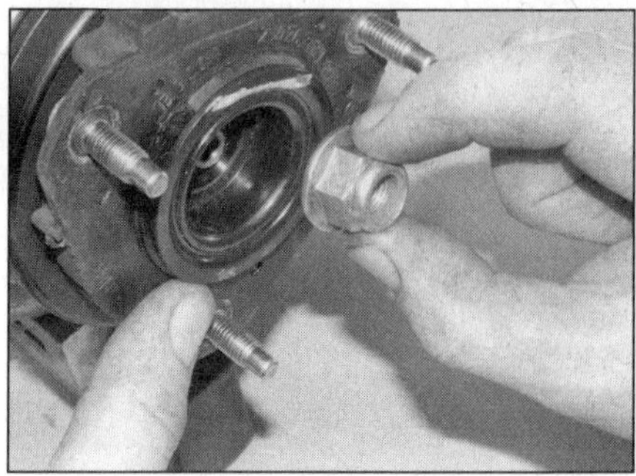

5.5a Remove the nut . . .

not attempt to use makeshift methods. Uncontrolled release of the spring could cause damage and personal injury.

1 If the front struts exhibit signs of wear (leaking fluid, loss of damping capability, sagging or cracked coil springs) then they should be dismantled and overhauled as necessary. The struts themselves cannot be serviced, and should be renewed if faulty, but the springs and related components can be renewed. To maintain balanced characteristics on both sides of the car, the components on both sides should be renewed at the same time.

2 With the strut removed from the car, clean away all external dirt, then mount it in a vice **(see illustration)**.

3 Fit the coil spring compressor tools (ensuring they are fully engaged), and compress the spring until all tension is relieved from the upper mounting.

4 Hold the strut piston with an Allen key, and unscrew the thrust bearing retaining nut with a ring spanner **(see illustration)**. **Do not** attempt to undo this nut unless the spring is compressed as described in paragraph 3.

5 Withdraw the top mounting, thrust bearing, bump stop and upper spring seat, gaiter and coil spring **(see illustrations)**.

6 If a new spring is to be fitted, the original spring must now be carefully released from the compressor. If it is to be re-used, the spring can be left in compression.

7 With the strut assembly now completely dismantled, examine all the components for wear and damage, and check the bearing for smoothness of operation. Renew components as necessary.

8 Examine the strut for signs of fluid leakage. Check the strut piston for signs of pitting along its entire length, and check the strut body for signs of damage.

9 Test the operation of the strut, while holding it in an upright position, by moving the piston through a full stroke, and then through short strokes of 50 to 100 mm. In both cases, the resistance felt should be smooth and continuous. If the resistance is jerky, uneven, or if there is any visible sign of wear or damage to the strut, renewal is necessary.

10 Reassembly is a reversal of dismantling, noting the following points:

*a) Make sure that the coil spring ends are correctly located in the upper and lower seats before releasing the compressor **(see illustration)**.*

b) Check that the thrust bearing is correctly fitted to the upper mounting.

c) Tighten the thrust bearing retaining nut to the specified torque.

5.5b . . . followed by the top mounting . . .

5.5c . . . thrust bearing . . .

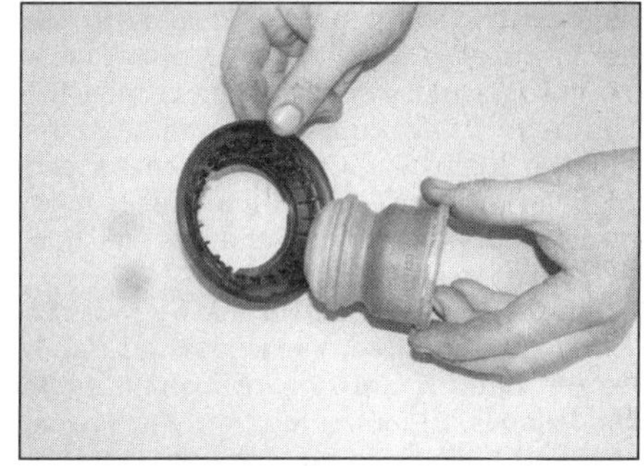

5.5d . . . bump stop and upper spring seat . . .

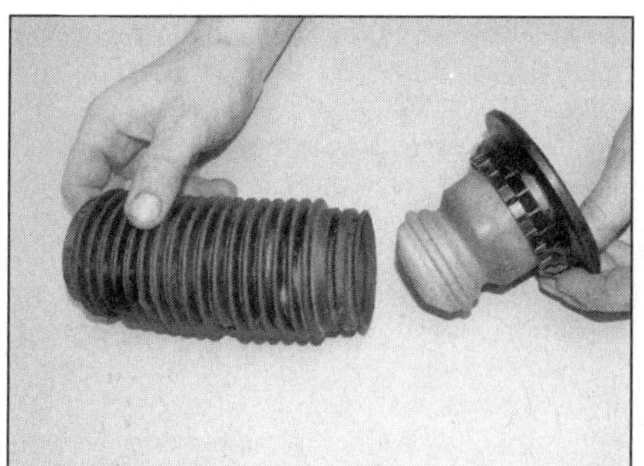

5.5e . . . gaiter . . .

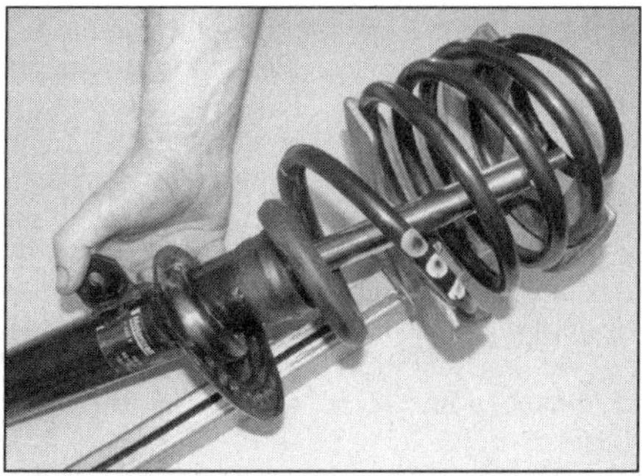

5.5f . . . and coil spring (with compressor tool)

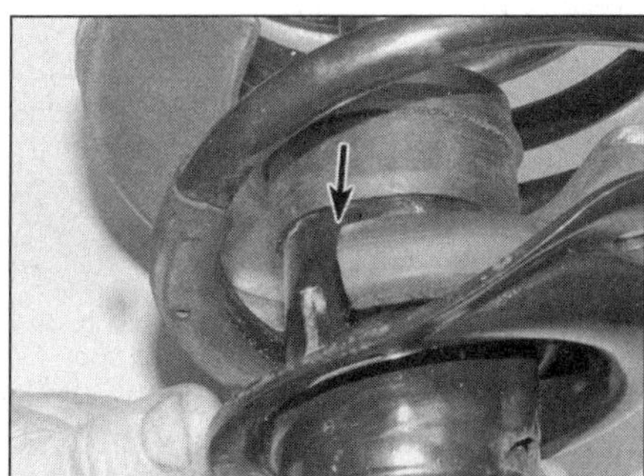

5.10 Make sure that the coil spring ends are located against the spring seats

6.21 Anti-roll bar mounting clamp

6 Front anti-roll bar and links - removal and refitting

Removal

1 Loosen the front wheel nuts. Apply the handbrake, then jack up the front of the car and support it on axle stands (see *Jacking and vehicle support*). Turn the steering to the straight-ahead position and lock it. Remove both front wheels.

2 Remove the driver's side lower facia trim panel, which is secured by four screws and two upper clips. Where applicable, unclip the diagnostic connector plug from the panel, and/or disconnect the wiring from the climate control sensor as the panel is removed.

3 Where applicable, remove the insulation pad from over the foot pedals.

4 Unscrew and remove the clamp bolt securing the steering inner column to the flexible coupling on the steering gear. Rotate the clamp plate clockwise and detach the clamp from the coupling. Note that the coupling stub has a triangular shape and the shaft may only be fitted in one of three positions. Discard the bolt as a new one must be fitted on reassembly.

Warning: Make sure that the steering wheel remains locked in its straight-ahead position while the clamp is disconnected from the flexible coupling. Failure to do this may result in damage to the airbag and clock spring, and subsequent personal injury in the event of an accident.

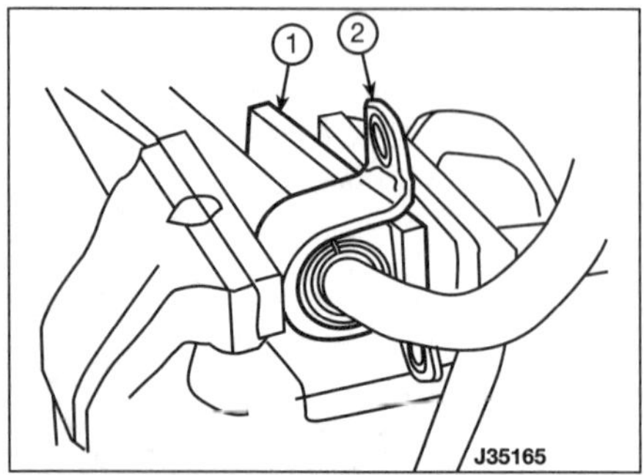

6.23 Press the clamps (2) onto the mounting rubbers in a vice, using a 10 mm thick metal bar (1) as a spacer

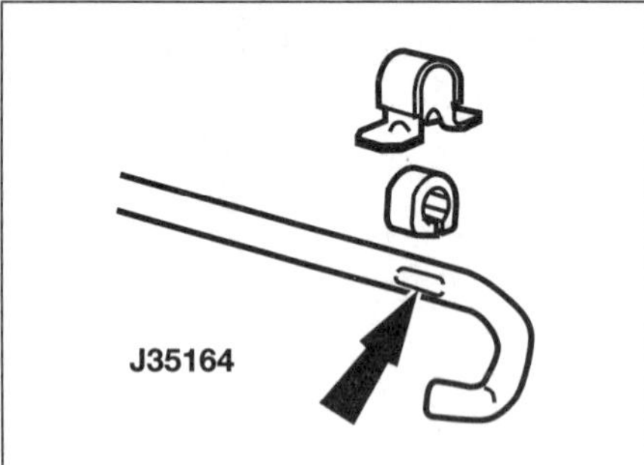

6.22 The anti-roll bar mounting rubbers are located on flats

5 Hold the radiator in the upper mountings using split pins inserted through the holes in the upper location pins. Access to the holes is gained through the apertures in the front crossmember.

6 Undo the screws and remove the splash shield from under the radiator position. On diesel models, also remove the engine undershield and left-hand wheel arch lower liner.

7 Under the front of the car, unbolt the hose bracket (where fitted) next to the left-hand radiator support bracket, then unbolt and remove both radiator support brackets.

8 Unscrew the nuts and disconnect the anti-roll bar links from the front struts. If necessary, use a 5 mm Allen key to hold the spindles while the nuts are loosened.

9 On 1.8 and 2.0 litre petrol engines, and all diesel engines, remove the exhaust flexible pipe from the front of the exhaust system with reference to the appropriate part of Chapter 4.

10 On V6 engines, remove the exhaust front lower Y-pipe as described in Chapter 4A.

11 Remove the engine rear mounting with reference to the appropriate part of Chapter 2.

12 As applicable, disconnect the second oxygen sensor wiring, and unclip the wiring from the subframe. On models with a diesel particulate filter, detach the associated wiring and pipework as necessary.

13 On models with xenon headlights, release the ties and detach the headlight-levelling sensor wiring harness from the subframe.

14 Release the radiator cooling fan wiring harness from the subframe.

15 Support the front subframe on one or two trolley jacks. If necessary, enlist the help of an assistant.

16 Carefully mark the position of the front subframe on the underbody to ensure correct refitting. **Note:** *Ford technicians use special alignment pins to locate the subframe accurately when refitting.* Unscrew and remove the subframe rear mounting bolts, then unbolt the rear brackets from the subframe.

17 Unscrew and remove the subframe front mounting bolts.

18 Keeping it level, lower the subframe about 150 mm, making sure that the lower arm rear hydro-bushes are not strained or damaged.

19 Unscrew the nuts and disconnect the anti-roll bar links from the anti-roll bar. If necessary, use a 5 mm Allen key to hold the spindles while the nuts are loosened.

20 Unbolt the steering gear from the subframe, then use cable ties to suspend the steering gear from the underbody.

21 Unscrew the mounting clamp bolts on both sides **(see illustration)**, then remove the anti-roll bar from the subframe and withdraw from one side of the car. Remove the clamps.

22 With the anti-roll bar on the bench, mark the location of the mounting rubbers and note how they are fitted to the flats on the bar, then remove them **(see illustration)**. Examine the rubbers for wear and damage, and renew them if necessary.

Refitting

23 Before refitting the anti-roll bar, the mounting rubbers and clamps must be pressed into position. Grip the anti-roll bar in a vice, and use a 10 mm thick metal bar measuring 30 mm by 100 mm as a spacer to press on the clamps **(see illustration)**.

24 Refitting is a reversal of the removal procedure, but tighten the nuts and bolts to the specified torques. When refitting the subframe, raise it against the underbody, and position it accurately with the marks made during removal. If available, use the special Ford alignment pins. Refit the rear brackets, then insert the mounting bolts and tighten to the specified torque. Make sure the subframe does not move when tightening the bolts. Always fit a new steering column-to-flexible coupling clamp bolt.

25 Have the front wheel alignment checked and adjusted at the earliest opportunity.

26 If on completion, the car pulls to one side, or abnormal tyre wear is noted, have the subframe alignment checked by a Ford dealer.

7 Front lower arm - removal and refitting

Removal

1 Loosen the relevant front wheel nuts. Apply the handbrake, then jack up the front of the car and support it on axle stands (see *Jacking and vehicle support*). Remove the relevant wheel.

2 Undo the screws securing the front splash undershield to the subframe. On diesel engine models, remove the engine undershield complete.

3 On models with xenon headlights, a headlight-levelling sensor is located on the left-hand lower arm. If removing this arm, remove the sensor by first disconnecting the wiring, then releasing the connecting rod and unbolting the sensor.

4 Support the subframe next to the relevant lower arm using a trolley jack. **Note:** *Only one*

side of the subframe needs to be lowered to remove the lower arm.

5 Carefully mark the position of the front subframe on the underbody to ensure correct relocation. **Note:** *Ford technicians use special alignment pins to locate the subframe accurately.*

6 Unbolt and remove the subframe-to-underbody rear mounting bracket on the side being worked on. Loosen the bolts of the remaining rear mounting bracket by five turns only.

7 Unscrew and remove the subframe front mounting bolt on the side being worked on. Loosen the remaining front mounting bolt by five turns.

8 Note which way round the front lower arm balljoint pinch-bolt is fitted, then unscrew and remove it from the knuckle assembly. **Do not** pull down on the lower arm at this stage, as the rear hydro-bush will be damaged.

9 Lower the subframe on the side being worked on, far enough to access the top of the lower arm rear mounting bolt; this will give the necessary room to disconnect the lower arm balljoint without damaging the rear hydro-bush.

Caution: The subframe MUST be lowered when removing the front lower arm, otherwise damage will occur to the lower arm rear hydro-bush.

10 Detach the lower arm balljoint from the steering knuckle, and remove the heat shield. If it is tight, carefully tap down the outer end of the arm with a mallet, or prise open the knuckle clamp using a wedge-shaped tool. Take care not to damage the balljoint rubber boot.

11 Support the lower arm, then unscrew and remove the front bolt and the rear mounting nut and bolt, and withdraw the arm from the subframe **(see illustrations)**. Take care not to damage the rear hydro-bush. Discard the bolts and nut, and obtain new ones.

12 The front lower arm is supplied complete with the rubber mountings and the balljoint, and it is not possible to obtain the mountings and balljoint separately.

Refitting

13 Refit the lower arm to the subframe and insert the new bolts and nut finger-tight at this stage. Final tightening is carried out with the weight of the car on the suspension.

14 Locate the heat shield on the bottom of the knuckle, then position the knuckle over the lower arm balljoint and lift the balljoint until the spindle is fully entered in the clamp. Tap up the end of the lower arm to make sure it is fully entered. Insert the pinch-bolt from the rear of the knuckle and tighten it to the specified torque.

15 Raise the subframe against the underbody, and position it accurately with the marks made during removal. If available, use the special Ford alignment pins. Refit the rear bracket, then insert the mounting bolts. Tighten all of the subframe and rear bracket bolts to the specified torque. Make sure the subframe does not move when tightening the bolts. If applicable, remove the Ford alignment pins.

7.11a Front lower arm front mounting . . .

7.11b . . . and rear mounting

16 On models with xenon headlights, refit the sensor to the lower arm and tighten the bolts. Reconnect the connecting rod and the wiring. **Note:** *After refitting, the headlight-levelling system must be initialised by a Ford dealer using a special setting instrument.*

17 Refit the wheel and lower the car to the ground.

18 With the weight of the car on its suspension, tighten the lower arm front and rear bolts to the specified torques. Also tighten the wheel nuts to the specified torque.

19 Raise and support the front of the car on axle stands again.

20 On diesel models, refit the complete engine undershield. On all models insert and tighten the screws securing the front splash undershield to the subframe.

21 Lower the car to the ground.

22 Have the front wheel alignment checked and adjusted at the earliest opportunity. On models with xenon headlights, have the levelling system initialised by a Ford dealer.

23 If on completion, the car pulls to one side, or abnormal tyre wear is noted, have the subframe alignment checked by a Ford dealer.

8 Front lower arm balljoint – renewal

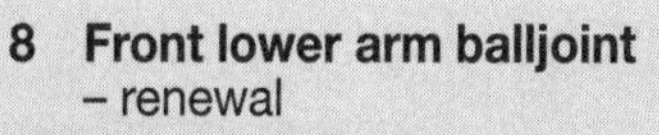

Note: *If the lower arm balljoint is worn, it appears at the time of writing that the complete lower arm must be renewed (see Section 7), although the balljoint was available separately on earlier models. Seek the advice of your Ford dealer or parts supplier to establish whether the balljoint is available separately. If the balljoint has already been renewed, it will be bolted in position; if the original balljoint is being renewed, then it will be riveted in position. This Section describes the renewal of a riveted balljoint.*

1 Remove the front lower arm as described in Section 7. It is not recommended that the balljoint be renewed with the lower arm in position on the car; the accurate drilling necessary may not be possible, and the holes in the arm may be enlarged.

2 With the lower arm on the bench, use a 3 mm drill to make a pilot hole through each of the three rivets **(see illustration)**. Now use a 9 mm drill to drill the rivets to a depth of 12 mm, then use a 7 or 8 mm drift to drive the rivets out of the arm.

3 Clean any rust or dirt from the rivet holes.

4 The new balljoint is supplied with a protective plastic cover over the rubber boot and stub, and it is recommended that this remains in position until it is time to connect the balljoint to the steering knuckle.

5 Locate the new balljoint on the lower arm, and use three new bolts to secure it, inserting the bolts from the top of the arm. Tighten the nuts to the specified torque. Make sure that the location lug on the balljoint engages the hole in the lower arm **(see illustration)**.

6 Refit the front lower arm as described in Section 7.

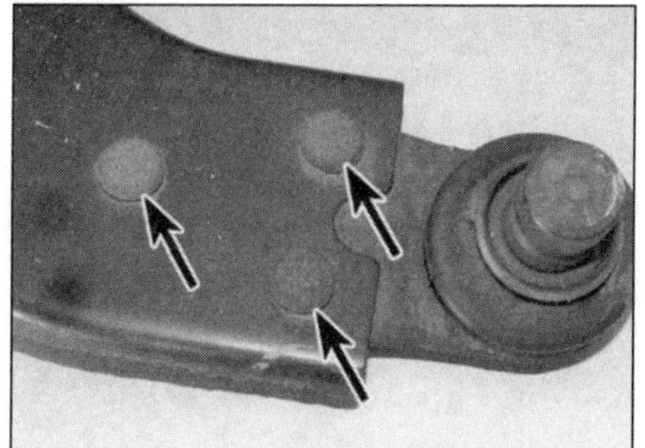

8.2 Front lower arm balljoint rivets

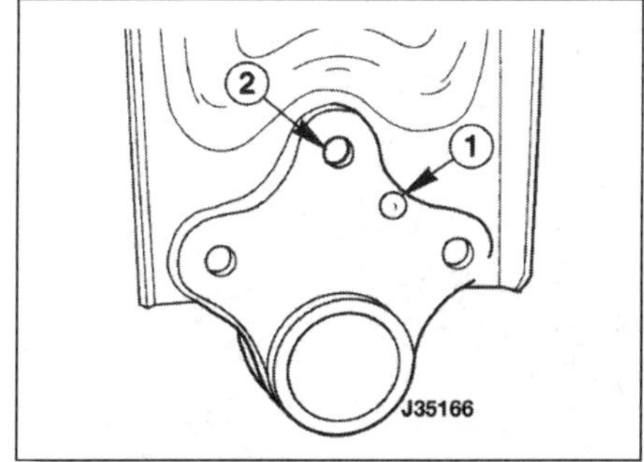

8.5 Location lug (1) and bolt hole (2) in the front lower arm balljoint

9.6a Use a 5 mm Allen key to hold the spindles while the nuts are loosened . . .

9.6b . . . then disconnect the anti-roll bar links from the struts

9.7a On 1.8 and 2.0 litre petrol engines, and all diesel engines, remove the bracket . . .

9.7b . . . unhook the rubber mountings . . .

9.7c . . . then remove the flexible pipe . . .

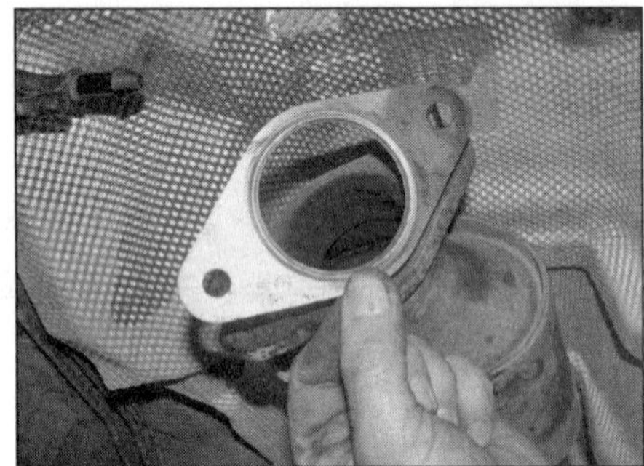
9.7d . . . and recover the gasket

9 Front subframe – removal and refitting

Removal

1 Loosen the front wheel nuts. Apply the handbrake, then jack up the front of the car and support it on axle stands (see *Jacking and vehicle support*). Turn the steering to the straight-ahead position and lock it. Remove both front wheels.

2 Working inside the car, unscrew and remove the clamp bolt securing the steering inner column to the flexible coupling on the steering gear. Rotate the clamp plate clockwise and detach the clamp from the coupling. Discard the bolt as a new one must be fitted on reassembly.

Warning: Make sure that the steering wheel remains locked in its straight-ahead position while the clamp is disconnected from the flexible coupling. Failure to do this may result in damage to the airbag and clock spring.

3 Hold or tie the radiator in the upper mountings – where necessary, use split pins inserted through the holes in the radiator upper location pins. Access to the holes is gained through the apertures in the front crossmember.

4 Undo the screws and remove the splash shield from under the radiator position. On diesel models, also remove the engine undershield.

5 Under the front of the car, unbolt the hose bracket (where fitted) next to the left-hand radiator support bracket, then unbolt and remove both radiator support brackets.

6 Unscrew the nuts and disconnect the anti-roll bar links from the front struts. If necessary, use a 5 mm Allen key to hold the spindles while the nuts are loosened **(see illustrations)**.

7 On 1.8 and 2.0 litre petrol engines, and all diesel engines, remove the exhaust flexible pipe from the front of the exhaust system with reference to the appropriate part of Chapter 4 **(see illustrations)**.

8 On V6 engines, remove the exhaust front lower Y-pipe as described in Chapter 4A.

9 Remove the engine rear mounting with reference to the appropriate part of Chapter 2 **(see illustration)**.

10 On petrol models, disconnect the second oxygen sensor wiring, and unclip the wiring from the subframe.

11 On models with xenon headlights, disconnect the wiring from the headlight-levelling sensor then release the ties and detach the wiring harness from the subframe.

12 Release the radiator cooling fan wiring harness from the subframe **(see illustration)**.

13 Support the front subframe on one or two trolley jacks. If necessary, enlist the help of an assistant **(see illustration)**.

14 Carefully mark the position of the front subframe on the underbody to ensure correct refitting. **Note:** *Ford technicians use special alignment pins to locate the subframe accurately when refitting.* Unscrew and remove the subframe rear mounting bolts, then unbolt the rear brackets from the subframe **(see illustrations)**.

15 Unscrew and remove the subframe front mounting bolts **(see illustration)**.

9.9 Removing the engine rear support/link

9.12 Removing the radiator cooling fan wiring from the subframe

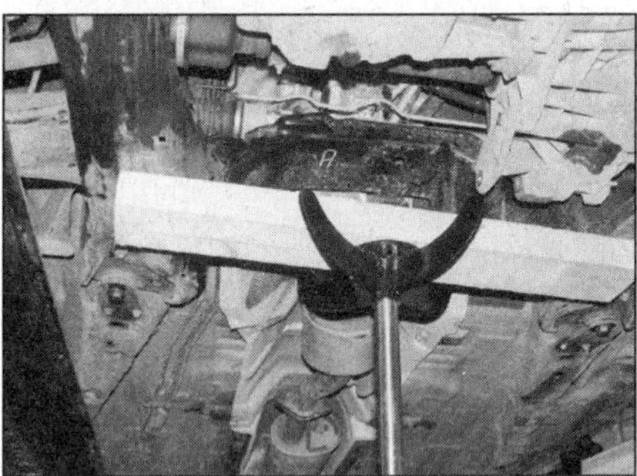
9.13 Support the subframe adequately

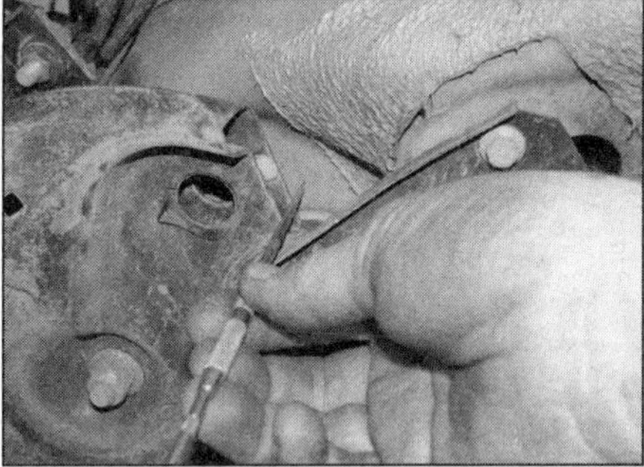
9.14a Mark the position of the subframe to ensure correct refitting

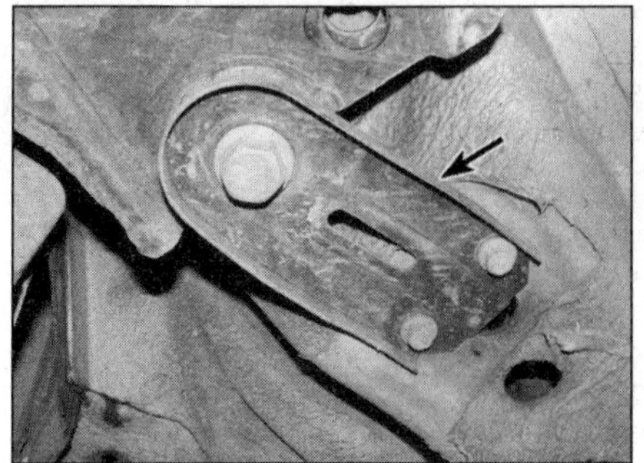
9.14b Subframe rear bracket

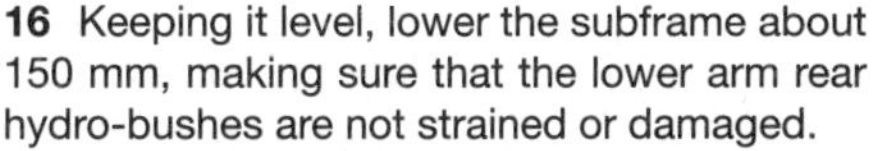
9.14c Using the special subframe alignment tool

9.15 Removing the subframe front mounting bolts

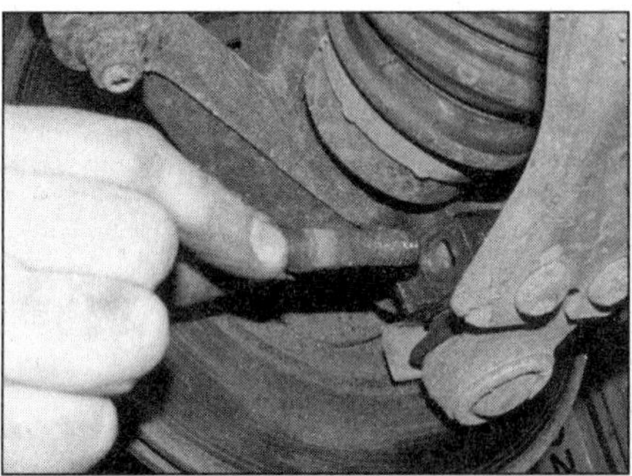
9.17 Removing the front lower arm balljoint pinch-bolts

16 Keeping it level, lower the subframe about 150 mm, making sure that the lower arm rear hydro-bushes are not strained or damaged.

17 Note which way round the front lower arm balljoint pinch-bolts are fitted, then unscrew and remove them from the knuckle assemblies on both sides **(see illustration)**.

18 Detach the lower arm balljoints from the steering knuckles, and remove the heat shields **(see illustration)**. If they are tight, carefully tap down the outer ends of the arms with a mallet, or prise open the knuckle clamps using a wedge-shaped tool. Take care not to damage the balljoint rubber boots.

19 Unbolt the steering gear from the subframe, then use cable ties to suspend the steering gear from the underbody. Alternatively, the steering gear may be left on the subframe if the power steering hose and pipe union is disconnected first **(see illustration)**. If this latter method is used, fit a hose clamp to the hydraulic flexible fluid lines to reduce fluid loss. Recover the O-ring seals.

20 Lower the subframe to the ground.

21 Unscrew the mounting clamp bolts on both sides, then remove the anti-roll bar from the subframe.

22 Remove the lower arms from the subframe with reference to Section 7. If necessary, the subframe mounting bushes may be renewed using a suitable puller **(see illustration)**.

23 If applicable, unbolt and remove the steering gear from the subframe.

Refitting

24 Refit the lower arms to the subframe with reference to Section 7.

25 Refit the anti-roll bar and tighten the mounting clamp bolts to the specified torque with reference to Section 6.

26 Raise and support the subframe to approximately 150 mm below the underbody.

27 Refit the steering gear and tighten the mounting bolts to the specified torque. Where applicable, refit the power steering hydraulic pipe union using new seals, and tighten to the specified torque **(see illustration)**. Remove the hose clamp.

28 Working on each side separately, locate

9.18 Removing the lower balljoint heat shields

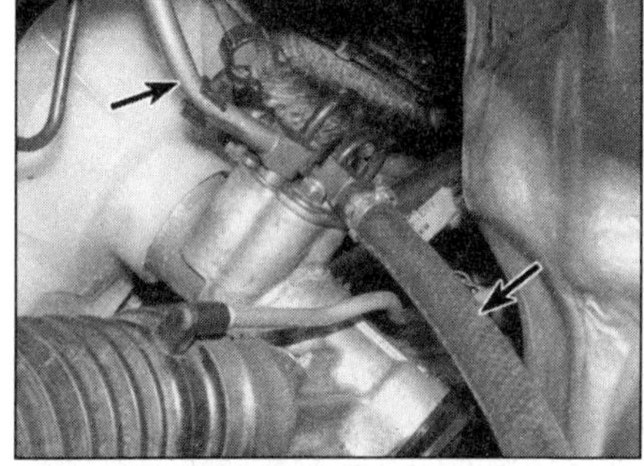
9.19 Power steering hose and pipe union on the steering gear

9.22 Subframe mounting bush

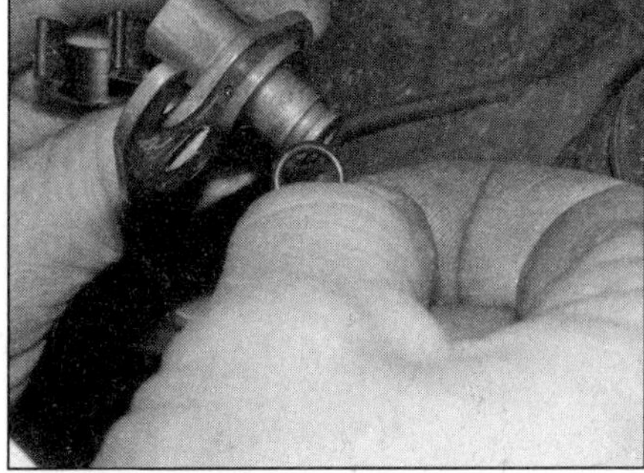
9.27 Fitting new O-ring seals to the power steering hydraulic union

10.3 Assessing rear wheel bearing play

10.7a Disconnect the wiring . . .

10.7b . . . then undo the mounting screw . . .

10.7c . . . and withdraw the sensor

the heat shield on the bottom of the knuckle, then position the knuckle over the lower arm balljoint, and lift the balljoint until the spindle is fully entered in the clamp. Tap up the end of the lower arm to make sure it is fully entered. Insert the pinch-bolt from the rear of the knuckle, and tighten to the specified torque.

29 Raise the subframe against the underbody, and position it accurately with the marks made during removal. If available, use the special Ford alignment pins. Refit the rear bracket, then insert the mounting bolts. Tighten all of the subframe and rear bracket bolts to the specified torque. Make sure the subframe does not move when tightening the bolts. If applicable, remove the Ford alignment pins.

30 Use a cable tie to attach the radiator cooling fan wiring harness to the subframe.

31 On models with xenon headlights, reconnect the wiring to the headlight-levelling sensor, then use cable ties to attach the wiring harness to the subframe.

32 On all petrol models, reconnect the second oxygen sensor wiring, and clip the wiring to the subframe.

33 Refit the engine rear mounting with reference to the appropriate part of Chapter 2.

34 On V6 engines, refit the exhaust front lower Y-pipe as described in Chapter 4A.

35 On 1.8 and 2.0 litre petrol engines, and all diesel engines, refit the exhaust flexible pipe to the front of the exhaust system with reference to the appropriate part of Chapter 4.

36 Reconnect the anti-roll bar links to the struts and tighten the nuts to the specified torque. If necessary, use a 5 mm Allen key to hold the spindles while tightening the nuts.

37 Refit the radiator support brackets and hose bracket to the subframe and tighten to the specified torque.

38 On diesel models, refit the complete engine undershield. On all models, insert and tighten the screws securing the front splash undershield to the subframe.

39 Remove the temporary retaining split pins from the radiator upper location pins.

40 Refit the steering inner column to the flexible coupling on the steering gear, rotate the clamp plate anti-clockwise, then insert a new clamp bolt and tighten to the specified torque.

41 Refit the front wheels and lower the car to the ground. Tighten the wheel nuts to the specified torque, then refit the wheel cover (or centre cover) to the wheels.

42 Have the front wheel alignment checked and adjusted at the earliest opportunity. On models with xenon headlights, have the levelling system initialised by a Ford dealer.

43 If on completion, the car pulls to one side, or abnormal tyre wear is noted, have the subframe alignment checked by a Ford dealer.

10 Rear hub and bearings – inspection, removal and refitting

Inspection

1 The rear hub bearings are non-adjustable, and are supplied complete with the hub and ABS wheel sensor ring. It is not possible to renew the bearings separately from the hub.

2 To check the bearings for excessive wear, chock the front wheels, then jack up the rear of the car and support on axle stands (see *Jacking and vehicle support*). Fully release the handbrake.

3 Grip the rear wheel at the top and bottom, and attempt to rock it **(see illustration)**. If excessive movement is noted, or if there is any roughness or vibration felt when the wheel is spun, it is indicative that the hub bearings are worn.

Removal

4 Remove the rear wheel.

5 Disconnect the handbrake cable from the rear brake caliper as follows. First push the lever forwards, then release the end of the inner cable from the fitting on the lever.

6 Release the handbrake outer cable from the caliper bracket and position it to one side. Where a plastic ferrule is fitted to the outer cable, it will be necessary to compress the plastic tangs in order to release it from the bracket.

7 Disconnect the wiring from the ABS wheel speed sensor located on the inner end of the hub. Access is gained through the hole in the rear lower arm. Undo the mounting screw, and withdraw the sensor **(see illustrations)**.

8 Remove the plastic covers, then unscrew the two bolts securing the brake caliper mounting bracket to the lower arm, and slide the caliper and brake pads off the brake disc. Alternatively, remove the brake pads first and unbolt the caliper from the bracket, then unbolt the bracket **(see illustrations)**. Note

10.8a Unbolt the caliper from the bracket . . .

10.8b . . . then remove the plastic covers . . .

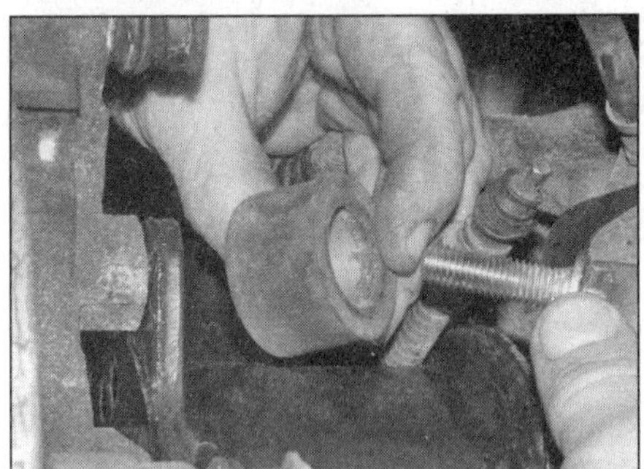
10.8c . . . unscrew the bolts and remove the dampers/spacers . . .

10.8d . . . and withdraw the bracket from the lower arm

10.10a Using a Torx socket through the holes in the hub drive flange . . .

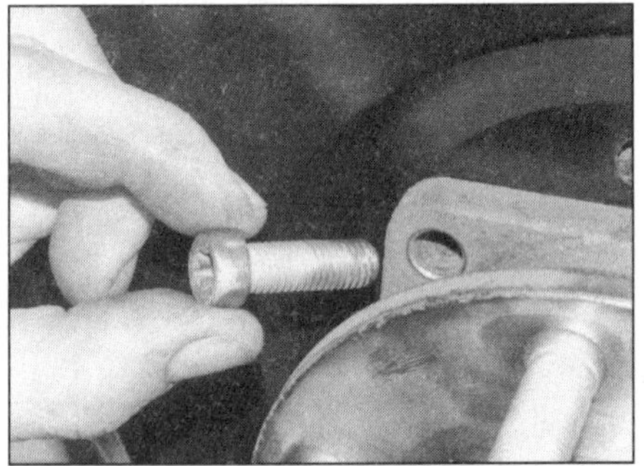
10.10b . . . remove the bolts . . .

10.10c . . . then withdraw the hub . . .

10.10d . . . and backplate

the dampers/spacers located beneath the bolts. Tie or support the caliper and bracket as necessary to one side, taking care not to strain the flexible hydraulic hose.
9 Remove the rear brake disc with reference to Chapter 9.
10 Using a socket through the holes in the hub drive flange, unscrew the bolts securing the hub to the lower arm. Withdraw the hub and backplate from the car **(see illustrations)**.

Refitting

11 Clean the contact surfaces of the hub and lower arm, then refit the hub and backplate, insert the bolts and tighten them to the specified torque.
12 Refit the rear brake disc with reference to Chapter 9.
13 Refit the caliper and brake pads, together with the mounting bracket, onto the brake disc, insert the two bolts, and tighten them to the specified torque. Apply a little locking fluid to the threads of the mounting bracket retaining bolts before refitting them **(see illustration)**.

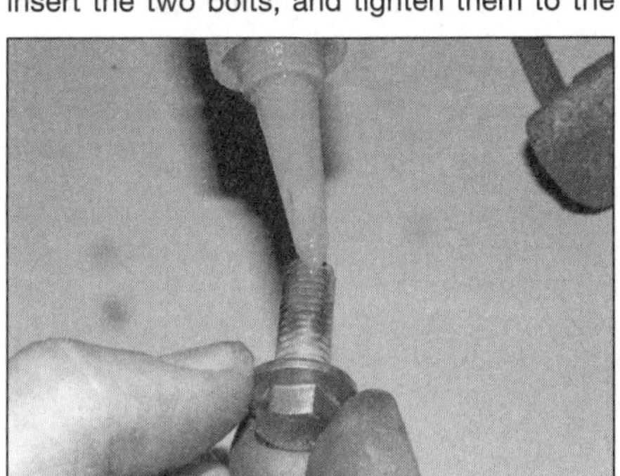
10.13 Apply locking fluid to the threads of the mounting bracket retaining bolts

14 Refit the ABS wheel speed sensor and tighten the bolt, then reconnect the wiring.
15 Refit the handbrake outer cable to the caliper bracket, then reconnect the inner cable to the caliper lever fitting.
16 Refit the rear wheel and lower the car to the ground. Tighten the wheel nuts to the specified torque.

11 Rear knuckle (Saloon/Hatchback) - removal and refitting

Removal

1 Remove the rear hub and backplate as described in Section 10.
2 Unbolt the front and rear lower arms from the rear knuckle, and move them to one side.
3 Unscrew the bolt and disconnect the rear of the tie-bar downwards from the bottom of the knuckle.
4 Unscrew the nut and disconnect the anti-roll bar link lower end from the anti-roll bar.
5 Support the knuckle, then unscrew and remove the clamp bolt securing the knuckle to the strut.
6 Prise the top of the knuckle apart carefully using a large flat-bladed tool, and withdraw the knuckle downwards from the strut. If necessary, tap the knuckle downwards with a soft-faced mallet. Withdraw the knuckle from under the rear wheel arch.

Refitting

7 Locate the knuckle fully on the strut, then insert the clamp bolt and tighten to the specified torque.
8 Refit the anti-roll bar link to the anti-roll bar, and tighten the nut to the specified torque.
9 Refit the tie-bar to the bottom of the knuckle, and insert the bolt finger-tight at this stage.
10 Refit the front and rear lower arms to the knuckle, and insert the bolts finger-tight at this stage.
11 Refit the rear hub and backplate with reference to Section 10.
12 With the weight of the car on the suspension, fully tighten the mounting bolts for the tie-bar and lower arms.

12 Rear strut (Saloon/Hatchback) - removal and refitting

Removal

1 Remove the rear knuckle as described in Section 11.
2 Unscrew the nut and disconnect the upper end of the anti-roll bar link from the rear strut.
3 The bottom of the strut rests on a crossmember ledge/bump stop when fully extended. Using a trolley jack, lift the strut above the ledge, move it outwards and lower it fully.
4 Reach up into the wheel housing and unscrew the strut mounting bolts. Lower the strut and withdraw it from under the car.

Refitting

5 Lift the strut into position, insert the mounting bolts and tighten to the specified torque.

6 Position the trolley jack under the strut, then raise the strut, move it inwards, and lower it onto the crossmember ledge/bump stop. The bump stop is tapered inwards, and the strut bracket should be fully engaged with it before releasing the jack.

7 Reconnect the anti-roll bar link on the strut and tighten the nut to the specified torque.

8 Refit the rear knuckle with reference to Section 11.

13 Rear strut (Saloon/Hatchback) – overhaul

Warning: Before attempting to dismantle the rear strut, a spring compressor tool is required to hold the coil spring in compression. Do not attempt to use makeshift methods. Uncontrolled release of the spring could cause damage and personal injury.

1 If the rear struts exhibit signs of wear (leaking fluid, loss of damping capability, sagging or cracked coil springs) then they should be dismantled and overhauled as necessary. The struts themselves cannot be serviced, and should be renewed if faulty, but the springs and related components can be renewed. To maintain balanced characteristics on both sides of the car, the components on both sides should be renewed at the same time.

2 With the strut removed from the car, clean away all external dirt, then mount it in a vice.

3 Fit the coil spring compressor tools (ensuring they are fully engaged), and compress the spring until all tension is relieved from the upper mounting.

4 Hold the strut piston with an Allen key, and unscrew the top mounting/thrust bearing retaining nut with a ring spanner. **Do not** attempt to undo this nut unless the spring is compressed as described in paragraph 3.

5 Withdraw the retaining cup, top mounting, upper spring seat and spring, followed by the gaiter and bump stop **(see illustration)**.

6 If a new spring is to be fitted, the original spring must now be carefully released from the compressor. If it is to be re-used, the spring can be left in compression.

7 With the strut assembly now completely dismantled, examine all the components for wear and damage, and check the bearing for smoothness of operation. Renew components as necessary.

8 Examine the strut for signs of fluid leakage. Check the strut piston for signs of pitting along its entire length, and check the strut body for signs of damage.

9 Test the operation of the strut, while holding it in an upright position, by moving the piston through a full stroke, and then through short strokes of 50 to 100 mm. In both cases, the resistance felt should be smooth and continuous. If the resistance is jerky, uneven, or if there is any visible sign of wear or damage to the strut, renewal is necessary.

10 Reassembly is a reversal of dismantling, noting the following points:

a) *Make sure that the coil spring ends are correctly located in the upper seat and strut before releasing the compressor.*

b) *Tighten the thrust bearing retaining nut to the specified torque.*

14 Rear anti-roll bar and links (Saloon/Hatchback) – removal and refitting

Removal

1 Loosen the rear wheel nuts, then chock the front wheels. Jack up the rear of the car and support on axle stands (see *Jacking and vehicle support*). Remove the rear wheel.

2 Unscrew the nuts securing the anti-roll bar links to the rear struts on both sides.

3 Unscrew the bolts securing the anti-roll bar mounting clamps to the rear crossmember **(see illustration)**, then unhook the clamps and withdraw the anti-roll bar from under the car. Identify the left- and right-hand sides of the bar to ensure correct refitting.

4 Unscrew the nuts and remove the links from the anti-roll bar.

5 Examine the rubber bushes for the mounting clamps and links, and if necessary renew them. The links are available individually.

Refitting

6 Locate the anti-roll bar on the rear crossmember, hook the mounting clamps in

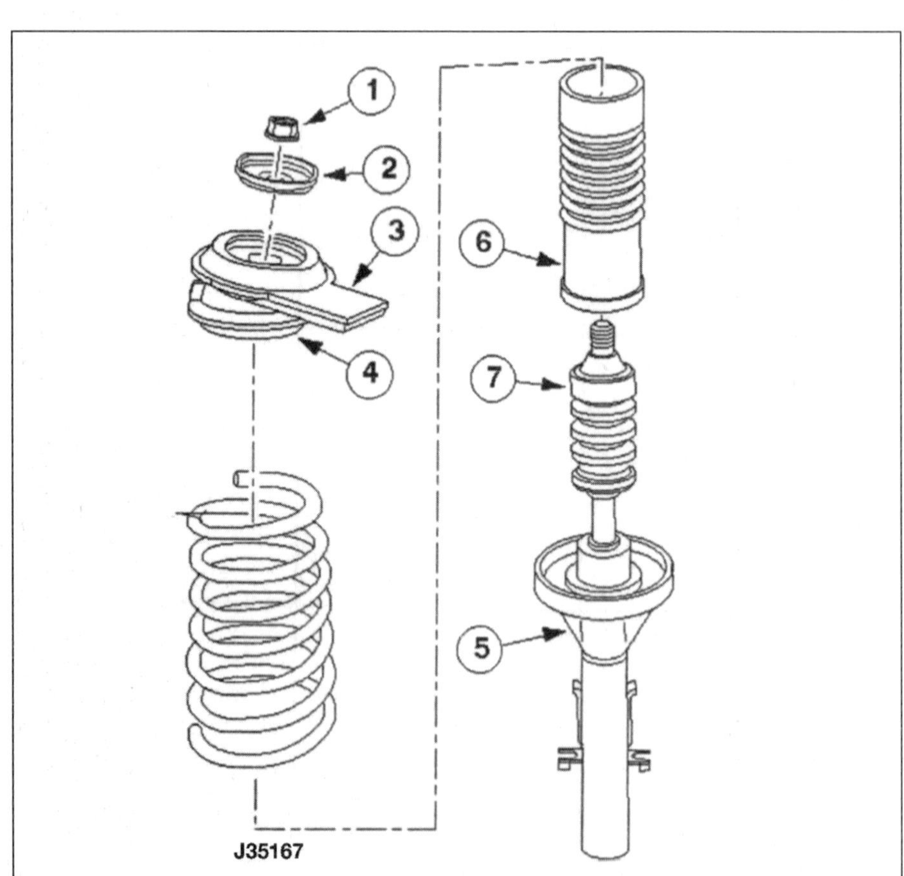

13.5 Rear strut components

1 *Top mounting/bearing retaining nut*
2 *Retaining cup*
3 *Top mounting/ bearing*
4 *Upper spring seat*
5 *Rear suspension strut*
6 *Gaiter*
7 *Bump stop*

14.3 Rear anti-roll bar mounting clamp bolts

position, and insert the bolts. Tighten the bolts to the specified torque.

7 Locate the anti-roll bar links on the struts and bar. Refit the nuts and tighten them to the specified torque.

8 Refit the rear wheels, and lower the car to the ground. Tighten the wheel nuts to the specified torque.

15 Rear lower arms (Saloon/Hatchback) – removal and refitting

Removal

1 Loosen the rear wheel nuts. Chock the front wheels, then jack up the rear of the car and support on axle stands (see *Jacking and vehicle support*). Remove the relevant rear wheel.

Front lower arm

2 On models with xenon headlights, a headlight-levelling sensor is located on the front left-hand lower arm. If removing this arm, remove the sensor by first disconnecting the wiring, then releasing the connecting rod and unbolting the sensor.

3 Release the rubber mounting supporting the intermediate exhaust system.

4 Release the rubber mounting supporting the rear exhaust system, then lower the exhaust system onto an axle stand. On models with the 2.5 litre V6 engine, release both rear rubber mountings.

5 Carefully mark the position of the rear subframe on the underbody to ensure correct relocation. **Note:** *Ford technicians use special alignment pins to locate the subframe accurately.*

6 Support the rear subframe using a trolley jack and block of wood.

7 Unscrew and remove the subframe mounting bolts.

8 Lower the subframe far enough to access the front lower arm retaining nut and bolt.

9 Check the markings on the lower arm to ensure correct refitting.

10 Unscrew the outer bolt securing the lower arm to the knuckle, then unscrew the inner bolt securing the lower arm to the subframe. Withdraw the arm from under the car.

Rear lower arm

11 Check the markings on the lower arm to ensure correct refitting.

12 Unscrew the outer bolt securing the lower arm to the knuckle, then unscrew the inner bolt securing the lower arm to the subframe. Withdraw the arm from under the car.

Refitting

13 Refitting is a reversal of the removal procedure, noting the following points:

a) *The arm mounting bolts should be finger-tightened initially, and only fully tightened after the car is lowered to the ground, so that its weight is on the rear suspension.*

b) *The rear toe setting should be checked, and if necessary adjusted, at the earliest opportunity.*

16 Rear tie-bar (Saloon/Hatchback) – removal and refitting

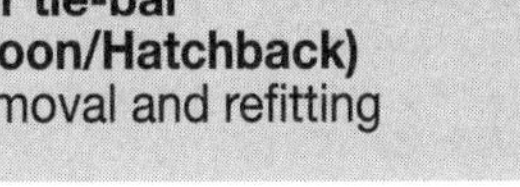

Removal

1 Loosen the rear wheel nuts. Chock the front wheels, then jack up the rear of the car and support on axle stands (see *Jacking and vehicle support*). Remove the relevant rear wheel.

2 Unbolt the cover from over the tie-bar.

3 Where applicable, unhook the exhaust mounting rubber from the tie-bar front mounting bracket.

4 On models with xenon headlights, the levelling sensor wiring is attached to the left-hand tie-bar. Release the wiring from the clips.

5 Release the handbrake cable from the clips on the tie-bar.

6 Release the ABS rear wheel speed sensor wiring from the tie-bar.

7 Unscrew and remove the bolt securing the tie-bar to the bottom of the knuckle.

8 At the front of the tie-bar, unscrew and remove the two bolts securing the mounting bracket to the underbody. Withdraw the tie-bar from under the car.

9 With the tie-bar on the bench, unscrew and remove the front pivot bolt and remove the bracket from the tie-bar.

10 It is not possible to renew the rubber bushes – if they are worn excessively, the tie-bar should be renewed complete.

Refitting

11 Refitting is a reversal of the removal procedure, noting the following points:

a) *The bracket-to-underbody bolts should be fully tightened to the specified torque before lowering the car.*

b) *The bolts securing the tie-bar to the bracket and knuckle should be finger-tightened initially, and only fully tightened after the car is lowered to the ground, so that its weight is on the rear suspension.*

17 Rear crossmember bushes (Saloon/Hatchback) – renewal

General information

1 The rear crossmember on Saloon and Hatchback models is attached to the floor by four bolts. Each of the four bolt holes in the crossmember has a bonded rubber bush fitted. Over time, the bonding may fail, or the rubber may perish and tear, causing the crossmember to detach itself partially from the floor (clearly dangerous, and an MOT failure point). If not caught in time, the increased movement can also cause wear in the suspension arm bushes.

2 A number of options are available if your Mondeo suffers this problem, and these are outlined in this Section. At the time of writing, there is no bush renewal procedure from Ford themselves.

3 First, and easiest, is to take the car to a Ford dealer. This problem occurs sufficiently often that many dealers perform this job on an 'exchange' basis. The dealer keeps a crossmember in the stores which has new bushes fitted, and when your car comes in, the mechanic takes off your crossmember complete, and fits the 'reconditioned' one, which saves time and, hopefully, money (your unit is kept, and new bushes are then fitted in time for the next customer). In theory, all you pay for are the bushes, and the labour to swap a crossmember.

4 Next, complete reconditioned crossmembers are available from some discount parts suppliers (the internet is a good place to start looking). However, if there's nothing wrong with the crossmember itself, other than the bushes being worn, all this avoids is the struggle removing the old bushes and fitting the new ones.

5 The bushes themselves are available from Ford dealers, motor factors, and other internet sources. We understand the genuine Ford bushes (and presumably, most pattern ones) have to be glued into place – check this point with your parts supplier when buying. The glue is available from Ford dealers (just enough to do the job) for a reasonable sum.

6 Some owners have opted for aftermarket polyurethane bushes, which it is felt may last better than the standard Ford items. As these are effectively non-standard parts, be sure to obtain fitting instructions when buying.

Bush renewal

7 Although it involves more work, we recommend removing the crossmember to fit new bushes, especially where gluing is required. This method gives total access for bush removal and renewal, and arguably, a better job will be done overall. Crossmember removal and refitting is covered in Section 18.

8 However, some owners report success renewing the bushes with the crossmember in place. If the car is well-supported on axle stands, and only one crossmember bolt at a time is removed, this could work. It seems the only real difficulty is cutting out all of the old bush (this can be achieved using a hacksaw blade – tape one end to make a 'handle'). The new bush can be pressed in from below using a thick block of wood, and a trolley jack.

9 Before removing the bushes, bear in mind that the originals are not identical – two have a metal core with flat sides, while the core on the other two has a V shape (or a 'corner'). Make a note of which fits where, and also of which way round the each metal core should be, relative to the car. The bushes are cone-shaped, so will only fit one way up.

10 As stated earlier, the original bushes were bonded (glued) in place. Before fitting the new bushes, the bush locations in the crossmember should be cleaned with a suitable solvent, and allowed to dry. If the bush locations are cleaned using abrasives of any kind, take care not to enlarge the holes.

11 If the new bushes are to be glued in place, current advice is that the glue is applied to the bushes and to the crossmember locations, and the bushes are then fitted straight away. On completion, they should be left for 24 hours before refitting the crossmember (or before fully tightening the crossmember bolts).

12 This last point presents a problem if the work is carried out *in situ*. Mark the crossmember's position relative to the floor before starting, support the crossmember with another trolley jack or axle stand in the centre, and only refit the removed bolts hand-tight until the glue has dried. **Do not** fully remove more than one bolt at a time – working under the car with all four bolts removed could be dangerous, as could removing both bolts on the same side.

13 Pressing the bushes into place is likely to prove difficult (see paragraph 8 if working *in situ*). Don't be tempted to apply any kind of oil or grease to rubber bushes, however, as this may lead to accelerated wear. A little washing-up liquid can safely be used on any bush which does not have to be glued in place.

14 If the crossmember has been removed, the new bushes can be pressed into place using a combination of threaded bar, two nuts, and a selection of washers, etc. If the bar is passed through the crossmember hole and the new bush, with washers and a nut at either end, the nuts can be tightened to draw the bush into position. It may also be possible to use a large vice for this job.

15 Bush-fitting tools specific to the Mondeo are also available, but these are unlikely to be cost-effective for the DIY mechanic.

16 On completion, where applicable, align the crossmember marks made at the start before tightening the bolts to the specified torque. Alternatively, refit the crossmember as described in Section 18. **Note:** *Especially if non-standard bushes have been fitted, make sure that the bushes do not pull through when tightening the bolts.*

18 Rear crossmember (Saloon/Hatchback) – removal and refitting

Removal

1 Loosen the rear wheel nuts. Chock the front wheels, then jack up the rear of the car and support on axle stands (see *Jacking and vehicle support*). Remove both rear wheels.

2 On models with xenon headlights, a headlight-levelling sensor is located on the left-hand lower arm. Remove the sensor by first disconnecting the wiring, then releasing the connecting rod and unbolting the sensor.

3 Unscrew the nuts and disconnect the catalytic converter from the exhaust front pipe. Where applicable, the front flexible section must be protected with a temporary splint (refer to the appropriate part of Chapter 4). It is recommended that the gasket/ring and nuts are renewed on refitting.

4 Release the front, intermediate and rear rubber exhaust mountings, then lower the exhaust as far as possible (ensure that, where applicable, the oxygen sensor wiring is not strained) and support it on axle stands.

5 Unscrew the nuts and disconnect both anti-roll bar links from the anti-roll bar.

6 Reach in behind the rear hubs and disconnect the wiring from the ABS wheel speed sensors on both sides.

7 At each rear brake caliper, push the handbrake lever forwards then unhook the inner cable from the fitting.

8 Release the handbrake outer cables from the caliper brackets. Where a plastic ferrule is fitted to the outer cable, it will be necessary to compress the plastic tangs in order to release it from the bracket.

9 Working on both sides, unscrew the mounting bolts securing the brake caliper bracket to the strut, and slide the caliper complete with pads from the discs. Support the calipers to one side on axle stands, taking care not to strain the flexible brake hoses.

10 Unscrew the bolts and remove the front and rear lower arms from the knuckles on both sides.

11 Unscrew the bolts and remove each tie-bar from the bottom of the struts.

12 Working on each side in turn, use a trolley jack to raise the strut and move it outwards from the ledges on the crossmember. Lower the jack to release the tension on the strut coil springs.

13 Support the crossmember using two trolley jacks. It is recommended that an assistant be available for the removal of the crossmember, as it is heavy.

14 Carefully mark the exact position of the crossmember on the underbody to ensure correct refitting. **Note:** *Ford technicians use special alignment pins to locate the subframe accurately.*

15 Unscrew the mounting bolts (two each side) then lower the crossmember to the ground.

Refitting

16 Raise the crossmember against the underbody, and position it accurately with the marks made during removal. If available, use the special Ford alignment pins. Insert the mounting bolts and tighten to the specified torque.

17 Working on each side in turn, use a trolley jack to raise the struts and position them on the crossmember ledges.

18 Refit each tie-bar to the bottom of the struts, and insert the bolts finger-tight. All suspension bolts are fully tightened with the car weight on the suspension.

19 Refit the front and rear lower arms to the knuckles, and insert the bolts finger-tight.

20 Refit the brake calipers complete with pads to the struts, and tighten the mounting bracket bolts to the specified torque.

21 Refit the handbrake outer cables, and hook the inner cables onto the caliper levers.

22 Reconnect the wiring to the ABS wheel speed sensors on both sides.

23 Reconnect the anti-roll bar links to the anti-roll bar, and tighten the nuts to the specified torque.

24 Relocate the exhaust system on the rubber mountings and reconnect to the front pipe using a new gasket/ring and nuts. Refer to the appropriate part of Chapter 4 if necessary, and apply anti-seize grease to the studs before refitting the nuts. Where applicable, remove the temporary splint from the exhaust flexible section.

25 On models with xenon headlights, refit the sensor to the lower arm and tighten the bolts. Reconnect the connecting rod and the wiring. **Note:** *After refitting, the headlight-levelling system must be initialised by a Ford dealer using a special setting instrument.*

26 Refit the rear wheels and lower the car to the ground. Tighten the wheel nuts to the specified torque.

27 Fully tighten the front and rear arm and tie-bar mounting bolts/nuts to the specified torque.

28 Have the rear wheel toe setting checked and adjusted at the earliest opportunity (see Section 36).

19 Rear tie-bar/knuckle (Estate) – removal and refitting

Removal

1 Remove the rear hub as described in Section 10.

2 On models with xenon headlights, a headlight-levelling sensor is located on the front left-hand lower arm. Disconnect the wiring from the sensor and release it from the knuckle.

3 Release the ABS wheel speed sensor wiring from the tie-bar/knuckle.

4 Pull the handbrake cable through the aperture in the tie-bar/knuckle.

5 Unbolt the cover from the front of the tie-bar/knuckle.

6 Release the handbrake cable from the clip on the front of the tie-bar/knuckle.

7 Where applicable, unhook the exhaust system rubber mounting from the tie-bar/knuckle.

8 A suitable rod or bar must now be fabricated in order to hold the rear of the tie-bar/knuckle at its design height setting. This will prevent damage to the rubber mountings, and enable the mounting bolts to be tightened to their specified torque before lowering the car to the ground. Fabricate a 20 mm by 186 mm long metal bar for this purpose.

9 Using a socket through the hole in the bottom of the rear lower arm, unscrew the anti-roll bar link securing nut.
10 Refer to Section 22 and remove the coil spring. Only use a purpose-made coil spring compressor to do this.
11 With the coil spring removed, raise the rear lower arm and position the bar described in paragraph 8 as shown **(see illustration)**.
12 Unbolt the front lower arm from the tie-bar/knuckle.
13 Unbolt the upper arm from the tie-bar/knuckle.
14 Unbolt the shock absorber from the tie-bar/knuckle.
15 Unbolt the rear lower arm from the tie-bar/knuckle.
16 Support the weight of the tie-bar/knuckle, then unbolt the front bracket from the underbody and lower the tie-bar/knuckle to the ground.
17 Unscrew the front pivot bolt and separate the bracket from the tie-bar/knuckle.

Refitting

18 Refitting is a reversal of the removal procedure, but tighten all nuts and bolts to the specified torque. Finally, check and if necessary adjust the rear wheel toe setting as described in Section 36.

20 Rear shock absorber (Estate) – removal, testing and refitting

Removal

1 Loosen the rear wheel nuts. Chock the front wheels, then jack up the rear of the car and support on axle stands (see *Jacking and vehicle support*). Remove the relevant rear wheel.
2 Position a trolley jack under the coil spring area of the rear lower arm, to keep the coil spring in compression.
3 Unscrew and remove the shock absorber lower mounting bolt **(see illustration)**.
4 Unscrew and remove the upper mounting bolt, and withdraw the shock absorber from under the car. Access to the upper bolt is difficult, and a socket drive with universal joint may be required **(see illustration)**.

Testing

5 Check the mounting rubbers for damage and deterioration. If they are worn, the complete shock absorber must be renewed, as they are not available separately.
6 Mount the shock absorber in a vice, gripping it by the lower mounting. Examine the shock absorber for signs of fluid leakage. Test the operation of the shock absorber by moving it through a full stroke, and then through short strokes of 50 to 100 mm. In both cases, the resistance felt should be smooth and continuous. If the resistance is jerky or uneven, the shock absorber should be renewed.

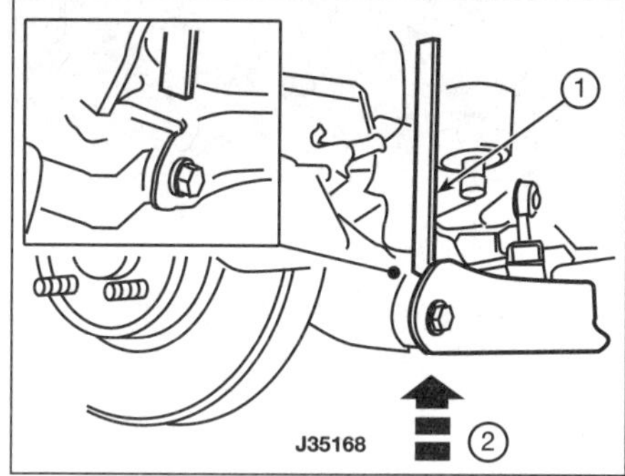

19.11 Position the spacer (1) as shown and raise the rear lower arm (2)

Refitting

7 Refitting is a reversal of the removal procedure, however, do not fully tighten the mounting bolts to the specified torque until the full weight of the car is on its suspension. Note that on models fitted with load-levelling shock absorbers, the tab on the upper mounting must point outwards.

21 Rear anti-roll bar and links (Estate) – removal and refitting

Removal

1 Loosen the rear wheel nuts. Chock the front wheels, then jack up the rear of the car and support on axle stands (see *Jacking and vehicle support*). Remove both rear wheels.
2 Unscrew the nuts securing the anti-roll bar links to the rear lower arms. The nuts are accessed through the holes in the bottom of the arms.
3 Unscrew the bolts securing the anti-roll bar mounting clamps to the rear crossmember **(see illustration)**. Release the clamps, and withdraw the anti-roll bar from under the car.
4 Unscrew the nuts and remove the links from the anti-roll bar **(see illustration)**.
5 Examine the rubber bushes for the mounting clamps and links, and if necessary renew them. The links are available individually, and the rubbers can be pulled from the ends of the bar.

Refitting

6 Where removed, fit the new rubbers in position on the bar, with their flat surfaces facing upwards. Also refit the links to the bar and tighten the upper mounting nuts to the specified torque.
7 Locate the anti-roll bar on the rear crossmember, then refit the clamps and tighten the bolts to the specified torque.
8 Refit the anti-roll bar links to the rear lower arms, and tighten the nuts to the specified torque, while holding the links stationary in their central position.
9 Refit the rear wheels, and lower the car to the ground.

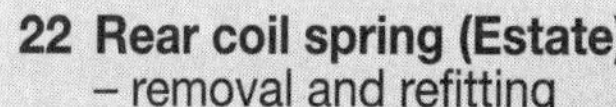

22 Rear coil spring (Estate) – removal and refitting

Note: *Before attempting to remove the rear*

20.3 Removing the shock absorber lower mounting bolt (Estate)

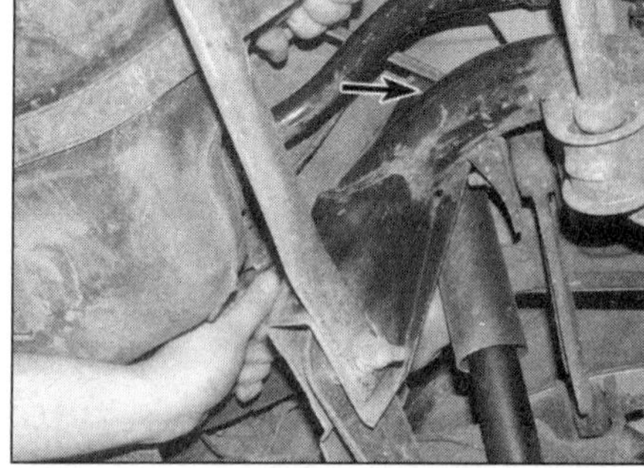
20.4 Access to the shock absorber upper bolt is difficult

21.3 Rear anti-roll bar mounting clamp

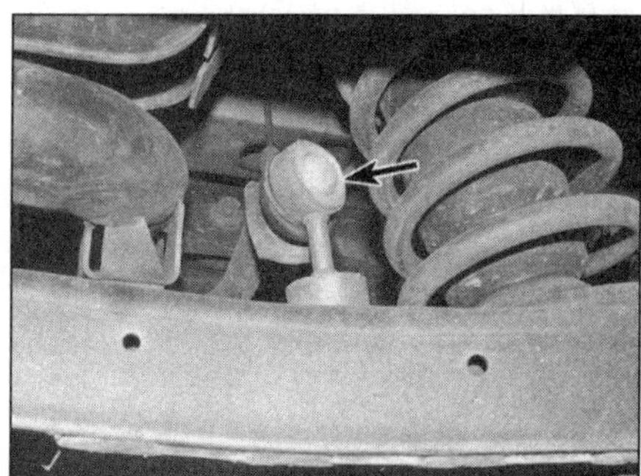
21.4 Anti-roll bar links

22.2 Rear coil spring (Estate)

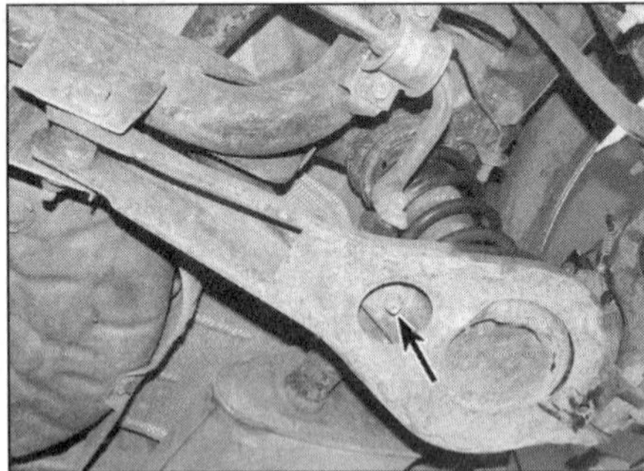
23.6 Nut securing the anti-roll bar link to the rear lower arm

23.9 Eccentric bolt securing the lower arm to the crossmember

coil spring, a tool to hold the coil spring in compression must be obtained. Careful use of conventional coil spring compressors will prove satisfactory.

Removal

1 Loosen the rear wheel nuts. Chock the front wheels, then jack up the rear of the car and support on axle stands (see *Jacking and vehicle support*). Remove the relevant rear wheel.

2 With no weight on the rear suspension, the shock absorber will be fully extended and will support the lower arm. Mark the spring to ensure it is refitted correctly **(see illustration)**.

3 Fit the coil spring compressor tools (ensuring they are fully engaged), and compress the coil spring until all tension is relieved from the upper mounting.

Warning: The coil spring will be under extreme tension; make sure that the compressor tools are fitted correctly.

4 Release the bump stop from the crossmember, then withdraw it together with the coil spring from under the car.

5 If a new coil spring is to be fitted, the original coil spring must be released from the compressor. If it is to be re-used, the coil spring can be left in compression.

Refitting

6 Refitting is a reversal of the removal procedure, but make sure that the bump stop is located correctly on the crossmember, and that the ends of the coil spring are correctly located in the crossmember and lower arm before releasing the spring tension.

24.2 Brace securing nut

23 Rear lower arm (rear) (Estate) – removal and refitting

Removal

1 Loosen the rear wheel nuts. Chock the front wheels, then jack up the rear of the car and support on axle stands (see *Jacking and vehicle support*). Remove the relevant wheel.

2 The bolt securing the rear lower arm to the crossmember has an eccentric head and spacer, which are used to adjust the rear toe setting. Before removing this bolt, mark its position, using a scriber or similar sharp instrument.

3 Remove the rear coil spring as described in Section 22.

4 A suitable rod or bar must now be fabricated in order to hold the rear of the tie-bar/knuckle at its design height setting. This will prevent damage to the rubber mountings, and enable the mounting bolts to be tightened to their specified torque before lowering the car to the ground. Fabricate a 20 mm by 186 mm long metal bar for this purpose.

5 With the coil spring removed, raise the rear lower arm and position the bar as described in Section 19 **(see illustration 19.11)**.

6 Unscrew the nut securing the anti-roll bar link to the rear lower arm. The nut is accessed through the hole in the bottom of the arm **(see illustration)**.

24.4 Front lower arm outer mounting

7 On models with xenon headlights, a headlight-levelling sensor is located on the left-hand lower arm. Disconnect the wiring from the sensor and unclip it from the lower arm.

8 Unscrew and remove the bolt securing the rear lower arm to the tie-bar knuckle.

9 Unscrew and remove the eccentric bolt and withdraw the lower arm from the crossmember **(see illustration)**.

Refitting

10 Refitting is a reversal of the removal procedure, but tighten all nuts and bolts to the specified torque. Finally, check and if necessary adjust the rear wheel toe setting as described in Section 36.

24 Rear lower arm (front) and brace (Estate) – removal and refitting

Removal

1 Loosen the rear wheel nuts. Chock the front wheels, then jack up the rear of the car and support on axle stands (see *Jacking and vehicle support*). Remove the rear wheels.

2 The brace is fitted across the crossmember, between the two inner pivots of the front lower arms. To remove the brace, unscrew the two nuts and withdraw the brace from the crossmember **(see illustration)**. Do not remove the bolts from the crossmember.

3 To remove a front lower arm, first remove the brace, then remove the inner pivot bolt from the crossmember. Note which way round the mounting bolts are fitted.

4 Unscrew and remove the outer pivot bolt, and withdraw the arm from the crossmember and knuckle **(see illustration)**.

Refitting

5 Refitting is a reversal of the removal procedure, but delay fully tightening the mounting bolts until the weight of the car is on the rear suspension. Note that the bolts are fitted with their heads facing forwards.

25 Rear upper arm (Estate) – removal and refitting

Removal

1 Loosen the rear wheel nuts. Chock the front wheels, then jack up the rear of the car and support on axle stands (see *Jacking and vehicle support*). Remove the relevant wheel.
2 Support the rear tie-bar/knuckle on a trolley jack. Note which way round the mounting bolts are fitted.
3 Unscrew and remove the mounting bolts, and withdraw the arm from the tie-bar/knuckle and crossmember **(see illustration)**.

Refitting

4 Refitting is a reversal of the removal procedure, but delay fully tightening the mounting bolts until the weight of the car is on the rear suspension. Note that the outer bolt is fitted with its head facing forwards, whereas the inner bolt is fitted with its head facing rearwards.

26 Rear crossmember (Estate) – removal and refitting

Removal

1 Remove both rear tie-bars/knuckles as described in Section 19.
2 On models with xenon headlights, a headlight-levelling sensor is located on the left-hand lower arm. Remove the sensor by first disconnecting the wiring, then releasing the connecting rod and unbolting the sensor.
3 Working on each side in turn, remove the brake calipers and mounting brackets as described in Chapter 9, however, disconnect the flexible hoses at the crossmember brackets instead of at the calipers. To do this, unscrew the rigid brake line union nuts, then pull out the retaining clips and remove the hoses from the crossmember. Plug or tape over the brake pipes and hoses to prevent entry of dust and dirt.
4 The bolts securing the rear lower arms to the crossmember have eccentric heads and spacers, which are used to adjust the rear toe setting. Before removing these bolts, mark their positions, using a scriber or similar sharp instrument.
5 Unscrew and remove the inner pivot bolts and disconnect the lower arms from the crossmember.
6 With the help of an assistant, support the rear crossmember on one or two trolley jacks.
7 Unscrew the three mounting bolts on each side, then carefully lower the crossmember to the ground. Note that guide pins are incorporated in the crossmember to ensure correct refitting.
8 If necessary, remove the suspension components from the crossmember as described in the appropriate Sections of this Chapter.

Refitting

9 Refitting is a reversal of the removal procedure, noting the following points:
a) When raising the crossmember, locate the guide pins in the holes provided in the underbody, then insert and fully tighten the mounting bolts.
b) Delay fully tightening the suspension arm mounting bolts until the weight of the car is on the rear suspension.
c) Tighten all bolts to the specified torque.
d) Bleed the brake hydraulic system as described in Chapter 9.
e) Check, and if necessary adjust, the rear wheel toe setting as described in Section 36.

27 Steering wheel – removal and refitting

Warning: All models are equipped with an airbag system. Make sure that the safety recommendations given in Chapter 12 are followed, to prevent personal injury.

Removal

1 Disconnect the battery negative lead (refer to *Disconnecting the battery* at the end of this manual).

Warning: Before proceeding, wait a minimum of one minute after disconnecting the battery, as a precaution against accidental firing of the airbag unit. This period ensures that any stored energy in the back-up capacitor is dissipated. We suggest you wait several minutes.

2 Turn the steering wheel so that the front wheels are in the straight-ahead position.
3 Remove the airbag unit from the steering wheel as described in Chapter 12.

Warning: Position the airbag module in a safe place, with the airbag and trim cover facing up as a precaution against accidental operation.

4 Make sure that the steering lock is not engaged, by inserting the ignition key. Identify the top of the steering wheel to aid refitting (note the steering wheel can only be fitted in three positions). Unscrew the retaining bolt from the centre of the steering wheel **(see illustration)**.
5 Remove the steering wheel from the top of the column, while feeding the horn and airbag wiring through the hole in the steering wheel hub **(see illustration)**.

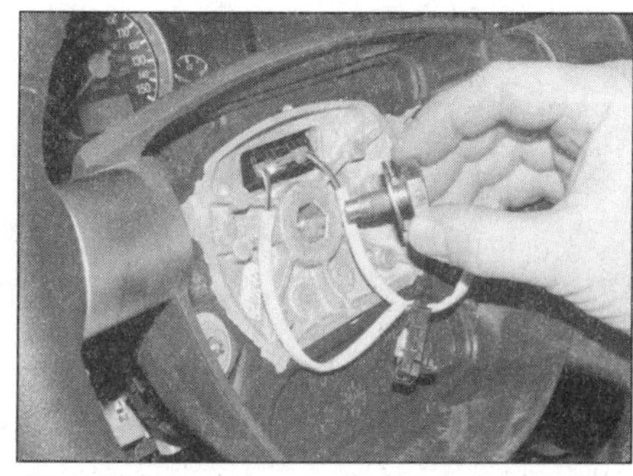

27.4 Unscrew the steering wheel retaining bolt . . .

25.3 Rear upper arm (Estate)

Refitting

6 Make sure that the front wheels are still facing straight-ahead, then locate the steering wheel on the top of the steering column while feeding the horn and airbag wiring through the centre hole.
7 Refit the retaining bolt, and tighten it to the specified torque while holding the steering wheel. Do not tighten the bolt with the steering lock engaged, as this may damage the lock.
8 Refit the airbag unit with reference to Chapter 12.
9 Make sure that the ignition is switched off (remove the key). Reconnect the battery negative lead (refer to *Disconnecting the battery* at the end of this manual).

28 Steering column – removal, inspection and refitting

Warning: All models are equipped with an airbag system. Make sure that the safety recommendations given in Chapter 12 are followed, to prevent personal injury.

27.5 . . . and remove the steering wheel from the top of the column

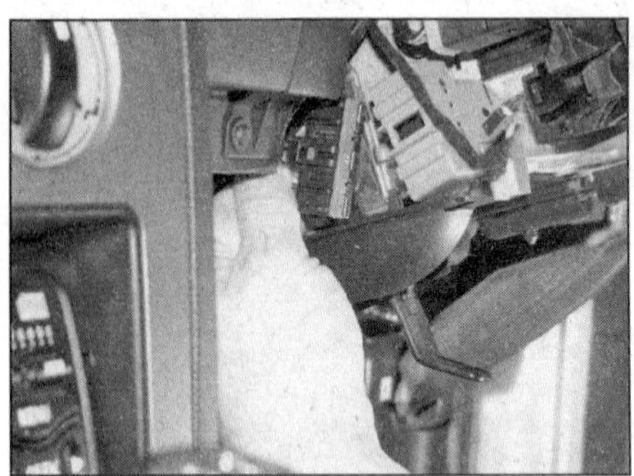
28.8a Disconnecting the ignition switch wiring . . .

28.8b . . . and turn signal switch wiring

28.9a Disconnecting the passive anti-theft system (PATS) wiring . . .

28.9b . . . and wiper/washer switch wiring

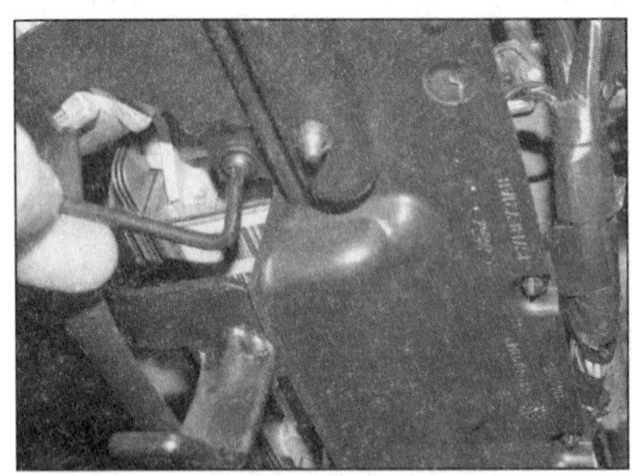
28.10a Undo the screws . . .

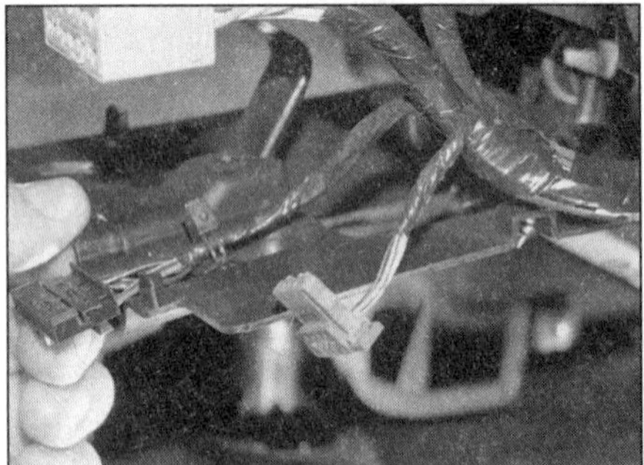
28.10b . . . and remove the spreader plate from under the column

Removal

1 Disconnect the battery negative lead (refer to *Disconnecting the battery* at the end of this manual).

Warning: Before proceeding, wait a minimum of one minute after disconnecting the battery, as a precaution against accidental firing of the airbag unit. This period ensures that any stored energy in the back-up capacitor is dissipated. We suggest you wait several minutes.

2 Turn the steering wheel so that the front wheels are in the straight-ahead position. At this stage, the steering wheel can be removed as described in Section 27, or alternatively left in position and removed together with the column.

Warning: If the steering wheel is left in situ, use adhesive tape to hold it in the straight-ahead position. Failure to do this may result in damage to the airbag and clock spring.

3 Remove the driver's side lower facia trim panel, which is secured by four screws and two upper clips. Where applicable, unclip the diagnostic connector plug from the panel, and/or disconnect the wiring from the climate control sensor as the panel is removed.

4 Where applicable, remove the insulation pad from over the foot pedals.

5 Where fitted, remove the audio control switch from the steering column lower shroud. Use a small screwdriver to release the locking tang, then lift the switch from the column and disconnect the wiring.

6 Remove the steering column upper shroud from the lower shroud by inserting a thin screwdriver between the clip on each side.

7 Undo the three screws and remove the lower shroud.

8 Disconnect the ignition switch and turn signal switch wiring connectors **(see illustrations)**.

9 On the right-hand side of the steering column, disconnect the wiring connectors for the passive anti-theft system (PATS) transceiver, wiper/washer switch and airbag clock spring **(see illustrations)**.

10 Note the routing of the airbag clock spring wiring, then undo the screw and remove the spreader plate from under the column **(see illustrations)**.

11 On models with Electronic Stability Programme (ESP), disconnect the wiring from the steering wheel rotation sensor at the bottom of the column.

12 Unscrew and remove the clamp bolt securing the column intermediate shaft to the flexible coupling on the steering gear. Rotate the clamp plate through 180°, and release the shaft from the coupling **(see illustrations)**. Note that the coupling has a triangular shape, and the shaft may only be fitted in one of three positions. Discard the clamp bolt and obtain a new one.

13 Support the steering column, then unscrew the four mounting bolts with a Torx key. Slide the column upwards to disengage the retaining tab from the groove in the crossbeam then lower the column from the bulkhead crossbar bracket **(see illustrations)**. Discard the bolts and obtain new ones.

28.12a Unscrew the clamp bolt . . .

28.12b . . . and rotate the clamp plate through 180°

Inspection

14 With the steering column removed, check the universal joints for wear, and examine the column upper and lower shafts for any signs of damage or distortion. Where evident, the column should be renewed complete.

15 Examine the height adjustment lever mechanism for wear and damage. Lock the mechanism before refitting the column.

16 With the steering lock disengaged, turn the inner column, and check the upper and lower bearings for smooth operation. At the time of writing it was not possible to obtain the column bearings separately, so if excessive wear is evident, the column assembly must be renewed complete.

Refitting

17 Before refitting the steering column, the inner safety telescopic tube must be set to 70 mm by temporarily fitting a metal spacer. First apply some silicone grease to the inner tube, and fully extend and retract the column several times. Now make up the spacer and attach it to the inner column with two plastic cable ties **(see illustration)**.

18 Locate the steering column on its bracket, making sure that the tab slides down into the groove correctly, then insert the **new** mounting bolts and tighten to the specified torque.

19 With the front wheels and steering wheel still in their straight-ahead positions, locate the steering column shaft on the flexible coupling, swivel the clamp plate anti-clockwise, then insert a **new** bolt and tighten to the specified torque.

20 Remove the temporary spacer from the inner column.

Warning: Failure to remove the temporary spacer could result in personal injury in the event of an accident.

21 On models with Electronic Stability Programme (ESP), reconnect the wiring to the steering wheel rotation sensor at the bottom of the column.

22 Make sure that the clock spring wiring loom is routed inside the spreader plate depression, then refit the spreader plate to the column and tighten the retaining screw.

23 On the right-hand side of the steering column, reconnect the wiring connectors for the passive anti-theft system (PATS) transceiver, wiper/washer switch and airbag clock spring.

24 Beneath the steering column, reconnect the ignition switch and turn signal switch wiring connectors.

25 Refit the column lower shroud and tighten the three screws.

26 Refit the column upper shroud. Press down on the shroud to engage the clips.

27 Where fitted, refit the audio control switch to the steering column, and reconnect the wiring.

28 Where applicable, refit the insulation pad over the foot pedals.

29 Refit the driver's side lower facia trim panel. Where applicable, clip the diagnostic connector plug back into place, and/or reconnect the climate control sensor.

30 If removed, refit the steering wheel with reference to Section 27.

31 Reconnect the battery negative lead (refer to *Disconnecting the battery* at the end of this manual), and initialise the door window motors as described in Chapter 11.

32 On models with Electronic Stability Programme (ESP), have the steering wheel rotation sensor initialised by a Ford dealer.

28.13a Steering column mounting bolt locations

28.13b Using a Torx key to unscrew the steering column mounting bolts

28.13c Lowering the steering column from the bulkhead

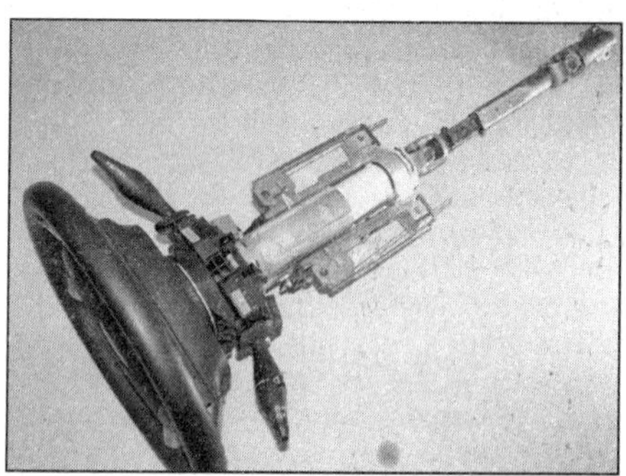

28.13d The steering column removed from the car

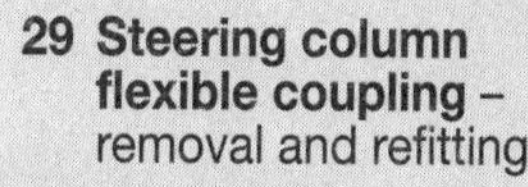

29 Steering column flexible coupling – removal and refitting

Removal

1 Loosen the front wheel nuts. Apply the handbrake, then jack up the front of the car and support it on axle stands (see *Jacking and vehicle support*). Turn the steering to the straight-ahead position and lock it. Remove both front wheels.

2 Working in the driver's footwell, undo the four retaining screws and unclip the lower facia panel from under the steering column. Where applicable, unclip the diagnostic connector plug from the panel, and/or disconnect the wiring from the climate control sensor as the panel is removed.

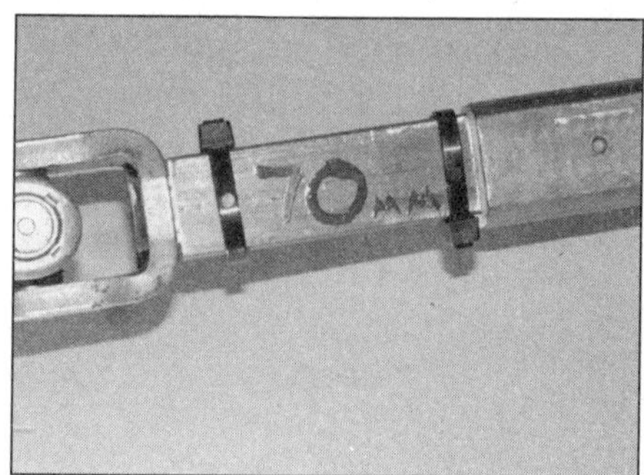

28.17 The 70 mm spacer attached to the steering column with cable-ties

3 Where applicable, remove the insulation pad from over the foot pedals.

4 Unscrew and remove the clamp bolt securing the steering inner column to the flexible coupling on the steering gear. Rotate the clamp plate clockwise and detach the clamp from the coupling. Note that the coupling stub has a triangular shape, and the shaft may only be fitted in one of three positions. Discard the bolt as a new one must be fitted on reassembly.

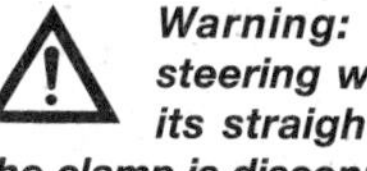

Warning: Make sure that the steering wheel remains locked in its straight-ahead position while the clamp is disconnected from the flexible coupling. Failure to do this may result in damage to the airbag and clock spring, and subsequent personal injury in the event of an accident.

5 Hold the radiator in the upper mountings using temporary split pins inserted through the holes in the upper location pins. Access to the holes is gained through the apertures in the front crossmember.

6 Undo the screws and remove the splash shield from under the radiator position. On diesel models, also remove the engine under-shield and left-hand wheel arch lower liner.

7 Under the front of the car, unbolt the hose bracket (where fitted) next to the left-hand radiator support bracket, then unbolt and remove both radiator support brackets.

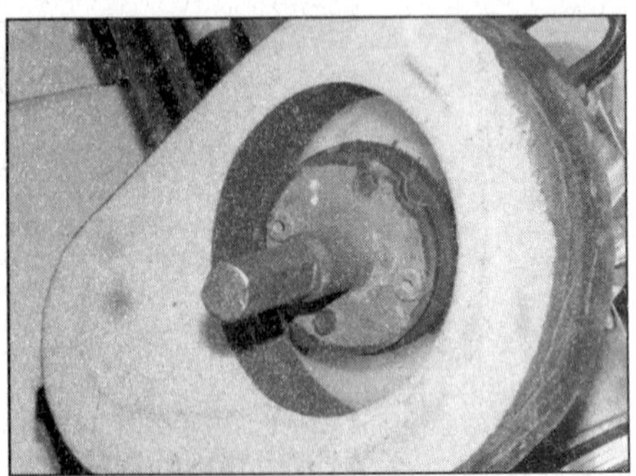
30.3 Bulkhead seal on the steering gear

8 Unscrew the nuts and disconnect the anti-roll bar links from the front struts. If necessary, use a 5 mm Allen key to hold the spindles while the nuts are loosened.
9 On 1.8 and 2.0 litre petrol engines, and all diesel engines, remove the exhaust flexible pipe from the front of the exhaust system with reference to the appropriate part of Chapter 4.
10 On V6 engines, remove the exhaust front lower Y-pipe as described in Chapter 4A.
11 Remove the engine rear mounting with reference to the appropriate part of Chapter 2.
12 As applicable, disconnect the second oxygen sensor wiring, and unclip the wiring from the subframe. On models with a diesel particulate filter, detach the associated wiring and pipework as necessary.
13 On models with xenon headlights, release the ties and detach the headlight-levelling sensor wiring harness from the subframe.
14 Release the radiator cooling fan wiring harness from the subframe.
15 Support the front subframe on one or two trolley jacks. If necessary, enlist the help of an assistant.
16 Carefully mark the position of the front subframe on the underbody to ensure correct refitting. **Note:** *Ford technicians use special alignment pins to locate the subframe accurately when refitting.* Unscrew and remove the subframe rear mounting bolts, then unbolt the rear brackets from the subframe.
17 Unscrew and remove the subframe front mounting bolts.
18 Keeping it level, lower the subframe about 150 mm, making sure that the lower arm rear hydro-bushes are not strained or damaged.

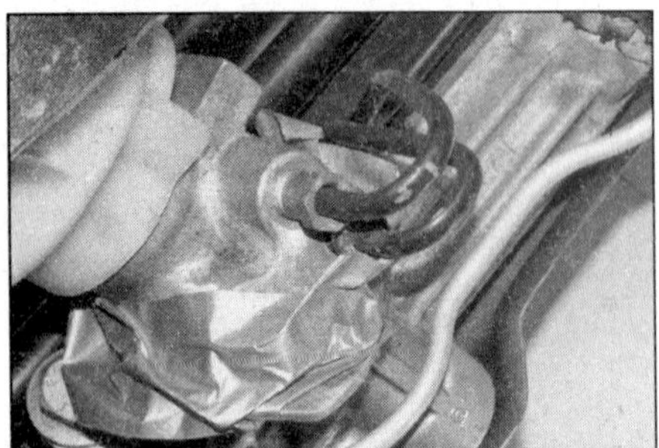
30.6a Hydraulic lines to the control valve on the steering gear (tape over the open lines)

19 Mark the coupling in relation to the steering gear pinion shaft to aid refitting, then use an Allen key to unscrew the clamp bolt and withdraw the coupling from the splines on the pinion shaft. Discard the bolt and obtain a new one. On right-hand drive models, also withdraw the seal from the bulkhead.

Refitting

20 On right-hand drive models, locate the seal on the bulkhead.
21 Locate the coupling on the pinion shaft splines making sure that the clamp bolt hole is aligned with the annular groove. Insert the new bolt, and tighten to the specified torque.
22 Raise the subframe against the underbody, and position it accurately with the marks made during removal. If available, use the special Ford alignment pins. Refit the rear bracket, then insert the mounting bolts. Tighten all of the subframe and rear bracket bolts to the specified torque. Make sure the subframe does not move during tightening of the bolts. If applicable, remove the Ford alignment pins.
23 Secure the radiator cooling fan wiring harness to the subframe with plastic cable ties.
24 On models with xenon headlights, secure the headlight-levelling sensor wiring to the subframe clips.
25 On petrol models, reconnect the second oxygen sensor wiring and secure with the clips.
26 Refit the engine rear mounting with reference to the appropriate part of Chapter 2.
27 On 1.8 and 2.0 litre petrol engines, and all diesel engines, refit the exhaust flexible pipe to the front of the exhaust system with reference to the appropriate part of Chapter 4.
28 On V6 engines, refit the exhaust front lower Y-pipe as described in Chapter 4A.
29 Reconnect the anti-roll bar links to the front struts and tighten the nuts to the specified torque. If necessary, use a 5 mm Allen key to hold the spindles while the nuts are loosened.
30 Refit the hose bracket (where fitted) and the two radiator support brackets, and tighten the bolts to the specified torque.
31 Refit the splash shield under the radiator position and tighten the screws. On diesel models, also refit the engine undershield and left-hand wheel arch lower liner.

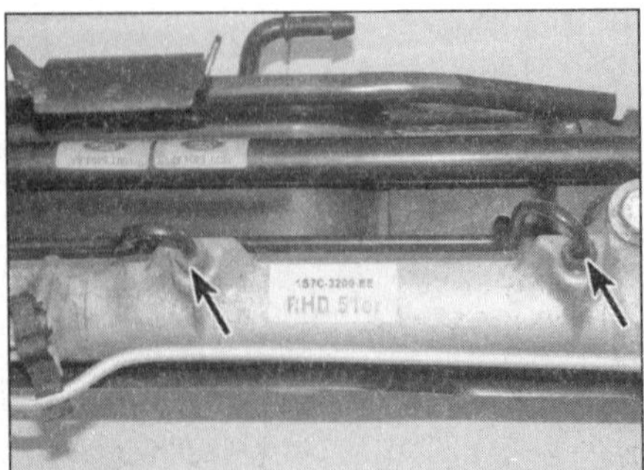
30.6b Hydraulic line to power steering ram

32 Remove the temporary split pins holding the radiator to its upper mountings.
33 Apply some silicone grease to the steering column inner tube and fully extend and retract the column several times. Before refitting the steering column to the flexible coupling, the inner safety telescopic tube must be set to 70.00 mm by temporarily fitting a metal spacer. Make up the spacer and attach it to the inner column with two plastic cable ties (refer to Section 28 if necessary).
34 Locate the steering column shaft on the flexible coupling, swivel the clamp plate anti-clockwise, then insert a **new** bolt and tighten to the specified torque.
35 Remove the temporary spacer from the inner column.

Warning: Failure to remove the temporary spacer could result in personal injury in the event of an accident.

36 Where applicable, refit the insulation pad over the foot pedals.
37 Refit the lower facia panel beneath the steering column. Where applicable, clip the diagnostic connector back into place, and/or reconnect the climate control sensor.
38 Refit the front wheels, then lower the car to the ground. Tighten the wheel nuts to the specified torque.
39 Have the front wheel alignment checked and adjusted at the earliest opportunity.
40 If on completion, the car pulls to one side, or abnormal tyre wear is noted, have the subframe alignment checked by a Ford dealer.

30 Steering gear – removal and refitting

Removal

1 Remove the steering column flexible coupling as described in Section 29. This procedure includes lowering the front subframe by 150 mm.
2 Loosen the nuts securing the steering track rod ends to the knuckle steering arms on each side. Using a balljoint separator tool, release the balljoints from the steering arms. Fully unscrew the nuts and disconnect the track rod ends from the arms. If necessary, use a 5 mm Allen key to hold the balljoints stationary while the nuts are loosened. Discard the nuts as new ones must be used on refitting.
3 Remove the bulkhead seal from the steering gear pinion shaft **(see illustration)**.
4 To reduce the loss of hydraulic fluid from the power steering circuit, either syphon the fluid from the reservoir, or fit a hose clamp to the supply and return hoses.
5 Release the power steering hydraulic lines from the retaining clips on the steering gear.
6 Note the location of each hydraulic line on the steering gear, then unscrew the union bolt, and pull the lines a short distance away from

the steering gear. Be prepared for some loss of hydraulic fluid by positioning a suitable container beneath the steering gear. Tape over or plug the lines and apertures to prevent entry of dust and dirt **(see illustrations)**. Remove and discard the O-ring seals and the bolt, and obtain new ones.

7 Unscrew and remove the steering gear mounting bolts. The bolts are located on top of the steering gear, and are difficult to reach. If available, the special U-shaped Ford spanner should be used, but it is just possible to reach them with a normal spanner **(see illustrations)**. Discard the bolts and obtain new ones.

8 Carefully withdraw the steering gear to one side, taking care not to damage the brake lines and components on the underbody.

Refitting

9 Locate the steering gear on the subframe, and insert the two **new** mounting bolts. Tighten the bolts to the specified torque. Note that, if the special Ford tool is being used, the bottom of the tool must be turned anti-clockwise in order to tighten the mounting bolts.

10 Using new O-ring seals, reconnect the hydraulic lines to the steering gear. Use a new union bolt, tightened to the specified torque. Where applicable, remove the clamp from the fluid supply and return hoses.

11 Secure the hydraulic lines in the retaining clips on the steering gear.

12 Refit the bulkhead seal to the steering gear pinion shaft.

13 Refit the track rod end balljoints to the steering knuckles, and tighten the **new** nuts to the specified torque. If necessary, use a 5 mm Allen key to hold the balljoints stationary while the nuts are tightened.

14 Refit the steering column flexible coupling with reference to Section 29.

15 Fill and bleed the power steering hydraulic system as described in Section 33.

16 Have the front wheel alignment checked, and if necessary adjusted, at the earliest opportunity (refer to Section 36).

17 On models with Electronic Stability Programme (ESP), have the steering wheel rotation sensor initialised by a Ford dealer.

31 Power steering gear rubber gaiter – renewal

1 Loosen the front wheel nuts. Apply the handbrake, then jack up the front of the car and support it on axle stands (see *Jacking and vehicle support*). Remove the relevant wheel.

2 On diesel models, remove the engine undershield, and also remove the wheel arch lower liner from the left-hand side.

3 Remove the track rod end and its locknut from the track rod, as described in Section 32. Note the exact position of the track rod end on the track rod, in order to retain the front wheel alignment setting on refitting.

30.7a Steering gear right-hand mounting bolt . . .

30.7b . . . and left-hand mounting bolt

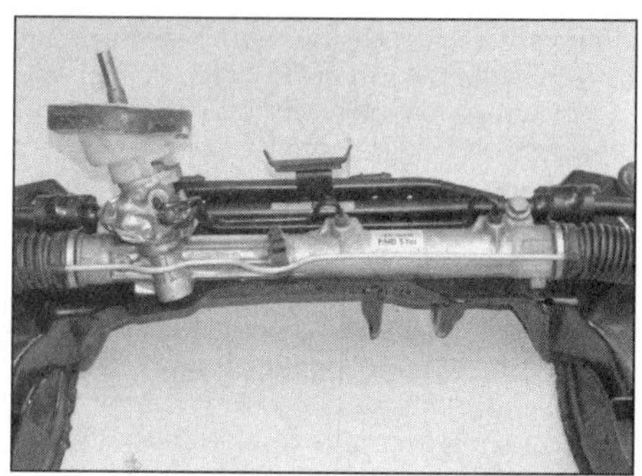

30.7c Steering gear on the subframe

30.7d The steering gear mounting bolts are just accessible with a normal spanner

4 Wipe clean the outer surfaces of the rubber gaiter, then disconnect the breather pipe. Note the location of the breather pipe stub for correct refitting. Also clean the track rod.

5 Release the inner and outer retaining clips securing the gaiter to the steering gear and track rod. Note the position of the gaiter on the track rod.

6 Disconnect the inner end of the gaiter from the steering gear housing, then pull the outer end from the track rod.

7 Remove the gaiter clips and discard them. New clips are supplied with the new gaiter.

8 Scrape off all grease from the old gaiter, and apply to the track rod inner joint. Wipe clean the seating areas on the steering gear housing and track rod.

9 Apply a little grease to the track rod, then slide the new gaiter into position. Position the inner end on the steering gear housing, and the outer end at its previously-noted position on the track rod.

10 Position the breather pipe stub at the top as previously-noted, then refit and tighten the inner and outer retaining clips. If crimp-type clips are supplied, tighten them with a pair of pincers.

11 Reconnect the breather pipe.

12 Refit the track rod end with reference to Section 32.

13 On diesel models, refit the wheel arch lower liner and engine undershield.

14 Refit the wheel and lower the car to the ground. Tighten the wheel nuts to the specified torque.

15 Have the front wheel alignment checked, and if necessary adjusted, at the earliest opportunity (refer to Section 36).

32.2 Steering track rod end

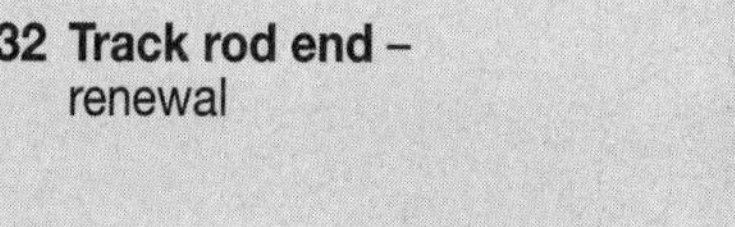

32 Track rod end – renewal

Removal

1 Loosen the front wheel nuts. Apply the handbrake, then jack up the front of the car and support it on axle stands (see *Jacking and vehicle support*). Remove the relevant front roadwheel.

2 Slacken the locknut on the track rod by a quarter-turn **(see illustration)**. Hold the track rod end stationary with another spanner engaged with the special flats while loosening the locknut.

3 Loosen the nut securing the steering track rod end to the knuckle steering arm. Do not remove the nut at this stage as it will protect the balljoint threads. If necessary, use an Allen key to hold the balljoint shaft while loosening the nut **(see illustration)**.

4 Using a balljoint separator tool, release the balljoint from the steering arm **(see illustration)**. If the balljoint is to be re-used, take care not to damage the dust cover when using the separator tool. Fully unscrew the nut and disconnect the track rod end from the arm. If necessary, use a 5 mm Allen key to hold the balljoint stationary while the nut is loosened. Discard the nut as a new one must be used on refitting.

5 Count the number of exposed threads visible on the inner section of the track rod, and record this figure.

6 Unscrew the track rod end from the track rod, counting the number of turns necessary to remove it. If necessary, hold the track rod stationary with grips.

Refitting

7 Screw the track rod end onto the track rod by the number of turns noted during removal, until it just contacts the locknut.

8 Engage the shank of the balljoint with the steering knuckle arm, and refit the **new** nut. Tighten the nut to the specified torque. If the balljoint shank turns while the nut is being tightened, use a 5 mm Allen key to hold the shank, or alternatively press down on the track rod. The tapered fit of the shank will lock it, and prevent rotation as the nut is tightened.

9 Hold the track rod stationary with one spanner, then tighten the track rod end locknut to the specified torque.

10 Refit the roadwheel, and lower the car to the ground. Tighten the wheel nuts to the specified torque.

11 Finally check, and if necessary adjust, the front wheel alignment as described in Section 36.

33 Power steering hydraulic system – bleeding and flushing

1 Following any operation in which the power steering fluid lines have been disconnected, the power steering system must be bled, to remove any trapped air. If the car has covered a high mileage and the fluid is noticeably discoloured or dirty, the old fluid must be flushed and new fluid installed.

Bleeding

2 With the front wheels in the straight-ahead position, check the power steering fluid level in the reservoir and, if low, add fresh fluid until it reaches the MAX mark. Pour the fluid slowly, to prevent air bubbles forming, and use only the specified fluid (refer to *Weekly checks*).

3 Start the engine, and allow it to run at idle speed. Check the hoses and connections for leaks.

4 Stop the engine, and recheck the fluid level. Add more if necessary, up to the MAX mark.

5 Start the engine again, allow it to idle, then bleed the system by slowly turning the steering wheel from side-to-side several times. This should purge the system of all internal air. However, if air remains in the system (indicated by the steering operation being very noisy), leave the car overnight, and repeat the procedure again the next day.

6 If air still remains in the system, it may be necessary to resort to the Ford method of bleeding, which uses a hand-operated vacuum pump. Turn the steering to the right until it is near the stop, then switch off the engine. Fit the vacuum pump to the fluid reservoir, and apply 15.0 in Hg of vacuum. Maintain the vacuum for a minimum of 5 minutes, then repeat the procedure with the steering turned to the left. If the vacuum decreases by more than 2.0 in Hg in the 5 minutes, check the hoses for leaks.

7 Keep the fluid level topped-up throughout the bleeding procedure. Note that, as the fluid temperature increases, the level will rise in the reservoir.

Flushing

Note: *This procedure involves turning the engine on the starter motor.*

8 Apply the handbrake, then jack up the front of the car and support it on axle stands (see *Jacking and vehicle support*).

Petrol models

9 Remove the engine top cover.

10 Position a suitable container beneath the hydraulic fluid reservoir. Have ready a cap to fit onto the reservoir return stub. Loosen the clip and disconnect the return hose, then allow the fluid to drain from the reservoir and hose into the container. Position the cap on the reservoir return stub.

11 Disconnect the crankshaft position sensor wiring from the right-hand end of the engine (this is necessary to temporarily prevent the fuel injection and ignition systems from working). If necessary, remove the lower plastic cover from the right-hand wheel arch for access to the sensor.

12 Disconnect the HT wiring from the spark plugs, then unscrew and remove the spark plugs. Refer to Chapter 1A if necessary.

Diesel models

13 Remove the oil filler cap and the oil level dipstick, then remove the engine top cover. Refit the filler cap and dipstick to prevent dust and dirt entry into the lubrication system.

14 Remove the glow plug relay from the fusebox with reference to Chapter 12.

15 Disconnect the injector wiring, and also disconnect the wiring from the fuel pressure sensor and camshaft position sensor.

16 Unscrew the nuts and disconnect the wiring from the glow plugs, then unscrew and remove them (refer to Chapter 5C if necessary).

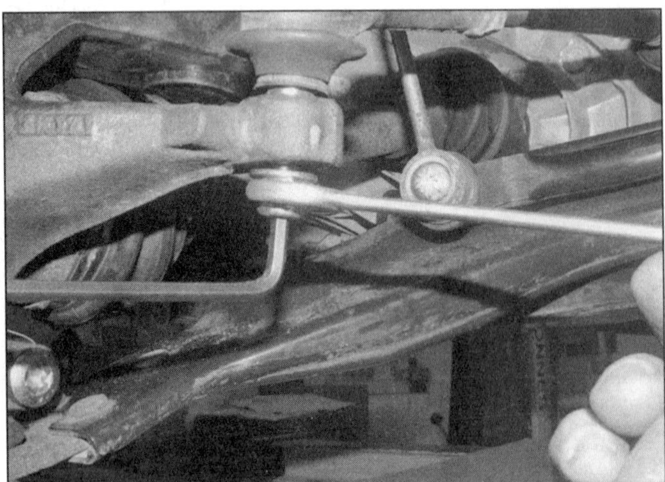

32.3 Loosen (only) the nut while using an Allen key to hold the balljoint shaft . . .

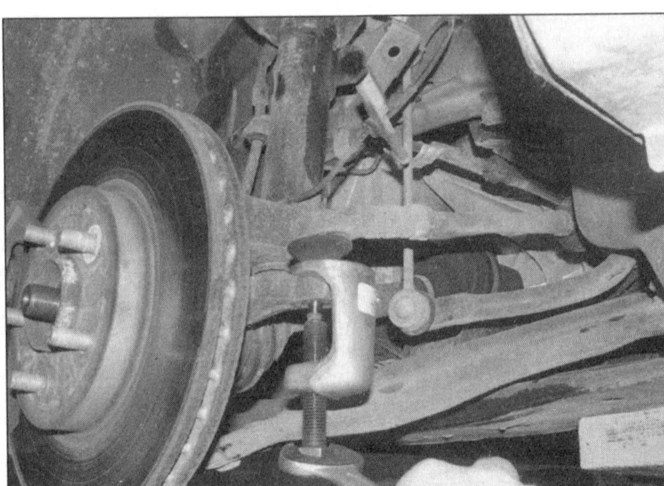

32.4 . . . then use a balljoint separator tool to release the balljoint from the steering arm

17 Unclip and remove the radiator grille from the engine compartment front cross-member.

18 Unscrew the mounting bolt securing the power steering fluid reservoir to the inner wheel arch panel.

19 Position a suitable container beneath the hydraulic fluid reservoir. Have ready a cap to fit onto the reservoir return stub. Loosen the clip and disconnect the return hose, then allow the fluid to drain from the reservoir and hose into the container. Position the cap on the reservoir return stub.

All models

20 Pour fresh fluid into the reservoir up to the MAX mark. Do not agitate the fluid prior to pouring it, as air may be introduced.

21 An assistant will be required for this procedure. Do not allow the level of fluid to drop below the MIN mark on the reservoir.

22 While directing the fluid from the return hose into the container, have the assistant crank the engine on the starter motor for 30 seconds and turn the steering wheel slowly from lock-to-lock. **Note:** *Do not exceed 30 seconds, as the starter motor may overheat, causing internal damage. Wait at least 60 seconds before activating the starter motor again.*

23 Top up the fluid to the MAX mark on the reservoir.

24 Repeat the procedure described in the last two paragraphs, using 1.0 litre of fresh fluid. Turn off the ignition switch.

25 Remove the cap from the fluid reservoir, and immediately reconnect the return hose. Tighten the retaining clip.

26 Refit and reconnect the relevant components as applicable for petrol or diesel models, then bleed the system again as described above.

34 Power steering pump – removal and refitting

Removal

1.8 and 2.0 litre petrol models

Note: *New power steering pumps may not be supplied with the pulley fitted. The pulley is a press-fit on the pump driveshaft, so a puller and fitting tool will be needed to transfer the old pulley to the new pump.*

1 Disconnect the battery negative lead (refer to *Disconnecting the battery* at the end of this manual).

2 Loosen the front wheel nuts. Apply the handbrake, then jack up the front of the car and support it on axle stands (see *Jacking and vehicle support*). Remove the right-hand roadwheel.

3 Unbolt and remove the splash shield for access to the crankshaft pulley. Note the routing of the auxiliary drivebelt, and mark it with an arrow to indicate its normal (clockwise) rotational direction. Turn the auxiliary drivebelt tensioner clockwise using a spanner on the centre bolt, then slip the drivebelt from the pulleys and remove from under the wheel arch.

4 At this stage, removal of the power steering pump will be made easier if the pulley is first removed using a suitable puller, as this will allow access to the high pressure line union, however, it is just possible to remove the pump without loosening the union and leaving the pulley in position. The following paragraphs describe removal leaving the pulley in position.

5 Syphon the hydraulic fluid from the power steering fluid reservoir. Position cloth rags beneath the pump, then loosen the clip and disconnect the fluid outlet (cooler) hose. Fit a cap to the reservoir stub and plug the hose, and tie the hose to one side **(see illustration)**. Recover the two seals.

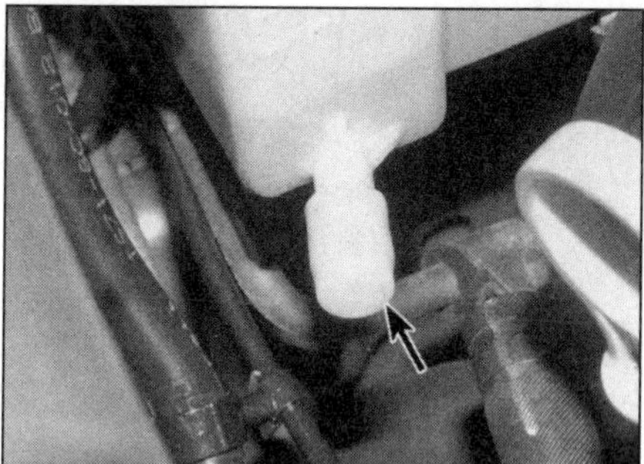

34.5 Fit a cap to the reservoir stub

34.6 Removing the plastic clip at the rear of the hydraulic fluid reservoir

6 Release the wiring loom from the plastic clip at the rear of the hydraulic fluid reservoir, then remove the plastic clip **(see illustration)**.

7 Unscrew the fluid reservoir mounting stud/bolts (one rear stud and a front bolt either side), then tilt the reservoir back and remove it from the pump **(see illustrations)**. Plug the reservoir outlet and pump aperture to prevent entry of dust and dirt. Remove the O-ring seals from the reservoir and discard them; obtain new ones for refitting. **Note:** *The reservoir contains a filter which must not be contaminated. Make sure the filler cap is tightened firmly.*

8 If the pulley has not been removed, it will not be possible to unscrew the high pressure outlet union, and in this case the in-line union at the flexible hose-to-pressure switch near the pump should be unscrewed. If the pulley has been removed, unscrew the outlet union securing the high pressure pipe to the pump. Tape over or plug the line and aperture.

9 Unscrew the hydraulic line support bracket retaining nut, disconnect the wiring from the hydraulic line pressure switch, then unscrew the four mounting bolts and studs and withdraw the power steering pump from the engine. Where applicable, unscrew the high-pressure union nut and disconnect the line **(see illustrations)**.

V6 models

10 Disconnect the battery negative lead (refer to *Disconnecting the battery* at the end of this manual).

34.7a Remove the rear mounting stud . . .

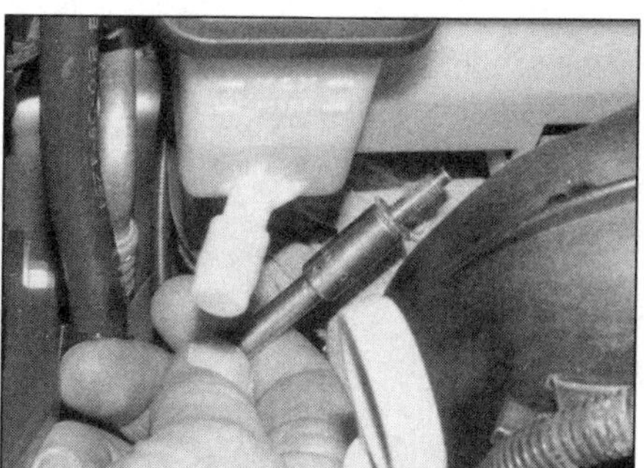

34.7b . . . and side mounting bolts . . .

34.7c . . . then remove the hydraulic fluid reservoir from the power steering pump

34.9a Unscrew the hydraulic line support bracket retaining nut . . .

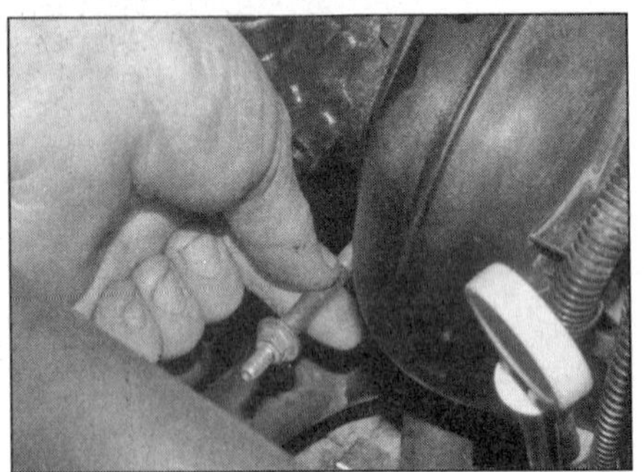

34.9d . . . and studs

11 Loosen the front wheel nuts. Apply the hand-brake, then jack up the front of the car and support it on axle stands (see *Jacking and vehicle support*). Remove the right-hand roadwheel.

12 Unbolt and remove the splash shield for access to the crankshaft pulley. Note the routing of the auxiliary drivebelt, and mark it with an arrow to indicate its normal rotational direction. Turn the auxiliary drivebelt tensioner clockwise using a spanner on the centre bolt, then slip the drivebelt from the pulleys and remove from under the wheel arch.

13 Position a suitable container beneath the power steering pump, then unscrew the union nut securing the high-pressure line to the pump. Unbolt the support bracket and disconnect the hydraulic fluid high-pressure line from the pump. Allow the fluid to drain, then tape over or plug the end of the line and the aperture in the pump to prevent entry of dust and dirt.

34.31 Power steering hydraulic fluid high-pressure line support bracket

34.9b . . . disconnect the wiring from the pressure switch . . .

34.9e Power steering pump removed from the engine (2.0 litre petrol)

14 Syphon the hydraulic fluid from the power steering fluid reservoir, or alternatively fit a hose clamp to the reservoir hose leading to the pump. Loosen the clip and disconnect the hose.

15 Unscrew the power steering fluid reservoir mounting bolt from the inner wheel arch, and move the reservoir to one side.

16 Unscrew the coolant expansion tank mounting bolts from the inner wheel arch, and move the tank to one side.

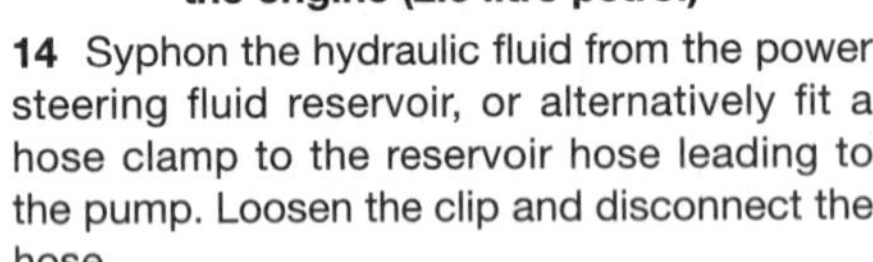

17 Release the spark plug HT leads and plastic holder from the right-hand engine mounting.

18 Using a trolley jack and block of wood beneath the sump, temporarily support the weight of the engine. Make sure the engine is supported safely.

19 Unscrew the nuts securing the engine right-hand mounting bracket to the engine, and also unscrew the bolts securing the bracket to the inner wheel arch. Remove the bracket.

34.33 High-pressure line to the top of the power steering pump

34.9c . . . then unscrew the mounting bolts . . .

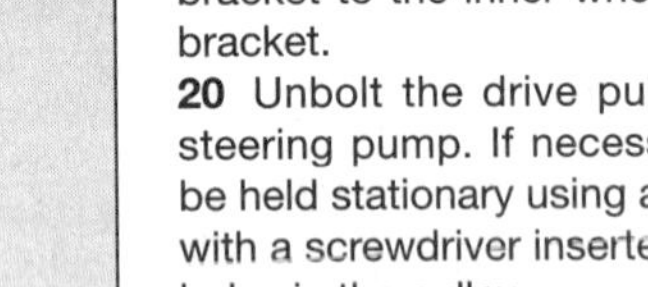

20 Unbolt the drive pulley from the power steering pump. If necessary, the pulley may be held stationary using an 8 mm Allen key, or with a screwdriver inserted through one of the holes in the pulley.

21 At the front of the power steering pump, unscrew the mounting bracket retaining bolt.

22 Unscrew the small nuts from the retaining plate, then unscrew the two main bolts from the retaining plate.

23 Unscrew the two mounting bolts, then remove the retaining plate, followed by the pump itself.

24 If fitting a new pump, unbolt the elbow and union from the old pump. Discard the O-ring seals and obtain new ones.

Diesel engine models

25 Disconnect the battery negative lead (refer to *Disconnecting the battery* at the end of this manual).

26 Undo the fasteners and remove the engine plastic top cover.

27 Release the coolant hose from the plastic clip, then loosen the clips and remove the air inlet elbow.

28 Unscrew and remove the two bolts securing the air inlet pipe and exhaust gas recirculation (EGR) tube.

29 Note the routing of the power steering pump drivebelt, and mark it with an arrow to indicate its normal rotational direction.

30 Using a suitable square tool in the special hole at the top of the drivebelt tensioner, rotate the tensioner clockwise then slip the drivebelt from the camshaft and pump pulleys. Release the tensioner.

31 Unscrew the bolt securing the fluid high-pressure line bracket to the left-hand end of the cylinder head **(see illustration)**.

32 Position a suitable container beneath the power steering pump, then loosen the clip and disconnect the return hose from the bottom of the pump. Allow the fluid to drain into the container. Alternatively, fit a hose clamp to the hose.

33 Unscrew the union and disconnect the high-pressure line from the top of the pump **(see illustration)**. Counterhold the union with a second spanner, to prevent damage to

34.34 The power steering pump support bracket bolts

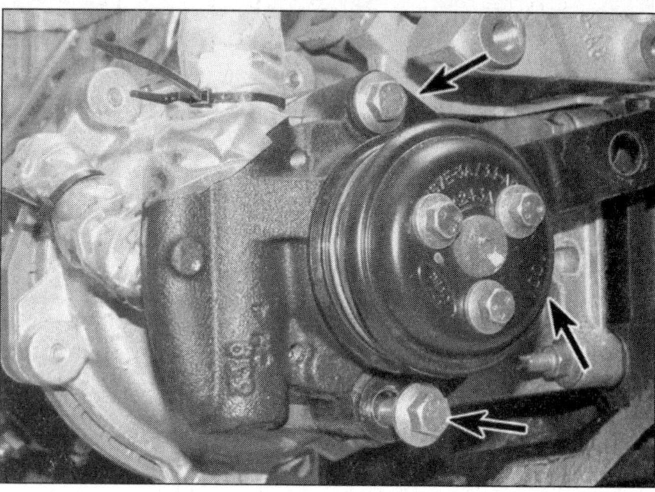
34.35a Unscrew the mounting bolts . . .

the pipe. Be prepared for some loss of fluid. Remove the union O-ring seal and discard it; a new one must be fitted on refitting.

34 Unscrew and remove the power steering pump support bracket bolts **(see illustration)**.

35 Unscrew the mounting bolts and remove the pump from the water pump housing **(see illustrations)**. Remove and discard the small O-ring from the water pump driveshaft – a new one should be used when refitting.

36 If fitting a new pump, unbolt the pulley from the old unit.

Refitting

1.8 and 2.0 litre petrol models

37 If necessary, the sealing ring on the high-pressure outlet union nut should be renewed. Ideally, the special Ford sleeve should be used to prevent damage to the ring as it passes over the union threads, however, a suitable alternative can be made out of plastic tubing or by wrapping suitable tape over the threads. Note that new pumps are supplied with new unions.

38 If the drive pulley is already fitted to the pump, connect the high-pressure line and screw on the union. Tighten the union to the specified torque.

39 Locate the pump on the engine, insert the mounting bolts and studs, and tighten them to the specified torque.

40 If the drive pulley has not been fitted at this stage, refit the high-pressure pipe and tighten the union to the specified torque.

41 Refit the hydraulic line support bracket and tighten the retaining nut securely.

42 Fit new O-ring seals to the hydraulic fluid reservoir outlet, then refit the reservoir to the pump **(see illustrations)**. Insert the reservoir mounting stud/bolts and tighten to the specified torque.

43 Refit the plastic clip to the rear of the reservoir, then locate the wiring loom in it.

44 Reconnect the fluid outlet (cooler) hose to the reservoir and tighten the clip.

45 At this stage, if a new pump is being fitted, the new pulley should be pressed onto the pump driveshaft using the special Ford tool or similar. The pulley must be pressed on flush with the end of the shaft.

46 Turn the auxiliary drivebelt tensioner clockwise, then locate the drivebelt on the pulleys and release the tensioner. Make sure the multi-vee serrations of the belt locate correctly on the pulleys. If the original belt is being refitted, make sure it is fitted the same way around as noted on removal.

47 Refit the crankshaft pulley splash shield, then refit the roadwheel and lower the car to the ground. Tighten the wheel nuts to the specified torque.

34.35b . . . and remove the power steering pump from the water pump housing bracket

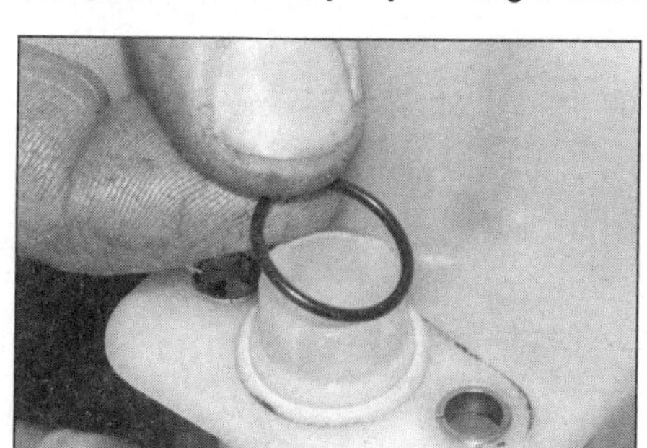
34.42b . . . and small diameter seal to the power steering hydraulic fluid reservoir outlet . . .

V6 models

48 Where applicable, fit the elbow and union to the power steering pump, using new O-ring seals, and tighten the bolts and union to the specified torque.

49 Refit the retaining plate to the pump, and tighten the nuts and two main bolts to the specified torque.

50 Locate the pump on the engine, refit the mounting bolts and tighten to the specified torque. Also refit and tighten the mounting bracket retaining bolt at the front of the pump.

51 Refit the pulley and tighten to the specified torque while holding it stationary as for removal.

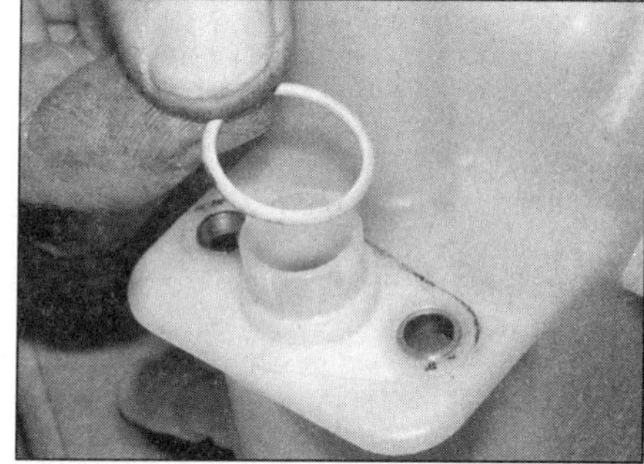
34.42a Fit a new large diameter seal . . .

34.42c . . . then refit the reservoir to the pump

35.3 Fluid hose connection to the power steering fluid cooler

35.4 Power steering fluid cooler mounting screw

52 Refit the engine right-hand mounting bracket, and tighten the nuts and bolts to the specified torque. Remove the trolley jack from under the engine.
53 Refit the spark plug HT leads and plastic holder to the right-hand engine mounting.
54 Refit the coolant expansion tank and tighten the mounting bolts.
55 Refit the power steering fluid reservoir and tighten the mounting bolt.
56 Reconnect the fluid hose to the pump and tighten the clip.
57 If necessary, the sealing ring on the high-pressure outlet union nut should be renewed. Ideally, the special Ford sleeve should be used to prevent damage to the ring as it passes over the union threads, however, a suitable alternative can be made out of plastic tubing or by wrapping suitable tape over the threads. Note that new pumps are supplied with new unions.
58 Reconnect the high-pressure line to the pump, and tighten the union to the specified torque. Refit the support bracket bolt and tighten securely.
59 Turn the auxiliary drivebelt tensioner clockwise, then locate the drivebelt on the pulleys and release the tensioner. Make sure the belt ribs locate correctly on the pulleys. If the original belt is being refitted, make sure it is fitted the same way around as noted on removal.
60 Refit the crankshaft pulley splash shield, then refit the roadwheel and lower the car to the ground. Tighten the wheel nuts to the specified torque.

Diesel models

61 Where applicable, fit the pulley to the pump and tighten the bolts to the specified torque.
62 If necessary, the sealing ring on the high-pressure outlet union nut should be renewed. Ideally, the special Ford sleeve should be used to prevent damage to the ring as it passes over the union threads, however, a suitable alternative can be made out of plastic tubing or by wrapping suitable tape over the threads. Note that new pumps are supplied with new unions.
63 On the rear of the pump, apply spline lubricant (Ford part number WSS-M12A4-A2, or equivalent) to the water pump driveshaft splines, and fit a new O-ring to the driveshaft groove.
64 Refit the power steering pump to the water pump housing, then insert the mounting bolts and tighten to the specified torque.
65 Refit the support bracket and tighten the bolts securely.
66 Reconnect the high-pressure line, and tighten the union to the specified torque – counterhold the union with a second spanner, to prevent damage to the pipe.
67 Reconnect the fluid return hose and tighten the clip.
68 Refit the fluid high-pressure line bracket to the left-hand end of the cylinder head, and tighten the bolt securely.
69 Locate the auxiliary drivebelt on the camshaft and pump pulleys. Using the special tool, rotate the tensioner clockwise and position the belt on the tensioner pulley. Release the tensioner and check that the belt is correctly located on each pulley.

All models

70 Reconnect the battery negative lead (refer to *Disconnecting the battery* at the end of this manual).
71 Fill and bleed the power steering system with reference to Section 33.

35 Power steering fluid cooler – removal and refitting

Removal

1 Disconnect the battery negative (earth) lead (refer to *Disconnecting the battery* at the end of this manual).
2 Apply the handbrake, then jack up the front of the car and support it on axle stands (see *Jacking and vehicle support*).
3 The fluid hoses to and from the cooler must now be disconnected. The connections at the cooler itself are inaccessible with the unit in place, so trace the hoses back from the cooler, and disconnect them at the front of the subframe. Alternatively, remove the front bumper as described in Chapter 11 for access **(see illustration)**. Have a container ready to catch spilt fluid, and plug the open hose ends quickly, to prevent fluid loss and dirt entry.
4 Unscrew and remove the cooler mounting screws, taking care not to damage the radiator (or the air conditioning condenser). Slide the cooler (and where applicable, its hoses) out of position **(see illustration)**. Handle the unit carefully, as the cooling fins are easily damaged.

Refitting

5 Refitting is a reversal of removal. It may be wise to replace the spring-type hose clips with screw-type items when reconnecting the fluid hoses. On completion, fill and bleed the power steering system as described in Section 33.

36 Wheel alignment and steering angles – general information

1 Accurate front wheel alignment is essential to provide positive steering, and to prevent excessive tyre wear. Before considering the steering/suspension geometry, check that the tyres are correctly inflated, that the front wheels are not buckled, and that the steering linkage and suspension joints are in good order, without slackness or wear. Alignment of the front subframe is also critical to the front suspension geometry – refer to a Ford dealer for accurate setting-up.
2 Wheel alignment consists of four factors **(see illustration)**:

Camber is the angle at which the front wheels are set from the vertical, when viewed from the front of the car. 'Positive camber' is the amount (in degrees) that the wheels are tilted outward at the top of the vertical.

Castor is the angle between the steering axis and a vertical line, when viewed from each side of the car. 'Positive castor' is when the steering axis is inclined rearward at the top.

Steering axis inclination is the angle (when viewed from the front of the car) between the vertical and an imaginary line drawn through the suspension strut upper mounting and the lower arm balljoint.

Toe setting is the amount by which the distance between the front inside edges of the roadwheels (measured at hub height) differs from the diametrically-opposite distance measured between the rear inside edges of the front roadwheels.

3 With the exception of the toe setting, all other steering angles are set during manufacture, and no adjustment is possible. It can be assumed, therefore, that unless the car has suffered accident damage, all the preset steering angles will be correct. Should there be some doubt about their accuracy, it will be necessary to seek the help of a Ford dealer, as special gauges are needed to check the steering angles.

4 Two methods are available to the home mechanic for checking the front wheel toe setting. One method is to use a gauge to measure the distance between the front and rear inside edges of the roadwheels. The other method is to use a scuff plate, in which each front wheel is rolled across a movable plate which records any deviation, or scuff, of the tyre from the straight-ahead position as it moves across the plate. Relatively-inexpensive equipment of both types is available from accessory outlets.

5 If, after checking the toe setting using whichever method is preferable, it is found that adjustment is necessary, proceed as follows.

6 Turn the steering wheel onto full-left lock, and record the number of exposed threads on the right-hand track rod. Now turn the steering onto full-right lock, and record the number of threads on the left-hand track rod. If there are the same number of threads visible on both sides, then subsequent adjustment can be made equally on both sides. If there are more threads visible on one side than the other, it will be necessary to compensate for this during adjustment. After adjustment, there must be the same number of threads visible on each track rod. This is most important.

7 To alter the toe setting, slacken the locknut on the track rod, and turn the track rod using self-locking pliers to achieve the desired setting. When viewed from the side of the car, turning the rod clockwise will increase the toe-in, turning it anti-clockwise will increase the toe-out. Only turn the track rods by a quarter of a turn each time, and then recheck the setting.

8 After adjustment, tighten the locknuts. Reposition the steering gear rubber gaiters, to remove any twist caused by turning the track rods.

9 The rear wheel toe setting may also be checked and adjusted, but as this additionally requires alignment with the front wheels, it should be left to a Ford dealer or specialist having the required equipment.

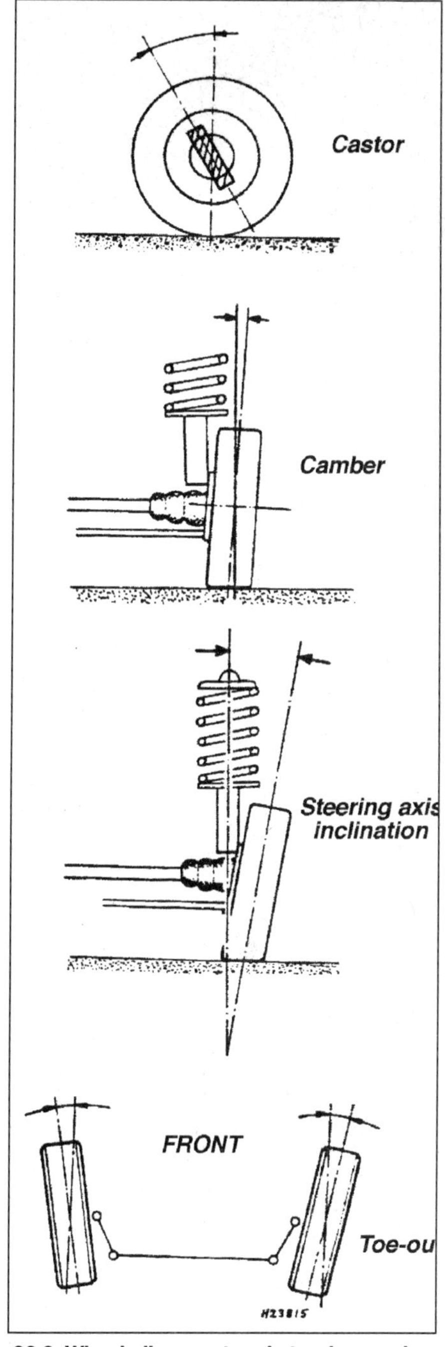

36.2 Wheel alignment and steering angles

Chapter 11
Bodywork and fittings

Contents

Degrees of difficulty

Easy, suitable for novice with little experience 	**Fairly easy,** suitable for beginner with some experience	**Fairly difficult,** suitable for competent DIY mechanic	**Difficult,** suitable for experienced DIY mechanic	**Very difficult,** suitable for expert DIY or professional

Specifications

Torque wrench settings

Torque wrench settings	Nm	lbf ft
Bonnet hinge to body and bonnet	25	18
Bonnet latch	8	6
Boot lid hinge to body	23	17
Boot lid to hinge	23	17
Bumper mounting to body	15	11
Door check strap to door	6	4
Door check strap to door pillar	23	17
Door striker	28	21
Exterior mirror	2	1
Front seat belt height adjuster	25	18
Front seat belt stalk and pretensioner	50	37
Front seat mounting bolts	25	18
Rear bumper to mounting bracket	20	15
Rear seat backrest (Saloon)	25	18
Rear seat backrest centre hinge pin	20	15
Rear seat backrest centre locking plate	25	18
Rear seat backrest hinge bolts	55	41
Rear seat backrest latch	30	22
Rear seat belt centre stalk (Saloon)	55	41
Rear seat cushion	25	18
Seat belt anchor bolts	38	28
Seat belt inertia reels	38	28
Tailgate hinge bolts	23	17

1 General information

The bodyshell and underframe on all models is of all-steel welded construction, incorporating progressive crumple zones at the front and rear, and a rigid centre safety cell.

The bulkhead behind the engine compartment incorporates crash grooves which determine its energy-absorption characteristics, and special beams to prevent the intrusion of the front wheels into the passenger compartment during a serious accident. All passenger doors incorporate side impact bars.

All sheet metal surfaces which are prone to corrosion are galvanised. The painting process includes a base colour which closely matches the final topcoat, so that any stone damage is not as noticeable.

The door hinges are bolted to both the door and body, and the striker plates have integral contact switches.

The front and rear bumpers have foam elements built into them, which spread the forces to the crumple zones in the event of an accident. The front seats have 'active' headrests – in the event of a rear end crash, pressure against the seat back causes the headrest to be pushed forwards and upwards, to keep the neck supported. The front seats are also of anti-submarining design – in the event of a severe frontal collision, the front edge of the seat lifts as it moves forwards, to prevent the occupant sliding forward into the footwell.

Inertia reel seat belts are fitted, and the front seat belt stalks are mounted on automatic tensioners. In the event of a serious front impact, the system is triggered and pulls the stalk buckle downwards to tension the seat belt. It is not possible to reset the tensioner once fired, and it must therefore be renewed. The tensioners are fired by an explosive charge similar to that used in the airbag, and are triggered via the airbag control module. A seat belt reminder system alerts the driver by warning light and warning chime if the seat belt has not been done up – this system can be deactivated by a Ford dealer if desired.

Central locking with 'double-locking' is fitted as standard. When the car is locked normally (single locking) the interior door handles can still be used to open the doors. When the double locking feature is used, the door lock mechanism is disconnected, making it impossible to open any of the doors or the tailgate/boot lid from inside the car. This means that, even if a thief should break a side window, he will not be able to open the door using the interior handle. In the event of a serious accident, a crash sensor unlocks all doors if they were previously locked. The central locking system is monitored and controlled by the Generic Electronic Module (GEM) which also synchronises the locking functions of the doors. If the car is unlocked with the remote control but no door is opened and the ignition not switched on within 45 seconds, the GEM automatically relocks the car. All windows and the sunroof may be closed by pressing the remote control locking button for approximately 2 seconds, but the action is interrupted if an object becomes trapped. The bonnet is unlocked with the ignition key, after swivelling the Ford badge on the radiator grille anti-clockwise.

Many of the procedures in this Chapter require the battery to be disconnected (refer to *Disconnecting the battery* at the end of this manual).

2 Maintenance – bodywork and underframe

The general condition of a car's bodywork is the one thing that significantly affects its value. Maintenance is easy, but needs to be regular. Neglect, particularly after minor damage, can lead quickly to further deterioration and costly repair bills. It is important also to keep watch on those parts of the car not immediately visible, for instance the underside, inside all the wheel arches, and the lower part of the engine compartment.

The basic maintenance routine for the bodywork is washing – preferably with a lot of water, from a hose. This will remove all the loose solids which may have stuck to the car. It is important to flush these off in such a way as to prevent grit from scratching the finish. The wheel arches and underside need washing in the same way, to remove any accumulated mud which will retain moisture and tend to encourage rust. Strange as it sounds, the best time to clean the underside and wheel arches is in wet weather, when the mud is thoroughly wet and soft. In very wet weather, the underside is usually cleaned of large accumulations automatically, and this is a good time for inspection.

Periodically, except on cars with a wax-based underbody protective coating, it is a good idea to have the whole of the underframe of the car steam-cleaned, engine compartment included, so that a thorough inspection can be carried out to see what minor repairs and renovations are necessary. Steam-cleaning is available at many garages, and is necessary for the removal of the accumulation of oily grime, which sometimes is allowed to become thick in certain areas. If steam-cleaning facilities are not available, grease solvents are available, which can be brush-applied; the dirt can then be simply hosed off. Note that these methods should not be used on cars with wax-based underbody protective coating, or the coating will be removed. Such cars should be inspected annually, preferably just prior to Winter, when the underbody should be washed down, and any damage to the wax coating repaired. Ideally, a completely fresh coat should be applied. It would also be worth considering the use of such wax-based protection for injection into door panels, sills, box sections, etc, as an additional safeguard against rust damage, where such protection is not provided by the car manufacturer.

After washing the paintwork, wipe off with a chamois leather to give an unspotted clear finish. A coat of clear protective wax polish will give added protection against chemical pollutants in the air. If the paintwork sheen has dulled or oxidised, use a cleaner/polisher combination to restore the brilliance of the shine. This requires a little effort, but such dulling is usually caused because regular washing has been neglected. Care needs to be taken with metallic paintwork, as special non-abrasive cleaner/polisher is required to avoid damage to the lacquer top coat (although actually, several coats of lacquer are normally applied, and the finish is quite durable). Always check that the door and ventilator opening drain holes and pipes are completely clear, so that water can be drained out. Brightwork should be treated in the same way as paintwork. Windscreens and windows can be kept clear of the smeary film which often appears, by the use of proprietary glass cleaner. Never use wax polish on the windscreen.

3 Maintenance – upholstery, trim and carpets

Mats and carpets should be brushed or vacuum-cleaned regularly, to keep them free of grit. If they are badly stained, remove them from the car for scrubbing or sponging, and make quite sure they are dry before refitting.

Cloth or velour seats and interior trim panels can be kept clean by wiping with a damp cloth. If they do become stained (which can be more apparent on light-coloured cloth or velour upholstery), use a little liquid detergent and a soft nail brush to scour the grime out of the grain of the material. Keep the headlining clean in the same way as the upholstery

When using liquid cleaners inside the car, do not over-wet the surfaces being cleaned. Excessive damp could get into the seams and padded interior, causing stains, offensive odours or even rot. If the inside of the car gets wet accidentally, it is worthwhile taking some trouble to dry it out properly, particularly where carpets are involved. *Do not leave oil or electric heaters inside the car for this purpose.*

In the case of leather upholstery, a whole range of different products exist to clean, feed and generally restore the leather, and it is recommended that these are used exclusively. Ordinary detergents should be avoided, as they will prematurely dry out leather, causing it to crack and split.

The plastic trim panels inside the car can also be cleaned successfully using liquid detergent, if they have become badly ingrained with dirt, but it may be worth testing a small area of the panel first. Otherwise, various sprays exist to restore shine and colour to plastics, but while these are very effective, they should be used with a little caution. First, it's better to spray them onto a cloth and wipe them on, as this produces a more even shine and colour. Don't let the spray get on the inside of the windscreen (it smears, making it hard to see through), and don't use it on the steering wheel or foot pedals (it makes their surfaces dangerously slippery).

4 Minor body damage – repair

Repair of minor scratches

If the scratch is very superficial, and does not penetrate to the metal of the bodywork, repair is very simple. Lightly rub the area of the scratch with a paintwork renovator, or a very fine cutting paste, to remove loose paint from the scratch, and to clear the surrounding bodywork of wax polish. Rinse the area with clean water.

In the case of metallic paint, the most commonly-found scratches are not in the paint, but in the lacquer top coat, and appear white. First note that damage to the lacquer coat will show up worse if (white) polish residue collects in the chip or scratch – clean any suspected area thoroughly, with perhaps a toothbrush. Fine scratches can sometimes be rendered less obvious by very careful use of paintwork renovator (which would otherwise not be used on metallic paintwork). Deeper scratches in the lacquer can be treated by applying lacquer with a fine brush – after several days, this can be blended into the panel, again by carefully using a paint cutting product.

Where paint is needed, apply it to the scratch using a fine paint brush; continue to apply fine layers of paint (allowing each one time to dry) until the surface of the paint in the scratch is level with the surrounding paintwork. Allow the new paint at least two weeks to harden, then blend it into the surrounding paintwork by rubbing the scratch area with a paintwork renovator or a very fine cutting paste. Finally, apply wax polish.

Where the scratch has penetrated right through to the metal of the bodywork, causing the metal to rust, a different repair technique is required. Remove any loose rust from the bottom of the scratch with a penknife, then apply rust-inhibiting paint, to prevent the formation of rust in the future. Using a rubber or nylon applicator, fill the scratch with bodystopper paste. If required, this paste can be mixed with cellulose thinners, to provide a very thin paste which is ideal for filling narrow scratches. Before the stopper-paste in the scratch hardens, wrap a piece of smooth cotton rag around the top of a finger. Dip the finger in cellulose thinners, and quickly sweep it across the surface of the stopper-paste in the scratch; this will ensure that the surface of the stopper-paste is slightly hollowed. The scratch can now be painted over as described earlier in this Section.

Repair of dents

If the dent is shallow, and the paint has not been broken, it may be possible to have the dent repaired professionally, by one of the specialist mobile dent repair companies.

When deep denting of the car's bodywork has taken place, the first task is to pull the dent out, until the affected bodywork almost attains its original shape. There is little point in trying to restore the original shape completely, as the metal in the damaged area will have stretched on impact, and cannot be reshaped fully to its original contour. It is better to bring the level of the dent up to a point which is about 3 mm below the level of the surrounding bodywork. In cases where the dent is very shallow anyway, it is not worth trying to pull it out at all. If the underside of the dent is accessible, it can be hammered out gently from behind, using a mallet with a wooden or plastic head. Whilst doing this, hold a block of wood firmly against the outside of the panel, to absorb the impact from the hammer blows and thus prevent a large area of the bodywork from being 'belled-out'.

Should the dent be in a section of the bodywork which has a double skin, or some other factor making it inaccessible from behind, a different technique is called for. Drill several small holes through the metal inside the area – particularly in the deeper section. Then screw long self-tapping screws into the holes, just sufficiently for them to gain a good purchase in the metal. Now the dent can be pulled out by pulling on the protruding heads of the screws with a pair of pliers.

The next stage of the repair is the removal of the paint from the damaged area, and from an inch or so of the surrounding 'sound' bodywork. This is accomplished most easily by using a wire brush or abrasive pad on a power drill, although it can be done just as effectively by hand, using sheets of abrasive paper. To complete the preparation for filling, score the surface of the bare metal with a screwdriver or the tang of a file, or alternatively, drill small holes in the affected area. This will provide a really good 'key' for the filler paste.

To complete the repair, see the Section on filling and respraying.

Repair of rust holes or gashes

Remove all paint from the affected area, and from an inch or so of the surrounding 'sound' bodywork, using an abrasive pad or a wire brush on a power drill. If these are not available, a few sheets of abrasive paper will do the job most effectively. With the paint removed, you will be able to judge the severity of the corrosion, and therefore decide whether to renew the whole panel (if this is possible) or to repair the affected area. New body panels are not as expensive as most people think, and it is often quicker and more satisfactory to fit a new panel than to attempt to repair large areas of corrosion.

Remove all fittings from the affected area, except those which will act as a guide to the original shape of the damaged bodywork (e.g. light units). Then, using tin snips or a hacksaw blade, remove all loose metal and any other metal badly affected by corrosion. Hammer the edges of the hole inwards, in order to create a slight depression for the filler paste.

Wire-brush the affected area to remove the powdery rust from the surface of the remaining metal. Paint the affected area with rust-inhibiting paint; if the back of the rusted area is accessible, treat this also.

Before filling can take place, it will be necessary to block the hole in some way. This can be achieved by the use of aluminium or plastic mesh, or aluminium tape.

Aluminium or plastic mesh, or glass-fibre matting is probably the best material to use for a large hole. Cut a piece to the approximate size and shape of the hole to be filled, then position it in the hole so that its edges are below the level of the surrounding bodywork. It can be retained in position by several blobs of filler paste around its periphery.

Aluminium tape should be used for small or very narrow holes. Pull a piece off the roll, trim it to the approximate size and shape required, then pull off the backing paper (if used) and stick the tape over the hole; it can be overlapped if the thickness of one piece is insufficient. Burnish down the edges of the tape with the handle of a screwdriver or similar, to ensure that the tape is securely attached to the metal underneath.

Filling and respraying

Before using this Section, see the Sections on dent, deep scratch, rust holes and gash repairs.

Many types of bodyfiller are available, but generally speaking, those proprietary kits which contain a tin of filler paste and a tube of resin hardener are best for this type of repair. A wide, flexible plastic or nylon applicator will be found invaluable for imparting a smooth and well-contoured finish to the surface of the filler.

Mix up a little filler on a clean piece of card or board – measure the hardener carefully (follow the maker's instructions on the pack), otherwise the filler will set too rapidly or too slowly. Using the applicator, apply the filler paste to the prepared area; draw the applicator across the surface of the filler to achieve the correct contour and to level the surface. As soon as a contour that approximates to the correct one is achieved, stop working the paste – if you carry on too long, the paste will become sticky and begin to 'pick-up' on the applicator. Continue to add thin layers of filler paste at 20-minute intervals, until the level of the filler is just proud of the surrounding bodywork.

Once the filler has hardened, the excess can be removed using a metal plane or file. From then on, progressively-finer grades of abrasive paper should be used, starting with a 40-grade production paper, and finishing with an 800-grade wet-and-dry paper. Always wrap the abrasive paper around a flat rubber, cork, or wooden block – otherwise the surface of the filler will not be completely flat. During the smoothing of the filler surface, the wet-and-dry paper should be periodically rinsed in water. This will ensure that a very smooth finish is imparted to the filler at the final stage.

At this stage, the 'dent' should be surrounded by a ring of bare metal, which in turn should be encircled by the finely 'feathered' edge of the good paintwork. Rinse the repair area with clean water, until all of the dust produced by the rubbing-down operation has gone.

Spray the whole area with a light coat of primer – this will show up any imperfections in the surface of the filler. Repair these imperfections with fresh filler paste or bodystopper, and once more smooth the surface with abrasive paper. If bodystopper is used, it can be mixed with cellulose thinners, to form a really thin paste which is ideal for filling small holes. Repeat this spray-and-repair procedure until you are satisfied that the surface of the filler, and the feathered edge of the paintwork, are perfect. Clean the repair area with clean water, and allow to dry fully.

The repair area is now ready for final spraying. Paint spraying must be carried out in a warm, dry, windless and dust-free atmosphere. This condition can be created artificially if you have access to a large indoor working area, but if you are forced to work in the open, you will have to pick your day very carefully. If you are working indoors, dousing the floor in the work area with water will help to settle the dust which would otherwise be in the atmosphere. If the repair area is confined to one body panel, mask off the surrounding panels; this will help to minimise the effects of a slight mis-match in paint colours. Bodywork fittings (e.g. chrome strips, door handles etc) will also need to be masked off. Use genuine masking tape, and several thicknesses of newspaper, for the masking operations.

Before commencing to spray, agitate the aerosol can thoroughly, then spray a test area (an old tin, or similar) until the technique is mastered. Cover the repair area with a thick coat of primer; the thickness should be built up using several thin layers of paint, rather than one thick one. Using 800-grade wet-and-dry paper, rub down the surface of the primer until it is really smooth. While doing this, the work area should be thoroughly doused with water, and the wet-and-dry paper periodically rinsed in water. Allow to dry before spraying on more paint.

Spray on the top coat, again building up the thickness by using several thin layers of paint. Start spraying at the top of the repair area, and then, using a side-to-side motion, work downwards until the whole repair area and about 2 inches of the surrounding original paintwork is covered. Remove all masking material 10 to 15 minutes after spraying on the final coat of paint.

Allow the new paint at least two weeks to harden, then, using a paintwork renovator or a very fine cutting paste, blend the edges of the paint into the existing paintwork. Finally, apply wax polish.

Plastic components

With the use of more and more plastic body components by the car manufacturers (e.g. bumpers, spoilers, and in some cases major body panels), rectification of more serious damage to such items has become a matter of either entrusting repair work to a specialist in this field, or renewing complete components. Repair of such damage by the DIY owner is not really feasible, owing to the cost of the equipment and materials required for effecting such repairs. The basic technique involves making a groove along the line of the crack in the plastic, using a rotary burr in a power drill. The damaged part is then welded back together, using a hot air gun to heat up and fuse a plastic filler rod into the groove. Any excess plastic is then removed, and the area rubbed down to a smooth finish. It is important that a filler rod of the correct plastic is used, as body components can be made of a variety of different types (e.g. polycarbonate, ABS, polypropylene).

Damage of a less serious nature (abrasions, minor cracks etc) can be repaired by the DIY owner using a two-part epoxy filler repair. Once mixed in equal, this is used in similar fashion to the bodywork filler used on metal panels. The filler is usually cured in twenty to thirty minutes, ready for sanding and painting.

If the owner is renewing a complete component himself, or if he has repaired it with epoxy filler, he will be left with the problem of finding a suitable paint for finishing which is compatible with the type of plastic used. At one time, the use of a universal paint was not possible, owing to the complex range of plastics encountered in body component applications. Standard paints, generally speaking, will not bond to plastic or rubber satisfactorily, but suitable paints to match any plastic or rubber finish, can be obtained from dealers. However, it is now possible to obtain a plastic body parts finishing kit which consists of a pre-primer treatment, a primer and coloured top coat. Full instructions are normally supplied with a kit, but basically, the method of use is to first apply the pre-primer to the component concerned, and allow it to dry for up to 30 minutes. Then the primer is applied, and left to dry for about an hour before finally applying the special-coloured top coat. The result is a correctly-coloured component, where the paint will flex with the plastic or rubber, a property that standard paint does not normally possess.

5 Major body damage – repair

Where serious damage has occurred, or large areas need renewal due to neglect, it means that complete new panels will need welding-in; this is best left to professionals. If the damage is due to impact, it will also be necessary to check completely the alignment of the bodyshell; this can only be carried out accurately by a Ford dealer, using special jigs. If the body is left misaligned, it is primarily dangerous, as the car will not handle properly, and secondly, uneven stresses will be imposed on the steering, suspension and possibly transmission, causing abnormal wear or complete failure, particularly to items such as the tyres.

6 Bumpers – removal and refitting

Front bumper

Removal

1 Remove the radiator grille as described in Section 7, then remove both headlights as described in Chapter 12.

2 Where applicable, prise the headlight washer covers from the front bumper.

3 Apply the handbrake, then jack up the front of the car and support it on axle stands (see *Jacking and vehicle support*).

4 Undo a total of seven screws and remove the plastic splash shield from beneath the radiator **(see illustrations)**.

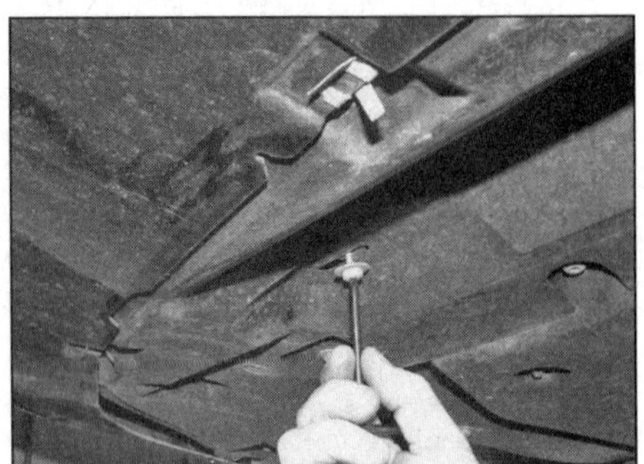

6.4a Remove seven screws . . .

6.4b . . . and lower out the splash shield under the radiator

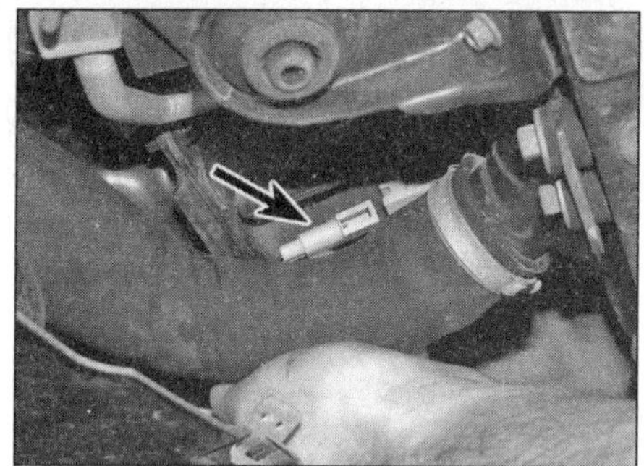
6.5a Disconnect the frost/ice sensor wiring plug above the foglight . . .

6.5b . . . or unclip the sensor (arrowed) from the bumper

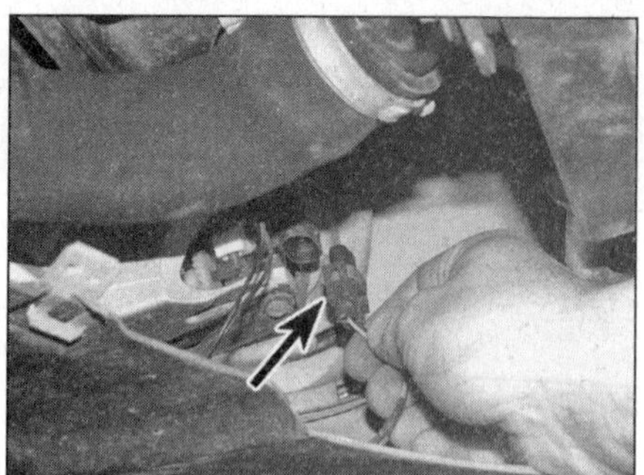
6.6 Disconnect the front foglight wiring plugs

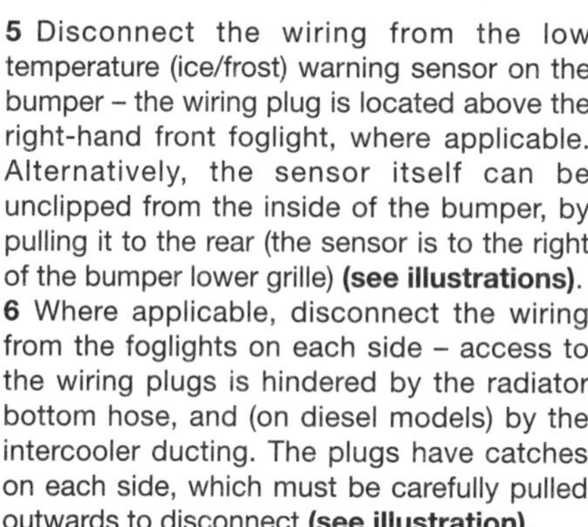

5 Disconnect the wiring from the low temperature (ice/frost) warning sensor on the bumper – the wiring plug is located above the right-hand front foglight, where applicable. Alternatively, the sensor itself can be unclipped from the inside of the bumper, by pulling it to the rear (the sensor is to the right of the bumper lower grille) **(see illustrations)**.

6 Where applicable, disconnect the wiring from the foglights on each side – access to the wiring plugs is hindered by the radiator bottom hose, and (on diesel models) by the intercooler ducting. The plugs have catches on each side, which must be carefully pulled outwards to disconnect **(see illustration)**.

7 Working on each side in turn, undo the three screws securing the wheel arch liners to the front bumper **(see illustrations)**.

8 Pull out the rear edge of the bumper on both sides, then pull back the wheel arch liner and unscrew the bumper mounting bolts from below, where the bumper joins the front wing. Depending on model, there may be two, three or four bolts **(see illustration)**. Access is limited – if necessary, remove more of the wheel arch liner screws, or even remove the liner completely.

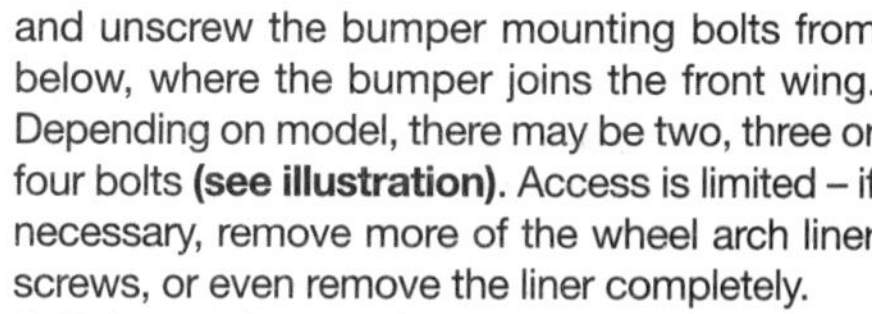

9 Release the two bumper locating legs in each headlight aperture by pressing the tabs downwards, or by tilting the bumper upwards. With the aid of an assistant, carefully lift the front bumper away from the car **(see illustrations)**.

Refitting

10 Refitting is a reversal of removal.

Rear bumper

Removal

11 Open the tailgate or boot lid, according to model.

12 On Saloon models, remove the two bumper upper retaining screws in the corners of the boot lid opening.

13 Chock the front wheels, then jack up the rear of the car and support on axle stands (see *Jacking and vehicle support*).

14 Working in the rear wheel arches, remove the three screws securing the wheel arch liner to the edge of the bumper. Pull back the liner, then reach inside and unscrew the two bumper mounting screws each side **(see illustrations)**.

15 Carefully pull the sides of the bumper outwards, to release the side clips **(see illustration)**.

16 On models equipped with a reverse parking aid, disconnect the wiring from the sensors behind the bumper – there should be four plugs on all, colour-coded to avoid confusion when refitting **(see illustration)**.

6.7a Undo the screws securing the wheel arch liners to the front bumper . . .

6.7b . . . noting that one of them is fitted from underneath

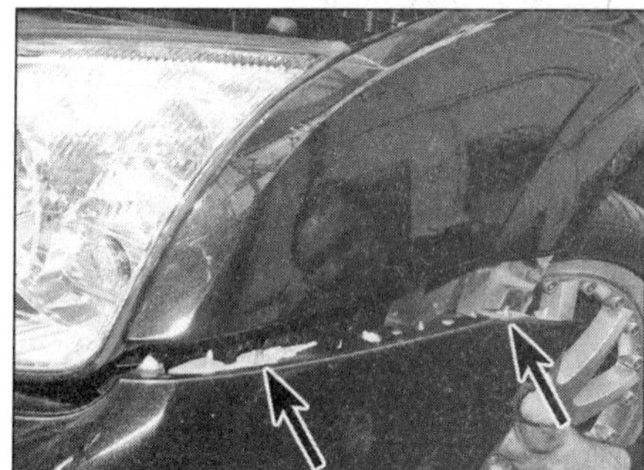
6.8 Bumper separated from wing, showing mounting bolt locations (arrowed)

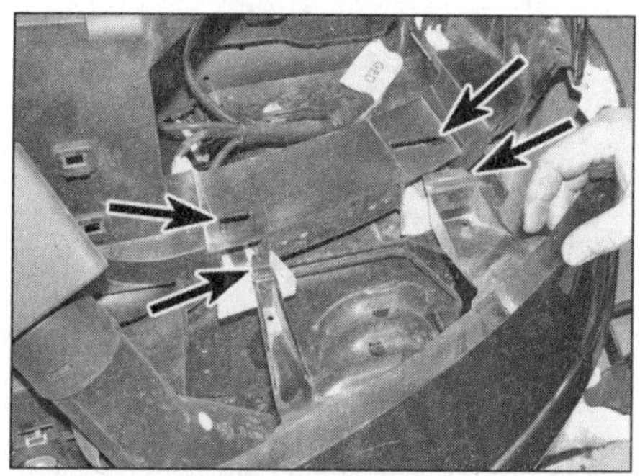
6.9a Unhook the two locating legs in the headlight apertures . . .

6.9b . . . and withdraw the bumper from the car

6.14a Unscrew the rear bumper-to-wheel arch liner screws . . .

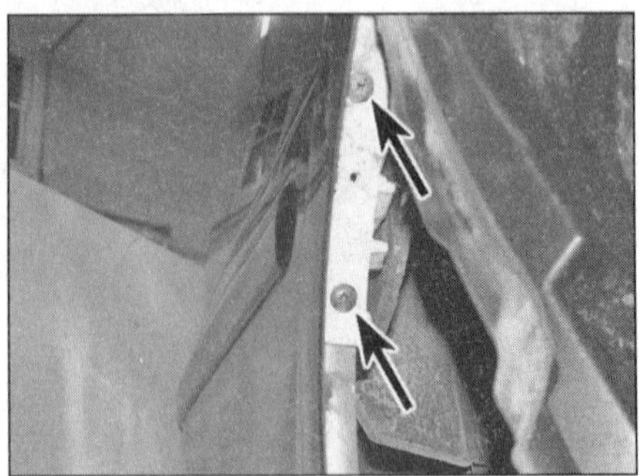
6.14b . . . then reach inside and unscrew the bumper mounting screws

6.15 Pull the bumper ends outwards to release the side clips

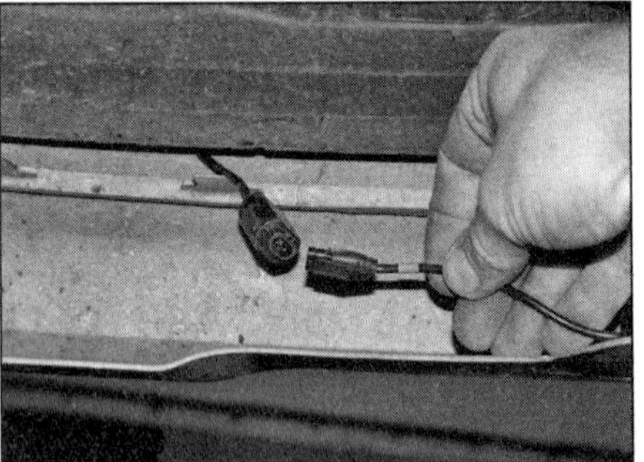
6.16 Where applicable, disconnect the reverse parking sensors

6.17 Unscrew the bumper mounting nuts under the car

6.18 Removing the rear bumper

17 Working under the car, undo the nuts securing the lower edge of the bumper to the spare wheel well – there will be four nuts on Saloon and Hatchback models, only two on Estates **(see illustration)**. On 3.0 litre ST models, the lower edge of the bumper is secured by a row of five screws across the back.

18 With the aid of an assistant, carefully lift the rear bumper away from the car **(see illustration)**.

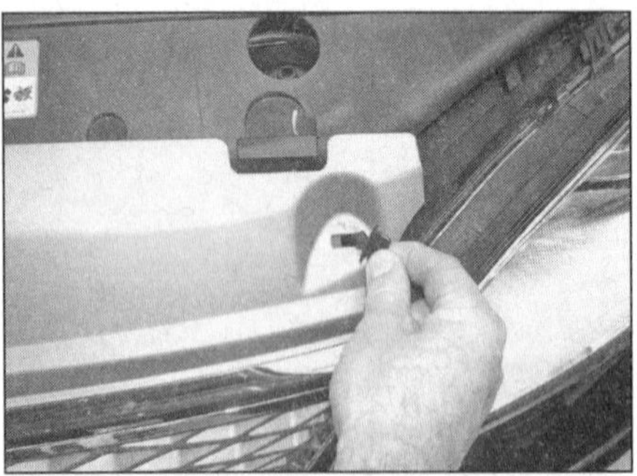
7.2 Twist the fasteners through a quarter-turn to remove them

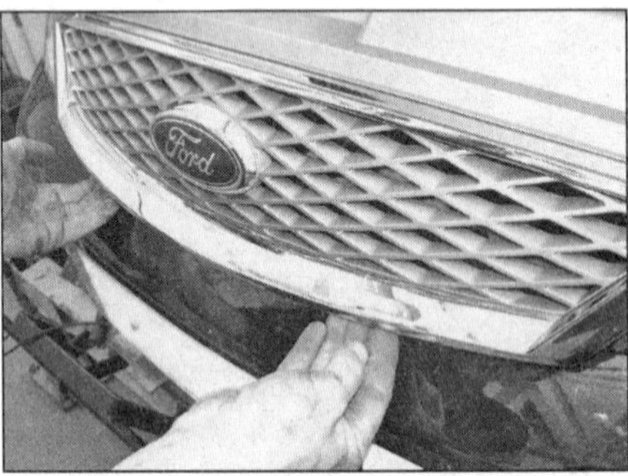

7.3 Pull the grille bottom edge forwards . . .

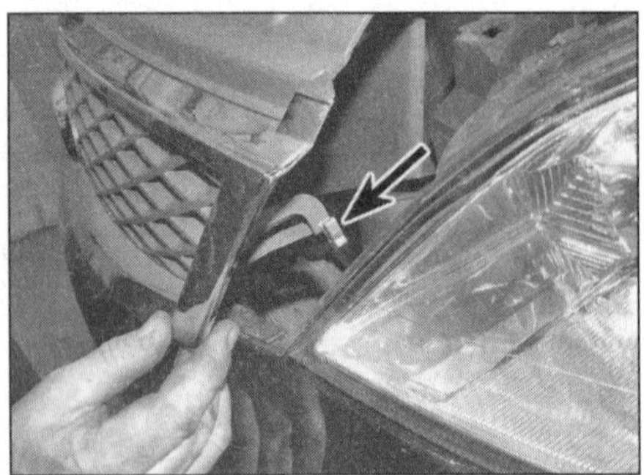
7.4 . . . and unhook the side lugs at the rear

8.2a Undo the screws . . .

Refitting

19 Refitting is a reversal of removal.

7 Radiator grille – removal and refitting

Removal

1 Support the bonnet in the open position.

2 Release the fasteners at each upper corner of the radiator grille. Twist the fasteners a quarter-turn to release them **(see illustration)**.

3 Hold the bumper back with one hand, and carefully pull the bottom edge of the grille forwards, to release a row of small tabs which locate the grille into the bumper **(see illustration)**.

4 The grille also has two side lugs at the back, which loosely hook round the edges of the headlights – once the bottom of the grille is free, unhook the side lugs, and the grille can be removed **(see illustration)**.

Refitting

5 Offer the grille loosely into place, and first hook the side lugs around the headlights.

6 Ensure that the grille is lined up with the top of the bumper, then press the lower edge backwards to engage the lower tabs through the slots in the bumper.

7 Finally, secure the top corners of the grille by inserting and turning the two fasteners.

8 Bonnet – removal, refitting and adjustment

Removal

1 Open the bonnet. The help of an assistant will be necessary when the support struts are disconnected.

2 Undo the screws and remove the plastic resonator from the bonnet **(see illustrations)**.

3 Prise out the clips from the insulator panel on the underside of the bonnet, for access to the windscreen washer hoses **(see illustration)**. It is not necessary to completely remove the insulator.

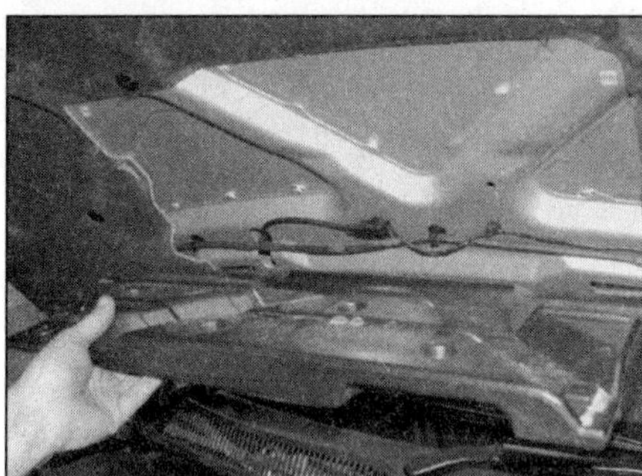

8.2b . . . and remove the plastic resonator from the underside of the bonnet

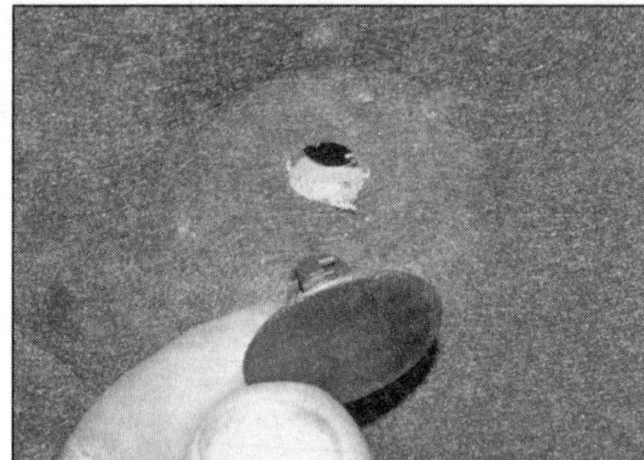

8.3 Prise out the clips securing the insulator panel to the bonnet

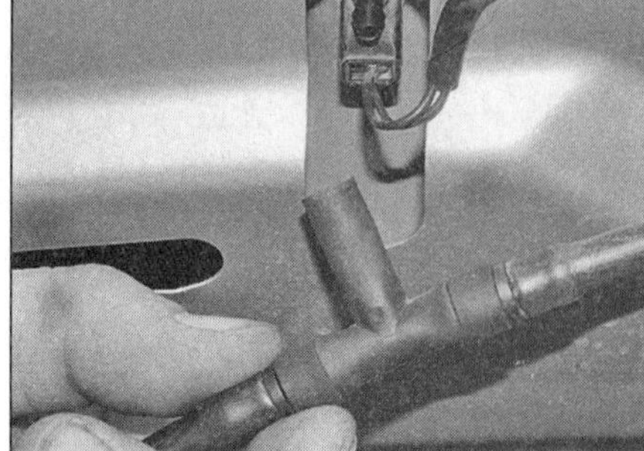

8.4 Disconnecting the hoses from the washer jets

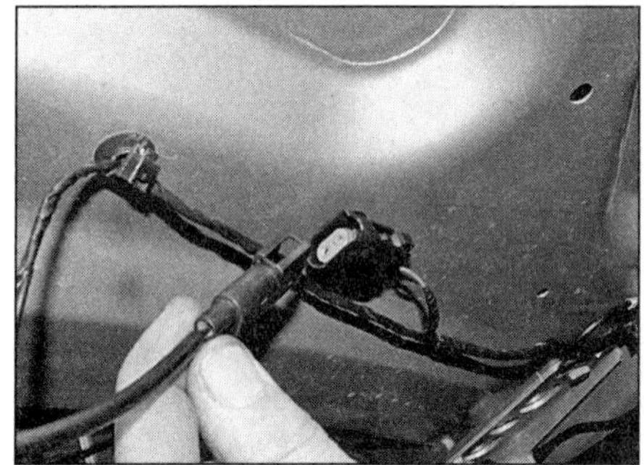

8.5 Disconnecting the washer jet heater wiring

8.7 Support strut and bonnet bracket

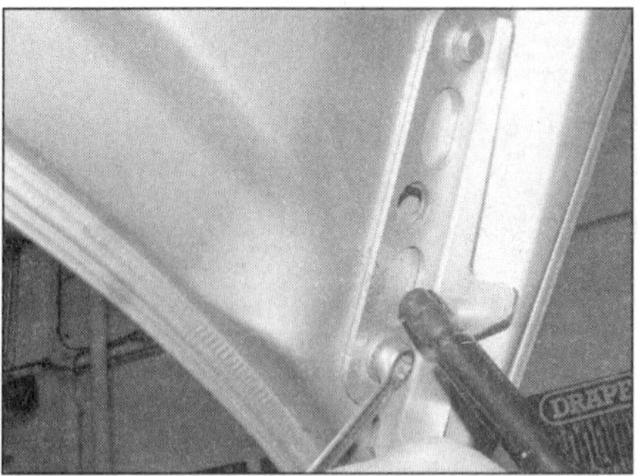

8.8 Unscrewing the bonnet-to-hinge mounting bolts

4 Carefully pull the hoses from the washer jets and release them from the retaining clips **(see illustration)**.

5 Disconnect the washer jet heater wiring, and release it from the retaining clips **(see illustration)**.

6 To assist in correctly realigning the bonnet when refitting it, mark the outline of the hinges with a soft pencil.

7 While an assistant supports the bonnet in its fully open position, prise off the spring clips and disconnect the support struts **(see illustration)**.

8 With the help of an assistant, unscrew the four bolts and lift the bonnet from the car **(see illustration)**.

Refitting and adjustment

9 Refitting is a reversal of the removal procedure. If the original bonnet is being refitted, and the hinge positions were carefully noted, there should be no need to carry out a full adjustment procedure.

10 Before refitting the support struts, slowly close the bonnet and check that the striker enters the lock centrally **(see illustration)**. Also check that, when closed, the bonnet is level with the front wings and windscreen scuttle cowl. If the adjustment is complete, reconnect the support struts – if not, set the bonnet position as described below.

11 According to Ford, the bonnet lock should be removed prior to any substantial bonnet adjustment is carried out – this will allow the bonnet to be closed completely without engaging the lock, which should make adjustment easier. Remove the two bolts securing the lock to the front panel, as described in Section 9. Alternatively, unbolt and remove the lock striker from the bonnet.

12 If necessary, adjust the position of the bonnet at the hinge bolts, and adjust its front height using the bump stop rubbers, which screw in and out of the front panel.

13 When the bonnet is aligned satisfactorily with the wings and headlights, etc, tighten the hinge bolts and refit the lock (or striker). Adjust the position of the lock (or striker) so that the striker enters the lock centrally. Refit any other removed components to complete.

9 Bonnet lock – removal, refitting and adjustment

Removal

1 Remove the radiator grille as described in Section 7.

2 The cylinder private lock assembly is attached to the security housing by shear-bolts, and it will be necessary to drill these out for access to the lock **(see illustration)**. Obtain new shear-bolts for refitting.

3 Use a soft pencil to mark the position of the

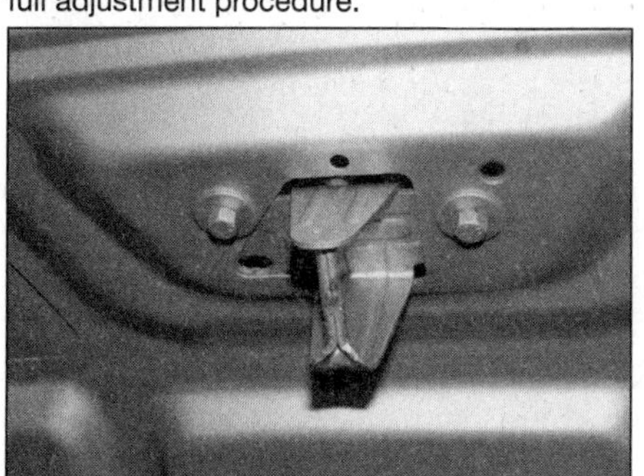

8.10 Bonnet striker

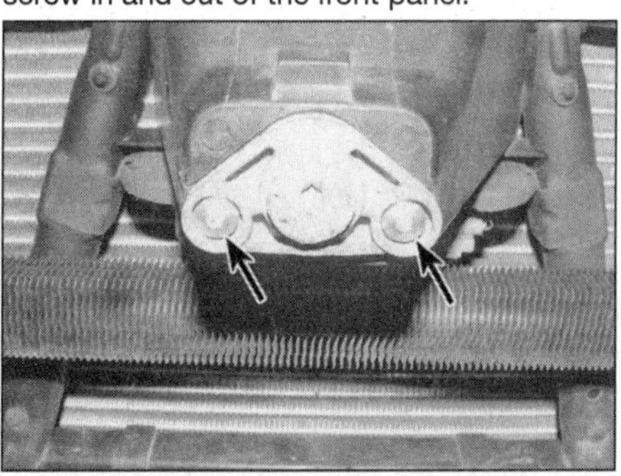

9.2 Shear-bolts securing the cylinder private lock to the housing

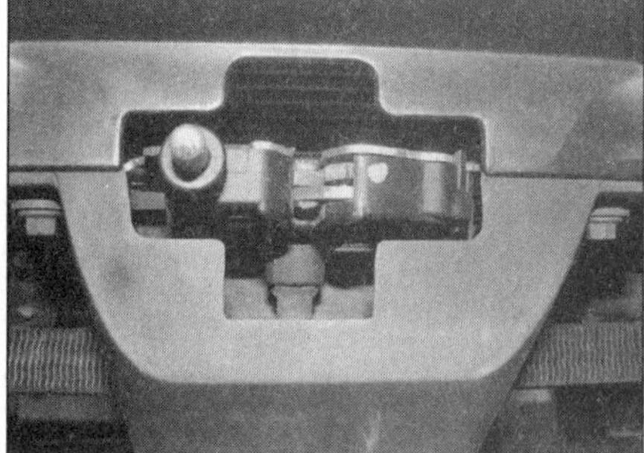

9.3 Top view of the bonnet lock

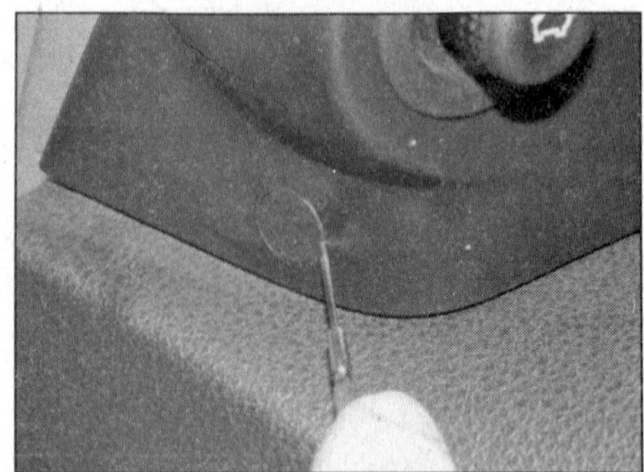
10.2a Prise out the plastic cover . . .

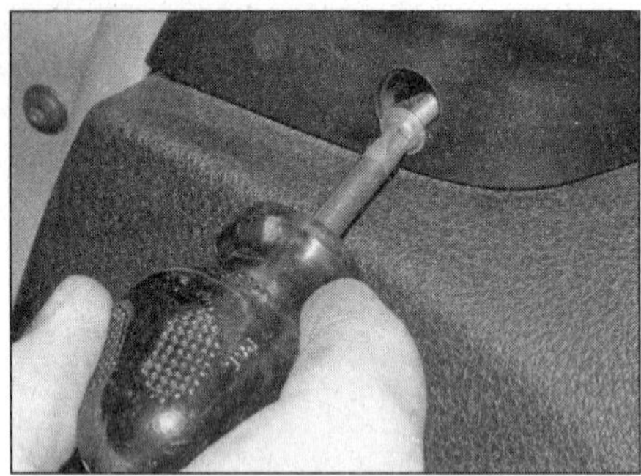
10.2b . . . then undo the screw . . .

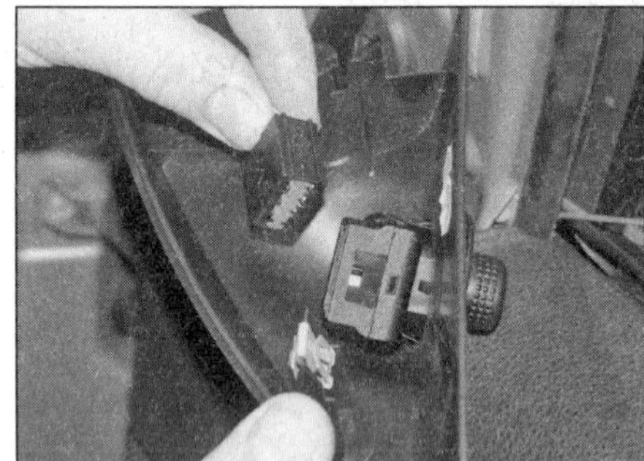
10.2c . . . and disconnect the exterior mirror wiring

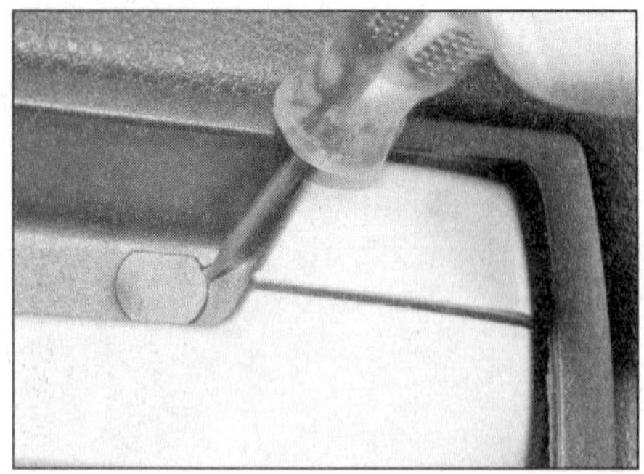
10.3a Prise out the plastic cover . . .

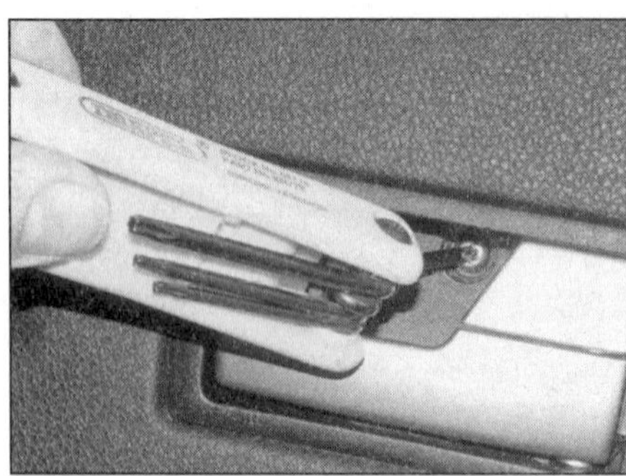
10.3b . . . then undo the screw . . .

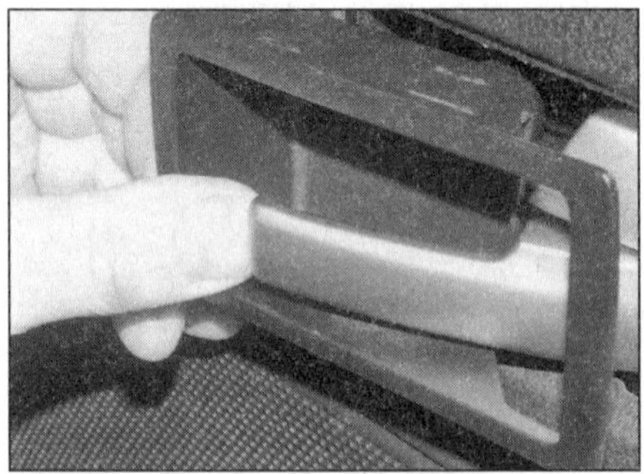
10.3c . . . and slide off the bezel

bonnet lock on the front crossmember, then unscrew the mounting bolts and remove the lock **(see illustration)**.

Refitting and adjustment

4 Refitting is a reversal of the removal procedure, but position the lock as previously noted before tightening the bolts. Check that the bonnet striker enters the lock centrally. When refitting the cylinder private lock, tighten the new shear-bolts until their heads break off. Check that the front edge of the bonnet is level with the front wings, and if necessary, align the bonnet as described in Section 8.

10.4a Prise out the cover . . .

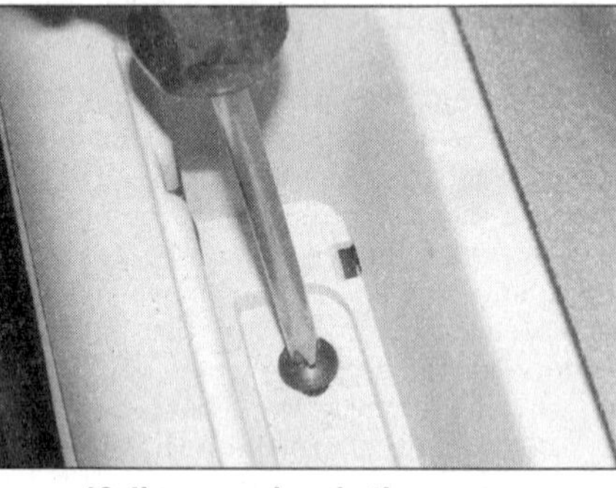
10.4b . . . and undo the screws

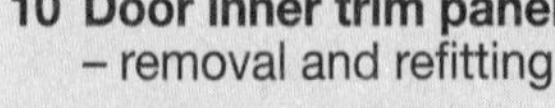

10 Door inner trim panel – removal and refitting

Removal

Front door

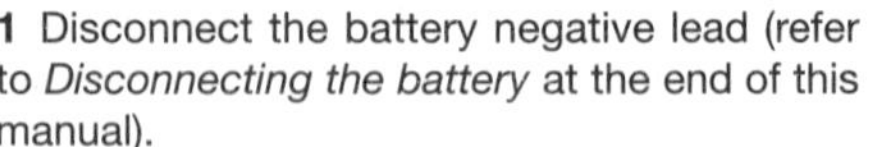

1 Disconnect the battery negative lead (refer to *Disconnecting the battery* at the end of this manual).

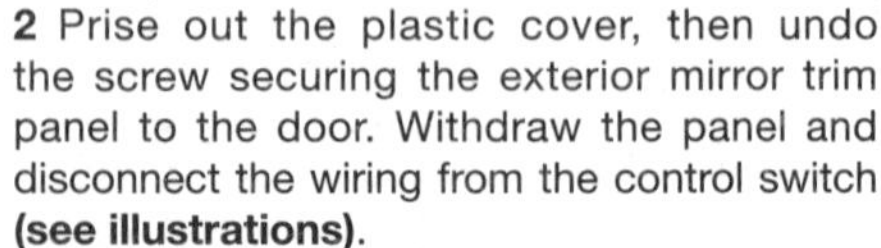

2 Prise out the plastic cover, then undo the screw securing the exterior mirror trim panel to the door. Withdraw the panel and disconnect the wiring from the control switch **(see illustrations)**.

3 Prise out the plastic cover, then use an Allen key to undo the screw securing the inner handle bezel to the door. Slide the bezel to one side over the inner door handle **(see illustrations)**.

4 Carefully prise out the cover from inside the door pull handle, then undo the exposed screws securing the trim panel to the door **(see illustrations)**.

5 Undo the trim panel securing screws. There are two at the front, two at the rear and two at the bottom **(see illustration)**.

6 Lift the trim panel slightly to release the upper edge, then withdraw the panel from the door far enough to disconnect the wiring from the electric window switch **(see illustration)**.

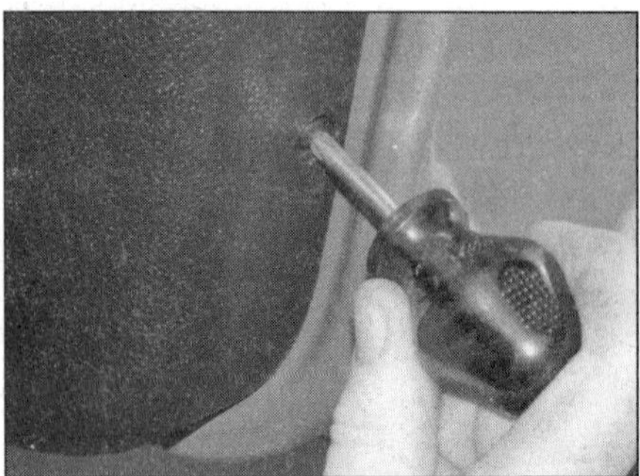
10.5 Removing the trim panel securing screws

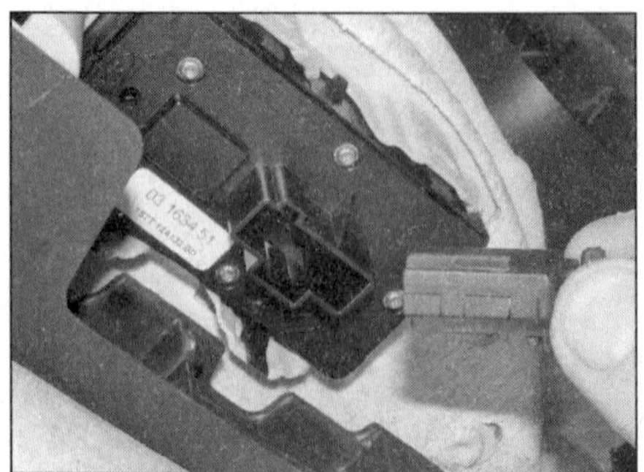
10.6 Disconnecting the wiring from the electric window switch

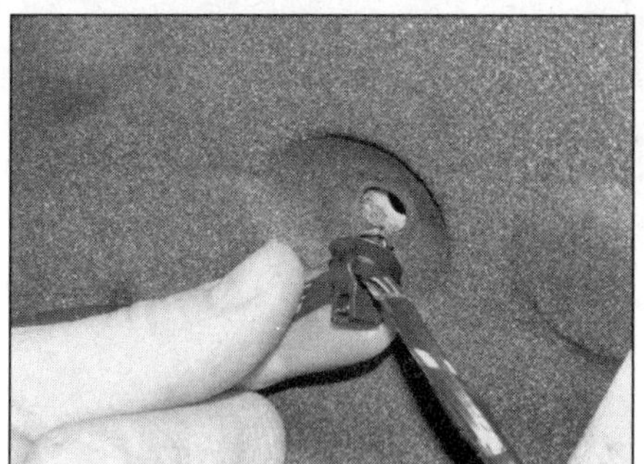
10.7a Prise out the loom clip . . .

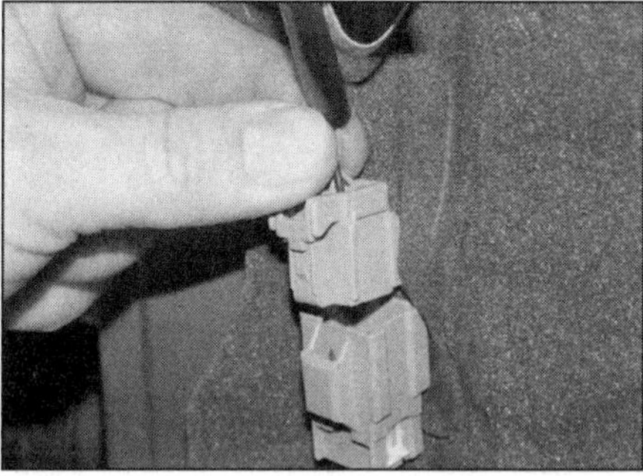
10.7b . . . disconnect the exterior mirror wiring . . .

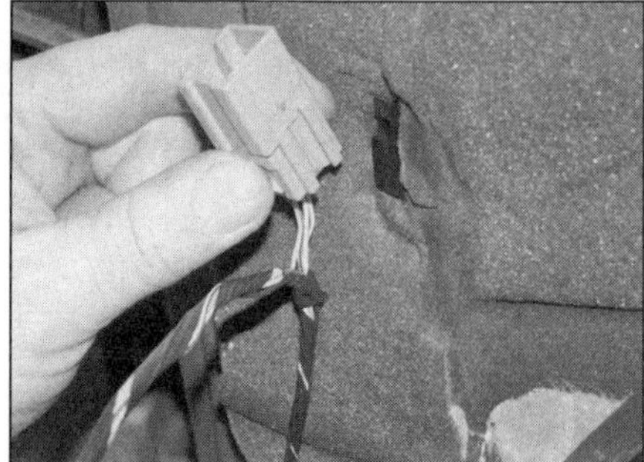
10.7c . . . slide the connector from the support . . .

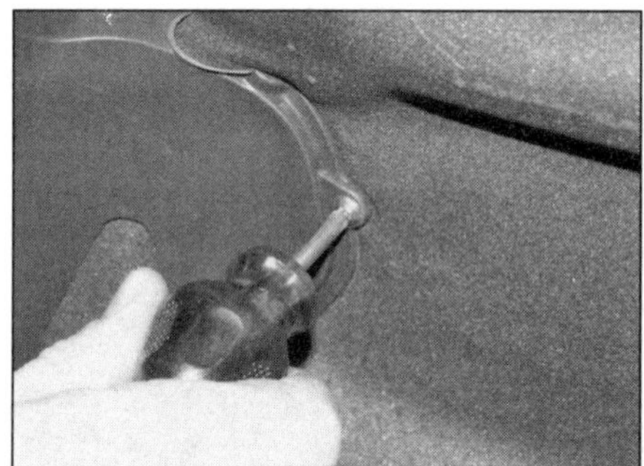
10.7d . . . remove the speaker . . .

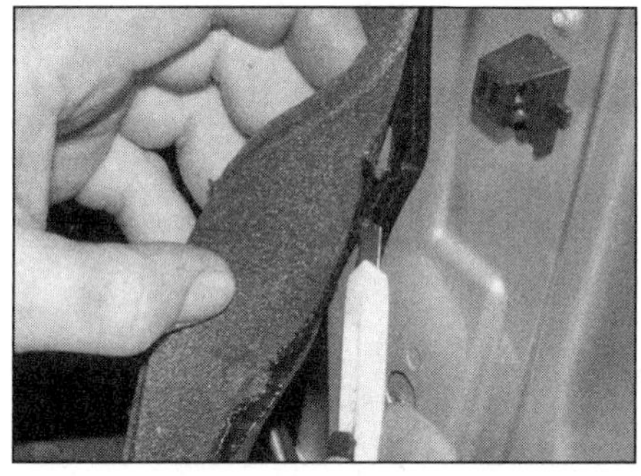
10.7e . . . and cut the adhesive with a knife

10.10a Prise out the plastic cover . . .

7 If further dismantling of the door is required, remove the waterproof membrane as follows. Prise out the electric window wiring loom retaining clip, then disconnect the exterior mirror wiring and slide the connector from the support. Undo the screws and remove the speaker from the door, then disconnect the wiring. The membrane is attached to the inner door panel with a bead of mastic adhesive – carefully pull back the membrane without tearing it, while using a knife to cut along the bead of adhesive **(see illustrations)**.

8 Place the membrane to one side, and protect the adhesive from dust and dirt so it can be used again.

Rear door

9 Disconnect the battery negative lead (refer to *Disconnecting the battery* at the end of this manual).

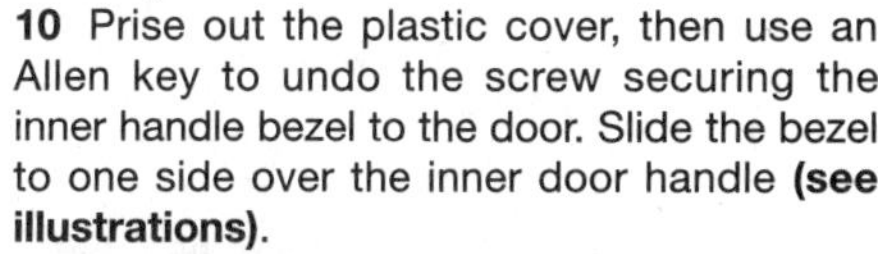

10 Prise out the plastic cover, then use an Allen key to undo the screw securing the inner handle bezel to the door. Slide the bezel to one side over the inner door handle **(see illustrations)**.

11 Carefully prise out the cover from inside the door pull handle, then undo the exposed screw securing the trim panel to the door **(see illustrations)**.

12 On models fitted with manual (ie, non-electric) windows, fully shut the window, and note the position of the regulator handle. Release the spring clip by inserting a clean cloth between the handle and the door trim. Using a 'sawing' action, pull the cloth against the open ends of the clip to release it, at the same time pulling the handle from the regulator shaft splines. Withdraw the handle (and where fitted, the spacer) and recover the clip.

13 Undo the trim panel securing screws. There are two at the front edge and two at the rear edge **(see illustration)**.

14 Lift the trim panel slightly to release the upper edge, then withdraw the panel from the door. On models with electric windows, disconnect the wiring from the electric window switch **(see illustration)**.

15 If further dismantling of the door is required, remove the waterproof membrane as

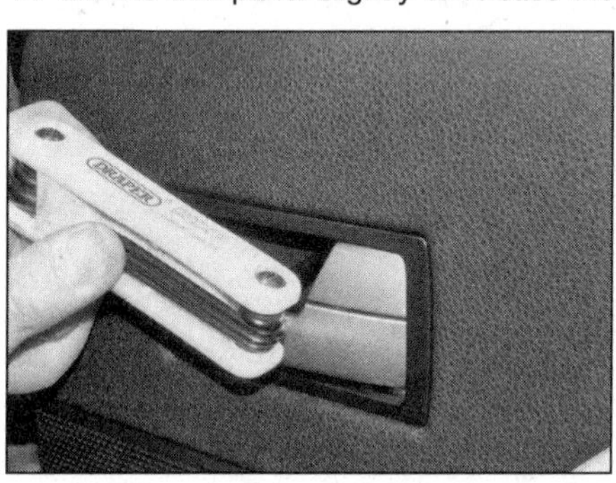
10.10b . . . then undo the screw . . .

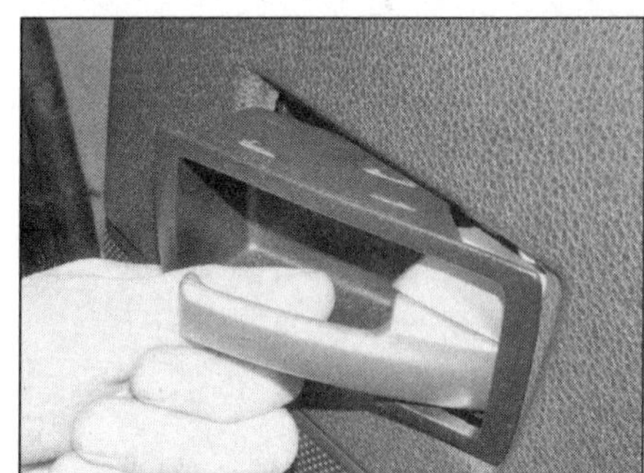
10.10c . . . and remove the bezel

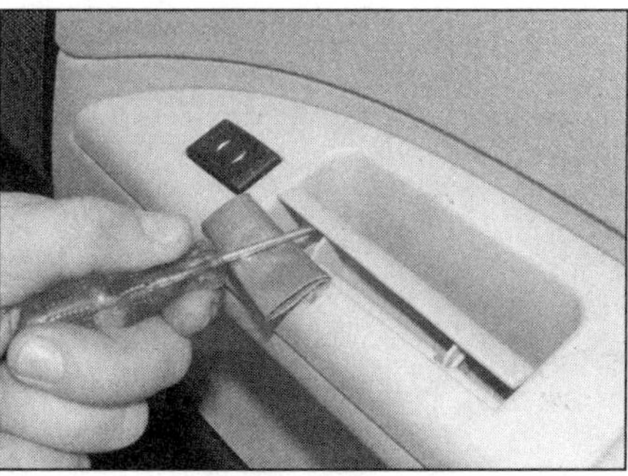
10.11a Prise out the cover . . .

10.11b . . . and undo the screw

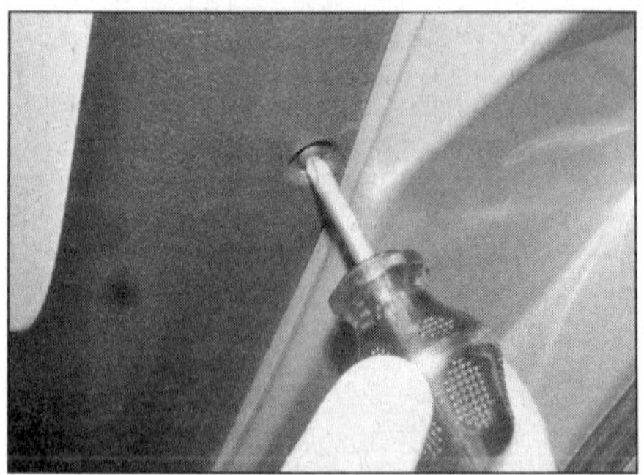

10.13 Removing the trim panel securing screws

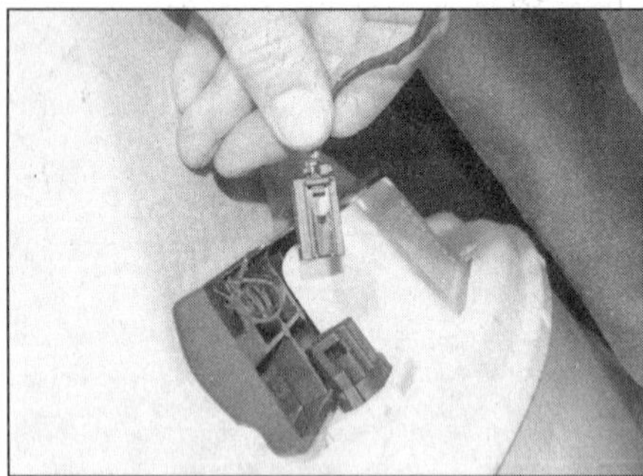

10.14 Disconnecting the wiring from the electric window switch

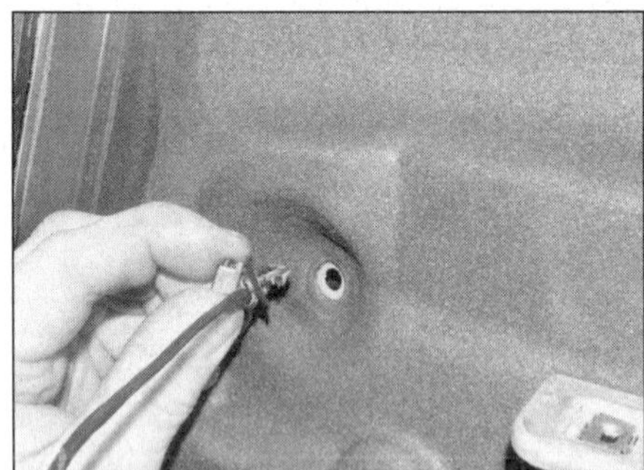

10.15a Prise out the loom clip . . .

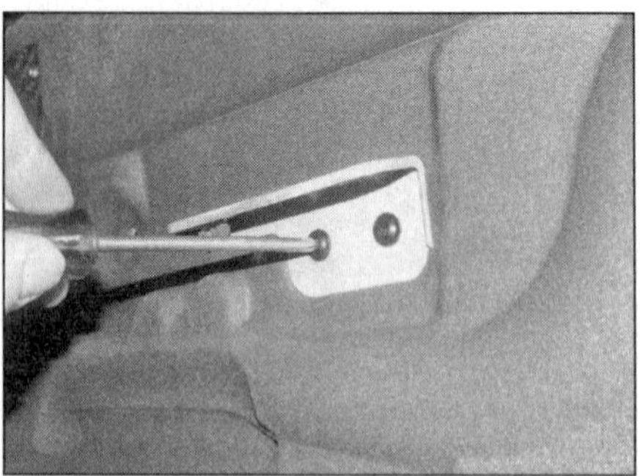

10.15b . . . remove the support bracket . . .

10.15c . . . remove the speaker . . .

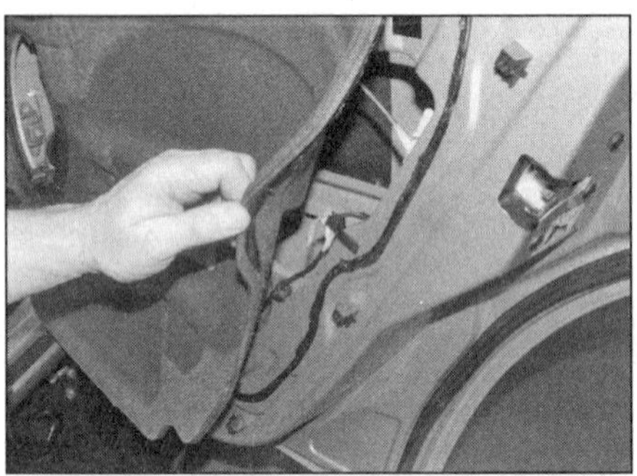

10.15d . . . then pull back the waterproof membrane

follows. Prise out the electric window wiring loom retaining clip, then undo the screws and remove the door handle support bracket. Undo the screws and remove the speaker from the door, then disconnect the wiring. The membrane is attached to the inner door panel with a bead of mastic adhesive – carefully pull back the membrane without tearing it, while using a knife to cut along the bead of adhesive **(see illustrations)**.

16 Place the membrane to one side, and protect the adhesive from dust and dirt so it can be used again.

Refitting

17 Refitting is a reversal of removal.

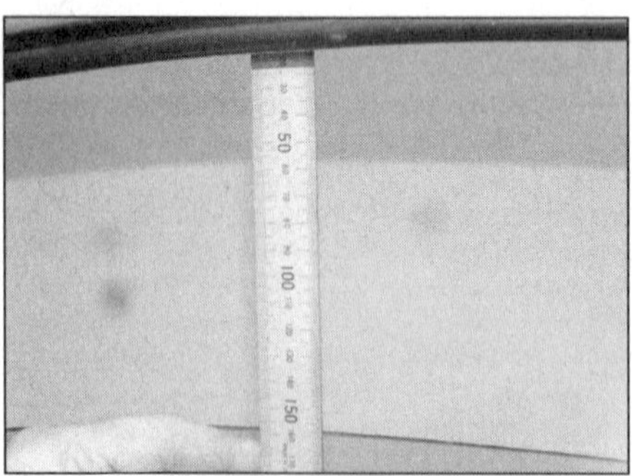

11.1 Lower the window glass 160 mm . . .

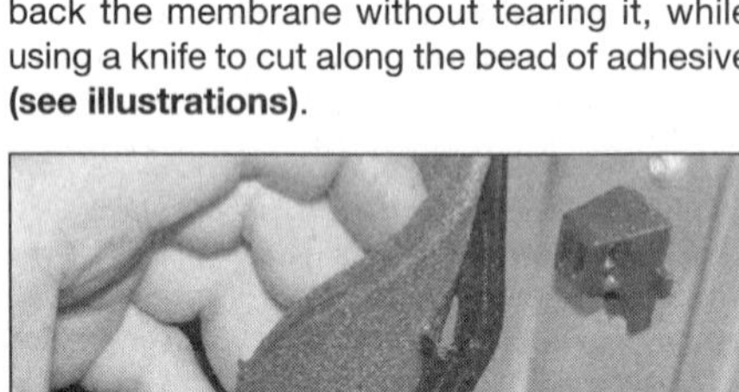

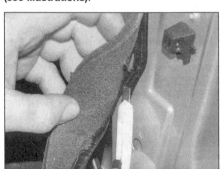

11.2 . . . remove the door inner trim panel and waterproof membrane . . .

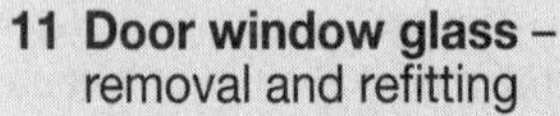

11 Door window glass – removal and refitting

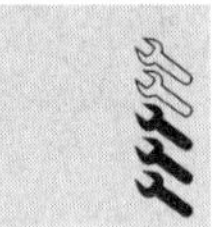

Removal

Front door

1 With the ignition temporarily switched on, lower the front door window glass 160 mm from its closed position **(see illustration)**.

2 Remove the front door inner trim panel and waterproof membrane as described in Section 10 **(see illustration)**.

3 Using a socket through the inner door panel apertures, loosen the clamp bolts securing the window regulator to the glass **(see illustration)**.

4 Carefully prise out the inner glass weatherstrip from the inner door panel **(see illustration)**.

5 Lift the rear edge of the glass, then tilt the glass forwards and remove it upwards from the outside of the door **(see illustration)**.

Rear door

6 Lower the rear door window glass 160 mm from its closed position **(see illustration)**. On models with electric windows, it will be necessary to temporarily switch on the ignition.

11.3 . . . loosen the clamp bolts securing the window regulator to the glass . . .

11.4 . . . remove the inner glass weatherstrip . . .

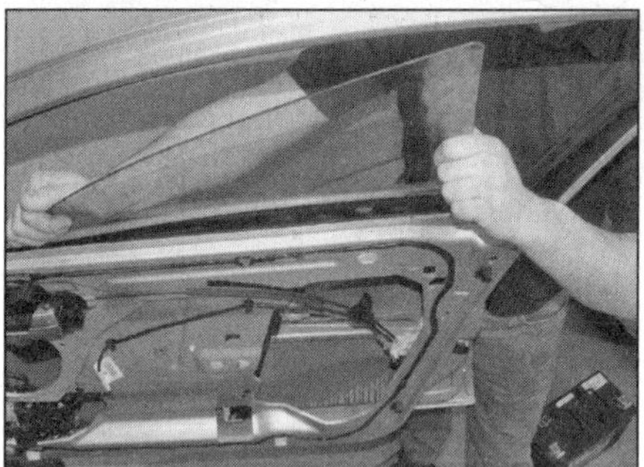

11.5 . . . and lift the glass from the outside of the front door

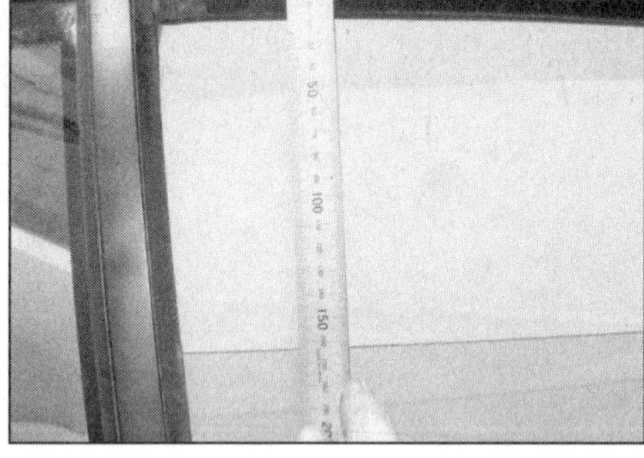

11.6 Lower the window glass 160 mm . . .

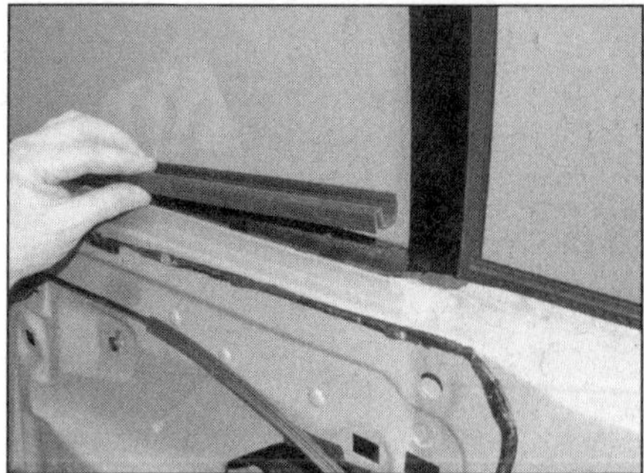

11.8 . . . and remove the inner glass weatherstrip

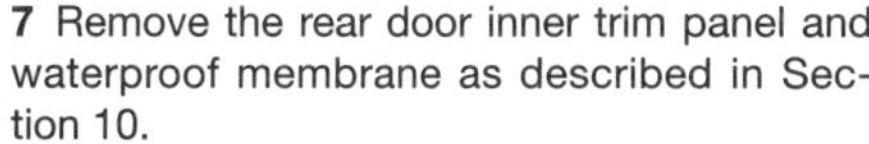

7 Remove the rear door inner trim panel and waterproof membrane as described in Section 10.

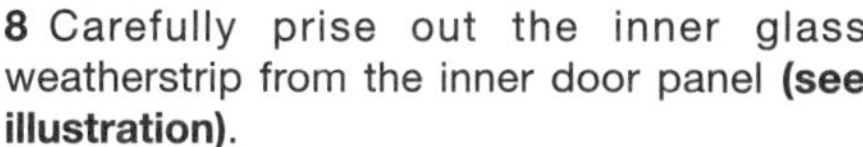

8 Carefully prise out the inner glass weatherstrip from the inner door panel **(see illustration)**.

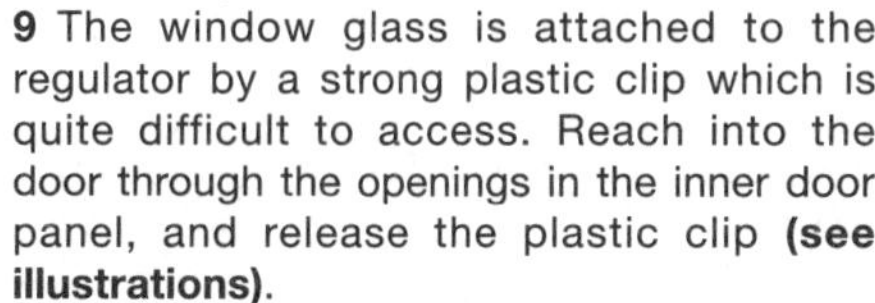

9 The window glass is attached to the regulator by a strong plastic clip which is quite difficult to access. Reach into the door through the openings in the inner door panel, and release the plastic clip **(see illustrations)**.

10 On Estate models, the rear quarter light must be removed from the rear door before removing the window glass. It is suggested that the window regulator is also removed to provide additional working room. Pull back the window channel rubber weatherstrip and remove the glass outer weatherstrip, then unclip the plastic outer cover, undo the retaining screws and withdraw the quarter light from the door **(see illustrations)**.

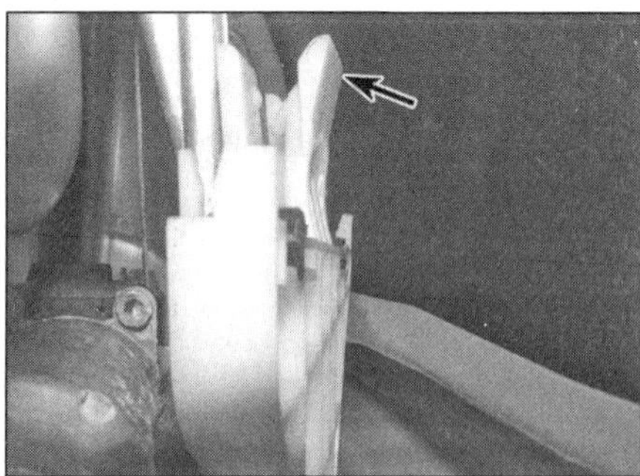

11.9a Plastic clip securing the window glass to the regulator

11 Tilt the window glass forwards, and carefully lift it from the outside of the door **(see illustration)**.

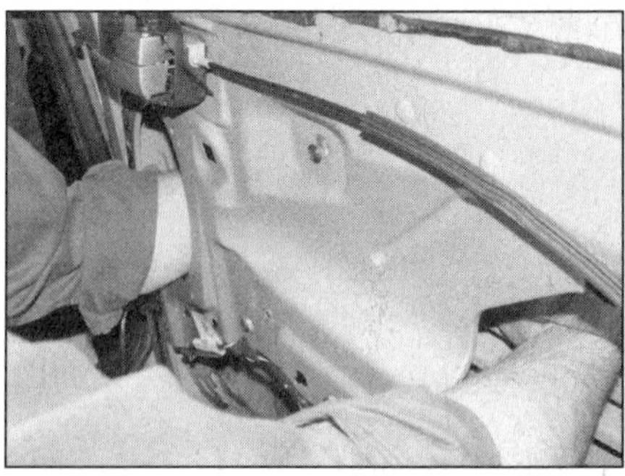

11.9b Reach through the two apertures to disconnect the clip

Refitting

12 Refitting is a reversal of the removal procedure, but initialise the electric windows as described in Section 12.

11.10a Pull back the window channel rubber weatherstrip . . .

11.10b . . . remove the glass outer weatherstrip . . .

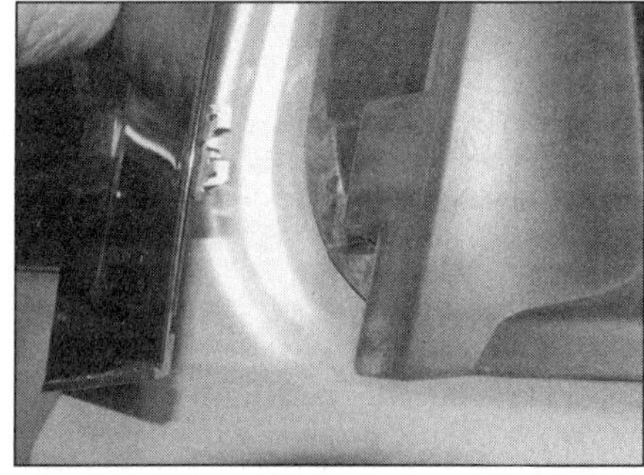

11.10c . . . unclip the plastic outer cover . . .

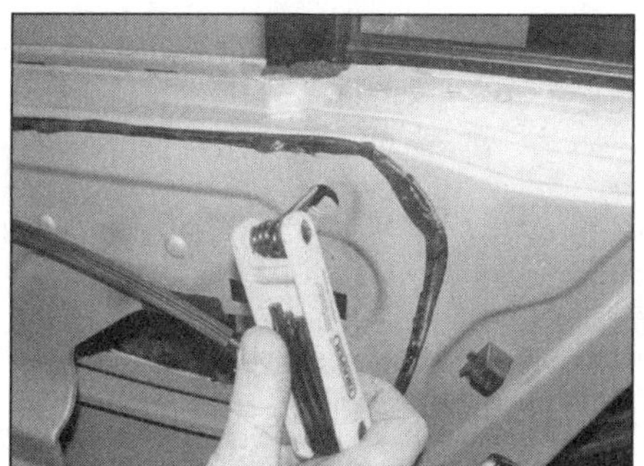

11.10d . . . undo the retaining screws . . .

11.10e . . . and withdraw the quarter light from the rear door

11.11 Removing the window glass from the rear door

12.2 Disconnecting the window regulator wiring

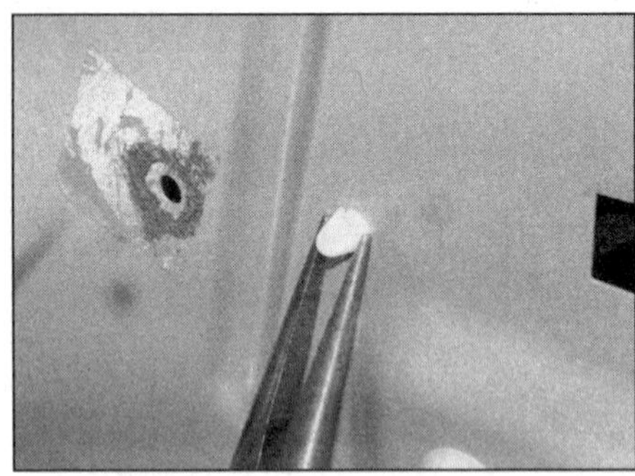
12.3a Release the plastic clip . . .

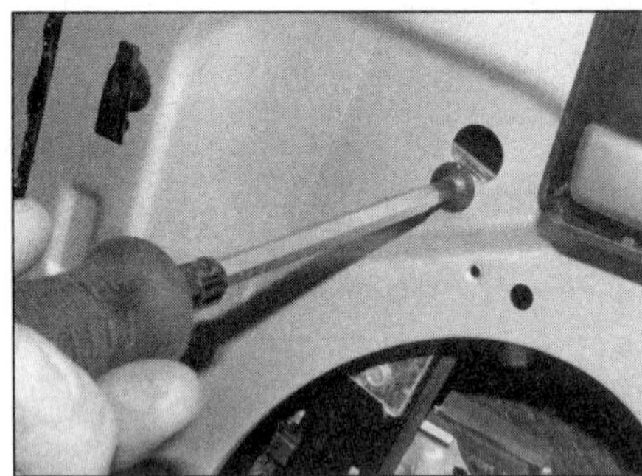
12.3b . . . then loosen the screws . . .

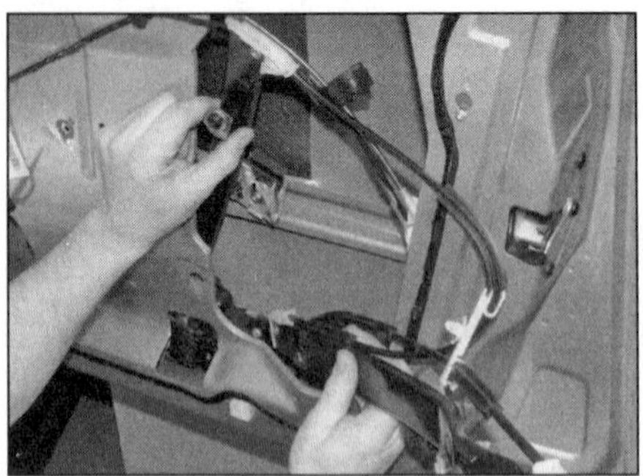
12.3c . . . and withdraw the regulator through the aperture in the inner door panel

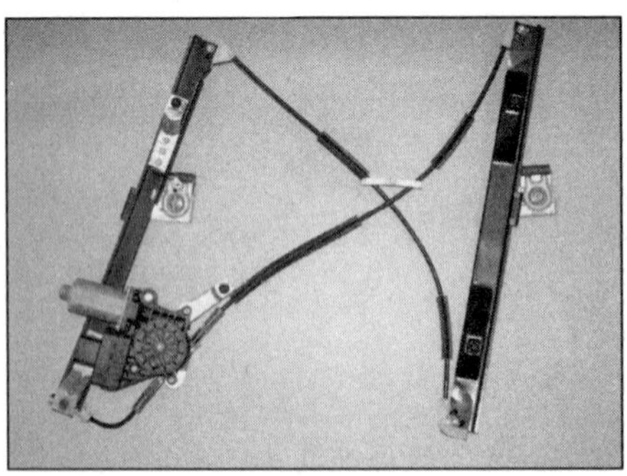
12.3d Window regulator removed from the front door

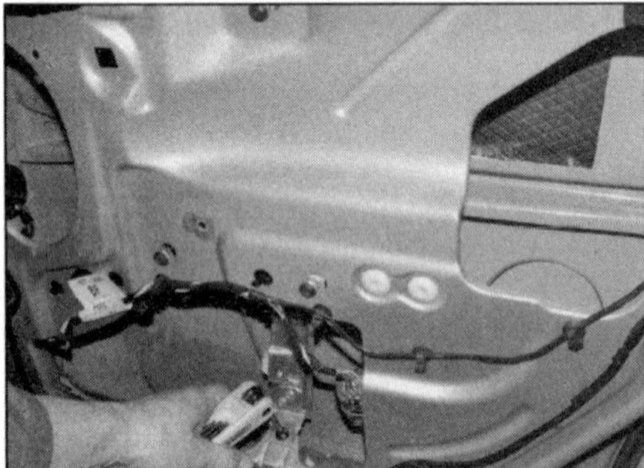
12.5 Unscrew the single lower mounting bolt . . .

12 Door window regulator and motor – removal, refitting and initialisation

Removal

Front door

1 Remove the front door window glass as described in Section 11.

2 Disconnect the wiring from the door window regulator **(see illustration)**.

3 Release the plastic clip, loosen (but do not remove) the five regulator retaining screws, then lift the regulator and move the screws through the larger holes in the inner panel. Carefully withdraw the regulator from the rear aperture in the door **(see illustrations)**.

Rear door

4 Remove the rear door window glass as described in Section 11.

5 If the regulator is still mounted, loosen (but do not remove) the three upper regulator mounting bolts, then unscrew and remove the single lower mounting bolt securing the regulator to the bottom of the door **(see illustration)**.

6 Disconnect the wiring from the regulator motor, then lift the regulator and move the bolts through the larger holes in the inner panel. Carefully withdraw the regulator from the bottom aperture in the door **(see illustrations)**.

Refitting and initialisation

7 Refitting is a reversal of the removal procedure. Tighten the mounting bolts securely and initialise each of the door window motors as follows.

8 First, make sure that there is no obstruction in the window aperture. With the ignition switched on, press the switch close button until the window is fully closed, then hold the button in the closed position for a further second. Release the close button, then depress again for one second, so that the system 'learns' the closed position.

9 Press the switch open button until the window is fully open, then release. Press the switch open button again for one second, to allow the system to 'learn' the open position.

10 Check that the window now opens and closes automatically, with just a brief touch on the switch – if not, repeat the initialisation procedure. Repeat the initialisation for the remaining window motors.

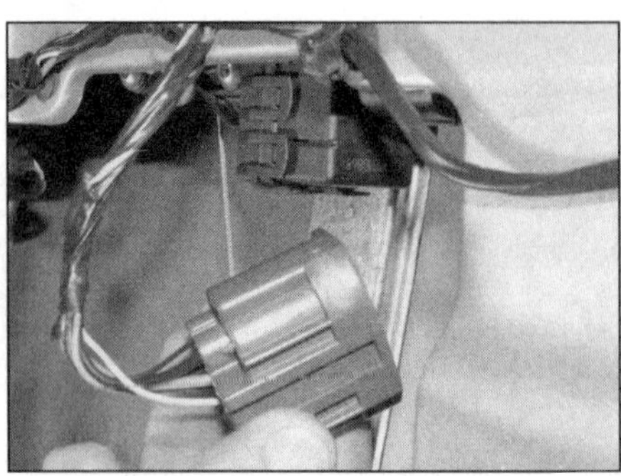
12.6a . . . then disconnect the wiring . . .

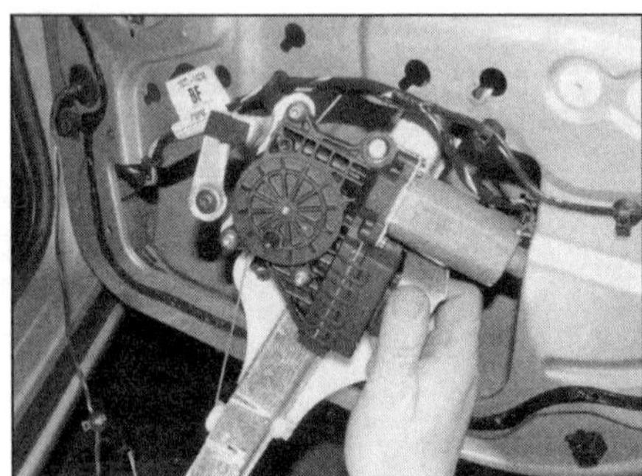
12.6b . . . and withdraw the regulator from the bottom aperture of the door

13 Door handle and lock components – removal and refitting

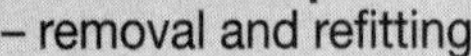

Front door lock and handle

Removal

1 With the door open, prise out the grommet from the rear edge of the door. Pull out and hold the exterior handle, then loosen the handle retaining screw using an Allen key **(see illustrations)**.

2 On the driver's side, lift out the private lock cover **(see illustration)**.

13.1a Prise out the grommet . . .

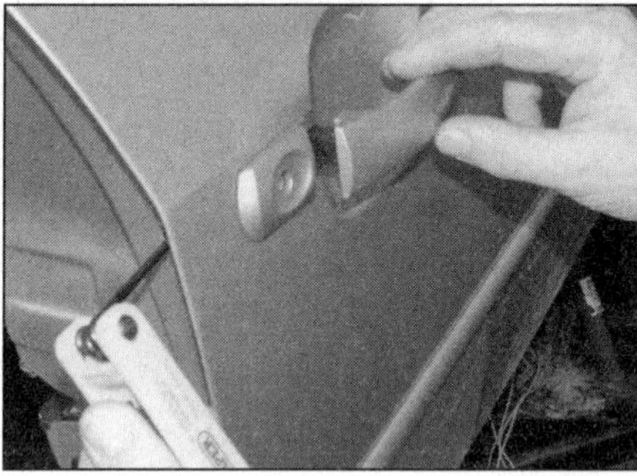
13.1b . . . pull out the exterior handle, and loosen the retaining screw with an Allen key

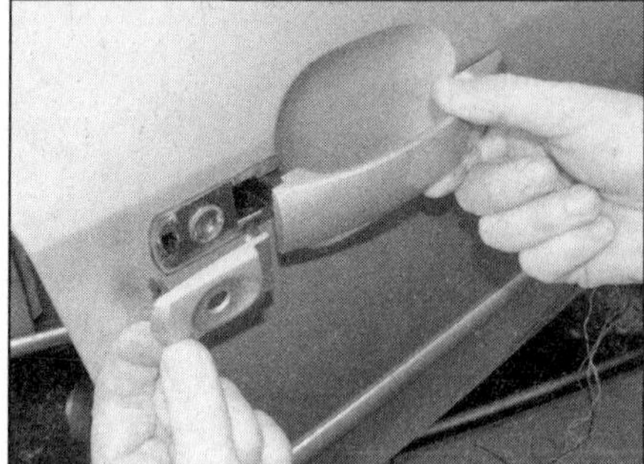
13.2 Remove the private lock cover from the driver's side

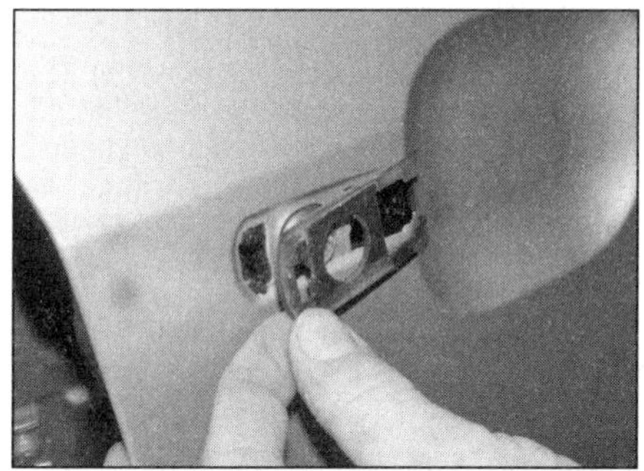
13.3 Removing the exterior handle rubber gasket

13.5a Undo the screw and remove the spacer . . .

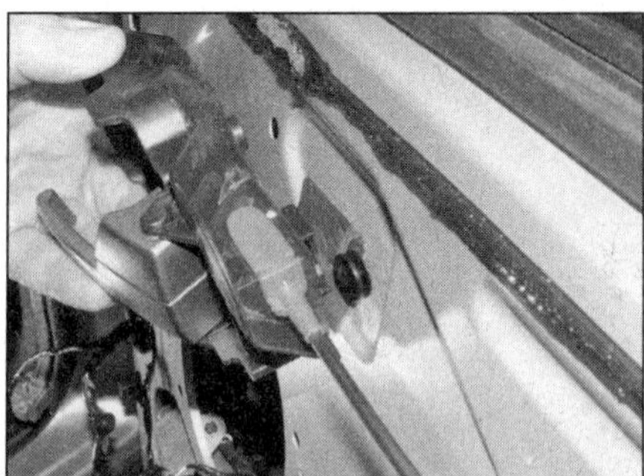
13.5b . . . and release the inner door handle from the door

3 Slide the door handle rearwards and withdraw it from the door. Recover the rubber gasket **(see illustration)**.

4 Remove the door inner trim panel and waterproof membrane as described in Section 10.

5 Undo the screw securing the inner door handle to the door, remove the spacer, and release the handle from the door **(see illustrations)**.

6 Disconnect the wiring from the door lock actuator **(see illustration)**.

7 Working through the aperture in the inner door panel, loosen (do not remove completely) the screw from the reinforcement plate **(see illustration)**. Slide the plate towards the front of the door and release the locking tangs from the slots in the outer door panel.

8 Unscrew the lock retaining screws from the rear edge of the door, and withdraw the lock complete with inner handle from the door **(see illustrations)**.

9 With the lock assembly on the bench, undo the screws and remove the security shield **(see illustration)**. Some 3.0 litre ST models have a security shield which is riveted on.

10 Release the clips and disconnect the connecting rods from the lock. Where

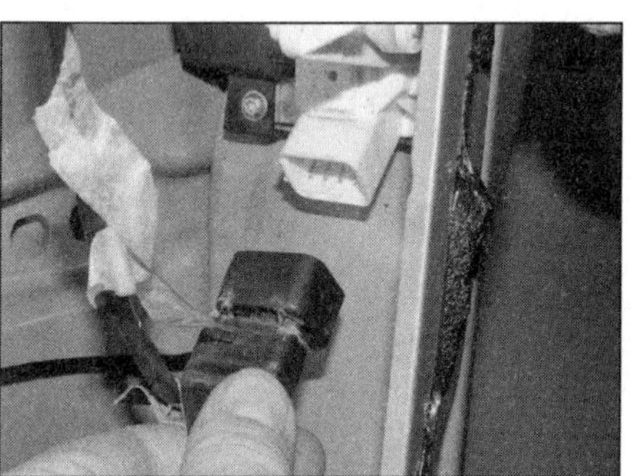
13.6 Disconnecting the wiring from the door lock actuator

13.7 Loosen the screw from the reinforcement plate

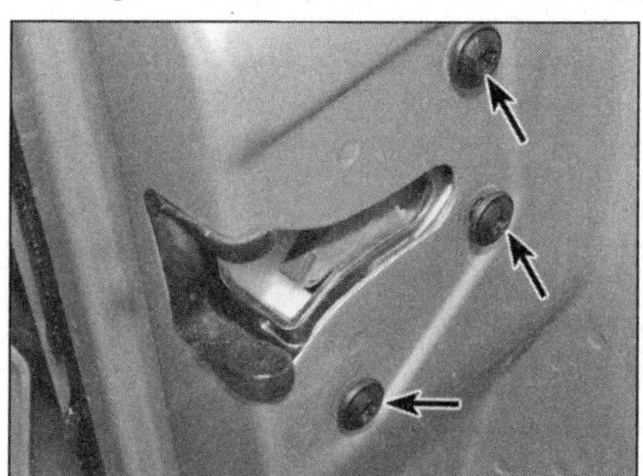
13.8a Undo the retaining screws . . .

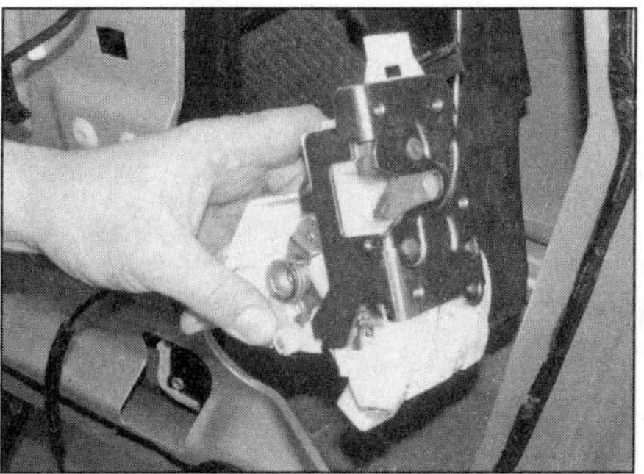
13.8b . . . and withdraw the lock and inner handle from the door

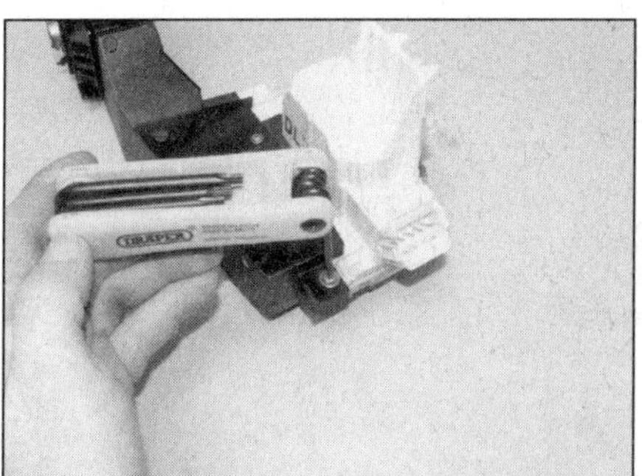

13.9 Undo the screws and remove the security shield

13.10a Disconnecting the rods . . .

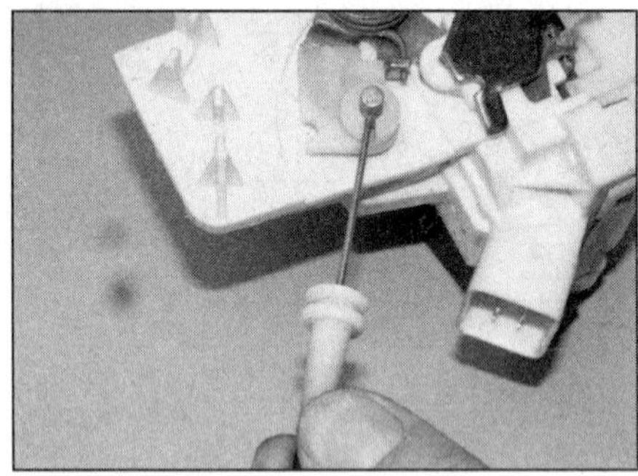
13.10b . . . and cable

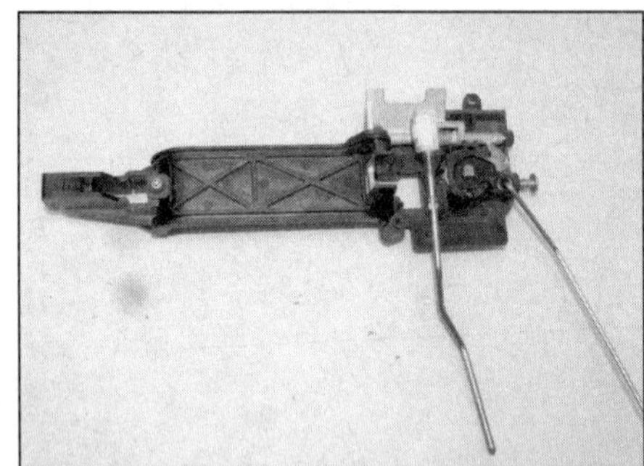
13.10c Private lock and security housing

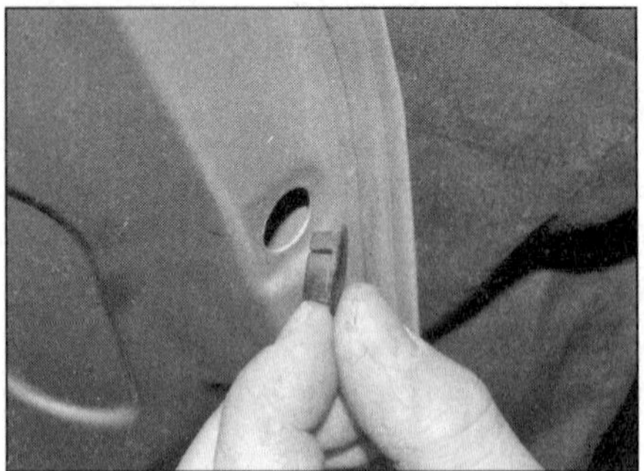
13.15a Prise out the grommet . . .

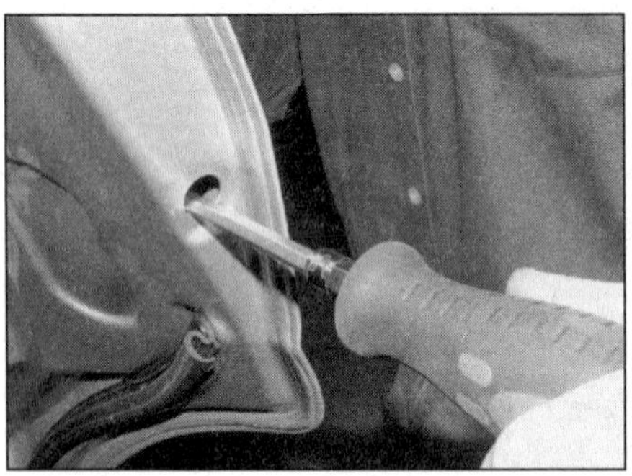
13.15b . . . and loosen the handle retaining screw

necessary, rotate the rod through 90° to align the tab with the cut-out. Also disconnect the inner handle cable **(see illustrations)**.

11 Unclip the adjustment clip from the reinforcement plate. **Note:** *Ford recommend that the clip is renewed.*

12 It is not possible to remove the private lock cylinder separately.

Refitting

13 Refitting is a reversal of removal. The adjustment clip should be fitted so that the lock is released after the exterior handle has moved approximately 22.0 mm from its closed position. There should then be approximately 5.0 to 6.0 mm of handle movement after the lock has been released. When closing the door slowly, there must be two audible clicks as the lock engages.

Rear door lock and handle

Removal

14 Remove the door inner trim panel and waterproof membrane as described in Section 10.

15 Prise out the grommet from the rear edge of the door. Pull out and hold the exterior handle, then loosen the handle retaining screw using an Allen key **(see illustrations)**.

16 Slide the door handle rearwards and withdraw it from the door. Remove the cover and rubber gasket **(see illustrations)**.

17 Undo the screw securing the inner door handle to the door, remove the spacer, and release the handle from the door **(see illustrations)**.

18 Disconnect the wiring from the door lock actuator **(see illustration)**.

19 Working through the aperture in the inner door panel, loosen (do not remove completely) the screw from the reinforcement plate. Slide the plate towards the front of the door and release the locking tangs from the slots in the door **(see illustrations)**.

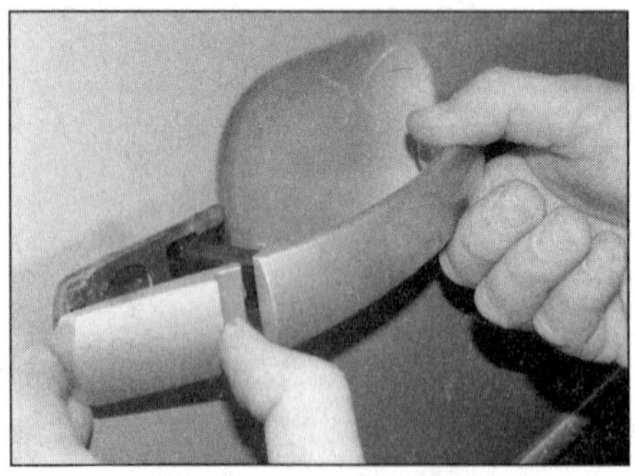
13.16a Remove the handle and cover . . .

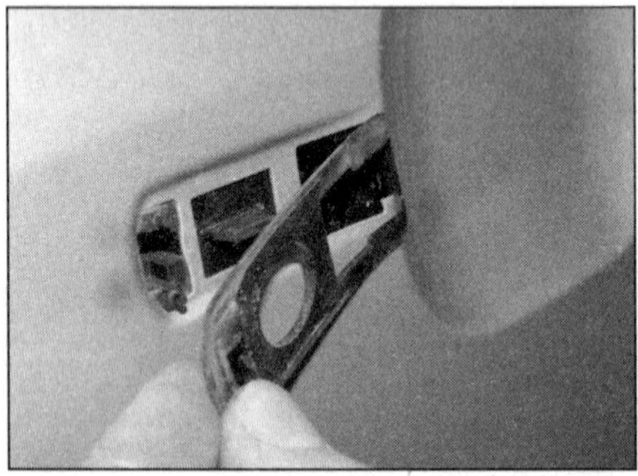
13.16b . . . followed by the rubber gasket

13.17a Undo the screw . . .

13.17b . . . remove the spacer . . .

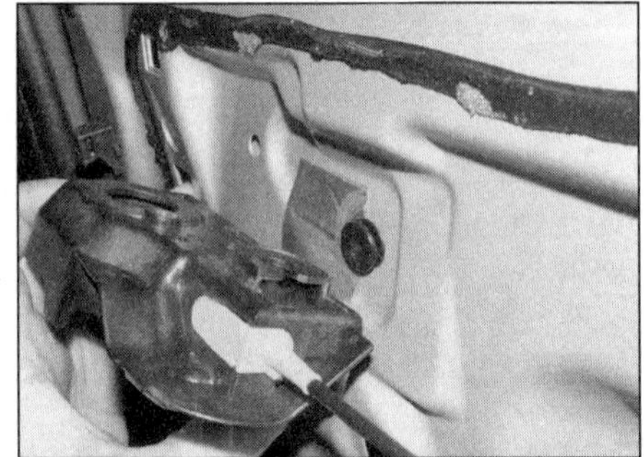
13.17c . . . and release the inner handle from the door

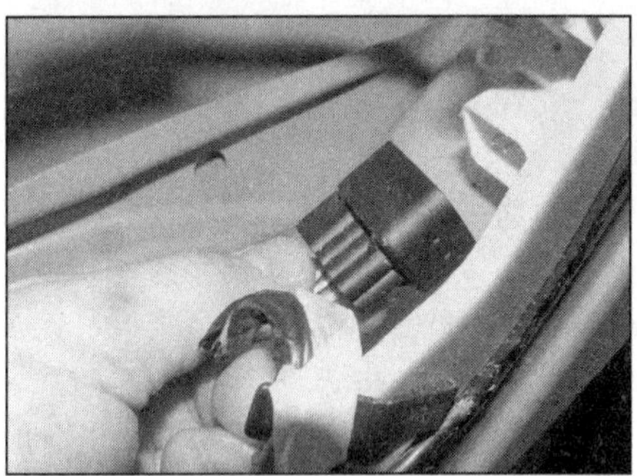

13.18 Disconnect the door lock actuator wiring . . .

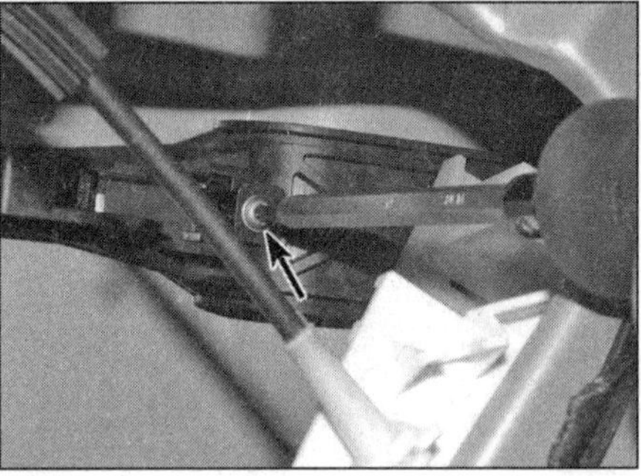

13.19a . . . loosen the reinforcement plate screw . . .

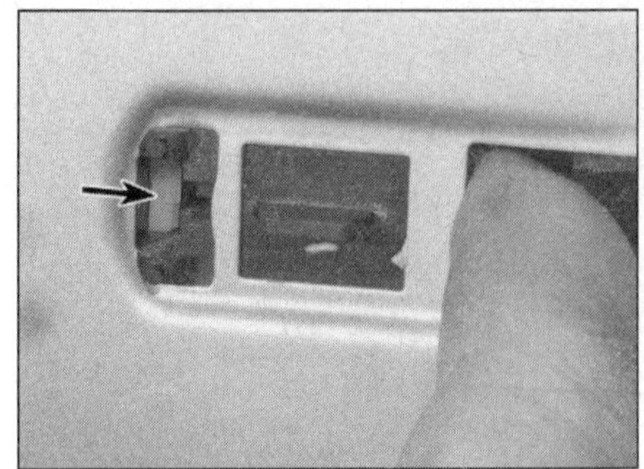

13.19b . . . and slide the plate to release the locking tangs from the door

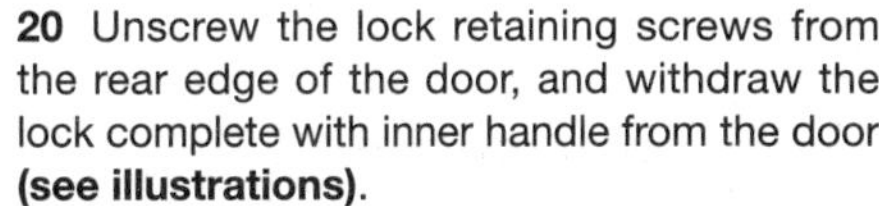

20 Unscrew the lock retaining screws from the rear edge of the door, and withdraw the lock complete with inner handle from the door **(see illustrations)**.

21 With the lock assembly on the bench, use a pair of pliers to squeeze the plastic clip, then remove the reinforcement plate from the lock **(see illustrations)**.

22 Release the clips and disconnect the connecting rods from the lock. Where necessary, rotate the rod through 90° to align the tab with the cut-out. Also disconnect the inner handle cable **(see illustrations)**.

23 Unclip the adjustment clip from the connecting rod. **Note:** *Ford recommend that the clip is renewed.*

Refitting

24 Refitting is a reversal of removal. The adjustment clip should be fitted so that the lock is released after the exterior handle has moved approximately 22.0 mm from its closed position **(see illustrations)**. There should then be approximately 5.0 to 6.0 mm of handle movement after the lock has been released. When closing the door slowly, there must be two audible clicks as the lock engages.

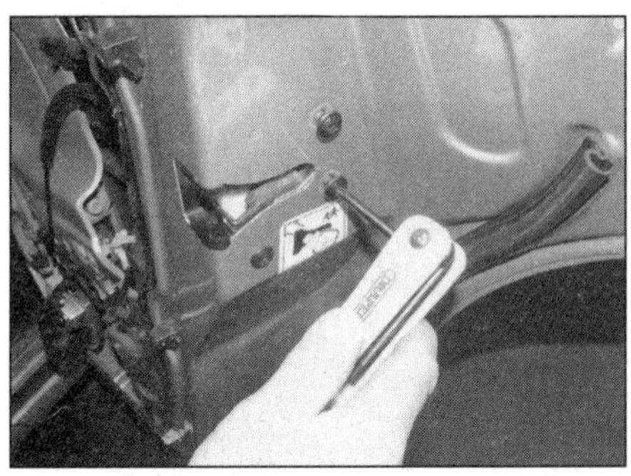

13.20a Unscrew the lock retaining screws . . .

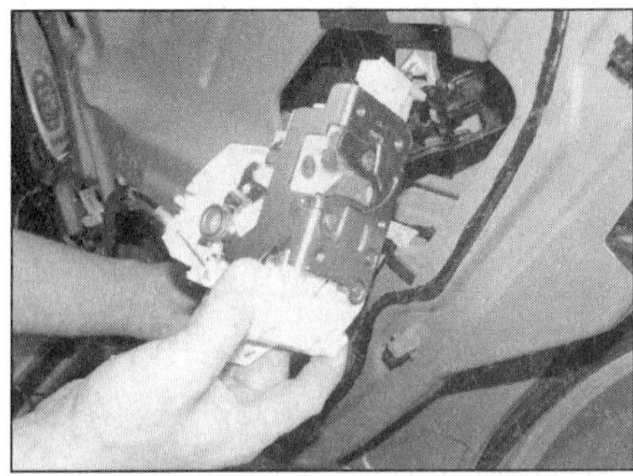

13.20b . . . and withdraw the lock complete with inner handle from the door

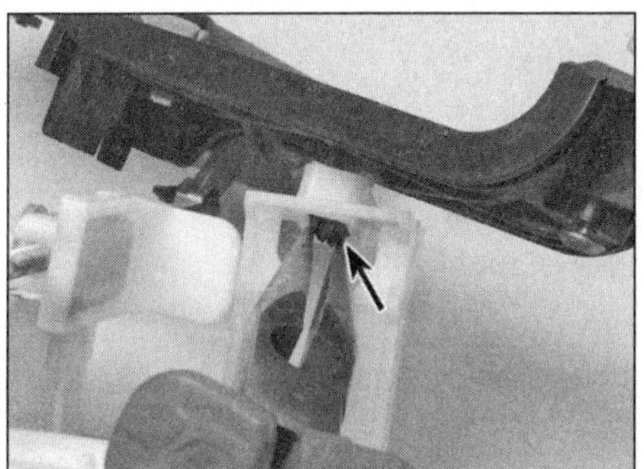

13.21a Squeeze the plastic clip . . .

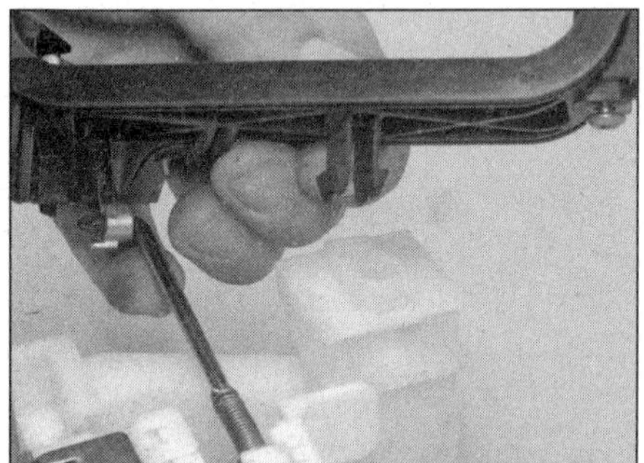

13.21b . . . and disconnect the reinforcement plate from the lock

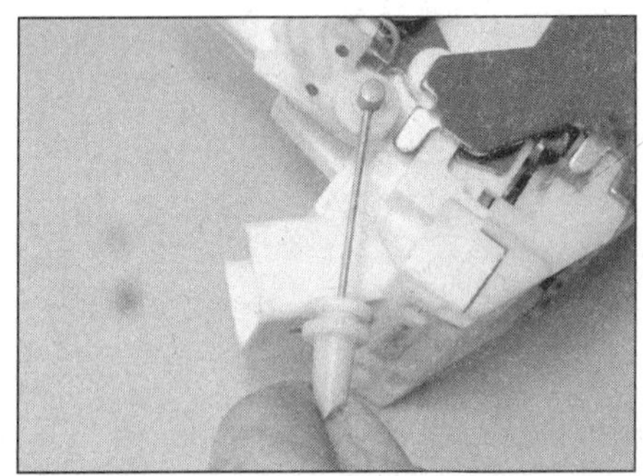

13.22a Disconnecting the cable from the lock . . .

13.22b . . . and interior door handle

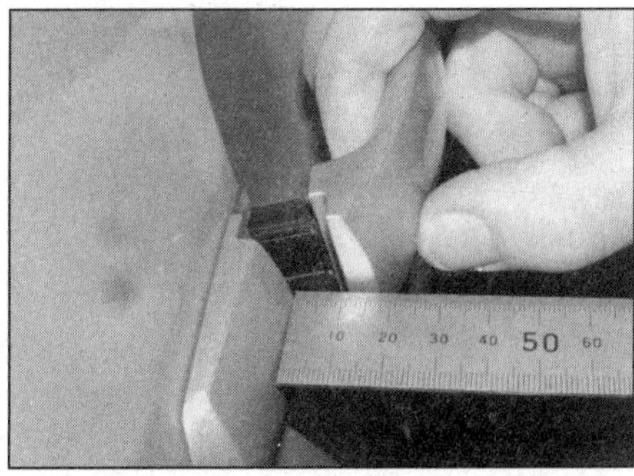

13.24a The lock must release with the handle 22.0 mm from its closed position

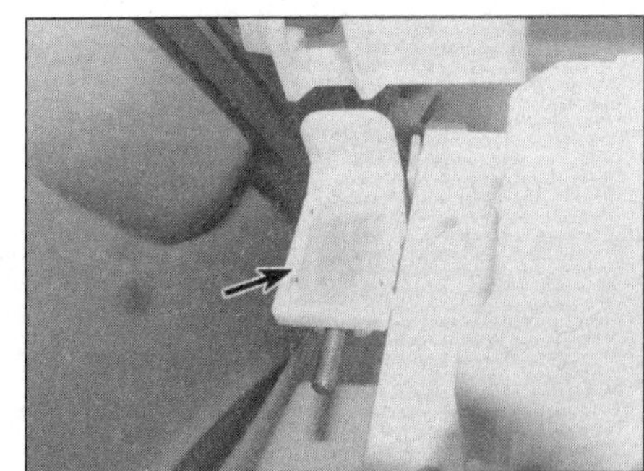

13.24b The lock adjustment clip

13.25 Front door striker on the B-pillar

13.26a Remove the kick panel . . .

13.26b . . . then unscrew the striker mounting bolts

13.27 The striker can be adjusted with the kick panel in position

13.29 Torx bolt securing the check strap to the door pillar

Strikers

Removal

25 To remove a door striker, first mark its position with a pencil to assist refitting. Use an Allen key to undo the retaining screws and remove the striker from the door pillar **(see illustration)**.

26 To remove the tailgate striker, first undo the screws and remove the kick panel. Mark the position of the striker with a pencil, then undo the screws and remove it from the rear valance **(see illustrations)**.

Refitting

27 Refitting is a reversal of removal. Adjust the position of the striker so that it enters the lock centrally. Note that on Estate models, the position of the striker may be adjusted without removing the kick panel **(see illustration)**.

Check straps

Removal

28 Remove the door inner trim panel as described in Section 10.

29 Using a Torx key, unscrew the bolt securing the strap to the door pillar **(see illustration)**.

30 Unscrew the mounting nuts and withdraw the check strap from inside the door.

Refitting

31 Refitting is a reversal of removal.

14.2 Door check strap

14.3 Wiring connector on the door pillar

14.4 Small circlip retaining the pin in the hinge brackets

14.6 Bolts securing the hinge bracket to the door pillar

14 Door – removal and refitting

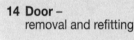

Removal

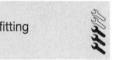

1 Disconnect the battery negative lead (refer to *Disconnecting the battery* at the end of this manual).

2 Using a Torx key, unscrew and remove the check strap mounting screw from the door pillar **(see illustration)**.

3 Disconnect the wiring connector by twisting it anti-clockwise **(see illustration)**.

4 Extract the small circlips from the upper and lower hinge pins. The upper circlip is at the top of the pin, whereas the lower circlip is at the bottom of the pin **(see illustration)**.

5 Have an assistant support the weight of the door, then drive the hinge pins through the hinges using a small drift. Carefully lift the door from the hinges.

6 If required, the hinge brackets can be unbolted from the door and pillar **(see illustration)**. Access to the inner bolt will require the inner trim to be removed.

14.7 Front door striker on the B-pillar

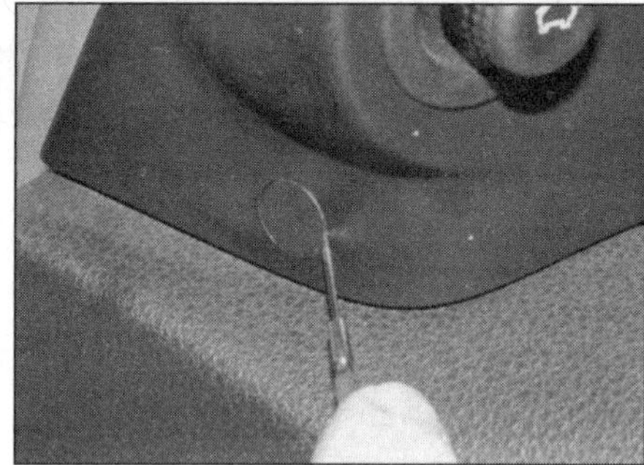

15.1a Prise out the plastic cover . . .

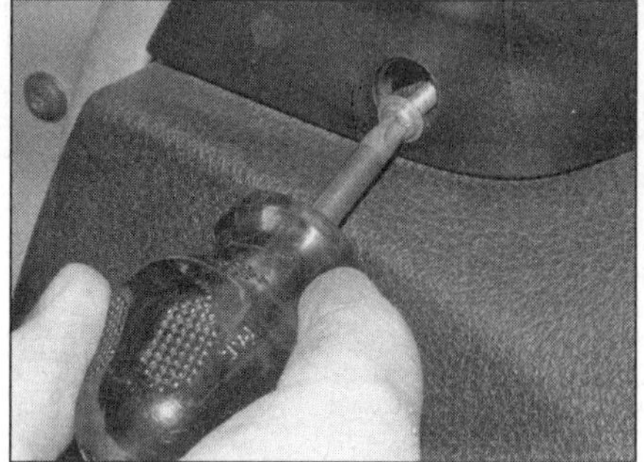

15.1b . . . undo the screw . . .

Refitting

7 Refitting is a reversal of the removal procedure, but check that the door lock passes over the striker centrally **(see illustration)**. If necessary, reposition the striker.

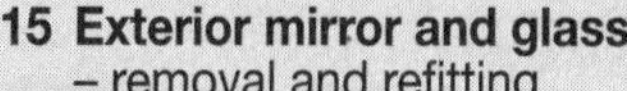

15 Exterior mirror and glass – removal and refitting

Exterior mirror

Removal

1 Prise out the plastic cover, then undo the screw securing the inner trim and switch to the door panel. Disconnect the switch wiring and remove the trim **(see illustrations)**. Remove the door inner trim panel as described in Section 10 and disconnect the mirror wiring.

2 Support the exterior mirror, then undo the retaining screws using an Allen key **(see illustration)**.

3 Withdraw the mirror from the outside of the door while feeding the wiring through the hole **(see illustration)**.

Refitting

4 Refitting is a reversal of removal.

Exterior mirror glass

Removal

5 Position the glass so that its outer edge is towards the rear of the car.

6 Using a screwdriver, carefully depress the plastic tags and release the mirror and holder from the articulated base **(see illustrations)**.

Refitting

7 Locate the mirror on the base, and, using a wad of cloth, carefully press on the mirror until the plastic tags engage.

16 Interior mirror – removal and refitting

Removal

1 Where applicable for models with auto-dimming, disconnect the wiring from the base of the interior mirror.

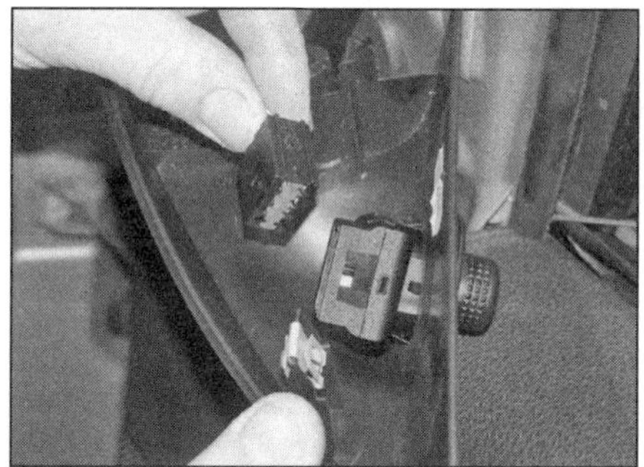

15.1c . . . then remove the trim and disconnect the wiring

15.2 Undo the screws . . .

2 Ford technicians use a special puller tool to release the locking tag holding the mirror joint housing on the windscreen bracket. The tool is tightened onto the housing then pushed upwards to release the locking tag, however, careful use of a screwdriver will release the tag **(see illustration)**.

3 With the locking tag released, support the

15.3 . . . and withdraw the exterior mirror from the door

15.6a Depress the plastic tags to release the mirror from its base

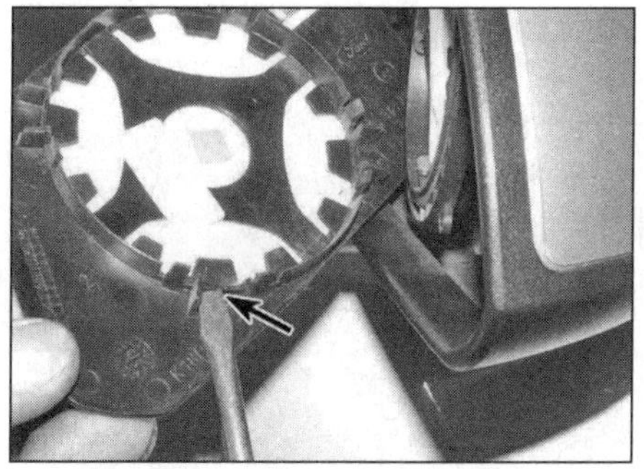

15.6b Plastic tag shown with the mirror removed

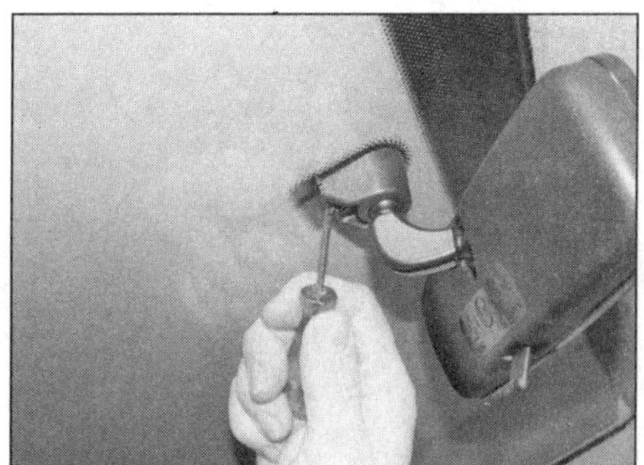

16.2 Release the tag . . .

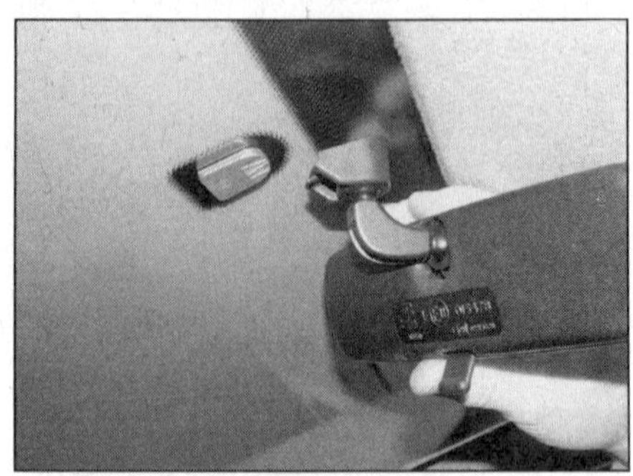

16.3 . . . then withdraw the interior mirror

interior mirror, then, if necessary, use a wooden block and hammer to tap the housing from the windscreen bracket **(see illustration)**.

Caution: Only tap the bracket lightly, to prevent damage/breakage to the windscreen.

Refitting

4 Locate the mirror socket housing on the mounting bracket, and push it downwards until it locks into position. It may be necessary to use the wooden block and hammer to ensure the housing is locked onto the bracket.

5 Where applicable, reconnect the auto-dimming wiring.

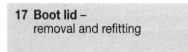

17 Boot lid – removal and refitting

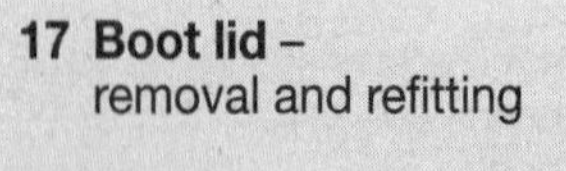

Removal

1 Disconnect the battery negative lead (refer to *Disconnecting the battery* at the end of this manual), and open the boot lid.

2 Have an assistant support the open boot lid, then disconnect the support strut from the ball on the hinge.

3 Where fitted, remove the trim from inside the boot lid.

4 Disconnect the wiring at the connectors visible through the boot lid inner skin aperture.

5 Attach a length of strong cord to the end of the wires in the aperture, to act as an aid to guiding the wiring through the lid when it is refitted.

6 Withdraw the wiring loom through the boot lid apertures. Untie the cord, and leave it in the boot lid.

7 Mark the position of the hinge arms with a pencil.

8 Place rags beneath each corner of the boot lid, to prevent damage to the paintwork.

9 With the help of an assistant, unscrew the mounting bolts and lift the boot lid from the car.

Refitting

10 Refitting is a reversal of the removal procedure, but check that the boot lid is correctly aligned with the surrounding bodywork, with equal clearance around its edge. Adjustment is made by loosening the hinge bolts and moving the boot lid within the elongated mounting holes. Check that the striker enters the lock centrally when the boot lid is closed. If necessary, loosen the striker retaining bolts, reposition the striker, then retighten them. If new components have been fitted, carry out the following adjustment procedure.

11 Loosen the three striker mounting bolts, then pull off the weatherstrip from the boot lid opening.

12 Unscrew and remove the bump stops from the boot lid. Have an assistant support the boot lid, then prise out the spring clips and remove the support struts.

13 Loosen the bolts securing the hinges to the body, adjust the hinges to the centre of the elongated holes, and retighten the bolts.

14 Loosen the bolts securing the hinges to the boot lid, then finger-tighten them to allow adjustment of the boot lid position.

15 Lower the boot lid and adjust its position so that equal clearances exist on each side. It should be possible to insert a 4.0 mm thick spacer between the boot lid and rear quarter panel on each side.

16 Carefully open the boot lid, taking care not to move the hinges, then fully tighten the boot lid-to-hinge bolts to the specified torque.

17 Loosen the two hinge-to-body bolts on each side, then finger-tighten them. Close the boot lid and position the boot so that it is 2.0 mm below the rear quarter panels. Carefully raise the boot lid, then fully tighten the bolts to the specified torque.

18 Refit the support struts, bump stops and weatherstrip, then check the striker as described in paragraph 10 and tighten the retaining bolts.

18 Boot lid lock – removal and refitting

Removal

1 Disconnect the battery negative lead (refer to *Disconnecting the battery* at the end of this manual).

2 With the boot lid open, remove the inner trim panels.

3 Undo the screws and remove the cover from the boot lid lock.

4 Disconnect the wiring and cable.

5 Mark the position of the lock, for use when refitting. Using a Torx key, unscrew the lock mounting screws, and withdraw the lock.

Refitting

6 Refitting is a reversal of removal, but use the alignment marks made on removal to ensure that the lock is positioned accurately.

19 Tailgate – removal and refitting

Removal

1 Disconnect the battery negative lead (refer to *Disconnecting the battery* at the end of this manual).

2 With the tailgate open, undo the screws and remove the handgrip **(see illustration)**.

3 Using a wide-bladed screwdriver, carefully prise away the window surround trim, then similarly prise away the tailgate trim **(see illustrations)**. Locate the screwdriver near the retaining clips when releasing the clips.

4 Note the location and routing of the wiring loom, then disconnect it from each component in the tailgate, including the heated rear window **(see illustration)**.

5 Prise out the wiring rubber gaiter from the top edge of the tailgate, and carefully remove the wiring loom. Also disconnect and remove the tailgate washer tubing.

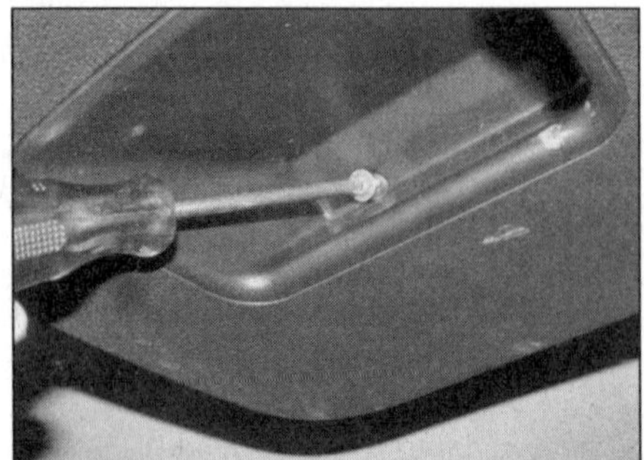

19.2 Removing the handgrip from the tailgate

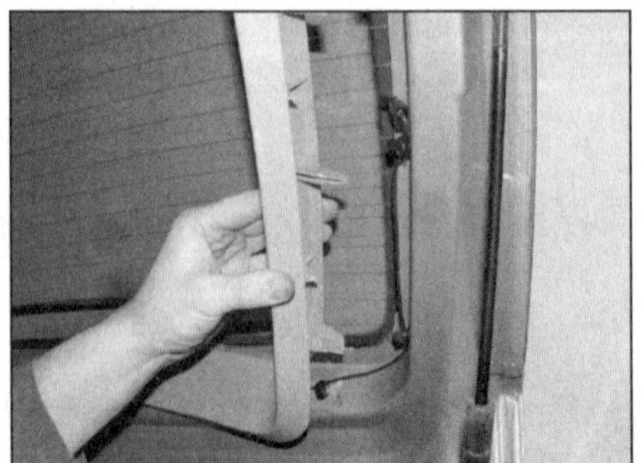

19.3a Removing the window surround trim . . .

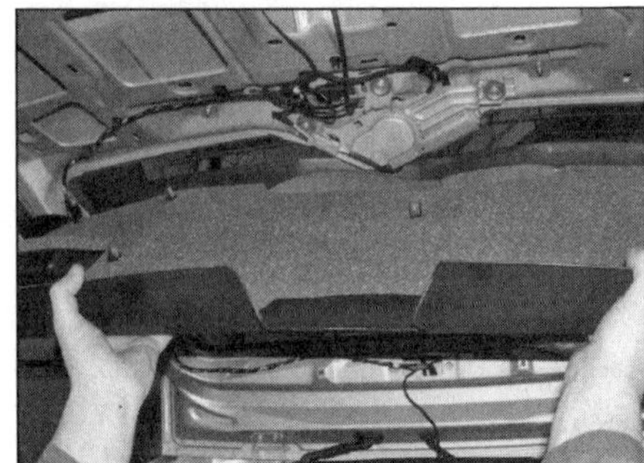

19.3b . . . and tailgate trim

6 Have an assistant support the tailgate. Using a screwdriver, prise out the spring clips and disconnect the support struts from the tailgate. Lower the struts into the rear luggage compartment.
7 Use a pencil to mark the position of the hinges on the tailgate, then unscrew the bolts and lift away the tailgate **(see illustration)**.

Refitting

8 Refitting is a reversal of the removal procedure, but check that the tailgate is located centrally in the body aperture, and that the striker enters the lock centrally. If necessary, loosen the mounting bolts and reposition the tailgate as required.

19.4 Wiring to the heated rear window

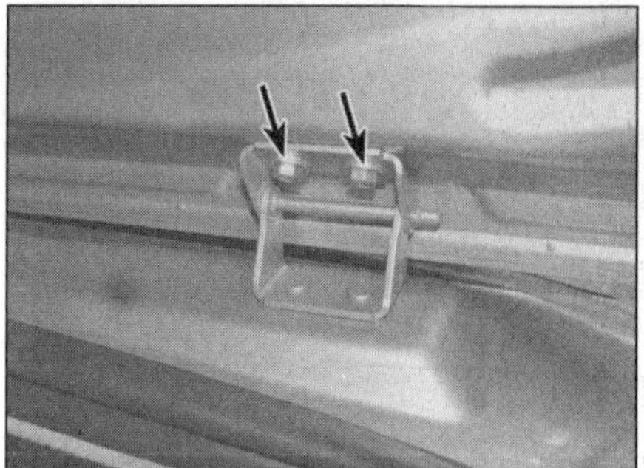

19.7 Bolts securing the tailgate to the hinges

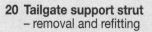

20 Tailgate support strut – removal and refitting

Removal

1 Support the tailgate in its open position.
2 Prise off the upper spring clip securing the strut to the tailgate, then pull the socket from the ball-stud **(see illustration)**.
3 Similarly prise off the bottom clip, and pull the socket from the ball-stud. Withdraw the strut.

Refitting

4 Refitting is a reversal of the removal procedure, but make sure that the narrow (piston) end of the strut is fitted on the tailgate (ie, upwards).

20.2 Prising off the tailgate support strut upper spring clip

21 Tailgate lock components – removal and refitting

Private lock

Removal

1 With the tailgate open, undo the trim retaining screws, noting that some are located within the handgrips and some are beneath plastic covers **(see illustration)**.
2 Using a wide-bladed screwdriver, carefully prise away the window surround trim, then similarly prise away the tailgate trim. Locate the screwdriver near the retaining clips when releasing the clips **(see illustrations)**.
3 Disconnect the wiring from the rear of the number plate illumination cross-panel. Undo the retaining nuts and withdraw the panel from the tailgate, and at the same time disconnect the wiring from the number plate illumination lights. Disconnect the wiring and cable, then unscrew the mounting nuts and remove the private lock from the tailgate **(see illustrations)**. It is not possible to remove the lock cylinder separately.

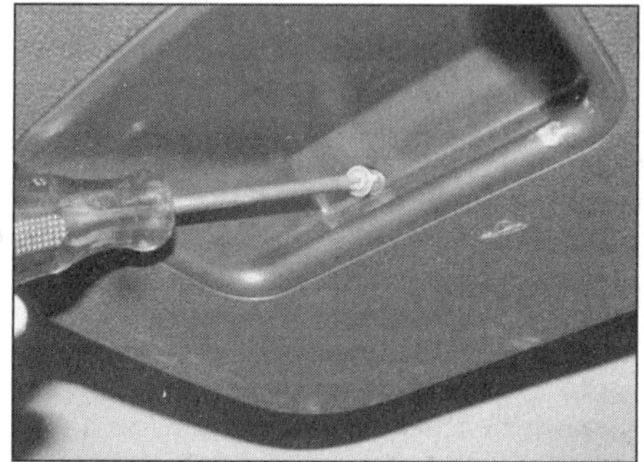

21.1 Removing the handgrip from the tailgate trim

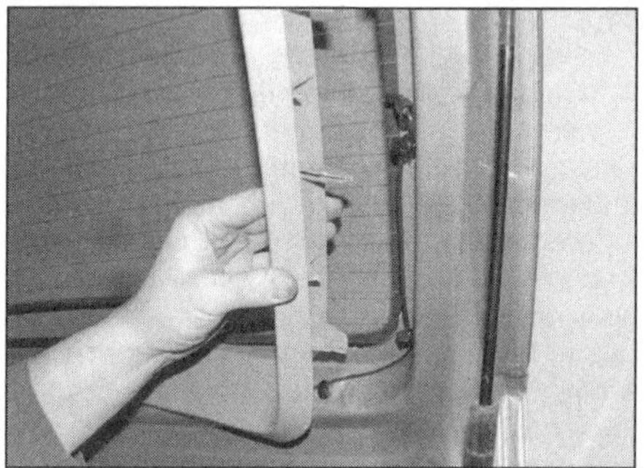

21.2a Removing the window surround trim . . .

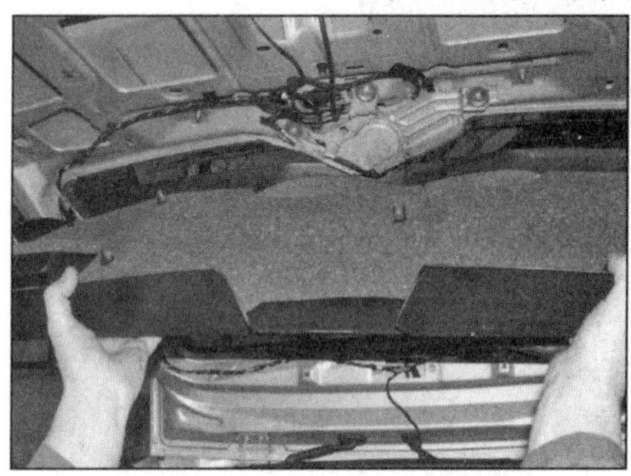

21.2b . . . and the tailgate trim

21.3a Disconnect the wiring . . .

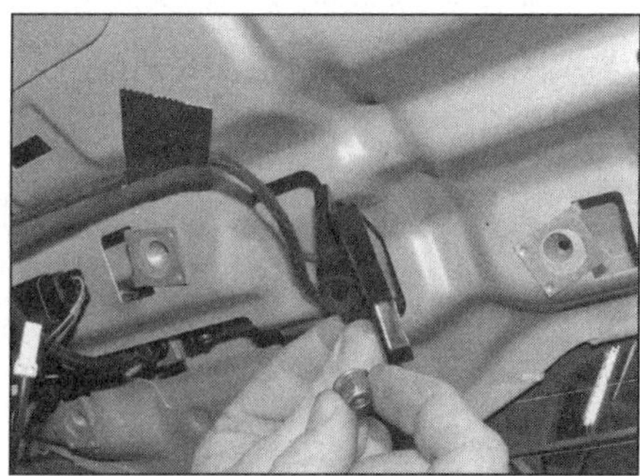

21.3b . . . then unscrew the mounting nuts . . .

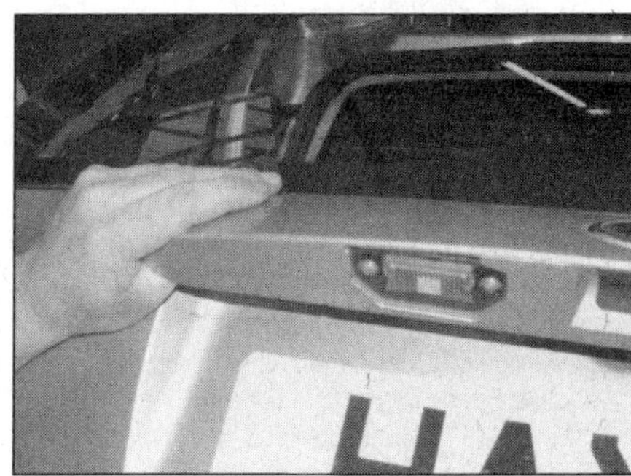

21.3c . . . withdraw the number plate illumination cross-panel . . .

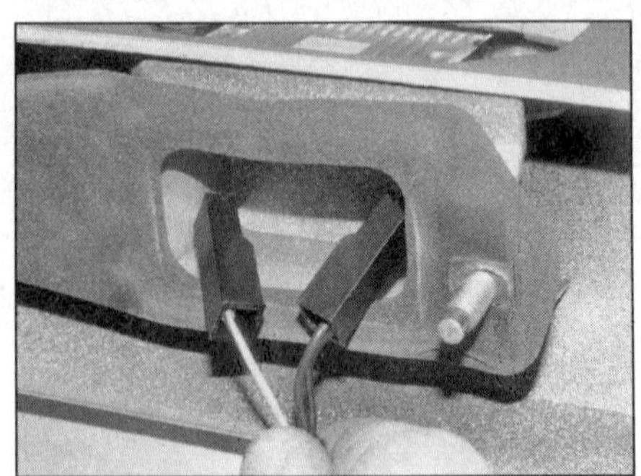
21.3d . . . disconnect the wiring

21.3e Unscrew the nuts . . .

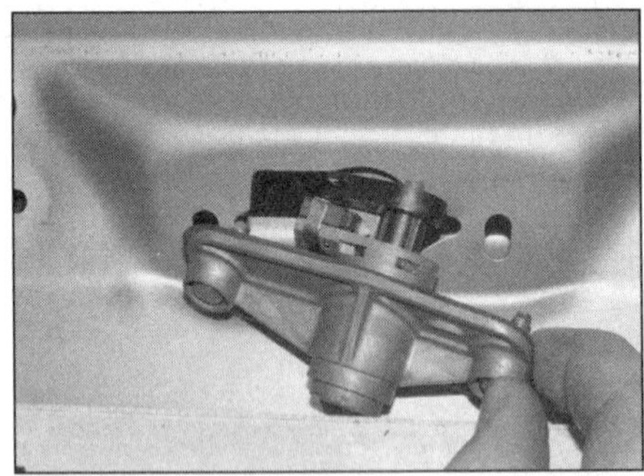
21.3f . . . and remove the private lock

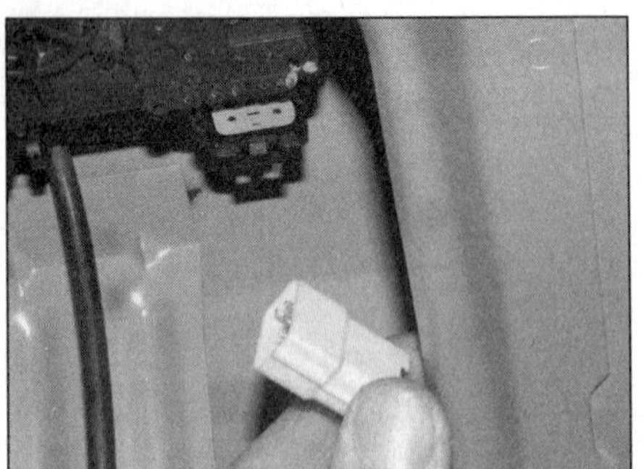
21.7a Disconnect the wiring and cable . . .

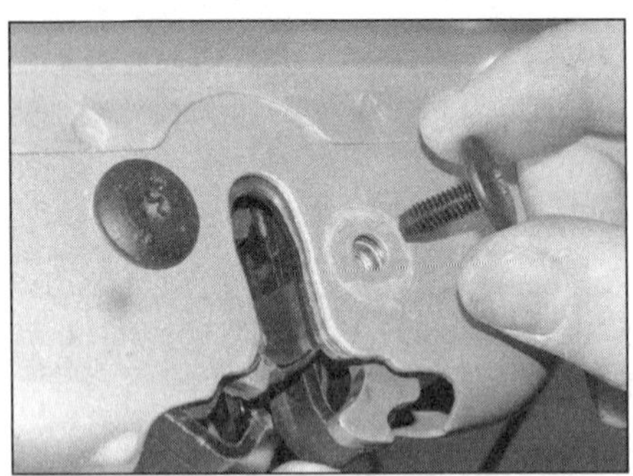
21.7b . . . then unscrew the mounting screws . . .

21.7c . . . and withdraw the lock

Refitting

4 Refitting is a reversal of removal.

Tailgate lock

Removal

5 With the tailgate open, undo the screws and remove the handgrip.

6 Using a wide-bladed screwdriver, carefully prise away the window surround trim, then similarly prise away the tailgate trim. Locate the screwdriver near the retaining clips when releasing the clips.

7 Disconnect the wiring and cable, then unscrew the mounting screws and withdraw the lock through the aperture in the tailgate inner panel **(see illustrations)**.

Refitting

8 Refitting is a reversal of removal.

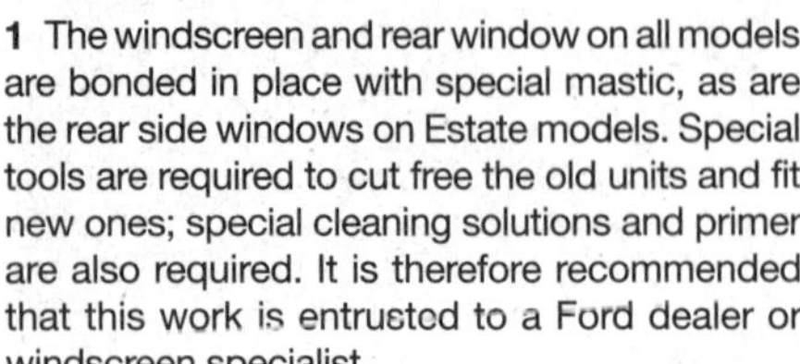

22 Windscreen and fixed windows – removal and refitting

1 The windscreen and rear window on all models are bonded in place with special mastic, as are the rear side windows on Estate models. Special tools are required to cut free the old units and fit new ones; special cleaning solutions and primer are also required. It is therefore recommended that this work is entrusted to a Ford dealer or windscreen specialist.

2 Note that the windscreen contributes towards the structural strength of the car as a whole, so it is important that it is fitted correctly.

23 Body side mouldings and badges – removal and refitting

Removal

1 Insert a length of strong cord (fishing line is ideal) behind the moulding or emblem concerned. With a sawing action, break the adhesive bond between the moulding or emblem and the panel.

2 Thoroughly clean all traces of adhesive from the panel using methylated spirit, and allow the location to dry. If necessary, the tape residue can be removed with a pinstripe removal tool, which mounts in a power drill, and should be available from larger motor factors or bodyshops.

Refitting

3 Peel back the protective paper from the rear face of the new moulding or emblem. Carefully fit it into position on the panel concerned, but take care not to touch the adhesive. When in position, apply hand pressure to the moulding/emblem for a short period, to ensure maximum adhesion to the panel.

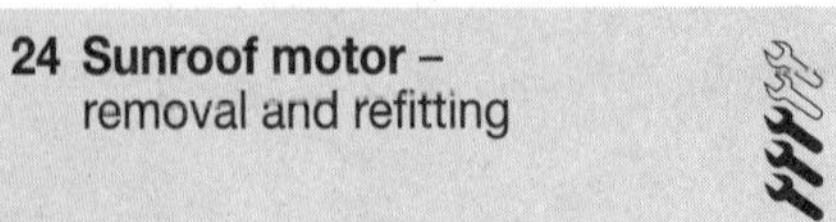

24 Sunroof motor – removal and refitting

Note: *With the exception of the sunroof motor and glass panel, work on the sunroof is considered outside the scope of the home mechanic as it involves removal of the headlining.*

Removal

1 Disconnect the battery negative lead (refer to *Disconnecting the battery* at the end of this manual).

2 Remove the overhead console as described in Section 30.

3 Disconnect the wiring from the sunroof motor.

4 Unscrew the three mounting bolts, then withdraw the motor.

Refitting

5 Remove the panel guide arm covers from the front of the sunroof opening.

6 Check that the left- and right-hand cable guide pins are aligned centrally between the lugs on the guides **(see illustration)**. Depress the bar in order to view the pins.

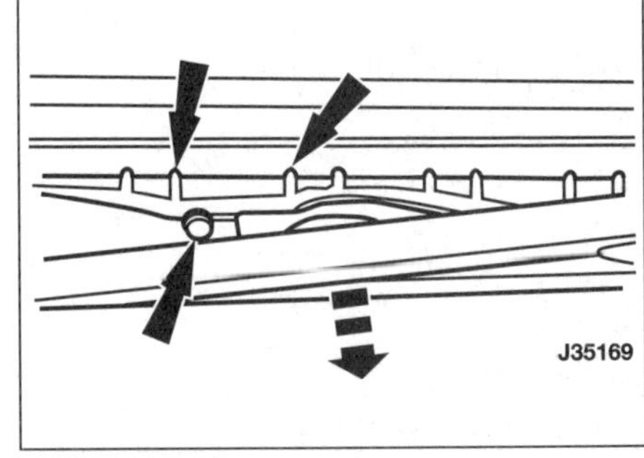

24.6 Depress the bar, and check that the guide pins are aligned

7 If adjustment of guide pins is necessary, use a screwdriver to move the cable in the required direction.

8 Refit the sunroof panel guide arm covers.

9 Support the motor and reconnect the wiring.

10 Reconnect the battery negative lead and the sunroof control switch connector.

Motor initialisation

Updating

Warning: The anti-trap function will not operate during initialisation. Make sure that foreign material, fingers, etc, are kept away from the sunroof opening.

11 If refitting the original motor, carry out the following updating motor initialisation procedure. If a new motor is being fitted, proceed to paragraph 16.

12 With the sunroof panel guide arm covers removed, close the sunroof, then position a 1.0 to 1.2 mm thick, 150.0 mm long spacer (a strip of plastic or card should do) between the rear edge of the sunroof panel glass and the roof panel opening.

13 With the help of an assistant, loosen the screws and adjust the rear edge of the glass so that it is flush with, or no more than 1.0 mm above the rear roof panel. Check that the glass is central in the opening, then tighten the rear retaining screws. Similarly, adjust the front edge of the glass so that it is flush with, or no more than 1.0 mm below, the roof panel.

14 Make sure all the screws are tight, then refit the guide arm covers and remove the spacer.

15 Fully open the sunroof then release the switch. Close the sunroof and hold the switch for 30 seconds until there is a small movement of approximately 2.0 mm and the motor stops. Release the switch and immediately close the sunroof within 0.5 seconds until the panel stops. This completes one initialisation cycle.

Initial

Warning: The anti-trap function will not operate during initialisation. Make sure that foreign material, fingers, etc, are kept away from the sunroof opening.

16 Align the sunroof as described in paragraphs 12 to 14.

17 Fully close the sunroof, then release the switch and immediately re-press the close switch within 0.5 seconds until the panels stops. This completes one initialisation cycle.

Erasure

Note: *This is necessary only when the motor has been detached from the sunroof panel, and must also be carried out before fitting a previously used motor (ie, before removing the used motor).*

18 With the wiring connected to the motor, operate the close switch until the motor stops, then release it.

19 Operate the close switch again and hold it for 30 seconds. The motor will turn in one direction. Release the switch, then attempt to operate the open switch – if the motor does not turn, the erasing procedure has been carried out correctly. If the motor turns, repeat the erasing procedure.

25 Sunroof glass panel – removal, refitting and adjustment

Removal

1 Slide the sunroof blind fully to the rear, and open the panel to the tilt position.

2 Unclip the plastic covers from the guide arm on each side of the panel.

3 Unscrew and remove the two panel securing screws from the guide arm on each side.

4 Remove the glass panel from outside the car – lift it clear, taking care not to scratch the roof.

Refitting

5 Fit the panel loosely in position, and align the mounting holes with those in the guide arms. Fit the two securing screws each side, but only tighten them by hand at this stage.

6 Close the roof gently, then adjust the position of the glass panel as described below.

Adjustment

7 If not already done, unclip the guide arm plastic covers each side, and loosen both pairs of securing screws so that the panel can be moved.

8 Close the sunroof, then position a 1.0 to 1.2 mm thick, 150.0 mm long spacer (a strip of plastic or card should do) between the rear edge of the sunroof panel glass and the roof panel opening.

9 With the help of an assistant, adjust the rear edge of the glass so that it is flush with, or no more than 1.0 mm above the rear roof panel. Check that the glass is central in the opening, then tighten the rear retaining screws. Similarly, adjust the front edge of the glass so that it is flush with, or no more than 1.0 mm below, the roof panel.

10 Make sure all the screws are tight, then refit the guide arm covers and remove the spacer.

11 Check the operation of the sunroof on completion.

26 Seats – removal and refitting

Front seat

Removal

1 Disconnect the battery negative lead (refer to *Disconnecting the battery* at the end of this manual).

Warning: Before proceeding, wait a minimum of one minute, as a precaution against accidental firing of the side airbag unit, which is located inside the seat. This period ensures that any stored energy in the back-up capacitor is dissipated.

2 Move the seat fully rearwards.

3 Disconnect the wiring from under the front seat – depending on model, this may only be one large wiring connector, or one large one and several smaller ones. Where applicable, unscrew the connector mounting bolt **(see illustrations)**.

4 Unscrew and remove the seat front mounting bolts **(see illustration)**.

5 Move the seat fully forwards.

6 Unbolt the seat belt lower anchor from the underside of the front seat **(see illustration)**.

26.3a Undo the bolt . . .

26.3b . . . and remove the front seat wiring connector

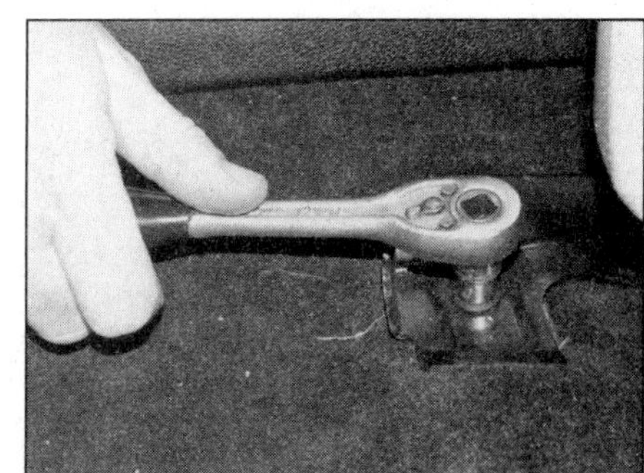

26.4 Removing the front mounting bolts

26.6 Unbolting the seat belt lower anchor from the front seat

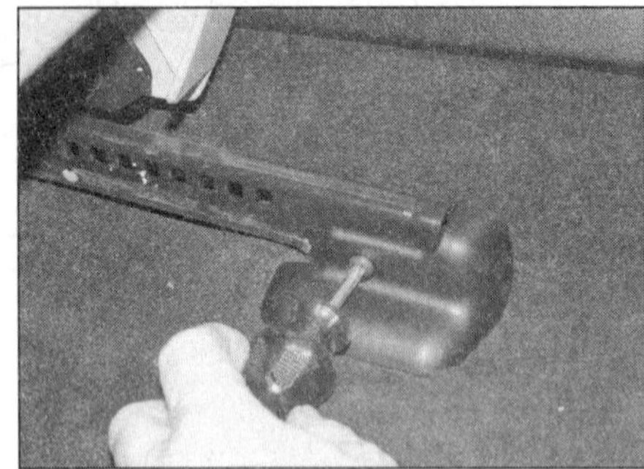

26.7a Undo the screws . . .

26.7b . . . and remove the rear mounting bolt covers

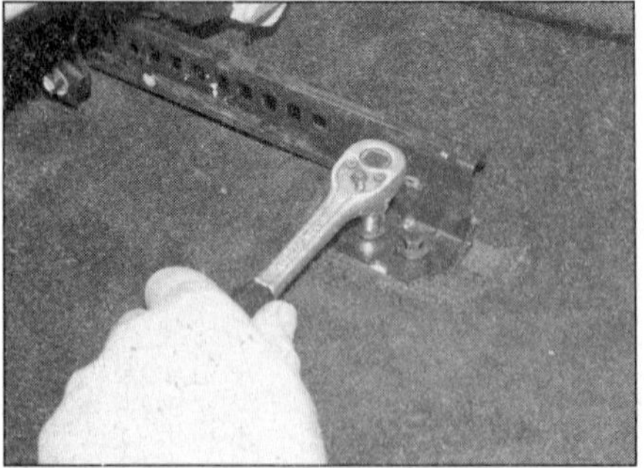

26.8a Removing the rear mounting bolts

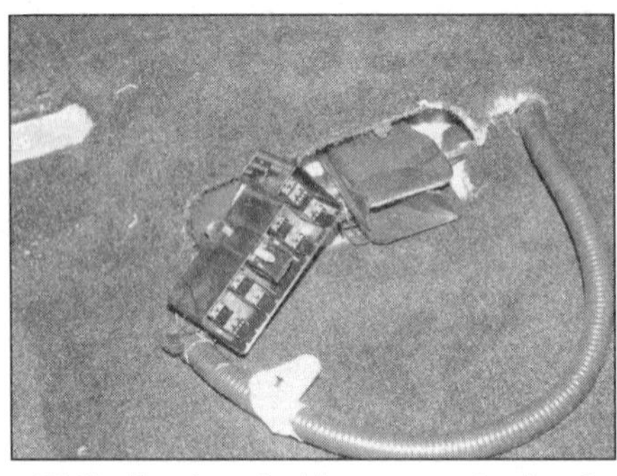

26.8b Front seat wiring connector (seat removed)

7 Undo the screws and remove the rear mounting bolt covers **(see illustrations)**.

8 Unscrew and remove the rear mounting bolts, then carefully withdraw the seat from the car **(see illustrations)**.

Refitting

9 Refitting is a reversal of removal, but tighten the mounting bolts to the specified torque.

Rear seat

Removal

10 On Saloon and Estate models, pull out the retaining clips from the front edge of the seat, then lift the cushion and remove from the inside of the car. Ford recommend that the clips are renewed whenever removed.

11 On Hatchback models, simply raise the rear edge of the cushion, and withdraw it from the car.

12 Pull out the centre seat belt by approximately 200 mm from its stop, and ensure that it cannot retract by attaching a clip of some kind around it. Take care not to damage the seat belt in achieving this – it may be possible to wrap carpet tape around, instead of a clip.

13 Unbolt the centre safety belt stalk from the rear floor.

14 On Saloon models, fold the rear seat backrests forwards, then unscrew the four hinge bolts on each backrest.

15 On Hatchback and Estate models, fold the rear seat backrest forwards, then unscrew the bolt from the centre hinge locking plate. Remove the backrest outer hinge retaining clip, and withdraw the backrest from the car.

Refitting

16 Refitting is a reversal of removal, but tighten the mounting bolts to the specified torque.

27 Seat belts - removal and refitting

Front seat belt

1 Move the front seat fully forwards.

2 Unbolt the seat belt anchor from the rear underside of the seat.

3 Pull back the rubber weatherstrips from each side of the door B-pillar, for access to the seat belt shoulder height adjuster **(see illustration)**. Move the adjuster to its lowest position.

4 Carefully pull out (sideways) the lower edges of the trim panel and release the locating tangs.

5 Prise off the cover, then undo the screw securing the top of the trim to the B-pillar **(see illustrations)**.

6 Remove the upper section trim panel and, at the same time, feed the seat belt through the slot **(see illustrations)**.

7 Undo the screws, then release the clips and remove the lower section of the B-pillar trim **(see illustrations)**.

8 Undo the screws, then release the clips and remove the inner sill kickplate **(see illustrations)**.

9 Unscrew the bolt and remove the seat belt upper anchor from the shoulder height adjuster **(see illustration)**.

Caution: A special washer is fitted to the bolt to retain it on the anchor plate. The washer must remain on the bolt at all times with the seat belt removed.

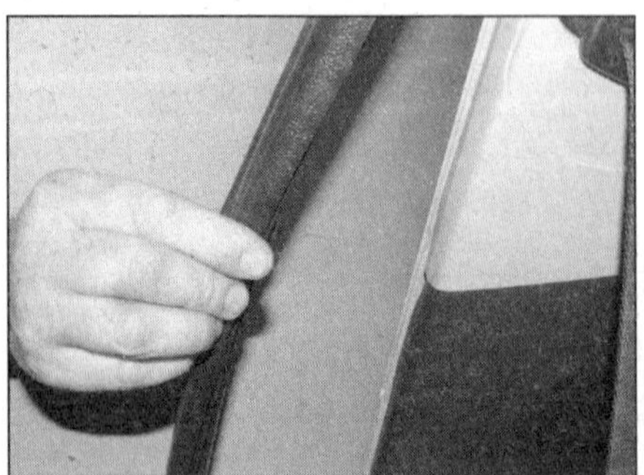

27.3 Pull back the weatherstrips from the B-pillar

27.5a Prise off the cover . . .

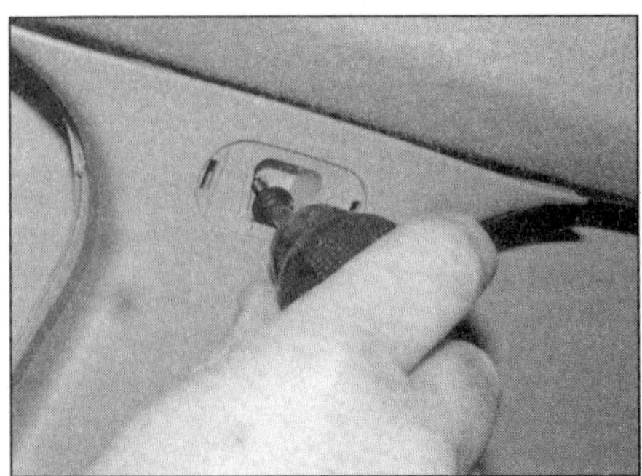

27.5b . . . and undo the screw from the B-pillar trim

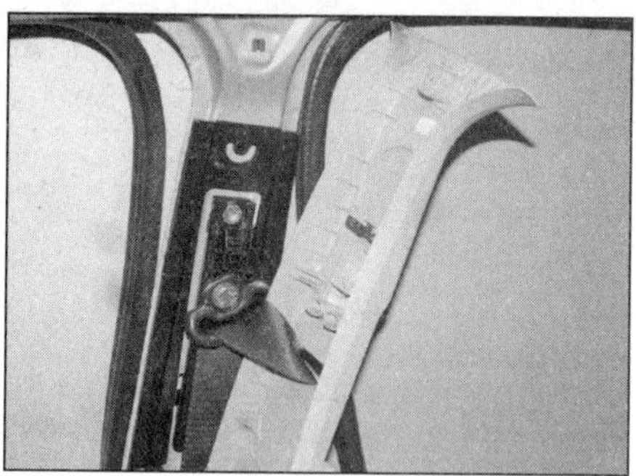

27.6a Remove the upper section of the B-pillar trim . . .

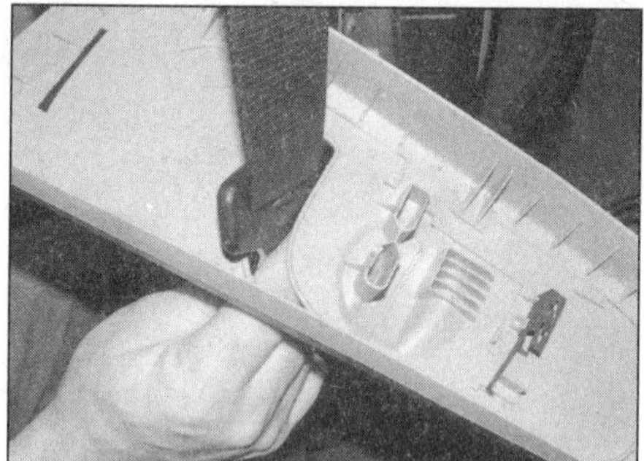

27.6b . . . and feed the seat belt through the slot

27.7a Undo the screws . . .

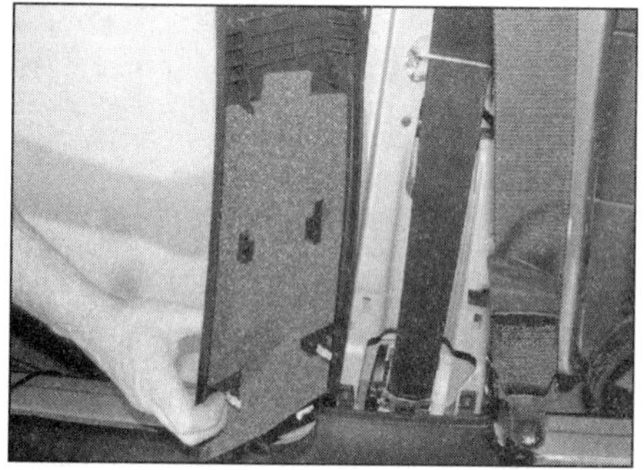

27.7b . . . and remove the lower section of the B-pillar trim

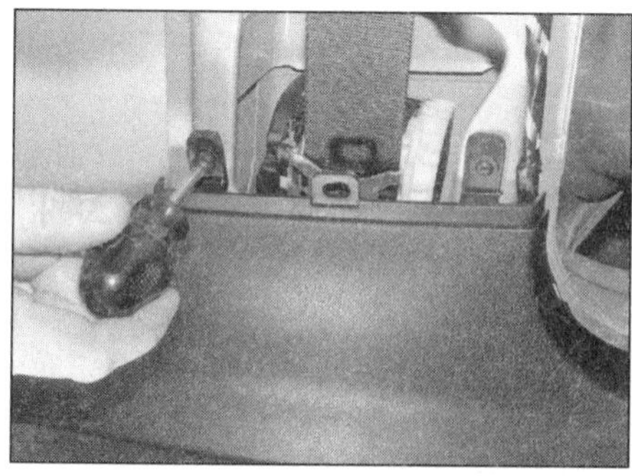

27.8a Remove the centre screws . . .

27.8b . . . and end screws . . .

10 Unbolt the guide loop from the B-pillar **(see illustration)**.

11 Unscrew the bolt and lift the inertia reel from inside the B-pillar **(see illustration)**. Note the locating tang on the reel.

12 Refitting is a reversal of removal, but tighten all bolts to the specified torque. Ensure the tang on the reel is correctly located.

Front belt stalk

⚠ ***Warning: Take extreme care when handling the seat belt pretensioning device. It contains a small explosive charge (pyrotechnic device), and injury may occur if the device is accidentally deployed. Once fired, the tensioner cannot be reset, and must be renewed. Note also that seat belts and associated components which have been subject to impact loads must be renewed at the same time.***

13 Remove the front seat as described in Section 26.

14 Disconnect the wiring from the seat belt buckle switch and pretensioner.

15 Note the location of the pretensioner wiring harnesses, then release them from the underside of the front seat.

16 Unscrew the mounting bolt, and remove the stalk from the front seat **(see illustration)**. ***Caution: Do not probe any of the wiring,***

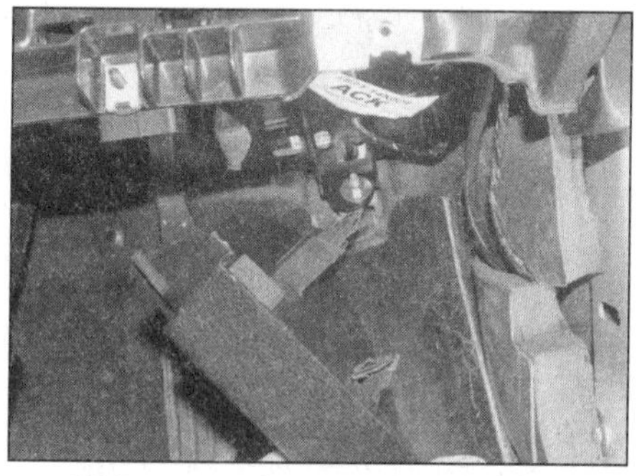

27.8c . . . and remove the inner sill kickplate

27.9 Bolt securing the seat belt upper anchor to the shoulder height adjuster

27.10 Bolt securing the seat belt guide loop to the B-pillar

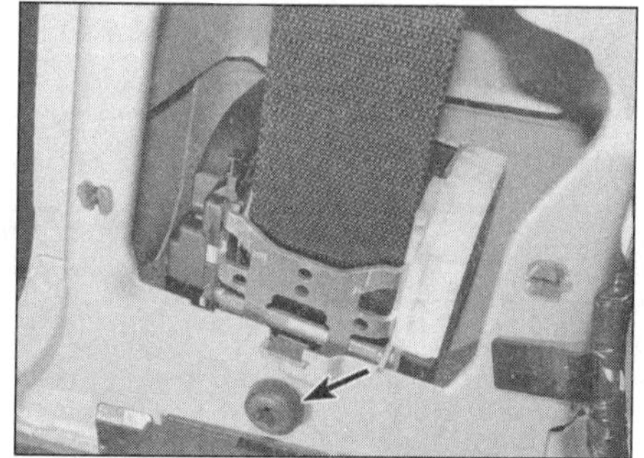

27.11 Bolt securing the seat belt reel to the B-pillar

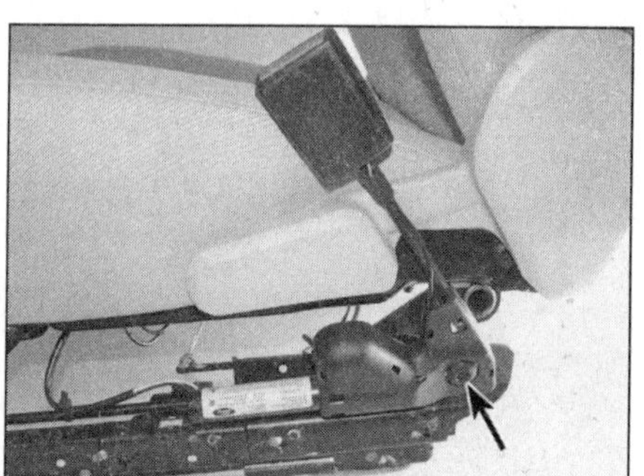

27.16 Front seat belt stalk mounting bolt

27.19 Rear seat belt floor anchor

27.20a Undo the screws . . .

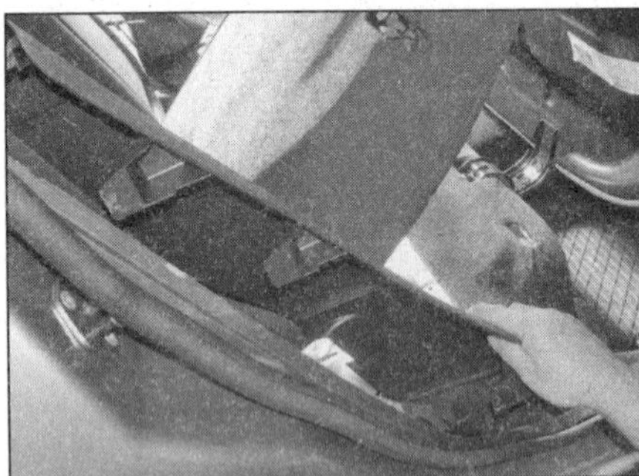
27.20b . . . and remove the lower trim panel from the C-pillar

27.22a On Hatchback models, remove the rear shelf side panel . . .

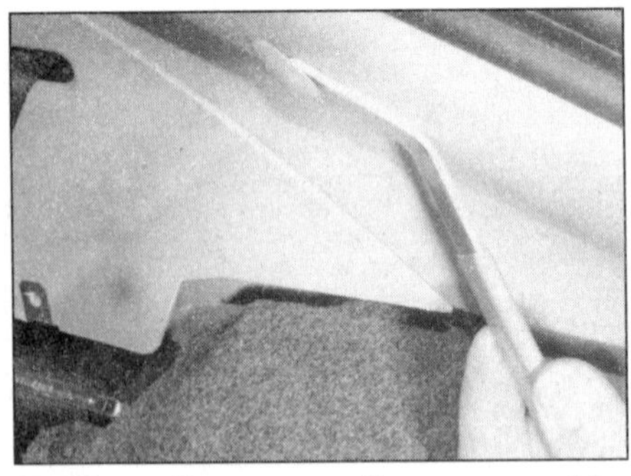
27.22b . . . then remove the rear upper trim panel . . .

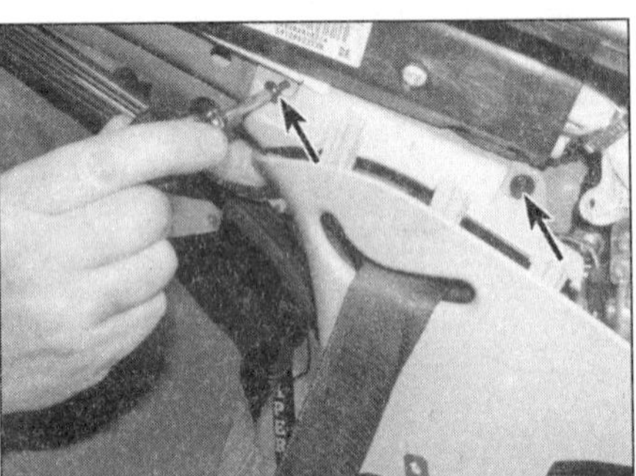
27.22c . . . undo the screws . . .

as static electricity may activate the pretensioner.

17 Refitting is a reversal of removal, but tighten all mounting bolts to the specified torque.

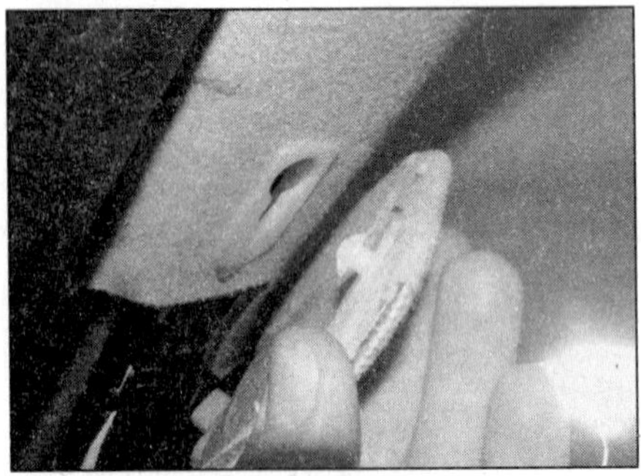
27.22d . . . release the clip . . .

27.23 Rear seat belt upper anchor bolt

Rear outer belt

Saloon and Hatchback models

18 Pull the rear door weatherstrip from the C-pillar, and remove the rear seat cushion.

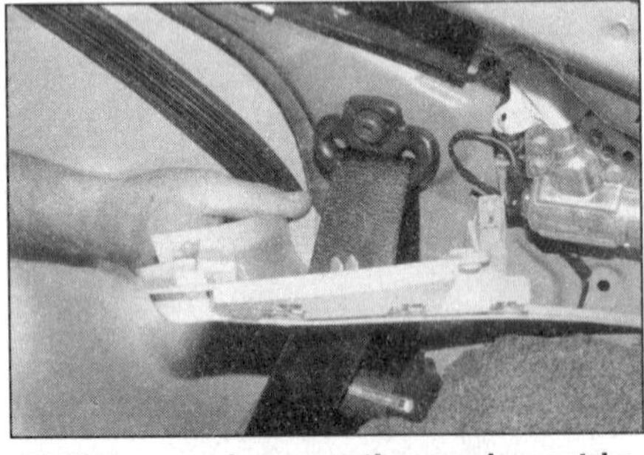
27.22e . . . and remove the rear lower trim panel while feeding the seat belt through the slot

27.24 Rear seat belt reel retaining bolt

19 Using a Torx key, unscrew the bolt securing the rear seat belt anchor to the floor **(see illustration)**.

20 Undo the screws and remove the lower trim panel from the C-pillar **(see illustrations)**.

21 On Saloon models, prise out the plastic covers, then undo the screws and remove the rear trim panel. Feed the seat belt through the slot in the panel.

22 On Hatchback models, where necessary remove the rear shelf side panel, then prise out the plastic covers and undo the screws securing the rear upper trim panel. Release the retaining clips and withdraw the panel. If working on the right-hand seat belt, disconnect the rear window washer tube from the panel. Undo the screws securing the rear lower trim panel, then release the clip and withdraw the panel while feeding the seat belt through the slot **(see illustrations)**.

23 On all models, unscrew the bolt and remove the seat belt upper anchor from the C-pillar **(see illustration)**.

Caution: A special washer is fitted to the bolt to retain it on the anchor plate. The washer must remain on the bolt at all times with the seat belt removed.

24 Unscrew the bolt and lift the retractor from inside the C-pillar **(see illustration)**. Note the locating tang on the retractor.

25 Refitting is a reversal of removal, but tighten all bolts to the specified torque. Ensure the retractor tang is correctly located.

Estate models

26 With the tailgate open, pull away the

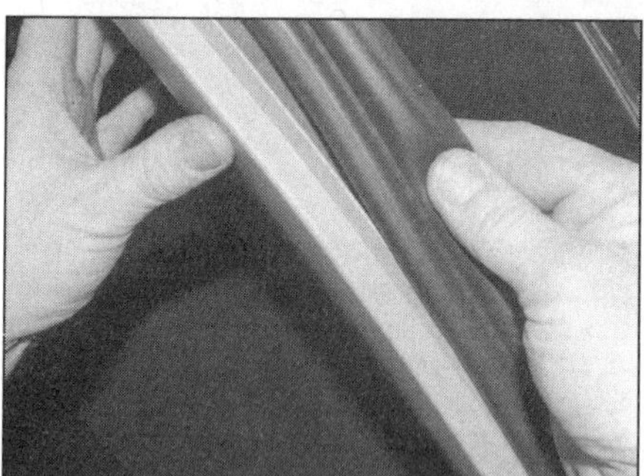
27.26 Pull away the weatherstrip . . .

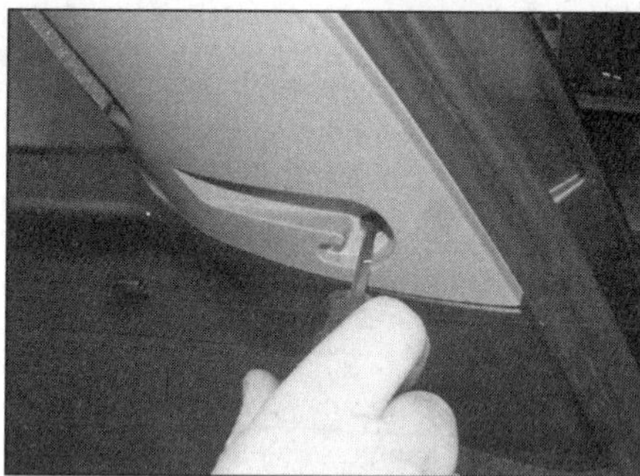
27.27a . . . then undo the screw . . .

27.27b . . . and remove the trim panel from the D-pillar

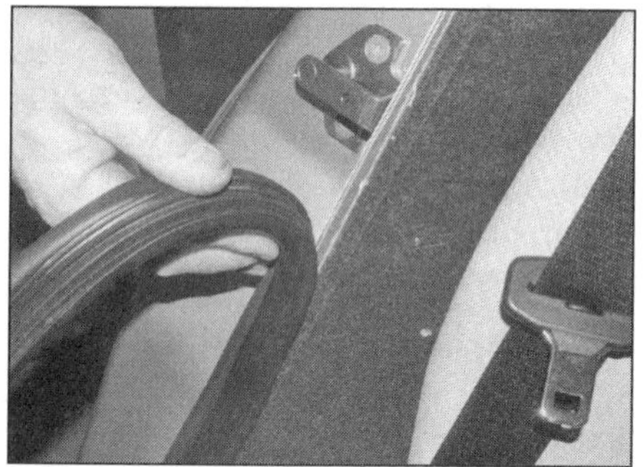
27.28a Pull away the weatherstrip . . .

27.28b . . . then undo the screws . . .

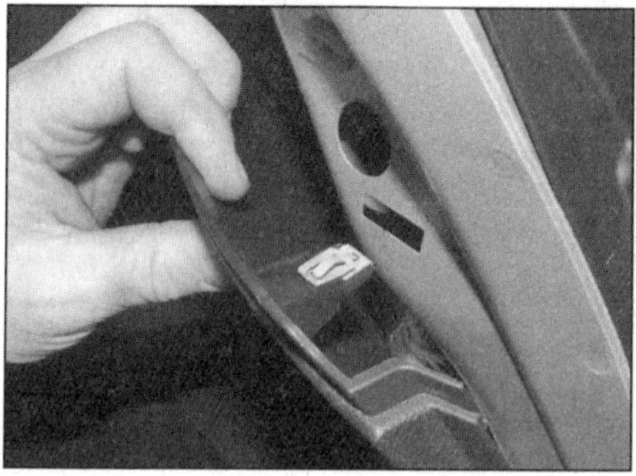
27.28c . . . and remove the load space upper trim panel

weatherstrip from the D-pillar trim panel **(see illustration)**.

27 Undo the screw and remove the trim panel from the D-pillar **(see illustrations)**. If removing the right-hand panel, disconnect the rear washer tube.

28 Pull away the weatherstrip from the C-pillar, then undo the screws and remove the load space upper trim panel located beneath the rear quarter window. Where necessary, disconnect the wiring for the auxiliary 12 volt supply **(see illustrations)**.

29 Using a Torx key, unscrew the seat belt lower anchor bolt from the floor **(see illustration)**.

30 Prise off the cover and unscrew the seat belt upper anchor bolt from the C-pillar. If necessary, unclip and remove the upper trim panel **(see illustrations)**.

Caution: A special washer is fitted to the bolt to retain it on the anchor plate. The washer must remain on the bolt at all times with the seat belt removed.

31 Pull back the carpet, then unscrew the mounting bolt and withdraw the inertia reel from the C-pillar. Note the reel's locating tang **(see illustration)**.

32 To remove the centre stalk, first remove

27.28d Disconnecting the wiring from the auxiliary 12 volt supply

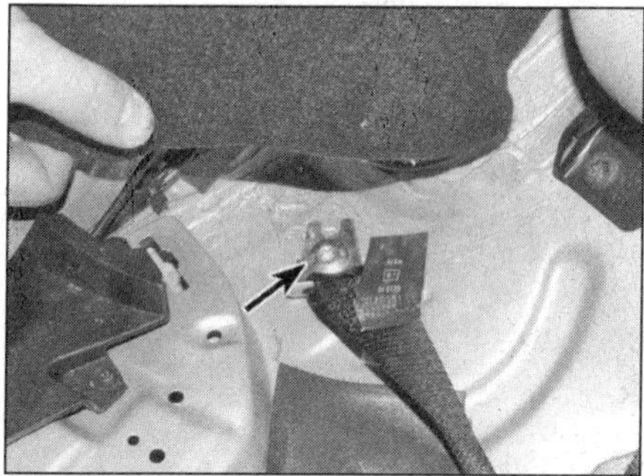
27.29 Bolt securing the rear seat belt lower anchor to the floor

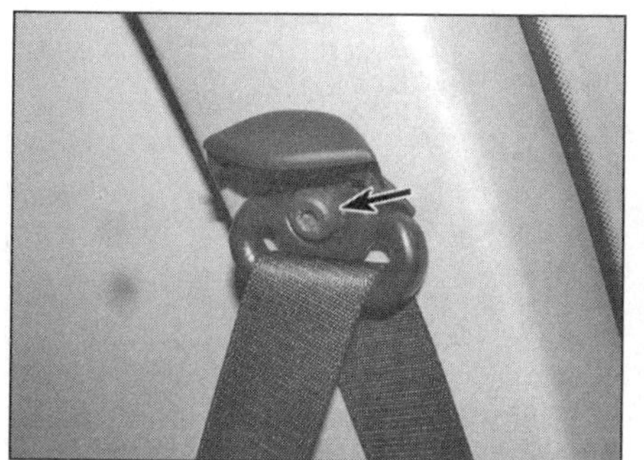
27.30a Bolt securing the rear seat belt upper anchor bolt to the C-pillar

27.30b Removing the upper trim panel

27.31 Outer rear seat belt reel mounting bolt (Estate)

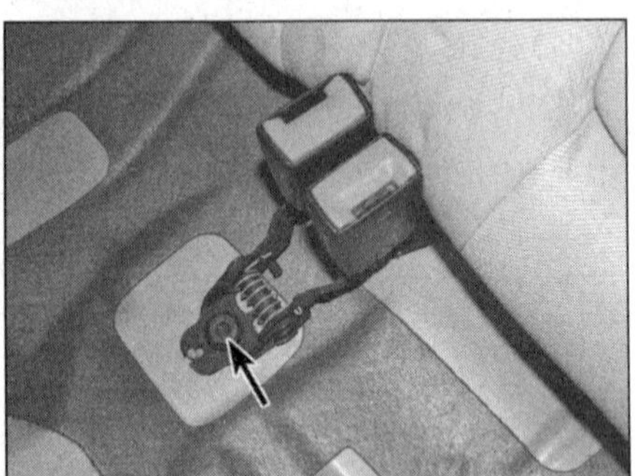

27.32 Rear seat centre stalk mounting bolt (Estate)

the cushion by pulling out the retaining clips, then unscrew the mounting bolt and remove the stalks **(see illustration)**.

33 Refitting is a reversal of removal, but tighten all bolts to the specified torque. Ensure the inertia reel tang is correctly located.

Rear centre belt

Saloon models

34 Pull the rear door weatherstrip from the C-pillar.

35 Prise out the plastic covers, then undo the screw and remove the lower trim panel from the C-pillar.

36 Remove the rear seat cushion.

37 Unscrew the Torx bolt and remove the centre stalk from the floor.

38 Fold down the rear seat backrests.

39 Remove the centre seat belt plastic guide.

40 Remove the backrest retaining latch trim panels.

41 Prise out the plastic covers, then undo the screws and remove the rear parcel shelf, while feeding the seat belt through the slot.

42 Unscrew the mounting bolt and remove the centre seat belt reel.

43 Refitting is a reversal of removal, but tighten the mounting bolts to the specified torque.

Hatchback and Estate models

44 Remove the rear seat backrest, then lock the backrest latch.

45 Note the location of the backrest latch cable, then remove it from the retractor.

46 Using a knife, make a cut in the carpet over the reel mounting bolt in the backrest. Unscrew the bolt and remove the reel while feeding the seat belt through the guide.

47 Refitting is a reversal of removal, but tighten the mounting bolt to the specified torque, and apply suitable adhesive to the rear carpet to stick it to the backrest.

28 Interior trim panels – removal and refitting

Removal

Sun visor

1 Using a Torx key, unscrew the two screws securing the sun visor to the roof/headlining, and withdraw it **(see illustration)**.

2 Prise up the cover, unscrew the inner bracket mounting screws, and remove the bracket.

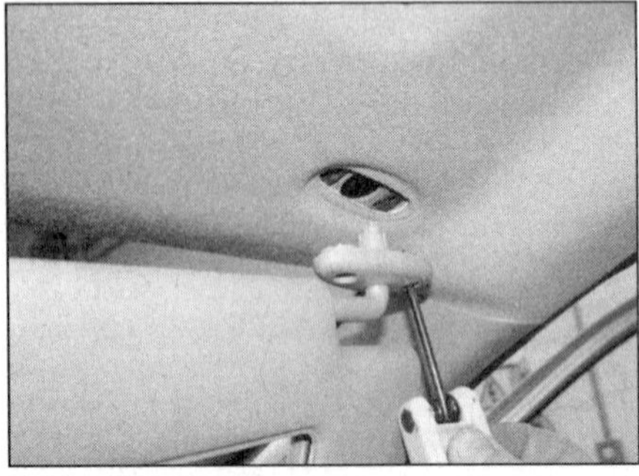

28.1 Removing the sun visor

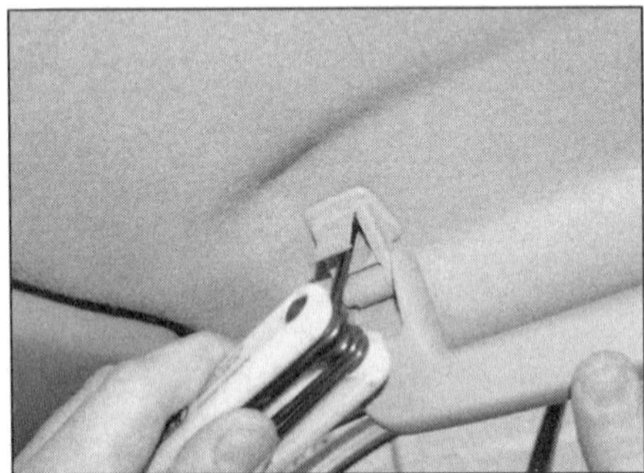

28.3 Removing the passenger grab handle

Passenger grab handle

3 Prise up the covers, then unscrew the mounting screws and remove the grab handle **(see illustration)**.

A-pillar trim

4 Note that on models fitted with curtain airbags, the A-pillar trim is attached to the top of the A-pillar by a special yellow strap which forms part of the airbag system, and retains the black cord from the air curtain. It is important that this strap is not damaged and is always refitted correctly.

5 Pull away the door weatherstrip in the area of the trim.

6 Carefully pull away the top of the trim and release the clips. Where applicable, note the location of the curtain airbag cord strap, then release it from the trim. Withdraw the trim panel **(see illustrations)**.

B-pillar and cowl side trim

7 The procedure is described in Section 27 as the first part of the removal of the front seat belt.

C-pillar trim (Hatchback and Estate)

8 Pull away the rear door weatherstrip in the area of the trim.

9 On Estate models, unbolt the rear seat belt upper anchor from the C-pillar with reference to Section 27. On Hatchback models, prise out the covers and undo the trim panel retaining screws.

10 Release the retaining clips, then withdraw the C-pillar trim in a forwards and upwards direction **(see illustration)**.

C-pillar trim (Saloon)

11 Pull away the rear door weatherstrip in the area of the trim.

12 Undo the single screw and remove the lower trim panel from the C-pillar.

13 Fold down the rear seat backrests, and remove the latch covers.

14 Undo the screws and remove the parcel shelf trim panel.

15 Prise out the covers, then undo the screws securing the C-pillar trim. Where necessary, remove the rear seat belt upper anchor (see Section 27). Withdraw the trim panel.

D-pillar trim (Estate)

16 With the tailgate open, pull away the

28.6a The curtain airbag strap must be correctly located in the yellow plastic holder

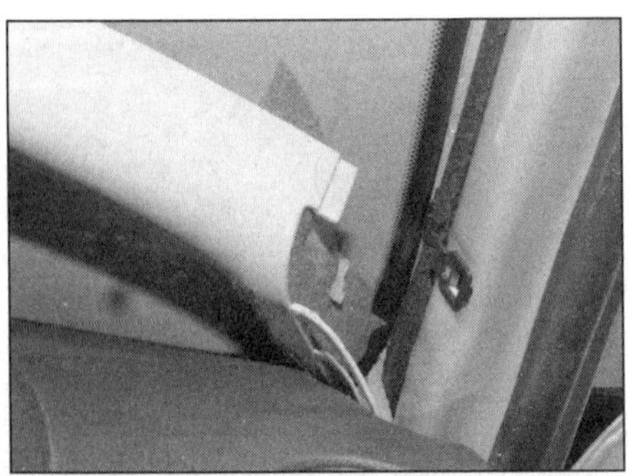

28.6b Releasing the bottom end of the trim panel from the A-pillar

28.10 Removing the C-pillar trim panel (Estate)

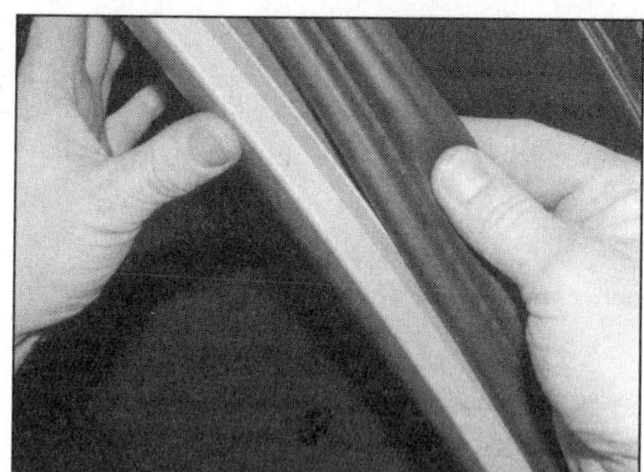

28.16 Pull away the weatherstrip . . .

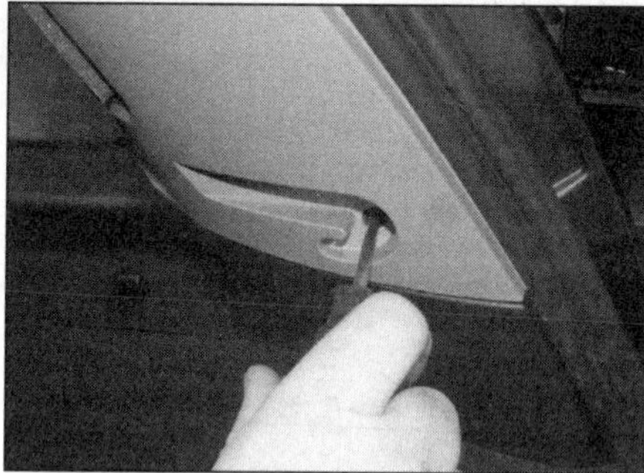

28.17 . . . then undo the screw . . .

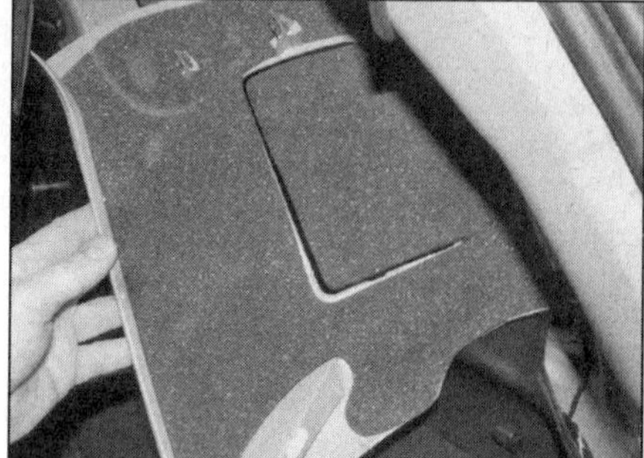

28.18 . . . and remove the trim panel from the D-pillar (Estate)

28.20a Undo the upper screws . . .

28.20b . . . and lower screws . . .

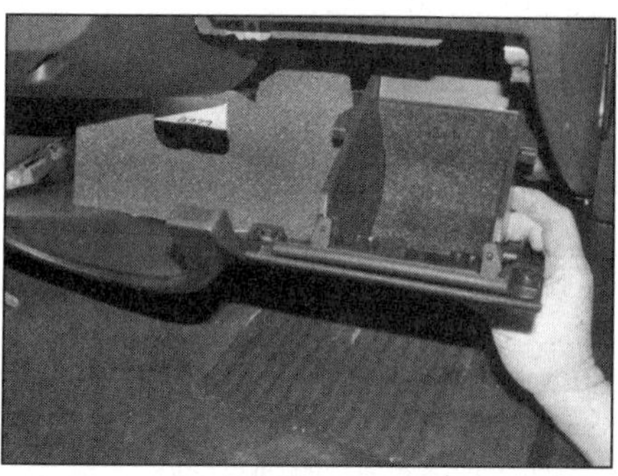

28.20c . . . and withdraw the lower facia panel from the facia

weatherstrip in the area of the trim **(see illustration)**.

17 Undo the screw securing the trim to the D-pillar **(see illustration)**.

18 Release the retaining clips, then withdraw the D-pillar trim **(see illustration)**. If removing the right-hand panel, release the rear window washer tube.

Lower facia panel

19 Remove the steering column top and bottom shrouds.

20 Unscrew the mounting screws from the upper corners and above the coin tray position, and withdraw the lower facia panel from the facia **(see illustrations)**. Where applicable, detach the diagnostic plug connector from the panel.

Lower centre panels

21 Release the two screws or clips each side, and withdraw the panels from the front of the centre console **(see illustration)**.

Refitting

22 Refitting is a reversal of the removal procedure. Where seat belt fastenings have been disturbed, make sure that they are tightened to the specified torque.

29 Centre console – removal and refitting

Removal

1 Working in the footwell on each side, remove the console front side panels. To do this, prise out the cover and undo the front screw located near the bulkhead, then carefully release the five upper clips and one lower clip. Withdraw the panels **(see illustrations)**.

2 Where applicable, disconnect the phone speaker wiring connector at the front of the console, on the driver's side.

3 On models equipped with Ford's satellite navigation system, the display unit must be withdrawn from the facia. The proper Ford removal tools will be required for this, to avoid damage – they may have been supplied with the car when new (and may be found in the glovebox). Insert the tools at the four corners of the panel, observing their markings (TOP L is the top left tool), and withdraw the panel by about 30 mm, taking care not to strain the wiring. Ideally, remove the unit completely.

4 On manual transmission models, prise up the gear lever trim panel at the rear to release the clips, then pull it backwards to release the front clips – the clips are quite tight. To make the job easier, the gaiter can be pulled out separately, so you can reach inside to pull up the panel. Turn the gaiter inside-out, and feed the panel up the gear lever, clear of the working

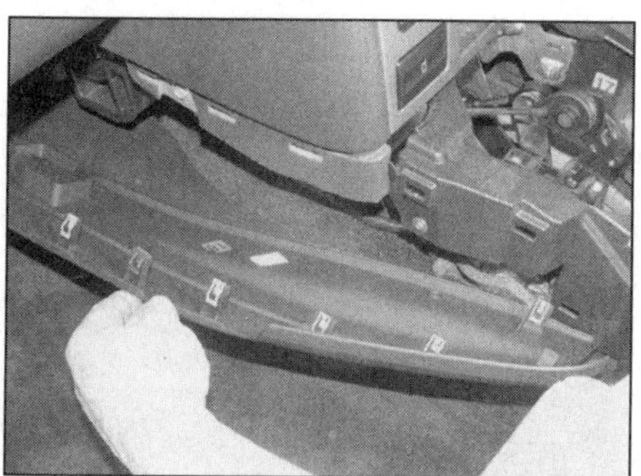

28.21 Removing the lower centre panels

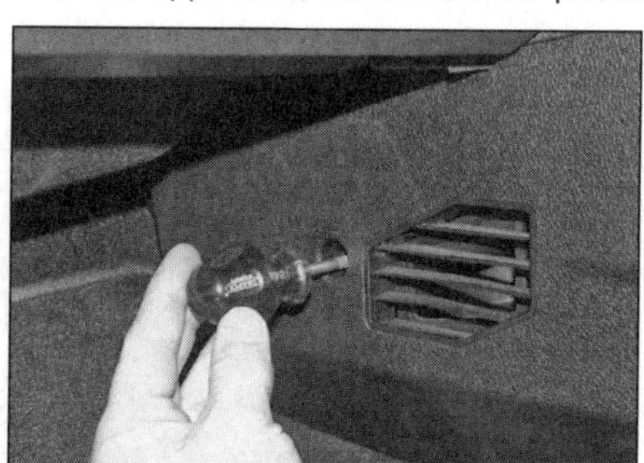

29.1a Remove the front screw . . .

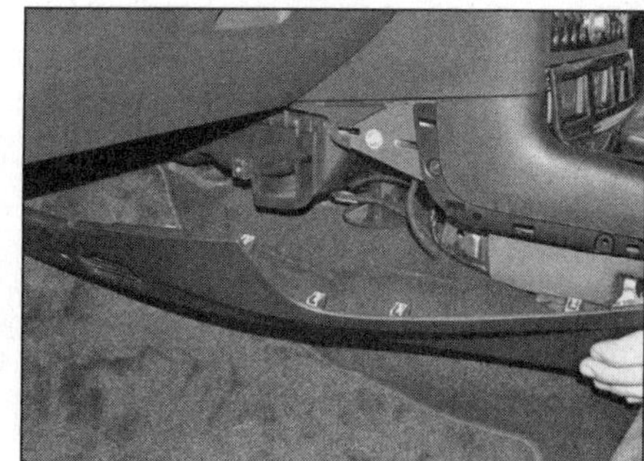

29.1b . . . then unclip and remove the centre console side panels

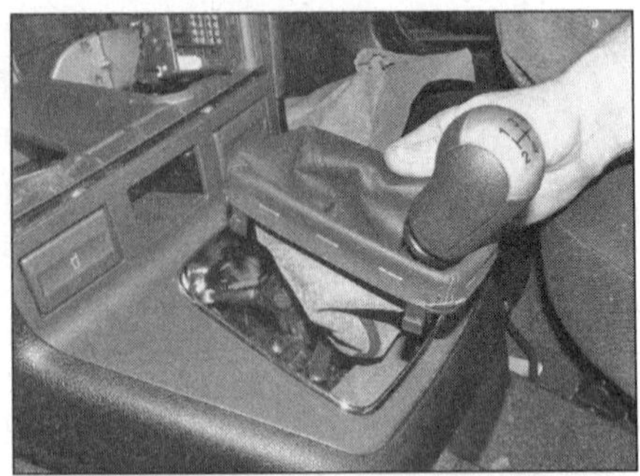

29.4a The gear lever gaiter can be unclipped separately if preferred

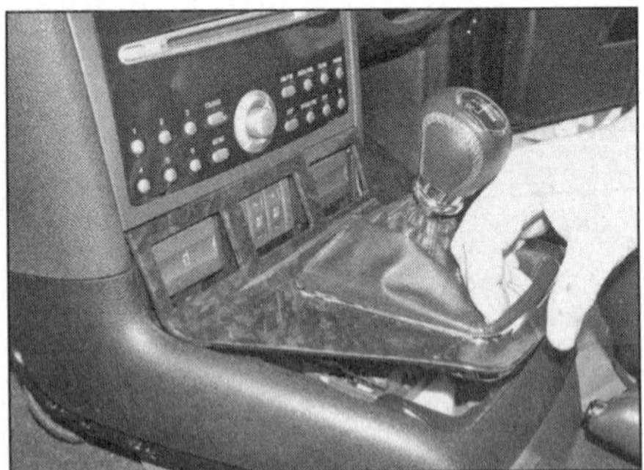

29.4b Unclip the gear lever trim panel, starting at the rear . . .

29.4c . . . then lift the panel up and off the gear lever

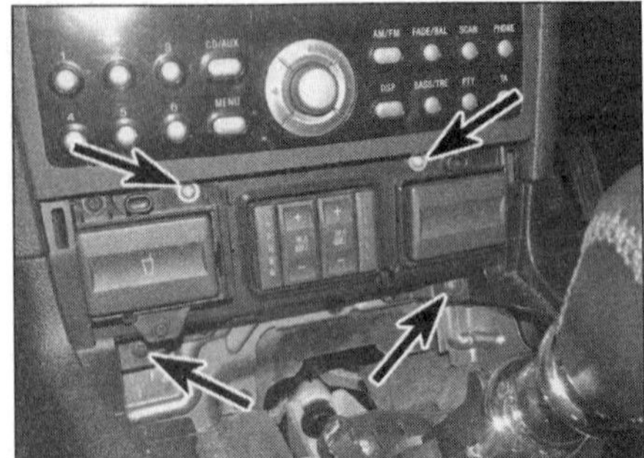

29.6a Remove the four screws at the front . . .

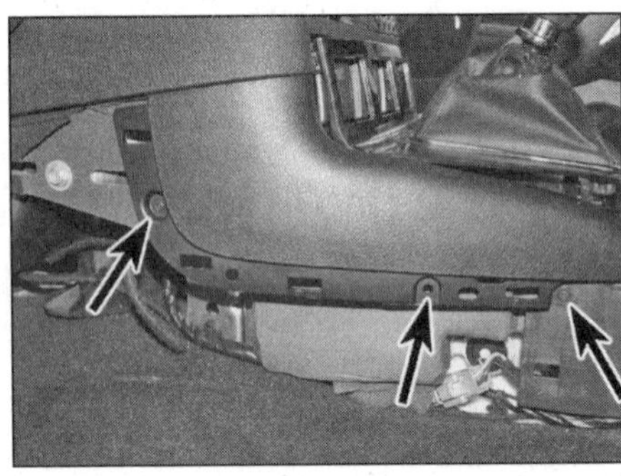

29.6b . . . two (or three) more at the sides . . .

29.6c . . . then release the upper trim panel . . .

area. To remove the panel completely (which is useful but not strictly necessary), carefully stretch the elasticated top of the gaiter up and over the gear knob **(see illustrations)**.

5 On automatic transmission models, move the selector lever to the N position. Starting with the clip on either side at the front, unclip and lift off the selector lever trim panel.

6 Remove the console upper trim panel, which is secured by four screws at the front and centre, with two (or possibly three) more on each side. Reach in behind the switch panel at the front, and disconnect the wiring plugs from the ESP switch and heated seat switches (as applicable) **(see illustrations)**.

7 Carefully prise out the ashtray and cup holder (and phone cradle, where applicable) from the centre console, and disconnect the cigar lighter wiring underneath **(see illustrations)**. On models with phone equipment, trace the wiring forwards and disconnect it in the centre of the facia panel.

8 Where applicable, use a small screwdriver to release the side clips, and prise out the rear passenger entertainment panel from the back of the console. Disconnect the wiring plug.

9 Undo the centre console retaining screws and bolts – there's one either side at the front, one in the middle, and three in the base of the console storage box (remove the box 'carpet' for access to the screws) **(see illustrations)**.

29.6d . . . and disconnect any switch wiring from behind

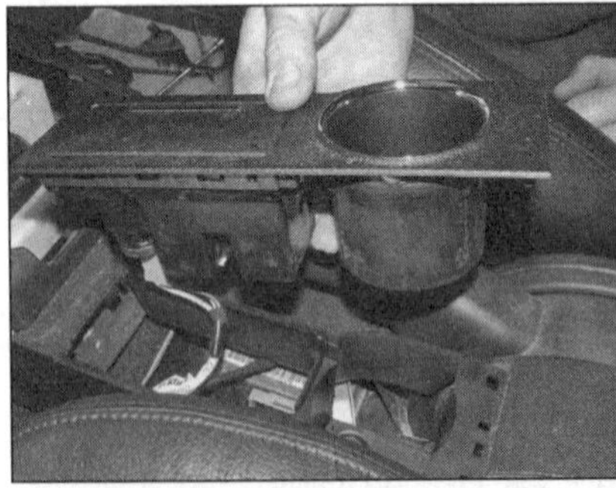

29.7a Lift out the ashtray and cup holder from the centre console . . .

29.7b . . . then disconnect the cigar lighter wiring plugs

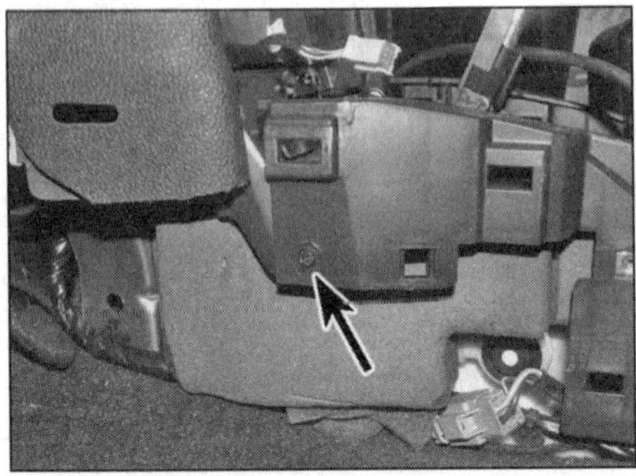

29.9a Remove the console screws at the sides . . .

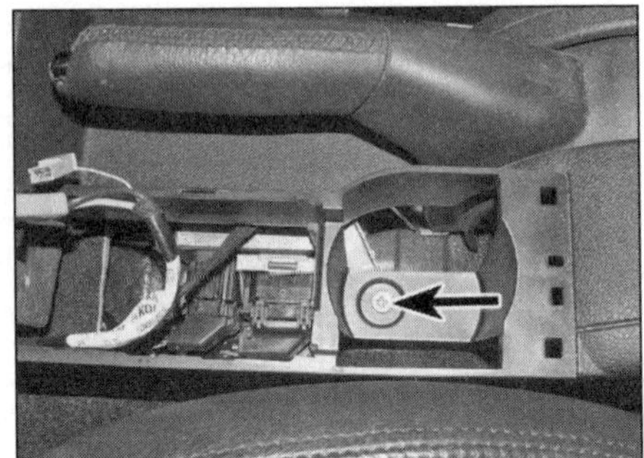

29.9b . . . one in the middle . . .

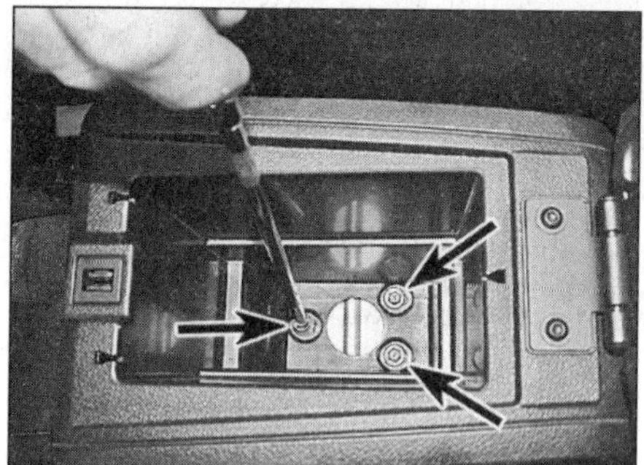

29.9c . . . and at the rear, in the storage box

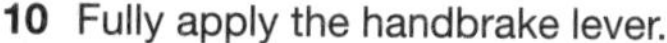

10 Fully apply the handbrake lever.

11 Reach in under the driver's side of the console, and disconnect the handbrake-on warning light switch wiring plug. Where applicable, also disconnect the two wiring plugs for the heated rear seats.

12 Raise the front of the centre console, and feel inside for any remaining wiring which may still be clipped to it. Remove the console from between the front seats **(see illustration)**.

Refitting

13 Refitting is a reversal of the removal procedure.

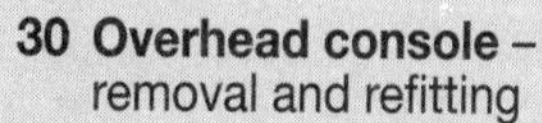

30 Overhead console – removal and refitting

Removal

1 Disconnect the battery negative lead (refer to *Disconnecting the battery* at the end of this manual).

2 Using a screwdriver, carefully prise the interior light from the overhead console, then disconnect the wiring **(see illustration)**.

3 On models equipped with a sunroof, prise up the covers and turn the front retaining clips through 90°. Lower the front of the overhead console, then move it forwards and release the rear retaining clips. Disconnect the wiring and remove the sunroof control switch.

4 On models without a sunroof, open the storage compartment, then carefully pull down the rear of the compartment, using a screwdriver to release the retaining clips. Take care not to damage the compartment or console.

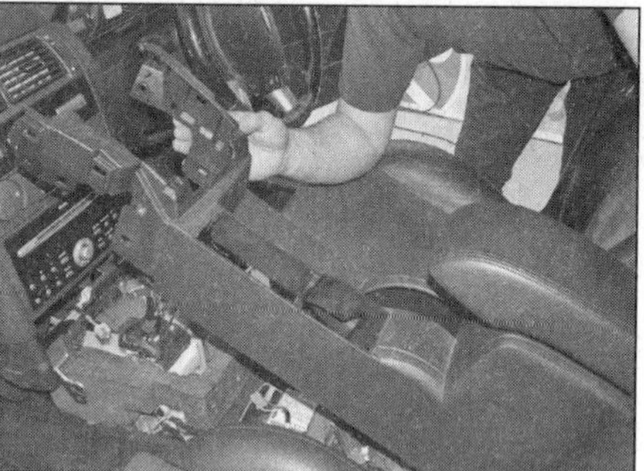

29.12 Removing the centre console

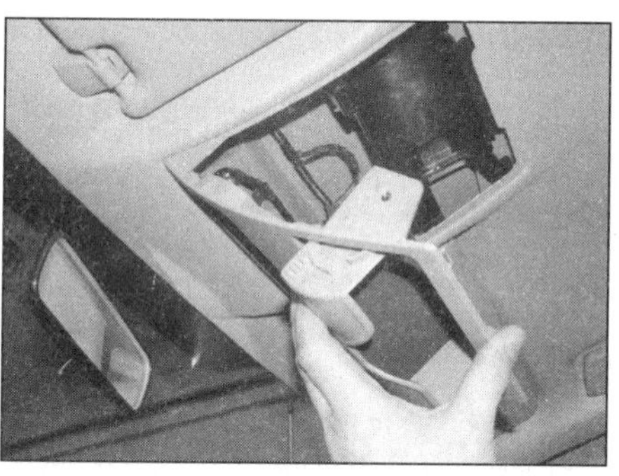

30.5a Removing the overhead console from the headlining

5 On all models, carefully prise down the rear of the console, then pull it to the rear to release the front retaining clips **(see illustrations)**.

6 Release the Velcro and withdraw the storage compartment cover downwards.

7 On models with telematics, note the location of the microphone, then remove it from the console as follows. Release the adhesive tape from the electrical connector and wiring harness. Detach the microphone wiring connector followed by the microphone and foam pad.

Refitting

8 Refitting is a reversal of removal, but initialise the electric windows as described in Section 12. Do not refit the Velcro tape until after the storage compartment has been refitted; with the compartment fitted, push up the console and refit the tape.

30.2 Removing the interior lamp from the overhead console

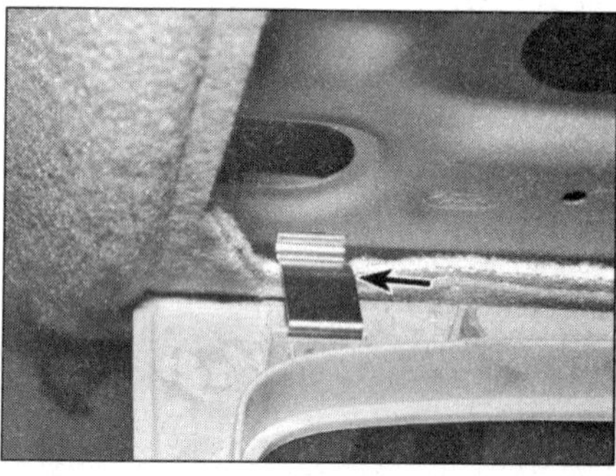

30.5b Front retaining clip on the overhead console

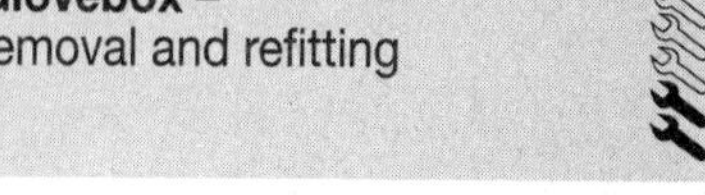

31 Glovebox – removal and refitting

Removal

1 Open the glovebox, then disconnect the damper from the outer side of the glovebox – this unclips towards the left **(see illustration)**.

2 Press in both sides of the glovebox to release the stops, and fully open the glovebox **(see illustration)**.

3 Release the bottom hinges by pulling the base of the glovebox towards you, and withdraw the glovebox from the facia panel **(see illustration)**.

31.1 Disconnect the damper . . .

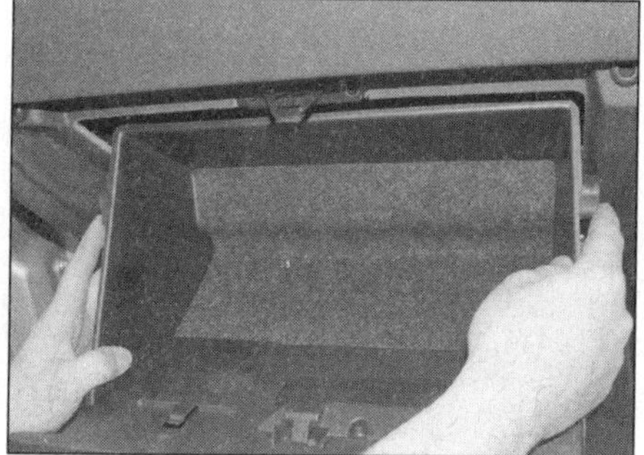

31.2 . . . press in both sides . . .

31.3 . . . then release the hinges and withdraw the glovebox

31.4a Undo the screws . . .

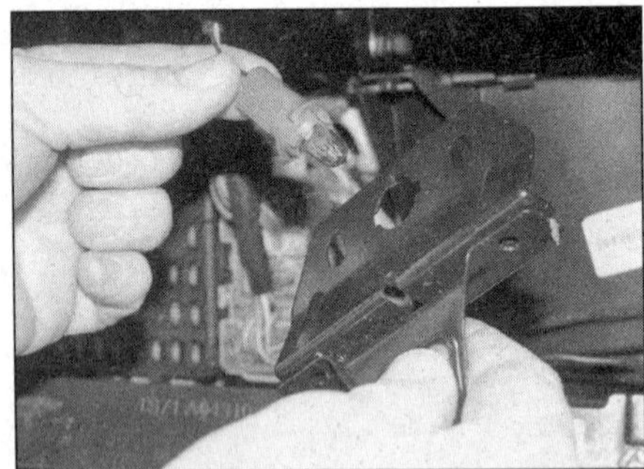

31.4b . . . and disconnect the illumination light bulbholder . . .

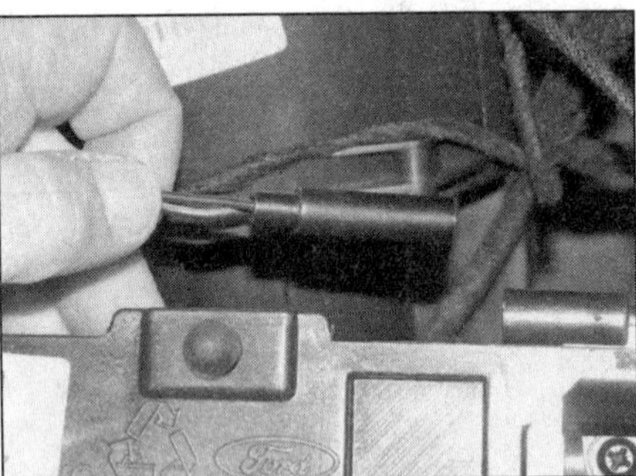

31.4c . . . then disconnect the wiring and withdraw the latch

4 To remove the glovebox latch, first undo the two retaining screws. Withdraw the latch and disconnect the illumination light bulbholder. Disconnect the illumination light wiring at the connector **(see illustrations)**.

Refitting

5 Refitting is a reversal of removal.

32 Facia – removal and refitting

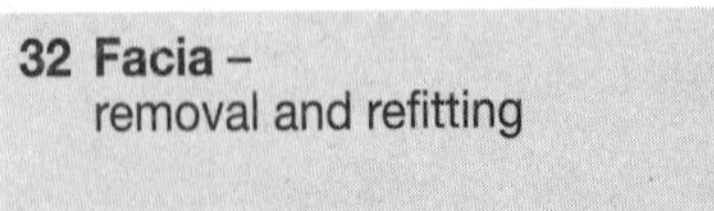

Removal

1 Disconnect the battery negative lead (refer to *Disconnecting the battery* at the end of this manual).

2 Remove the centre console as described in Section 29.

3 Remove the radio unit from the centre of the facia as described in Chapter 12.

4 Remove the heater control panel as described in Chapter 3.

5 Remove the steering column as described in Chapter 10.

6 Unclip the facia lower trim panels above the driver's and passenger's footwells. Where applicable, disconnect the wiring plugs from the footwell lights.

7 Remove the screw securing the diagnostic connector plug to the driver's side of the facia panel **(see illustrations)**.

8 Remove the glovebox as described in Section 31, then unclip the glovebox light switch from the facia panel.

9 Remove the internal temperature sensor from the lower facia on the driver's side.

10 Reach up under the facia on the passenger's side, and disconnect the wiring from the passenger airbag module.

11 Undo the two bolts securing the passenger airbag to the facia crossmember.

Caution: The passenger airbag module retaining bolts must only be used a maximum of three times. Use a centre-punch to mark the bolts.

12 Remove the instrument panel from the facia as described in Chapter 12.

Caution: The instrument panel must be kept upright, to prevent silicone liquid leaking from the gauges.

13 On models equipped with remote central locking, carefully prise out the grille from the front of the facia (beneath the windscreen) and disconnect the wiring from the sensor **(see illustration)**. The sensor is visible on top of the grille if remote locking is fitted, otherwise it is not necessary to remove the grille.

14 In the centre of the facia, undo the four screws and remove the support bracket. Also in the centre, unscrew the support bracket retaining nut **(see illustration)**.

15 Unscrew the nuts/bolts securing each end of the facia to the facia crossmember **(see illustration)**.

16 Remove the trim panels from each A-pillar as described in Section 28.

17 Pull back the A-pillar weatherstrips in the area of the facia, then remove the side trim panels, and unscrew the facia side mounting bolts **(see illustrations)**.

18 On automatic transmission models, move the selector lever to position P.

19 With the help of an assistant, carefully lift the facia away from the bulkhead and

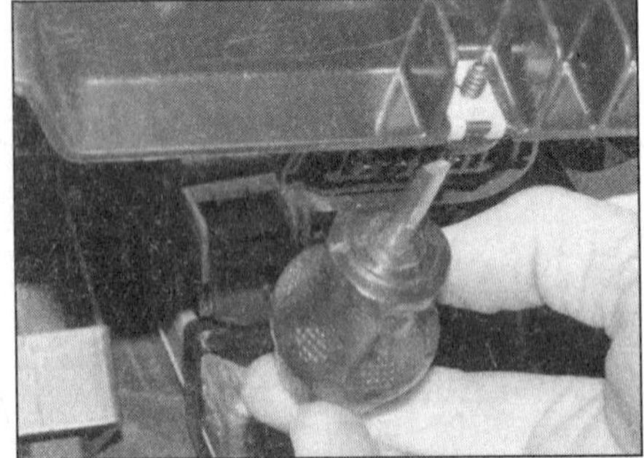

32.7a Undo the screw . . .

32.7b . . . and remove the diagnostic plug

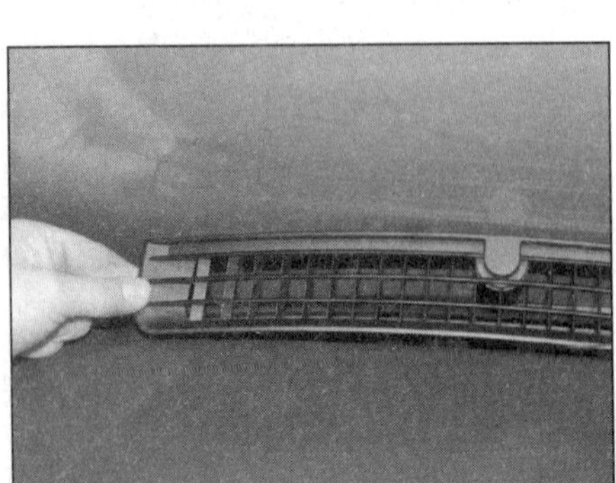

32.13 Removing the grille from the front of the facia

32.14 Removing a support bracket from the centre of the facia

32.15 Unscrewing the nuts/bolts securing each end of the facia to the bulkhead crossbeam

withdraw it from one side of the car **(see illustration)**.

Refitting

20 Refitting is a reversal of removal, but tighten nuts and bolts to the specified torque where this is given in the appropriate Chapter. In particular, observe the refitting procedure for the passenger airbag, A-pillar trim and steering column. On completion, check the operation of all electrical components.

33 Wheel arch liner – removal and refitting

Removal

Front

1 Apply the handbrake, then jack up the front of the car and support it on axle stands (see *Jacking and vehicle support*). Remove the relevant roadwheel.
2 Undo the retaining screws located on the outer edge of the wheel arch.
3 Unscrew the two bolts located on the rear lower edge of the liner.
4 Remove the three plastic fasteners by pressing out the central locking pins.
5 Remove the wheel arch liner from the car, while guiding it around the front suspension strut.

Rear

6 Chock the front wheels, then jack up the rear of the car and support on axle stands (see *Jacking and vehicle support*). Remove the relevant roadwheel.
7 Remove the screws and clips securing the liner to the outer edge of the wheel arch.
8 Unscrew and remove the screws securing the liner to the inner wheel arch, and withdraw the liner from under the car.

Refitting

9 Refitting is a reversal of the removal procedure, but tighten the wheel nuts to the specified torque.

34 Fuel filler flap release cable – removal and refitting

Removal

1 Working in the luggage compartment, remove the trim from the right-hand side for access to the fuel flap release cable.
2 Reach into the inner panel aperture and disconnect the cable from the release pin **(see illustration)**.
3 With the filler flap open, prise out the release pin.
4 The filler flap cable is routed over the rear wheel arch and along the inner sill panel to the control lever next to the driver's seat **(see

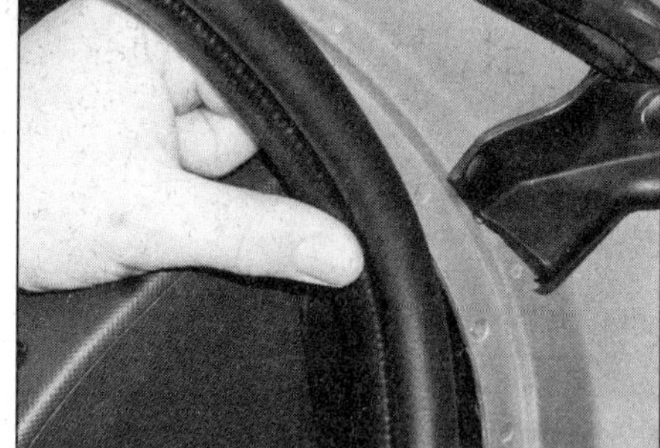

32.17a Pull back the weatherstrips . . .

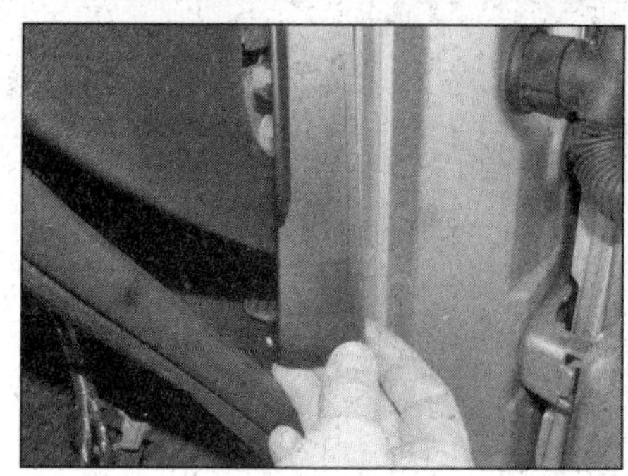

32.17b . . . remove the side trim panels . . .

32.17c . . . and unscrew the facia side mounting bolts

32.19 Removing the facia

illustration)**. Remove the interior trim panels with reference to Section 28.
5 Release the cable from the retaining clips and withdraw from the car.
6 The release lever is bolted to the inner sill panel with two bolts **(see illustration)**.
7 The fuel tank filler neck is retained by a single bolt to the body panel.

Refitting

8 Refitting is a reversal of removal.

35 Cup holder – removal and refitting

Removal

1 On manual transmission models, prise up the gear lever trim panel at the rear to release the clips, then pull it backwards to release the front clips – the clips are quite tight. Turn the gaiter inside-out, and feed the panel up the gear lever, clear of the working area. To remove the panel completely (which is useful but not strictly necessary), carefully stretch the elasticated top of the gaiter up and over the gear knob.

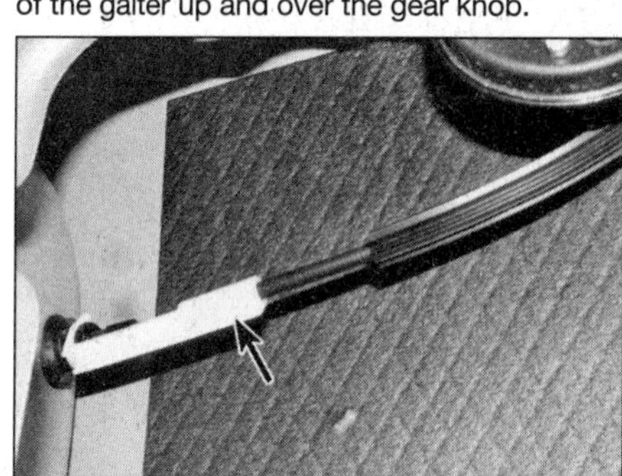

34.2 Fuel filler flap release pin and cable

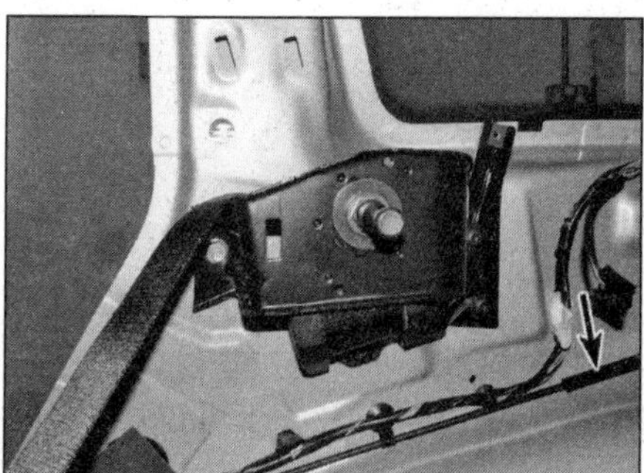

34.4 Fuel filler flap release cable routed over the rear wheel arch

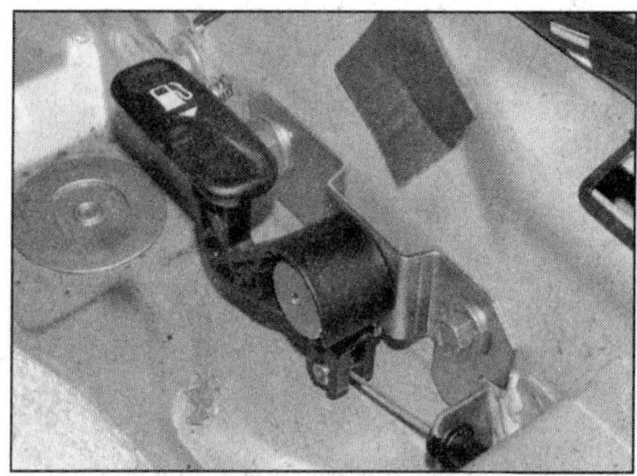

34.6 Fuel filler flap release lever

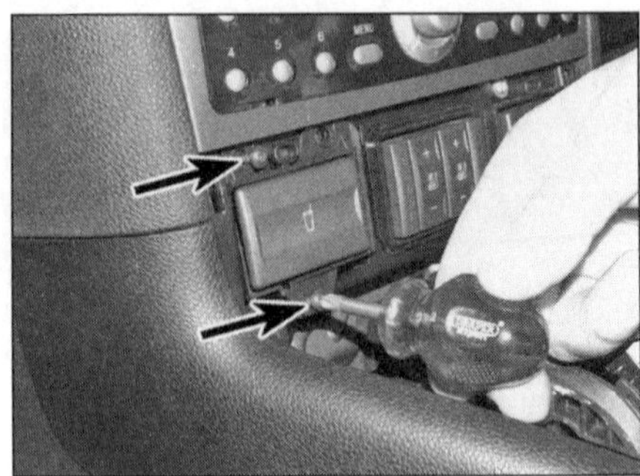
35.3a Remove the two screws . . .

35.3b . . . and withdraw the cup holder from the facia

2 On automatic transmission models, move the selector lever to the N position. Starting with the clip on either side at the front, unclip and lift off the selector lever trim panel.

3 Remove the two screws securing the cup holder to the facia, then carefully withdraw it – it is quite a long unit **(see illustrations)**.

Refitting

4 Refitting is a reversal of removal. The cup holder unit is fitted with a foam section at the front, which can be quite fiddly to feed into place – it make take a few tries before it will seat properly.

Chapter 12
Body electrical system

Contents

Degrees of difficulty

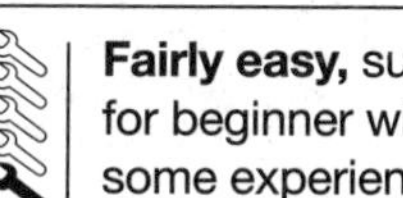

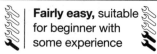

Easy, suitable for novice with little experience	**Fairly easy,** suitable for beginner with some experience	**Fairly difficult,** suitable for competent DIY mechanic	**Difficult,** suitable for experienced DIY mechanic	**Very difficult,** suitable for expert DIY or professional

Specifications

Fuses and relays
Refer to the wiring diagrams at the end of this Chapter.

Note: *Fuse ratings and circuits are liable to change from year to year. Consult the handbook supplied with the car, or consult a Ford dealer, for the latest information.*

Bulbs	**Wattage**	**Type**
Direction indicator lights	21	Bayonet, orange
Footwell	5	Wedge
Front foglight:		
Standard	55	H11 Halogen
Sports bumper	55	H3 Halogen
ST models	55	H7 Halogen
Glove compartment	5	Wedge
Headlight:		
Main beam	55	H1 Halogen
Dipped beam	55	H7 Halogen
High-level stop-light (x5)	5	Wedge
Interior light	10	Festoon
Luggage compartment	10	Festoon
Number plate light	5	Festoon
Reading light	5	Wedge
Rear fog/tail lights (Estate)	21/4	Bayonet
Rear foglight (Saloon)	21	Bayonet
Rear tail light (Saloon and Hatchback)	5	Bayonet
Reversing light:		
Saloon and Hatchback	21 (special bulb)	Bayonet, halogen
Estate	21	Bayonet
Side repeater light	5	Wedge, orange
Sidelight	5	Wedge
Sun visor	5	Wedge

Torque wrench settings	Nm	lbf ft
Airbag control module	7	5
Driver's airbag	5	4
Front crash sensor	8	6
Front suspension strut top mounting brace:		
To cowl	8	6
To inner wing panel	25	18
Front suspension strut upper mounting	30	22
Passenger's airbag	7	5
Side impact sensor	7	5
Windscreen wiper motor crank to motor shaft	26	19
Windscreen wiper motor linkage/bracket to bulkhead	8	6
Windscreen wiper motor to bracket	8	6
Wiper arm nuts	15	11

1 General information

Warning: Before carrying out any work on the electrical system, read through the precautions given in Safety first! at the beginning of this manual.

The electrical system is of 12 volt negative-earth type. Power for the lights and all electrical accessories is supplied by a lead-calcium or lead-acid battery which is charged by the alternator. The lead-calcium battery is identified by the letters 'Ca' on the information label, and the manufacturers recommend that an identical battery is fitted when renewing the battery.

This Chapter covers repair and service procedures for the various electrical components not associated with the engine. Information on the battery, alternator, and starter motor can be found in Chapter 5A; the ignition system is covered in Chapter 5B.

All models are fitted with a two-stage driver's airbag mounted in the steering wheel, which is designed to prevent serious chest and head injuries to the driver during a frontal accident (of sufficient force) within 30° from the left or right of the vehicle's centre-line. A similar bag for the front seat passenger is also fitted in the facia. Side airbags, which are built into the sides of the front seats, and side curtain airbags, located on each side of the roof headlining, are fitted to offer greater passenger protection in a side impact. The control unit for the airbag system is located under the centre console; it triggers the seat belt pretensioners in the event of an accident, as well as the airbags. A crash sensor is located at the front of the vehicle and a side impact sensor is located behind the trim panels at the base of each B-pillar. A seat position sensor is fitted to the driver's seat track, and a seat occupancy sensor is fitted to the front passenger seat **(see illustration)**.

The airbag system control unit (the Restraints Control Module) contains a back-up capacitor, crash sensor, decelerometer, safety sensor, integrated circuit and microprocessor. Each airbag is inflated by a gas generator, which forces the bag out of the cover in the steering wheel, facia panel, seat side cushion or headlining – care must be taken not to hinder the deployment of the side airbags by fitting aftermarket seat covers or by hanging articles of clothing over the seat backs. On the driver's airbag (which turns with the steering wheel) a 'clock spring' connector ensures that a good electrical connection is maintained with the airbag module at all times – as the steering wheel is turned in each direction, the spring winds and unwinds. The front passenger seat occupancy sensor forms part of the seat cushion and cannot be renewed separately.

The airbag system is known as the Intelligent Protection System as it has an adaptive capability – it can adjust the level of protection according to circumstances, and to the number of passengers (or lack of them). If the system's crash sensors detect a less-severe impact, the front airbags may only deploy their first stage, or may not fire at all, while the seat belt pretensioners (see Chapter 11) can, in fact, deploy independently – at lower impact levels than the airbags. A seat position sensor is fitted to the driver's seat track to inform the system how far forward the seat is set by the driver – when the seat is close to the steering wheel, the driver's airbag's second stage of firing is disabled, to prevent neck injuries. Thanks to the front passenger seat occupancy sensor, the system knows if a passenger is using the front seat – when the seat is empty, the passenger front and side airbags are disabled – to show this, if the front passenger seat is empty and its seat belt is buckled, the airbag deactivation light (where fitted) in the facia illuminates; normally, this light illuminates only briefly (as a check of its operation) on switching on the ignition, and then goes out. Although all airbags are linked, the separate side impact sensors are used to detect major lateral collisions – the side and curtain airbags will only deploy if the car is struck from the side with 'serious' force. The unit performs continual system diagnostics; on switching on the ignition the airbag warning light in the instrument panel will illuminate briefly (as a check of its operation) and then go out if all is well. If the airbag warning light illuminates, whether intermittently or continuously, at any other time (or if it does not illuminate on switching on the ignition), this indicates the presence of a fault which must be checked as soon as possible by a Ford dealer.

Warning: The passenger airbag cannot be disabled manually. Babies and small children should never be carried – especially in rearward-facing child seats – in the front passenger seat; there is a very high risk of injury to the baby if the airbag should deploy. Furthermore, they should never be carried on the lap of a person occupying that seat.

Warning: When working on the airbag system, always wait at least one minute after disconnecting the battery, as a precaution against accidental deployment of the airbag unit. This period ensures that any stored energy in the back-up capacitor is dissipated. Do not use battery-operated radio key code savers, as this may cause the airbag to be deployed, with the possibility of personal injury.

On models with xenon dipped headlights, an automatic headlight-levelling system is fitted to comply with current legislation. The system consists of sensors fitted to the front

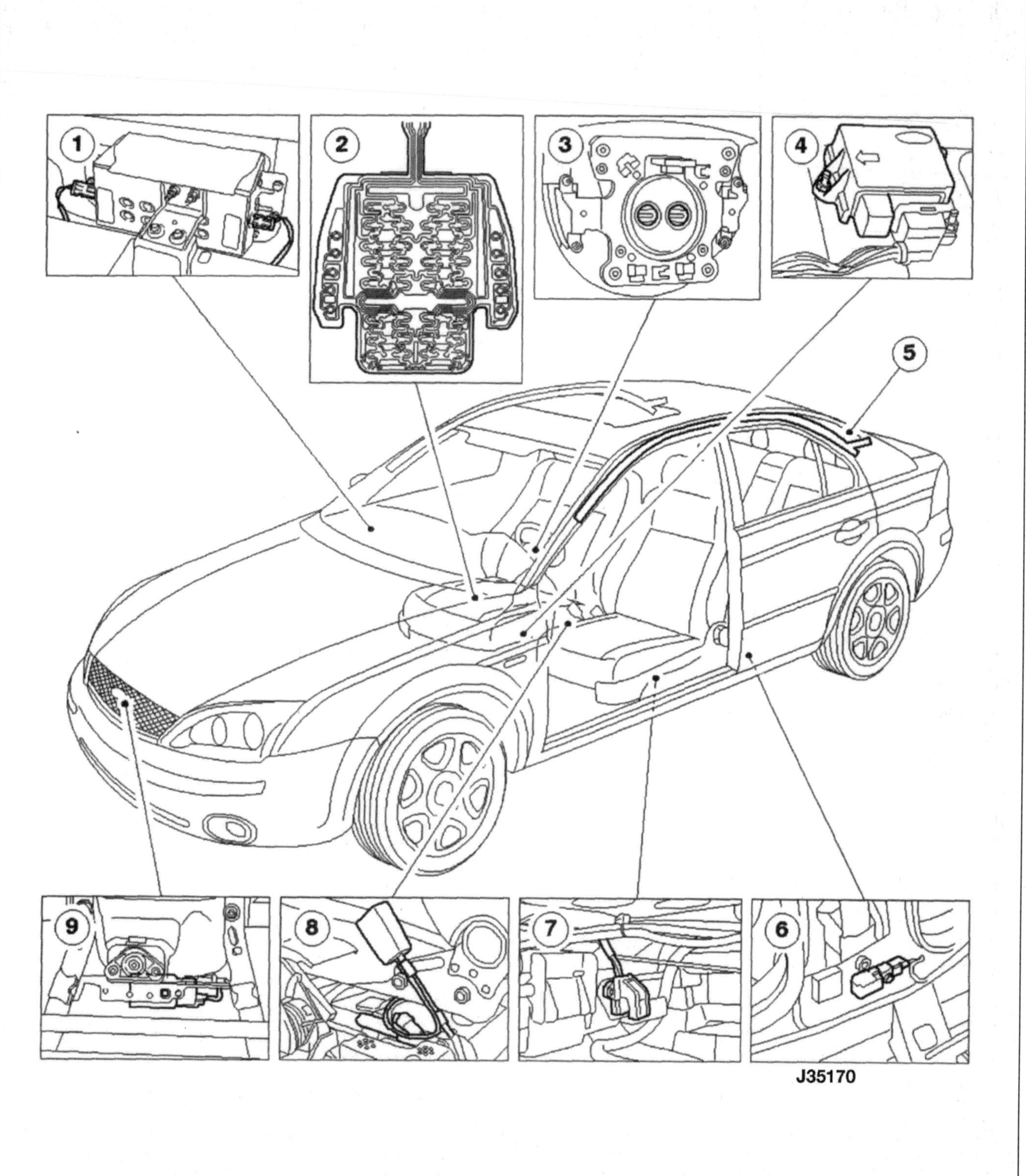

1.3 Airbag and safety belt pretensioner supplemental restraint system (SRS)

1 *Passenger airbag module*
2 *Occupant classification sensor*
3 *Driver airbag module*
4 *Airbag control module*
5 *Curtain airbag module*
6 *Side impact sensor*
7 *Seat position sensor*
8 *Safety belt buckle switch*
9 *Crash sensor*

and rear axles, a master control module on the left-hand headlight housing, a slave control module fitted on the right-hand headlight housing, and headlight-levelling motors fitted to both headlight housings. When the ignition is switched on, the system automatically adjusts the headlight beam to avoid dazzling of oncoming traffic. Note that the system must be initialised whenever a sensor is removed, or after disconnecting the system electrical wiring. Note that xenon bulbs are designed to last the life of the car.

Models with conventional headlights are fitted with a manually-controlled headlight-levelling system, with a facia-mounted control. On position 0, the headlights are in their base (normal) position – from here, turn the control to lower the aim of the headlights according to the load being carried.

All UK models are fitted with an alarm system incorporating an engine immobiliser. On Saloon and Hatchback models, the alarm system horn is located on the left-hand side of the luggage compartment, but on Estate models, it is on the right-hand side.

It should be noted that, when portions of the electrical system are serviced, the lead should be disconnected from the battery negative terminal, to prevent electrical shorts and fires (refer to *Disconnecting the battery* at the end of this manual).

2 Electrical fault finding – general information

Note: *Refer to the precautions given in Safety first! and in Section 1 of this Chapter before starting work. The following tests relate to testing of the main electrical circuits, and should not be used to test delicate electronic circuits (such as engine management systems, anti-lock braking systems, etc), particularly where an electronic control unit (ECU) is used.*

General

A typical electrical circuit consists of an electrical component, any switches, relays, motors, fuses, fusible links or circuit breakers related to that component, and the wiring and connectors which link the component to both the battery and the body. To help pinpoint a problem in an electrical circuit, wiring diagrams are included at the end of this Chapter.

Before attempting to diagnose an electrical fault, first study the appropriate wiring diagram, to obtain a complete understanding of the components included in the particular circuit concerned. The possible sources of a fault can be narrowed down by noting if other components related to the circuit are operating properly. If several components or circuits fail at one time, the problem is likely to be related to a shared fuse or earth connection.

Electrical problems usually stem from simple causes, such as loose or corroded connections, a faulty earth connection, a blown fuse, a melted fusible link, or a faulty relay (refer to Section 3 for details of testing relays). Visually inspect the condition of all fuses, wires and connections in a problem circuit before testing the components. Use the wiring diagrams to determine which terminal connections will need to be checked in order to pinpoint the trouble spot.

The basic tools required for electrical fault finding include a circuit tester or voltmeter (a 12 volt bulb with a set of test leads can also be used for certain tests), an ohmmeter (to measure resistance and check for continuity), a battery and set of test leads, and a jumper wire (preferably with a circuit breaker or fuse incorporated), which can be used to bypass suspect wires or electrical components. Before attempting to locate a problem with test instruments, use the wiring diagram to determine where to make the connections.

To find the source of an intermittent wiring fault (usually due to a poor or dirty connection, or damaged wiring insulation), a 'wiggle' test can be performed on the wiring. This involves wiggling the wiring by hand to see if the fault occurs as the wiring is moved. It should be possible to narrow down the source of the fault to a particular section of wiring. This method of testing can be used in conjunction with any of the tests described in the following sub-Sections.

Apart from problems due to poor connections, two basic types of fault can occur in an electrical circuit – open-circuit, or short-circuit.

Open circuit faults are caused by a break somewhere in the circuit, which prevents current from flowing. An open circuit fault will prevent a component from working, but will not cause the relevant circuit fuse to blow.

Short circuit faults are caused by a 'short' somewhere in the circuit, which allows the current flowing in the circuit to 'escape' along an alternative route, usually to earth. Short circuit faults are normally caused by a breakdown in wiring insulation, which allows a feed wire to touch either another wire, or an earthed component such as the bodyshell. A short circuit fault will normally cause the relevant circuit fuse to blow.

Finding an open-circuit

To check for an open circuit, connect one lead of a circuit tester or the negative lead of a voltmeter either to the battery negative terminal or to a known good earth.

Connect the other lead to a connector in the circuit being tested, preferably nearest to the battery or fuse.

Switch on the circuit, bearing in mind that some circuits are live only when the ignition switch is moved to a particular position.

If voltage is present (indicated either by the tester bulb lighting or a voltmeter reading, as applicable), this means that the section of the circuit between the relevant connector and the switch is problem-free.

Continue to check the remainder of the circuit in the same fashion.

When a point is reached at which no voltage is present, the problem must lie between that point and the previous test point with voltage. Most problems can be traced to a broken, corroded or loose connection.

Finding a short-circuit

To check for a short circuit, first disconnect the load(s) from the circuit (loads are the components which draw current from a circuit, such as bulbs, motors, heating elements, etc).

Remove the relevant fuse from the circuit, and connect a circuit tester or voltmeter to the fuse connections.

Switch on the circuit, bearing in mind that some circuits are live only when the ignition switch is moved to a particular position.

If voltage is present (indicated either by the tester bulb lighting or a voltmeter reading, as applicable), this means that there is a short circuit.

If no voltage is present during this test, but the fuse still blows with the load(s) reconnected, this indicates an internal fault in the load(s).

Finding an earth fault

The battery negative terminal is connected to 'earth' – the metal of the engine/transmission and the body – and many systems are wired so that they only receive a positive feed, the current returning via the metal of the car body. This means that the component mounting and the body form part of that circuit. Loose or corroded mountings can therefore cause a range of electrical faults, ranging from total failure of a circuit, to a puzzling partial failure. In particular, lights may shine dimly (especially when another circuit sharing the same earth point is in operation), motors (eg, wiper motors or the radiator cooling fan motor) may run slowly, and the operation of one circuit may have an apparently-unrelated effect on another. Note that on many vehicles, earth straps are used between certain components, such as the engine/transmission and the body, usually where there is no metal-to-metal contact between components, due to flexible rubber mountings, etc.

To check whether a component is properly earthed, disconnect the battery and connect one lead of an ohmmeter to a known good earth point. Connect the other lead to the wire or earth connection being tested. The resistance reading should be zero; if not, check the connection as follows.

If an earth connection is thought to be faulty, dismantle the connection, and clean back to bare metal both the bodyshell and the wire terminal or the component earth connection mating surface. Be careful to remove all traces of dirt and corrosion, then use a knife to trim away any paint, so that a clean metal-to-metal joint is made. On reassembly, tighten the joint fasteners securely; if a wire terminal is being refitted, use serrated washers between the

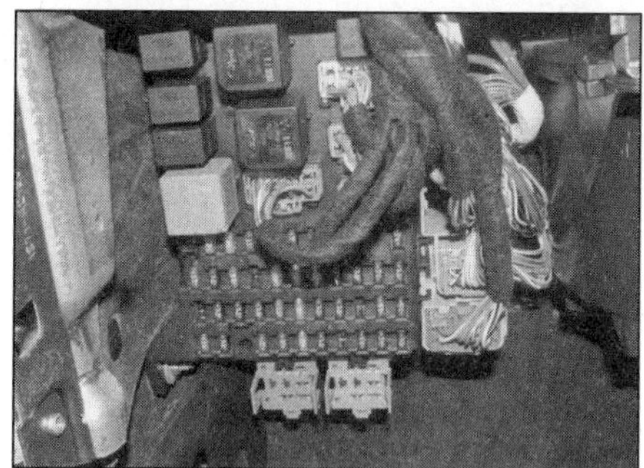

3.1 Main fusebox and relay location behind the glovebox

terminal and the bodyshell, to ensure a clean and secure connection. When the connection is remade, prevent the onset of corrosion in the future by applying a coat of petroleum jelly or silicone-based grease, or by spraying on (at regular intervals) a proprietary ignition sealer or a water-dispersant lubricant.

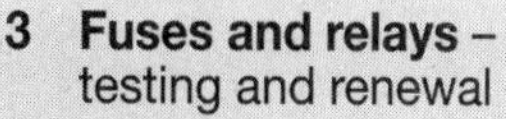

3 Fuses and relays – testing and renewal

Fuses

1 Fuses are designed to break a circuit when a predetermined current is reached, in order to protect components and wiring which could be damaged by excessive current flow. Any excessive current flow will be due to a fault in the circuit, usually a short-circuit. The main fusebox, which also carries some relays, is located inside the car behind the glovebox **(see illustration)**; remove the glovebox, or simply disconnect the damper and fully open the glovebox as described in Chapter 11.

2 The auxiliary fusebox is located in the engine compartment, on the left-hand side of the battery **(see illustration)**, and is accessed by first unclipping and removing the battery cover, then releasing the catch and lifting the fusebox cover. The auxiliary fusebox also contains some relays. Each circuit is identified on the outside of the removed glovebox and on the inside of the auxiliary fusebox cover. Plastic tweezers are attached to the inside face of the auxiliary fusebox to remove and fit the fuses.

3 To remove a fuse, use the tweezers provided or pliers to pull it out of the holder. Slide the fuse sideways from the tweezers. The wire within the fuse is clearly visible, and it will be broken if the fuse is blown **(see illustrations)**.

4 Always renew a fuse with one of an identical rating. Never substitute a fuse of a higher rating, or make temporary repairs using wire or metal foil; more serious damage, or even fire, could result. The fuse rating is stamped on top of the fuse. Never renew a fuse more than once without tracing the source of the trouble.

5 Spare fuses of various current ratings are provided in the cover of the auxiliary fusebox.

3.2 Auxiliary fusebox in the engine compartment

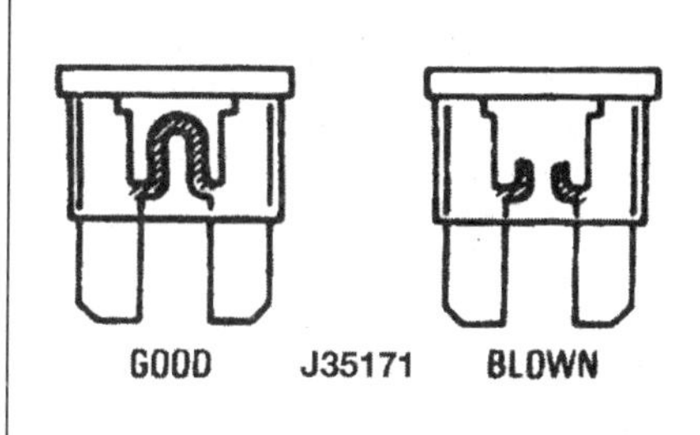

3.3b The fuses can be checked visually to determine if they are blown

Relays

6 Relays are electrically-operated switches, which are used in certain circuits. The various relays can be removed from their respective locations by carefully pulling them from the sockets.

7 If a component controlled by a relay becomes inoperative and the relay is suspect, listen to the relay as the circuit is operated. If the relay is functioning, it should be possible to hear it click as it is energised. If the relay proves satisfactory, the fault lies with the components or wiring of the system. If the relay is not being energised, then either the relay is not receiving a switching voltage, or the relay itself is faulty. Do not overlook the relay socket terminals when tracing faults. Testing is by the substitution of a known good unit, but be careful; some relays are identical in appearance and in operation, others look similar, but perform different functions.

4.1 Disconnecting the battery negative lead

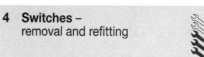

3.3a Removing a fuse

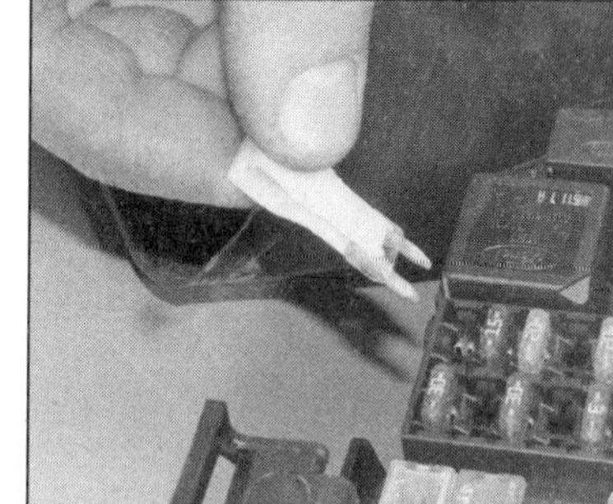

3.3c Using the special tweezers to remove a fuse

8 To renew a relay first ensure that the ignition switch is off. The relay can then simply be pulled out from the socket and the new relay pressed in.

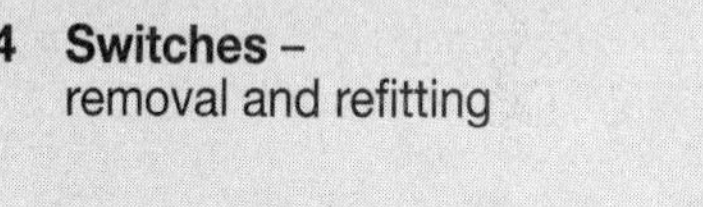

4 Switches – removal and refitting

Ignition switch and lock

Removal

1 Disconnect the battery negative lead (refer to *Disconnecting the battery* at the end of this manual) **(see illustration)**.

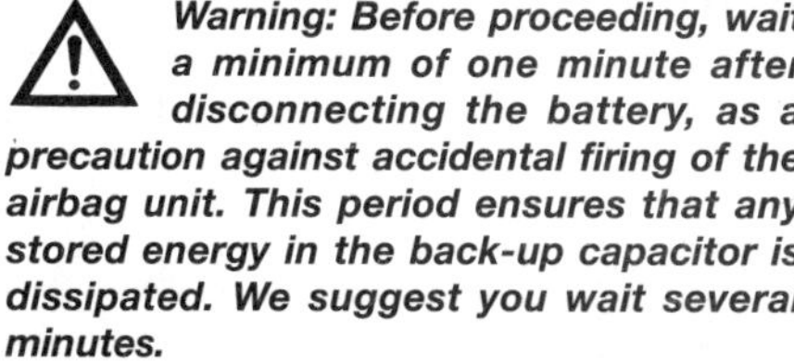

Warning: Before proceeding, wait a minimum of one minute after disconnecting the battery, as a precaution against accidental firing of the airbag unit. This period ensures that any stored energy in the back-up capacitor is dissipated. We suggest you wait several minutes.

2 With the front wheels in the straight-ahead position, remove the steering wheel as described in Chapter 10.

Caution: Make sure that the airbag clock spring is retained in its straight-ahead position using tape.

3 Remove the driver's side lower facia trim panel, which is secured by four screws and two upper clips. Where applicable, unclip the diagnostic connector plug from the panel, and/or disconnect the wiring from the climate control sensor as the panel is removed.

4 Where fitted, remove the audio control

4.7a Undo the screw . . .

4.7b . . . and remove the Passive Anti-Theft System (PATS) transceiver

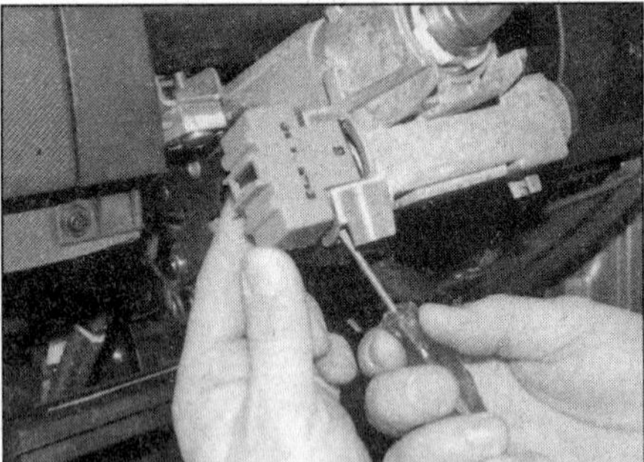
4.8a Release the clips . . .

4.8b . . . and remove the ignition switch

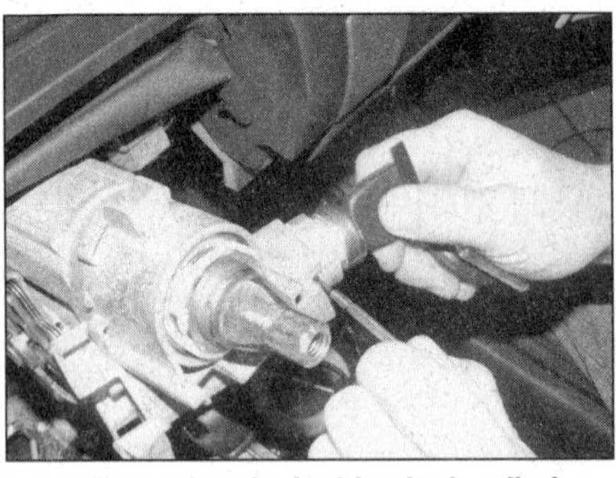
4.9 Removing the ignition lock cylinder

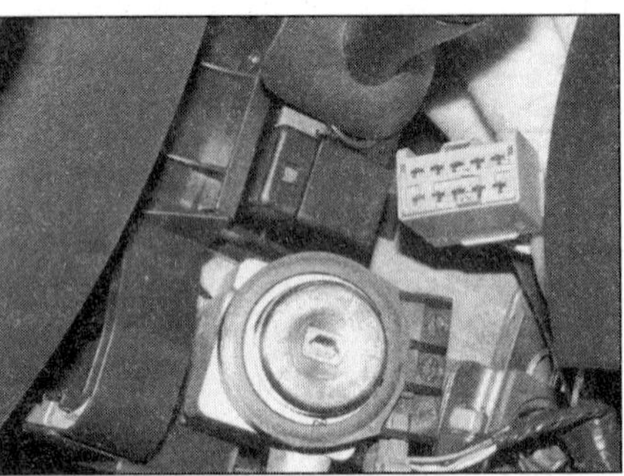
4.13 Disconnect the wiring . . .

switch from the steering column lower shroud. To do this, use a small screwdriver to release the plastic locking clip. Disconnect the wiring.

5 Remove the steering column upper shroud from the lower shroud by inserting a thin screwdriver between the clip on each side.

4.14a . . . then release the clip . . .

4.16a Removing the lower facia panel . . .

6 Undo the three screws and remove the lower shroud.

7 Undo the screw and remove the Passive Anti-Theft System (PATS) transceiver from the ignition/steering lock **(see illustrations)**.

8 Using a screwdriver, release the clips and remove the ignition switch **(see illustrations)**. Disconnect the wiring connector.

9 Insert the ignition key and turn it to position I, then, using a small screwdriver, depress the detent in the lock housing and withdraw the lock cylinder **(see illustration)**.

4.14b . . . and slide the windscreen wiper multifunction switch up from the steering column

4.16b . . . and vent

Refitting

10 Refitting is a reversal of removal, with reference to Chapter 10 when refitting the steering wheel. Also initialise the door window motors as described in Chapter 11.

Wiper/washer switch

Removal

11 Remove the steering column upper shroud from the lower shroud by inserting a thin screwdriver between the clip on each side.

12 Undo the three screws and remove the lower shroud.

13 Disconnect the wiring at the multiplug **(see illustration)**.

14 Using a screwdriver, release the clip then slide the windscreen wiper/washer multifunction switch up from the steering column **(see illustrations)**.

Refitting

15 Refitting is a reversal of removal.

Lights and foglights switch

Removal

16 Open the coin box lid. Remove the driver's side lower facia trim panel, which is secured by four screws and two upper clips. Where applicable, unclip the diagnostic connector plug from the panel, and/or disconnect

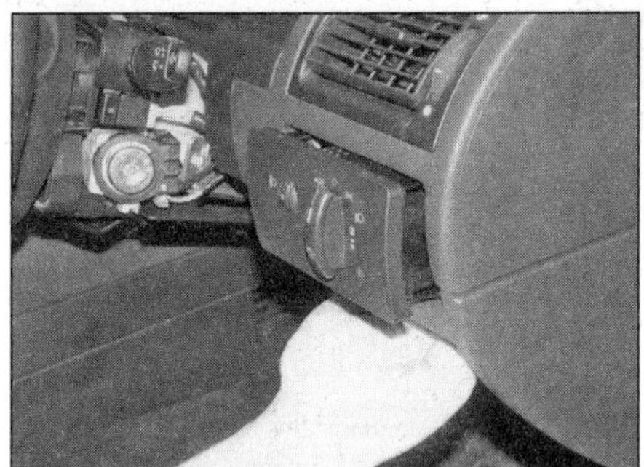
4.17 Press out the main lights and foglights combination switch from the facia . . .

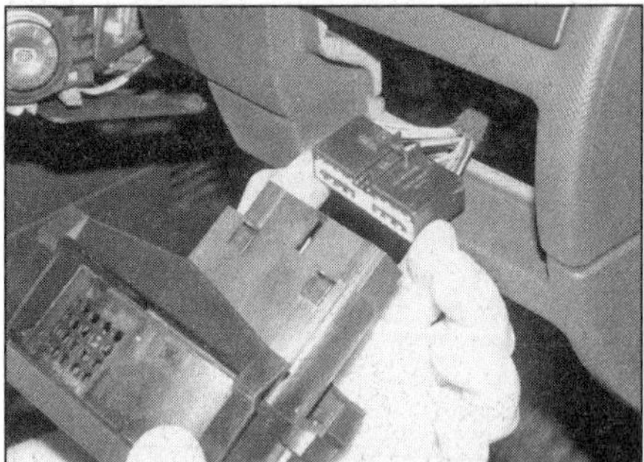
4.18 . . . then disconnect the wiring

4.20 Prise out the switch panel top corners . . .

the wiring from the climate control sensor as the panel is removed. Also remove the vent located above the switch position **(see illustrations)**.

17 Reach up behind the facia and carefully press out the combination switch **(see illustration)**. The retaining plastic clips should release, however, it may be necessary to squeeze them together.

18 Disconnect the wiring from the rear of the switch **(see illustration)**.

Refitting

19 Refitting is a reversal of removal.

Heated screen switches

Removal

20 Using a small screwdriver, and taking care to protect the surrounding panels from damage, carefully prise out the switch surround panel at the top corners **(see illustration)**.

21 The switch surround panel bottom clips are located either side of the clock, at the base. The only way we found to release these clips was to slide a very thin-bladed screwdriver along the base of the panel, then lift and prise out the panel to release the clip on either side **(see illustration)**. Great care must be taken to avoid scratching the heater control panel as this is done.

22 Alternatively, removing the glovebox as described in Chapter 11 does give some access to the back of the switch surround panel, which may make removal easier.

23 With the panel released, disconnect the three wiring plugs on the back, noting their locations, and remove it completely **(see illustration)**.

24 The switches are in one unit, which is clipped into the panel at the rear **(see illustration)**. Once the clips are released, the switch assembly is pushed out from behind the panel.

Refitting

25 Refitting is a reversal of removal.

Hazard warning light switch

26 This switch is removed in the same way as the heated screen switches, described earlier in this Section.

4.21 . . . then release the bottom edge

4.23 Disconnect the wiring plugs on the back of the panel

Heated seat and ESP switches

Removal

27 Referring to Chapter 11, Section 29, paragraphs 4 to 6, remove the gear/selector lever trim panel, and the centre console upper trim panel.

28 Release the clips, and push the switch out of the panel from behind **(see illustration)**.

Refitting

29 Refitting is a reversal of removal.

Door mirror control switch

Removal

30 Prise the plastic cover from the door mirror inner trim, then undo the retaining screw.

31 Remove the trim and disconnect the wiring from the mirror control switch.

32 Carefully push the switch from the trim.

Refitting

33 Refitting is a reversal of removal.

Indicator and main/dip switch

Removal

34 Where fitted, remove the audio control switch from the steering column lower shroud. Use a small screwdriver to release the locking tang, then lift the switch from the column and disconnect the wiring.

35 Remove the steering column upper shroud from the lower shroud by inserting a thin screwdriver between the clip on each side.

36 Undo the three screws and remove the lower shroud.

37 Disconnect the multiplug, the depress the retaining lug and withdraw the switch assembly **(see illustrations)**.

38 With the switch assembly removed, pull

4.24 Release the clips at the rear, and push out the switch

4.28 Push the heated seat switch out from behind the trim panel

4.37a Disconnect the wiring . . .

4.37b . . . then release the clip . . .

4.37c . . . and slide the direction indicator/dipped beam multifunction switch up from the steering column

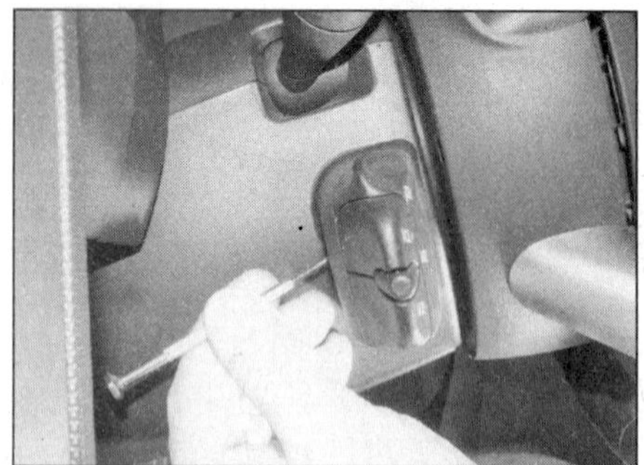
4.44a Release the locking tang . . .

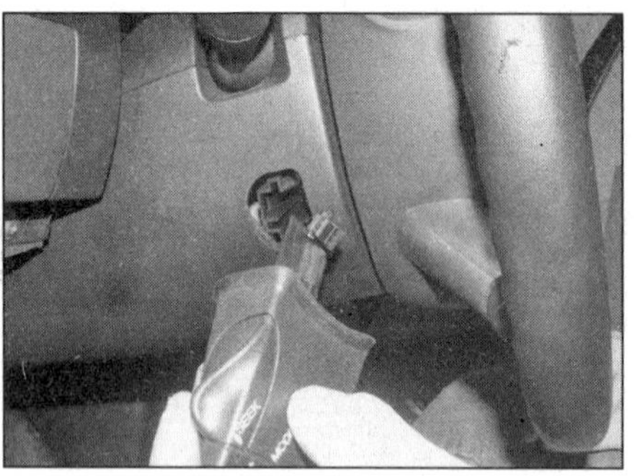
4.44b . . . and lift the switch from the shroud

4.52 Removing the handbrake-on warning switch from the handbrake lever

out the direction indicator relay (flasher unit) if required.

Refitting

39 Refitting is a reversal of removal.

Horn switch

Removal

40 Remove the airbag unit from the steering wheel as described in Section 28.
41 On models with cruise control, remove the switch components as described in Section 22.
42 Disconnect the wiring connector, then (where applicable) remove the two securing screws and carefully prise out the switch assembly.

Refitting

43 Refitting is a reversal of removal.

Radio remote control switch

Removal

44 Remove the audio control switch from the steering column lower shroud. Use a small screwdriver to release the locking tang, then lift the switch from the column shroud **(see illustrations)**.
45 Disconnect the wiring and remove the switch.

Refitting

46 Refitting is a reversal of removal.

Cruise control switches

47 Refer to Section 22.

Electric window switch

Removal

48 Carefully prise out the switch from the door inner trim panel, using a cloth pad to prevent damage to the trim.
49 Disconnect the multiplug and remove the switch.

Refitting

50 Refitting is a reversal of removal.

Handbrake-on warning switch

Removal

51 Remove the centre console as described in Chapter 11.
52 Disconnect the wiring, then remove the screw and withdraw the switch from the handbrake lever mounting bracket **(see illustration)**.

Refitting

53 Refitting is a reversal of removal.

5 Bulbs (exterior lights) – renewal

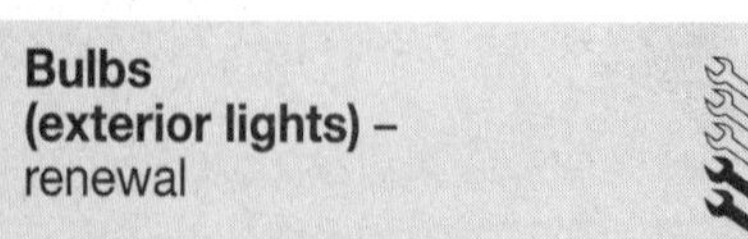

1 Whenever a bulb is renewed, note the following points:

- *Switch off all exterior lights and the ignition.*
- *Remember that if the light has just been in use, the bulb may be extremely hot.*
- *Always check the bulb contacts and holder, ensuring that there is clean metal-to-metal contact.*
- *Where bayonet-type bulbs are fitted, ensure that the contact springs bear firmly against the bulb contacts.*
- *Always ensure that the new bulb is of the correct rating and that it is completely clean before fitting it.*
- *Do not touch the glass of halogen-type bulbs (headlights, front foglights, reversing lights) with the fingers, as this may lead to premature failure of the new bulb; if the glass is accidentally touched, clean it with methylated spirit.*

Warning: Ford recommend the wearing of protective gloves and safety glasses when renewing xenon headlight bulbs. Do not switch on the headlights with the bulb removed – high voltages are present which could cause personal injury.

Headlight (main beam)

2 Remove the headlight unit as described in Section 7.
3 With the headlight unit on the bench, release the plastic clips and remove the cover for access to the headlight bulb **(see illustration)**. On models with xenon bulbs, undo the screws and release the locking tab to remove the cover.
4 Disconnect the wiring connector from the headlight main beam bulb (the inner one), then release the spring clip and withdraw the bulb, noting how it is fitted **(see illustrations)**.
5 Fit the new bulb using a reversal of the removal procedure.

5.3 Removing the cover for access to the headlight bulb

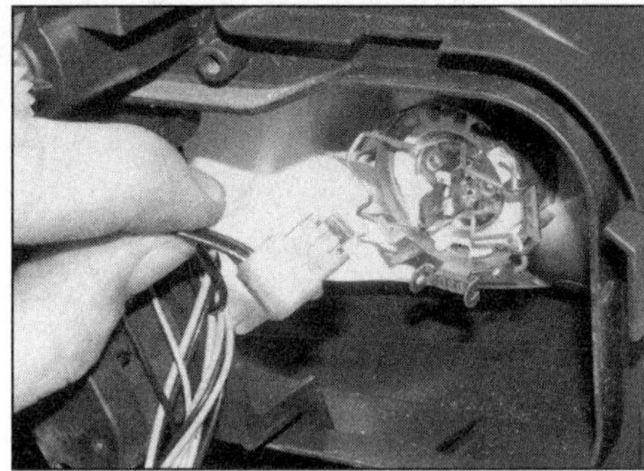
5.4a Disconnect the wiring connector . . .

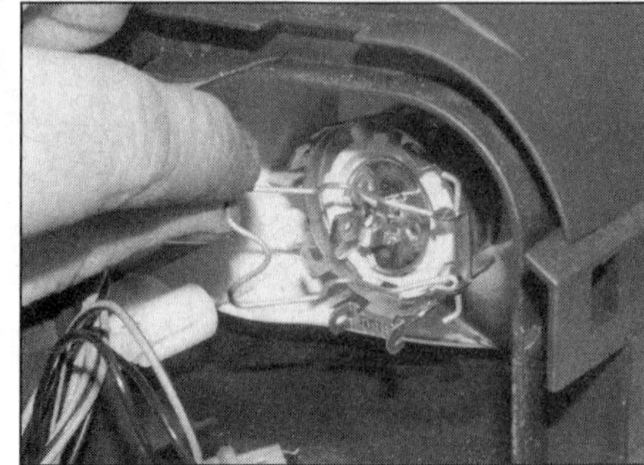
5.4b . . . then release the spring clip . . .

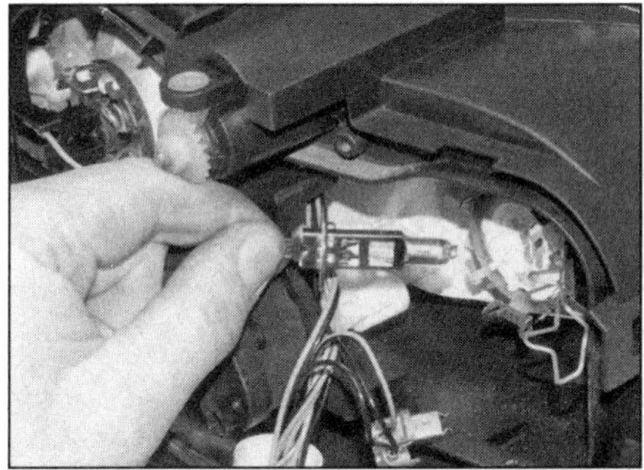
5.4c . . . and withdraw the headlight main beam bulb

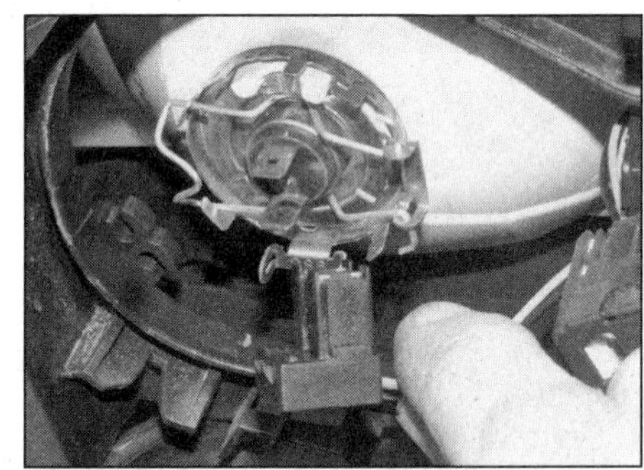
5.8a Disconnect the wiring connector . . .

5.8b . . . then release the spring clip . . .

Headlight (dipped beam)

6 Remove the headlight unit as described in Section 7.

7 With the headlight unit on the bench, release the plastic clips and remove the cover for access to the headlight bulb. On models with xenon bulbs, undo the screws and release the locking tab to remove the cover.

8 Disconnect the wiring connector from the headlight dipped beam bulb (the outer one), then release the spring clip and withdraw the bulb, noting how it is fitted **(see illustrations)**.

9 Fit the new bulb using a reversal of the removal procedure.

Front sidelight

10 Remove the headlight unit as described in Section 7.

11 With the headlight unit on the bench, twist the cover anti-clockwise to remove it **(see illustration)**.

12 Prise out the bulbholder, if necessary using a screwdriver **(see illustration)**.

13 Pull out the wedge-type bulb **(see illustration)**.

14 Fit the new bulb using a reversal of the removal procedure.

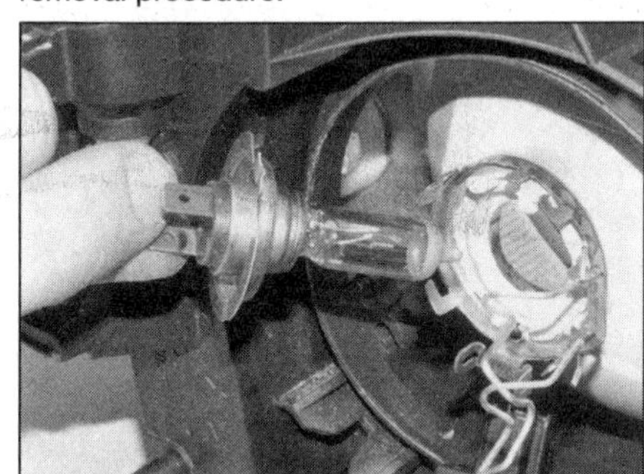
5.8c . . . and withdraw the headlight dipped beam bulb

Front direction indicator

15 Remove the headlight unit as described in Section 7.

16 With the headlight unit on the bench, turn the bulbholder anti-clockwise and remove

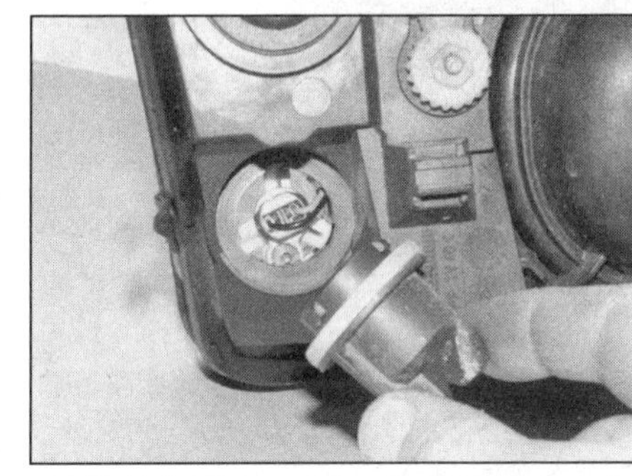
5.11 Twist the cover anti-clockwise and remove it . . .

5.12 . . . then prise out the bulbholder . . .

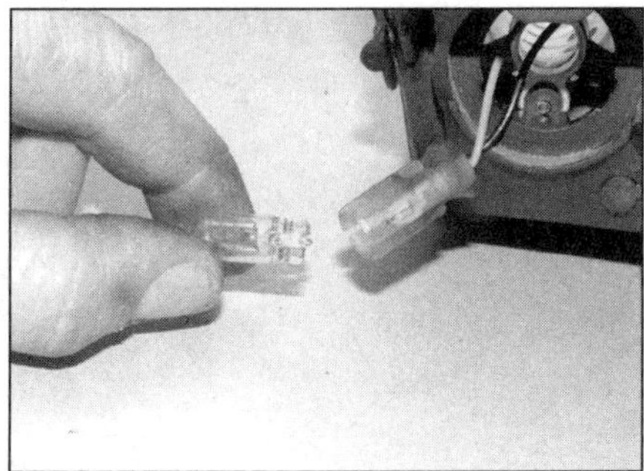
5.13 . . . and pull out the wedge-type front sidelight bulb

5.16 Turn the front direction indicator bulbholder anti-clockwise to remove it from the headlight unit

5.17 Depress and twist the bulb to remove it from the bulbholder

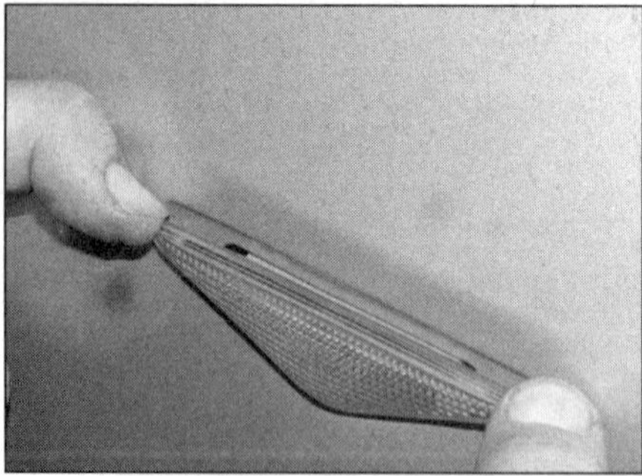

5.19a Press down the ends of the side repeater lens . . .

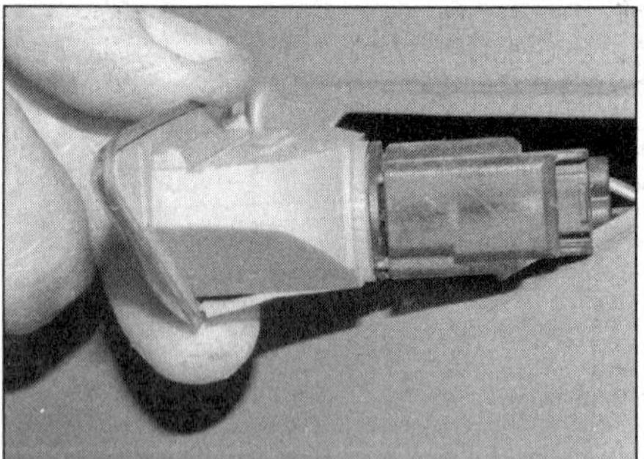

5.19b . . . then pull it out from the front wing

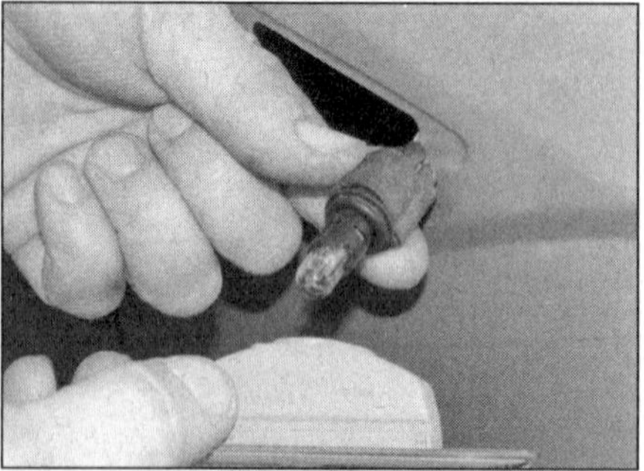

5.20 Twist the bulbholder anti-clockwise from the lens . . .

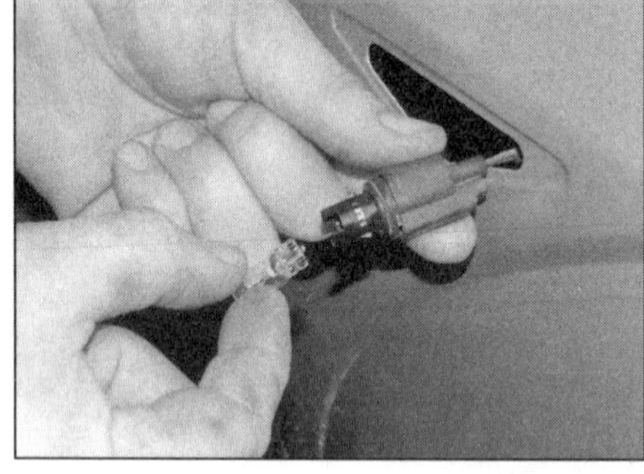

5.21 . . . then pull out the wedge-type bulb

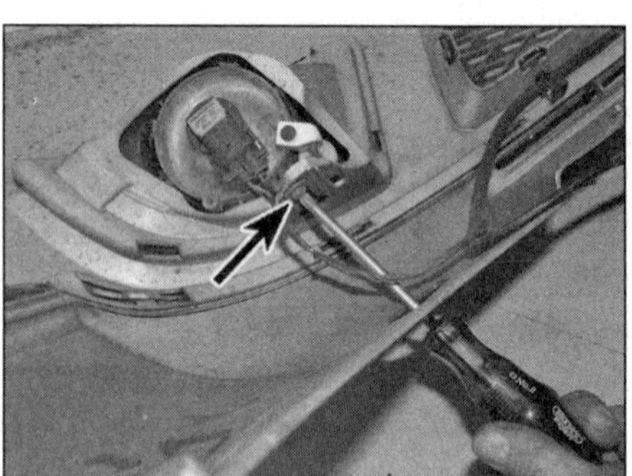

5.23 Remove the foglight mounting screw through the access hole in the bumper

it together with the bulb from the rear of the headlight unit **(see illustration).**

17 Depress and twist the bulb to remove it from the bulbholder **(see illustration).**

18 Fit the new bulb using a reversal of the removal procedure.

Side repeater

19 Carefully press down on the ends of the side repeater lens, then pull it out from the front wing **(see illustrations).**

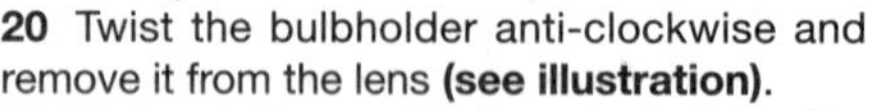

20 Twist the bulbholder anti-clockwise and remove it from the lens **(see illustration).**

21 Pull out the wedge-type bulb from the bulbholder **(see illustration).**

22 Fit the new bulb using a reversal of the removal procedure.

Front foglight

Except round light units

23 Remove the single cross-head screw underneath the light unit, working through the access hole provided in the bottom of the bumper **(see illustration).**

24 Using a small flat-bladed screwdriver, and taking care not to damage the bumper paintwork, release the two catches at the top of the light unit, and prise it forwards from the bumper **(see illustrations).**

25 Twist the bulbholder anti-clockwise and remove it from the light unit **(see illustration).**

26 Release the catches on either side of the wiring plug, and disconnect it from the bulb **(see illustration).**

27 Fit the new bulb using a reversal of the removal procedure.

Round light units

28 Remove the screw securing the foglight surround panel, and carefully prise out the panel from the front of the bumper. Remove the three screws behind, and pull out the light unit.

29 Release the catches, then pull the wiring plug on the back of the unit downwards to disconnect it. Twist the bulbholder anti-

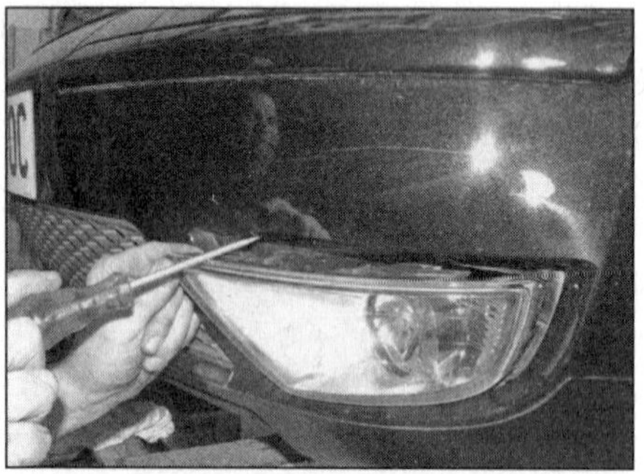

5.24a Carefully prise the foglight forwards at the top . . .

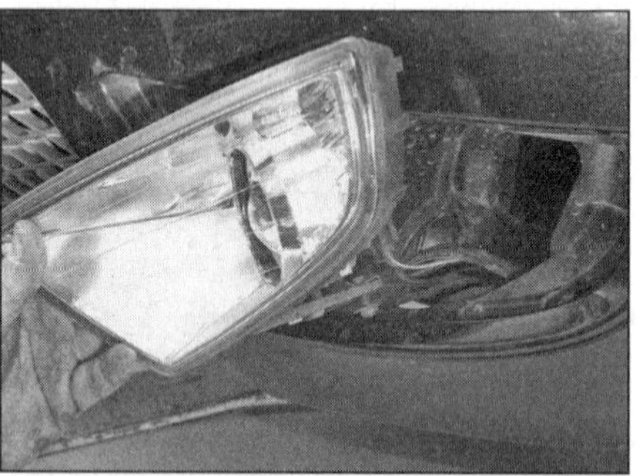

5.24b . . . and withdraw it from the bumper

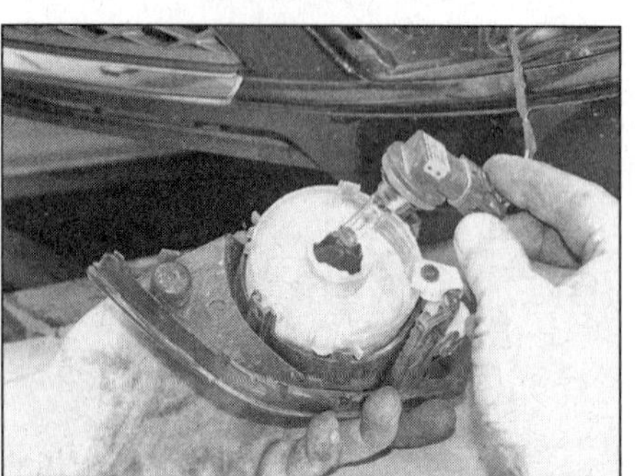

5.25 Twist the bulbholder anti-clockwise and withdraw from the light

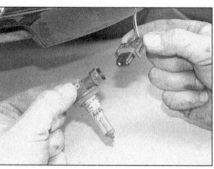

5.26 Disconnect the wiring plug from the bulb

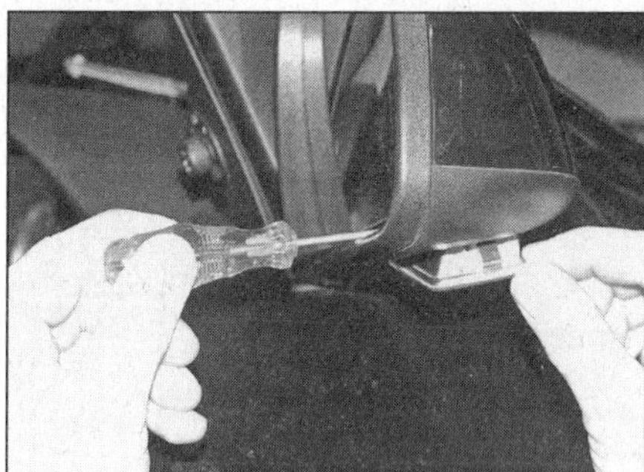
5.31 Use a small screwdriver as shown to release the approach light

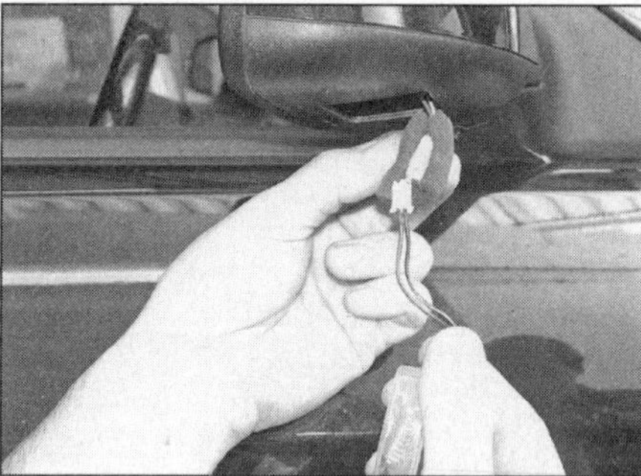
5.32 Disconnect the light's wiring plug

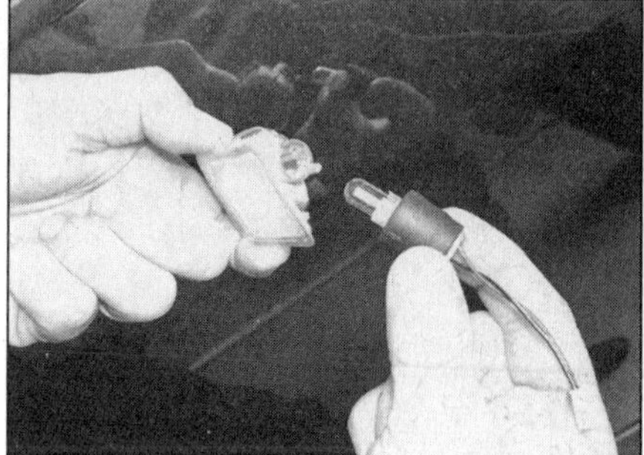
5.33 Release the bulbholder's rubber boot to remove

5.34 Pull out the wedge-base bulb

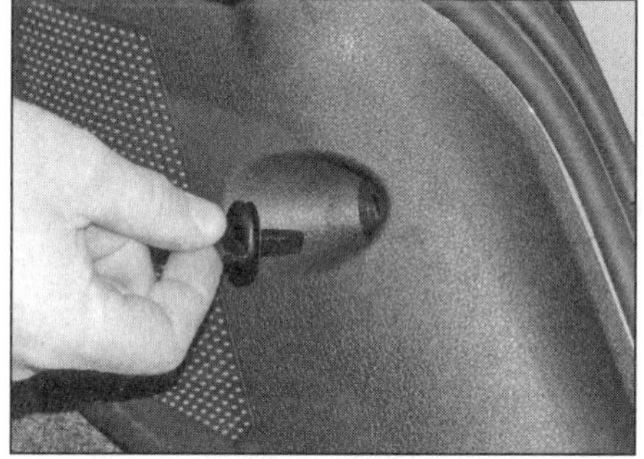
5.36a Twist off the fasteners . . .

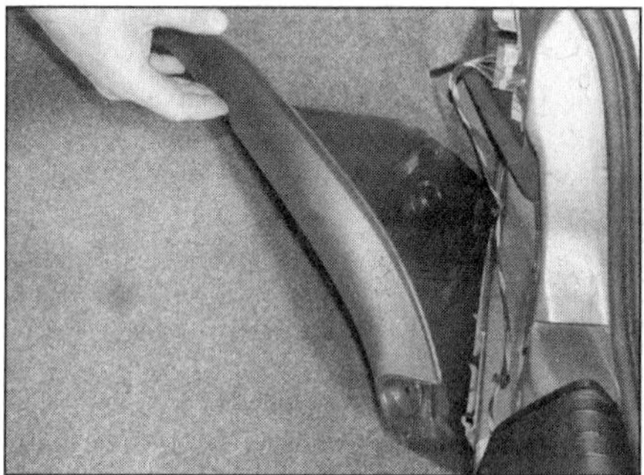
5.36b . . . and remove the rear light cluster cover . . .

clockwise and remove it from the light unit. Pull out the bulb, noting the position of the locating tab or flat.

30 Fit the new bulb using a reversal of the removal procedure.

Door mirror approach light

31 Using a small flat-bladed screwdriver inserted between the base of the mirror glass and the mirror housing/shell, release the spring clip at the outer side of the light, and swing it down from the mirror **(see illustration)**.

32 Disconnect the small wiring plug, and remove the light from the mirror **(see illustration)**.

33 The bulbholder has a tight-fitting rubber boot fitted between it and the light itself, which makes pulling out the bulbholder more difficult. However, by gently lifting the edge of the rubber with a screwdriver, it will release, and the bulbholder can be pulled out **(see illustration)**.

34 The bulb is a push-fit wedge-base type, and simply pulls out of the bulbholder **(see illustration)**.

35 Fit the new bulb using a reversal of the removal procedure. Ensure that the rubber boot is refitted correctly, as this keeps water out of the bulbholder. When refitting the light unit, engage the lugs on the inner end of the light with the mirror shell, then swing the outer end upwards and press to engage the spring clip.

Rear light cluster

Saloon and Hatchback

36 Open the boot lid and turn the three fasteners anti-clockwise to remove the relevant rear light cluster cover **(see illustrations)**.

37 Squeeze together the two red tabs to separate the bulbholder assembly from the light housing **(see illustrations)**.

38 Depress and twist the relevant bulb to remove it **(see illustrations)**. Note that the reversing light bulb is a special bayonet-fit

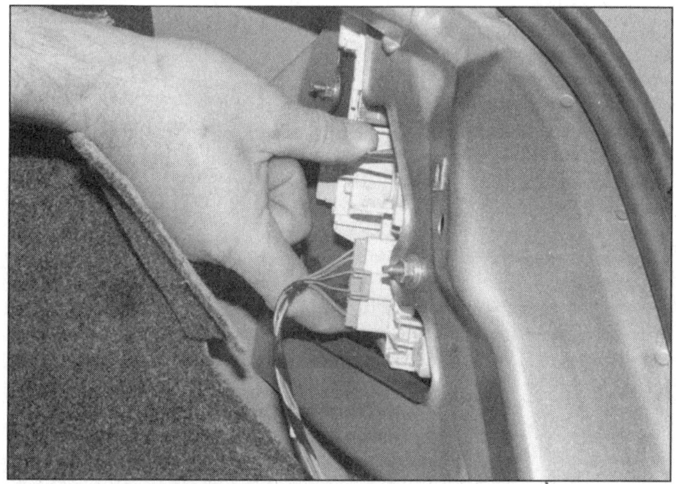
5.37a . . . then squeeze together the red tabs . . .

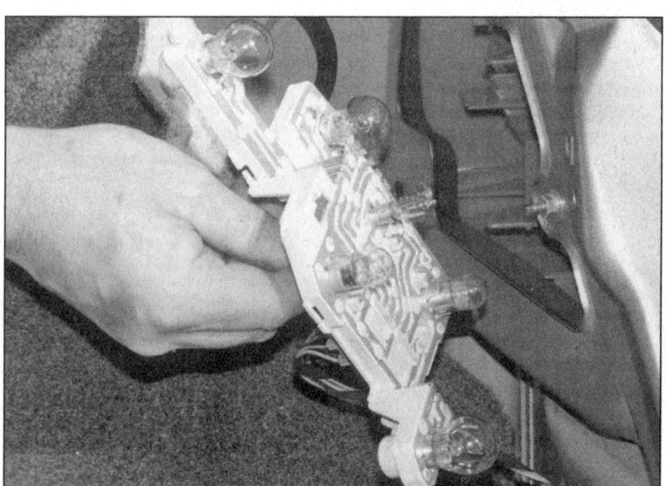
5.37b . . . and remove the bulbholder assembly

5.38a Removing a bulb

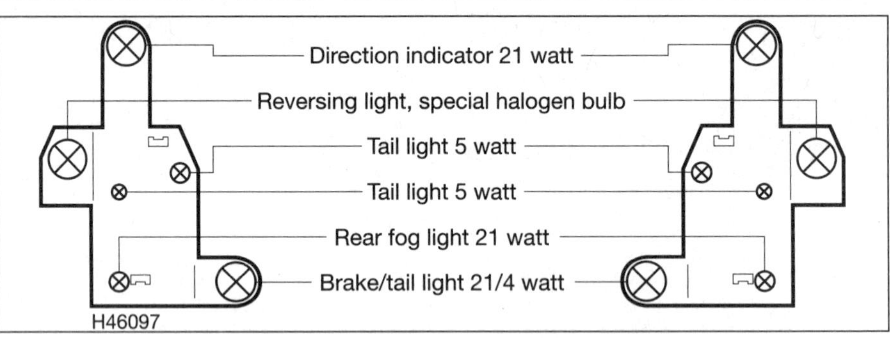

5.38b Rear light cluster bulb locations (Saloon and Hatchback)

5.40a Remove the upper cover (which is a speaker grille) . . .

5.40b . . . and lower cover, for access to the rear light cluster retaining wing nuts (Estate)

5.41 Unscrew the wing nuts . . .

5.42 . . . and withdraw the rear light cluster from the outside

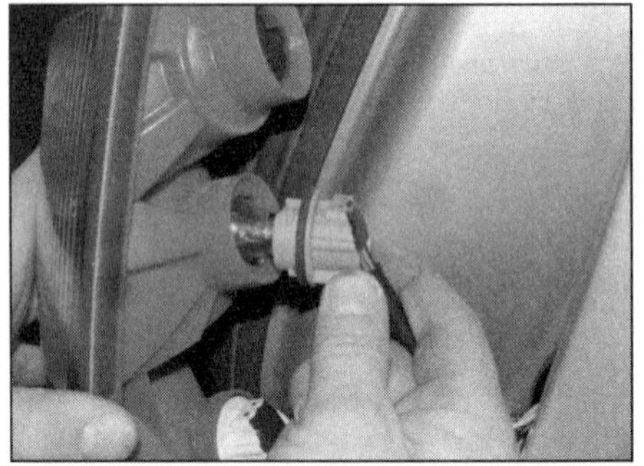

5.43a Twist the bulbholder from the light cluster . . .

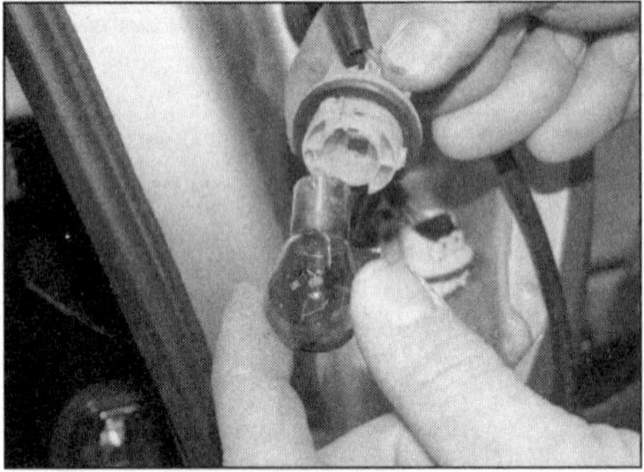

5.43b . . . then depress and twist the bulb to remove it

halogen bulb, which may only be available from a Ford dealer.

39 Fit the new bulb using a reversal of the removal procedure.

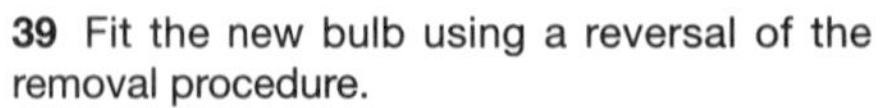

5.43c Rear light cluster bulb locations (Estate)

Estate

40 With the tailgate open, remove the upper and lower covers for access to the rear light cluster wing nuts. The upper cover is a speaker grille, which can be unclipped using a small flat-bladed screwdriver. The lower one is released using the turn-buckle fastener, though on some models, the lower cover is secured with Velcro **(see illustrations)**.

41 Support the rear light cluster from outside, then unscrew and remove the upper and lower wing nuts from inside the cover apertures **(see illustration)**. Take care not to drop the nuts inside the inner cavity.

42 Withdraw the rear light cluster from outside **(see illustration)**.

43 Twist the relevant bulbholder anti-clockwise from the rear of the light cluster, then depress and twist the bulb to remove it **(see illustrations)**.

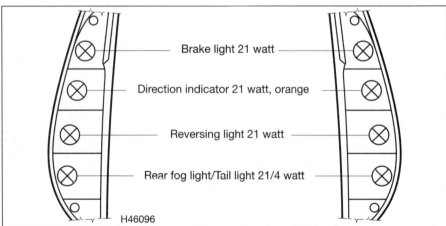

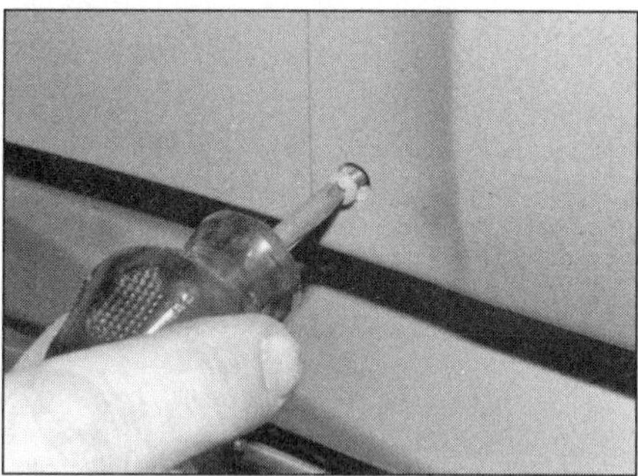
5.49a Undo the screws . . .

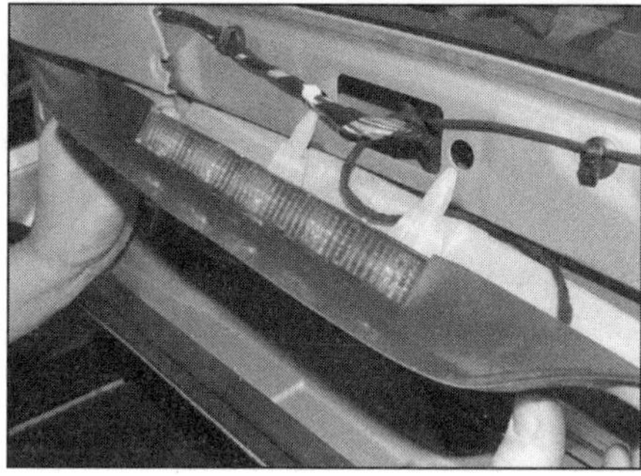
5.49b . . . and remove the high-level stop-light and cover

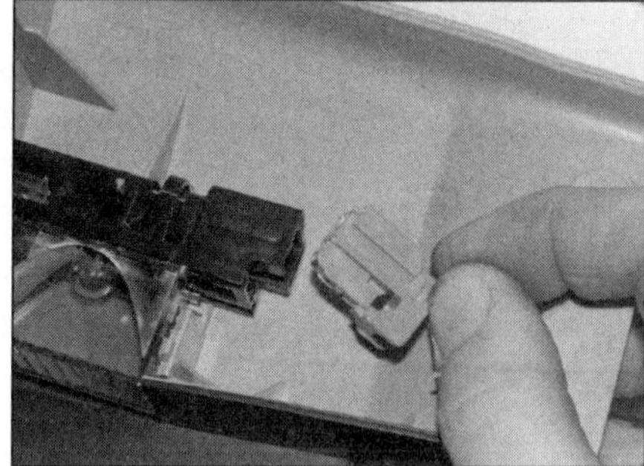
5.50a Disconnect the wiring . . .

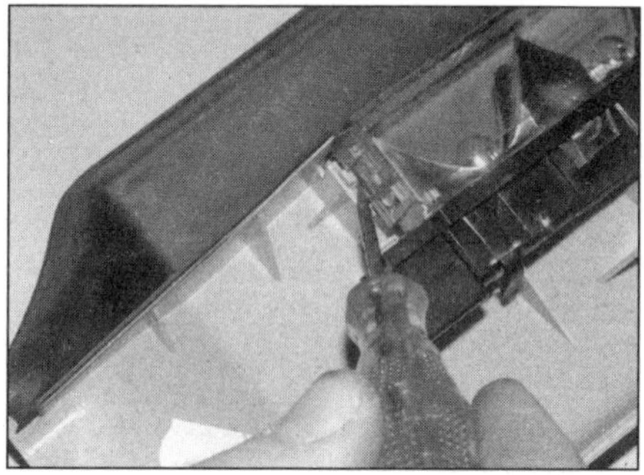
5.50b . . . and prise out the light unit

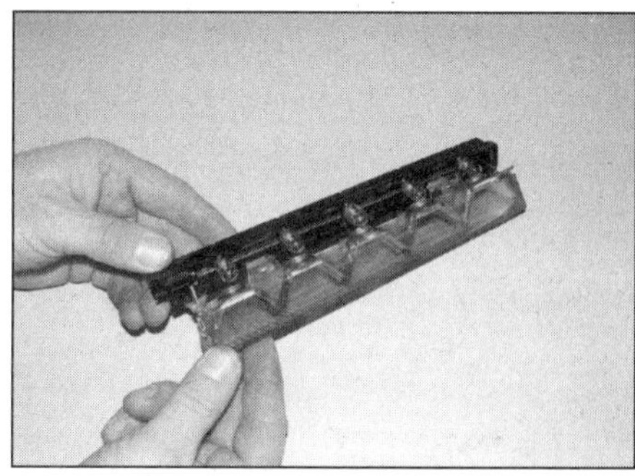
5.51a Remove the cover . . .

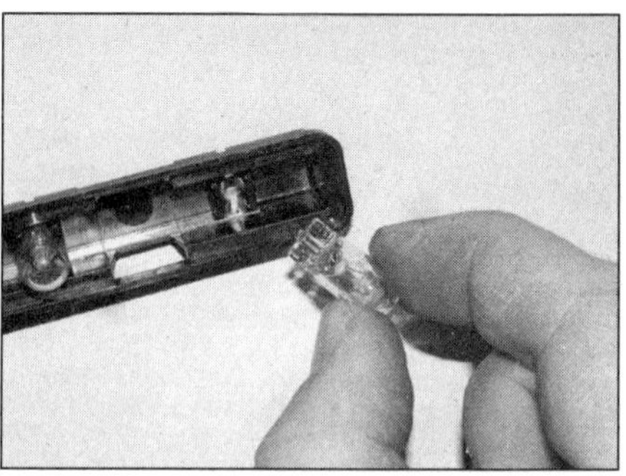
5.51b . . . and pull out the wedge-type bulb

44 Fit the new bulb using a reversal of the removal procedure.

Number plate light

45 Undo the retaining screws and lower the number plate light unit from the tailgate/boot lid.

46 Remove the festoon-type bulb from the contact springs.

47 Fit the new bulb using a reversal of the removal procedure. Make sure that the tension of the contact springs is sufficient to hold the bulb firmly.

High-level stop-light

48 On Saloon models, carefully pull off the cover from inside the car.

49 On Estate and Hatchback models, open the tailgate. Undo the two mounting screws and remove the high-level stop-light and cover **(see illustrations)**.

50 On all models, disconnect the wiring connector and prise out the high-level stop-light unit with a screwdriver **(see illustrations)**.

51 Depress the catches and remove the cover, then pull out the relevant wedge-type bulb **(see illustrations)**.

52 Fit the new bulb using a reversal of the removal procedure.

6 Bulbs (interior lights) – renewal

1 Whenever a bulb is renewed, note the following points:

- *Switch off all interior lights.*
- *Remember that if the light has just been in use, the bulb may be extremely hot.*
- *Always check the bulb contacts and holder, ensuring that there is clean metal-to-metal contact.*
- *Where bayonet-type bulbs are fitted, ensure that the contact springs bear firmly against the bulb contacts.*
- *Always ensure that the new bulb is of the correct rating and that it is completely clean before fitting it.*

Sun visor/vanity mirror light

2 Pull down the sun visor.

3 Using a screwdriver, prise out the light from the headlining **(see illustration)**.

4 Pull out the wedge-type bulb from the light **(see illustration)**.

5 Fit the new bulb using a reversal of the removal procedure.

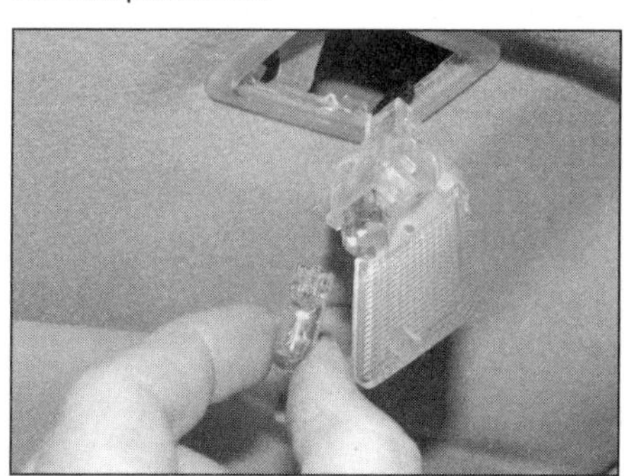
6.4 . . . then pull out the wedge-type bulb

Map reading light

6 Prise out the map reading light using a small screwdriver inserted in the recess opposite the switch **(see illustration)**.

6.3 Prise out the sun visor/vanity light from the headlining . . .

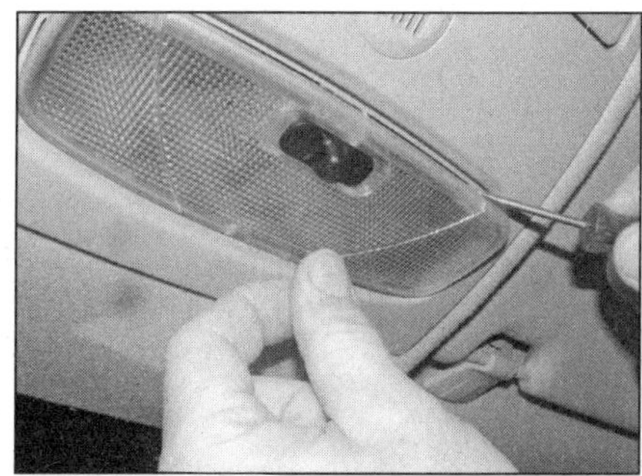
6.6 Prise out the map reading light . . .

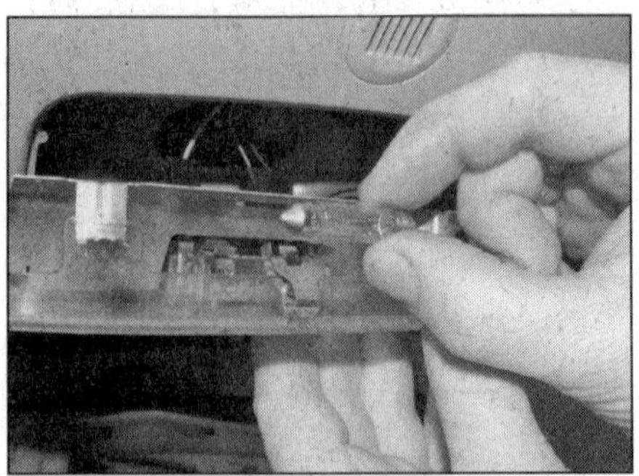

6.7 . . . and release the festoon-type bulb from the contact springs

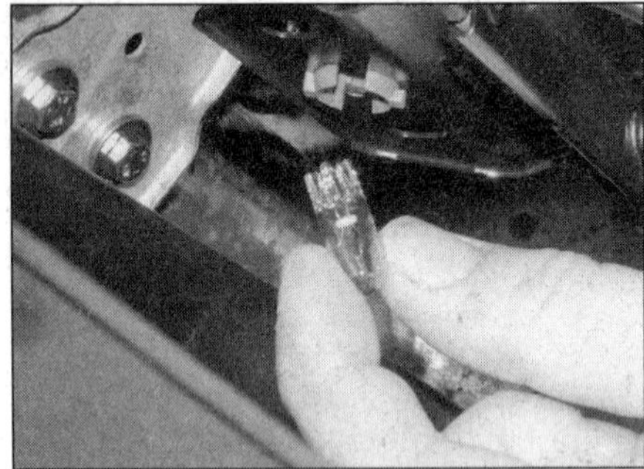

6.10 Removing the glovebox illumination bulb

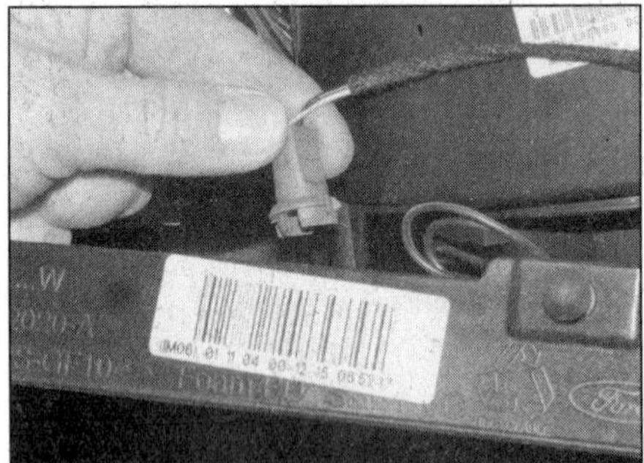

6.12 Press the bulbholder into the top of the glovebox latch

6.13 Removing the luggage compartment light from the headlining

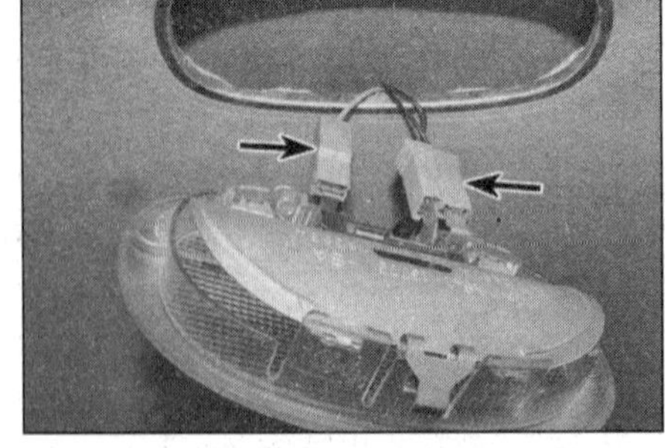

6.14a Disconnect the wiring, if necessary . . .

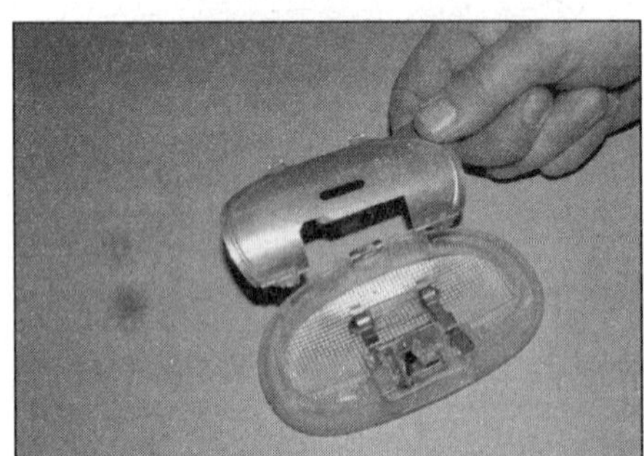

6.14b . . . and unclip the reflector

7 Release the festoon-type bulb from the contact springs **(see illustration)**.

8 Fit the new bulb using a reversal of the removal procedure. Make sure that the tension of the contact springs is sufficient to hold the bulb firmly.

Glovebox light

9 Remove the glovebox as described in Chapter 11.

10 Reach up under the glovebox latch, and pull out the wedge-type bulb from the bulbholder **(see illustration)**.

11 Fit the new bulb using a reversal of the removal procedure.

12 If the bulbholder becomes detached from the latch, remove the latch as follows. Undo the retaining screws and withdraw the glovebox latch and bulbholder from the facia. Press the bulbholder into the hole on top of the latch, then refit the latch **(see illustration)**.

Luggage compartment light

13 Prise out the light from the headlining using a small screwdriver **(see illustration)**.

14 Where applicable, unclip the reflector from the light unit, and if necessary, disconnect the wiring and remove the light unit from the headlining **(see illustrations)**.

15 Release the festoon-type bulb from the contact springs **(see illustration)**.

16 Fit the new bulb using a reversal of the removal procedure. Make sure that the tension of the contact springs is sufficient to hold the bulb firmly.

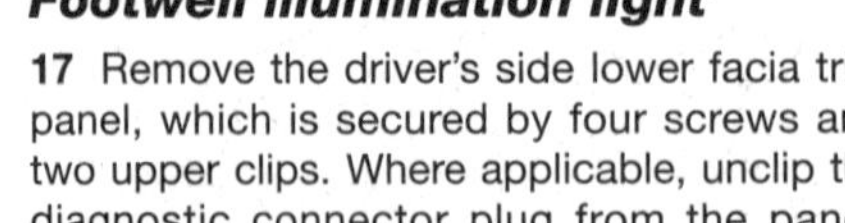

Footwell illumination light

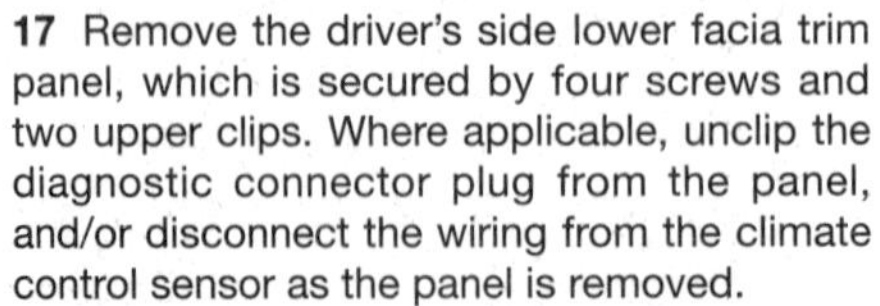

17 Remove the driver's side lower facia trim panel, which is secured by four screws and two upper clips. Where applicable, unclip the diagnostic connector plug from the panel, and/or disconnect the wiring from the climate control sensor as the panel is removed.

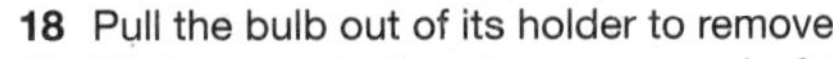

18 Pull the bulb out of its holder to remove.

19 Fit the new bulb using a reversal of the removal procedure.

Instruments and warning lights

20 Remove the instrument panel as described in Section 11.

21 Twist the bulbholder anti-clockwise to remove it **(see illustration)**.

22 Pull out the wedge-type bulb **(see illustration)**. **Note:** *The Ford bulb is only available together with the bulbholder.*

23 Fit the new bulb using a reversal of the removal procedure.

Cigar lighter illumination

24 Carefully prise out the ashtray and cup holder from the centre console, and disconnect the wiring from the cigar lighter.

25 Use a screwdriver to release the tag, then

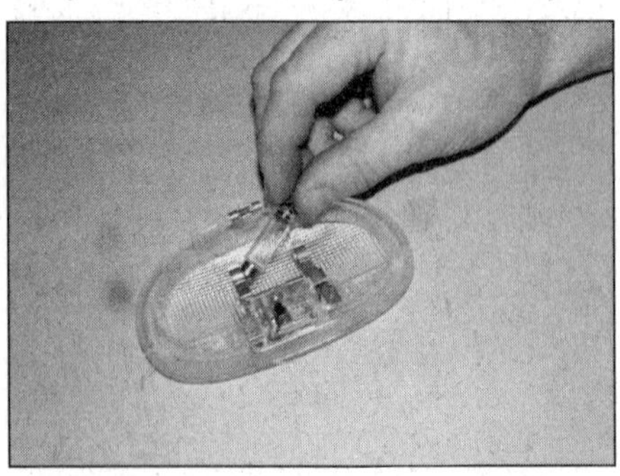

6.15 Removing the festoon-type bulb from the luggage compartment light

6.21 Twist the bulbholder anti-clockwise to remove it . . .

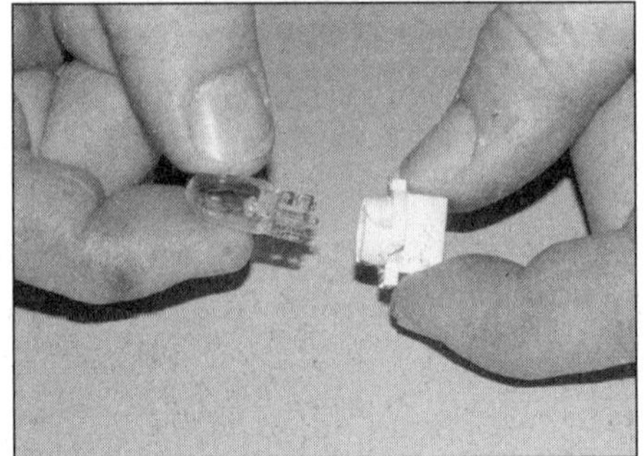

6.22 . . . then pull out the wedge-type bulb

6.25a Release the tag . . .

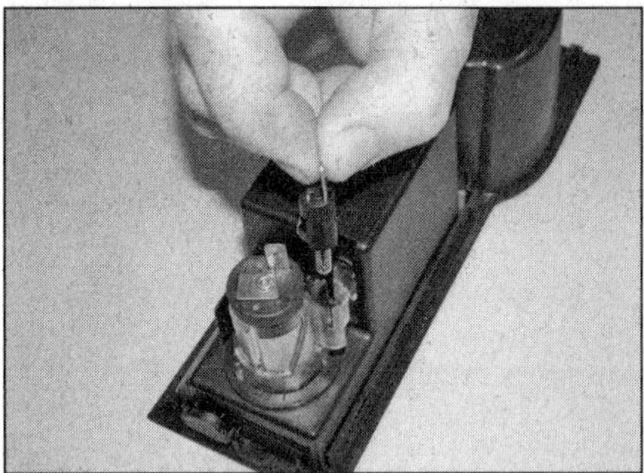
6.25b . . . then pull the bulbholder from the cigar lighter

6.26 Pull the wedge-type bulb from the bulbholder

pull the bulbholder from the side of the cigar lighter **(see illustrations)**.

26 Pull the wedge-type bulb from the bulbholder **(see illustration)**.

27 Fit the new bulb using a reversal of the removal procedure.

Automatic transmission selector illumination

28 Select position N, then prise out the panel from the centre console.

29 Disconnect the bulbholder and pull out the wedge-type bulb.

30 Fit the new bulb using a reversal of the removal procedure.

Heater control illumination

31 The heater control panel can be removed as described in Chapter 3. However, there are no separate bulbs which are accessible once the panel is removed.

7 Exterior light units – removal and refitting

1 Before removing any light unit, note the following points:

- *Ensure that the light is switched off.*
- *Remember that if the light has just been in use, the bulb and lens may be extremely hot.*

Headlight and indicator

2 Remove the radiator grille as described in Chapter 11. The two retaining fasteners are located next to the headlight units.

3 Pull up the two headlight locking bars, then carefully withdraw the headlight unit from the front of the car. The inner bar is located next to the radiator grille fastener bracket, and the outer bar is located near the wing panel **(see illustrations)**.

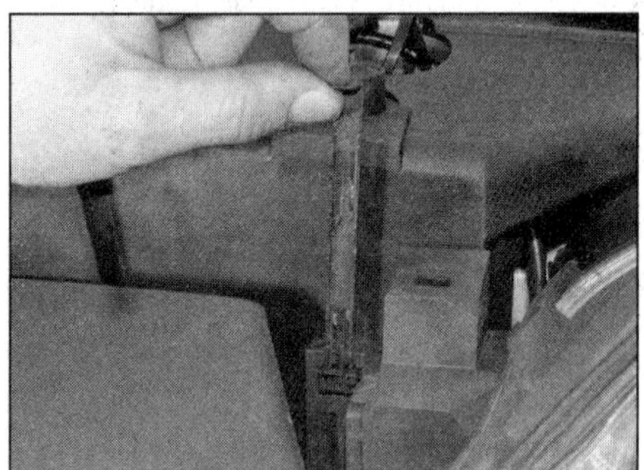
7.3a To remove the headlight, pull up the inner . . .

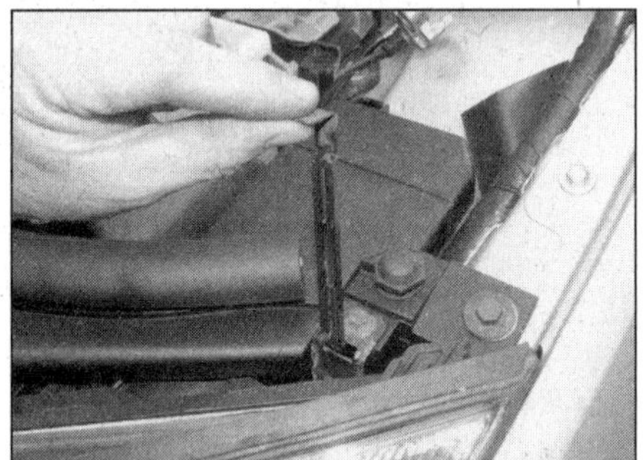
7.3b . . . and outer locking bars . . .

4 Disconnect the wiring multiplug from the rear of the headlight unit **(see illustration)**.

5 Refitting is a reversal of the removal procedure. Have the beam alignment checked or adjusted as described in the next Section.

Front foglight

6 Removing the front foglight is covered in the bulb renewal procedure in Section 5. Note that there are two different designs of foglight fitted on the Mondeo.

Door mirror approach light

7 Removing the approach lights fitted to the base of the door mirrors is covered in the bulb renewal procedure in Section 5.

Rear light cluster

Saloon and Hatchback

8 Open the boot lid and turn the fasteners anti-clockwise to remove the relevant rear light cluster cover.

9 Squeeze together the two red tabs to separate the bulbholder assembly from the light housing.

10 Support the rear light cluster, then undo the retaining screws and remove the unit from the rear of the car. Recover the gasket **(see illustrations)**.

11 Refitting is a reversal of removal. Check the condition of the gasket, and renew it if necessary.

Estate

12 With the tailgate open, remove the upper

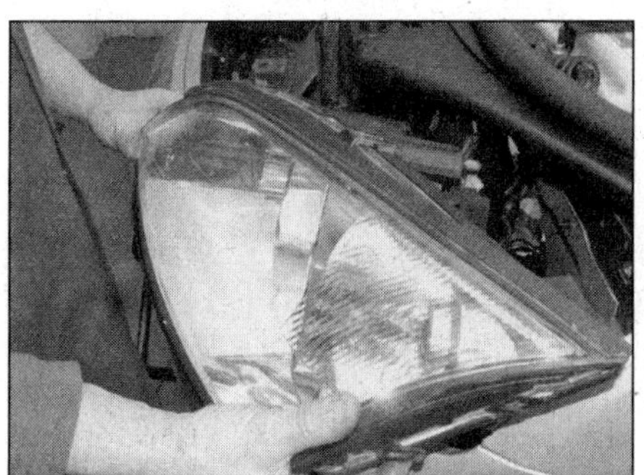
7.3c . . . and withdraw the headlight

7.4 Disconnecting the wiring from the headlight unit

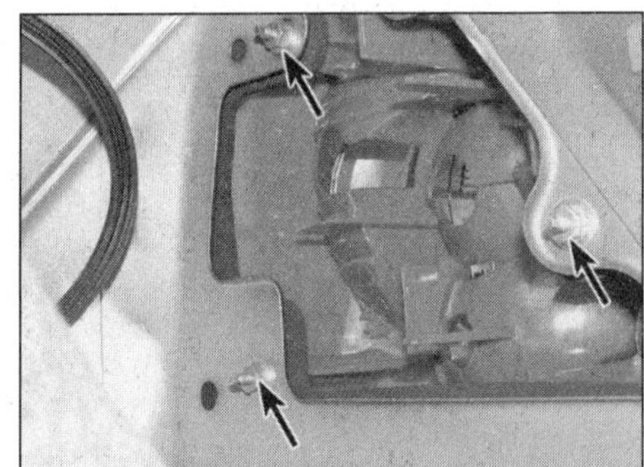
7.10a Undo the retaining screws . . .

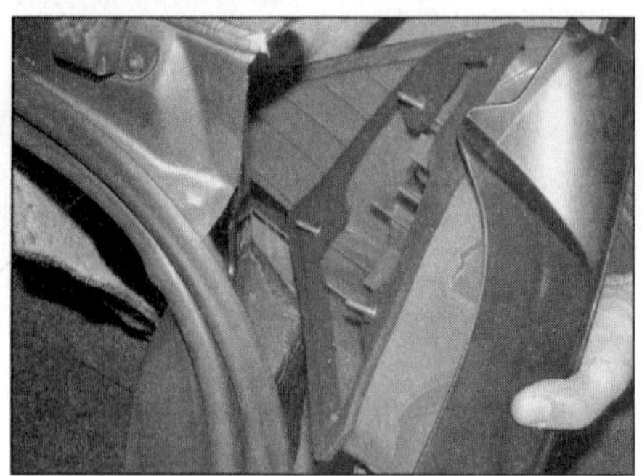

7.10b . . . and withdraw the rear light cluster (Hatchback)

7.13 Unscrew the wing nuts . . .

7.14 . . . and withdraw the rear light cluster

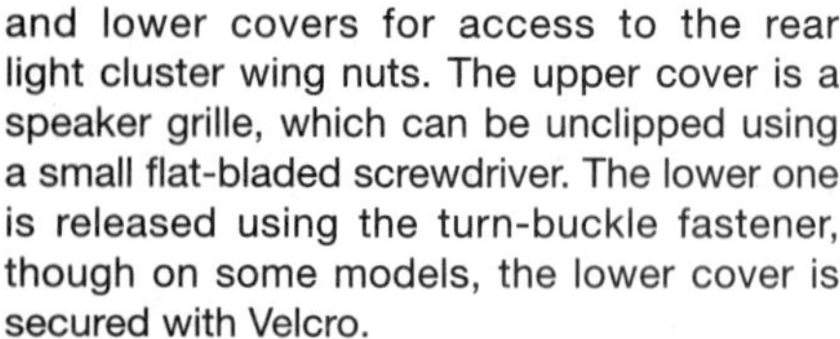

and lower covers for access to the rear light cluster wing nuts. The upper cover is a speaker grille, which can be unclipped using a small flat-bladed screwdriver. The lower one is released using the turn-buckle fastener, though on some models, the lower cover is secured with Velcro.

13 Support the rear light cluster from outside, then unscrew and remove the upper and lower wing nuts from inside the cover apertures **(see illustration)**. Take care not to drop the nuts inside the inner cavity.

14 Withdraw the rear light cluster from outside, then twist the bulbholders anti-clockwise and remove them from the light cluster unit **(see illustration)**.

15 Refitting is a reversal of removal.

Number plate light

16 Undo the retaining screws and lower the number plate light unit from the tailgate/boot lid.

17 Disconnect the wiring and remove the number plate light.

18 Refitting is a reversal of removal.

High-level stop-light

19 On Saloon models, carefully pull off the cover from inside the car.

20 On Estate and Hatchback models, open the tailgate. Undo the mounting screws, and remove the high-level stop-light and cover.

21 On all models, disconnect the wiring connector and prise out the high-level stop-light unit with a screwdriver.

22 Depress the catches and remove the cover.

23 Refitting is a reversal of removal.

8 Headlight and front foglight beam alignment – checking and adjustment

1 Accurate adjustment of the headlight or front foglight beams is only possible using optical beam-setting equipment. This work should therefore be carried out by a Ford dealer, or other service station with the necessary facilities.

2 Temporary adjustment as follows can be made as an emergency measure if the alignment is incorrect following accident damage.

Headlight adjustment

3 Park the car (unladen) on a level surface, with the tyres at the correct pressure. Bounce the front of the car a few times.

4 On models fitted with load-levelling shock absorbers, leave the car to settle for at least one minute.

5 Switch on the ignition and operate the headlight-levelling system several times, then set it to position 0. Switch off the ignition.

6 Ideally, headlight beam alignment equipment should now be positioned in front of the headlights, however, this equipment is not usually available to the average home mechanic. Alternatively, to make a temporary adjustment, position the car 5 metres in front of a wall or garage door, and make a horizontal line at the height of the headlight centres. Mark this line with the position of the headlights as a focal point to make the main beam adjustment. Make a further line slightly below.

7 Switch on the headlights and select main beam. Check that the area of light concentration is centred on the main beam focal points marked on the wall.

8 Now switch the headlights on dipped beam, and check that the beam boundary line touches the lower line on the wall, with the 15° riser commencing directly beneath the main beam mark.

9 If adjustment is necessary, use a screwdriver inserted onto the two adjustment knobs from the top of the unit. These rotate the adjustment turnwheels on the rear of the headlight units. Note that the 'inner' headlights are the main beams, and the 'outer' headlights are the dipped beams.

9.3 Headlight-levelling motor

10 Note that on models equipped with xenon dipped headlights, adjustment is possible for driving on the left or right-hand side of the road. However, this adjustment must be carried out by a Ford dealer.

Front foglight adjustment

11 Park the car (unladen) on a level surface, with the tyres at the correct pressure. Bounce the front of the car a few times.

12 On models fitted with load-levelling shock absorbers, leave the car to settle for at least one minute.

13 Ideally, foglight beam alignment equipment should now be positioned in front of the foglights, however, this equipment is not usually available to the average home mechanic. Alternatively, to make a temporary adjustment, position the car 5 metres in front of a wall or garage door, and make a horizontal line slightly below the height of the foglight centres. Mark this line with the position of the foglights as a focal point to make the beam adjustment.

14 Carefully prise out the bezel from the front of the foglight, for access to the single adjustment screw.

15 Switch on the foglights and check that the beam boundary line touches the line on the wall, with the 15° riser commencing at the positional mark.

16 If necessary, turn the adjustment screw as required.

9 Headlight-levelling motor – removal and refitting

Removal

1 Remove the headlight as described in Section 7.

2 With the headlight unit on the bench, release the plastic clips and remove the rear cover.

3 Twist or undo the screws and disconnect the pushrod ball from the socket **(see illustration)**. Remove the motor from the headlight.

Refitting

4 Refitting is a reversal of removal.

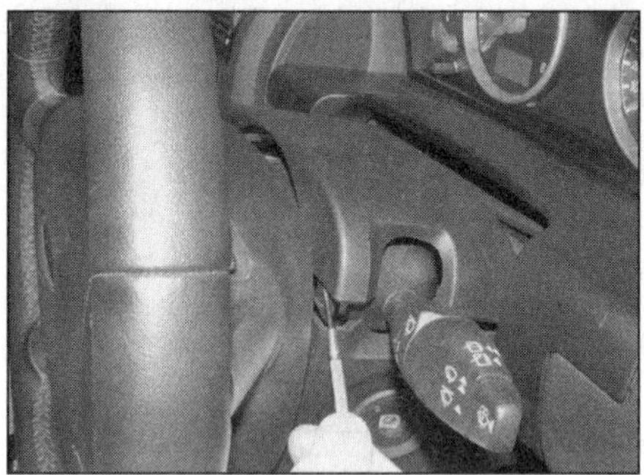

11.4 Removing the steering column upper shroud

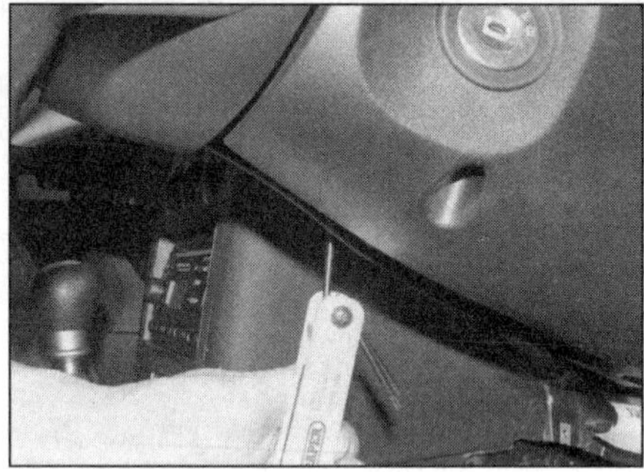

11.5a Undo the screws . . .

11.5b . . . and remove the lower shroud

11.6a Undo the screws . . .

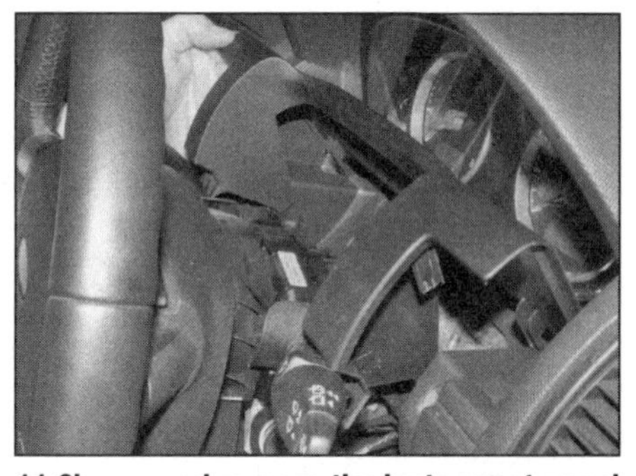

11.6b . . . and remove the instrument panel surround

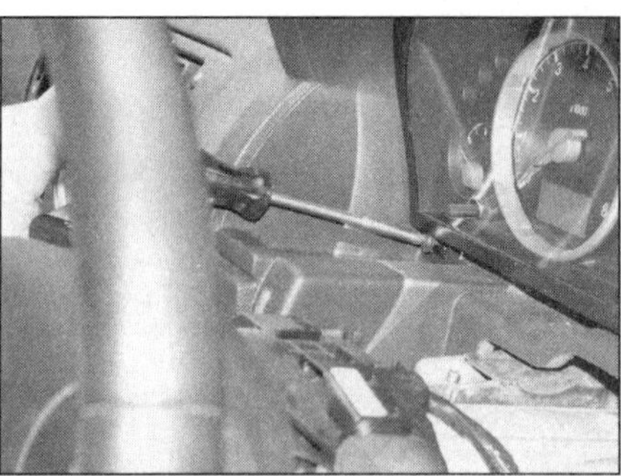

11.7a Undo the screws . . .

10 Headlight-levelling sensor – removal and refitting

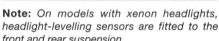

Note: *On models with xenon headlights, headlight-levelling sensors are fitted to the front and rear suspension.*

Removal

1 Raise the relevant front or rear of the car, and support on axle stands (see *Jacking and vehicle support*). Remove the roadwheel.

2 Disconnect the wiring from the headlight-levelling sensor. Note that the sensor is connected to the suspension arm by a short link.

3 Disconnect the link from the sensor arm by prising it from the ball fitting.

4 Undo the mounting screws and withdraw the sensor.

Refitting

5 Refitting is a reversal of removal. On completion, have the headlight-levelling system initialised by a Ford dealer.

11 Instrument panel – removal and refitting

Note: *If a **new** instrument panel is being fitted, the existing instrument panel configuration must first be uploaded so that the new unit can be programmed with the same configuration. This can only be carried out by a Ford dealer using specialised equipment. Note that Ford operate a 'new for old' scheme whereby the old instrument panel can be exchanged.*

Removal

1 Disconnect the battery negative lead (refer to *Disconnecting the battery* at the end of this manual).

Warning: The airbag warning light on the panel forms part of the airbag circuit. Before proceeding, wait a minimum of one minute after disconnecting the battery, as a precaution against accidental firing of the airbag. This period ensures that any stored energy in the back-up capacitor is dissipated. We suggest you wait several minutes.

2 Remove the driver's side lower facia trim panel, which is secured by four screws and two upper clips. Where applicable, unclip the diagnostic connector plug from the panel, and/or disconnect the wiring from the climate control sensor as the panel is removed.

3 Where fitted, remove the audio control switch from the steering column. Use a small screwdriver to release the locking tang, then lift the switch from the column and disconnect the wiring.

4 Release the steering column upper shroud from the lower shroud by inserting a thin screwdriver between the clip on each side **(see illustration)**. Pull the upper shroud out, and unhook its rear edge to remove it.

5 Undo the three screws and remove the lower shroud **(see illustrations)**.

6 Undo the two lower screws each side, and remove the instrument panel surround **(see illustrations)**.

7 Undo the lower screw each side, and withdraw the instrument panel from the facia far enough for access to the wiring. Pull out the top of the panel first, before removing it **(see illustrations)**.

8 Release the locking tang, and disconnect the wiring from the rear of the instrument panel **(see illustration)**.

11.7b . . . and withdraw the instrument panel

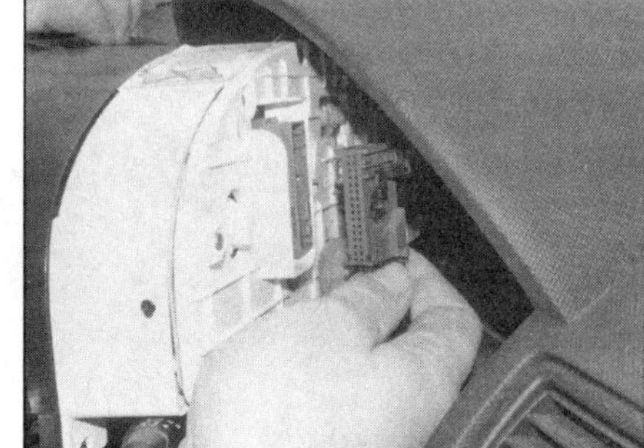

11.8 Disconnecting the wiring from the instrument panel

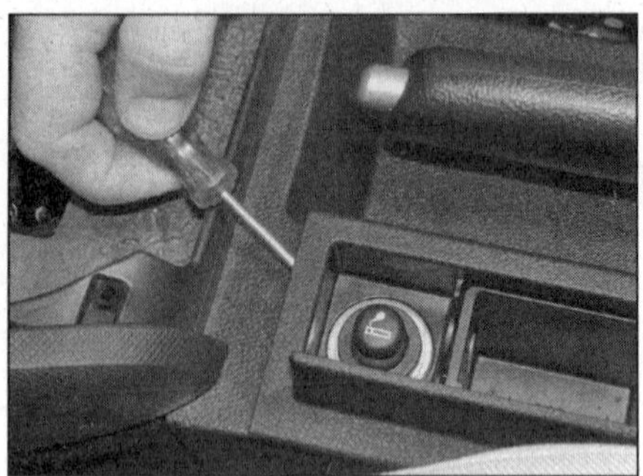
13.1a Prise out the ashtray . . .

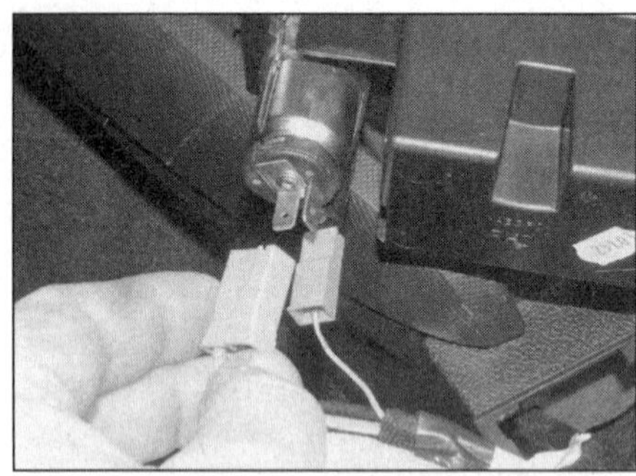
13.1b . . . and disconnect the wiring from the cigar lighter

13.2a Release the tang . . .

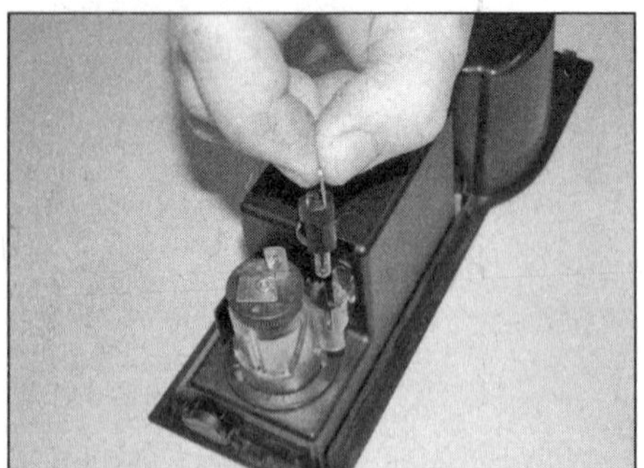
13.2b . . . and remove the cigar lighter illumination light bulbholder

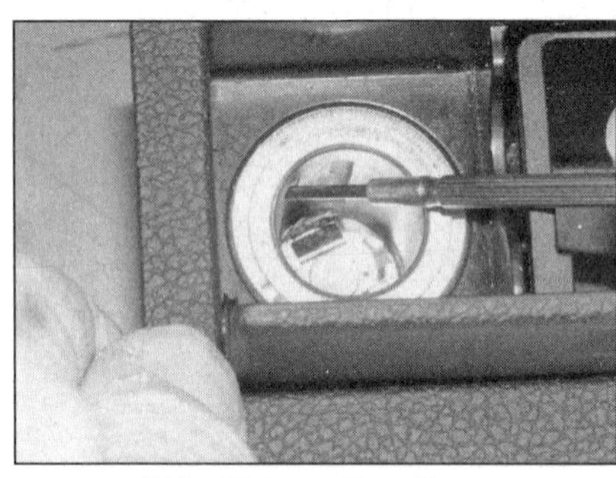
13.3a Release the clip . . .

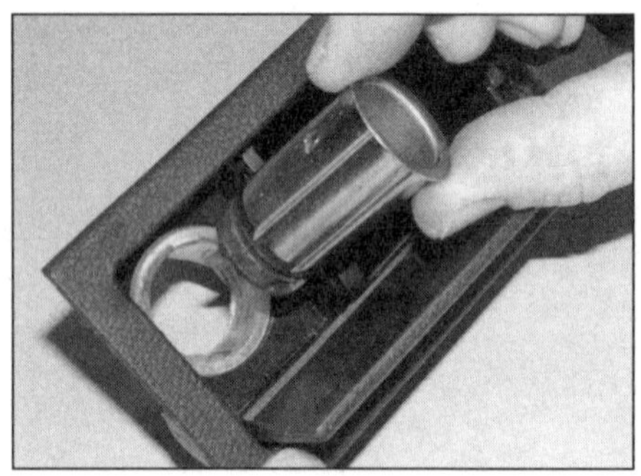
13.3b . . . and remove the holder from the ashtray

9 Withdraw the instrument panel from the facia, and to one side of the steering wheel. ***Caution: Keep the cluster as upright as possible while it is removed, otherwise the silicone fluid used to damp the gauges may leak out.***

Refitting

10 Refitting is a reversal of removal.

12 Instrument panel components – general information

General information

1 The instrument panel is connected to the airbag system, powertrain control module (PCM), anti-lock brake system (ABS), traction control system (TCS), and electronic stability program (ESP), by a control area network (CAN) bus. When the ignition is switched on, a display test is carried out to verify that all warning and indicator bulbs are functioning correctly.

2 The instrument panel incorporates a self-diagnosis mode. To enter the mode, depress and hold the tripmeter reset button, then turn the ignition switch to position II. When TEST is displayed, release the tripmeter reset button; the self-diagnosis test will now commence. Press the reset button to navigate through or skip any of the options. To cancel the test, depress and hold the reset button for 5 seconds, or switch off the ignition.

3 The instrument panel is a solid-state unit, with no individual renewable parts. If proved faulty, a new (or exchange) unit will be needed – however, check very carefully first that the problem is not due to a faulty sensor (fuel tank sender unit, temperature sensor, etc).

13.4 Removing the plastic illumination ring

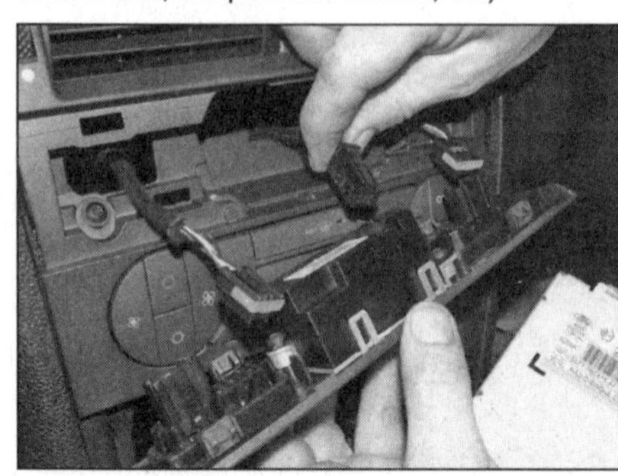
14.1 Disconnect the clock wiring plug

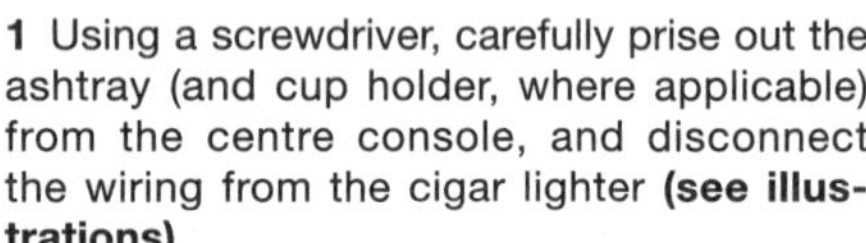

13 Cigar lighter – removal and refitting

Removal

1 Using a screwdriver, carefully prise out the ashtray (and cup holder, where applicable) from the centre console, and disconnect the wiring from the cigar lighter **(see illustrations)**.

2 From the rear of the unit, release the tang and remove the illumination light bulbholder **(see illustrations)**.

3 Remove the cigar lighter element, then use a screwdriver to release the clip, and remove the holder from the ashtray **(see illustrations)**.

4 Release the clip and remove the plastic illumination ring **(see illustration)**.

Refitting

5 Refitting is a reversal of removal.

14 Clock – removal and refitting

Removal

1 Working as described in Section 4 for heated screen switches removal, unclip and remove the switch and clock surround panel, disconnecting the clock wiring plug as this is done **(see illustration)**.

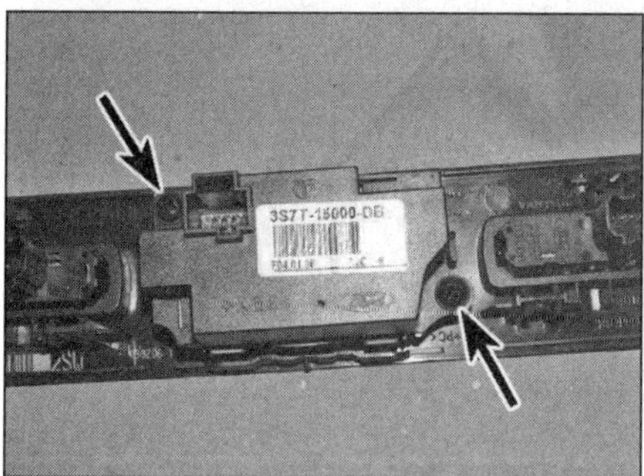

14.2 Clock mounting screws

15.2 Twin horns are fitted to some models

15.4 Horn and mounting bracket

2 With the surround panel on the bench, undo the two screws and withdraw the clock **(see illustration)**.

Refitting

3 Refitting is a reversal of removal. Reset the clock on completion by pressing the button on the front.

15 Horn – removal and refitting

Note: *When attempting to diagnose a non-operating horn, remember that the airbag clock spring (Section 30) forms part of the horn wiring circuit.*

Removal

1 Apply the handbrake, then jack up the front of the car and support it on axle stands (see *Jacking and vehicle support*).

2 Remove the undertray/splash shield for access to the horns located on the front valance **(see illustration)**.

3 Disconnect the wiring from the horn terminal.

4 Unscrew the mounting bolt, and withdraw the horn with its mounting bracket from under the car **(see illustration)**.

Refitting

5 Refitting is a reversal of the removal procedure. Tighten the horn unit mounting bolt securely.

16 Wiper arms – removal and refitting

Removal

1 With the wipers 'parked' (ie, in the normal at-rest position), mark the positions of the blades on the screen/rear window, using a wax crayon or strips of masking tape.

2 Lift up the plastic cap from the bottom of the wiper arm, and loosen the nut one or two turns.

3 Lift the wiper arm, and release it from the taper on the spindle by easing it from side-to-side. If necessary use a puller to release it **(see illustrations)**.

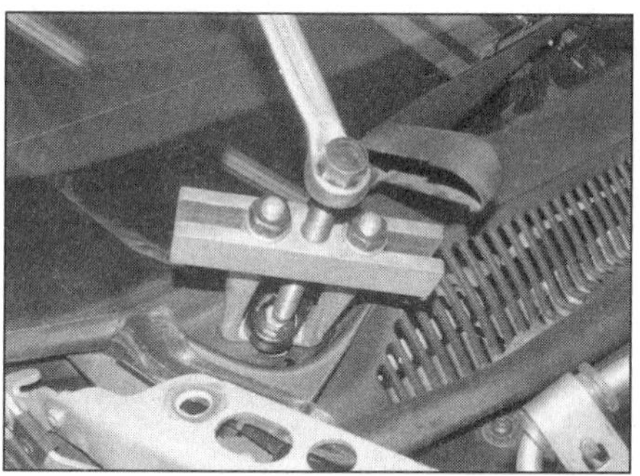
16.3a Using a puller to release the wiper arm from its taper

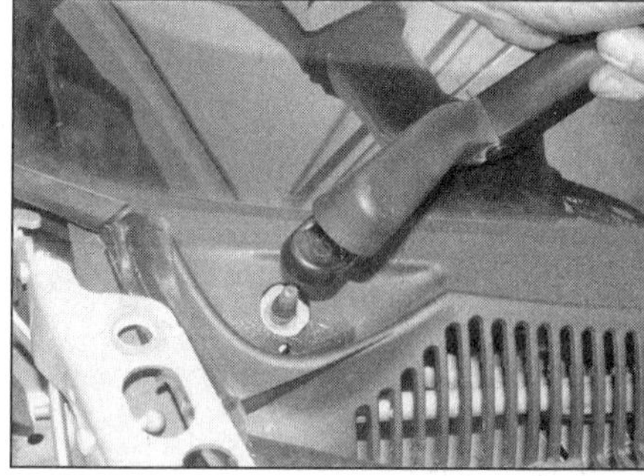
16.3b Removing a wiper arm

4 Completely remove the nut, and withdraw the wiper arm from the spindle. If necessary, remove the blade from the arm as described in *Weekly checks* at the beginning of this Manual.

Refitting

5 Refitting is a reversal of the removal procedure. Make sure that the arm is fitted in its previously-noted position before tightening the nut to the specified torque.

17 Windscreen wiper components – removal and refitting

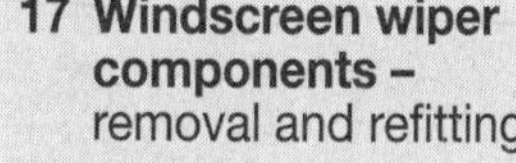

Wiper arms

1 See Section 16.

Wiper motor and linkage

2 Make sure that the ignition is switched off. Be aware, however, that there is a live wire supply in the wiring connector to the windscreen wiper motor, which operates the 'park' function. Provided the connector is positioned to one side when the wiper motor is being removed, there is no need to disconnect the battery.

3 Remove the wiper arms as described in Section 16.

4 Undo the screws securing the heat shield and the plastic cowls in front of the windscreen, then lift the rear of the cowl from the retaining groove **(see illustrations)**.

5 Disconnect the wiring from the wiper motor **(see illustration)**.

6 Unscrew the three bolts and remove the wiper motor complete with linkage from the bulkhead **(see illustrations)**. Where applicable, also disconnect the wiring plug

17.4a Undo the screws . . .

17.4b . . . then remove the left-hand cowl . . .

17.4c . . . and right-hand cowl

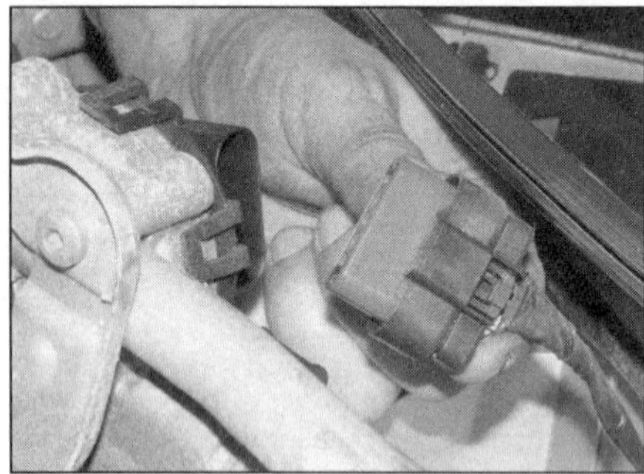

17.5 Disconnect the wiring . . .

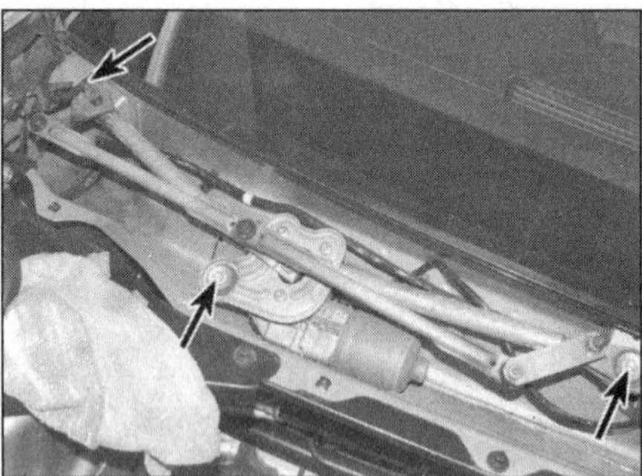

17.6a . . . then unscrew the mounting bolts . . .

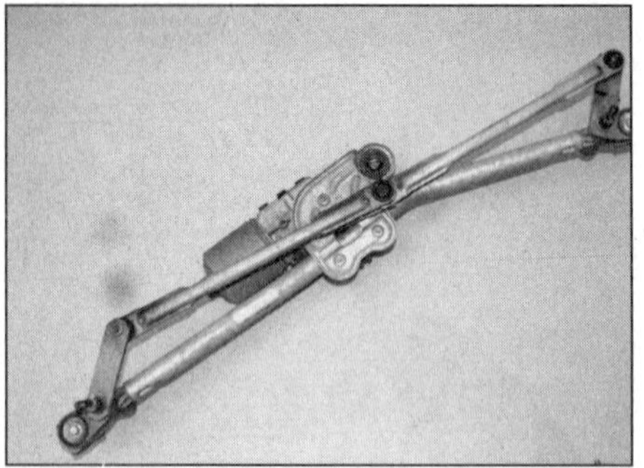

17.6b . . . and remove the wiper motor and linkage

17.7 The wiper motor crank

from the alarm's back-up battery unit, which is attached to the wiper frame.

7 Mark the wiper crank in relation to the motor bracket to ensure correct refitting, then unscrew the retaining nut and remove the crank from the splines on the motor shaft **(see illustration)**.

8 Undo the three mounting bolts and remove the motor from the bracket.

9 Refitting is a reversal of the removal procedure, but tighten the nuts/bolts to the specified torque. Make sure that the crank is refitted in its previously-noted position, and also make sure that the wiper motor is in its 'parked' position.

Rain/light sensor

10 The rain sensor is located in front of the interior mirror, inside the windscreen. It is a light-sensitive device which detects the presence of rain drops on the screen, and signals the wipers to come on automatically. The same sensor is used to operate the headlights at low light levels.

11 The control unit for the system is located to the right of the steering column, under the instrument panel – it should be accessible after removing the driver's lower facia trim panel, which is secured by four screws and two upper clips.

12 On models from October 2004, the sensitivity of the sensor can be adjusted using a six-position column switch which was previously used for setting the intermittent wipe delay. The washer/wiper switch is a one-piece assembly, removal and refitting of which is covered in Section 4.

13 To remove the sensor, first unclip and remove both halves of the trim fitted over the interior mirror mount. The upper half is removed first – squeeze the trim at the sides where the halves join, and slide it upwards. The lower half of the trim unclips downwards into the car **(see illustrations)**.

14 Disconnect the sensor wiring plug, then unclip the sensor from its bracket and remove it. The sensor has hinged metal clips at each side, which are released by pressing the catches at the corners. Swing the clips fully

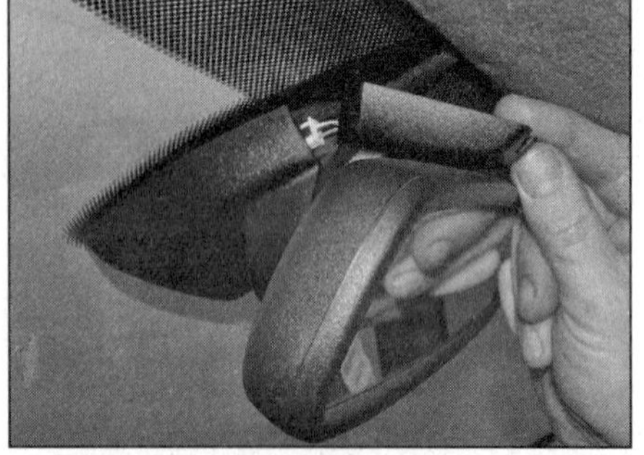

17.13a Unclip the upper half of the mirror trim panel upwards . . .

17.13b . . . the lower half unclips down into the car

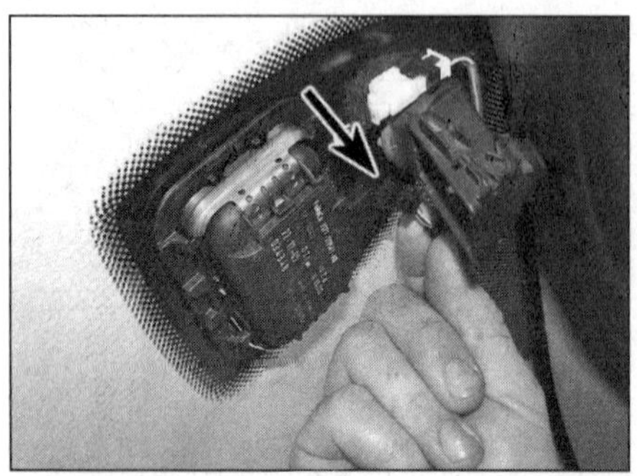

17.14a Disconnect the sensor wiring plug . . .

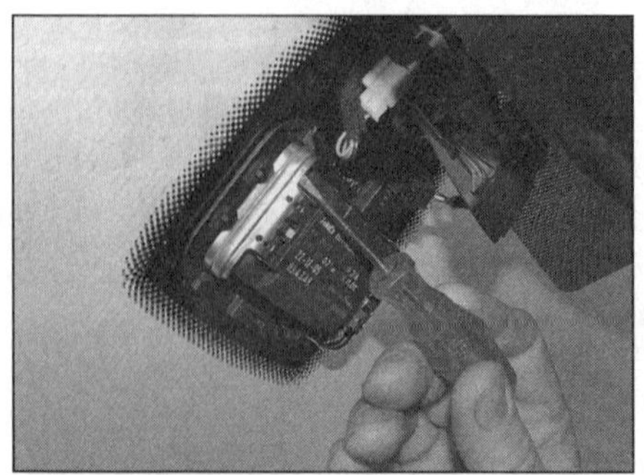

17.14b . . . then swing down the metal side clips . . .

17.14c . . . release the sensor side clips with a screwdriver . . .

downwards, then release a further clip on each side of the sensor itself, and remove it from the screen mounting plate **(see illustrations)**. The mounting plate is bonded to the windscreen.
Caution: Do not touch the upper surface of the sensor cells, nor the inside of the lens fitted to the screen, as this may affect its operation.

15 When refitting, ensure that no dust or dirt whatsoever gets trapped inside, otherwise the sensor's operation will be affected. Ensure that the sensor is secured correctly with the mounting clips. The operation of the system can be checked by sprinkling water onto the outside of the screen near the sensor.

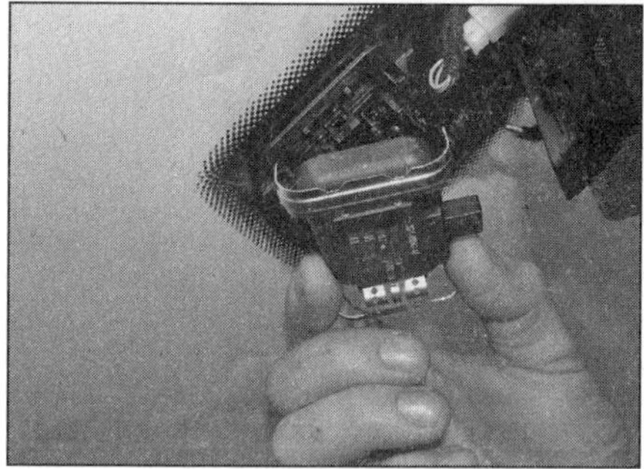

17.14d . . . and remove the sensor from the screen mount

18.2 Removing the tailgate wiper arm

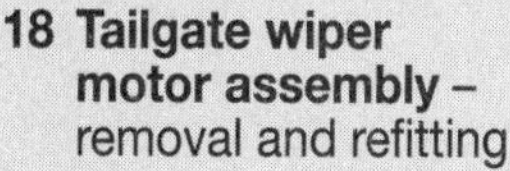

18 Tailgate wiper motor assembly – removal and refitting

Removal

1 Make sure that the ignition is switched off. Be aware, however, that there is a live wire supply in the wiring connector to the rear window wiper motor, which operates the 'park' function. Provided the connector is positioned to one side when the wiper motor is being removed, there is no need to disconnect the battery.

2 Remove the tailgate wiper arm as described in Section 16 **(see illustration)**.

3 Open the tailgate, then undo the trim panel retaining screws, noting that some are located beneath plastic covers. On Hatchback models remove the lock cover first. On Estate models, some of the screws are located in the handgrip recesses **(see illustrations)**.

4 Using a wide-bladed screwdriver, carefully prise the trim panel from the tailgate. Insert the screwdriver next to the retaining clips to prevent damage from the clip being torn from the panel.

5 Disconnect the wiring from the wiper motor **(see illustration)**.

6 Undo the three mounting screws and withdraw the wiper motor from the tailgate, while guiding the spindle through the rubber grommet **(see illustrations)**.

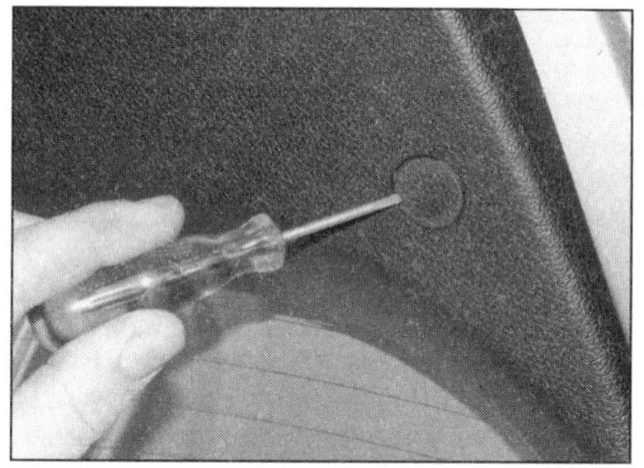

18.3a Where necessary, prise out the plastic cover . . .

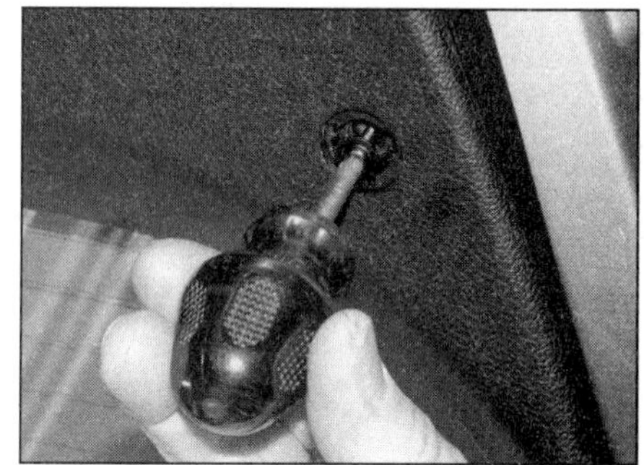

18.3b . . . for access to the screws

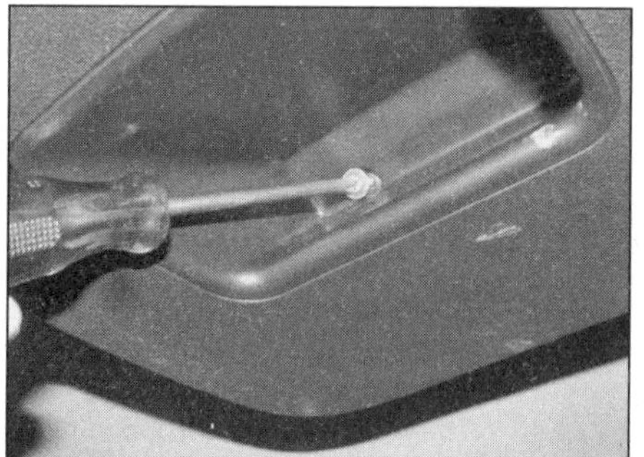

18.3c Retaining screws located in the handgrip recesses on Estate models

18.3d Removing the lock cover on Hatchback models

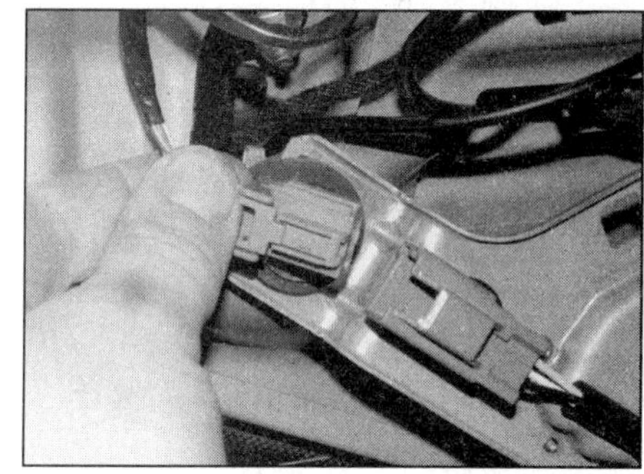

18.5 Disconnect the wiring . . .

18.6a . . . then undo the mounting screws . . .

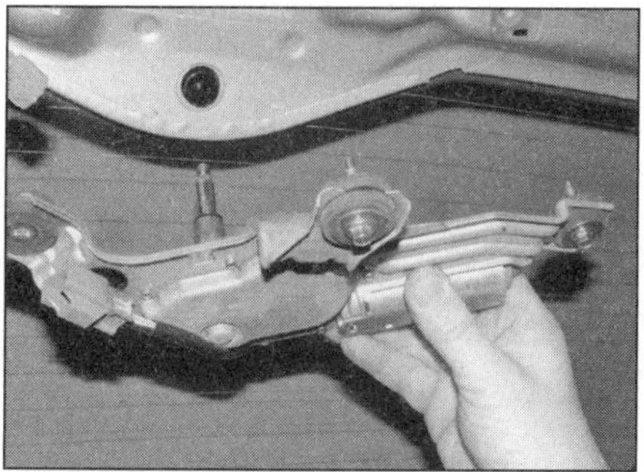

18.6b . . . and withdraw the wiper motor from the tailgate

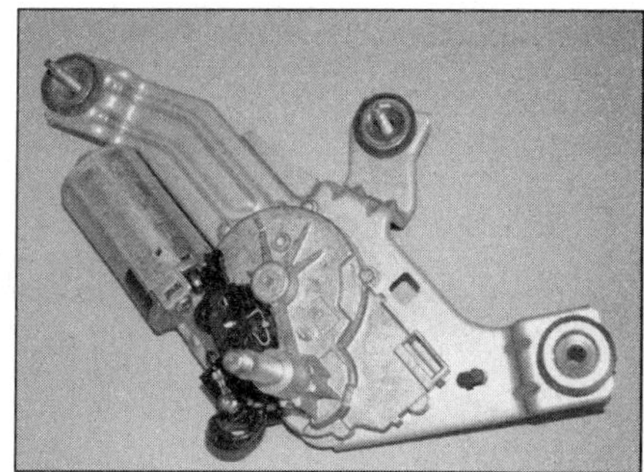

18.6c Wiper motor on the bench

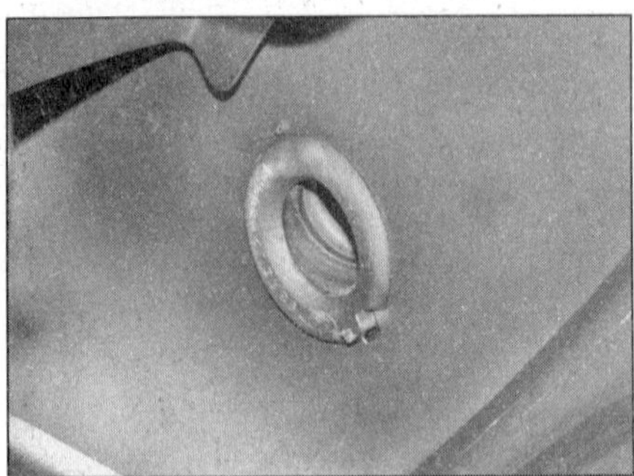

18.7 Wiper motor rubber grommet in the tailgate

7 If necessary, remove the rubber grommet from the tailgate **(see illustration)**.

Refitting

8 Refitting is a reversal of the removal procedure. Make sure that the wiper motor is in its 'parked' position before fitting the wiper arm.

19 Generic electronic module – information, testing, removal and refitting

Note: *The Generic electronic module is also known as the Central timer unit.*

General information

1 A generic electronic module (GEM) is fitted to control the following functions:

- *Direction indicator/hazard warning light control.*
- *Interior light control.*
- *Instrument panel dimmer control.*
- *Heated windscreen and rear window deactivation control.*
- *Wiper interval and washer control.*
- *Lights-on warning.*
- *Door-open warning.*
- *Automatic transmission PRNDL warning.*
- *Generation of warning and confirmation tones.*
- *Battery protection function (switching off interior lights after a predetermined delay).*
- *Window/sunroof closing system control.*
- *Checking that doors and tailgate are closed, and activating a warning buzzer.*

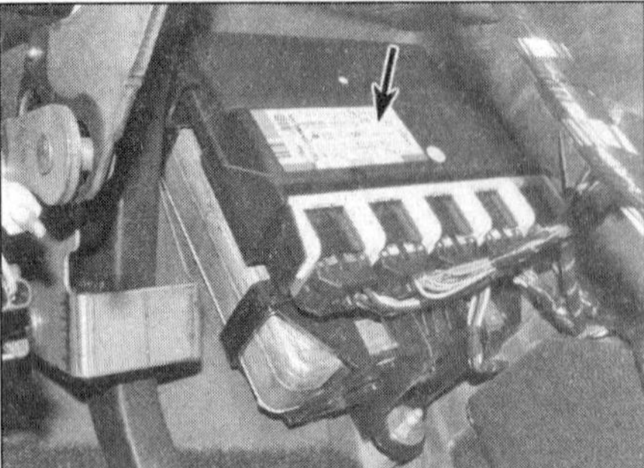

19.15 The generic electronic module (GEM)

- *Window regulator and sliding roof closing control.*
- *Vehicle static condition monitoring (anti-theft warning system).*

2 The generic electronic module will automatically activate the rear wiper if reverse gear is engaged when the windscreen wipers are switched on. The mode of operation is adapted to the windscreen wipers; if the windscreen wipers are in continual mode, the rear wiper will also be in continual mode, and similarly, if the windscreen wipers are in intermittent mode, likewise the rear wiper will be in intermittent mode. Note, however, that the rear wiper has only one intermittent speed.

3 The remote central locking aerial is attached to the generic electronic module and is located in the wiring harness along the facia carrier.

4 Fault diagnosis of the GEM can be performed by a Ford dealer using a WDS diagnostic instrument, however, it is possible to carry out a limited check of the system as described below.

5 The GEM is programmable and includes a self-diagnosis function. If a new unit is fitted, it must be programmed specifically for the car, as otherwise functions which are not available are recognised as faults and are stored in the memory.

Testing

6 The GEM self-diagnosis system can be activated either by a Ford dealer using the WDS equipment, or by using the integrated service mode. To enable the integrated service mode, first switch off the ignition and all electrical systems, apply the handbrake, engage neutral (or P on automatic transmission models), and close all doors.

7 Note that if the anti-theft alarm sounds, the service mode cannot be activated. First switch the ignition on then off. Press and hold the rear window heater switch, then switch on the ignition and release the rear window heater switch. At this point, a signal sounds and the indicator lights come on to indicate that the service mode has been entered.

8 Switch the wiper switch to the 'off' position to test the input signals, then check the following components (in no particular order). An acoustic signal sounds and the direction indicator lights flash to indicate receipt of each input signal by the GEM:

- *Direction indicators (right, left, hazard warning lights).*
- *Sidelights.*
- *Intermittent wipe, windscreen.*
- *Wash/wipe system, windscreen.*
- *Rear wiper.*
- *Wash/wipe system, rear window.*
- *Doors open/closed.*
- *Remote release switch in the centre console for the tailgate/luggage compartment lid.*
- *Tailgate/luggage compartment lid release button in the tailgate/luggage compartment lid.*
- *Open the tailgate/luggage compartment lid with a key.*
- *Locking key on the remote control (the ignition key must not be in the ignition during the test).*
- *Release key on the remote control (the ignition key must not be in the ignition during the test).*
- *Tailgate/luggage compartment lid release key on the remote control (the ignition key must not be in the ignition during the test).*
- *Bonnet open/closed (models with an anti-theft alarm system).*
- *Heated rear window.*
- *Heated windscreen (where fitted).*
- *Ignition on.*
- *Automatic transmission, selector lever position P.*

9 Switch the wiper switch to the 'intermittent' position to test the output signals – pressing the rear window heater switch activates or deactivates the output signals in the following order:

a) *Front wipers (a signal sounds and the direction indicator lights flash when the Park position is reached).*
b) *Rear window heater.*
c) *Interior lights (the switch for the interior lights must be in the 'door contact' setting).*
d) *'Door ajar' warning light in the instrument panel.*
e) *Rear window wiper.*
f) *Windscreen heater (when the engine is running only).*

10 The GEM automatically exits the service mode 20 seconds after the last input or if the car is driven. This is indicated by three acoustic signals and by the direction indicator lights flashing.

11 If a fault is indicated, first check all wiring and connectors for damage, then if necessary check the component.

Removal

Note: *The GEM must be initialised by a Ford dealer after refitting.*

12 The GEM is located on top of the engine management powertrain control module (PCM) behind the right-hand side of the facia.

13 On left-hand drive models, remove the passenger side lower facia trim. Open the glovebox and disconnect the damper, then squeeze the top of the glovebox and detach the hinges to remove it from the facia.

14 On right-hand drive models, remove the facia lower trim panel.

15 Note the location of the five wiring connectors, then disconnect them from the GEM unit **(see illustration)**.

16 Depress the clip and slide the GEM from the top of the PCM.

Refitting

17 Refitting is a reversal of removal, but have the GEM initialised by a Ford dealer as soon as possible.

20 Telematics control module – general information, removal and refitting

General information

1 The telematics system allows the driver to select the following functions:

- *Emergency calls.*
- *Roadside assistance service.*
- *GPS location of the car.*
- *Voice communications.*
- *Route finder system.*
- *Traffic information.*
- *Ordering services (hotel, theatre, car parking, etc).*

2 The microphone for the telematics system is attached to the overhead console.

3 The control module is located beneath the right-hand side of the facia, and includes a SIM (subscriber identification module), GSM module, GPS receiver, and telematics processor.

Removal

4 On left-hand drive models, remove the passenger side lower facia trim. Open the glovebox and disconnect the damper, then squeeze the top of the glovebox and detach the hinges to remove it from the facia.

5 On right-hand drive models, remove the facia lower trim panel.

6 Unscrew the telematics control module support bracket mounting screw.

7 Push the module retaining bracket from the support bracket for access to the top mounting screw, then undo all the mounting screws and lower the control module.

8 Disconnect the wiring from the module, then disconnect the GPS and GSM aerial leads.

9 Withdraw the module from inside the car.

Refitting

10 Refitting is a reversal of removal.

21 Anti-theft alarm system – general information

1 All UK models are fitted with an anti-theft alarm system, incorporating an engine immobiliser. The system is activated when the car is locked, and has both active and passive capabilities. The active section includes the generic electronic module (GEM – described in Section 19), door and luggage compartment lock actuators, bonnet latch, audio unit security, and the alarm horn. The passive section includes the ignition key transponder, passive anti-theft system (PATS) transceiver and LED, starter relay, fuel injection pump control unit (diesel models), and the powertrain control module (PCM).

2 The alarm fitted to all models features ultrasonic sensors which, when armed, monitor the interior of the car. This means that a thief cannot gain entry by breaking a window, without setting off the alarm. However, it would also mean that the car cannot be left with the windows open, as the alarm will sound. For this reason, the ultrasonic interior monitoring is only set when the car is double-locked.

3 Certain models are equipped with a higher-grade 'Cat 1' alarm, which has extra security features such as a back-up battery to keep it active, even if the car's main battery is disconnected.

4 When activating the anti-theft alarm system, there is a 20 second delay during which time it is still possible to open the car without triggering the alarm. After the 20 second delay, the system monitors all doors, bonnet and tailgate, provided they are closed. If one of these items is closed later, the system will monitor it after the 20 second delay.

5 If the alarm is triggered, the alarm horn will sound for a period of 30 seconds, and the hazard lights will flash for a period of 5 minutes. An attempt to start the engine or remove the radio automatically triggers the alarm horn.

6 To deactivate the alarm system, the driver's door must be unlocked with the ignition key or remote control. The tailgate may be unlocked with the ignition key or remote control with the alarm system still activated, however, the alarm is again reactivated when the tailgate is locked.

7 The PATS includes a start inhibitor circuit, which makes it impossible to start the engine with the system armed. The immobiliser is deactivated by a transponder chip built into the ignition key.

8 The PATS transceiver unit is fitted around the ignition switch, and it 'reads' the code from a microchip in the ignition key. This means that any new or duplicate keys must be obtained through a Ford dealer – any key cut locally will not contain the microchip, and will therefore not disarm the immobiliser.

9 If an attempt is made to remove the radio unit while the alarm is active, the alarm will sound.

22 Cruise control system – general information and component renewal

General information

1 Cruise control is available as an option on some models **(see illustration)**.

2 The system is active at roadspeeds above

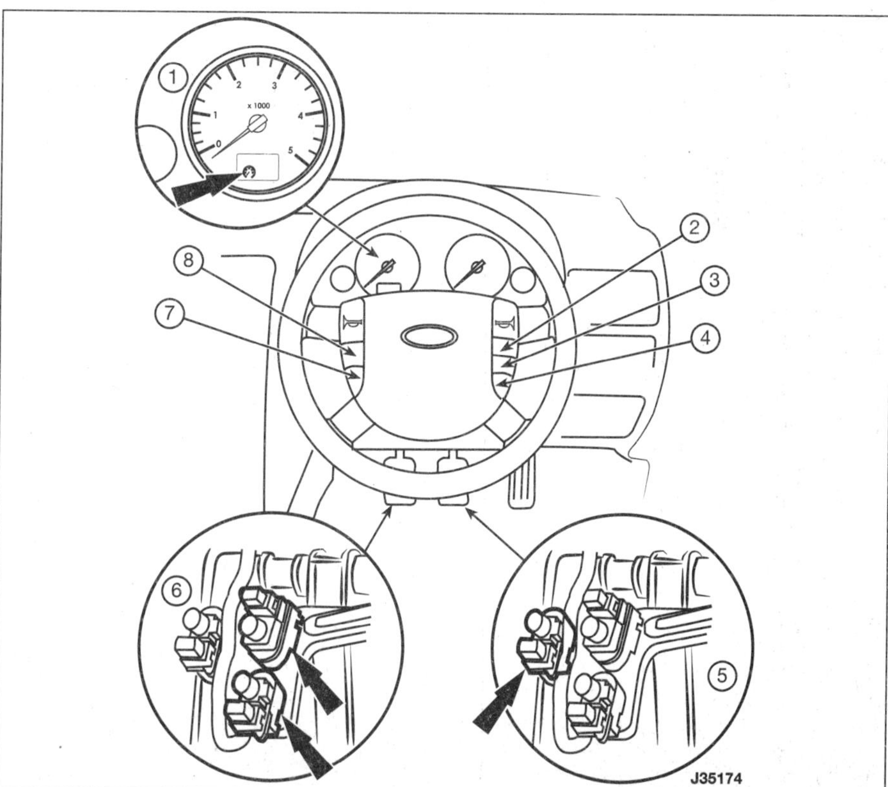

22.1 Cruise control system components

1 *Speed control status indicator*
2 *Speed control resume switch*
3 *Speed control set/accelerate and tap up switch*
4 *Speed control coast and tap down switch*
5 *Speed control de-activator switch (clutch pedal)*
6 *Speed control de-activator switches (brake pedal)*
7 *Speed control de-activate switch*
8 *Speed control activate switch*

23.3a Washer reservoir front mounting bolts . . .

23.3b . . . and rear mounting bolt

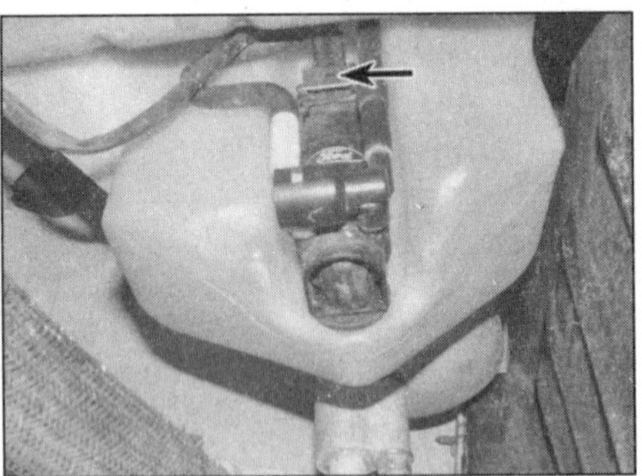
23.4 Washer pump wiring plug

26 mph. Additionally, on diesel models, the transmission must be in third gear or higher (manual) or in D (automatic).

3 The system comprises an electronic speed control unit with integral actuator and switches, mounted in the engine compartment, a control cable connected to the throttle valve actuator, steering wheel switches, brake and clutch pedal switches, a warning light, and the speed signal from the ABS wheel sensors.

4 The steering wheel switches allow the driver to control the various functions.

5 The vehicle speed signal is taken from the ABS wheel sensors, and is supplied to the cruise control unit via the ABS ECU.

6 The brake stop-light switch and clutch pedal switches are used to disable the cruise control system.

7 A warning light on the instrument panel is illuminated when the system is in operation.

Steering wheel switches

Removal

8 Remove the airbag unit from the steering wheel as described in Section 28.

9 Disconnect the wiring plugs from the horn switch, noting the location of each plug and how the wiring is routed for refitting.

10 Remove the two screws each side securing the operating switches, and remove them as required from the steering wheel.

11 If required (for access to the horn switch, for example), the switch contact plates and springs can be removed, after unscrewing the two retaining screws each side.

Refitting

12 Refitting is a reversal of removal.

Brake and clutch pedal switches

Removal

13 Remove the driver's side lower facia trim panel, which is secured by four screws and two upper clips. Where applicable, unclip the diagnostic connector plug from the panel, and/or disconnect the wiring from the climate control sensor as the panel is removed.

14 Disconnect the multiplugs from the clutch switch, brake pedal switch and stop-light switch.

15 To remove the clutch and brake pedal switches, twist them anti-clockwise. To remove the stop-light switch, twist it clockwise.

Refitting

16 Refitting is the reverse of removal. To ensure correct operation of the switches, reset the switch by fully extending its plunger. Fully depress the pedal and hold it in this position, then clip the switch securely into position and slowly release the pedal. This will automatically set the position of the switch.

Speed control actuator

Removal

17 Detach the crankcase ventilation hose and vacuum hose from the clips on the engine top cover. Remove the top cover.

18 Remove the cover from the left-hand front suspension strut top mounting brace, then unscrew the three nuts securing the strut to the body and brace.

19 Unscrew the nuts from the cowl and inner wing panel, then remove the strut top mounting brace.

20 Disconnect the speed control cable from the throttle linkage, then unclip the speed control cable from the throttle body.

21 Note the routing and fixing of the speed control cable around the air cleaner and left-hand suspension strut tower, then release it.

22 Behind the left-hand suspension strut tower, unscrew and remove the speed control actuator retaining bolt.

23 Detach the speed control actuator inwards from the retaining bracket, then disconnect the wiring plug.

24 Withdraw the actuator outwards from the engine compartment.

25 To detach the cable from the actuator, press and hold the locking clip, and turn the cap anti-clockwise 90°. Carefully release the locking spring, then push the cable out of the pulley slot.

Refitting

26 Engage the inner cable with the pulley slot in the actuator, then pull the inner cable to ensure there is no free play at the actuator end of the cable.

27 Refit the cable cap and rotate it 90° to secure.

28 Locate the actuator on the bulkhead and reconnect the wiring.

29 Insert and tighten the mounting bolt, then locate the cable in its clips and reconnect it to the throttle body and linkage.

30 Refit the strut top mounting brace and tighten the bolts to the specified torque.

31 Refit the nuts securing the strut to the mounting brace and tighten to the specified torque. Refit the cover.

32 Refit the engine top cover, then locate the crankcase ventilation hose and vacuum hose in their clips.

23 Windscreen/tailgate washer system components – removal and refitting

Removal

Washer reservoir and pump

1 Apply the handbrake and loosen the right-hand front wheel nuts. Jack up the front of the car and support on axle stands. Remove the front wheel.

2 Unscrew the bolts, and release the clips to remove the radiator lower cover. Release the wheel arch liner fasteners as necessary for access to the reservoir.

3 Unscrew the two mounting bolts, and pull the reservoir forwards slightly **(see illustrations)**. For better access, it may be necessary to remove the front bumper.

4 Disconnect the multiplugs for the windscreen washer pump and fluid level sensor **(see illustration)**.

5 Disconnect the hoses from the windscreen washer pump and (where applicable) from the headlight washer pump. Anticipate some loss of fluid by placing a container beneath the reservoir. The pump is attached to the inner face of the reservoir.

6 Withdraw the reservoir from the car.

7 Pull the level sensor, the windscreen washer pump, and (where applicable) the headlight washer pump, from the reservoir.

8 Remove the rubber seals.

Washer nozzle (windscreen)

9 With the bonnet supported in its open position, remove the screws and fasteners,

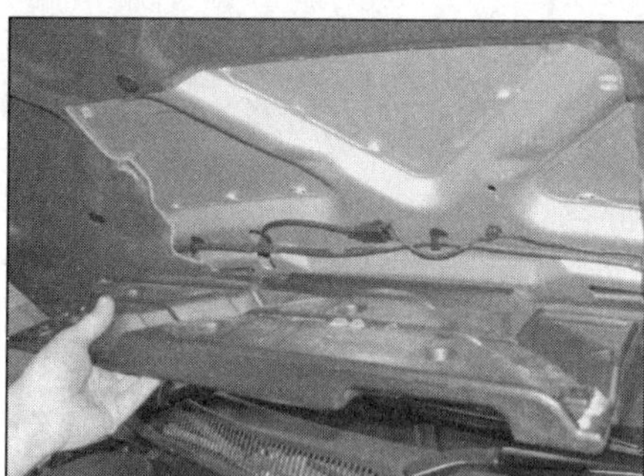

23.9a Remove the sound-deadening cover . . .

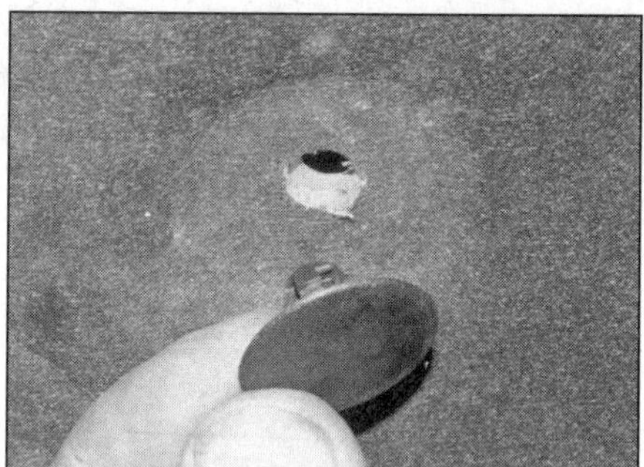

23.9b . . . and material . . .

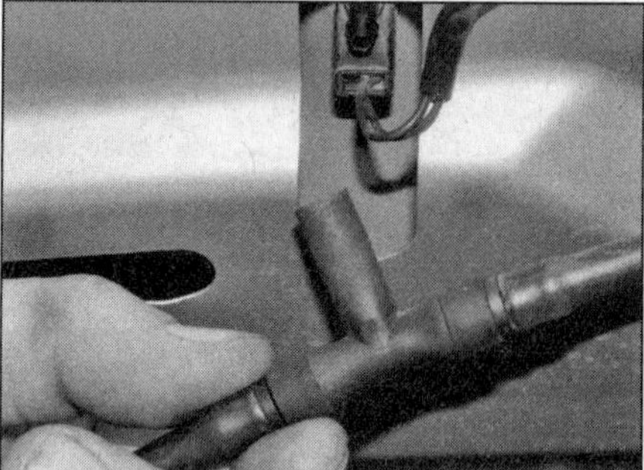

23.9c . . . then disconnect the washer tube . . .

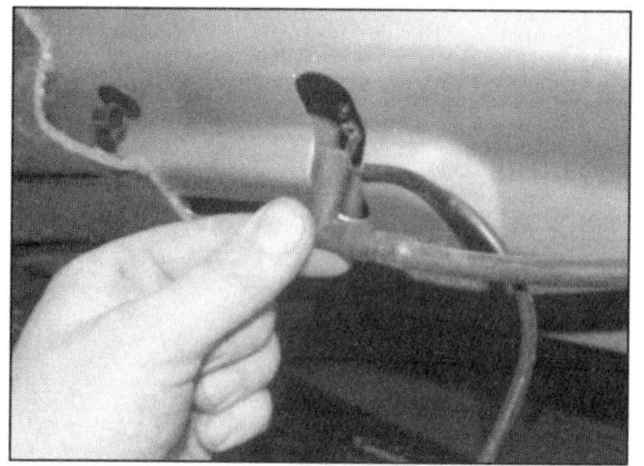

23.10a . . . disconnect the jet heater wiring . . .

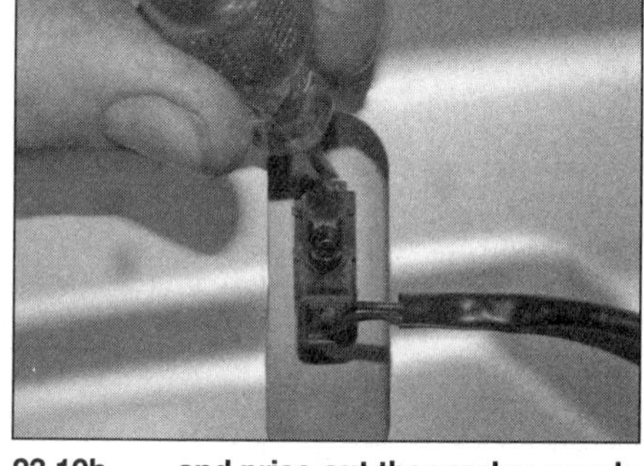

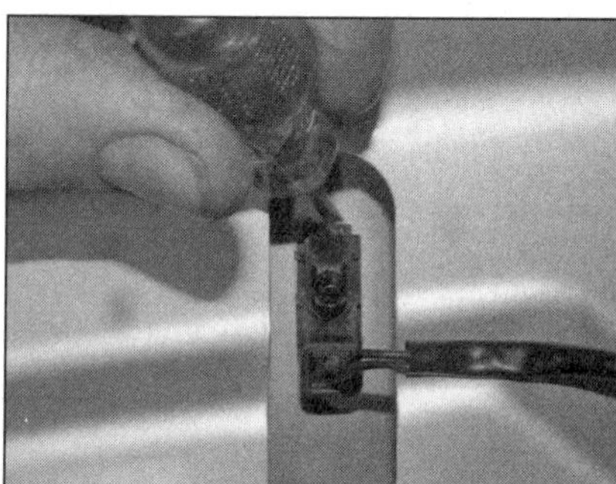

23.10b . . . and prise out the washer nozzle

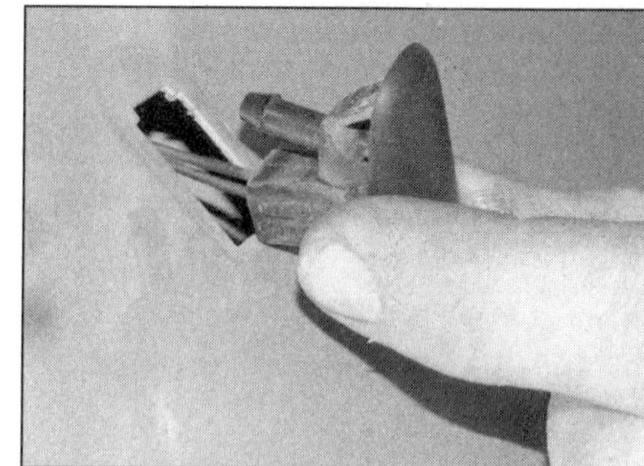

23.10c Removing the nozzle from the bonnet

and withdraw the sound-deadening cover and material from the area beneath the washer nozzles. Disconnect the washer tube from the bottom of the nozzle **(see illustrations)**.

10 Using a screwdriver and working from under the bonnet, carefully prise out the nozzle. Where necessary, disconnect the wiring for the nozzle heater **(see illustrations)**.

Washer nozzle (rear window)

11 With the tailgate open, carefully pull off the inner trim panel from the top of the tailgate.

12 Pull the washer tube from the bottom of the nozzle.

13 Carefully prise the nozzle out of the tailgate glass **(see illustration)**, then prise out the rubber grommet. Where necessary, disconnect the wiring for the nozzle heater.

Washer nozzle (headlight)

14 Remove the headlight on the side concerned, as described in Section 7.

15 Carefully unclip and remove the front cover from the nozzle.

16 Disconnect the washer tube from the base of the assembly.

> **HAYNES HiNT** *To make disconnecting the washer tubes easier, gently heat the tube where it connects to the nozzle, using a hot-air gun or hairdryer. This will soften the tube, making it easier to prise off the tube.*

17 Remove the two mounting screws and withdraw the assembly from the front of the car.

18 Pull off the nozzle retaining clip and withdraw the nozzle from the bumper.

Refitting

19 Refitting is a reversal of the removal procedure, noting the following points:

a) *In the case of the screen washer nozzles, press them in until they are fully engaged.*

b) *The rear window washer nozzle must rest against the rubber seal.*

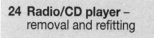

24 Radio/CD player – removal and refitting

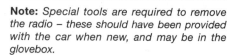

Note: *Special tools are required to remove the radio – these should have been provided with the car when new, and may be in the glovebox.*

1 If a Ford 'Keycode' unit is fitted, and the unit and/or the battery is disconnected, the unit will not function again on reconnection until the correct security code is entered. Details of this procedure are given in the 'Ford Audio Systems Operating Guide' supplied with the car when new, with the code itself being given in a 'Radio Passport' and/or a 'Keycode Label' at the same time.

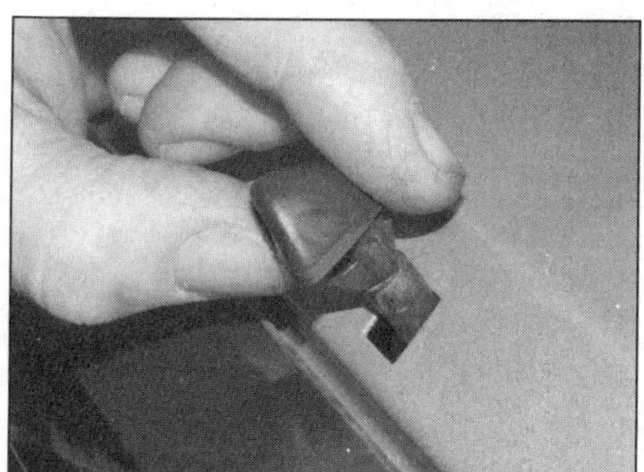

23.13 Removing the rear window washer nozzle

2 For obvious security reasons, the recoding procedure is not given in this manual – if you do not have the code or details of the correct procedure, but can supply proof of ownership and a legitimate reason for wanting this information, the car's selling dealer may be able to help.

3 Note that these units will allow only ten attempts at entering the code – any further attempts will render the unit permanently inoperative until it has been reprogrammed by Ford themselves. At first, three consecutive attempts are allowed; if all three are incorrect, a 30 minute delay is required before another attempt can be made. Each of any subsequent attempts (up to the maximum of ten) can be made only after a similar delay.

Removal

4 Disconnect the battery negative lead (refer to *Disconnecting the battery* at the end of this manual).

5 Four special removal keys are required to remove the unit (see the note at the start of this Section). The keys are marked for position – eg, TOP L is the top left-hand key – and the markings should face upwards when in position. Where no markings are present, the flat sides of the key handles should face to the outside. Slide the keys into place until they click.

24.6 Removing the radio using the four special keys

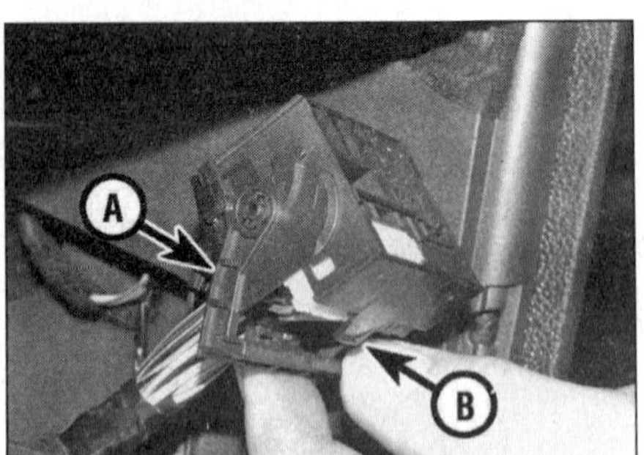

24.7b Main wiring plug hinged locking lever (A) and retaining tab (B)

6 Using the rings on the removal keys, pull the unit squarely from its aperture **(see illustration)**.

7 With the unit partly withdrawn, disconnect the aerial lead and the main wiring multiplug. The main wiring plug has a locking lever at the base, secured on a retaining tab – unclip the lever, and swing it upwards to release the wiring plug **(see illustrations)**. Where applicable, also detach and remove the plastic support bracket from the rear of the unit.

8 Once the set is free, the removal keys can be released from it by depressing the side clips **(see illustration)**.

Refitting

9 Refitting is a reversal of removal. With the wiring reconnected to the rear of the unit, press it into position until the retaining clips are felt to engage. Reactivate the unit by entering the correct code (see paragraphs 1 to 3).

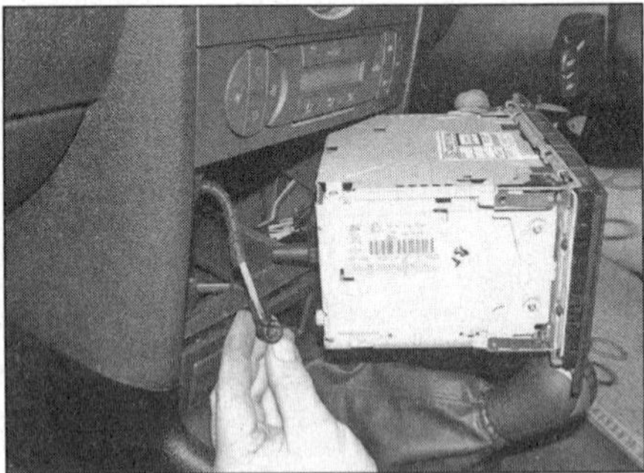

24.7a Disconnecting the aerial lead

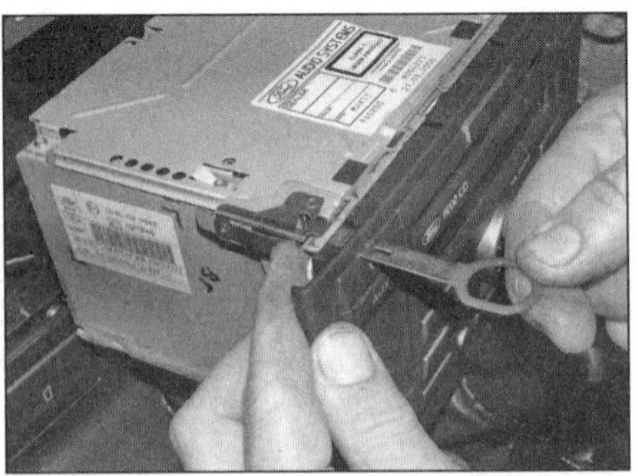

24.8 Depress the side clip and pull out the removal tool

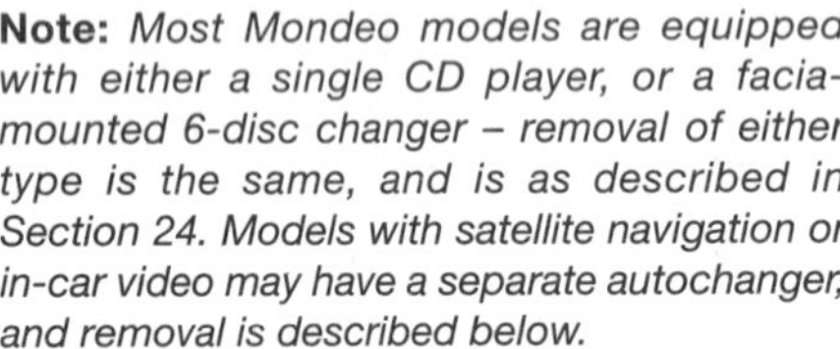

25 CD autochanger – removal and refitting

Note: *Most Mondeo models are equipped with either a single CD player, or a facia-mounted 6-disc changer – removal of either type is the same, and is as described in Section 24. Models with satellite navigation or in-car video may have a separate autochanger, and removal is described below.*

1 A compact disc (CD) changer is available as an optional extra on most models. The unit is located in the boot, on the left-hand side.

2 Disconnect the battery negative lead (refer to *Disconnecting the battery* at the end of this manual).

3 On the left-hand side of the boot, there is a cover/storage panel to remove first, which is secured by four screws. Inside, remove four screws each side securing the changer to its mounting bracket, and withdraw it. Disconnect the wiring plug from the back of the unit, and remove it completely.

4 Refitting is a reversal of removal. According to Ford, if a new unit is fitted, it has to be configured using Ford's WDS2000 diagnostic tool before it will work properly.

26 Speakers – removal and refitting

Removal

1 To remove the door-mounted speakers, first remove the door trim panel as described in Chapter 11.

2 Unscrew the cross-head screws, and withdraw the speaker from the door inner panel **(see illustration)**.

3 Disconnect the wiring and remove the speaker **(see illustration)**.

Refitting

4 Refitting is a reversal of the removal procedure.

27 Radio aerial and lead – removal and refitting

Removal

1 If just the aerial mast is to be removed, this can be unscrewed from the base, from outside.

2 To remove the aerial base, first remove the overhead console as described in Chapter 11, then unbolt the lead and remove the base from the roof **(see illustration)**.

3 To remove the complete aerial lead, remove the radio unit (Section 24) and overhead console (Chapter 11), then unbolt the aerial lead from the aerial base.

4 Remove the right-hand A-pillar trim panel and the centre console right-hand trim panel, then lift up the right-hand front door weatherstrip and remove the right-hand cowl trim.

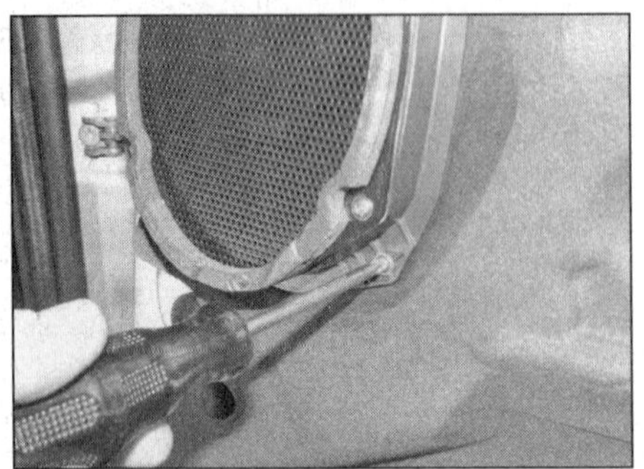

26.2 Undo the mounting screws, and withdraw the speaker . . .

26.3 . . . then disconnect the wiring

27.2 Aerial mounting bolt on the roof

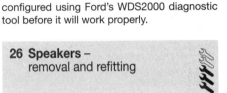

5 Remove the right-hand rear door weather-strip, cowl panel, B-pillar trim panel, and remove the carpet from the right-hand front footwell.

6 Detach the aerial lead from the floor, then attach a piece of string to the roof end of the aerial lead. Pull the aerial lead down the A-pillar, disconnect the string, and remove it from inside the car.

Refitting

7 Refitting is a reversal of the removal procedure.

28 Airbag units – removal and refitting

Warning: Handle any airbag unit with extreme care, as a precaution against personal injury, and always hold it with the cover facing away from the body. If in doubt concerning any proposed work involving an airbag unit or its control circuitry, consult a Ford dealer or other qualified specialist. Stand the airbag with the cover uppermost, and do not expose it to heat sources in excess of 100°C. Do not attempt to open or repair an airbag unit, or apply any electrical current to it. Do not use any airbag unit which is visibly damaged or which has been tampered with. It is recommended that safety glasses are worn when working on the airbag unit.

Driver's airbag

1 Disconnect the battery negative lead (refer to *Disconnecting the battery* at the end of this manual).

Warning: Before proceeding, wait a minimum of one minute, as a precaution against accidental firing of the airbag unit. This period ensures that any stored energy in the back-up capacitor is dissipated. We suggest you wait several minutes.

2 Rotate the steering wheel so that one of the airbag mounting bolt holes (at the rear of the steering wheel boss) is visible above the steering column upper shroud. Alternatively, remove the multifunction switches as described in Section 4.

3 Unscrew and remove the first mounting bolt, then turn the steering wheel through 180° and remove the remaining mounting bolt **(see illustration)**.

4 Carefully withdraw the airbag unit from the steering wheel far enough to disconnect the airbag and horn push wiring, then remove it from inside the car **(see illustrations)**.

5 If a new airbag module is being fitted, the horn switch must be transferred from the old unit. Disconnect the wiring from the switch, then detach the connectors, undo the nuts and remove the switch and contact plate from the module.

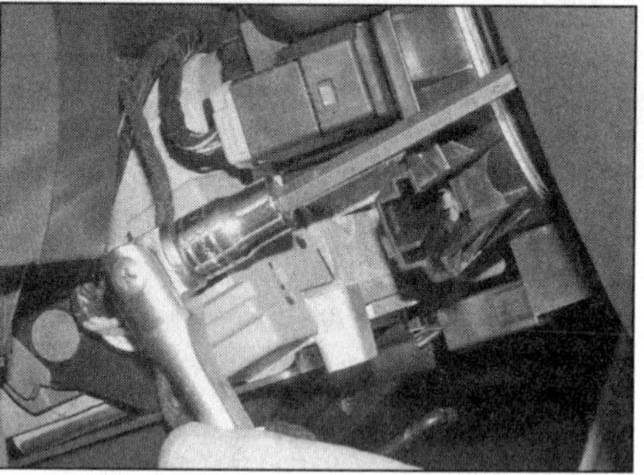

28.3 Unscrew the mounting bolts . . .

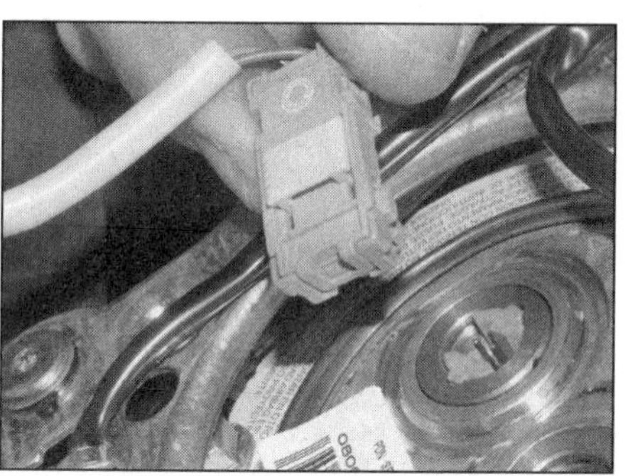

28.4b . . . and airbag wiring

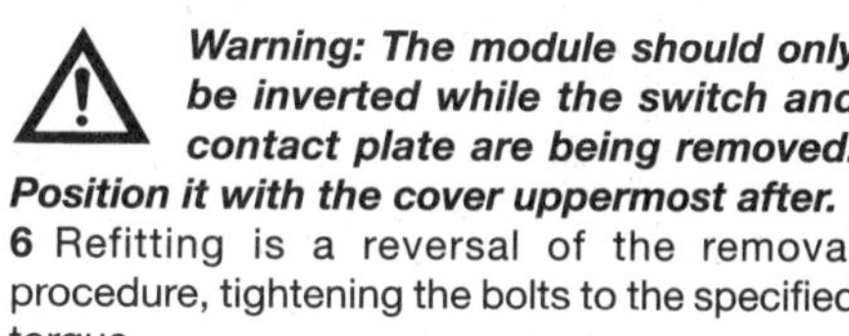

Warning: The module should only be inverted while the switch and contact plate are being removed. Position it with the cover uppermost after.

6 Refitting is a reversal of the removal procedure, tightening the bolts to the specified torque.

Passenger's airbag

7 Disconnect the battery negative lead (refer to *Disconnecting the battery* at the end of this manual).

Warning: Before proceeding, wait a minimum of one minute, as a precaution against accidental firing of the airbag unit. This period ensures that any stored energy in the back-up capacitor is dissipated. We suggest you wait several minutes.

8 Remove the glovebox and latch as described in Chapter 11.

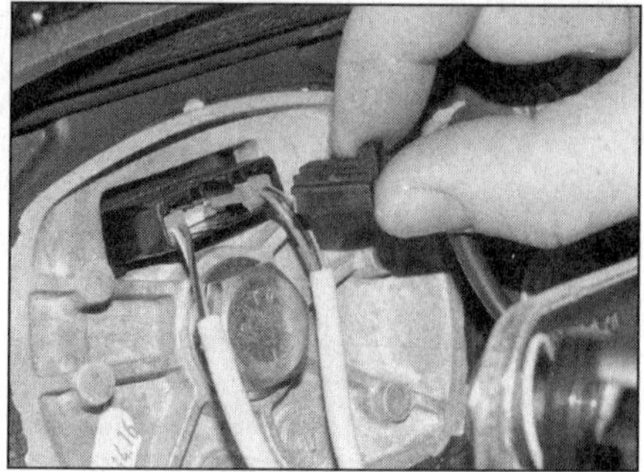

28.4a . . . then disconnect the horn wiring . . .

28.4c Driver's airbag module removed from the steering wheel

9 Disconnect the wiring from the passenger airbag module **(see illustration)**. To do this, slide the clips away from the module.

10 Unscrew the retaining bolts and remove the airbag module from the facia crossmember **(see illustration)**.

Warning: The retaining bolts must only be used a maximum of three times. Centre-punch them to indicate the number of times they have been unscrewed.

11 Refitting is a reversal of the removal procedure, but tighten the bolts to the specified torque, and initialise the electric window motors as described in Chapter 11.

Side airbag and curtain airbag

12 Removal of the side airbag and curtain airbag units requires work which is not considered to be within the scope of the

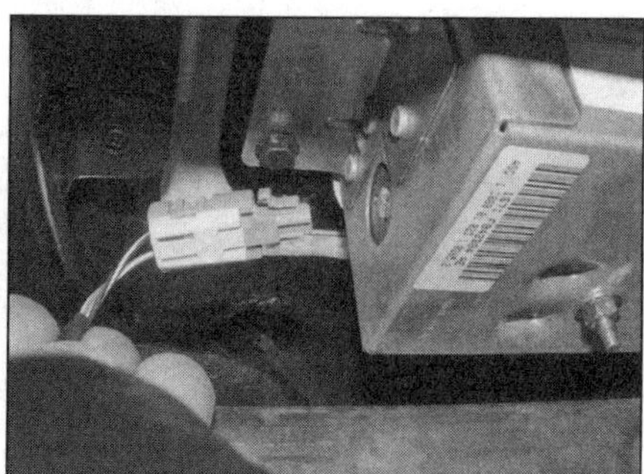

28.9 Disconnecting the wiring from the passenger's airbag

28.10 Unscrewing the passenger's airbag mounting bolts

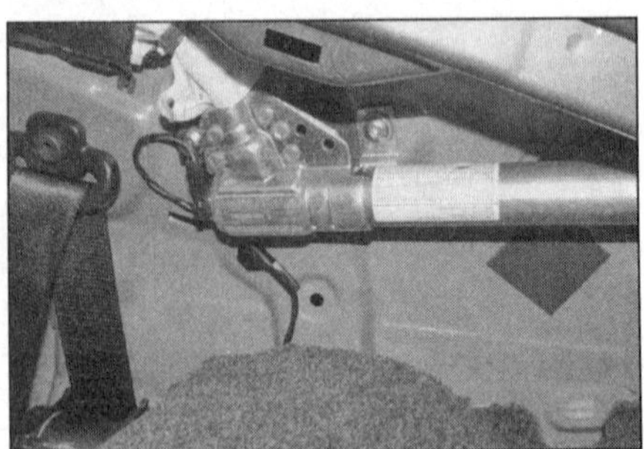
28.12 The curtain airbag module is located behind the rear luggage compartment side panel

home mechanic. The car should be taken to a Ford dealer for this work to be undertaken **(see illustration)**.

29 Airbag control module - removal and refitting

Caution: New airbag modules must be configured following installation. This work must be carried out by a Ford dealer, using specialist equipment.

Removal

1 Disconnect the battery negative lead (refer to *Disconnecting the battery* at the end of this manual).

Warning: Before proceeding, wait a minimum of one minute, as a precaution against accidental firing of the airbag unit. This period ensures that any stored energy in the back-up capacitor is dissipated. We suggest you wait several minutes.

2 Remove the centre console as described in Chapter 11.

3 Disconnect the wiring from the airbag control module **(see illustration)**.

29.3 Airbag control module located beneath the centre console

4 Unscrew the nuts and remove the module from the floor. Note the forward-pointing arrow on the upper face of the module.

Refitting

5 Refitting is a reversal of the removal procedure, but tighten the mounting nuts to the specified torque.

30 Airbag clock spring - removal and refitting

Removal

1 Disconnect the battery negative lead (refer to *Disconnecting the battery* at the end of this manual).

Warning: Before proceeding, wait a minimum of one minute, as a precaution against accidental firing of the airbag unit. This period ensures that any stored energy in the back-up capacitor is dissipated. We suggest you wait several minutes.

2 Remove the lower trim panel from beneath the steering column, which is secured by four screws and two upper clips.

3 Remove the steering wheel as described in Chapter 10, then remove the large coil spring. Make sure the front wheels are in their straight-ahead position. Ensure the airbag clock spring remains in its straight-ahead position using adhesive tape **(see illustrations)**.

4 Where fitted, remove the audio control switch from the steering column lower shroud using a thin screwdriver to release the locking tang. Disconnect the wiring.

5 Using a screwdriver, release the clips and remove the steering column upper shroud, then undo the screws and remove the lower shroud.

6 Remove both multifunction switches from the steering column as described in Section 4.

7 If necessary, undo the screw and remove the spreader plate from under the steering column and position it to one side. Note that it is possible to remove the clock spring leaving the plate in position.

8 Disconnect the wiring from the clock spring **(see illustration)**.

9 Using a screwdriver, carefully release the plastic locking clips and withdraw the clock spring from the steering column **(see illustrations)**.

Refitting

10 Refitting is a reversal of removal, but make sure that all wiring is connected correctly. If the spreader plate was removed, ensure that the clock spring wiring is routed down the special depression. **Note:** *The clock spring must be fitted in its central position, with the special alignment arrows aligned* ***(see illustration)****. To check for this position, turn the clock spring housing anti-clockwise until resistance is felt, then turn in the opposite direction by two-*

30.3a Removing the large coil spring

30.3b Use adhesive tape to keep the clock spring in its straight-ahead position

30.8 Disconnect the wiring from the airbag clock spring

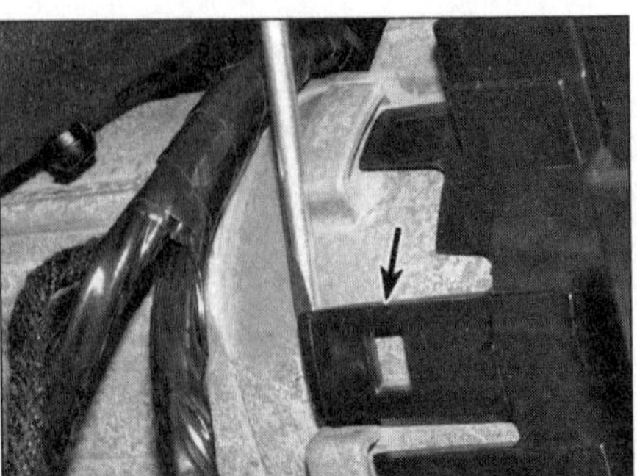
30.9a Use a screwdriver to release the plastic locking clips . . .

30.9b . . . then withdraw the clock spring from the steering column

and-a-half turns. The front wheels must still be in their straight-ahead position before refitting the clock spring.

31 Airbag side impact sensor – removal and refitting

Removal

1 Disconnect the battery negative lead (refer to *Disconnecting the battery* at the end of this manual).

Warning: Before proceeding, wait a minimum of one minute, as a precaution against accidental firing of the airbag unit. This period ensures that any stored energy in the back-up capacitor is dissipated. We suggest you wait several minutes.

2 With the relevant side doors open, pull the rubber weatherstrips away from the B-pillar for access to the trim panel.

3 Adjust the seat belt height to its lowest position. Prise out the cover and undo the uppermost screw, then unclip the trim panel from the B-pillar. Undo the screws and unclip the lower trim panel from the B-pillar.

4 Undo the screws then unclip the sill inner trim panel.

5 Disconnect the wiring from the side impact sensor located at the bottom of the B-pillar.

6 Unscrew the bolt and withdraw the sensor **(see illustration)**.

Refitting

7 Refitting is a reversal of removal, but tighten the mounting bolt to the specified torque.

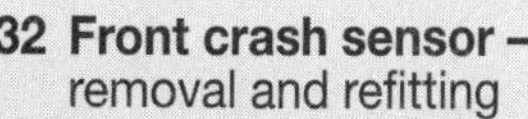

32 Front crash sensor – removal and refitting

Removal

1 Disconnect the battery negative lead (refer to *Disconnecting the battery* at the end of this manual).

Warning: Before proceeding, wait a minimum of one minute, as a precaution against accidental firing of the airbag unit. This period ensures that any stored energy in the back-up capacitor is dissipated. We suggest you wait several minutes.

30.10 Airbag clock spring alignment arrows

2 Remove the radiator grille as described in Chapter 11.

3 Disconnect the wiring from the crash sensor located below the bonnet lock **(see illustration)**.

4 Unscrew the bolt and withdraw the sensor.

Refitting

5 Refitting is a reversal of removal, but tighten the mounting bolt to the specified torque.

33 Reverse parking aid system – general information

Where fitted as an option, the park reverse aid is an ultrasonic proximity detection system, intended to help avoid rear collisions when reversing.

The system consists of four ultrasonic sensors mounted in the rear bumper, a display/buzzer unit mounted in the C-pillar trim panel, and an ECU mounted behind the left-hand side trim panel in the luggage compartment.

The system is only operational when reverse gear is engaged; changing audible and visual signals warn the driver of impending contact as the car reverses towards an object in its path.

The sensors in the bumper can be unclipped and disconnected once the rear bumper is removed, and the display/buzzer unit can be removed after removal of the C-pillar trim panel. Refer to Chapter 11 for this procedure.

31.6 Airbag side impact sensor mounting bolt

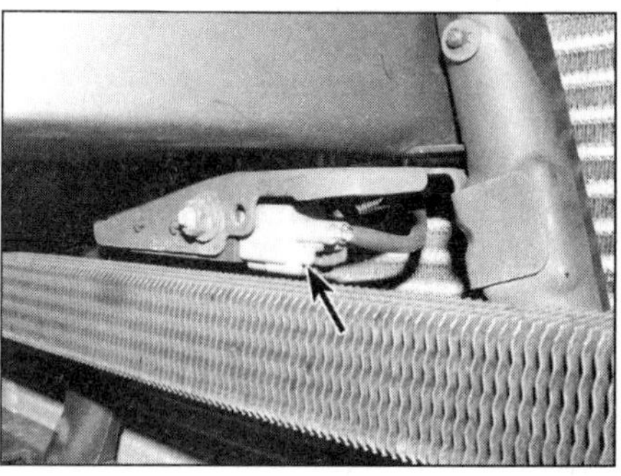

32.3 The crash sensor is located beneath the bonnet lock

The system ECU can be disconnected once the luggage area left-hand trim panel is removed.

34 Ice/frost warning sensor – removal and refitting

Removal

1 Apply the handbrake, then jack up the front of the car and support it on axle stands (see *Jacking and vehicle support*).

2 Undo a total of seven screws and remove the plastic splash shield from beneath the radiator.

3 The sensor is mounted inside the bumper, to the right of the lower grille. Pull the sensor rearwards off its mounting lug, then reach up above the right-hand foglight and disconnect the wiring plug **(see illustrations)**.

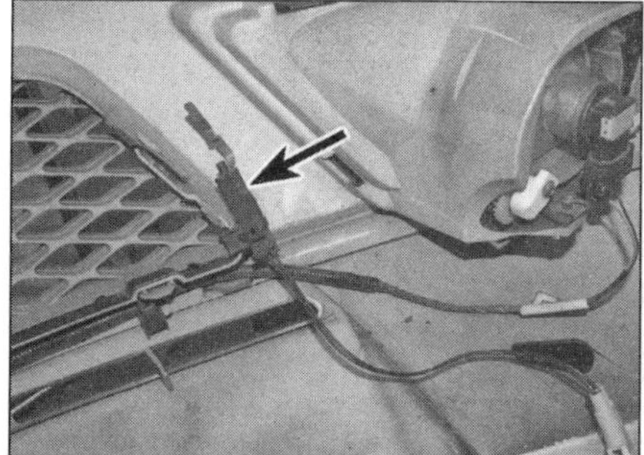

34.3a The sensor is inside the bumper, to the right of the grille

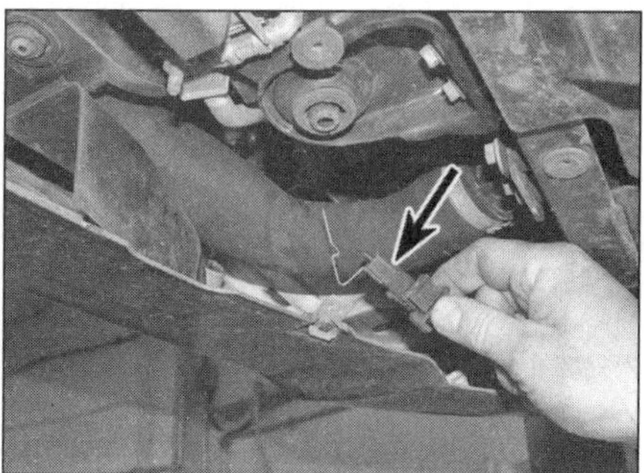

34.3b Unclipping the ice/frost warning sensor from the front bumper

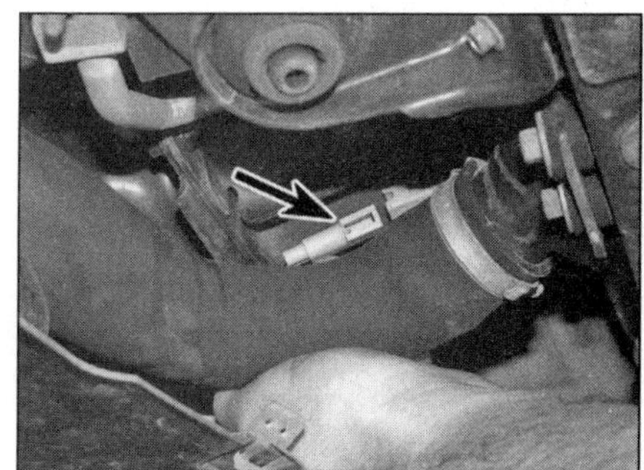

34.3c The sensor wiring plug is above the right-hand foglight

Refitting

4 Refitting is a reversal of removal.

35 Satellite navigation system – general information

The satellite navigation system uses Global Positioning System (GPS) satellites to track the car against a digital map stored on disc. The antenna for the AM/FM radio and telematics system (where applicable) is also used for the satellite navigation system. The system receives input signals from the reversing light switch and the ABS hydraulic control unit. The reversing light switch allows the system module to determine whether the car is moving forward or backward. The ABS rear wheel sensors provide the system with data on how far the car has travelled, and a compass is fitted.

The navigation module is the heart of the system, processing all data received from the antenna, wheel sensors, compass and map disc, and providing instructions which are displayed on the system's display panel.

Two systems are available on the Mondeo – a basic CD-based version known as Ford Travel Pilot, which has a small monochrome screen, and a high-end DVD-based system with a larger, colour touchscreen. Both systems read from a map disc in either a CD autochanger or DVD player which is usually mounted in the boot.

Removal and refitting of the facia-mounted unit and the autochanger are as described in Sections 24 and 25 respectively. Where applicable, the boot-mounted DVD player is removed in a similar way to the autochanger, but is secured by two bolts on either side. On some models, the DVD unit may be located under the front passenger seat. Seat removal and refitting is covered in Chapter 11, but it appears that the seat has to be dismantled to access the unit, making this a job for a Ford dealer.

Any problems with the system should be referred to a Ford dealer for diagnosis, after the usual checks have been made for loose or damaged wiring, etc.

36 Electric seat components – removal and refitting

Heated seats

1 If heated seats are fitted, both driver's and front passenger seats have heating elements built into the seat cushion and backrest. Certain models may be equipped with 'climate-control' seats, which feature heating elements and cooling fans, giving the occupants a 'micro-climate' of their own choosing.

2 No repairs can be made to the heating elements or fan motors without dismantling the seat and removing the seat fabric – therefore this work should be left to a Ford dealer or other specialist.

3 The heated seat switches are removed as described in Section 4.

Seat adjustment components

4 Only the driver's seat is equipped with motors, and only the highest specification models have anything other than a height adjustment motor.

5 To gain access to the motors, remove the driver's seat as described in Chapter 11.

6 The motors are bolted to a mounting frame, which in turn is bolted to the seat base. Before removing a motor, trace its wiring back from the motor to its wiring plug, and disconnect it.

7 Remove the mounting frame bolts or the motor mounting bolts, as applicable, and remove the components from the seat base.

8 Refitting is a reversal of removal. It is worth periodically greasing the worm-drive components and seat runners, to ensure trouble-free operation.

9 For further diagnosis of any problems with the system, refer to Sections 2 and 3, and to the wiring diagrams at the end of this Chapter.

FORD MONDEO wiring diagrams

Diagram 1

Engine fusebox 5

Fuse	Rating	Circuit protected
F1	30A	ABS
F2	50A	Ignition relay
F3	60A	Auxiliary coolant heater
F4	30A	Heated rear window relay
F5	20A	Ignition relay 2
F6	40A	Heater blower relay
F7	50A	Main supply
F8	60A	Engine cooling fan, preheating
F9	20A	Engine management relay
F10	40A	Engine cooling fan
F11	30A	LH heated screen element
F12	-	Not used
F13	30A	RH heated screen element
F14	-	Not used
F15	3A	Heated front/rear screen switch
F16	7.5/20A	LH dipped beam
F17	10A	Automatic transmission
F18	7.5/20A	RH dipped beam
F19	-	Not used
F20	20A	ABS
F21	15A	Sidelights
F22	20A	Headlight washer
F23	7.5/20A	Alarm sounder (petrol), booster heater (Diesel)
F24	20A	Generic electronic control unit
F25	15A	Generic electronic control unit
F26	20A	Horn relay, heated screen relay
F27	15A	Engine management
F28	20A	Ignition switch
F29	30A	Starter relay
F30	7.5A	Alternator
F31	7.5A	Air conditioning wide open throttle relay
F32	3A	Automatic transmission
F33	7.5A	Engine management control unit
F37	15A	Engine management
F38	-	Not used
F39	-	Not used
F40	7.5A	Engine management
F41	7.5A	Engine management
F42	10/15A	Engine management

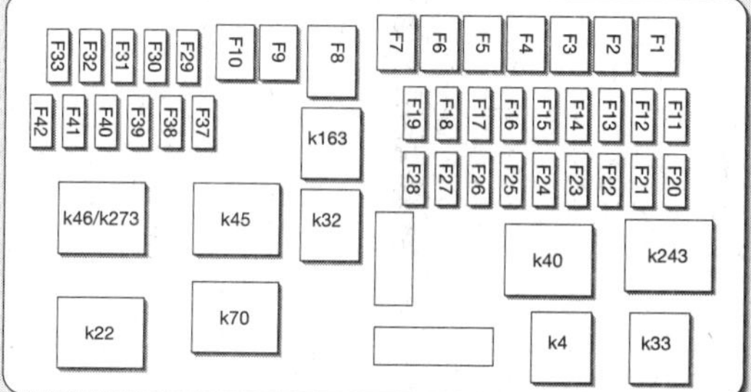

Passenger fusebox 6

Fuse	Rating	Circuit protected
F60	25A	Electric windows
F61	25A	Electric windows
F62	15A	Fog lights
F63	7.5A	Instrument cluster, sidelights, sidelight warning light
F64	7.5A	Sidelights
F65	7.5A	Heated seats, air conditioning
F66	30A	Powered seats
F67	7.5A	Engine management, warning devices, alarm
F68	15A	Instrument cluster, cigar lighter
F69	7.5A	ABS, audio system, instrument cluster, navigation, phone
F70	15A	Instrument cluster
F71	10A	Audio/video system, navigation, phone
F72	20A	Audio/video system, navigation, phone, diagnostic socket
F73	20A	Sunroof
F74	20A	Exterior lighting
F75	7.5A	Electric mirrors, clock, instrument cluster
F76	7.5A	Heater control
F77	7.5A	ABS
F78	7.5A	Instrument cluster
F79	-	Not used
F80	7.5A	Reversing lights
F81	7.5A	Automatic transmission, heated seats
F82	7.5A	Heated washer jets, air conditioning, engine management
F83	15A	Heated seats, air conditioning
F84	-	Not used
F85	7.5A	LH main beam
F86	7.5A	RH main beam
F87	-	Not used
F88	15A	Headlights
F89	7.5A	SRS system
F90	15A	Rear wiper
F91	7.5A	Electric windows
F92	10A	Rear fog light cut-off
F93	10A	Stop lights, heater blower
F94	20A	Wash/wipe
F95	7.5A	Dipped beam
F96	-	Not used
F97	7.5A	Interior lighting, number plate lights
F98	7.5A	Heated front screen, heated mirrors
F99	10A	Interior lighting

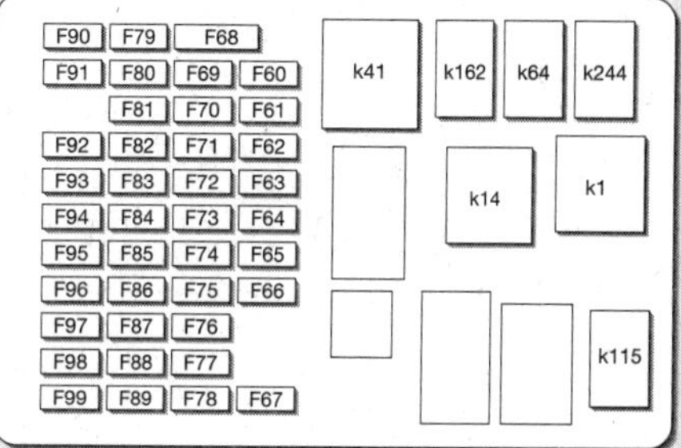

Key to symbols

Bulb

Flashing bulb

Switch

Multiple contact switch (ganged)

Fuse/fusible link and current rating — F5 30A

Item no. — 2

Pump/motor

Gauge/meter

Earth point — E4

Diode

Light emitting diode (LED)

Resistor

Variable resistor

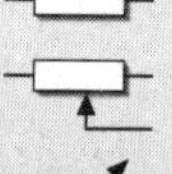

Variable resistor

Heating element

Solenoid actuator

Connecting wires

Wire splice, soldered joint or unspecified connector

Plug & socket contact

Wire colour (green with red tracer), bracket denotes alternative wiring. — Gn/Rd

Dashed outline denotes part of a larger item, containing in this case an electronic or solid state device. e.g. connector no. 429, pin 2.

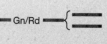

H33527

Diagram 2

Wire colours

Bk	Black	**Vt**	Violet
Gn	Green	**Rd**	Red
Pk	Pink	**Gy**	Grey
Lg	Light green	**Bu**	Blue
Bn	Brown	**Wh**	White
Og	Orange	**Ye**	Yellow
Na	Natural	**Sr**	Silver

Key to items

1 Battery
2 Starter motor
3 Alternator
4 Ignition switch
5 Engine fusebox
   K22 = starter relay
   K33 = horn relay
   K45 = cooling fan relay
   k163 = engine management relay
6 Passenger fusebox
7 Clock
8 Generic electronic control unit
9 Instrument cluster
   a = alternator warning light
10 Cooling temperature sensor
11 Cooling fan motor
12 Steering wheel multifunction switch
   a = horn switch
13 Steering wheel clock springs
14 Automatic transmission control unit
15 Horn
16 Horn (low pitch)
17 Horn (high pitch)
18 Cigar lighter

H33528

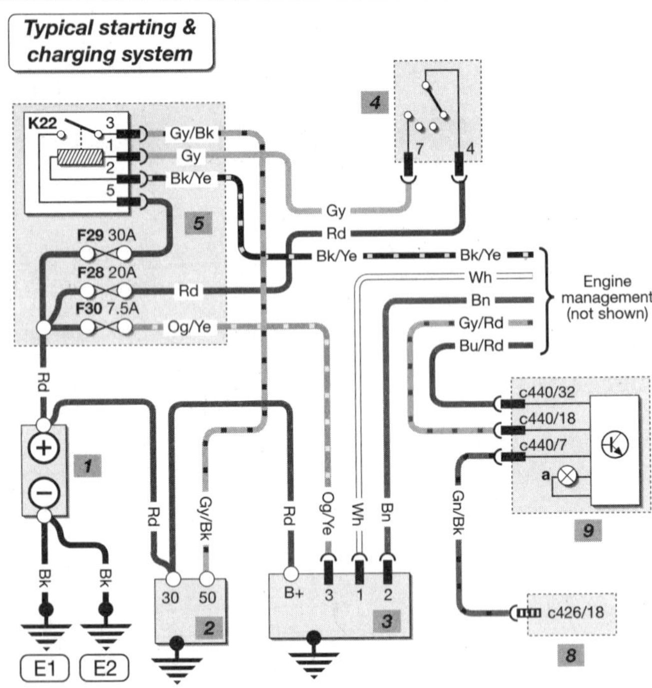

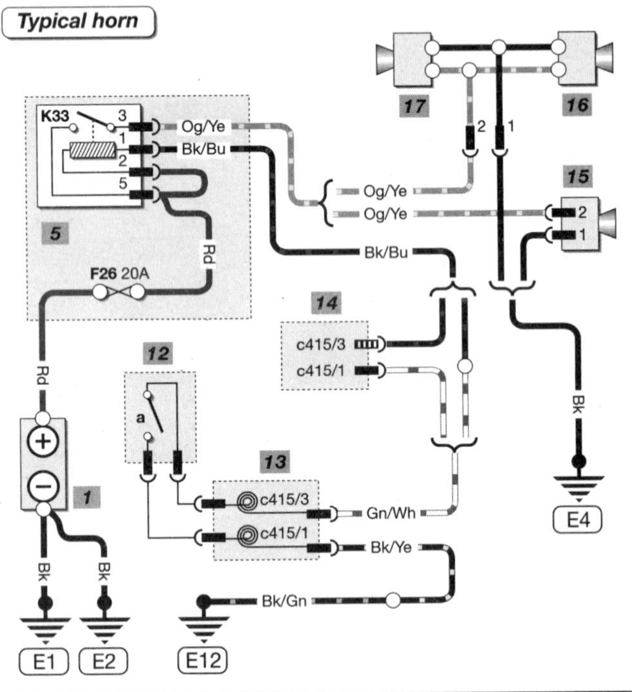

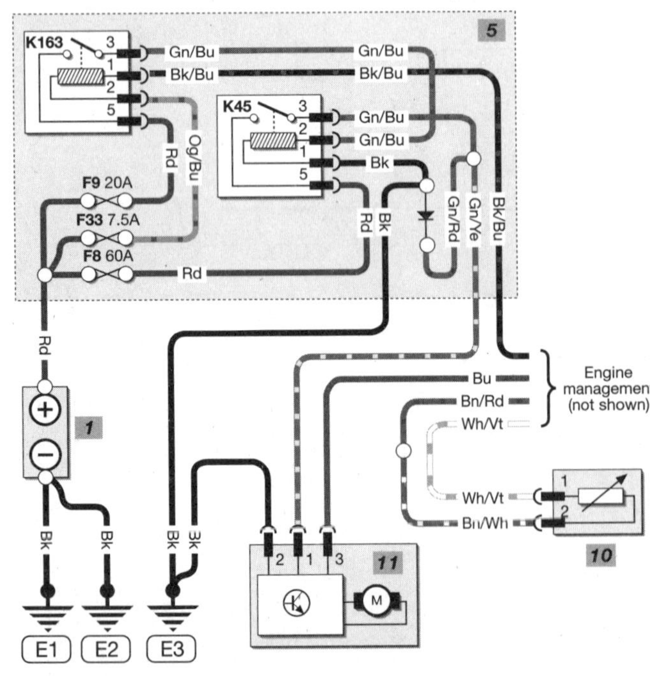

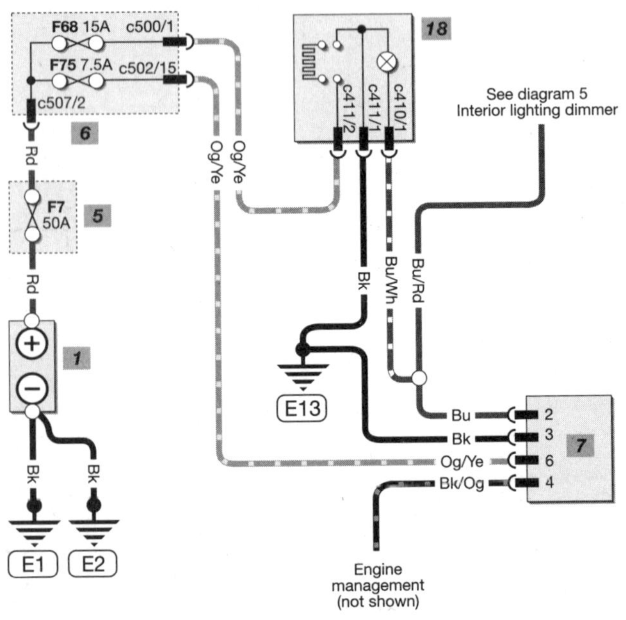

Diagram 3

Wire colours

- **Bk** Black
- **Gn** Green
- **Pk** Pink
- **Lg** Light green
- **Bn** Brown
- **Og** Orange
- **Na** Natural
- **Vt** Violet
- **Rd** Red
- **Gy** Grey
- **Bu** Blue
- **Wh** White
- **Ye** Yellow
- **Sr** Silver

* 5-door models

Key to items

1 Battery
4 Ignition switch
5 Engine fusebox
6 Passenger fusebox
K41 = ignition relay
8 Generic electronic control unit
9 Instrument cluster
b = LH indicator warning light
c = RH indicator warning light
22 Stop light switch
23 Reversing light switch (manual)
24 Transmission range selector (auto)
25 LH rear light unit
a = stop/tail light
b = reversing light
c = fog light
d = direction indicator
26 RH rear light unit
(as above)
27 High level stop light
28 Light switch
a = front/rear fog light
29 LH front foglight
30 RH front foglight
31 LH multifunction switch
a = direction indicators
b = audible warning
32 Hazard warning switch
33 LH front light unit
a = direction indicator
34 RH front light unit
b = direction indicator
35 LH front side repeater
36 RH front side repeater

H33529

Typical stop & reversing lights

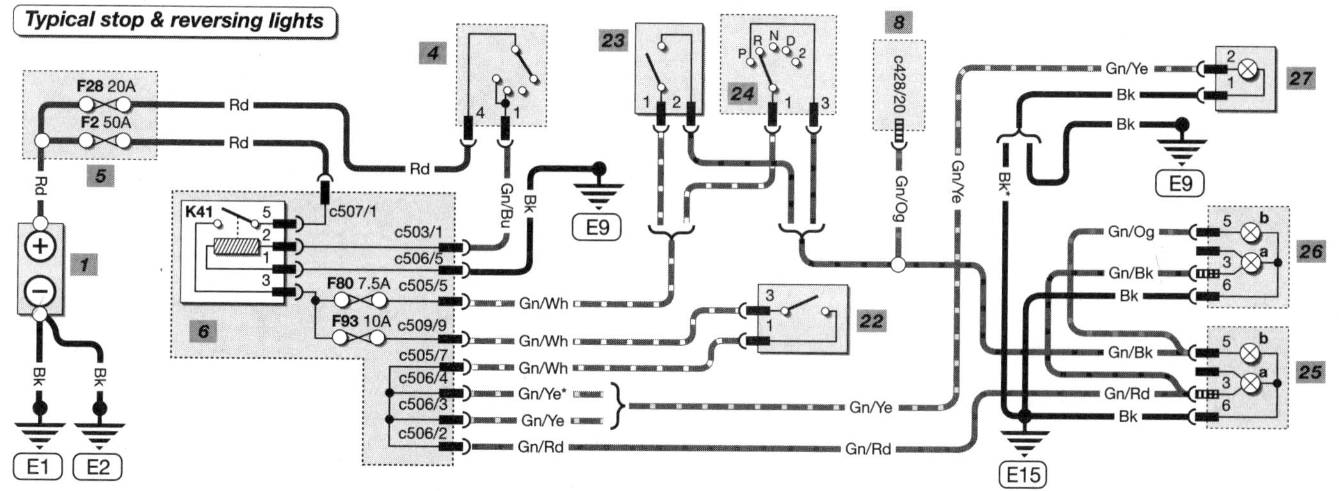

Typical front & rear fog lights

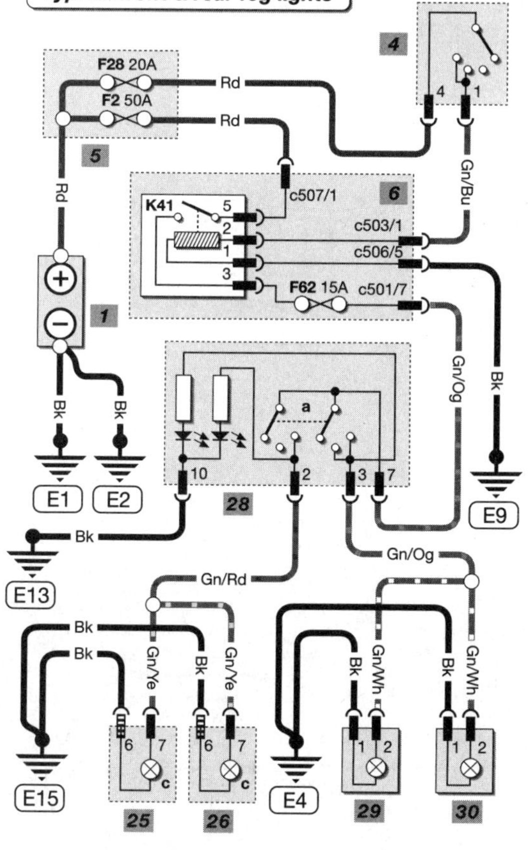

Typical direction indicators & hazard warning lights

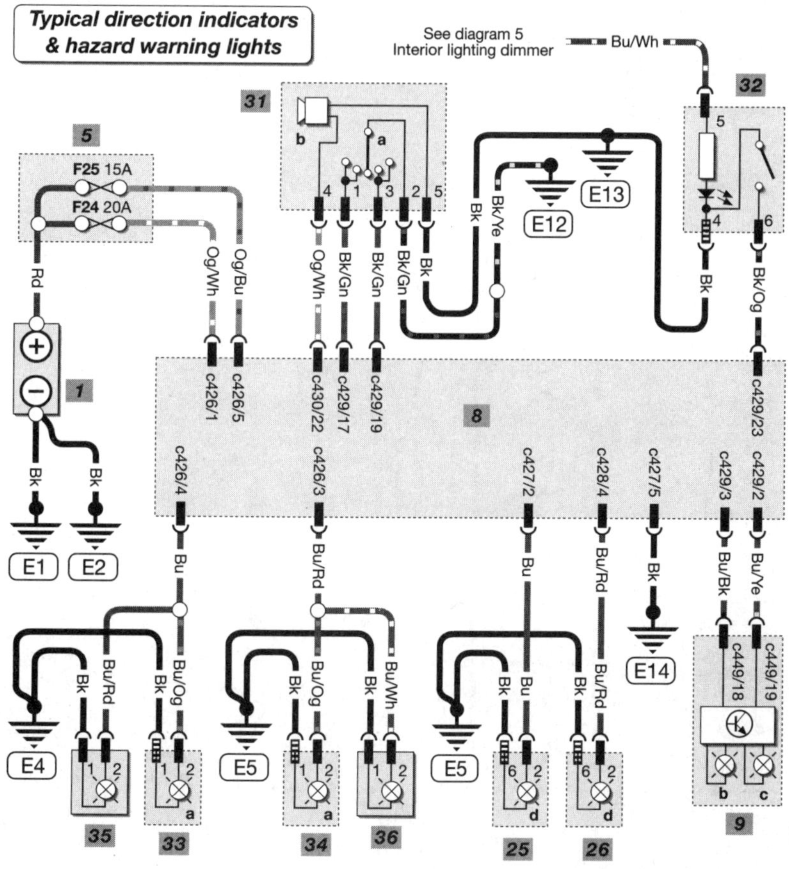

See diagram 5 Interior lighting dimmer

Diagram 4

Wire colours

Bk	Black	**Vt**	Violet
Gn	Green	**Rd**	Red
Pk	Pink	**Gy**	Grey
Lg	Light green	**Bu**	Blue
Bn	Brown	**Wh**	White
Og	Orange	**Ye**	Yellow
Na	Natural	**Sr**	Silver

Key to items

1 Battery
4 Ignition switch
5 Engine fusebox
K243 = dipped beam relay
K244 = main beam relay
6 Passenger fusebox
8 Generic electronic control unit
9 Instrument cluster
d = side/headlight warning light
e = main beam warning light
25 LH rear light unit
a = stop/tail light
26 RH rear light unit
(as above)
28 Light switch
b = parking/side/headlight
31 LH multifunction switch
c = headlight dip/flash
33 LH front light unit
b = sidelight
c = dip beam
d = main beam
34 RH front light unit
(as above)
40 LH number plate light
41 RH nimber plate light

H33530

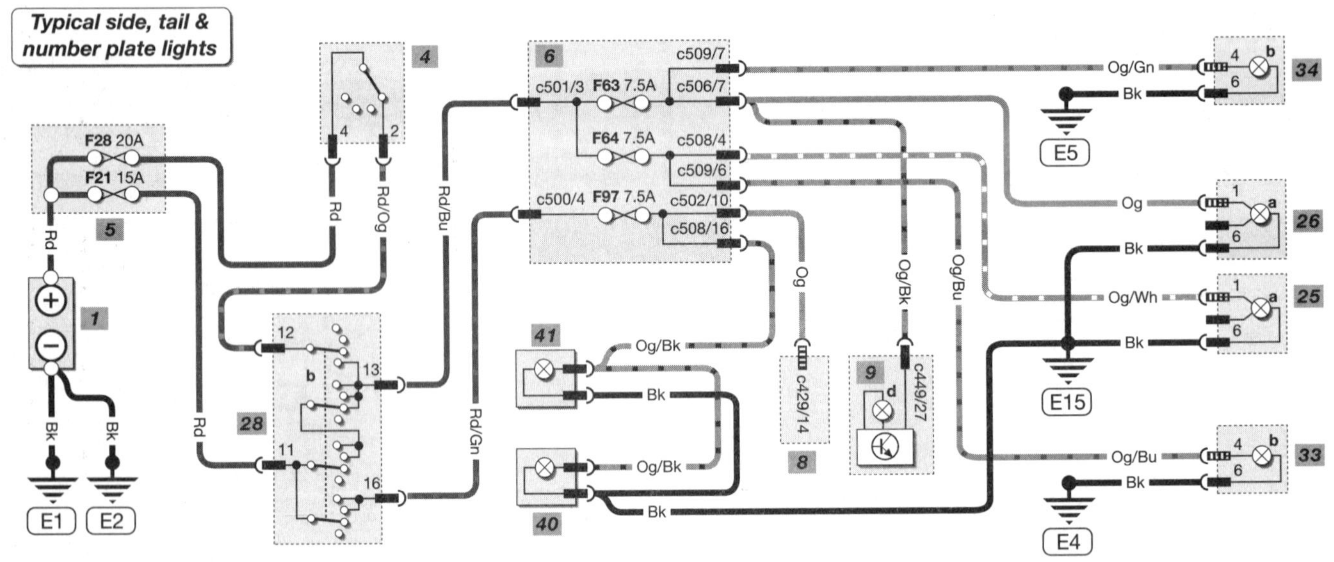

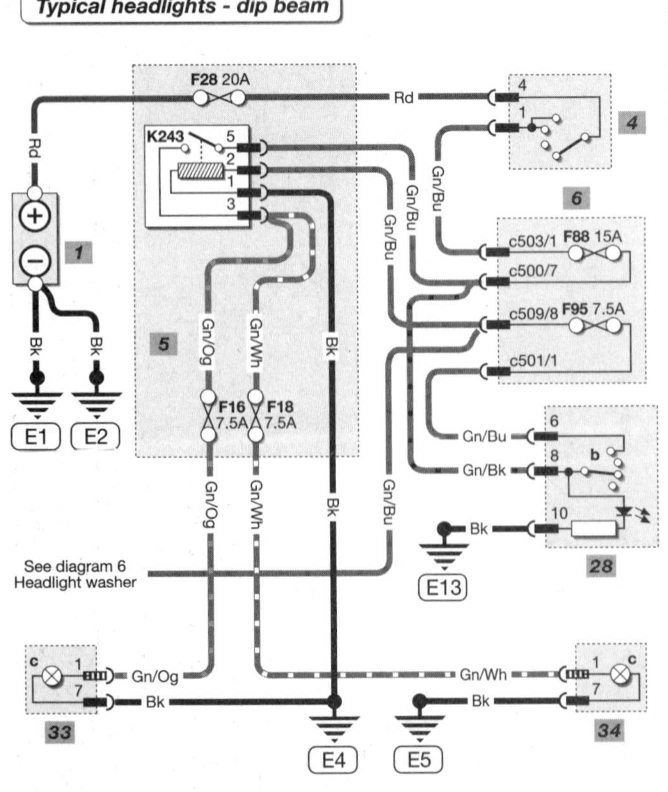

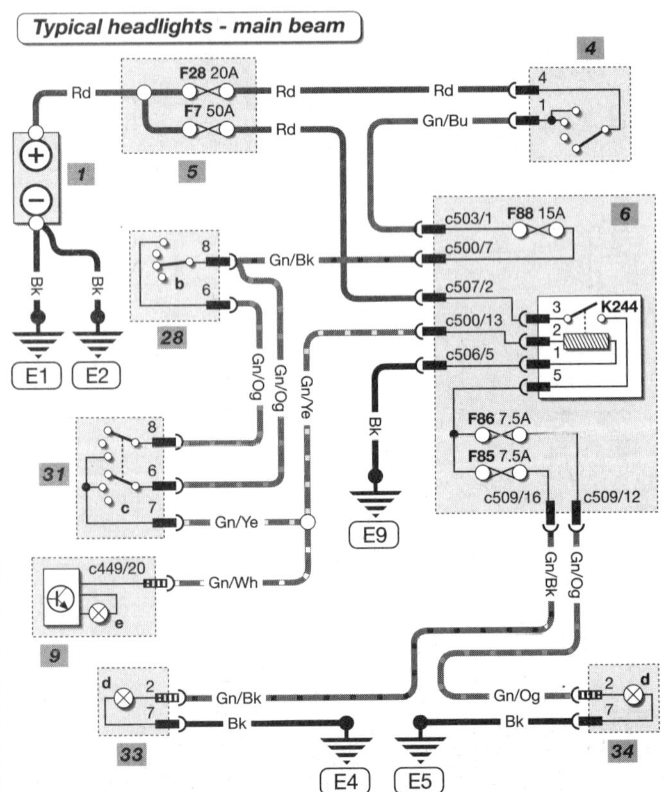

Wire colours

Bk	Black	**Vt**	Violet
Gn	Green	**Rd**	Red
Pk	Pink	**Gy**	Grey
Lg	Light green	**Bu**	Blue
Bn	Brown	**Wh**	White
Og	Orange	**Ye**	Yellow
Na	Natural	**Sr**	Silver

Key to items

1 Battery
4 Ignition switch
5 Engine fusebox
6 Passenger fusebox
8 Generic electronic control unit
28 Light switch
 b = parking/side/headlight
 c = headlight levelling
 d = interior lighting dimmer
33 LH front light unit
 e = headlight levelling
34 RH front light unit (as above)
45 LH front door switch
46 LH rear door switch
47 RH front door switch
48 RH rear door switch
49 Front interior light
50 Rear interior light
51 Glovebox light
52 Glovebox light switch
53 LH vanity mirror
54 RH vanity mirror
55 LH door mirror assembly
 a = puddle light
56 RH door mirror assembly (as above)
57 LH front footwell light
58 RH front footwell light
59 Luggage compartment light (estate)
60 Luggage compartment light 4/5 door)
61 Tailgate lock motor

Diagram 5

H33531

Typical headlight levelling & interior lighting dimmer

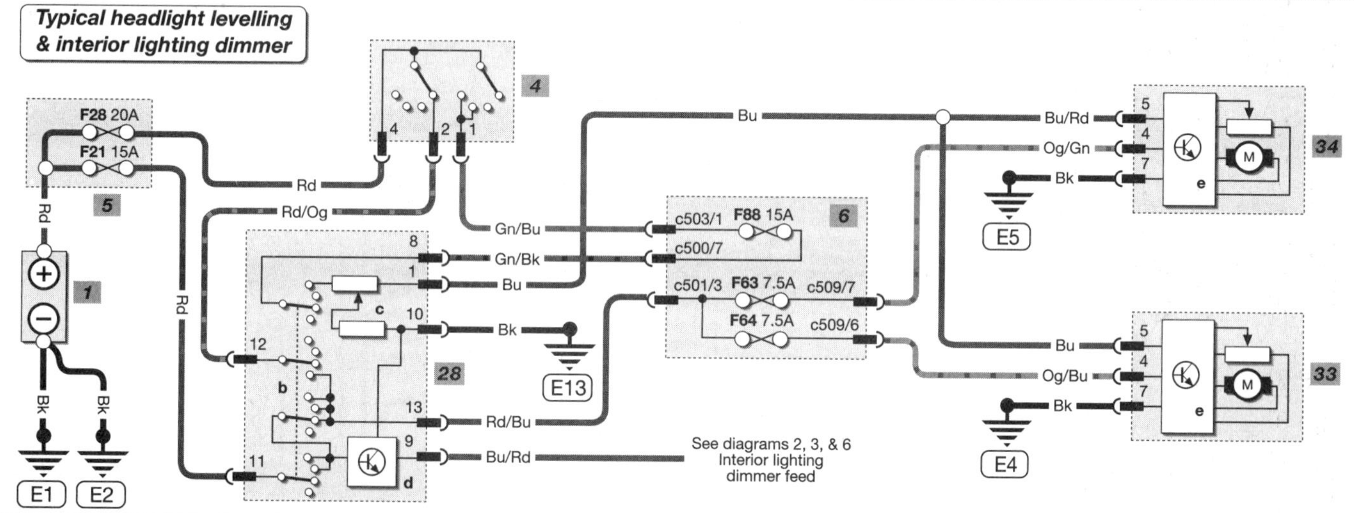

Typical interior lighting

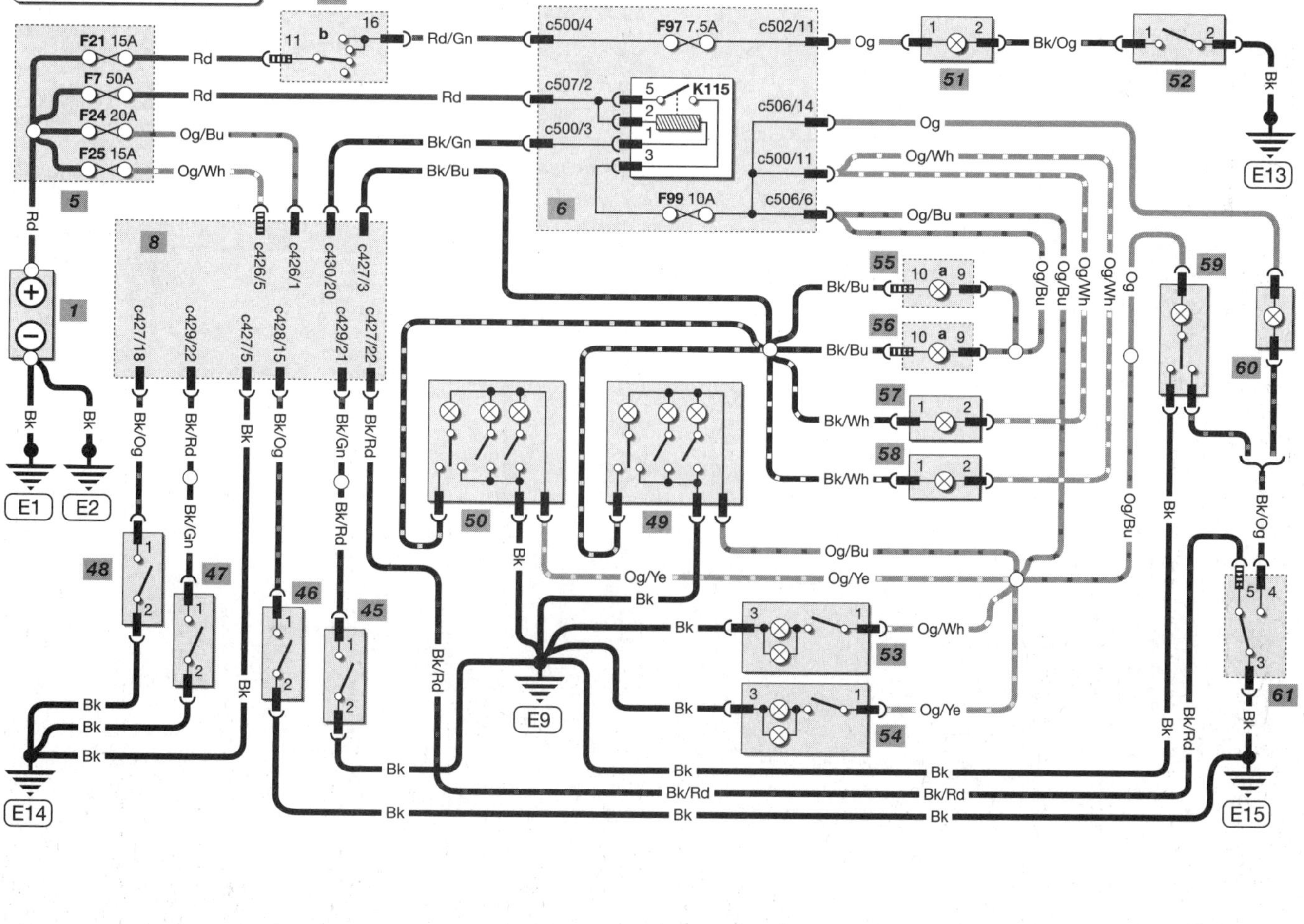

28
11 b 16
Rd/Gn
F21 15A
F7 50A
F24 20A
F25 15A
Rd
Rd
Og/Bu
Og/Wh
5
1
Bk
Bk
E1
E2
c500/4
F97 7.5A
c502/11
Og
Bk/Og
51
52
Bk
E13
c507/2
K115
Rd
c500/3
Bk/Gn
Bk/Bu
c506/14
c500/11
F99 10A
c506/6
6
Og
Og/Wh
Og/Bu
8
c426/5
c426/1
c430/20
c427/3
c427/18
c429/22
c427/5
c428/15
c429/21
c427/22
Bk/Og
Bk/Rd
Bk/Gn
Bk
Bk/Og
Bk/Gn
Bk/Rd
55
10 a 9
Bk/Bu
56
10 a 9
Bk/Bu
57
Bk/Wh
58
Bk/Wh
59
60
Og/Bu
Og/Bu
Og/Wh
Og/Wh
Og
50
49
48
47
46
45
Og/Bu
Og/Ye
Og/Ye
Bk
Bk
Og/Wh
53
Bk
Og/Ye
54
E9
Bk/Rd
Bk/Og
61
Bk
Bk/Rd
Bk
Bk
Bk
Bk
E14
Bk
Bk
Bk/Rd
Bk/Rd
Bk
Bk
Bk
E15

Diagram 6

Wire colours

Bk	Black	**Vt**	Violet
Gn	Green	**Rd**	Red
Pk	Pink	**Gy**	Grey
Lg	Light green	**Bu**	Blue
Bn	Brown	**Wh**	White
Og	Orange	**Ye**	Yellow
Na	Natural	**Sr**	Silver

* 4-door models

Key to items

1 Battery
4 Ignition switch
5 Engine fusebox
 k40 = heated front screen relay
6 Passenger fusebox
 k1 = heated rear window relay
 k14 = blower motor relay
 k41 = ignition relay
8 Generic electronic control unit
9 Instrument cluster
55 LH door mirror asssembly
 b = heating element
56 RH door mirror assembly
 b = heating element
65 Heater blower motor
66 Heater blower resistors
67 Heater blower switch
68 Heater/air conditioning control unit
69 Heated rear window
70 LH front screen heating element
71 RH front screen heating element
72 Heated front/rear window switch
 a = switch illumination
 b = heated rear window switch/indicator
 c = heated front screen switch/indicator
73 Wash/wipe switch
 a = front washer
74 Headlight washer relay
75 Headlight washer pump

H33532

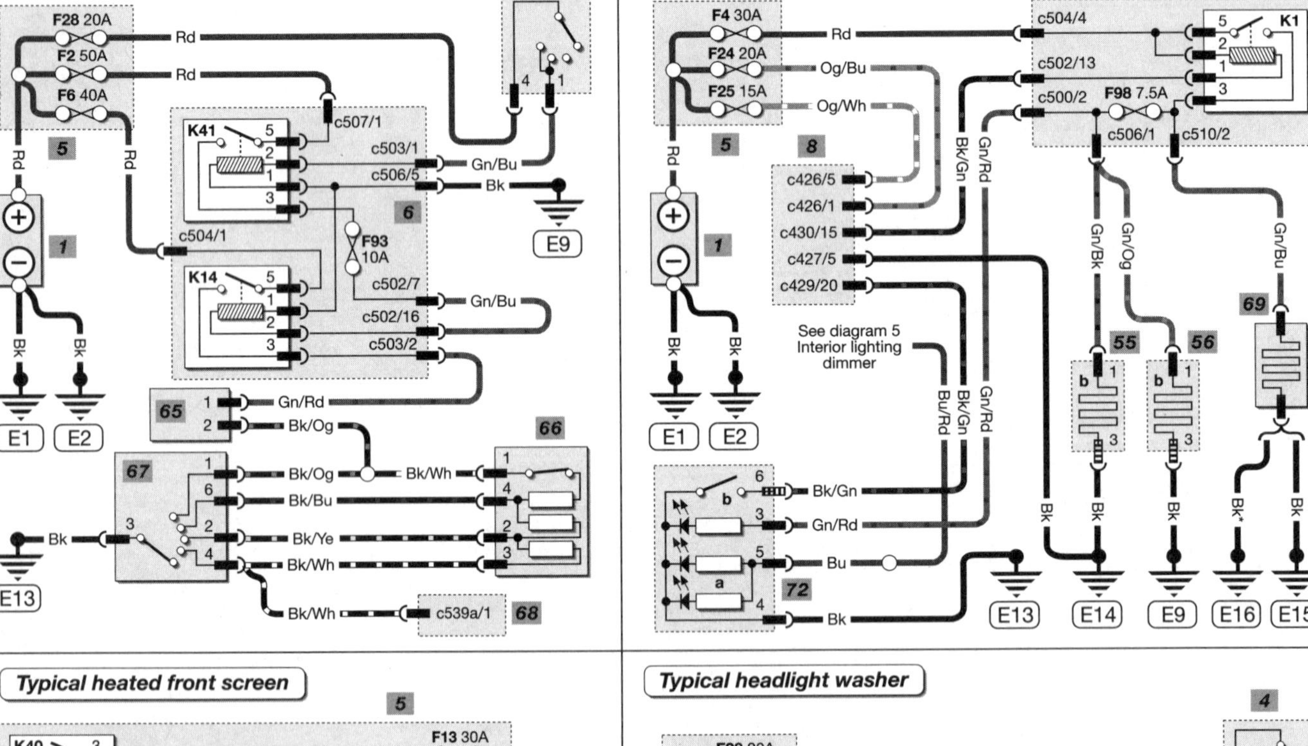

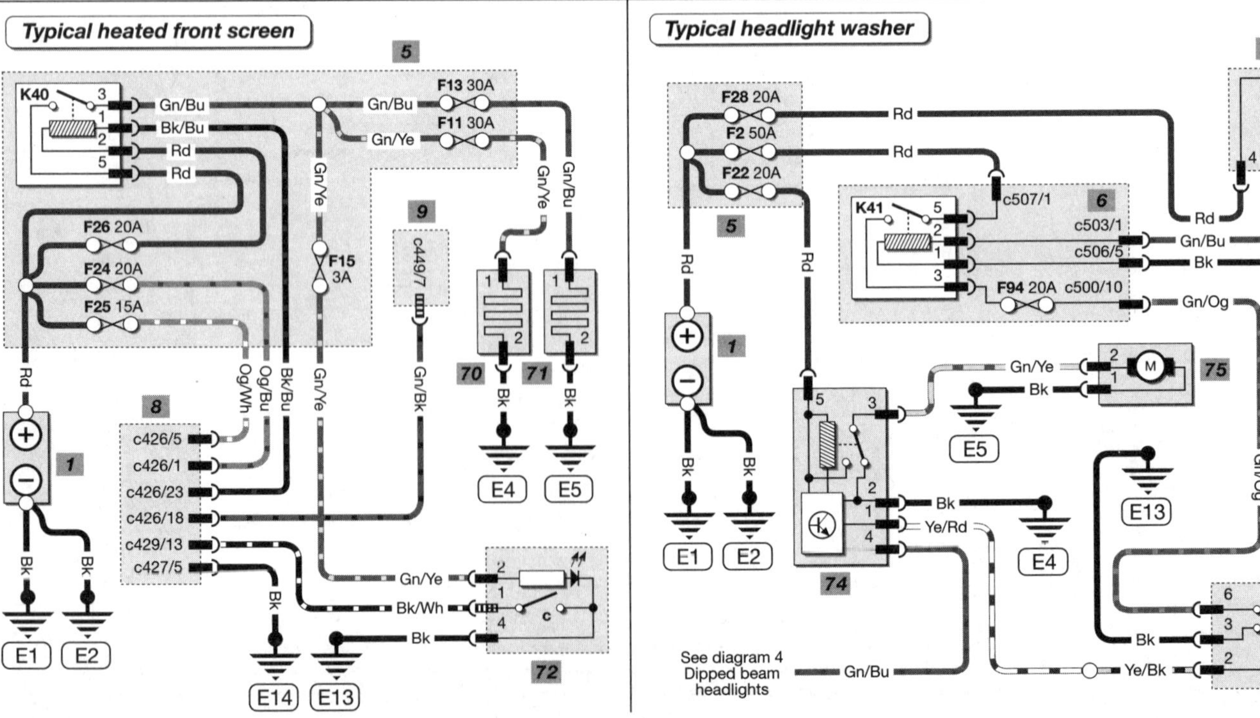

Wire colours

Bk	Black	**Vt**	Violet
Gn	Green	**Rd**	Red
Pk	Pink	**Gy**	Grey
Lg	Light green	**Bu**	Blue
Bn	Brown	**Wh**	White
Og	Orange	**Ye**	Yellow
Na	Natural	**Sr**	Silver

Key to items

Diagram 7

1 Battery
4 Ignition switch
5 Engine fusebox
6 Passenger fusebox
  k41 = ignition relay
  k64 = rear wiper relay
  k162 = front wiper relay
8 Generic electronic control unit
55 LH door mirror assembly
  c = mirror retraction motor
  d = up/down motor
  e = left/right motor
56 RH door mirror assembly (as above)
73 Wash/wipe switch
  a = front washer
  b = rear wash/wipe
  c = front wiper
74 Headlight washer relay
78 Front/rear washer pump
79 Front wiper motor
80 Rear wiper motor
81 Mirror retraction control unit
82 Mirror control switch
  a = left/right switch
  b = up/down switch
  c = changeover switch

H33533

Typical front & rear wash/wipe

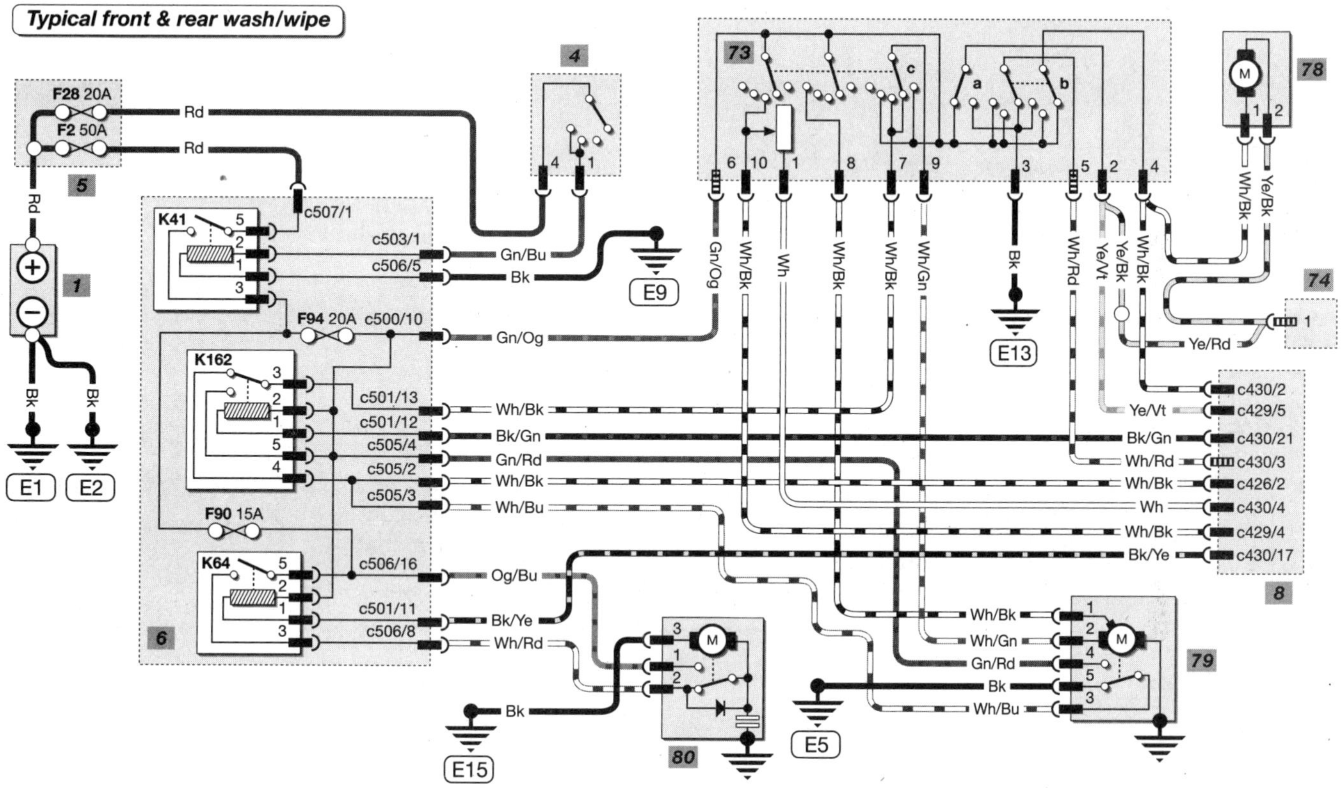

Typical electric mirrors

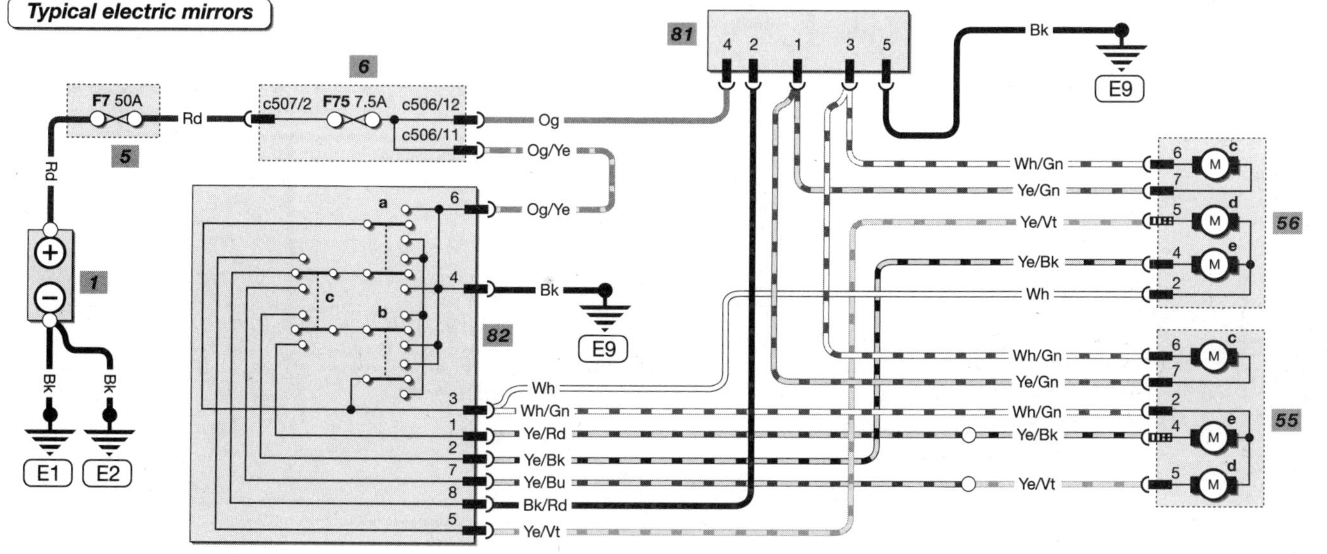

Diagram 8

Wire colours

Bk	Black	**Vt**	Violet
Gn	Green	**Rd**	Red
Pk	Pink	**Gy**	Grey
Lg	Light green	**Bu**	Blue
Bn	Brown	**Wh**	White
Og	Orange	**Ye**	Yellow
Na	Natural	**Sr**	Silver

Key to items

1 Battery
5 Engine fusebox
6 Passenger fusebox
 k41 = ignition relay
8 Generic electronic control unit
9 Instrument cluster
 f = door ajar warning light
45 LH front door switch
46 LH rear door switch
47 RH front door switch
48 RH rear door switch
61 Tailgate lock motor
85 Bootlid anti-theft switch (4 door models)
86 ESP/tailgate release switch
87 Tailgate release switch
88 LH rear door lock assembly
89 RH rear door lock assembly
90 LH front door lock assembly
91 RH front door lock assembly
92 LH front window motor
93 RH front window motor
94 LH window switch
95 RH window switch

H33534

Typical central locking

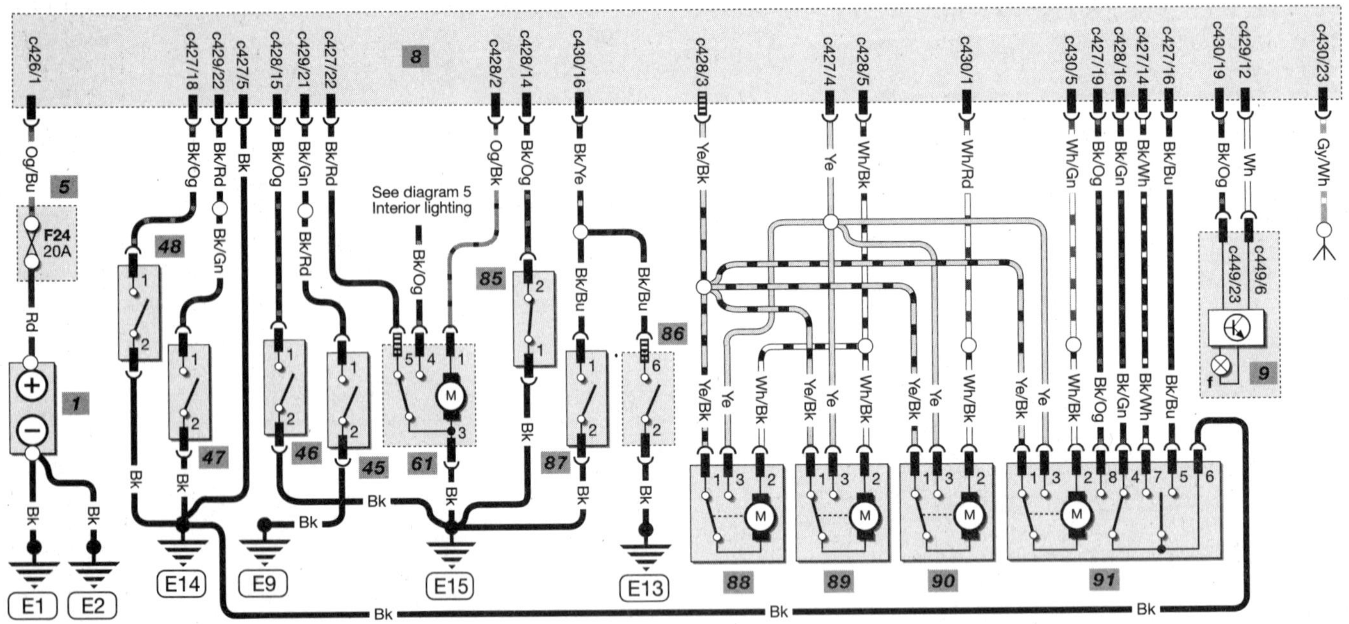

Typical electric windows

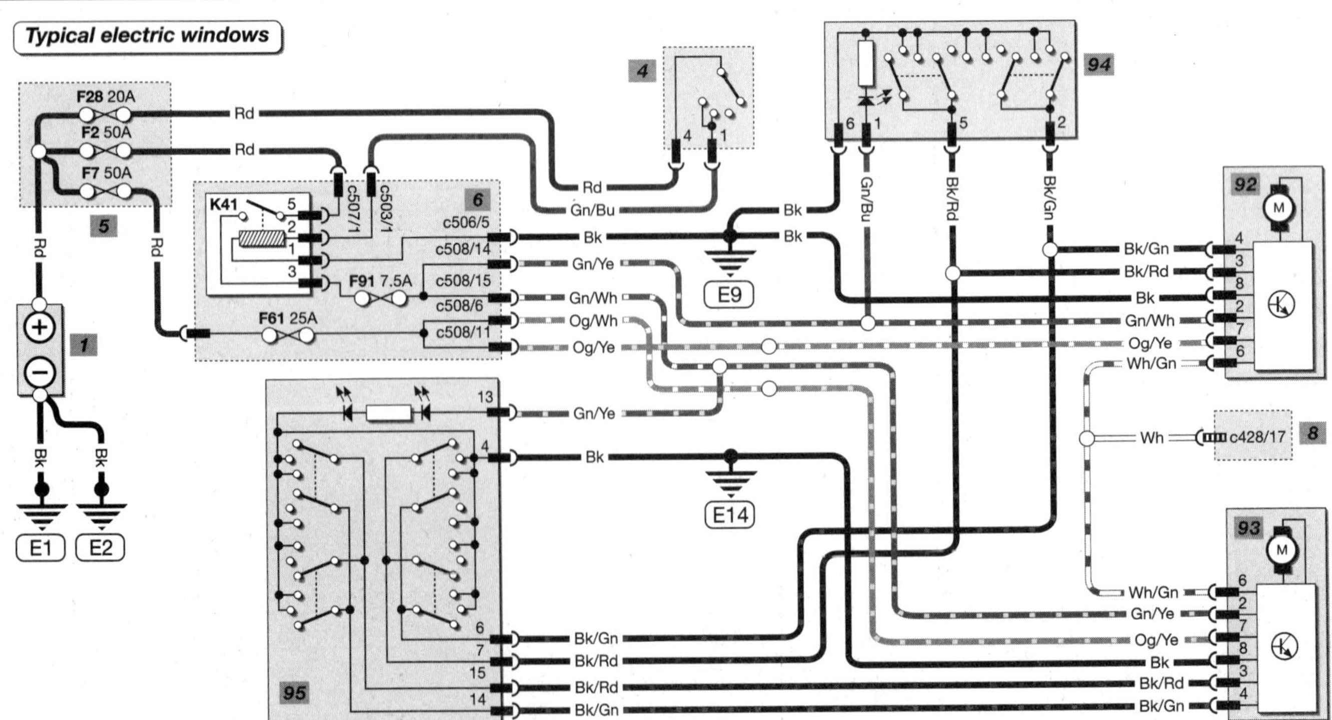

Dimensions and weights

Note: *All figures are approximate, and vary according to model. Refer to manufacturer's data for exact figures*

Dimensions

Overall length:	
Saloon and Hatchback	4731 mm (4753 mm with body kit)
Estate	4804 mm (4831 mm with body kit)
Overall width – including mirrors	1958 mm
Overall height – at kerb weight:	
Saloon/Hatchback	1415 to 1459 mm
Estate:	
Including roof rails	1427 to 1514 mm
Without roof rails	1427 to 1474 mm
Wheelbase	2754 mm

Weights

	Saloon/Hatchback	**Estate**
Kerb weight:		
1.8 and 2.0 litre petrol engines	1360 to 1411 kg	1434 to 1470 kg
V6 engines	1450 to 1490 kg	1511 to 1552 kg
Diesel engines	1472 to 1536 kg	1545 to 1595 kg
Maximum roof rack load	75 kg	

Conversion factors

Length (distance)

Inches (in)	x 25.4	= Millimetres (mm)	x 0.0394	= Inches (in)
Feet (ft)	x 0.305	= Metres (m)	x 3.281	= Feet (ft)
Miles	x 1.609	= Kilometres (km)	x 0.621	= Miles

Volume (capacity)

Cubic inches (cu in; in^3)	x 16.387	= Cubic centimetres (cc; cm^3)	x 0.061	= Cubic inches (cu in; in^3)
Imperial pints (Imp pt)	x 0.568	= Litres (l)	x 1.76	= Imperial pints (Imp pt)
Imperial quarts (Imp qt)	x 1.137	= Litres (l)	x 0.88	= Imperial quarts (Imp qt)
Imperial quarts (Imp qt)	x 1.201	= US quarts (US qt)	x 0.833	= Imperial quarts (Imp qt)
US quarts (US qt)	x 0.946	= Litres (l)	x 1.057	= US quarts (US qt)
Imperial gallons (Imp gal)	x 4.546	= Litres (l)	x 0.22	= Imperial gallons (Imp gal)
Imperial gallons (Imp gal)	x 1.201	= US gallons (US gal)	x 0.833	= Imperial gallons (Imp gal)
US gallons (US gal)	x 3.785	= Litres (l)	x 0.264	= US gallons (US gal)

Mass (weight)

Ounces (oz)	x 28.35	= Grams (g)	x 0.035	= Ounces (oz)
Pounds (lb)	x 0.454	= Kilograms (kg)	x 2.205	= Pounds (lb)

Force

Ounces-force (ozf; oz)	x 0.278	= Newtons (N)	x 3.6	= Ounces-force (ozf; oz)
Pounds-force (lbf; lb)	x 4.448	= Newtons (N)	x 0.225	= Pounds-force (lbf; lb)
Newtons (N)	x 0.1	= Kilograms-force (kgf; kg)	x 9.81	= Newtons (N)

Pressure

Pounds-force per square inch (psi; lbf/in^2; lb/in^2)	x 0.070	= Kilograms-force per square centimetre (kgf/cm^2; kg/cm^2)	x 14.223	= Pounds-force per square inch (psi; lbf/in^2; lb/in^2)
Pounds-force per square inch (psi; lbf/in^2; lb/in^2)	x 0.068	= Atmospheres (atm)	x 14.696	= Pounds-force per square inch (psi; lbf/in^2; lb/in^2)
Pounds-force per square inch (psi; lbf/in^2; lb/in^2)	x 0.069	= Bars	x 14.5	= Pounds-force per square inch (psi; lbf/in^2; lb/in^2)
Pounds-force per square inch (psi; lbf/in^2; lb/in^2)	x 6.895	= Kilopascals (kPa)	x 0.145	= Pounds-force per square inch (psi; lbf/in^2; lb/in^2)
Kilopascals (kPa)	x 0.01	= Kilograms-force per square centimetre (kgf/cm^2; kg/cm^2)	x 98.1	= Kilopascals (kPa)
Millibar (mbar)	x 100	= Pascals (Pa)	x 0.01	= Millibar (mbar)
Millibar (mbar)	x 0.0145	= Pounds-force per square inch (psi; lbf/in^2; lb/in^2)	x 68.947	= Millibar (mbar)
Millibar (mbar)	x 0.75	= Millimetres of mercury (mmHg)	x 1.333	= Millibar (mbar)
Millibar (mbar)	x 0.401	= Inches of water (inH_2O)	x 2.491	= Millibar (mbar)
Millimetres of mercury (mmHg)	x 0.535	= Inches of water (inH_2O)	x 1.868	= Millimetres of mercury (mmHg)
Inches of water (inH_2O)	x 0.036	= Pounds-force per square inch (psi; lbf/in^2; lb/in^2)	x 27.68	= Inches of water (inH_2O)

Torque (moment of force)

Pounds-force inches (lbf in; lb in)	x 1.152	= Kilograms-force centimetre (kgf cm; kg cm)	x 0.868	= Pounds-force inches (lbf in; lb in)
Pounds-force inches (lbf in; lb in)	x 0.113	= Newton metres (Nm)	x 8.85	= Pounds-force inches (lbf in; lb in)
Pounds-force inches (lbf in; lb in)	x 0.083	= Pounds-force feet (lbf ft; lb ft)	x 12	= Pounds-force inches (lbf in; lb in)
Pounds-force feet (lbf ft; lb ft)	x 0.138	= Kilograms-force metres (kgf m; kg m)	x 7.233	= Pounds-force feet (lbf ft; lb ft)
Pounds-force feet (lbf ft; lb ft)	x 1.356	= Newton metres (Nm)	x 0.738	= Pounds-force feet (lbf ft; lb ft)
Newton metres (Nm)	x 0.102	= Kilograms-force metres (kgf m; kg m)	x 9.804	= Newton metres (Nm)

Power

Horsepower (hp)	x 745.7	= Watts (W)	x 0.0013	= Horsepower (hp)

Velocity (speed)

Miles per hour (miles/hr; mph)	x 1.609	= Kilometres per hour (km/hr; kph)	x 0.621	= Miles per hour (miles/hr; mph)

Fuel consumption*

Miles per gallon, Imperial (mpg)	x 0.354	= Kilometres per litre (km/l)	x 2.825	= Miles per gallon, Imperial (mpg)
Miles per gallon, US (mpg)	x 0.425	= Kilometres per litre (km/l)	x 2.352	= Miles per gallon, US (mpg)

Temperature

Degrees Fahrenheit = (°C x 1.8) + 32

Degrees Celsius (Degrees Centigrade; °C) = (°F - 32) x 0.56

** It is common practice to convert from miles per gallon (mpg) to litres/100 kilometres (l/100km), where mpg x l/100 km = 282*

Spare parts are available from many sources, including maker's appointed garages, accessory shops, and motor factors. To be sure of obtaining the correct parts, it will sometimes be necessary to quote the vehicle identification number (see *Vehicle identification*). If possible, it can also be useful to take the old parts along for positive identification. Items such as starter motors and alternators may be available under a service exchange scheme – any parts returned should always be clean.

Our advice regarding spare part sources is as follows.

Officially-appointed garages

This is the best source of parts which are peculiar to your car, and which are not otherwise generally available (eg, badges, interior trim, certain body panels, etc). It is also the only place at which you should buy parts if the car is still under warranty.

Accessory shops

These are very good places to buy materials and components needed for the maintenance of your car (oil, air and fuel filters, light bulbs, drivebelts, greases, brake pads, touch-up paint, etc). Components of this nature sold by a reputable shop are of the same standard as those used by the car manufacturer.

Besides components, these shops also sell tools and general accessories, usually have convenient opening hours, charge lower prices, and can often be found close to home. Some accessory shops have parts counters where components needed for almost any repair job can be purchased or ordered.

Motor factors

Good factors will stock all the more important components which wear out comparatively quickly, and can sometimes supply individual components needed for the overhaul of a larger assembly (eg, brake seals and hydraulic parts, bearing shells, pistons, valves). They may also handle work such as cylinder block reboring, crankshaft regrinding, etc.

Tyre and exhaust specialists

These outlets may be independent, or members of a local or national chain. They frequently offer competitive prices when compared with a main dealer or local garage, but it will pay to obtain several quotes before making a decision. When researching prices, also ask what 'extras' may be added – for instance fitting a new valve and balancing the wheel are both commonly charged on top of the price of a new tyre.

Other sources

Beware of parts or materials obtained from market stalls, car boot sales or similar outlets. Such items are not invariably sub-standard, but there is little chance of compensation if they do prove unsatisfactory. In the case of safety-critical components such as brake pads, there is the risk not only of financial loss, but also of an accident causing injury or death.

Second-hand components or assemblies obtained from a car breaker can be a good buy in some circumstances, but his sort of purchase is best made by the experienced DIY mechanic.

Vehicle identification

Modifications are a continuing and unpublicised process in vehicle manufacture, quite apart from major model changes. Spare parts manuals and lists are compiled upon a numerical basis, the individual vehicle identification numbers being essential to correct identification of the component concerned.

When ordering spare parts, always give as much information as possible. Quote the car model, year of manufacture, body and engine numbers as appropriate.

The *vehicle identification plate* is located on the lower section of the right-hand front door pillar **(see illustration)**. In addition to many other details, it carries the Vehicle Identification Number (VIN), maximum vehicle weight information, and codes for interior trim and body colours.

The *Vehicle Identification Number (VIN)* is given on the vehicle identification plate. It is also stamped on the engine compartment bulkhead, and on a tag on the left-hand side of the facia, so that it can be seen through the bottom left-hand corner of the windscreen **(see illustrations)**. A symbol on the tag indicates how many air bags are fitted to the car.

The *engine number* is stamped on the cylinder block/crankcase. On 1.8 and 2.0 litre petrol engines, it is also on a sticker attached to the timing chain cover. On the V6 engine, it is at the front of the engine compartment and on the left-hand cam cover. On diesel engines, it is on the right-hand side, adjacent to the timing chain cover **(see illustration)**.

Vehicle identification plate on the right-hand front door pillar

Vehicle identification number stamped on the engine compartment bulkhead

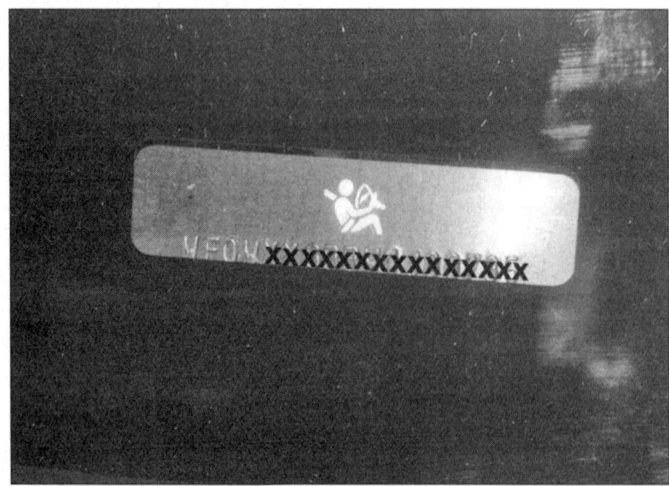

Vehicle identification number visible through the bottom left-hand corner of the windscreen

Engine number (diesel)

Whenever servicing, repair or overhaul work is carried out on the car or its components, observe the following procedures and instructions. This will assist in carrying out the operation efficiently and to a professional standard of workmanship.

Joint mating faces and gaskets

When separating components at their mating faces, never insert screwdrivers or similar implements into the joint between the faces in order to prise them apart. This can cause severe damage which results in oil leaks, coolant leaks, etc upon reassembly. Separation is usually achieved by tapping along the joint with a soft-faced hammer in order to break the seal. However, note that this method may not be suitable where dowels are used for component location.

Where a gasket is used between the mating faces of two components, a new one must be fitted on reassembly; fit it dry unless otherwise stated in the repair procedure. Make sure that the mating faces are clean and dry, with all traces of old gasket removed. When cleaning a joint face, use a tool which is unlikely to score or damage the face, and remove any burrs or nicks with an oilstone or fine file.

Make sure that tapped holes are cleaned with a pipe cleaner, and keep them free of jointing compound, if this is being used, unless specifically instructed otherwise.

Ensure that all orifices, channels or pipes are clear, and blow through them, preferably using compressed air.

Oil seals

Oil seals can be removed by levering them out with a wide flat-bladed screwdriver or similar implement. Alternatively, a number of self-tapping screws may be screwed into the seal, and these used as a purchase for pliers or some similar device in order to pull the seal free.

Whenever an oil seal is removed from its working location, either individually or as part of an assembly, it should be renewed.

The very fine sealing lip of the seal is easily damaged, and will not seal if the surface it contacts is not completely clean and free from scratches, nicks or grooves. If the original sealing surface of the component cannot be restored, and the manufacturer has not made provision for slight relocation of the seal relative to the sealing surface, the component should be renewed.

Protect the lips of the seal from any surface which may damage them in the course of fitting. Use tape or a conical sleeve where possible. Lubricate the seal lips with oil before fitting and, on dual-lipped seals, fill the space between the lips with grease.

Unless otherwise stated, oil seals must be fitted with their sealing lips toward the lubricant to be sealed.

Use a tubular drift or block of wood of the appropriate size to install the seal and, if the seal housing is shouldered, drive the seal down to the shoulder. If the seal housing is unshouldered, the seal should be fitted with its face flush with the housing top face (unless otherwise instructed).

Screw threads and fastenings

Seized nuts, bolts and screws are quite a common occurrence where corrosion has set in, and the use of penetrating oil or releasing fluid will often overcome this problem if the offending item is soaked for a while before attempting to release it. The use of an impact driver may also provide a means of releasing such stubborn fastening devices, when used in conjunction with the appropriate screwdriver bit or socket. If none of these methods works, it may be necessary to resort to the careful application of heat, or the use of a hacksaw or nut splitter device.

Studs are usually removed by locking two nuts together on the threaded part, and then using a spanner on the lower nut to unscrew the stud. Studs or bolts which have broken off below the surface of the component in which they are mounted can sometimes be removed using a stud extractor. Always ensure that a blind tapped hole is completely free from oil, grease, water or other fluid before installing the bolt or stud. Failure to do this could cause the housing to crack due to the hydraulic action of the bolt or stud as it is screwed in.

When tightening a castellated nut to accept a split pin, tighten the nut to the specified torque, where applicable, and then tighten further to the next split pin hole. Never slacken the nut to align the split pin hole, unless stated in the repair procedure.

When checking or retightening a nut or bolt to a specified torque setting, slacken the nut or bolt by a quarter of a turn, and then retighten to the specified setting. However, this should not be attempted where angular tightening has been used.

For some screw fastenings, notably cylinder head bolts or nuts, torque wrench settings are no longer specified for the latter stages of tightening, "angle-tightening" being called up instead. Typically, a fairly low torque wrench setting will be applied to the bolts/nuts in the correct sequence, followed by one or more stages of tightening through specified angles.

Locknuts, locktabs and washers

Any fastening which will rotate against a component or housing during tightening should always have a washer between it and the relevant component or housing.

Spring or split washers should always be renewed when they are used to lock a critical component such as a big-end bearing retaining bolt or nut. Locktabs which are folded over to retain a nut or bolt should always be renewed.

Self-locking nuts can be re-used in non-critical areas, providing resistance can be felt when the locking portion passes over the bolt or stud thread. However, it should be noted that self-locking stiffnuts tend to lose their effectiveness after long periods of use, and should then be renewed as a matter of course.

Split pins must always be replaced with new ones of the correct size for the hole.

When thread-locking compound is found on the threads of a fastener which is to be re-used, it should be cleaned off with a wire brush and solvent, and fresh compound applied on reassembly.

Special tools

Some repair procedures in this manual entail the use of special tools such as a press, two or three-legged pullers, spring compressors, etc. Wherever possible, suitable readily-available alternatives to the manufacturer's special tools are described, and are shown in use. In some instances, where no alternative is possible, it has been necessary to resort to the use of a manufacturer's tool, and this has been done for reasons of safety as well as the efficient completion of the repair operation. Unless you are highly-skilled and have a thorough understanding of the procedures described, never attempt to bypass the use of any special tool when the procedure described specifies its use. Not only is there a very great risk of personal injury, but expensive damage could be caused to the components involved.

Environmental considerations

When disposing of used engine oil, brake fluid, antifreeze, etc, give due consideration to any detrimental environmental effects. Do not, for instance, pour any of the above liquids down drains into the general sewage system, or onto the ground to soak away. Many local council refuse tips provide a facility for waste oil disposal, as do some garages. If none of these facilities are available, consult your local Environmental Health Department, or the National Rivers Authority, for further advice.

With the universal tightening-up of legislation regarding the emission of environmentally-harmful substances from motor vehicles, most vehicles have tamperproof devices fitted to the main adjustment points of the fuel system. These devices are primarily designed to prevent unqualified persons from adjusting the fuel/air mixture, with the chance of a consequent increase in toxic emissions. If such devices are found during servicing or overhaul, they should, wherever possible, be renewed or refitted in accordance with the manufacturer's requirements or current legislation.

OIL CARE
FOLLOW THE CODE
OIL BANK LINE
0800 66 33 66
www.oilbankline.org.uk

Note: It is antisocial and illegal to dump oil down the drain. To find the location of your local oil recycling bank, call this number free.

Jacking and vehicle support

The jack supplied with the car's tool kit should only be used for changing the roadwheels - see *Wheel changing* at the front of this book. When carrying out any other kind of work, raise the car using a hydraulic (or 'trolley') jack, and always supplement the jack with axle stands positioned under the jacking/support points. If the roadwheels do not have to be removed, consider using wheel ramps - if wished, these can be placed under the wheels once the car has been raised using a hydraulic jack, and then lowered onto the ramps so that it is resting on its wheels.

Only ever jack the car up on a solid, level surface. If there is even a slight slope, take great care that the car cannot move as the wheels are lifted off the ground. Jacking up on an uneven or gravelled surface is not recommended, as the weight of the car will not be evenly distributed, and the jack may slip as the car is raised.

As far as possible, do not leave the car unattended once it has been raised, particularly if children are playing nearby.

Before jacking up the front of the car, ensure that the handbrake is firmly applied. When jacking up the rear of the car, place wooden chocks in front of the front wheels, and engage first gear (or P). Either place the jack head under the front jacking points on the door sill, with a block of wood to prevent damage, or use the two front support points, and lift the car evenly **(see illustrations)**. Note that the front jacking point is located approximately 27.0 cm from the front end of the sills; the height of this Haynes Manual is approximately 27.0 cm.

To raise the rear of the car, chock the front wheels and engage a gear (or select P). Use the two rear jacking points on the door sill, with a block of wood to prevent damage **(see illustration)**. The rear jacking points are located approximately 10.0 cm from the rear end of the sills; approximately half the width of a page in this Haynes Manual.

To raise the side of the car, prepare the car as described for front AND rear lifting. Place the jack head under the appropriate point. If a trolley jack or similar is used on the points provided for the car's own jack, make up a wooden spacer with a groove cut in it to accept the underbody flange, so that there is no risk of the jack slipping or buckling the flange.

Do not jack the car under any other part of the sill, sump, floor pan, or directly under any of the steering or suspension components.

Never work under, around, or near a raised car, unless it is adequately supported on stands. Do not rely on a jack alone, as even a hydraulic jack could fail under load.

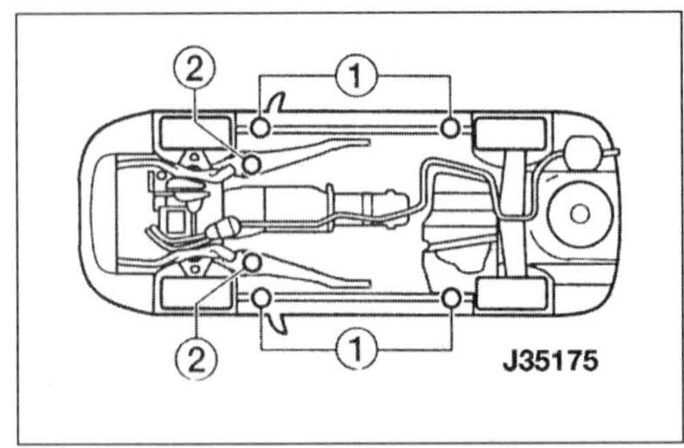

Jacking and supporting points

1 *Jacking points for vehicle jack in roadside use. May also be used as support points with axle stands*
2 *Jacking points for trolley jack. May be used as additional support points with axle stands*

Using the front jacking point and support point (with wooden blocks) to raise the front of the car

Using the rear jacking point to raise the rear of the car

Several systems fitted to the car require battery power to be available at all times, either to ensure their continued operation (such as the clock), or to maintain electronic memory settings which would otherwise be erased. Whenever the battery is to be disconnected, first note the following points, to ensure there are no unforeseen consequences:

a) *First, on any car with central door locking, it is a wise precaution to remove the key from the ignition, and to keep it with you, so that it does not get locked in if the central locking engages when the battery is reconnected.*

b) *The car's powertrain control module (PCM) will lose the information stored in its memory when the battery is disconnected. This includes idling and operating values, and any fault codes detected – in the case of the fault codes, if it is thought likely that the system has developed a fault for which the corresponding code has been logged, the car must be taken to a suitably-equipped garage for the codes to be read, using the special diagnostic equipment necessary for this. Whenever the battery is disconnected, the information relating to idle speed control and other operating values will have to be re-programmed into the unit's memory. The PCM does this by itself, but until then, there may be surging, hesitation, erratic idle and a generally inferior level of performance. To allow the PCM to relearn these values, start the engine and let it run as close to idle speed as possible until it reaches its normal operating temperature, then run it for approximately two minutes at 1200 rpm. Next, drive the car as far as necessary – approximately 5 miles of varied driving conditions is usually sufficient – to complete the relearning process.*

c) *If the battery is disconnected while the alarm system is armed or activated, the alarm will remain in the same state when the battery is reconnected. The same applies to the engine immobiliser system.*

d) *If a security-coded audio unit is fitted, and the unit and/or the battery is disconnected, the unit will not function again on reconnection until the correct security code is entered. Details of this procedure, which varies according to the unit fitted and model, are given in the owner's handbook. Where necessary, ensure you have the correct code before you disconnect the battery. If you do not have the code or details of the correct procedure, but can supply proof of ownership and a legitimate reason for wanting this information, a Ford dealer may be able to help.*

e) *Where electric windows with 'one-touch' operation are fitted, this function may not work correctly until each window has been reset. This is done by fully opening the window with the button pressed, keeping the button pressed for a few seconds after opening, then pressing it open once more so the system can 'learn' the fully-open position. Close the window, keep the button pressed for a few seconds, then press it closed once more.*

Warning: Battery-operated radio key code savers claim to avoid a lot of these problems, but they should be avoided as the current may cause the airbag to be deployed, with the possibility of personal injury.

Introduction

A selection of good tools is a fundamental requirement for anyone contemplating the maintenance and repair of a motor vehicle. For the owner who does not possess any, their purchase will prove a considerable expense, offsetting some of the savings made by doing-it-yourself. However, provided that the tools purchased meet the relevant national safety standards and are of good quality, they will last for many years and prove an extremely worthwhile investment.

To help the average owner to decide which tools are needed to carry out the various tasks detailed in this manual, we have compiled three lists of tools under the following headings: *Maintenance and minor repair*, *Repair and overhaul*, and *Special*. Newcomers to practical mechanics should start off with the *Maintenance and minor repair* tool kit, and confine themselves to the simpler jobs around the vehicle. Then, as confidence and experience grow, more difficult tasks can be undertaken, with extra tools being purchased as, and when, they are needed. In this way, a *Maintenance and minor repair* tool kit can be built up into a *Repair and overhaul* tool kit over a considerable period of time, without any major cash outlays. The experienced do-it-yourselfer will have a tool kit good enough for most repair and overhaul procedures, and will add tools from the *Special* category when it is felt that the expense is justified by the amount of use to which these tools will be put.

Maintenance and minor repair tool kit

The tools given in this list should be considered as a minimum requirement if routine maintenance, servicing and minor repair operations are to be undertaken. We recommend the purchase of combination spanners (ring one end, open-ended the other); although more expensive than open-ended ones, they do give the advantages of both types of spanner.

- ☐ *Combination spanners:*
  Metric - 8 to 19 mm inclusive
- ☐ *Adjustable spanner - 35 mm jaw (approx.)*
- ☐ *Spark plug spanner (with rubber insert) - petrol models*
- ☐ *Spark plug gap adjustment tool - petrol models*
- ☐ *Set of feeler gauges*
- ☐ *Brake bleed nipple spanner*
- ☐ *Screwdrivers:*
  Flat blade - 100 mm long x 6 mm dia
  Cross blade - 100 mm long x 6 mm dia
  Torx - various sizes (not all vehicles)
- ☐ *Combination pliers*
- ☐ *Hacksaw (junior)*
- ☐ *Tyre pump*
- ☐ *Tyre pressure gauge*
- ☐ *Oil can*
- ☐ *Oil filter removal tool*
- ☐ *Fine emery cloth*
- ☐ *Wire brush (small)*
- ☐ *Funnel (medium size)*
- ☐ *Sump drain plug key (not all vehicles)*

Repair and overhaul tool kit

These tools are virtually essential for anyone undertaking any major repairs to a motor vehicle, and are additional to those given in the *Maintenance and minor repair* list. Included in this list is a comprehensive set of sockets. Although these are expensive, they will be found invaluable as they are so versatile - particularly if various drives are included in the set. We recommend the half-inch square-drive type, as this can be used with most proprietary torque wrenches.

The tools in this list will sometimes need to be supplemented by tools from the *Special* list:

- ☐ *Sockets (or box spanners) to cover range in previous list (including Torx sockets)*
- ☐ *Reversible ratchet drive (for use with sockets)*
- ☐ *Extension piece, 250 mm (for use with sockets)*
- ☐ *Universal joint (for use with sockets)*
- ☐ *Flexible handle or sliding T "breaker bar" (for use with sockets)*
- ☐ *Torque wrench (for use with sockets)*
- ☐ *Self-locking grips*
- ☐ *Ball pein hammer*
- ☐ *Soft-faced mallet (plastic or rubber)*
- ☐ *Screwdrivers:*
  Flat blade - long & sturdy, short (chubby), and narrow (electrician's) types
  Cross blade – long & sturdy, and short (chubby) types
- ☐ *Pliers:*
  Long-nosed
  Side cutters (electrician's)
  Circlip (internal and external)
- ☐ *Cold chisel - 25 mm*
- ☐ *Scriber*
- ☐ *Scraper*
- ☐ *Centre-punch*
- ☐ *Pin punch*
- ☐ *Hacksaw*
- ☐ *Brake hose clamp*
- ☐ *Brake/clutch bleeding kit*
- ☐ *Selection of twist drills*
- ☐ *Steel rule/straight-edge*
- ☐ *Allen keys (inc. splined/Torx type)*
- ☐ *Selection of files*
- ☐ *Wire brush*
- ☐ *Axle stands*
- ☐ *Jack (strong trolley or hydraulic type)*
- ☐ *Light with extension lead*
- ☐ *Universal electrical multi-meter*

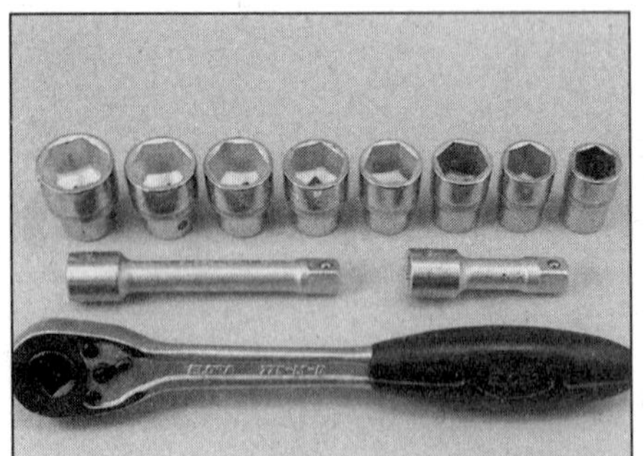

Sockets and reversible ratchet drive

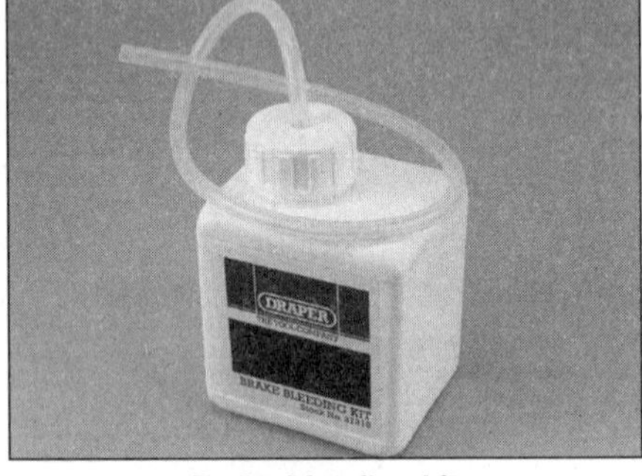

Brake bleeding kit

Torx key, socket and bit

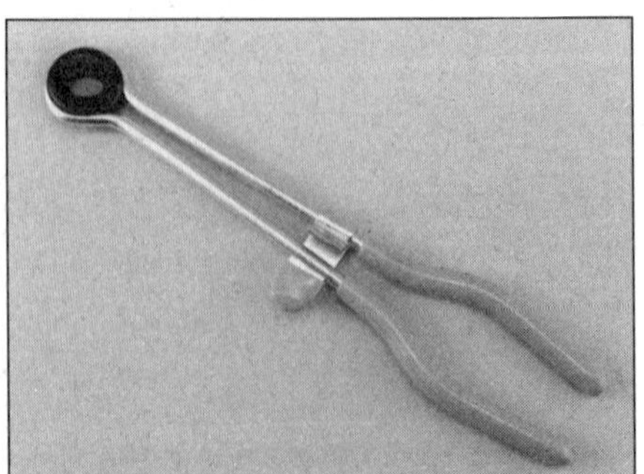

Hose clamp

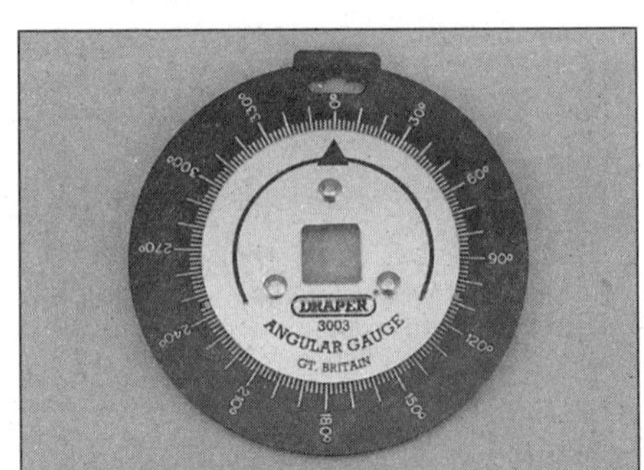

Angular-tightening gauge

Special tools

The tools in this list are those which are not used regularly, are expensive to buy, or which need to be used in accordance with their manufacturers' instructions. Unless relatively difficult mechanical jobs are undertaken frequently, it will not be economic to buy many of these tools. Where this is the case, you could consider clubbing together with friends (or joining a motorists' club) to make a joint purchase, or borrowing the tools against a deposit from a local garage or tool hire specialist. It is worth noting that many of the larger DIY superstores now carry a large range of special tools for hire at modest rates.

The following list contains only those tools and instruments freely available to the public, and not those special tools produced by the vehicle manufacturer specifically for its dealer network. You will find occasional references to these manufacturers' special tools in the text of this manual. Generally, an alternative method of doing the job without the vehicle manufacturers' special tool is given. However, sometimes there is no alternative to using them. Where this is the case and the relevant tool cannot be bought or borrowed, you will have to entrust the work to a dealer.

- ☐ *Angular-tightening gauge*
- ☐ *Valve spring compressor*
- ☐ *Valve grinding tool*
- ☐ *Piston ring compressor*
- ☐ *Piston ring removal/installation tool*
- ☐ *Cylinder bore hone*
- ☐ *Balljoint separator*
- ☐ *Coil spring compressors (where applicable)*
- ☐ *Two/three-legged hub and bearing puller*
- ☐ *Impact screwdriver*
- ☐ *Micrometer and/or vernier calipers*
- ☐ *Dial gauge*
- ☐ *Stroboscopic timing light*
- ☐ *Dwell angle meter/tachometer*
- ☐ *Fault code reader*
- ☐ *Cylinder compression gauge*
- ☐ *Hand-operated vacuum pump and gauge*
- ☐ *Clutch plate alignment set*
- ☐ *Brake shoe steady spring cup removal tool*
- ☐ *Bush and bearing removal/installation set*
- ☐ *Stud extractors*
- ☐ *Tap and die set*
- ☐ *Lifting tackle*
- ☐ *Trolley jack*

Buying tools

Reputable motor accessory shops and superstores often offer excellent quality tools at discount prices, so it pays to shop around.

Remember, you don't have to buy the most expensive items on the shelf, but it is always advisable to steer clear of the very cheap tools. Beware of 'bargains' offered on market stalls or at car boot sales. There are plenty of good tools around at reasonable prices, but always aim to purchase items which meet the relevant national safety standards. If in doubt, ask the proprietor or manager of the shop for advice before making a purchase.

Care and maintenance of tools

Having purchased a reasonable tool kit, it is necessary to keep the tools in a clean and serviceable condition. After use, always wipe off any dirt, grease and metal particles using a clean, dry cloth, before putting the tools away. Never leave them lying around after they have been used. A simple tool rack on the garage or workshop wall for items such as screwdrivers and pliers is a good idea. Store all normal spanners and sockets in a metal box. Any measuring instruments, gauges, meters, etc, must be carefully stored where they cannot be damaged or become rusty.

Take a little care when tools are used. Hammer heads inevitably become marked, and screwdrivers lose the keen edge on their blades from time to time. A little timely attention with emery cloth or a file will soon restore items like this to a good finish.

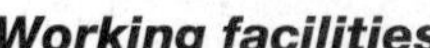

Working facilities

Not to be forgotten when discussing tools is the workshop itself. If anything more than routine maintenance is to be carried out, a suitable working area becomes essential.

It is appreciated that many an owner-mechanic is forced by circumstances to remove an engine or similar item without the benefit of a garage or workshop. Having done this, any repairs should always be done under the cover of a roof.

Wherever possible, any dismantling should be done on a clean, flat workbench or table at a suitable working height.

Any workbench needs a vice; one with a jaw opening of 100 mm is suitable for most jobs. As mentioned previously, some clean dry storage space is also required for tools, as well as for any lubricants, cleaning fluids, touch-up paints etc, which become necessary.

Another item which may be required, and which has a much more general usage, is an electric drill with a chuck capacity of at least 8 mm. This, together with a good range of twist drills, is virtually essential for fitting accessories.

Last, but not least, always keep a supply of old newspapers and clean, lint-free rags available, and try to keep any working area as clean as possible.

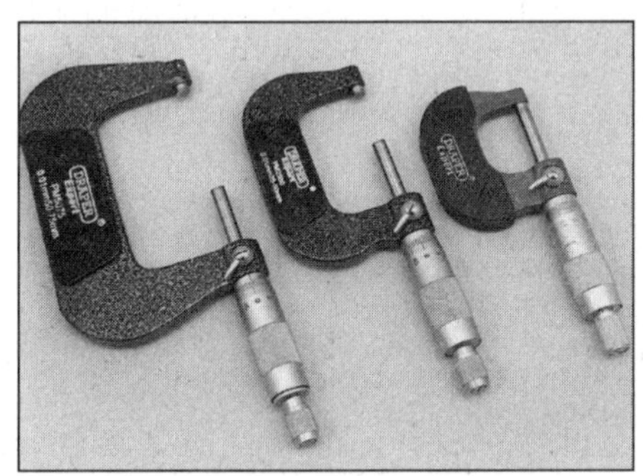

Micrometers

Dial test indicator ("dial gauge")

Strap wrench

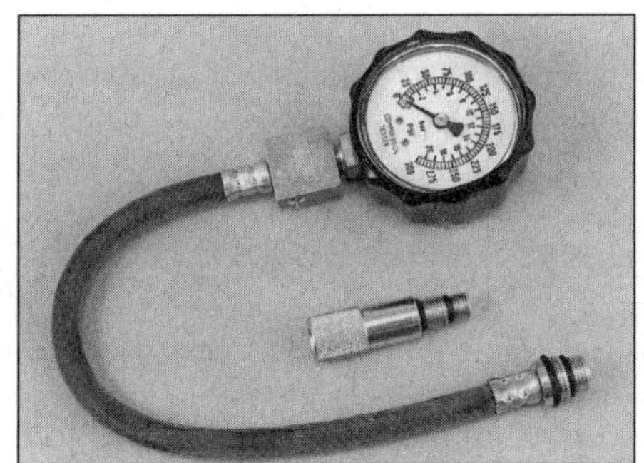

Compression tester

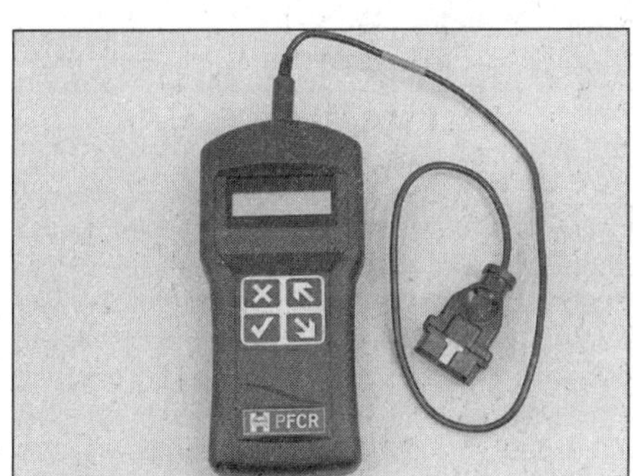

Fault code reader

This is a guide to getting your vehicle through the MOT test. Obviously it will not be possible to examine the vehicle to the same standard as the professional MOT tester. However, working through the following checks will enable you to identify any problem areas before submitting the vehicle for the test.

It has only been possible to summarise the test requirements here, based on the regulations in force at the time of printing. Test standards are becoming increasingly stringent, although there are some exemptions for older vehicles.

An assistant will be needed to help carry out some of these checks.

The checks have been sub-divided into four categories, as follows:

1 Checks carried out **FROM THE DRIVER'S SEAT**

2 Checks carried out **WITH THE VEHICLE ON THE GROUND**

3 Checks carried out **WITH THE VEHICLE RAISED AND THE WHEELS FREE TO TURN**

4 Checks carried out on **YOUR VEHICLE'S EXHAUST EMISSION SYSTEM**

1 Checks carried out FROM THE DRIVER'S SEAT

Handbrake

☐ Test the operation of the handbrake. Excessive travel (too many clicks) indicates incorrect brake or cable adjustment.

☐ Check that the handbrake cannot be released by tapping the lever sideways. Check the security of the lever mountings.

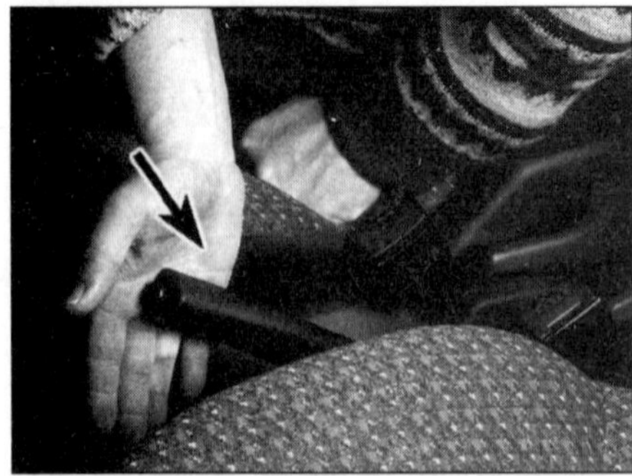

Footbrake

☐ Depress the brake pedal and check that it does not creep down to the floor, indicating a master cylinder fault. Release the pedal, wait a few seconds, then depress it again. If the pedal travels nearly to the floor before firm resistance is felt, brake adjustment or repair is necessary. If the pedal feels spongy, there is air in the hydraulic system which must be removed by bleeding.

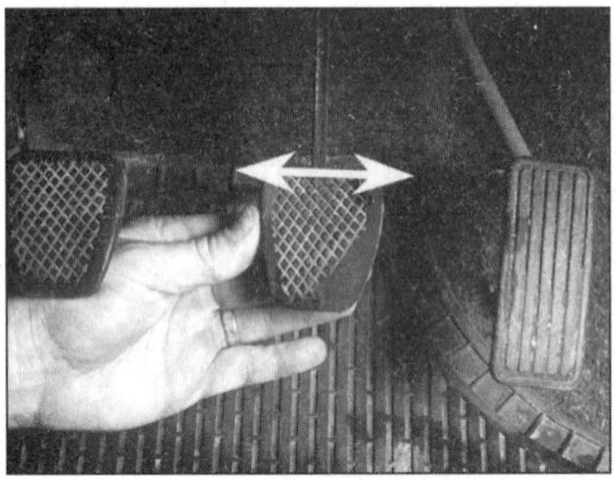

☐ Check that the brake pedal is secure and in good condition. Check also for signs of fluid leaks on the pedal, floor or carpets, which would indicate failed seals in the brake master cylinder.

☐ Check the servo unit (when applicable) by operating the brake pedal several times, then keeping the pedal depressed and starting the engine. As the engine starts, the pedal will move down slightly. If not, the vacuum hose or the servo itself may be faulty.

Steering wheel and column

☐ Examine the steering wheel for fractures or looseness of the hub, spokes or rim.

☐ Move the steering wheel from side to side and then up and down. Check that the steering wheel is not loose on the column, indicating wear or a loose retaining nut. Continue moving the steering wheel as before, but also turn it slightly from left to right.

☐ Check that the steering wheel is not loose on the column, and that there is no abnormal

movement of the steering wheel, indicating wear in the column support bearings or couplings.

Windscreen, mirrors and sunvisor

☐ The windscreen must be free of cracks or other significant damage within the driver's field of view. (Small stone chips are acceptable.) Rear view mirrors must be secure, intact, and capable of being adjusted.

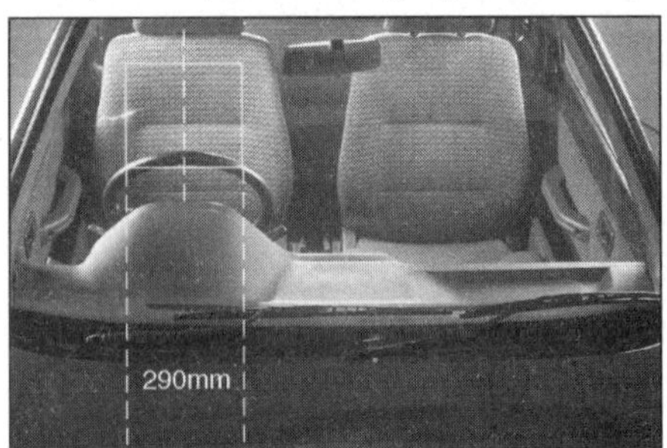

☐ The driver's sunvisor must be capable of being stored in the "up" position.

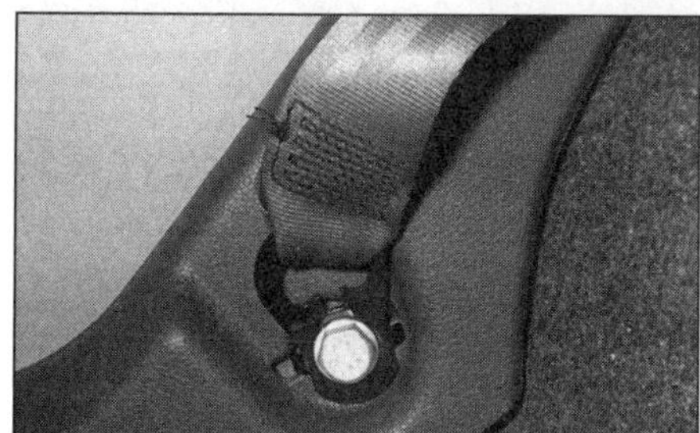

Seat belts and seats

Note: *The following checks are applicable to all seat belts, front and rear.*

☐ Examine the webbing of all the belts (including rear belts if fitted) for cuts, serious fraying or deterioration. Fasten and unfasten each belt to check the buckles. If applicable, check the retracting mechanism. Check the security of all seat belt mountings accessible from inside the vehicle.

☐ Seat belts with pre-tensioners, once activated, have a "flag" or similar showing on the seat belt stalk. This, in itself, is not a reason for test failure.

☐ The front seats themselves must be securely attached and the backrests must lock in the upright position.

Doors

☐ Both front doors must be able to be opened and closed from outside and inside, and must latch securely when closed.

2 Checks carried out WITH THE VEHICLE ON THE GROUND

Vehicle identification

☐ Number plates must be in good condition, secure and legible, with letters and numbers correctly spaced – spacing at (A) should be at least twice that at (B).

☐ The VIN plate and/or homologation plate must be legible.

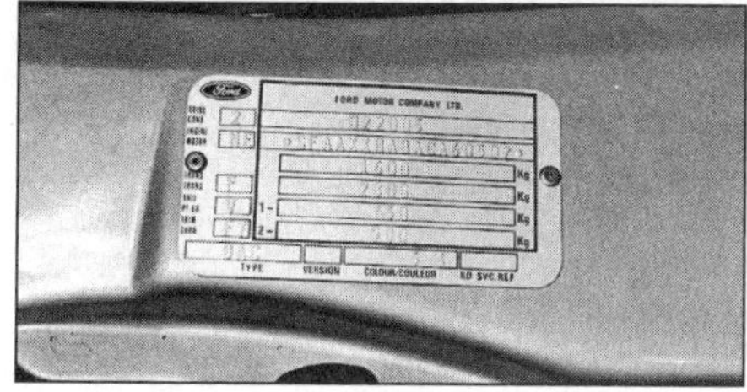

Electrical equipment

☐ Switch on the ignition and check the operation of the horn.

☐ Check the windscreen washers and wipers, examining the wiper blades; renew damaged or perished blades. Also check the operation of the stop-lights.

☐ Check the operation of the sidelights and number plate lights. The lenses and reflectors must be secure, clean and undamaged.

☐ Check the operation and alignment of the headlights. The headlight reflectors must not be tarnished and the lenses must be undamaged.

☐ Switch on the ignition and check the operation of the direction indicators (including the instrument panel tell-tale) and the hazard warning lights. Operation of the sidelights and stop-lights must not affect the indicators - if it does, the cause is usually a bad earth at the rear light cluster.

☐ Check the operation of the rear foglight(s), including the warning light on the instrument panel or in the switch.

☐ The ABS warning light must illuminate in accordance with the manufacturers' design. For most vehicles, the ABS warning light should illuminate when the ignition is switched on, and (if the system is operating properly) extinguish after a few seconds. Refer to the owner's handbook.

Footbrake

☐ Examine the master cylinder, brake pipes and servo unit for leaks, loose mountings, corrosion or other damage.

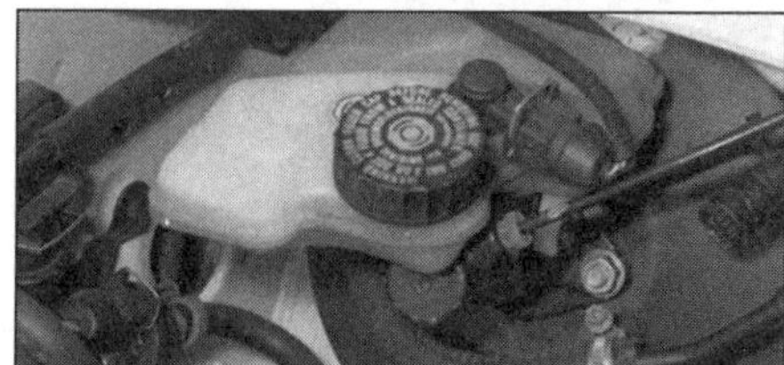

☐ The fluid reservoir must be secure and the fluid level must be between the upper (**A**) and lower (**B**) markings.

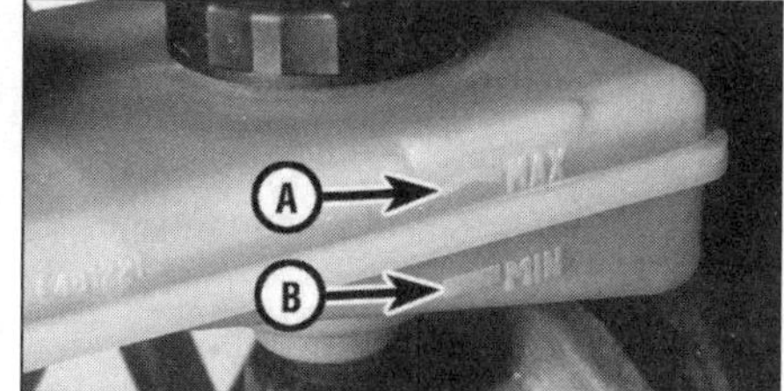

☐ Inspect both front brake flexible hoses for cracks or deterioration of the rubber. Turn the steering from lock to lock, and ensure that the hoses do not contact the wheel, tyre, or any part of the steering or suspension mechanism. With the brake pedal firmly depressed, check the hoses for bulges or leaks under pressure.

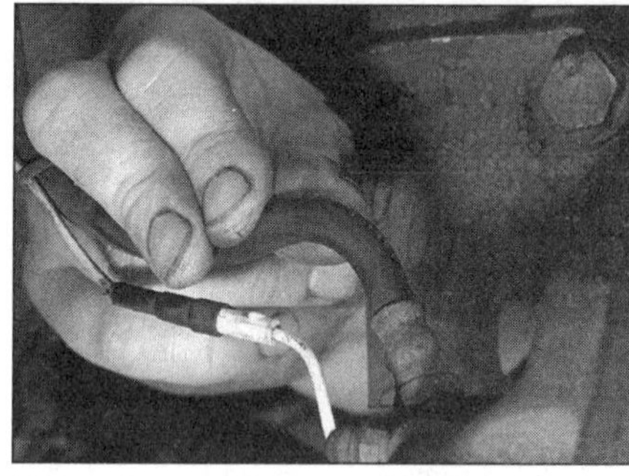

Steering and suspension

☐ Have your assistant turn the steering wheel from side to side slightly, up to the point where the steering gear just begins to transmit this movement to the roadwheels. Check for excessive free play between the steering wheel and the steering gear, indicating wear or insecurity of the steering column joints, the column-to-steering gear coupling, or the steering gear itself.

☐ Have your assistant turn the steering wheel more vigorously in each direction, so that the roadwheels just begin to turn. As this is done, examine all the steering joints, linkages, fittings and attachments. Renew any component that shows signs of wear or damage. On vehicles with power steering, check the security and condition of the steering pump, drivebelt and hoses.

☐ Check that the vehicle is standing level, and at approximately the correct ride height.

Shock absorbers

☐ Depress each corner of the vehicle in turn, then release it. The vehicle should rise and then settle in its normal position. If the vehicle continues to rise and fall, the shock absorber is defective. A shock absorber which has seized will also cause the vehicle to fail.

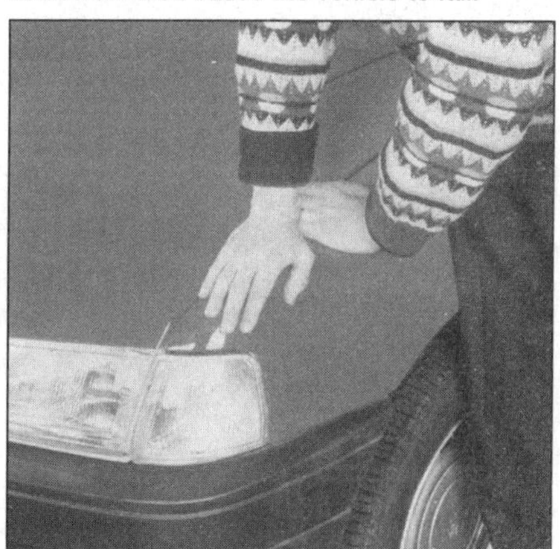

Exhaust system

☐ Start the engine. With your assistant holding a rag over the tailpipe, check the entire system for leaks. Repair or renew leaking sections.

3 Checks carried out WITH THE VEHICLE RAISED AND THE WHEELS FREE TO TURN

Jack up the front and rear of the vehicle, and securely support it on axle stands. Position the stands clear of the suspension assemblies. Ensure that the wheels are clear of the ground and that the steering can be turned from lock to lock.

Steering mechanism

☐ Have your assistant turn the steering from lock to lock. Check that the steering turns smoothly, and that no part of the steering mechanism, including a wheel or tyre, fouls any brake hose or pipe or any part of the body structure.

☐ Examine the steering rack rubber gaiters for damage or insecurity of the retaining clips. If power steering is fitted, check for signs of damage or leakage of the fluid hoses, pipes or connections. Also check for excessive stiffness or binding of the steering, a missing split pin or locking device, or severe corrosion of the body structure within 30 cm of any steering component attachment point.

Front and rear suspension and wheel bearings

☐ Starting at the front right-hand side, grasp the roadwheel at the 3 o'clock and 9 o'clock positions and rock gently but firmly. Check for free play or insecurity at the wheel bearings, suspension balljoints, or suspension mountings, pivots and attachments.

☐ Now grasp the wheel at the 12 o'clock and 6 o'clock positions and repeat the previous inspection. Spin the wheel, and check for roughness or tightness of the front wheel bearing.

☐ If excess free play is suspected at a component pivot point, this can be confirmed by using a large screwdriver or similar tool and levering between the mounting and the component attachment. This will confirm whether the wear is in the pivot bush, its retaining bolt, or in the mounting itself (the bolt holes can often become elongated).

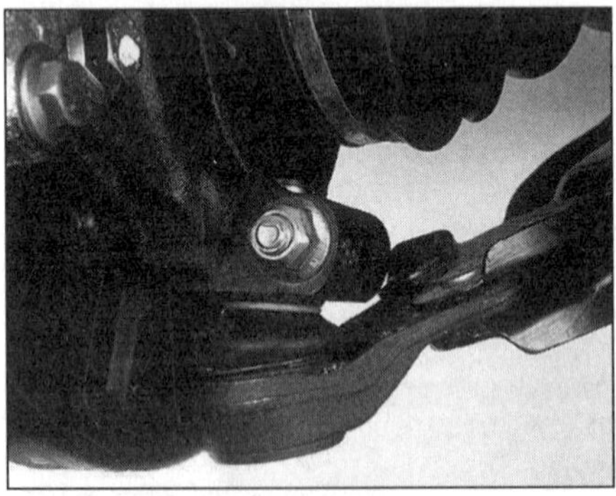

☐ Carry out all the above checks at the other front wheel, and then at both rear wheels.

Springs and shock absorbers

☐ Examine the suspension struts (when applicable) for serious fluid leakage, corrosion, or damage to the casing. Also check the security of the mounting points.

☐ If coil springs are fitted, check that the spring ends locate in their seats, and that the spring is not corroded, cracked or broken.

☐ If leaf springs are fitted, check that all leaves are intact, that the axle is securely attached to each spring, and that there is no deterioration of the spring eye mountings, bushes, and shackles.

☐ The same general checks apply to vehicles fitted with other suspension types, such as torsion bars, hydraulic displacer units, etc. Ensure that all mountings and attachments are secure, that there are no signs of excessive wear, corrosion or damage, and (on hydraulic types) that there are no fluid leaks or damaged pipes.

☐ Inspect the shock absorbers for signs of serious fluid leakage. Check for wear of the mounting bushes or attachments, or damage to the body of the unit.

Driveshafts (fwd vehicles only)

☐ Rotate each front wheel in turn and inspect the constant velocity joint gaiters for splits or damage. Also check that each driveshaft is straight and undamaged.

Braking system

☐ If possible without dismantling, check brake pad wear and disc condition. Ensure that the friction lining material has not worn excessively, (A) and that the discs are not fractured, pitted, scored or badly worn (B).

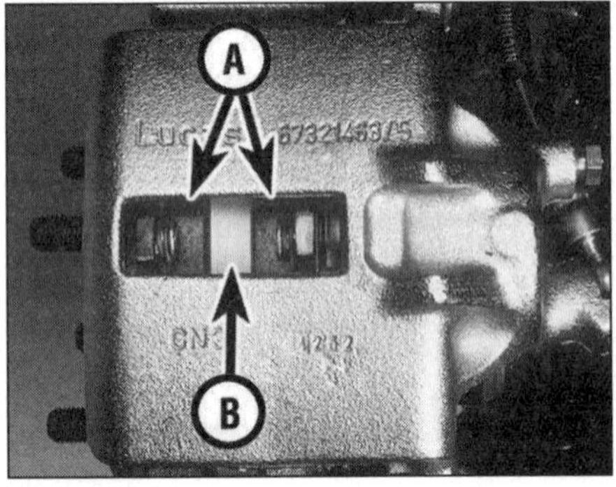

☐ Examine all the rigid brake pipes underneath the vehicle, and the flexible hose(s) at the rear. Look for corrosion, chafing or insecurity of the pipes, and for signs of bulging under pressure, chafing, splits or deterioration of the flexible hoses.

☐ Look for signs of fluid leaks at the brake calipers or on the brake backplates. Repair or renew leaking components.

☐ Slowly spin each wheel, while your assistant depresses and releases the footbrake. Ensure that each brake is operating and does not bind when the pedal is released.

☐ Examine the handbrake mechanism, checking for frayed or broken cables, excessive corrosion, or wear or insecurity of the linkage. Check that the mechanism works on each relevant wheel, and releases fully, without binding.

☐ It is not possible to test brake efficiency without special equipment, but a road test can be carried out later to check that the vehicle pulls up in a straight line.

Fuel and exhaust systems

☐ Inspect the fuel tank (including the filler cap), fuel pipes, hoses and unions. All components must be secure and free from leaks.

☐ Examine the exhaust system over its entire length, checking for any damaged, broken or missing mountings, security of the retaining clamps and rust or corrosion.

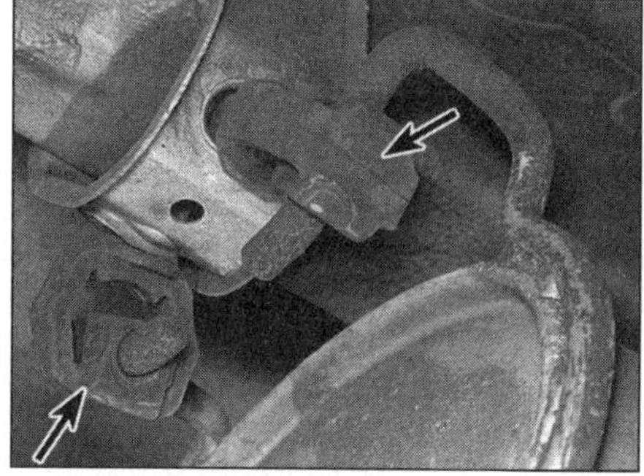

Wheels and tyres

☐ Examine the sidewalls and tread area of each tyre in turn. Check for cuts, tears, lumps, bulges, separation of the tread, and exposure of the ply or cord due to wear or damage. Check that the tyre bead is correctly seated on the wheel rim, that the valve is sound and properly seated, and that the wheel is not distorted or damaged.

☐ Check that the tyres are of the correct size for the vehicle, that they are of the same size and type on each axle, and that the pressures are correct.

☐ Check the tyre tread depth. The legal minimum at the time of writing is 1.6 mm over at least three-quarters of the tread width. Abnormal tread wear may indicate incorrect front wheel alignment.

Body corrosion

☐ Check the condition of the entire vehicle structure for signs of corrosion in load-bearing areas. (These include chassis box sections, side sills, cross-members, pillars, and all suspension, steering, braking system and seat belt mountings and anchorages.) Any corrosion which has seriously reduced the thickness of a load-bearing area is likely to cause the vehicle to fail. In this case professional repairs are likely to be needed.

☐ Damage or corrosion which causes sharp or otherwise dangerous edges to be exposed will also cause the vehicle to fail.

4 Checks carried out on **YOUR VEHICLE'S EXHAUST EMISSION SYSTEM**

Petrol models

☐ The engine should be warmed up, and running well (ignition system in good order, air filter element clean, etc).

☐ Before testing, run the engine at around 2500 rpm for 20 seconds. Let the engine drop to idle, and watch for smoke from the exhaust. If the idle speed is too high, or if dense blue or black smoke emerges for more than 5 seconds, the vehicle will fail. Typically, blue smoke signifies oil burning (engine wear); black smoke means unburnt fuel (dirty air cleaner element, or other fuel system fault).

☐ An exhaust gas analyser for measuring carbon monoxide (CO) and hydrocarbons (HC) is now needed. If one cannot be hired or borrowed, have a local garage perform the check.

CO emissions (mixture)

☐ The MOT tester has access to the CO limits for all vehicles. The CO level is measured at idle speed, and at 'fast idle' (2500 to 3000 rpm). The following limits are given as a general guide:

At idle speed – Less than 0.5% CO
At 'fast idle' – Less than 0.3% CO
Lambda reading – 0.97 to 1.03

☐ If the CO level is too high, this may point to poor maintenance, a fuel injection system problem, faulty lambda (oxygen) sensor or catalytic converter. Try an injector cleaning treatment, and check the vehicle's ECU for fault codes.

HC emissions

☐ The MOT tester has access to HC limits for all vehicles. The HC level is measured at 'fast idle' (2500 to 3000 rpm). The following limits are given as a general guide:

At 'fast idle' – Less then 200 ppm

☐ Excessive HC emissions are typically caused by oil being burnt (worn engine), or by a blocked crankcase ventilation system ('breather'). If the engine oil is old and thin, an oil change may help. If the engine is running badly, check the vehicle's ECU for fault codes.

Diesel models

☐ The only emission test for diesel engines is measuring exhaust smoke density, using a calibrated smoke meter. The test involves accelerating the engine at least 3 times to its maximum unloaded speed.

Note: *On engines with a timing belt, it is VITAL that the belt is in good condition before the test is carried out.*

☐ With the engine warmed up, it is first purged by running at around 2500 rpm for 20 seconds. A governor check is then carried out, by slowly accelerating the engine to its maximum speed. After this, the smoke meter is connected, and the engine is accelerated quickly to maximum speed three times. If the smoke density is less than the limits given below, the vehicle will pass:

Non-turbo vehicles: 2.5m-1
Turbocharged vehicles: 3.0m-1

☐ If excess smoke is produced, try fitting a new air cleaner element, or using an injector cleaning treatment. If the engine is running badly, where applicable, check the vehicle's ECU for fault codes. Also check the vehicle's EGR system, where applicable. At high mileages, the injectors may require professional attention.

Engine

- ☐ Engine fails to rotate when attempting to start
- ☐ Engine rotates, but will not start
- ☐ Engine difficult to start when cold
- ☐ Engine difficult to start when hot
- ☐ Starter motor noisy or excessively-rough in engagement
- ☐ Engine starts, but stops immediately
- ☐ Engine idles erratically
- ☐ Engine misfires at idle speed
- ☐ Engine misfires throughout the driving speed range
- ☐ Engine hesitates on acceleration
- ☐ Engine stalls
- ☐ Engine lacks power
- ☐ Engine backfires
- ☐ Oil pressure warning light illuminated with engine running
- ☐ Engine runs-on after switching off
- ☐ Engine noises

Cooling system

- ☐ Overheating
- ☐ Overcooling
- ☐ External coolant leakage
- ☐ Internal coolant leakage
- ☐ Corrosion

Fuel and exhaust systems

- ☐ Excessive fuel consumption
- ☐ Fuel leakage and/or fuel odour
- ☐ Excessive noise or fumes from exhaust system

Clutch

- ☐ Pedal travels to floor – no pressure or very little resistance
- ☐ Clutch fails to disengage (unable to select gears)
- ☐ Clutch slips (engine speed increases, with no increase in vehicle speed)
- ☐ Judder as clutch is engaged
- ☐ Noise when depressing or releasing clutch pedal

Manual transmission

- ☐ Noisy in neutral with engine running
- ☐ Noisy in one particular gear
- ☐ Difficulty engaging gears
- ☐ Jumps out of gear
- ☐ Vibration
- ☐ Lubricant leaks

Automatic transmission

- ☐ Fluid leakage
- ☐ Transmission fluid brown, or has burned smell
- ☐ General gear selection problems
- ☐ Transmission will not downshift (kickdown) with accelerator pedal fully depressed
- ☐ Engine will not start in any gear, or starts in gears other than Park or Neutral
- ☐ Transmission slips, shifts roughly, is noisy, or has no drive in forward or reverse gears

Driveshafts

- ☐ Vibration when accelerating or decelerating
- ☐ Clicking or knocking noise on turns (at slow speed on full-lock)

Braking system

- ☐ Car pulls to one side under braking
- ☐ Noise (grinding or high-pitched squeal) when brakes applied
- ☐ Excessive brake pedal travel
- ☐ Brake pedal feels spongy when depressed
- ☐ Excessive brake pedal effort required to stop car
- ☐ Judder felt through brake pedal or steering wheel when braking
- ☐ Brakes binding
- ☐ Rear wheels locking under normal braking
- ☐ ABS warning light stays on

Suspension and steering

- ☐ Car pulls to one side
- ☐ Wheel wobble and vibration
- ☐ Excessive pitching and/or rolling around corners, or during braking
- ☐ Wandering or general instability
- ☐ Excessively-stiff steering
- ☐ Excessive play in steering
- ☐ Lack of power assistance
- ☐ Tyre wear excessive

Electrical system

- ☐ Battery will not hold a charge for more than a few days
- ☐ Ignition/no-charge warning light remains illuminated with engine running
- ☐ Ignition/no-charge warning light fails to come on
- ☐ Lights inoperative
- ☐ Instrument readings inaccurate or erratic
- ☐ Horn inoperative, or unsatisfactory in operation
- ☐ Windscreen wipers inoperative, or unsatisfactory in operation
- ☐ Windscreen washers inoperative, or unsatisfactory in operation
- ☐ Electric windows inoperative, or unsatisfactory in operation
- ☐ Central locking system inoperative, or unsatisfactory in operation

Introduction

The car owner who does his or her own maintenance according to the recommended service schedules should not have to use this section of the manual very often. Modern component reliability is such that, provided those items subject to wear or deterioration are inspected or renewed at the specified intervals, sudden failure is comparatively rare. Faults do not usually just happen as a result of sudden failure, but develop over a period of time. Major mechanical failures in particular are usually preceded by characteristic symptoms over hundreds or even thousands of miles. Those components which do occasionally fail without warning are often small and easily carried in the car.

With any fault-finding, the first step is to decide where to begin investigations. Sometimes this is obvious, but on other occasions, a little detective work will be necessary. The owner who makes half a dozen haphazard adjustments or replacements may be successful in curing a fault (or its symptoms), but will be none the wiser if the fault recurs, and ultimately may have spent more time and money than was necessary. A calm and logical approach will be found to be more satisfactory in the long run. Always take into account any warning signs or abnormalities that may have been noticed in the period preceding the fault – power loss, high or low gauge readings, unusual smells, etc – and remember that failure of components such as fuses or spark plugs may only be pointers to some underlying fault.

The pages which follow provide an easy-reference guide to the more common problems which may occur during the operation of the vehicle. These problems and their possible causes are grouped under headings denoting various components or systems, such as Engine, Cooling system, etc. The general

Chapter which deals with the problem is also shown in brackets; refer to the relevant part of that Chapter for system-specific information. Whatever the fault, certain basic principles apply. These are as follows:

Verify the fault. This is simply a matter of being sure that you know what the symptoms are before starting work. This is particularly important if you are investigating a fault for someone else, who may not have described it very accurately.

Don't overlook the obvious. For example, if the car won't start, is there fuel in the tank? (Don't take anyone else's word on this particular point, and don't trust the fuel gauge either!) If an electrical fault is indicated, look for loose or broken wires before digging out the test gear.

Cure the disease, not the symptom. Substituting a flat battery with a fully-charged one will get you off the hard shoulder, but if the underlying cause is not attended to, the new battery will go the same way. Similarly, changing oil-fouled spark plugs for a new set will get you moving again, but remember that the reason for the fouling (if it wasn't simply an incorrect grade of plug) will have to be established and corrected.

Don't take anything for granted. Particularly, don't forget that a 'new' component may itself be defective (especially if it's been rattling around in the boot for months), and don't leave components out of a fault diagnosis sequence just because they are new or recently-fitted. When you do finally diagnose a difficult fault, you'll probably realise that all the evidence was there from the start.

Consider what work, if any, has recently been carried out. Many faults arise through careless or hurried work. For instance, if any work has been performed under the bonnet, could some of the wiring have been dislodged or incorrectly routed, or a hose trapped? Have all the fasteners been properly tightened? Were new, genuine parts and new gaskets used? There is often a certain amount of detective work to be done in this case, as an apparently-unrelated task can have far-reaching consequences.

Diesel fault diagnosis

The majority of starting problems on small diesel engines are electrical in origin. The mechanic who is familiar with petrol engines but less so with diesel may be inclined to view the diesel's injectors and pump in the same light as the spark plugs and distributor, but this is generally a mistake.

When investigating complaints of difficult starting for someone else, make sure that the correct starting procedure is understood and is being followed. Some drivers are unaware of the significance of the preheating warning light – many modern engines are sufficiently forgiving for this not to matter in mild weather, but with the onset of winter, problems begin.

As a rule of thumb, if the engine is difficult to start but runs well when it has finally got going, the problem is electrical (battery, starter motor or preheating system). If poor performance is combined with difficult starting, the problem is likely to be in the fuel system. The low-pressure (supply) side of the fuel system should be checked before suspecting the injectors and high-pressure pump. The most common fuel supply problem is air getting into the system, and any pipe from the fuel tank forwards must be scrutinised if air leakage is suspected. Normally the pump is the last item to suspect, since unless it has been tampered with, there is no reason for it to be at fault.

Engine

Engine fails to rotate when attempting to start

- ☐ Battery terminal connections loose or corroded (see *Weekly checks*)
- ☐ Battery discharged or faulty (Chapter 5A)
- ☐ Broken, loose or disconnected wiring in the starting circuit (Chapter 5A)
- ☐ Defective starter solenoid or ignition switch (Chapter 5A or 12)
- ☐ Defective starter motor (Chapter 5A)
- ☐ Starter pinion or flywheel ring gear teeth loose or broken (Chapter 2 or 5A)
- ☐ Engine earth strap broken or disconnected (Chapter 5A)
- ☐ Engine suffering 'hydraulic lock' (eg, from water ingested after driving through a flood, or from a serious internal coolant leak) – consult a Ford dealer for advice
- ☐ Automatic transmission not in position P or N (Chapter 7B)

Engine rotates, but will not start

- ☐ Fuel cut-off switch energised (Chapter 4A)
- ☐ Fuel tank empty
- ☐ Battery discharged (engine rotates slowly) (Chapter 5A)
- ☐ Battery terminal connections loose or corroded (see *Weekly checks*)
- ☐ Ignition components damp or damaged – petrol models (Chapter 1A or 5B)
- ☐ Immobiliser fault, or 'uncoded' ignition key being used (Chapter 12 or *Roadside repairs*)
- ☐ Crankshaft sensor fault (Chapter 4A or 4B)
- ☐ Broken, loose or disconnected wiring in the ignition circuit – petrol models (Chapter 1A or 5B)
- ☐ Worn, faulty or incorrectly-gapped spark plugs – petrol models (Chapter 1A)
- ☐ Preheating system faulty – diesel models (Chapter 5C)
- ☐ Fuel injection system fault (Chapter 4A or 4B)
- ☐ Air in fuel system – diesel models (Chapter 4B)
- ☐ Major mechanical failure (eg, timing chain snapped) (Chapter 2A, 2B or 2C)

Engine difficult to start when cold

- ☐ Battery discharged (Chapter 5A)
- ☐ Battery terminal connections loose or corroded (see *Weekly checks*)
- ☐ Worn, faulty or incorrectly-gapped spark plugs – petrol models (Chapter 1A)
- ☐ Other ignition system fault – petrol models (Chapter 1A or 5B)
- ☐ Preheating system faulty – diesel models (Chapter 5C)
- ☐ Fuel injection system fault (Chapter 4A or 4B)
- ☐ Wrong grade of engine oil used (*Weekly checks*, Chapter 1A or 1B)
- ☐ Low cylinder compression (Chapter 2A, 2B or 2C)

Engine difficult to start when hot

- ☐ Air filter element dirty or clogged (Chapter 1A or 1B)
- ☐ Fuel injection system fault (Chapter 4A or 4B)
- ☐ Low cylinder compression (Chapter 2A, 2B or 2C)

Starter motor noisy or excessively-rough in engagement

- ☐ Starter pinion or flywheel ring gear teeth loose or broken (Chapter 2 or 5A)
- ☐ Starter motor mounting bolts loose or missing (Chapter 5A)
- ☐ Starter motor internal components worn or damaged (Chapter 5A)

Engine (continued)

Engine starts, but stops immediately

- ☐ Loose or faulty electrical connections in the ignition circuit – petrol models (Chapter 1A or 5B)
- ☐ Vacuum leak at the throttle body or inlet manifold – petrol models (Chapter 4A)
- ☐ Blocked injectors/fuel injection system fault (Chapter 4A or 4B)
- ☐ Air in fuel, possibly due to loose fuel line connection – diesel models (Chapter 4B)

Engine idles erratically

- ☐ Air filter element clogged (Chapter 1A or 1B)
- ☐ Vacuum leak at the throttle body, inlet manifold or associated hoses – petrol models (Chapter 4A)
- ☐ Worn, faulty or incorrectly-gapped spark plugs – petrol models (Chapter 1A)
- ☐ Valve clearances incorrect (Chapter 2A, 2B or 2C)
- ☐ Uneven or low cylinder compression (Chapter 2A, 2B or 2C)
- ☐ Camshaft lobes worn (Chapter 2A, 2B or 2C)
- ☐ Blocked injectors/fuel injection system fault (Chapter 4A or 4B)
- ☐ Air in fuel, possibly due to damaged or loose fuel line connection – diesel models (Chapter 1B or 4B)

Engine misfires at idle speed

- ☐ Worn, faulty or incorrectly-gapped spark plugs – petrol models (Chapter 1A)
- ☐ Faulty spark plug HT leads, or ignition coil – petrol models (Chapter 1A or 5B)
- ☐ Vacuum leak at the throttle body, inlet manifold or associated hoses – petrol models (Chapter 4A)
- ☐ Blocked injectors/fuel injection system fault (Chapter 4A or 4B)
- ☐ Faulty injector(s) – diesel models (Chapter 4B)
- ☐ Uneven or low cylinder compression (Chapter 2A, 2B or 2C)
- ☐ Disconnected, leaking, or perished crankcase ventilation hoses (Chapter 4C)

Engine misfires throughout the driving speed range

- ☐ Fuel filter choked (Chapter 1A or 1B)
- ☐ Fuel pump faulty, or delivery pressure low – petrol models (Chapter 4A)
- ☐ Fuel tank vent blocked, or fuel pipes restricted (Chapter 4A or 4B)
- ☐ Vacuum leak at the throttle body, inlet manifold or associated hoses – petrol models (Chapter 4A)
- ☐ Worn, faulty or incorrectly-gapped spark plugs – petrol models (Chapter 1A)
- ☐ Faulty spark plug HT leads, or ignition coil – petrol models (Chapter 1A or 5B)
- ☐ Faulty injector(s) – diesel models (Chapter 4B)
- ☐ Uneven or low cylinder compression (Chapter 2A, 2B or 2C)
- ☐ Blocked injector/fuel injection system fault (Chapter 4A or 4B)
- ☐ Blocked catalytic converter (Chapter 4A or 4B)
- ☐ Engine overheating – petrol models (Chapter 3)
- ☐ Fuel tank level low – diesel models (Chapter 4B)

Engine hesitates on acceleration

- ☐ Worn, faulty or incorrectly-gapped spark plugs – petrol models (Chapter 1A)
- ☐ Vacuum leak at the throttle body, inlet manifold or associated hoses – petrol models (Chapter 4A)
- ☐ Blocked injectors/fuel injection system fault (Chapter 4A or 4B)
- ☐ Faulty injector(s) – diesel models (Chapter 4B)
- ☐ Faulty clutch pedal switch (Chapter 4A or 4B)

Engine stalls

- ☐ Vacuum leak at the throttle body, inlet manifold or associated hoses – petrol models (Chapter 4A)
- ☐ Fuel filter choked (Chapter 1A or 1B)
- ☐ Fuel pump faulty, or delivery pressure low – petrol models (Chapter 4A)
- ☐ Fuel tank vent blocked, or fuel pipes restricted (Chapter 4A or 4B)
- ☐ Blocked injectors/fuel injection system fault (Chapter 4A or 4B)
- ☐ Faulty injector(s) – diesel models (Chapter 4B)

Engine lacks power

- ☐ Air filter element blocked (Chapter 1A or 1B)
- ☐ Fuel filter choked (Chapter 1A or 1B)
- ☐ Fuel pipes blocked or restricted (Chapter 4A or 4B)
- ☐ Valve clearances incorrect (Chapter 2A, 2B or 2C)
- ☐ Worn, faulty or incorrectly-gapped spark plugs – petrol models (Chapter 1A)
- ☐ Engine overheating – petrol models (Chapter 4A)
- ☐ Fuel tank level low – diesel models (Chapter 4B)
- ☐ Accelerator cable problem – petrol models (Chapter 4A)
- ☐ Accelerator position sensor faulty – diesel models (Chapter 4B)
- ☐ Vacuum leak at the throttle body, inlet manifold or associated hoses – petrol models (Chapter 4A)
- ☐ Blocked injectors/fuel injection system fault (Chapter 4A or 4B)
- ☐ Faulty injector(s) – diesel models (Chapter 4B)
- ☐ Fuel pump faulty, or delivery pressure low – petrol models (Chapter 4A)
- ☐ Uneven or low cylinder compression (Chapter 2A, 2B or 2C)
- ☐ Blocked catalytic converter or diesel particulate filter (Chapter 4A, 4B or 4C)
- ☐ Brakes binding (Chapter 1A, 1B or 9)
- ☐ Clutch slipping (Chapter 6)

Engine backfires

- ☐ Vacuum leak at the throttle body, inlet manifold or associated hoses – petrol models (Chapter 4A)
- ☐ Blocked injectors/fuel injection system fault (Chapter 4A or 4B)
- ☐ Blocked catalytic converter or diesel particulate filter (Chapter 4A, 4B or 4C)
- ☐ Spark plug HT leads incorrectly fitted – petrol models (Chapter 1A or 5B)
- ☐ Ignition coil unit faulty – petrol models (Chapter 5B)

Oil pressure warning light illuminated with engine running

- ☐ Low oil level, or incorrect oil grade (see *Weekly checks*)
- ☐ Faulty oil pressure sensor, or wiring damaged (Chapter 5A)
- ☐ Worn engine bearings and/or oil pump (Chapter 2A, 2B, 2C or 2D)
- ☐ High engine operating temperature (Chapter 3)
- ☐ Oil pump pressure relief valve defective (Chapter 2A, 2B or 2C)
- ☐ Oil pump pick-up strainer clogged (Chapter 2A, 2B or 2C)

Engine runs-on after switching off

- ☐ Excessive carbon build-up in engine (Chapter 2)
- ☐ High engine operating temperature (Chapter 3)
- ☐ Fuel injection system fault (Chapter 4A or 4B)

Engine (continued)

Engine noises

Pre-ignition (pinking) or knocking during acceleration or under load

- ☐ Ignition timing incorrect/ignition system fault – petrol models (Chapter 1A or 5B)
- ☐ Incorrect grade of spark plug – petrol models (Chapter 1A)
- ☐ Incorrect grade of fuel (Chapter 4)
- ☐ Knock sensor faulty – some petrol models (Chapter 4A)
- ☐ Vacuum leak at the throttle body, inlet manifold or associated hoses – petrol models (Chapter 4A)
- ☐ Excessive carbon build-up in engine (Chapter 2A, 2B, 2C or 2D)
- ☐ Blocked injector/fuel injection system fault (Chapter 4A or 4B)
- ☐ Faulty injector(s) – diesel models (Chapter 4B)

Whistling or wheezing noises

- ☐ Leaking inlet manifold or throttle body gasket – petrol models (Chapter 4A)
- ☐ Leaking exhaust manifold gasket or pipe-to-manifold joint (Chapter 4A or 4B)
- ☐ Leaking vacuum hose (Chapter 4, 5 or 9)
- ☐ Blowing cylinder head gasket (Chapter 2A, 2B or 2C)
- ☐ Partially blocked or leaking crankcase ventilation system (Chapter 4C)

Tapping or rattling noises

- ☐ Valve clearances incorrect (Chapter 2A, 2B or 2C)
- ☐ Worn valve gear or camshaft (Chapter 2A, 2B or 2C)
- ☐ Ancillary component fault (coolant pump, alternator, etc) (Chapter 3, 5A, etc)

Knocking or thumping noises

- ☐ Worn big-end bearings (regular heavy knocking, perhaps less under load) (Chapter 2D)
- ☐ Worn main bearings (rumbling and knocking, perhaps worsening under load) (Chapter 2D)
- ☐ Piston slap – most noticeable when cold, caused by piston/bore wear (Chapter 2D)
- ☐ Ancillary component fault (coolant pump, alternator, etc) (Chapter 3, 5A, etc)
- ☐ Engine mountings worn or defective (Chapter 2A, 2B or 2C)
- ☐ Front suspension or steering components worn (Chapter 10)

Cooling system

Overheating

- ☐ Insufficient coolant in system (see *Weekly checks*)
- ☐ Thermostat faulty (Chapter 3)
- ☐ Radiator core blocked, or grille restricted (Chapter 3)
- ☐ Cooling fan faulty, or resistor pack fault on models with twin fans (Chapter 3)
- ☐ Inaccurate cylinder head temperature sender (Chapter 3, 4A or 4B)
- ☐ Airlock in cooling system (Chapter 3)
- ☐ Expansion tank pressure cap faulty (Chapter 3)
- ☐ Engine management system fault (Chapter 4A or 4B)

Overcooling

- ☐ Thermostat faulty (Chapter 3)
- ☐ Inaccurate cylinder head temperature sender (Chapter 3, 4A or 4B)
- ☐ Cooling fan faulty (Chapter 3)
- ☐ Engine management system fault (Chapter 4A or 4B)

External coolant leakage

- ☐ Deteriorated or damaged hoses or hose clips (Chapter 1A or 1B)
- ☐ Radiator core or heater matrix leaking (Chapter 3)
- ☐ Expansion tank pressure cap faulty (Chapter 1A or 1B)
- ☐ Coolant pump internal seal leaking (Chapter 3)
- ☐ Coolant pump gasket leaking (Chapter 3)
- ☐ Boiling due to overheating (Chapter 3)
- ☐ Cylinder block core plug leaking (Chapter 2D)

Internal coolant leakage

- ☐ Leaking cylinder head gasket (Chapter 2A, 2B or 2C)
- ☐ Cracked cylinder head or cylinder block (Chapter 2A, 2B, 2C or 2D)

Corrosion

- ☐ Infrequent draining and flushing (Chapter 1A or 1B)
- ☐ Incorrect coolant mixture or inappropriate coolant type (see *Weekly checks*)

Fuel and exhaust systems

Excessive fuel consumption

- ☐ Air filter element dirty or clogged (Chapter 1A or 1B)
- ☐ Fuel injection system fault (Chapter 4A or 4B)
- ☐ Engine management system fault (Chapter 4A or 4B)
- ☐ Crankcase ventilation system blocked (Chapter 4C)
- ☐ Tyres under-inflated (see *Weekly checks*)
- ☐ Brakes binding (Chapter 1A, 1B or 9)
- ☐ Fuel leak, causing apparent high consumption (Chapter 1A, 1B, 4A or 4B)

Fuel leakage and/or fuel odour

- ☐ Damaged or corroded fuel tank, pipes or connections (Chapter 4A or 4B)
- ☐ Evaporative emissions system fault – petrol models (Chapter 4C)

Excessive noise or fumes from exhaust system

- ☐ Leaking exhaust system or manifold joints (Chapter 1A, 1B, 4A or 4B)
- ☐ Leaking, corroded or damaged silencers or pipe (Chapter 1A, 1B, 4A or 4B)
- ☐ Broken mountings causing body or suspension contact (Chapter 1A or 1B)

Clutch

Pedal travels to floor – no pressure or very little resistance

- ☐ Air in hydraulic system/faulty master or slave cylinder (Chapter 6)
- ☐ Faulty hydraulic release system (Chapter 6)
- ☐ Clutch pedal return spring detached or broken (Chapter 6)
- ☐ Broken clutch release bearing or fork (Chapter 6)
- ☐ Broken diaphragm spring in clutch pressure plate (Chapter 6)

Clutch fails to disengage (unable to select gears)

- ☐ Air in hydraulic system/faulty master or slave cylinder (Chapter 6)
- ☐ Faulty hydraulic release system (Chapter 6)
- ☐ Clutch disc sticking on transmission input shaft splines (Chapter 6)
- ☐ Clutch disc sticking to flywheel or pressure plate (Chapter 6)
- ☐ Faulty pressure plate assembly (Chapter 6)
- ☐ Clutch release mechanism worn or incorrectly assembled (Chapter 6)

Clutch slips (engine speed increases, with no increase in vehicle speed)

- ☐ Faulty hydraulic release system (Chapter 6)
- ☐ Clutch disc linings excessively worn (Chapter 6)
- ☐ Clutch disc linings contaminated with oil or grease (Chapter 6)
- ☐ Faulty pressure plate or weak diaphragm spring (Chapter 6)

Judder as clutch is engaged

- ☐ Clutch disc linings contaminated with oil or grease (Chapter 6)
- ☐ Clutch disc linings excessively worn (Chapter 6)
- ☐ Faulty or distorted pressure plate or diaphragm spring (Chapter 6).
- ☐ Worn or loose engine or transmission mountings (Chapter 2A, 2B or 2C)
- ☐ Clutch disc hub or transmission input shaft splines worn (Chapter 6)
- ☐ Faulty dual-mass flywheel, where applicable (Chapter 2A, 2B or 2C)

Noise when depressing or releasing clutch pedal

- ☐ Worn clutch release bearing (Chapter 6)
- ☐ Worn or dry clutch pedal bushes (Chapter 6)
- ☐ Worn or dry clutch master cylinder piston (Chapter 6)
- ☐ Faulty pressure plate assembly (Chapter 6)
- ☐ Pressure plate diaphragm spring broken (Chapter 6)
- ☐ Broken clutch disc cushioning springs (Chapter 6)
- ☐ Faulty dual-mass flywheel, where applicable (Chapter 2A, 2B or 2C)

Manual transmission

Noisy in neutral with engine running

- ☐ Lack of oil (Chapter 1A or 1B)
- ☐ Input shaft bearings worn (noise apparent with clutch pedal released, but not when depressed) (Chapter 7A)*
- ☐ Clutch release bearing worn (noise apparent with clutch pedal depressed, possibly less when released) (Chapter 6)

Noisy in one particular gear

- ☐ Worn, damaged or chipped gear teeth (Chapter 7A)*

Difficulty engaging gears

- ☐ Clutch fault (Chapter 6)
- ☐ Worn, damaged, or poorly-adjusted gearchange cables (Chapter 7A)
- ☐ Lack of oil (Chapter 1A or 1B)
- ☐ Worn synchroniser units (Chapter 7A)*

Jumps out of gear

- ☐ Worn, damaged, or poorly-adjusted gearchange cables (Chapter 7A)
- ☐ Worn synchroniser units (Chapter 7A)*
- ☐ Worn selector forks (Chapter 7A)*

Vibration

- ☐ Lack of oil (Chapter 1A or 1B)
- ☐ Worn bearings (Chapter 7A)*

Lubricant leaks

- ☐ Leaking driveshaft or selector shaft oil seal (Chapter 7A)
- ☐ Leaking housing joint (Chapter 7A)*
- ☐ Leaking input shaft oil seal (Chapter 7A)*

** Although the corrective action necessary to remedy the symptoms described is beyond the scope of the home mechanic, the above information should be helpful in isolating the cause of the condition, so that the owner can communicate clearly with a professional mechanic.*

Automatic transmission

Note: *Due to the complexity of the automatic transmission, it is difficult for the home mechanic to properly diagnose and service this unit. For problems other than the following, the car should be taken to a dealer service department or automatic transmission specialist. Do not be too hasty in removing the transmission if a fault is suspected, as most of the testing is carried out with the unit still fitted. Remember that, besides the sensors specific to the transmission, many of the engine management system sensors described in Chapter 4A or 4B are essential to the correct operation of the transmission.*

Fluid leakage

- ☐ Automatic transmission fluid is usually dark red in colour. Fluid leaks should not be confused with engine oil, which can easily be blown onto the transmission by airflow.
- ☐ To determine the source of a leak, first remove all built-up dirt and grime from the transmission housing and surrounding areas using a degreasing agent, or by steam-cleaning. Drive the car at low speed, so airflow will not blow the leak far from its source. Raise and support the car, and determine where the leak is coming from. The following are common areas of leakage:

a) Fluid pan
b) Dipstick tube – 4-speed transmission only (Chapter 1A or 1B)
c) Transmission-to-fluid cooler unions (Chapter 7B)

Transmission fluid brown, or has burned smell

- ☐ Transmission fluid level low (Chapter 1A or 1B)

General gear selection problems

- ☐ Chapter 7B deals with checking the selector cable on automatic transmissions. The following are common problems which may be caused by a faulty selector cable or lever position sensor:

a) Engine starting in gears other than Park or Neutral.
b) Indicator panel indicating a gear other than the one actually being used.
c) Car moves when in Park or Neutral.
d) Poor gear shift quality or erratic gear changes.

Transmission will not downshift (kickdown) with accelerator pedal fully depressed

- ☐ Low transmission fluid level (Chapter 1A or 1B)
- ☐ Engine management system fault (Chapter 4A or 4B)
- ☐ Faulty transmission sensor or wiring (Chapter 7B)
- ☐ Incorrect selector cable adjustment (Chapter 7B)

Engine will not start in any gear, or starts in gears other than Park or Neutral

- ☐ Faulty transmission sensor or wiring (Chapter 7B)
- ☐ Engine management system fault (Chapter 4A or 4B)
- ☐ Incorrect selector cable adjustment (Chapter 7B)

Transmission slips, shifts roughly, is noisy, or has no drive in forward or reverse gears

- ☐ Transmission fluid level low (Chapter 1A or 1B)
- ☐ Faulty transmission sensor or wiring (Chapter 7B)
- ☐ Engine management system fault (Chapter 4A or 4B)

Note: *There are many probable causes for the above problems, but diagnosing and correcting them is considered beyond the scope of this manual. Having checked the fluid level and all the wiring as far as possible, a dealer or transmission specialist should be consulted if the problem persists.*

Driveshafts

Vibration when accelerating or decelerating

- ☐ Worn inner constant velocity joint (Chapter 8)
- ☐ Bent or distorted driveshaft (Chapter 8)
- ☐ Worn intermediate bearing (Chapter 8)

Clicking or knocking noise on turns (at slow speed on full-lock)

- ☐ Worn outer constant velocity joint (Chapter 8)
- ☐ Lack of constant velocity joint lubricant, possibly due to damaged gaiter (Chapter 8)
- ☐ Worn intermediate bearing (Chapter 8)

Braking system

Note: *Before assuming that a brake problem exists, make sure that the tyres are in good condition and correctly inflated, that the front wheel alignment is correct, and that the car is not loaded with weight in an unequal manner. Apart from checking the condition of all pipe and hose connections, any faults occurring on the anti-lock braking system should be referred to a Ford dealer for diagnosis.*

Car pulls to one side under braking

- ☐ Worn, defective, damaged or contaminated brake pads on one side (Chapter 1A, 1B or 9)
- ☐ Seized or partially-seized brake caliper piston (Chapter 1A, 1B or 9)
- ☐ A mixture of brake pad materials fitted between sides (Chapter 1A, 1B or 9)
- ☐ Brake caliper mounting bolts loose (Chapter 9)
- ☐ Worn or damaged steering or suspension components (Chapter 1A, 1B or 10)

Noise (grinding or high-pitched squeal) when brakes applied

- ☐ Brake pad material worn down to metal backing (Chapter 1A, 1B or 9)
- ☐ Excessive corrosion of brake disc (may be apparent after the car has been standing for some time (Chapter 1A, 1B or 9)
- ☐ Foreign object (stone chipping, etc) trapped between brake disc and shield (Chapter 1A, 1B or 9)

Excessive brake pedal travel

- ☐ Faulty master cylinder (Chapter 9)
- ☐ Air in hydraulic system (Chapter 1A, 1B, 6 or 9)
- ☐ Faulty vacuum servo unit (Chapter 9)

Brake pedal feels spongy when depressed

- ☐ Air in hydraulic system (Chapter 1A, 1B, 6 or 9)
- ☐ Deteriorated flexible rubber brake hoses (Chapter 1A, 1B or 9)
- ☐ Master cylinder mounting nuts loose (Chapter 9)
- ☐ Faulty master cylinder (Chapter 9)

Excessive brake pedal effort required to stop car

- ☐ Faulty vacuum servo unit (Chapter 9)
- ☐ Faulty vacuum pump – diesel models (Chapter 9)
- ☐ Disconnected, damaged or insecure brake servo vacuum hose (Chapter 9)
- ☐ Primary or secondary hydraulic circuit failure (Chapter 9)
- ☐ Seized brake caliper piston (Chapter 9)
- ☐ Brake pads incorrectly fitted (Chapter 9)
- ☐ Incorrect grade of brake pads fitted (Chapter 9)
- ☐ Brake pads contaminated (Chapter 1A, 1B or 9)

Judder felt through brake pedal or steering wheel when braking

Note: *Under heavy braking on models equipped with ABS, vibration may be felt through the brake pedal. This is a normal feature of ABS operation, and does not constitute a fault*

- ☐ Excessive run-out or distortion of discs (Chapter 1A, 1B or 9)
- ☐ Brake pads worn (Chapter 1A, 1B or 9)
- ☐ Brake caliper mounting bolts loose (Chapter 9)
- ☐ Wear in suspension or steering components or mountings (Chapter 1A, 1B or 10)
- ☐ Front wheels out of balance (see *Weekly checks*)

Brakes binding

- ☐ Seized brake caliper piston (Chapter 9)
- ☐ Incorrectly-adjusted handbrake mechanism (Chapter 9)
- ☐ Faulty master cylinder (Chapter 9)

Rear wheels locking under normal braking

- ☐ Rear brake pads contaminated or damaged (Chapter 1 or 9)
- ☐ Rear brake discs warped (Chapter 1 or 9)
- ☐ ABS fault (Chapter 9)

ABS warning light stays on

- ☐ Wheel sensor wiring plug corroded, or wiring damaged (Chapter 9)
- ☐ Other wiring fault – check ABS hydraulic unit in engine compartment (Chapter 9)
- ☐ ABS fuse blown (Chapter 12)
- ☐ Low brake fluid level, possibly due to a leak, or system needs bleeding (Chapter 1A, 1B or 9)
- ☐ Incompatible 'new' parts fitted, or system requires setup with Ford WDS2000 (Chapter 9)

Suspension and steering

Note: *Before diagnosing suspension or steering faults, be sure that the trouble is not due to incorrect tyre pressures, mixtures of tyre types, or binding brakes.*

Car pulls to one side

- ☐ Defective tyre (see *Weekly checks*)
- ☐ Excessive wear in suspension or steering components (Chapter 1A, 1B or 10)
- ☐ Incorrect front wheel alignment (Chapter 10)
- ☐ Accident damage to steering or suspension components (Chapter 1A or 1B)

Wheel wobble and vibration

- ☐ Front wheels out of balance (vibration felt mainly through the steering wheel) (see *Weekly checks*)
- ☐ Rear wheels out of balance (vibration felt throughout the car) (see *Weekly checks*)
- ☐ Roadwheels damaged or distorted (see *Weekly checks*)
- ☐ Faulty or damaged tyre (see *Weekly checks*)
- ☐ Worn steering or suspension joints, bushes or components (Chapter 1A, 1B or 10)
- ☐ Wheel nuts loose (Chapter 1A or 1B)

Excessive pitching and/or rolling around corners, or during braking

- ☐ Defective shock absorbers (Chapter 1A, 1B or 10)
- ☐ Broken or weak spring and/or suspension component (Chapter 1A, 1B or 10)
- ☐ Worn or damaged anti-roll bar or mountings (Chapter 1A, 1B or 10)

Wandering or general instability

- ☐ Incorrect front wheel alignment (Chapter 10)
- ☐ Worn steering or suspension joints, bushes or components (Chapter 1A, 1B or 10)
- ☐ Roadwheels out of balance (see *Weekly checks*)
- ☐ Faulty or damaged tyre (see *Weekly checks*)
- ☐ Wheel nuts loose (Chapter 1A or 1B)
- ☐ Defective shock absorbers (Chapter 1A, 1B or 10)
- ☐ Rear crossmember bushes worn – Saloon and Hatchback models (Chapter 10)

Excessively-stiff steering

- ☐ Seized steering linkage balljoint or suspension balljoint (Chapter 1A, 1B or 10)
- ☐ Broken or slipping auxiliary drivebelt (Chapter 1A or 1B)
- ☐ Incorrect front wheel alignment (Chapter 10)
- ☐ Steering rack damaged (Chapter 10)

Excessive play in steering

- ☐ Worn steering column/intermediate shaft joints (Chapter 10)
- ☐ Worn track rod balljoints (Chapter 1A, 1B or 10)
- ☐ Worn steering rack (Chapter 10)
- ☐ Worn steering or suspension joints, bushes or components (Chapter 1A, 1B or 10)

Lack of power assistance

- ☐ Broken or slipping auxiliary drivebelt (Chapter 1A or 1B)
- ☐ Incorrect power steering fluid level (see *Weekly checks*)
- ☐ Restriction in power steering fluid hoses (Chapter 1A or 1B)
- ☐ Faulty power steering pump (Chapter 10)
- ☐ Faulty steering rack (Chapter 10)

Tyre wear excessive

Tyres worn on inside or outside edges

- ☐ Tyres under-inflated (wear on both edges) (see *Weekly checks*)
- ☐ Incorrect camber or castor angles (wear on one edge only) (Chapter 10)
- ☐ Worn steering or suspension joints, bushes or components (Chapter 1A, 1B or 10)
- ☐ Excessively-hard cornering or braking
- ☐ Accident damage

Tyre treads exhibit feathered edges

- ☐ Incorrect toe setting (tracking) (Chapter 10)

Tyres worn in centre of tread

- ☐ Tyres over-inflated (see *Weekly checks*)

Tyres worn on inside and outside edges

- ☐ Tyres under-inflated (see *Weekly checks*)

Tyres worn unevenly

- ☐ Tyres/wheels out of balance (see *Weekly checks*)
- ☐ Excessive wheel or tyre run-out
- ☐ Worn shock absorbers (Chapter 1A, 1B or 10)
- ☐ Faulty tyre (see *Weekly checks*)

Electrical system

Note: *For problems associated with the starting system, refer to the faults listed under* **Engine** *earlier in this Section.*

Battery will not hold a charge for more than a few days

- ☐ Battery defective internally (Chapter 5A)
- ☐ Battery terminal connections loose or corroded (see *Weekly checks*)
- ☐ Auxiliary drivebelt worn or slipping (Chapter 1A or 1B)
- ☐ Alternator not charging at correct output (Chapter 5A)
- ☐ Alternator or voltage regulator faulty (Chapter 5A)
- ☐ Short-circuit causing continual battery drain (Chapter 5A or 12)

Ignition/no-charge warning light remains illuminated with engine running

- ☐ Auxiliary drivebelt broken, worn, or slipping (Chapter 1A or 1B)
- ☐ Internal fault in alternator or voltage regulator (Chapter 5A)
- ☐ Broken, disconnected, or loose wiring in charging circuit (Chapter 5A or 12)

Ignition/no-charge warning light fails to come on

- ☐ Warning light bulb blown (Chapter 12)
- ☐ Broken, disconnected, or loose wiring in warning light circuit (Chapter 5A or 12)
- ☐ Alternator faulty (Chapter 5A)

Lights inoperative

- ☐ Bulb blown (Chapter 12)
- ☐ Corrosion of bulb or bulbholder contacts (Chapter 12)
- ☐ Blown fuse (Chapter 12)
- ☐ Faulty relay (Chapter 12)
- ☐ Broken, loose, or disconnected wiring (Chapter 12)
- ☐ Faulty switch (Chapter 12)

Automatic headlights not operating correctly

- ☐ Windscreen dirty or damaged in area of rain/light sensor
- ☐ Windscreen wiper switch faulty (Chapter 12)
- ☐ Windscreen wiper rain sensor faulty – possibly due to trapped dirt or condensation (Chapter 12)
- ☐ Generic electronic module fault (Chapter 12)

Instrument readings inaccurate or erratic

Instrument readings increase with engine speed

- ☐ Faulty instrument panel voltage regulator (Chapter 12)

Fuel or temperature gauges give no reading

- ☐ Faulty gauge sender unit (Chapter 3, 4A or 4B)
- ☐ Wiring open-circuit (Chapter 12)
- ☐ Faulty gauge (Chapter 12)

Fuel or temperature gauges give continuous maximum reading

- ☐ Faulty gauge sender unit (Chapter 3, 4A or 4B)
- ☐ Wiring short-circuit (Chapter 12)
- ☐ Faulty gauge (Chapter 12)

Horn inoperative, or unsatisfactory in operation

Horn operates all the time

- ☐ Horn push either earthed or stuck down (Chapter 12)
- ☐ Horn cable-to-horn push earthed (Chapter 12)

Horn fails to operate

- ☐ Blown fuse (Chapter 12)
- ☐ Cable or connections loose, broken or disconnected (Chapter 12)
- ☐ Faulty horn (Chapter 12)

Horn emits intermittent or unsatisfactory sound

- ☐ Cable connections loose (Chapter 12)
- ☐ Horn mountings loose (Chapter 12)
- ☐ Faulty horn (Chapter 12)

Windscreen wipers inoperative, or unsatisfactory in operation

Wipers fail to operate, or operate very slowly

- ☐ Wiper blades stuck to screen, or linkage seized or binding (Chapter 12)
- ☐ Blown fuse (Chapter 12)
- ☐ Battery discharged (Chapter 5A)
- ☐ Cable or connections loose, broken or disconnected (Chapter 12)
- ☐ Faulty relay (Chapter 12)
- ☐ Faulty wiper motor (Chapter 12)

Automatic wipers not operating correctly

- ☐ Windscreen dirty or damaged in area of rain/light sensor
- ☐ Windscreen wiper switch faulty (Chapter 12)
- ☐ Rain sensor faulty – possibly due to trapped dirt or condensation (Chapter 12)
- ☐ Generic electronic module fault (Chapter 12)

Wiper blades sweep over too large or too small an area of the glass

- ☐ Wiper blades incorrectly fitted, or wrong size used (see *Weekly checks*)
- ☐ Wiper arms incorrectly positioned on spindles (Chapter 12)
- ☐ Excessive wear of wiper linkage (Chapter 12)
- ☐ Wiper motor or linkage mountings loose or insecure (Chapter 12)

Wiper blades fail to clean the glass effectively

- ☐ Wiper blade rubbers dirty, worn or perished (see *Weekly checks*)
- ☐ Wiper blades incorrectly fitted, or wrong size used (see *Weekly checks*)
- ☐ Wiper arm tension springs broken, or arm pivots seized (Chapter 12)
- ☐ Insufficient windscreen washer additive to adequately remove road film (see *Weekly checks*)

Electrical system (continued)

Windscreen washers inoperative, or unsatisfactory in operation

One or more washer jets inoperative

- ☐ Blocked (or frozen) washer jet
- ☐ Disconnected, kinked or restricted fluid hose (Chapter 12)
- ☐ Insufficient fluid in washer reservoir (see *Weekly checks*)

Washer pump fails to operate

- ☐ Broken or disconnected wiring or connections (Chapter 12)
- ☐ Blown fuse (Chapter 12)
- ☐ Faulty washer switch (Chapter 12)
- ☐ Faulty washer pump (Chapter 12)

Washer pump runs for some time before fluid is emitted from jets

- ☐ Faulty one-way valve in fluid supply hose (Chapter 12)
- ☐ Fluid supply hose leaking (check under or inside car), or partially blocked (Chapter 12)

Electric windows inoperative, or unsatisfactory in operation

Window glass will only move in one direction

- ☐ Faulty switch (Chapter 12)

Window glass slow to move

- ☐ Battery discharged (Chapter 5A)
- ☐ Regulator seized or damaged, or in need of lubrication (Chapter 11)
- ☐ Door internal components or trim fouling regulator (Chapter 11)
- ☐ Faulty motor (Chapter 11)

Window glass fails to move

- ☐ Blown fuse (Chapter 12)
- ☐ Faulty relay (Chapter 12)
- ☐ Broken or disconnected wiring or connections (Chapter 12)
- ☐ Faulty motor (Chapter 11)

One-touch feature not working

- ☐ Switch needs resetting after battery disconnection (see *Disconnecting the battery*)

Central locking system inoperative, or unsatisfactory in operation

Complete system failure

- ☐ Remote handset battery discharged, where applicable
- ☐ Blown fuse (Chapter 12)
- ☐ Faulty relay (Chapter 12)
- ☐ Broken or disconnected wiring or connections (Chapter 12)
- ☐ Faulty motor (Chapter 11)

Latch locks but will not unlock, or unlocks but will not lock

- ☐ Remote handset battery discharged, where applicable
- ☐ Faulty master switch (Chapter 12)
- ☐ Broken or disconnected latch operating rods or levers (Chapter 11)
- ☐ Faulty relay (Chapter 12)
- ☐ Faulty motor (Chapter 11)

One solenoid/motor fails to operate

- ☐ Broken or disconnected wiring or connections (Chapter 12)
- ☐ Faulty operating assembly (Chapter 11)
- ☐ Broken, binding or disconnected latch operating rods or levers (Chapter 11)
- ☐ Fault in door latch (Chapter 11)

Fuel economy

Although depreciation is still the biggest part of the cost of motoring for most car owners, the cost of fuel is more immediately noticeable. These pages give some tips on how to get the best fuel economy.

Working it out

Manufacturer's figures

Car manufacturers are required by law to provide fuel consumption information on all new vehicles sold. These 'official' figures are obtained by simulating various driving conditions on a rolling road or a test track. Real life conditions are different, so the fuel consumption actually achieved may not bear much resemblance to the quoted figures.

How to calculate it

Many cars now have trip computers which will display fuel consumption, both instantaneous and average. Refer to the owner's handbook for details of how to use these.

To calculate consumption yourself (and maybe to check that the trip computer is accurate), proceed as follows.

1. Fill up with fuel and note the mileage, or zero the trip recorder.
2. Drive as usual until you need to fill up again.
3. Note the amount of fuel required to refill the tank, and the mileage covered since the previous fill-up.
4. Divide the mileage by the amount of fuel used to obtain the consumption figure.

For example:

Mileage at first fill-up (a) = 27,903
Mileage at second fill-up (b) = 28,346
Mileage covered (b - a) = 443
Fuel required at second fill-up = 48.6 litres

The half-completed changeover to metric units in the UK means that we buy our fuel in litres, measure distances in miles and talk about fuel consumption in miles per gallon. There are two ways round this: the first is to convert the litres to gallons before doing the calculation (by dividing by 4.546, or see Table 1). So in the example:

48.6 litres ÷ 4.546 = 10.69 gallons
443 miles ÷ 10.69 gallons = 41.4 mpg

The second way is to calculate the consumption in miles per litre, then multiply that figure by 4.546 (or see Table 2).

So in the example, fuel consumption is:

443 miles ÷ 48.6 litres = 9.1 mpl
9.1 mpl x 4.546 = 41.4 mpg

The rest of Europe expresses fuel consumption in litres of fuel required to travel 100 km (l/100 km). For interest, the conversions are given in Table 3. In practice it doesn't matter what units you use, provided you know what your normal consumption is and can spot if it's getting better or worse.

Table 1: conversion of litres to Imperial gallons

litres	1	2	3	4	5	10	20	30	40	50	60	70
gallons	0.22	0.44	0.66	0.88	1.10	2.24	4.49	6.73	8.98	11.22	13.47	15.71

Table 2: conversion of miles per litre to miles per gallon

miles per litre	5	6	7	8	9	10	11	12	13	14
miles per gallon	23	27	32	36	41	46	50	55	59	64

Table 3: conversion of litres per 100 km to miles per gallon

litres per 100 km	4	4.5	5	5.5	6	6.5	7	8	9	10
miles per gallon	71	63	56	51	47	43	40	35	31	28

Maintenance

A well-maintained car uses less fuel and creates less pollution. In particular:

Filters

Change air and fuel filters at the specified intervals.

Oil

Use a good quality oil of the lowest viscosity specified by the vehicle manufacturer (see *Lubricants and fluids*). Check the level often and be careful not to overfill.

Spark plugs

When applicable, renew at the specified intervals.

Tyres

Check tyre pressures regularly. Under-inflated tyres have an increased rolling resistance. It is generally safe to use the higher pressures specified for full load conditions even when not fully laden, but keep an eye on the centre band of tread for signs of wear due to over-inflation.

When buying new tyres, consider the 'fuel saving' models which most manufacturers include in their ranges.

Driving style

Acceleration

Acceleration uses more fuel than driving at a steady speed. The best technique with modern cars is to accelerate reasonably briskly to the desired speed, changing up through the gears as soon as possible without making the engine labour.

Air conditioning

Air conditioning absorbs quite a bit of energy from the engine – typically 3 kW (4 hp) or so. The effect on fuel consumption is at its worst in slow traffic. Switch it off when not required.

Anticipation

Drive smoothly and try to read the traffic flow so as to avoid unnecessary acceleration and braking.

Automatic transmission

When accelerating in an automatic, avoid depressing the throttle so far as to make the transmission hold onto lower gears at higher speeds. Don't use the 'Sport' setting, if applicable.

When stationary with the engine running, select 'N' or 'P'. When moving, keep your left foot away from the brake.

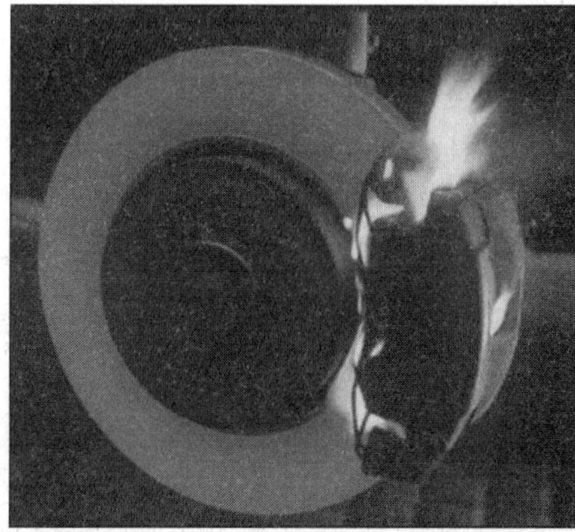

Braking

Braking converts the car's energy of motion into heat – essentially, it is wasted. Obviously some braking is always going to be necessary, but with good anticipation it is surprising how much can be avoided, especially on routes that you know well.

Carshare

Consider sharing lifts to work or to the shops. Even once a week will make a difference.

Electrical loads

Electricity is 'fuel' too; the alternator which charges the battery does so by converting some of the engine's energy of motion into electrical energy. The more electrical accessories are in use, the greater the load on the alternator. Switch off big consumers like the heated rear window when not required.

Freewheeling

Freewheeling (coasting) in neutral with the engine switched off is dangerous. The effort required to operate power-assisted brakes and steering increases when the engine is not running, with a potential lack of control in emergency situations.

In any case, modern fuel injection systems automatically cut off the engine's fuel supply on the overrun (moving and in gear, but with the accelerator pedal released).

Gadgets

Bolt-on devices claiming to save fuel have been around for nearly as long as the motor car itself. Those which worked were rapidly adopted as standard equipment by the vehicle manufacturers. Others worked only in certain situations, or saved fuel only at the expense of unacceptable effects on performance, driveability or the life of engine components.

The most effective fuel saving gadget is the driver's right foot.

Journey planning

Combine (eg) a trip to the supermarket with a visit to the recycling centre and the DIY store, rather than making separate journeys.

When possible choose a travelling time outside rush hours.

Load

The more heavily a car is laden, the greater the energy required to accelerate it to a given speed. Remove heavy items which you don't need to carry.

One load which is often overlooked is the contents of the fuel tank. A tankful of fuel (55 litres / 12 gallons) weighs 45 kg (100 lb) or so. Just half filling it may be worthwhile.

Lost?

At the risk of stating the obvious, if you're going somewhere new, have details of the route to hand. There's not much point in achieving record mpg if you also go miles out of your way.

Parking

If possible, carry out any reversing or turning manoeuvres when you arrive at a parking space so that you can drive straight out when you leave. Manoeuvering when the engine is cold uses a lot more fuel.

Driving around looking for free on-street parking may cost more in fuel than buying a car park ticket.

Premium fuel

Most major oil companies (and some supermarkets) have premium grades of fuel which are several pence a litre dearer than the standard grades. Reports vary, but the consensus seems to be that if these fuels improve economy at all, they do not do so by enough to justify their extra cost.

Roof rack

When loading a roof rack, try to produce a wedge shape with the narrow end at the front. Any cover should be securely fastened – if it flaps it's creating turbulence and absorbing energy.

Remove roof racks and boxes when not in use – they increase air resistance and can create a surprising amount of noise.

Short journeys

The engine is at its least efficient, and wear is highest, during the first few miles after a cold start. Consider walking, cycling or using public transport.

Speed

The engine is at its most efficient when running at a steady speed and load at the rpm where it develops maximum torque. (You can find this figure in the car's handbook.) For most cars this corresponds to between 55 and 65 mph in top gear.

Above the optimum cruising speed, fuel consumption starts to rise quite sharply. A car travelling at 80 mph will typically be using 30% more fuel than at 60 mph.

Supermarket fuel

It may be cheap but is it any good? In the UK all supermarket fuel must meet the relevant British Standard. The major oil companies will say that their branded fuels have better additive packages which may stop carbon and other deposits building up. A reasonable compromise might be to use one tank of branded fuel to three or four from the supermarket.

Switch off when stationary

Switch off the engine if you look like being stationary for more than 30 seconds or so. This is good for the environment as well as for your pocket. Be aware though that frequent restarts are hard on the battery and the starter motor.

Windows

Driving with the windows open increases air turbulence around the vehicle. Closing the windows promotes smooth airflow and reduced resistance. The faster you go, the more significant this is.

And finally . . .

Driving techniques associated with good fuel economy tend to involve moderate acceleration and low top speeds. Be considerate to the needs of other road users who may need to make brisker progress; even if you do not agree with them this is not an excuse to be obstructive.

Safety must always take precedence over economy, whether it is a question of accelerating hard to complete an overtaking manoeuvre, killing your speed when confronted with a potential hazard or switching the lights on when it starts to get dark.

Note: *References throughout this index are in the form* **"Chapter number" • "Page number"**. *So, for example, 2C•15 refers to page 15 of Chapter 2C.*

A

B

C

Note: *References throughout this index are in the form* **"Chapter number" • "Page number"**. *So, for example, 2C•15 refers to page 15 of Chapter 2C.*

D

Note: *References throughout this index are in the form* "**Chapter number**" • "**Page number**". *So, for example, 2C•15 refers to page 15 of Chapter 2C.*

E

F

Note: *References throughout this index are in the form* **"Chapter number" • "Page number"**. *So, for example, 2C•15 refers to page 15 of Chapter 2C.*

Note: *References throughout this index are in the form* **"Chapter number" • "Page number"**. *So, for example, 2C•15 refers to page 15 of Chapter 2C.*

I

J

K

L

M

N

Note: *References throughout this index are in the form* **"Chapter number"** • **"Page number"**. *So, for example, 2C•15 refers to page 15 of Chapter 2C.*

O

P

R

Note: *References throughout this index are in the form* **"Chapter number" • "Page number"**. *So, for example, 2C•15 refers to page 15 of Chapter 2C.*

S

T

Note: *References throughout this index are in the form* **"Chapter number" • "Page number"***. So, for example, 2C•15 refers to page 15 of Chapter 2C.*

Haynes Manuals – The Complete UK Car List

Title	Book No.
ALFA ROMEO Alfasud/Sprint (74 - 88) up to F *	0292
Alfa Romeo Alfetta (73 - 87) up to E *	0531
AUDI 80, 90 & Coupe Petrol (79 - Nov 88) up to F	0605
Audi 80, 90 & Coupe Petrol (Oct 86 - 90) D to H	1491
Audi 100 & 200 Petrol (Oct 82 - 90) up to H	0907
Audi 100 & A6 Petrol & Diesel (May 91 - May 97) H to P	3504
Audi A3 Petrol & Diesel (96 - May 03) P to 03	4253
Audi A4 Petrol & Diesel (95 - 00) M to X	3575
Audi A4 Petrol & Diesel (01 - 04) X to 54	4609
AUSTIN A35 & A40 (56 - 67) up to F *	0118
Austin/MG/Rover Maestro 1.3 & 1.6 Petrol (83 - 95) up to M	0922
Austin/MG Metro (80 - May 90) up to G	0718
Austin/Rover Montego 1.3 & 1.6 Petrol (84 - 94) A to L	1066
Austin/MG/Rover Montego 2.0 Petrol (84 - 95) A to M	1067
Mini (59 - 69) up to H *	0527
Mini (69 - 01) up to X	0646
Austin/Rover 2.0 litre Diesel Engine (86 - 93) C to L	1857
Austin Healey 100/6 & 3000 (56 - 68) up to G *	0049
BEDFORD CF Petrol (69 - 87) up to E	0163
Bedford/Vauxhall Rascal & Suzuki Supercarry (86 - Oct 94) C to M	3015
BMW 316, 320 & 320i (4-cyl) (75 - Feb 83) up to Y *	0276
BMW 320, 320i, 323i & 325i (6-cyl) (Oct 77 - Sept 87) up to E	0815
BMW 3- & 5-Series Petrol (81 - 91) up to J	1948
BMW 3-Series Petrol (Apr 91 - 99) H to V	3210
BMW 3-Series Petrol (Sept 98 - 03) S to 53	4067
BMW 520i & 525e (Oct 81 - June 88) up to E	1560
BMW 525, 528 & 528i (73 - Sept 81) up to X *	0632
BMW 5-Series 6-cyl Petrol (April 96 - Aug 03) N to 03	4151
BMW 1500, 1502, 1600, 1602, 2000 & 2002 (59 - 77) up to S *	0240
CHRYSLER PT Cruiser Petrol (00 - 03) W to 53	4058
CITROËN 2CV, Ami & Dyane (67 - 90) up to H	0196
Citroën AX Petrol & Diesel (87 - 97) D to P	3014
Citroën Berlingo & Peugeot Partner Petrol & Diesel (96 - 05) P to 55	4281
Citroën BX Petrol (83 - 94) A to L	0908
Citroën C15 Van Petrol & Diesel (89 - Oct 98) F to S	3509
Citroën C3 Petrol & Diesel (02 - 05) 51 to 05	4197
Citroen C5 Petrol & Diesel (01-08) Y to 08	4745
Citroën CX Petrol (75 - 88) up to F	0528
Citroën Saxo Petrol & Diesel (96 - 04) N to 54	3506
Citroën Visa Petrol (79 - 88) up to F	0620
Citroën Xantia Petrol & Diesel (93 - 01) K to Y	3082
Citroën XM Petrol & Diesel (89 - 00) G to X	3451
Citroën Xsara Petrol & Diesel (97 - Sept 00) R to W	3751
Citroën Xsara Picasso Petrol & Diesel (00 - 02) W to 52	3944
Citroen Xsara Picasso (03-08)	4784
Citroën ZX Diesel (91 - 98) J to S	1922
Citroën ZX Petrol (91 - 98) H to S	1881
Citroën 1.7 & 1.9 litre Diesel Engine (84 - 96) A to N	1379
FIAT 126 (73 - 87) up to E *	0305
Fiat 500 (57 - 73) up to M *	0090
Fiat Bravo & Brava Petrol (95 - 00) N to W	3572
Fiat Cinquecento (93 - 98) K to R	3501
Fiat Panda (81 - 95) up to M	0793
Fiat Punto Petrol & Diesel (94 - Oct 99) L to V	3251
Fiat Punto Petrol (Oct 99 - July 03) V to 03	4066
Fiat Punto Petrol (03-07) 03 to 07	4746
Fiat Regata Petrol (84 - 88) A to F	1167
Fiat Tipo Petrol (88 - 91) E to J	1625
Fiat Uno Petrol (83 - 95) up to M	0923
Fiat X1/9 (74 - 89) up to G *	0273
FORD Anglia (59 - 68) up to G *	0001

Title	Book No.
Ford Capri II (& III) 1.6 & 2.0 (74 - 87) up to E *	0283
Ford Capri II (& III) 2.8 & 3.0 V6 (74 - 87) up to E	1309
Ford Cortina Mk I & Corsair 1500 ('62 - '66) up to D*	0214
Ford Cortina Mk III 1300 & 1600 (70 - 76) up to P *	0070
Ford Escort Mk I 1100 & 1300 (68 - 74) up to N *	0171
Ford Escort Mk I Mexico, RS 1600 & RS 2000 (70 - 74) up to N *	0139
Ford Escort Mk II Mexico, RS 1800 & RS 2000 (75 - 80) up to W *	0735
Ford Escort (75 - Aug 80) up to V *	0280
Ford Escort Petrol (Sept 80 - Sept 90) up to H	0686
Ford Escort & Orion Petrol (Sept 90 - 00) H to X	1737
Ford Escort & Orion Diesel (Sept 90 - 00) H to X	4081
Ford Fiesta (76 - Aug 83) up to Y	0334
Ford Fiesta Petrol (Aug 83 - Feb 89) A to F	1030
Ford Fiesta Petrol (Feb 89 - Oct 95) F to N	1595
Ford Fiesta Petrol & Diesel (Oct 95 - Mar 02) N to 02	3397
Ford Fiesta Petrol & Diesel (Apr 02 - 07) 02 to 57	4170
Ford Focus Petrol & Diesel (98 - 01) S to Y	3759
Ford Focus Petrol & Diesel (Oct 01 - 05) 51 to 05	4167
Ford Galaxy Petrol & Diesel (95 - Aug 00) M to W	3984
Ford Granada Petrol (Sept 77 - Feb 85) up to B *	0481
Ford Granada & Scorpio Petrol (Mar 85 - 94) B to M	1245
Ford Ka (96 - 02) P to 52	3570
Ford Mondeo Petrol (93 - Sept 00) K to X	1923
Ford Mondeo Petrol & Diesel (Oct 00 - Jul 03) X to 03	3990
Ford Mondeo Petrol & Diesel (July 03 - 07) 03 to 56	4619
Ford Mondeo Diesel (93 - 96) L to N	3465
Ford Orion Petrol (83 - Sept 90) up to H	1009
Ford Sierra 4-cyl Petrol (82 - 93) up to K	0903
Ford Sierra V6 Petrol (82 - 91) up to J	0904
Ford Transit Petrol (Mk 2) (78 - Jan 86) up to C	0719
Ford Transit Petrol (Mk 3) (Feb 86 - 89) C to G	1468
Ford Transit Diesel (Feb 86 - 99) C to T	3019
Ford Transit Diesel (00-06)	4775
Ford 1.6 & 1.8 litre Diesel Engine (84 - 96) A to N	1172
Ford 2.1, 2.3 & 2.5 litre Diesel Engine (77 - 90) up to H	1606
FREIGHT ROVER Sherpa Petrol (74 - 87) up to E	0463
HILLMAN Avenger (70 - 82) up to Y	0037
Hillman Imp (63 - 76) up to R *	0022
HONDA Civic (Feb 84 - Oct 87) A to E	1226
Honda Civic (Nov 91 - 96) J to N	3199
Honda Civic Petrol (Mar 95 - 00) M to X	4050
Honda Civic Petrol & Diesel (01 - 05) X to 55	4611
Honda CR-V Petrol & Diesel (01-06)	4747
Honda Jazz (01 - Feb 08) 51 - 57	4735
HYUNDAI Pony (85 - 94) C to M	3398
JAGUAR E Type (61 - 72) up to L *	0140
Jaguar MkI & II, 240 & 340 (55 - 69) up to H *	0098
Jaguar XJ6, XJ & Sovereign; Daimler Sovereign (68 - Oct 86) up to D	0242
Jaguar XJ6 & Sovereign (Oct 86 - Sept 94) D to M	3261
Jaguar XJ12, XJS & Sovereign; Daimler Double Six (72 - 88) up to F	0478
JEEP Cherokee Petrol (93 - 96) K to N	1943
LADA 1200, 1300, 1500 & 1600 (74 - 91) up to J	0413
Lada Samara (87 - 91) D to J	1610
LAND ROVER 90, 110 & Defender Diesel (83 - 07) up to 56	3017
Land Rover Discovery Petrol & Diesel (89 - 98) G to S	3016
Land Rover Discovery Diesel (Nov 98 - Jul 04) S to 04	4606
Land Rover Freelander Petrol & Diesel (97 - Sept 03) R to 53	3929
Land Rover Freelander Petrol & Diesel (Oct 03 - Oct 06) 53 to 56	4623

Title	Book No.
Land Rover Series IIA & III Diesel (58 - 85) up to C	0529
Land Rover Series II, IIA & III 4-cyl Petrol (58 - 85) up to C	0314
MAZDA 323 (Mar 81 - Oct 89) up to G	1608
Mazda 323 (Oct 89 - 98) G to R	3455
Mazda 626 (May 83 - Sept 87) up to E	0929
Mazda B1600, B1800 & B2000 Pick-up Petrol (72 - 88) up to F	0267
Mazda RX-7 (79 - 85) up to C *	0460
MERCEDES-BENZ 190, 190E & 190D Petrol & Diesel (83 - 93) A to L	3450
Mercedes-Benz 200D, 240D, 240TD, 300D & 300TD 123 Series Diesel (Oct 76 - 85)	1114
Mercedes-Benz 250 & 280 (68 - 72) up to L *	0346
Mercedes-Benz 250 & 280 123 Series Petrol (Oct 76 - 84) up to B *	0677
Mercedes-Benz 124 Series Petrol & Diesel (85 - Aug 93) C to K	3253
Mercedes-Benz A-Class Petrol & Diesel (98-04) S to 54)	4748
Mercedes-Benz C-Class Petrol & Diesel (93 - Aug 00) L to W	3511
Mercedes-Benz C-Class (00-06)	4780
MGA (55 - 62) *	0475
MGB (62 - 80) up to W	0111
MG Midget & Austin-Healey Sprite (58 - 80) up to W *	0265
MINI Petrol (July 01 - 05) Y to 05	4273
MITSUBISHI Shogun & L200 Pick-Ups Petrol (83 - 94) up to M	1944
MORRIS Ital 1.3 (80 - 84) up to B	0705
Morris Minor 1000 (56 - 71) up to K	0024
NISSAN Almera Petrol (95 - Feb 00) N to V	4053
Nissan Almera & Tino Petrol (Feb 00 - 07) V to 56	4612
Nissan Bluebird (May 84 - Mar 86) A to C	1223
Nissan Bluebird Petrol (Mar 86 - 90) C to H	1473
Nissan Cherry (Sept 82 - 86) up to D	1031
Nissan Micra (83 - Jan 93) up to K	0931
Nissan Micra (93 - 02) K to 52	3254
Nissan Micra Petrol (03-07) 52 to 57	4734
Nissan Primera Petrol (90 - Aug 99) H to T	1851
Nissan Stanza (82 - 86) up to D	0824
Nissan Sunny Petrol (May 82 - Oct 86) up to D	0895
Nissan Sunny Petrol (Oct 86 - Mar 91) D to H	1378
Nissan Sunny Petrol (Apr 91 - 95) H to N	3219
OPEL Ascona & Manta (B Series) (Sept 75 - 88) up to F *	0316
Opel Ascona Petrol (81 - 88)	3215
Opel Astra Petrol (Oct 91 - Feb 98)	3156
Opel Corsa Petrol (83 - Mar 93)	3160
Opel Corsa Petrol (Mar 93 - 97)	3159
Opel Kadett Petrol (Nov 79 - Oct 84) up to B	0634
Opel Kadett Petrol (Oct 84 - Oct 91)	3196
Opel Omega & Senator Petrol (Nov 86 - 94)	3157
Opel Rekord Petrol (Feb 78 - Oct 86) up to D	0543
Opel Vectra Petrol (Oct 88 - Oct 95)	3158
PEUGEOT 106 Petrol & Diesel (91 - 04) J to 53	1882
Peugeot 205 Petrol (83 - 97) A to P	0932
Peugeot 206 Petrol & Diesel (98 - 01) S to X	3757
Peugeot 206 Petrol & Diesel (02 - 06) 51 to 06	4613
Peugeot 306 Petrol & Diesel (93 - 02) K to 02	3073
Peugeot 307 Petrol & Diesel (01 - 04) Y to 54	4147
Peugeot 309 Petrol (86 - 93) C to K	1266
Peugeot 405 Petrol (88 - 97) E to P	1559
Peugeot 405 Diesel (88 - 97) E to P	3198
Peugeot 406 Petrol & Diesel (96 - Mar 99) N to T	3394
Peugeot 406 Petrol & Diesel (Mar 99 - 02) T to 52	3982

* Classic reprint

Title	Book No.
Peugeot 505 Petrol (79 - 89) up to G	0762
Peugeot 1.7/1.8 & 1.9 litre Diesel Engine (82 - 96) up to N	0950
Peugeot 2.0, 2.1, 2.3 & 2.5 litre Diesel Engines (74 - 90) up to H	1607
PORSCHE 911 (65 - 85) up to C	0264
Porsche 924 & 924 Turbo (76 - 85) up to C	0397
PROTON (89 - 97) F to P	3255
RANGE ROVER V8 Petrol (70 - Oct 92) up to K	0606
RELIANT Robin & Kitten (73 - 83) up to A *	0436
RENAULT 4 (61 - 86) up to D *	0072
Renault 5 Petrol (Feb 85 - 96) B to N	1219
Renault 9 & 11 Petrol (82 - 89) up to F	0822
Renault 18 Petrol (79 - 86) up to D	0598
Renault 19 Petrol (89 - 96) F to N	1646
Renault 19 Diesel (89 - 96) F to N	1946
Renault 21 Petrol (86 - 94) C to M	1397
Renault 25 Petrol & Diesel (84 - 92) B to K	1228
Renault Clio Petrol (91 - May 98) H to R	1853
Renault Clio Diesel (91 - June 96) H to N	3031
Renault Clio Petrol & Diesel (May 98 - May 01) R to Y	3906
Renault Clio Petrol & Diesel (June '01 - '05) Y to 55	4168
Renault Espace Petrol & Diesel (85 - 96) C to N	3197
Renault Laguna Petrol & Diesel (94 - 00) L to W	3252
Renault Laguna Petrol & Diesel (Feb 01 - Feb 05) X to 54	4283
Renault Mégane & Scénic Petrol & Diesel (96 - 99) N to T	3395
Renault Mégane & Scénic Petrol & Diesel (Apr 99 - 02) T to 52	3916
Renault Megane Petrol & Diesel (Oct 02 - 05) 52 to 55	4284
Renault Scenic Petrol & Diesel (Sept 03 - 06) 53 to 06	4297
ROVER 213 & 216 (84 - 89) A to G	1116
Rover 214 & 414 Petrol (89 - 96) G to N	1689
Rover 216 & 416 Petrol (89 - 96) G to N	1830
Rover 211, 214, 216, 218 & 220 Petrol & Diesel (Dec 95 - 99) N to V	3399
Rover 25 & MG ZR Petrol & Diesel (Oct 99 - 04) V to 54	4145
Rover 414, 416 & 420 Petrol & Diesel (May 95 - 98) M to R	3453
Rover 45 / MG ZS Petrol & Diesel (99 - 05) V to 55	4384
Rover 618, 620 & 623 Petrol (93 - 97) K to P	3257
Rover 75 / MG ZT Petrol & Diesel (99 - 06) S to 06	4292
Rover 820, 825 & 827 Petrol (86 - 95) D to N	1380
Rover 3500 (76 - 87) up to E *	0365
Rover Metro, 111 & 114 Petrol (May 90 - 98) G to S	1711
SAAB 95 & 96 (66 - 76) up to R *	0198
Saab 90, 99 & 900 (79 - Oct 93) up to L	0765
Saab 900 (Oct 93 - 98) L to R	3512
Saab 9000 (4-cyl) (85 - 98) C to S	1686
Saab 9-3 Petrol & Diesel (98 - Aug 02) R to 02	4614
Saab 9-3 Petrol & Diesel (02-07) 52 to 57	4749
Saab 9-5 4-cyl Petrol (97 - 04) R to 54	4156
SEAT Ibiza & Cordoba Petrol & Diesel (Oct 93 - Oct 99) L to V	3571
Seat Ibiza & Malaga Petrol (85 - 92) B to K	1609
SKODA Estelle (77 - 89) up to G	0604
Skoda Fabia Petrol & Diesel (00 - 06) W to 06	4376
Skoda Favorit (89 - 96) F to N	1801
Skoda Felicia Petrol & Diesel (95 - 01) M to X	3505
Skoda Octavia Petrol & Diesel (98 - Apr 04) R to 04	4285
SUBARU 1600 & 1800 (Nov 79 - 90) up to H *	0995

Title	Book No.
SUNBEAM Alpine, Rapier & H120 (67 - 74) up to N *	0051
SUZUKI SJ Series, Samurai & Vitara (4-cyl) Petrol (82 - 97) up to P	1942
Suzuki Supercarry & Bedford/Vauxhall Rascal (86 - Oct 94) C to M	3015
TALBOT Alpine, Solara, Minx & Rapier (75 - 86) up to D	0337
Talbot Horizon Petrol (78 - 86) up to D	0473
Talbot Samba (82 - 86) up to D	0823
TOYOTA Avensis Petrol (98 - Jan 03) R to 52	4264
Toyota Carina E Petrol (May 92 - 97) J to P	3256
Toyota Corolla (80 - 85) up to C	0683
Toyota Corolla (Sept 83 - Sept 87) A to E	1024
Toyota Corolla (Sept 87 - Aug 92) E to K	1683
Toyota Corolla Petrol (Aug 92 - 97) K to P	3259
Toyota Corolla Petrol (July 97 - Feb 02) P to 51	4286
Toyota Hi-Ace & Hi-Lux Petrol (69 - Oct 83) up to A	0304
Toyota RAV4 Petrol & Diesel (94-06) L to 55	4750
Toyota Yaris Petrol (99 - 05) T to 05	4265
TRIUMPH GT6 & Vitesse (62 - 74) up to N *	0112
Triumph Herald (59 - 71) up to K *	0010
Triumph Spitfire (62 - 81) up to X	0113
Triumph Stag (70 - 78) up to T *	0441
Triumph TR2, TR3, TR3A, TR4 & TR4A (52 - 67) up to F *	0028
Triumph TR5 & 6 (67 - 75) up to P *	0031
Triumph TR7 (75 - 82) up to Y *	0322
VAUXHALL Astra Petrol (80 - Oct 84) up to B	0635
Vauxhall Astra & Belmont Petrol (Oct 84 - Oct 91) B to J	1136
Vauxhall Astra Petrol (Oct 91 - Feb 98) J to R	1832
Vauxhall/Opel Astra & Zafira Petrol (Feb 98 - Apr 04) R to 04	3758
Vauxhall/Opel Astra & Zafira Diesel (Feb 98 - Apr 04) R to 04	3797
Vauxhall/Opel Astra Petrol (04 - 08)	4732
Vauxhall/Opel Astra Diesel (04 - 08)	4733
Vauxhall/Opel Calibra (90 - 98) G to S	3502
Vauxhall Carlton Petrol (Oct 78 - Oct 86) up to D	0480
Vauxhall Carlton & Senator Petrol (Nov 86 - 94) D to L	1469
Vauxhall Cavalier Petrol (81 - Oct 88) up to F	0812
Vauxhall Cavalier Petrol (Oct 88 - 95) F to N	1570
Vauxhall Chevette (75 - 84) up to B	0285
Vauxhall/Opel Corsa Diesel (Mar 93 - Oct 00) K to X	4087
Vauxhall Corsa Petrol (Mar 93 - 97) K to R	1985
Vauxhall/Opel Corsa Petrol (Apr 97 - Oct 00) P to X	3921
Vauxhall/Opel Corsa Petrol & Diesel (Oct 00 - Sept 03) X to 53	4079
Vauxhall/Opel Corsa Petrol & Diesel (Oct 03 - Aug 06) 53 to 06	4617
Vauxhall/Opel Frontera Petrol & Diesel (91 - Sept 98) J to S	3454
Vauxhall Nova Petrol (83 - 93) up to K	0909
Vauxhall/Opel Omega Petrol (94 - 99) L to T	3510
Vauxhall/Opel Vectra Petrol & Diesel (95 - Feb 99) N to S	3396
Vauxhall/Opel Vectra Petrol & Diesel (Mar 99 - May 02) T to 02	3930
Vauxhall/Opel Vectra Petrol & Diesel (June 02 - Sept 05) 02 to 55	4618
Vauxhall/Opel 1.5, 1.6 & 1.7 litre Diesel Engine (82 - 96) up to N	1222
VW 411 & 412 (68 - 75) up to P *	0091
VW Beetle 1200 (54 - 77) up to S	0036
VW Beetle 1300 & 1500 (65 - 75) up to P	0039

Title	Book No.
VW 1302 & 1302S (70 - 72) up to L *	0110
VW Beetle 1303, 1303S & GT (72 - 75) up to P	0159
VW Beetle Petrol & Diesel (Apr 99 - 07) T to 57	3798
VW Golf & Jetta Mk 1 Petrol 1.1 & 1.3 (74 - 84) up to A	0716
VW Golf, Jetta & Scirocco Mk 1 Petrol 1.5, 1.6 & 1.8 (74 - 84) up to A	0726
VW Golf & Jetta Mk 1 Diesel (78 - 84) up to A	0451
VW Golf & Jetta Mk 2 Petrol (Mar 84 - Feb 92) A to J	1081
VW Golf & Vento Petrol & Diesel (Feb 92 - Mar 98) J to R	3097
VW Golf & Bora Petrol & Diesel (April 98 - 00) R to X	3727
VW Golf & Bora 4-cyl Petrol & Diesel (01 - 03) X to 53	4169
VW Golf & Jetta Petrol & Diesel (04 - 07) 53 to 07	4610
VW LT Petrol Vans & Light Trucks (76 - 87) up to E	0637
VW Passat & Santana Petrol (Sept 81 - May 88) up to E	0814
VW Passat 4-cyl Petrol & Diesel (May 88 - 96) E to P	3498
VW Passat 4-cyl Petrol & Diesel (Dec 96 - Nov 00) P to X	3917
VW Passat Petrol & Diesel (Dec 00 - May 05) X to 05	4279
VW Polo & Derby (76 - Jan 82) up to X	0335
VW Polo (82 - Oct 90) up to H	0813
VW Polo Petrol (Nov 90 - Aug 94) H to L	3245
VW Polo Hatchback Petrol & Diesel (94 - 99) M to S	3500
VW Polo Hatchback Petrol (00 - Jan 02) V to 51	4150
VW Polo Petrol & Diesel (02 - May 05) 51 to 05	4608
VW Scirocco (82 - 90) up to H *	1224
VW Transporter 1600 (68 - 79) up to V	0082
VW Transporter 1700, 1800 & 2000 (72 - 79) up to V *	0226
VW Transporter (air-cooled) Petrol (79 - 82) up to Y *	0638
VW Transporter (water-cooled) Petrol (82 - 90) up to H	3452
VW Type 3 (63 - 73) up to M *	0084
VOLVO 120 & 130 Series (& P1800) (61 - 73) up to M *	0203
Volvo 142, 144 & 145 (66 - 74) up to N *	0129
Volvo 240 Series Petrol (74 - 93) up to K	0270
Volvo 262, 264 & 260/265 (75 - 85) up to C *	0400
Volvo 340, 343, 345 & 360 (76 - 91) up to J	0715
Volvo 440, 460 & 480 Petrol (87 - 97) D to P	1691
Volvo 740 & 760 Petrol (82 - 91) up to J	1258
Volvo 850 Petrol (92 - 96) J to P	3260
Volvo 940 petrol (90 - 98) H to R	3249
Volvo S40 & V40 Petrol (96 - Mar 04) N to 04	3569
Volvo S40 & V50 Petrol & Diesel (Mar 04 - Jun 07) 04 to 07	4731
Volvo S60 Petrol & Diesel (01-08)	4793
Volvo S70, V70 & C70 Petrol (96 - 99) P to V	3573
Volvo V70 / S80 Petrol & Diesel (98 - 05) S to 55	4263

DIY MANUAL SERIES

Title	Book No.
The Haynes Air Conditioning Manual	4192
The Haynes Car Electrical Systems Manual	4251
The Haynes Manual on Bodywork	4198
The Haynes Manual on Brakes	4178
The Haynes Manual on Carburettors	4177
The Haynes Manual on Diesel Engines	4174
The Haynes Manual on Engine Management	4199
The Haynes Manual on Fault Codes	4175
The Haynes Manual on Practical Electrical Systems	4267
The Haynes Manual on Small Engines	4250
The Haynes Manual on Welding	4176

* Classic reprint

All the products featured on this page are available through most motor accessory shops, cycle shops and book stores. Our policy of continuous updating and development means that titles are being constantly added to the range. For up-to-date information on our complete list of titles, please telephone: (UK) +44 1963 442030 • (USA) +1 805 498 6703 • (Sweden) +46 18 124016 • (Australia) +61 3 9763 8100

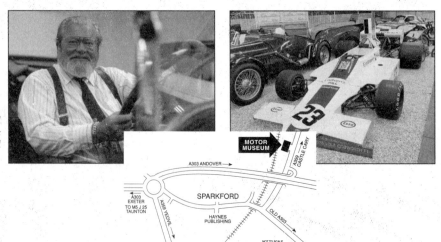

KU-580-937
B280 OLE
UNION P
HAWAII MARS
COULSON
N-40272
X4014
4014
TL
B
22
7435

PRIMARY EXPLORERS

CARS, PLANES AND TRAINS

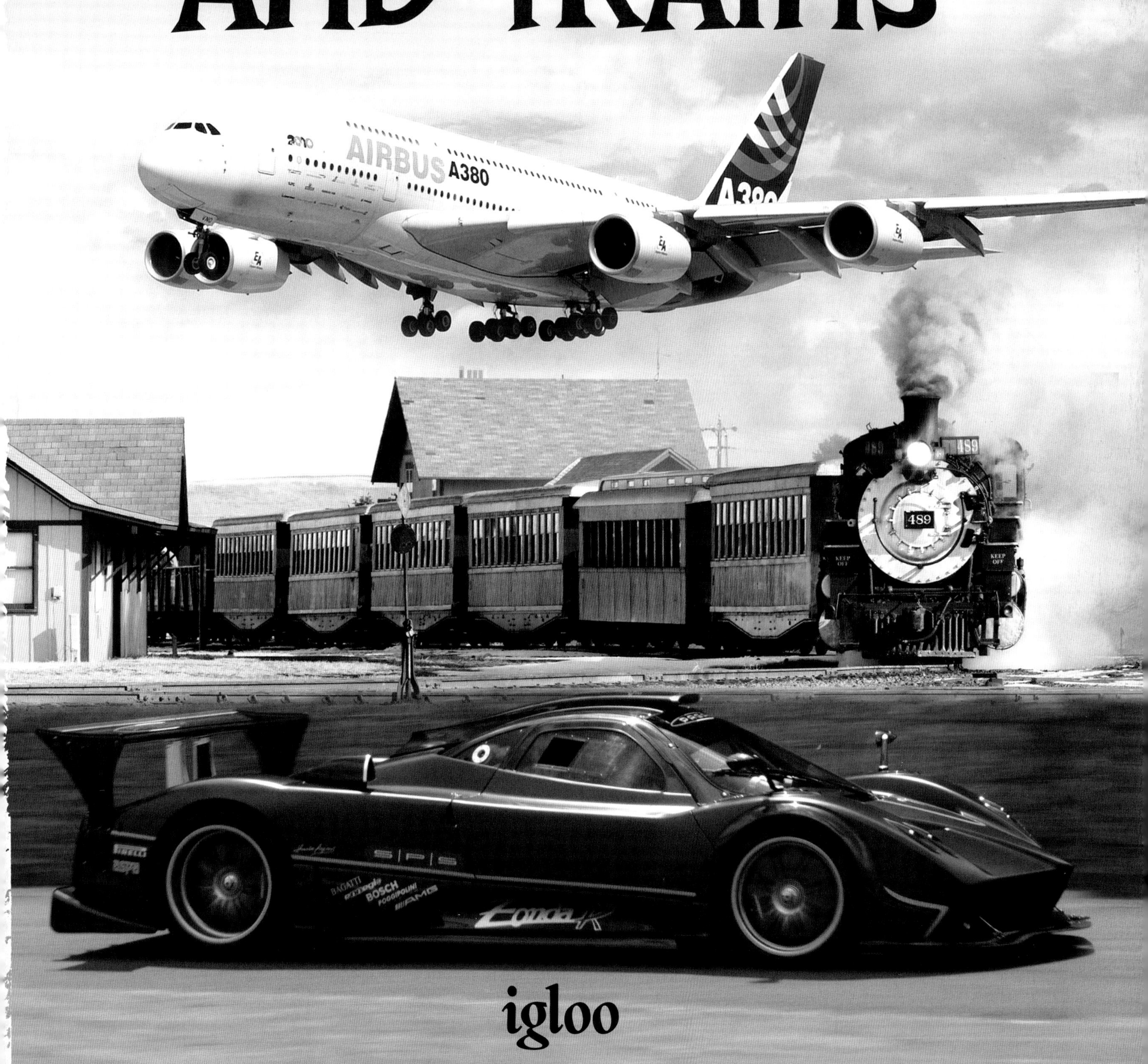

igloo

Contents

SNCF

TRANSPORT REVOLUTION

Rapid changes in transport between 1700 and 1900 made the world a much smaller place.

Many important advances in technology happened over quite a short period of time. This period is known as the Industrial Revolution. During the Industrial Revolution, more goods needed to be carried over longer distances. Roads were improved, canals built, the railways were developed and air travel followed soon afterwards.

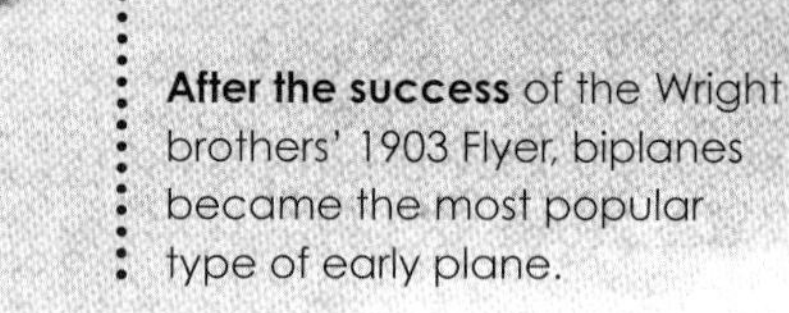

After the success of the Wright brothers' 1903 Flyer, biplanes became the most popular type of early plane.

THE INDUSTRIAL REVOLUTION

The Industrial Revolution changed the way people lived and worked. New methods of farming and types of machinery drove workers away from rural areas to the mines, mills and factories that were opening in larger towns and cities. Improved transport helped to make this large-scale movement of people, or migration, possible.

DID YOU KNOW?

Early railways were partly paid for by businesses and by wealthy people who had 'railway mania'!

THE SPIRIT OF INVENTION

The 19th century was a time of incredible inventions, from steam and internal combustion engines to propellers and electric motors. Each of these inventions helped to build new types of transport, but people weren't satisfied with new – they wanted to make things better, too. This constant desire to go further and faster, whether in a train, plane or car, drove the transport revolution forward.

British locomotives were built to be fast and reliable. Here, the locomotive *Experiment*, pulling the West Coast Express, is seen speeding past an early biplane in 1910.

The thousands of Navvies who were employed to build a new railway often had to live close to the line. They usually slept in damp, badly built huts next to the railway, because there weren't enough lodgings for them in nearby towns and villages.

The speed of travel opened up the world. People could travel across countries, continents and oceans faster than ever before.

HARD-WORKING NAVVIES

Another vital part of the transport revolution was hard manual work. First the canals and then the railways were built by workers, known as Navvies. Mechanical diggers were not used until the late 1800s, so most of the work was done with hand-tools. Tunnels were blasted using dangerous explosives, such as dynamite.

BENEFITS OF CHANGE

An improved transport system meant goods could be transported further, faster and more cheaply than before. It also made communication easier. Postal services became quicker and newspapers could be sent from cities out into the country.

The transport revolution changed the face of the world. Today, over 100 years later, roads, railways and airports are busier than ever.

INVENTING THE CAR

The history of the car dates back to the 18th century.

The earliest types of motor vehicle were powered by steam. The steam was created by a boiler outside the engine, which was sometimes so big it could tip the vehicle over! Slow and bulky, steam-powered vehicles were mostly used for farming, or carrying heavy goods.

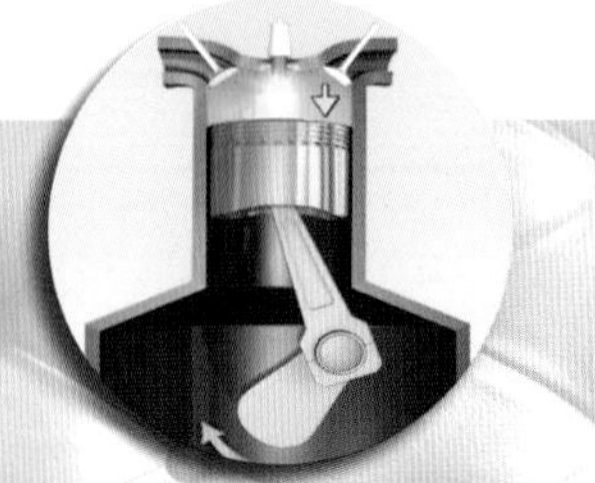

KEY STAGES IN DEVELOPMENT

As early as 1478, Leonardo da Vinci sketches plans for a clockwork car. It has three wheels, no seats and works like a wind-up toy.

1769 Nicolas-Joseph Cugnot invents the first successful self-propelling vehicle. His steam-powered cart has a top speed of 2.5 mph (4 km/h).

1825–29 Steam coaches are built by British inventor Sir Goldsworthy Gurney for commercial use.

1889 René Panhard and Emile Levassor are the first car manufacturers. Their 4 hp (horsepower) car, bulit in 1894, used a petrol motor invented by German engineer Gottlieb Daimler.

1927 Henry Ford sees the 15 millionth Model T roll off his production line.

Henry Ford's first car was built in a shed in his garden. It had a gas-powered engine and four bicycle wheels.

MOVING ON

It wasn't until the internal combustion engine was developed during the 19th century by various scientists and engineers, that cars became a serious alternative to horse-drawn vehicles. The internal combustion engine used petrol (gasoline), instead of coal, to power the engine – this meant it didn't need a boiler. Lighter and more powerful, these engines were fitted into specially-designed cars that carried passengers instead of goods.

German engineer Karl Benz designed this motor car in 1888. It was one of the first in the world to be put into production. In 1885, Benz had designed the first vehicle specifically to be powered by a motor.

MASS PRODUCTION

In 1908, the Ford Motor Company introduced a car called the Model T. It was built on the first assembly line ever to use a moving conveyor belt. This meant cars could be made twice as quickly and at a much lower cost. Now, more people than ever could afford to buy a car.

INTERNAL COMBUSTION ENGINE

Fuel and air are sprayed into the engine's cylinder, and squeezed by a piston. The spark plug then creates a spark, igniting the fuel. Hot, expanding gasses force the piston to move down, and a valve opens, releasing waste fumes. As the piston is forced up and down, it rotates a crankshaft, and this movement is passed to the wheels.

According to legend, Henry Ford famously insisted that the Model T Ford be "painted any color . . . so long as it is black", because black paint dried more quickly.

THE NEED FOR SPEED

Ever since cars were invented, people have wanted them to go faster.

The first recognized speed record was set in 1898 by a Frenchman, Count Gaston de Chasseloup-Laubat, as part of a competition organized by a motoring magazine. His electric car set the record at 39 mph (63 km/h). This was beaten many times over the following years, as cars changed and improved.

LAND SPEED RECORDS

1904 Henry Ford sets a record driving across a frozen lake.

1906 The Stanley Rocket Racer is the first car to travel faster than a train.

1964 Donald Campbell sets a land speed record of more than 400 mph (644 km/h).

Also in 1964 Jet-powered cars begin breaking records.

1997 Thrust SSC is the first land vehicle to break the sound barrier. Its speed is measured as a Mach number. Mach 1 is another name for the speed of sound.

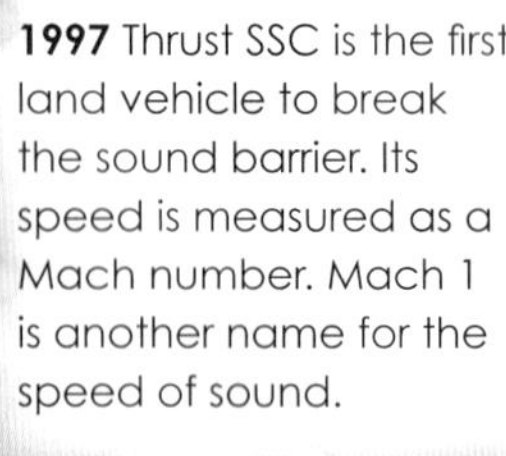

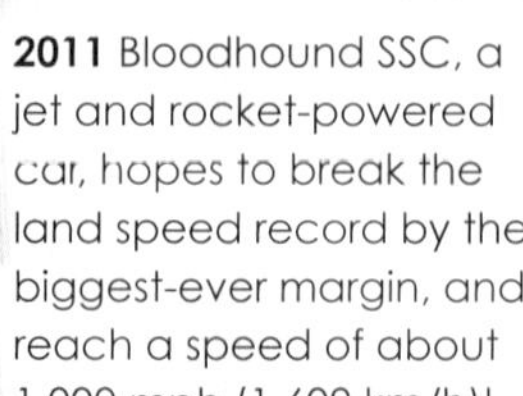

2011 Bloodhound SSC, a jet and rocket-powered car, hopes to break the land speed record by the biggest-ever margin, and reach a speed of about 1,000 mph (1,609 km/h)!

FASTEST MAN ON EARTH

Colonel John Stapp became known as the 'fastest man on Earth'. He was a doctor who carried out high-speed experiments on himself using a rocket-powered sled called Sonic Wind 1. During the 1950s, he achieved speeds of over 600 mph (1,017 km/h).

Donald Campbell's car, Bluebird-Proteus CN7, cost £1 million to build in 1960. Four years later, it set a land speed record at 403 mph (648 km/h) in Australia.

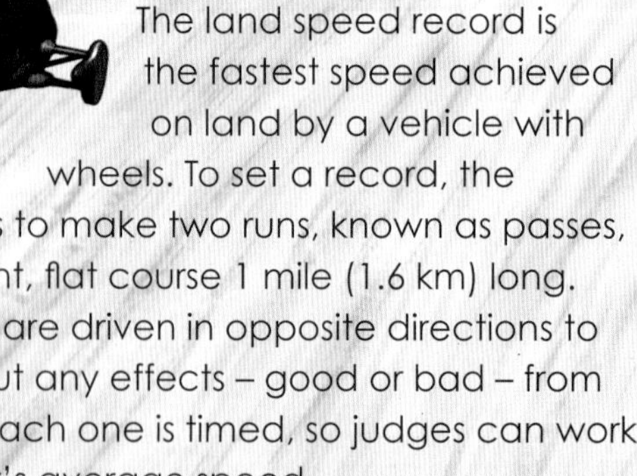

WORLD LAND SPEED RECORD

The land speed record is the fastest speed achieved on land by a vehicle with wheels. To set a record, the vehicle has to make two runs, known as passes, on a straight, flat course 1 mile (1.6 km) long. The passes are driven in opposite directions to balance out any effects – good or bad – from the wind. Each one is timed, so judges can work out the car's average speed.

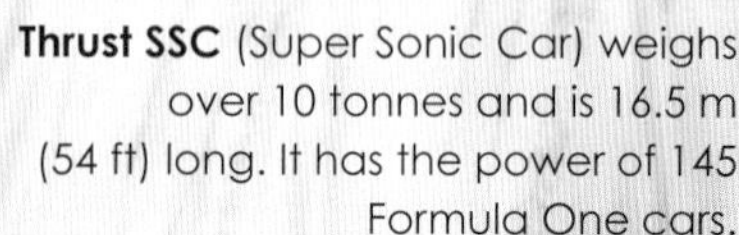

Thrust SSC (Super Sonic Car) weighs over 10 tonnes and is 16.5 m (54 ft) long. It has the power of 145 Formula One cars.

JETS AND ROCKETS

During the 1960s, high-speed cars were given powerful jet engines. Unlike a normal engine, which has pistons, a jet engine has a series of fan-blades to pull in and compress more air. This creates bigger explosions in the engine, giving the car extra energy, or thrust, so it can go much faster. Today, designers are using rocket engines, which are lighter and help vehicles, such as the supersonic Bloodhound, achieve even greater speeds.

STEAM-POWERED RECORD BREAKER

The land speed record for a steam-powered vehicle was set by the British car Inspiration in 2009. The record it set was 140 mph (225 km/h). Nicknamed the Flying Kettle, the car is powered by 12 suitcase-sized boilers, which produce enough heat to make 23 cups of tea every second!

The driver of Thrust SSC during its record-breaking run was an RAF fighter pilot. He achieved a speed of 763 mph (1,228 km/h), although the car can travel at up to 850 mph (1,368 km/h).

DID YOU KNOW?

In 1906, the women's world speed record was broken by motor-racing pioneer Dorothy Levitt. She also invented the rear-view mirror.

MOTOR RACING

Motor racing is one of the most popular spectator sports in the world.

Drivers have raced ever since the car was invented. Today, events include super-fast Formula One races, drag races along a short, straight track and long-distance endurance rallies.

FORMULA ONE

In Formula One (F1), drivers compete in a series of Grand Prix races around the world. The cars race on specially-built circuit tracks (or sometimes public roads) at up to 220 mph (360 km/h). In each race, the drivers compete to drive a set number of laps in the fastest time. They win points in each race, and at the end of the series the points are combined to find out who is the World Champion.

In an F1 racing car, almost all the controls and instruments are on the steering wheel.

Racing engines run on unleaded fuel almost identical to the petrol/ gasoline used in a normal car. The pistons move up and down 300 times a second (18,000 times a minute).

RALLY RACING

Some rally races are held on closed roads. The cars leave the starting point at intervals and are timed between chosen points. Off-road rallies are driven across dirt tracks, or even deserts.

THE HISTORY OF MOTOR RACING

The first serious motor race took place in 1895. Like most early races, it ran between two cities (Paris and Bordeaux). As cars became faster, however, road-racing grew more dangerous. The first purpose-built racetrack opened in England in 1907. Gradually, others were built around the world, and by the 1920s, most races took place on a track.

STOCK-CAR RACING

Stock cars combine the body of a normal road car with a more powerful, racing-style engine. They're much heavier than open-wheel cars (such as Formula and Indy cars), which have wheels to the sides of the car's body rather than below it. The extra weight makes them slower, but they can still reach speeds of 200 mph (320 km/h). Stock-car races take place on an oval track, or speedway.

Formula One drivers are supported by a huge team of people. At a pit stop during a race, a crew of 15 to 20 mechanics will change the wheels and make any small repairs needed. A pit stop can take less than 10 seconds.

DID YOU KNOW?

Indy-car racing is named after the famous Indianapolis 500-Mile Race, which first took place over 100 years ago.

A dragster, or drag car, speeds away from the start line. Drag cars can achieve speeds of 300 mph (480 km/h) by the time they cross the finish line at the end of the short, straight track. The fastest ones sometimes use a parachute to help them slow down.

SUPERCARS & SPORTS CARS

Many drivers dream of owning a sleek sports car or supercar.

Also known as performance cars, they're much more expensive than most road vehicles. Although they can be driven on public roads, drivers need to visit a race track to try out a performance car's top speed.

WHAT IS A SUPERCAR?

Supercars are fast, eye-catching and very expensive cars with powerful engines. Many are made as limited editions and they often have unusual features, such as doors that open from the top. As a road vehicle, they don't have the extra safety features of a racing car, and they also use more fuel than a normal car.

ICONIC SUPERCARS

The Lamborghini Gallardo can accelerate from 0 to 62 mph (100 km/h) in less than 4 seconds. Two of these cars are used by the Italian police during emergencies on the road.

The Ferrari 458 Italia was designed with the help of Formula One driver Michael Schumacher. Many of its controls are on the steering wheel, as in a racing car.

The Bugatti Veyron Super Sport is the fastest and most expensive road car in the world. It has a top speed of 268 mph (431 km/h) and costs about US $1,600,000.

TURBOCHARGER

A turbocharger uses exhaust gasses to spin a turbine. This is connected to a pump, which sucks in and compresses air. The air is then forced back into the engine, and increases its power.

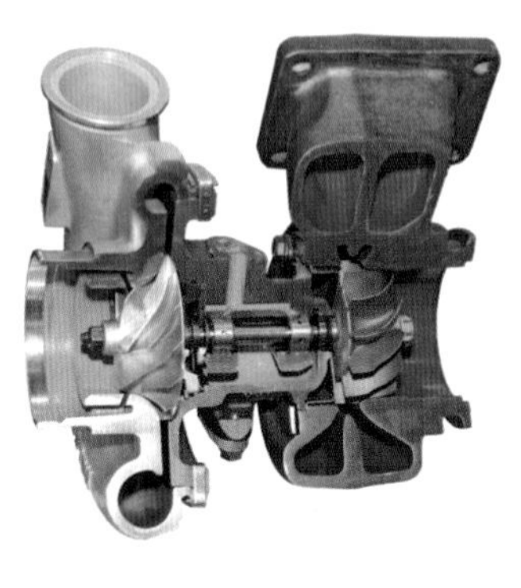

The Pagani Zonda R was the first road car in the world to have a body made from super-light carbon-titanium.

DID YOU KNOW?

The curvy, streamlined shape of a sports car allows air to flow smoothly around the body. This stops resistance, or 'drag', and helps the car to go faster.

The Jaguar E-type is a classic sports car and was the first to be mass-produced in Europe (1961–75). It is considered one of the most beautiful cars ever made.

SPORTS CARS

Small and lightweight, with just two seats, sports cars are often less powerful than supercars. A sports car's engine is at the front, while the back wheels 'drive' the car. This helps it to grip the road more firmly, especially when going round corners or driving at high speeds.

Every year in Italy, people celebrate the vintage sports cars that take part in the Mille Miglia, or Thousand Miles road race.

OFF-ROAD TYPES

Off-road vehicles have a wide range of uses. They can be driven on sand, mud, grass and snow.

Troop carriers armed with machine guns are used to transport soldiers.

A dune buggy has large, wide wheels for driving on sandy beaches.

The jeep is the oldest off-road vehicle still in use.

Land Rovers on safari handle lush grasslands and dusty dirt tracks.

Off-road vehicles

An off-road vehicle can drive both on and off the smooth surface of a public road.

Off-roaders are often used by farmers or people who live in the country and have to drive on rough tracks and muddy fields, as well as normal roads. For others, off-road driving is a hobby. Drivers enjoy the challenge of exploring hard-to-reach places in tough vehicles.

HOW DO THEY DO IT?

Off-road vehicles use gears called differentials that allow the wheels to turn at different speeds. This improves traction, or grip, and along with anti-locking brakes, helps prevent skidding. Off-roaders also have flexible suspension. This means the wheels move independently of each other, so even on the most uneven terrain all four wheels stay on the ground and drive the vehicle forward.

FOUR-WHEEL DRIVE

In a car with four-wheel drive, the engine sends turning force to all four wheels at the same time. This differs from a two-wheel drive car, in which only two wheels are powered at once.

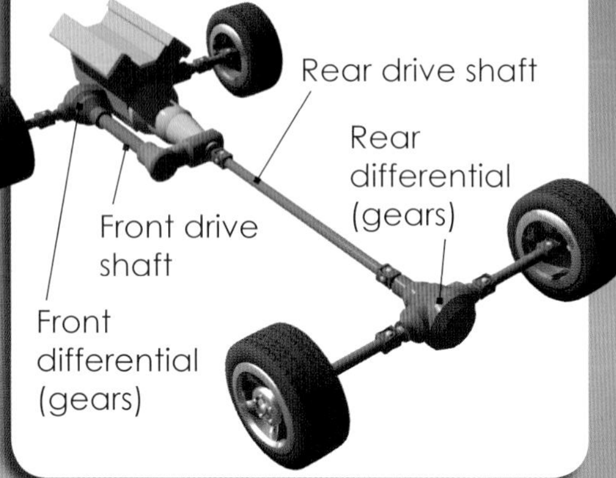

WHEELS AND TRACKS

Most off-road vehicles have special wheels so they don't sink or slide on difficult surfaces. These are often larger than normal, as the extra width, or thickness, provides better traction. In especially rough terrain, vehicles may use rubber or metal caterpillar tracks instead of wheels.

Amphibious vehicles can travel on land or in water. Some manage to use their wheels in the water, while others have propellers or a pump-jet.

In Rally Raid races, off-road vehicles drive up to 560 miles (900 km) a day over rough, difficult terrain.

Off-road races include mud-bogging (driving through mud or clay), dune-bashing (on sand dunes), rock racing (over rocks) and greenlaning (through forests).

DID YOU KNOW?

Off-roaders first became popular after World War 2. The army no longer needed many of its jeeps, so people bought them to use as utility vehicles.

ICONIC CARS

A famous, or iconic, car is popular, unique and easily recognized.

Sometimes known as classic cars, they are often typical of the era in which they were built. An iconic car might be well known for its appearance and styling, its performance, or setting a new motoring trend. Many are collectable and those which are rare, or especially popular, can be more expensive than the smartest new cars.

FAMOUS MODELS

Many different qualities can make a car famous, including speed, cost, design, production and even the number of wheels!

The Reliant Robin is famous for its three-wheeled design. The front wheel steers the car, while the engine drives the two rear wheels.

The Rolls Royce Silver Cloud (1955–66) was known as 'the best car in the world'. Many are still running today, often as wedding cars.

The Trabant is symbolic of the former communist East Germany. Its name, meaning satellite, was inspired by the Russian Sputnik satellite. It was the first car with a body made of recycled materials.

BEETLE MANIA

The first Volkswagen (which means 'people's car') was designed in 1938, by order of Germany's leader Adolf Hitler. VW Type 1 was quickly nicknamed the Beetle, or Bug. Over the next 65 years, more than 21 million were sold, making it the world's most-produced single design car.

Its iconic looks and reliable engine earned the VW Beetle fourth place on a list of the 20th century's most influential car designs. It came just behind the Ford Model T, Mini and Citroen DS.

A 'stretch limo' has an extended body – it can carry between five and ten passengers. It is usually driven by a chauffeur and is used to transport VIPs, or is hired out for special occasions. Some stretch limos contain a music system, a TV and even a cool box for drinks!

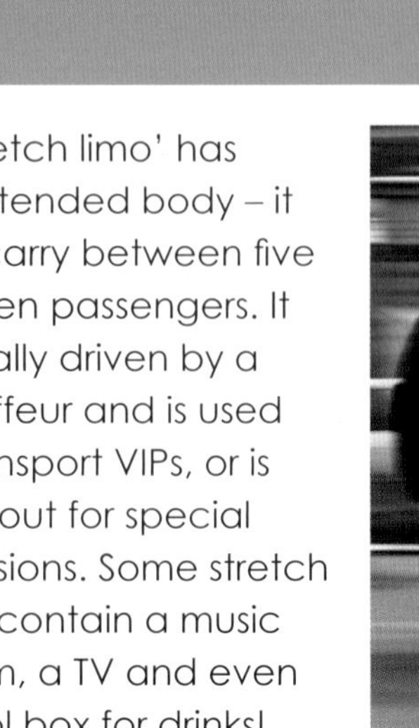

ON YOUR MARKS

Many iconic cars take part in race events around the world. Some of these are speed races. Others, sometimes known as classic rallies, give owners a chance to drive and show off their beautiful cars to other owners and fans.

Thousands of Minis join the London to Brighton Mini Run every year. In 2009, 1,450 cars broke a world record – the largest parade of Minis – at the event.

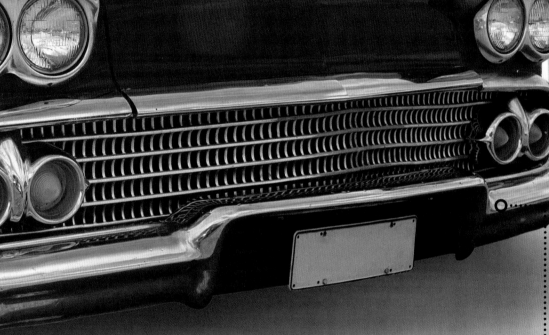

MIGHTY MINI

The two-door Mini is a classic British car. It was first produced in 1959, and became a design icon that inspired many other car-makers. Variations included a Mini truck, van and buggy, as well as the sporty Mini Cooper, which won the Monte Carlo Rally three times in the 1960s.

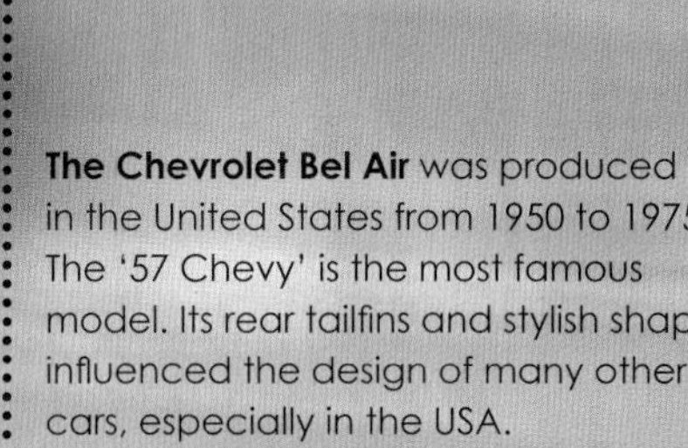

The Chevrolet Bel Air was produced in the United States from 1950 to 1975. The '57 Chevy' is the most famous model. Its rear tailfins and stylish shape influenced the design of many other cars, especially in the USA.

STRETCHED LIMOUSINE

21st-Century Cars Go Green

Could hybrid, electric or solar-powered cars soon become the cars of the future?

Fossil fuels, such as petrol/gasoline, won't last forever, so car designers are starting to consider alternative sources of power. Cars that use solar energy or renewable fuels, such as hydrogen, cause much less pollution than a petrol engine. This is better for the environment and may turn out to be a cheaper way of driving, too.

The hybrid car was invented in 1900, but it wasn't until the Toyota Prius was launched in 1997 that HEVs (Hybrid Electric Vehicles) become popular.

The sleek, smooth shape of the hybrid Porsche 918 RSR makes the car more aerodynamic (able to move through the wall of air that pushes against a vehicle at high speed). This helps it to save fuel.

DID YOU KNOW?

The most commonly used electric vehicle of the 20th century was the British milk float!

HYBRID ELECTRIC VEHICLES

A hybrid car, or HEV (Hybrid Electric Vehicle), combines the power of a petrol engine with the eco-friendliness of an electric car – in other words, it is better for the environment. It uses two smaller engines – usually an internal combustion engine and an electric motor – to drive the car. This makes it more efficient and less polluting.

POWER AND PLUG-INS

Electric cars, including hybrids, use a system called regenerative braking to keep their battery charged. In most vehicles, energy from the brakes is wasted, but in an HEV it's converted into power and stored in the battery.

Like most electric cars, the new Smart ED (Electric Drive) uses a rechargeable battery that is light and long-lasting. This neat car is great in cities, where it can be parked in small spaces.

DID YOU KNOW?

Most solar-powered cars can't carry passengers, or luggage. They need so many energy-collecting solar cells to power the engine that there's only room for one seat.

HYDROGEN FUEL CELL CARS

A hydrogen fuel cell is similar to a battery. Inside, hydrogen reacts with oxygen to make electricity, which is used to power a car engine. The cells are expensive to make, but very clean, producing water vapour instead of polluting gasses. One of the first fuel-cell cars to have been developed is the Honda FCX Clarity (below). As yet, not many places have hydrogen filling stations.

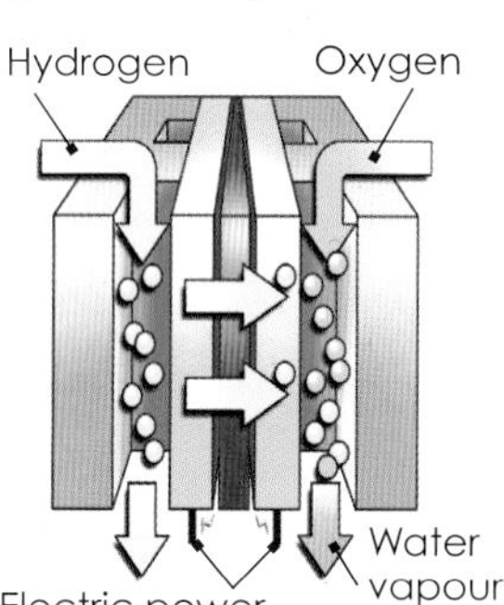

The Tokai Challenger is a solar-powered car. It won the World Solar Challenge race in 2009. The solar cells that cover the car make up about a third of its weight. The cells collect energy from the sun to power the car.

EARLY STEAM TRAINS

TIMELINE

About 1764 James Watt improves the steam engine invented by Thomas Newcomen. Smaller and more efficient, his version is able to power a vehicle.

1804 The first full-sized, working steam locomotive is built by English engineer Richard Trevithick.

1825 The first public railway opens, running between Stockton and Darlington in the north of England.

1829 George and Robert Stephenson's Rocket sets a speed record of 29 mph (47 km/h) at the Rainhill Trials.

1830 The first American-built locomotive, Tom Thumb, runs on the newly opened Baltimore and Ohio Railroad in the United States.

1830 The Liverpool and Manchester Railway operates the first passenger service. The Railway Age begins.

Steam trains were the world's most-used type of transport for over 100 years.

The earliest railways used horses to pull carts along a wooden track. During the 1760s, metal plates were fixed to the tracks to make them stronger and safer. Then, in 1764, Scottish engineer James Watt designed an improved version of the steam engine that paved the way for a new type of train. By 1804, the first successful steam locomotive had been invented.

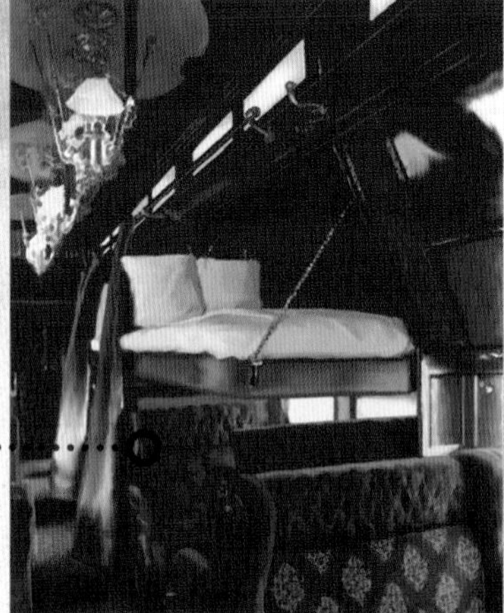

Sleeping cars were introduced in about 1838. By the 1860s, George Pullman's luxury sleeping cars had carpets, curtains, soft chairs and fold-down beds. Customers were looked after by the famously polite Pullman Porters.

Stephenson's Rocket won the Rainhill Trials, an important competition held to find the best steam engine for the Liverpool and Manchester Railway.

Firebox
Boiler
Driving rod
Piston

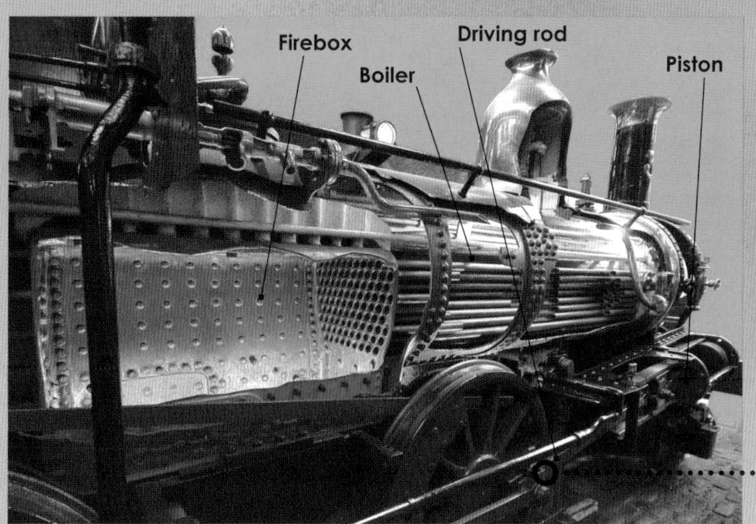

In a steam locomotive, coal is burned in a furnace, or firebox. This heats the water in the boiler, creating energy in the form of steam. The steam powers a piston, which is connected to a driving rod, and the driving rod turns the train's wheels.

TRACK GAUGES

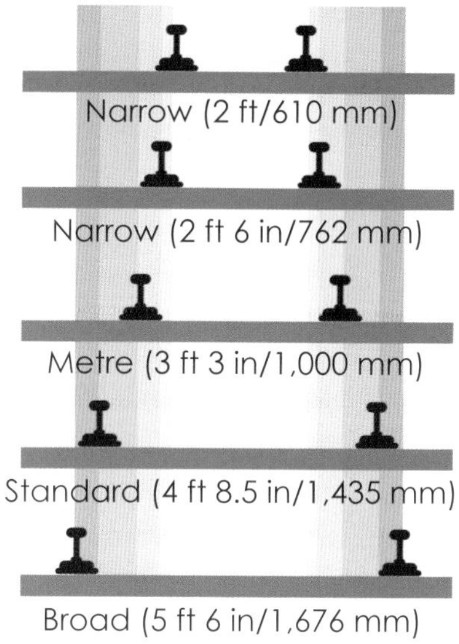

Narrow (2 ft/610 mm)
Narrow (2 ft 6 in/762 mm)
Metre (3 ft 3 in/1,000 mm)
Standard (4 ft 8.5 in/1,435 mm)
Broad (5 ft 6 in/1,676 mm)

Gauge is the inside distance between the two rails on a track. Over half of all rail tracks in the world use standard gauge, which was set by The Liverpool and Manchester Railway in 1830.

RAILWAY REVOLUTION

Trains soon proved to be a cheaper, faster and more effective way of transporting heavy goods and they became an important part of the Industrial Revolution. The first public railway, the Stockton and Darlington, carried coal to a river port over 20 miles (32 km) away.

PASSENGERS ON BOARD

As locomotive design improved and new railways opened, train companies were surprised to find they earned as much money from carrying passengers as they did from carrying goods. By the 1850s, many passenger trains included restaurant cars (carriages) and sleeping cars.

Built in 1829, the Rocket was the most advanced steam locomotive of its time.

LIVERPOOL
TRAVELLER
MANCHESTER
RAILWAY — COMPANY

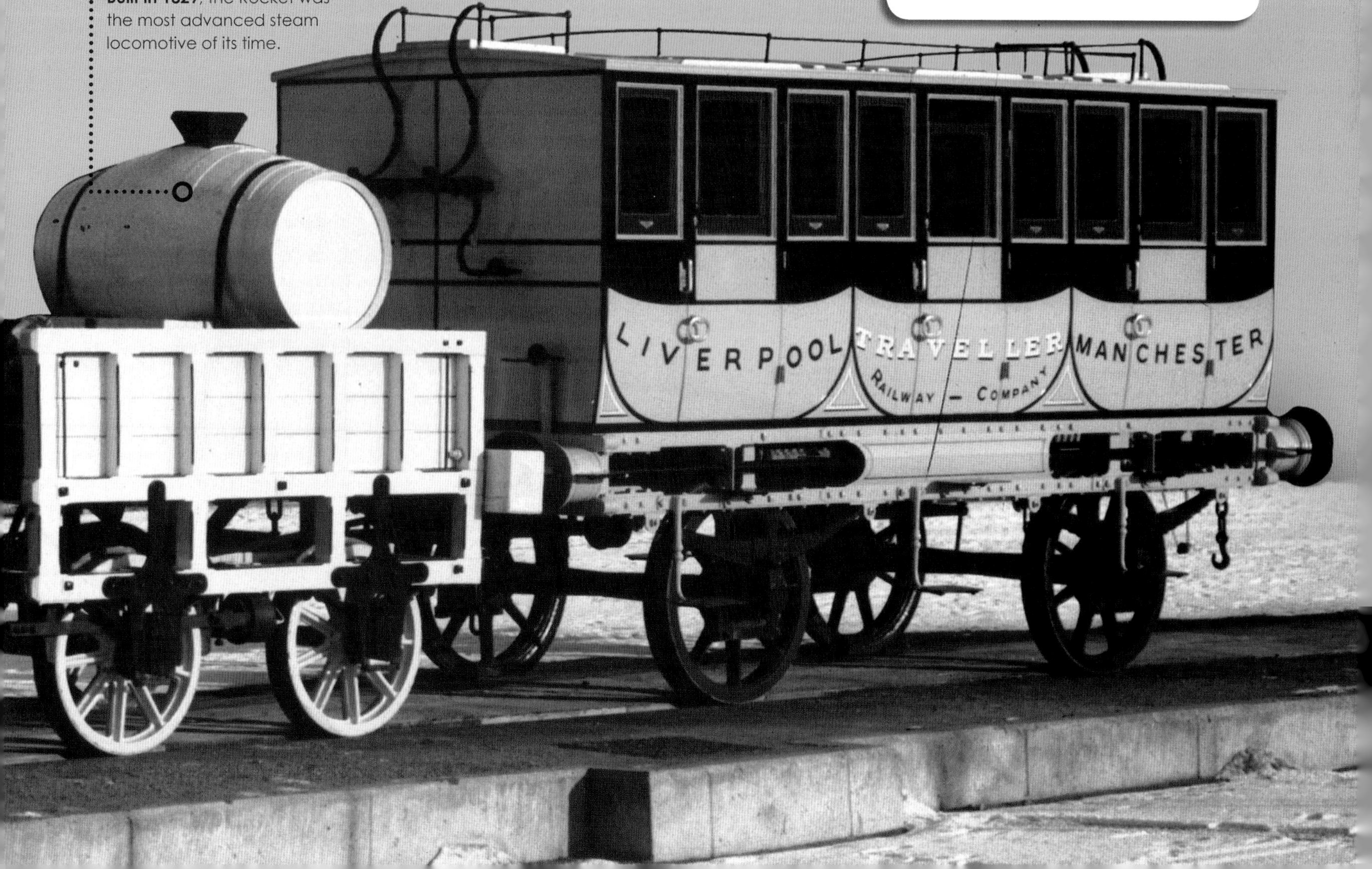

AMERICAN RAILROADS

TIMELINE

1830 There are just 23 miles (37 km) of railroad track in the United States.

1830–60 Railroad building booms in America.

1853 The first 'union station', shared by three train companies, opens in Indianapolis.

1861 The American Civil War begins. Railroads help transport soldiers and equipment.

1862 President Abraham Lincoln signs the Pacific Railroad Bill, allowing a transcontinental railroad to be built.

1865 The Pullman sleeping car is introduced.

1869 The first transcontinental railroad, connecting the East and West coasts, is completed.

1872 George Westinghouse patents the railway air brake.

1877 The Great Railroad Strike lasts 45 days – workers complain about wages.

1890 Some 164,000 miles (264,000 km) of railroad track have been built in the USA.

American railroad-building began in the 1830s.

In the South, routes were short, carrying cotton to sea and river ports. Further north, freight trains transported grain and livestock. The government helped pay for new railroads and by 1860, every city in the North and Midwest was connected by rail.

It was vital for steam locomotives to top up their water supply on long journeys. Water towers alongside the track allowed them to do this quickly and easily.

THE AGE OF TRAINS

Many locomotives featured distinctive metal 'cowcatchers' on the front. These pushed obstacles safely off the tracks, without the train needing to slow down. Faster and more reliable than canals and steamboats (their main rivals), trains were soon the most popular form of transport in North America.

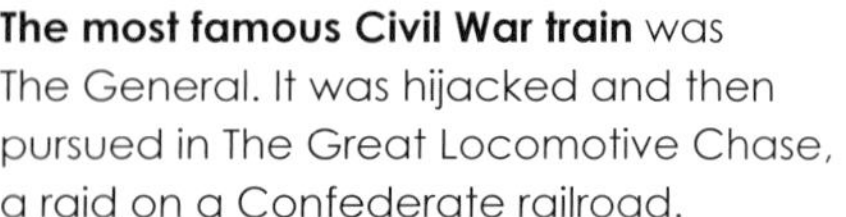

The most famous Civil War train was The General. It was hijacked and then pursued in The Great Locomotive Chase, a raid on a Confederate railroad.

From 1863 to 1869 two railroads were built to connect the existing eastern railroad network with the West coast. A journey across America that once took over four months could now be done in a week!

The two lines of the transcontinental railroad met at Promontory Summit, Utah, now preserved as a famous national park.

DID YOU KNOW?

After engineer George Westinghouse saw two trains crash, he invented a new braking system to stop it happening again. Modern train brakes are still based on his design.

THE AMERICAN CIVIL WAR

During the American Civil War, railroads transported Union soldiers and equipment in the North. In the South, Confederates had fewer trains and relied on factories in the North to supply tracks. When this stopped, they couldn't repair the railroads damaged by Union attacks. By the end of the war, the Confederate railroad network had collapsed.

NEW ROUTES

After the war, railroads in the South were rebuilt and linked to those in the North. They were extended into new territories, in both the South and the West. Railroad builders faced many dangers as they worked, including attack by Native Americans defending their land. Eventually, new towns and settlements grew up around the completed railroads.

The railroads allowed people to head West and build an exciting new life in unexplored parts of the country. This 1925 locomotive runs on a line built in 1880.

GREAT LOCOMOTIVES

Modern trains may be faster, but classic engines are still admired by many people.

Whether they were famous for being large, luxurious or for covering long distances, some of these great locomotives are now preserved in museums. Those in working order may also run along historic routes or take part in special railway events.

STEAM AND SPEED

Built in 1923, the Flying Scotsman was a long-distance express train, named after the non-stop service that runs between London and Edinburgh. It was the first steam locomotive to be officially recorded as reaching a speed of 100 mph (161 km/h), setting the land-speed record for a steam locomotive. This was beaten by another steam engine, the Mallard, in 1938. The Mallard set a new record of 126 mph (203 km/h), which has never been broken.

To keep a steam train running well, a man with a shovel had the hot, tiring task of stoking the engine – topping it up with coal and moving the coal around with a poker.

THE ORIENT EXPRESS

During the 1920s and 30s, the long-distance Orient Express passenger service was famous for its comfortable, luxurious trains, which included sleeping cars and a restaurant coach.

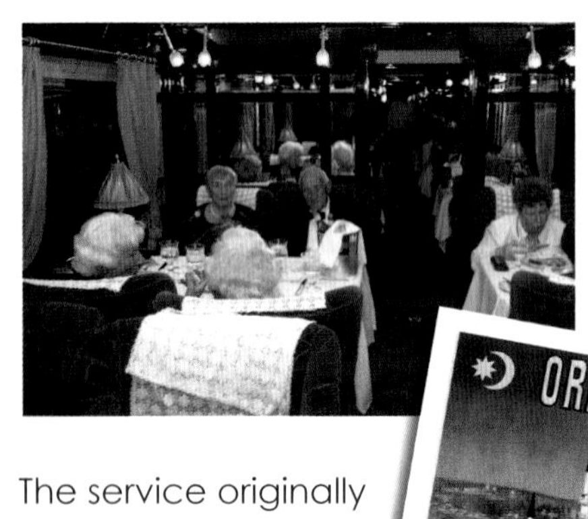

The service originally ran between Paris and Istanbul, carrying wealthy passengers, diplomats and even royalty. The service still runs today, following a similar route to the original.

The journey from London to Edinburgh took the Flying Scotsman eight hours. By the time it retired in 1963, the train had covered a distance of 2 million miles (3.2 million km).

THE UNION PACIFIC BIG BOYS

Steam locomotives known as Big Boys were built during the 1940s for the Union Pacific Railroad in the United States. The company needed trains that could climb the steep Wasatch Mountains in Utah without slowing down. The Big Boys were powerful enough to pull 100 freight wagons along the steep line, at speeds of up to 60 mph (97 km/h).

Only 25 Big Boy trains were ever built. They operated until 1962, burning coal from local mines, and were among the last steam locomotives in the USA taken out of service to be replaced by diesels.

DID YOU KNOW?

All of the daring stunts in the 1929 film *The Flying Scotsman* were performed on board the real train.

Diesels

During the 1930s, powerful diesel locomotives gradually began to replace older, less efficient steam trains.

The diesel engine was invented in 1892, at about the same time as the electric locomotive. At first, diesel engines were too heavy to power a train, and electricity was too expensive. Then, in 1924, diesel and electric were combined to create the diesel-electric train, which provided an alternative to steam.

THE BENEFITS OF DIESEL

As well as being cheaper and easier to run than steam locomotives, diesels were also cleaner. The trains used less fuel and didn't need as many repairs. They could safely be operated by just one person from a quieter and more comfortable engine room, and soon they were faster and more powerful than steam trains, too.

FREIGHT TRAINS

Specialized covered goods wagons, or box cars, are pulled by freight trains. Goods are loaded and unloaded at a cargo terminal.

Steel freight containers are loaded onto container cars by crane. They can also be transported by road or sea.

Bulky goods, such as wood, coal and grain, are carried in open-top hopper wagons that are easy to empty.

Gas products and liquids, including oil and milk, are carried in special cylinder-shaped tanker wagons.

AUTOMATIC CONTROL

Automatic Train Control (ATC) helps railways run more safely. A control computer sends information to the driver's cab, and to signals at the side of the track. It can also stop a train automatically if it's in danger.

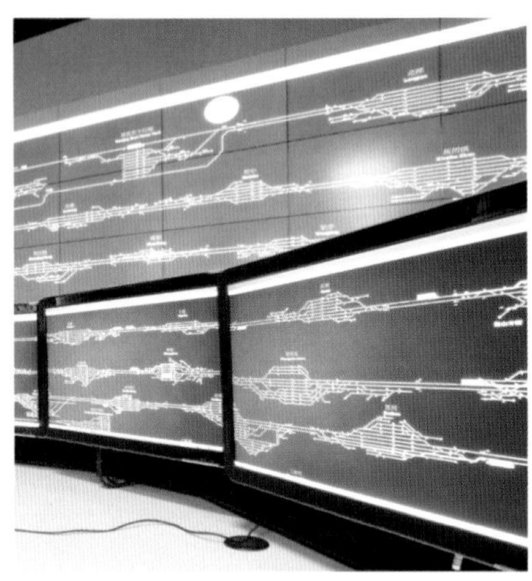

DID YOU KNOW?

The longest-ever freight train was made up of 682 wagons pulled by eight diesel-electric locomotives. It weighed almost 100,000 tonnes and was 4.6 miles (7.4 km) long!

The Trans-Siberian Express runs between Moscow and Vladivostok in Russia, on the world's longest railway. It takes 6 days to travel more than 5,600 miles (9,000 km), passing through 87 towns and cities.

In a diesel-electric locomotive, the diesel engine drives a generator, and the generator powers electric motors, called traction motors, that turn the wheels.

UNDERGROUND TRAINS AND TUNNELS

In busy cities, underground trains, also known as metro or subway trains, carry large numbers of people for short distances through tunnels.

Trains also run through long-distance tunnels under mountain ranges or beneath the sea bed. The earliest types of railway tunnels were made by digging a huge trench, then building a strong roof so roads could be reconstructed on top. Today, much deeper tube-shaped tunnels are built using enormous boring machines, nicknamed moles.

DID YOU KNOW?

Snow sheds are tunnels built around a surface-level track to protect the rails from avalanches.

THE LONDON UNDERGROUND

The world's oldest underground railway is the London Underground, or Tube. Despite delays caused by tunnel collapse and a flooded sewer, 40,000 passengers used the new railway on the day it opened in 1863. In 1890 the railway exchanged its smoky, steam-powered locomotives for one of the earliest types of electric train.

This part of the London Underground was built between 1866 and 1870. Building the line caused major disruption to the city.

WORLD SUBWAYS

With over 400 stations and a total of 842 miles (1,355 km) of track, the New York City Subway is the biggest underground railway in the world. The busiest is the Tokyo Metro, which carries more than 3 billion passengers a year.

Over 160 cities have an underground system. This sign is for the Paris Metro, the second-busiest metro system in Europe after Moscow.

Many metro stations, such as the São Paulo Metro in Brazil, feature platform screen doors in front of the track, for extra safety.

INSIDE A SUBWAY TRAIN

Most subway trains can hold 100 to 150 people per car. Plenty of standing room allows more people to fit inside. Trains on the Delhi Metro in India carry over 1 million passengers a day.

The Channel Tunnel took 15,000 people seven years to build, at a cost of over £3 million a day. During construction, many trains like this one ran in and out of the tunnel, carrying waste earth and rock, workers and equipment. The tunnel finally opened in 1994.

Eleven tunnel-boring machines were used to build the Channel Tunnel under the sea bed between England and France. The rail line connects London, Brussels and Paris.

HIGH-SPEED TRAINS

The fastest modern trains travel at speeds of more than 125 mph (200 km/h).

Most of them are powered by electricity from overhead cables and run on extra-smooth metal rails. The trains create less pollution than many other types of transport, including cars and planes. Although high-speed trains usually carry passengers, some are used for freight. In France, the post-office runs special TGV trains to transport mail more quickly.

DID YOU KNOW?

The fastest passenger train in daily service is the G1049 Harmony Express, which links Guangzhou to Wuhan in central China.

FASTEST TRAINS

The world's fastest trains are mostly found in Eastern Asia and Western Europe. They include Japan's Shinkansen and the Eurostar, which runs between London and Paris.

Spain's AVE can travel at up to 186 mph (300 km/h).

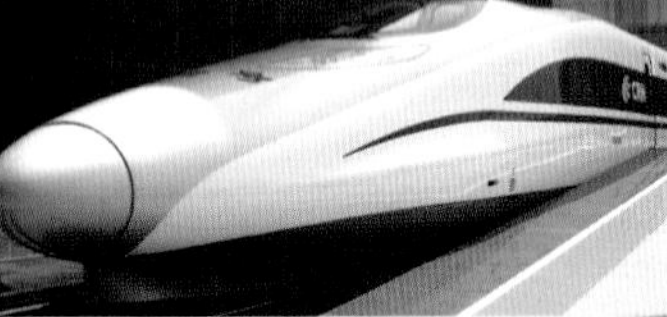

China's CRH2-380A cruises at 217.5 mph (350 km/h), but in December 2010 it achieved a top speed of 302 mph (486.1 km/h).

In 2009, an Italian ETR 500-AV set a new world speed record through a tunnel. It did 224.9 mph (362 km/h).

During a special test run in 2007, a French TGV achieved a top speed of 357.2 mph (574.8 km/h).

TILTING TRAINS

When a train passes along a curved section of track at high speed, the passengers inside may be thrown around or lose their balance. To make journeys more comfortable, many high-speed trains have a tilting mechanism. This allows the top part of the train to tilt sideways and travel around the curve without slowing down.

MAGLEV TRAINS

Magnetic levitation, or maglev, trains use powerful magnets to hover above a magnetic track. Magnetic fields generated by the electricity running through the track guide and push the train along.

Shanghai's maglev train (left) opened in China in 2003. It travels from the outskirts of the city to the airport at speeds of up to 267 mph (430 km/h).

The Chinese bullet train carries passengers between Beijing and Shanghai. It travels at speeds of 250–300 mph (400–483 km/h), making a journey that used to take ten hours now take just four.

SHINKANSEN

The world's busiest high-speed rail line is Japan's Shinkansen. It was opened in 1964 and is now used by over 150 million passengers a year. Ten trains an hour run on the line between Tokyo and Osaka, at speeds of up to 186 mph (300 km/h). The trains are well-known for being safe, fast and reliable.

TIMELINE

1267 Roger Bacon, English philosopher and monk, writes about flying machines.

1783 In France, two brothers, Joseph-Michel and Jacques-Étienne Montgolfier, invent the first hot-air balloon to carry a person.

1909 Louis Blériot flies across the English Channel from France to England.

1912 A French Deperdussin plane is the first plane to exceed 100 mph (160 km/h).

1919 Two English pilots, Captain John Alcock and Lieutenant Arthur Whitten Brown, are first to fly across the Atlantic non-stop. The flight, in a Vickers Vimy biplane, took 16 hours and 27 minutes.

1927 American Charles Lindbergh is first to fly solo from America to Europe.

1931 The Supermarine S6B is the first plane to fly at 400 mph (643 km/h).

1933 The 10-seater Boeing 247 is the first modern airliner, an all-metal monoplane with two engines.

Flying Machines

People first took to the air in 1783, when the Montgolfiers' hot-air balloon rose skywards.

Balloons led to airships that could cross oceans, but they were slow and at the mercy of the weather. In the 1890s, two American brothers, Wilbur and Orville Wright, experimented with gliders, and in 1903 they flew the first true airplane – a biplane called Flyer. The flying machine had arrived.

PLANES AT WAR

World War 1 (1914–18) transformed flying. The first planes were flimsy and slow, but in war, aircraft soon became deadly fighting machines. Air forces came into being. Ace fighter pilots fought battles in the skies, and large planes dropped bombs on cities. By 1919, aircraft could fly non-stop across the Atlantic Ocean.

The Red Baron, German ace Manfred von Richthofen, flew a Fokker triplane during World War 1. He shot down 80 planes before he was killed in 1918.

The Wright brothers in America made the first controlled, powered flight in an airplane. On 17 December, 1903, Orville piloted their plane, Flyer, for 12 seconds. Wilbur looked on as it covered a distance of 36.5 m (120 ft).

The Sopwith Camel of 1917 had a top speed of 115 mph (185 km/h). Only the best pilots could fly this very agile fighter.

DID YOU KNOW?

Sopwith Camels shot down at least 1,300 planes during World War 1. Some experts think it was 3,000!

A biplane such as the Sopwith Camel had two wings, braced by wooden struts and wires. The pilot sat in an open cockpit.

HOW A PLANE FLIES

Four forces act upon a plane in flight – lift, thrust, drag and gravity. Lift to push the plane upwards comes from air moving around the specially shaped (aerofoil/airfoil) wings. Thrust from the engine pushes the plane forwards. Drag from the air holds the plane back. The plane's weight, under the force of gravity, pulls it down.

DRAG AND LIFT

A plane's wings produce lift when they move through the air. If the plane's air speed falls too low, it may stall (start to fall). Air pushing against a plane as it moves forward causes drag (air resistance).

Flying boats and airships

Flying boats take off and land on water. Airships are gas-filled aircraft without wings, like giant balloons.

A flying boat is a plane that floats. It's a large aircraft with a boat-shaped fuselage (body) and small floats to balance the wings. Flying boats were popular passenger planes in the 1930s, when there were few airports. During World War 2, however, huge numbers of runways were built, and by the 1950s, the golden age of flying boats was over.

The Hughes H-4 Hercules flying boat, 'Spruce Goose', flew just once in 1947. It was the biggest propeller plane ever built.

DID YOU KNOW?

The Martin XP6M-1 SeaMaster (1955) was the fastest-ever flying boat. Its four jet engines gave it a top speed of more than 600 mph (965 km/h).

SEAPLANES

Seaplanes are smaller than flying boats. They have floats like giant water-skis that skim over the water at take-off and landing. Some of the very first planes were seaplanes – it was often safer to land on water than on land. Seaplanes are useful in remote regions with lakes and rivers but few airfields or runways.

When a seaplane takes off, it skims across the water on its floats until it lifts off and takes to the air.

This Martin Mars flying boat is used to fight forest fires in North America. It scoops up water into its tanks, flies over the fire and dumps the water onto the flames. The 1940s Mars was the biggest US Navy flying boat.

RECORD BALLOON JUMP

In 1960, Joseph Kittinger jumped from a balloon 31,333 m (102,800 ft) high. In free-fall for a record 4 mins 36 secs, he fell faster than any human (614 mph/988 km/h). He also flew across the Atlantic in a balloon, in 1984.

Germany's Hindenburg was the world's biggest airship. In 1937, it burst into flames as it came in to land in New Jersey, USA and was destroyed within 37 seconds. Of the 97 people on board, 62 survived.

The tailplane and wings of a seaplane are set high, well clear of spray and salt from the water.

GIANT AIRSHIPS

The first airship was Henri Giffard's steam-engined balloon (1852), but Germany's Zeppelins were the marvels of the airship age. Their huge metal frames were filled with gas-bags and driven by propellers. Zeppelins bombed England during World War 1, and flew passengers across the Atlantic. A series of crashes in the 1930s ended the great days of airship travel, but modern airships fly safely on non-burning gases.

DID YOU KNOW?
The US airship Akron (1931–33) flew with four fighter planes on board, and once carried a record 207 people.

FIGHTERS AND BOMBERS OF WW2

During World War 2 (1939–45), aircraft got faster and bigger and in 1944 the first jets roared into action.

Aircraft played a key part in most battles, from the German invasion of Poland (1939), throughout the Battle of Britain (1940) to the sea battles in the Pacific (1943–45). Heavy bombers and fast fighters poured off factory production lines and the first rocket planes and jets took to the skies.

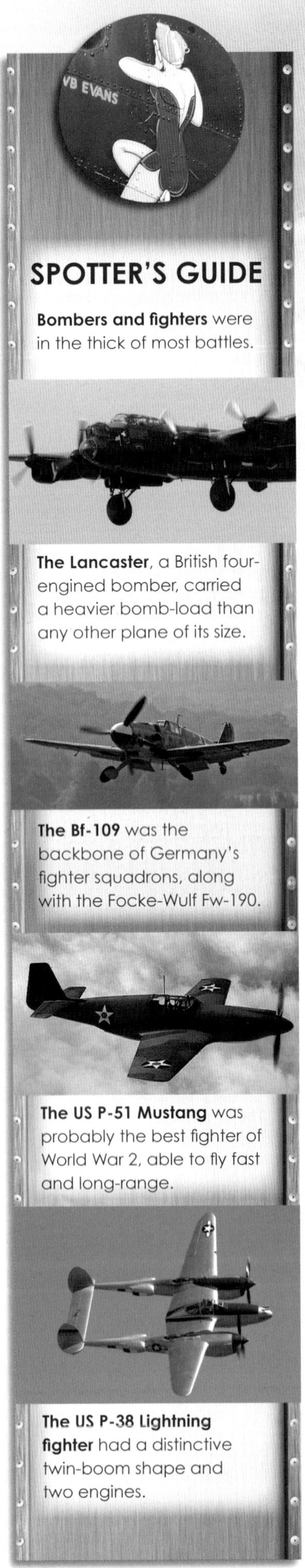

SPOTTER'S GUIDE

Bombers and fighters were in the thick of most battles.

The Lancaster, a British four-engined bomber, carried a heavier bomb-load than any other plane of its size.

The Bf-109 was the backbone of Germany's fighter squadrons, along with the Focke-Wulf Fw-190.

The US P-51 Mustang was probably the best fighter of World War 2, able to fly fast and long-range.

The US P-38 Lightning fighter had a distinctive twin-boom shape and two engines.

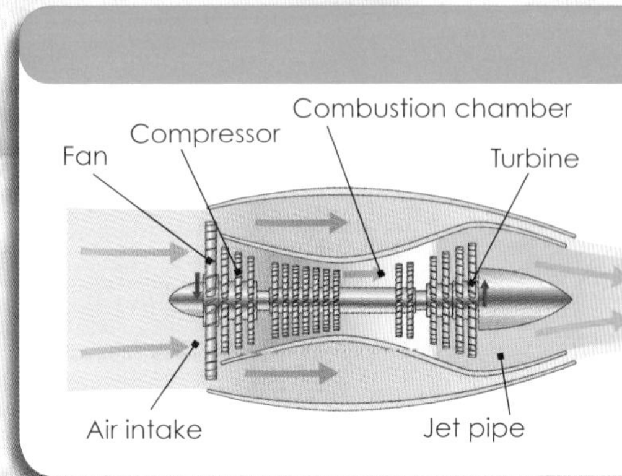

AIR POWER

Control of the air was vital to victory. The importance of air power at sea was shown in December 1941, when Japanese planes bombed the US fleet at Pearl Harbor. Aircraft flown from carriers fought mass air-sea battles in the Pacific, while in Europe, heavy bombers raided enemy targets by day and night.

The B-17 Flying Fortress bomber was armed with machine guns to shoot at enemy fighters. This B-17 is the famous 'Memphis Belle'.

The Me-262 was the first jet to see combat, in 1944. The German twin-jet fighter had a top speed of 540 mph (869 km/h) and could fly faster than any propeller plane.

HOW A JET ENGINE WORKS

A jet engine sucks in air. The air is compressed, mixed with fuel in the combustion chamber and burns. Hot gases rush through turbine blades, to drive the compressor, then stream out of the jet pipe, pushing the plane forwards.

The Spitfire is the most famous British aircraft of World War 2. It was the RAF's first all-metal monoplane fighter, and it first flew in 1936.

FIGHTER PILOTS

Many pilots who flew RAF Spitfires and Hurricanes were still teenagers. They had learned to fly on slow biplanes before switching to the faster, single-engined fighters. Spitfires and Hurricanes, armed with guns in their wings, fought off attacks by German planes during the Battle of Britain. More than 20,000 Spitfires were built in over 30 versions, and a number are still flying today.

DID YOU KNOW?

From its airfield in England, 'Memphis Belle' flew 25 bombing missions with the same crew during 1942–43.

Fastest flyers

Modern fast jets fly at two or three times the speed of sound.

Sound travels at roughly one mile in five seconds, or one kilometer in three seconds. A plane flying faster than the speed of sound is said to be supersonic. Supersonic flight is about 761 mph (1,225 km/h) at sea level. This is Mach 1. Mach 2 is twice the speed of sound, and so on. The first plane to 'break the sound barrier' in level flight was the US Bell X-1 in 1947. By 1956, test planes had reached Mach 3, and by the 1960s the X-15 had exceeded Mach 6.

DID YOU KNOW?

At 10,700 m (35,000 ft) high, the speed of sound is 660 mph (1,060 km/h) – about 100 mph less than at sea level.

Concorde was a luxury supersonic passenger airliner that flew between Europe and the United States, taking half the time of other airliners. It cruised at 15,545 m (51,000 ft), flying at 1,354 mph (2,179 km/h). Concorde retired from service in October 2003.

The SR-71 Blackbird spy plane flew at Mach 3 at up to 85,000 ft (25,930 m). It once flew across the Atlantic in under two hours!

GOING SUPERSONIC

Most airliners fly at just below Mach 1 – they are not supersonic. The only Mach 2 airliner, Concorde, flew from New York to London in 3 hours. Superfast military jets turn on extra engine power, or 'afterburn', to boost speed, but this uses up a lot of fuel. One of the fastest modern jets is the US F-22 Raptor. Its top speed (a secret) is between Mach 2 and Mach 3, without afterburn.

The F-22 Raptor is one of the fastest warplanes flying today. Its 'stealth' design helps cloak it from radar scanners.

The no-pilot X-43 was built to explore high-speed flight. Launched from a larger plane, it has an air-breathing scramjet engine (a jet engine that works best at very high speeds). In 2004, the X-43 set a new jet speed record of Mach 9.6 (almost 7,000 mph/11,265 km/h).

A plane makes a 'boom' sound as it breaks the 'sound barrier'. Because the plane is moving faster than sound, this 'sonic boom' is heard on the ground after the plane has passed. Air in front of a supersonic jet is squashed so much that it forms shock waves around the wings.

SECRET AIRCRAFT DESIGN

Some top-secret US military planes were designed by Boeing's 'Phantom Works' and Lockheed Martin's 'Skunk Works'. They include the SR-71 Blackbird, which holds the official air speed record of 2,192 mph (3,529 km/h) and the F-117 Nighthawk 'stealth' plane. Experimental planes are known in America as X-planes, and include the X-15 rocket plane and the X-43.

MiG-25

The Russian MiG-25 is one of the fastest and highest-flying jets in the world. In 1977 a version known as the E-266M reached a record height of 37,650 m (123,524 ft). Another MiG-25 variant, flown by Svetlana Savitskaya, set a women's speed record of 1,667 mph (2,683 km/h) in 1975. A number of countries still use MiG-25s today, in north Africa and Asia.

Airliners

Airliners carry passengers on short and long flights around the world.

Until the 1950s, all airliners had propellers and a top speed of about 340 mph (550 km/h). Then, in 1952, the world's first commercial jet airliner, the de Havilland DH 106 Comet, was introduced. A series of accidents followed, but in 1958 Boeing launched the Boeing 707, and air travel rapidly increased.

AT THE AIRPORT

The world's airports handle passengers and cargo. The biggest are like small cities.

Passengers check in at the airport terminal. People and baggage pass through security scans.

On the ground, planes are guided on and off the runway by airport workers.

Baggage from the plane's hold is unloaded onto a moving carousel, ready for collection by passengers.

Between flights, aircraft are cleaned, filled with fuel, checked and regularly serviced by engineers.

More than 1000 Boeing 747s have been built, including a specially adapted version, known as Air Force One, which is used to carry the President of the United States.

BIGGER AND BIGGER

As jet engines improved, bigger planes could be built, carrying more passengers in greater comfort and more quickly. In 1970, the first Boeing 747 'jumbo jet' came into airline service. The 747 weighed twice as much as any previous airliner and carried between 350 and 450 passengers. Bigger planes needed larger airports. Most airports have a single runway for take-offs and landings, but some have two.

DID YOU KNOW?

An airliner can fly non-stop from America to Australia, cruising at over 600 mph (965 km/h).

AIR TRAFFIC CONTROL

From the control tower, controllers use radar, computers and radio to direct planes and to tell pilots when it's safe to take off or land.

Air traffic controllers monitor the flight paths of all planes. Before flying, every pilot hands in a flight plan showing the plane's route.

Security checks are now part of life at airports. Trained sniffer dogs work alongside electronic scanners to detect explosives or illegal drugs that might be hidden in bags.

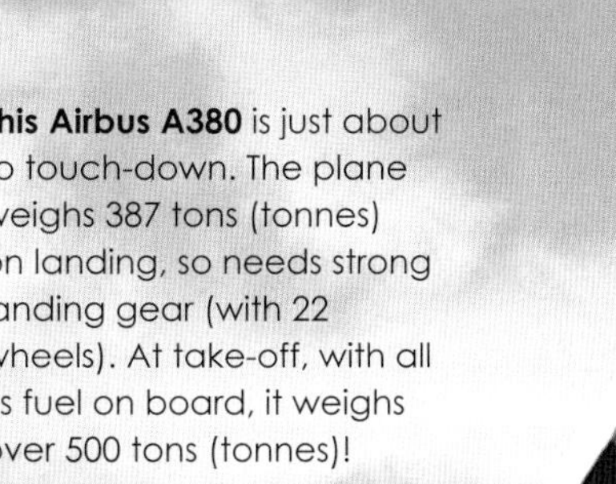

This Airbus A380 is just about to touch-down. The plane weighs 387 tons (tonnes) on landing, so needs strong landing gear (with 22 wheels). At take-off, with all its fuel on board, it weighs over 500 tons (tonnes)!

The A380 superjumbo has two passenger decks, 220 windows and 310 miles (500 km) of electrical wires.

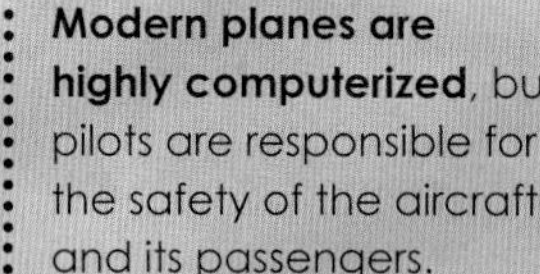

Modern planes are highly computerized, but pilots are responsible for the safety of the aircraft and its passengers.

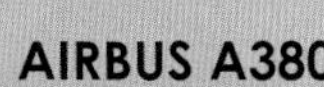

AIRBUS A380

The twin-deck Airbus A380 is 73 m (239 ft) long, and it has an upper deck extending the whole length of the plane. Normally the seats are arranged to carry 525 people, but they can be re-arranged to take 853 passengers. Both the A380 and the Boeing 747 can fly non-stop for more than 8,000 miles (almost 13,000 km).

Reaching for the Stars

Aircraft have flown to the edge of space, but only rocket-craft can explore further.

Aircraft need wings to fly in Earth's atmosphere, but wings are no use in space, where there is no air. Jet engines are also no use in space, because they need air to burn their fuel. Spacecraft instead have rocket motors that do not need air to burn fuel.

Specially converted 747 jets, known as Shuttle Carrier Aircraft (SCAs), were used to ferry space shuttles from their landing sites back to the launch complex at the Kennedy Space Center.

SpaceShipTwo (in the middle) is carried 10 miles (16 km) high by its carrier-plane White Knight Two. SpaceShipTwo then detaches and rockets up for a brief trip into space.

INTO SPACE

Some spacecraft, such as the US space shuttles, have wings so that they can glide back to Earth. Others, such as Russia's Progress and the European Space Agency's Automated Transfer Vehicle, carry cargo to the International Space Station, but are not designed to return to Earth.

The Russian Progress spacecraft is launched by rocket. After delivering its cargo to the space station, it burns up when it re-enters Earth's atmosphere.

SPACE PLANES

Space planes will give passengers brief trips into space. Virgin Galactic's SpaceShipTwo is built to carry six passengers and two pilots. The space trip begins when the plane takes off attached to a twin-fuselage carrier-plane, called White Knight Two. The two craft separate, and rocket motors boost the space plane to 110 km (68 miles) high. Other space plane projects include hypersonic aircraft that will 'skip' through the upper atmosphere at Mach 10.

THE SPACE SHUTTLE

The US space shuttle was a reusable vehicle. At launch, it used its own three main engines and two solid rocket boosters to which it was attached. In space, where wings are useless, it used two smaller orbital manoeuvring engines and a set of rocket thrusters to guide it. Returning to Earth, the space shuttle's wings and tail were essential for a soft landing. As it came down through Earth's atmosphere, the shuttle became a giant glider, relying on its wings to descend and land on a runway. The US space shuttle Atlantis retired from space flights in 2011.

White Knight Two, the carrier plane, has four jet engines. Like SpaceShipTwo, it can also carry passengers.

DID YOU KNOW?

The X-37B is a US Air Force reusable, unmanned space plane. It can remain in orbit for up to 270 days.

Remarkable facts

Have you ever wondered how long the longest traffic jam might be or just how small the smallest car is?

The world of planes, trains and automobiles never stands still for very long. With thousands of changes happening every year, it's sometimes good to get right to the facts, whether they're record breaking and incredible, or just plain strange!

DID YOU KNOW?
Cars are the world's most recycled product. About three-quarters of every scrapped car can be re-used, including the battery, metal parts and bodywork.

In 2004, British racing driver Fiona Leggate set a world record by competing in five different auto races in 24 hours.

Fighter pilots in World War 1 did not have parachutes, even though the first parachute had been used by André Jacques Garnerin as long ago as 1797.

In 1909 pioneer pilot, JTC Moore-Brabazon, flew with a piglet – to show that 'pigs might fly'!

In 1785 Jean-Pierre Blanchard and Dr John Jeffries crossed the English Channel in a balloon. In 1809, Blanchard had a heart attack while ballooning, fell out and later died from his injuries. His wife died when her balloon caught fire over Paris, France, in 1819.

Puffing Billy is the world's oldest surviving steam locomotive. It was built in 1813 to carry coal and had a top speed of 5 mph (8 km/h).

The world's worst traffic jam happened in Hebei province, in China, during August 2010. It was over 62 miles (100 km) long and took 12 days to clear.

The Darjeeling Himalayan Railway in India opened in 1881 and is still powered by steam locomotives today. Two men, riding on the train's front buffer, sprinkle sand to help the wheels grip the track as the train climbs over 2,100 m (6,890 ft).

TOP FIVE LONGEST TUNNELS

1. NAME: Gotthard Base Tunnel
   LOCATION: Beneath the Alps in Switzerland
   LENGTH: 35.4 miles (57 km)

2. NAME: Seikan Tunnel
   LOCATION: Under the Tsugaru Strait in Japan
   LENGTH: 33.5 miles (54 km)

3. NAME: Channel Tunnel
   LOCATION: Under the English Channel (between England and France)
   LENGTH: 31.4 miles (50.5 km)

4. NAME: Lötschberg Base Tunnel
   LOCATION: Through the Swiss Alps
   LENGTH: 21.5 miles (34.6 km)

5. NAME: Guadarrama Tunnel
   LOCATION: North-central Spain
   LENGTH: 17.6 miles (28.4 km)

Gotthard Base Tunnel

The RAF's Harrier jump jet can take-off and land vertically, or on short runways. This is known as V/STOL (vertical/short take-off and landing).

The largest railway station in the world is Grand Central Station in New York. The terminal has 44 platforms and over 100 tracks, above and below ground.

GlobalFlyer is the first jet aircraft built to fly non-stop around the globe. In 2005, solo pilot Steve Fossett did the trip in 67 hours.

The smallest roadworthy car ever produced is the Peel P50. It measures 104 cm (41 in) tall, 66 cm (26 in) wide and 132 cm (52 in) long and is about the same size as a washing machine!

A pedal-powered aircraft, the Gossamer Albatross, flew across the English Channel in 1979. In 1981, the solar-powered Solar Challenger made the same crossing, flying a total of 162 miles (262 km) in 5 hours and 23 minutes.

In 1853 Sir George Cayley sent his coachman up into the sky in a home-made glider. The coachman had to follow the order, but never flew again after his brief 'hop'.

Glossary

Accelerate To increase speed, or start to go faster.

Aerodynamic An object that has been designed and built to offer as little air-resistance as possible is said to be aerodynamic.

Aerofoil (or airfoil) An aeroplane wing that is rounded at the front edge and sharp at the back.

Assembly line A process that allows products to be made more quickly, by adding one piece or part at a time in an organized sequence.

Battle of Britain Air battle (1940) between British and German air forces in World War 2.

Biplane Aircraft with two wings set one above the other.

Combustion (burning) A chemical process in which fuel (such as petrol/gasoline) reacts with oxygen to produce heat.

Conveyor belt A continuously moving surface that carries objects from one place to another.

Earth's atmosphere The mixture of gasses that surround the Earth.

Emissions Waste or exhaust gasses from an engine that are released into the atmosphere.

Firebox The part of a steam locomotive (usually box-shaped) where fuel is burned.

Freight Cargo or goods transported by air, rail, road or sea.

Fuselage The main body of a plane, to which the wings, tail and engines are fixed.

Generator A piece of equipment that changes mechanical (moving) energy into electricity.

Horsepower A measurement of work done over a period of time. Originally, it was used as a way of comparing the power of a steam engine with that of draft horses pulling a mill wheel.

Hydrogen A very light gas, with no taste or smell.

Orbit The curved path of an object as it moves around a larger object, such as a star or planet.

Piston A solid, tube-shaped piece of metal that moves up and down inside the cylinder of an engine.

Pits The place alongside a race track where cars can be quickly repaired, adjusted or topped up with fuel during a race.

Pump jet A system, usually including a propeller and a nozzle, that creates a jet of water to power a boat or amphibious vehicle.

Radar System for tracking objects using reflected radio waves.

Rally A long-distance car or motorcycle race, usually run on closed public roads.

Resistance (or drag) A force that stops or slows the movement of an object, usually through air or water.

Rocket motor An engine that burns chemical fuel and does not need an air supply.

Sound barrier Term used by 1940s test pilots who felt planes shake as they approached the speed of sound (there is no real barrier).

Streamlined An object that has been designed and built with smooth, sleek lines to move as quickly and effectively as possible through air or water is said to be streamlined.

Terminal The airport building where passengers check in for departure and arrive after landing.

Terrain An area of land or ground with specific natural features or particular qualities.

Touch-down When an aircraft's wheels make contact with the ground on landing.

Traction A force that allows wheels to grip or hold firm on a surface without slipping.

Transcontinental Spanning or crossing an entire continent.

Transmission (or gearbox) A device that uses power from the engine of a vehicle to drive the wheels.

Upper atmosphere The four layers of Earth's atmosphere above the lowest layer, the troposphere, where Earth's weather occurs.

Utility vehicle An off-road vehicle with four-wheel drive, often used for towing or practical purposes.

Valve A device that controls the flow of air or liquid, often in one direction only, through a pipe.

Index

CREDITS
Text written by: Kirsty Neale and Brian Williams

PICTURES
SSPL = Science & Society Picture Library, Sh = Shutterstock.com, Th = Thinkstock.com.
t = top, b = bottom, l = left, r = right, c = centre.

Page 1t Sh/ © Graham Bloomfield, 1c Sh/ © PHB.cz (Richard Semik), 1b Sh/ © Margo Harrison, 2-3t Sh/ © PHB.cz (Richard Semik), 2-3t (left to right 1-11) 1. © Roger Stewart, 2. with thanks to Lynne Angel, © The Steam Car Company Limited, 3. Sh/ © B.Stefanov, 4. Sh/ © olgaru79, 5. Sh/ © Jerry Susoeff, 6. thanks to the Railway and Locomotive Historical Society's Southern California chapter at Pomona Fairplex, USA, 7. Sh/ © Stefan Ataman, 8. Sh/ © Kim D. French, 9. © Kogo, 10. Sh/ © James Steidl, 11. Sh/ © 1971yes, 2b Sh/ © Kosarev Alexander, 2-3 © Virgin Galactic/ Mark Greenberg, 3b Sh/ © Christopher Meder - Photography, pages 4-5 © National Railway Museum / SSPL, 5tl © National Railway Museum / SSPL, 5tr Sh/ © ArchMan, 5br Sh/ © iofoto, 6l (top to bottom 1-4) 1. Sh/ © Andrea Danti, 2. © Science Museum / SSPL, 3. © Science Museum / SSPL, 4. © Science Museum / SSPL, 6tr From "The Truth About Henry Ford" by Sarah T. Bushnell, 6bc © Science Museum / SSPL, 6-7 © Science Museum / SSPL, 7br Sh/ © Andrea Danti, 8l (top to bottom 1-3) 1. © Roger Stewart, 2. © Science Museum / SSPL, 3. © Roger Stewart, 8tr photo in public domain, 8c © Science Museum / SSPL, 8-9 © Roger Stewart, 9tr with thanks to Lynne Angel, © The Steam Car Company Limited, 10l (top to bottom 1-3) 1. stock.xchng/Ivan Raszl, 2. Sh/ © joyfull, 3. Sh/ © Bocos Benedict, 10tr Sh/ © B.Stefanov, 10bc Sh/ © cjmac, 10-11 Sh/ © Michael Stokes, 12l (top to bottom 1-4) 1. Sh/ © ANATOL, 2. Sh/ © olgaru79, 3. Sh/ © Naiyyer, 4. Sh/ © Max Earey, 12tr Sh/ © ANATOL, 12-13 Sh/ © Christoff, 13t Sh/ © magicinfoto, 13c Sh/ © Adriano Castelli, 14l (top to bottom 1-5) 1. Sh/ © Denton Rumsey, 2. Sh/ © yuri4u80, 3. Sh/ © Denton Rumsey, 4. Sh/ © bogdanhoda, 5. Sh/ © Josep Pena Llorens, 14tr © Roger Stewart, 14b Sh/ © BartlomiejMagierowski, 15 Sh/ © Pedro Jorge Henriques Monteiro, 16l (top to bottom 1-4) 1. Sh/ © Margo Harrison, 2. © Oxyman, 3. Sh/ © Rob Wilson, 4. Sh/ © Jessmine, 16bc Sh/ © Taras Vyshnya, 16-17c Sh/ © Margo Harrison, 16-17b Sh/ © SVLuma, 17tr Sh/ © Jacqueline Abromeit, 18t Sh/ © Jose Gil, 18c Sh/ © Darren Brode, 18-19 © Hideki Kimura, Kouhei Sagawa, 19tr Sh/ © Artem Kliatchkine, 19cr © Nick Leggett, 19br Sh/ © LovelaceMedia, 20l (top to bottom 1-3) 1. © National Railway Museum / SSPL, 2. © National Railway Museum / SSPL, 3. © NRM Pictorial Collection / SSPL, 20tr © Roger Stewart, 20-21 © National Railway Museum / SSPL, 21tl © Tom Jeffs, 21tr © Nick Leggett, 22tl © Roger Stewart, 22tr Sh/ © PHB.cz (Richard Semik), 22cl Sh/ © thatsmymop, 22cr © Roger Stewart, 22-23 Sh/ © PHB.cz (Richard Semik) 23t Sh/ © Jerry Susoeff, 23c © Nick Leggett, 24tr Sh/ © Theunis Jacobus Botha, 24cl Sh/ © Keith Levit, 24bl © NRM Pictorial Collection / SSPL, 24-25 © National Railway Museum / SSPL, 25t thanks to the Railway and Locomotive Historical Society's Southern California chapter at Pomona Fairplex, USA, 26l (top to bottom 1-5) 1. Sh/ © Konstantin Menshikov, 2. Sh/ © Evlakhov Valeriy, 3. Sh/ © Kenneth Sponsler, 4. Sh/ chrisdouglas123, 5. Sh/ © zcw, 26tr Sh/ © zhu difeng, 26-27 Sh/ © Konstantin Menshikov, 27t Sh/ © Christopher Meder - Photography, 28c © Science Museum Archive / SSPL, 28bl Sh/ © Clara, 28br © LeoMSantos, 28-29 © National Railway Museum / SSPL, 29t Sh/ © paul prescott, 29b © National Railway Museum / SSPL, 30l (top to bottom 1-5) 1. Sh/ © Lee Prince, 2. Sh/ © jorgedasi, 3. © Alancrh, 4. Sh/ © Pinosub, 5. Sh/ © Stefan Ataman, 30-31 Sh/ © chungking, 31tl Sh/ © Lee Prince, 31tr © Nick Leggett, 32tl Sh/ © Paul Fleet, 32cl © Science Museum / SSPL, 32tr Sh/ © Charles F McCarthy, 32bc © Science Museum / SSPL, 32-33 Sh/ © Paul Fleet, 33br Sh/ © Michael Ransburg, 34tr photo in public domain, 34bl Sh/ © Kim D. French, 34-35 Sh/ © Matsonashvili Mikhail, 35tl Sh/ © James Steidl, 35tr courtesy of the US Air Force, 36l (top to bottom 1-5) 1. Sh/ © Warren Parsons, 2. Sh/ © Tim Jenner, 3. © Kogo, 4. courtesy of Mark Sherwood, 5. Sh/ © Brandon Bourdages, 36tr © Roger Stewart, 36bc courtesy of Noop1958, 36-37 Sh/ © Warren Parsons, 37tr Sh/ © Paul Drabot, 38c Sh/ © Graham Bloomfield, 38b Sh/ © James Steidl, 38-39 Sh/ © Cristopher McRae, 39tr courtesy of NASA, 39br © Dmitry A. Mottl, 40l (top to bottom 1-5) 1. Sh/ © Steve Mann, 2. Sh/ © paul prescott, 3. Sh/ © Carlos E. Santa Maria, 4. Th/ © Digital Vision, 5. Sh/ © Ing. Schieder Markus, 40tr Sh/ © TechWizard, 40-41 Sh/ © Steve Mann, 41tl Sh/ © tepic, 41tc Th/ © Comstock, 41tr Th/ © Digital Vision, 41br Sh/ © Carlos E. Santa Maria, 42tr courtesy of NASA/Carla Thomas, 42bl courtesy of NASA/Crew of Expedition 11, 42-43 © Virgin Galactic/Mark Greenberg, 43tl courtesy of NASA, 43tr Sh/ © 1971yes, 44tr © Science Museum / SSPL, 44bl © Arne Hückelheim, 45tr Sh/ © A Periam Photography, 45c Sh/ © Jorg Hackemann, 45bl © AlpTransit Gotthard Ltd., 45br © Philip (flip) Kromer.

Poster: All poster images are taken from the book, as credited above, except for the Model T Ford (Sh/ © Richard Thornton), the Rocket (© Urmelbeauftragter) and the *Reno* steam locomotive (Sh/ © mrubcic).

489
AIRBUS
A380
Mobil 1